HANDBOOK ON FORMATIVE AND SUMMATIVE EVALUATION OF STUDENT LEARNING

BENJAMIN S. BLOOM
University of Chicago

J. THOMAS HASTINGS
University of Illinois

GEORGE F. MADAUS
Boston College

Handbook on Formative and Summative Evaluation of Student Learning

With chapters by

Thomas S. Baldwin
Courtney B. Cazden
Joseph J. Foley
Constance K. Kamii
Leopold E. Klopfer
Walter J. Moore and Larry D. Kennedy
Lisanio R. Orlandi
Alan C. Purves
Rebecca M. Valette
Brent G. Wilson
James W. Wilson

McGRAW-HILL BOOK COMPANY

New York St. Louis San Francisco Düsseldorf Johannesburg Kuala Lumpur London Mexico Montreal New Delhi Panama Rio de Janeiro Singapore Sydney Toronto

HANDBOOK ON FORMATIVE AND SUMMATIVE EVALUATION OF STUDENT LEARNING

Library of Congress Catalog Card Number 75-129488
07-006114-9

1 2 3 4 5 6 7 8 9 0 D O D O 7 9 8 7 6 5 4 3 2 1 0

This book was set in Melior by Progressive Typographers, Inc., and printed on permanent paper and bound by R. R. Donnelley & Sons Company. The designer was Paula Tuerk; the drawings were done by BMA Associates, Inc. The editors were Eliza Little, Nat LaMar, Susan Gamer, and Sally Abeles. Robert R. Laffler supervised production.

PREFACE

This is a book about the "state of the art" of evaluating student learning. It is intended primarily for present and future classroom teachers. Properly used, evaluation should enable teachers to make marked improvements in their students' learning. It is the improvement of student learning which is the central concern of this book.

The busy teacher, responsible for large classes with a great variety of students, has been so concerned with the instructional processes that he has given little time or attention to the evaluation processes. Furthermore, he has not been able to keep abreast of the growing literature on the art and science of evaluation. This handbook, by bringing together the best of evaluation techniques in general as well as in each of the major subject disciplines and levels of education, is intended to help the teacher use evaluation to improve both the teaching process and the learning process.

Part 1 consists of four sections dealing with the evaluation problems all teachers are likely to encounter. The first section, Education and Evaluation (Chapters 1 to 3), presents a point of view about education and educational objectives and describes in detail the ways in which evaluation may be used to help bring students up to mastery levels of learning.

The second section, Using Evaluation for Instruction Decisions (Chapters 4 to 6), is intended to help teachers become aware of the different purposes of evaluation and the ways in which different types of evaluation instruments can be developed for use in the classroom. The teacher will find ways of improving the summative evaluation he now uses; and the discussions of diagnostic and formative evaluation are likely to present new and very different ways in which evaluation can be used to improve teaching and learning.

The third section, Evaluation Techniques for Cognitive and Affective Objectives (Chapters 7 to 10), is organized around the *Taxonomy of Educational Objectives* (Bloom et al., 1956; Krathwohl et al., 1964); it presents models and techniques for constructing valid evaluation instruments for the different types of objectives found at all levels of education and in most subject fields.

The fourth section, Evaluation Systems (Chapters 11 and 12), suggests some of the ways in which cooperation by teachers and specialists can reduce the work involved in evaluation and improve the effectiveness of evaluation in the school situation. This section also considers some of the major new developments taking place in evaluation.

Part 2 consists of chapters dealing with evaluation in each of the major subject fields and levels of education. These chapters are intended to help teachers in each of these fields and levels find ways of using evaluation to improve learning in their own areas of interest.

While the book is primarily intended for teachers in schools, it is also designed for students in teacher-training programs and graduate programs in departments of education.

The reader should not regard this as a book to be read from cover to cover. It is, rather, a handbook to be used as the teacher (or student) encounters various evaluation problems at the beginning of the teaching cycle for an academic year and at each stage in this cycle, including the final summative stage. The reader should become familiar with the ideas contained in Part 1 so that he may return for a more careful reading to particular chapters that relate to specific evaluation problems he is attempting to solve.

The teacher will, however, find the relevant chapter (or chapters) in Part 2 of greatest interest, and undoubtedly he will return to the specific chapter repeatedly as he works through the curriculum and instructional and evaluation problems of the subjects he teaches.

The handbook should also prove useful to students in courses on test construction. For such students, Part I provides a framework and techniques for test construction, while a specific chapter in Part 2 will provide illustrations of objectives and testing techniques in the particular subject field for which he wants to develop evaluation instruments. Since the entire book is related to the *Taxonomy of Educational Objectives*, the test maker will be able to find a large number of evaluation techniques relevant to the objectives and behaviors he wants to evaluate. The detailed tables of contents and the index will enable the test constructor to find the models and illustrations he seeks.

The curriculum specialist should find this book useful in the range of objectives and behaviors which it defines and illustrates with evaluation techniques. The master table of specifications at the beginning of each of the chapters in Part 2 attempts to include the content and behaviors which curriculum makers have identified as relevant to the subject field. These tables identify what teachers and curriculum workers presently believe are the "possible" behaviors and content of the field. It is not likely that any specific curriculum, course of study, or program can accomplish the entire range of content and behaviors identified in the large table of specifications. In each chapter the writer has attempted to show how selected courses or programs emphasize particular sets of behaviors and content from the larger table of specifications. The authors of these chapters have illustrated the evaluation techniques relevant to the overall table of specifications and, in some cases, the ways in which the underlying philosophy and goals for a particular course or program alter both the way evaluation techniques are used and their place in the scheme of things in a particular instructional approach.

But the entire book is a handbook, to be used in a variety of teaching contexts and learning contexts. It is our hope that students in teacher-training institutions will secure the book early in their student careers, that they will refer to it in the curriculum courses they take, that they will use it to provide illustrations and models for evaluation courses, that they will find it useful in their methods courses as they attempt to relate instructional and learning approaches to the feasible objectives of courses in their field, and that the evaluation procedures will help them become clearer about the meaning and significance of the objectives. As they do their practice teaching, they should find the book helpful in improving their evaluation practices. Finally, we hope they find this book so useful that they continue to use it during their teaching careers as they face choices of curriculum and instructional approaches, improvement of evaluation procedures, and the maintenance and development of a point of view about education, mastery learning, and evaluation.

We believe that the skilled teacher may eventually go beyond the limits provided by this handbook—when this occurs, let us hope that it will no longer be needed or that new handbooks will be available. In the meantime, it is our hope that the full significance of what education can be is not lost in the details of translating tables of specifications into learning experiences and evaluation procedures. These are operations intended to enable more teachers to realize the seductive dream which drew them into education—the fullest educational development of their students.

Benjamin S. Bloom
J. Thomas Hastings
George F. Madaus

CONTENTS

HANDBOOK ON FORMATIVE AND SUMMATIVE EVALUATION OF STUDENT LEARNING

PART
1

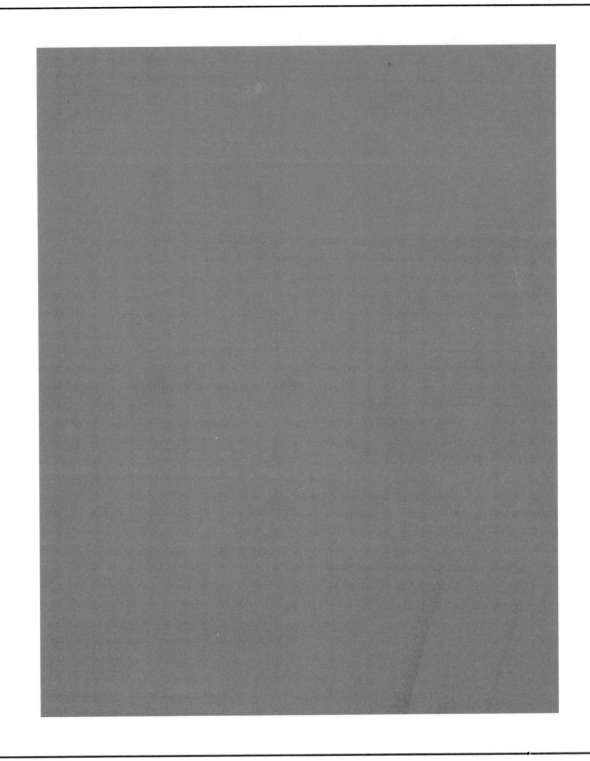

SECTION 1

Education and Evaluation

1
A View of Education

Selection versus development

Education throughout the world has for many centuries emphasized a selective function. Much of the energy of teachers and administrators has been devoted to determining the students to be dropped at each major stage of the education program. The culmination of the public education system has been conceived of as entrance into or completion of a university program. Thus, of 100 students entering into formal education, something on the order of 5 percent were regarded as fitted by nature or nurture for the rigors of higher education. Little interest was felt by educators in the 95 percent to be dropped at the different stages of the education system.

Back of this very wasteful procedure was the notion that it is the rare individual who is really equipped to complete secondary school or to enter and complete a college program. The basic task of education was assumed to be the identification of the few who were to be permitted to enter and complete the secondary school academic program and then admitted to higher education. The effect of this selection process, especially when the major decisions are made early—before age 12, was to weed out most of the children from the working-class group and to give special advantages to children of professional parents. While one may wish to argue about genetic differences between these children, it is becoming more and more evident that the observable differences between children of different social classes lie in the development of standard language, motivation to secure as much education as possible, willingness to work for teacher approval or long-term goals, and acceptance of the learning tasks set by the schools with a minimum of rebellion.

There is little doubt that appropriate home and school conditions can significantly modify these characteristics. And there is a rapidly growing body of evidence showing the effects of early modifications of these characteristics on later school learning (Bereiter & Engelmann, 1966; Bloom, Davis, & Hess, 1965; Klaus & Gray, 1963).

Quite in contrast to the notion of using schools for selection purposes is the view that education has as its primary function the development of the individual. Under this view, the central task of the schools is to develop those characteristics in students which will enable them to live effectively in a complex society. The underlying assumption is that talent can be developed by educational means, and that the major resources of the schools should be devoted to increasing the effectiveness of individuals rather than to predicting and selecting talent.

Many of the highly developed countries are rapidly moving into a situation where a greater proportion of the labor force than 5 percent will need some form of higher education. This movement is largely dictated by changes in the economic system and the need for more highly trained workers. It is in part a consequence of greater affluence and the desire of a broader segment of the population for upward social and economic mobility. In almost every country in the world, the demand for education at every level exceeds the facilities and opportunities presently available. One symptom of this demand is that, with few exceptions, the largest single expenditure of public moneys in almost every nation is devoted to education—and the demand is rising very rapidly for increased expenditures.

Two countries of the world are especially distinctive in the proportion of the age group that at present completes secondary education—the United States, with about 75 percent of the 18-year-olds finishing high school, and Japan, with approximately 60 percent of the 18-year-olds completing secondary education. It is likely that in the next decade, a sizable number of countries will have at least four-fifths of the age group completing secondary education.

In short, education, at least through secondary school, will be provided for the large majority of young people. Selection procedures, prediction, and other judgments to determine who is to be given educational opportunities are quite irrelevant when most young people complete secondary schooling (or, in the more distant future, two or four years of college). Education must be increasingly concerned about the fullest development of all children and youth, and it will be the responsibility of the schools to seek learning conditions which will enable each individual to reach the highest level of learning possible for him.

But education does not end with the completion of secondary or higher education. The nature of change in modern society requires that formal as well as informal education continue throughout life. Most workers at the skilled level or above must relearn their jobs many times throughout their career. The worker who desires to advance to another level of work (in terms of complexity of task or responsibility) must learn the new skills and duties required. One no longer plans a curriculum for any profession or occupation on the assumption that this will be the last time the learner will have to learn. Most occupational fields now recognize the need for continuing learning, and are finding ways of providing educational opportunities at different stages in the career of the worker.

However, continuing learning is not restricted to increased vocational competence. One must learn how to be an effective parent, citizen, and consumer (or producer) of the arts, and how to understand the changes in the world and their effects on each of us. Education, whether by the schools or other means, must be regarded as a process that never fully ceases.

If education is to serve youth and society under these new and very fluid conditions, it is evident that the schools and the teachers must learn to work in new ways. While this is a book about evaluation rather than curriculum and instruction, it is clear that both evaluation and teaching must undergo marked transformations if they are to be adequate to the new demands placed on them. It is the task of this chapter to delineate some of the new views of education (and evaluation) that appear to us to be in harmony with the new educational tasks.

The changing place of evaluation

Education throughout the world has been conceived of as a set of learning tasks which presumably are more difficult as one proceeds from the first to the last year of formal schooling. It has also been assumed that as students move up this education ladder, fewer and fewer will have the necessary native endowments or acquired skills and attitudes to negotiate the higher rungs successfully. Education has for centuries been thought of as a pyramid, with all or most of the younger age groups attending school at the bottom and very few ever reaching the apex.

Examinations of some kind have been used to make the decision about who is to be permitted to go to the next level. As part of the process, the results of examinations and teacher judgments have been turned into a grading system in which all students are classified annually or more frequently.

Thus, education has been viewed as having a fixed curriculum, a graded set of learning tasks, and a mixed group of learners to be classified at each major time unit in the system. Examinations or other evaluation procedures are used to make critical and often irreversible decisions about each student's worth and his future in the education system. These decisions and classifications frequently affect his entire career.

The consequences of this system for learning or for the welfare of the individual student have not been a major concern of the people running it—teachers and administrators. While there are rumblings from time to time in each society about the education system, rarely is there concerted action to do more than alter some small piece of the overall framework. The system does produce a small proportion of individuals who have successfully negotiated the hurdles provided—and some of these do make very significant contributions to society.

The effect of this system on the unsuccessful students—and the largest fraction of those who begin education are unsuccessful at some stage in the system—is not of central concern to teachers and administrators. The system of categorizing students is generally designed to approximate a normal distribution of marks (such as A, B, C, D, and F) at each grade or level. Since the system is highly consistent from one grade or level to the next, our research finds that some students are rewarded with an A or B at each grade, whereas others are reminded over and over again that they are D or F students (Bloom, 1964; Hicklin, 1962; Payne, 1963). The result of this method of categorizing individuals is to convince some that they are able, good, and desirable from the viewpoint of the system and others that they are deficient, bad, and undesirable. It is not likely that this continual labeling has beneficial consequences for the individual's educational development, and it is likely that it has an unfavorable influence on many a student's self-concept. To be physically (and legally) imprisoned in a school system for ten or twelve years and to receive negative classifications repeatedly for this period of time must have a major detrimental effect on personality and character development (Stringer & Glidewell, 1967).

The purpose of evaluation, as it is most frequently used in the existing education systems, is primarily the grading and classifying of students. It is designed to find those who have failed (D or F), those who have succeeded (A or B), and those who have gotten by (C). As testing and other forms of evaluation are commonly used in the schools, they contribute little to the improvement of teaching and learning, and they rarely serve to ensure that all (or almost all) learn what the school system regards as the important tasks and goals of the education process.

The intent of this book is to present a broader view of evaluation and its place in education. We are primarily concerned with its use to improve teaching and learning. Briefly, our view encompasses

1. Evaluation as a method of acquiring and processing the evidence needed to improve the student's learning and the teaching.
2. Evaluation as including a great variety of evidence beyond the usual final paper and pencil examination.
3. Evaluation as an aid in clarifying the significant goals

and objectives of education and as a process for determining the extent to which students are developing in these desired ways.

4. Evaluation as a system of quality control in which it may be determined at each step in the teaching-learning process whether the process is effective or not, and if not, what changes must be made to ensure its effectiveness before it is too late.
5. Finally, evaluation as a tool in education practice for ascertaining whether alternative procedures are equally effective or not in achieving a set of educational ends.

Education as a process of change

Education for us is a process which changes the learners. Given this view we expect each program, course, and unit of education to bring about some significant change or changes in the students. Students should be different at the end of a unit from what they were before it. Students who have completed a unit of education should be different from those who have not had it. Although it is true that some of the differences in a learner between the beginning and end of secondary school are to be attributed to maturation, growth, and the influences of varied experiences, we are here concerned with the changes produced by education and in the last analysis determined by the school, curriculum, and instruction.

It is here that we become concerned with means and ends. No doubt an individual student can be markedly affected by specific teachers, by the process of interaction among students, teachers, and subject matter, and by the particular combinations of experiences he has. For research purposes, it may be important to disentangle this great variety of processes and experiences in order to determine what has influenced each student. We are interested in evaluation, however, as an attempt to describe, appraise, and in part influence the changes which take place rather than to analyze all the processes which bring them about. Thus, we wish to distinguish the role of evaluation, whose primary purpose is to describe and influence change, from that of research methodology, which may seek an understanding of cause and effect or undertake a detailed analysis of the variables regarded as significant in producing change in learners. *Evaluation, as we see it, is the systematic collection of evidence to determine whether in fact certain changes are taking place in the learners as well as to determine the amount or degree of change in individual students.*

In proposing these views on the education process, we are registering our faith (and there is much evidence to support it) that education can produce significant changes in learners. This is not to say that all learners will change in exactly the same way and to the same degree. Nor is it to say that all teachers, curricula, and schools will be equally effective in changing their students or will do so in the same way and to the same degree.

If the role of education is to produce changes in learners, then someone must decide what changes are *possible* and what are *desirable*. Every teacher-student interaction is based on some implicit conviction on the part of both the teacher and the student about the possibility and desirability of certain changes. It is not really possible to ignore these basic questions. Each teaching act and each learning act come out of answers to them. The teacher who does not want to state his educational objectives is merely avoiding an explicit verbal answer to these questions. His actions and interactions with students are implicit answers.

However, making verbal formulations of goals does not ensure that the implicit goals are congruent with the explicit. Nor does it ensure that the explicit goals will be realized. This is one of the uses of evaluation—to relate the actualities of student change to the stated formulation of changes sought.

Establishing objectives

Having argued that the questions of possible and desirable changes cannot really be avoided, we still face the problem of who should answer these questions. There is no doubt that the student must be involved in the process of decision about educational goals and objectives. He must accept and to some degree understand the goals if he is to exert the appropriate learning effort. We recognize that this is difficult for the very young learner, who is less able to grasp or be moved by long-term goals than is the older learner, who may more readily accept distant aims and deferred rewards. We also recognize that many students are not in the best position to participate actively in setting goals which they find hard to comprehend fully before they have achieved them. At the very least, it is to be desired that the learner accept the goals. At the other extreme, it is to be desired that he have some sense of participation in setting them. However, we would argue that the full responsibility for setting goals cannot be placed on the student, who in most cases will not be able to foresee the alternatives available and in many cases cannot fully appreciate the implications of particular choices.

There is no doubt that the task of determining the objectives of instruction must rest largely with the teacher. It is on this assumption that much of our book is written. We believe that at the beginning of the year the teacher should make explicit to himself as well as to the students the changes that are expected to take place in them as a result of the course. With these goals in mind, he will consciously make his selection of materials, teaching procedures, and instruction strategies. With these goals in mind, he will use appropriate evaluation techniques, and will find ways of working with individual students and groups of students in order to accomplish the given aims. And as he works with particular groups of students, he will modify his goals as he must to adjust the plan to the actualities in the classroom.

The teacher is not alone in setting the goals for a particular course or subject. Whether we like it or not, textbooks and syllabi have always had a major effect on the aims of instruction. During the past three decades, a great deal of work has been done by teachers, curriculum teams, and professional associations and other expert groups in thinking through the goals of each subject in the school curriculum. In Part II of this book we have attempted to bring together some of the best work in selected fields. The teacher of a course in science, social studies, or literature, for example, will be guided in part by the work of others in thinking through both the content and objectives of instruction in his subject. However, it is not likely that he can simply borrow specifications created by others. He must deal with particular groups of learners and must find ways of modifying the curriculum specifications of others to suit the local conditions he faces. One may hope also that the individual teacher will find ways of going beyond such curriculum specifications to include objectives and procedures which are in some sense an advancement over what others have been able to do.

Teaching is a cycle which is repeated across groups of students. The cycle is repeated in subsequent years on new students or, if the teacher has several sections of the same course, concurrently with several groups. It is thus possible for the dedicated teacher to strive for more effective teaching and learning as he repeats the cycle. Evaluation, if used properly, gives him some of the necessary information to determine where improvement is necessary. Although it may give him clues as to where to make the improvement, he will usually have to find additional bases for determining how to remedy the situation. He may discover correctives by observing the variations in his students and by referring to the experience he has accumulated in dealing with individual differences. He may find possible answers by consulting with other teachers or experts. The literature on learning and psychology, on cultural differences in students, and on instruction in his own subject may furnish additional ideas for remedies. Supported by these resources, evaluation should provide the teacher with the evidence he needs on the effectiveness of the procedures he utilizes.

Thus, the professional growth of the teacher is dependent on his ability to secure the evaluation evidence and other information and material he needs to constantly improve his teaching and the students' learning. Repetition gives him the possibility of learning from one cycle for improvement in another. Also, evaluation can serve as a means of quality control to ensure that each new cycle secures results as good as or better than those in previous cycles.

However, the teacher working by himself must have a very limited set of objectives. Especially at the junior and senior high school levels, he has the students for only a fraction of their school time. Certain objectives can be realized in relation to a given subject matter, but others will undoubtedly transcend its boundaries. Here it is possible for a number of courses (and teachers) either to oppose each other or to reinforce and support each other. The cumulative effect of several courses with related objectives may be far more powerful than the mere sum of these courses taken one at a time. Especially in the so-called higher mental processes and the more deeply rooted attitudes and values, there is a necessity for educational goals to be determined by groups of teachers who work with the same group of students. This is necessary not only for subjects being taken simultaneously by the same students but also for those which will be taken over a period of years. There are complex problems of integration and sequence in learning which have a bearing on the selection of objectives; and here it is important to recognize that groups of teachers (and in fact the entire school) must be involved at one stage or another in decisions about the changes to be produced in students by the cumulative effect of learning experiences over a number of years.

At a more remote point from the classroom is the curriculum maker. A curriculum—whether it is a textbook, a complete set of materials and activities, or a whole school program—must have some ends in view. It must be constructed in relation to some purposes. Ideally, these should be formulated in terms of the changes in students the curriculum is intended to bring about. Without an explicit set of goals and specifications, the curriculum is primarily an artistic expression of its maker. We do believe that every curriculum and set of instructional materials must reflect the insights, special skills, and uniqueness of the designers. That is, they represent to some degree the artistry of those who create them. But they must also be designed to produce particular types of learning in selected groups of students. Explicit specifications of content and objectives define in part what the curriculum includes and what it is intended to accomplish. Unless the teachers or staff involved in selecting and using curriculum material are fully aware of the specifications it incorporates (and the evidence of its effectiveness in accomplishing given goals), they must accept or reject it on the basis of their views about the curriculum maker, their beliefs about what it may accomplish, or the salesmanship of its promoters. We are convinced that the users of curriculum programs and materials will increasingly be provided with explicit sets of specifications and with evaluative evidence of their effectiveness under prescribed conditions (see Tyler and Klein, 1967).

Sources of objectives

As we have said, there are two types of decisions about curriculum objectives which must be made by teachers and curriculum makers—what is *possible* and what is *desirable*. The first of these is somewhat easier to determine than the second.

What is *possible* is essentially a problem of what has already been accomplished elsewhere. It is here that the research literature in education can be very valuable. Objectives that are possible in particular subject areas have been summarized in the writings on each subject field. The two handbooks of the *Taxonomy of Educational Objectives—Cognitive Domain* and *Affective Domain*—do indicate some of the broad classifications of educational objectives which are possible of attainment by students (Bloom, 1956; Krathwohl, Bloom, & Masia, 1964).

In Part II of this book, we indicate the types of objectives which careful teachers and expert groups believe are possible in each field. But we must hasten to emphasize that this is what such experts believe (or have found to be the case) under present conditions. As new research is pursued and new curriculum procedures are devised, it is highly likely that present limits on objectives will have to be altered. Thus, educators are finding that when culturally deprived children are provided with appropriate learning conditions, they can be prepared to learn more rapidly and to achieve a greater range of educational objectives than seemed possible a few years ago. Also, in Chaps. 3 and 6 we describe how the careful use of formative (or diagnostic progress) evaluation devices, accompanied by a variety of instructional resources, makes it possible for the majority of students to achieve objectives which previously had been attained by only a small proportion of those in the same class or course.

That an educational objective may be possible for some students to attain does not mean that it is possible for all. Clearly age and level and type of previous learning are important factors here. The teacher confronted with a particular group of students, who have varying levels of ability and varying interests and attitudes toward learning tasks, must determine what is possible for them. He may seek some evidence in the literature which bears on students of the type he is teaching, but this is difficult to locate. In general, it is the teacher who in the last analysis will decide which objectives his students are likely to attain, and he will implement his decisions in his methods of instruction and interaction with students. He may err by expecting too much or too little, but he is the person whose expectations and procedures determine the objectives toward which the students will work and perhaps to a lesser degree the extent to which they attain them.

Many teachers believe that the decision about what is possible should be based not on the students' characteristics but on the teacher's—his teaching style, his ability, experience, and personality. We recognize that teachers do differ in their capabilities and especially in their self-confidence in relation to particular objectives. However, it is our considered judgment that most teachers can learn new ways of teaching students and that most can, if they will make the appropriate effort, help their students attain a great variety of educational objectives. The *teacher* does not, in our thinking, represent the major factor in determining the objectives which are possible. It is the *teaching* which determines the objectives which are possible. If teachers are convinced of the need and are provided with the necessary training and experience, they can become effective in teaching for most of the important objectives in their field.

A more difficult problem in determining objectives is what is *desirable*. This is a value problem which can be helped by the use of evidence but not answered by evidence alone (Bloom, 1966; Tyler, 1950). What is desirable for particular students and groups of students is in part dependent on their present characteristics and their goals and aspirations for the future. If we were able to know in advance a person's entire life pattern, there would be little doubt about the desirable educational objectives. This lacking, objectives must be selected which are likely to give him maximum flexibility in making a great variety of possible life decisions. Thus, what is desirable for the individual student may coincide with the greatest range of possibilities available in the light of his ability, previous achievement, and personality. If education is really to be development, objectives must be selected which maximize the range of possible developments.

Some help in determining the appropriate range of objectives for groups of students may be found in the study of the existing society. Social scientists have been attempting to determine the forces behind changes currently occurring and to foresee the likely changes in many aspects of the society. Not all of these have a direct impact on the work of the schools, but many of them have considerable relevance to the question of desirable objectives in education. It is clear that the nature of careers will be much affected by changes in the society; what implications do these have for desirable educational objectives? It is quite evident that increased leisure will be available to a large segment of the society in the near future; what implications does this have? Changes in social structure, government, communication and transportation, and other areas all bear on desirability of some objectives as contrasted with others.

While we do not believe that each teacher must function as a social scientist in order to determine desirable objectives, we do believe that teachers should become increasingly aware of the consequences of social trends for decisions about educational objectives. It will be more and more necessary for them to have concise statements available about social changes and their implications for the work of the schools. Perhaps national and regional commissions could assume the central task of helping schools and teachers to these ends.

Another source of decision on the desirability of particular objectives is the educational philosophy of the teachers and the school. While everyone involved in education, including parents, does have an implicit philosophy of education, it is difficult for people to spell it out explicitly. All too frequently such a statement seems so trivial and banal that the author hesitates to dignify it as a philosophical statement. However, an educational philosophy that makes clear the author's conception of the good man and the good life can be a powerful tool in determining what educational objectives are desirable. An educational philosophy that makes explicit the role of particular subjects and the role of personality and character in a society may be extremely useful in selecting objectives. Moreover, especially for a schoolwide committee, a statement of philosophic position can help determine the relations among courses and teachers with regard to the educational objectives (and instruction) which are desirable.

In Part II, where major objectives are described for each subject field as seen by experts, there are brief attempts to suggest the rationale for these—some from the viewpoint of the nature of the subject matter, some from societal conditions and trends, and some from a set of philosophic propositions about the school and the good life. The reader may find these useful as suggesting some of the bases for determining the desirability of particular objectives.

Structure of a subject versus structure of the learning process

A great deal is currently being written about the structure of a subject field. Many writers appear to believe that the structure of a field is synonymous with the proper structure of instruction in the subject field (Elam, 1964; Ford & Pugno, 1964). We take issue with this view on structure.

At a certain stage of sophistication in a subject, the scholar and the research worker are able to see relations among ideas and phenomena that form powerful conceptual tools for further study. Thus, Einstein's theory of relativity puts a great range of physical phenomena in a new perspective. Role theory in sociology and psychology is a very useful model for organizing a plethora of behavioral data, and constitutes a highly important set of ideas for new research. Set theory does much the same for mathematics. There is no doubt that the structuring of a subject field around a few theoretical formulations or conceptual models is extremely useful for the scholar and researcher. Whether in fact such ideas are useful for instruction is not to be decided upon by their usefulness for specialized scholarship.

There is no argument with the view that the learning in a subject field should have a structure which helps relate various aspects of the learning and gives increasingly deeper meaning to what otherwise might be a large number of unconnected specifics. There is much evidence in the research on learning to demonstrate that parts are more easily grasped and remembered in relationship to each other than in isolation.

The usefulness of a structure for learning has to do with the ability of students to comprehend it and to use it as an organizing factor in their learning. There is no clear relation between the usefulness of a structure for scholars and its usefulness (and meaningfulness) for students. Furthermore, when alternative structures are available in a subject field, it may well be that overlearning one structure will incapacitate the student to learn other structures later.

In contrast to the structure of a subject field is the structure of the learning process. The structure of the learning process should be one in which the student can successfully move from one phase of learning to another. He should continually be offered clues and stimuli which are meaningful to him at each stage. The student should be able to participate actively in the learning process and be repeatedly rewarded by successful mastery as he advances to increasingly more complex learning tasks. It is possible that the end result of the learning will be a structure of the subject that resembles one scholars find useful. As we said, however, the structure of teaching and learning must be based on pedagogical considerations and need not mirror the scholar's view of his field.

Components of the learning process

In both curriculum making and teaching, there is the act of breaking a subject and a set of behavioral objectives into a series of tasks and activities. If this is done properly, it will result in the student's developing the cognitive and affective characteristics which are the intended outcomes of the education process.

The art of teaching is the analysis of a complex final product into the components which must be attained separately and in some sequence. To teach anything is to have in view the final model to be attained while concentrating on one step at a time in the movement toward the goal. One gets a glimpse of the great power of pedagogy when it is applied to very complex new ideas in mathematics, the sciences, philosophy, the social sciences, and other fields. Einstein's theory of relativity, DNA genetic coding, and set theory are all examples of significant new ideas which, when first developed, could be understood only by a small number of scholars in the respective fields. Such ideas may now be understood by millions of students at the secondary level because curriculum workers and teachers have found ways of explaining them to a great variety of learners. Evidence of this is the fact that many parents have difficulty comprehending some concepts which their children can use with great facility.

The analysis and organization of the learning process is difficult to describe when one is dealing with such complex ideas as the above. It is easier to convey something of this work by describing a simple and readily observed learning procedure. One begins to teach a child how to ride a two-wheel bicycle with a mental picture of the child's operating the bicycle smoothly at the end of the learning process. Then the good teacher breaks the learning task into the steps of adjusting the bicycle to the child's size, the child's balancing, getting started and building sufficient momentum, braking the bicycle, steering it, and so forth. In addition, the teacher is likely to be concerned with special problems such as safety and signals to other vehicles. Given this breakdown, he then determines the appropriate sequence of learning steps. As he teaches the child, he is aware of the special problems the rider is having and the corrections needed. He also attempts to reward and reassure the learner whenever he can.

This learning task exemplifies the analysis of the parts to be mastered and the arrangement of those parts in the most appropriate sequence of learning steps. The teacher has subdivided the whole unit of learning into the equivalent of a breakdown chart or a blowup diagram with the conception of a naïve learner at the beginning and a competent cyclist at the end. Each of the parts has its own special learning characteristics. The diagram might look something like Fig. 1-1.

Other, more complex learning tasks may be viewed in much the same fashion, although the learning-time requirements may be years instead of hours.

Essentially, the structure of a learning process may be broken into several major parts: a model of outcomes, the diagnosis of the learner at the beginning of the learning unit, and the instructional process.

The model of outcomes and table of specifications

The teacher has in mind a model of the outcomes of instruction. While it may be rather general, the careful teacher is fully aware of many of the specifics in the model. He may even have worked it out to the point that he can list and check off an inventory of the characteristics of the end product. He also tries to help the student become aware of the final model and to strive to attain it as the goal of learning.

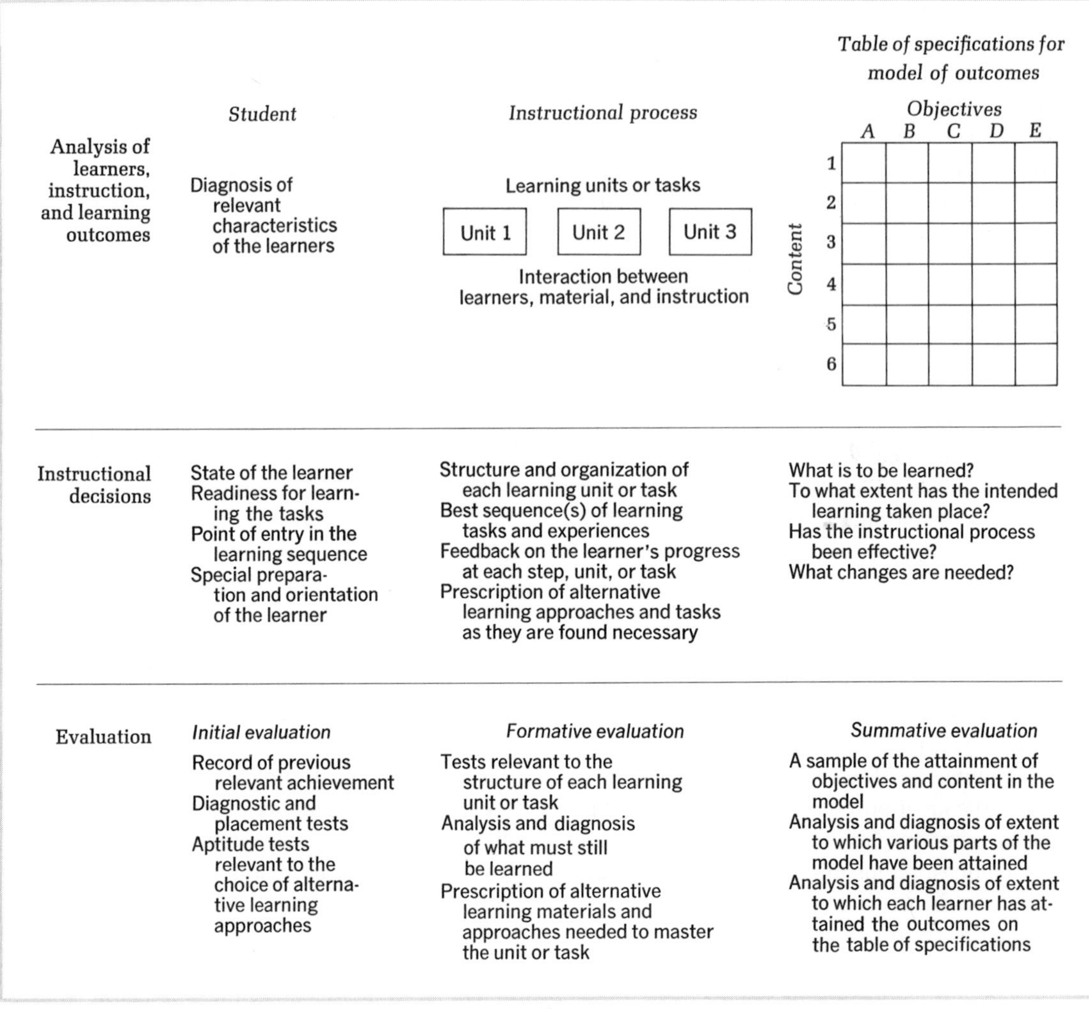

Table of specifications for model of outcomes
Student
Instructional process
Objectives
A B C D E
Analysis of learners, instruction, and learning outcomes
Diagnosis of relevant characteristics of the learners
Learning units or tasks
Unit 1
Unit 2
Unit 3
Interaction between learners, material, and instruction
Content
1
2
3
4
5
6
Instructional decisions
State of the learner
Readiness for learning the tasks
Point of entry in the learning sequence
Special preparation and orientation of the learner
Structure and organization of each learning unit or task
Best sequence(s) of learning tasks and experiences
Feedback on the learner's progress at each step, unit, or task
Prescription of alternative learning approaches and tasks as they are found necessary
What is to be learned?
To what extent has the intended learning taken place?
Has the instructional process been effective?
What changes are needed?
Evaluation
Initial evaluation
Record of previous relevant achievement
Diagnostic and placement tests
Aptitude tests relevant to the choice of alternative learning approaches
Formative evaluation
Tests relevant to the structure of each learning unit or task
Analysis and diagnosis of what must still be learned
Prescription of alternative learning materials and approaches needed to master the unit or task
Summative evaluation
A sample of the attainment of objectives and content in the model
Analysis and diagnosis of extent to which various parts of the model have been attained
Analysis and diagnosis of extent to which each learner has attained the outcomes on the table of specifications

FIGURE 1-1 The relation among evaluation, instructional decisions, and the analysis of learners, instruction, and learning outcomes.

The model of outcomes or objectives of instruction can be expressed in many ways. Some teachers (and courses of study) specify in great detail the subject matter or content the student should have learned by the end of the year, term, course, or other unit. This is very useful, but it does not specify in what sense the student should have "learned" the subject. In most contemporary developments of instruction and curriculum, there is some attempt to define the objectives or behaviors which the student should attain. These are statements of the ways in which students should be able to think, act, or feel about the subject matter. They may also be statements on how the student should be able to think, act, or feel about himself, about others, about social institutions, and so forth—that is, the objectives need not always be confined to a course or subject. We have found it useful to represent the relation of content and behaviors or objectives in the form of a two-dimensional table with the objectives on one axis, the content on the other. The cells in the table then represent the specific content in relation to a particular objective or behavior. The development and use of objectives is spelled out in greater detail in Chap. 2. In each chapter of Part II, we have attempted to describe in some detail possible models of outcomes for selected subjects and programs of instruction. Various users may refer to the tabular form of the model as the "master chart," "table of specifications," or "matrix of content and behaviors," among other titles; in the present volume, we will call it the "table of specifications."

We believe that one of the most difficult problems in stating the specifications in the model is to make them precise enough to convey clear ideas of what is intended not only to the person making the model but also to other teachers, education workers, and related professional people. All too frequently language fails us as we try to describe the characteristics we intend to develop in our students. The statements become bland and relatively meaningless, even to their author.

One way of making the objectives more detailed is to specify the behaviors the student should possess or exhibit if he has attained the objectives. The use of behavioral statements is developed further in Chaps. 2 and 4, in Chaps. 7 through 10 for each type of objective, and in each chapter of Part II for selected school subjects and programs of instruction.

Another way of giving further clarity to the specifications of outcomes is to represent them in the form of the problems, questions, tasks, and the like which the student should be able to do or the kinds of reactions he should give to specific questions or situations. What is being suggested here is that the summative evaluation instruments, when finally constructed, offer an operational definition of the model or specifications. To construct or select an appropriate evaluation instrument is to define something about what the student should learn and to give a detailed operational definition of a sample of the problems, questions, tasks, situations, and so on to which he should be able to respond in an appropriate manner. This idea will be further developed throughout the entire book and is treated in a very detailed way for the subjects included in Part II.

Diagnosis of the learner at the beginning of the learning unit

A teacher does attempt to determine what the learner has brought to the learning task that is relevant. He further determines what the special problems are that the student may have in relation to previous related learning. In our bicycle illustration, a very young learner will be seen as different from a much older learner. A child who can ride a tricycle will begin a bit differently from one who has never ridden any type of cycle.

When the teacher or curriculum maker is specifying the outcomes of instruction, he must have in mind the kinds of students or learners who are likely to be able to attain these outcomes in a reasonable period of time under the learning conditions he is planning to use. He may assume that his students possess certain characteristics when they enter his course or program. However, his assumptions may not be entirely accurate, and he may gradually learn to his regret that his students lack particular important characteristics that he had expected. Thus, he will be forced to revise his expectations or change the nature of the learning tasks he had planned, or both.

The teacher must be able to diagnose the relevant characteristics of his learners at the time they enter the course or program. He must know the readiness of his students for the learning tasks, he must know the point of entry into a learning sequence that is appropriate for individual learners or the group, and he must be able to determine what special preparation and orientation will be necessary before the students begin the sequence of learning tasks.

Evaluation can play a vital role in providing the teacher with the information he needs to make the necessary decisions about individual learners or about the entire group he plans to work with. Part of this initial evaluation will be provided by records of previous evaluations made on the students. Other aspects may require special diagnostic and placement tests or even the use of particular aptitude tests and other instruments, which may suggest alternative learning approaches. The use of initial evaluation procedures is discussed more fully in Chap. 5.

The instructional process

During each step of the learning there is interaction among the learner or learners, the material or problems, and the teacher. It is this interaction which is the heart of the instructional process.

The teacher, having selected a model of the outcomes of instruction, has to make decisions about what *materials* to use, what *methods* of teaching are appropriate, and what *activities* on the part of the learner are likely to help him attain the objectives desired. Although these topics are more properly a part of teaching and curriculum than of evaluation, we would be remiss if we did not communicate something about the nature of these decisions. We discuss this further in Chap. 3.

Materials Never before have teachers had the wealth of instructional materials now available. A quarter of a century ago, the primary (and usually the only) instructional materials were textbooks. Now the teacher may make use of readings, workbooks, programmed materials, games, films and other audiovisual media, concrete materials (including laboratory materials), problem materials (including pamphlets and readings giving the necessary background to a complex problem), carefully designed drill materials, and other types. Although these materials may be used by entire groups of students, the teacher is likely to find that a "learning laboratory" with a great range of alternative materials to fit the special needs of individual learners at particular stages in the learning will yield far greater results than those obtained under a single set of required materials for all.

The decisions on materials to be used will in part be determined by the experience the teacher has had in the past in working toward particular objectives. In general, materials which are purely descriptive are likely to be most useful for objectives of the knowledge and comprehension types, whereas problem materials are likely to be most useful for the higher cognitive objectives such as application and analysis (see Chaps. 8 and 9).

Methods of instruction Each teacher tends to use a single general method of instruction—lecture, recitation, or discussion, for example. However, as he clarifies the range of objectives he is seeking, he will find it necessary to use a greater variety of instructional methods. For some purposes he may see all instruction as ranging from didactic to dialectical (Ginther, 1964; Rippey, 1969); the first are largely one-way forms of communications from teacher to learners, and the second are predominantly interactive processes between learners and teachers around problems and questions. In other connections he may view instruction as including tutorial methods; problem sessions of the discovery type; small-group work sessions (with or without the aid of the teacher); larger-group methods such as having students read, listen, or work in some way; recitation to determine whether they have learned what was intended, with corrections as needed; and lectures to very large groups of students. While many other possibilities are available, these are likely to be combinations of the few methods already listed.

Again, the choice of method must be dependent on the objectives of the instruction. Didactic teaching is likely to be very effective for the lower mental processes, although dialectical teaching will probably be necessary for the higher mental processes. Methods which maximize the reinforcement of the learning and the students' success are likely to lead to greater interest in and more favorable attitudes toward the subject and learning in general.

When one considers the variety of students involved in a course and the size of the class which must be taught as a group, it is likely that the methods to be used will be dictated by the practical considerations confronting the teacher. It is, however, quite probable that the attainment of a range of objectives will require a variety of instructional methods. It is also likely that alternative methods must be provided for those students who are not showing the desired development under the instruction approaches being used for the group (see Chaps. 3 and 6).

Learning units or tasks Learning takes place over time, and the instructional material and process must be organized into smaller units than an entire course, grade, or program.

The instructor or curriculum maker must determine the learning steps by which he can help the students over a period of time to attain the outcomes he regards as important and desirable. This requires that there be an overview of the structure of the subject or ideas to be learned, a breakdown of this structure into a series of steps or units to be learned in some sequence, and a further analysis of what is included in each learning unit or task.

Each unit or task may be conceived of as comprising the learning to take place in a relatively short period of time—a day, a week, or a month, perhaps. Each learning unit may also be conceived of as a series of subtasks which can best be learned as a series of short steps, each related to the others, building from relatively simple and concrete elements (terms, facts, procedures) to more complex and abstract ideas (concepts, rules, principles, processes) to even more abstruse ideas (theories, models, applications, and analyses). The art of instruction, as we have pointed out, consists in large part in breaking down a relatively complex idea or process into a series of smaller elements or steps, and then finding a way of helping individual students learn these elements.

The breakdown of the learning task provides the specifications for formative evaluation tests or procedures (see Chap. 6). If such instruments are well used, they can furnish information to the teacher and the students about how adequately each unit is being learned as well as provide feedback on what is still necessary if the unit is to be mastered by individual students and the entire group. Formative evaluation may be utilized as one basis for decisions on alternative learning tasks and procedures (see Chaps. 3 and 6). Thus, we are suggesting that the proper use of formative evaluation—evaluation during the formation of learning—can do much to ensure that the outcomes of instruction are attained by the largest proportion of the learners. The breakdown of learning tasks and the construction of formative evaluation instruments are illustrated for each subject field in the chapters in Part II.

Summary

In this chapter we have attempted to spell out in some detail the point of view about teaching and learning which is central in this book. We take the position that the main task of the education process is to change the learners in desirable ways, and that it is the primary task of teachers and curriculum makers to specify in precise terms the ways in which students will be altered by the learning process.

There is a series of decisions which teachers must make if they are to be effective in helping learners change in the desired ways, and it is the role of evaluation to provide appropriate evidence to help both teachers and learners attain the goals of instruction. The remainder of the book attempts to delineate the specific evaluation procedures and techniques which may be utilized or constructed to provide the information needed at each step in the education process.

Part I deals with these procedures and techniques in a general way, and Part II provides the teacher of selected subjects and programs with illustrations of those procedures and techniques which are likely to have the greatest practical value in each subject field or program.

REFERENCES

Bereiter, C., & Engelmann, S. *Teaching disadvantaged children in the preschool.* Englewood Cliffs, N.J.: Prentice-Hall, 1966.

Bloom, B. S. (Ed.) *Taxonomy of educational objectives: The classification of educational goals.* Handbook 1. *Cognitive domain.* New York: McKay, 1956.

Bloom, B. S. *Stability and change in human characteristics.* New York: Wiley, 1964.

Bloom, B. S., Davis, A., & Hess, R. *Compensatory education for cultural deprivation.* New York: Holt, Rinehart and Winston, 1965.

Bloom, B. S. The role of the educational sciences in curriculum development. *International journal of educational sciences,* 1966, **1,** 5–16.

Elam, S. (Ed.) *Education and the structure of knowledge.* Chicago: Rand McNally, 1964.

Ford, G. W., & Pugno, L. (Eds.) *The structure of knowledge and the curriculum.* Chicago: Rand McNally, 1964.

Ginther, J. R. Conceptual model for analyzing instruction. In J. P. Lysaught (Ed.), *Programmed instruction in medical education.* Rochester, N.Y.: University of Rochester Clearing House, 1964.

Hicklin, W. J. A study of long-range techniques for predicting patterns of scholastic behavior. Unpublished doctoral dissertation, University of Chicago, 1962.

Klaus, R. A., & Gray, S. W. *Early Training Project: Interim report.* Nashville, Tenn.: George Peabody College for Teachers, November, 1963.

Krathwohl, D. R., Bloom, B. S., & Masia, B. B. *Taxonomy of educational objectives: The classification of educational goals.* Handbook 2. *Affective domain.* New York: McKay, 1964.

Payne, A. The selection and treatment of data for certain curriculum decision problems: A methodological study. Unpublished doctoral dissertation, University of Chicago, 1963.

Rippey, R. M. The Ginther model: Four dimensions of research on instruction. *Elementary School Journal,* 1969, **69,** 215–223.

Stringer, L. A., & Glidewell, J. C. *Early detection of emotional illnesses in school children.* (Final Rep.) St. Louis: St. Louis County Health Department, 1967.

Tyler, L. L., & Klein, M. F. Recommendations for curriculum and instructional materials. *Curriculum Theory Network,* 1968, **1,** 2–10.

Tyler, R. W. *Basic principles of curriculum and instruction.* Chicago: University of Chicago Press, 1950.

2 Defining Educational Objectives

In Chap. 1 we saw that a premise central to this book is that education is a process which helps the learner to change in many ways, some intentional, others quite unintentional. Given this premise, then one of the principal tasks of school administrators and teachers is to decide, as far as is possible, how they want the student to change and what part they can play in assisting him in the process. A second task arises both as instruction unfolds and upon its completion. That is to determine whether the student has changed in the desired ways and to try to define what kinds of unanticipated outcomes have been achieved.

The ways in which school officials would like to see the student change constitute the educational objectives or goals of instruction. These do not, however, comprise all of the outcomes of instruction since it is quite impossible in most subjects to anticipate the full range of results. As the course progresses, unanticipated outcomes, some positive, others unfortunately negative, often accrue. Some of these quickly become apparent; others may go unrecognized. Attempts to specify all the outcomes in advance can have a restrictive influence on both teaching and evaluation. This can happen if a teacher gets the mistaken impression that only the planned results are important and either neglects other outcomes in his teaching or evaluates only those explicitly detailed in advance.

This is not to imply that careful consideration should not be given before instruction to what outcomes are possible, desirable, and thus systematically to be sought; on the contrary, that is an essential step in instruction and evaluation, and this chapter deals with how to formulate maximally useful statements of educational objectives. However, it is important to realize also that other significant outcomes will become evident as instruction proceeds, and the teacher should be alert to such possibilities. We shall deal more directly in this book with the evaluation of anticipated goals. However, we wish to point out that techniques from sociology, anthropology, ethnology, and economics might also be useful in looking at some of the other outcomes of instruction.

In Chap. 1 we saw that in the planning of educational objectives, decisions must be made about what is possible and what is desirable. We saw that student and teacher characteristics must be considered when one is deciding whether an objective is possible, and that studying the existing society and philosophy of education is useful in determining whether a possible objective is desirable. This chapter deals with the formulation of useful statements of educational objectives once it has been established that an objective is both feasible and desirable. These decisions should not be neglected or hurried through, and the reader is referred back to the discussion in Chap. 1 of the various screens to be used in arriving at them.

Another premise outlined in Chap. 1 and running throughout this book is that evaluation should be both *formative* and *summative* in its scope. This distinction has been introduced primarily in hopes of bringing the evaluation process closer to the teaching and learning processes. Too often in the past, evaluation has been entirely summative in nature, taking place only at the end of the unit, chapter, course, or semester, when it is too late, at least for that particular group of students, to modify either process. Summative evaluation has as its primary goals grading or certifying students, judging the effectiveness of the teacher, and comparing curricula. Some teachers perform summative evaluation rather frequently. They may wish to grade student performance every few weeks or at the end of each chapter or unit of instruction. This intermediate assessment can be distinguished from evaluation that takes place at the end of a much longer period of time, such as a course or semester. Longer-term summative evaluation infers by sampling from the model the extent to which a student has realized the entire range of outcomes contained in the model. Intermediate summative evaluation, on the other hand, is concerned with more direct, less generalizable, and less transferable outcomes.

Both intermediate and longer-range summative evaluation are important and should not be minimized. However, if evaluation is to aid both the teaching and learning processes, it must take place not only at the termination of these processes but while they are still fluid and susceptible to modification. Formative evaluation, as the name implies, intervenes during the formation of the student, not when the process is thought to be completed. It points to areas of needed remediation so that immediately subsequent instruction and study can be made more pertinent and beneficial. Formative evaluation impinges on smaller, comparatively independent units of the curriculum within the model of outcomes described in Chap. 1, assessing in depth a relatively small number of objectives.

Formative and summative evaluation are covered in detail in Chaps. 6 and 4, respectively. This chapter concerns itself with the formulation of statements of objectives for both these types of evaluation.

A statement of an objective is an attempt by the teacher or curriculum maker to clarify within his own mind or communicate to others the sought-for changes in the learner. To accomplish this, the educator must choose words that convey the same meaning to all intended readers. Statements of objectives that can be interpreted differently by different readers give them no direction in selecting materials, organizing content, and describing obtained outcomes, nor do they provide a common basis for instruction or evaluation. This chapter deals then with the problem of arriving at meaningful, unambiguous statements of intended educational outcomes which can serve as models for formative evaluation, intermediate and long-range summative evaluation, and instruction.

Different approaches to defining education objectives

Much attention has been given to the statement of objectives in American education. There is probably no aspect of instruction about which more has been written. Books on teaching methods all stress the importance of definitions of educational objectives. Those in charge of teacher-training courses routinely require them as part of the lesson plans prepared by student teachers. National commissions, state and local curriculum groups, and individual classroom teachers have worked long and hard to delineate educational goals and objectives. Often, however, these efforts have had little impact on the instruction or evaluation practices of teachers. This in turn has led to confusion over the importance and worth of statements of objectives. Do they really help improve the education process, or is their formulation merely a rite of passage for the novice and a ritualistic exercise for the more experienced educator? In this book we maintain that the formulation and utilization of educational objectives should play a central and essential role in teaching and learning. We feel that once objectives are defined clearly, they can become models or plans that help shape and guide the instruction and evaluation processes.

To appreciate better the reasons for the confusion about the utility of statements of educational objectives, we may ask the question, Useful for what purpose? Let us examine the utility of the more common forms the statements can take.

Statements of educational objectives formulated by national curriculum groups or commissions are often very broad in scope—for example, "worthy use of leisure time," "the development of good citizenship," "to develop an appreciation of the value and power of mathematics in our technological society." Often broad concepts like these are criticized on the ground that they give no indication of the kinds of changes to look for in students who have purportedly reached the stipulated goals. While such attempts by blue-ribbon committees often result in excellent philosophic declarations of purpose that can give overall direction to a school system, they are too Delphian in nature to help the classroom teacher in the daily management of instruction. In other words, because of their vagueness, they cannot serve as an instruction or evaluation model or plan.

If the purpose of such statements was to guide instruction and evaluation, then of course this criticism would be valid. However, they are not intended for that use. They are designed rather to give direction to policy makers at the national, state, and local level. Though lofty, they are still explicit enough to suggest certain types of action to school boards and administrators. For example, if a board endorses "the development of good citizenship" as a statement of purpose for its schools, then it must consider curricula, programs, and activities for its students that will work toward the accomplishment of this intent.

Perhaps these general statements of purpose would be better labeled "goals" than "objectives." A goal is something broader, longer-range, and more visionary than an objective. It is

> . . . something presently out of reach; it is something to strive for, to move toward, or to become. It is an aim or purpose so stated that it excites the imagination and gives people something they want to work for, something they don't yet know how to do, something they can be proud of when they achieve it.
>
> (Kappel, 1960, p. 38)

Goals must of course be translated into school programs and activities. In turn, the explicit behaviors that a program will help the student develop are its immediate objectives and should be related to the statement of long-range purpose that initiated it. It is these more immediate aims that must be made precise enough to guide instruction and evaluation.

Educators can lose sight of the relationship between short-term objectives and long-range purposes. Thus, some teachers and administrators assert that their "real" objectives are intangible or unidentifiable and hence impossible to state in terms of student change. The claim is made that the student develops certain attitudes, values, or skills that are not immediately apparent and may not reveal themselves until much later in his life, long after he has finished school. The argument is sometimes lodged by a teacher that these are the only important objectives he has, and that he cannot anticipate even what form or direction these outcomes will take. This is sometimes summed up by the cliché "More is caught than taught."

Now, no one will deny that there are many intangible or unidentifiable long-term outcomes, good and bad, that result from instruction. Often more *is* "caught than taught." But to claim that these intangibles are the only important objectives for the classroom teacher is to adopt the untenable position of being unable to prove that one has ever taught anything. For purposes of meaningful evaluation at least, objectives must be stated in terms of more readily observable outcomes or changes on the student's part, so that one can determine whether he is making progress in learning during the course. The remainder of this chapter will concern itself with these more immediate objectives of instruction. The hope is that the outcomes sought in day-to-day instruction will work toward the realization of long-range goals. However, longitudinal data are needed to determine the ultimate success of a school's programs in fulfilling its broad declarations of purpose.

What are some of the ways the more immediate educational objectives have been stated? The following illustrate one approach:

To demonstrate the distributive properties of multiplication
To prove the pythagorean theorem
To discuss the nineteenth-century critics
To illustrate Bernoulli's law
To point out the causes of the Civil War
To parse compound sentences

In all these statements, the verb describes a teacher action, what the teacher intends to do. Thus, the model or plan is teacher-centered rather than pupil-centered. As discussed earlier, a basic premise of this book is that education is a systematic process which helps the learner change in various intended ways. Therefore, the desired changes in the pupil become the primary focus for the direction and evaluation of instruction. Statements of the teacher's intent are helpful in his planning of classroom tactics only after he has answered the question of why such actions are being performed in the first place. The teacher's activities are means to an end and not ends in themselves. Otherwise they could be performed in the absence of students. The reason a teacher carries out any instruction activity is to help the students change in some way, to assist them in developing a new ability or improving an existing one. This is the reason teachers prove, plan, demonstrate, read, lecture, and so forth; it is the change in the student that is the real reason, the objective, of the teacher's activity.

Another method of stating educational objectives is to detail the subject matter to be covered, as in the following examples:

Newton's law of motion
Mexico
The causes of the Civil War
Pages 59–68 of the text
Hamlet
The House of the Seven Gables
The Boston Tea Party

The teacher who states objectives in this fashion will tend to feel the model has been realized if the content area in question has been mentioned or "covered" in class or in assignments. But given that the end of education is to help the learner change in some intended way, then statements of content to be covered do not describe the variety of ways in which the content is to be learned.

Content by itself is often meaningless. What the student is supposed to be able to do with it should be the important issue. Subject matter is frequently used to develop intellectual skills or processes in the student and should not become an end in and of itself. Thus statements of content are incomplete as models for instruction and evaluation. Not only do they fail to convey the changes hoped for in the students, but often by themselves they are unimportant or trivial, and in fact serve merely as vehicles for developing certain abilities or skills in the students. Bruner (1966, p. 73) has put it this way:

> One must begin by setting forth the intellectual substance of what is to be taught, else there can be no sense of what challenges and shapes the curiosity of the student. Yet the moment one succumbs to the temptation to "get across" the subject, at that moment the ingredient of pedagogy is in jeopardy. For it is

only in a trivial sense that one gives a course to "get something across," merely to impart information. There are better means to that end than teaching. Unless the learner also masters himself, disciplines his taste, deepens his view of the world, the "something" that is got across is hardly worth the effort of transmission.

While some overemphasize the content to be covered in their statements of educational objectives, others overemphasize the desired pupil behavior divorced from content. Formulations such as "develop critical thinking," "develop problem-solving skills, and "increase the students' facility in interpreting data" are sometimes put forward as educational objectives. These statements do describe sought-for behaviors, albeit in a vague way, but they are much too general to give the classroom teacher direction in planning instruction or evaluation. Two immediate questions arise. The first is, Think critically about what? Here the content area must be specified. Critical thinking skills may differ from discipline to discipline; but more important, unless the content area is also specified, planning, selecting materials, and determining methods of presentation become impossible. The second question is, What is meant by critical thinking? Here the behavior must be further specified. That is, what evidence will one accept that critical thinking is taking place or has taken place?

In view of the preceding discussion, the characteristics of an acceptable model emerge. First, statements of educational objectives flow from broad, long-range, and visionary statements of goals. The short-term objectives must be stated in an unambiguous way so that they are clear not only to the teacher himself but also to his colleagues with whom he may wish to share his observations. In order to communicate objectives precisely and unambiguously, it is not enough to specify independently the content to be covered or the abilities and skills the student is expected to acquire. Communicability requires accurate statements of the expected behavioral changes related to a particular content area. If a teacher is successful in clarifying his objectives in his own mind and expressing them clearly to his colleagues, then it becomes possible to plan instruction and evaluation procedures more intelligently.

The remainder of this chapter will address itself to the problem of how to achieve suitable levels of communicability in statements of educational objectives.

Operationalism

In order to understand better the nature of a clear, unambiguous statement of an educational objective, a brief description of operationalism is in order at this point.

In 1927 Percy Bridgman, in his book *The Logic of Modern Physics*, pointed out the need for defining terms in physics not by furnishing dictionary synonyms but by describing the operations used to measure the construct. This concept was adopted by psychologists of the period, becoming an integral part of the school known as behaviorism. Behaviorism found it important to define psychological constructs in terms of those "point-at-able" behaviors of the subject which the psychologist would accept as evidence the construct was present.

Nominal definitions involve the use of synonyms. Thus "intelligence" is defined in *Webster's Seventh New Collegiate Dictionary* as follows:

in·tel·li·gence \in-'tel-ə-jən(t)s\ *n, often attrib* **1 a** (1) **:** the capacity to apprehend facts and propositions and their relations and to reason about them **:** REASON, INTELLECT; *also* **:** the use or exercise of the intellect esp. when carried on with considerable ability (2) *Christian Science* **:** the basic eternal quality of divine Mind **b :** mental acuteness **:** SHREWDNESS **2 :** an intelligent being; *esp* **:** ANGEL **3 :** the act of understanding **:** COMPREHENSION **4 a :** information communicated **:** NEWS **b :** information concerning an enemy or possible enemy or an area; *also* **:** an agency engaged in obtaining such information

By permission. From *Webster's Seventh New Collegiate Dictionary* © 1967 by G. & C. Merriam Co., Publishers of the Merriam-Webster Dictionaries.

One of the synonyms for "intelligence" in the above definition is "intellect," which in turn is defined as:

in·tel·lect \'int-ᵊl-,ekt\ *n* [ME, fr. MF or L; MF, fr L *intellectus*, fr. *intellectus*, pp. of *intellegere*] **1 a :** the power of knowing as distinguished from the power to feel and to will **:** the capacity for knowledge **b :** the capacity for rational or intelligent thought esp. when highly developed **2 :** a person of notable intellect

By permission. From *Webster's Seventh New Collegiate Dictionary* © 1967 by G. & C. Merriam Co., Publishers of the Merriam-Webster Dictionaries.

Now, one of the difficulties psychologists would have using a nominal definition of "intelligence" is that it lacks precision, since the words used in the definition are themselves synonyms open to various interpretations. For purposes of clear communication, psychologists desired an unambiguous statement of meaning, and turned to the operational definition. In this approach, the operations one performs to measure the construct become the definition of the construct. Operationally, then, "intelligence" might be defined as "a person's score resulting from the administration of the California Test of Mental Maturity." The shift in meaning between the two statements that follow illustrates the key difference between the definitions. "A person received a score of 130 on the California Test of Mental Maturity because *he is intelligent*." In this nonoperational statement, the descriptive concept "intelligent" is being used as an explanatory word; that is, intelligence is given as the reason for the performance. "A person is considered intelligent because *he received a score of 130* on the California Test of Mental Maturity." In this operational statement, "intelligent," a descriptive word, is being defined by the person's performance on a given task. While one may disagree, no latitude is left for different interpretations of the term. Thus, whenever the psychologist uses the word "intelligence" in his work, the reader has been apprised of the exact and limited meaning that can be properly attached to the construct. Further, anyone wishing to replicate the psychologist's findings can exactly reproduce the construct in other samples because the method for measuring it has been spelled out, and can be followed like a recipe in a cookbook.

Teachers often employ words like "understanding," "appreciation," "motivation," and "comprehension" in describing students or stating educational objectives. These terms, like "intelligence," are nominal or descriptive rather than explanatory constructs. Take the word "understanding." No one has ever seen "understanding"; instead this word is a construct invented to describe certain observable behavior patterns. For example, if a student applies a previously learned principle to solve a novel problem or successfully lists a series of dates or translates graphic information into his own words, the teacher may say he "understands." However, there is often confusion in the way these constructs are used. Consider the following statements: "The student has successfully solved the new problem in chemistry because he understands"; "He understands because he has successfully solved the problem." In the first statement, the descriptive concept "understands" is being used as an explanatory word; that is, understanding is given as the reason for successful completion of the problem. The second usage is an operational statement; "understands" is being defined by the student's performance on the problem.

Using operational rather than nominal definitions will make statements of educational objectives clear and easier to communicate to others. Words like "understanding," "comprehension," and "appreciation" will take on more precise behavioral meanings and will not be open to various interpretations.

The effects of operationalism on defining educational objectives

The effect of operationalism on the defining of educational objectives has been felt in two distinct but related quarters. The first influence can be seen in Ralph Tyler's work in curriculum and instruction. Tyler built on the premise that education is a systematic process designed to help produce behavioral changes in the learner through the vehicle of instruction. The function of evaluation, as he saw it, is primarily to determine the extent to which students have or have not changed in relation to the set of desired behaviors. Since evaluation data were used mainly to make judgments at the conclusion of the course, evaluation became largely summative in nature; it stressed grading, selecting, and certifying students and determining the effectiveness of the curriculum compared with alternative curricula.

While in charge of the Eight-year Study of secondary education for the Progressive Education Association, Tyler was one of the first people to emphasize successfully the need to define educational objectives clearly in terms of overt student behavior and content. A group of high schools labeled "progressive" were attempting to develop new curricula and approaches to instruction and learning. Those in charge of the programs anticipated that their graduates might find it difficult to gain admission to college. Since these students would not have followed "traditional" high school curricula, some colleges might feel that they lacked sufficient prerequisite credits. The Eight-year Study enlisted the cooperation of colleges to admit graduates of progressive high schools so that the development of the new programs could continue and be carefully evaluated longitudinally through the four years of higher education. For comparison purposes, students from traditional schools were also followed longitudinally. It became critical to the success of this study that the objectives of the new curricula be stated in clear, unambiguous terms so that appropriate evaluation instruments and techniques could be developed to appraise the effectiveness of the curricula. Smith and Tyler's book *Appraising and Recording Student Progress* (1942), one of five volumes describing the Eight-year Study, contains example after example of educational objectives operationalized in terms of content area and overt student behavior: that is, given a certain content area, how the student should think, feel, or act.

The current National Assessment Project, directed by Tyler, requires that educational objectives accepted as desirable by lay panels be further clarified by prototype exercises which give students an opportunity to demonstrate the behavior implied in the statement of the objective but not as yet fully operationalized. This requirement ensures that a panel's statements will not be so vague as to make their interpretation a matter of widely diverging opinions.

The importance of carefully defined educational objectives for the improvement of curricula and instruction is central to all of Tyler's work. In his rationale for curriculum development (1950), statements of objectives serve as the first step in the development of improved curriculum materials and instruction techniques. Further, these same statements serve as guides to teachers in building evaluation instruments to appraise the effectiveness of newly developed materials or techniques. Though Tyler's approach did include evaluation of instruction in progress, the main emphasis, as noted earlier, was summative—on appraising how well objectives had been obtained at the end of a course or curriculum. Unfortunately, it was this aspect of Tyler's thinking rather than the improvement of instruction and curriculum that received the greatest emphasis by those who subsequently used his work.

The centrality of clear statements of educational objectives in the designing and improvement of programmed and computer-assisted instruction is an outgrowth of the second influence of operational definitions. This influence was exerted by psychologists involved in the problems of education and particularly in problems of developing, sequencing, and testing new instruction units. Investigators like Gagné, Glaser, Stolurow, and Mager were chiefly interested in *why* rather than whether an instruction program worked or failed to work. Such an orientation allows for the improvement of the instruction package while it is in the development phase and avoids the necessity of introducing radical changes into a completed program. Each step in the program is evaluated in relation to very carefully defined behavioral criteria. Thus, from the point of view of evaluation, the emphasis is primarily formative rather than summative.

This trend can be traced to World War II and the Korean conflict, when the military turned to psychologists for help in training personnel. The psychologists were asked to develop efficient programs to equip trainees with identical, well-defined competences. It was clear what the desired skill was and how it was to be used. Further, barring changes in technology, the skill was meant to be fairly permanent. Thus, when the Army wished to train soldiers to assemble and disassemble an M-1 rifle, the psychologists began by specifying the training objectives through a technique that became known as task analysis. In task analysis, the skill desired at the end of the unit of instruction is described and then analyzed into "a repertoire of behavior structures" that must be sequentially built up to arrive at the terminal performance. In training, unlike education, the rote learning of a sequence of steps will assure that the trainee acquires the desired skill. Prescribing the most efficient set of hierarchial steps to be learned then becomes essential. The task description details the competence the trainee should have acquired at the end of the course; the task analysis goes beyond this to specify the conditions thought to be directly related to learning. Thus task analysis takes the "macro" performance and breaks it down into "micro" behavior components, which are the building blocks of instruction. Formative evaluation determines how well the students are assimilating these various intermediate components.

The techniques of the military psychologists were adopted with modifications by experimental psychologists investigating classroom learning, by those interested in programmed instruction, and more recently by those working in the area of computer-assisted instruction. The first step in the development of auto-instruction materials is a detailed description of the desired terminal behavior.

One of the purposes of the detailed task analysis is to bring principles derived from learning theory to bear on the sequencing of instruction. The school of learning theory the psychologist adheres to will of course determine the character of the resulting analysis and the methods used in the instruction sequence. For example, a developmental psychologist might begin by diagnosing the developmental level of the child and then apply the learning process associated with that level. Eleanor Gibson (1965), on the other hand, approaches the analysis of learning to read from a perceptual point of view. She postulates three sequential and to some degree overlapping phases in acquiring this skill: recognizing and making discriminative responses to printed letters, figures, and symbols; decoding letters into sounds; and utilizing higher order units of the previously learned structures. Various principles from perceptual psychology are then used in planning how to teach at each of these three stages.

Gagné (1963) offers an example of a task analysis done from a stimulus-response frame of reference. Figure 2-1 shows how he has analyzed two objectives in mathematics.

The two desired objectives in the figure have been broken into subordinate behaviors. Each element is thought to support the learning of each succeeding topic in the hierarchy, as indicated by the arrows. So, for example, it is hypothesized that the student must learn to use parentheses to group names for the same whole number (V*b*) before he can be expected to identify numerals for whole numbers, employing the closure property (IV*d*).

Regardless of the frame of reference, the educator can devise and carefully test instruction strategies based on experimental and theoretical psychology by analyzing the structure of the desired objective and postulating a hierarchy and sequence.

The technique of task analysis is not equally applicable to all areas of the curriculum. In education, unlike training, we do not expect all students to use the skills acquired in a course in exactly the same way. The higher one proceeds up the education ladder, the more apparent this becomes. For example, two students might learn to apply the principles of physics as a result of an introductory course in high school. However, one may use this ability only in his role as an intelligent citizen who reads with interest the progress being made in the space program, whereas the other may build on these same behaviors when he elects a college major in physics. At the elementary school level, on the other hand, certain skills, like the acquisition of the number facts, are prerequisites for later instruction. Here training techniques may be more appropriate, although even at this level some of the new curriculum projects do not stress the rote learning of the number facts.

From the point of view of evaluation, the work of the task analysis group is most helpful for an understanding of formative evaluation. The task

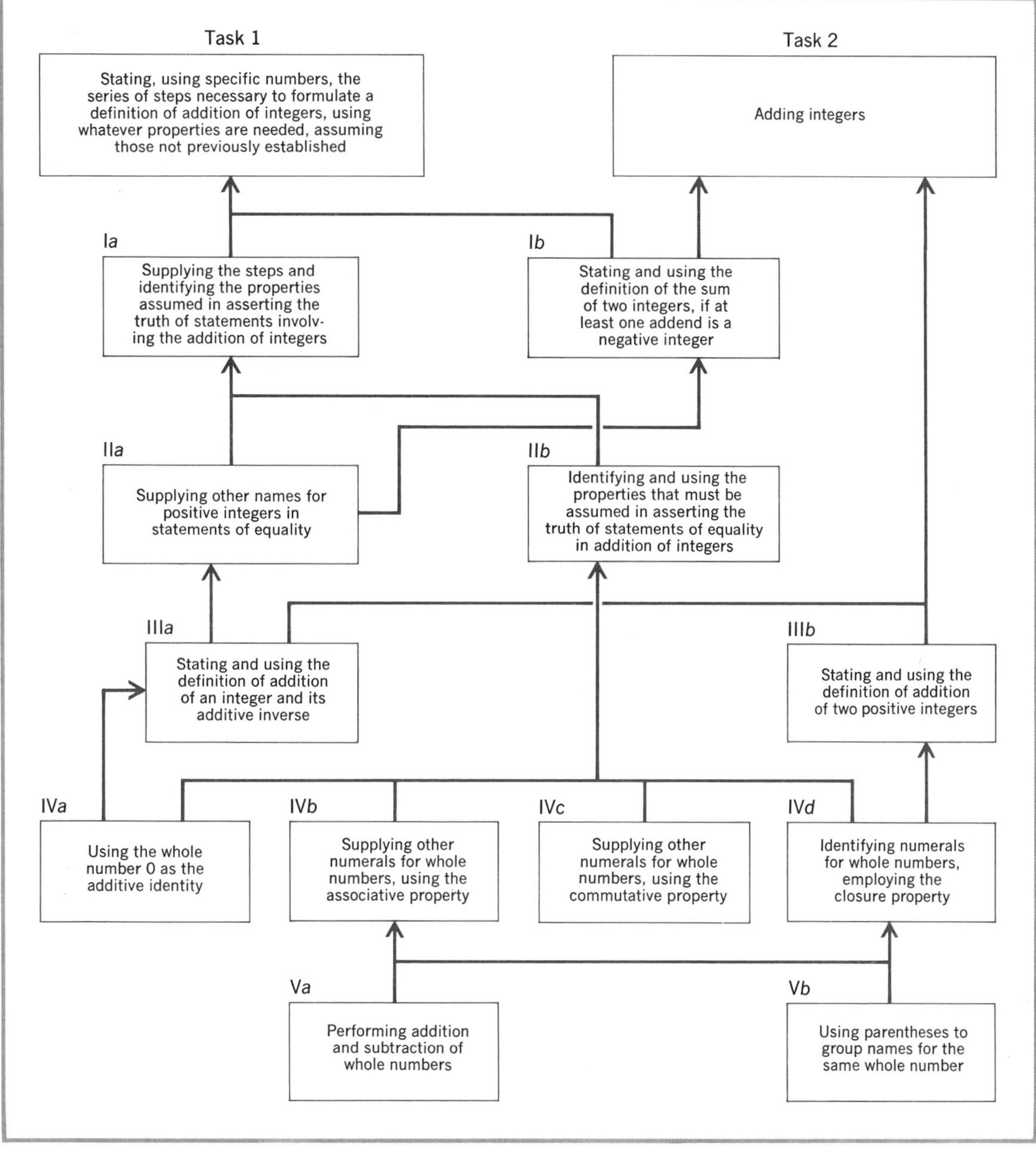

FIGURE 2-1. Task analysis of two objectives in mathematics. (R. M. Gagné. Learning and proficiency in mathematics. *Mathematics Teacher*, 1963, **56,** 623.)

analysis group evaluates students on whether or not they can correctly perform each of the behaviors subordinate to the final task that are contained in the instruction program. Tyler's work, on the other hand, is most useful for an understanding of summative evaluation since the emphasis is on the state of the individual after instruction in relation to a set of overall objectives.

One might justifiably ask at this point, How

does a formative unit of instruction differ from a summative unit? One can always discover units within units, depending how far away one stands to view "the curriculum." For example, while the topic of polynomials may be considered a section of an algebra course, it in turn might be broken down into smaller parts, such as the powers of X, factoring, the use of factoring to solve quadratic equations, and so forth. These may be considered as isolated units or, as is more common, they may be viewed as forming a hierarchy in which each element is part of an overall structure with definite relationships existing between the parts—for example, the powers of X must be understood before the definition of a polynomial is attempted. The work of Airasian (1968) demonstrates that in some cases these postulated relationships hold up under inspection while in others the sequencing is not so critical in the realization of the overall objectives.

The distinction, then, between a formative and a summative unit is not clear-cut. The major difference lies not in the amount of content covered, that is, how closely one stands in viewing the curriculum, but rather in the purpose of the evaluation. If the evaluation is performed to determine how well students have mastered various elements in a postulated hierarchy so that decisions can be made on how instruction should best proceed, then it is formative in nature. Chap. 6 discusses this aspect of evaluation in more detail. However, given the same amount of content material, if the purpose is simply to grade the student at the end of one unit before proceeding to the next, then the evaluation is summative.

The approaches of the task analysis school and the Tyler school complement and supplement one another despite their differences in emphasis. For example, Tyler stops at a description of the desired behavior, whereas task analysis goes on to prescribe a very detailed behavior repertoire. That is, the two viewpoints differ on the degree of specificity required in the statement of the objective. Tyler's approach does not require the specificity which Gagné's entails in his description of each small step in the instruction program.

The two points of view are in agreement, however, that any instruction program has as its goal helping students to change their behavior; the student must be able to do something after instruction that he could not do before. Further, they agree that the degree of success of a program must be assessed, and that this can be done only by an evaluation or measurement of student performance; hence the objectives must be stated in terms which are operational, involving reliable observation and allowing no leeway in interpretation. Both approaches feel formative and summative evaluation are important; the principal differences lie in emphasis. This can be most clearly seen if we consider a table or matrix of specifications.

Table of specifications

There are several approaches to building useful instruction and evaluation models. Figures 2-1 and 2-3 in the present chapter are examples of the task analysis approach. Chapter 6 presents still another alternative. A third method is basic in Tyler's approach to curriculum development: the construction of a table of specifications, which presents the course objectives in the form of a two-dimensional matrix. There are three steps involved in arriving at a table of specifications.

First, general objectives stated temporarily in rather broad terms must be decided upon by the teacher or curriculum builder. The next step is to break each of these objectives down into a content component and a behavior component. The content area refers to the specific subject matter to be conveyed. The behavior refers to what we want the student to do with the material. A later section of this chapter (see pages 30 to 37) will describe in more detail procedures that can be used in specifying behaviors. The determination of content components is naturally a function of the subject-matter specialist.

Once the first two steps have been accomplished, a table of specifications can be drawn up. This is a two-dimensional matrix or chart. Each behavior is listed along one dimension and the different content areas are specified along the

	BEHAVIORS													
CONTENT	A.0 *Recall and recognition of materials learned*	A.1 *Terminology*	A.2 *Specific facts*	A.3 *Conventions*	A.4 *Trends and sequences*	A.5 *Classifications and categories*	A.6 *Criteria*	A.7 *Methodolgy*	A.8 *Principles and generalizations*	A.9 *Theories and structures*	B.0 *Application of knowledge to new concrete situations*	B.1 *Nonquantitative*	B.2 *Quantitative*	C.0 *Use of skills involved in understanding science problems*
1.0 Evolution														
1.1 Data of Change														
1.2 Theories of Change														
2.0 Diversity of Types and Unity of Pattern														
3.0 Genetic Continuity														
4.0 Complementarity of Organisms and Environment														

FIGURE 2-2. Section of Table of Specifications for Secondary-level Biological Sciences. [Adapted from E. Klinckmann. The BSCS grid for test analysis. *BSCS Newsletter*, 1963, No. 19, p. 20 (Biological Sciences Curriculum Study, University of Colorado). Reproduced in Chap. 4 of this book, pages 64–65.]

second axis. The intersection of each behavior (*B*) with each content area (*C*) results in a chart composed of $C \times B$, or *n* behavior-content cells. Figure 2-2, taken from Chap. 4, contains a section of a master Table of Specifications for Secondary-level Biological Sciences.

Several cells in a matrix may well be empty, meaning that the specific behavior for that particular content is not an objective of the course. Chap. 4 discusses in detail various ways of assigning values to instructional objectives represented by target cells in a table of specifications. However, no matter how these values are assigned, the relative value afforded each cell in the matrix helps to assure that any test instrument built will have content validity. This may be accomplished by having the number of test items written to measure each objective in the matrix approximate the value assigned to each cell.

The way in which the table of specifications is used points up the distinction between formative and summative evaluation and between formative and summative objectives. Each target cell of the specifications matrix is a summative objective, and the students' attainment of the objectives is evaluated at the end of the course or sequence. Generally it is not possible to evaluate the student on the total matrix in one summative test; therefore, evaluation at the end of the course usually is directed at a sample of the cells with the view of making inferences about the students' performance on the whole table.

Formative evaluation, on the other hand, deals with only a segment rather than the total specifications matrix, but in a detailed and exhaustive fashion. Parts of the table have a separable existence in that they can be learned in relative isolation from other parts. Thus, it is conceivable that one cell may be treated independently as a learning unit, or it may be that a row or column of cells naturally go together in the learning process. Once a separable learning unit has been identified, it is necessary then to identify the components of the more broadly conceived objectives in that part of the matrix.

An example of analyzing a broader objective into formative components is contained in Fig. 2-1. Another example can be seen in the work of Glaser and Reynolds (1964), illustrated in Fig. 2-3.

The top box in Fig. 2-3, "Telling time to the nearest minute," can be considered as one objective in a large first-grade arithmetic specifications table, and hence a summative objective. It is divided into three subobjectives: writing the hour and minute in sequence, saying the minutes and hours in sequence, and saying "o'clock" on the hour. In turn, each of these is broken down into component behaviors, which are arranged hierarchically (designated by the symbols A1, A2, A3, etc.). These separate components are also related to the task horizontally (indicated by the lateral lines in the flowchart). The analysis continues backward from the overall objective until the curriculum builder is willing to accept certain behaviors as assumed at this particular age or grade.

Such a flowchart serves as an instruction model by detailing the sequence of steps which must be followed to reach the overall objective, telling time. Steps A1 and A2 are prerequisites for step A3, which must be accomplished before step A4 is taken. From the analysis of the overall behavior a set of programmed materials can be developed and tested.

At each point in the programmed material, the students' progress toward the overall objective can be evaluated and the results used to determine whether they should go on to the next step or be remedied at the present level. If a considerable number have not attained step A3 after exposure to the programmed material, a new approach to steps A1 and A2 might be developed and tried out.

The illustrations from Gagné and Glaser and Reynolds are exemplars, formidable in scope and detail. Because of constraints of time and training, classroom teachers may not be able to produce such expert plans. Furthermore, the average teacher is generally not called upon to develop a programmed text, a computer-aided instruction program, or even new curriculum material. Instead an existing curriculum is given, generally in the form of a textbook and accompanying teacher's guide. Thus for formative evaluation the task facing the classroom teacher is one of inferring the specific objectives of the curriculum builder from the materials. Chapter 6 details methods the teacher may use in analyzing given instruction material.

Up to this point, we have dealt with the concepts of formative and summative evaluation and with formative and summative objectives, and have described the development and use of a table of specifications. Further, we have characterized the set of statements of objectives as an instruction model. Certain pitfalls that destroy the model's usefulness have been discussed. Let us now consider the actual writing of objectives, formative and summative, that qualify as parts of a useful instruction model.

Defining objectives

The teacher concerned with good instruction and evaluation faces the following basic tasks, each of which necessitates a clear statement of objectives:

1. He must decide upon the goals and summative objectives he hopes to obtain at the end of his course.
2. He must select commercially available materials (textbooks, teacher guides, filmstrips, topics, etc.) or himself create materials to provide the learning experiences which will help the student attain these goals. This involves developing formative objectives.
3. He must provide continuity and sequence to help the student integrate sometimes apparently isolated experiences.
4. He must measure or evaluate the student's performance in relation to the goals originally chosen.

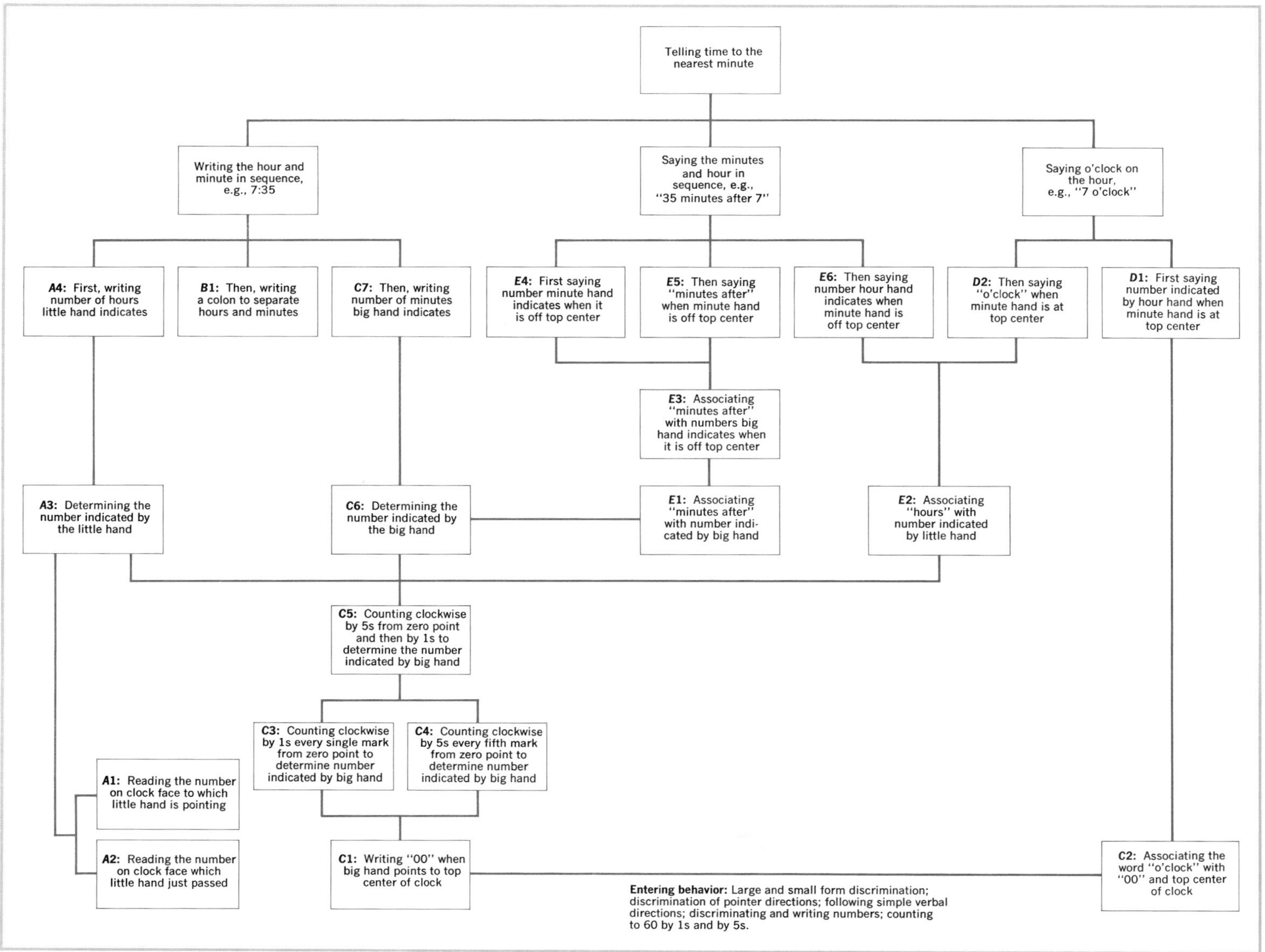

FIGURE 2-3 An example of breaking an overall objective into component behaviors. [R. Glaser & J. Reynolds. Instructional objectives and programmed instruction: A case study. In C. M. Lindvall (Ed.), *Defining educational objectives*. Pittsburgh: University of Pittsburgh Press, 1964. P. 64.]

How does one go about stating an educational objective? A statement of an objective describes the ways in which students are to be changed by their interaction with the process and materials of instruction. It should be expressed in terms of desired student behavior and content areas. More importantly, it must succeed in communicating the teacher's intent. Communicating is successful when any knowledgeable person in the same area can look at a student's behavior or products and decide whether or not the objective has been reached. In fact, the degree to which different people can agree on whether a performance reflects an operational statement has been suggested by Dodd (1943) as an index of the reliability or clarity of the statement.

It must be firmly kept in mind, however, that success in communicating an objective does not mean the objective is necessarily desirable or possible. These attributes must be determined using the criteria suggested in Chap. 1. Proper formulation of an objective makes accurate observation possible but does not necessarily assure its educational worth or guarantee that students can attain it.

There has been considerable disagreement over the degree of specificity or level of precision necessary in the statement of an objective. We would hold that this should be determined at least partly by the learning experiences planned for the student and partly by the generalizability of the behavior sought for. If the student is expected to interact almost exclusively with learning materials contained in a programmed text or computer, then the objectives must be stated very specifically. This is true if for no other reason than that such materials cannot be built without a detailed task description. However, as the variables in the learning situation increase (teacher, number of students, and type of materials among others), it becomes more difficult to arrive at highly specific formulations. Statements of the objectives hoped for at the end of a course or year would transcend the particulars of the content used during instruction and instead describe more generalizable and transferable skills. For example, "analysis of dramatic works" may be a long-term objective. Notice the statement refers to all rather than to any single dramatic work. In order to achieve this aim, the teacher will undoubtedly start out with a particular play, perhaps one in which the development of plot and character are sharp. He then may proceed to another and more complex work. However, the objective is the ability to analyze many types of dramatic works, not merely the two or three studied in class. Each of the master tables of specifications in Part II gives examples of long-term objectives. For example, *Analysis of organizational principles of punctuation* in Table 21-1, the Table of Specifications for Writing (see page 770), is a generalized statement applicable to a wide range of writings, such as letters, essays, and articles.

The following are statements of long-range objectives:

The ability to apply social science generalizations and conclusions to actual social problems.

The ability to present ideas (orally or in writing) in accordance with the principles of grammar.

The ability to apply principles of propaganda to political arguments.

The ability to apply the principles of the number system.

The ability to relate principles of civil liberties and civil rights to current events.

Each of these statements subsumes several major principles and literally millions of possible applications of them. The objectives imply that though the student was given practice in the various principles on only a small number of illustrations, this should result in his acquiring the more generalizable and transferable skills associated with the higher mental processes described above.

The specificity of the content and behavior of the skill can vary, of course. Occasionally the content description of a long-term objective is relatively detailed. This is particularly true of courses that are sequential and therefore require knowledge or comprehension of specifics to build on, perhaps in hopes of subsequently developing more generalizable skills. Further, if the subject matter is viewed as more or less closed and not likely to change much in the future, the objectives may stress knowledge or comprehension. If, on the other hand, the content of the discipline is expanding rapidly, then the aims may stress transferable competences.

Ultimately, of course, the generalized behavior described in statements of long-term objectives must be operationalized for evaluation purposes. Some would do this by indicating precisely the kinds of evidence they would accept as establishing the presence of the behavior. As mentioned above, the National Assessment Project uses this technique.

Describing observable manifestations of the general aim ensures that teachers are in fact communicating with one another about the same outcome. For example, a fairly common statement of objective in social studies is that "The student understands the Bill of Rights." The behavior sought for is understanding; the content, the Bill of Rights. However, if this objective was given to a large group of social studies teachers and they were asked to tell what evidence they would accept that the student "understands," there would be almost as many interpretations as teachers. Some would accept the student's ability to recite the Bill of Rights as evidence of understanding, whereas others would ask that he apply its principles to situations he has not previously encountered in classwork. If the word "understands" were used alone, without further specification, two teachers in adjoining classrooms could think they were attempting to realize the same objectives when in fact both the desired and the actual student outcomes in the two classes were entirely different. Thus, in discussing a supposedly common objective, two teachers might very well engage in conversation without communication.

The reason for the failure in communication is that many words teachers use to describe student behavior are subject to various interpretations. The following are examples of such terms:

1. Knowledge
2. Comprehension
3. Critical thinking
4. Understanding
5. Appreciation
6. Has an interest in
7. Fully appreciates
8. Grasps the significance of
9. Learns
10. Respects
11. Expands his horizons
12. Works effectively
13. Speaks effectively
14. Speaks correctly
15. Reads with ease
16. Uses basic skills

The difficulty with terms such as the first eleven listed above is that the behaviors involved cannot be directly observed. One cannot see "understanding" or observe "critical thinking" or hear or feel "appreciation." The presence or absence of such actions can only be inferred from an overt, observable performance or manifest product of the student's. One says in effect, "If I observe the student doing a certain thing after instruction that he could not do before, I will call this action knowledge." Similarly, one might say, "I will accept this product of the student's as evidence of the existence of critical thinking."

In examples 12 to 16, while the behavior is observable in that one can directly witness reading, speaking, and working, misinterpretations arise because of the modifier or object of the verb. The criteria for correctness, effectiveness, and ease differ from person to person, as does the meaning of "basic skills."

To define objectives so that they are not open to multiple interpretations involves translating the verbs that are open to inference into action verbs that entail direct observation and, when appropriate, specifying the criteria to be used in interpreting adverbs. The overt behavior or the procedure for observing it must be described so that all who read the description can agree whether or not a given student's performance or product testifies to the presence of the objective in question.

Thus, while "understands," "appreciates," "learns," and the like are perfectly good words and can be used in an initial, general statement of an objective, they should be further clarified by the use of active or operational verbs not open to misinterpretation. The following are examples of such "point-at-able" verbs:

1. To state
2. To recognize
3. To distinguish true statements from false
4. To match dates with battles
5. To put into one's own words
6. To evaluate
7. To predict
8. To volunteer answers
9. To use conventional grammatical forms
10. To punctuate according to conventional rules
11. To compute
12. To select correct answers from several alternatives
13. To take out library books about the Civil War
14. To name the instruments in a band
15. To state relationships existing between data
16. To list the consequences of a course of action

These verbs describe what the student does to demonstrate that he has achieved the objective in question. Any intelligent person, given the opportunity to observe his performance, can decide whether what he is doing or has produced is acceptable evidence that the objective has been realized. When there is reliable agreement among readers on the behaviors that are acceptable, then the objective has been satisfactorily stated. Again, it must be borne in mind that the use of action verbs does not by itself mean the objective is desirable or possible. Chapters 7 to 10 illustrate further how behavioral statements can be made more specific, precise, and operational.

Lysaught and Williams (1963) demonstrate how a generally defined objective, "to acquire a basic understanding of earth-sun relationships," is made more specific by listing operations and overt, observable behaviors (see Table 2-1). As the degree of specificity increases, so does the reliability of the observations.

The action verb used to specify one's objectives can help determine the instruction sequence and the evaluation procedures to be used. For example, suppose the objective is stated, "The student has knowledge of the decimal system." Until "has knowledge" is further defined, this objective is subject to various interpretations. One teacher might decide that he will accept as evidence of knowledge the student's ability to write numerals in expanded notation. Another teacher may expect the student to be able to perform addition operations involving carrying in bases other than ten.

The first teacher might want the instruction sequence to emphasize practice in breaking numerals into units, tens, hundreds, and onward, using exponential notation for each position. The evaluation procedure used might simply present the student with a set of numerals and ask him to write them using expanded notation. The fact that a place system will work with any base need not be taught and other bases need not be introduced. The behaviors sought by the second teacher would call for practice in a system of notation with a different base, say, base two or seven, as well as in addition. The evaluation procedure might require the student to perform addition which involves carrying on a set of numerals in a base not specifically studied, say, base three. The point is that since the behaviors accepted as evidence of knowledge differ, the instruction sequences will probably differ, as will the situation planned to allow the student to demonstrate his mastery of the objective.

It should be pointed out that a teacher might define "has knowledge" by using not one but multiple action verbs. For example, the broadly stated objective "The student has knowledge of the causes of the Civil War" might be further specified as follows:

The student can list the causes of the Civil War.
The student can distinguish true causes from false ones.
The student can explain the causes in his own words.

Since these behaviors appear to differ, each should be considered separately in planning instruction and evaluating outcomes. Whether in fact they are separate behaviors may be determined from an inspection of how a student performs on items designed to measure each of the three.

In addition to describing behavior in terms of operational verbs, some would urge even further specification in the stating of objectives. For

Table 2-1 An Example of Further Specifying of a Generally Defined Objective

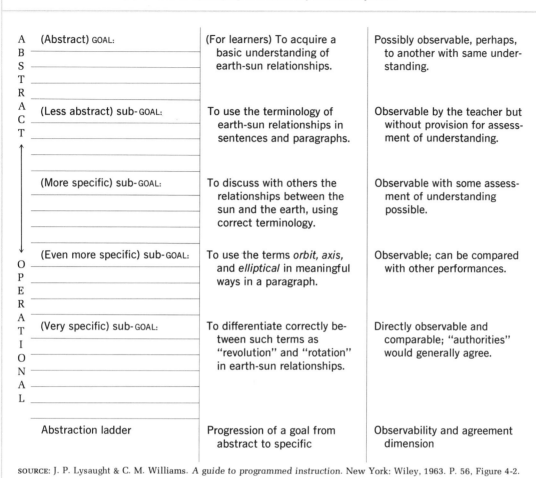

ABSTRACT ↕ OPERATIONAL		
(Abstract) GOAL:	(For learners) To acquire a basic understanding of earth-sun relationships.	Possibly observable, perhaps, to another with same understanding.
(Less abstract) sub-GOAL:	To use the terminology of earth-sun relationships in sentences and paragraphs.	Observable by the teacher but without provision for assessment of understanding.
(More specific) sub-GOAL:	To discuss with others the relationships between the sun and the earth, using correct terminology.	Observable with some assessment of understanding possible.
(Even more specific) sub-GOAL:	To use the terms *orbit, axis,* and *elliptical* in meaningful ways in a paragraph.	Observable; can be compared with other performances.
(Very specific) sub-GOAL:	To differentiate correctly between such terms as "revolution" and "rotation" in earth-sun relationships.	Directly observable and comparable; "authorities" would generally agree.
Abstraction ladder	Progression of a goal from abstract to specific	Observability and agreement dimension

SOURCE: J. P. Lysaught & C. M. Williams. *A guide to programmed instruction.* New York: Wiley, 1963. P. 56, Figure 4-2.

example, two additional characteristics of a good statement have been pointed out by Mager (1962). The first of these is that the important conditions under which the behavior is expected to occur are described. Consider this objective: "Given a sketch and map of the world, the learner must be able to correctly mark the ocean currents with arrows on the map." Here the details of the evaluation situation and what is expected of the student in it are contained in the statement of the objective.

The second characteristic Mager requires is a designation of how accurate the performance must be. Thus the previous objective could be further clarified by stating it this way: "Given a sketch and map of the world, the student must be able to correctly mark *six* ocean currents with arrows on the map in a fifteen-minute time period." Here the number of correct responses is indicated along with the time in which the student must finish. A minimal acceptable performance is described, giving further specificity to the statement of the objectives.

Gagné (1965, p. 34), summarizing the high degree of specificity described in the work of Mager (1962) and Miller (1961), breaks a statement of an objective into four basic components. The four are illustrated in this sentence taken from Gagné: "Given two numerals connected by the sign +, the student states orally the name of the number which is the sum of the two." First, the statement contains words denoting the stimulus situation which initiates the performance ("Given two numerals connected by the sign +"). Second, there is an action word or verb which denotes observable behavior ("states"). Third, there is a term denoting the object acted upon (which sometimes is simply implied). Finally, there is a phrase indicating the characteristics of the performance that determine its correctness ("the name of the number which is the sum of the two").

It is not necessary, of course, to state all objectives in a format as precise as that described above. Not all require the degree of specificity called for in Gagné's four steps. Certainly it is not necessary to follow any one approach in clarifying objectives. (Other approaches are discussed later in the chapter; see pages 38 to 40.) What level of clarity *is* called for? When the objective has been operationalized in terms of behaviors so that readers can reliably agree on whether a student's performance or product fulfills the objective, then the objective is sufficiently specific. Thus the criterion is effectiveness of communication. The following are behavioral statements of varying degrees of specificity used to clarify educational objectives:

Translate unorganized data into groups, tables, or charts.
To read a clock and be able to tell time by saying the time aloud with accuracy at one-minute intervals.
The student can describe the causes of some current problems of American society.
To write two examples of verse in iambic pentameter.
To read an oral thermometer correctly to the nearest tenth of a degree.
Match given names with given events in American history.
The student can apply the principles of physics.
Given a situation new to the student, he can solve it correctly by applying previously learned principles of Newton's laws of motion in one class period.
The pupil can correctly print his name, keeping all the letters between the given lines on the paper.
Given a car with any induced disability in the motor so that the car will not start, the student can identify the trouble, requisition the correct parts, and make the necessary repairs so that the car is operable again in two class periods.
The student can disassemble and assemble a carburetor correctly in one class period.
The pupil sings songs learned in class during free play time.
The student composes his own songs.
The student can support his preference for a given poem by citing evidence of structural properties in the work itself.
Given fifty true-false questions regarding communism, the student can correctly answer forty-five.
The student can do twenty push-ups in ninety seconds.
Given dictation, the student can transcribe shorthand notes on the typewriter with a maximum of two errors.
Given basic arithmetical formulas for area, volume, and distance, the student can choose a suitable translation from alternatives supplied.
The student can expand a number expressed in base seven.
The student asks for additional references to works by an author.
Given a number expressed in base two, the student can translate the number into base ten.

Thus there are various levels of precision with which one can specify an objective and still succeed in communicating the intention of instruction.

In the above examples, one cannot always determine from the statement itself whether it embodies a formative, a long-term summative, or an intermediate summative objective. Generally, however, statements of long-term summative objectives are less specific in regard to content and describe more generalized and transferable abilities than formative, which define both the behaviors sought and the content required much more explicitly.

Further, statements of formative and short-term summative aims are indistinguishable from one another more often than not. The time point at which the evaluation takes place (while instruction is still going on rather than after it has been concluded) and the reason for the evaluation (diagnosis, remediation, and planning rather than grading or judging) would have to be known before one could classify a statement as either formative or short-term summative in nature.

Objectives by national curriculum groups

During the past ten years, various groups, composed mainly of university scholars and skilled teachers who are interested in curriculum reforms, have produced new statements of objectives for almost all the subjects taught in the elementary and secondary schools. The objectives of some of these curriculum projects are discussed for each of the separate disciplines in Part II of this book. In the case of a few projects, the Cambridge Conference on School Mathematics (1963), for example, the goals have been visionary and long-range so that educators may have some informed notion of the direction in which they should be moving. However, in most cases these groups have translated their objectives into curriculum materials for classroom use.

Since many classroom teachers are using these materials, the question of the relation between teachers' objectives and the nationally developed objectives arises.

First, the statements from the national curriculum groups serve as a frame of reference for the teacher, indicating what a selected body of experts regards as important in the discipline. The teacher can then compare his objectives—what he thinks is important—with those of the national group, which thus provide him with a basis for informed choice.

Second, the teacher must carefully study the objectives of the given curriculum in relation to his particular situation. Knowledge of previous instruction, available time for teaching, the specific needs of a group of students, the interest or qualifications of the teacher may individually or collectively militate against the inclusion of selected objectives contained in the curriculum.

Third, since the text and materials are the embodiment of the objectives of the curriculum, the teacher should carefully study the content. The reader is referred to Chap. 6, which describes techniques for discovering the structure and hence the actual objectives contained in instruction units.

The benefits of cooperation in defining objectives

The stating of educational objectives so they are useful in the planning and evaluation of instruction is not a particularly easy job. It takes a great deal of careful thought and analysis, which in turn requires large amounts of time. The job can be made easier if teachers in the same department or grade level within a school or system develop the objectives in common. Cooperation among colleagues yields at least three benefits.

Time savings An individual teacher seldom has the necessary time to write the objectives for all his courses with clarity and reliability. A group of teachers can benefit, therefore, if they divide the labor. In this way, formative and summative objectives can be more meaningfully stated in a much shorter period of time. Once again we should emphasize that it is impossible and sometimes not very desirable to state all the objectives for a course behaviorally. Many worthy results can only be incompletely formulated at best, and others develop as the course unfolds. However, in the planning of instruction and evaluation, it is desirable to specify as many of the anticipated outcomes behaviorally as possible. A collective effort by teachers will minimize the time and work entailed in specifying the objectives.

A common core of objectives Group participation in the formulation of objectives also helps ensure that students in the same school system, taking the same course of study from different teachers, are working toward the attainment of an identical core of objectives. Too often classes taking the "same" course from different teachers demonstrate entirely different behaviors at its end. Not that there is no longer room for individual teachers to have unique educational objectives; however, the determination of *all* the objectives for a common course cannot be left entirely to the discretion of each instructor. Within the framework of a common set of objectives, there is still sufficient leeway for the teacher to work toward certain goals unique to his class. Further, in realizing the unified aims, he can follow many paths. Common objectives do not have to imply common methods and thus need not stifle the creativity of the individual teacher. Admittedly some capable and conscientious educators may not value the idea of an identical core of objectives. They may instead place a premium on diversity and differences between their own and others' objectives. But to the extent that equivalence is seen as valuable, cooperative development of objectives is highly recommended.

Formation of item pools A further benefit of group participation in the writing of objectives is that the cooperation can lead to the formation of a common item pool. An item pool consists of a large number of test items, each coded by behavioral aim, content, and approximate grade level, that are used to build tests to evaluate student outcomes. A full discussion of the formation and use of item pools is given in Chap. 11. Suffice it to say at this point that cooperation among teachers in the specification of objectives is a necessary first step in the development of an item pool.

Strategies in developing educational objectives

A group of teachers beginning the job of formulating common course objectives might start with a discussion of the desired terminal behaviors and content areas or, as suggested in Chap. 6, with an analysis of the text and materials used in the course. This will probably result in broadly stated goals that will have to be further specified as previously described. There are three other strategies that may be employed in identifying and detailing course objectives: analysis of teacher tests, classroom observation, and use of the *Taxonomies of Educational Objectives.*

Analysis of teacher tests The group might well begin with an analysis of the tests used by various teachers to evaluate course outcomes. By analyzing test items in the light of the instruction experiences of the learners, one can draw inferences about the kinds of behaviors required of them in answering each question. It must be emphasized that the validity of such inferences depends on an accurate knowledge of the background the student brings to the item, because the same item may elicit entirely different behaviors from different people. For example, a test question may involve simple recall of memorized facts for students who have previously discussed the specific material in class, while it may require high-level analysis and application for those who have never seen the material but have covered principles that relate to the solution of the problem during the instruction period.

Despite differences in student backgrounds, however, this first strategy can give insights into the actual behaviors intended by the teachers, thereby providing some guidelines for specifying objectives.

Classroom observation for unexpected outcomes Another way to begin the formulation of objectives is by observing classes for the purpose of identifying student changes *actually* taking place. Actual student performance reveals the objectives of instruction. Often these are quite different from the objectives stated at the outset of the course.

In this strategy, the observer looks not only for expected terminal behaviors but also for unanticipated outcomes. The procedure is based on the assumption that while the text or course materials have content validity, it is difficult to envision *all* the resulting behaviors beforehand. Too often unexpected negative and positive outcomes of the course are overlooked because evaluation is concentrated exclusively on the previously formulated objectives. Course improvement can be obtained more readily when the picture of the outcomes is complete. The Illinois Elementary School Science Project utilizes such an approach in assessing its strengths and weaknesses. As J. Myron Atkin (1963), then Project Director, put it,

> Project personnel are beginning a series of classroom observations in an attempt to identify unexpected behavioral changes in students. In the customary methods of course development and evaluation, such a procedure seems backwards. The standard practice is to identify the changes desired in the students, then see if the course is effective in producing the changes. Instead we are observing classes for the purpose of identifying changes that are not predicted or recognized at the start [p. 132].

Classroom observation, then, not only helps identify post hoc "objectives" but also results in more comprehensive and reliable evaluation. Evaluation involves a description of course outcomes. To be valid, this description must be complete. It must detail not only the extent to which desired objectives have been obtained but also the positive and negative effects that their realization has on students. For example, in the "traditional" arithmetic curricula of the 1930s and 1940s, great emphasis was placed on computational skills and social utility. It was not realized that such objectives were often obtained at the expense of positive attitudes toward mathematics as well as of higher-level understandings of its structure and properties until the "modern" math groups began to look at a wider range of mathematical behaviors. Thus, while expected outcomes often can be realized, the teacher should always try to determine what is unexpectedly forfeited or gained by his decisions about objectives. Classroom observation can give a teacher these needed insights.

The Taxonomy of Educational Objectives The third strategy in developing objectives is the use of the *Taxonomy of Educational Objectives* (Bloom, 1956; Krathwohl, Bloom, & Masia, 1964). The two parts of the work will each be summarized in the Appendix to Part I of this book and will be treated more fully in Chaps. 7 to 10 and in the chapters in Part II. However, a brief description of the volumes is in order here.

Handbook 1, *Cognitive Domain*, was published in 1956. The *Cognitive Domain* classifies objectives which involve intellectual tasks. For some of these objectives the student has to do little more than remember; for others he must determine the essential problem and then reorder given material or combine it with ideas, methods, or procedures previously learned. Handbook 2, *Affective Domain*, was completed in 1964, and categorizes objectives which emphasize a feeling line, an emotion, or a degree of acceptance or rejection. A third volume, on the psychomotor domain, has not yet been started.

The *Taxonomy* is a result of the work of a group of college examiners who developed the classification system for educational objectives to facilitate communication among themselves and with colleagues about objectives, test items, and test procedures. They were aware that the lack of such a systematically operationalized procedure for classification was responsible for much of the ambiguity, misinterpretation, and conversation without communication which greeted educators' attempts to share ideas about objectives and testing.

In the definition of educational objectives, as we have seen, both the behavior and the content must be specified. The *Taxonomy* places the behavioral aspect of the objective within a hierarchical framework: each category is assumed to include behavior more complex, abstract, or internalized than the previous category. These categories are arranged along a continuum from simple to complex in the *Cognitive Domain*. In the *Affective Domain*, the continuum is one of internalization; that is, the ordering describes the process by which a given phenomenon or value progresses from a level of bare awareness to a position of some power to guide or control a person's actions.

Each of the hierarchial categories in both volumes is illustrated by examples of educational objectives taken from the literature, a description of the behaviors involved at the particular level, and sample test items designed to measure the described behaviors.

Teachers may use the *Taxonomy* in various ways. First, if a group of teachers have a set of objectives stated in broad terms, the *Taxonomy* can help specify them operationally. Thus, if one of the objectives is that "The student understands economic information present in graphic form," the teachers can translate this statement into more precise terms by choosing various behaviors specified in the categories of the *Taxonomy* or by using the illustrative test items as operational statements. Either way, the *Taxonomy* provides teachers struggling over the problems of stating objectives with a common point of reference on which to center their discussions.

Second, the test items in the *Taxonomy* can be used by teachers as models in building similar items peculiar to their content-area needs. The *Taxonomy* abounds in model items designed to measure all types of behavior from simple to very complex. Teachers generally have little difficulty testing straightforward recall of facts but are not so adept at building items to measure higher-order mental processes or affective outcomes of instruction. One of the main criticisms teachers level at objective tests is that they examine only very simple skills. The model items in the *Taxonomy* should disabuse them of this notion and give them direction in constructing items measuring more complex behavior. In fact, one of the principal values of the cognitive *Taxonomy* has been that it has called teachers' attention to the fact that it is possible to measure more complex objectives than recall of facts.

Third, the *Taxonomy* can suggest classes of objectives not previously considered. Used in this manner, it becomes a guide for a more comprehensive evaluation of course outcomes by proposing behaviors to be looked for that may not be anticipated at the outset of the course. This generates a more valid description of the results of a particular instruction sequence, which in turn should lead to improved instruction in the future.

Fourth, the *Taxonomy* can be used to help teachers analyze standardized tests. As Krathwohl (1964) has said, teachers have the feeling that standardized tests are

> . . . put together by experts who know more than they do, and though they may feel a vague discontent with the test, too often they do not analyze the content of these tests against their objectives to determine how well they match. Here again, by using the taxonomy as a translating framework one can compare the test with the teachers' goals. In its simplest form this may be a determination of the proportion of items in each of the major taxonomy categories. This alone is often enough information to help a teacher determine a test's relevance [p. 34].

Finally, if a teacher is interested in building a valid achievement test himself, he should try to have his test items reflect the relative emphasis instruction has placed on the various taxonomic categories.

REFERENCES

Airasian, P. W. Formative evaluation instruments: A construction and validation of tests to evaluate learning over short time periods. Unpublished doctoral dissertation, University of Chicago, 1968.

Atkin, J. M. Some evaluation problems in a course content improvement project. *Journal of Research in Science Teaching*, 1963, **1**, 129–132.

Bloom, B. S. (Ed.) *Taxonomy of educational objectives: The classification of educational goals.* Handbook 1. *Cognitive domain.* New York: McKay, 1956.

Bridgman, P. *The logic of modern physics.* New York: Macmillan, 1927.

Bruner, J. S. *Toward a theory of instruction.* Cambridge, Mass.: The Belknap Press of Harvard University Press, 1966.

Cambridge Conference on School Mathematics. *Goals for school mathematics: The report of the Cambridge Conference on School Mathematics.* Boston: Houghton Mifflin, 1963.

Dodd, S. C. Operational definitions operationally defined. *American Journal of Sociology,* 1943, **48,** 482–489.

Gagné, R. M. Learning and proficiency in mathematics. *Mathematics Teacher,* 1963, **56,** 620–626.

Gagné, R. M. The analysis of instructional objectives for the design of instruction. In R. Glaser (Ed.), *Teaching machines and programmed learning.* Vol. 2. *Data and directions.* Washington, D.C.: National Education Association, 1965. Pp. 21–65.

Gibson, E. J. Learning to read. *Science,* 1965, **148,** 1066.

Glaser, R., & Reynolds, J. Instructional objectives and programmed instruction: A case study. In C. M. Lindvall (Ed.), *Defining educational objectives.* Pittsburgh: University of Pittsburgh Press, 1964. Pp. 47–76.

Kappel, F. R. *Vitality in a business enterprise.* New York: McGraw-Hill, 1960.

Klinckmann, E. The BSCS grid for test analysis. *BSCS Newsletter,* 1963, No. 19, pp. 17–21 (Biological Sciences Curriculum Study, University of Colorado).

Krathwohl, D. R. The taxonomy of educational objectives: Use of the cognitive and affective domains. In C. M. Lindvall (Ed.), *Defining educational objectives.* Pittsburgh: University of Pittsburgh Press, 1964. Pp. 19–36.

Krathwohl, D. R., Bloom, B. S., & Masia, B. B. *Taxonomy of educational objectives: The classification of educational goals.* Handbook 2. *Affective domain.* New York: McKay, 1964.

Lindvall, C. M. (Ed.) *Defining educational objectives.* Pittsburgh: University of Pittsburgh Press, 1964.

Lysaught, J. P., & Williams, C. M. *A guide to programmed instruction.* New York: Wiley, 1963.

Mager, R. F. *Preparing objectives for programmed instruction.* San Francisco: Fearon, 1962.

Miller, R. B. The newer roles of the industrial psychologist. In B. Gilner (Ed.), *Industrial psychology.* New York: McGraw-Hill, 1961. Pp. 353–380.

Smith, E. R., & Tyler, R. W. *Appraising and recording student progress.* (Adventure in American Education Ser., Vol. 3) New York: Harper, 1942.

Tyler, R. W. *Basic principles of curriculum and instruction.* Chicago: University of Chicago Press, 1950.

3
Learning for Mastery

Introduction

Each teacher begins a new term or course with the expectation that about a third of his students will adequately learn what he has to teach. He expects about a third to fail or to just "get by." Finally, he expects another third to learn a good deal of what he has to teach, but not enough to be regarded as "good students." This set of expectations, supported by school policies and practices in grading, is transmitted to the students through the grading procedures and through the methods and materials of instruction. This system creates a self-fulfilling prophecy such that the final sorting of students through the grading process becomes approximately equivalent to the original expectations.

This set of expectations, which fixes the academic goals of teachers and students, is the most wasteful and destructive aspect of the present education system. It reduces the aspirations of both teachers and students, it reduces motivation for learning in students, and it systematically destroys the ego and self-concept of a sizable group of the students who are legally required to attend school for ten to twelve years under conditions which are frustrating and humiliating year after year. The cost of this system in reducing opportunities for further learning and in alienating youth from both school and the community at large is so great that no society can tolerate it for long.

Most students (perhaps more than 90 percent) can master what we have to teach them, and it is the task of instruction to find the means which will enable them to master the subject under consideration. A basic task is to determine what we mean by "mastery of the subject" and to search for the methods and materials which will enable the largest proportion of our students to attain such mastery.

In this chapter we will consider one approach to learning for mastery and the underlying theoretical concepts, research findings, and techniques required. Basically, the problem of developing a strategy for mastery learning is one of determining how individual differences in learners can be related to the learning and teaching processes.

Background

Some societies can utilize only a small number of highly educated people in the economy and can provide the economic support for only a small proportion of the students to complete secondary or higher education. Under such conditions, much of the effort of the schools and the external examining system is devoted to finding ways of rejecting the majority of students at various points in the education system and to discovering the talented few who are to be given advanced educational opportunities. Such societies invest a great deal more in predicting and selecting talent than in developing it.

The complexities of the skills required by the work force in the United States and in other highly developed nations mean that we can no longer operate on the assumption that completion of secondary and advanced education is for the few. The increasing evidence (Bowman, 1966; Schultz, 1963) that investment in the education of humans pays off at a greater rate than does capital investment suggests that we cannot return to an economy of scarcity of educational opportunity.

Whatever might have been the case previously, highly developed nations must seek to find ways to increase the proportion of the age group that can successfully complete both secondary and higher education. The question is no longer one of finding the few who can succeed. The basic problem is to determine how the largest proportion of the age group can learn effectively the skills and subject matter regarded as essential for their own development in a complex society.

However, given another set of philosophic and psychological presuppositions, we may express our concern over the consequences for intellect and personality of a lack of clear success in the learning tasks of the school. Learning throughout life (continuing learning) will become necessary for an increasingly larger segment of the work force. If school learning is regarded as frustrating and even impossible by a sizable proportion of students, then little can be done at later levels to kindle a genuine interest in further learning. School learning must be successful and rewarding as one basis for ensuring that learning can continue throughout life as needed.

Even more important in modern society is the malaise about values. As the secular society becomes more and more central, the values remaining for the individual have to do with hedonism, interpersonal relations, self-development, and ideas. If the schools frustrate the students in the latter two areas, only the first two are available to them. Whatever the case may be for each of these values, the schools must strive to assure all students of successful learning experiences in the realms of ideas and self-development.

There is little question that the schools now do provide successful learning experiences for some students—perhaps as many as one-third. If the schools are to provide successful and satisfying learning experiences for at least 90 percent of the students, major changes must take place in the attitudes of students, teachers, and administrators as well as in teaching strategies and the role of evaluation.

The normal curve

As educators we have used the normal curve in grading students for so long that we have come to believe in it. Achievement measures are designed to detect differences among our learners—even if the differences are trivial in terms of the subject matter. We then distribute our grades in a normal fashion. In any group of students we expect to have some small percentage receive A grades. We are surprised when the figure differs greatly from about 10 percent. We are also prepared to fail an equal proportion of students. Quite frequently this failure is determined by the rank order of the students in the group rather than by their failure to grasp the essential ideas of the course. Thus, we have become accustomed to classifying students in about five levels of performance and assigning grades in some relative fashion. It matters not that the failures of one year performed at about the same level as the C students of another year. Nor does it matter that the A students of one school do about as well as the F students of another.

Having become "conditioned" to the normal distribution, we set grade policies in these terms and are horrified when some teacher attempts to recommend a very different distribution of marks. Administrators are constantly on the alert to control teachers who are "too easy" or "too hard" in their grading. A teacher whose grade distribution is normal will avoid difficulties with administrators. But even more important, we effectively convince students that they can only do C or D work by our grading system and even by our system of quizzes and progress testing. Finally, we proceed in our teaching as though only the minority of our students should be able to learn what we have to teach.

There is nothing sacred about the normal curve. It is the distribution most appropriate to chance and random activity. Education is a purposeful activity, and we seek to have the students learn what we have to teach. If we are effective in our instruction, the distribution of achievement should be very different from the normal curve. In fact, we may even insist that our educational efforts have been *unsuccessful* to the extent that the distribution of achievement approximates the normal distribution.

"Individual differences" in learners are facts that can be demonstrated in many ways. That students vary in many ways can never be forgotten. The notion that these variations must shape learning standards and achievement criteria is a reflection more of our policies and practices than of the necessities of the case. The basic task in education is to find strategies which will take individual differences into consideration but which will do so in such a way as to promote the fullest development of the individual.

The variables for mastery-learning strategies

A learning strategy for mastery may be derived from the work of Carroll (1963), supported by the ideas of Bruner (1966), Glaser (1968), Goodlad and Anderson (1959), Morrison (1926), Skinner (1954), and Suppes (1966). In presenting these ideas, we will refer to some of the research findings which bear on them. However, our main concern here is with the major variables in a model of school learning and the ways in which these variables may be utilized in a strategy for mastery learning.

Put in its briefest form, the model proposed by Carroll (1963) makes it clear that if the students are normally distributed with respect to *aptitude* for some subject (mathematics, science, literature, or history, for example) and all the students are provided with exactly the *same instruction* (same in terms of amount and quality of instruction and time available for learning), the end result will be a normal distribution on an appropriate measure of achievement. Furthermore, the relation between aptitude and achievement will be fairly high (a correlation of +.70 or higher is to be expected if the aptitude and achievement measures are valid and reliable). Conversely, if the students are normally distributed with respect to aptitude but the kind and quality of instruction and the amount of time available for learning are made appropriate to the characteristics and needs of *each* student, the majority of students may be expected to achieve mastery of the subject. And the relation between aptitude and achievement should approach zero. It is this basic set of ideas we wish to develop in the following discussion.

Aptitude for particular kinds of learning

Teachers have come to recognize that individuals do differ in their aptitudes for particular kinds of learning, and over the years test makers have developed a large number of instruments to measure these differences. In study after study, it has been found that aptitude tests are relatively good predictors of achievement criteria (achievement tests or teacher judgments). Thus, for example, a good set of mathematics aptitude tests given at the beginning of a course in algebra will bear a correlation of as high as +.70 with the achievement tests given at the end of the year.

The use of aptitude tests for predictive purposes and the high correlations between such tests and achievement criteria have led many of us to the view that high levels of achievement are possible only for the most able students. From this it is an easy step to some notion of a causal connection between aptitude and achievement. The simplest notion of causality is that the students with high levels of aptitude can learn the complex ideas of the subject while the students with low levels of aptitude can learn only the simplest ideas of the subject.

Quite in contrast to this is Carroll's view that *aptitude is the amount of time required by the learner to attain mastery of a learning task*. Implicit in this formulation is the assumption that, given enough time, all students can conceivably attain mastery of a learning task. If Carroll is right, then learning to mastery is theoretically available to all, if we can find the means for helping each student. This formulation of Carroll's has the most fundamental implications for education.

One type of support for this view is to be found in the grade norms for many standardized achievement tests. These norms demonstrate that selected criterion scores achieved by the top students at one grade level are achieved by the majority of students at a later grade level. Further support is provided by studies of students who are allowed to learn at their own rate. These show that although most students eventually reach mastery of each learning task, some achieve it much sooner than do others. (Atkinson, 1967; Glaser, 1968).

Can all students learn a subject equally well? That is, can all master a learning task at a high level of complexity? From a study of aptitude distributions in relation to student performance, we have become convinced that there are differences between the learners at the extremes and the remainder of the population. At the top of the aptitude distribution (the upper 1 to 5 percent), there are likely to be some students who have an unusual talent for the subject. These are able to learn and use the subject with greater fluency than others. The student with special aptitudes for music or foreign languages can learn these subjects in ways not available to most other people. Whether this is a matter of native endowment or the effect of previous training is not clear, although this must vary from subject to subject. It is likely that some people are born with sensory organs better attuned to sounds (music, language, and so forth) than are others, and that these constitutional characteristics give them special advantages in learning the related subjects. For other areas of study, such factors as special training and particular interests may develop these high-level aptitudes.

At the other extreme of the aptitude distribution, there are students with special disabilities for particular kinds of learning. The tone-deaf will have great difficulty learning music; the color-blind will have special problems in learning art; and the individual who thinks in concrete forms will be at a disadvantage in learning highly abstract conceptual systems, as in philosophy. Again, it is believed these may constitute less than 5 percent of the distribution, but this will vary with the subject and the aptitudes.

In between are approximately 90 percent of the learners, about whom the writers believe (as does Carroll) that aptitudes are predictive of rate of learning rather than the level or complexity of learning that is possible. Thus, we are expressing the view that, given sufficient time and appropriate types of help, 95 percent of students (the top 5 percent plus the next 90 percent) can learn a subject with a high degree of mastery. To say it another way, we are convinced that the grade of A as an index of mastery of a subject can, under appropriate conditions, be achieved by up to 95 percent of the students in a class.

It is assumed that it will take some students more effort, time, and help to achieve this level than it will others. There will be those for whom the effort and help required may make it prohibitive. Thus, to learn high school algebra to a point of mastery may require more than a year for some students but only a fraction of a year for others. Whether mastery learning is worth the great effort the first group must invest is highly problematic. A basic problem for a mastery-learning strategy is to find ways of reducing the amount of time the slower students require to a point where it is not prohibitively long.

It is not assumed that aptitude for particular learning tasks is completely stable. There is evidence (Bloom, 1964; Hunt, 1961) that aptitudes may be modified by environmental conditions or learning experiences in the school and the home. The major task of education programs concerned with learning to learn and general education should be to produce positive changes in the students' basic aptitudes. It is likely that these aptitudes can be most markedly affected during the early years in the home and during the elementary school period. Undoubtedly, however, some changes can take place at later points in a learner's career.

However, even if marked changes do not occur in the individual's aptitudes, it is highly probable that more effective learning conditions can reduce the amount of time which all students and especially those with lower aptitudes require to master a subject. It is this problem which must be directly attacked by strategies for mastery learning.

Quality of instruction

The schools have usually proceeded on the assumption that there is a standard classroom situation for all students. Typically, this has been expressed in the teacher-student ratio of 1 to 30, with group instruction as the central means of teaching. There is the expectation that each teacher will present the subject in much the same way as other teachers. The standardization is further emphasized by the adoption of a textbook which specifies the instructional material to be provided each class. Closely related to this is the extensive research during the past fifty years which has sought to find the one instructional method, material, or curriculum program that is best for all students.

Thus, over the years, researchers have fallen into the "educational trap" of specifying quality of instruction in terms of good and poor teachers, teaching, instructional materials, curriculum—all as related to group results. They persist in asking such questions as, What is the best teacher for the group? What is the best method of instruction for the group? What is the best instructional material for the group?

One may start with the very different assumption that individual students may need very different types and qualities of instruction to achieve mastery. That is, the same content and objectives of instruction may be learned by different students as the result of very different types of instruction. Carroll (1963) defines the *quality of instruction in terms of the degree to which the presentation, explanation, and ordering of elements of the task to be learned approach the optimum for a given learner.*

Much research is needed to determine how individual differences in learners can be related to variations in the quality of instruction. There is evidence that some students learn quite well through independent study while others need highly structured teaching-learning situations (Congreve, 1965). It seems reasonable to expect that some students will need more concrete illustrations and explanations than will others, some will need more examples to get an idea than others, some will need more approval and reinforcement than others, and some may need to have several repetitions of the explanation while others may be able to get it the first time.

We believe that if every student had a very good tutor, most of them would be able to learn a particular subject to a high degree. The good tutor attempts to find the qualities of instruction (and motivation) best suited to a given learner. And there is some evidence (Dave, 1963) that middle-class parents do make an effort to tutor their children when they believe that the quality of instruction in school does not enable their children to learn a particular subject. In an unpublished study, one of the writers found that one-third of the students in an algebra course in a middle-class school were receiving as much tutorial instruction at home in the subject as group instruction at school. Their grades for the course were comparatively high, and the relationship between their mathematics aptitude scores at the beginning of the year and their achievement in algebra at the end was almost zero. In contrast, for the students who received no instruction other than the regular classroom instruction, the relationship between their mathematics aptitude scores and their algebra achievement scores was very high (+.90). While this type of research needs to be replicated, this small study makes it evident that the home-tutoring help was providing the quality of instruction needed by the recipients to learn the algebra—that is, the instruction was adapted to the needs of the individual learners.

The point to be stressed is that the quality of instruction should be assessed in terms of its effects on individual learners rather than on random groups of learners. We may hope that the research of the future will lead to the definition of the qualities and kinds of instruction needed by various *types* of learners. Such research may suggest more effective group instruction, since it is unlikely that the schools will be able to provide instruction for each learner separately.

Ability to understand instruction

In most courses at the high school and college levels, there are a single teacher and a single set of instructional materials. If the student finds it easy to understand the teacher's communications about the learning and the instructional material (usually a textbook), he has little difficulty learning the subject. If he finds it hard to understand the instruction, the material, or both, he is likely to have great difficulty learning the subject. *The ability to understand instruction may be defined as the ability of the learner to understand the nature of the task he is to learn and the procedures he is to follow in the learning of the task.*

Here is a point at which the students' abilities interact with the instructional materials and the instructor's skill in teaching. For the student in our highly verbal schools, it is likely that the ability to understand instruction is determined primarily by verbal ability and reading comprehension. These two measures of language proficiency are significantly related to achievement in the majority of subjects, and they are highly correlated (+.50 to +.60) with grade-point averages at the high school or college level. What this suggests is that verbal ability (independent of specific aptitudes for each subject) determines some general ability to learn from teachers and instructional materials.

While it is possible to alter an individual's verbal ability by appropriate training, there are limits to the amount of change that can be produced. Most change in verbal ability can be produced at the preschool and elementary school levels, with less and less change being likely as the student gets older (Bloom, 1964). However, vocabulary and reading skill may be improved to some extent at all age levels, even though the utility of this approach diminishes with increasing age. Improvements in verbal proficiency should result in improvements in the learner's ability to understand instruction.

The greatest immediate payoff in dealing with this ability is likely to come from modifications in instruction to meet the needs of individual students. There is no doubt that some teachers do attempt to tailor their instruction to a given group of students. Many focus on the middle group of their students, others on the top or bottom group. However, these are reflections of teachers' habits and attitudes, and are by no means determinants of what it is *possible* for them to do. Given help and various types of aids, individual teachers can find ways of modifying their instruction to fit the differing needs of their students.

Group study Group study procedures should be available to students as they need it. In our own experience we have found that small groups (two or three students) meeting regularly to go over points of difficulty in the learning process were most effective, especially when the students could help each other without any danger of giving each other special advantages in a competitive situation. Where learning can be turned into a cooperative process with everyone likely to gain from it, small-group learning procedures can be very effective. Much depends on the composition of the group and the opportunities it affords each person to expose his difficulties and have them corrected without demeaning one member and elevating another. The group process provides occasions for the more able students to strengthen their own learning as they help others grasp an idea through alternative explanations and applications.

Tutorial help The one-to-one relationship between teacher and learner represents the most costly type of help, and should be used only where alternative procedures are not effective. However, tutoring should be available to students as they need it. Ideally, the tutor should be someone other than the teacher, since he should provide a fresh way of viewing an idea or process. He must be skillful in detecting the points of difficulty in the student's learning, and should help him in such a way as to free the student from continued dependence on him.

Another approach to differences in students' ability to understand instruction is to vary the instructional material.

Textbooks Textbooks vary in the clarity with which they explain a particular idea or process. The fact that one text has been adopted by the school or the teacher does not necessarily mean that others cannot be used at particular points in the instruction when they would be helpful to a student who can't grasp the idea from the adopted book. The task here is to determine where a learner is having difficulty understanding the instruction, and then provide alternative textbook explanations if they are more effective at that point.

Workbooks and programmed instruction units These may be especially helpful for some students who can't grasp the ideas or a procedure in the textbook form. Some students need the drill and specific tasks which workbooks can provide. Others need the small steps and frequent reinforcement built into programmed units. Such materials may be used in the initial instruction or as students encounter specific difficulties in learning a given unit or section of the course.

Audiovisual methods and academic games Some students may learn a particular idea best through concrete illustrations and vivid graphic explanations. For these learners, filmstrips and short motion pictures which can be used by individual students as needed may be very effective. Others may need concrete experiences as with laboratory experiments, simple demonstrations, and blocks and other relevant apparatus in order to comprehend an idea or task. Academic games, puzzles, and other interesting but not threatening devices may be useful. Here again, the point is that some ways of communicating and comprehending an idea, problem, or task may be especially effective for some students although others may not use or need such materials and methods. We need not place the highest priority for all on abstract and verbal ways of instructing.

With regard to instructional materials, the suggestion is not that particular materials be used by particular students throughout the course. It is that each type of material may serve as a means of helping individual students at selected points in the learning process—and that each student may use whatever variety of materials he finds useful as he encounters difficulties in his learning.

In all use of alternative methods and materials of instruction, the essential point to be borne in mind is that these are attempts to improve the *quality of instruction* in relation to the ability of each student to *understand the instruction*. As feedback methods inform teachers of particular errors and difficulties the majority of students are having, it is to be expected that the regular group instruction will be modified so as to correct these problems. As particular students are helped, the goal should be not only to help the student over specific learning difficulties but also to enable him to become more independent in his learning and to help him identify the alternative ways by which he can comprehend new ideas. But most important, the presence of a great variety of instructional materials and procedures should help both teachers and students to overcome feelings of defeatism and passivity about learning. If the student can't learn in one way, he should be reassured that alternatives are available to him. The teacher should come to recognize that it is the learning which is important, and that alternatives exist to enable all or almost all the students to learn the subject to a high level.

Perseverance

Carroll defines perseverance as *the time the learner is willing to spend in learning*. Obviously, if a student needs a certain amount of time to master a particular task and he spends less than this amount in active learning, he is not likely to learn the task to the level of mastery. Carroll attempts to differentiate between spending time at learning and the amount of time he is actively engaged in the learning.

Perseverance does appear to be related to attitudes toward and interest in learning. In the *International Study of Educational Achievement in Mathematics* (Husén, 1967), the relationship between number of hours of homework per week reported by students (a crude index of perseverance) and the number of years of further education desired by them is +.25.

There is no doubt that students vary in the amount of perseverance they bring to a specific learning task. However, they appear to approach different learning tasks with different degrees of persistence. The student who gives up quickly in his efforts to learn an academic subject may persevere an unusually long time in learning to repair an automobile or play a musical instrument. It would appear to us that as a student finds the effort rewarding, he is likely to spend more time on a particular learning task. If, on the other hand, he is frustrated in his learning, he must in self-defense reduce the amount of time he devotes to it. Though the frustration level of students may vary, we believe that all must sooner or later give up a task if it is too painful for them.

While efforts may be made to increase the amount of perseverance in students, it is likely that manipulation of the instruction and learning materials will be more effective in helping them master a given learning task, regardless of their present level of perseverance. Frequency of reward and evidence of success in learning can increase the student's perseverance in a learning situation. As he attains mastery of a given task, his perseverance in a related learning task is likely to increase.

In research at the University of Chicago, it is being found that the demand for perseverance may be sharply reduced if students are provided with the instructional resources most appropriate for them. Frequent feedback accompanied by specific help in instruction and material as needed can decrease the time (and perseverance) required. Improvement in the quality of instruction (explanations and illustrations) may lessen the amount of persistence necessary for a given learning task.

There seems to be little reason to make learning so difficult that only a small proportion of the students can persevere to mastery. Endurance and unusual perseverance may be appropriate for long-distance running; they are not great virtues in their own right. The emphasis should be on learning, not on vague ideas of discipline.

Time allowed for learning

Throughout the world, schools are organized to give group instruction with definite periods of time allocated for particular learning tasks. A course in history at the secondary level may be planned for an academic year, another course may be planned for a semester, and the amount of instruction time allocated for a subject like arithmetic at the fifth grade may be fixed. Whatever the amount of time allowed by the school and the curriculum for particular subjects or learning tasks, it is likely to be too much for some students and not enough for others.

For Carroll, the time spent on learning is the key to mastery. His basic assumption is that aptitude determines the rate of learning, and that most if not all students can achieve mastery if they devote the amount of time needed to the learning. This implies that the student must be *allowed* enough time for the learning to take place.

There seems to be little doubt that students with high levels of aptitude are likely to be more efficient in their learning and to require less time for it than those with lower levels of aptitude. Whether most students can be helped to become highly efficient learners in general is a problem for future research.

The amount of time students need for a particular kind of learning has not been studied directly. One indication comes from studies of the amount of time they spend on homework. In reviewing the data from the *International Study of Educational Achievement in Mathematics* (Husén, 1967) on how long 13-year-old students worked on mathematics homework, we find that if we omit the extreme 5 percent of the subjects, the ratio is roughly 6 to 1. That is, some students spend six times as much time on mathematics homework as do others. Other studies of student use of time suggest that this is roughly the order of magnitude to be expected.

If instruction and student use of time become more effective, it is likely that most students will need less time to master a subject, and the ratio of time required by the slower learners to that needed by the faster learners may be reduced from about 6 to 1 to perhaps 3 to 1.

In general, we find a zero or a slightly negative relationship between final grades and amount of time spent on homework. In the International Study just mentioned, the average correlation for twelve countries at the 13-year-old level is approximately −.05 between achievement test scores in mathematics and number of hours per week of homework in mathematics as reported by students. Thus, the amount of time spent on homework does not seem to be a very good predictor of achievement in the subject.

We are convinced that it is not the sheer amount of time spent in learning (either in or out of school) that accounts for the level of learning. Each student should be allowed the time he needs to learn a subject. And the time he needs is likely to be affected by his aptitudes, his verbal ability, the quality of instruction he receives in class, and the quality of the help he receives out of class. The task of a strategy for mastery learning is to find ways of altering the time individual students need for learning as well as ways of providing whatever time is needed by each. Thus, a strategy for mastery learning must find some way of solving the problems of instruction as well as of school organization (including the question of time).

One strategy for mastery learning

There are many feasible strategies for mastery learning. Each must incorporate some way of dealing with individual differences in learners by relating the instruction to their needs and characteristics. Each strategy must find some way of dealing with the five variables discussed in the foregoing section.

Were it not so costly in human resources, the provision of a good tutor for each student might be an ideal strategy. In any case, the tutor-student relationship is a useful model to consider when one attempts to work out the details of a less costly strategy. Also, the tutor strategy is not so far-fetched as it may seem at first glance. In the preschool period, most of the child's instruction is tutorial—usually provided by the mother. In many middle-class homes, the parents continue to give tutorial help as needed by the child during much of his school career.

Other strategies include permitting students to go at their own pace, guiding students with respect to courses they should or should not take, and establishing different tracks or streams for different groups of learners. The nongraded school (Goodlad & Anderson, 1959) represents one attempt to provide an organizational structure that permits and encourages mastery learning.

A group at the University of Chicago working with Bloom has been doing research on the variables discussed on the previous pages. In addition, members of this group have been attempting to develop a strategy of teaching and learning which will bring all or almost all students to a level of mastery in the learning of any subject. The approach has been to supplement regular group instruction by using diagnostic procedures and alternative instructional methods and materials in such a way as to bring a large proportion of the students to a predetermined standard of achievement. In this approach, the goal is for most of the students to reach mastery levels of achievement within the regular term, semester, or calendar period in which the course is usually taught. Undoubtedly, some students will spend more time than others in learning the subject, but if the majority reach mastery levels at the end of the time allocated for the subject, this will have affective as well as cognitive consequences.

There have been some successes and some dismal failures with this approach. The group has been trying to learn from both. It hopes to have some of these ideas applied in the near future to a large number of classrooms in selected school systems. Initially, the work is on subjects which have few prerequisites (algebra and science, for example) because it is easier to secure mastery learning in a given time period in such courses. In contrast are subjects which are late in a long sequence of learning (sixth-grade reading, eighth-grade arithmetic, advanced mathematics, and the like). In such courses, it is unlikely that mastery learning can be attained within a term by a group of students who have had a long history of cumulative learning difficulties in the specific subject field.

In working on this strategy, the group has attempted to spell out some of the preconditions necessary, develop the operating procedures required, and evaluate some of the outcomes of the strategy.

Preconditions

In order to develop mastery learning in students, one must be able to recognize when they have achieved it. Teachers must be able to define what they mean by mastery, and they must be able to collect the necessary evidence to establish whether or not a student has attained it.

The specification of the objectives and content of instruction is one necessary means of informing both teachers and students of the learning that is expected. The translation of the specifications into evaluation procedures helps define further what it is that the student should be able to do when he has completed the course. The evaluation procedures used to appraise the outcomes of instruction (summative evaluation) help the teacher and student know when the instruction has been effective.

Implicit in this way of defining the outcomes and preparing evaluation instruments is a distinction between the teaching-learning process and the evaluation process. At some point in time, the results of teaching and learning can be reflected in the evaluation of the students. But these are *separate* processes. That is, teaching and learning are intended to prepare the student in an area of learning, while summative evaluation is intended to appraise the extent to which the student has developed in the desired ways. Both the teacher and the learner must have some understanding of what the achievement criteria are, and both must be able to secure evidence of progress toward these criteria.

If the achievement criteria are primarily competitive, that is, if the student is to be judged in terms of his relative position in the group, then he is likely to seek evidence on his rank order in the group as he progresses through the learning tasks. It is recognized that competition may be a spur to students who view others in competitive terms, but much of learning and development may be destroyed by a primary emphasis on competition.

Much more preferable in terms of intrinsic motivation for learning is the setting of standards of mastery and excellence apart from interstudent competition, followed by appropriate efforts to bring as many students up to these standards as possible. This suggests some notion of absolute criteria and the use of grades or marks which will reflect them. Thus, it is conceivable that all students will achieve mastery and the grade of A. It is also possible in a particular year in a specific course for few or none of the students to attain mastery or a grade of A.

While it would be desirable to use absolute standards carefully worked out for a subject, we recognize the enormous difficulty of arriving at them. In some of the work of the Chicago group, they have made use of standards derived from previous experience with students in a selected course. In one course, students in 1966 were informed that the grades for that year would be based on *standards* arrived at in 1965. The grades of A, B, C, D, and F would be given on an examination parallel to that used in 1965 and would be set at the same performance levels as those established in 1965. The class was informed that the proportion of students receiving each grade was to be determined by their performance levels rather than by their rank order in the group. Thus, the students were not competing with each other for grades; they were to be judged on the basis of levels of mastery used in 1965.

This is not the only way of arriving at achievement standards, but the point is that students must feel they are being judged in terms of level of performance rather than on a normal curve or some other arbitrary and relative set of standards. This is not a recommendation for national achievement standards. What is being recommended are realistic performance criteria developed for each school or group, followed by instruction procedures which will enable the majority of students to attain them.

One result of this method of setting achievement standards was that it enabled the students to work with and help each other without being concerned about giving special advantages (or disadvantages) to others. Cooperation in learning rather than competition was a clear result from this method of setting achievement criteria.

In its work, the Chicago group has attempted to have the instructor teach the course in much the same way as previously. That is, the materials, methods of instruction, and time schedule during the course in the current year were about the same as in earlier years. The operating procedures to be discussed in the next section *supplemented* the regular instruction of the teacher. The Chicago investigators have proceeded in this way because a useful strategy for mastery learning should be widely applicable. If extensive training of teachers is necessary for a particular strategy, it will be less likely to receive widespread use.

Operating procedures

The operating procedures used are intended to provide detailed feedback to teachers and students and to furnish specific supplementary instructional resources as needed. These procedures are devised to ensure mastery of each learning unit in such a way as to reduce the time required while directly affecting both the quality of the instruction and the student's ability to understand the instruction.

Formative evaluation One useful operating procedure is to break a course or subject into smaller units of learning. The unit may correspond with a chapter in a textbook, a well-defined content portion of a course, or a particular time unit of the course. We have tended to think of units as involving a week or two of learning activity.

Using some of the ideas of Gagné (1965) and Bloom (1956), the Chicago group analyzed each unit into a number of elements ranging from specific terms or facts, through more complex and abstract ideas such as concepts and principles, to still more complex processes such as application of principles and analysis of theoretical statements. It is assumed that such elements form a hierarchy of learning tasks.

Brief diagnostic progress tests were constructed and used to determine whether each student had mastered the unit and, if not, what he still had to do to master it. We have borrowed the term "formative evaluation" from Scriven (1967) to refer to these tests.

Frequent formative evaluation tests pace the students' learning and help motivate them to put forth the necessary effort at the proper time. The appropriate use of these tests helps ensure that each set of learning tasks has been thoroughly mastered before subsequent tasks are started.

Each formative test is administered after the completion of the appropriate learning unit. While the frequency of the progress tests may vary throughout the course, it is likely that some portions of the course—and especially the early sections—may need more frequent formative tests than later ones. Where some of the learning units are basic and thus prerequisite for others, the tests should be administered frequently enough to ensure thorough mastery of the material.

For the student who has thoroughly mastered the unit, the formative tests should reinforce the learning and assure him that his present mode of learning and approach to study are adequate. The student who consistently demonstrates mastery on the recurring tests should be able to reduce his anxiety about his course achievement.

For the student who lacks mastery of the unit, the formative test should reveal the particular points of difficulty—that is, the specific questions he answered incorrectly and the ideas, skills, and processes he still needs to work on. It is most helpful when the diagnosis shows the elements in a learning hierarchy that he has not yet mastered. It has been observed that students respond best to the formative test results when they are referred to particular instructional materials or processes intended to help them clear up their difficulties. The *diagnosis* should be accompanied by a very specific *prescription* if the students are to do anything about it.

Although there is limited evidence on this point, we are of the opinion that formative tests should not be assigned grades or quality points. The tests are marked to show *mastery* and *nonmastery*. The nonmastery evaluation is accompanied by a detailed diagnosis and prescription of what has still to be done before mastery is complete. It is likely that the use of grades on repeated progress tests prepares students for the acceptance of less than mastery. To be graded C repeatedly, for instance, inclines a learner to accept a C as his "fate" for the course, especially when the grades on progress tests are averaged in as part of the final mark. Under such conditions, there must come a point when it is impossible to do better than a particular grade in the course—and there is little value in striving to improve. Formative evaluation tests should be regarded as part of the learning process, and should in no way be confused with the judgment of the student's capabilities or included in the grading process.

Formative tests can also give feedback to the teacher, because they can be used to identify particular points in the instruction that need modification. They can serve too as a quality control in future cycles of the course: the students' performance on each test may be compared with the norms for previous years to ensure that they are doing as well or better. Such comparisons can be used as well to make certain that changes in instruction or materials are not producing more error and difficulty than was the case in a previous cycle.

The development and use of formative evaluation are discussed in some detail in Chap. 6 of this book and are treated in each chapter in Part II.

Alternative learning resources It is one thing to diagnose the specific learning difficulties a student has and to suggest the steps he should take to overcome them. It is quite another to get him to do anything about it. By itself, the frequent use of progress tests can improve achievement to a small degree. If in addition the student can be motivated to expend further effort on correcting his errors, the gains in achievement can be very great.

It has been found in our work at the University of Chicago on mastery learning that students do attempt to work on their difficulties when they are given specific suggestions (usually based on the formative evaluation results) about precisely what they need to do.

The most effective procedure found thus far is

to have small groups of students—two or three, as noted above—meet regularly for as long as an hour a week to review the results of their formative evaluation tests and to help each other overcome the difficulties identified on the tests.

Tutorial help has been offered as students desired it, but so far those at the secondary or higher education level do not seek this kind of help frequently.

Other types of learning resources that have been prescribed for students include (1) rereading particular pages of the original instructional materials, (2) reading or studying specific pages in alternative textbooks or other materials, (3) using specific pages of workbooks or programmed texts, and (4) using selected audiovisual materials.

We suspect that no specific learning material or process is indispensable. The presence of a great variety of instructional materials and procedures and specific suggestions regarding which ones he might use help the student recognize that if he can't learn in one way, alternatives are available to him. Perhaps further research will reveal the best match between individuals and alternative learning resources. At present, we do not have firm evidence on the relations between student characteristics and instructional material or procedures.

Outcomes

What are the results of a strategy for mastery learning? So far we have limited evidence. However, the findings to date are very encouraging. We are in the process of securing more data on a variety of situations at the elementary, secondary, and higher education levels.

Cognitive outcomes of a mastery strategy The work to date has provided some evidence of the effectiveness of a strategy for mastery learning. The best results have been found in a course on test theory (Airasian, 1967), where it has been possible to use parallel achievement tests from 1965 to 1967. In 1965, before the strategy was used, approximately 20 percent of the students received the grade of A on the final examination. In 1966, after the strategy was employed, 80 percent reached this same level of mastery on the parallel examination and were given the grade of A. The difference in the mean performance of the two groups represents about two standard deviations on the 1965 achievement test and is highly significant.

In 1967, the same formative evaluation tests were used as in 1966, so that it was possible to compare the results from the two years after each unit of learning. Thus the tests became quality control measures. Where there were significant negative differences between the results of a particular test from 1966 to 1967, the instructor reviewed the specific learning difficulties and attempted to explain the ideas in a different way. The final outcome on the 1967 summative evaluation instrument, which was parallel to the final achievement tests in 1965 and 1966, was that 90 percent of the students achieved mastery and were given grades of A. The results were comparable in 1968.

Similar studies are underway at different levels of education. We expect to have many failures and a few successes. But the point is that no single strategy of mastery learning can be used mechanically to achieve a given set of results. Rather, the problem is to determine what procedures will prove effective in helping particular students learn the subject under consideration. It is to be hoped that each time a strategy is used, it will be studied to find where it is succeeding and where it is not. For which students is it effective and for which students is it not? It is also to be hoped that the strategy in a particular year will take advantage of the experience accumulated during previous years.

Affective consequences of mastery As we have pointed out, educators for the past century have conceived of mastery of a subject as being possible for only a minority of students. With this assumption, they have adjusted the grading system so as to certify that only a small percentage of the students, no matter how carefully selected, are awarded a grade of A. If a group of students learns a subject better than a previous group, teachers persist in awarding the A to only the top 10 or 15 percent. They grudgingly award grades of D and C to the majority of students, whom they see as having merely "gotten by." Mastery and recognition of mastery under the present relative grading system is unattainable for the majority—but this is the result of the way the education system has been "rigged."

Mastery must be both a subjective recognition by the student of his competence and a public recognition by the school or society. The public recognition must be in the form of appropriate certification by the teacher or the school. If this is denied him, then no matter how much he has learned, the student must come to believe that *he* is inadequate, rather than the system of grading or the instruction. Subjectively, the student needs to gain feelings of control over ideas and skills. He must come to recognize that he "knows" and can do what the subject requires.

If the system of formative evaluation (diagnostic-progress tests) and summative evaluation (achievement examinations) informs the student of his mastery of the subject, he will come to believe in his own competence. He may be informed by the grading system as well as by the discovery that he can adequately cope with the variety of tasks and problems in the evaluation instruments.

When the student has mastered a subject and when he receives both objective and subjective indications of this, there are profound changes in his view of himself and of the outer world.

Perhaps the clearest evidence of affective change is the interest the student develops for the subject he has mastered. He begins to "like" it and to want more of it. To do well in a subject opens up further avenues for exploring it. Conversely, to do poorly in a subject closes an area to further voluntary study. The student desires some control over his environment, and mastery of a subject gives him some feeling of control over a part of his environment. Interest in a subject is both a cause of mastery of the subject and a result of mastery. Motivation for further learning is one of the more important consequences of mastery.

At a deeper level is the student's self-concept. Each person searches for positive recognition of his worth, and he comes to view himself as adequate in those areas where he receives assurance of his competence or success. For a student to see himself in a positive light, he must be given many opportunities to be rewarded. Mastery and its public recognition provide the necessary reassurance and reinforcement to help him look upon himself as adequate. One of the more positive aids to mental health is frequent and objective indications of self-development. Mastery learning can be one of the more powerful sources of mental health. We are convinced that many of the neurotic symptoms displayed by high school and college students are exacerbated by painful and frustrating experiences in school learning. If 90 percent of the students are given positive indications of adequacy in learning, one might expect them to need less and less in the way of emotional therapy and psychological help. Contrarily, frequent indications of failure and learning inadequacy are bound to be accompanied by increased self-doubt in the student and a search for reassurance and adequacy outside the school.

Finally, modern society requires continual learning throughout life. If the schools do not promote adequate learning and reassurance of progress, the student must come to reject learning—both in the school and in later life. Mastery learning can give zest to school learning and can develop a lifelong interest in learning. It is this continual learning which should be the major goal of the education system.

REFERENCES

Airasian, P. W. An application of a modified version of John Carroll's model of school learning. Unpublished master's dissertation, University of Chicago, 1967.

Atkinson, R. C. *Computerized instruction and the learning process.* (Tech. Rep. No. 122) Stanford, Calif.: Institute for Mathematical Studies in the Social Sciences, 1967.

Bloom, B. S. *Stability and change in human characteristics.* New York: Wiley, 1964.

Bloom, B. S. (Ed.) *Taxonomy of educational objectives: The classification of educational goals.* Handbook 1. *Cognitive domain.* New York: McKay, 1956.

Bowman, M. J. The new economics of education. *International Journal of Educational Sciences,* 1966, **1,** 29–46.

Bruner, J. S. *Toward a theory of instruction.* Cambridge, Mass.: Harvard University Press, 1966.

Carroll, J. A model of school learning. *Teachers College Record,* 1963, **64,** 723–733.

Congreve, W. J. *Independent learning. North Central Association Quarterly,* 1965, **40,** 222–228.

Dave, R. H. The identification and measurement of environmental process variables that are related to educational achievement. Unpublished doctoral dissertation, University of Chicago, 1963.

Gagné, R. M. *The conditions of learning.* New York: Holt, Rinehart and Winston, 1965.

Glaser, R. Adapting the elementary school curriculum to individual performance. In *Proceedings of the 1967 Invitational Conference on Testing Problems.* Princeton, N. J.: Educational Testing Service, 1968. Pp. 3–36.

Goodlad, J. I., & Anderson, R. H. *The nongraded elementary school.* New York: Harcourt, Brace, 1959.

Hunt, J. McV. *Intelligence and experience.* New York: Ronald Press, 1961.

Husén, T. (Ed.) *International Study of Educational Achievement in Mathematics: A comparison of twelve countries.* New York: Wiley, 1967. 2 vols.

Morrison, H. C. *The practice of teaching in the secondary school.* Chicago: University of Chicago Press, 1926.

Schultz, T. W. *The economic value of education.* New York: Columbia University Press, 1963.

Scriven, M. The methodology of evaluation. *AERA Monograph Series on Curriculum Evaluation,* 1967, No. 1, pp. 39–83.

Skinner, B. F. The science of learning and the art of teaching. *Harvard Educational Review,* 1954, **24**(2), 86–97.

Suppes, P. The uses of computers in education. *Scientific American,* 1966, **215**(51), 206–221.

SECTION 2

Using Evaluation for Instructional Decisions

4
Summative Evaluation

In the previous chapters distinctions were made between formative and summative evaluation of student learning. The distinguishing characteristics have to do with purpose (expected uses), portion of course covered (time), and level of generalization sought by the items in the examination used to collect data for the evaluation. Since these characteristics are not absolute, it seems useful to give some examples of the differences.

The main *purpose* of formative observations (there are other useful ways of observing behavior besides testing) is to determine the degree of mastery of a given learning task and to pinpoint the part of the task not mastered. Perhaps a negative description will make it even clearer. The purpose is not to grade or certify the learner; it is to help both the learner and the teacher focus upon the particular learning necessary for movement toward mastery. On the other hand, summative evaluation is directed toward a much more general assessment of the degree to which the larger outcomes have been attained over the entire course or some substantial part of it. In fifth-grade arithmetic, for example, summative evaluation would have as its major purpose to determine the degree to which a student can translate word problems into quantitative solutions or his accuracy and rapidity in handling division. Further purposes would be to grade pupils and to report to parents or administrators. In formative evaluation the concern is with seeing whether a deficiency in translating word problems is due to vocabulary inadequacies or to inability to demonstrate arithmetic formulations; and the division question would focus on type of error. Here the purpose would be to direct both the student and the teacher to specific learnings needed for mastery.

It is quite true that a teacher might wish to try deriving both kinds of evaluation from one examination. There is a danger that such a combination will give the learner a different total stimulus from what a formative test alone would provide (see Chaps. 3 and 6). Also, the attempt would very likely demand a test which was much longer and more complex than advisable.

The characteristic of *timing* (position along the time line of the instruction-learning process) also enters into the differentiation of summative from formative evaluation of student learning. Tests for formative purposes tend to be given at much more frequent intervals than are the summative variety. It follows from the purposes described in the foregoing paragraphs that formative tests should be utilized whenever the preliminary instruction on a new skill or concept is completed. At least several skills or concepts which combine to make a broader ability should have been presented before a summative examination is administered. This sort of test is *not* intended solely for the end of a course, although certainly the final examinations given in most colleges and some secondary schools are summative—usually intended only for grading and certification. More frequently, tests of a summative nature are used two or three times within a course. In the elementary situation it is more common to see teacher-made tests given for grading purposes every four to six weeks. In some cases published tests, usually standardized, are administered in January or February or in May or June. These are summative. On the other hand, relatively short tests which come at the end of a short unit of instruction tend to have the other characteristics of formative evaluation also.

Perhaps *level of generalization* is the factor which differentiates summative from formative evaluation most sharply. Chapter 2 discussed, among other things, the contributions to statements of behavioral objectives by Tyler and Gagné. It was suggested that the Tylerian approach tends to produce descriptions of desired behaviors (Gagné speaks of them as "expected capabilities"), while Gagné's task analysis produces very detailed "prerequisite capabilities" for each large aim. The difference is one of generalizability or transferability. For example, in algebra one might have as an objective "the ability to construct and interpret graphs dealing with linear data." This implies the possession of a number of skills and knowledges—for example, the ability to locate points in a coordinate system and the ability to use signed numbers correctly. In formative evaluation an attempt would be made to observe the underlying prerequisite behaviors; summative evaluation would focus much more on the broad ability represented by the phrase "construct and interpret."

General steps in constructing tests

Regardless of one's point of view on education and appropriate instruction procedures, there are a few general steps which can be of help in the construction of a test for summative evaluation. Later in this chapter we will discuss alternatives tailored to special uses. Chapter 2 describes ways of defining instruction objectives. In Chaps. 7 to 10, certain types of skills, knowledges, and abilities are connected with the development of test items. In the second part of the book, Chaps. 13 to 23 treat specific contents and education levels. Each of these chapters introduces a table of specifications which relates content to behaviors. This is the beginning point for the construction of tests.

In Table 4-1 we present a specifications chart for convenience in the following discussion, the Table of Specifications for Secondary-level Biological Sciences. Though it deals with specific contents and behaviors, illustrations from it are readily applicable to other subject areas and levels. In this chapter attention is directed to the use of such a table for developing tests for the summative evaluation of student learning. No matter what combination we have of the three characteristics discussed in the preceding paragraphs, a summative examination should be built on the basis of a table of specifications.

The general procedures for constructing test items are discussed in Chaps. 7 to 10. The development of a summative test from the items is the focus of the present chapter. The steps, explained more fully in the next section of this chapter, are the following:

1. Develop (or borrow and adapt) a table of specifications for the subject area and education level of your concern. (See Chap. 2 for the general procedure and Chaps. 13 to 23 for particular subject areas.)

Although the idea of developing a specifications matrix is treated more fully elsewhere in this book, it seems good here to suggest to readers who are classroom teachers that there are a few sources and rules which can be of help. The principal rule, which is very general, is that you should look at your content area in terms of large categories of subject material. You may wish to use such homogenizing dimensions as the "themes" of the Biological Sciences Curriculum Study's test grid (adapted in Table 4-1), or you might prefer to use subject-matter breakdowns such as physiological systems, biological functions, and zoological considerations. In Part II you will find special suggestions for particular subject areas. For behaviors, you will perhaps want to consult the book by J. Raymond Gerberich (1956) on *Specimen Objective Test Items*. You will certainly wish to refer to Nolan C. Kearney (1953) and Will French and associates (1957) for suggestions on objectives for elementary and secondary schools, respectively.

2. Develop test items (or use those already developed—see Chaps. 7 to 10 for general suggestions and Chaps. 13 to 23 for specific subject areas) which fit the applicable cells of the matrix.
3. Choose items which test the various cells by sampling in some rational way. A sampling across the whole table is one possibility. A highly select sampling of complex end behaviors is another.

You can obtain a sampling across the entire table of specifications by assigning numbers to all test items, along whatever lines you wish, and using the numbers for a sampling across content or themes, or both. If you have the notion that each outcome is as important as the next, then your selection will follow the rules of random sampling of all possible items.

If, on the other hand, you see the purpose of your summative evaluation as that of testing a few generalized objectives, then you should decide which cells you should sample. For example, working from Table 4-1, you might want to use only items representing behavior category *D*.0, *Demonstration of relationships between bodies of knowledge*. You would put together a random sample of items which test behaviors *D*.1, *D*.2, *D*.3, and so on for the particular contents or themes you choose.

As discussed more fully after step 5, for grading purposes you might wish to sample across the content rows and down the behavior columns; for certification purposes a more appropriate sampling might cover only ultimate behaviors which are desirable for the job or the next course in question—for instance, *B*.0-5.0 and *C*.1-7.0.

4. Assemble the items according to some systematic plan. In certain cases it may be desirable to assemble them within the examination by subgroups representing types of behavior. In other cases the items may be grouped by content. When the choice of items is such that they are relatively homogeneous with respect to content and behavior, it may be well to assemble them along a scale ranging from relatively easy (many passing) to relatively difficult (few passing). With different types of items—multiple-choice, matching, true-false—it is generally useful to group by types simply because directions are easier for the teacher to give and the student to remember.
5. Develop a scoring scheme which will furnish the most useful information or the examination purpose or purposes.

In assignments of *grades* a single score—even though it is the sum of several others—is most useful. In *certification* a score may be obtained on each special skill or on particular abilities across specific subject areas. (In Table 4-1 the subject areas are themes; in Chaps. 13 to 23 they deal with education level and content.) For *prediction* purposes a single score is most useful for empirical tests, although multiple forecasts (see any good statistics book available) allow the teacher to assess whether the various behavior-control cells should be weighted differently for the best possible prediction. For the *initiation of instruction* in subsequent courses, the scoring system should afford a range of scores applicable to the things which can be done in the next course. For *feedback* to students the scheme should tell them the things on which they can realistically operate—which skill or ability with which content; therefore, separate scores should be given for different behaviors. When you are *comparing the*

TABLE 4-1 TABLE OF SPECIFICATIONS FOR SECONDARY-LEVEL BIOLOG

	BEHAVIORS													
	Recall and recognition of materials learned	*Terminology*	*Specific facts*	*Conventions*	*Trends and sequences*	*Classifications and categories*	*Criteria*	*Methodolgy*	*Principles and generalizations*	*Theories and structures*	*Application of knowledge to new concrete situations*	*Nonquantitative*	*Quantitative*	*Use of skills involved in understanding science problems*
CONTENT	*A.0*	*A.1*	*A.2*	*A.3*	*A.4*	*A.5*	*A.6*	*A.7*	*A.8*	*A.9*	*B.0*	*B.1*	*B.2*	*C.0*
1.0 Evolution														
1.1 Data of Change														
1.2 Theories of Change														
2.0 Diversity of Types and Unity of Pattern														
3.0 Genetic Continuity														
4.0 Complementarity of Organisms and Environment														
5.0 Biological Roots of Behavior														
6.0 Complementarity of Structure and Function														
7.0 Homeostasis and Regulation														
8.0 Intellectual History of Biological Function														
9.0 Science as Inquiry														

SOURCE: Adapted from E. Klinckmann, The BSCS grid for test analysis, *BSCS Newsletter*, 1963, No. 19. P. 20. (Biological Sciences Curriculum Study, University of Colorado.)

outcomes of different groups or treatments, it would be well to use a scoring system which reflects differences in abilities and skills and knowledges across subject areas or themes. These ideas are treated in the next chapter section, Test Uses and Test Construction.

6. Develop directions for the examinee which unambiguously tell him the ground rules. These will cover such matters as whether he is expected to try all items or to work only on those he feels he knows; what moves he should make in matching items; whether he is to choose the one best answer or to look for a correct response; how much time he has for

BEHAVIORS															
Interpretation of qualitative data	*Interpretation of quantitative data*	*Understanding of the relevance of data to problems*	*Screening and judging of the design of experiments*	*Screening of hypotheses*	*Identification of problems*	*Identification of assumptions and unanswered questions*	*Analysis of scientific reports*	*Demonstration of relationships between bodies of knowledge*	*Comparison*	*Extrapolation*	*Application to another biological area*	*Application to other fields*	*Analysis of relationships*	*Interrelating of facts, principles, and phenomena in a new way*	*Development of a new set of interrelated concepts*
C.1	*C.2*	*C.3*	*C.4*	*C.5*	*C.6*	*C.7*	*C.8*	*D.0*	*D.1*	*D.2*	*D.3*	*D.4*	*D.5*	*D.6*	*D.7*

the test or each subpart; whether, in cases in which he writes out a response, he will be marked for substance only or also for spelling, grammar, and style.

These general steps in summative test construction, with the exception of 1 and 2 (which are discussed in other chapters), are reexamined in the following section. They deal with the original construction of a test from some rational selection of items. There are steps which should be taken in the revision and improvement of any test which has been used. Suggestions for these steps appear after the discussion of uses and construction.

Test uses and test construction

Formative tests are discussed in Chap. 6. In this chapter we are ignoring the uses of formative instruments. The word "test" or "examination" occurs frequently in this chapter without the adjective "summative"; but unless it explicitly states otherwise, the discussion at all times concerns tests intended as a basis for summative evaluation of student learning.

The summative examination may serve a variety of functions. There are steps in the construction and scoring of tests which help optimize each of these uses. It is quite true that the results of a given test may be employed in several different ways rather than one only. In either case, if the intended aim or aims are established clearly before the test is constructed, the results can be utilized more satisfactorily.

Test outcomes are not equally applicable to all uses at all levels of schooling or in all subject areas. Among the most commonly mentioned uses of test results are the following:

Assigning of grades
Certification of skills and abilities
Prediction of success in subsequent courses
Initiation point of instruction in a subsequent course
Feedback to students
Comparisons of outcomes of different groups

Each of these is discussed in the following pages with reference to test development and to cautions to be observed in carrying out the intended uses.

Assigning of grades

The most prevalent use of summative tests, from elementary school through college and graduate work, is as a basis for assigning grades, represented either by letters or by numbers. Grading usually attempts to categorize each student in terms of his amount or level of learning in relation to other students. This purpose most often reflects the view that courses are designed to spread individuals out so that in the usual class there are a few in the top category, some more in a second group, a larger number who are "average," and fewer in the lower categories. If this is the intent, then there is a way of optimizing the spread in the process of constructing the test. A new criterion must be added to the steps dealing with the selection of items which represent specific cells—given behaviors with given contents. This criterion concerns item difficulty and item discrimination.

Item difficulty is the percentage of examinees who pass the item. A good spread in results can be obtained if the average difficulty of items is around 50 or 60 percent and if the items vary in difficulty from about 20 to 80 percent. Obviously, test questions which are passed by all or nearly all students do nothing to differentiate the examinees—that is, spread them out. The same can be said for items which none or almost none pass.

Item discrimination is an index comparing the percentage of top students with the percentage of poorer students who pass the same item. The words "top" and "poorer" or "more capable" and "less capable" usually have their reference to a total score on the test. However, other measures of quality (for example, the teacher's estimate from classroom observations) can be used. Given a separation of the students into two such sets, the measure works as follows: If 50 percent of each group passes the item, it is said that the item does not discriminate. The same is true with any other close pair of percentages. If, on the other hand, 50 percent of the better group passes the item while only 30 percent of the poorer group does, the item is said to discriminate positively. If the total test score has been used to divide the examinees, this merely means that the item is spreading students in the same direction as does the whole test. Finally, if on another item 60 percent of the top students but 80 percent of the poorer students pass, the item is working in the opposite direction from the total test. To spread the students' scores for the purpose of grading to "weed some out," the discrimination index of all items should be positive (that is, more of the better students should pass the item); and difficulty (proportion passing) should vary from about 20 to 80 percent, with the average around 50 or 60.

The foregoing discussion implies that every test must be tried out with the same or similar students before it is used for grading. Obviously this is impracticable. However, there are several ways of estimating the difficulty and discrimination indexes. For example, the difficulty index can be approximated by teachers with experience in the particular area of learning. This is by no means a perfect substitute for trying out the items, but it is better than no estimate. Another method is that of slowly accumulating an item pool, an idea discussed in Chaps. 2 and 11. The aim here is to suggest that the teacher who wishes to hold to the notion of grading as a selective function may, over a period of time, build a pool of items with the characteristics of difficulty and discrimination needed to spread results, providing that the instruction which underlies the items remains relatively constant.

An alternative is possible. An examination may be developed according to the best estimates available (experienced judgments of other teachers and past experience with items) and given to the students being evaluated. On the basis of the results, the indexes of difficulty and discrimination are computed for each item. Then the final score for each student is based only upon the items which meet the criteria of difficulty and discrimination. This solution of the problem is costly in terms of items dropped because they fail to meet the criteria. However, if what is wanted is spread of scores with most being in the center category, the expense in lost items must be weighed against the purpose. In the ordinary setting, you will not lose more than 10 percent of the items.

For those who view education as being directed at mastery, at whatever level or in whatever subject, and who will undertake changes in instruction time and procedures to accomplish this, the two criteria just discussed are of far less or no import. They may select behaviors and contents from a specifications table or task analysis chart in accordance with the value they attach to them. All or almost all students may pass the items constructed to test these outcomes, in which case the examinees are assigned the highest category of grades. It may happen that a large number do not pass some of the items, in which case the teacher may conclude that the instruction procedures are at fault. As the instruction improves, more students get more items correct. This is the view which formative evaluation espouses (see Chaps. 3 and 6).

The foregoing discussion does not purport to cover all aspects of the use of test results for assigning grades. It is intended to alert the teacher to some of the considerations involved in this particular application. Most published tests are built upon the assumption of the need to spread the students over several grade categories. However, one can think of tests and grades on a different basis.

If the purpose is assignment of grades, then some attention should be given to the various suggestions in construction steps 3, 4, and 5. Referring to Table 4-1, the Table of Specifications for Secondary-level Biological Sciences, the teacher might wish the test at the end of the course to include items which sample each of the behavioral categories, *A*.0 to *D*.0, across all of the content themes. If so, his procedure should probably be to assemble the items according to type or format (step 4) and to assign one score (step 5) to the whole test. This is so simply because a sampling of the entire table (unless the test is extremely long) would not furnish enough items for each of the content areas to allow a reliable score on a given behavior or theme. Within the format groups, he might wish to arrange items from easy to difficult. The score from such a test would have to be interpreted as a general index of ability in the course as a whole. The fact that two students obtaining the same score might not have been successful on many of the same items, sometimes called the compensatory principle in scoring, would make the score useless for feedback or diagnosis.

To make the point clearer, let us take a different example. Suppose another teacher decides that a summative examination at the end of a course should focus upon behavior categories C.0 and D.0, *Use of skills involved in understanding science problems* and *Demonstration of relationships between bodies of knowledge.* Let us say he decides also that the themes of *Evolution* (1.0) and *Complementarity of organisms and environment* (4.0) are the crucial ones. Sampling from these restricted areas of the table of specifications, he could score four subgroups of items, one set for each of the categories of behavior with each of the two content aspects. In this approach he should plan on having at least twelve or fifteen items in each subgroup—forty-eight to sixty items in the test—in order to feel somewhat secure about the reliability of the scores. In general, the more items per score, the more reliable, or stable, it is.

A teacher might use a summative test for grading purposes during the course, say, at the end of a couple of chapters or two units. The same designs mentioned in the first two examples could apply. He might wish to sample from all subelements of behavior categories A.0 and B.0, *Recall and recognition of materials learned* and *Application of knowledge to new concrete situations,* even though he would do this for only two themes (perhaps Genetic continuity, 3.0, and Biological roots of behavior, 5.0). If so, he could plan to have either one score, for the whole test, or two, one for each theme. With eleven themes (see Table 4-1), he could scarcely expect to have enough items for meaningful separate scores in each.

It should be noted in this connection that when the design of the test (step 4) and the plan for scoring (step 5) afford more than one overall score, the chances of using the test results for purposes of feedback, initiation of later instruction, and certification are improved. The multiple scores will carry more meaning than will a single score representing biology accomplishment generally across the entire specifications table or some part of it.

Standards The question of the standards to be adopted is a very real topic in the assigning of grades, the use just discussed, as well as in certification, which will be examined next. There are at least three types of standards: (1) empirical norms, (2) estimated norms, and (3) criterion-based performance. The latter two are frequently labeled "absolute" standards, as contrasted with "normative." They are, however, quite different sorts of standards.

Normative, or *empirical, standards* are most frequently used with published tests. They are based upon the responses of a sample of examinees of the type for whom the test was designed. For example, as the Natural Science Reading Comprehensive Test (Illinois Statewide High School Testing Program, 1956) was being developed, it was decided that the test should be standardized (or "normed") on a representative sample of eleventh-graders in such a way that the scores would spread students out from high to low. The early forms were subsequently administered to samples of students in selected Illinois schools. Items which all passed or all failed were deleted, as were items which did not discriminate (see pages 74 to 75). The scoring system which was developed for the "functional" items placed the examinee *in order* among his peers who took the test—a distribution, therefore, made on an empirical basis. For the classroom teacher to do this requires that he give the same test to a usefully large sample of students similar to those whom he wishes to grade or certify.

Estimated norms result in the same sort of relative standing, except that they are not based upon an actual tryout of the examination. Rather, experts in the subject area who are also experienced with students of the level or educational condition for which the test is being built try to answer the question, What would these students be expected to do with these items? The question may be altered to ask, What percentage of the items would better students answer correctly, or What percentage would the average student answer correctly? As a classroom teacher, you can ask the question of yourself in order to establish estimated norms. You will probably feel more confident of the results if you pose it to several other teachers who know the subject and have worked with students at the given level. Our experience with this type of standard is that the estimate is perhaps 10 to 15 percent above empirical results on the proportion of items passed by a sample of students. Nevertheless, the technique does establish a standard which is useful in grading and certification.

Criterion-based standards are established by the kind of task analysis discussed in Chap. 2 (the Gagné model), or by mastery ideas like those expressed in Chap. 3. They differ from standards which mirror estimated norms in that they derive from the performance desired on given tasks. As a classroom teacher you would decide, with whatever help from specialists you require, what specific performances should be demanded for a grade of A or for certification for a given job or a subsequent course. For example, you might decide that in order for the student to do a particular kind of multiplication, he must know and be able to use certain addition facts. The implication of such a statement is obviously that someone has collected empirical evidence on the proposition—has made a real tryout of it—and found it to be true.

Certification of skills and abilities

There are occasions on which the main purpose of a summative examination is to certify that a given student possesses, at least at that time, certain skills, knowledges, and abilities. These situations are perhaps most likely to occur in technical training in the secondary school or junior college. See Chap. 23, Evaluation of Learning in Industrial Education, for important considerations in these areas. However, the general idea of certification is present in other settings: he is able, from the standpoint of reading skills, to handle social studies reading material of this sort; she has mathematical skills and concepts which are needed for a beginning course in education statistics; the applicant has skills in the science laboratory and the ability to attack science problems which permit him to handle the assistantship.

In each of these settings, the focus is mainly upon the level of behavior with a given content. The implication of this is that the test items must be so selected that specific behavior-content cells of a known table of specifications may be scored. There is the further assumption that a known level of performance exists, above which most students can do the specified job and below which most cannot (Cronbach, 1960). As we will note also in the discussion of prediction, empirical evidence is highly desirable if not necessary for confidence. It is true that careful subjective judgments by those who have experience with performers may substitute as estimates until empirical evidence is collected.

Certification, as described in the foregoing paragraphs, is a legitimate use of summative evaluation of student learning. Let us caution that the development of tests for this purpose may require consultation with specialists for the technical aspects. Such people are available in sizable school systems, nearby colleges and universities, and some state offices of public instruction. The teacher, however, is the one who must decide the purposes of the examination. The special consultant should not be expected to make that decision.

Prediction of success in subsequent courses

For purposes of academic guidance, it is sometimes claimed, a summative test (especially at the end of a course) has as an important function the prediction of success in a subsequent, related course. For example, it is suggested that an eighth-grade arithmetic examination may be quite helpful in the prediction of a student's success in ninth-grade algebra or general mathematics. The first caveat to be observed regarding this use is that it assumes two things: (1) there is empirical evidence of the relationship, and (2) the subsequent course does not alter in method, content, or students' learning characteristics. These are broad assumptions, but they may indeed hold in a setting in which the teachers see the subject (in the example, algebra) as relatively known and stable.

Ideally, the teacher or the examination construction group should try various plans reflecting combinations of behavior and content in a series of tests. The reason for this may be illustrated from Table 4-1: knowledge of terminology, *A*.1, and knowledge of conventions, *A*.3, may be good predictors for a more advanced biology course, but the use of skills involved in understanding science problems, *C*.0, may be a better predictor than these for subsequent work in physics or chemistry. In the example of arithmetic and algebra, skill with computation may be a good predictor for *some* algebra courses, whereas ability to translate verbal problems into conventional formulas may provide a better forecast for others—depending on the contents, methods, and purposes the two courses embody.

In very general terms, students who score high on summative examinations in any academic field tend to score high in other fields. In this connection, however, many questions are still unanswered; it is not yet known whether this pattern is due to a general factor (such as intelligence), a special ability (as in test taking), or some relationship in learning between the subject areas involved.

It is our view that great care must be taken in using summative examination results for predictions regarding subsequent courses, and that technical help should be sought for the task, as recommended in the discussion of certification. It is highly questionable whether a single test could effectively serve the purpose of prediction in combination with other summative evaluation intents.

Initiation point of instruction in a subsequent course

Especially at the elementary school level, there are those who see an important use of summative examinations—usually given at the end of the year—in the decision by the teacher of the next grade level on where to begin the instruction of individuals or groups. From one perspective this is much like formative evaluation in a continuing instruction situation. From another it represents some of the suggested strategies in Chap. 5, Placement and Diagnostic Evaluation.

In the present discussion, which deals with steps and decisions in the construction of summative tests, a point to be noted is that the rules governing this use are much the same as for the use of tests for feedback to students, treated in the following section. Certainly a single score in, for example, third-grade arithmetic is of little use to the next teacher in establishing a behavior-content point at which to begin instruction. A table of specifications should be agreed upon, for the most part, by the two teachers. Steps 3, 4, and 5 of the general procedures for constructing a test must be so handled that there will be several scores representing important behavior-content cells. The teacher who is to use the results for locating the point at which to begin instruction in arithmetic—to stick with the example—must fully understand the score categories.

Feedback to students

The communication to the student of information about his progress (with some immediacy, it is hoped) is the very essence of formative evaluation. Summative evaluation of learning can be used in this fashion also. As stated before, summative tests may be given at various points within a course and cover relatively large units, or they may be finals at the end of a course. If it is truly the end of a unit or course ("Well, we'll never touch that again!"), the feedback of score or grade information may have little effect in terms of changing the student's behavior. It is something like telling a person who has arrived at La Guardia Airport in New York which wrong plane he boarded at O'Hare Field in Chicago. If he ever makes the same trip again, he will know better—if and *only* if the schedules do not change in the meantime. Unfortunately, the analogy truly falls short since the probability of a traveler's taking the same plane trip twice is much higher than the probability of a student's taking a course twice!

If the examination is intended for feedback to students, then it should be so constructed that the interpretations of scores will direct the student's attention to useful things he may do to make up for deficiencies. A simple communication of a single grade of C, let us say, merely tells him that in some fashion or other he was not such a "big egg" as others. It gives him little information with which he can do anything. A similar statement can be made about numerical scores as a total report on a final examination. A mark of 76, whether it refers to percentage of items, a percentile score, or an actual count of right or wrong answers, gives the student very little guidance for making corrections in his behavior—other than that frequently used admonition, "Try harder." The test at the end of the course described in the section on Assigning of Grades (see pages 66 to 68) would be comparatively useless for feedback. In the example following it, the examination with four scores, relatively interpretable in terms of behavior, would furnish more useful information to students.

If a summative test is built and scored astutely, we may infer from the results that the student did reasonably well in aspects which involved, for example, vocabulary but rather poorly in those which demanded recognition of relationships between concepts. It is possible that the student will find the information of some use for future learning. Even this is difficult to establish for an end-of-course examination unless one can point out that other courses which he might take require some of the same processes. The first statement implies that the test items are so built that they can reveal various processes which are reasonably generalizable, and the second presupposes some sort of community agreement within the school across several courses or curricula regarding desirable behavior.

Providing feedback to students is a legitimate purpose of summative evaluation of student learning, even though formative evaluation focuses on this intent. However, the results of summative tests are more likely to be useful for feedback if careful attention is paid to the decisions and alternatives described in steps 3, 4, and 5 of the general test construction procedures. Multiple scores, particularly on behavior categories related to the cells tested, can be helpful to the student if they are based upon a sufficient number of items for reliability (discussed further on pages 75 to 76).

Comparisons of outcomes of different groups

The use of summative measures to compare outcomes is different from the other applications in one particular respect: it has to do not with the evaluation of learning by individual students but rather with the evaluation of outcomes from different methods, materials, or types of students. It is oftentimes the express purpose of examinations to compare groups of students, versions of a course, or sections of courses when taught by different teachers. In such a case it is rather obvious immediately that certain kinds of antecedents are needed to make useful interpretations possible. For example, one must know the entry behavior of students in terms of ability and motivation; or one should have an index of the familiarity of the teachers with the course.

Beyond this observation, it is also true that, when the essential purpose of the exam is to compare outcomes, one might be going about the project inefficiently if he gave all the students exactly the same questions or test items. In all the uses pointed out earlier, the concern was with individual students. When we wish to compare one learner with others, it is obviously necessary to give them all identical tasks or items. On the other hand, if our sights are trained on group outcomes across an entire course or large unit, then our hope should be to get as much information as we can about the whole class.

Any one class is a sample of students. If we break that class into fourths, we have four samples. Therefore, we can administer four separate tests and greatly increase the number of items given. Most courses include a rather large variety of objectives. There should be a number of different items which test each objective. Tables 4-2 and 4-3 represent a scheme which is supposed to suggest the possibility of sampling across various objectives with differing sets of tasks or items.

Assume that a battery of items has been pulled from a pool which has several items for each of the behavior-content cells represented in the BSCS grid shown in Table 4-1, page 64. In Table 4-2 we have numbered thirty-four such items consecutively. The first nine items deal with behavior denoting knowledge of terminology in connection with the content of evolution; items 10 to 14 sample recall of trends and sequences in the content associated with diversity of types and unity of pattern. The remaining twenty items test three other cells of the table of specifications. Items are numbered serially for simplicity in later assignment to the four subtests illustrated in Table 4-3. It should be noted that there may or may not be equal numbers of items for the different cells. This choice depends upon the emphasis which the test maker wishes to place on the particular behavior and content. Also, the number of items (or some multiple) representing a given cell need not equal the number of subtests (or some multiple).

Table 4-3 suggests how the thirty-four items can be assigned to the four subtests, with the first column on the left giving the new item number in each. Note that certain items do appear in all four subtests (original numbers 9 and 14) or in two (original numbers 23, 24, 33, and 34). This overlap is desirable because it provides a check on the extent to which the groups behave alike as groups. They are spoken of as "anchor items." If two of the student samples do quite differently on all of the anchor items common to them, there is some question of how representative these examinees are of the whole group.

By giving four largely different subtests of only eleven items each to subgroups of the total class, we have managed to obtain information on thirty-four items and thus on a wider range of objectives. Of course one might want to include forty to sixty items in a subtest; we used a smaller number in the example for simplicity in showing method. Also, there is nothing mandatory about the division into four subgroups. For a very large group of students, say, two or three hundred, one might want to have five or six subgroups. For a small class, of perhaps twenty students, it would probably be better to use only two sets of students and items.

The advantages of this kind of sampling for the purpose of making comparisons are rather obvious. The teacher does not have to limit the final examination because of time or other

Table 4-2 Item Numbers of Items Testing Certain Objectives from Table 4-1, Table of Specifications for Secondary-level Biological Sciences

Behavior-content cells	*Item numbers in sample*									
A.1–1.0	1	2	3	4	5	6	7	8	9	
A.4–2.0	10	11	12	13	14					
A.7–6.0	15	16	17	18	19	20	21	22	23	24
B.2–1.0	25	26	27	28						
C.2–4.0	29	30	31	32	33	34				

Table 4-3 Items from Table 4-2 Assigned to Subgroups and Renumbered as Subtests

Item number in subgroup test	*Subgroup tests* A	B	C	D
1	1	2	3	4
2	5	6	7	8
3	9	9	9	9
4	10	11	12	13
5	*14*	*14*	*14*	*14*
6	15	16	17	18
7	19	20	21	22
8	*23*	*23*	*24*	*24*
9	25	26	27	28
10	29	30	31	32
11	*33*	*33*	*34*	*34*

demands to a fifty-item sampling of a whole course. Instead, he can obtain information from his subgroups of students concerning several times the number of items he would have been able to cover in a single classwide test of the same length. There are certainly disadvantages from this procedure as well. One is the fact that comparisons between students are treacherous indeed. Another important one, which is not very clearly seen by people in testing, is that there is interdependence among test items in certain areas; this means that it may make a difference whether item 5 appears with items 6 and 7 or with items 15 and 23. This is equally true, however, if one changes the order of items in a regular test.

In summary, the intent of this section has been to raise questions about the purpose of giving summative examinations. It is possible for one examination to serve two or three different uses, though in general not efficiently. It must be remembered that the rules concerning objectives set forth in Chap. 2 apply to every instrument, whatever purpose it serves. Those rules stipulate that objectives should be stated in terms of observable and replicable acts. Summative examinations do not differ from formative or diagnostic examinations in the requirement that they be based on clearly stated objectives.

General steps in revising tests

In the second section of this chapter, we listed six steps for the construction of tests. In the section following it, we pointed out that the various purposes for administering summative examinations require somewhat different approaches in the steps. Such concepts as item difficulty and item discrimination were explained in connection with using tests to assign grades. The idea of reliable multiple scores was discussed, especially under the heading Feedback to Students. Some characteristics of test responses—discrimination, difficulty, and reliability—have been described in connection with test purposes in this chapter.

Now is the time to draw some of these elements together in a few steps which should be taken in the revision of tests. It would be useful if a test could always be tried out with a representative group before it was given to the intended examinees. For many reasons this is seldom possible for the classroom teacher. It should be a bit easier to arrange with a test which will be used by a number of different teachers in a given department or school system. Tryout is a must for tests which are to be published (see American Educational Research Association & National Council on Measurements Used in Education, 1955). Each of the following steps should be considered when an instrument is to be revised. Some of them suggest modifications directly; others provide information which can be used in working toward revision. Chapter 11 discusses using the computer to procure the necessary data and computations for some of these steps.

1. Give the test individually to a small number of students and ask each one to do his reading, thinking, and answering orally. Take rather full notes (or use a recorder) so that you can have a record of his item-answering behavior. From the data on the whole group you can make inferences concerning the clarity of the vocabulary and the graphic material in the directions and questions. If the students are chosen to represent a fairly broad band of ability, testing only five to eight can give you considerable help in picking out points at which revision is needed in order to improve the two-way communication. We have used this technique at all levels very beneficially, even when the students selected for tryout were only remotely equivalent to those for whom the test was ultimately slated. For example, we have used sixth-graders for a fifth-grade test in arithmetic; we have used graduate students for a test intended for upper-division undergraduates. One can do this with individual items, but it helps to try out the complete test since there are frequently interrelationships among items. The student responses provided by this step are likely to give the teacher clues for revision which he could not have had during the original test construction.
2. Show the items of the test and the specifications table to a competent judge (preferably several)—another specialist in the same area—and ask him to indicate the cell or cells of the table which he would connect with each item. As stated at a number of places later

in this book, if the judge is not familiar with the actual instruction, he may misconnect some items because he assumes that something which you are calling "application" was taught in class and is therefore "knowledge," or that something which you classify as "knowledge" is "translation." Nevertheless, if points of disagreement are discussed, the finished test will generally be improved. Both the test maker and the judge will find it helpful to have each item set forth on a separate card (3 by 5 or 4 by 6 inches), with full directions for each type of item written on another card. The card system will also be helpful in the development of an item pool for use in constructing new tests.

Very simply, the *median* (Md.) is the score which divides the tested group into two parts, the score above and below which are one-half of the cases. To obtain this measure, arrange the scores in order from highest to lowest and count from the bottom up (or the top down) to the middle score. If there are an even number of scores, choose a point between the two middle scores. If these are tied, they represent the median.

The *mean* (M) is found by adding all scores and dividing that sum by the number of scores. If a test is administered to 50 students and their scores add up to 1,500, the mean is 30—1,500 divided by 50.

FIGURE 4-1 Computation of median and mean.

The steps for computing standard deviation, *s*, are as follows. First, square every score. Second, add the squares to obtain a total. Third, divide this total by the number of scores in the group. Fourth, subtract from this total the square of the mean (see Fig. 4-1). Fifth, take the square root of the difference you obtain in the fourth computation. That square root is the standard deviation, *s*, for the sample of test scores. The formula for the five computations, if you prefer an equation to prose, is

$$s = \sqrt{\frac{\Sigma X^2}{N} - M^2}$$

where Σ = "the sum of"
X = a score
X^2 = the score squared
N = the number of scores
M = the mean
$\sqrt{\ }$ = "the square root of"

FIGURE 4-2 Computation of standard deviation.

3. Compute the median and mean of the test scores obtained from the tryout group. Both can be used in later steps for revision. The median can be used in figuring the discrimination index, which was discussed under the heading Assigning of Grades. The mean is necessary for the procedures described in steps 4 and 7, which concern standard deviation and reliability. These measures of "central tendency" are useful also in comparing the performances of different groups on the same test (Fig. 4-1.)
4. Compute the standard deviation of the test scores. This group measure is useful, along with the mean, in the procedures for obtaining an estimate of reliability (see step 7). It is useful too in comparisons between groups and comparisons of tests. The standard deviation, usually denoted by the letter *s*, is a measure of dispersion of scores. Two groups might take the same test and have approximately equal means or medians, and at the same time the sets of scores for the two groups might spread out above and below the mean or median quite differently. For example, suppose two groups take an arithmetic test of fifty items. Suppose further that group A's scores vary from 10 to 48 and group B's from 25 to 40. Group A would have the larger dispersion as measured by the standard deviation.

   For the meaning of the concept of standard deviations, it suggested that you consult a beginning statistics book (for example, Adkins, 1964; Blommers & Lindquist, 1960; Walker & Lev, 1958). However, the computation of *s* is not difficult, especially if one has access to a calculator. The method is outlined in Fig. 4-2.
5. Obtain a measure of difficulty for each item. The difficulty index of an item was discussed in the section Test Uses and Test Construction, first in connection with the assigning of grades. It is a figure which represents the proportion of students getting an item right. To obtain it one merely divides the number of students passing the item by the total number of students trying it. For test revision it is very helpful to know the difficulty of each item. If you are using a test to spread students out (rather than to assess mastery), you will want to reject items which everyone or almost everyone either passes or fails to pass. Neither sort of item helps spread the students. The difficulty index is also needed in computing the discrimination index (see step 6).

   Rejecting an item which is very high or very low in difficulty is not always necessary. You can alter its difficulty by changing some of the alternatives in a multiple-choice question or by altering the language of the item. When you make such changes, however, it is very important to make sure that the item is still measuring the same behavior (see the discussion of validity in the section Technical Characteristics, and see steps 1 and 2 in this section).

6. Determine the discriminating power of each item. Discrimination was discussed first along with the topic of assigning grades in the section on test purposes. The index of discrimination at its simplest level involves obtaining the difficulty index for each of two groups of the students tested: those who do well on the test and those who do poorly. A common method calls for calculating the difficulty index for those above and below the median separately. If the index for the better students is larger than that for the poorer students—that is, if more of the better ones pass the item—the item discriminates positively and hence properly. This merely reflects in numbers the fact that we expect good students on the average to do better with each item than do poor students.

   If an item does not discriminate properly, it can be discarded. This, however, is expensive. Some time and energy have gone into every item. Therefore, it is indeed wiser to attempt to revise the item so that it will discriminate as you want it to. A common reason for negative discrimination is that the item contains subtle language which misleads the better students but is ignored by the poorer. Further use of the procedures suggested in revision step 1 will help you locate the trouble. Again, however, as stated in step 5, care must be taken in revising an item to ensure that its meaningfulness and validity are not lost. There are more precise (and more intricate) ways of indexing discrimination power of items. The interested reader should see Ebel (1965).

7. Look at the reliability of the test results. The meaning and importance of reliability are discussed in the following section, Technical Characteristics. At this point let us see how to obtain a reliability measure when the test has been given and steps are being taken to revise it.

   There are a number of different types of reliability and a number of different formulas for obtaining a reliability coefficient. We will present just one type of reliability—consistency across different samples of items with the testing procedures used—and two formulas for computing it. The reader who wishes to go more deeply into reliability (and we would urge it) should refer to Ebel (1965).

   Our choice of these two procedures out of the many available was not made by chance. In regard to achievement tests in the classroom, the main concern is whether the items selected from the many possible ones for the same cell constitute a good sample. The formulas afford a coefficient for consistency across different samples of items with the testing procedures used. Also, they are relatively easy to use if one is already collecting item-difficulty information. Procedures which estimate stability of performance across time interest us less in the present setting than do the ones we have chosen.

Kuder-Richardson formula number 20 uses two measures discussed in revision steps 4 and 5. The formula is

$$r = \frac{k}{k-1}\left(1 - \frac{\Sigma pq}{s^2}\right)$$

In this formula r is the reliability coefficient. The letter k represents the number of items in the test. Σ, as in Fig. 4-2, means "the sum of." The letter p stands for the proportion of students passing (giving the correct answer on) a given item, and q represents the proportion not passing (giving the wrong answer). The figures for p and q must add up to 1.00; or, stated another way, q is obtained by subtracting p from 1.00. The symbol s^2 stands for the square of the standard deviation, s, for which a formula was given in Fig. 4-2. Since we took the square root of a certain quantity to obtain s, that quantity is the same as s^2. Therefore, $s^2 = (\Sigma X^2/N) - M$. To use K-R number 20, first obtain the item difficulty (p) for each item. Then multiply this proportion by q (which is $1.00 - p$) and add the products together for all items in the test (Σpq). Then divide this figure by s^2 and subtract the quotient from 1.00. Multiply the remainder by the quotient of the number of items divided by one less than the number of items. The resulting figure is r, the index of reliability.

FIGURE 4-3 Computation of reliability (K-R no. 20).

Kuder and Richardson present another formula, number 21, which somewhat simplifies the calculation. This formula uses only the number of items in the test, k; the mean of the set of scores (see Fig. 4-1); and the square of the standard deviation, s^2. It is

$$r = \frac{k}{k-1}\left(1 - \frac{M(k-M)}{ks^2}\right)$$

In this formula it is assumed that the difficulty index is approximately the same for all items, varying from only about 0.3 to 0.7. If the p values vary much more than this, the r will be a serious underestimate of the "true" index of consistency. Either number 20 or number 21 overestimates the consistency if speed is a large factor in the test, that is, if many of the examinees do not have time to attempt each item. These formulas probably should not be used unless 90 to 95 percent of the students are able to complete the examination.

FIGURE 4-4 Computation of reliability (K-R no. 21).

In 1937 G. Frederic Kuder and Marion W. Richardson published an article, "The Theory of the Estimation of Test Reliability." They presented a number of formulas for the reliability coefficient—ordered in general from highly abstract and generalizable to rather specific. It is two of these, K-R numbers 20 and 21, that we have chosen to demonstrate. They appear in Figs. 4-3 and 4-4.

Technical characteristics

The technical characteristics of any examination include validity, reliability, and scoring objectivity. They certainly apply to summative examinations. There are, however, some special considerations which apply to summative testing and which arise from the purpose it is to serve. In the immediately following pages the three general characteristics will be discussed in the order in which they were just mentioned, and any special considerations will be taken up under these headings.

Validity

The literature on testing abounds in excellent discussions of the characteristic which we label "validity." In them the word is most frequently preceded by a modifier, such as "content," "construct," "predictive," or "concurrent."

Content validity generally refers to the correspondence between achievement test items and the instruction for which the test is built. For example, an item in a mathematics test which samples recall of trigonometric functions would not have content validity in an achievement test used for a course in which that skill was not meant to be taught. The insistence in this book that both instruction and examinations to evaluate learning should be tied to the same table of behavior-content specifications is really an insistence on content validity.

An appropriate technique for checking the compliance of examination items with the rule just stated involves the use of judges. The judges you choose to look at your test items should have competence in your subject area. Perhaps they will be fellow teachers, or they may be specialists from a nearby college or university. They must also have as full explanations as possible of the meaning of the content rows and behavior columns in your table of specifications. Given these things, they should be asked to match the items to cells in the table. There is bound to be some disagreement over designations among the judges or between them and you. However, if you get 75 percent agreement or better, you can feel comfortable about content validity. If the agreement is less than 50 percent, you should reexamine your item choices or discuss instruction expectations with the judges. It may be, for example, that items which you expect to measure application to new situations will impress them as measuring knowledge—simply because they think the instruction includes these particular applications.

Construct validity is a characteristic most frequently attributed to ability (for instance, intelligence) tests or personality tests. Very generally it means that hypotheses about the relatedness of behaviors prove correct. Suppose that we develop test X (say, on rigidity of attitudes), and hypothesize that those who score high on it will respond differently to test Y (say, on economic liberalism) from those who score low. Empirical evidence that this occurs is used as support for construct validity—meaning that the two sets of test scores are related as we believe the two traits are. This is not the same as saying that students who are creative in graphic arts are probably more creative in poetry than are those who are not. In this case the construct, creativity, is the same in both cases and we would be talking about generalizability of the trait.

Perhaps the closest thing in achievement testing to the notion of construct validity relates to the use of several different types of items—true-false, matching, multiple-choice, essay—to test the same cell of a specifications table. For example, if we look at cell *B*.0-4.0 in Table 4-1, we surely could think of several types of items which would measure the students' ability to apply the principles of complementarity to new concrete instances of organisms in their environments. We might ask a question about a given relationship and request the student to supply a short paragraph detailing how the principles would apply. Or the items might be of the choice type, in which the student selects the best of several alternatives. Or again, we might list several principles on one side of the paper and several situations on the other, and ask the student to match the applicable principle to the situation (organism and environment) it best fits. The question here is the extent to which the three types of items measure the same behavior. One may answer this question by determining the correlation between types of items—that is, the extent to which students who score high on one type also score high on another, and similarly for low scorers. The degree of correlation suggests the degree to which the desired behavior, as such, is being measured. Low correlations suggest that the construct to which the behavior refers may be less useful than was hoped. For those who wish to go farther into this approach to validity, we recommend an article by D. T. Campbell and D. W. Fiske (1959) which deals with the relationships among tests using a variety of methods for measuring a number of traits.

Predictive validity, a term usually applied to ability measures, is requisite in summative tests being used for prediction. We were writing about predictive validity when we suggested above that empirical data (real tryouts) were necessary to support the notion that prediction is an important function of summative testing (see pages 69 to 70).

It is possibly useful to view performance on formative tests (see Chap. 6) as predicting performance on a summative test or tests. The purpose of formative examinations is to determine whether the student has attained mastery and, if not, to discover what is missing in his knowledge, skills, and abilities. Since summative examinations are intended to test the larger behaviors which rest upon these kinds of learning, we would expect overall performance on the series of formative instruments to predict the results of the summative measures. Obviously, if the instruction is so successful that all students do very well on all of the mastery tests, the correlation between these and the summative examination scores will tend toward zero, since dispersion of scores is a necessary condition for a positive or negative relationship. On the other hand, if all do well on the formative tests but there is a sizable number of poor scores on the summative, this should lead to a reexamination of the assumptions underlying both sets of examinations and their logical relationships.

Concurrent validity is demonstrated by evidence that students maintain the same rank order on one test (for example, an arithmetic examination) as they have on another which purportedly measures the same capabilities. This sort of validity has been relied on widely by test developers who want to show that a new test they have developed measures the same powers as a respected intelligence test, such as the Binet. This approach is seldom helpful with achievement tests since it is difficult to decide which test one is validating if both tests consist of samples of items from a table of specifications.

The notion of concurrent validity can be of use if we wish to inquire into the relation between an indirect and a more direct measure of some behavior. A straightforward example of this occurs in composition skills. Most teachers will say that a direct measure of writing ability can be had only when the student actually prepares a composition. On the other hand, a device which is widely used is a composition with known errors which the student is asked to "proofread and correct." There are advantages in this approach in that it saves time and allows all students to be given the same task. However, the proofreading instrument is useful only if it correlates substantially with carefully developed scores on compositions written by the students. This, in effect, is the application of the idea of concurrent validity to two tests developed for the same purpose when one offers a less direct measure than does the other.

A very useful discussion appears in Norman E. Gronlund's *Measurement and Evaluation in Teaching* (1965), which the reader who is planning to develop tests would do well to read. The heart of his argument concerns not the adjective preceding the word "validity" but rather the qualifying phrase following it—validity *for what.* He points out that validity pertains to the uses made of an instrument and the results of the test use, not to the instrument itself. Two examples follow.

If a final examination in a particular course is intended to determine at what point in a subsequent course to begin with each of the students, then it is valid if and only if it works. The expression "it works" means that if on the basis of the test we start with student X on instruction A and student Y on instruction B, each ultimately learns more than had he started at some other point. In terms of predictive validity, discussed a few paragraphs earlier, we are judging the validity of the test by its usefulness in predicting an appropriate starting point. What we are talking about here is discussed at some length in Chap. 5, on diagnosis. The reason for alluding to it here is that this use is mentioned fairly frequently in connection with subject areas which are seen as sequential.

As another example, it is obvious that if the final examination is given simply for the purpose of assigning categories of overall quality (grades) to the students' work, then the test is valid only if the category in which a student is placed corresponds with a real category of worth. That statement is merely a roundabout way of saying that the test must consist of items representing the actual behaviors which are operational definitions of the objectives of the course. Again, the defining of instruction objectives was described in detail in Chap. 2.

Since this book emphasizes the appropriate use of a table of specifications as affording the main support for validity, it seems good in this section to discuss some ways of selecting items for a summative test. Now, it is reasonably obvious that in a broad subject area, which is what we are generally dealing with when we talk about final examinations, the actual number of available recall and recognition or application items will be exceedingly large. Certainly there will be far too many to include in any one examination. This then puts us in the position of wondering how to decide which ones to use. As we will see a little later on, a prior question of how one expects to score the test and use the results is of importance here. In the meantime, let us look at two general criteria by which this sampling within given abilities might be decided.

First, as always in testing, there is the issue of value. Using our familiar Table 4-1, a given instructor might consider that the material on *Diversity of types and unity of pattern* (2.0) and *Intellectual history of biological function* (8.0) are together more important than are the materials indicated by the other themes of the specifications matrix. In this value weighting, then most assuredly more items for these content areas should be sampled. Moreover, it should be understood that even if a teacher does not pay explicit attention to values, he is valuing the various content areas. For example, if he chooses items randomly, he is saying that *he* values the various rows equally.

The question is properly raised at this point of how one places values on content areas. Some seem to have no trouble with this at all in their own fields. They *know* which of the subject's categories are most valuable. Their conviction is based on such things as what seemed to be good for them as they went through their own training, what the textbooks emphasize in terms of pages devoted to the topics, or what another authority has said.

Some teachers find it useful or even necessary to adopt a value order which stems from the department or school curriculum guide. They prefer and possibly should prefer to rely on the judgment of certain local authorities, such as the department head or the supervisor or the committee on curriculum organization.

There are those who attack the problem of valuing the content areas from the standpoint of logical connections with later courses or with the total subject. The people in this group may use their own knowledge of the field as a basis for determining which categories of content and behavior have the most mileage—that is, have the greatest number of connections with other areas in the subject. As an example, the concepts involved in a number line probably have more connections with other mathematics than do the operations of multiplication. On the other hand, a teacher may investigate the literature available in his subject to see which concepts and topics are most frequently objects of concern. In cases where the final examination is viewed as an instrument for sampling broadly across all the content categories of the specifications matrix in terms of any one behavior, the first criterion is that of the value attached to the specific content.

A second criterion used in sampling across the learning areas in a subject is that of equivalence among the tasks involved. For example, if a biology teacher knows that the terminology and symbols used in the study of circulation are used also in another area, such as respiration, he will do well to avoid sampling from both if he is limited in the number of items he can use.

Or again, a teacher concerned with arithmetic at the lower intermediate level may be sampling from a specifications table which has a behavior column called *Speed and accuracy in computation* and content rows which include addition, subtraction, multiplication, and division. For the purpose of sampling, he may decide that division problems provide evidence concerning subtraction and multiplication, and he may therefore sample more heavily from division items.

In any attempt at weighting items in a whole test, it must be recognized that part of the task is necessarily empirical. To take a simple case related to the example just used, let us suppose that an arithmetic teacher includes ten items each on the four fundamental operations in a test. The equal numbers of items do not necessarily mean that each part contributes the same weight to the total score. Let us say that for some reason the class has learned the operations of addition and multiplication well, whereas various pupils have learned subtraction and division to differing degrees of mastery. If these two facts are reflected in the test results, it may be that all the pupils will make the same scores on multiplication and addition but will vary considerably in their scores on subtraction and division.

One has only to try a simple case to illustrate the effect on weighting of this example. Let us write down that each of the pupils makes either a 9 or a 10 on both the multiplication and the addition items. This means that everyone has a total score on these two parts of 18 to 20. If we further propose that, because of the variability in the learning of subtraction and division, the examinees make scores on each of these sets of items ranging from 4 to 10, we can see that the total score of these two parts will vary from 8 to 20.

Now, if we look at the total score for all four parts, we see that it varies from a minimum of 26 to a maximum of 40, a spread of fourteen points. However, the main differences among the pupils across this range are due to the wider variations in scores on the division and subtraction items—a reflection of the differential learning. The addition and multiplication items can separate the pupils only by two points, whereas the other parts of the test can separate them by many more.

An extreme case of this same sort would be one in which all pupils make exactly the same score on one part of the test but vary considerably on the other. Then the total score will differ from pupil to pupil only as much as they differ on the second part. The first part, on which they have all performed alike, adds nothing but a constant to scores on the second part.

What the foregoing says to us is that even though the maker of an examination does think through the sampling of items in terms of the value of various concepts or behaviors, he can only be sure that he has those relative weightings after he has administered the test and has determined the weight actually given to the total score by the students' responses. The relative numbers of items in the various parts will not guarantee appropriate relative weighting. The spread in scores will.

Another empirical idea enters into weighting. Let us assume this time that in the sample of items representing the themes in Table 4-1, it is decided that C.4, C.5, and C.8 have equal value. Let us assume further that *Screening and judging of the design of experiments* (C.4) and *Screening of hypotheses* (C.5) are highly correlated. That is, students who do well with one also do well with the other, and similarly, students who do poorly with one do poorly with the other. Moreover, let us say that the items testing C.8, *Analysis of scientific reports*, are not correlated so strongly with the items from the other two behaviors. That is, not always do students score comparably on C.8 and on C.4 and C.5 items. In such a case, then, the items most highly correlated will add more weight to the total score than the number of those items would suggest.

From the examples given above, it becomes apparent that the weight or value given to the components of any test—that is, to the number of items from various rows and columns in the specifications table—reflects the weighting of these components in the total score if and *only* if the examinees are equally variable in their responses to the components and if the relationships among the components, as reflected in their correlations, are the same. These two conditions are rarely met in any test. This does not preclude the necessity, however, for the maker of a summative examination to consider carefully the weightings which he *wishes* to give to various parts of a test if he has decided to sample from the whole specifications matrix.

Reliability

A test characteristic which may be considered separately from validity, but upon which validity in part depends, is reliability. The reliability of a set of test scores refers to the consistency with which the results place students in the same relative position to other students if the test is given repeatedly. If the same test were administered to a given group twice, once in the morning and again in the afternoon, we would ordinarily expect the ordering of the examinees to be much the same for the two different times. If this were not so, we would say that the results were not consistent. Similarly, if two samples of items representing the same content-behavior cells were given one after the other and the results were not approximately the same in terms of the relative ranking of the examinees, we would say the results were not consistent. To help clarify the idea, let us look at a third example: if the same students take a given test again—or a different one sampling the same ability—after a lapse of six months and do not come out in about the same order, we would say that the results lacked consistency. However, in this last example, we might claim that we did not expect a high degree of consistency because the students had received instruction during the six months. The three examples suggest at least three types of reliability.

The first example—of the same test given twice within a very short time interval—reflects consistency in the testing procedure or instrument. Such things as ambiguities in items may cause examinees to interpret the questions or the instructions differently at different times. The scoring procedures—a real part of the testing procedure—may be such that the same responses are scored differently on the two occasions. This is more likely to be true of supply items, for which the student supplies his own answers and the scorer must judge correctness, than of multiple-choice items, for which one scoring key can be used identically by a number of judges or by the same judge on a number of occasions. The ways in which one may improve reliability here are rather obvious. Any ambiguities in questions and directions can be decreased by the use of steps 1 and 2 discussed in the preceding section, General Steps in Revising Tests. In the case of scoring inconsistencies, greater care can be taken in scoring with a key, and greater agreement can be sought between judges or from one scorer judging at two different times. Some suggestions are made in this connection in the next section, Scoring Objectivity.

The second example described above—of two samples of items representing the same content-behavior cells which are given with a very short or no time lag—may also reflect consistency in the testing procedure or instruments. However, a new factor enters here: the equivalence of the samples, or how well they represent all possible items testing that cell. Generally one can increase reliability, that is, decrease inconsistency in results, by adding more items to a sample. Very simply, if a teacher wanted to test the ability to divide a three-digit numeral by a two-digit numeral, he would expect to get more reliable results from six items than from two. Obviously, he would have to concern himself also with ambiguities in the items and with consistency in scoring procedures, as in the earlier example.

The third example—of a relatively long time lag before a second testing with the same or a different sample of items—reflects a third type of reliability: stability of the trait or ability in the students. If we are dealing with student interests for purposes of predicting vocational success, we expect some stability over time. However, if we are dealing with writing ability during a period when instruction is being given, we do not expect high stability. In summative evaluation of student learning, this sort of reliability seldom has major importance. In the use of tests for certification or prediction of success, stability should be of real concern. For a fuller treatment of stability and methods of estimating it, the reader should see Ebel (1965). It remains to be said that reliability even of this third sort is affected by the factors discussed regarding the first two examples.

The opening sentence of this discussion stated that validity depends in part upon reliability. The converse is not true. One could construct a test which was quite invalid (such as one for measuring the ability to interpret data which consists solely of questions on knowledge of terminology!) but highly reliable in terms of both testing procedure and item sampling. However, even if a test maker found general agreement among appropriate judges that a certain set of items measured ability to interpret data, thus establishing content validity, he could not think of his test as valid if he discovered that its reliability was low. Reliability limits validity. A measure which gives inconsistent results cannot give valid results.

Just as there are several types of reliability, there are a number of quantitative estimates of the various types (see Ebel, 1965; Gronlund, 1965). Figures 4-3 and 4-4 give two such formulas, fairly easy ones to compute, which estimate consistency in the testing procedure and across samples of items. These are the characteristics which we have said are most generally of concern to those who deal with examinations for summative evaluation of student learning.

Several suggestions have been made in this section for improving the reliability of a test. Let us enumerate these and a few additional ones:

1. Clarifying any ambiguities in items and directions (revision step 1) will generally improve both reliability and validity.
2. Increasing the agreement among scorers or from a single scorer on different occasions (see the section Scoring Objectivity, below) will improve reliability, but unless this is done in a very rational and careful manner—certainly not by mere "voting counts"—it can decrease validity.
3. Adding more items of similar content-behavior validity to the test or subtest will increase the reliability of the resultant scores, as long as attention is paid to quality of items and scoring (1 and 2, above).
4. Improving the discrimination power of items (revision step 6), other things being equal, will increase reliability. In heightening discrimination, one must be careful not to make alterations which are irrelevant to the content-behavior intent lest he lower

validity. It would be irrelevant, for example, to increase the reading difficulty of an item not measuring reading, to word the correct alternative in a multiple-choice item in esoteric terms, or to shorten the time for answering an item when speed is not part of the behavior desired.

Scoring objectivity

Objective scoring of examinations is not a topic which pertains solely to summative evaluation. However, there are reasons for special concern with objectivity in the scoring of the final test for a given course. When one is doing diagnostic examining or the kind of formative evaluation which takes place during the course, there are always opportunities for correcting the conclusions derived from the data by later testing. With a final examination—at the end of a course or a large unit—the general expectation is that we will have no further data for correcting the inferences we have drawn.

Objectivity in scoring has to do not only with fairness but with validity and reliability. No matter how well the items of a test match the table of specifications of intended outcomes, if any element of the scoring brings about inaccuracies in its application, then content validity is lowered. If any bias in the scoring causes the same relevant behavior to be scored differently for different examinees, then both the validity and the reliability of the results are lowered.

Now we need to look at examples to illustrate these observations. Let us first take a reasonably simple case in which we have a choice test. If the teacher keying the test has somewhat different notions from his colleagues on which alternatives are right and wrong for each item, then there is question whether the test is being scored objectively even though the same scores will be given to all students choosing the same alternatives. There are many cases in the biological sciences, for example, in which competent biology teachers will key different alternatives for the same item as the best response. When the key for a final examination lacks professionwide uniformity, the validity of the results is affected. The implication of these statements is that, even when items correspond closely with a specifications matrix, the results of the test will not necessarily have content validity unless there is agreement on the keying of responses. This is another case in which it is important to have the agreement of competent judges (other teachers, subject-matter experts, people with training and experience in testing). This does not mean a mere "nose count" of opinions, but a discussion of the reasons for choosing the alternative associated with the intended behavior. If agreement cannot be reached on a given test item, it is doubtful whether the item should be used. It may be possible, however, to alter the wording of the item without departing from the intent of the content-behavior cell in a way that meets with the judges' approval. Altering the item for the sake of agreement per se will probably only decrease validity.

In a choice test, once the key is made, the only reason for different scorings of examinees who have given the same responses is pure error in using the scoring key. If this happens, we do have lowered reliability and validity. About the only corrective for this kind of error is independent scorings, either by different scorers or by the same scorer at different times, using the same key.

With supply items the case is different, whether the student is called on to give a one-word answer, as in a simple completion or blank-filling test, or to write a page or two, an operation frequently referred to as an essay answer. Unfortunately, the terminology which designates choice tests as "objective" and supply tests as "essay" was developed quite a number of years ago and obtains to this day. In the sense used here, "objective tests" are merely tests without bias in scoring once the key is set.

Most readers will be familiar with the fact that "essay tests" are quite frequently not essays in the literary meaning of the term. It should be noted that with proper safeguards, the responses on a supply test can be as objectively scored as those on a choice test. It should also be noted that in a choice test, some person or group must judge which responses afford the best answer.

In the scoring of a supply test which calls for one-word or one-phrase completions, there are those who will accept a rather liberal range of terms as long as it seems that the meaning is "within the ball park." For example, the following item was culled from a ninth-grade algebra final examination:

> What name do we attach to the following set of equations?
>
> $3X + 2Y = 18$
>
> $X - 4Y = 6$

The keyed response for this item was "a set of simultaneous linear equations." Some students filled the blank with exactly that phrase. Many supplied statements which were clearly incorrect. A number of students wrote in "a set of equations in two unknowns." In this particular example, some teachers scoring the test accepted only the expression "a set of simultaneous linear equations" as the one to mark correct. Anything else was marked wrong. Other teachers also accepted the response "a set of equations in two unknowns" as correct, but somewhat differentially, seeming to judge according to who was answering. As a hypothetical example, if Mary, a student who had repeatedly been unable to understand various concepts in algebra, gave this response, she was marked as incorrect. If on the other hand Alice gave exactly the same response, she was marked as correct simply because her teacher knew that she was highly familiar with the concept. Other factors which bring about bias are poor handwriting from the student and fatigue on the part of the scorer. These bias factors can be decreased if one remains aware of them.

There are two things in the foregoing example which bear upon the idea of objective scoring. First, even when a group of teachers agree that a given supplied response is the only one which will be accepted, there is still a danger that the item will be rendered invalid by a student's thinking of another way to state the idea accurately. Second, in the latter part of the example, identical responses by different students were marked differently because of additional knowledge which the scorer held concerning the students. Even if this additional knowledge is perfectly valid, it remains that such differential scoring (nonobjectivity) lowers the reliability and the validity of the test.

This fault is much more likely to occur when several sentences or paragraphs are to be written in response to a given item. The scorers, even when in the closest agreement on the aspects of the response to look for in marking, are apt to be diverted by extraneous information. There are two main sources of bias.

First, the scorer may be influenced as he moves from paper to paper by irrelevant errors in the responses. If a paper consists of some paragraphs written about generalizations which may be drawn from certain anthropological data, and the sentences themselves are carelessly constructed grammatically, he may give the response a lower score than he does a paper which contains the same conclusions but stated more appropriately in acceptable style. An effective way to correct this kind of bias is to mark the item independently for grammar or spelling or penmanship. A score separate from the one reflecting the value of the intended response can be useful without being relevant to the specifications table. By pulling off the facets of each response that do not pertain to the purpose of the item, the scorer should be able to concentrate more fully upon those which were intended to be scored.

The other source of bias most common in scoring supply items is the knowledge the scorer has of how a particular student did on earlier items in a test. For example, let's say that there is an item on which a number of different responses are correct, some less explicitly than others. Some teachers, in looking at the less correct answers, will tend to score according to how well the student has seemed to do on preceding items. One who has missed many items probably "does not know what he is writing about." One who has been quite successful on previous items possibly "grasped the correct idea but doesn't express himself very well." This kind of bias is perhaps best overcome by the use of the following procedure:

1. Remove the identifying name or set of initials from each response sheet, perhaps by cutting it off, after numbering the two sections of the sheet with the same number.
2. Shuffle the response sheets for the entire group before starting to mark any of them. Since they now carry no names, it is very difficult to identify who wrote a given sheet unless the number of students is exceedingly small.
3. If there are several items, score all papers on one item only. Then reshuffle the sheets so that they are not in the same order and proceed to score the next item on all papers.
4. Enter the score for each item either on a separate sheet or on the response sheet in such a fashion that it cannot be seen when you are scoring the next item.

The foregoing suggestions may seem to entail an excessive amount of work. However, insofar as they prevent irrelevant judgments from biasing the scoring, they will also prevent lack of objectivity from decreasing both the validity and the reliability of the test results.

Summary

This chapter has suggested that summative examinations may have a variety of purposes, one being simply to give grades and another being to certify competence in a given area. A test may serve to provide feedback for students or predictions of later success, among other uses. We have suggested that as the purposes vary, so will some of the procedures for developing and scoring the test. We have laid strong emphasis on the notion that content validity will come only from the appropriate valuing of the behavior-content cells in a table of specifications. After all, it is easily argued that content validity is the sine qua non of a final examination. The chapter was intended to give some help with ways in which one might set about weighting the parts of a test. In that section of the discussion, it was pointed out that the actual weight of elements of a test in the total score does depend upon the empirical characteristics of variance and correlation. Finally, it was argued that objectivity can be controlled in either choice or supply items, and steps were suggested for doing this.

REFERENCES

Adkins, D. C. *Statistics: An introduction for students in the behavioral sciences.* Columbus: Merrill, 1964.

American Educational Research Association & National Council on Measurements Used in Education, Committees on Test Standards. *Technical recommendations for achievement tests.* Washington, D.C.: AERA and NCMUE, 1955.

Blommers, P., & Lindquist, E. F. *Elementary statistical methods.* Boston: Houghton Mifflin, 1960.

Campbell, D. T., & Fiske, D. W. Convergent and discriminant validation by the multitrait-multimethod matrix. *Psychological Bulletin,* 1959, **56,** 81–105.

Cronbach, L. J. *Essentials of psychological testing.* (2nd ed.) New York: Harper, 1960.

Ebel, R. L. *Measuring educational achievement.* Englewood Cliffs, N.J.: Prentice-Hall, 1965.

French, W., and associates. *Behavioral goals of general education in high school.* New York: Russell Sage Foundation, 1957.

Furst, E. J. *Constructing evaluation instruments.* New York: Longmans, Green, 1958.

Gerberich, J. R. *Specimen objective test items: A guide to achievement test construction.* New York: Longmans, Green, 1956.

Gronlund, N. E. *Measurement and evaluation in teaching.* New York: Macmillan, 1965.

Illinois Statewide High School Testing Program. *Natural Science Reading Comprehension Test.* Urbana, Ill.: Center for Instructional Research and Curriculum Evaluation, University of Illinois at Urbana-Champaign, 1956.

Kearney, N. C. *Elementary school objectives.* New York: Russell Sage Foundation, 1953.

Klinckmann, E. The BSCS grid for test analysis. *BSCS Newsletter,* 1963, No. 19, pp. 17–21. (Biological Sciences Curriculum Study, University of Colorado.)

Kuder, G. F., & Richardson, M. W. The theory of the estimation of test reliability. *Psychometrica,* 1937, **2,** 151–160.

Walker, H. M., & Lev, J. *Elementary statistical methods.* (Rev. ed.) New York: Holt, 1958.

5

Evaluation for Placement and Diagnosis

Chapter 2 introduced the basic distinction between formative and summative evaluation. Chapters 4 and 6 are given over respectively to a detailed treatment of each approach. The present discussion deals with a third type—diagnostic evaluation—distinct in many ways from but at the same time closely related to both formative and summative evaluation. Like all forms of evaluation, diagnosis involves a valuing, determination, description, and classification of some aspect of student behavior. However, the two purposes of diagnosis—either to place the student properly at the outset of instruction or to discover the underlying causes of deficiencies in student learning as instruction unfolds—distinguish it from other forms of evaluation.

Diagnostic evaluation performed prior to instruction has placement as its primary function; that is, it attempts to focus instruction by locating the proper starting point. Diagnosis for this purpose may take several forms. First, it may seek to determine whether or not a student possesses certain entry behaviors or skills judged to be prerequisite to the attainment of the objectives of the planned unit. Second, it may attempt to establish whether the student already has mastery over the objectives of a given unit or course, thereby allowing him to enroll in a more advanced program. Finally, it may aim to classify students according to certain characteristics, such as interest, personality, background, aptitude, skill, and prior instructional history, hypothesized or known to be related to a particular teaching strategy or instructional method.

Diagnostic evaluation performed while instruction is underway has as its primary function determining the underlying circumstances or causes of repeated deficiencies in a student's learning that have not responded to the usual form of remedial instruction. The causes for a student's failure in a formative unit may be unrelated to the instructional methods and materials per se, but may instead be physical, emotional, cultural, or environmental in nature. Diagnosis tries to pinpoint the reasons for observed symptoms of learning disorder so that, when possible, remedial action can be taken to correct or remove these blocks to progress.

Diagnostic evaluation, especially in its placement function, is closely related to the question of educational "grouping." There are three categories of grouping (Yates, 1966). The first is interschool grouping, according to which students are assigned to different types of schools—vocational, commercial, college preparatory, and so forth. The second category, intraschool grouping, can result in the same kind of gross streaming as does interschool grouping; that is, within a comprehensive high school a student can be placed in the vocational, commercial, or college preparatory track. Intraschool grouping can also involve the placing of students in the proper instructional group according to their level of prerequisite entry behaviors, their prior degree of mastery of course objectives, or other student variables known or thought to be related to a particular teaching strategy or instructional method. The third category, intraclass grouping, like intraschool, can place students in rather broad tracks, such as "bright," "average," or "slow"; or it too can try to place students in the proper instructional group on the basis of student diagnosis. To borrow a term from Thelen (1967), this last type of grouping results in the formation of "teachability groups."

This chapter will not discuss the pros and cons of grouping in itself. The reader is referred to Yates (1966) or Thelen (1967) for a complete discussion of the various grouping practices currently employed in education. Instead, the present discussion will emphasize the diagnosis of the individual student, which is different from though related to grouping and group diagnosis per se.

The remainder of this chapter will point out similarities and differences between diagnostic evaluation and both formative and summative evaluation, describe the various functions of diagnostic evaluation and many of the techniques presently available to help the teacher fulfill these functions, and discuss some of the limitations and gaps in present diagnostic methodology.

Similarities and Differences between Diagnostic Evaluation and Formative and Summative Evaluation

As we pointed out above, diagnostic evaluation is closely related to while at the same time being distinct from both formative and summative evaluation.

Diagnostic evaluation for placement purposes performed before instruction begins often depends heavily on the results of summative evaluation or can employ instruments designed for summative purposes. Summative evaluation takes place at the end of a period of instruction in order to grade or certify students on the unit, chapter, course, or semester's work, among other things.

Typically in education, summative evaluation has resulted in the student's being assigned a single score or grade for the course or subject. The summative grades are sometimes used diagnostically from primary school through college to group or track students. Thus in September a fifth-grade teacher, on the basis of summative grades in fourth-grade arithmetic, might divide his class into three groups—advanced, average, and slow—for differential instruction in arithmetic.

In Chap. 4 and later in this chapter, we describe ways in which the results of a summative evaluation can be reported so that they can be intelligently employed in subsequent diagnosis for placement purposes. At this point, however, a caution is in order. The practice of using summative results for diagnosis, if not planned and judiciously monitored, has dubious validity at best and can cause irreparable harm by trapping some students in the vise of a self-fulfilling prophecy of failure. A principal difficulty with such a procedure is that an important placement decision is made on the basis of a single letter or numerical grade that is often unreliable. Moreover, whatever its administrative convenience, a single grade precludes an adequate description of the student's performance on each of the objectives of the course. It is unlikely that a student performed consistently at the same level of competence on all of the objectives of the course. In other words, the single grade hides more than it shows. It does not reveal the variation in learning from objective to objective, and therefore does not provide adequate diagnostic information for intelligent placement.

Chapter 3, Learning for Mastery, discussed the adverse results the use of such gross summative measures for subsequent placement have had in the past on a child's self-concept. Even first-graders quickly learn the expectation level the teacher has for the different reading groups in the room. For a more detailed discussion of the adverse effects poor grouping practices can have on a child, see Yates (1966) and Thelen (1967). Suffice it to recall here that repeated failure or even continued grouping in a track for which there is a low expectation of success can destroy a student's faith in his ability to perform. Therefore, placement decisions must be carefully made with the end in view of entering the student into an instructional sequence that will lead him eventually to mastery rather than some watered-down level of achievement or outright failure.

Summative examinations can be used in diagnostic evaluation for placement decisions. For example, if a student can demonstrate at the beginning of the year a satisfactory level of mastery on a summative exam in French I, he might be awarded the credits for French I and be allowed to pursue the next French course in the foreign-language sequence.

Diagnostic evaluation can be quite distinct from or closely related to formative evaluation, depending on the function it seeks to fulfill. If ten formative units are planned for a semester's work in a given subject, diagnostic evaluation can, as we have already seen, try to place the student at the most appropriate starting point. This type of diagnosis takes place prior to instruction and focuses on the student's status in relation to prerequisite behaviors, level of mastery of each unit, or some other variable, such as aptitude or interest, thought to be pertinent to a particular type of instruction. In this way diagnostic evaluation differs from formative, which has as its function providing the learner and teacher with feedback information as the learner progresses through any one of the ten units. Further, diagnosis used for placement does not concern itself, as does formative evaluation, with the relationships or lack of them between elements in a given unit and among the ten units themselves. Thus diagnosis for placement purposes is a before-the-fact operation, while formative evaluation is an ongoing process designed to provide the student and teacher with continual feedback on their effectiveness as they proceed through the instructional hierarchy.

However, we have seen that diagnostic evaluation can also be an ongoing process carried on in conjunction with formative evaluation to try to determine whether factors unconnected with instruction are the cause of the breakdown in learning which has been pinpointed by formative testing. Formative evaluation determines whether the student has mastered each step in the instructional hierarchy, and if not prescribes alternative or remedial instruction designed to lead the majority of students to mastery. If, however, the student does not profit from these prescriptions and continues to exhibit symptoms of failure or disinterest, diagnostic evaluation probes deeper to try to discover the cause. We shall see later in the chapter that this type of diagnosis involves forming hypotheses about the reasons for these persistent learning difficulties based on observation, and then systematically checking each hypothesis, often by referring the student to medical, psychological, guidance, or remedial specialists.

Another important difference between diagnostic and formative evaluation lies in the characteristics of the instruments used by each. Diagnostic tests, particularly those available commercially, usually are designed to measure more generalized skills and traits than are formative instruments. In many ways they resemble aptitude tests, particularly in that they give subscale scores for important skills and abilities related to the performance being diagnosed. The total score in each of the subscales is considered independently, and the individual test items making up each scale are not considered by themselves. For example, the Gates

Reading Diagnostic Tests (Gates, 1945) give scores for the following important general characteristics of reading performance: Silent Reading, Oral Reading (which in turn is divided into eleven subscores), Oral Vocabulary, Reversals, Phrase Perception, Word Perception Analysis (two subscores), Spelling, seven scores on Visual Perception Technique, and four on Auditory Technique.

Formative tests, on the other hand, are designed specifically for a particular unit of instruction and are intended to locate *exactly* where in the unit the student is experiencing difficulty. Further, a total score on a formative test is not very meaningful; instead item response patterns in terms of mastery or nonmastery of the skills and content measured by the items are used to check progress through each and every step in the unit. Thus formative tests are criterion-referenced measures. Glaser (1963) has described the characteristics of criterion-referenced tests in the following manner:

> Underlying the concept of achievement measurements is the notion of a continuum of knowledge acquisition ranging from no proficiency at all to perfect performance. An individual's achievement level falls at some point on this continuum as indicated by the behaviors he displays during testing. The degree to which his achievement resembles desired performance at any specified level is assessed by criterion-referenced measures of achievement or proficiency. The standard against which a student's performance is compared when measured in this manner is the behavior which defines each point along the achievement continuum. The point is that the specific behaviors implied at each level of proficiency can be identified and used to describe the specific tasks a student must be capable of performing before he achieves one of these knowledge levels. It is in this sense that measures of proficiency can be criterion-referenced [p. 519].

Commercial diagnostic tests, however, are generally norm-referenced instruments. That is, the performance of the student on the group of items making up a given subscale is compared with the performance of a normative group of some kind. The student's score may be in terms of how his performance compares with that of students at various age or grade levels or in terms of his rank or standing in some comparison group. Basically, one is told that he is more or less proficient than others in each of the characteristics being measured.

The interpretation of criterion-referenced scores is automatic in that the score itself details what the student actually can do and what skills and content he has still to master. The use and appraisal of norm-referenced feedback, by contrast, will differ according to makeup of the norm group. For example, scoring higher than 90 percent of a group consisting of students who are apathetic and not particularly academically oriented or able will have different implications from ranking at the 40th percentile in a group consisting of the hardest-working, academically eager college-bound students. However, as we shall presently see, norm-referenced diagnostic tests are extremely valuable in placing the student at the proper instructional starting point.

The report of information gained as a result of diagnostic placement evaluation usually takes the form of an individual profile, criterion- or norm-referenced, on the cognitive, affective, or psychomotor objectives being evaluated. Formative criterion-referenced results are reported as patterns of passes and failures on each cognitive objective making up the structure of the unit (see Chap. 6, page 130). Summative results are generally reported in terms of a total score or some norm-referenced score, although subscores for various cognitive and psychomotor and occasionally affective objectives making up the test are sometimes given.

Table 5-1 summarizes the similarities and differences between diagnostic, formative, and summative evaluation.

Let us now consider ways in which diagnostic evaluation can be carried out and at the same time some of the limitations and gaps in present diagnostic methodology. We shall first treat diagnosis performed prior to instruction for placement purposes, and then deal with diagnosis performed during ongoing instruction to determine the more deep-seated causes of learning difficulties.

Table 5-1 Similarities and Differences between Diagnostic, Formative, and Summative Evaluation

	Type of Evaluation		
	Diagnostic	*Formative*	*Summative*
Function	Placement: Determining the presence or absence of prerequisite skills; Determining the student's prior level of mastery; Classifying the student according to various characteristics known or thought to be related to alternative modes of instruction Determination of underlying causes of repeated learning difficulties	Feedback to student and teacher on student progress through a unit Location of errors in terms of the structure of a unit so that remedial alternative instruction techniques can be prescribed	Certification or grading of students at the end of a unit, semester, or course
Time	For placement at the outset of a unit, semester, or year's work During instruction when student evidences repeated inability to profit fully from ordinary instruction	During instruction	At the end of a unit, semester, or year's work
Emphasis in evaluation	Cognitive, affective, and psychomotor behaviors Physical, psychological, and environmental factors	Cognitive behaviors	Generally cognitive behaviors; depending on subject matter, sometimes psychomotor; occasionally affective behaviors
Type of instrumentation	Formative and summative instruments for pretests Standardized achievement tests Standardized diagnostic tests Teacher-made instruments Observation and checklists	Specially designed formative instruments	Final or summative examinations

(Continues on page 92.)

Table 5-1 Similarities and Differences between Diagnostic, Formative, and Summative Evaluation (Continued)

	Type of Evaluation		
	Diagnostic	*Formative*	*Summative*
How objectives of evaluation are sampled	Specific sample of each prerequisite entry behavior Sample of weighted course objectives Sample of student variables hypothesized or known to be related to a particular type of instruction Sample of physically, emotionally, or environmentally related behaviors	Specific sample of all related tasks in the hierarchy of the unit	A sample of weighted course objectives
Item difficulty	Diagnosis of prerequisite skills and abilities: a large number of easy items, 65% difficulty or higher	Cannot be specified beforehand	Average difficulty, ranging from 35% to 70%, with some very easy and some very difficult items
Scoring	Norm- and criterion-referenced	Criterion-referenced	Generally norm-referenced but can be criterion-referenced
Method of reporting scores	Individual profile by subskills	Individual pattern of pass-fail scores on each task in the hierarchy	Total score or subscores by objectives

Diagnostic evaluation for placement purposes

Very often as a course begins, the instruction starts at the same point for all members of the class. This practice assumes, at least implicitly, that everyone in the class is at the same point on an achievement continuum—an imaginary zero point in terms of mastery of the planned objectives. The assumption of homogeneity of education backgrounds might have been safer in the past, at least at the elementary and secondary levels, before our society became so highly mobile. However, most classes today, particularly in our urban and suburban schools, are made up of students with a wide variety of educational backgrounds, lacking complete uniformity in their patterns of achievement and differing with respect to the nature, amount, and depth of independent study and reading. As this diversification of backgrounds increases, the variance from an imaginary zero point increases. Students who actually fall at that point are those who have not yet mastered any of the objectives of the planned course but who do possess all of the entry behaviors, skills, and content prerequisite to the attainment of the objectives. In fact, some students may be well beyond the zero point, already having mastered all or many of the competences the course has been designed to develop. On the other hand, some students fall below it—that is, they possess few or none of the entry behaviors, skills, and content judged to be prerequisite for future progress.

One of the principal purposes of diagnostic evaluation is to determine the position of the student on the imaginary continuum so that he can be placed at the proper step in the instruction sequence. If instruction for all students starts at the same point, the result can be that those who have already mastered objectives well beyond this point fast become bored and disinterested while those who do not yet possess the prerequisites fast become discouraged and frustrated.

Diagnosis of prerequisite entry behaviors and skills

A crucial function of diagnostic evaluation is the identification of students who fall below the imaginary zero point discussed above. One of the problems of students who have not been successful in school, and in particular disadvantaged children, is that they have often been placed in instructional sequences without having mastered basic skills or prerequisite abilities taught at a lower grade. We should not expect materials and methods developed for average or successful students to work with those lacking the necessary previous learning. For example, a student would most likely be prevented from mastering the objectives of a fourth-grade social studies course if he has not yet acquired such a basic beginning reading skill as the command of sound-symbol relationships. With some students, and particularly with disadvantaged children, it may be necessary to adapt the instruction so that the child first acquires these prerequisite skills, especially in the reading and language arts. This, of course, is the area of many of the compensatory education programs developed under Title I of the Elementary and Secondary Education Act.

This diagnostic function, while particularly critical in compensatory education programs, is by no means limited to culturally disadvantaged students. Within any grade, wide variation can be found in the achievement levels of students in basic subjects such as reading, arithmetic, and language skills. Goodlad and Anderson (1959) have shown that even as early as the second grade, some students are reading at a fourth-grade level while some fall below the norm for the second grade. Balow (1962) shows that by the fifth grade proficiency in overall reading can vary in grade equivalent from grades 2 to 9, and that the variation on reading subtests can be even greater. Even when students are homogeneously grouped on the basis of a particular variable, they can still differ somewhat on that variable and widely on related subskills (Yates, 1966). Such findings demonstrate the fallacy of assuming that all students in a given grade possess certain basic skills and abilities equally, and that therefore the same starting point in instruction is appropriate for all or at least most. Many students have not yet in fact mastered skills taught at the lower grades, and identifying these students is a primary function of diagnostic evaluation.

The use of standardized achievement tests in the diagnosis of prerequisite entry behaviors and skills

The diagnosis of weaknesses in the relatively general prerequisite abilities can begin with the administration of a standardized achievement test battery. Such a battery can help a teacher identify general levels of a student's performance in the common aspects of the elementary school curriculum. The tests allow the teacher to compare the performance of a child of a given grade level or age with that of a normative group in such basic areas as vocabulary, reading, spelling, language usage, arithmetic computation, and arithmetic problem solving. Most major test makers give the teacher the option of filling out individual profile charts for each student. These provide a graphic picture of the student's overall level of achievement in relation to either his age or his grade group.

Figures 5-1, 5-2, and 5-3 present examples of individual profile charts prepared by three major test makers.

Basically the charts allow the teacher to compare a student's performance on various subtests visually with the performance of a norm group. On all the profiles pictured in the figures, the student's raw score is transformed into one or more converted scores. With the SRA Pupil Profile (Fig. 5-1), the teacher can write the grade equivalent and the percentile rank directly under each subtest and then plot the grade equivalents. The Metropolitan Individual Profile Chart pictured in Fig. 5-3 uses standard scores, grade equivalents (percentile ranks could be used instead), and stanines. It also allows the teacher to plot the student's stanine from each subtest. The California Individual Test Record, example (Fig. 5-2), uses grade equivalents (standard scores could be used instead), the student's anticipated achieve-

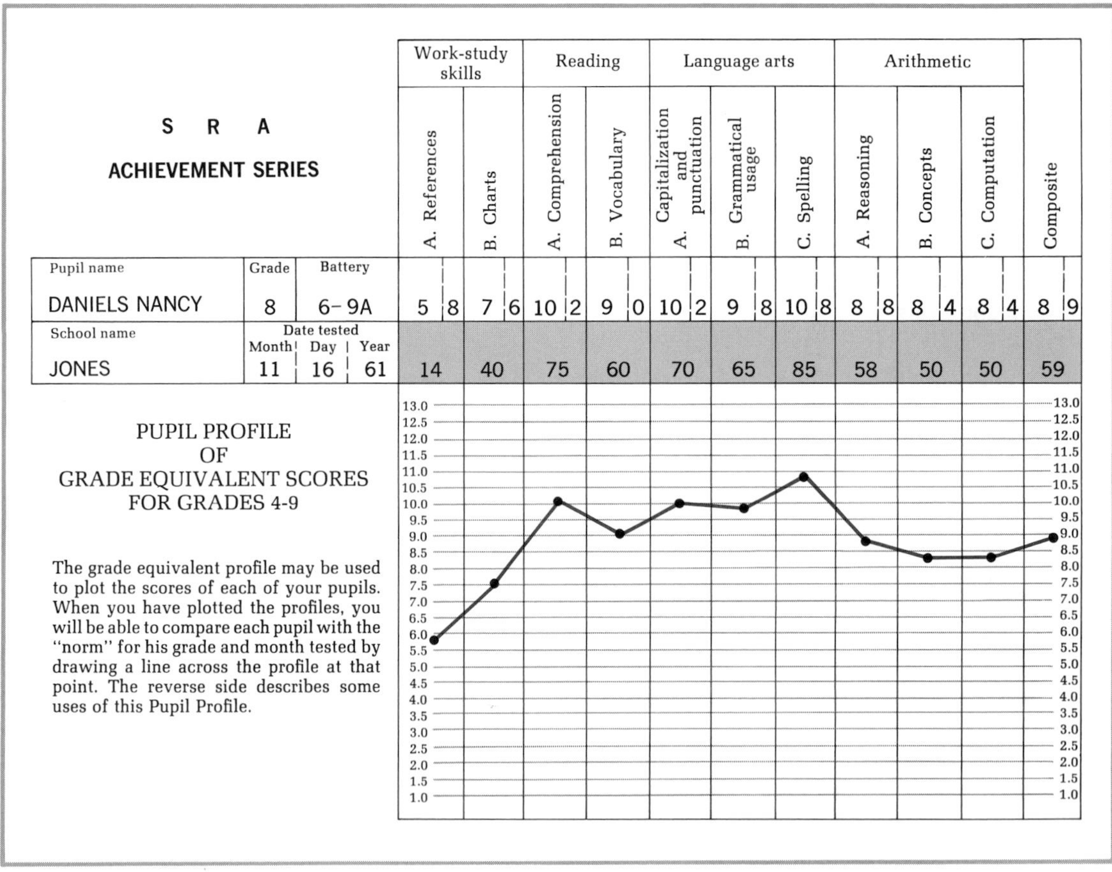

FIGURE 5-1. An adaptation of the Science Research Associates pupil profile chart. (L. P. Thorpe, D. W. Lefever, & R. A. Naslund. *How to use the SRA Achievement Series.* (2nd ed.) Chicago: Science Research Associates, 1962. P. 21. The chart is copyright © 1961 by Science Research Associates, Inc., 259 East Erie Street, Chicago, Illinois; All Rights Reserved.)

CTB INDIVIDUAL TEST RECORD

COMPREHENSIVE TESTS OF BASIC SKILLS

C T B S

ROBERTS ANN	◄ NAME	TEACHER ►	JONES	DATE OF TESTING ►
CENTRAL	◄ SCHOOL	GRADE ►	5.1	5374-011 10 68
ANY TOWN	◄ CITY	LEVEL ►	Q2	

AREA Test	RS	GE or SS	AAGE or AASS	DIFFERENCE	NAT'L %ILE
READING Vocabulary	26	5.1	5.5		52
READING Comprehension	31	5.7	5.5		60
TOTAL Reading	57	5.4	5.6		57
LANGUAGE Mechanics	11	4.2	5.1		34
LANGUAGE Expression	18	5.3	5.6		54
LANGUAGE Spelling	27	8.4	5.4	+3.0	93
TOTAL Language	56	5.4	5.3		58
ARITHMETIC Computation	16	3.4	4.8	−1.4	7
ARITHMETIC Concepts	10	3.2	4.8	−1.6	13
ARITHMETIC Applications	6	3.4	4.5		18
TOTAL Arithmetic	32	3.3	4.7	−1.4	8
TOTAL BATTERY	145	4.4	5.0		35
STUDY SKILLS Reference materials	9	4.6	5.2		41
STUDY SKILLS Graphic materials	12	4.0	4.9		27
TOTAL Study skills	21	4.2	5.0		32

NATIONAL PERCENTILE

1 2 5 10 20 30 40 50 60 70 80 90 95 98 99

READING Vocabulary

A. RECOGNITION AND / OR APPLICATION OF TECHNIQUES — Vocabulary (items 1–40)

READING Comprehension

A. RECOGNITION — Literal meaning; B. TRANSLATION — Simple rewording, Paraphrasing; C. INTERPRETATION — Main idea, Relationships, Conclusions, Inferences; D. ANALYSIS — Extended meaning

LANGUAGE Mechanics

A. RECOGNITION AND / OR APPLICATION OF TECHNIQUES — Punctuation (items 1–13), Capitalization (items 14–25)

LANGUAGE Expression

A. RECOGNITION / APPLICATION — Correct usage (items 26–35); B. TRANSLATION — Economy / clarity (items 51–55); C. INTERPRETATION — Word choice (items 36–50)

LANGUAGE Spelling

A. RECOGNITION AND / OR APPLICATION OF TECHNIQUES — Spelling (items 1–30)

ARITHMETIC Computation

A. RECOGNITION AND / OR APPLICATION OF TECHNIQUES — Addition, Subtraction, Multiplication, Division

ARITHMETIC Concepts

A. RECOGNITION / APPLICATION — Recognition of concept; B. TRANSLATION — Converting form; C. INTERPRETATION — Equations, Comparisons, Other relationships; D. ANALYSIS — Organization

ARITHMETIC Applications

C. INTERPRETATION — Selecting method, Solving problem; D. ANALYSIS — Organization

STUDY SKILLS Reference materials

A. RECOGNITION / APPLICATION OF TECHNIQUES — Parts of books, Dictionary use, Library use

STUDY SKILLS Graphic materials

B. TRANSLATION — Converting symbols; C. INTERPRETATION — Relationships, Conclusions; D. ANALYSIS — Extended meaning

Q2

FIGURE 5-2. An adaptation of the California Test Bureau pupil profile chart. (California Test Bureau. *Comprehensive Tests of Basic Skills: CTB Individual Test Record*. Monterey, Calif.: CTB, A Division of McGraw-Hill Book Company, undated.)

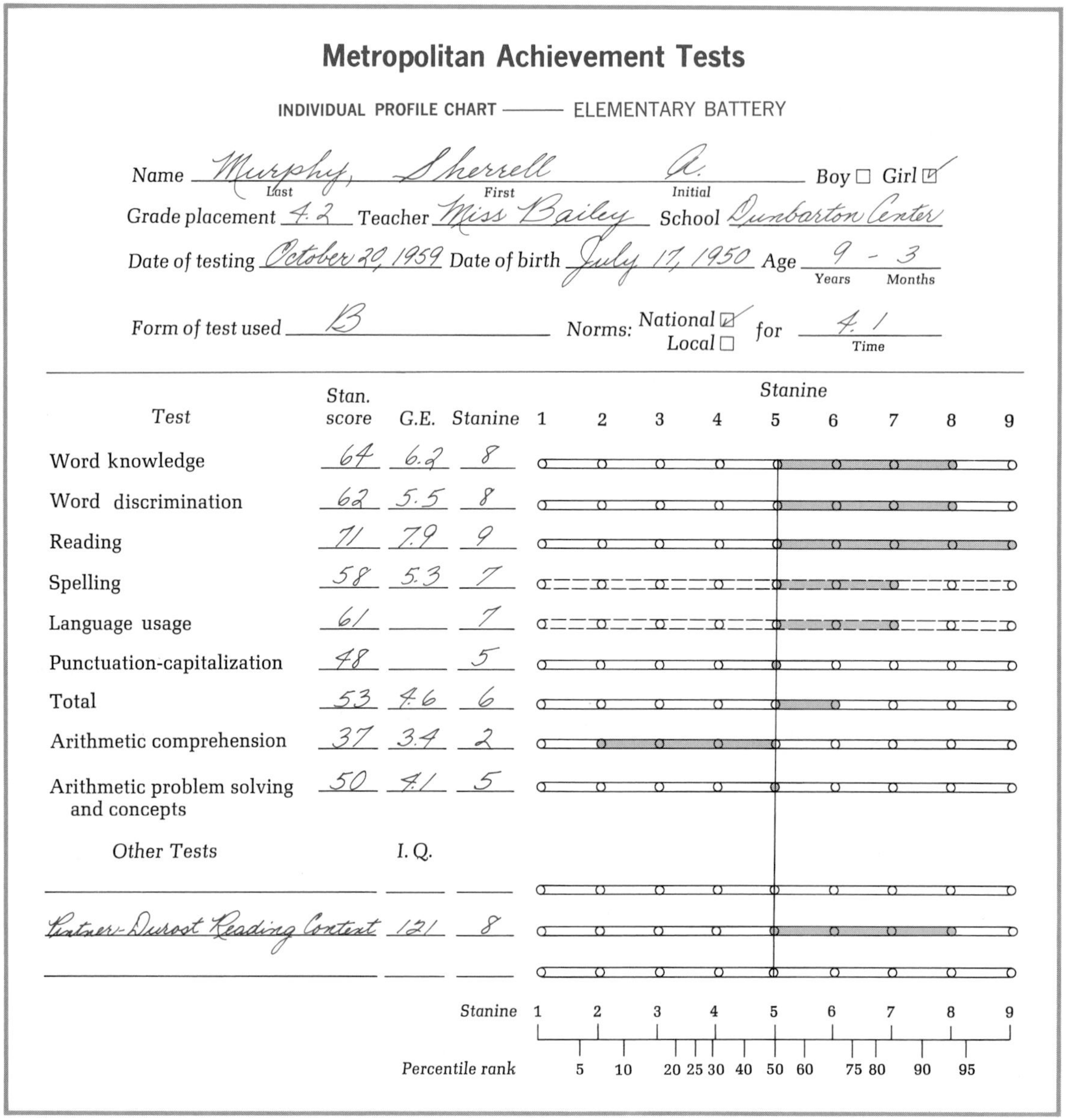

Metropolitan Achievement Tests

INDIVIDUAL PROFILE CHART —— ELEMENTARY BATTERY

Name Murphy, (Last) Sherrell (First) A. (Initial) Boy ☐ Girl ☑

Grade placement 4.2 Teacher Miss Bailey School Dunbarton Center

Date of testing October 20, 1959 Date of birth July 17, 1950 Age 9 (Years) - 3 (Months)

Form of test used B Norms: National ☑ Local ☐ for 4.1 (Time)

Test	Stan. score	G.E.	Stanine
Word knowledge	64	6.2	8
Word discrimination	62	5.5	8
Reading	71	7.9	9
Spelling	58	5.3	7
Language usage	61		7
Punctuation-capitalization	48		5
Total	53	4.6	6
Arithmetic comprehension	37	3.4	2
Arithmetic problem solving and concepts	50	4.1	5
Other Tests	I. Q.		
Pintner-Durost Reading Content	121		8

Stanine 1 2 3 4 5 6 7 8 9

Percentile rank 5 10 20 25 30 40 50 60 75 80 90 95

FIGURE 5-3. An adaptation of the Metropolitan Achievement Tests pupil profile chart. (*Metropolitan Achievement Tests: Directions for completing Individual Profile Chart, all batteries.* New York: Harcourt, Brace, 1960. Copyright © 1960 by Harcourt, Brace & World, Inc.; All Rights Reserved.)

ment grade equivalent, the difference between her obtained grade equivalent and her anticipated achievement grade equivalent (if the difference is significant), and her national percentile rank. The national percentiles are then plotted in the form of percentile ranks to picture the range within which the student's true score falls sixty-eight times out of one hundred. In addition, the California profile shows how the student answered each item in each subtest by using a plus sign for items answered correctly and a minus for items answered incorrectly.

The creators of the Metropolitan chart present a typical diagnosis of a general deficiency revealed in the student's Individual Profile Chart pictured in Fig. 5-3:

> It would seem to be quite clear that Sherrell is a handicapped child in the area of arithmetic. The very low stanine of 2 in Arithmetic Computation suggests that the difficulty lies in her failure to master fundamentals. Her performance is just average in Arithmetic Problem Solving. Since this test involves more reasoning ability, it is logical for her stanine to be higher here than in Computation. [Sherrell's IQ stanine was 8.] One cannot tell from the profile alone the nature of her difficulty, but an alert teacher would consider this to be a danger signal calling for careful study.
>
> (*Metropolitan Achievement Tests*, 1960)

The important caution contained in the above description should not be overlooked: the standardized achievement test can alert the teacher to the fact that a student is weak in a certain general area like reading or arithmetic computation when compared with some normative group, but it does not reveal the exact nature and cause of the difficulty. More sensitive diagnostic instruments are needed for this task.

In order to achieve a somewhat finer diagnosis of weaknesses on a particular subtest, some test publishers suggest using item data. This technique involves examining the item response pattern of a student. If a student misses several items all dealing with the principle of carrying in addition, then a workable hypothesis might be that the student needs remedial instruction in this skill. The California Individual Test Record pictured in Fig. 5-2 shows an item analysis of each subtest in the battery taken by a student. Other test makers also provide various types of item analysis charts. However, it is a simple matter for a teacher to construct one himself that gives an individual or group item analysis profile on how each item was answered. Table 5-2 is an example of part of such a chart.

The teacher simply lists the name of each student in his class (the patterns for only six students are shown in Table 5-2). Along the top of the chart he lists the item numbers, arranged according to subtest, objective, content, or behavior; vertical lines enclose each group of related items. A plus sign indicates that the item was answered correctly and a zero that it was answered incorrectly. If the chart is read across, the individual's pattern of responses on the related items is revealed; if the chart is read down, the pattern of the class response is shown. These patterns can then be examined to determine whether it appears that an individual or the class as a whole is consistently missing a certain type of item and therefore might be in need of remedial instruction.

While the practice of examining item response patterns on standardized tests can be helpful, it often lacks the refinement needed for an accurate

Table 5-2 An Example of Part of an Item Analysis Chart that Could Be Constructed by a Classroom Teacher

	1	2	7	9	10	12	14	3	4	5	6	11	13	15	16	18	19	20	21	22	23	24	25	26
Mary Ryan	+	+	+	+	+	+	+	+	+	+	0	0	+	0	0	0	0	0	+	+	+	+	0	+
Martha Smith	+	0	+	0	0	0	0	0	0	0	+	+	0	0	0	0	0	0	+	0	+	+	0	+
Joseph O'Brien	0	+	+	0	+	+	+	0	+	+	0	0	+	+	0	+	+	0	+	+	+	+	+	+
George Carlson	+	+	+	+	0	0	+	0	0	0	+	0	+	0	0	0	0	0	+	0	+	+	0	+
Eileen Jones	0	0	0	+	0	+	+	0	+	0	0	0	+	+	0	0	0	0	+	0	+	+	0	+
Sarah Allen	+	+	+	0	+	+	+	0	0	0	0	+	0	0	0	+	+	0	0	0	+	+	0	+

Table 5-3 Remedial Charts for Use with the Greene-Stapp Language Abilities Test

Test 1: Capitalization, and Test 4: Punctuation

Possible causes of low test scores	*Evidence indicating specific deficiency*	*Suggested remedial treatment*
1. Lack of knowledge of specific capitalization and punctuation situations.	1. Types of errors made on this test and in student's other written work.	1. Compare specific capitalization and punctuation errors with skills emphasized in textbook and local course of study to determine those areas in which remedial training is needed. Provide dictation and proofreading exercises involving skills in these areas. Exercises should require insertion of capitals and punctuation as well as avoidance of overcapitalization and overpunctuation. Emphasize the need of critical editing of own copy.
2. Tendency to overcapitalize or overpunctuate.	2. High proportion of errors involving overuse of capitals or punctuation.	2. Use dictation and proofreading exercises designed to emphasize elimination of improper or excessive punctuation and capitalization.
3. Carelessness in proofreading.	3. Erratic and careless work in daily written expression in other subjects; limited ability to detect errors in written copy.	3. Emphasize the development of a critical attitude toward own written work. Provide proofreading exercises related to the types of situations in which the student shows weakness.
4. Poorly developed sentence sense.	4. Low score on Test 3; tendency to use incomplete sentences in writing.	4. See suggestions for Test 3.
5. Carelessness in handwriting and other matters of form.	5. Careless formation of letters and punctuation marks in daily work.	5. Give practice in writing properly those letters and punctuation marks which cause difficulty. Stress the essentials of good form in written work. Insist that the student edit and proofread his own papers before submitting them.

Test 2: Spelling

Possible causes of low test scores	*Evidence indicating specific deficiency*	*Suggested remedial treatment*
1. Specific learning difficulties:	1.	1.
a. Faulty pronunciation.	a. Poor speech habits; results of informal pronunciation tests based on spelling vocabulary.	a. Give practice in repeating correctly pronounced word while looking at the written form.
b. Failure to associate sounds of letters and syllables with spelling of words.	b. Results of individual informal test; types of spelling errors in daily work.	b. Teach basic phonetic combinations and methods of analyzing words.

Test 2: Spelling (Continued)

Possible causes of low test scores	*Evidence indicating specific deficiency*	*Suggested remedial treatment*
c. Tendency to transpose, add, or omit letters.	c. Errors observed in daily work.	c. Emphasize visual recall of words. Have student practice writing the words, exaggerating the formation of letters. Underline individual hard spots.
d. Limited power to visualize word forms.	d. Results of individual interview or informal test.	d. Emphasize the practice of learning new words by looking at the word, closing the eyes, and attempting to recall or reproduce the word.
e. Tendency to spell unphonetic words phonetically.	e. Types of errors made, especially insertion or omission of letters.	e. Show that all words are not spelled as they sound. Emphasize steps in learning to spell.
f. Difficulties in writing; poor letter formation.	f. Errors in daily written work; low rating on handwriting scale.	f. Give practice in writing difficult letter formations and combinations. Emphasize need to form carefully such letters as *i* and *e*, *u* and *n*.
g. Failure to master a method of learning to spell.	g. Poor methods of studying spelling.	g. Teach steps in learning to spell. Suggested steps: (1) Look at word. (2) Listen while teacher pronounces it. (3) Pronounce it. (4) Say it by syllables. (5) Use it in a sentence. (6) Close eyes and visualize the word. (7) Write it. (8) Close eyes and recall it. (9) Write it again. (10) Repeat steps as necessary.
2. Lack of teaching emphasis on individual's spelling difficulties.	2. Student's misspellings as observed in daily written work.	2. Have each student keep a list of words misspelled as a basis for individual study.
3. Careless in proofreading.	3. Erratic work in daily written expression.	3. Emphasize accuracy in writing and insist on careful proofreading of own written work.
4. Lack of experience with the testing technique.	4. Low score on test contrasted with high score when the same words are dictated.	4. Give practice in choosing correctly spelled words from lists of words, some of which are spelled incorrectly. Emphasize proofreading own written work correctly.
5. Instructional emphasis on different vocabulary.	5. Low score on test in contrast with good record for spelling in daily work.	5. Check the words taught locally with lists of known social utility.
6. Difficulties in seeing and hearing.	6. Handicaps detected by observation or medical examination.	6. Refer to doctor for medical advice. Have student sit near window and blackboard. Make special effort to speak and write clearly.

Table 5-3 Remedial Charts for Use with the Greene-Stapp Language Abilities Test (Continued)

Test 3: Sentence Structure and Applied Grammar, and Test 5: Usage and Applied Grammar

Possible causes of low test scores	*Evidence indicating specific deficiency*	*Suggested remedial treatment*
1. Lack of adequate grammatical background.	1. Difficulty with grammatical aspects of work in language.	1. Compare student's sources of difficulty with local course of study to determine those areas in which remedial training is needed.
2. Lack of knowledge of specific correct usages.	2. Specific errors in daily oral and written expression.	2. Supplement written exercises with oral practice in correct usage.
3. Poor language background.	3. Careless and inaccurate usage in oral and written expression; poor enunciation and pronunciation.	3. Select for emphasis a limited number of important usages. Check oral and written expression carefully for errors in these aspects of language.
4. Foreign language in the home.	4. Difficulty in pronunciation of English; evidence of use of two languages at home.	4. Give corrective instruction to overcome a limited number of specific errors at a time.
5. Careless language habits.	5. Observed carelessness in expression, particularly in informal situations.	5. Encourage a critical attitude toward oral and written expression. Have student proofread all written work before submitting it.
6. Inability to sense what is missing in sentence fragments.	6. Tendency to use incomplete sentences in own writing; inability to recognize subjects and predicates.	6. Give practice in identifying complete subjects and complete predicates, particularly in own writing. Provide exercises requiring recognition and completion of sentence fragments.
7. Lack of ability to recognize "run-on" sentences; overuse of *and.*	7. Poor sentence structure in student's writing.	7. Give practice in identifying poor sentence structure and in recasting poor sentences. Stress individual practice in writing good sentences.
8. Poor reading comprehension.	8. Low scores on standardized reading comprehension tests.	8. Provide instruction in vocabulary and reading comprehension at level suggested by test results.
9. Low mental ability.	9. Low IQ as shown by reliable mental test.	9. Emphasize functional rather than formal aspects of sentence structure and usage.

SOURCE: H. A. Greene & H. I. Stapp. *Greene-Stapp Language Abilities Test.* Yonkers-on-Hudson, N.Y.: World Book, 1954. Pp. 11–12.

diagnosis of specific learning disabilities in a given content area. The reason is that often there are not enough items of a specific type to make a reliable judgment on mastery. Further, some skills within a subject field may not be measured at all. This, of course, is not the fault of the test; no standardized test can hope to have a sufficient number of items for all the local objectives contained in a unit of instruction. The practice of analyzing item responses on standardized tests, if used with caution, can at least provide the teacher with testable hypotheses about the instructional needs of students. However, more sensitive diagnostic instruments are required to pinpoint the exact nature and cause of the difficulty.

Some standardized tests provide remedial charts designed to suggest possible causes of low scores on various subtests of the battery.

Examples of such charts, dealing with five subtests of the Greene-Stapp Language Abilities Test, are contained in Table 5-3.

Charts similar to those in Table 5-3 can help the teacher form hypotheses concerning the nature of the difficulties signaled by scores which fall below the average score for the grade or age level of the student. However, the validity of the hypotheses can be determined only by more sensitive diagnostic measures. Standardized achievement tests and their accompanying diagnostic charts and suggestions, then, are useful primarily in giving the teacher an initial, general picture of the areas where a student is performing above, at, or below the average level for a grade or age.

The use of standardized diagnostic tests to identify weaknesses in prerequisite skills and abilities

Once general deficiencies have been identified, more analytical diagnostic instruments should be employed to try to pinpoint the nature of the learning retardation. (Possible causes of such retardation will be discussed presently.) The diagnostic test evaluates a particular subskill in much greater detail than is possible for an achievement test, which must cover many general areas rather broadly. Likewise, since a diagnostic test is designed to assess the weaknesses of students performing below average on a subskill, these instruments have many more easy items than do achievement tests, which are designed to measure the entire range of performance. Beatty, Madden, and Gardner (1966) point out that this relative ease of diagnostic items means that

> . . . pupils who may be frustrated by even a well-developed achievement test should experience a good deal of success on the diagnostic test. Furthermore, more accurate, reliable measurement of below average performance is afforded by the less difficult nature of a diagnostic test. In order to increase the reliability of measurement in identifying weaknesses of pupils and still keep the test administration time within reasonable limits, precision in measurement for the upper levels of performance is sacrificed in a substantial number of subtests. A high level of performance on a diagnostic subtest indicates that a certain area is *not* a weakness for a pupil or group, although it may not indicate exactly how strong the pupil or group is in that area [p. 3].

An example of a standardized diagnostic test is the Stanford Diagnostic Arithmetic Test (SDAT). The SDAT measures key arithmetic subskills in detail. Level I, for example, evaluates the areas of Number System Counting, Operations, Decimal Place Value, and Computation and Number Facts for Addition, Subtraction, Multiplication, and Division.

The interpretation of a diagnostic test like the SDAT involves looking for patterns of responses while scoring the booklet by hand. Once scored, the pupils' stanines are plotted on a pupil profile chart. If a student receives a low stanine on a subskill, the teacher should go back to specific responses to begin the diagnosis. Figure 5-4 presents a pupil profile prepared by the makers of the SDAT and the accompanying observations and suggestions based on the profile.

There have been very few standardized diagnostic instruments developed for most areas of the curriculum. Arithmetic, of course, is one exception. Another is reading; this important language art has been provided with many fine standardized individual and group tests designed for more analytical diagnosis than is available from the usual standardized achievement test. The interested reader is referred to the books by Bond and Tinker (1968) and Wilson (1967), each of which contains an excellent treatment of these tests as well as a description of some informal methods that can be employed to diagnose reading difficulties. Another noteworthy exception to this paucity of standardized diagnostic instruments is the Illinois Test of Psycholinguistic Abilities, or ITPA (McCarthy & Kirk, 1961). The ITPA is a diagnostic test which helps identify nine specific psycholinguistic abilities and disabilities in children between 2½ and 9 years of age. This instrument is discussed further in Chap. 14. Other standardized tests applicable to or specifically designed for diagnosis are described in the standardized test section in each chapter of Part II.

Grade 3. Age: 8 years, 4 months. Tested with SDAT Level I, Form W, in November of grade 3. Otis IQ: 85.

TEST	1. Concepts			2. Computation				3. No. Facts	Add.	Subt.	Mult.	Div.
	Number system counting	Operations	Decimal place value	Add.	Subt.	Mult.	Div.	Set 1	19	18	16	
								Set 2	5	3	4	
Raw score	10	4	9	3	1	1	not given	Total raw sc.	24	21	20	not given
	9	9	9	9	9	9	9					
S	8	8	8	8	8	8	8		A	A	A	A
T	7	7	7	7	7	7	7	R				
A	6	6	6	6	6	6	6	A				
N	5	5	5	5	5	5	5	T	B	B	B	B
I	4	4	4	4	4	4	4	I				
N	3	3	3	3	3	3	3	N				
E	2	2	2	2	2	2	2	G	C	C	C	C
	1	1	1	1	1	1	1					

Total scores		Raw score	Grade score	Stanine		Raw score	Grade score	Stanine
	Test 1	23	16	2	Test 2 (A+B or A+B+C+D)	4	19	1

Eddie's ability level suggests that he probably learns slowly and needs considerable help. Analysis of his test booklet may suggest ways in which help may be provided.

On Test 1, Part A, Eddie correctly named cardinal numbers of sets of dots. He counted forward correctly by ones below hundreds, by tens, and by hundreds. All other responses were incorrect. On Part B, he responded correctly to sets of dots related to division (25 and 26). The other two correct responses were probably obtained through knowledge of the number facts, $4 + 2 = \square + 4$, and if $2 + 4 = 6$, then $6 - 4 = 2$. On Part C he wrote dictated numerals correctly, compared two-place numbers correctly, correctly selected "the numeral that stands for," and interpreted 4 tens and 3 ones as 43. Other responses were incorrect.

The three items correctly answered on the Addition test were 10, 11, and 12: all one-place examples in column addition. The responses to 2-place and 3-place examples are all incorrect. Sums have no discernible relation to addends. The first example on the Subtraction test is correct. Other answers again seem to be numerals written at random, as do the answers on the Multiplication test.

Eddie responded correctly to all but one item of Set 1, Addition Facts, all but two of Set 1, Subtraction Facts, and all but 4 of Set 1, Multiplication Facts.

One infers that Eddie has very little understanding of number and depends on rote memorization for recall of number facts. Work with sets of objects, the number line, a ten tens chart, place value pockets, and an abacus should help him improve his ability to work with numbers. Such experiences are generally quite interesting for young boys. As with Andy (above), activities that emphasize relationships and the expression of ideas in appropriate symbolism should be used. A few examples done slowly, with opportunity to explain what he is doing, should help him in making progress.

FIGURE 5-4. An adaptation of the pupil profile and diagnosis for a student named Eddie on the Stanford Diagnostic Arithmetic Test, Level 1. (L. S. Beatty, R. Madden, & E. F. Gardner. *Manual for administering and interpreting Stanford Diagnostic Arithmetic Test.* New York: Harcourt, Brace & World, 1966. P. 25.)

The use of teacher-made tests for diagnosis

As we pointed out in Chap. 3, the student's ability to understand verbal communication and to express himself verbally are closely related to his ability to profit from the highly verbal-conceptual type of instruction that characterizes our schools. Remedial instruction in basic vocabulary, reading, and expressive skills may be necessary before a student can hope to master the curriculum. Whether the subject is seventh-grade arithmetic, preparatory physics, or automobile mechanics, learning can be effectively blocked if he lacks these basic skills. Failure to remedy faulty verbal abilities can result in the student's experiencing nothing but frustration in his learning, setting up the vicious cycle of failure, frustration, hostility, and failure. The degree to which a student's poor verbal skills can be altered is conversely related to the age at which remediation begins. Only the most powerful environmental conditions are likely to produce significant changes in later grades (Bloom, 1964). Therefore, it behooves school systems to provide remedial programs in the primary grades.

The new programs in compensatory education have been faced with large numbers of children retarded in the language arts. The usual methods of teaching these children individually or in small groups outside the classroom proved to be no longer feasible. Further, commercially available standardized diagnostic tests were either lacking or too complex to administer and interpret for teachers forced to deal with large classes lacking basic language skills. Therefore, teacher-built diagnostic instruments were needed which were easy to administer and interpret and which could point out the specific language needs of children in terms of mastery rather than only in terms of their relative standing in a somewhat unrepresentative norm group.

The Gary, Indiana, Program in Compensatory Education—Intensive Language Arts, under the direction of Mrs. Sophie Bloom (see Bloom, 1967), affords examples of easy-to-interpret teacher-made group diagnostic tests. This program has developed oral and written diagnostic instruments for both the receptive and the expressive language skills. The language skill in question is broken down into a hierarchy of sequential subskills. Techniques for the development of formative tests outlined in Chap. 6 are followed, and the reader is referred to that chapter for a description of these techniques.

The results of the tests are reported in color-coded charts which show each student's level of mastery over each of the subskills being examined rather than the grade or age level of his performance. Only three colors are required to give teachers the necessary detailed information concerning the children's specific needs. Blue indicates mastery, yellow near mastery, and red a skill which has not been learned. Table 5-4 presents a portion of one of these diagnostic charts. Colors have been replaced by three different shadings.

Coded charts like this one show at a glance the strong and weak subskills of the children. When the chart is read vertically, the coding indicates groups in the class which have mastered various subskills. When the pattern is inspected horizontally, it conveys to the teacher the status of an individual child. The teachers and children can see specific weaknesses more clearly and where instruction might most effectively begin.

The child receives his portion of the outcome map, and keeps track of his progress toward mastery of subskills during the ensuing formative units by removing red tags and replacing them with yellow and then blue. The concept of "pass" or "fail" is avoided by the use of terms like "has learned" and "still to be learned" in connection with the tags. The students are told they can master each skill and are allowed to arrive at mastery according to their own schedule. The issue is not passing or failing but only when the last "still to be learned" tag can be replaced by a blue tag signifying mastery.

Here is an example of how the schools, while unable to remove the environmental and cultural causes of underdeveloped language skills, can intervene with necessary remedial instruction to help ensure that the students will acquire the verbal skills prerequisite to profiting from later verbally dependent learning experiences.

The color-coded diagnostic report form of the

Table 5-4 Diagnostic Chart for Word-attack Skills, Gary Public Schools

	Word-attack skills								
	Beginning sounds	*Final sounds*	*Blends*	*Rhyming*	*Long-short vowels*	*Other vowels*	*Syllabication*	*Prefixes and suffixes*	*Root words*
Ricardo	Near mastery	Near mastery	Near mastery	Near mastery	Skill not learned yet	Skill not learned yet	Mastery	Skill not learned yet	Near mastery
Anthony	Skill not learned yet	Skill not learned yet	Skill not learned yet	Skill not learned yet	Skill not learned yet	Skill not learned yet	Near mastery	Skill not learned yet	Near mastery
Sharon	Skill not learned yet	Skill not learned yet	Skill not learned yet	Skill not learned yet	Skill not learned yet	Skill not learned yet	Skill not learned yet	Skill not learned yet	Skill not learned yet
Brenda	Skill not learned yet	Skill not learned yet	Skill not learned yet	Skill not learned yet	Near mastery	Skill not learned yet	Near mastery	Skill not learned yet	Mastery
Barbara	Skill not learned yet	Near mastery	Skill not learned yet	Skill not learned yet	Skill not learned yet	Skill not learned yet	Skill not learned yet	Skill not learned yet	Mastery
Earlie	Near mastery	Near mastery	Skill not learned yet	Skill not learned yet	Skill not learned yet	Skill not learned yet	Skill not learned yet	Skill not learned yet	Near mastery

[shaded] = Mastery [cross-hatched] = Near mastery [dotted] = Skill not learned yet

SOURCE: Adapted from S. Bloom. Using continuous evaluation in the elementary program. Paper presented at the Annual Convention of the International Reading Association, Seattle, Wash., August 1967.

Gary Public Schools is of course adaptable to other areas of the curriculum, such as arithmetic. The strength of such reports lies in the fact that they are easy to interpret and they indicate levels of mastery for each subskill or objective. Further, the Gary example shows that with proper direction teachers can build highly analytical diagnostic instruments to determine whether a student possesses the necessary skills, abilities, and content judged prerequisite to their own particular course.

Summative reports designed to aid diagnosis

As we indicated earlier in this chapter, one of the difficulties with using summative grades for placement purposes is that a single grade—letter or numerical—does not adequately describe the student's performance or mastery level on each of the objectives of the course. It is possible, however, to design record files and report cards that do report levels of mastery on various objectives and subskills. The Mathematics Goal Record Card of the Winnetka, Illinois, Public Schools shown in Fig. 5-5 is an example.

The boxes on the two sides of the goal card which the teacher checks (or marks with some other arbitrary symbol) indicate arithmetic abilities, skills, or content which the student has mastered. Lack of a check indicates that the student has yet to master the objective in question.

Such a report form has both immediate and long-range benefits. Immediately it gives parents (and learners when they get a bit older) a clear picture of the child's strengths and weaknesses in his arithmetic progress. It conveys with greater clarity than could a single overall grade where the parent can work to help his child improve.

Perhaps even more important, this card follows the child to the next grade. The second-grade

Winnetka Public Schools

MATHEMATICS GOAL RECORD CARD 1

*Pupil*__________ *Teacher* __________ *Year*____

	Check
Recognizes number groups up to 5	
Recognizes patterns of objects to 10	
Can count objects to 100	
Recognizes numbers to 100	
Can read and write numerals to 50	
Recognizes addition and subtraction symbols	
Understands meaning of the equality sign	
Understands meaning of the inequality signs	
Can count objects:	
By 2s to 20	
By 5s to 100	
By 10s to 100	
Recognizes geometric figures:	
Triangle	
Circle	
Quadrilateral	
Recognizes coins (1¢, 5¢, 10¢, 25¢)	
Knows addition combinations 10 and under using objects	
Knows subtraction combinations 10 and under using objects	
Recognizes addition and subtraction vertically and horizontally	
Shows understanding of numbers and number combinations (check one)	
1. Using concrete objects	
2. Beginning to visualize and abstract	
3. Making automatic responses without concrete objects	
Can tell time	
1. Hour	
2. Half hour	
3. Quarter hour	

	Check
Addition combinations 10 and under (automatic response)	
Subtraction combinations 10 and under (automatic response)	
Can count to 200	
Can understand zero as a number	
Can understand place value to tens	
Can read and write numerals to 200	
Can read and write number words to 20	
Uses facts in 2-digit column addition (no carrying)	
Roman numerals to XII	

CARD 2

*Pupil*__________ *Teacher*__________ *Year*____

	Check
Calendar (months, days of week, dates)	
Coins and their equivalent value to 25¢	
Recognizes 50¢ coin and $1.00	
Recognizes and uses 1/2, 1/4, 1/3 of a whole	
Addition facts to 18 (aim for mastery)	
Subtraction facts to 18 (aim for mastery)	
Word problems: (check one)	
1. Can set the problem up	
2. Can understand the process involved	
3. Can notate word problems	

Comments:

FIGURE 5-5. Adaptation of Winnetka Public Schools Mathematics Goal Record Card. (Winnetka Public Schools. *Mathematics Goal Record Card.* Winnetka, Ill.: WPS, undated. Sides 1 and 2.)

teacher is provided with information about what the pupil has mastered and what he still needs to learn. Grouping according to learners' behavioral needs is facilitated. Individual and group instructional needs are pinpointed in terms of observable arithmetic abilities. Instead of spending several weeks trying to determine student proficiency in many diverse skills, the teacher has placement and diagnostic information upon which to begin his instructional program immediately. Data in this criterion-referenced form are of more value to the new teacher than the single letter grade or percentage so often used by school systems to report progress or lack of it at the end of the year.

It might be argued at first that these relatively detailed, criterion-related reports are more feasible at the primary school level where subject areas are sequential and hierarchical. However, it is possible to design records that report degrees of mastery for any subject at any level.

The report booklet designed by the University Examiners' Office of the University of Chicago is a case in point. Figure 5-6 presents a double page from the Humanities section of the report.

A performance grade of "high," "above average," "average," "below average," or "low" is placed beside each of the objectives listed in Fig. 5-6. These grading terms report the student's degree of mastery of the stated objectives of the course. However, as the terms indicate, mastery in this case is related to the performance levels of past classes and therefore is not criterion-referenced. If Humanities 2 is viewed as being sequential to and in some measure as building on the Humanities 1 course, then an instructor beginning the Humanities 2 course can examine this report form to determine the behavioral level of students on the objectives for Humanities 1.

Diagnosis to determine the extent of prior mastery of course objectives

The previous discussion of placement diagnosis has dealt almost exclusively with the diagnosis of weaknesses in prerequisite entry behaviors that would lessen a student's chances of profiting from the planned instruction. Another form of placement diagnosis involves the determination of the degree to which a student already has mastery over the objectives planned for a course. Students who have already achieved all or a number of planned objectives should either be allowed to elect another course or have instruction start at the most appropriate place.

Diagnostic evaluation for this type of placement can begin by pretesting the students with an alternative form of the summative examination designed for the course. If the student reaches some previously determined level of mastery on the test, he could be given credit for the course and be placed in a more advanced one, or, in the case of nonsequential courses, be allowed to elect another course. Such a system works particularly well at higher levels of education where scheduling and elective courses allow for more individualization of a student's program. In self-contained classrooms or in systems that do not permit flexible scheduling, the teacher can at least make provisions for an enrichment program of more advanced work for students who have displayed an adequate level of mastery on the summative pretest. Techniques for constructing summative examinations are discussed in Chaps. 4, 7, 8, 9, and 10 and will therefore not be taken up here.

Some students might not display the required level of mastery on the summative pretest but still possess some of the competences the course seeks to develop. If this is the case, it may be possible to tailor the course more intelligently by locating the optimum starting point for instruction. If a teacher has broken the course down into formative units and has built formative tests for each unit as described in Chap. 6, then these tests may be used to diagnose not only the appropriate unit at which instruction should begin but also the proper starting point within the structure of that unit.

When formative tests are not yet available, a teacher can gain valuable diagnostic information through a careful analysis of errors on more traditional types of teacher-made tests used as pretests for placement purposes. Chapter 16 in Part II describes item types that permit the analysis of patterns of errors made in interpreting data. The key to this type of item is designed response

HUMANITIES 1

Performance Part

_______ 1 Music—total objective items.

_______ 2 Music—essay, a *synthesis* of observations about words and music of a song.

_______ 3 Art—total objective items.

_______ 4 Art—essay, a *synthesis* of observations about certain works of various date and in various media by a single artist.

_______ 5 Literature—total objective items.

_______ 6 Literature—essay, a *synthesis* of observations about the use and effect of a particular narrative device in two very different novels.

Knowledge

_______ 7 Demonstration of factual information about a work or about the history or the processes of an art (measured here by a relatively very small number of items in which information as such is not primarily subordinated to one of the abilities listed below).

Comprehension

_______ 8 Ability to translate into verbal communication specific details of what is seen in a painting, print, building, or work of sculpture, or what is heard in a work of music or read in musical notation; ability to paraphrase or summarize accurately what is asserted or what occurs in a work of literature. (AM, items 7, 8, 10, 11, 14, 31, 62, 62, 66, 78, 79; PM, items 106-112)*

Application

_______ 9 Ability to apply general concepts of the elements of the arts, or of certain materials and processes and types, or of the style of certain men or periods, to the differentiation or identification of particular works. (AM, items 18, 20, 38, 40, 41, 46, 49, 50, 68, 76-77, 80-81, 91-92, 96, 121, 124; PM, 26-30, 121-131)*

Analysis

_______ 10 Ability to relate parts of a work to each other and to the whole—to grasp, that is, the work's organization. (AM, items 1-6, 19, 33-36, 42-43, 67, 113-120; PM, 1-25, 36-97)*

Parts 1-6 make up the total score of the examination.

Parts 7-10 (like Parts 1, 3, 5) make up the total score of the objective sections.

*Illustrative items to be found in the June, 1951, Humanities 1 comprehensive examination.

HUMANITIES 2

Performance Part

Skills of analysis and interpretation:

_______ 1 As applied to historical and rhetorical writings.

_______ 2 As applied to fictional works.

_______ 3 As applied to philosophical writings.

Acquaintance with texts assigned on the course reading list:

_______ 4 Elementary familiarity with all the works assigned for reading in the course.

Skills in formulating an interpretation in writing:

_______ 5 In presenting an interpretation of a work of rhetoric.

Skills and abilities as applied to the work of the entire year:

Knowledge

_______ 6 The recall of specific facts from the works studied both in and out of class.

Comprehension

_______ 7 The ability to understand and interpret works as a whole or passages from works. This includes the ability to translate difficult passages into other words or to summarize the essential meaning of long passages or whole works. This is applied to works studied in and out of class.

Analysis

_______ 8 The ability to identify the parts of a work, to determine the relations among these parts or between part and whole, and to recognize the principles which account for the organization of whole works. Part 8 applies only to works studied in class.

_______ 9 The same as Part 8, but applied only to works read out of class.

FIGURE 5-6. A criterion-referenced report form, adapted. (University of Chicago, College. *Diagnostic reports in comprehensive examinations*. Chicago: UCC, Spring 1952. Pp. 4–5.)

categories that permit multidimensional scoring. The scoring scheme for the interpretation-of-data tests developed during the Eight-year Study for the Progressive Education Association (see Smith & Tyler, 1942) is a classic example of how well-designed response categories permit the teacher to analyze errors and thereby be better able to individualize future instruction. Table 5-5 shows the scoring scheme of keyed responses with which the student's answers are compared.

The table shows that student responses can be described in terms of four scores:

1. A *general accuracy* score indicates how well the student's response matches the keyed response: cells *a*, g, m, s, and y. This number is expressed as a percent of the total number of possible correct responses. Subscores for accuracy in each response category are also derived.
2. The *caution* score indicates the extent to which a student will not attribute as much to a statement as will the key: cells *f*, k, *l*, n, o, and *t*.
3. The score on *going beyond the data* indicates the degree to which a student is giving an interpretation with greater certainty than is warranted by the data: cells b, c, h, r, *w*, and x.
4. The *crude error* score indicates the extent to which the student marks probably true or true statements as false or probably false and vice versa: cells *d*, e, i, *j*, p, q, u, and v. This type of error can be accounted for by carelessness or misunderstanding of the data.

Table 5-5 Scoring Scheme for an Interpretation-of-data Test

Jury key / Student responses	*True*	*Probably true*	*Insufficient data*	*Probably false*	*False*
True	Accurate *a*	Beyond data *b*	Beyond data *c*	Crude error *d*	Crude error *e*
Probably true	Caution *f*	Accurate *g*	Beyond data *h*	Crude error *i*	Crude error *j*
Insufficient data	Caution *k*	Caution *l*	Accurate *m*	Caution *n*	Caution *o*
Probably false	Crude error *p*	Crude error *q*	Beyond data *r*	Accurate *s*	Caution *t*
False	Crude error *u*	Crude error *v*	Beyond data *w*	Beyond data *x*	Accurate *y*

SOURCE: Reprinted by permission from *Appraising and recording student progress*, by Eugene R. Smith & Ralph W. Tyler, The Progressive Education Association. Copyright 1942 by McGraw-Hill, Inc. P. 54.

Table 5-6 **A Summary Chart for Interpretation-of-data Test Scores**

SCHOOL A

GRADE 12

SUMMARY FOR TEST 2.52
INTERPRETATION OF DATA
DATE TEST GIVEN 6-2-39

SEVEN STUDENTS SELECTED FROM A GROUP OF 69

Students	General accuracy	Accuracy: P. T. P. F.	Accuracy: Insufficient data	Accuracy: True-false	Omit	Caution	Beyond data	Crude errors
Students	1	2	3	4	5	6	7	8
1. Peggy	34	20	30	52	0	13	60	32
2. Joseph	71	66	69	71	0	20	23	7
3. William	64	65	54	68	0	7	38	14
4. Homer	51	18	74	52	0	53	22	10
5. Andrew	71	74	60	78	0	6	33	8
6. George	47	11	60	75	0	41	38	8
7. Faye	57	46	53	75	0	21	37	11
Maximum possible	100 percent in all columns							
Lowest score	21	11	11	11	0	6	22	5
Highest score	71	74	74	78	24	53	64	32
Group median	51	43	45	65	0	22	42	13
Group mean	50.0	42.2	45.0	60.0	1.3	22.2	43.4	13.9

Scores in all columns are percents.

SOURCE: E. R. Smith & R. W. Tyler. *Appraising and recording student progress.* (Adventure in American Education Ser., Vol. 3) New York: Harper, 1942. P. 57.

The feedback to both student and teacher can be seen in the summary chart in Table 5-6, also developed during the Eight-year Study.

The chart is divided by a double line. The upper part gives information on individual students. The bottom of the chart contains group statistics. An examination of Table 5-6 shows that different students need different kinds of training in the interpretation of data. Homer tends to be overcautious. Peggy's general accuracy score is too low, and she has a tendency to go beyond the data. Although Joseph and Andrew have identical accuracy scores, Andrew tends to go beyond the data more often than does Joseph.

While the best examples of analysis of error patterns generally deal with interpretive exercises, teachers interested in other skills or behaviors should try when possible to develop response categories or scoring techniques that will allow them to examine different types of errors committed by students.

An analysis of error patterns like that described above has obvious value in formative evaluation for prescribing remedial experiences. However, using such a technique as a pretest could also be of considerable benefit in determining the extent of a student's prior ability to interpret data, resulting in a more reasonable placement or individualization of instruction.

Thus, when administered as pretests, summative and formative instruments can be used to determine the extent to which the student already has mastered the behavior the course seeks to develop, and thereby to locate the proper starting point for instruction.

Placement diagnosis for alternative teaching strategies

Teachers in the same subject, reflecting differences in experiences, training, interests, and personality, have always shown variation in the way they approach their instruction. Thus one teacher may approach a first course in statistics from a simple arithmetic point of view while another equally effective instructor may employ calculus or matrix algebra in his approach. A student could fail the course taught with the latter emphasis not because he is unable to master statistics but because he does not have the necessary calculus and matrix algebra assumed by the instructor. Thus in a sense the student really "fails" the prerequisite subjects, not statistics.

A simple pretest in calculus and matrix algebra may very accurately predict the degree of success a student can expect in the course. The instructor should administer such a pretest to determine which students do not yet possess these skills. He can then make provisions to help those who lack the skills develop them before he begins his instruction, or he can use an alternative teaching strategy that does not depend on calculus or matrix algebra with such students.

Thelen's concept of "teachability grouping" also recognizes that some students are more successful with certain types of teachers than with others. This concept of placement is based on the proposition that

> . . . a teacher does a better job with some pupils than with others, and that therefore it makes sense to assign him a class composed of the sort of students with whom he has been found to do a better job. An obvious corollary is that the students to assign to each teacher must be determined in some way that takes each teacher into account.
>
> (Thelen, 1967, p. 191)

The method of assigning students to teachability groups involves three basic steps. First, the teacher lists the students whom he has found to be teachable and unteachable. Second, a group of teachers compare these high and low teachables to try to determine recognizable characteristics of each category. These traits must be described clearly and unambiguously so that one can recognize their presence or absence in other students. Finally, the descriptions are sent to the teachers in the grade below so that they can rate the upcoming students on how well they fit the model "teachable" student. As a result, those who most resemble the model constructed by a teacher will be placed in that teacher's room the next year. The reader is referred to Thelen (1967) for a more detailed treatment of each step and for a description of one strategy of teachability grouping. Suffice it to say that Thelen's concept of teachability groups involves a type of diagnosis to place students with instructors whose teaching strategy has been successful in the past with similar types of learners.

Placement diagnosis for alternative curricula

One of the outgrowths of the major new curriculum projects has been the recognition that there is no single best way to organize or approach the development of a new course. These groups have perceived the need to offer diversity and variation in their approaches and materials so that alternative routes to the same goal are open to both teachers and students. A statement by F. James Rutherford describes the rationale underlying one large project's decision to design alternative approaches and is equally applicable to other areas of the curriculum:

> Practical considerations, as well as educational and psychological theory, suggested the direction taken by Project Physics. As you look out at the real world

> of students, teachers, and schools in this country you see that great diversity exists; and there [appear] to be no imminent educational or social developments likely to change that situation in the foreseeable future. It seems a matter of practical good sense, therefore, to accept diversity as a fact of life, and to build enough flexibility into our physics course to accommodate and even to take advantage of that diversity. This acceptance was neither reluctant nor despairing. Far from being disturbed by the existence of diversity, we applaud and foster it. Thus the Project set out to design a course that permitted and indeed *encouraged* variation. We have been trying to develop a flexible physics course that allows a teacher to complement his strengths and supplement his weaknesses, that makes it possible for him to take into account student differences, and that is workable within a wide variety of school situations.
>
> (Rutherford, 1967, p. 215)

Many new curriculum projects have designed alternative curriculum packages to be used as different approaches to the achievement of the same goal. Other projects working more or less independently of each other have produced a wealth of packages in the same subject area but each with a different approach or emphasis.

The fact that alternative curricula containing diverse and varied materials are now available to schools raises the possibility of placing students according to some characteristic in the curriculum that would be maximally beneficial. This type of placement goes beyond the usual homogeneous ability grouping in the fast, average, and slow or the college preparatory, commercial, and vocational tracks. As was pointed out earlier, the heterogeneity of aptitudes, interests, educational backgrounds, aspirations, and countless other characteristics within these "homogeneous" groups argues against using the single criterion of track or level to determine the type of instruction a pupil receives. Instead the more sophisticated approach asks, Which students, regardless of track or level, can best profit from the various approaches available in the same subject field?

Ideally, it should be possible to match instructional techniques and materials with individual student characteristics so that the achievement of all students seeking a given objective of instruction will be greater than would have been realized had a single method been employed. Research in instruction is now seeking to establish whether or not interactions exist between various treatment variables and student characteristics. A researcher merely comparing one curriculum or instructional method with another may be unable to demonstrate any differences in learners' achievements until he takes certain student characteristics into consideration. In other words, a single variable (for example, type of treatment or curriculum) can fail to reveal the total pattern of the influence of differential student characteristics. An ideal, hypothetical pattern of interaction between pupil characteristics and type of instructional treatment is presented in Fig. 5-7.

In the figure, those who fall to the left of X_0 on the student characteristics axis receive the highest criterion achievement scores when they have treatment *B* rather than *A*. Those to the right of X_0 would benefit most from treatment *A*. A test

FIGURE 5-7. An idealized example of an interaction effect between student characteristics and differential instructional treatments.

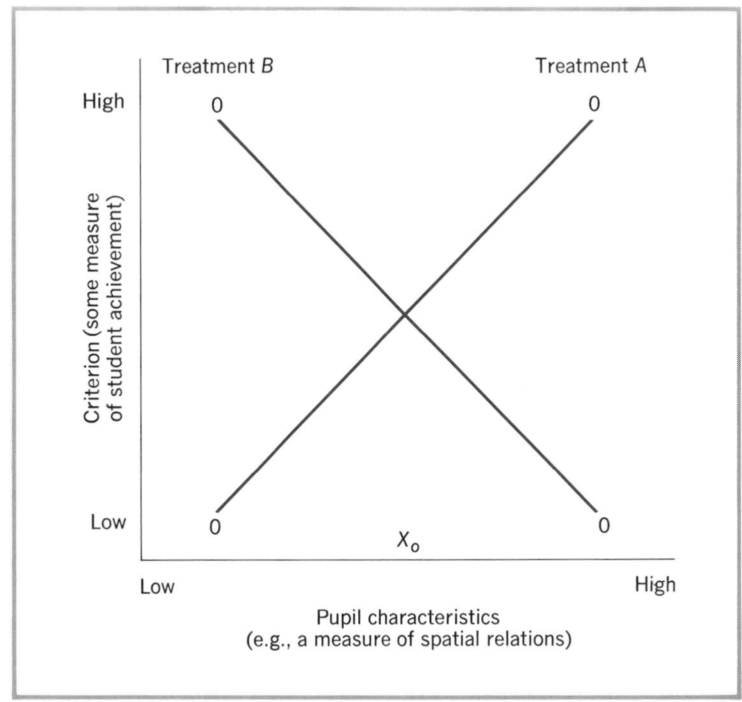

on the characteristic variable, *X*, could be used to place students in either treatment *A* or treatment *B*. Unfortunately, the ideal and precise pattern shown in Fig. 5-7 is not yet found in instruction research. The exact kind of differential placement pictured awaits further theoretical speculation on the adaptation of instruction for different types of pupils and practical research in curriculum development.

While the sophistication of the approach pictured in the figure is not possible, it is possible to take into consideration a student's existing academic background or ability level in making decisions about the appropriateness of a particular curriculum or version of a multiversion curriculum. First, published evaluations, studies, and reviews of a new curriculum often offer suggestions as to the type of student who benefits most from the new offering. Second, a teacher's personal experience and the shared experiences of his colleagues give insights into whether students with different academic backgrounds or abilities profit equally well from each of several alternative approaches to a subject. Biological Sciences Curriculum Study (BSCS) materials will be used to illustrate how intelligent decisions can be arrived at in attempting to place students in the most appropriate version of a multiversion curriculum. The techniques to be described are as applicable to other subject areas that have alternative curricula as they are to the BSCS materials.

The BSCS decided that there was no *one* best approach to a high school biology course and therefore developed three models, the Yellow, Blue, and Green Versions, each approaching the subject field differently. While the models had different emphases, each was designed as a balanced first course in high school biology for average and above-average tenth-graders. Further, the BSCS group developed a fourth set of instructional materials for lower-ability students who could not profit from the regular BSCS versions.

Published studies of these materials offer suggestions that should be carefully considered when placement decisions are to be made. For example, Cain (1967, p. 258) reports that a student's "mathematical aptitude as measured by the Differential Aptitude Test of Numerical Ability may be a more important factor to success in the BSCS biology program than it is in a traditional biology program." He concludes that a student's mathematical aptitude should be considered when he enrolls in high school biology. A student with low math aptitude should perhaps be placed in a more traditional biology course, or a special remedial class in math should be made a prerequisite to enrollment in a BSCS course. Biology teachers experienced with both the BSCS materials and traditional biology curricula should consider such research in the light of their own observations, successes, and failures to determine whether they wish to *experiment* with using a measure of mathematical aptitude as *one* aid in making placement decisions.

A content analysis of the alternative versions of a curriculum may indicate that one version presupposes a higher level of sophistication in the subject on the student's part than do the other versions. For example, Ausubel (1966), after analyzing the three sets of BSCS materials, argues that the Blue Version presupposes an introductory biology course as well as courses in chemistry and physics, whereas the Green Version gives the impression of being at an appropriate level for a beginning course. The validity of Ausubel's critique is not at issue here; the reader can judge this for himself after studying the article. The point is that a detailed content analysis by knowledgeable teachers, coupled with analyses by content experts when available, may lead to the conclusion that certain students should be enrolled in one version of a curriculum rather than another. This process is of course little different from the content analysis employed by curriculum committees in screening various textbooks for adoption, the difference being that alternative curricula may be adopted instead of a single text and students placed in the version most suitable to their educational histories, aptitudes, and interests.

Often a particular curriculum group makes recommendations concerning the type of student best suited to alternative versions of materials. For example, the three versions of BSCS High

School Biology were designed for tenth-grade students of average or above-average ability. However, the BSCS people recognized that the almost one million tenth-graders who were at or below the 40th percentile on a test of general intellectual ability probably would not profit from these materials. Grobman (1965a) observed that in the past

> . . . such students generally either fulfilled their science requirement in a ninth grade or tenth grade general science course (often a watered-down physiology and general health course), were placed in a special high school biology course which was non-laboratory oriented and which might be primarily nature study, or were placed in with students in regular biology classes and experienced repeated failures. Many observers believe that because of such repeated failures these lower-ability students are more likely to become high school drop-outs [p. 16].

In an attempt to reverse this record of the past, the BSCS proceeded to build a Special Materials (SM) curriculum for lower-ability students. After careful research, the following placement information was offered:

> The class mean [for SM classes] should not exceed the 40th percentile on a general ability test or a test of reading comprehension; and, for any individual in the class with an ability test score of over the 50th percentile, . . . there [should] be a written explanation of his/her presence in the class.
>
> (Grobman, 1965b, p. 764)

With this kind of direction, diagnosis for correct placement would involve administering either a general ability test or a reading comprehension test, or both, and placing students in the SM track in biology who fall below the 50th percentile. In situations where a regular BSCS version has been adopted and students are experiencing difficulty, they could be tested to determine which among them are trying to cope with unsuitable materials and which should be designated as underachievers for various psychological, motivational, or other reasons but not candidates for SM.

Thus various kinds of differential placement are often possible. Teachers must keep abreast of instructional research in their subject field as one guide to the kinds of diagnosis necessary. They also should carefully study any placement recommendations made by the curriculum group that designed alternative versions of a course. Even if no information or direction for improved placement of students is available from these two sources, interested teachers within a department can pool their own observations and experiences with different materials or perform a detailed content analysis of the alternative curricula to try to determine whether these different provisions, all designed to reach the same goal, suppose different educational backgrounds or skills on the part of the student. Such a cooperative venture can lead to the design of diagnostic instruments for matching student characteristics with the appropriate curriculum and materials.

Diagnosis of noneducational causes of inability to profit from instruction

Up to this point we have discussed diagnosis primarily in terms of placement. We saw that it is possible to determine whether a student possesses the necessary general and specific abilities, skills, behaviors, or content judged to be prerequisite for a given curriculum. Further, we saw that instruments can be developed or existing ones used for an accurate analytical diagnosis of the nature and extent of learning disabilities. We discussed the use of summative and formative tests for determining the extent to which a student already possesses the planned objectives of a curriculum. We saw also that it is possible in some instances to fit alternative versions of a curriculum to the student's educational history or intellectual capacity.

Every teacher recognizes that despite this type of diagnosis, some students who are properly placed according to the above criteria are still unsuccessful learners. For these students alternative modes of instruction and different materials and methods still fail to produce the expected level of mastery. When this occurs, a teacher must try to diagnose the noneducational causes of the student's inability to profit from instruction in the hope that they can be corrected.

Noneducational causes of learning disability may be classified as physical, psychological, or environmental in nature. These categories sometimes overlap or are closely related to one another. For example, a student's poor general health may in turn be caused by the parents' inability to provide an adequate diet. Again, a student may be emotionally upset over a long period of time because of some abnormal condition in the home.

If a teacher suspects a noneducational factor to be the cause of learning disabilities, he should look for behavior symptomatic of physical, psychological, or environmental problems. If he observes several such symptoms, he may use available screening devices to check his hypothesis further. If these support his conjectures, he should then refer the student to the proper authorities or agency for additional diagnosis and remedy. If the screening devices do not sustain his hypothesis, he should search for alternative explanations for the symptoms. Some other rather simple factor may account for the observed behavior. Failing to find an alternative explanation, the teacher should refer the student to the proper authorities or agency for further diagnosis.

For example, Mary, a third-grade pupil of normal intelligence and achievement, has been having difficulties with reading. The teacher suspects some noneducational factor is causing the difficulty. Observing Mary's behavior, he notices that Mary is tense during reading class, loses her place easily, and seems to hold her book close to her face when reading. Since these are all symptoms of a visual abnormality, the teacher may administer or ask the school nurse to administer a simple eye test. If Mary fails the test, the teacher should refer her to the school medical authorities, who can either make further tests or notify the parents of the need for a more detailed eye examination. If Mary performs satisfactorily on the screening test, the teacher might explore other possible explanations for her symptoms. She may be nervous or upset because of some condition in the home, she may not be getting enough sleep, or she may be seeking more attention. Screens for these explanations would involve the teacher's talking with Mary or asking the school guidance counselor to talk with her. In any event, the teacher should be alert for symptoms of physical, psychological, or environmental problems and refer the student to the proper specialist for help if they appear.

In the category of physical problems, visual, auditory, motor, speech, dietary, general health, glandular, or neurological conditions may cause or contribute to a student's learning disability.

Under the classification of psychological problems are a host of emotional factors which could impair a student's ability to profit from instruction. Poor self-concept, the negative emotional effects of a broken home, neurosis or more debilitating mental disorders, or simply the tensions concomitant with adolescence can all complicate the control function of teaching and may make it impossible for a student to profit from the usual type of learning experiences.

Similarly, the category of environmental problems includes many factors which can contribute to a student's learning difficulties. As we saw previously, some of these, especially those caused by cultural deprivation, such as poor language and reading skills, can be detected, and the student can be placed in the proper compensatory class. Other environmental factors, ranging from marital difficulties between the child's parents to a bilingual problem, will not necessarily be picked up by ordinary placement diagnosis.

We shall not go into a detailed treatment of each of the noneducational causes of learning problems as there are several excellent sources available. The reader is referred to Bond and Tinker (1968), Kessler (1966), and Wilson (1967) for detailed discussions of the classroom symptoms of physical, psychological, and environmental causes of learning disabilities. These books contain descriptions of symptoms, screening devices, and referral agencies for the various types of causes.

Several cautions are in order. First, the teacher is not expected to be an expert on deep-seated noneducational causes of learning disabilities. He should, however, recognize the symptoms associated with such causes. Second, he should be aware of the special agencies available to him if he observes these symptoms in a student. Third, he should keep in mind the tragic but inexorable fact that the school may not be able to help some students suffering from certain kinds of physical, psychological, or environmental problems, and therefore should not blame himself if these students continue to do poorly in ordinary classroom interaction.

REFERENCES

Ausubel, D. P. An evaluation of the BSCS approach to high school biology. *American Biology Teacher*, 1966, **28**(3), 176–186.

Balow, I. H. Does homogeneous grouping give homogeneous groups? *Elementary School Journal*, 1962, **63**(1), 28–32.

Beatty, L. S., Madden, R., & Gardner, E. F. *Manual for administering and interpreting Stanford Diagnostic Arithmetic Test.* New York: Harcourt, Brace & World, 1966.

Bloom, B. S. *Stability and change in human characteristics.* New York: Wiley, 1964.

Bloom, S. Using continuous evaluation in the elementary program. Paper presented at the Annual Convention of the International Reading Association, Seattle, Wash., August 1967.

Bond, G., & Tinker, M. A. *Reading difficulties: Their diagnosis and correction.* (2nd ed.) New York: Appleton-Century-Crofts, 1968.

Cain, R. W. An analysis of relationships between achievement in high school biology and mathematical aptitude and achievement. *Science Education*, 1967, **51**(3), 255–259.

California Test Bureau. *Comprehensive Tests of Basic Skills: CTB Individual Test Record.* Monterey, Calif.: CTB, undated.

Gates, A. I. *Gates Reading Diagnostic Tests.* New York: Teachers College, Columbia University, Bureau of Publications, 1945.

Glaser, R. Instructional technology and the measurement of learning outcomes. *American Psychologist*, 1963, **18,** 519–522.

Goodlad, J. I., & Anderson, R. H. *The nongraded elementary school.* New York: Harcourt, Brace, 1959.

Greene, H. A., & Stapp, H. I. *Greene-Stapp Language Abilities Test.* Yonkers-on-Hudson, N.Y.: World Book, 1954.

Grobman, H. Background of the 1963–64 evaluation. *BSCS Newsletter*, 1965, No. 24, pp. 16–24. (a)

Grobman, H. Assignment of students to tracks in biology. *American Biology Teacher*, 1965, **27,** 762–764. (b)

Kessler, J. W. *Psychopathology of childhood.* Englewood Cliffs, N.J.: Prentice-Hall, 1966.

McCarthy, J. J., & Kirk, S. A. *Examiner's manual, ITPA.* Urbana, Ill.: University of Illinois Press, 1961.

Metropolitan Achievement Tests: Directions for completing Individual Profile Chart, all batteries. New York: Harcourt, Brace, 1960.

Rutherford, F. J. Flexibility and variety in physics. *Physics Teacher*, 1967, **5,** 215–221.

Smith, E. R., & Tyler, R. W. *Appraising and recording student progress.* (Adventure in American Education Ser., Vol. 3) New York: Harper, 1942.

Thelen, H. A. *Classroom grouping for teachability.* New York: Wiley, 1967.

Thorpe, L. P., Lefever, D. W., & Naslund, R. A. *How to use the SRA Achievement Series.* (2nd ed.) Chicago: Science Research Associates, 1962.

University of Chicago, College. *Diagnostic reports in comprehensive examinations.* Chicago: UCC, Spring 1952.

Wilson, R. M. *Diagnostic and remedial reading for classroom and clinic.* Columbus: Merrill, 1967.

Winnetka Public Schools. *Mathematics Goal Record Card.* Winnetka, Ill.: WPS, undated.

Yates, A. (Ed.) *Grouping in education.* New York: Wiley, 1966.

6
Formative Evaluation

We have chosen the term "summative evaluation" to indicate the type of evaluation used at the end of a term, course, or program for purposes of grading, certification, evaluation of progress, or research on the effectiveness of a curriculum, course of study, or educational plan. In Chap. 4 we considered in some detail the special problems of constructing tests and using test data for this type of evaluation. Perhaps the essential characteristic of summative evaluation is that a judgment is made about the student, teacher, or curriculum with regard to the effectiveness of learning or instruction, after the learning or instruction has taken place. It is this act of judgment which produces so much anxiety and defensiveness in students, teachers, and curriculum makers. We do not believe it is possible to escape from the use of summative evaluation, nor would we wish to do so. However, there is another type of evaluation which all who are involved—student, teacher, curriculum maker—would welcome because they find it so useful in helping them improve what they wish to do.

In searching around for a term to describe this other type of evaluation, we found "formative evaluation" first used by Scriven (1967) in connection with curriculum improvement. Scriven points out that once a curriculum has been put in final form, everyone connected with it resists evidence which would make for major alterations. It is his view that formative evaluation involves the collection of appropriate evidence *during* the construction and trying out of a new curriculum in such a way that revisions of the curriculum can be based on this evidence.

We regard formative evaluation as useful not only for curriculum construction but also for instruction and student learning. Formative evaluation is for us the use of systematic evaluation in the process of curriculum construction, teaching, and learning for the purpose of improving any of these three processes. Since formative evaluation takes place during the formation stage, every effort should be made to use it to improve the process. This means that in formative evaluation one must strive to develop the kinds of evidence that will be most useful in the process, seek the most useful method of reporting the evidence, and search for ways of reducing the negative effect associated with evaluation—perhaps by reducing the judgmental aspects of evaluation or, at the least, by having the users of the formative evaluation (teachers, students, curriculum makers) make the judgments. The hope is that the users of the formative evaluation will find ways of relating the results of the evaluation to the learning and instructional goals they regard as important and worthwhile.

Analysis of learning units

The unit of learning

Most fundamental to the use of formative evaluation is the selection of a unit of learning. Within a course or education program there are parts or divisions which have a separable existence such that they can, at least for analytic purposes, be considered in relative isolation from other parts. While these parts may be interrelated in various ways so that the learning (or level of learning) of one part has consequences for the learning of others, it is still possible to consider the parts separately.

The nature of the unit may vary for different purposes. In curriculum construction it may be desirable to regard the unit as a single lesson or learning session. However, for the practical purposes of instruction and learning, it appears to us that a useful unit would be something larger than the single session. In some of our work we have found that a unit of learning could be the content covered in a chapter of a textbook or the material covered in one to two weeks of instruction. The delineation of the unit may be arbitrary; ideally it should be determined by natural breaks in the subject matter or by the content that makes a meaningful whole.

Specifications for the unit

A unit of learning, however conceived, consists of subject matter to be learned over a given period of time. For the purposes of formative evaluation, it is necessary to analyze the components of this unit. The task of determining the specifications for formative evaluation is much the same as that of creating specifications for summative evaluation.

It is possible for the curriculum maker to construct a unit by beginning with a set of specifications in which he outlines in some detail the content to be included as well as the student behaviors or objectives to be achieved in relation to this content. Ideally the curriculum maker may also determine the standards he desires to be met in the attainment of the specifications. Given the set of specifications, *instructional materials personnel* attempt to create the material and set the learning experiences which will enable students to develop in the ways specified. The same types of specifications can be used by *evaluation specialists* or *teachers* to construct formative evaluation instruments which can be used to determine when students have attained the competence defined by the specifications as well as to indicate in which aspects of the specifications the students' development is satisfactory or unsatisfactory.

Content

In our own work at the University of Chicago on formative evaluation, we have begun with existing instructional material and have attempted to analyze a learning unit into its components. The first step, which in some ways is the simplest, is to determine what *new* content or subject matter has been introduced in the new unit. What are the new terms, facts, relations, procedures which have been explained, defined, illustrated, or otherwise presented in the learning material?

We find that the usual textbook is relatively clear in signaling the new content that has been developed in a particular chapter. In either the textbook or the teacher's guide the new material is indicated by changes in print or color, comments in the margin, the summary at the end of the chapter, and the index.

Two or more independent judges who know the

subject field rarely have difficulty agreeing on the new elements of content or subject matter that are included in a particular learning unit. In our work with teachers and graduate students, we find agreement between judges to be on the order of 90 percent or higher when they independently list the details of content that have been introduced in a particular textbook chapter or set of instructional materials.

Behaviors

A second type of analysis is undertaken to determine the student behaviors or learning outcomes related to each new element of content. That is, given a new idea, relation, statement of truth, or other information, what is the student expected to learn? What is the student expected to remember? What is he expected to be able to do with the specific subject matter introduced in the learning unit?

We have found it useful to classify the new elements of subject matter or content according to some of the categories in the *Taxonomy of Educational Objectives*, Handbook 1, *Cognitive Domain* (Bloom, 1956). These classifications attempt to define a hierarchy of levels of behavior that relate to the difficulty and complexity levels of the learning process. We have used the following levels:

Knowledge of terms The "terms" are the specific vocabulary of a subject that the student is to learn. He may be expected to define the term, recognize illustrations of it, determine when the term is used correctly or incorrectly, or recognize synonyms. This category represents the lowest or simplest behavior level in the *Taxonomy*. (*Knowledge of terms* is defined in more detail in Chap. 7.)

Knowledge of facts "Facts" are the specific types of information which the student is expected to remember. They may include dates, names of persons or events, and descriptions; in general they are the particular details which are to be known simply because someone regards them as important in their own right or as essential for other kinds of learning. The student is expected to recall or remember these as discrete and separable content elements. He may be expected to recall the specific bit of information, to distinguish between accurate and inaccurate statements of it, and to remember the correct fact when asked about it in a relatively direct manner. (This category is also defined in more detail in Chap. 7.)

Knowledge of rules and principles This classification entails recall of the major ideas, schemes, and patterns by which the phenomena and ideas in a subject area are organized. Rules and principles bring together a large number of facts or describe the interrelationships among many specifics in such a way that the student can organize a large body of information in a parsimonious manner. The student is expected to know the rule or principle, to remember the illustrations of it used in the instruction, to recall situations in which it is applicable, and to remember the conditions under which it is or is not applicable. Rules and principles are likely to be more abstract and more difficult to learn than specific terms and facts. However, it is important to recognize that this category deals only with the recollection of the rules and principles and not with their application. (See Chap. 7 for a fuller definition and illustrations of this category.)

Skill in using processes and procedures This category is not included in the *Taxonomy*. We found, after inspecting a number of courses and especially some of the newer curriculum materials, that students are frequently expected to be able to use certain procedures and operations accurately and rapidly. Quite frequently these are particular steps in a process which the student learns in the appropriate sequence. It is sometimes possible for the student to learn a process before he has a name or rule to identify it—for example, he may be able to speak correctly before he has grammatical rules, or to take the square root of a number by following correct steps before he has a rule or principle which "explains" the operation. In this category the emphasis is on the student's being able to use the process or procedure accurately. That is, the student can do the steps in the procedure in the correct order, he can perform the operation in an appropriate manner, and he can get the correct result with a minimum of awkward or extraneous activity.

Ability to make translations This category involves the transformation of a term, fact, rule or principle, or process or procedure from one form to another. In translation the student can put the idea in his own words; he can take a phenomenon or event presented in one mode or form and represent it by an equivalent form or mode. For example, the representation may move from a verbal to a symbolic form, from a concrete to a more abstract form, or from a general to a more specific illustration, and vice versa. The student will be able to use new illustrations of a term, fact, rule, or other matter, and determine when a new illustration is an appropriate or inappropriate one for it. In general, translation is being employed when the student puts an idea in his own words or uses relatively new examples of what he has already learned. (This category is further defined and illustrated in Chap. 7.)

Ability to make applications "Application" is the use of rules and principles to solve problems presented in situations which are new or unfamiliar to the student. The primary behavior required at the application level is the use of a rule or principle learned in one context to solve a problem presented in a new context. If a problem is one the student has encountered many times previously except that new data are substituted, the behavior to be performed can be classified as translation rather than application. It is difficult to identify examples which represent true application without some knowledge of the learning materials or context within which the student originally encountered the relevant rules and principles. In application the student must recognize the essentials of the problem; determine the rules, principles, generalizations, and so forth which are relevant; and then use these ideas to solve a problem which is different from those previously encountered in the instruction or instructional materials. This is the most complex of the categories in that it depends on some of the previous classifications but requires the student to apply the ideas in new situations or problems. (This category is further defined and illustrated in Chap. 8.)

The classification of the detailed content according to these categories of behavior is more difficult than the identification of the content. However, we find that after a little explanation and some practice in applying the behaviors to given material, judges (teachers, psychologists, researchers) can agree on 85 percent or more of the classifications, with most of the errors having to do with distinctions between facts and rules or principles and between translations and applications (Airasian, 1968). It is evident that teachers of a subject have less difficulty making these distinctions than do psychologists and research workers who have never taught the subject. The teachers are familiar with the content, they are more clearly aware of what the instructional material is intended to do, and they have a clearer model of what the student should be able to do after he has completed the learning unit. In general, teachers are able to apply these categories to a specific learning unit with a few hours of practice.

Table of specifications

We have found it useful to organize the specifications for a unit of learning and for formative evaluation in tabular form. On one axis of this table we place the major behavior categories. Under each of these we list the appropriate subject-matter elements or details. Then, by using connecting lines, we attempt to show the interrelations among the elements. That is, if an element at one level is necessary for an element at a more complex level, this is shown by a line connecting the two elements. In Tables 6-1, 6-2, and 6-3 we illustrate the use of tables of specifications in analyzing units of learning in chemistry,

TABLE 6-1 TABLE OF SPECIFICATIONS FOR A CHEMISTRY UNIT

A. Knowledge of terms	*B. Knowledge of facts*	*C. Knowledge of rules and principles*	*D. Skill in using processes and procedures*	*E. Ability to make translations*	*F. Ability to make applications*
Atom (1)		Boyle's law (12)			
Molecule (2)		Properties of a gas (13)			
Element (3)				Substance into diagram	
Compound (4)		Atomic theory (16)		(22)	Writing and solving equations to fit experimental situations
Diatomic (5)	Diatomic gases (11)			Compound into formula	
		Chemical formula (19)		(21)	(28)
Chemical formula (6)		Avogadro's hypothesis (14)			(23)
Avogadro's number (7)		Gay-Lussac's law (15)			
Mole (8)					(24)
		Grams to moles (18)			(25)
					(26)
			Molecular weight (20)		(27)
Atomic weight (9)		Molecular weight (17)			(29)
Molecular weight (10)					

TABLE 6-2 TABLE OF SPECIFICATIONS FOR A BIOLOGY UNIT

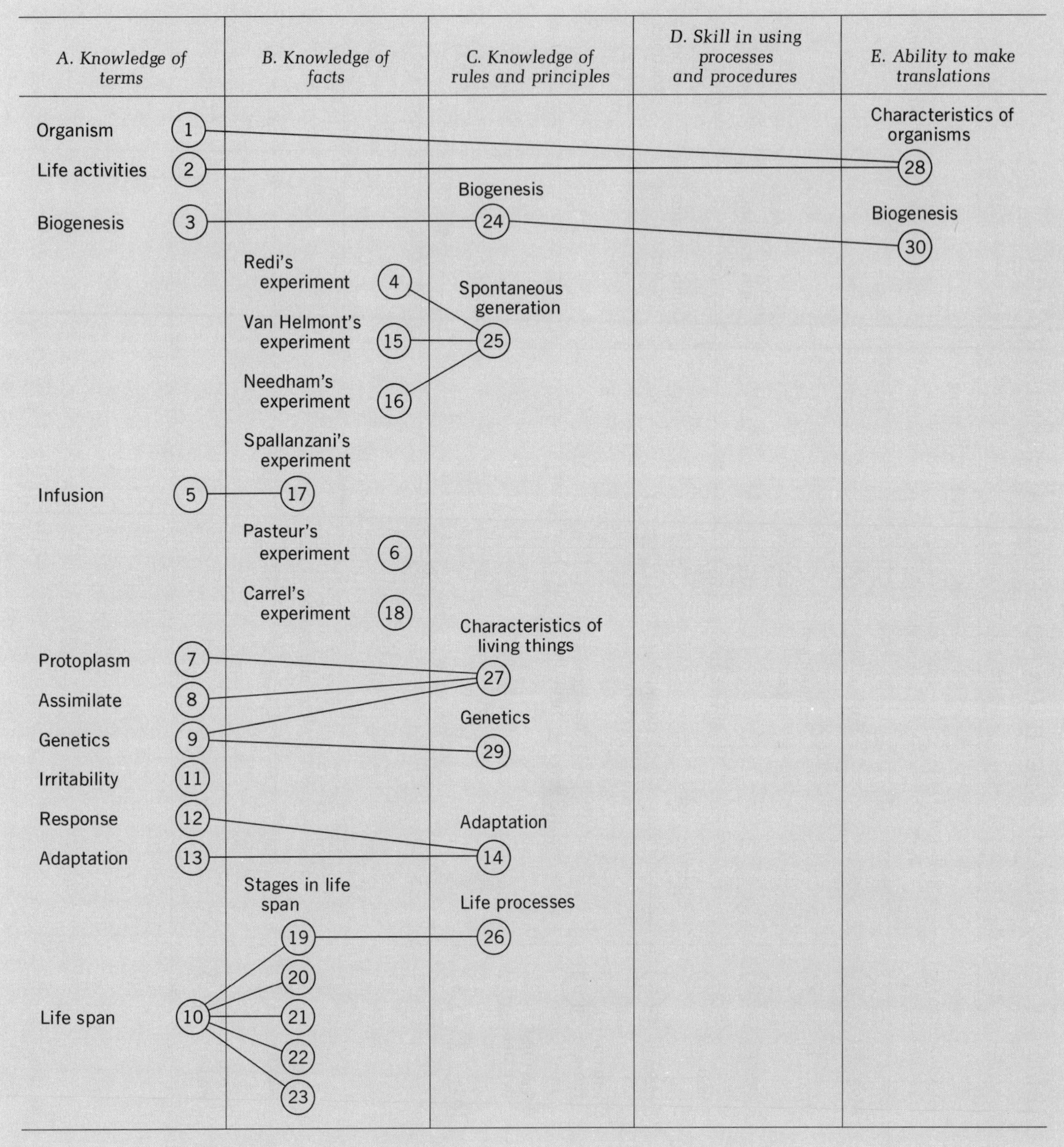

TABLE 6-3 TABLE OF SPECIFICATIONS FOR AN ALGEBRA UNIT

A. Knowledge of terms		*B. Knowledge of facts*	*C. Knowledge of rules and principles*	*D. Skill in using processes and procedures*	*E. Ability to make translations*	*F. Ability to make applications*
Variable	(1)					
Replacement set	(2)					
Variable expression	(3)					
Term	(4)					
Factor	(5)					
Coefficient	(6)				Identifying coefficients (16)	
Exponent	(7)			Evaluating an expression (15)		
Base	(8)			(18)		
Power	(9)					
Open sentence	(10)			Solving open sentences (14)		
Root	(11)			(17)	Problem statements into algebraic sentences	Solving problems with open sentences
Solution set	(12)			(19)	(21)	(24)
Inequality	(13)			(20)	(22) (23)	(25)

biology, and algebra. On each chart we have indicated in circles the numbers of relevant formative test items, some of which will be given in the following section, Formative Test Construction.

The process of developing specifications in this manner is highly revealing to teachers since it enables them to see in a very compact form the elements in a unit of learning as well as the relations among these elements as developed in the unit. Teachers and curriculum workers are especially sensitive to gaps revealed by the specifications table—it immediately shows terms, facts, or rules which are to be learned without being used in translations or applications. Quite frequently a unit of learning will consist of simply a large number of terms or facts to be learned with a minimum of interrelation. The specifications describe the elements, behaviors, and interrelationships as they are developed in the instructional material. If most of the elements fall under a particular category of behavior, this becomes apparent. If the elements are introduced in isolation from each other, this becomes apparent also. The teacher or curriculum worker may have some views about what can or should be done with a particular unit of learning, and he can compare his model of what might be with the material as it is organized in the learning unit. The teacher especially can see what he must do with the instructional materials if he is to achieve the outcomes he desires.

The specifications table is useful in the construction of formative evaluation instruments in that one can determine what should be included in the formative test and something about the hypothesized relations among the test items.

Formative test construction

After the unit is appropriately analyzed into content and behavior, the constructor of a formative evaluation instrument (teacher, evaluation expert, curriculum maker, or other professional) must determine which elements in the unit are important or essential and which are unimportant or useful only as background for the essential material. For example, in a chemistry unit, the name of the originator of an idea, the dates when he lived, or the country of his birth may be useful as interesting background for presenting the idea but may be of little cognitive importance in the unit. Such specific facts may be included in the specifications but dropped at the time of testing. The point is that not everything included in the specifications is of equal importance, and the curriculum maker, the teacher, or the formative evaluator must apply some judgment and draw on experience to determine what is essential in the unit and what is trivial—that is, what may be omitted without impairing the student's mastery of the unit.

General principles of formative evaluation test construction

Formative evaluation should include all the important elements in a unit as detailed by the table of specifications. Thus, if there are twenty-five important elements in the table, all twenty-five should be represented by one or more test items. This is in contrast with summative evaluation, where it is feasible, in the testing time available, only to sample the range of contents and behaviors outlined in a table of specifications.

The formative evaluation should include items at each of the behavior levels specified. Virtually the same subject matter may be included as a term, specific fact, rule, process, translation, and application, if all are included in the specifications. This means that the tester must clearly distinguish an item that appraises the student's knowledge of a term or fact from the item that determines whether or not he can translate an idea into a new form or whether he can apply a rule or principle to a new problem. In Tables 6-4, 6-5, and 6-6 we present structural diagrams for formative tests in the three units of learning for which detailed specifications were indicated in Tables 6-1 to 6-3.

TABLE 6-4 STRUCTURAL DIAGRAM FOR A FORMATIVE TEST IN THE CHEMISTRY UNIT

A. Terms	*B. Facts*	*C. Rules and principles*	*D. Processes*	*E. Translations*	*F. Applications*
1					
		12			
2					
		13			
3					
		16		22	
4					
		19		21	28
5	11				
		14			23
6					
		15			
					24
7					
		18			25
8					
					26
			20		
9					27
		17			29
10					

Although Chaps. 7 to 10 and Part II of this book go into more detail on appropriate classifications of behavior and testing techniques, we have illustrated those used at each level of the specifications in formative tests constructed for learning units in chemistry, biology, and algebra. So that the reader may relate the test items to their place in the structure of these units (see Tables 6-1, 6-2, and 6-3), we have used the same numbers in the charts and in the cell codes of the following illustrative questions. Although all these items are in the multiple-choice form for rapid administration and ease of scoring, it is of course possible to use other testing forms as appropriate to the content and behaviors being examined.

Knowledge of terms (A)

Chemistry: A-5

1. A molecule that contains only two atoms, both of the same element, is called a(n)
   - a. monatomic molecule
   - b. noble gas
   - c. diatomic molecule
   - d. ionic compound

Biology: A-1

2. Complete and entire living things composed of living substances and performing life activities are
   - a. organisms
   - b. frogs and grasses
   - c. rock and water
   - d. nonliving things
   - e. protoplasm

TABLE 6-5 STRUCTURAL DIAGRAM FOR A FORMATIVE TEST IN THE BIOLOGY UNIT

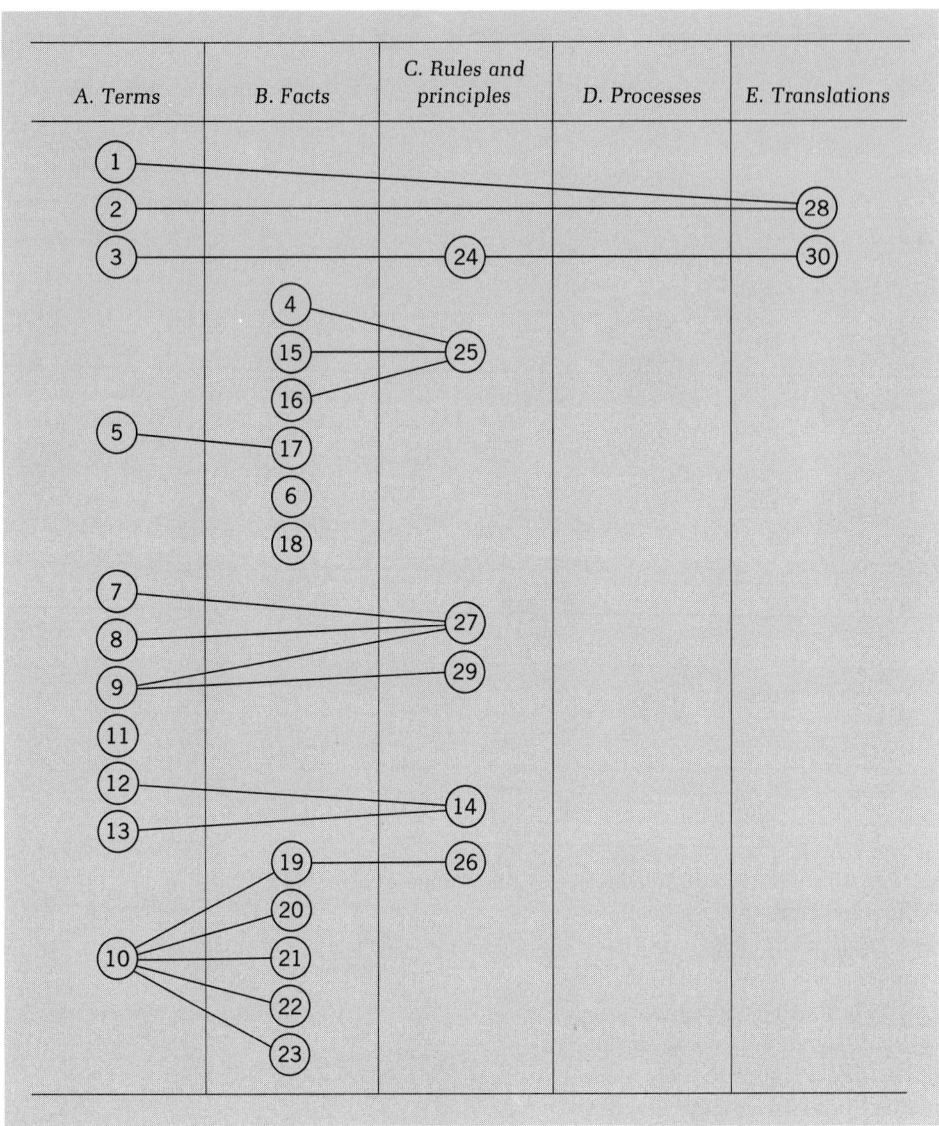

Algebra: A-10

3. Which of the following is an open sentence?

 a. 3x
 b. 3x + 1
 c. 3x + 1 = 8
 d. 7 + 1 = 4 + 4
 e. none of these

Algebra: A-12

4. The set whose members make an open sentence true is called the ______ of the open sentence.
 a. replacement set
 b. solution set
 c. variable set
 d. erector set
 e. none of these

Knowledge of facts (B)

Chemistry: B-11

5. Hydrogen, oxygen, and nitrogen are
   a. noble gases
   b. compounds
   c. diatomic gases
   d. monatomic gases

Biology: B-15

6. The outline of a method of producing mice from grains of wheat and human sweat was given by
   a. Jan van Helmont
   b. Francesco Redi
   c. John Needham
   d. Lazzaro Spallanzani
   e. Louis Pasteur

Knowledge of rules and principles (C)

Chemistry: C-19

7. In order to write a chemical formula, you have to know
   a. only the symbols of the elements that are in the compound
   b. only the proportions in which the atoms of elements combine

TABLE 6-6 STRUCTURAL DIAGRAM FOR A FORMATIVE TEST IN THE ALGEBRA UNIT

A. Terms	*B. Facts*	*C. Rules and principles*	*D. Processes*	*E. Translations*	*F. Applications*
1					
2					
3					
4					
5					
6				16	
7			15		
8					
			18		
9					
10			14		
11					
12			17		
13					
				21	
			19	22	24
			20		25
				23	

c. both the symbols of the elements that are in the compound and the proportions in which the atoms of elements combine
d. the atomic weight of the elements that form the compound

Biology: C-24

8. The principle of biogenesis states that
   a. living things have a cellular organization
   b. life arises from nonliving materials
   c. living things are capable of response
   d. organisms are capable of growth
   e. life arises from life

Skill in using processes and procedures (D)

Chemistry: D-20

9. The molecular weight of a gas can be determined experimentally by
   a. weighing 22.4 liters of the gas
   b. comparing the weight of a known volume of the gas with the weight of a different volume of another gas of known molecular weight
   c. comparing the weight of a known volume of the gas with the weight of 22.4 liters of the same gas
   d. comparing the weight of a known volume of the gas with the weight of the same volume of another gas of known molecular weight

Algebra: D-19

10. Find the roots of $3x + 5 = 8$ and $y - 2 = 11$. The *sum* of their roots is
   a. 10
   b. 14
   c. 40/3
   d. 52/3

Ability to make translations (E)

Chemistry: E-21

11. The correct formula for the compound dinitrogen tetroxide is
   a. N_4O_2
   b. NO_4
   c. NO_2
   d. N_2O_4

Biology: E-30

12. Select an example of the principle of biogenesis:
   a. puppy growing into a dog
   b. bud blooming into a flower
   c. moth hatching from a cocoon
   d. flies coming from meat
   e. salmon laying eggs

Algebra: E-23

13. A notebook costs 28 cents more than a pencil. The pencil costs x cents. Five pencils and two notebooks cost 91 cents. Which of the following describes the situation?
   a. $x + (x + 28) = 91$
   b. $2x + 5(x + 28) = 91$
   c. $5x + 2(x + 28) = 91$
   d. $5x + 2x + 28 = 91$
   e. $2x + 5x + 140 = 91$

Ability to make applications (F)

Questions 14 and 15 are based on the following new situation.

An evacuated container was weighed, then filled with oxygen and weighed again. The container was evacuated, filled with an unknown gas, and weighed again. Both gases were weighed at the same temperature and pressure. The following data were obtained:

Container empty	150.10/g
Container + oxygen gas	151.41/g
Container + unknown gas	151.82/g

Chemistry: F-26

14. What is the weight of one molecule of the unknown gas as compared to one molecule of oxygen?
   a. .761
   b. 1.01
   c. 1.30
   d. 1.00

Chemistry: F-28

15. It is determined experimentally that the unknown gas contains carbon and hydrogen atoms in the ratio of 1 to 2. What is the simplest formula?
   a. CH
   b. C_2H
   c. C_2H_2
   d. CH_2

Algebra: F-24

16. A team won three times as many games as it lost. It played 172 games. The *difference* between the number won and the number lost is
   a. 28
   b. 38
   c. 48
   d. 86

If there is a hierarchy in learning difficulty (see Gagné, 1965, 1968), then the responses of students to the test should reveal this hierarchy.

That is, the test items for knowledge of specific facts or terms should be passed by more students than those for knowledge of rules and principles or skill in the use of processes. Also, the test items involving translation and application are likely to be more difficult, and thus to be passed by fewer students.

The items in the test may also form a hierarchy in that passing the lower-level item is necessary for the mastery of the higher-level item (if this is indicated by the specifications). The item analysis might then conform with a pattern such as this:

		Higher-level item	
		Fail	Pass
Lower-level item	Pass	35%	35%
	Fail	30%	0%

That is, if the lower-level item is necessary for success on the higher-level item, then those students who fail the lower item should also fail the higher item—none who fail the first should be able to pass the second (except by chance or guessing). On the other hand, it is possible for some of the students who pass the lower item to fail the higher one, if the lower item is *necessary but not sufficient* for mastery of the higher item. Appropriate item analysis procedures can be used to determine whether the hierarchy of items established by the table of specifications is in fact borne out by student performance. In an unpublished doctoral dissertation (1968), Airasian found that three-fourths or more of the student responses showed the pattern of correct and incorrect responses indicated in the specifications for a chemistry and an algebra unit.

One analysis of the formative evaluation test should be made in terms of mastery or nonmastery. We have used accuracy levels of 80 to 85 percent on each formative test as an indication of mastery. This is arbitrary, however, and individual teachers may want to set the score for mastery higher or lower. If the accuracy level is too high (95 to 100 percent), it is likely to be obtained by only a few students, and there will be little positive reinforcement for mastery for very many students. On the other hand, if the mastery level is too low (50 to 60 percent), then a large number of students may have the illusion that they have mastered the unit of learning when in fact they have made many errors.

Another type of analysis of formative evaluation tests should reveal to the students the errors they have made. We have found it useful to provide the student with an answer sheet on which he can mark his errors. The back carries a diagram on which he can indicate his mistakes so that he may see the relations among the items he has answered incorrectly. Table 6-7 shows diagrams marked with errors made by two students on the chemistry unit formative test illustrated in Table 6-4. The value of such a diagram is that the student can trace the pattern of his errors in relation to the behaviors involved. He can also relate these errors to the content included by reference to the actual items in the test.

Where possible, the record of errors should be accompanied by a detailed prescription of the instructional materials (textbooks, workbooks, programmed instruction, films, and so forth) he should consult to correct the errors and strengthen his mastery of the unit under consideration. These remedial suggestions might appear on the front of the answer sheet, as outlined in Fig. 6-1. It is desirable to make the prescription very specific with regard to pages to be read, films to be seen, and the like.

The use of formative evaluation by students

The most important value of formative evaluation, in our view, is the aid it can give the student in his learning of the subject matter and behaviors for each unit of learning. As has been indicated in Chap. 3, Learning for Mastery, it is possible to have the large majority of students attain mastery of the subject if instruction is appropriately individualized. One step in individualizing instruction can be formative evaluation accompanied by a variety of materials and instructional procedures for the student to use in remedying the particular gaps in his learning of a specific unit.

The pacing of students

Probably the most effective use of formative evaluation is in pacing student learning. When subject matter is sequential in a course, that is, when learning units 1 and 2 are prerequisites to subsequent units, it is of importance that the student master units 1 and 2 before 3 and 4, 3 and 4 before 5 and 6, and so forth. This is most evident in subjects like algebra, where the first three or four units of the subject are basic to everything that follows. In such a subject, poor learning of the early units is likely to result in poor learning of all ensuing ones.

In sequential subjects, formative evaluation can set goals for student learning as well as a time schedule for each unit. There is some educational literature, summarized by Anthony (1967), Merkhofer (1954), and Stephens (1951), indicating that the frequency of quizzes and other testing, when accompanied by detailed feedback to the examinee, is related to the performance level of the students. One way in which this operates is by pressing students to put the appropriate effort into studying the subject for each of the periods covered by the quizzes. The student is always faced with conflicting demands on his time, and he is likely to postpone work and study

TABLE 6-7 ERRORS MADE BY TWO STUDENTS ON THE FORMATIVE TEST IN THE CHEMISTRY UNIT

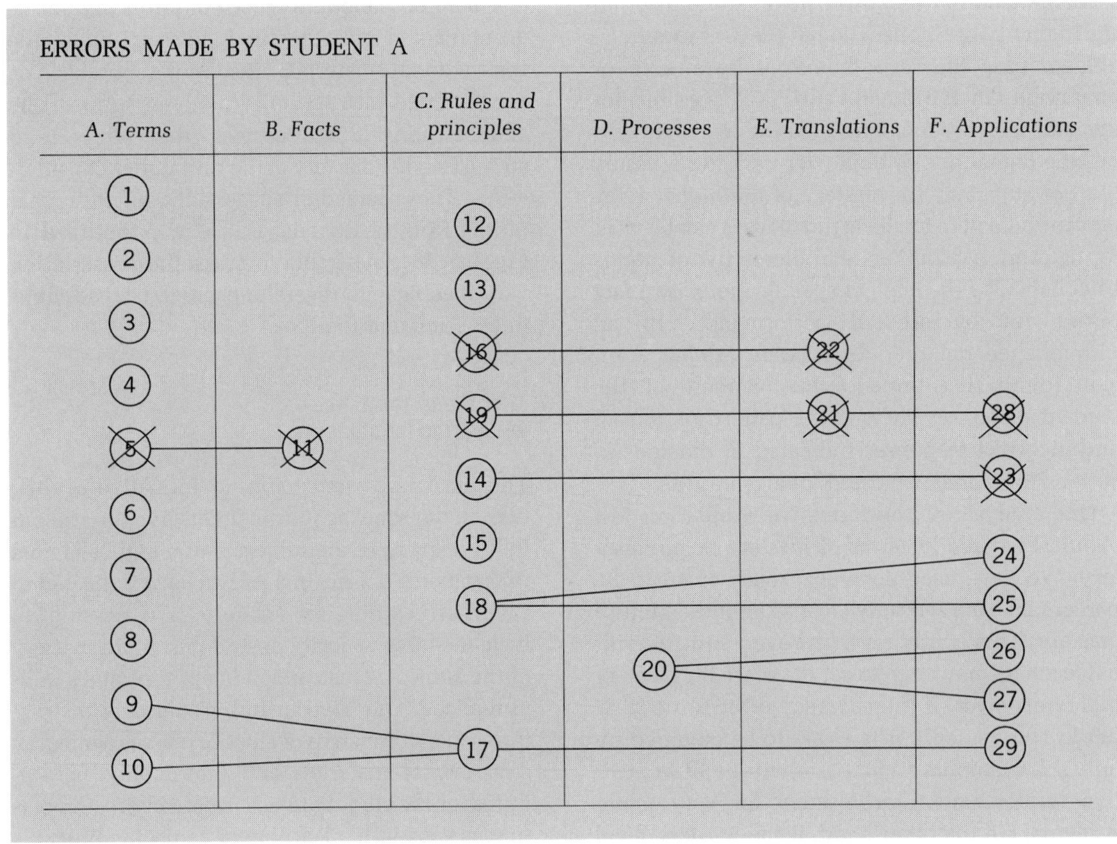

where the demands are less urgent. If he anticipates a quiz or a progress test, he is likely to make the appropriate preparation before the test.

Thus formative evaluation helps the student by breaking the entire learning sequence into smaller units and by pressing him to make more adequate preparation while he and others are learning a particular unit. Although pacing the students is of the utmost importance when the learning units form a hierarchical sequence, it is still of some importance for the student to learn in a scheduled way even if the units are not arranged hierarchically. Especially is this true when there is a great deal to be learned, so that students who postpone their study too long will be faced with an overwhelming amount of material, usually too great to be learned well just before the final summative evaluation.

It is difficult for students to determine whether their learning is satisfactory, particularly with an instructor and a subject new to them. For students who have achieved mastery or near mastery of a unit of learning, the results of the formative evaluation can be an effective reward or reinforcement. This is especially useful for providing the student with positive reinforcement over small units of learning. The repeated evidence of mastery is a powerful reinforcement which will help ensure that the student will continue to invest the appropriate effort and interest in the subject.

It is less certain that grading students on quizzes or formative evaluation is a useful reinforcement. If the student is given a C repeatedly on a series of tests, he comes to believe that C is

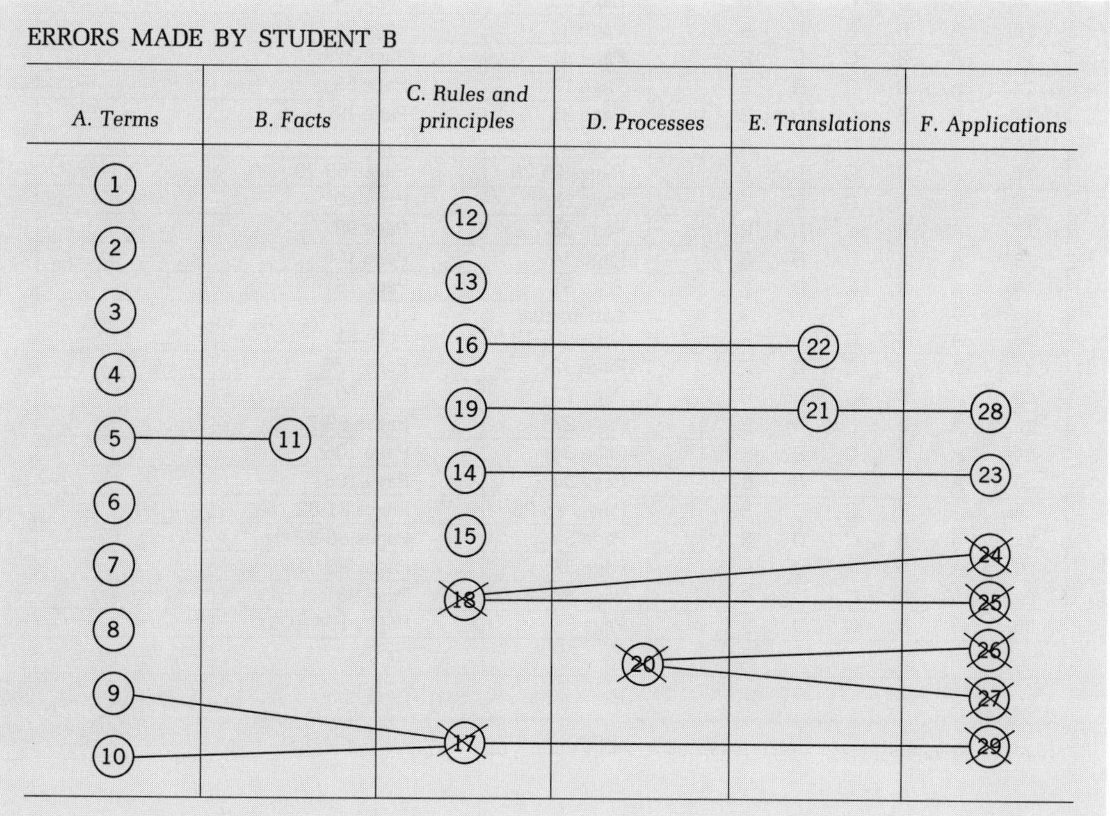

CHEMISTRY TEST

Answer sheet

Name ______________________

Date ______ *Test number* ___2___

CIRCLE your answer for each question. When you score this test, put an R beside each correct answer. Leave your incorrect answers blank.

Alternative learning resources: This test is designed to inform you of your learning difficulties. This test will not count as part of your final grade. Below is a list of learning materials which will explain the ideas you still need to learn. For each item you did not get right, read across to find where the correct answer or idea is explained.

	Right (R)	Textbook: *Chemistry: An Experimental Science*	*Chemistry: A Science of Matter, Energy, & Change* by Choppin and Jaffe	
1. A B C D E		Page 21	Page 19	
2. A B C D E		Page 21	Page 18	
3. A B C D E		Page 28	Page 14	
4. A B C D E		Page 28	Page 15	
5. A B C D E		Page 31	Page 76	
6. A B C D E		Page 31	Page 16	
7. A B C D E		Page 33	Page 86	
8. A B C D E		Page 32	Page 84	
9. A B C D E		Page 33	Page 84	
10. A B C D E		Page 33	Page 84	
11. A B C D E		Page 31	Page 77	
12. A B C D E		Page 17	Page 53	
13. A B C D E		Page 21	Page 19	
14. A B C D E		Page 25	Page 71	
15. A B C D E		Pages 25-26	Pages 69-70	
16. A B C D E		Page 28	Page 50	
17. A B C D E		Page 33	Page 98	
18. A B C D E		Page 34	Page 105	
19. A B C D E		Page 31	Page 16	
20. A B C D E		*Lab manual* Pages 14-18	Page 81	
21. A B C D E		Page 32	Page 136	
22. A B C D E		Page 28	Page 50	
23. A B C D E		Page 27	Pages 69-71	
24. A B C D E		Page 34	Page 106	
25. A B C D E		Page 34	Page 106	
26. A B C D E		Pages 25-26	Pages 81-82	
27. A B C D E		Page 34	Pages 86-87	
28. A B C D E		Page 37	Pages 88-91	
29. A B C D E		Page 33	Page 98	
30. A B C D E		Page 38	Pages 104-105	

FIGURE 6-1 Remedial instructional materials keyed to items on a formative chemistry test.

the mark he will finally receive in the course; and this is highly probable if the quiz grades are averaged and counted as part of the final grade. The C student must defend his self-concept by investing an amount of time and effort commensurate with getting a C. Thus it is highly likely that students who receive frequent Cs or lower grades on quizzes will adjust their investment in the subject so as to protect their ego when they finally get C for the course. They must convince themselves that it is impossible for them to get a higher grade, they could never learn this subject, they didn't really try, and so on.[1]

For this reason, we believe formative evaluation should simply inform the student whether he has or has not mastered the unit, and if he has not, indicate that there are certain steps he should take before leaving the unit.

In sequential units we have found that many students become progressively more able as they master the essential earlier units. That is, if students do the necessary learning or relearning over the first few units, the attainment of mastery levels on later units becomes more probable. This progressive development of mastery as well as the repeated evidence of mastery serves as a very powerful reinforcement, and the student comes to look forward to this reassurance and to the tests which provide it. Furthermore, the student is likely to anticipate the tests and make the necessary preparation for them in advance.

Even the student who hasn't achieved mastery on a particular formative test may be assured of what he has learned and what he still needs to work on. If the results can be put in positive terms, he can be reinforced for what he has learned. If necessary, a parallel form of the formative test can be given to those who did not attain mastery on the first form of the test but who did attempt to relearn those parts of the content and behaviors they missed the first time. The repeated administration of the formative evaluation test can then further reinforce those who attained mastery on the second administration.

[1] It is to be noted that some students may reduce their learning effort when their test results are not graded. One possibility for such students is to grade them on both formative and summative tests but to give them the alternative of having the final grade in the course be the average of both formative and summative tests or of only the summative tests, whichever is higher.

Diagnosis of difficulties

As has been mentioned before, a *score* on a formative evaluation test has little value in the learning process other than to reassure some students and to make others aware that they have more to learn. What the student needs is feedback which informs him of what he has learned and what he still needs to learn.

If the student, after taking a formative test, is shown which items he got right (presumably he has mastered the ideas which these items represent) and which he got wrong, he will have information about which ideas he still needs to learn or review. If the formative test does include most of the important terms, facts, principles, and other elements in the unit of learning, the student can use the items he got right as a useful inventory of what he has already learned and the items he got wrong as indications of what he still needs to learn. Locating his difficulties provides a useful type of feedback to him, especially if he is motivated to do the additional learning or review necessary to master the items (or ideas) that he did not get right.

But even more useful to the student, if it can be obtained, is an analysis of the causes of his difficulties—that is, an analysis not only of where but also *why* he had difficulties. We believe that eventually (especially with the use of computers and more carefully devised formative tests) it should be possible to write a very complete diagnosis of the student's difficulties and their probable causes. However, for some time to come, such an analysis may need to be done by a specialist who has a great deal of information available about the student, his study habits, his motivations, his aptitudes and skills, and other factors. (The reader may wish to refer again to Chap. 5 for a more extensive treatment of diagnostic evaluation procedures.)

Yet we believe that the use of a structural analysis of a unit of learning in relation to his errors on the formative test may provide the student with one type of diagnosis of the sources of his difficulty. On the answer sheets we have used in our own work we have presented a chart which shows the relations among the terms, facts, principles, processes, translations, and applications in selected learning units (see Tables 6-4, 6-5, and 6-6). We have had the students mark their wrong answers on the diagrams so that they may determine the pattern of their errors in terms of this structural analysis (see Table 6-7). There is some evidence in the work that has been done (Airasian, 1968) that the lower items in a series have a necessary (but not sufficient) relation to the higher items in the series. That is, if a student makes an error on a lower item, it is unlikely that he will be able (except by chance or guessing) to answer a related higher item correctly. While this evidence does not establish a clear causal connection among the items, it does suggest that errors on the higher items are in part the result of errors on the lower items. Such evidence must eventually be secured in other subjects, although we have found that when two subject specialists in chemistry or algebra are agreed on the hierarchical relation among the items, empirical evidence on student performance appears to support them.

The point is that one type of diagnosis is the finding of a pattern of errors on the formative test, and the student can do this by marking a diagram with his errors on a particular formative test and noticing the patterns that emerge.

This type of diagnosis is useful in that it suggests that the student who needs to relearn or review the subject should proceed from the lowest items in a series (terms or facts) to the next higher items (rules or processes) to the highest (translation or application). That is, if he has not mastered the lower items, he will have difficulty mastering the higher ones in a series.

It is to be hoped that the art of formative testing will evolve in such a way that the particular error a student makes on a specific test item can also be used to help him find what he is doing wrong in his answer to the question or in his learning about the particular idea. Much must still be done to develop formative testing so that it pinpoints not only the mistakes and difficulties a student is having but also their source or cause.

Prescription of alternative remedial measures

While the formative evaluation test can only locate the problems the student is having, it is possible to relate these diagnostic aspects of the test results to alternative ways in which he may overcome his difficulties.

It will be noticed that the illustrative answer sheet in Fig. 6-1 refers the student in each case to the appropriate page or pages in the textbook and laboratory manual assigned to the class and an alternative textbook. Other types of material might be suggested as well, such as a programmed unit and a workbook.

These represent relatively simple alternative instructional materials. Ideally each alternative should have some qualities not possessed by the others, such as clearer or simpler explanations, concrete illustrations, and drill and practice work on specific problems. It would be desirable to create special remedial materials—for example, short motion pictures explaining specific ideas, sound recordings, and even games or other devices—to help the student over a particular difficulty. We can even imagine the possibility of developing a set of cards each of which contains a test problem with a brief discussion of why certain answers are wrong, an explanation of why a particular answer is correct, and a short exposition of the idea being tested.

Two alternatives that are not included on the answer sheet are tutorial assistance and special group cooperation. In our own work, as we pointed out in Chap. 3, we have found that small groups of two or three students, meeting on a scheduled basis (a special study period, a regular meeting time, or the like) after each formative test, are most effective in helping each other overcome specific learning difficulties as pointed up by the test results. While not all groupings of students work equally effectively (and some groups may need reorganization from time to time), we are especially convinced that all students can profit from reviewing particular ideas together, and that this is of greatest value when the review is focused by the results of formative tests. When able students help less able ones, they gain increased understanding of the ideas as well as increased social sensitivity and cooperativeness. The less able students frequently get a new way of comprehending an idea since it must be explained in a form they can understand. We believe the time is well spent for all who participate in these helping relations.

It is likely that there will be individual differences in students which will make given alternatives more effective for some than for others. At this state in our work, we are not able to indicate which of various remedial measures is likely to be of greatest value to a student. Perhaps in the future it will be possible to accumulate data on each student as to the effectiveness of each alternative and to prescribe the one or two remedial measures that are likely to work best for him. However, it is possible that the greatest value in providing alternative procedures is that students will come to believe that if they can't learn the ideas from one instructional method or set of materials, they can learn them from another. This would enable them, we may hope, to come to see that it is the learning which is central rather than a particular textbook, teacher, or instructional method. We may hope also that each student will come to recognize the particular approach to learning which is most effective for him.

The use of formative evaluation by teachers

Scriven (1967) has proposed the use of formative evaluation by curriculum makers. He recommends that they try out their materials and methods with selected samples of students and teachers, and that they secure evidence on the effectiveness of these materials as well as on the specific aspects of the curriculum that are in need of revision. The type of formative testing we have suggested in this chapter is likely to be of great value in this tryout process since it can be used to locate specific difficulties that students are having with a particular portion of a curriculum. However, it is clear from Scriven's article that he would not confine his formative evaluation for curriculum development purposes to testing procedures; nor would we. Teachers' comments, subject specialists' criticisms, interest and attitudinal reactions of students are all relevant for formative evaluation. The advantages of the type of cognitive formative test we have stressed in this chapter are that it can accurately represent the structure of a curriculum unit, it can show the difficulties students are having, and it can represent the behavioral hierarchies and patterns of student responses. The appropriate use of such tests enables the curriculum maker to test hypotheses and hunches about specific aspects of a curriculum and the relations among the elements in a particular unit of learning. We will not dwell on the use of formative evaluation for curriculum development since we are primarily concerned in this book with student learning and instruction.

Feedback to teachers

Teachers have usually made use of quizzes, progress tests, and other evaluation techniques over brief periods of learning. However, though these are to some degree formative instruments, they are primarily used to motivate students and to mark their work at frequent intervals. For the most part these teacher-made tests are summarized to show the scores or marks of individual students. Only rarely does a teacher use them as a basis for modifying instruction. The primary change in the teacher's use of formative testing proposed here is that they be directed to yielding information which he can use to alter instruction or to review those ideas on which students are having great difficulty.

It is suggested that at the end of each learning unit, the teacher prepare an analysis of the errors students in a particular class have made on each item in the formative test. This can be done in a few minutes if the teacher places the students' answer sheets side by side and counts the number of correct or incorrect answers made on each item by the group. For items answered incorrectly by a sizable portion of the students, the teacher may want to count the number of times students made a specific wrong answer on a particular item, since this can give him an understanding of some of the confusions or types of difficulties the students are having.[2]

The results of this item analysis can be used to identify terms, facts, rules, and so forth, with which the students are having difficulty. If the majority of students answer a particular item incorrectly, this would appear to represent an element of the learning unit which has not been adequately mastered by the class. It is suggested that the teacher regard errors made by a substantial proportion of the students (we suggest 60 percent or more, but each teacher may have his own criterion of what constitutes a "substantial proportion") as stemming from difficulties in the instructional material or the instructional process. Such items should be reviewed at the next session of the class and efforts be made to find a different approach in explaining these ideas. One might expect the teacher to use different illustrations, to attempt to discover what the stumbling block was and remove it, or to relate the idea to other ideas which the majority have adequately learned, among other techniques. The teacher may get clues to the cause of the difficulty by noting the kinds of errors made by the students as well as the place of these items in the entire structure of the unit (see Tables 6-4, 6-5, and 6-6).

In sum, then, errors on a formative test made by less than the majority of a class are errors to be corrected by individual students. In contrast, errors made by the majority of students are regarded as difficulties in the instructional material or process and should be corrected by group instructional procedures. Some teachers believe that these group errors should be resolved in the same session as that in which the test was taken. In any case, they should be corrected as soon as possible after the time the formative test is taken.

[2] If the class is relatively large, the teacher may wish to make the item analysis of a sample of twenty to twenty-five answer sheets. If the sample is selected at random, or if the answer sheets are arranged in order of total score and every second, third, or fourth answer sheet is taken (depending on the number of examinees and the size of the sample to be analyzed), the sample should be quite representative of the entire group.

Quality control

Each new cycle of a course is in some respects related to previous cycles. That is, each time the course is given to a new group of students, the teacher may make use of his previous experience with it.

If the course is similar in content and objectives and includes some of the same units as before, the teacher may use the formative tests of an earlier term or year, with or without modification. Since the tests are to be used to help the students in the learning process (rather than for grading purposes), there is little danger that a student will be given any great advantage by consulting previous students in order to get help on the tests in advance of their distribution to the class.

The teacher may compare the results from the new group of students with those obtained previously for quality control purposes. Thus the proportion of students attaining mastery on test 1 in the formative test series may be compared from one year to another. When the results are lower for the current term, the teacher may wish to study the item analysis of test outcomes in the two terms to note where the difficulties lie. If the results are equal, or if the current performance shows an improvement over that of the previous class, the teacher may expect that, if succeeding test results are equally favorable, the final results on the summative tests will be at least as good as those in the previous term.

Especially in sequential units, the formative tests used as quality-control indices can be used to determine whether the current class is doing as well as previous classes or better. Also, the teacher can use the results of formative tests to seek ways of improving the current class's achievement over that of previous classes who took the same course.

Where an earlier group of students had special

difficulties with particular ideas or units, the teacher may wish to try a different instructional approach to these and to note whether the formative test results are indicative of the desired improvement in the learning process.

All this is to suggest that a teacher maintain a record of the formative test results of a particular year and use them as a set of norms or expectancies for new classes taking the same course. It is to be hoped that each new cycle of the course can be improved through an analysis of the results from a previous cycle, and that the improvement can be discerned through a comparison of the formative test results on each unit with the previous results as well as with the results on parallel summative examinations over several years.

Forecasting summative evaluation results

Formative tests are achievement tests over particular units of learning. Summative tests are achievement tests over a number of units of learning. Since there is usually some overlap between the two tests with regard to subject matter, behaviors, and even evaluation procedures, it is likely that the two types of test results will be related. In our own work we have found relatively high relationships between the performance of students on two or more formative tests and their performance on summative tests given several months later.

From these relationships, which appear to hold for individual students as well as groups of students, it is possible to predict results on summative tests several months in advance. That is, it is possible to anticipate results on summative tests while the instruction and learning process is still going on. And if the teachers and learners desire, it is possible to change the forecast.

In Fig. 6-2 we show several possible curves of results on a series of formative tests. Curves *A*, *B*, and *C* have actually been obtained in particular classes. Curve *D* is theoretically possible but has not as yet been observed.

Curve *A* represents a series of formative tests in which the same proportion of students achieve mastery on each test. It is not likely that more than about a fourth of the students will achieve mastery on the summative tests.

Curve *B* is one we have observed in a course where the formative tests were used for feedback and each student attempted to learn what he had missed on each of the tests. In this course students helped each other in small groups under the supervision of the teachers. On the summative tests more than two-thirds of the students achieved mastery.

We have observed curve *C* when students received the results of each formative test but were not motivated to do the necessary additional learning. It is obvious that a group of students like this one will do very poorly on the summative tests, and that the rate of failure will be very high.

Curves such as these may give the teacher a good picture of what is happening to a class, and may serve to sensitize the teacher or students to some of the learning problems they are encounter-

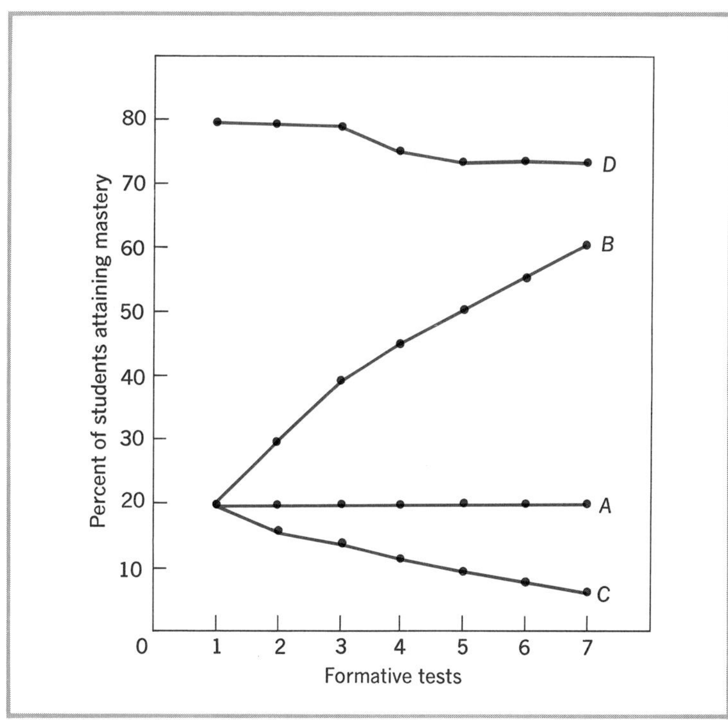

FIGURE 6-2 Some possible curves of results on formative tests.

ing. Especially with curves *A* and *C*, it is clear that something should have been done to alter the situation, perhaps after the second or third formative test. It is obvious that the methods of teaching and learning in the classes represented by curves *A* and *C* were not working very well. While it is less obvious what new methods should have been introduced, it is likely that more systematic review of particular ideas, more effective assistance for students in difficulty, and improvement of attitudes toward the subject would have been helpful.

Curve *D* is only theoretical. However, it is one which is likely to occur where the students have overlearned the first three units of the course and as a result are able to learn the later units to mastery with little difficulty.

We believe that formative tests can be of vital importance in helping the teacher and students determine the quality of learning that is taking place, and can allow them to forecast the results of summative tests some time in advance of the summative testing. Such results may be used as a basis for altering the teaching-learning situation early enough to change the immediate learning as well as to alter the forecast.

Learning is a process which can be observed and evaluated as it is taking place. Formative evaluation can be used to make the process more effective long before the summative evaluation. Recognition of the interactions among formative evaluation, teaching and learning, and summative evaluation can do much to improve teaching and learning before it is too late.

REFERENCES

Airasian, P. W. Formative evaluation instruments: A construction and validation of tests to evaluate learning over short time periods. Unpublished doctoral dissertation, University of Chicago, 1968.

Anthony, B. C. The identification and measurement of classroom environmental process variables related to academic achievement. Unpublished doctoral dissertation, University of Chicago, 1967.

Bloom, B. S. (Ed.) *Taxonomy of educational objectives: The classification of educational goals.* Handbook 1. *Cognitive domain.* New York: McKay, 1956.

Gagné, R. M. *The conditions of learning.* New York: Holt, Rinehart and Winston, 1965.

Gagné, R. M. Learning hierarchies. *Educational Psychologist,* 1968, **6,** 1–9.

Merkhofer, B. E. College students' study behavior. Unpublished doctoral dissertation, University of Chicago, 1954.

Scriven, M. The methodology of evaluation. *AERA Monograph Series on Curriculum Evaluation,* 1967, No. 1, pp. 39–83.

Stephens, J. M. *Educational psychology: The study of educational growth.* New York: Holt, 1951.

SECTION 3

Evaluation Techniques for Cognitive and Affective Objectives

7

Evaluation Techniques for Knowledge and Comprehension Objectives

The goals or objectives defined as "knowledge" have held a precarious position in American education for forty years. Not so "comprehension"! The difference is this: "knowledge" gets put down (to use a current phrase) every decade or so on the ground that it implies recall or recognition of myriad inconsequential details, with no understanding or systematization of those details; "comprehension," on the other hand, suggests that the learner "understands"—or internalizes and systematizes the "knowledges." However, if one looks at almost any of the various tables of specifications of content-behavior outcomes in this book (see Chaps. 4 and 6 and the subject-area chapters in Part II), he finds that knowledge of such things as terminology, principles, and rules appears as part of the behavior-content objectives. This situation is not peculiar to this book; statewide and local courses of study include knowledge as a basic part of the curriculum.

Knowledge objectives

The importance of knowledge objectives

The phrase "knowledge objectives," as used in this book, implies recall or recognition of specific elements in a subject area. Perhaps the widest range of types of things which are taught for the purpose of immediate recall appears in the *Taxonomy of Educational Objectives,* Handbook 1, *Cognitive Domain* (Bloom, 1956, pp. 62–77). In that treatise there are examples of knowledge objectives as disparate in content as "the recall of major facts about particular cultures" (p. 66) and "knowledge of a relatively complete formulation of the theory of evolution" (p. 77). Terminology, conventions, and criteria can each be the substance of knowledge.

The objective of the ability to recall does not in

itself suggest either the existence or the nonexistence of the capability of using or applying that knowledge. Certainly any self-respecting educator—or education system—would expect acquired knowledge to be useful in some fashion, whether for the solution of problems (knowledge of the relationship between temperature and pressure) or for personal enjoyment (recall of lines from a poem by E. A. Robinson). It is true that much of what we term "knowledge" is forgotten after a period of disuse, but this does not deny that such knowledge was a worthy outcome at the time it was learned. For example, most readers of this book had a course in algebra at one time which required recall of the general quadratic equation, $ax_2 + bx + c = 0$. Unless you have been engaged in work (or games) which use it or you are a mathematics buff, the chances are that you could not have recalled it exactly at this point. However, when you took algebra, it was important to *know* it both for the solving of exercises and for the more general purpose of acquiring usable concepts about relationships between first-order and second-order equations.

Although many of the specifics which we learn to recall or recognize during our formal instruction are forgotten within a few months or years, knowledge of them at the time of learning is *extremely important* for the development of ideas which do stay with us for interpretive and associational uses. Therefore, *during* the instruction period it is important for the teacher to test such knowledge as one facet of the evaluation of student learning. In many cases assessment of recall of specific facts is more a function of formative evaluation (Chap. 6) than of summative (Chap. 4). We need to have evidence of whether the student can recall certain terms, facts, or methods in order to make inferences about difficulties or next treatments.

If we turn to Gagné's method of defining educational objectives, discussed in Chap. 2 (see page 26 to 27 and Fig. 2-1), we will find time after time that knowledge of a particular term, relationship, or operation is an essential part of the pyramid of prerequisite capabilities for the desired terminal behavior. In some cases, perhaps in many, the underlying knowledges may be important only during the learning process, but at that point they are *essential.* Thus testing for them is highly desirable if one is to understand what is happening to his students.

Statements of knowledge objectives

As noted before, knowledge objectives abound in curriculum guides at all levels, in books on the pedagogy of particular subjects, and in books on the measurement of educational outcomes. The following statements are typical of the manner in which such objectives are worded:

1. "Knowledge of reliable sources of information for wise purchasing" (Bloom, 1956, p. 67).
2. "Knowledge of the standard representational devices and symbols in maps and charts" (Bloom, 1956, p. 70).
3. "To define technical terms by giving their attributes, properties, or relations" (Bloom, 1956, p. 64).
4. ". . . recall the specific definition of negative camber . . ." (Baldwin, Chap. 23 of this book, page 872).
5. ". . . to recognize a Shakespearean sonnet" in "a group of sonnets" (Purves, Chap. 20 of this book, page 707).
6. "Know biographical information" (Purves, Chap. 20 of this book, page 724).
7. "To identify letters of the alphabet" (Cleveland Heights School District, 1964, p. 18).
8. "The differentiation and discrimination among patterns and elements . . ." (Valette, Chap. 22 of this book, page 823).
9. "The ability to recognize the meanings or the definitions of words and of those terms which are necessary for study in the language arts" (Moore & Kennedy, Chap. 15 of this book, page 412).

Any reader who is at all familiar with education can list many more statements of knowledge objectives. The reason for the selection of the few foregoing ones is to present the common forms in which they appear. Those just stated differ from each other in two obvious ways—first, in the objects of the behaviors, and second, in the verbs or implied verbs (for example, "knowledge" meaning "to know"). There are other differences which are not quite so obvious but which are very important when it comes to evaluating student learning. These are the differences in specificity and type of content and observability and type of behavior.

In terms of specificity of content, perhaps statements 4 and 7 are the most explicit. Number 4 deals with one definition of one term. It is easy to see several clear ways of testing for this objective; for example, the teacher need only ask the student to state orally or in writing the definition wanted. For the statement dealing with letters of the alphabet, there would be more items, certainly, since there are twenty-six letters, but the area of content is clear and finite.

Numbers 1 and 9 indeed present limited content, but for either there would be some question of the limits. Some procedure would have to be used to determine which are the "*reliable* sources of information for *wise* purchasing," but even then the number of specific ones might be so large that the evaluator would find it desirable to sample only a few of them in order to estimate the extent of the student's knowledge. Much the same thing can be said about number 9, but with the additional note that the statement includes as content "the meanings or the definitions." The act of implementing this statement in testing situations would have to take into account the possible differences between "meanings" and "definitions." One way to obviate this latter concern is to cut one or the other of the two words out of the statement. We would argue against doing so on the ground that intended outcomes would be altered *in order to make it easier to test for them.* This should never be the criterion. On the other hand, one simply must not overlook the difference in meaning between the two words.

In content statement 5 deals with sonnets by Shakespeare and sonnets by others. This may suggest a field which is functionally infinite, since one could presumably write sonnets for this purpose. However, the necessary decision here, different from those in 1 and 9, concerns the dimensions along which one wants the student to differentiate and the closeness of the differentiation. One could say that the comparisons should treat subject matter or word choice or word orders—or all of these and others. None of this is meant to suggest that this particular statement of a knowledge objective is poorly stated or is less than useful; it does imply that the teacher who is attempting to evaluate student learning outcomes in the light of such an objective must keep these possible concerns in mind.

The final observation about the content end of statements of knowledge objectives is directed at number 3. At first glance this statement may seem to deal with much the same order of things as do numbers 4 (the definition of negative camber) and 9 (definitions of words in the language arts). On second reading it is clear that the real content is *not* subject matter in any restrictive sense; rather it is a method or technique. The "knowledge" required is how to define technical terms by citing attributes, properties, or relations of the things to which the terms refer. There are other ways in which to show "knowledge" of a term—for example, by using it in a sentence, identifying an incorrect use of it, and giving an example of the class to which it refers. We must assume that the objective in statement 3 is not intended to entail any single subject matter or groups of subject areas. The intent is to develop in students a particular way of defining technical terms. Therefore, if one wishes to assess the extent to which learners have developed this ability, sampling across technical terms in various areas (at their level of learning) would seem to be demanded.

Several paragraphs earlier it was stated that the list of statements of knowledge objectives also illustrates differences in observability and type of behavior. Chapter 2 has discussed differences in the behavioral aspect of behavior-content objectives as formulated by various people, among them Tyler and Gagné. The nine statements of knowledge objectives illustrate certain concerns for the teacher who is assessing student learning. For instance, number 4 (to recall a specific definition) and number 8 (to differentiate and discriminate) suggest or imply different behaviors. As an example, if we ask you to differentiate and discriminate between the terms "square" and "parallelogram" and you simply list the characteristics of each, you are scarcely delivering the behavior we requested. This doesn't mean that you are naughty—or that you can't distinguish between the two. It means that you didn't give evidence of the sort of behavior which was solicited.

Statement 1 in the list implies that the student "knows" the reliable sources. When we wish to convert this statement into a test item, we must decide what act or behavior on his part satisfies our meaning of "knowing." It could be that if he *lists* the sources either orally or in writing when requested, we will be satisfied he knows them. If he does not do this, we may have a question as to whether he does not know the sources or does not—for whatever reason—wish to comply with our request. This is why in Chap. 3, on Learning for Mastery, and Chap. 6, Formative Evaluation, it was suggested that the emphasis on grading students be dropped in many circumstances, and that student learning be assessed for the sole purpose of improving the instruction. Under such circumstances, if the student can be taught to believe in these ground rules, he will be much more willing to respond to our requests to "list the sources." Then the fact that one student lists fewer than does another or that one lists less acceptable sources means that the one so doing needs more help to arrive at mastery.

Statement 1 might mean that the student is given a list of possible sources of information on which he checks those which are reliable for wise purchasing and leaves blank those which do not fit this category. Such behavior is observable. One can see whether or not the student checks a certain alternative; one cannot see whether or not he *knows*. Similarly, with a literal meaning attached to statement 4, one cannot observe whether a student "recalls" but can observe whether he lists, writes, states, or chooses a given definition.

There are those (Mager, 1962; Popham, 1969) who demand that any statement of an objective be put in terms of "observable behavior." The authors of this book feel that in general it is useful to express objectives in terms of such categories as "recall," "recognize," and "remember," with the expectation that each teacher or other evaluator of student learning will look for several possible ways of observing the behavior. We feel that different students may express their "knowing" in different ways; we also believe that our collective knowledge of the contingencies among different acts (explicit behaviors) is not yet strong enough to allow for a prescription of the *best* way of expressing "knowing."

Both number 5 and number 9 use the word "recognize." Ordinarily this means something different from "recalling." In the former case one expects to deal with a choice item, defined in Chap. 4 as one in which the student is asked to select from among alternatives which are given. The word "recall," on the other hand, more frequently carries the meaning of having the student respond to a supply item, that is, one in which he is asked to provide a response instead of select among several. (In the next section of this chapter, examples are given of both supply and choice items.) It is true, however, that if he chooses a response from among several which are given—whether he selects the "correct" one or not—he is *recalling* something. One could say also that when the student supplies an answer ("List the five most reliable sources") instead of choosing among sources given ("From the following ten sources select the five most reliable"), he is *recognizing* the appropriate responses among the several or many which come to his mind.

In other words, the terms "recognize" and "recall" do not in themselves explicate the observable behavior which is intended any more than does the expression "to know." The person who is developing tests for these objectives must think of the various observable behaviors which could be used to demonstrate "recognizing," "recalling," and "knowing." He may be satisfied with using one such behavior for all students for a given knowledge objective. On the other hand, he may wish to use several different types of behavior and require that the student demonstrate competence with each. Finally, he may wish to use several different ones but require that the student be competent only with any one of them.

Illustrative test items for knowledge objectives

The intent of this section is to give the reader examples of a few of the main item formats and indicate the knowledge behaviors for which they are appropriate. Items designed to test knowledge have been more prevalent in tests—teacher-made or published—in almost all fields of study than have items directed at application, analysis, and other uses of knowledge. Examples of types of items which can be used to test knowledge abound both in such tests and in books whose purpose is to present item types and functions. Perhaps one of the most complete sets of illustrations of various item types is in the book by J. Raymond Gerberich, *Specimen Objective Test Items* (1956). Another excellent source of item types, ordered according to subcategories of knowledge (for example, knowledge of conventions, knowledge of trends and sequences, and knowledge of methodology), is the *Taxonomy of Educational Objectives* (Bloom, 1956). Some of the illustrations in this section have been chosen from other works. In each case where the item was not written specially for this chapter, the source is indicated.

There are two very important characteristics of good knowledge items. First, a good item is at a level of exactness and discrimination which is very similar to the level used in the original learning. If one is teaching at a beginning level for knowledge of conventions in language usage or knowledge of methodology in history, his test items on the material should never call for finer discrimination or more exact usage than that for which the teaching might account. If they do, he is necessarily testing for some behavior beyond knowledge; the student must in some way use other principles, generalizations, criteria to respond correctly. This is not to say that such testing is not useful; it simply suggests that it does not fall in the knowledge category.

The second characteristic is that items should not be couched in terms or settings which are new to the student. This is just the opposite of the rule for testing application or analysis (see Chap. 8). If one has taught the child that the materials deep inside the earth are hot, then he should not test for this knowledge with an item using terms like "interior" and "igneous fusion" unless he knows that these are familiar to the child. If he uses terms which are unfamiliar, he is not testing for the knowledge taught—he is testing for unfamiliar vocabulary.

As stated earlier, the two main classes of knowledge items are *supply* and *choice*.

Perhaps the simplest form of the supply type is the completion item.

1. The name of the third President of the United States is ________.
2. The Crimean War took place in the years ________ to ________.
3. If 6 is multiplied by 8, the answer is ____________.
4. Two triangles are congruent if they have ________ and ________ of one equal respectively to ________ and ________ of the other.

Items such as these are usually best for testing knowledge of specific names, technical terms, and definitions. In building them one must be sure to leave enough space for the word or words which are to be placed in the blanks. Also, it should be obvious that great care must be taken to phrase the statement so that it is unambiguous. For example, if the second item were worded "The Crimean War took place in ________," an appropriate answer might be any of the following: "1853 to 1856," "the Crimea," "the nineteenth century," "southern Russia."

There are those who contend that this type of item leads more directly to rote learning or verbalization without meaning than do other types. Because of the two characteristics cited a few paragraphs earlier, knowledge items in general can motivate students toward rote learning and verbalization if the instruction sets the stage for this and if there is no testing for other capabilities, such as translation, application, and synthesis. One must remember that knowledge items are intended to discover whether the student recalls certain important things—in much the same form as he learned them. If he is taught these things in a meaningless fashion, if there is no attempt to measure understanding in addition to knowledge, the result may well be mere verbalization. This is scarcely the fault of the type of item.

Another kind of supply item which is familiar to most teachers is the direct request for a definition, the statement of a principle or convention, or the steps of a method.

5. State the law relating temperature, pressure, and volume of a gas.
6. List in order the steps which should be taken in adjusting the timer on a six-cylinder engine.
7. Write the definition for similar triangles.

One of the main difficulties with this type of item is that the decisions on scoring them may be very complex. How many different wordings of the response to item 5 should be accepted as satisfactory? What differential scoring should be used on the responses to item 6 if the ordering of the steps differs from that desired? Should the student's response be counted as all wrong if he fails to describe one of the steps adequately? Does a slight misstatement in a student's reply to item 7 mean that he does not know the definition, or does it mean that although he knows it his ability to express himself is not good? There can be answers to such questions, but the process is time-consuming for both the examinees and the teacher. When the rules are set up for scoring, it would be well to check them out with someone else in the subject area. It is also important that every attempt be made in the directions to convey the ground rules—the exact limits of responses—to the students.

The type of completion item for which the response consists of one to three words obviates some of the difficulties with scoring. The choice item (see below) is usually more efficient in amount of information gained in a set period of time and in scoring time. However, it must be recognized that the examiner is not demanding the same behavior in the supply items just illustrated as in completion or choice types. The one who is evaluating the student learning must decide which sort of behavior satisfies his knowledge objective.

There is one other type of supply item which bears mentioning. This is one in which the stimulus for recall is visual or auditory.

8. For each of the following figures, write the name below the figure.

9. I will play parts of each of six musical selections on the record player. At the end of each selection I will pause while you write the name of the composer on the line for that selection.
   a. ____________
   b. ____________
   c. ____________
   d. ____________
   e. ____________
   f. ____________

Obvious variations on this item would be to ask for the name of the composition or the type of musical selection.

10. As I show you certain pieces of laboratory equipment one at a time, write down the name of the equipment on the lines provided.
   a. ____________
   b. ____________
   c. ____________
   d. ____________

One could ask instead for the function of the equipment or for an example of use.

Such items as these elicit a type of behavior which is valued in many kinds of learning. The form itself can be adapted to many different subject areas, but it is probably best suited to use in the fine arts classroom, the laboratory, and the shop. It should be noted that the choice of a written answer as opposed to an oral one is not required by the intent of the item. The written response and the prescribed places for responses allow for group use and for standardization of procedure. One should recognize that in this item, as in the preceding set, scoring requires decisions about limits of acceptability of responses. For example, in item 8 should one accept for the second figure both "parallelogram" and "quadrilateral"? In item 9 should one allow an approximate phonic spelling of names—as long as they are "recognizable"—or demand something more exact? It seems to us that the answers to these sorts of questions rest upon a careful determination of the behavior and content meaning of the knowledge objective.

Choice items for knowledge objectives take many different forms to fit special needs. We will present several of the most common ones, again with comments on some benefits and some dangers involved in using them for testing knowledge objectives. Perhaps the reader can best satisfy his requirements by practicing with a few of these forms. Then, if he wants more detailed information on particular rules and on statistical techniques for improving tests, he can refer to some of the books designed especially for test construction, such as those by Ahmann and Glock (1963), Ebel (1965), and Gronlund (1965).

One of the most commonly used forms is that in which the examinee is asked a question and then presented with several alternatives from which he must select one correct answer. Here is one which parallels item 1, above.

11. Who was the third President of the United States? (Circle the letter of the correct name.)
    a. Adams
    b. Clay
    c. Jackson
    d. Jefferson
    e. Madison

The advantages that this type of item has over the completion form are that there can be no room for ambiguity and in general more items can be sampled in a given time period. Studies have indicated that when the same students are given a large sample of each type testing the same material, the results for the students, in terms of their standing on the tests, is very nearly the same. There may be reasons in a given situation for wanting to sample the supply behavior instead of the choice type, but if the two place students in about the same order, it is usually more efficient to use the choice type.

This multiple-choice form is quite well suited to testing for knowledge of terminology or specific facts, as is illustrated in the following:

12. A synapse can best be described as
    1. a mass or layer of protoplasm having many nuclei but lacking distinct cell boundaries.
    2. a lapse of memory caused by inadequate circulation of blood to the brain.
    3. the pairing of maternal with paternal chromosomes during maturation of the germ cell.
    4. the long cylindrical portion of an axon.
    5. the point at which the nervous impulse passes from one neuron to another.

(Bloom, 1956, p. 79, item 1.)

13. Negative camber is the
    a. inward tilt of the kingpin at the top
    b. outward tilt of the kingpin at the top
    c. forward tilt of the kingpin
    d. backward tilt of the kingpin

(Baldwin, Chap. 23 of this book, page 872, item 1.)

In most multiple-choice items, the distracters (nonpreferred alternatives) provided can make discrimination between them and the "correct" choice more or less difficult. If in item 11 we make the alternatives to "Jefferson" such names as "Kalderwehki" and "Kawakami," the student is apt to make his choice on other grounds than knowledge of the third President's name. It should also be recognized that one can ask for a "best choice" from among those given as opposed to "the correct choice." This possibility is frequently needed in the social sciences and humanities, but it is certainly applicable to other areas. Take this example:

14. An important difference between a trapezoid and a parallelogram is that the latter has
    a. angles which sum to 360 degrees
    b. sides of equal length
    c. opposite angles which are equal
    d. two angles which are obtuse

Alternative c is not necessarily the only correct difference or the best of all possible answers, but it is the best alternative given.

Another design of choice item which is useful for the rapid sampling of many knowledge objectives is the true-false format.

15. For each of the following statements, put a T or an F on the blank in front of the statement according to whether you believe it is true (T) or false (F).
    a. ________ The opposite sides of a parallelogram are equal.
    b. ________ A quadrilateral has four equal angles.
    c. ________ An isosceles triangle has three equal sides.

The list may continue with many statements.

This type of item demands that the student match his memory of a fact, a convention, a definition, or some other statement with the one presented to him. It should be recognized that this is exactly what many multiple-choice items do except that they test one piece of knowledge with several statements and ask the student to identify only the one which is "true." A great difficulty with this type is that in many subject areas it is very difficult to make true or false statements without the use of such conditioners as "usually," "in general," "always," and "never." In statements like "Elm trees are usually found in temperate climates" and "Cacti never grow outside of subtropical or tropical climates," the student, particularly the clever student, is quite apt to react to the words "usually" and "never," marking the former "true" and the latter "false." His chances of being correct are increased, but you are not testing for the knowledge behavior you intended. This does not mean that the true-false item type is poor; it merely means that great care must be taken in writing such items.

The third type of choice item is called the matching item.

16. On the line to the left of each phrase in *Column A*, write the letter of the word in *Column B* that best matches the phrase. Each word in *Column B* may be used once, more than once, or not at all.

Column A	Column B
__1. Name of the *answer* in addition problems.	a. Difference
	b. Dividend
__2. Name of the *answer* in subtraction problems.	c. Multiplicand
	d. Product
__3. Name of the *answer* in multiplication problems.	e. Quotient
	f. Subtrahend
__4. Name of the *answer* in division problems.	g. Sum

(Gronlund, 1965, p. 134.)

17. Identify the author of each title in the left-hand column by putting the letter which appears before the name in the right-hand column in the blank before the title. One author may have written several of the works named or none of them.

__1. *The Taming of the Shrew*	a. Benét
__2. *Ode on a Grecian Urn*	b. Byron
__3. *Talifer*	c. Longfellow
__4. *Moby Dick*	d. Melville
__5. *John Brown's Body*	e. Robinson
__6. *Tristram*	f. Shakespeare
	g. Tennyson

Items in this category, like true-false items, provide efficiency in terms of coverage per unit of time. They are, however, very difficult to construct. For example, the terminology of the title should not suggest the period or school of the author. In general there should be more choices in the right-hand column than things to be identified in the left-hand column. Otherwise the student responding may select one or two on some principle of elimination, not on the basis of knowledge.

In summary, when testing for knowledge objectives, one resorts to either the supply item, in which the student affords the answer *out of his memory*, or choice items, in which he selects from some set of *given alternatives*. There are several ways in which to ask for either. If units of information per period of time are important, some of the item formats are more likely to be useful than are others. Supply items are likely to be more difficult to score than are the choice type. On the other hand, they are easier to invent. The final question which a teacher should ask himself, however, is, "What observable behavior will satisfy my objective of knowledge of . . . ?"

Comprehension objectives

The foregoing section on knowledge objectives dealt with behavior that could be (educators forbid!) mere rote learning or verbalization. In 1946 the National Society for the Study of Education issued a yearbook devoted to the measurement of understanding as opposed to rote memory and verbalization (Henry, 1946). The idea of the publication was to emphasize that knowledge alone is not enough; use of the knowledge is more important. The authors of the chapters treated understanding operationally as any behavior from stating a proposition in words different from those of the original statement through giving examples of a referent in a definition to applying a principle in a situation new to the learner. Ten years after that publication, the *Taxonomy of Educational Objectives*, Handbook 1, *Cognitive Domain* (Bloom, 1956), treated many of the same operations and some additional ones, but classified them into levels of cognition. In the scheme presented in the *Taxonomy*, the category called "comprehension" is the first level beyond the category of "knowledge."

"Comprehension" is described in terms of three different operations. The lowest order is that of *translation*, in which the known concept or message is put in different words or changed from one kind of symbology to another. Evidence of translation is present when a person puts into words the parts of a graph which shows trends over time in the cost of living. He expresses points of the graph in words. Obviously, if one changes a statement in French to its equivalent in English, he is engaging in translation. The ability to translate is frequently very important in such tasks as applying principles of physics to a mechanical problem, analyzing a document, or creating a work of art.

The second level of comprehension is *interpretation*. Evidence of this behavior is present when a student can go beyond recognizing the separate parts of a communication—translating the graph mentioned in the preceding paragraph—and see the interrelations among the parts. He can relate the various parts of the graph to actual events. Also, he must be able to differentiate the essentials of the message from such unimportant (to the message) aspects as the color of the graph or the size of the time-scale units.

The third level of comprehension is *extrapolation*. In this category the receiver of a communication is expected to go beyond the literal communication itself and make inferences about consequences or perceptibly extend the time dimensions, the sample, or the topic. In the example of the graph showing cost-of-living trends, extrapolation would demand such behaviors as inferring what the next time unit—beyond the graph—might show, suggesting the possible meaning of the graph for different sorts of commodities, or presenting the effects which the situation described by the message might have on wages or taxes. In this sense extrapolation is much akin to interpretation, but it exceeds the literal limits of the message.

Although it is very useful for both instructional and evaluative purposes for the teacher to be concerned with each of the three subcategories independently, they are highly interrelated. In certain tasks and behaviors, one may draw a line too fine if he attempts to say, "This is translation and not interpretation" or "That is interpretation but not extrapolation." There are cases, however, in which the distinctions are clear. Therefore, in the remainder of this chapter we will present objectives, test items, and discussions of the items under the more general heading of "comprehension," although the subcategories are indicated where appropriate.

Statements of comprehension objectives

Objectives in this area appear in courses of study and in methods books in various subject areas almost as frequently as do statements of knowledge objectives. Some rather typically worded statements are these:

1. "The ability to translate an abstraction, such as some general principle, by giving an illustration or sample" (Bloom, 1956, p. 92).
2. "The ability to read musical scores" (Bloom, 1956, p. 92).
3. "The ability to comprehend the connotative value in words" in a literary work (Purves, Chap. 20 of this book, page 737).
4. "Give a literal translation [of a sentence from French into English] and a meaningful English equivalent" (Valette, Chap. 22 of this book, page 832).
5. "A major aspect of reading in the social sciences is geared to the interpretation of maps, globes, graphs, tables, and charts, and cartoons" (Orlandi, Chap. 16 of this book, page 476).
6. "To write a one- or two-paragraph summary based on reading material, observation, or listening" (Cleveland Heights School District, 1964, p. 37).
7. ". . . the ability to comprehend the significance of particular words in a poem in the light of the context of the poem" (Moore & Kennedy, Chap. 15 of this book, page 412).
8. "The ability to recognize puns or verbal ambiguities . . ." (Purves, Chap. 20 of this book, page 736).
9. The ability "to extrapolate from data presented in a table" (Orlandi, Chap. 16 of this book, page 476).
10. "The ability to estimate or predict consequences of courses of action described in a communication" (Bloom, 1956, p. 96).
11. "Skill in predicting continuation of trends" (Bloom, 1956, p. 96).
12. "The ability to be sensitive to factors which may render predictions inaccurate" (Bloom, 1956, p. 96).

Any reader would do well to spend some time looking through methods books and courses of study or curriculum guidelines in his own field in order to find statements like the foregoing. If you are a teacher and have not developed statements like these for your own class, you should try your hand at some right now. Note that statements 1 and 2 concern translation. Statements 3 and 4 certainly involve translation as a main ingredient, but each may entail some interpretation in that an assessment of the relationship among elements of the message *may* be demanded. Interpretation is clearly the level of statements 5 to 8, whereas extrapolation is the focus of 9 to 12.

Even a cursory study of the list above will show that comprehension, as defined in this setting, is not the sole property of one or two fields of study. For example, statements 5 and 2 represent geography and music respectively; language arts, literature, and foreign language are the subject areas of statements 3, 4, and 6 to 8; and science, social studies, and mathematics can be the contents of statements 1, 9, and 12 in that order.

In the preceding section, it was pointed out that items built for the purpose of evaluating knowledge outcomes should stick as nearly as possible to the form and the level of precision used in instruction. In comprehension items—ranging from translation to extrapolation—the opposite is true. If the student is asked to translate in *exactly* the same situation as the one in which he was taught to translate, he may be working much more at the knowledge level than in the comprehension category. For example, if we teach for statement 1 by using certain principles accompanied by particular illustrations and then assess his learning by items which use those same principles and allow the identical illustrations, the student's correct response is more likely to be direct recall than it is a generalized translation ability.

On the other hand, items which call for interpretation in a totally different setting from the one in which instruction was given probably come much nearer to testing application and analysis than to measuring interpretation in the meaning which is used here. For instance, if we have instructed a student along the lines suggested by statement 7 above, and then we test him on his ability to comprehend objects in a cartoon in the light of the total cartoon, we are probably asking him to use higher-order abilities than we had intended.

In many ways statements of comprehension objectives provide more direction in their very wording for writing questions and examination items than do statements of knowledge objectives. Note statement 2, which deals with music. The obvious way of testing for this is by giving students musical scores and asking them to translate the symbols into actual notes. However, it would still be translation if the student were required to write in words the notes, phrasing, and other characteristics. Or again, statement 5 suggests that one give the examinee a map and then ask him questions about how to get from here to there, or ask him to describe the terrain. However, if the objective is statement 11, there may be several routes to the evaluation of the outcomes. One could set up a situation in which the "continuation" has occurred—inflation in the 1880s—and judge the student response against the fact. Unfortunately, this might be a knowledge item for some students. An alternative would be to use current data and expert judgments on the probability of the choice of trends.

The main consideration with comprehension objectives is to see whether students can go beyond the *knowledge* objectives—which are highly specific—to *understanding* (Henry, 1946). If the student can translate, interpret, and extrapolate from messages which are used as input, he has gone beyond verbalization of knowledge. He has to some extent a "command of substantive knowledge" (Ebel, 1965, p. 38).

Illustrative test items for comprehension objectives

The characteristics of comprehension items are fairly clear. The material for translation, interpretation, or extrapolation must *not* be the same as was used in instruction, but it should have similar characteristics in terms of language or symbology, complexity, and content. Translation should involve elements instead of the relationships between elements in the message to be translated. Interpretation items will involve the translation of elements with the additional requirement that the student see interrelationships among elements of the total message. Extrapolation items will call for going beyond the limits of the literal message and will involve both translation and interpretation.

18. The following sentence is stated as a definition, but the underlined words are fictitious. Your task is to read the definition and choose the formula below the statement which states the same thing. "The *calong* (C) is equal to the sum over the entire set of the squared differences between the *lorang* (L) and the *beland* (B) divided by twice the number of *graks* (G)."

    a. __ $C = \frac{\Sigma(B^2 - L)}{G^2}$

    b. __ $C = \frac{\Sigma(L - B)^2}{2G}$

    c. __ $C = \frac{\Sigma L^2 - \Sigma B^2}{2G}$

    d. __ $C = \frac{\Sigma(L - B)}{G^2}$

This sort of item could be built around a real law or definition and still require the student to translate from words to symbols. The difficulty with using a real definition is that the students may have memorized the formula, in which case this is likely to become a knowledge item.

19. A group of examiners is engaged in the production of a taxonomy of educational objectives. In ordinary English, what are these persons doing?
    a. Evaluating the progress of education
    b. Classifying teaching goals
    c. Preparing a curriculum
    d. Constructing learning exercises

(Bloom, 1956, p. 99, item 1.)

Item 19 requires a simple translation of the word "taxonomy" into "classification" and of "educational objectives" into "teaching goals." This item illustrates that translation can be at a very simple level. It should be noted that if the student has been instructed that "classification" can substitute for "taxonomy," the item will represent the knowledge category.

20. When a current is induced by the relative motion of a conductor and a magnetic field, the direction of the induced current is such as to establish a magnetic field that opposes the motion. This principle is illustrated by
    A. a magnet attracting a nail.
    B. an electric generator or dynamo.
    C. the motion of a compass needle.
    D. an electric doorbell.

(Bloom, 1956, p. 99, item 3.)

This item requires a student to translate from a formal and fairly abstract definition into a specific example. If the example had been used in the instructional setting, then one might be testing straight recall of a verbal tie.

21. While listening to lectures in physical science you have heard the following terms frequently used: "hypotheses," "theories," "scientific laws," "scientific method," and "scientific attitude." In a series of paragraphs, indicate in your own words and in terms of everyday experiences what these terms mean to you.

(Bloom, 1956, p. 99, item 4.)

Item 21 illustrates that supply (as opposed to choice) situations can be very useful for evaluating translation. It should be recognized that item 18, above, could have been put in supply form. As a matter of fact, giving an item such as that in supply form to a small group of learners is one way to generate alternatives for the choice item.

22. A comparatively easy achievement test was given to a group of good learners. Which of the following graphs—in which *f* represents the frequency of a score among the examinees and *s* represents the score scale from low to high—shows the distribution you would expect?

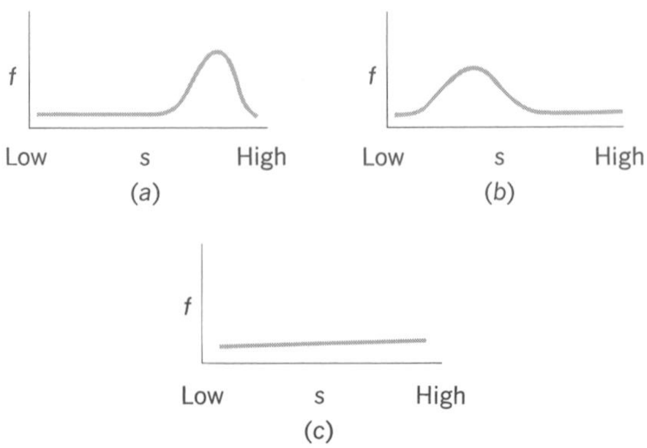

Translation of an idea into graphic form is an important behavior in many subject areas. One could turn the direction of translation around by giving a graph and then requesting the student to choose among several verbal descriptions.

DIRECTIONS: Use the following numbers to indicate your answer [to each of the questions concerning Fig. 7-1].

1. The statement is supported by the evidence given in the chart.
2. Whether the statement is correct or incorrect cannot be determined by the evidence in the chart.
3. The statement is contradicted by the evidence given in the chart.

Questions on [Fig. 7-1]

23. The total farm economy of the United States depends upon exports.
24. Less than 50 percent of exports of agricultural products are government sponsored.
25. The American farmer would suffer great loss of income if government-sponsored programs were to be dropped.
26. Rice was the largest item in government-sponsored programs.
27. The United States consumes about two-thirds of the tobacco produced.
28. The United States keeps for its own use over half of the rice and wheat grown.
29. The graph demonstrates that economic health in the United States depends upon the economic health of the countries that import our products.

30. Cotton exports would suffer least from the withdrawal of government-sponsored programs.

(Morse & McCune, 1964, pp. 62–63, items 33–40, quoted in Orlandi, Chap. 16 of this book, pages 476–477, items 36–43.)

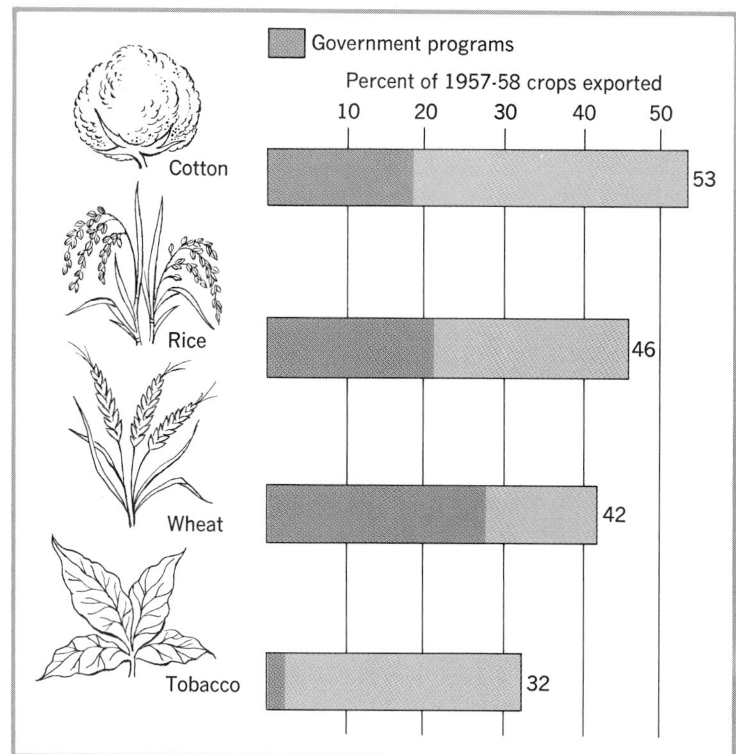

FIGURE 7-1 U.S. agriculture depends on exports. [U.S. Department of State, U.S. Department of Defense, & International Cooperation Administration. *Mutual security program, fiscal year 1960: A summary presentation.* Washington, D.C.: USDS, USDD, and ICA, March 1959. (Reprinted: In H. T. Morse & G. H. McCune. *Selected items for the testing of study skills and critical thinking.* [Bull. No. 15, 4th ed.] Washington, D.C.: National Council for the Social Sciences, 1964, P. 62) Reproduced in Chap. 16 of this book, page 476.]

This kind of complex item can be very useful for evaluating comprehension. Most of these statements appear to involve all three levels of comprehension, although some focus more upon one level than another. Statements 27 and 28 call mostly for translation from graphics into words—if we assume that what is not exported is used within the country. Statements 24 and 30 emphasize interpretation, since the student must interrelate various elements in the graph. Extrapolation is clearly demanded in statements 25 and 29, which ask the examinee to go beyond the limits of the message.

A scientist cultivated a large colony of disease-producing bacteria. From them, he extracted a bacteria-free material referred to as substance X. A *large* dose of substance X was then injected into each of a group of animals (group A). These animals promptly developed some of the symptoms normally produced in infection by the bacteria in question. Then, into each of a number of other animals (group B), the scientist made a series of injections of *small* doses of substance X. Three weeks after this series of injections, and continuing for two years thereafter, this group of animals (group B) could be made to develop the disease by injecting them with several thousand times the number of bacteria which was fatal to untreated animals.

After the item number on the answer sheet, blacken space

A—if the data given above definitely show that the item correctly completes the introductory statement.

B—if the data given above do not definitely show that the item correctly completes the introductory statement.

(Be careful to make your judgments in terms of the data given in the description of the experiment.)

Substance X acted upon the animals of group A as if it were a

31. poison.
32. destroyer of poisons.
33. stimulator causing animals of group A to produce destroyers of the bacterial poison.

With reference to its effect upon the animals of group B, substance X appeared to act as

34. a means of counteracting the effects of the disease-producing bacteria.
35. if it were a destroyer of the bacteria or of their poisonous products.
36. if it were a poisonous product of the bacteria.

Ten months after the series of injections described above, the scientist prepared serum from the blood of the animals of group B. He injected this serum into each of a large group (group C) of animals infected with the disease. A control group, also infected with the disease, was given no serum. There was a higher percentage of prompt recoveries in group C than in the control group.

Serum from the animals of group B acted in the animals of group C to

37. stimulate the animals of group C to produce a destroyer of the disease-producing bacteria or their poisonous products.
38. destroy the disease-producing bacteria or their poisonous products.
39. hasten the deleterious effects of the disease-producing bacteria upon animals of group C.

(Bloom, 1956, pp. 111–112, items 40–48.)

This group of items is an excellent example of testing for both translation and interpretation. Although the group appears in the *Taxonomy* with examples of interpretation items, it is obvious that parts of it (for example, items 31 to 33) are almost completely translation from one set of terms to another. One could increase or decrease the translation behavior by making the statements to be judged less or more similar in language to the descriptions of the experiments. Again, as in items 23 to 30, one could test for extrapolation using this item form by simply going outside the exact boundaries of the message (the descriptions) and asking for predictions or estimates of related events.

Each of the following selections concerns a mathematical situation. The activities described and the numbers used are correct, but in some cases the wrong term (mathematical word) is used. You are to read the selection and *underline* the terms which you believe have been used incorrectly.

40. In a problem which John was working, it was necessary to add 618, 431, and 215. He added them and found their product to be 1,264. He checked by re-adding in the other direction.
41. In making arrangements to redecorate his home, Mr. Gray found that he needed to use some mathematics. The ratio between the height, 12 feet, and the width, 10 feet, of a certain room was 2 feet. It was also necessary to find the area of the air in the room for purposes of heating. To solve the problem of lighting the room, Mr. Gray had to determine certain angles formed by lines drawn from various points in the room to the center of each window.

This sort of item set is intended basically for translation, but it does have some characteristics of interpretation, since the successful student must be aware of relationships between elements of the message. The selections can be made more difficult by increasing the number of relationships to be noted.

In this problem you are to follow the directions in the box below to judge the statements about the accompanying table

Public Debt of the United States

Year	*Total national debt, dollars*	*Per capita debt, dollars*
1900	1,263,416,913	16.60
1905	1,132,357,095	13.51
1910	1,146,939,969	12.41
1915	1,191,264,068	11.85
1920	24,299,321,467	228.23
1925	20,516,193,888	167.12
1930	16,185,309,831	131.51
1935	28,700,892,625	225.55
1940	42,967,531,038	325.59
1945	258,682,187,410	1,853.21

The figures in the table were compiled and published by the United States Treasury Department. The column headed "Per capita debt" shows the amount of money each person living in the United States that year would have owed if the national debt had been divided equally.

Make a decision about each of the numbered statements on the basis of the above information and the graphs, and indicate your decisions on the answer sheet as follows:

1. It is *true*.
2. It is *probably true*.
3. The facts alone are *not sufficient* to indicate whether there is any degree of truth or falsity in the statement.
4. It is *probably false*.
5. It is *false*.

42. In 1940 the per capita debt in the United States was approximately two times as great as in 1925.
43. This table shows that the United States needs a better system of taxation.

44. The total national debt was greater in 1916 than in 1911.
45. In 1948 the people of the United States had lowered the per capita debt to about the 1935 level.
46. The reason for the decrease in the total debt between 1920 and 1930 was that during those years the United States had Presidents who were excellent administrators of the national wealth.
47. For those years shown in the period from 1905 to 1915 inclusive, the size of the total national debt decreased.
48. The dollar amount of the debt resulting from the programs of national defense and relief was greater in 1940 than in 1935. (About 65 percent of the debt was due to these programs.)
49. There was a sharp drop in the per capita debt in 1942.
50. The decrease in the per capita debt from 1910 to 1915 was much greater than the decrease from 1900 to 1905.
51. From 1920 to 1945 there was a steady and continuous increase in the total national debt.
52. In 1947 the per capita debt was less than it was in 1940.
53. The United States Treasury Department published these facts to show people how greatly wars increase the national debt. (A large part of the debt in 1945 was caused by military expenditures.)
54. The total debt of the United States was somewhat greater in 1900 than in 1915.
55. Poor administration of government funds caused the heavily increased per capita debt in 1935.
56. In 1890 the per capita debt was less than in 1920.

In this problem you are to follow the directions in the box [in the next column] in judging the statements which are made about the graphs [in Fig. 7-2].

The graphs were published by the Safety Council of Middleburg, West Virginia. The information plotted for each given hour is the total number of accidents in the year 1949 in the three-hour span from one and one-half hours before to one and one-half hours after the hour stated. For example, a point at "3 A.M." represents the total number of accidents that occurred during the year in that part of the day from 1:30 A.M. to 4:30 A.M.

Of the registered drivers in Middleburg, 70 percent were men and 30 percent were women.

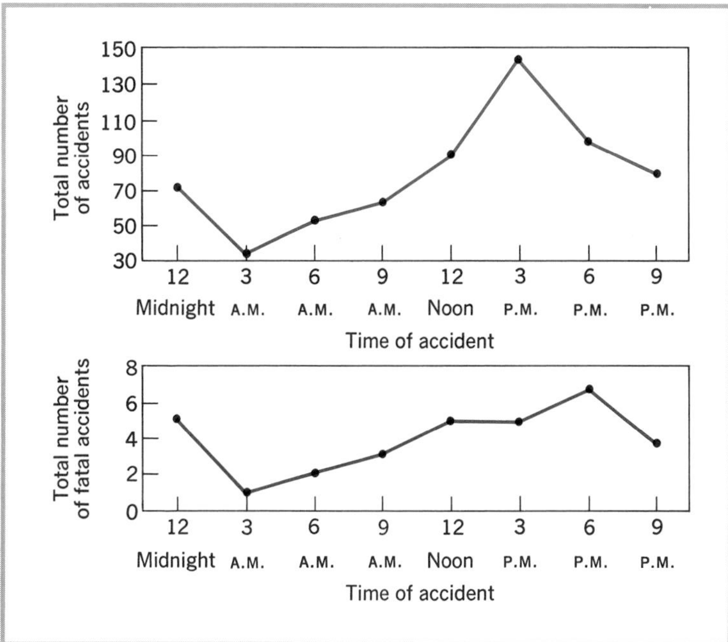

FIGURE 7-2 Number of traffic accidents at given hours in the city of Middleburg, West Virginia, for 1949.

> Make a decision about each of the numbered statements on the basis of the above information and the graph, and indicate your decisions on the answer sheet as follows:
> 1. It is *true.*
> 2. It is *probably true.*
> 3. The facts alone are *not sufficient* to indicate whether there is any degree of truth or falsity in the statement.
> 4. It is *probably false.*
> 5. It is *false.*

57. The total number of accidents showed a sharp drop between midnight and 3 A.M.
58. Most of the fatal accidents which occurred between midnight and 3 A.M. were a result of drunken driving.
59. The accident rate at 10 A.M. was less than the rate at 11 A.M.
60. The greatest number of fatal accidents occurred at midnight.
61. Over half of the drivers involved in the accidents between noon and midnight were men.

62. In the downtown area, the accident rate was slightly lower in the afternoon than in the morning. (A recent traffic count revealed that a large majority of the car owners drive in the downtown area each day.)
63. There were fewer fatal accidents between midnight and 6 A.M. than there were between 3 P.M. and 9 P.M.
64. This chart was published to show that people ought to drive more carefully. (Ten percent of the drivers in Middleburg were involved in a traffic accident in 1949.)
65. In many other cities of this size in the United States, there are more fatal traffic accidents in the late afternoon hours than in the early morning.
66. Between midnight and noon the total number of accidents showed a steady increase.
67. The total number of accidents per hour was greater at 5 A.M. than at 1 A.M.
68. More women than men were involved in the accidents which occurred during the late afternoon period.
69. The Police Department of Middleburg ought to increase their traffic force.
70. The total number of accidents at 12:30 A.M. was greater than the number which occurred at 2:30 A.M.
71. Any person who causes and survives an accident fatal to someone else should have his driver's license suspended.

Although the approach used in both sets of item complexes, 42 to 56 and 57 to 71, is especially useful for testing comprehension in the social and natural sciences, the idea can be adapted to industrial arts, business education, and even certain areas of the humanities. The item groups obviously call for interpretation of a message. Translation from one set of symbols to another is especially prominent in items 57 to 71 because most of the message is given in graph form. It should be noted that such items as 52 and 56 call for extrapolation in time. Item 70 requires the learner to be sensitive to how far he can estimate beyond the data.

The last two sets of items, 42 to 56 and 57 to 71, also afford some interesting and useful scoring possibilities. Each statement about the data is keyed as true (T), probably true (PT), not sufficiently indicated by the data (NS), probably false (PF), or false (F). Thus, item 42 would be keyed as T, 43 as NS, 44 (representing a variety of the extrapolation-level item) as PT, 45 as PF, and 47 as F. Obviously a student's responses could be scored, as on most tests, by a mark of either correct (like the key) or incorrect (unlike the key) on each response. However, the evaluation staff of the Eight-year Study of Secondary Education (Smith & Tyler, 1942, pp. 48–56) worked out a scoring scheme which gives more detailed information. The chart in Table 7-1 is basic to the system. A fuller explanation of this system is presented in Chap. 5 (page 108).

The letter "A" in the body of the chart represents an *accurate* response; that is, the student's response matches the key. "C" stands for a *cautious* answer. If the statement is in fact true but the student responds with "PT" or "NS," he is not using or interpreting all the data available—he is being cautious. "CE" represents a *crude error;* the student who says that a statement keyed "T" is either probably false or false is really missing the translation, interpretation, or extrapolation.

If a student indicates that he believes a statement keyed "PT" or "NS" is in fact true, "T," he is going *beyond the data,* "BD." Also, he can go beyond the data in his interpretation at the "false" end of the scale.

Table 7-1 Chart Showing How Scores Are Derived

		Student's response to statement				
		T	*PT*	*NS*	*PF*	*F*
Key	T	A	C	C	CE	CE
	PT	BD	A	C	CE	CE
	NS	BD	BD	A	BD	BD
	PF	CE	CE	C	A	BD
	F	CE	CE	C	C	A

SOURCE: Adapted from Table 5-5, page 108, which is reprinted by permission from *Appraising and recording student progress,* by Eugene R. Smith & Ralph W. Tyler, The Progressive Education Association. Copyright 1942 by McGraw-Hill, Inc. P. 54.

Any response a student makes can be put into one of these four categories: accurate answer, cautious answer, crude error, or answer beyond the data. For example, if a student responded to most statements with "NS" when all five types of statements appear in the problem, he would be classified as cautious in his ability to comprehend the data. On the other hand, were he always—or almost always—to say "true" or "false" to statements many of which were only probably true or probably false and for some of which there were not sufficient data to say either way, we would certainly have evidence that his tendency was to go beyond the data, that is, to overinterpret.

This type of scoring could be very useful in either summative evaluation (Chap. 4) or formative evaluation (Chap. 6). It is also possible with this type of item to score in terms of the three levels of comprehension—translation, interpretation, and extrapolation—if the test maker sees to it that all three types of statements are present. For example, item 57 calls mainly for translation, since the elements to be related are so close together and the descending line translates to "drop." Item 63, however, puts most of the weight on the interrelations between several elements and is therefore interpretation. Any item, such as 70, which asks for information not explicitly plotted on the graph is dealing with extrapolation.

REFERENCES

Ahmann, J. S., & Glock, M. D. *Evaluating pupil growth.* Boston: Allyn & Bacon, 1963.

Bloom, B. S. (Ed.) *Taxonomy of educational objectives: The classification of educational goals.* Handbook 1. *Cognitive domain.* New York: McKay, 1956.

Cleveland Heights School District. *A sequential program in composition.* Cleveland: CHSD, 1964.

Ebel, R. L. *Measuring educational achievement,* Englewood Cliffs, N.J.: Prentice-Hall, 1965.

Gerberich, J. R. *Specimen objective test items: A guide to achievement test construction.* New York: Longmans, Green, 1956.

Gronlund, N. E. *Measurement and evaluation in teaching.* New York: Macmillan, 1965.

Henry, N. B. (Ed.) *The measurement of understanding: The forty-fifth yearbook of the National Society for the Study of Education.* Chicago: University of Chicago Press, 1946.

Mager, R. F. *Preparing objectives for programmed instruction.* San Francisco: Fearon, 1962.

Morse, H. T., & McCune, G. H. *Selected items for the testing of study skills and critical thinking.* (Bull. No. 15, 4th ed.) Washington, D.C.: National Council for the Social Sciences, 1964.

Popham, J. W. Objectives and instruction. *AERA Monograph Series on Curriculum Evaluation,* 1969, No. 3, pp. 32–52.

Smith, E. R., & Tyler, R. W. *Appraising and recording student progress.* The Progressive Education Association. New York: McGraw-Hill, 1942.

8

Evaluation Techniques for Application and Analysis Objectives

Application of principles and generalizations

Application is "the use of abstractions in particular and concrete situations. The abstractions may be in the form of general ideas, rules of procedures, or generalized methods. The abstractions may also be technical principles, ideas, and theories which must be remembered and applied" (Bloom, 1956, p. 205).

The ability to apply principles and generalizations to new problems and situations is a type of educational objective which is found in most courses of instruction beginning with the elementary school and is increasingly stressed at the high school, college, graduate, and professional school levels.

Teachers and curriculum makers have long recognized that a student doesn't really "understand" an idea or principle unless he can use it in new problem situations. Thus, application is frequently regarded as an indication that a subject has been adequately mastered. More commonly, teachers and curriculum makers have stressed this objective in its own right. They have regarded the ability to apply principles and generalizations to new problems and situations as one of the more complex and difficult objectives of education. They may see it as important because it makes the learning constantly useful in problem solving, it enables the student to gain some degree of control over various aspects of his environment and the problems it poses, or it represents one of the learning outcomes which enable a student to cope with conditions and problems in a complex and rapidly changing society. Then too, the student who has demonstrated a high level of ability in this type of objective has acquired an intellectual independence which in part frees him from continued dependence on teachers, experts, and other adult authorities. Finally, there is some evidence that once the ability to make applications is developed, it is likely to be one of the more permanent acquisitions in learning. If the ability is

The ability to present ideas [orally or in writing] in accordance with the principles of grammar (1, p. 18).

The ability to present ideas [in written form] in accordance with the principles of rhetoric [e.g., principles relating to coherence, transition, unity, and emphasis] (1, p. 19).

To consistently apply scientific knowledge and understandings in the solution of personal and social problems (1, p. 42).

To apply the generalizations [facts, and theories established by the investigations] to explain phenomena (1, p. 54).

To apply a scientific generalization [or method] to interpret the natural phenomena related to the social or personal problem (1, p. 54).

To judge the probable applicability of the generalization or method by evaluating its warranted assertability as an explanation of natural phenomena (1, p. 54).

Application to the phenomena discussed by a paper, of the scientific terms and concepts used in other papers (2, p. 124).

The ability to apply social science generalizations and conclusions to actual social problems (2, p. 124).

The ability to predict the probable effect of a change in a factor on a biological situation previously at equilibrium (2, p. 124).

The ability to apply science principles, postulates, theorems, or other abstractions to new situations (2, p. 124).

Apply principles of psychology in identifying the characteristics of a new social situation (2, p. 124).

The ability to relate principles of civil liberties and civil rights to current events (2, p. 124).

Skill in applying principles of democratic group action to participation in group and social situations (2, p. 124).

The ability to apply the laws of trigonometry to practical situations (2, p. 124).

To develop some skill in applying Mendel's laws of inheritance to experimental findings on plant genetic problems (2, p. 124).

To apply the major principles, concepts and ideas of Civics to specific new situations (3, p. 25).

To apply the principles of Social Studies to the solution of social problems.... (3, p. 25).

To relate geographic principles and knowledge to problems involving the development of material resources (3, p. 77).

Explains events in daily life in terms of scientific principles, concepts and theories (3, p. 105).

Recognises the limits within which a scientific principle is applicable (3, p. 105).

Applies the principles of science to determine appropriate courses of action in gardening and other home activities (3, p. 105).

The ability to apply principles of Physics to new situations (3, p. 133).

The student will develop the ability to apply economic knowledge to problems of economic policy (4, p. 59).

(continued)

[1] Tyler, 1954.

[2] Bloom, 1956.

[3] All India Council, 1958.

[4] University Grants Commission, 1961.

[5] French, 1957.

FIGURE 8-1 Statements of objectives for *Application*.

The student will develop the ability to apply knowledge of political science to solve current problems in politics and administration (4, p. 95).

The student should develop the ability to apply the facts, concepts and theories to actual life situations (4, p. 123).

The student should know the limitation of the applications of psychology (4, p. 123).

The students are able to apply chemistry to daily life (4, p. 185).

The student will develop the ability to apply the physical laws to explain various natural phenomena (4, p. 207).

The student will develop the ability to apply basic principles in solving physical problems (4, p. 207).

The student should be able to apply the principles of botany to new problems (4, p. 229).

The student should become aware of the limitations in the applicability of botany (4, p. 229).

The student will develop the ability to solve problems on the basis of the theories and methods learned (4, p. 247).

Ability to apply scientific fact and principle (5, p. 107).

[1] Tyler, 1954.

[2] Bloom, 1956.

[3] All India Council, 1958.

[4] University Grants Commission, 1961.

[5] French, 1957.

FIGURE 8-1 Continued.

retained well, in part because it is so serviceable, then it becomes an especially important objective for education, wherever it is appropriate.

Whatever the reasons for stressing this objective, its importance for evaluation can be demonstrated by the frequency with which it is stated in various courses and programs at the elementary, secondary, and higher education levels. In Fig. 8-1 we have listed objectives which may be classified under the general category of *Application* established in the *Taxonomy of Educational Objectives* (see the Appendix to Part I, page 271).

It will be seen from this list that the application objectives generally include or imply three phrases which are in need of further refinement and definition. These are *ability to apply, principles and generalizations*, and *new problems and situations*. In the following discussion we will attempt to clarify each of these three phrases. However, we will do this in reverse order.

New problems and situations

By "new problems and situations" we mean problems and situations which are *likely* to be new to the student. These are similar to those which were included in the instruction but have some elements of newness or unfamiliarity for the student. He should not be able to solve the new problems and situations merely by remembering the solution to or the precise method of solving a similar problem in class. It is not a new problem or situation if it is exactly like others solved in class except that new quantities or symbols are used (as in mathematics or physics). It is not a new problem or situation if it is the same as one solved in class with only some new names or other slight changes altering the original form.

It is a new problem or situation if the student has not been given instruction or help on a given problem and he must do some of the following with the statement of the problem before he can solve it:

1. The statement of the problem must be modified in some way before it can be attacked.
   a. The student must search through the statement to find exactly what is given and what is needed before it can be attacked or solved.
   b. He must recognize that there are extraneous or irrelevant elements in the statement which he must delete or ignore.
   c. He must recast the problem by putting its parts in a different order from that found in the statement.
   d. The student may have to restate or redefine the problem before it becomes clear to him exactly what he is to do to solve it.
2. The statement of the problem must be put in the form of some paradigm or model before the student can bring the principles or generalizations previously learned to bear on it. This is especially true of mathematics and science problems where the student has previously been given problem types and models and some practice in using them. It is more difficult to find such forms and structures in the social sciences and humanities.
3. The statement of the problem requires the student to search through his memory of principles and generalizations to find those which are relevant to it. Furthermore, it is a new problem if the student must use the principles and generalizations somewhat differently from the way he has used them previously.

The posing of new problems and situations is a difficult art in evaluation. It requires the evaluator to find or make new problems and situations within the grasp of his students. It is especially useful if the problems are real ones rather than contrived ones, with artificial or fictitious elements. Students find real problems more satisfying to attack than patently contrived problems, which can seem rather like puzzles and tricks to be solved. Problems occurring in real life, problems found in the specialized literature of a given subject, and problems encountered by specialists in the field are more likely to be interesting and useful to solve than problems dreamed up by a teacher or evaluator just for the purposes of testing the students. Then too, the relations between the principles and the problem are more likely to be the real or natural relations rather than those imposed by the evaluator.

In one case in which the students were given examinations with obviously contrived and artificial problem situations requiring the application of principles, the students expressed some resentment and were of the opinion that they were supposed to outwit the examiners. They indicated that solving such problems depended mainly on their ability to figure out just what the tester was up to. When the problems were more real, they had a sense of working on worthwhile questions, and even when they had difficulty, they expressed some satisfaction with the meaningfulness of attempting to solve such problems.

Principles and generalizations

In each subject field there are some basic ideas which summarize much of what scholars have learned over the long history of the field. These ideas give meaning to much that has been learned, and they provide the basic ideas for dealing with many new problems as they are encountered by people who have learned what the field has to offer. We believe that it is the primary obligation of the scholars as well as the teachers of the subject to search constantly for these abstractions, to find ways of helping students learn them, and especially to help students learn how to use them in a great variety of problem situations. To learn such principles and generalizations adequately is to become a very different human being. Through them one comes to appreciate the beauty and orderliness of the universe. Through them one learns to appreciate the great power of the human mind. To learn to use such principles is to possess a powerful way of dealing with the world.

For example, the student who has learned the law of gravity has possession of an abstraction which applies to phenomena throughout the universe. It is as applicable to the movement of a baseball as it is to the movement of a planet. With it he can understand the special problems of sending a rocket into space or of throwing a discus in an athletic contest. He also becomes aware of the enormous feat of conceptualizing and using such a powerful law of nature.

We distinguish several levels of abstractions which can be applied to new problems.

Principles By "principle" we mean a statement about a process or relation which describes a fundamental truth, or a law accepted and used by the scholars in a field. Some examples are

The pressure of a given quantity of gas increases with an increase of temperature.
A learned act is not repeated unless it is reinforced.
The capacity of air to hold water increases with an increase in temperature.
A body remains at rest or in a state of uniform motion in a straight line unless a force acts on it.

These principles are statements which hold under a great range of conditions. They represent relatively precise inferences from a large body of observations and experiments, or are deductions from a body of theory or accepted assumptions.

Generalizations By "generalizations" we mean general statements or inferences which summarize a body of information or other particulars and which can be applied in new situations. Some examples are

Frustration increases anxiety.
Crime is greatest among individuals who are alienated from society.
The educational aspirations of students are related to their parents' socioeconomic status.
Institutional patterns exercise strong control over conduct.
Japanese children are disciplined by being made fun of.
Hybrids are more vigorous than closely inbred individuals.
In undisturbed sedimentary rocks, the youngest layer is on top.

A generalization holds under limited conditions, and the special problem it poses to the student is to recognize its tentativeness, the particular circumstances under which it may hold true, and its value in quickly ordering new phenomena. One hopes that the student will be able to understand the basis for the generalization, the underlying phenomena at work, and the restricted truth which the generalization summarizes.

We recognize that the distinctions between principles and generalizations are not always clear, and we must leave it to the different subjects to determine the types of abstractions they may have which are basic to their own fields. It is clear that the sciences have some of the most powerful principles, whereas the social sciences and the humanities have great difficulty formulating generalizations which are more than common-sense statements. When such generalizations are stated, they seem so obvious that few would disagree with them—but it is difficult to determine just how they help summarize our present knowledge. Or there are so many exceptions to the generalization that we do not find them very helpful in dealing with new problems.

Principles and generalizations are developed in a number of different ways. Some are developed by definition and convention. Workers in the field agree on a rule, definition, or relationship.

The circumference of a circle equals $2\pi r$.
Force = mass × acceleration.
Friction exists between any two bodies in contact with each other.

Such abstractions are conventions which are very effective in classifying and organizing a great many specific phenomena in their respective fields. There is an arbitrary quality about these generalizations since they are true only by definition. What the student must learn about them is what they include and what they do not include. He must also learn what specific phenomena, concrete objects, and events illustrate the rule and which ones do not. He may also be expected to know various relations among the abstractions—whether the relations are chronological, superordinate and subordinate, concomitant variation, or cause and effect. He may also be expected to know whether the abstractions are parts of a theory, taxonomy, or classification scheme.

Since these abstractions are true by definition, it is not possible for the student to discover them on his own. While he may come to see the specific phenomena on his own, he must find the term and definitions by reference to the history of the subject. One might speculate that among other approaches, an effective way for the student to learn about such abstractions would be for him to begin with situations in which he must recognize specific, clear instances of the abstraction. Then he can be given opportunities to learn the use of the abstraction to name, classify, or organize such phenomena. Finally, he should be helped to explore the range of phenomena included in the abstraction.

Another set of abstractions are the result of empirical research and scholarship. Boyle's law, the effects of combinations of genes, and the relationship between intelligence and academic achievement are examples of principles and generalizations discovered through investigations of existing phenomena. These generalizations are true—within certain limits—and they can be used to organize many specific events, actions, facts, and so forth. Abstractions of this type may be "discovered" afresh by each student if the phenomena and the necessary measuring and observational techniques are available. The student who has "discovered" the abstraction is likely to find the exact statement of the generalization useful as a more precise and parsimonious formulation of the relationship among the phenomena. In any case, learning experiences must somehow help the student relate specific and concrete phenomena to the statement of the abstraction. One without the other is unlikely to be very useful or meaningful to the student.

A third type is a more limited set of generalizations derived from observation. The following are illustrations of this type:

Hemingway's heroes usually overcome conflicts between man and nature.
Frustrated children tend to show regressive behavior.
Smoking cigarettes may cause cancer.
Too rigid toilet training may produce personality disorders.
High interest rates reduce capital investment.

These generalizations may be statements of trends, tendencies, and regularities which are far from universal laws and principles; that is, they may occur frequently but there are many exceptions. They may be examples of an effect which may also be produced by quite different causes, or illustrations of phenomena which have multiple causation. For example, although smoking may cause cancer, there are many other causes of the disease, and smoking does not always cause it. Many of these generalizations concern phenomena and events for which there is not a full understanding of the reasons that they occur or the process which relates one part of the statement to the other. Such generalizations have so many exceptions to them that the student must learn to be cautious in using them. Here also, the student may discover some of these generalizations on his own, but he must be alerted to their limited nature. Again, he must be given opportunities to relate the abstract statement to specific and concrete examples.

A final set represent generalizations which are deductions from a larger theory, model, or point of view. Such generalizations may rarely describe existing phenomena but are statements of what would occur under special circumstances or ideal conditions. Examples are

If children are given sufficient love and attention, they will not develop anxiety.
Children's ego identity gains real strength only from consistent recognition of real accomplishment.
Dialectic methods attempt to remove or transcend some contradiction.
Equal volumes of gases at the same temperature and pressure contain about the same number of molecules.
Population tends to multiply faster than its means of subsistence.

Such generalizations represent a particular (and somewhat restricted) view of the world, and they are true if a particular set of assumptions are accepted. In learning such generalizations the student must clearly recognize the point of view which they represent, and he should be helped to understand that they represent one alternative when others may also exist.

Gagné (1965) has emphasized that there is a hierarchical process in the learning of principles, generalizations, and concepts. He believes that these are best learned as a result of a movement from concrete phenomena to higher-order abstractions. In his model the student is expected to move from specific facts and terms to relationships among them to the eventual development of the larger abstraction. If a student has failed to understand and master some of the lower-order phenomena, Gagné believes he will have difficulty in understanding the generalization or abstraction. In Chap. 6 we have indicated the way in which formative tests may be developed to determine where the student has difficulty in Gagné's model of learning and what learning problems are posed by specific difficulties at different levels of the model.

The ability to apply

The "ability to apply" implies that with appropriate training, practice, and other kinds of help the student becomes able to apply principles and generalizations to new problems and situations. That is, he can appropriately use principles and generalizations in solving problems that are new to him. The implication is that there is a generalized ability which grows out of the student's learning experiences such that, when faced with new problems and situations, he can make use of the ability to apply principles and generalizations.

In terms of student behaviors, the ability to apply might include some of the following:

The student can determine which principles or generalizations are appropriate or relevant in dealing with a new problem situation (*A*).

The student can restate a problem so as to determine which principles or generalizations are necessary for its solution (*B*).

The student can specify the limits within which a particular principle or generalization is true or relevant (*C*).

The student can recognize the exceptions to a particular generalization and the reasons for them (*D*).

The student can explain new phenomena in terms of known principles or generalizations (*E*).

The student can predict what will happen in a new situation by the use of appropriate principles or generalizations (*F*).

The student can determine or justify a particular course of action or decision in a new situation by the use of appropriate principles and generalizations (*G*).

The student can state the reasoning he employs to support the use of one or more principles or generalizations in a given problem situation (*H*).

These behaviors will be discussed in the next section as we attempt to define them further and illustrate testing techniques appropriate to them.

Testing for application

It is possible to determine the requirements or rules for making test items for the application of principles and generalizations from the foregoing analysis of the three phrases "ability to apply," "principles and generalizations," and "new problems and situations."

Some of the requirements are these:

1. The problem situation must be new, unfamiliar, or in some way different from those used in the instruction. The difficulty of the problem will be determined in part by how different it is from problems encountered in the instruction.
2. The problem should be solvable in part by the use of the appropriate principles or generalizations.
3. One or more of the behaviors listed above under the subsection Ability to Apply should be sampled by the test problem.

Since the behaviors discussed under Ability to Apply give useful clues to how questions might be formed, our test illustrations will follow that listing. Most of the test illustrations have been drawn from the files of the University Examiner's Office of the University of Chicago. We have used these because they illustrate a variety of test forms in a number of different subject areas. When the source of the illustration is not the Examiner's Office, we have accompanied the item with indications of the specific source. Additional illustrations for each subject field will be found in the appropriate chapter in Part II of this book.

Test problems for application behaviors A and B

The student can determine which principles or generalizations are appropriate or relevant in dealing with a new problem situation (A).

The student can restate a problem so as to determine which principles or generalizations are necessary for its solution (B).

In this type of problem, the student does not actually have to solve the problem completely; all he needs to do is determine the principles or generalizations which are appropriate. In the following examples, it will be noted that the examinee must do little more than exhibit his grasp of what the problem is about and what principles or generalizations are relevant, useful, or pertinent. One cannot be sure from such problems that the student could actually solve the problem in a detailed way, but one can be sure that he has some grasp of what is required. The great value of this type of problem is the efficiency with which one can sample a great variety of problems and principles or generalizations.

1. The following are some of the basic principles upon which our [Canadian] federal government has been built:

   A. majority rule

   B. the federal government having primary responsibility only in certain areas

   C. responsible government

   D. other principles not listed above

   For each of the following practices . . . indicate the principle involved. Mark D if none of the above principles are involved.

   (1) Mr. Pearson as leader of the Liberal Party is Prime Minister.

   (2) The federal government provides unemployment insurance.

   (3) The federal government collects excise taxes.

   (4) The governor-general may request the leader of the opposition to form a government.

   (Ayers, 1966.)

In this set of questions, the principles are stated and the student has only to determine which ones are relevant to each governmental practice. He may have to reformulate some of the practices in order to determine which of the given principles is relevant. It would be a more difficult task if the student was not given a list of principles but had to state the political principles underlying each statement.

2. DIRECTIONS: For each statement of fact below, blacken the answer space corresponding to the one explanatory principle, from the list preceding the statements, which is most directly useful in explaining the fact. If none of the principles listed is applicable, blacken answer space E. NOTE THAT EACH ITEM REQUIRES ONE ANSWER ONLY.

   Explanatory Principles

   A. Force is equal to mass times acceleration.

   B. Friction exists between any two bodies in contact with each other.

   C. Conservation of momentum.

   D. Conservation of energy.

   E. None of the foregoing.

   (1) To be opened slowly a given door requires a small force; to be opened quickly it requires a much greater force.

   (2) The velocity of a body moving along a curve cannot be constant.

   (3) A brick can be pulled along a fairly smooth surface by means of a string; the string would break, however, if jerked sharply.

In the set of questions above, two of the principles are named rather than stated in a more complete form. (1) and (3) require the student to restate the problem before he can determine the appropriate principle, whereas (2) is likely to be stated in the form in which he originally learned it and to require little more than remembering what it was supposed to illustrate. The set of questions would probably be more difficult (and realistic) if some of the problems required more than a single explanatory principle.

3. DIRECTIONS: *Blacken* the answer space corresponding to the *one* principle which is most useful in explaining each statement of fact.

   Explanatory Principles

   A. Force is equal to mass times acceleration.
   B. The momentum of a body tends to remain constant.
   C. The moment or turning effect of a force is proportional to its distance from the axis of rotation.
   D. Friction exists between bodies in contact and moving with respect to one another.
   E. The sum of kinetic and potential energies in an isolated system is a constant.

   (1) Shears used to cut sheet metal have long handles.
   (2) The force exerted on a brake by the driver's foot is much less than that exerted on the brake drums.
   (3) A rocket can propel itself in a vacuum.
   (4) If a rapidly rotating grindstone bursts, the fragments fly outward in straight lines.
   (5) Streamlining an automobile reduces the amount of power necessary to maintain a speed of 60 miles per hour.

This set of questions is very similar to the preceding set. However, the problems are more likely to be different from the illustrations used in the instruction given to explain the principles. It would be slightly more difficult if the student was asked to supply new illustrations for the principles or if he were asked to state the principles relevant to each fact or observation.

4. The trend in the United States is toward greater concentration of power in the national government as compared to state and local governments. It is sometimes argued that this is both *inevitable* and *desirable*.

   DIRECTIONS: The following statements represent various points of view concerning this issue. *Blacken* answer space

   A—if the statement presents a *valid* argument *supporting* the inevitability or desirability of this trend

   B—if the statement presents a *valid* argument *questioning* either the inevitability or desirability of this trend

   C—if the statement is *invalid* or *irrelevant* to the issue

   (1) Increasing industrial and economic centralization makes local regulation of economic affairs largely ineffective.
   (2) Decentralization of authority permits more adequate experimentation in various forms of political control.
   (3) The policies of decentralized governmental units coincide more closely with public opinion then do the policies of centralized government.
   (4) If local areas were redefined to correspond to industrial or social units, decentralized authority could be made more effective.

In this type of question, the student must determine the validity of the generalization, its relevance, and whether it supports or questions the trend. Note that it is possible to have several generalizations which are applicable to the trend. The trend could have been presented in more detail in the form of observations about governmental practices at different levels and at different times. This would have made the problem less familiar to the student and somewhat more realistic.

5. DIRECTIONS: *Consider the following statement:*

   "A writer on Russia asserted that Communism cannot suppress the Russian peasant's instinct of religion. He later pointed to the recognition of the Greek Catholic Church by the Soviet Union as evidence to support his opinion that there was such an instinct, which could not be suppressed."

Following are some comments on this statement. For each item, *blacken* answer space

A—if you think it is a *good* comment

B—if you think it is a *bad* comment

NOTE: A good comment is one which shows informed understanding of the subject under discussion.

(1) Strongly entrenched habits are often mistaken for instincts.

(2) Institutional patterns exercise strong control over conduct.

The use of "good comment" (which had to be further defined in a note) makes this an academic exercise. It might be more effective if the student was merely asked which generalizations are relevant or had to determine which generalizations are relevant to some predictions or particular events or practices in Russia. In the original test problem, there were many more generalizations than those included here.

6. DIRECTIONS: For each of the following statements, *blacken* answer space

A—if the statement is consistent with the *Darwinian* conception of evolution, but *not* with the *Lamarckian* conception of evolution or the hypothesis of *special creation*

B—if the statement is consistent with both the *Darwinian* and *Lamarckian* evolutionary conceptions, but *not* with the hypothesis of *special creation*

C—if the statement is consistent with the *Darwinian* conception and *special creation* hypothesis, but *not* with the *Lamarckian*

D—if the statement is consistent with *all three* conceptions

E—if the statement is inconsistent with the *Darwinian* conception

(1) The wolf and the fox have a common ancestor.

(2) Trees growing along the Pacific coast often bend inland away from the wind, whether grown there from seed or planted there as small trees.

(3) The descendants of the trees in item [2], which have been grown for many generations in this windy place, if reared in a calm site grow as erect as trees native to that calm site.

(4) A breeding experiment is conducted with many generations of rats. Short-haired animals are selectively mated to each other, and only that half of each generation with shorter hair is retained in the experiment. The laboratory, however, is kept at a temperature well below that of the natural habitat of these rats. At the end of the experiment, the average length of hair based on all the individuals in the *last* generation is very much less than the average hair length based on all individuals in the *first* generation.

(5) While the Carlsbad caverns are inhabited primarily by blind animals, successive generations of mice reared there in a small laboratory in total darkness have eyesight as good as that of their normal forebears.

(6) In both plant and animal kingdoms, offspring tend to resemble their parents.

(7) The serum of a rabbit which has been inoculated with the serum of a pig is agglutinated less strongly by chicken serum than horse serum, still less strongly by shark serum, imperceptibly by earthworm serum. Other similar experiments reveal that, in each case, the serum of a rabbit which has been sensitized to that of a particular animal is more strongly agglutinated by the sera of animals thought to be closely related phylogenetically to the sensitizing animal than by the sera of animals thought to be more distantly related.

(8) It is impossible to improve the commercial value of domestic plants and animals by breeding.

(9) The birth rate among residents of upper- and middle-class urban areas is much lower than among slum residents.

In this set of questions, each of the three conceptions of evolution includes several principles which are not differentiated. The questions might have been more searching if the directions had stated the specific principles instead of merely naming the theory. The list of alternatives requires the student to make very clear distinctions. Perhaps this set would have been less searching had the student had only to determine consistency with each of the conceptions. It is evident that a great range of phenomena might be sampled in this type of problem.

Test problems for application behaviors C and D

The student can specify the limits within which a particular principle or generalization is true or relevant (C).

The student can recognize the exceptions to a particular generalization and the reasons for them (D).

When these behaviors are being tested, the problems should include applications which go beyond the limits of the generalization or principle as well as applications where the generalization or principle is applicable. It should be remembered that these problems have the purpose of determining whether or not the student is aware of the boundary conditions under which the principles or generalizations are operative. For the most part, the evaluation procedures for these behaviors can be relatively simple, and the student may be asked to do little more than recognize or supply illustrations which are within or outside the limits and in some cases to indicate the reasons the application or illustration is outside the limits within which the principle or generalization is true, useful, or relevant.

7. DIRECTIONS: In each of the following items, you are given a fact followed by a conclusion. *Blacken* answer space

   A—if the fact is good evidence to *support* the conclusion

   B—if the fact is good evidence to *disprove* the conclusion

   C—if neither A nor B clearly applies

   (1) FACT: The native tribes of Australia have a very complex social organization and a very simple technology.

   CONCLUSION: The complexity of nonmaterial culture is not dependent upon high technological development.

   (2) FACT: The number of shareholders in most large corporations has increased considerably during the last 30 years.

   CONCLUSION: Control of corporations has become more democratic in the last thirty years.

   (3) FACT: The machine has stimulated a progressively greater division of labor with an emphasis upon more and more minutely detailed operations.

   CONCLUSION: The individual worker in modern society is typically without insight into the workings of the total social mechanism.

If the conclusions are generalizations, this type of question can be used to determine whether the student can recognize situations which question or support the generalization. The use of "C—if neither A nor B clearly applies" is a further check on the relevance of the generalization to the situation.

8. The statement is made that the altitude of the celestial pole is equal to the geographic latitude of the observer. This is correct

   A. if the diameter of the earth is considered negligible compared to the distances to the stars
   B. only if the earth is considered spherical
   C. only if the altitude is measured from the plane of the ecliptic
   D. if the observation is made at 12:00 noon
   E. only if the altitude of the celestial pole is equal to its zenith distance

9. In using the equation $s = \frac{1}{2}gt^2$ to calculate the time it takes a given body to fall from a height h to the ground, which of the two factors [below] would introduce the greater error?

   A. Factor 1 (Variation in gravity).
   B. Factor 2 (Variation in air resistance).
   C. Factor 1 for heights above a certain value; Factor 2 for lesser heights.
   D. Factor 2 for heights above a certain value; Factor 1 for lesser heights.

10. Lobachevsky based his geometry on the assumption that through a given external point any number of straight lines can be drawn parallel to a given straight line. This assumption
    A. has been found true under certain circumstances and is now considered a basic law of nature
    B. is obviously incorrect but is useful in checking the accuracy of other geometries
    C. can be shown to be incorrect by drawing lines through the point and demonstrating that all but one line intersects the given line
    D. cannot be established or disproved experimentally
    E. is entirely arbitrary, having no relation to the other assumptions and theorems of Lobachevsky's geometry

11. A defect of Rousseau's generalization that those laws are compatible with liberty which are in accordance with the "general will" is that
    A. it makes no provision for the liberty of minority groups
    B. it offers no criterion by which we can decide when the commands of government are an expression of the "general will"
    C. it does not recognize that a government must have the sanction of force behind its commands
    D. it fails to recognize that to consent willingly to a government, knowing it necessarily to have imperfections, is to consent to the imperfections

12. "The best economic system is that one which allows individuals the most freedom to pursue their own interests. In so doing, they will compete one with another, the end result being to the benefit of society."
    (1) A necessary condition if the theory stated in the quotation is to be true is that
        A. government regulate the prices of a few basic commodities and let individuals make their decisions accordingly
        B. individuals have access to the necessary information
        C. individuals be morally sound
        D. government be made up of experts
    (2) If true, which of the following is the best evidence *against* the application of the theory stated in the quotation?
        A. Individuals, when left free to pursue their own interests, have unequal incomes.
        B. Ever increasing concentration of capital is accompanied by continuous reduction in prices.
        C. Individuals have other motivations in addition to the desire for profit.
        D. Governments with unlimited power tend toward corruption.

In each of the above, the student is to recognize the limits, special conditions, or assumptions under which the generalization or principle may be true or useful. This type of student behavior is especially useful in subjects where principles or generalizations have limited applicability. The forms suggested here are the simple forms for testing this behavior.

Test problems for application behavior E

The student can explain new phenomena in terms of known principles or generalizations (E).

The problems testing for this behavior should include new phenomena, new illustrations, or new situations which must be explained by the use of principles or generalizations. The explanations most frequently take the form "A occurs because of Y," where Y is a principle or generalization. The explanation may use the principle or generalization to show *why* something happens, *how* it happens, or *under what conditions* it occurs.

13. If one frequently raises the cover of a vessel in which a liquid is being heated, the liquid takes longer to boil because
    A. boiling occurs at a higher temperature if the pressure is increased
    B. escaping vapor carries heat away from the liquid
    C. permitting the vapor to escape decreases the volume of the liquid

D. the temperature of a vapor is proportional to its volume at constant temperature

E. permitting more air to enter results in increased pressure on the liquid

14. Dilute sulfuric acid reacts readily with iron strips and yet concentrated sulfuric acid can be safely stored in iron vessels. This is because

A. concentrated sulfuric acid is less ionized than dilute sulfuric acid

B. iron is above hydrogen in the activity series

C. the iron vessel, being more massive, conducts away the heat of reaction

D. iron contains carbon which is not affected by sulfuric acid

E. the sulfur in the sulfuric acid coats the iron and protects it

15. The steps leading to a swimming pool appear bent where they enter the water. Which *one* of the following gives the best explanation of this phenomenon?

A. Diffraction of light by the surface of the water

B. Dispersion of light on entering water

C. Refraction of light due to difference in speed of light in air and water

D. Light does not travel in straight lines in water

E. Suspended particles in the water

The questions above require a relatively precise recognition of the principles or generalizations which can explain the given phenomena. These simple test forms are useful for a wide range of application problems.

16. PRINCIPLE: A metal owes its magnetism to an orderly arrangement of relatively large units (called "domains") each composed of thousands of atoms. In a magnetized material these domains may be compared to tiny magnets all pointing in the same direction.

DIRECTIONS: For each statement below, blacken answer space

A—if it is supported by the principle

B—if it is contradicted by the principle

C—if it is neither supported nor contradicted by the principle

(1) A current of electricity flowing in a nearby wire *cannot* cause a bar of metal to become magnetic.

(2) A hot bar of iron is harder to magnetize than a cold bar.

(3) The best conductors are also capable of the strongest magnetization.

17. DIRECTIONS: In these questions, select the one best *numbered* response and then select the one best *lettered* response.

The radial velocities of a star can be detected by

(1) photographing the stars at two different times

(2) comparing their spectra with spectra obtained in the laboratory

(3) measuring variations in the angle of parallax

This method depends upon the principle that: (A- Radial motion is very minute. B- The apparent motions of such distant objects is small. C- Relative motion of source of waves and observer alters the frequency. D- Parallax measurements yield the distances of stars. E- The radius of a star varies with temperature and therefore with spectral type.)

These questions require the student to relate a principle or generalization to the problem situation and to indicate the particular way in which the principle or generalization relates to the situation.

18. DIRECTIONS: Below you are given a group of statements about the culture of the Japanese. These statements are followed by comments which describe certain personality or behaviour traits of the Japanese and questions about each comment. Read the statements as if they were a paragraph description of the Japanese. Then answer the questions following each comment.

STATEMENTS:

A. Japanese children are teased a great deal by their parents. In fact, the child is disciplined by being made fun of.

B. There is a marked discontinuity in the upbringing of Japanese boys. As infants, all satisfactions are possible to them and they are treated like little gods. But at the age of six or seven increasingly heavy responsibility is placed on them and this responsibility is upheld by the most drastic sanctions.

C. There is very little in Japanese life that permits the harmless diffusion of emotion. There is everything that locks it in, represses it, frustrates it, chokes it.

D. If a boy is disrespectful to his teachers, his family may cast him out. He is made to realize that he is his family's representative before the world.

E. Japanese children are taught that they owe a great debt to their parents.

Consider the above statements in the light of what you have learned regarding the analysis of culture. Unless otherwise directed, *blacken* the answer space corresponding to the letter of the above statement which supplies the *one best answer* to the question following the comments.

COMMENT: In Japan the individual is sure of support from his own group only as long as approval is given by other groups.

(1) Which statement above furnishes data for this comment?

COMMENT: The great moral decisions of the Japanese have hinged not on the battle of good and evil of the individual's inner consciousness, but on the opposition between the individual's personal inclinations and his social duty.

(2) Which *two* statements above describe a fact of Japanese life which would be likely to produce the phenomenon described in the comment?

COMMENT: In Japan, the approval of the "outside world" takes on an importance probably unparalleled in any other society.

(3) Which statement most strikingly exemplifies this comment?

COMMENT: Japanese behaviour is full of contradictions and gives evidence of a deeply implanted dualism.

(4) Which statement describes a condition which would be likely to produce the behaviour described in the comment?

COMMENT: Fear of ridicule is one of the strongest social restraints.

(5) Which statement describes a fact which would be likely to produce the attitude described in the comment?

While this is a relatively complex test form, it lends itself to the examination of a great variety of relations between generalizations and phenomena, including the use of generalizations to explain given phenomena.

Test problems for application behavior F

The student can predict what will happen in a new situation by the use of appropriate principles or generalizations (F).

In tests for this behavior, the new situation may be a common observation, or it may be a situation in which something has happened or will happen and for which the student is to predict the outcome. The predictions may involve qualitative or quantitative changes likely to occur. With respect to the quantitative changes, the predictions may be very precise or only according to rough orders of magnitude. The difficulty of the problem may be determined by the precision with which the change must be estimated or calculated. In many of the problems, the student must use a principle or generalization to predict but may not be asked to state or cite the basis for the prediction. In other problems, he must not only predict but also indicate the basis on which he made the prediction.

19. Suppose an elevator is descending with a constant acceleration of gravity "g." If a passenger attempts to throw a rubber ball upward, what will be the motion of the ball with respect to the elevator? The ball will

    A. remain fixed at a point the passenger releases it
    B. rise to the top of the elevator and remain there
    C. not rise at all, but will fall to the floor
    D. rise, bounce, then move toward the floor at a constant speed
    E. rise, bounce, then move toward the floor at an increasing speed

20. If the temperature of the sun were suddenly to change from 6,000° to 12,000°, while the mass, radius, and position in relation to the earth remained the same, the following effects would be noted:

(1) The color of the sun would be (A- more blue; B- more red; C- essentially unchanged).

(2) The sun would appear (A- brighter; B- about as bright; C- appreciably less bright).

(3) More molecular bands (A- would; B- would not) appear in the solar spectrum.

21. DIRECTIONS: Following are some predictions. For each item, *blacken*

answer space A if it is highly probable;

answer space B if it is highly improbable;

answer space C if neither of these judgments can be made.

(1) State governments will take over most of the functions now exercised by the federal government within the next fifty years.

(2) Productivity of labor will increase in the United States within the next thirty years.

(3) The influence of the small stockholder on the management of corporations will increase after the war.

(4) During the next decade net reproduction rates in large American cities will be sufficiently high to replace their present population.

22. For each hypothetical experimental modification of the normal functioning of an animal described below, a series of statements of possible consequences is given.

DIRECTIONS: For each numbered statement, *blacken answer space*

A—if the consequence described would be expected *to follow*

B—if the consequence described would be *expected not to follow*

The thyroid gland is removed from a rabbit. Examination of the animal is made five weeks after recovery from the operation.

(1) In a cold room body temperature will be lower than in normal rabbits in the same room.

(2) Vasoconstriction of skin blood vessels when the animal is in an environment of 40°F. will be greater than before the operation.

(3) Average amount of carbon dioxide exhaled is found to be lower than before the operation.

(4) Urine production is found to be lower than before the operation.

(5) Body weight of the animal is found to be lower than before the operation.

A dog is placed in a chamber, the air of which is maintained at the normal concentration of oxygen but with a concentration of carbon dioxide 100 times the normal concentration in the atmosphere.

(6) Rate of division of red cells in the circulating blood will increase.

(7) Rate of division of cells in the red bone marrow will increase.

(8) Rate of respiration will rise above the average rate before the experiment.

23. DIRECTIONS: In the following items you are to judge the effects of a particular policy on the distribution of income. In each case assume that there are no other changes in policy which would counteract the effects of the policy described in the item. For each item, *blacken* answer space

A—if the policy described would tend to *reduce* the existing degree of inequality in the distribution of income

B—if the policy described would tend to *increase* the existing degree of inequality in the distribution of income

C—if the policy described would have no effect, or an indeterminate effect, on the distribution of income

(1) Increasingly progressive income taxes

(2) Introduction of a national sales tax

(3) Provision of educational and medical services, and low cost public housing

(4) Reduction in the degree of business monopoly

(5) Increasing taxes in periods of prosperity and decreasing them in periods when depressions threaten

24. DIRECTIONS: In each of the following items a certain social or economic condition or policy is described and a certain group or groups mentioned. You are to judge the effect of this condition or policy on consensus *within* the group, if only one group is mentioned; or on consensus *between* the two groups, if two groups are mentioned. *Blacken* answer space

A—if the policy or condition is likely to result in *increased* consensus.

B—if the policy or condition is likely to result in *decreased* consensus.

C—if the policy or condition is likely to have no effect or an indeterminate effect on the level of consensus.

Condition or policy	Group or groups involved
(1) Decentralization of urban centers	Farmers and urban dwellers
(2) Teaching of morality, based on individual self-interest	Student body of a university
(3) Voluntary sharing of responsibility for factory administration	Shop foremen and shop stewards
(4) More stringent divorce laws	Newly married couples
(5) Administration of local school system by combined boards of educational specialists and representatives from various civic and labor groups	School teachers and parents of community

In all of the above sets, the student must use an unstated principle or generalization in order to make the prediction. These would be more searching questions if the student also had to indicate the principle he used to make the prediction. The following items illustrate the latter point.

25. Would the air in a closed room be heated or cooled by the operation of an electric refrigerator in the room with the refrigerator door open?
    A. heated, because the heat given off by the motor and the compressed gas would exceed the heat absorbed
    B. cooled, because the refrigerator is a cooling device
    C. cooled, because compressed gases expand in the refrigerator
    D. cooled, because liquids absorb heat when they evaporate
    E. neither heated nor cooled

(Ayers, 1965.)

26. A car having a mass of 2,000 pounds is given the maximum acceleration which the motor can produce. If a load of 2,000 pounds is now placed in the car, the maximum acceleration that can be given to the car is
    (1) twice as great
    (2) the same
    (3) one-half as great

    In solving this problem, which of the following was used directly? (A- Newton's First Law of Motion B- Newton's Second Law of Motion C- Newton's Law of Gravitation D- Law of Falling Bodies E- Definition.)

27. Regions lying 10 degrees to the north or south of the equator and near to the coast are normally
    (1) subject to heavy rains (in excess of 60 inches per year)
    (2) desert
    (3) subject to only moderate rains (30 to 40 inches per year)

    because (A- air currents are dominantly descending B- the rate of evaporation in the tropics is low C- cyclonic storms occur every few weeks D- air currents are dominantly ascending E- dry winds blow in from the deserts to the north and south).

28. A body of air with temperature of 60°F. has a relative humidity of 40 percent. If the temperature of this body is raised to 80° without addition of any water, the relative humidity will be:
    (1) increased
    (2) decreased
    (3) unaffected

    because (A- the capacity of air to hold water decreases with increase in temperature B- the capacity of air to hold water is independent of the temperature of the air C- the capacity of air to hold water increases with the increase of temperature D- the rate of evaporation will be increased E- the ratio of the weight of water vapor to the weight of air remains the same).

In these questions, the student has to make a prediction as well as indicate the principle or generalization which is applicable.

Test problems for application behavior G

The student can determine or justify a particular course of action or decision in a new situation by the use of appropriate principles and generalizations (G).

This behavior involves decision making of some type—on policy, practical courses of action, ways of correcting a particular situation, and so forth—and the use of principles or generalizations to support or justify the action or decision. Behavior G is especially relevant to policy decisions in the social sciences. The illustrations given below all deal with social policy problems.

29. Which *two* of the following state possible weaknesses in the application of banking and monetary policy as the sole means of stabilizing the economy? (TWO ANSWERS)
    A. Monetary policies do not affect the real rate of return on investment.
    B. "Cheap money" policies may not be sufficient to encourage pessimistic enterprisers and householders to take credit.
    C. Inflationary tendencies may start long before a satisfactory level of employment and prosperity is reached.
    D. In the causation of cumulative changes in total effective demand, the quantity of money is unimportant compared with the velocity of its circulation.
    E. Creditors will apply political pressures to promote inflationary policies and debtors will try to promote deflationary tendencies.

30. Which of the following constitutes the most important objection against relying primarily upon changes in tax rates as a means to counteract a downswing?
    A. Increases in income and corporation tax rates tend to discourage the investment of "venture capital."
    B. Reductions in tax rates leave too much purchasing power in the hands of business or consumers and will tend to cause an inflation.
    C. While reductions in tax rates leave more purchasing power in the hands of the public, there is no assurance that these funds would be spent.
    D. Increases in income and corporation tax rates are sure to raise costs and therefore prices.
    E. There is no need to decrease tax rates in a downswing, for tax revenue will fall anyway.

In these questions the course of action is stated, and the student has only to indicate the principles or generalizations which support or oppose it.

31. DIRECTIONS: Many people predict that there will be an extreme inflationary period following the war. If you were a financial adviser to the Treasury Department, under the conditions described above, what would be your advice about the following policies? For each numbered item, *blacken* answer space
    A—if you would *advocate* it, if you wished to retard the trend described above
    B—if you would *not advocate* it, if you wished to retard the trend described above

    (1) Raising the rediscount rate
    (2) Increasing facilities by which more firms could borrow money at fair terms
    (3) Get people to cash their bonds immediately
    (4) Forced savings
    (5) Expansion of a public works program
    (6) Decrease taxes drastically

In this problem the student has only to indicate the course of action which would bring about a particular result. It would be a more searching set of questions if the student had also to cite the principle or generalization which he is using as a basis for the policy decisions.

Test problems for application behavior H

The student can state the reasoning he employs to support the use of one or more principles or generalizations in a given problem situation (H).

This is the most complex behavior under *Application,* since it requires the examinee to explain the reasoning used as well as to determine the principles and generalizations relevant to a given situation. It is likely that essay forms could be well used in testing for this type of behavior, although the illustrations below are of the recognition type.

32. Assume that the principle of national self-determination can be stated as follows: "Every nation has a right to choose freely the political, social, and economic arrangements under which it will live."

DIRECTIONS: Before each of the following items write

A—if it is a logical consequence of the principle of self-determination

B—if it is a logical consequence of the principle, but if carried into effect by only one country, would tend to destroy or weaken the conditions under which other countries could apply the principle

C—if it is a logical contradiction of the principle

D—if it is neither a logical consequence nor a logical contradiction of the principle but an empirical condition that would facilitate the universal application of the principle

E—if it is neither a logical consequence nor a contradiction of the principle but an empirical condition that would tend to obstruct the universal application of the principle

(1) The world should be dominated by those national or racial groups best fitted to rule.

(2) A substantial inequality in the distribution of military and economic power as between large states and small states.

(3) The right to depreciate the national currency.

(4) The unlimited right of a representative government to declare war.

(5) Establishment of a separate political unit for every linguistic or ethnic group.

33. The water supply for a certain big city is obtained from a large lake, and sewage is disposed of in a river flowing from the lake. This river at one time flowed into the lake, but during the glacial period its direction of flow was reversed. Occasionally, during heavy rains in the spring, water from the river backs up into the lake. What should be done to safeguard effectively and economically the health of the people living in this city?

DIRECTIONS: Choose the conclusion which you believe is most consistent with the facts given above and most reasonable in the light of whatever knowledge you may have, and mark the appropriate space on the Answer Sheet. . . .

CONCLUSIONS:

A. During the spring season, the amount of chemicals used in purifying the water should be increased.

B. A permanent system of treating the sewage before it is dumped into the river should be provided.

C. During the spring season, water should be taken from the lake at a point some distance from the origin of the river.

DIRECTIONS: Choose the reasons you would use to explain or support your conclusion and fill in the appropriate spaces on your Answer Sheet. Be sure that your marks are in one column only—the same column in which you marked the conclusion. . . .

REASONS:

(1) In light of the fact that bacteria cannot survive in salted meat, we may say that they cannot survive in chlorinated water.

(2) Many bacteria in sewage are not harmful to man.

(3) Chlorination of water is one of the least expensive methods of eliminating harmful bacteria from a water supply.

(4) An enlightened individual would know that the best way to kill bacteria is to use chlorine.

(5) A sewage treatment system is cheaper than the use of chlorine.

(6) Bacteriologists say that bacteria can be best controlled with chlorine.

(7) As the number of micro-organisms increases in a given amount of water, the quantity of chlorine necessary to kill the organisms must be increased.

(8) A sewage treatment system is the only means known by which water can be made absolutely safe.

(9) By increasing the amount of chlorine in the water supply, the health of the people in this city will be protected.

(10) Harmful bacteria in water are killed when a small amount of chlorine is placed in the water.

(11) When bacteria come in contact with chlorine they move out of the chlorinated area in order to survive.

(12) Untreated sewage contains vast numbers of bacteria, many of which may cause disease in man.

(13) In most cities it is customary to use chlorine to control harmful bacteria in the water supply.

(14) Sewage deposited in a lake tends to remain in an area close to the point of entry.

(Progressive Education Association, 1939, p. 8, problem VII.)

This type of problem is very complex in form and requires very specific directions. However, it lends itself to a detailed analysis of the quality of the reasoning used by the student in support of particular decisions or courses of action chosen. The errors made by students may include the use of inappropriate generalizations and principles; or the examinees may show weakness by using irrelevant arguments. Such problems require a good deal of testing time, and their use may be justified best when a detailed diagnosis of the students' thinking and reasoning is to be made for formative testing purposes.

Analysis

Analysis is "The breakdown of a communication into its constituent elements or parts such that the relative hierarchy of ideas is made clear and/or the relations between the ideas expressed are made explicit. Such analyses are intended to clarify the communication, to indicate how the communication is organized, and the way in which it manages to convey its effects, as well as its basis and arrangement" (Bloom, 1956, p. 205).

The ability to analyze a problem, communication, or approach to attacking a problem is a complex ability which makes use of knowledge, comprehension, and application but goes beyond them. Such an ability may be regarded as a further step in the "comprehension" of an idea, problem, or document, as a prelude to a complex evaluation of the idea or document, or as a preliminary step to a creative synthesis for a problem of some complexity.

Analysis is not frequently found in elementary school objectives; it is more common at the secondary school and higher education levels. Some justification of this may be found in Piaget's work, which questions how far preadolescents can pursue the kind of reasoning and the analytic processes which are so central in what we have termed "analysis." Analysis presupposes that the individual not only can comprehend what has been stated in a document (literally as well as figuratively) but also can separate himself from the message to view it in terms of how it does what it does.

In a real sense, analysis requires the student to "see" the underlying machinery, devices, and ideas employed in a document, which can only be inferred from what the author of the communication has done. Quite frequently the author himself will not have been fully aware of what he did, and the reader is expected to detect the underlying framework with little explicit help from the author.

There is little doubt that analysis objectives are very difficult to teach and to learn. Instructors and curriculum makers may stress such objectives because of the greater understanding they give the student about a problem, approach to a problem, or document. In a society where changes in ideas, problems, and methods are so rapid, analytic abilities are necessary in order to go below surface manifestations to explore the basis for these changes and distinguish those which are real and fundamental from those which are not. While analysis is a slower and more difficult process than comprehension, it is very important to use where a deeper understanding is required before decisions are reached, problems are attacked, or significant evaluations are made. Especially in a society where complex problems and issues must be faced and attacked in a deeper way, analytic abilities must be developed if the problems and issues are to be dealt with in more than a superficial way.

It is likely that once analytic abilities are developed in a number of fields of knowledge, they can be applied to new problems in a creative way. It is also likely that once such abilities are developed to a reasonable degree, they will be retained and will be available to the individual long after he has forgotten much of the detailed knowledge. What the student must learn is both how to make analyses and under what conditions the analytic abilities can and should be employed.

In Figs. 8-2 to 8-4 we have listed objectives which may be classified under the general taxonomy category of *Analysis*. We have distinguished among these objectives using the analysis subcategories of the *Taxonomy of Educational Objectives* (Bloom, 1956; see the Appendix to Part I of the present book).

Figure 8-2 presents some objectives which emphasize the taxonomic classification *Analysis of elements*. These are primarily concerned with the identification of the underlying elements in a communication, such as the assumptions, values, and views being used by the author of the communication. Analysis of elements may also be used to determine the nature and function of particular statements in the communication.

In Fig. 8-3 the objectives emphasize the taxonomic subcategory *Analysis of relationships*. These are primarily concerned with the interrelationships of elements and parts of a communication, such as the relationship of hypotheses to evidence, assumptions to arguments, causal relationships, and sequential relationships. They also include the logical or necessary relationships among the elements or parts.

A third group of objectives, like those shown in Fig. 8-4, primarily emphasize *Analysis of organizational principles*. These objectives involve the ability to deal with the organization, systematic arrangement, and structure which hold an entire work together. The taxonomic subcategory includes analyses of the way in which the entire work is predicated on a particular form, point of view, purpose, or conception of the author's.

It will be seen by scanning the lists of analysis objectives in the figures that all involve some

[The ability to recognize] basic terms and their interrelationships; supporting evidence; the difference between subjective and objective statements, etc. (1, p. 39).

The ability to distinguish factual from normative statements (2, p. 146).

Ability to distinguish a conclusion from statements which support it (2, p. 146).

The ability to recognize unstated assumptions (2, p. 146).

Skill in identifying motives and in discriminating between mechanisms of behavior with reference to individuals and groups (3, p. 35).

Recognize both defensible and indefensible techniques used in attempts to influence thought and behavior: propaganda, rumors, stereotypes, emotional appeals, etc. (4, p. 101).

[1] Tyler, 1954.

[2] Bloom, 1956.

[3] American Council on Education Studies, 1944.

[4] French, 1957.

FIGURE 8-2 Statements of objectives for *Analysis of elements*.

[The ability to recognize] basic terms and their interrelationship; the problem or question; the author's argument and his conclusions; supporting evidence; the purpose, assumptions, and pre-suppositions of the author (1, p. 29).

Ability to check the consistency of hypotheses with given information and assumptions (2, p. 147).

Ability to recognize which facts or assumptions are essential to a main thesis or to the argument in support of that thesis (2, p. 147).

...To identify unstated assumptions which are necessary to a line of argument (3, p. 101).

Ability to recognize what particulars are relevant to the validation of a judgment (2, p. 147).

Ability to recognize the causal relations and the important and unimportant details in an historical account (2, p. 147).

[The habit of thinking] critically (i.e. to recognize untoward emotional appeal, detect false inferences or unsubstantiated generalizations) (1, p. 20).

[Development of skill in recognizing] the assumptions underlying [theoretical economic] models (4, p. 81).

The ability to establish cause and effect relationships in economic phenomena (4, p. 59).

[The ability to distinguish] cause and effect relationships from other sequential relationships (5).

[1] Tyler, 1954.

[2] Bloom, 1956.

[3] French, 1957.

[4] University Grants Commission, 1961.

[5] Ayers, 1966.

FIGURE 8-3 Statements of objectives for *Analysis of relationships.*

The ability to infer the author's purpose, point of view, or traits of thought and feeling as exhibited in his work (1, p. 148).

The ability to recognize the tone, mood, and purpose of the author (2, p. 17).

[The ability to detect] the purpose, point of view, attitude, or general conception of the author (3).

Ability to analyze, in a particular work of art, the relation of materials and means of production to the "elements" and to the organization (1, p. 148).

The ability to recognize form and pattern in literary works as a means of understanding their meaning (4, p. 44).

Ability to recognize the point of view or bias of a writer in an historical account (1, p. 148).

[The ability to recognize] such different methods of scientific inquiry as classification, relational or analogical, inquiry, causal inquiry, etc. (2, p. 52).

[1] Bloom, 1956.

[2] Tyler, 1954.

[3] Ayers, 1965.

[4] American Council on Education Studies, 1944.

FIGURE 8-4 Statements of objectives for *Analysis of organizational principles.*

ability to recognize, identify, classify, distinguish, discriminate, or relate particular qualities or characteristics of a work. It can be inferred from these statements that the ability or skill is to be used on *new problems, materials, or situations,* and that the adequacy of the student's analysis is to be judged against the ability of some expert or experts to make a similar analysis with the same givens. We will attempt to clarify these two italicized terms.

New problems, materials, or situations

One learns to make analyses of the kinds suggested in these objectives by actually engaging in the process with selected materials and problems. Thus, "the ability to recognize unstated assumptions" or "to distinguish factual from normative statements" is likely to be developed by practice in *doing* what is suggested by the objective with real material in a learning situation. The teacher would undoubtedly begin with relatively easy materials, in which the unstated assumptions or factual as against normative statements are relatively evident to many students, and gradually move to more complex materials, in which more effort and skill are required to discern, distinguish, or recognize the assumptions or types of statements.

Obviously the evaluation of analysis abilities and skills requires that the student demonstrate the appropriate behaviors in a *new problem or situation.* Otherwise he would be doing no more than revealing his memory or knowledge of an analysis carried out by the students or the teacher in the learning situation. By "new" we mean material that is new to the student, or at least material that is unlikely to have been analyzed in this way by or for him previously.

The selection of new materials and situations on which the student is to be evaluated entails fine judgment on the part of the teacher or other evaluator. One can imagine a range of materials from examples so simple that almost all students could make the appropriate discriminations to others so complex that only the most skilled analyst could discern the relationships and qualities sought. No simple rule can be given for this selection other than that the analysis required should be at the level of complexity and difficulty expected of the students at the appropriate level in their learning of this set of skills—whether the evaluation is formative or summative. At least the new task should be as complex as the material used at this stage in the student's learning experiences for analysis purposes.

Ideally the new problem, material, or situation should be real; that is, it should be selected from work or documents that already exist rather than prepared expressly for the evaluation exercise. As we said earlier, real materials are more likely to be of interest to the students, who in our experience prefer to exercise their analytic skills on genuine problems rather than on puzzle solving, in which the task is to figure out where or how the evaluator "hid" the required assumptions, types of statements, and so forth.

The ability to analyze

The ability to analyze is a complex set of skills and behaviors which the student can learn through practice with a variety of materials. It is assumed that this practice requires help from the teacher in order for the student to focus on the particular qualities desired, to develop and recognize systematic ways of proceeding to make the analysis, to learn the symptoms or cues that are helpful in distinguishing assumptions, relations, and other elements of a problem, and to learn the criteria by which one can judge the adequacy of the analysis. Practice without guidance, help, and corrections is not likely to be very effective. Practice on materials which vary in difficulty, complexity, form, and other aspects is likely to be more effective for learning these skills than is repeated practice on the same kinds of materials.

In terms of student behaviors, the ability to analyze might include the following:

The student can classify words, phrases, and statements in a document using given analytic criteria; this is the taxonomic subcategory *Analysis of elements* (*A*).

The student can infer particular qualities or characteristics not directly stated from clues available in the document; this is also *Analysis of elements* (*B*).

The student can infer from the criteria and relations of material in a document what underlying qualities, assumptions, or conditions must be implicit, required, or necessary; the taxonomic subcategory is *Analysis of relationships* (*C*).

The student can use criteria (such as relevance, causation, and sequence) to discern a pattern, order, or arrangement of material in a document; *Analysis of organizational principles* is involved here (*D*).

The student can recognize the organizational principles or patterns on which an entire document or work is based—again, an instance of *Analysis of organizational principles* (*E*).

The student can infer the particular framework, purpose, and point of view on which the document is based; this is another form of *Analysis of organizational principles* (*F*).

Testing for analysis

It is possible to determine the requirements for making analysis test items from the foregoing exposition of behaviors and new situations. Some of the requirements are these:

1. The problem situation, document, or material to be analyzed must be new, unfamiliar, or in some way different from that used in instruction.
2. The new situation, document, or material should be available to the student as he makes the analysis, and he should be able to refer to it as he attempts to answer the questions or solve the problems posed by the evaluator.
3. One or more of the behaviors listed in the subsection on Ability to Analyze should be sampled by the test problem.
4. The adequacy of a particular analysis should be determined by a comparison with that made by competent persons in the field or by a judgment of the adequacy with which evidence is used to infer particular unstated qualities or characteristics.

In the following subsections, we will attempt to illustrate some of the testing procedures which have been used to evaluate analytic abilities. We will organize these illustrations under the six types of behavior listed above because these appear to provide a useful way of making clear what the test problem is attempting to evaluate and because the behaviors provide a rough scale of complexity of the analytic tasks. Most of the illustrations are in objective test form because such forms make it very clear what skills are being tested. However, there is no doubt that essay or completion forms could be used to evaluate the same skills. As was true of the *Application* illustrations, most of the examples are drawn from the extensive files of the Examiner's Office of the University of Chicago, which provides the richest and most varied collection of illustrations for our purpose. Where examples are drawn from other sources, this is indicated in the note accompanying the illustration.

Test problems for analysis behavior A

The student can classify words, phrases, and statements in a document using given analytic criteria (A).

This is the simplest type of analysis, in which the student, given analytic criteria or suggestions, can distinguish, classify, code, recognize, or otherwise discern particular elements of the material, document, or statement which are appropriate. Such elements are explicitly stated or contained in the communication, and the student's only task is to recognize and classify them appropriately. It is believed that this type of analysis is a first step in an overall analysis because it is necessary to sort or classify those elements explicit in the document before one can move to the more difficult task of inferring what is implicit in or underlying the material contained in the document.

It should be pointed out that this type of analytic problem need not directly test the student's comprehension of the statements or his evaluation of them. Rather, the questions attempt to determine whether or not the student recognizes the *function, purpose,* or *use* made of the particular elements in the document.

34. DIRECTIONS: Each statement below is to be marked on the answer sheet as

    A—if it is *factual* and has been found *true* by experiment or observation

    B—if it is *factual* and has been found *false* by experiment or observation

    C—if it is a *part* of an accepted theory

    D—if it is in *contradiction* to an accepted *theory*

    E—if it is true merely by *definition* of a word or words used

    (1) Water freezes at 0° Centigrade.

    (2) The interior of an atom is mostly empty space.

    (3) Pressure exerted by a gas is due to the weight of molecules.

    (4) Iron rusts by combining with oxygen.

    (5) Equal volumes of gases at the same temperature and pressure have the same weight.

    (6) The resistance of two conductors in series is greater than their resistance in parallel.

In these items the student is expected to know what is meant by the terms "experiment," "theory," and "definition" and to be able to recognize or classify statements in relation to these terms. He is also expected to know enough about the phenomena described by each of the statements to determine the type of evidence or support on which it is based as well as its truth or falsity. This problem does test the student's knowledge as well as his ability to use the criteria.

35. A biological situation is listed below. In each situation, a *specific phenomenon* is *underlined* [*italicized*]. After each situation is a numbered list of statements, each of which may or may not be directly related to the specific phenomenon.

    DIRECTIONS: For each numbered statement *blacken* the answer space, in accordance with the series of choices given below, which best characterizes the statement.

    Blacken answer space

    A—if the statement helps to *explain* the cause of the phenomenon

    B—if it *merely describes* the phenomenon

    C—if it describes a *consequence* of the phenomenon

    D—if the statement does not directly relate to the phenomenon

    A flower box is kept near a south window. All the plants in the box *bend toward the window.*

    (1) The plants were exposed to unequal illumination on opposite sides.

    (2) Growth rates differ on the exposed and shaded portions of the stems.

    (3) Cell division proceeds at a greater rate on the shaded side.

    (4) The rate of photosynthesis is greater on the exposed side.

    (5) The plants receive an increased illumination due to the bending.

    (6) The plants exhibit positive phototropism.

    (7) Within certain limits, cell elongation is directly proportional to the quantity of active auxin present.

In these items the student must determine the way in which the statements are related to the phenomena described, only one of which has been included above. It is clear that the student must have a good deal of knowledge about each phenomenon before he can make the relatively simple type of analysis required here.

36. DIRECTIONS: For items 1–6, mark the answer spaces to indicate whether each of the statements about the Benedictine monastic movement refers to

    A—its fundamental purpose

    B—achievements that were incidental to its fundamental purpose

    C—evidence of regard for the movement on the part of the laity

    D—evidence of corruption within the movement

    E—none of the above

    (1) The scholarly interests of monks assured the preservation of arts and letters.

(2) The monasteries came into possession of great landed estates stocked with serf labor.
(3) The monks did much to bring about the improvement of agriculture.
(4) The monks' day and night were organized about periods of prayer and worship.
(5) By forbidding the monks to hold personal property, the Benedictine rule demonstrated the idea of communal ownership of property.
(6) Travellers seeking shelter at monasteries kept the monks informed of current news.

In this problem the student is expected to have information about the historical events in order to proceed to the type of analysis required. He may fail it if he lacks the information, if he can't use the criteria, or both.

[Students were given a selection from a social science study in advance of the test.]

37. DIRECTIONS: You may refer to the reading material and to your own notes as frequently as you wish in answering these questions. For each of the statements below which refer to the study, *blacken* answer space

A—if the statement is an hypothesis whose validity the author seeks to investigate in his study
B—if the statement is an assumption on which this study is based *but not an hypothesis* which the study was designed to test
C—if the statement is a finding of the study *but was not an hypothesis which the study was designed to test*
D—if none of the above clearly applies.

(1) An individual's social and economic attitudes are closely related to his class identification and both are related to his role in the economic system.
(2) Some middle-class persons are more radical in terms of the author's definition than some working-class persons.
(3) A majority of Americans believe themselves to be members of the working class.
(4) An individual's social class position can be determined with reasonable accuracy by knowing the amount and steadiness of his income.
(5) The reactions of members of different social classes to questionnaires are sufficiently comparable so that different responses can be taken to represent different opinions.
(6) A social class is characterized by common attitudes and beliefs.
(7) It is possible to state the issues involved in a liberal or conservative socio-economic attitude in terms having substantially the same meaning for all Americans.
(8) Results obtained from a sample of eleven hundred persons are valid when generalized to the American people as a whole.

This is a more difficult problem of analysis, in which the student must distinguish among hypothesis, assumption, and finding and must determine which of these are being referred to in a relatively complex report of a social sciences investigation. While this type of test approaches that of the next type of behavior (*B*), the relatively straightforward distinctions above require relatively few clues to the underlying structure of the document.

Test problems for analysis behavior B

The student can infer particular qualities or characteristics not directly stated from clues available in the document (B).

In general this type of behavior requires the student to recognize a variety of clues in the document and to use these as the basis of his inferences. Here he must do more than classify explicit statements; he must infer the qualities rather than merely recognize them. However, the emphasis in this behavior is primarily on *specific* qualities, characteristics, or elements.

It is clear that for an evaluation of this behavior, it is necessary for the student to have the document or material available to refer to as frequently as he needs. While it may in some instances be possible for the student to remember the document well enough to refer to it in his memory, it is likely that analytic problems based on this condition will be very rare.

Passage A (written in 1789)

> "A plural Legislature is as necessary to good Government as a single Executive. It is not enough that your Legislature should be numerous; it should also be divided. Numbers alone are not a sufficient Barrier against the Impulses of Passion, the Combinations of Interest, the intrigues of Faction, the Haste of Folly, or Spirit of Encroachment. . . .
>
> "Hence it is that the two Branches should be elected by Persons differently qualified; and in short, that, as far as possible, they should be made to represent different Interests. Under this Reasoning I would establish a Legislature of two Houses. The Upper should represent the Property; the Lower the Population of the State. The Upper should be chosen by Freemen possessing in Lands and Houses one thousand Pounds; the Lower by all such as had resided four years in the Country, and paid Taxes. The first should be chosen for four, the last for two years. They should in Authority be coequal."
>
> —*An anonymous author writing on the Pennsylvania Constitution*

38. DIRECTIONS: The following questions refer to Passage A. For each question *blacken* the answer space corresponding to the *one best* answer or completion.

    (1) Of the assumption which the writer of the passage makes, one is that

    A. decisions made by a government in which there is a heavy representation of property will always be wise decisions.

    B. the principle basic to politics is that various groups strive to achieve their own economic ends.

    C. under a good form of government, "factions" will be eliminated.

    D. under a good form of government the drives which people have of using government to promote their own economic ends will be eliminated.

In this example, the student must recognize the underlying assumption which the writer was making. Note that the assumption must be derived from several clues in the document. In the actual test in which this passage was used, there were a number of questions to evaluate the student's *comprehension* of the document. In general questions on a lengthy passage will rarely be restricted to analysis. Analytic questions are likely to be part of a set of items dealing with comprehension, application, evaluation, and so forth.

[The student has the paper available for reference during the examination.]

39. (1) In Leibnitz' discussion of "quantity of motion," his first assumption establishes

    A. a definition of the term "force" acquired by a body in falling from height *A*.

    B. a relationship between falling bodies and bodies projected upward against gravity.

    C. that the momentum acquired by a body falling from height *h* is sufficient to carry it back to height *h*.

    D. the equivalence of weight and motive force.

    (2) His second assumption establishes

    A. a definition of the term "force."

    B. a relationship between height of fall and velocity acquired.

    C. a relationship between height of fall and weight of body.

    D. the special case arising in consideration of machines.

    (3) In discussing the separation of particles, Lavoisier does *not* assert or assume that

    A. any body expanded by heating can be contracted by cooling.

    B. there is a range of attainable temperature below the point at which bodies remain constant in size despite further cooling.

    C. the size of the individual particles is unaffected by heat.

    D. there is a point on the temperature scale below which further markings are meaningless.

In this example it is to be noted that the student is to determine the effect of the assumptions made by the writer. While these questions relate to the entire document or investigation, they deal primarily with the more immediate effect of particular elements in the paper.

40. [The students are presented with a letter from Thomas Jefferson to James Madison. They can refer to it repeatedly as they attempt to answer a series of questions related to it.]

    (1) A fundamental political tenet underlying Jefferson's argument is that

        A. a little liberty is a dangerous thing: men must choose between complete freedom and unlimited authority.
        B. anarchy is a better state than tyranny, and possibly the best state for man; but it is not a real alternative for American society.
        C. rebellions are a wholesome, if rather bitter, medicine for government, since they generally lead men a little closer to the ideal of society without government.
        D. government is a necessary evil, but it should be stripped of power, since all power tends to corrupt.
        E. all of the above.

    (2) A further underlying proposition is that

        A. the perils of extensive liberty in the hands of the people, however great, are less serious than the perils of arbitrary power in the hands of officials, whether royal or republican.
        B. men in general have the capacity for self-government.
        C. rebellions in general are a sign of public health, showing that men care enough about their rights to defend them at great risk.
        D. rebellions in general are a sign of public degeneracy, in that they testify to governmental encroachments on popular liberties.
        E. all of the above.

In this example the student is probably helped by his general knowledge of Jefferson's political position. However, he must answer these analytic questions primarily from a careful reading of the letter from Jefferson to Madison. These two questions illustrate the rather close relation between comprehension and analysis. In one sense both deal with conclusions that may be inferred from Jefferson's arguments. In another sense both deal with propositions or assumptions underlying these arguments.

41. DIRECTIONS: Read the following poem carefully; then consider items 1 to 3, which refer to it, blackening the answer space corresponding to the *one* best completion.

POEM II

Go, go, quaint follies, sugared sin,
Shadow no more my door;
I will no longer cobwebs spin,
I'm too much on the score.

For since amidst my youth and night
My great preserver smiles,
We'll make a match, my only light,
And join against their wiles;

Blind, desp'rate fits, that study how
To dress and trim our shame,
That gild rank poison, and allow
Vice in a fairer name;

The purls of youthful blood and bowels,
Lust in the robes of love,
The idle talk of fev'rish souls,
Sick with a scarf or glove;

Let it suffice my warmer days
Simpered and shined on you,
Twist not my cypress with your bays,
Or roses with my yew;

Go, go, seek out some greener thing,
It snows and freezeth here;
Let nightingales attend the spring,
Winter is all my year.

    (1) In addressing "quaint follies" and "sugared sin" (stanza 1), the speaker expresses his specific purpose of

        A. reconciling himself to the physical limitations of old age.
        B. rejecting his earlier practice of amorous versifying.
        C. rejecting his earlier indolent habits in favor of industrious and constructive activity.
        D. abandoning his former attitude of toleration toward the sinful, and adopting a policy of positive denunciation.

(2) The smiling of the "great preserver" (line 6) symbolizes

A. God's grateful recognition and acceptance of a life spent serving Him and hating His enemies.

B. the nearness of death (i.e., heavenly bliss) for the speaker.

C. the love of God for man, and God's consequent willingness to redeem man from eternal damnation.

D. the benevolent attitude toward the author of the poem of an unidentified patron.

(3) Among the meanings for "match" (line 7) which were in use at the time of the composition of Poem II . . . , the poet has drawn especially upon two, namely:

A. "a compact or agreement" and "an article furnishing illumination."

B. "a contest or competition" and "an article furnishing illumination."

C. "a compact or agreement" and "a similarity or sameness."

D. "a contest or competition" and "a similarity or sameness."

In these three questions, the student is called upon to analyze specific words and phrases in the poem. He is expected to use clues throughout the poem in answering these relatively simple analytic questions. It is evident that this type of analysis can only be made if the material (the poem in this case) is available at the time of the evaluation.

Test problems for analysis behavior C

The student can infer from the criteria and relations of material in a document what underlying qualities, assumptions, or conditions must be implicit, required, or necessary (C).

In behaviors *A* and *B* the student is expected to use analytic criteria on parts or elements of the document, passage, poem, or other material. For the most part, behaviors *A* and *B* could be evidenced in the handling of excerpts from the larger document, since the necessary clues are usually available within the excerpt itself. In behavior C the emphasis is on the entire document or idea, although the analysis still deals with particulars which have bearing on the document as a whole.

42. DIRECTIONS: In each of the following items, *blacken* answer space

A—if the conclusion logically follows;

B—if the conclusion does *not* logically follow.

(1) STATEMENTS: If X exists, then Y exists. X exists.

CONCLUSION: Y exists.

(2) STATEMENTS: If X exists, then Y exists. X does not exist.

CONCLUSION: Y does not exist.

DIRECTIONS: In each of the following items, select the best lettered response.

43. STATEMENTS: No lover of sophistry respects the truth. All skeptics love sophistry.

CONCLUSIONS:

A. All skeptics respect the truth.

B. Some skeptics respect the truth.

C. None who respect the truth are non-skeptics.

D. Some skeptics do not respect the truth.

E. None of the foregoing.

44. STATEMENTS: It is true that, if perfect competition exists, the cost of production inevitably equals selling price. But perfect competition never did exist, does not exist, and never will exist.

CONCLUSION: Cost of production cannot equal selling price.

COMMENTS:

A. The conclusion follows logically.

B. It is impossible to be sure that competition never did and never will exist.

C. It is not stated that perfect competition is the only condition that permits cost of production to equal selling price.

D. An argument that begins with "if" cannot lead to any certain conclusion.

E. The argument sounds plausible but contains an important fallacy.

45. STATEMENTS: Let me explain how you can establish whether one thing or event is the cause of another. We will speak of two things or events, x and y. If you begin at any time, and observe when x happens, and after that you notice that y always follows x, and y never happens except after x, then you can say with certainty that x is the cause of y.

I began once to make such observations and noticed that whenever the sun set, it was followed later by the rising of the sun, and the sun never rose without being preceded by the setting of the sun.

CONCLUSION: The setting of the sun is the cause of the rising of the sun.

COMMENTS:

A. The conclusion follows logically.
B. The second part of the "statements" is an unfair use of the first part; this is an exceptional case.
C. An important assumption has been omitted from the statements.
D. The conclusion is absurd, so it cannot be logical.
E. The statement about "cause" is somewhat fallacious.

A relatively simple type of analysis is evidenced in the use of logical relations. Although the document or idea as a whole is relatively restricted, we see these illustrations as examples of behavior C. There are many forms in which syllogistic reasoning can be demonstrated; these are only a few of the possible variations.

46. Light has wave characteristics. Which one of the following offers the best experimental support for this statement?

A. Light can be reflected by a mirror.
B. A beam of light spreads out on passing through a small opening.
C. A beam of light can be broken into colors by a prism.
D. Light causes a current to flow in a photoelectric cell circuit.
E. Light carries energy.

47. Geologists subscribe to the hypothesis that the earth has been shrinking. Which of the following is the best evidence for this hypothesis?

A. The earth is not a perfect sphere.
B. The density of the interior of the earth is considerably higher than that of the surface layers.
C. The force of gravity varies in different parts of the earth.
D. The earth came originally from the sun as heterogeneous material and has been readjusting to the force of gravity.
E. Mountain ranges consist of series of folds.

48. In the past, glaciers covered the Great Lakes region. Which of the following offers the most direct experimental support for this statement?

A. The region is relatively cool in the summer.
B. Unsorted deposits are found in the region.
C. Igneous rocks are found in the region.
D. Ice sheets are still present in Greenland.
E. Tropical vegetation is absent in the region.

49. Two theories are advanced to explain the burning of material in air. Both theories assume that no substance can have negative mass or weight.

Theory A. During combustion, the burning material unites with a certain component of the air.

Theory B. During combustion, a substance escapes from the burning material into the surrounding air. The capacity of air to take up this escaping substance is limited.

DIRECTIONS: Consider each fact below and decide whether the fact *taken by itself* constitutes better evidence for one theory than for the other, is nearly equally good evidence for either theory, or furnishes no evidence for either theory. For each of the facts given below, *blacken* answer space

A—if the fact lends more direct support to Theory A than to Theory B;
B—if the fact lends more direct support to Theory B than to Theory A;
C—if the fact supports the two theories about equally well;
D—if the fact could not be used to support either theory.

Facts

(1) A candle in a closed jar containing air stops burning before the candle is used up.
(2) The product formed by burning iron in air weighs more than the original iron.

(3) Some products of combustion, when heated in air which no longer supports combustion, restore the original properties of the air.

(4) A candle burns more brightly in a breeze than in still air.

(5) Illuminating gas burns more brightly in chlorine than in air.

In these examples the student is to determine which type of evidence supports a particular theoretical statement. The problem of relating evidence to theory could be put in different forms. The simplest form is that of selecting the best evidence for a statement. The most complex is probably that of determining the criteria which must be met for evidence or experimental findings to support or refute a particular theoretical position. In the problems above, the student must have a good deal of prior knowledge about the theoretical statements before he can make the type of analysis required. It is to be noted that the student is not asked to determine the truth or falsity of the different choices—only their relevance to the theoretical statement. In some items all the choices are true, but they differ in the criteria specified in the test question.

50. (1) Assume that the definition of mass developed in the excerpt [based on a writing by Galileo] is the only definition of mass utilized by the author. In order then to have his theory of mechanics cover the common experience of the varying *weights* of bodies, he must establish a relationship between

A. weight and force.

B. weight and inertia.

C. weight and acceleration.

(2) One postulate necessary to the logical development of the excerpt is contained in the statement (do *not* assume that *postulate* necessarily means *unreal*)

A. bodies differ in weight.

B. two bodies mutually affect the acceleration of each other.

C. mass is a ratio of two accelerations.

D. acceleration is inversely proportional to inertia.

(3) In the excerpt, the use of the acceleration of a particle due solely to the mutual action of it and one other particle in determining masses is justifiable

A. only if no other particles affect the two particles considered.

B. only if the initial acceleration of each particle is used, since the acceleration of each particle will depend on the distance between the particles.

C. only if the total acceleration of a particle is analyzable into component accelerations each of which can be considered as affecting the particle independently.

D. since acceleration is itself a directly measurable quantity.

In these items the student must determine the necessary relations, definitions, and conditions for the logical and theoretical developments in Galileo's writing.

51. Which one of the following statements best explains the diction of lines 7–11 [from *King Lear*]?

A. Only the language used in these lines is really appropriate to a king.

B. The language reveals Lear's innate tendency to exaggeration in circumstances that excite his anger.

C. The language, chosen by the playwright primarily with a view to the effect on the spectator or reader, achieves a skillful contrast by the creation of emotional stress after the emotional relaxation in lines 1–6.

D. The imaginative quality of the language vividly shows Lear's awareness, as a result of his own painful experience, of the suffering of the poor in general.

52. (1) The author [of a social science paper] is assuming as *basic* to his argument the idea that

A. the main problem of government is to get common action even though people are divided on their basic interests.

B. public discussion is important in that it allows an opportunity for the "experts" to inform the public of its true interests.

C. government is good to the degree that it achieves the welfare of the people.

D. true democracy consists of rule by the majority.

(2) A belief basic to the author's argument is that

A. under the correct conditions, what the public wants is the best clue to what will be for the public good.

B. the importance of intelligence has been overemphasized in discussion of how public policy should be made.

C. the democratic movement was essentially transitional and . . . another means for determining public policy must be discovered.

D. experts are specialists and have nothing to do with how public policy is formed.

53. *The Theme and Variation 1 will each be played ONCE.*

The livelier effect of Variation 1 as compared with the Theme is due to

A. the faster tempo of Variation 1.

B. the more rapid succession of notes of Variation 1.

C. both faster tempo and more rapid succession of notes.

D. neither faster tempo nor more rapid succession of notes.

Additional examples of behavior C are afforded by these examples from literature, the social sciences, and music. These are isolated questions from a series of questions based on a work in each subject. In each case the student must base his answer on a comprehension of the entire work, although the specific clues are for the most part to be found in a particular excerpt.

Test problems for analysis behaviors D, E, and F

The student can use criteria (such as relevance, causation, and sequence) to discern a pattern, order, or arrangement of material in a document (D).

The student can recognize the organizational principles or patterns on which an entire document or work is based (E).

The student can infer the particular framework, purpose, and point of view on which the document is based (F).

All three types of behavior require the student to make particular kinds of analysis in which he is able to discern the pattern, organizational principle, framework, or point of view on which an entire work is based. Appropriate test problems for these types of analysis behaviors require the student to relate the entire work to a given analytic question or problem.

54. (1) The poet shows [in the poem given to the students with the examination] that his frustrated desire to aid the sufferers on the ship is due to

A. his inexperience and lack of wisdom.

B. his inability to get himself accepted as one of them.

C. his inability to move the oppressors to pity.

D. a combination of A and C.

E. a combination of B and C.

(2) Stanza 8 serves chiefly

A. to relieve the emotional strain aroused by stanza 7.

B. to intensify the distress of the men before the mast who were "reckless" or "aghast."

C. to sharpen by constrast the reader's picture of the situation in the noisome hold.

D. to give a more definite idea of injustice in the situation on the ship.

(3) Stanza 9 serves the purpose chiefly of

A. giving the reader a realistic picture of the return of the fishing fleet.

B. returning the reader to the scene established in stanza 1.

C. providing material for extending the simile of the ship to a final point.

D. delaying the end to make the poem symmetrical.

(4) Which of the following describes the progression of thought in the poem most accurately and most completely?

A. The beauty of a particular spot suggests the harmony of the motion of the Earth in the universe; pleasure in this idea is marred by the sins of men against each other and the inequalities in their lots. Reflection on these evils causes fear for the ultimate destiny of Earth.

B. The sight of boats at sea suggests that Earth is like a ship carrying all sorts of men. The poet reflects that unless men unite in brotherhood, the ship will be wrecked and he implores us to right the ship before it is too late.

C. The poet feels that Earth, like ships at sea, is in constant danger both from tyrants (captains) and from labor agitators (slavers in the hold). There are some passengers but these are thwarted by the selfish men.

D. The poet contemplates the beauty of Earth and prays to God that this beauty may be kept intact among men as it is in nature.

In these items the student must relate parts of a poem to the entire work. The second and third questions attempt to determine whether the student can discern pattern in the relation between several of the stanzas (behavior *D*). The fourth question attempts to determine whether the student can analyze the progression of thought or pattern in the entire work (*E*). The first question attempts to determine the poet's point of view in the entire work (*F*). Typically questions of this type would come toward the end of a set of questions on a particular work since they depend in part on knowledge, comprehension, and application as well as on more specific kinds of analysis of details of the work. They thus form the more complex behaviors or questions in a hierarchy of cognitive abilities and skills as applied to a new work.

55. (1) The feeling of mass in the work [a sculpture] results from
    A. the material.
    B. the color.
    C. the form.
    D. the treatment of surfaces.

(2) The sculpture is unified chiefly by
    A. repetition of parallel planes.
    B. color, texture, and repetition of lines and volumes.
    C. bilateral symmetry.
    D. repetition of identical shapes.

(3) One principal movement in the sculpture is created by
    A. the parallel turning of front and back planes of the figure.
    B. a single cylindrical volume running from top to base.
    C. an unbroken curve encircling the figure.
    D. a vertical core-line extending from top to base.

(4) Linear movements felt in this work are
    A. vertical.
    B. diagonal.
    C. horizontal
    D. all of these.

(5) The principal linear movements in the sculpture are
    A. repeated by the volumes, and repeated by the grain of the wood.
    B. repeated by the volumes, but opposed by the grain of the wood.
    C. opposed by the volumes, but repeated by the grain of the wood.
    D. opposed by the volumes, and opposed by the grain of the wood.

(6) The medium affects the work chiefly
    A. by limiting the nature of the design.
    B. by its color and grain.
    C. by its structure and hardness.
    D. by the difficulty of carving it.

(7) This work is best described as
    A. close representation of the natural object.
    B. selective representation of the natural object.
    C. abstraction based upon geometrical principles.
    D. nearly nonobjective.

These questions are all related to a new work of sculpture presented to the students at the time of the examination. The first two questions attempt to evaluate the student's ability to discern particular aspects of the arrangement of material and form (behavior *D*). The next four test the student's recognition of some of the organizational principles underlying the work (*E*), while the last question focuses on the overall framework or quality of the sculpture (*F*).

56. Consider the following statement [relating to an excerpt shown on the test]:
"1) Hamlet is given a command by the ghost of his murdered father to take vengeance upon the murderer, Claudius. 2) He is not able to do so immediately because he does not have sufficient proof that Claudius has murdered his father. 3) In the process of finding this proof, Hamlet unwittingly allows the king to discover his suspicions. 4) As the action proceeds, Hamlet cannot take vengeance because he never has a real opportunity to do so. 5) As the action ends, Hamlet becomes involved in a duel arranged by Claudius which has as its consequences the death of the hero and his adversary as well as the more important of the subordinate characters."

(1) This statement may best be described as
A. an *interpretation* of the play (as the word "interpretation" is used in the syllabus for the course).
B. an analysis of *character* (as the word "character" is used in the syllabus for the course).
C. a summary of the *thought* of the play (as the word "thought" is used in the syllabus for the course).
D. an analysis of the *mode of dramatic representation* (as that phrase is used in the syllabus for the course).
E. an account of the events in *Hamlet* which are presented *on stage*.

(2) An inference could be made from this statement as to the *element* which the writer of the statement takes to be the *organizing principle* of the play (as these concepts are defined in the syllabus for the course). Judging by this statement, we may say that for its writer, the play seems to be organized by
A. action.
B. character.
C. thought.
D. diction.
E. manner of presentation.

(3) A consideration of the problems raised throughout this play leads to
A. the view that Hamlet is not "essentially a speculative person" but, on the contrary, essentially a man of *action*.
B. the view that Hamlet delays in carrying out the ghost's command because he has *moral scruples* against the act of murder.
C. a serious doubt of the validity of *characterizing* Hamlet as "the kind of man who is always substituting thinking for acting."
D. a serious doubt of the validity of the final "except-clause" of the statement ("except when he is forced by external circumstances to act on the instant").

In this set of questions, the student is expected to analyze a statement about Hamlet against his own knowledge of the play. Item 3 gets at the student's ability to analyze the overall pattern of the play (*D*). Item 2 attempts to have him discern the organizing principle to be inferred from the quoted passage (*E*), while item 1 concerns the point of view adopted by the writer of the passage (*F*).

REFERENCES

All India Council for Secondary Education. *Evaluation in secondary schools.* New Delhi: AICSE, 1958.

American Council on Education Studies. *A design for general education.* Washington, D.C.: ACE, 1944.

Ayers, J. D., et al. *Summary description of grade nine science objectives and test items.* Edmonton, Alberta, Can.: Department of Education, High School Entrance Examinations Board, 1965.

Ayers, J. D., et al. *Summary description of grade nine social studies objectives and test items.* Edmonton, Alberta, Can.: Department of Education, Examinations Board, 1966.

Bloom, B. S. (Ed.) *Taxonomy of educational objectives: The classification of educational goals.* Handbook 1. *Cognitive domain.* New York: McKay, 1956.

French, W., and associates. *Behavioral goals of general education in high school.* New York: Russell Sage Foundation, 1957.

Gagné, R. M. *The conditions of learning.* New York: Holt, Rinehart and Winston, 1965.

Progressive Education Association. *Test 1.3a: Application of principles in science. Evaluation in the eight-year study.* Chicago: PEA, 1939.

Tyler, R. W. The fact-finding study of the testing program of the United States Armed Forces Institute, 1952–1954. Report to the USAFI, University of Chicago, July, 1954.

University Grants Commission. *Evaluation in higher education.* New Delhi: UGC, 1961.

9

Evaluation Techniques for Synthesis and Evaluation Objectives

Synthesis

Synthesis is "The putting together of elements and parts so as to form a whole. This involves the process of working with pieces, parts, elements, etc., and arranging and combining them in such a way as to constitute a pattern or structure not clearly there before" (Bloom, 1956, p. 206).

There has been much discussion and research on creativity during the past decade (see summaries in Taylor & Barron, 1963). Creativity has been regarded as one of the more important types of educational outcome, especially for the academically gifted. It has also been viewed as a kind of self-expression in which a student is urged and helped to produce something novel or different, bearing the stamp of his personal uniqueness and individuality. Much of the emphasis on creativity has undoubtedly come as a reaction against authoritarian modes of teaching and highly structured educational programs. It is also a reaction against the relatively extreme type of rote learning frequently emphasized in such teaching or educational programs.

Creativity has also been deemed to emphasize divergent thinking in contrast with convergent thinking. In divergent thinking the answer to a problem cannot be fixed in advance (as in multiple-choice questions), and each person may be expected or desired to produce a unique answer. In convergent thinking the correct answer to a problem or question can be known in advance since it is fixed by the requirements of the subject matter or the problem or both. For the most part, the categories of the *Taxonomy of Educational Objectives* (Bloom, 1956) up to the level of *Synthesis—Knowledge, Comprehension, Application,* and *Analysis*—can be regarded as convergent thinking, and the test illustrations for the majority of these behaviors can be of a form in which the correct or best answer can be determined in advance.

Synthesis, however, appears to be a type of divergent thinking in that it is unlikely that the right solution to a problem can be set in advance. In synthesis each student may provide a unique response to the questions or problems posed, and it is the task of the teacher or evaluator to determine the merits of the responses in terms of the process exhibited, the quality of the product, or the quality of evidence and arguments supporting the synthetic work.

Whether or not we identify creativity with synthesis, we can justify the development of objectives involving synthesis. As a form of divergent thinking, synthesis represents one of the terminal outcomes of education. No longer is the student displaying to the teacher the particular types of knowledge or skills and abilities he has developed; he is now producing ideas, plans, and products which are uniquely his. Thus synthesis is one of the culminating objectives of education in that the individual becomes a scholarly or artistic craftsman in his own right.

Synthesis can also be regarded as educationally important because of the pride of authorship, sense of creativity, and sense of communication and relevance which accompany the creation of something unique—especially when the student feels that he has done an adequate job with the materials and ideas at his command.

In a world of rapidly changing problems and answers, the schools are largely organized around fixed problems and set answers. Education emphasizing synthetic problems that can be approached in highly individual ways represents a clear departure from the catechisms under the control of curriculum makers and teachers. Eventually the individual will be placed in positions where he is expected to make unique contributions in the industrial world, in the professions, in the arts, or in scholarship. Synthesis is what is frequently expected of the mature worker, and the sooner the student is given opportunities to make syntheses on his own, the sooner he will feel that the world of the school has something to contribute to him and to the life he will live in the wider society.

That synthesis has been recognized as important can be seen by the educational objectives included in Part II of this book. In each subject from the preschool level on, objectives will be found which can be included under the taxonomy category of *Synthesis*.

Skill in writing, using an excellent organization of ideas and statements (1, p. 169).

Ability to write creatively a story, essay, or verse . . . (1, p. 169).

To develop effective written expression—the ability to adapt . . . material to a level of language and form suitable to the purpose and situation (2, p. 19).

Expresses his ideas in speech, writing, or in some artistic form with increasing clarity and correctness (3, p. 97).

Ability to write simple musical compositions, as in setting a short poem to music (1, p. 169).

The ability to participate [effectively] . . . in at least one of the arts or crafts or in some form of musical expression (4, p. 45).

The ability to participate effectively in group discussions of social problems . . . coordinating different suggestions, suggesting solutions, and orienting these solutions to the goals of the group (2, p. 28).

Skill in constructing . . . graphic materials (2, p. 49).

---

[1] Bloom, 1956.

[2] Tyler, 1954.

[3] French, 1957.

[4] American Council on Education Studies, 1944.

FIGURE 9-1 Statements of objectives for *Production of a unique communication.*

Ability to propose ways of testing hypotheses (1, p. 170).

Devising . . . suitable experiments for testing hypotheses; providing controls for experimental variables; recognizing and allowing for uncontrolled variables; setting up . . . laboratory equipment needed (2, p. 39).

Ability to plan a unit of instruction for a particular teaching situation (1, p. 171).

Ability to design a building according to given specifications (1, p. 171).

[1] Bloom, 1956.

[2] Tyler, 1954.

FIGURE 9-2 Statements of objectives for *Production of a plan or proposed set of operations.*

In Figs. 9-1 to 9-3 we list a series of objectives which are included in the large category of *Synthesis*. We differentiate these objectives using the subcategories developed in the *Taxonomy of Educational Objectives* (Bloom, 1956; see the Appendix to Part I of this book).

In Fig. 9-1 are some synthesis objectives which emphasize the *Production of a unique communication*. These are primarily concerned with the development of a communication in which the author—writer, speaker, artist—attempts to convey ideas, feelings, relationships, or experiences to others. The communication may be in the form of a verbal statement (written or oral), a poem, a painting, a musical composition, or a mathematical statement, among others.

Figure 9-2 contains some synthesis objectives which emphasize the *Production of a plan or proposed set of operations*. These are primarily concerned with the development of a plan of work or the proposal of a plan of operations. The plan should satisfy the requirements of a task which may be given to the student or which he may select or develop for himself.

In Fig. 9-3 the synthesis objectives listed emphasize the *Derivation of a set of abstract relations*. These are concerned with the development of a set of abstract relations to classify or explain particular data or phenomena. They may also include the deduction of propositions and relations from a set of basic propositions or symbolic representations.

Development of a tentative hypothesis based on the data at hand (1, p. 39).

Ability to formulate appropriate hypotheses based upon an analysis of factors involved, and to modify such hypotheses in the light of new factors and considerations (2, p. 172).

Ability to make mathematical discoveries and generalizations (2, p. 172).

Makes logical experiments; i.e. assumes the truth of a proposition which he suspects is false, and then makes logical deductions from this proposition (as in certain proofs in demonstrative geometry) (3, p. 98).

Ability to perceive possible ways in which experience may be organized to form a conceptual structure (2, p. 172).

[1] Tyler, 1954.

[2] Bloom, 1956.

[3] French, 1957.

FIGURE 9-3 Statements of objectives for *Derivation of a set of abstract relations.*

The reader will see by scanning the lists of synthesis objectives in these figures that they all involve the student's developing some new organization of material and ideas to meet the requirements of a problem or task or to express some feelings or ideas.

It is evident that the problem or task must be a new one for the student; otherwise the outcome might be a remembered synthesis rather than a new one produced by the student. It also seems likely that the student must have a great deal of latitude in defining the problem or task if he is to relate his own ideas, feelings, or experiences to it. While a common task or problem may be given to a group, the redefinition of the problem and the approach of each student may be quite unique. It is also possible for the student to set his own synthesis task or problem.

It is not necessary that the problem be new and original in the field involved—only that it be new to the student. Nor must the synthetic solution be a new development, creation, or discovery for the field involved—only a unique development as far as the student is concerned.

Synthesis objectives like those in Figs. 9-1 to 9-3 require new views and roles from both teachers and students. The student is expected to produce something which is unique and different. He is expected to produce this when provided with a task or problem, a set of specifications, or a collection of materials. In doing this he must have a goal in view, a prospective audience in mind, and some criteria of what constitutes an adequate job. In contrast, the teacher for synthesis objectives is no longer a pedagogue. He is more a coach, guide, or master craftsman working with an apprentice. The teacher may also form the audience or critic for whom the unique production is intended. Ideally his judgments about the products are not pass-fail or a series of letter grades. Rather, like most formative judgments, they are directed to helping the student find aspects of his work which are adequate as well as aspects which could be improved or strengthened. The point is that no synthesis is ever really perfect but that each one opens up vistas of future products and syntheses. This requires that teacher and student move from the pedagogue-pupil to the master-apprentice relationship—a most difficult new relationship which demands much from both teacher and student.

For the other categories of the *Taxonomy*, we have been able to state relatively specific student behaviors. For *Synthesis*, the emphasis is on the quality of the products created rather than on the specific processes or behaviors involved in their creation. However, since it does seem that somewhat different products are involved in the three subcategories, we will present test illustrations under these subcategories:

Production of a unique communication (A)
Production of a plan or proposed set of operations (B)
Derivation of a set of abstract relations (C)

Testing for synthesis

Some of the requirements for developing synthesis problems and tests may be summarized briefly.

1. The problem, task, or situation involving synthesis should be new or in some way different from those used in the instruction. The student may set the task or problem for himself or at least have considerable freedom in redefining it.
2. The student may attack the problem with a variety of references or other materials available to him as he needs them. Thus, synthesis problems may be open-book examinations, in which the student may use his notes, references, the library, and other resources as he finds them appropriate. Ideally synthesis problems should be as close as possible to the scholar (or artist, engineer, and so forth) attacking a problem he is interested in. The time allowed, conditions of work, and other stipulations should be as far from the typical, controlled examination situation as possible.
3. The type of product developed may be one of the types listed under the general category of *Synthesis* or any other which is appropriate to the particular educational objective being evaluated.
4. The adequacy of the final product may be judged in terms of the effect it has on the reader, observer, or

audience; the adequacy with which it has accomplished the task; or evidence on the adequacy of the process by which it was developed.

Most of the examples to be presented in the following sections are drawn from the files of the Examiner's Office of the University of Chicago. With a few exceptions these illustrations are of the essay type or involve the production of a new set of materials, work, or other product. It is unlikely that recognition test forms would be of great value in testing for this category of objective. Additional synthesis test illustrations and objectives will be found in the relevant subject chapters in Part II of this book.

Test problems for synthesis A: production of a unique communication

In the type of synthesis classified as *Production of a unique communication,* the student is attempting to convey an idea, feeling, or experience to others. In doing this he must have in mind the effects to be achieved, the nature of the audience he is attempting to influence or affect, the particular medium or form to be used (written or spoken, painted, expressed in scientific symbols, and so forth), and the ideas, feelings, or experiences to be communicated.

It is obvious that the student must have considerable freedom in defining the task for himself or in redefining the problem or task set for him.

Session III (3 hours)

1. DIRECTIONS: On many campuses a favorite target for student criticism is the university newspaper. At Harvard or Chicago, for example, the charge is sometimes made that the *Crimson* or the *Maroon* is unfair or inaccurate, that it is too radical or too conservative, that the staff is limited to a clique, that the style is bad and the articles dull, that too much or too little space is given to sports or music or to this or that group of campus politicians, and so on. To such complaints the editor of the college paper often rejoins that student criticism is merely unconstructive griping and that students don't know what they want of their paper anyway.

   This afternoon you are to explain and describe what you want a college or university paper to be. You may center your discussion on a particular newspaper on a particular campus—say the *Chicago Maroon*—or you may, if you prefer, discuss college papers in general. In any case, present your ideas about the characteristics that you believe a college paper ought to possess and develop these ideas out of a clearly expressed and coherently formulated conception of the proper role of college and university newspapers and of the interests and conditions which they should reflect. What should be the purpose or purposes of the paper? What needs should it serve? By what standards should it be judged? For instance, should a college newspaper limit itself to articles and editorials dealing only with campus events, issues, and personalities, or should it also deal with national and international news? Or, again, are certain responsibilities and duties rightly to be expected of a college paper because on most campuses it has no competitor?

   Do not write merely a series of answers to these questions. They are intended to help you think about the problem. After you have done your thinking and planning, write an essay that will have a beginning, a middle, and an end, in which the parts will be linked by some principle of progression. Reserve time toward the close of the examination for proofreading what you have written. Write on every other line of the essay booklet so you can make corrections and insertions neatly and legibly.

In this example of the typical English essay problem, the student is given a relatively general task which he must further define for himself. He is offered a number of suggestions to help him get started. However, he is provided with little in the way of criteria or standards he must meet in his paper.

2. DIRECTIONS: Write a unified paper on some restricted aspect of the question of the future of private property in America. The paper may be either an argument in support of some form of ownership which you favor, or an attack upon some form which you oppose, or both. It must, however, observe the following stipulations:

(1) It must include a discussion of the *moral bases* and *social effects* of the kind of ownership which you favor or wish to attack. For example, what ultimate right has anyone to claim anything as his own? What should he be allowed to do with what he owns? How should such rights be achieved, or protected, or limited? What will be the effects on society of the policies which you discuss?

(2) It must relate to your thesis the arguments pro and con . . . the *passages* distributed before the examination which are relevant to your position. It must not merely report what these passages said in the order in which they were printed. In the course of developing your own position you must make use of the arguments which support it and refute the arguments which oppose it.

(3) It must show some *application* of your theoretical position to one or more examples of property rights drawn from your own experience, observation, or reading. The following examples may suggest possibilities: private property in the family, or in the dormitory; rented, owned, and cooperative housing; public and private schools; independent, chain, and cooperative stores; making the University Bookstore a cooperative; municipal ownership of utilities and transportation; nationalization of banks, coal mines, railroads, and communications; national developments such as TVA; the rights of capital, management, labor, and consumers in the control of large corporations, etc.

(4) In form, the paper must be an *argument*. It must not be a mere assertion of your opinions supported by a description of the practices which you favor. It must give reasons for the position which you favor and against the positions which you oppose. The reasoning must be logical, but it need not make explicit reference to logical forms.

(5) The argument should be clear, interesting, and acceptable to the *audience* to which it is addressed. In a preliminary paragraph, separate from the rest of the paper, describe briefly the traits of your audience which you intend to keep in mind while writing your paper.

(6) The paper must be effectively organized and well written. It must not follow the points given above as a writing outline. It must not ignore them, however. Students are expected to deal with the assignment.

(7) The nature of the opinions expressed in this paper will have no effect on grades, and will never be revealed. Papers will be read only by members of the English 3 staff, and only after the names of the writers have been removed.

In preparation for this essay, the student is given a series of brief articles which deal with various aspects of the subject. Here he is given relatively detailed specifications for his paper, with some suggestions of the criteria to be used in judging it. Note in point 7 the provisions for objectivity and the attempt to encourage the student to use wide latitude in expressing his opinions.

Essay (Suggested time: 2–2½ hours)

3. DIRECTIONS: Read the following Comment on Selections I and II of the Reading Materials and answer the question based on them.

COMMENT: "Each of the three statements—of a leading American policy planner, of Britain's (1951) Foreign Secretary, and of one of the Soviet Union's official newspapers—claims to prescribe indispensable conditions for the achievement of peace. But no one of the statements really deals with the crucial factors which underlie the conflict between East and West. No one of them indicates the fundamental policies, both domestic and foreign, which are necessary to achieve peace."

QUESTION: Do you agree or disagree with this Comment? In defending your answer, make clear your own view of the indispensable conditions, both within and between nations, of lasting peace, and describe and defend a major line of policy which the United States might now employ.

[Your essay will be judged *not* in terms of the particular view which you accept but in terms of the thoughtfulness and consistency of your essay as a whole, and the adequacy of the information which you bring to bear upon the issues with which you deal. Refer, when appropriate, to authors read in the Social Sciences 3 Course, but do not use such references as a substitute for presenting your own consistent, coherent point of view.]

In preparation for this social science problem, the student is provided with several readings relevant to the problem. The "Comment" is intended to help him get started as well as to state the problem.

Essay (40 minutes)

4. Write an essay in which you consider the relationship between words and music in the song "Orpheus with His Lute" by Sir Arthur Sullivan. The text and the vocal line of the song are printed on Music Plate XIX. The text is taken from Act III, Scene 1, of *King Henry the Eighth*.

   The song will be played once as you begin work on this essay, and twice more thereafter, at ten-minute intervals.

   It is recommended that you first spend about ten minutes of the time allotted to this essay in planning your remarks.

   Although the text is printed on the music plate, it may be useful for you to see how it appears when printed as verse.

   Orpheus with his lute made trees,
   And the mountain tops that freeze
   Bow themselves when he did sing.
   To his music plants and flowers
   Ever sprung, as sun and showers
   There had made a lasting spring.
   Every thing that heard him play,
   Even the billows of the sea,
   Hung their heads, and then lay by.
   In sweet music is such art,
   Killing care and grief of heart
   Fall asleep, or hearing die.

This is an interesting problem in that the student is provided with both the words and the music during the examination and must now relate them. However, this is a relatively restricted synthesis problem with very little freedom for the student to develop a unique communication of his own.

Test problems for synthesis B: production of a plan or proposed set of operations

In this type of synthesis, the student is to develop a plan or propose some procedures for dealing with a task or problem. The plan or proposed set of operations should, in the view of the student, meet the requirements of the task, provide for the specifications or data to be taken into account, and satisfy the standards and criteria generally accepted in the subject field. It is important to remember that the student is not actually executing the plan; he is only making the plan or proposing the operations necessary.

5. FACTS: Gases X and Y react readily when mixed in a glass flask. If, however, just before the gases are introduced, the flask is heated strongly and cooled, no reaction takes place. If a copper container is used, no reaction occurs.

   DIRECTIONS: Consider each hypothesis below in the light of the facts above. If the hypothesis is untenable or is not stated in a way that could be tested experimentally, blacken answer space A. Otherwise choose the experiment which will best test the hypothesis and blacken the corresponding answer space.

   (1) Water is a *necessary* participant in the reaction.
      A. Hypothesis is not tenable or cannot be tested experimentally.
      B. Dry the flask without heating it before introducing the gases.
      C. Leave the flask open after mixing the gases.
      D. Moisten the walls of the copper container before introducing the gases.
      E. Heat the glass flask strongly, allow it to cool, and leave it open for several days before introducing the gases.

   (2) When glass is present, molecules are absorbed in the glass in such a way that their active portions project inward.
      A. Hypothesis is not tenable or cannot be tested experimentally.
      B. Fill the container with broken glass and note any change in the rate of reaction.
      C. Dry the flask without heating it before introducing the gases.
      D. Cover the interior of the flask with paraffin.
      E. Examine the inside walls of the container with a microscope during the reaction.

   (3) Copper forms a stable compound with the gas X and prevents reaction with the other gas.

A. Hypothesis is not tenable or cannot be tested experimentally.

B. Analyze the interior surface of the copper container.

C. Increase the gas concentration of gas X in a glass flask and note whether the rate finally reaches a constant limiting value.

D. Moisten the walls of the copper container before introducing the gases.

(4) The reaction takes place by a simple collision of X and Y in the body of the gas.

A. Hypothesis is not tenable or cannot be tested experimentally.

B. Fill the container with broken glass and note any change in the rate of reaction.

C. Carry out the reaction with gases X and Y dissolved in water.

D. Cover the interior of the flask with paraffin.

E. Increase the gas concentrations of gas X in a glass flask and note whether the rate finally reaches a constant limiting value.

6. A measurement is to be made of the heat evolved in the complete combustion of a certain type of coal. The sample of coal is placed in a thin metal capsule; oxygen is admitted; and the capsule is sealed. The capsule is immersed in water contained in an insulated vessel and the contents are ignited by means of an electric spark. The amount of heat evolved in the capsule is determined from the rise of the temperature of the surrounding water.

DIRECTIONS: Keeping in mind the purpose of the determination described above, choose the *one* best alternative for each of the following items and *blacken* the corresponding answer space.

(1) The weight of the coal sample

A. must be known accurately

B. need only be known approximately, i.e. to about 50%

C. need not be known, but must at least equal the weight of water

D. is entirely immaterial

(2) The amount of the water in the vessel

A. must be known accurately

B. must be known only well enough to permit addition of water to balance evaporation

C. is immaterial as long as it covers the capsule completely

D. is immaterial but should not cover the capsule completely

7. An experiment is being planned to determine the amount of radiation emitted through a 25 sq. ft. opening in a furnace during a one-minute period. A paper-thin flat sheet of metal one foot square is held in the path of the radiation at a distance of five feet from the opening. Its rise in temperature is measured by means of a thermocouple.

DIRECTIONS: You are to decide which of the following factors are important in this experiment. For each factor below, *blacken*

answer space *A*—if the factor must be taken into account before even a rough estimate of the amount of radiation emitted can be made

answer space *B*—if the factor need be taken into account only if a fairly accurate estimate is to be made

answer space *C*—if the factor is not likely to affect the estimate to any measurable degree

(1) The shape of the metal sheet

(2) The angle at which it is held relative to the opening

(3) Whether the surface of the metal is blackened or shiny

(4) The temperature of the room

In these three illustrations the student is not required to make his own synthesis—only to judge particular details of a proposed set of operations. The value of this test form is that it can sample a variety of details in a brief amount of time. However, these would be clearer illustrations of synthesis if the student were asked to propose the hypotheses and state how he would test them.

8. A hitherto unknown ray has been discovered in the Arctic regions but in spite of diligent investigation no trace has been found elsewhere. On exposure to this ray, salt acquires a considerable charge; the odor of chlorine can be detected in the vicinity. Water, on like treatment, also assumes a powerful

charge and becomes quite sour in taste; no other changes are observed.

DIRECTIONS: In the *first* blank at the left of each of the items below, classify the following hypotheses concerning the nature of the ray as:

A. possibly correct and capable of experimental verification
B. possibly correct but expressed in terms which are not specific enough to lend themselves to experimental verification
C. untenable in the light of the facts given above

Next, for each statement which you have marked "A," select from the list below that *one* experiment which is the most direct test of that statement. Place its number in the remaining blank to the right of "A." If no appropriate experiment is listed, write a zero sign (0) in the blank.

List of Experiments

(1) Determine whether chlorine can be detected in water after the water has been irradiated.
(2) Pass the ray between charged condenser plates.
(3) Examine the ray with a spectroscope.
(4) Determine the intensity of the ray at different altitudes.
(5) Analyze irradiated salt for traces of hydrogen.
(6) Determine whether the ray will pass through an evacuated space.
(7) Carry out experiments on the ray in the tropics.
(8) Determine whether the ray is attracted toward one of the poles of a magnet.
(9) Determine the direction of the path of the ray.
(10) Determine whether the ray can be focused by means of a lens.
(11) Determine the penetrating power of the ray.
(12) Determine whether interference patterns can be produced on a screen covered with salt crystals.

Hypotheses

___ ___ The ray originates in outer space.
___ ___ The ray is a stream of high velocity sodium ions.
___ ___ The ray contains a transverse wave motion of frequency beyond the ultraviolet.
___ ___ The ray contains a longitudinal (compression) wave motion.
___ ___ The ray is a stream of high velocity protons.
___ ___ The ray is a stream of particles having no mass and no charge.

This is another illustration of the use of the objective test form to get at the student's ability to propose a plan to solve a problem. In this case it might have been simpler to have the student state his own hypotheses and describe the experiments he would propose.

Directions for Essay (Suggested time: 2–2½ hours)

9. COMMENT: "It is true that nowadays any program for American domestic policy must take account of the limitations imposed by the present international situation and proper goals with respect to it. But similarly, any proposals with respect to American foreign policy must reckon with their implications for domestic policies, including the limits imposed by current domestic conditions and by the values we seek in our domestic life. Regarded either individually or collectively, the proposals of Lippmann, Stevenson, and Eisenhower do not take adequate account of the second half of this circle."

   In terms of the above comment write an essay on American foreign policy. In the course of your essay, describe the principles which, in your view, should guide current policy; describe and defend the objectives which current policy should seek and the particular policies which should be followed (in case of doubt, intensive treatment of a limited policy problem, the broader ramifications of which have been made clear, is preferable to a broader, but superficial coverage of policies); and make it clear which characteristics of the contemporary domestic and international situation you regard as important to the justification of your policy proposals.

   Your essay will be judged not on the basis of the particular view you adopt but on the basis of its thoughtfulness and consistency as a whole, the adequacy of the information and analytical skill which you bring to bear upon the issues with which you deal, and the appropriateness with which you organize what you have to say. When appropriate, refer to authors read in the Social Sciences 3 Course, but do not use such references as a substitute for presenting clearly your own point of view.

Here the student is provided with relevant readings. He is now asked to propose a set of foreign policy objectives and principles and to defend them by reference to particular characteristics of the contemporary situation. It is possible that this would be better tested in a term paper or essay written over a more extended period of time. In some ways this synthesis task is as appropriate to subcategory *A* (unique communication) as it is to subcategory *B* (production of a plan).

Test problems for synthesis C: derivation of a set of abstract relations

The student is to produce a set of hypotheses or explanations to account for given phenomena; to create a classification scheme, explanatory model, conceptual scheme, or theory to account for a range of phenomena, data, and observations; or to determine the logical statements and hypotheses which can be deduced from a theory, set of propositions, or set of abstract relations. The student's work must meet the requirements of the phenomena and the logical possibilities inherent in the relationships among the phenomena or propositions.

10. A physiologist found that:

(1) Even with all nerves to the pancreas cut, pancreatic enzymes were secreted when food entered the intestine.

(2) When a wash from a piece of small intestine from an unfed dog was injected into the blood of normal animals no pancreatic enzyme secretion occurred. When intestinal tissue was first treated with hydrochloric acid, and a wash then made and injected into normal animals, pancreatic enzyme secretion occurred.

(3) Intestinal tissue was first treated with pure starch, fat, and protein. A wash from the treated intestine, when injected into the blood of a normal unfed animal, resulted in no pancreatic stimulation.

(4) Injection of hydrochloric acid alone into the blood of normal animals did not stimulate pancreatic secretion.

(5) The stomach of normal animals secretes hydrochloric acid.

From these facts, the physiologist formed the tentative hypothesis that

pancreatic secretion is stimulated by a hormone produced by the small intestine; the presence of hydrochloric acid is the necessary and sufficient condition under which the small intestine will secrete its pancreas-stimulating hormone.

He then performed another experiment, as follows:

The stomach was removed from a number of animals and the esophagus connected directly to the small intestine. From such animals he discovered four additional facts.

(6) When the animal was fed a meal consisting of starch, pure fat, and pure protein, pancreatic enzyme secretion, though delayed, nevertheless occurred.

(7) Blood taken from such animals 1 hour after they were fed a diet of pure starch, pure fat, and pure protein, would, when injected into normal animals, stimulate a flow of pancreatic juice.

(8) Blood taken from such animals after 24 hours without food did not stimulate secretion of pancreatic juice when injected into normal animals.

(9) In such stomach-less animals, the duct from pancreas to small intestine was tied off. After recovery, the animals were given a meal of pure protein, pure fat, and pure starch. One hour later the contents of the small intestine were removed and found to contain not only the pure foods previously ingested, but also small amounts of the digestion-products of protein, fat, and starch.

In the light of these new data carefully devise and state a refined and expanded hypothesis concerning stimulation of pancreatic enzyme secretion. Be sure that your answer (1) corrects any statements in the tentative hypothesis which the new data indicate to have been false or overstated; (2) accounts for stimulation of pancreatic secretion in *normal* animals; (3) accounts for all cases of pancreatic stimulation in the experimental animals above.

11. A physiologist found that:

(1) bile salts break up fats into fine droplets:

(2) the lymph leaving the small intestine contains fine droplets of fats;

(3) the absorbing cells of the intestine contain small fat droplets.

From these facts, the physiologist formed the tentative hypothesis that:

fats are emulsified by the bile salts and are absorbed and carried away from the intestine in this form.

He then found in addition that:

(4) in the absence of pancreatic juice, no fat is absorbed from the intestine (even when the fat has been emulsified by bile);

(5) pancreatic juice transforms fats into glycerol and fatty acids;

(6) careful examination of the absorbing cells of the intestine showed that there were no fat droplets in that part of each absorbing cell that projects into the intestine, but that the fat droplets were confined to that portion of each absorbing cell farthest from the cavity of the intestine.

Carefully devise and state a refined and expanded hypothesis concerning the digestion and absorption of fat. Explain clearly the successive steps necessary to account for all the facts presented above.

In both these illustrations, the student is to develop a set of hypotheses to account for the phenomena and findings in a series of experiments.

12. The experiments described below have actually been performed, with the results which are given. They are basic to the theories which have been proposed to account for the manner in which cells accomplish chemical transformations which either do not occur spontaneously or which occur spontaneously at extremely slow rates.

In answering the questions following these experiments, you are to use the evidence given by the experiments themselves, interpreting these as nearly as possible in the terms considered appropriate by cell physiologists such as Potter and Dixon.

To understand the methods employed in these experiments, you will need the following preliminary information.

INFORMATION: Methylene blue is a synthetic dye whose blue color disappears when its solution is treated with a mild reducing agent. Hydrogen gas itself does not decolorize methylene blue solution. When reduced methylene blue solution is shaken with air or oxygen gas, the solution absorbs oxygen and becomes blue again. The absorbed oxygen has combined with hydrogen from the reduced methylene blue to form water. Thus, methylene blue can act as a hydrogen acceptor in some cases, and, after having received the hydrogen, can yield it to oxygen to form water.

NOTE: Many of the necessary technical details in these experiments have been omitted from the descriptions. One such detail is that the mixtures for the experiments are made up with neutral buffer substances which keep the mixtures neutral even though an acid or a base is added in reasonable amounts.

Experiment A: Methylene blue solution was placed in a closed flask filled with helium, an inert gas. *Lactic acid* solution was added to the mixture without opening the flask. No color change was observed. Analysis of a sample showed that the lactic acid was still present.

Experiment B: A living frog was decapitated. One of its larger leg muscles was finely chopped, washed in several changes of physiological salt solution. The washed muscle was mixed with a methylene blue solution in helium gas as in *A*. No color change was observed.

Experiment C: The mixture from *A* was added to the flask in *B*. The blue color disappeared and analysis showed much less lactic acid than had been used in *A*.

Experiment D: When a similar muscle was heated to the boiling temperature before chopping, no change occurred and no lactic acid disappeared, in a test situation such as in C.

1. What kind of atoms were probably added to or removed from the lactic acid?
2. Use your knowledge of living tissues to invent an explanation for the difference between the results in *A*, *B*, *C*, and *D*.

Experiment E: Minced fresh frog muscle was washed in physiological salt solution *much longer* than in Experiment *B*. Then, Experiment *C* was repeated, using the more thoroughly washed muscle tissue. On this occasion the muscle produced almost no change in the color of methylene blue or in the quantity of lactic acid.

Experiment F: Juice from cooked minced frog muscle was added to the mixture from *E*. The methylene blue color now disappeared and the quantity of lactic acid was greatly lessened.

3. In the light of your knowledge of cell chemistry, what hypothesis or modification of your earlier hypothesis would best explain the results in *E* and *F*?

Experiment G: Experiments *A* through *D* were repeated, using *succinic acid* instead of lactic acid. The results obtained were similar.

Experiment H: A solution of succinic acid and methylene blue was placed in a closed flask, the space above the solution being filled with *oxygen* gas. The flask was attached to an apparatus arranged to measure changes in gas volume. During a period of an hour, no oxygen was used, no succinic acid had disappeared, and the color remained blue.

Experiment I: Fresh, chopped frog muscle was prepared *as in B*, except that no methylene blue solution was used. The mixture was placed in a flask such as was used in *H*, the space above the mixture being filled with oxygen. During a period of an hour, very little oxygen was used.

Experiment J: Succinic acid solution (with no methylene blue) was added to the mixture in *I*. At once, oxygen began to disappear relatively rapidly and continued until practically all the succinic acid had been used.

4. What hypothesis or hypotheses would satisfactorily explain these results?

Here the student is expected to take more and more data and observations into consideration as the experiments proceed. His hypotheses and explanations are to account for an increasingly complex set of results.

Social Sciences Essay

13. Imagine that you are able to travel into the future and study the culture of the United States two thousand years from now. You find that at that time the majority of positions of influence and honor are filled by women. When you question people, they tell you that intelligence, kindness, and a respect for creative work are the ideal human attributes and that women, by nature, excel men in these matters.

    Write an essay in which you describe what other significant social changes might accompany the change described above.

Here the student is given more freedom to develop and illustrate a simple theory about the social changes that might take place.

Evaluation

"Evaluation is defined as the making of judgments about the value, for some purpose, of ideas, works, solutions, methods, material, etc. It involves the use of criteria as well as standards for appraising the extent to which particulars are accurate, effective, economical, or satisfying. The judgments may be either quantitative or qualitative, and the criteria may be either those determined by the student or those which are given to him" (Bloom, 1956, p. 185).

Judgments such as "good-bad," "like-dislike," and "desirable-undesirable" are constantly being made by all of us. We have difficulty refraining from making a judgment about anything that comes within our view, whether it is a person, a thing, an idea, or a situation.

Many of these judgments are expressions of taste, whim, convention, or habit—"I like this," "I don't like that," "I have always liked this type of music," and so on. While such expressions of personal taste and feeling are real and important to the one making them, they are not illustrations of the types of evaluation found in educational objectives. Judgments which are primarily dictated by taste and habit are relatively simple; they are rarely examined; they are private; and they are rarely based on criteria and standards which can be made explicit.

In contrast, the types of evaluation found in educational objectives appear to us to be among the most complex cognitive behaviors. In the *Taxonomy of Educational Objectives* (Bloom, 1956), *Evaluation* is placed as the last category of objectives. Implicit in this placement of evaluation in the cognitive domain is the assumption that objectives in this category require some competence in all the previous categories—*Knowledge, Comprehension, Application, Analysis*, and *Synthesis*. Evaluation, however, goes beyond these in that the student is presumably required to make judgments about something he knows, analyzes, synthesizes, and so forth on the basis of criteria which can be made explicit.

Educational objectives involving evaluation, as defined in the *Taxonomy*, are found mainly at the secondary school and higher education levels. This type of informed judgment is likely to be so complex that teachers and curriculum makers include it relatively late in the education process. Perhaps it is so difficult to teach because it requires a temporary suspension of one's own quick judgment about something (for example, a work of art or a social policy) while he systematically appraises it by means of explicit and relatively complex criteria.

In spite of its complexity, evaluation appears to be one of the most important categories of educational objectives in our society. Increasingly, the citizen in a democracy is called upon to participate in making evaluations of social policies, political decisions, and governmental actions. Problems of pollution, war and peace, and urban conditions are so complex that the citizen must be exceedingly well informed if he is to participate meaningfully in the appraisal and evaluation of past as well as future decisions and actions. Given the increasingly complex and difficult set of problems posed in modern society, it seems evident that evaluation as defined here is most relevant for the education of citizens throughout the world.

So too the nature of music, art, literature, and even the substantive disciplines of the sciences and social sciences places more and more emphasis on evaluation. Rapid changes in the arts, new approaches to the sciences and the social sciences, and rapid communication about these developments require that a person be able to suspend his judgments about the new while he makes appropriate analyses and evaluations of it. To reject the new and different because it is new and different is to reject the opportunity of participating in the modern world. On the other hand, to accept the new and different because it is the current fad and fashion is not adaptive either. Thus, we are expressing the view that the development of adequate evaluative behavior is especially required for a person's well-being in a rapidly changing society where new choices, decisions, and consequences are ever present. Effective participation in a rapidly changing society continually requires evaluative behaviors of a very high order.

In Figs. 9-4 and 9-5 we list objectives which may be classified under the general taxonomy category of *Evaluation*. We again distinguish among these objectives according to the evaluation subcategories of the *Taxonomy of Educational Objectives* (Bloom, 1956).

In Fig. 9-4 are some evaluation objectives which emphasize *Judgments in terms of internal evidence*. These are primarily concerned with judgments of the accuracy of a communication from such evidence as logical accuracy and consistency.

Figure 9-5 presents some evaluation objectives which emphasize *Judgments in terms of external criteria*. They primarily entail evaluation of materials, objects, and policies by reference to selected criteria. These may be criteria developed by the student, criteria in the form of other related works, or standards and criteria formulated by specialists in the relevant fields.

It will be seen from the two lists of objectives in these figures that they all involve some *ability to*

Judging by internal standards, the ability to assess general probability of accuracy in reporting facts from the care given to exactness of statement, documentation, proof, etc. (1, p. 189).

The ability to apply given criteria (based on internal standards) to the judgment of the work (1, p. 189).

The ability to recognize the accuracy, completeness and relevance of data (2, p. 17).

The ability to distinguish between valid and invalid inferences, generalizations, arguments, judgments, and implications (2, p. 17).

The ability to verify the accuracy of the computations and check the validity of the inferences by examining the logic of the inductive or deductive proof [mathematics] (2, p. 48).

[The ability] to determine if the data, method of inquiry, and argument support the conclusions (2, p. 53).

[The ability] to evaluate a proposition about natural phenomena; to recognize the accuracy and reliability of the observations warranted by the nature of the problem, the chosen procedure, and the instruments used (2, p. 53).

[The ability to] recognize bias and emotional factors in a presentation and in his own thinking (3, p. 101).

The ability to distinguish between valid and invalid arguments and conclusions; recognizing adequacy, completeness and relevance of data; recognizing misrepresentation of data, partial truths, and incompleteness in over-all treatment of an issue (2, p. 29).

The student will be able to recognize gaps, contradictions, and redundance in a given set of postulates and to detect fallacies in mathematical arguments (4, p. 254).

[1] Bloom, 1956.

[2] Tyler, 1954.

[3] French, 1957.

[4] University Grants Commission, 1961.

FIGURE 9-4 Statements of objectives for *Judgments in terms of internal evidence.*

evaluate works, policies, or situations, among other things. It can be inferred from these statements that the ability or skill is to be used on *new problems, materials, or situations,* and that the adequacy of the student's evaluation is to be judged against the ability of some expert or experts to make a similar evaluation with the same material or against an expert judgment about the adequacy of the criteria used and the process by which the evaluation has been made. The two italicized phrases are further developed in the following discussion.

New problems, materials, or situations

It is obvious that evaluations made by the students should be related to new works not treated this way in the classroom. Otherwise the evaluations would represent little more than memory or knowledge of evaluations already made by the students or the teacher in the learning situation. By "new" we mean material which is new to the student or which is unlikely to have been evaluated in the same way by or for the student previously.

No simple rule can be given for the selection of new material for evaluation. One might expect that the new material, problems, and so forth might be similar to those evaluated in the learning situation in terms of difficulty or complexity.

Ideally the new material should be real in that it is selected from works, documents, situations, or other sources that already exist rather than expressly developed for the evaluation problems. As we have pointed out previously, students are likely to find real evaluation problems more interesting than obviously contrived ones. The type of material to be evaluated is in large part dictated by the statement of the objective (see Figs. 9-4 and 9-5) and by the particular behaviors deemed relevant.

Ability to evaluate

The ability to evaluate or judge works or other givens is a complex set of skills and behaviors which the student is expected to learn through practice with a variety of works and problems. While the ability is dependent on the student's acquisition of prior types of learning—knowledge, comprehension, application, analysis, and synthesis—it includes in addition specific behaviors involving judgments and evaluation.

In terms of student behaviors, evaluation includes the following:

The ability to apply self-developed [aesthetic] standards to the choice and use of the ordinary objects of the everyday environment (1, p. 192).

The ability to recognize artistic quality in contemporary works of music and art (2, p. 45).

[The ability to] distinguish between art objects which represent good design, line, color, and texture and those which do not (3, p. 111).

The ability to judge the overall literary quality of the work (4, p. 17).

Judging by external standards, the ability to compare a work with the highest known standards in the field—especially with other works of recognized excellence (1, p. 192).

Skill in recognizing and weighing values involved in alternative courses of action (1, p. 192).

The ability to identify and appraise judgments and values that are involved in the choice of a course of action (1, p. 192).

[The ability] to recognize those instances in which a scientific finding supports or is in conflict with doctrines explaining the constitution and processes of the physical world (4, p. 55).

[The ability] to evaluate a proposition about natural phenomena (4, p. 53).

The comparison of major theories, generalizations, and facts about particular cultures (1, p. 192).

The ability to evaluate the adequacy of the solution reached for the settlement of the original problematic situation [mathematics] (4, p. 48).

The student will develop the ability to critically assess traditional beliefs, institutions, and behavior patterns in relation to the functions of the state (5, p. 95).

The student will develop the ability . . . to formulate judgments [about controversial political problems] (5, p. 95).

The student will develop the ability to . . . evaluate current developments in politics at the national and international level (5, p. 95).

[Develops the ability to] evaluate his community government in terms of its contribution to the quality of living for families who reside there: protection, cultural stimulation, educational and recreational opportunities (3, p. 179).

[1] Bloom, 1956.

[2] American Council on Education Studies, 1944.

[3] French, 1957.

[4] Tyler, 1954.

[5] University Grants Commission, 1961.

FIGURE 9-5 Statements of objectives for *Judgments in terms of external criteria.*

The student can make judgments of a document or work in terms of the accuracy, precision, and care with which it has been made (internal accuracy; *A*).

The student can make judgments of a document or work in terms of the consistency of the arguments; the relations among assumptions, evidence, and conclusions; and the internal consistency of the logic and organization (internal consistency; *B*).

The student can recognize the values and points of view used in a particular judgment of a work (internal criteria; *C*).

The student can make judgments of a work by comparing it with other relevant works (external criteria; *D*).

The student can make judgments of a work by using a given set of criteria or standards (external criteria; *E*).

The student can make judgments of a work by using his own explicit set of criteria or standards (external criteria; *F*).

Testing for evaluation

It is possible to determine the requirements for making evaluation test problems from the foregoing analyses of behaviors and situations.

Some of the requirements are the following:

1. The problem situation, document, work, or material to be evaluated must be new, unfamiliar, or in some way different from those used in instruction.
2. The new problem situation, work, or other matter should be available to the student as he makes the evaluation, and he should be able to refer to it as he attempts to answer the evaluative questions or problems posed by the evaluator (or himself).
3. One or more of the behaviors listed in the foregoing subsection, Ability to Evaluate, should be sampled in the test situation.
4. The adequacy of a particular evaluation should be determined by a comparison of it with that made by competent experts in the field or by a judgment on the adequacy with which a particular evaluation is explained, argued, or defended.

In the following sections we will attempt to illustrate some of the testing procedures which have been used to appraise evaluative abilities. The illustrations will be grouped under the six types of behavior listed above, since these behaviors provide a useful way of making clear what the test problem is attempting to do and furnish a rough scale of complexity of the evaluative tasks. The test illustrations will be of both the objective and the essay form. In some ways it does seem that the essay form is superior to the recognition forms for testing evaluation. However, for purposes of illustrating the behaviors being tested, the objective form is simpler and somewhat clearer because it provides both the questions and the possible answers. It would take too much space to indicate the possible answers or scoring procedures for the essay problems.

The examples are drawn from the files of the Examiner's Office of the University of Chicago because of the care with which these test materials were constructed and because of the great variety of illustrations available in these files. Additional examples of evaluative test situations and educational objectives will be found in the chapters in Part II of this book.

Test problems for evaluation behavior A

The student can make judgments of a document or work in terms of the accuracy, precision, and care with which it has been made (internal accuracy; A).

This is the simplest type of evaluation, calling on the student to recognize the extent to which particular details of a document or work are accurate, precise, or carefully done. While this behavior does resemble some aspects of knowledge, comprehension, and analysis, these illustrations should emphasize not only the recognition of accuracy (or inaccuracy) in details but also a judgment on the adequacy of the work in terms of its internal accuracy. (We have provided only a single illustration of this behavior because we believe there should be little difficulty in constructing tests for this type of evaluation.)

14. Two investigators, Smith and Jones, after studying the foregoing data, tested their conclusions in the laboratory.

    Investigator Smith collected eggs from lake H and performed the following experiment:

    He distributed the eggs equally into each of 10 tanks which were known to be identical in all respects except temperature. Each tank was held at a *different, constant* temperature in a range of 5°C to 30°C. He recorded the number of fin-rays of the fish which developed in each tank.

    Investigator Jones performed a series of six experiments. Each experiment was just like that one experiment performed by investigator Smith, but in this case the eggs for

    experiment 1 were taken from lake L,
    experiment 2 were taken from lake I,
    experiment 3 were taken from lake G,
    experiment 4 were taken from lake H,
    experiment 5 were taken from lake B,
    experiment 6 were taken from lake A.

    Now state explicitly what biological factor is uncontrolled in Smith's experiment, but well-sampled by those of Jones.

In this illustration the student is to determine the features of the experiments which make one investigation more accurate and valid than the other.

Test problems for evaluation behavior B

The student can make judgments of a document or work in terms of the consistency of the arguments; the relations among assumptions, evidence, and conclusions; and the internal consistency of the logic and organization (internal consistency; B).

This type of behavior requires the student to recognize the ways in which the details and parts of a work fit together in terms of consistency, order, and organization. He must recognize the internal consistency of a work, the parts and details which are not consistent, and the ways in which the parts relate to each other. While the emphasis in this behavior is primarily on specific details and their internal logic, it is also expected that the student will make some final judgment about the work in terms of consistency among these details.

It is clear that in the tests for this behavior, the student will need to have the document or work available to him as he makes the necessary distinctions and judgments. Only rarely can the student be expected to make such judgments on the basis of his memory of the work.

15. DIRECTIONS: A dissolved substance lowers the freezing point of the solvent because of a mechanical hindrance offered by solute molecules to the process of the assumption of regular lattice arrangement by the solvent molecules during crystal formation. The lowering of the freezing point is a linear function of the hindrance, that is, of the concentration of solute molecules only. Mark each of the following factors as

    A—if the factor is *not* likely to interfere with accurate applicability of the theory

    B—if the factor is such that the theory is applicable if great accuracy is unimportant

    C—if the factor makes the theory not applicable

    D—if the information given is not sufficient to decide between A, B, and C

    (1) The dissolved substance has a very small vapor pressure.

    (2) The dissolved substance consists of charged particles.

    (3) The substance has a great tendency to unite chemically with the solvent.

    (4) The crystal lattice formed upon freezing contains alternating solute and solvent molecules.

    (5) The solution is concentrated.

    (6) The atmospheric pressure varies from one determination to the next.

16. The existence of complexly folded rock strata can be used as evidence for a shrinking earth

    A. provided this fact is supplemented by evidence that compensating tensions have not existed in other regions.

B. provided the rock folds are in a general north-south direction.

C. provided similarly folded rock strata can be found at great depths, i.e. over 100 miles.

D. provided one assumes that the earth is undergoing a cooling process.

E. without reservations; folding must always result in a surface shortening.

In these illustrations the student is judging the relations between parts of an argument or between a conclusion and evidence. While the problem may be new to the student, it is likely that some aspects of it have been previously learned. These would be clearer illustrations of evaluation if the detailed judgments were followed by some overall judgment about the theory or situation. These illustrations overlap considerably with some that we have considered under the category of analysis. However, the emphasis here is on the validity and consistency of the details and parts.

17. DIRECTIONS: Following is a series of pairs of propositions dealing with a single topic. In the case of each pair of propositions, you are to locate the source of their 'opposition,' real or apparent, by *blackening* the letter of the completion which best accounts for it. You will need, of course, to consider the context of each quotation as it appeared in your readings.

(1) (a) "Scientific discovery must ever depend upon some happy thought, of which we cannot trace the origin; in some fortunate cast of intellect, rising above all rules."

(b) "For my way of discovering the sciences goes far to level men's wits, and leaves but little to individual excellence."

The 'opposition' between these two statements is

A. merely verbal.

B. ascribable to the fact that while (a) refers to 'scientific discovery,' (b) refers to 'discovering sciences.'

C. ascribable to the fact that (a) has to do with induction, whereas (b) is concerned with deduction.

D. ascribable to different underlying notions of the relation between data and ideas.

E. ascribable to different underlying notions of the relation between observation and experiment.

(2) (a) "In any other case, it is no evidence of the truth of the hypothesis that we are able to deduce the phenomena from it."

(b) "The doctrine which is the *hypothesis* of the deductive reasoning, is the *inference* of the inductive process. . . . And in this manner the deduction establishes the induction. The principle which we gather from the facts is true, because the facts can be derived from it by rigorous demonstration."

The 'opposition' between these two statements is

A. merely verbal.

B. ascribable to the distinction implied in (a) between 'phenomena' and 'causes.'

C. ascribable to different underlying conceptions of the relation between sense and intellect.

D. ascribable to different underlying conceptions of the relation between deductive truths and prediction of unobserved cases.

E. ascribable to different underlying conceptions of the nature and role of proof in 'the science of discovery.'

(3) (a) "Human beings in society have no properties but those which are derived from, and may be resolved into, the laws of the nature of individual men."

(b) "Thus the great movements of enthusiasm, indignation, and pity in a crowd do not originate in any one of the individual consciousnesses."

The 'opposition' between these two statements is

A. merely verbal.

B. implies opposing conceptions of the psychology of individual men.

C. is ascribable to the inclusion of the 'social phenomena' cited in (b) within the scope of the 'laws of the nature of individual men' cited in (a).

D. is ascribable to the difference between the

'nature' of (a) and the 'consciousnesses' of (b).

E. expresses opposing attitudes toward Mill's conception of the 'Chemical' method in the social sciences.

In these examples the student is to judge the consistency or lack of consistency between pairs of statements as well as the basis on which the two statements may be related to each other.

18. Early in 1951, the public became aware that the Federal Reserve authorities and the Treasury had for some time been in conflict regarding the proper open market policy of the Federal Reserve Banks and regarding the proper related "debt management" policy to be pursued by the U. S. Treasury. The Federal Reserve authorities have insisted that the Treasury's "pressure" on them to buy government securities has interfered with their aims of counteracting credit expansion. Treasury officials, supported by other high government officials, in turn have charged the Federal Reserve system with attempting to sabotage the Treasury's debt-management policy; i.e., the policy of keeping the market price for government bonds stable and the interest rate on the public debt relatively constant at the low level of about 2½%. The Treasury stresses this point in view of the imminent need to refund a large amount of maturing bond issues.

DIRECTIONS: For each of the following items, you are asked to decide whether

A. the argument tends to support the Treasury's policy;

B. the argument tends to support the Federal Reserve authorities' policy;

C. the argument is likely to be accepted by both participants in the struggle and does *not* support either side in the issue at stake more than the other;

D. the argument is likely to be rejected by both groups in the struggle.

NOTE: Give only the *one best* answer.

(1) Holding down the yields and supporting the prices of Government bonds keeps down interest payments on the Federal debt; this is particularly important in a period in which tax revenue is urgently needed for armaments.

(2) If we fight inflation largely by price controls, we will curtail freedom and efficiency. If we rely primarily on sharp tax increases, we will find that they are politically unobtainable, or if attained, would produce undesirable economic effects. We must not confine ourselves to these strategies.

(3) The maintenance of government security prices at a constant level is desirable because it protects investors, including commercial banks, against depreciation of their investments.

(4) If the policy of maintaining stable prices of government bonds contributes significantly to the continuation of an inflationary process, such a policy will not be in the interest of actual or prospective bondholders. They will tend to consider the decrease in the *real* purchasing power of their principal and interest earnings more important than the maintenance of the dollar bond price.

(5) An increase in the level of interest rates, though fairly ineffective as a direct anti-inflationary measure, might have a negative effect on productive investment, especially in durable capital goods.

The primary task in this illustration is to determine the consistency between arguments and selected policies. Again, it would be a clearer evaluation problem if there was a final question on the soundness of the two policies in terms of the arguments presented.

Test problems for evaluation behavior C

The student can recognize the values and points of view used in a particular judgment of a work (internal criteria; C).

Here the student is not expected to make a judgment. Rather he is to identify the values, points of view, and assumptions on which the judgments given are based. Again, the behavior must be regarded as only one aspect of a more complex behavior—the final process of judgment. We place it here primarily because it appears to be one step toward the more complex behaviors *D*, *E*, and *F*. It is likely that a student who can demonstrate this behavior can also recognize the values he is using when he makes an evaluative judgment.

19. (1) The statement is often made, "Physics and chemistry are basic sciences; astronomy and geology are derived sciences." Which of the following is the best interpretation of the statement?

    A. Physics and chemistry rest on a sound foundation of proven laws; much of astronomy and geology is pure speculation.

    B. The development of astronomy and geology necessitates the use of physics and chemistry; the converse is not true.

    C. The entire subject matter of astronomy and geology could have been derived by using the laws and methods of physics and chemistry.

    D. Physics and chemistry are of more basic importance to human activity than are astronomy and geology.

    E. It is possible to carry out laboratory experiments in physics and chemistry but not in astronomy or geology.

    (2) Which of the following best interprets and clarifies the statement: "Geology for the most part is an observational science rather than an experimental science?"

    A. The phenomena of geology are usually too vast in time and scale for investigation under controlled conditions.

    B. It is impossible to investigate geological phenomena in the laboratory.

    C. An open mind can better be retained by observing nature as it is than as it performs under artificial conditions.

    D. As long as geological processes are easily visible, it is unnecessary to carry out experiments.

    E. The statement is based on the erroneous distinction between direct evidence such as that obtained through our senses and inference obtained by reasoning from facts; the statement is self-contradictory.

The student is provided with brief evaluative statements and is to determine the point of view or assumptions on which they could be based. It is clear that this type of test item could be used in many subject fields besides science.

20. The following questions are based on Tennyson's narrative poem, "The Revenge," which was printed in full in the original examination.

    DIRECTIONS: The following sentences are characteristic of the kinds of critical remarks people make about literary works. Read each statement carefully and mark in the space at the LEFT:

    (1) if the statement concerns the relation of the author to his work;

    (2) if the statement concerns the organization of the poem as a relationship of parts to the whole;

    (3) if the statement concerns the relationship between historical events and events treated in the poem;

    (4) if the statement is an evaluation made by the reader in terms of his own ideas;

    (5) if the statement is concerned with the classification of poems or with their metrical form.

    ___ The history of the ship, Revenge, unifies the poem.

    ___ Grenville's reputation as a naval commander makes him an appropriate hero for the poem.

    ___ The poem is written in imitation of the traditional ballad form.

    ___ The poem is bad because it does not arouse sympathy for the Spanish.

    ___ The poem was written from the English point of view because Tennyson was an Englishman.

    ___ Grenville's decision to fight the superior Spanish fleet initiates the actions which follow.

    ___ The action is improbable because no man with only one ship would fight a fleet of fifty-three.

    ___ The poem is written in trochaic metre.

    ___ The Revenge had been commanded by Drake in the fight against the Armada in 1588.

    ___ Grenville's devotion to "Queen and Faith" explains his actions throughout the poem.

The poem "The Revenge" is available to the student as he answers these questions. The questions are intended to determine whether the student recognizes the point of view or type of detail on which the critical remarks are based.

21. Two Critics on *A Farewell to Arms*

DIRECTIONS: The following statements are taken from . . . book reviews written at the time of the first publication of *A Farewell to Arms*. . . .

Critic I

In its depiction of war, the novel bears comparison with its best predecessors. But it is in the hero's perhaps unethical quitting of the battle line to be with the woman he has gotten with child that it achieves its greatest significance. Love is more maligned in literature than any other emotion, by romantic distortion on the one hand, by carnal diminution on the other. But Author Hemingway knows it at its best to be a blend of desire, serenity, and wordless sympathy. His man and woman stand incoherently together against a shattered, dissolving world. They express their feelings by such superficially trivial things as a joke, a gesture in the night, an endearment as trite as "darling." And as they make their escape from Italy in a rowboat, survey the Alps from their hillside lodgings, move on to Lausanne where there are hospitals, gaze at each other in torment by the deathbed of Catherine, their tiny shapes on the vast landscape are expressive of the pity, beauty, and doom of mankind.

Critic II

It is not the plot that counts, it is the circumstance and the complete realization of the characters. In this book you get your own times in typical essence to wonder about and interpret. Yet I do not believe that Hemingway's strength lies in character creation. His Catherine and his Henry have nothing strange or novel in their personalities. Catherine is a fine girl who needs a lover. Henry is an individualist who acts by instinct rationalized, not by principle, and makes his friends love him. Hemingway's art is to make such not unfamiliar characters articulate when he finds them. . . . It isn't *what* they are, it is *how* they are that seems important, and of course that is a true principle in art. Anyone can outline a psychology, but how many can give you, whole and self-interpreting, just a darky crossing the road, or a man nursing his first wound! Hemingway works almost entirely through a simple record of incident and dialogue which he stretches to include meditation in the rhythm of thought. . . . He is after voice rhythms and voice contrasts. It is the way these people talk, not what they say that lifts the scene into reality.

DIRECTIONS: Items [1 to 9] are based on the passages [above]. . . . For [these items] blacken the answer space corresponding to the *one* best completion.

(1) Critic I finds the "significance" of the novel to lie especially in

A. its account of the psychology of a deserter
B. its evocation of pity and fear
C. its representation of the true nature of love
D. its combination of realistic fatalism and symbolic beauty

(2) In support of this view, Critic I directs attention to certain details in the novel. When he describes the characters' methods of expressing their feelings as "superficially trivial," one understands that he must mean that

A. these "things" are trivial only on the surface
B. the characters are mediocre and lacking in depth
C. the novelist has been deficient in invention
D. there is a clear, but unimportant, weakness in the diction of the novel

(3) The last sentence of the passage implies that

A. the human figures are distorted by the romantic setting of the action
B. the emotions of the characters, being the common experience of all men, are shared by the reader
C. the particulars of the novel stand for universal propositions about life
D. the inevitable consequence of errors in conduct is symbolized in the outcome of this action

(4) Consequently, it is apparent that Critic I is judging the novel primarily as

A. an imitation of life
B. an interpretation of life
C. a means to the end of good conduct
D. an extension of the reader's experience

(5) Critic II, on the other hand, is judging the novel primarily as

A. an imitation of life

B. an interpretation of life

C. a source of aesthetic pleasure

D. an extension of the reader's experience

(6) From what he says about plot, character, and dialogue, it may be inferred that this critic is concerned, before judging a novel, with

A. determining the organizing principle of the whole

B. determining what aspect of reality the writer is trying to imitate

C. analyzing the personalities of the characters

D. analyzing his own subjective reactions to the book

(7) His criteria for judgment, so far as this excerpt indicates them, are primarily concerned with

A. the truth and novelty of the subject matter

B. the complete realism of the diction

C. the adequacy of execution to conception

D. the complete convincingness of the imitation

If these two critics were to analyze the function of the narrator in *A Farewell to Arms*, each would emphasize, it is assumed in the next two items, different points. You are warned to consider in these items, not only whether the completion is *appropriate* to the critic, but also whether it is *accurate* for the novel.

(8) Critic I would emphasize the fact that

A. the apparent incompleteness of emotional expression is accounted for by the character of the narrator and his involvement in the action

B. the apparent incompleteness of emotional expression is accounted for by the limited knowledge available to a narrator-observer

C. the symbolic significance of the action is heightened by the narrator's use of elaborate descriptive details, as in allegory

D. the symbolic significance of the action is brought to the attention of the reader by the narrator's comments on the symbols

(9) Critic II would emphasize the fact that

A. unity is achieved by the use of a single, limited point of view

B. the selection of a central character as narrator almost automatically gives one a "self-interpreting" action

C. the narrator's habit of directly addressing the reader makes the whole action seem more immediate

D. the first-person point of view, if well handled, gives one the most natural view of an action—as it really seems to a particular individual

In these items the student, who has studied Hemingway's *A Farewell to Arms*, is provided with statements taken from book reviews written by four critics (only two are illustrated here). What the student must do is to recognize the values, points of views, and assumptions made by each of the critics. The last two questions determine whether the student can extend the critics' points of view to other sets of details about the book. This is a relatively complex test situation which can be used to get at relatively subtle aspects of evaluation.

Test problems for evaluation behaviors D and E

The student can make judgments of a work by comparing it with other relevant works (external criteria; D).
The student can make judgments of a work by using a given set of criteria or standards (external criteria; E).

In both of these behaviors, the student is making judgments about a work by the use of some external criteria—another work, a set of criteria, or a known standard. In most of the illustrations that follow, the student is expected to analyze and judge a specific *new* subject—a work, document, proposal, policy—by relating it to some other works, books, positions, standards, and so forth which he has *previously studied* in connection with a relevant course.

ESSAY II—Time: 30 minutes

22. "If we will grant that what we want is *peace*, and that *justice* is the only way to peace, then we may begin dimly to perceive both the outlines of a policy for the present and the *constitutional* foundations of a future world order. We are required to abandon a policy of power and purchase and pursue a policy of justice at home and abroad."

    DIRECTIONS: Analyze and evaluate this position, using the principles and ideas in Kennan's *American Diplomacy*.

The students have read and discussed the Kennan work and are to use it in evaluating the position stated in the quotation. The directions are rather general and the student is given little guidance on what he is to do.

23. DIRECTIONS: The United States is confronted with international tensions which, as policy is now being carried out, require a large outlay for goods and services that will not find their way into consumers' markets.

    Various techniques have been proposed for financing this outlay and for determining the items to be produced. These techniques may serve or conflict with various values. For example, some techniques may (I) place serious restrictions on at least some economic freedoms which Simons (*Positive Program for Laissez-faire*) regards as essential to the maintenance of a free enterprise system. These same or other techniques may (II) conflict with goals of economic policy (other than freedom) in that they (i) would have "adverse effects" on the distribution of income (i.e., making it more unequal), (ii) would hamper the defense effort itself by intensifying the dangers of inflation, or (iii) would hamper the defense effort by failing to bring about production of the type and quantity of goods needed for the defense effort. For items (1) to (6) you are to judge the consequences of various policies for (I) freedom on the one hand vs. their effects on (II) these other goals of economic policy. A policy is to be considered as "conflicting with other goals of economic policy" if it appears to conflict significantly with *any one* of the goals listed in (II) above. For each item blacken answer space

    A—if the policy would be *compatible with* the maintenance of the *economic freedoms* which Simons regards as essential to the maintenance of a free enterprise system and *would not conflict* with other goals of economic policy

    B—if the policy would be *compatible with* the maintenance of the *economic freedoms* which Simons regards as essential to the maintenance of a free enterprise system but *would conflict* with other goals of economic policy

    C—if the policy would involve at least *some restriction on the economic freedoms* which Simons regards as essential to the maintenance of a free enterprise system but *would not conflict* with other goals of economic policy

    D—if the policy would involve at least *some restriction on the economic freedoms* which Simons regards as essential to the maintenance of a free enterprise system and *would also conflict* with other goals of economic policy

    E—if none of the above clearly applies

    NOTE: In answering these items, judge the effects of the policy in terms of the current situation as described in the *President's Economic Report*. In answering each item assume that the policy stated is not counteracted by other policies or devices employed at the same time.

    (1) A moderate increase in income taxes (the increase to be of a type which does not change the progressiveness of the present tax structure).
    (2) Legislation to prohibit automobile manufacturers from mass producing new models during the crisis.
    (3) A policy of permitting wages to rise in defense industries to the extent necessary to attract a sufficient number of workers to such jobs.
    (4) An increase of social security deductions so that less purchasing power finds its way into consumers' hands, and higher pension payments may be made when the crisis is over.
    (5) Imposition on all finished consumer goods of a uniform general sales tax sufficient to balance the budget.
    (6) A policy of government subsidization of all families earning an income of less than $2,500 for four people, where such an amount is clearly necessary for the maintenance of minimum living standards.

The students are to relate the President's Economic Report to Simons's book. The judgments concern the effects of particular economic policies. The test form and directions are relatively complex.

24. DIRECTIONS: Let us suppose that in 1952 the school board of Centerville, an American city of 50,000, prescribes for all teachers and students of all its elementary and secondary public schools a compulsory oath which is to be recited at regular intervals at such occasions as assemblies and class meetings. The oath is to include the conventional pledge of allegiance and also to affirm that the speaker "does not subscribe, will never subscribe, and has never in the past subscribed to any principles of any organization advocating a form of government alien to that of the United States or advocating violence as a means of changing the government."

    We may conceive at least four different views of such a regulation:

    A. The regulation is thoroughly improper.
    B. The regulation is proper as regards students but not as regards teachers.
    C. The regulation is proper as regards teachers but not as regards students.
    D. The regulation is thoroughly proper.

    The statements which follow were made by various speakers at a town meeting to discuss the regulation. For items (1) to (8) blacken the answer space corresponding to the letter of the above view which is most similar to that expressed by the speaker. *Blacken answer space E if no one of the above clearly applies.*

    (1) Hobbes is the only accurate philosopher of loyalty.
    (2) In his essay on *Civil Government* Locke, in contrast with Hobbes, advised citizens properly in regard to what they should do about arbitrary government.
    (3) Plato's standards for education are essentially sound.
    (4) Education is, as Mill said, a process in which free men help others to become free.
    (5) Mill was right in arguing that political conclusions require deliberations upon experience.
    (6) The clue to all loyalty oath questions is to be found in Mill's doctrine on the difference between thoughts and actions as proper objects of social control.
    (7) The requirement of an oath would violate the First Amendment by not making exceptions on religious grounds.
    (8) The principles underlying the Supreme Court's decisions in the second of the flag salute cases before it in 1940–43 are the correct ones.

Here is a simpler test form. The students are to judge a particular regulation using the views of selected philosophers and documents studied in the course.

25. Questions [1 to 4] deal with the following passage, concerning the general nature of science.

    At bottom, science admits only one test of the validity of its theories, namely *concordance:* consequences drawn by purely deductive reasoning from observations together with the theories of science must not contradict one another.

    The purpose of science is to discover order in the world, that is, to find relations connecting the various observed phenomena. For this purpose it is necessary to construct theories. These theories always postulate the existence of entities (such as atoms, fields of force, or the mass of the sun) which cannot be directly perceived in any observations, but which serve to unify our picture of the world behind our observations. The unification consists in the circumstance that by means of the nonobservable entities and the relations which are postulated to hold among them, we can draw conclusions from one set of observations concerning another such set.

    In particular, scientific theories are often quantitative in form, the postulated entities are characterized by numbers, and the relations which hold among them are mathematical. In this case, the "theoretical" quantities must be capable of being computed on the basis of observations, and the observations themselves must, therefore, be quantitative—i.e., they must be measurements. Furthermore, each "theoretical" quantity must, at least in some situations, be computable independently from *more than one* set of measurements. The agreement among the results of independent measurements is the concordance which tests the theory; if such independent determinations are impossible, there can be no test of the theoretic results; the theoretic quantity involved serves no useful function and is therefore redundant.

(1) Which of the following observations, taken by itself, provides a test of the "concordance" achieved by Newton's particle theory of light?

A. observation of the path of a particle, under the conditions described in Newton's first theorem concerning "very small bodies"

B. measurement of the angle of incidence and the angle of refraction for a single ray of light passing from one medium to another

C. measurement of the angle of incidence and the angle of reflection for a single ray of light reflected from a surface separating two media

D. measurement of the angle at which total reflection occurs for a single ray of light passing from water into air

(2) Which of the following is the most probable judgment of the author of the above passage, concerning the relative merits of a treatment of light which takes such generalizations as the laws of reflection and refraction as its basic premises, and a treatment like that of Newton's "On Very Small Bodies" or Huygens' *Treatise*?

A. A theory of light like Newton's or Huygens' is to be desired, because it is concerned not merely to describe but to *explain* the properties of light.

B. A theory of light like Newton's or Huygens' is relatively valueless if it postulates entities (like light rays) whose properties cannot be tested by any observations; since all the optical phenomena can be comprehended by laws like those of reflection and refraction, the "concordance" of optical phenomena can be fully achieved by a treatment based on such laws.

C. A treatment of light based upon the laws of reflection and refraction is not sufficiently mathematical to serve the purposes of science as well as a theory like Huygens' or Newton's.

D. A theory of light like Huygens' or Newton's is superior, because it relates optical phenomena to a wider class of phenomena (mechanical phenomena), and because it provides general principles in terms of which it should be possible to investigate the behavior of light in situations not covered by the known generalizations.

E. A treatment of light based on generalizations like the law of refraction is preferable, because it is more directly concerned with expressing the order found in observed phenomena, which is the true purpose of science.

(3) Which of the following would the author of the above passage be most likely to regard as a decisive reason for rejecting a scientific theory?

A. The theory is not quantitative.

B. The theory is not concordant with certain phenomena.

C. The theory contains redundant elements.

D. The theory contains postulates which assign to certain entities properties which differ from any that have ever been found in visible objects or processes.

E. Each of the above would probably constitute a decisive reason for rejecting the theory.

(4) Which of the following is *not* a reason for regarding Young's work as a scientific advance, from the point of view of the above passage?

A. Young discovered a new optical phenomenon, previously unknown, namely the "internal fringes" in a shadow; this is an advance because a new phenomenon involves new relations of this phenomenon to others.

B. Young discovered a quantitative relation previously undiscerned in phenomena which Newton had observed.

C. Young applied to light a theoretical conception—that of wave-length—in terms of which a much wider concordance of optical phenomena was achieved than had been previously.

D. Young devised a way of determining the ratio of the velocities of light in two media independently of the law of refraction.

E. Each of the above correctly states a reason regarding Young's work as an advance.

In this illustration a new set of criteria for scientific theories is given, and the student is to use it in making particular judgments about scientific theories he has studied. Note the relatively simple test form which has been used to get at very complex judgments.

26. Now we will attempt to apply to this poem the doctrines of three of the critics you have studied this year.

I. Aristotle's *Poetics:*

(1) If a critic were to apply the principles of the *Poetics* to a study of this poem, he would be most likely to regard the *object* of imitation as

A. the "subject." . . .
B. the poet's universal idea about this "subject."
C. the speaker going through an emotional response to this "subject."
D. the nature of mankind.
E. the poet's moral character.

(2) And he would regard the *manner* of imitation as

A. lyric.
B. dramatic.
C. narrative.
D. mixed.
E. sonnet.

(3) Viewing the poem as a whole, he would be most likely to *praise* it *primarily* for

A. its clear and convincing demonstration of a universal truth of human nature.
B. its forceful warning to its readers to avoid a very great danger—a danger to which man, because of his basic nature, is especially susceptible.
C. its unified plot.
D. its vivid and moving rendition of a recognizably human action.
E. its evocation and purgation of the audience's pity and fear.

II. Elder Olson's *Prolegomena to a Poetics of the Lyric:*

(4) A critic applying the principles of Olson to a study of this poem would come to a different conclusion. One important reason for this difference can be found in Olson's general conception of poetry, for Olson, *unlike* Aristotle, believes that

A. poetry must be judged without regard to the character of the poet.
B. poetry has no reference to the real world.
C. a poem is a whole composed of mutually related parts.
D. the purpose of poetry is to state universal truths.
E. the purpose of poetry is not to state universal truths.

(5) Because of this belief, a critic using Olson's principles would be most likely to regard the poem before us as

A. a complex structure of related terms.
B. the imitation of a human action.
C. a warning to the readers.
D. the expression of the poet's feelings.
E. the expression of a universal truth about the "subject." . . .

(6) Because of this view, he might very well *censure* the last two lines of this poem because

A. they inculcate an attitude of resignation toward a great evil.
B. "the world" did not appear in the situation the poet originally set up.
C. it is in fact false that no one "knows well to shun the heaven that leads men to this hell."
D. they are not "in character" for the speaker of the poem.
E. they violate the rules of the particular poetic "form" within which the poet is working.

III. Plato's *Phaedrus:*

(7) A critic using the principles of the *Phaedrus* would emerge with still a third view of this poem. One important reason for his difference from the two preceding critics can be found in Plato's general conception of poetry, for Plato, *unlike either* Aristotle or Olson, believes that

A. a poem is a whole composed of mutually related parts.
B. poetry is related to real life.
C. poetry must not be judged by cold, logical criteria.
D. poetry must be judged without regard to the character of the poet.
E. poetry is a form of moral activity.

(8) Because of this belief, a critic using Plato's principles would most likely *censure* the last two lines of this poem because they

A. are not "in character" for the speaker of the poem.
B. are written rather than spoken aloud.
C. fail to state a general conclusion about the "subject." . . .
D. inculcate an attitude of resignation toward a great evil.
E. violate the rules of the particular poetic "form" within which the poet is working.

(9) The deficiency of these last two lines (indicated in the correct response to the preceding item), this critic might say, really results from the poet's improper handling of his subject in the rest of the poem. We can see, from the way Plato handles a similar subject in the *Phaedrus*, that a "Platonic" critic would claim this poet has erred because he

A. has never risen above the lowest level of his subject, the level of "excess."
B. has risen from the level of "excess" to that of "temperance," but has failed to go on to the highest level on which his subject can be viewed.
C. has begun on the highest level of his subject and worked down, instead of moving in the opposite and more correct direction.
D. has tried to grapple with a high level of his subject without going through the necessary preliminary investigation of the lower levels.
E. is treating his subject on a level that is not befitting the conversation of a moral dialectician.

This part of a much larger test in which the student is given a new poem and then asked a series of questions to elicit particular elements of knowledge, comprehension, and analysis. In the above questions he is asked to judge specific aspects of the poem, using three critical points of view. The students study the three critics Aristotle, Plato, and Olson in the course and are now using them as bases for their judgments.

FULL AND STABLE EMPLOYMENT POLICIES

27. The following two sets of items deal with (I) some of the basic *objectives* and underlying values stressed by different participants in the Senate discussion of the Murray Bill leading to the Employment Act of 1946; and (II) *methods* of policy appropriate for different stabilization objectives under specified conditions. . . .

I. Basic goals stressed by different groups in the 1945 Senate hearings on S. 380 (Murray, Full Employment Bill).

DIRECTIONS: For each item, blacken the answer space corresponding to the letter of the *one* group which would accept the formulation of basic values or goals stated in the item. Note: Give only the *one best answer*.

(1) "Full and stable employment means security and security is such an outstanding value that we should be prepared to pay *any* price for it." This statement would be accepted by

A. proponents of the Full Employment Bill.
B. at least some of the businessmen testifying.
C. all representatives of organized labor.
D. all of the above.
E. none of the above.

(2) "Freedom and security are largely mutually compatible and even supporting goals. But they can conflict if either is pursued too exclusively. Full and stable employment should be pursued only to the degree and by such methods as are compatible with the maintenance of basic economic and political freedoms." This statement would be accepted by

A. sponsors of the Full Employment Bill.
B. at least some of the businessmen testifying.

C. all representatives of organized labor.

D. all of the above.

E. none of the above.

(3) "Freedom, in the traditional American sense of the free enterprise system including economic and political freedoms, is the best, and in principle, sufficient condition for the achievement and maintenance of a reasonable level of employment and degree of stability. Government should normally confine itself to the removal of obstacles and the protection of traditional freedoms." This statement would be accepted by

A. sponsors of the Full Employment Bill.

B. at least some spokesmen for business or farmers.

C. other spokesmen for business and farmers, *and* representatives of organized labor.

D. all of the above.

II. Methods appropriate to different stabilization objectives.

Assuming general agreement about the desirability both of stabilizing employment at a high level and of the preservation of the freedoms accepted by all participants in the Hearings on S. 380 as basic to a "free enterprise economy," we may distinguish several more specific policy objectives and methods appropriate to these specific objectives. Specific policy objectives may be classified as

A. *Structural Reform:* Those policies which aim at long-range structural reforms (including institutions and rules of the game) which would (i) decrease the economy's disposition toward cumulative processes of contraction and unemployment or of overexpansion and inflation, and (ii) strengthen its capacity to sustain a high and stable rate of progressive expansion.

B. *Anti-depression* or *Recovery:* Those policies which aim at counteracting an incipient or already developed depression and stimulating a process of recovery in the direction of "full employment."

C. *Anti-inflation:* Those policies which aim at preventing or counteracting an incipient or already developed inflationary boom.

DIRECTIONS: The following items describe methods which may be appropriate to one or another of the above objectives. For each item, blacken the answer space corresponding to the letter of the above objective to which it is most appropriate. In answering the items assume that the method described is not counteracted by simultaneous methods which would have opposite effects and that freedoms basic to a "free enterprise economy" are to be preserved. Since almost all methods may be said to curtail at least some freedoms of some individuals or groups, the condition of "preservation of essential freedoms" means that the method should be such that its probable *net* results for the economy as a whole would not involve serious curtailment of the basic freedoms designated above. Blacken answer space

D. if none of the above apply (i.e., the method would not contribute to any of the objectives, or would violate the freedom condition).

(4) Increase in expenditures for public works financed by government borrowing from banks or by the use of public funds accumulated in previous years.

(5) Policies aiming at a reduction of monopoly power which is likely to be used for restriction of output.

(6) Increase in the reserve requirements for member banks of the Federal Reserve System towards legal maxima.

(7) Initiation of a "cheap money" policy by reduction in interest rates.

(8) Comprehensive planning and permanent direct controls on all prices, wages, production and jobs.

(9) Replacement of the fractional reserve system by a 100% reserve requirement for commercial banks.

In this set of questions, the students have the Senate hearings available to them. The first set of questions involve relating particular judgments to specific positions taken by representatives of different groups during the hearings. The second set of questions require the use of particular criteria and standards in making judgments about selected methods of dealing with the problem.

Test problems for evaluation behavior F

The student can make judgments of a work by using his own explicit set of criteria or standards (external criteria; F).

The final type of behavior for evaluation is the student's use of his own standards or criteria. In this type of behavior, he is to make his criteria or standards explicit and to demonstrate how they are relevant to judgments he evolves about a particular work, document, policy, or situation. Since each student may have his own criteria or standards, it is not likely that objective or recognition types of question forms could be used in testing for this behavior. Thus the major problem of the evaluator is to judge the adequacy of the student's use of his own criteria in evaluating a particular work or other material. The evaluator may in passing also judge the adequacy of the student's critical criteria or standards.

Essay Question (one hour, 40 points)

28. Write an essay of 400 to 600 words on one of the four poems assigned for outside reading during the third quarter:

    Bridges, *Nightingales;*
    Frost, *The Death of the Hired Man;*
    Housman, *To an Athlete Dying Young;*
    Tate, *Ode to the Confederate Dead.*

    Your essay should meet the following three conditions:

    (1) It should offer one or more judgments about the poem (e.g., the value of its intention, the success of its means to that end, its truth, its beauty, etc.).

    (2) It should make explicit the nature of each criterion employed, and explain what assumptions concerning the nature or ends of poetry make this criterion a significant basis for judgment.

    (3) It should discuss in considerable detail (the major part of your essay) whatever parts or aspects of the poem are pertinent to the judgment made—as proof that your conclusions are justified.

This essay requires the student to make his own criteria explicit and to apply them in judging a poem which was assigned for reading but not discussed in the course. The directions given to the student make it clear what he is to do and the basis on which his essay is to be judged.

Essay in Criticism: Madame Bovary (Time: 2 hours)

29. A critic has said of *Madame Bovary:*

    "Whatever virtues *Madame Bovary* may have, it certainly does not possess that of unity. This is supposed to be the story of Emma Bovary, yet it begins, not with her early life (which we learn of later only from a few brief comments), but with a detailed description of Charles' history from childhood on. Nor does the novel end where it should, but goes on after Emma's death to recount the subsequent fortunes of Charles and M. Homais. And why, even before Emma's death, is so much attention devoted to Homais? Or, for that matter, to Hippolyte, the club foot, or to the hideous blind beggar? Clearly, none of these characters plays a very significant part in Emma's catastrophe."

    Do you agree or disagree with the above judgment of the unity of *Madame Bovary*? In a well-organized, coherent essay of from 300 to 600 words, expound and defend your position, supporting your argument with specific references to the novel wherever possible. Your discussion *must* take into account all the episodes and characters mentioned by the above critic, although you should feel free to deal with them in any order you wish, and to bring in any others that you consider relevant. While your treatment of this problem will consider all these particulars, it should be directed to a judgment of the novel as a whole of some sort. Your essay should reveal your general critical position; but your understanding of this position should be demonstrated by your intelligent and sensitive *application* of it to the critical problem here presented, rather than by any elaborate excursion into esthetic theory.

    You are to assume that you are writing for a literature reader, who has read *Madame Bovary* and the critical texts of Humanities 3, but who must be *convinced* of your judgment of the novel.

    Remember that you will be judged, not only on what you say, but on how effectively you say it. It is suggested that you give at least 20 minutes to the careful planning of your essay before beginning to write, 80 minutes to the actual writing, and 20 minutes at the end to proofreading and revision, so that the essay in its final form represents your best intention.

This test item requires the student to relate a critic's position to his own with respect to a particular characteristic of the novel *Madame Bovary*. Again, the directions make it clear what the student is expected to do in his evaluation.

Essay in Critical Evaluation (Time: 2 hours)

30. Write an essay on *The Bewitched Mill* (1913), an oil painting by the 20th century German artist Franz Marc (1880–1916), in which you express your own critical evaluation of the picture, supporting your evaluation by specific discussion of the work.

During the course of your essay indicate the criteria you have used in your judgments, and reveal the assumptions about art on which your views are based. You may, if you wish, refer to various authors whose works have been studied in the course; this should be undertaken only as a natural and connected part of your essay and should not appear as a parade of knowledge or authority. These references should not be a substitute for the exposition of your own views, since your essay must stand by itself.

This essay question is somewhat more general than the preceding illustrations. Here the student may select what he wishes in presenting his evaluation of the picture. The picture is available to him during this part of the examination.

Critical Essay (Time: 2 hours)

31. Write a well-organized, coherent essay of from 300 to 600 words on the song entitled "Nocturne" from Benjamin Britten's *Serenade* for tenor solo, horn, and strings. Your essay should consist of three parts: the "Nocturne" (1) as viewed from the critical position of James Beattie, (2) as viewed from the critical position of Ernest Newman; and (3) your own critical evaluation and conclusion.

In writing the first two parts of your essay, bear in mind in each case the problems that it would be appropriate to pose. Do not rehearse the critical principles of Beattie and Newman; rather, write freely in what you consider to be their vein.

Throughout your essay you should concentrate upon the most significant and compelling points that can be made, and should support your argument with explicit references to the song wherever possible. The principles upon which your judgment is based should be demonstrated rather by your intelligent and sensitive *application* of them to the song than by any elaborate excursion into esthetic theory.

In this illustration the student is to judge the song from the position of two critics as well as from his own position. Note that he is not asked to write about his own standards and criteria. Instead he is to be judged on the basis of the application of his critical principles to the music. The student has the score of the *Serenade* available to him as he prepares the essay.

Essay on the Comparison of Two Lyric Poems (Time: 2 hours)

32. Below are printed two complete poems with certain similarities of subject. Write a well-organized, coherent essay of from 300 to 600 words, comparing the two poems, indicating which one you consider to be superior, and justifying your choice with as forceful an argument as you can produce. Although many things can be said about the two poems, you should concentrate upon the most significant and compelling points which can be made, and should support your argument with explicit references to the texts wherever possible. You should recognize, too, that appropriate treatment of this problem, while it will consider all significant details, will be directed to a judgment of the two poems as poetic wholes. Your essay should reveal the principles upon which your judgment is based, but your understanding of these principles should be demonstrated by your intelligent and sensitive *application* of them to the critical problem here presented, rather than by any elaborate excursion into esthetic theory.

Remember that you will be judged, not only on what you say, but on how effectively you say it. It is suggested that you give at least 20 minutes to the careful planning of your essay before beginning to write, 80 minutes to the actual writing, and 20 minutes at the end to proofreading and revision, so that the essay in its final form represents your best work.

Write legibly in ink, skipping every other line.

POEM A

I taste a liquor never brewed,
From tankards scooped in pearl;
Not all the vats upon the Rhine
Yield such an alcohol!

Inebriate of air am I,
And debauchee of dew,
Reeling, through endless summer days,
From inns of molten blue.

When landlords turn the drunken bee
Out of the foxglove's door,
When butterflies renounce their drams,
I shall but drink the more!

Till seraphs swing their snowy hats,
And saints to windows run,
To see the little tippler
Leaning against the sun!

POEM B

Away, where leaves scarce grown are strown,
O'er the hills by the dewdrops known,
Across the dales by the dewdrops known,
Away from the city I'll flee.

I'll seek me a hilly throne of stone,
Where summer flowers by the winds are blown,
Where woodland smells by the winds are blown,
And free as the winds I'll be.

There on my hilly throne alone,
Where skies of blue to me are shown,
Where wonderful shrubs to me are shown,
Laurel tree and buzzing bee.

In this illustration the student is asked to compare two poems as well as to make explicit the criteria on which he is judging them.

REFERENCES

American Council on Education Studies. *A design for general education.* Washington, D.C.: ACE, 1944.

Bloom, B. S. (Ed.) *Taxonomy of educational objectives: The classification of educational goals.* Handbook 1. *Cognitive domain.* New York: McKay, 1956.

French, W., and associates. *Behavioral goals of general education in high school.* New York: Russell Sage Foundation, 1957.

Taylor, C. W., & Barron, F. *Scientific creativity: Its recognition and development.* New York: Wiley, 1963.

Tyler, R. W. The fact-finding study of the testing program of the United States Armed Forces Institute, 1952–1954. Report to the USAFI, University of Chicago, July, 1954.

University Grants Commission. *Evaluation in higher education.* New Delhi: UGC, 1961.

10

Evaluation Techniques for Affective Objectives

. . . we must ask whether in immersing ourselves so exclusively in this cognitive function of education—in education for verbal-conceptual abilities—we have not severely neglected other important and sometimes simpler facets of personality and life—the esthetic pleasures, for instance, that accrue from sharpening the instruments of sensory perception, or the intrinsic values in the appreciation of poetry and art which are available to those whose education has cultivated their intuitive powers and refined their capacities for sympathy and feeling. [McMurrin, 1967, p. 42. Reprinted from the *Saturday Review*, January 14, 1967, a special issue produced in cooperation with the Committee for Economic Development, by permission of the publisher.]

Introduction

Throughout the years American education has maintained that among its most important ideals is the development of such attributes as interests, desirable attitudes, appreciation, values, commitment, and willpower. McMurrin's quote, however, documents the reality that the types of outcomes which in fact receive the highest priorities in our schools, to the detriment of these affective goals, are verbal-conceptual in nature.

The reasons for this emphasis on the cognitive in preference to the affective are several and interactive. Our system of education is geared to producing people who can deal with the words, concepts, and mathematical or scientific symbols so necessary for success in our technological society. These skills can be achieved through the communication of both specific and generalized knowledge and through the development of deductive and inductive habits of thought.

Such outcomes lend themselves to the well-developed verbal-conceptual methods of lectures, conversations, demonstrations, discussions, and the printed word, all so widely used in our schools. In contrast the techniques a teacher might use to help a pupil change his attitude toward a minority group, develop an aesthetic sensibility, or learn to enjoy studying mathematics are not nearly so well defined. And they are certainly not identical to the pedagogic techniques used in the development of cognition.

This is not to imply that the realizations of cognitive outcomes are not accompanied by changes in affect—quite the contrary; these separate outcomes may be very closely related. As B. O. Smith points out (1966, p. 53), ". . . to teach any concept, principle, or theory is to teach not only for its comprehension, but also for an attitude toward it—the acceptance or rejection of it as useful, dependable, and so forth." Indeed, certain established pedagogic techniques for producing acceptable cognitive outcomes can destroy any positive feeling a student might have toward a subject area. Suffice it to say it is possible for a learner to understand and be quite proficient in a subject matter area and still have a deep aversion or other negative affect toward the discipline. Before discussing evaluation techniques for affective outcomes, let us first examine some of the reasons American education has failed to emphasize affective goals.

Reasons for the neglect of affective outcomes

Fear of indoctrination

One of the reasons for the failure to give instructional emphasis to affective outcomes is related to the Orwellian overtones which attitudinal and value-oriented instruction often conjures up in the minds of teachers and the public. Can we teach values without engaging in indoctrination or brainwashing techniques so foreign to our concepts of education? Scriven deals specifically with this problem in his excellent paper "Student Values as Educational Objectives" (1966). He makes a distinction between values acquired in conjunction with cognitive learning, such as the valuing of objectivity and the scientific methods, and moral values, such as empathy and sympathy, which cannot be taught with cognitive techniques.

In regard to cognitive-related values, Scriven points out (1966, p. 42) that not teaching these is "not just cowardice but *incompetence, professional* incompetence." On the subject of moral behavior and conclusions, he points out that there is a moral imperative to instruct in these areas so that students will not be "ignorant of the empirical punch behind the morality behind the law and the institutions which incorporate this country's virtues and permit its vices."

The teaching of both cognitive and moral values can, however, avoid the charge of brainwashing if three notions are held in mind:

1. We teach as facts only those assertions which can really be objectively established . . . ; others we teach as hypotheses. Hence, we do not violate the rights of others to make their own choices where choice is rationally possible, nor their right to know the truth where it is known.
2. Good teaching does not consist primarily in requiring the memorization of conclusions the teacher thinks are true, but in developing the skills needed to arrive at and test conclusions. . . .
3. That certain conclusions should now be treated as established does not mean they cannot ever turn out to be wrong. . . .

(Scriven, 1966, pp. 44–45)

Contrary, then, to fears of accusations of brainwashing or indoctrination, if the dangers of a *1984* society are to be avoided, schools have an obligation to work toward the realization of affective objectives.

Failure to evaluate affective outcomes

Other reasons for which teachers neglect to give instructional emphasis to their often stated affective objectives are similar to the reasons for their failure to evaluate the student on affective outcomes. Teacher-made tests used to assess student performance are geared almost exclusively to cognitive outcomes. Standardized tests used by the schools compare student performance with that of some national norm group, and lay stress on intellectual tasks involving recognition or recall of previously learned knowledge and the reordering or application of this knowledge to solve problems posed by the examination.

There are cogent explanations given for the failure to evaluate the affective objectives. First, it is often assumed that, unlike most cognitive objectives, affective objectives cannot be attained in the relatively short instructional period of a week, month, semester, or year, and that therefore they cannot be evaluated in the school setting. This belief is implied in the statements of teachers who claim their goals are intangible or so long range that the attitudes, values, interests, and appreciations they have tried to develop in their students may not reveal themselves until much later in life—long after formal education has been completed. If this assumption were correct, then it would indeed be difficult to evaluate affective objectives. While the time it takes to bring about an affective behavioral change is undoubtedly a function of the complexity of the behavior being sought, this is also true for desired changes in cognitive behavior. There is evidence that, like certain cognitive objectives, many affective objectives can be attained relatively quickly and are therefore amenable to evaluation.

A second reason for hesitancy to evaluate affective objectives is that characteristics of this kind, unlike achievement competences, are considered to be a private rather than a public matter. A person's attitudes on social issues, his religious beliefs or lack of them, his political preferences are private concerns, this privacy guaranteed by our Constitution. How one spends his leisure time, the type of literature, art, music, or cinema he likes are considered questions of personal preference in our society. Because of this private quality of the affective life, teachers are hesitant to make evaluative judgments in these areas.

Closely related to this is the fact that most educators do not consider it appropriate to record a grade for a student's attitudes, values, interests, or appreciations. Thus, though such affective characteristics may impinge, favorably or unfavorably, in an unofficial way on the grade a student receives for his performance on a cognitive achievement test, for most teachers an examination to grade them directly would be unthinkable.

The need to evaluate affective objectives

Despite the reasons for hesitancy just given, if the aims of the school include in addition to cognitive objectives such affective outcomes as "a spirit of inquiry," "compliance with the law and school regulations," "ability to appreciate the structure of the real number system," "listens with pleasure to good music," and "increased appetite and taste for what is good in literature," it then has the obligation to evaluate the effectiveness of the curriculum in forming those behaviors. If it does not evaluate them, it has no evidence on which to base modifications of its curriculum and pedagogic methods. Further, a failure to evaluate leads, as we have previously stated, to the eventual disregard of the affective aspect of education and an overemphasis on verbal-conceptual instruction. This failure is due in part to a narrow view of the concept of evaluation and to a disregard of the distinction between the *formative* and *summative* evaluation of both the student and the curriculum. Evaluation should not be equated with assigning a grade or giving an examination, for it is a much broader practice that employs a multitude of evidence-gathering techniques to help in decisions about the quality of an individual's or a group's performance or the success of a curriculum in relation to stated objectives.

Although it may not be a good practice to assign a summative grade for affective behavior, it is often desirable to evaluate a student's affective behavior formatively. Such an evaluation is diagnostic in that it can indicate to the student his progress toward the attainment of such outcomes; it can be educational, for example, when he is given a profile of his academic and vocational interest patterns. The point is, however, that feedback to the student, not the assignment of a grade, should be the purpose of making a formative evaluation of affective objectives.

If a curriculum purports to bring about affective outcomes, then formative and summative evaluation of it should provide an assessment of its progress toward and final success in fostering these outcomes. Information on how the group reacts to certain techniques or methods used in the hope of modifying an attitude can give formative direction for course improvement. That a large proportion of the class, contrary to the course objective, still holds an undesirable attitude on a social issue at the end of the course gives summative information on the effectiveness of the curriculum.

In both cases, techniques that assure anonymity can be used to gather group information. Thus it is possible to evaluate a curriculum's affective objectives both formatively and summatively without grading an individual's private and personal affective behavior.

This chapter will outline some typical affective objectives and illustrate them by giving behavioral definitions and techniques of measurement. In addition, a wide range of methods will be presented which a classroom teacher could use for the formative evaluation of a student and the formative and summative evaluation of a curriculum on the affective objectives of instruction.

Defining affective objectives in behavioral terms

The necessity for clear unambiguous, operational statements as the first step in instructional planning and evaluation was pointed out in Chap. 2. This need is no less important for affective than for cognitive objectives. However, because of the numerous interpretations people can place on affective concepts, the behavioral specification of these concepts is often neglected. Further, because of the hesitancy noted earlier to evaluate affective outcomes, the specification of behavioral manifestations of affective concepts is very seldom carried out.

This is not to imply that affective objectives cannot be stated in behavioral terms, but only to point out that teachers often neglect to give careful thought to the problem of what behaviors will lead them to infer the presence or absence of some affective construct in the student.

Many teachers find it more difficult to define affective objectives behaviorally than to operationalize cognitive ones. Furthermore, the large number of affective objectives found in the literature use concepts such as "attitudes," "values," "appreciation," and "interest" in a wide variety of ways. For example, objectives dealing with interest can encompass behaviors ranging from mere awareness that a given phenomenon exists to avid pursuit of experience of the phenomenon. "Appreciation" can also refer to a simple behavior such as mere perception of a phenomenon or to such a complex, emotionally toned behavior as active enjoyment when experiencing the phenomenon.

Taxonomy of educational objectives: Affective domain

The *Taxonomy of Educational Objectives*, Handbook 2, *Affective Domain* (Krathwohl, Bloom, & Masia, 1964), provides the teacher with a useful guide for operationalizing and classifying educational objectives which emphasize a feeling line, an emotion, or a degree of acceptance or rejection. The affective *Taxonomy* is summarized in the Appendix to Part I of this book along with Handbook 1, *Cognitive Domain*.

At the outset it should be mentioned that a close relationship exists between the cognitive and affective *Taxonomies;* as noted earlier, there is an intimate relationship between cognitive and affective behavioral changes. This relationship is operative at the instructional as well as the evaluation level. As the authors of the affective *Taxonomy* point out,

> Each affective behavior has a cognitive behavior counterpart of some kind and vice versa. An objective in one domain has a counterpart in the opposite domain, though often we do not take cognizance of it. . . . Each domain is sometimes used as a means to the other, though the more common route is from the cognitive to the affective. Theory statements exist which permit us to express one in terms of the other and vice versa.
>
> (Krathwohl, Bloom, & Masia, 1964, p. 62)

As this quotation indicates, affective qualities may be assessed indirectly through the use of traditional cognitive techniques. B. O. Smith (1966) incorporates knowledge and ability explicitly and such other cognitive behaviors as comprehension and evaluation implicitly in his list of six procedures for measuring value achievement. While these cognitive techniques will shed light on certain kinds of affective behavior, more direct affective techniques must also be employed in a well-developed, comprehensive evaluation of a curriculum.

The affective *Taxonomy* arranges objectives along a hierarchical continuum. At the lowest point on this continuum, the subject is merely aware of a phenomenon, simply able to perceive it. At the next level he is willing to attend to the phenomenon. The next step finds him responding to the phenomenon with feeling. At the next point the subject goes out of his way to respond to the phenomenon. Next he conceptualizes his behavior and feelings and organizes these into a structure. The subject reaches the highest point in the hierarchy when the structure becomes his life outlook.

The authors of the *Taxonomy* describe this continuum as one of internalization, in which the affective component passes from a level of bare awareness to a position of some power and then to control of a person's behavior. The five categories of internalization, arranged in order of degree, are these:

1.0 Receiving (attending) The first category is defined as sensitivity to the existence of certain phenomena and stimuli, that is, the willingness to receive or attend to them. A typical objective at this level would be: "The student develops a tolerance for a variety of types of music."

2.0 Responding "Responding" refers to a behavior which goes beyond merely attending to the phenomena; it implies active attending, doing something with or about the phenomena, and not merely perceiving them. Here a typical objective would be: "The student voluntarily reads magazines and newspapers designed for young children."

3.0 Valuing Behavior which belongs to this level of the taxonomy goes beyond merely doing something with or about certain phenomena. It implies perceiving them as having worth and consequently revealing consistency in behavior related to these phenomena. A typical objective at this level would be: "Writes letters to the press on issues he feels strongly about."

4.0 Organization Organization is defined as the conceptualization of values and the employment of these concepts for determining the interrelationship among values. Here a typical objective might be: "Begins to form judgments as to the major directions in which American society should move."

5.0 Characterization The organization of values, beliefs, ideas, and attitudes into an internally consistent system is called "characterization." This goes beyond merely determining interrelationships among various values; it implies their organization into a total philosophy or world view. Here a typical objective would include: "Develops a consistent philosophy of life" [Krathwohl et al., 1964, pp. 176–185].

As noted earlier, commonly used terms such as "interest," "appreciation," "attitude," "value," and "adjustment" take on a variety of meanings in relation to the taxonomic categories. Thus an attitudinal objective, when translated into behavioral terms, can range from responding behavior, in which ". . . the student was expected to display a particular behavior, especially with a certain amount of emotion (enthusiasm, warmth, or even disgust, if appropriate)," to organization, "in which he might go out of his way to display the value or to communicate to others about it" (Krathwohl et al., 1964, p. 36).

The use of the word "appreciation" offers another example of the varying degrees of internalization of behavior that are possible in specifications of affective objectives. "Appreciation of literature" is a common objective among English teachers, and it illustrates two points. First, the objective needs to be clarified further in terms of the behaviors which will be accepted as evidence that the student does appreciate literature. In other words, the objectives must be operationalized; the term "appreciation" must be more fully specified and defined. The second point is contingent on the further operationalization of the objective: the degree of internalization needs to be stated. The reason is appreciation behaviors cut across at least three taxonomic categories of internalization.

The Eight-year Study

The experience of the Evaluation Committee of the Eight-year Study (Smith & Tyler, 1942) with the objective "appreciation of literature" illustrates the need both for further specificity in the statement of the behavior and for definition of the degree of internalization involved once the behavior has been detailed. The committee members selected seven general behaviors they felt were central to appreciation; they specified these further in turn by listing examples of overt acts and verbal responses which they would accept as evidence of the presence or absence of each of the seven general behaviors. The resulting behavior list was as follows; note the various levels of internalization represented in the behavior statements:

1. SATISFACTION IN THE THING APPRECIATED
   - 1.1. He reads aloud to others, or simply to himself, passages which he finds unusually interesting.
   - 1.2. He reads straight through without stopping, or with a minimum of interruption.
   - 1.3. He reads for considerable periods of time.
2. DESIRE FOR MORE OF THE THING APPRECIATED
   - 2.1. He asks other people to recommend reading which is more or less similar to the thing appreciated.
   - 2.2. He commences this reading of similar things as soon after reading the first as possible.
   - 2.3. He reads subsequently several books, plays, or poems by the same author.
3. DESIRE TO KNOW MORE ABOUT THE THING APPRECIATED
   - 3.1. He asks other people for information or sources of information about what he has read.
   - 3.2. He reads supplementary materials, such as biographies, history, criticism, etc.
   - 3.3. He attends literary meetings devoted to reviews, criticisms, discussions, etc.
4. DESIRE TO EXPRESS ONE'S SELF CREATIVELY
   - 4.1. He produces, or at least undertakes to produce, a creative project more or less after the manner of the thing appreciated.
   - 4.2. He writes critical appreciations.
   - 4.3. He illustrates what he has read in some one of the graphic, spatial, musical or dramatic arts.
5. IDENTIFICATION OF ONE'S SELF WITH THE THING APPRECIATED
   - 5.1. He accepts, at least while he is reading, the persons, places, situations, events, etc., as real.
   - 5.2. He dramatizes, formally or informally, various passages.
   - 5.3. He imitates, consciously and unconsciously, the speech and actions of various characters in the story.
6. DESIRE TO CLARIFY ONE'S OWN THINKING WITH REGARD TO THE LIFE PROBLEMS RAISED BY THE THING APPRECIATED
   - 6.1. He attempts to state, either orally or in writing, his own ideas, feelings, or information concerning the life problems with which his reading deals.
   - 6.2. He examines other sources for more information about these problems.
   - 6.3. He reads other works dealing with similar problems.
7. DESIRE TO EVALUATE THE THING APPRECIATED
   - 7.1. He points out, both orally and in writing, the elements which in his opinion make it good literature.
   - 7.2. He explains how certain unacceptable elements (if any) could be improved.
   - 7.3. He consults published criticisms.

(Smith & Tyler, 1942, pp. 251–252)

Additional clarification of an objective such as "appreciation of literature" occurs when items are developed for inclusion in an inventory. Items taken from the Literature Questionnaire: the Novel, Test 3.22, of the Eight-year Study (Progressive Education Association, 1940) illustrate for each of the seven appreciation categories how the process of definition is carried through to the item-development stage.

The student was instructed to mark each question in the following manner:

A. means that you answer the question *Yes*
U. means that you are unable to answer *Yes* or *No* to the question
D. means that your answer to the question is *No*

[Derives satisfaction from reading]

1. After you had started this novel were you more interested in finishing it than in doing almost anything else?

[Wants to read more]

2. Do you have any desire to read this novel or any parts of it again?

[Becomes curious about reading]

3. Would you like to know more about the life of the author?

[Expresses himself creatively]

4. If you were an artist, would you like to illustrate this novel?

[Identifies himself with reading]

5. Were you able to picture in your mind how some of the characters in the novel must have looked?

[Relates his reading to life]

6. Do you feel that reading this novel has helped you to understand more clearly why people act as they do in various circumstances?

[Evaluates his reading]

7. Did you read this novel without giving much thought to the merits or defects of the plot?

(Progressive Education Association, 1940, items 55, 27, 11, 16, 6, 63, 21.)

A classroom teacher or group of teachers preparing an affective inventory would do well to follow the criteria used by the participants in the Eight-year Study in selecting the above items. First, the teachers judged the item to be a definition of what they meant by each behavior category. Thus each item became a further operational definition of each of the appreciation categories. The second criterion was that each item describe a behavior which high school students are apt to exhibit or a situation they are apt to find themselves in. The final criterion for item selection was that the behavior or situation described deal only with things which the student might be expected to report honestly. If the instrument is designed primarily for evaluating the student, this last criterion becomes extremely important. As has been previously pointed out, if formative or summative curriculum evaluation is desired, group data are sufficient. Anonymity can therefore be guaranteed to the respondents, which lessens further the chance of their giving dishonest answers, unconsciously or consciously.

One subject-matter area with many affective objectives is reading. For example, a common objective among teachers today is that "the student develop an interest in reading." The Evaluation Committee of the Eight-year Study posited the following four behaviors as central to the realization of this objective (suggested ways of gathering evidence about each included in brackets after each behavior):

1. The reading should be abundant. [An item that asks "How many books have you read within the past month?" might be one of several used to determine the extent of a respondent's reading.]
2. The reading should be varied as to type and content. It should include, for example, both fiction and nonfiction; it should reflect a wide range of human experience, and deal with many subjects. [An item that asks "Do you care to balance your reading program by including in it various types of books, like books from American and foreign authors?" would be one of several used to determine the variety of one's reading.]
3. The reading should be selective, showing some concentration of interest upon subjects or types of reading suited to the reader. [An item that asks "Does reading a book often make you want to read books which deal with the same topic from another point of view?" could be used with similar items to determine the selectivity of one's reading program.]
4. The reading should be increasingly mature, gradually increasing in difficulty, complexity, and depth of insight. [An item that asks students to "List the authors and works you have read during the past semester" could be used to measure this.]

(Smith & Tyler, 1942, p. 319)

There are, of course, numerous techniques that could be used to measure an objective such as interest in reading. A wide range of methods for measuring affect will be discussed later in this chapter. The questionnaire items suggested for the reading objectives above are meant primarily to illustrate further behaviors that would be acceptable as evidence of reading interest as well as to indicate measuring techniques that could be employed.

Lewy's survey of affective objectives

Lewy (1966) has carefully screened several published curricula in reading, and has selected the following four affective objectives common to most reading curricula and independent of experience with specific cognitive content:

1. The student should develop a life-long habit of reading good books of fiction and non-fiction.
2. The student should use reading as a tool for acquiring information.
3. The student should find relaxation and enjoyment in reading good books.
4. The student should develop a sense of the importance of evaluating and planning his reading program.

(Lewy, 1966, p. 58)

In developing a series of instruments to measure aspects of these affective reading objectives at four taxonomic levels of internalization, Lewy gives further specificity to the objectives. For example, objective 3, "The student should find relaxation and enjoyment in reading good books," can be further operationalized at different levels of internalization by the following questionnaire items, to be answered "yes" or "no":

1.0 Receiving

8. Would you be presently interested in joining a club which meets frequently to discuss books?

2.0 Responding

9. Is it usually impossible for you to read for as long as an hour without being bored?

3.0 Valuing

10. Do you often become so absorbed in your reading of a book that you are almost unaware of what is going on around you?

4.0 Organization

11. Has your reading of books or articles ever led you to take up any new hobbies or interests?

(Lewy, 1966, pp. 168–174, from items 3–78)

Items 12 to 27 contain additional forced-choice (yes-or-no) questions used by Lewy to measure aspects of his affective reading objectives. These items are further classified by levels on internalization of the *Taxonomy*.

1.0 Receiving

12. Do you wish you had more time to devote to reading?
13. Do you have in mind one or two books which you would like to read sometime soon?
14. Would you like to have a collection of books?
15. Would you like to know more about famous American contemporary authors?

2.0 Responding

16. If you see some books in the rooms of your friends when you visit them, do you often read their titles or the descriptions printed on their jackets?
17. Walking in the streets in your leisure time, do you like to stop before the windows of the bookstores and read the titles of the books?
18. Once you have begun a book, do you usually finish it within a few days' time?
19. Is it unusual for you to spend a whole afternoon or evening reading a book?

3.0 Valuing

20. Do you ever spend time browsing in a library or book store?
21. Is it very unusual for you to become so enthusiastic about a book that you urge several of your friends to read it?
22. Do you have a collection of your own books, not counting school textbooks?
23. If some book is not available in your school library, would it be unusual for you to try to borrow it from some other library?

4.0 Organization

24. Do you like to listen to opinions expressed by other people on books which you read?

25. Have any of the books you read markedly influenced your choice of a life's vocation?
26. Have any of the books which you read markedly influenced your views about social problems like unemployment?
27. Have any of the books you read markedly influenced your views about marriage or family life?

(Lewy, 1966, pp. 168–170, items 1, 2, 4, 5, 6, 8, 9, 10, 11, 12, 18, 34, 38, 39, 40.)

After reviewing published curricula, Lewy also chose common affective objectives for the fields of music and mathematics. In music he found that the following were the three most common affective objectives:

1. The student should gain a lasting enjoyment of good music.
2. The student should cultivate a taste for good music.
3. The student should become aware of music as an important part of our cultural heritage.

(Lewy, 1966, pp. 57–58)

As is the case with his affective reading objectives, items used by Lewy to measure these affective music objectives at four levels of internalization define these objectives more clearly. For example, objective 3, "The student should become aware of music as an important part of our cultural heritage," is further specified by the following questionnaire items, the first three to be answered "true" or "not true," the last "yes" or "no":

1.0 Receiving

28. I have never had the wish to improve my understanding of music.

2.0 Responding

29. It is not unusual for me to talk about topics related to music.

3.0 Valuing

30. I like to listen to records which contain explanations or discussion of the music played.

4.0 Organization

31. Have you ever had to explain or discuss the [question,] What makes a musical composition immortal?

(Lewy, 1966, pp. 160, 163, 165, items 4, 43, 74, 77.)

The items below, arranged by taxonomic level of internalization, are examples of additional forced-choice (true–not true) questions chosen by Lewy to measure aspects of his music objectives.

1.0 Receiving

32. I have never had the desire to go to a concert.
33. It is very unusual for me to play the radio for the purpose of listening to music. (Do not forget what the word music stands for in this questionnaire!)
34. If my parents or friends play the radio and listen to music, I prefer to leave the room.
35. I have never had the wish to improve my understanding of music.
36. I would like to devote some time to listening to good music.

2.0 Responding

37. Being with friends, or in a party, I usually welcome suggestions to listen to records of classical music.
38. There are several musical pieces which I like so much that I would like to hear them performed by various musicians.
39. It is unusual for me to listen to music continuously for a period of two hours.
40. I do attend concerts at least once a year.
41. When I attend a concert, it is usually at the urging of somebody else (my parents or friends).

3.0 Valuing

42. It is not unusual for me to talk about topics related to music.
43. If I like a certain musical piece, I often recommend it to my friends for the purpose of listening to it.
44. In several instances I tried to convince my friends that they should devote some time for listening to music.
45. Quite often I read articles [on music] with great interest.

4.0 Organization

46. When listening to music, I usually try to make judgments about the quality of the performance.

47. It is not unusual for me to compare performance of the same music by different musicians.
48. I like to exchange views on the quality of performance with others who have heard the same program.
49. In forming an opinion on performance, I consider the technique of the performers.

(Lewy, 1966, pp. 160–166, from items 1–86.)

In the field of mathematics, Lewy found the two most common affective objectives to be these:

1. The student should appreciate the function of mathematics in our society.
2. The student should perceive mathematics as a discipline which enhances logical thinking and reasoning.

(Lewy, 1966, p. 58)

The second objective is further delineated at four levels of internalization by the following items:

1.0 Receiving

50. People sometimes try to find better ways to do things, such as using logarithms for simplifying arithmetical computations. Would you be interested in hearing the idea explained? [Yes or no]

2.0 Responding

51. Do you frequently use diagrams in presenting your thoughts? [Yes or no]

3.0 Valuing

52. Would you spend some time intensively studying the meaning of a complex design? [Yes or no]

4.0 Organization

53. Have you ever thought about what is the meaning of "beauty in mathematics"? [Yes or no].

(Lewy, 1966, pp. 151–157, items 15, 40, 42, 65.)

Items 54 to 70 are additional forced-choice questions (true–false and yes–no) chosen by Lewy to measure aspects of his affective mathematics objectives. These items are further arranged by taxonomic levels of internalization.

1.0 Receiving

54. Do you feel that [the designs shown] are just a lot of uninteresting lines and shapes?
55. Do you think that [either] of these designs [is] attractive?
56. Would you like to see more designs of this kind?
57. Would you like to know more details about these kinds of designs, such as when were they prepared, by whom, etc.?

2.0 Responding

You probably had to prove geometric problems like the following:

Prove that if a pentagon inscribed in a circle has equal angles, then its sides are equal.

58. Did you often wish you should not have to bother with problems like this?
59. Would it be unusual for you to try to solve problems like this on your own accord?
60. Would you enjoy helping students to solve problems like this?

61. Would you feel bored if one would speak about problems like this?

62. Have you read some popular books dealing with mathematics?

3.0 Valuing

63. Mathematics is a very good field for creative people to enter.

64. Unless one is planning to become a mathematician or scientist, the study of advanced mathematics is not very important.

65. Almost anyone can learn mathematics if he is willing to study.

66. Mathematics (Algebra, Geometry, etc.) is not useful for problems of everyday life.

67. In the near future most jobs will require a knowledge of advanced mathematics.

4.0 Organization

The following is a quotation:

"No music nor poem, no painting, no other work of art gives me a greater sense of the beauty of harmony than a well developed body of mathematical doctrine, and I cannot avoid the feeling that there are many people who are able in some measure to add the same pleasure to their life."

68. Have you ever experienced a sense of beauty in mathematics as described in this statement?

69. In your writing or speeches, have you ever tried expressing your opinion on the importance of mathematics in our life?

70. Do you agree that the word "elegance" is suitable for describing some solution to mathematical problems?

(Lewy, 1966, pp. 150–158, from items 1–71.)

The examples above, from the Eight-year Study and Lewy's work, illustrate the fact that affective objectives can be stated in terms of student behaviors that are acceptable as evidence of the presence or absence of the affective construct. As pointed out in Chap 2, defining any objective, cognitive or affective, takes careful thought, and can often be best accomplished by interested teachers working cooperatively to state objectives. The illustrations used above are for the most part forced-choice questionnaire items; however, as noted earlier, there are numerous additional techniques available to those interested in evaluating affective outcomes. The remainder of this chapter considers various alternative methods of making formative and summative evaluations of affective outcomes.

Methods of evaluating affective outcomes

The next step in the evaluation process for the teacher who has defined his objectives in behavioral terms is that of devising situations and techniques which will allow the student to manifest the desired affective behavior. This important step is not so easy with affective outcomes as it is with cognitive behaviors, which lend themselves more readily to evaluation through the traditional paper and pencil achievement test. In fact, if the students feel that the evaluation techniques used are tests, in that grade penalties or rewards are associated with their performance on the instrument, the validity of the results will be highly questionable. That is, if a student feels his affective behavior is subject to either criticism or grading, there is a possibility that he will "fake" the desired behavior.

We have noted earlier the justifiable hesitancy teachers feel about grading affective behavior. However, summative and formative evaluation of the affective goals of the curriculum is another matter. Group data on affective behavior are all that is required for curriculum decisions. If a large proportion of the students have not achieved the affective behaviors sought for in the course, then action can be taken to change deficient methods or materials as needed.

The acceptability of group results for the evaluation of outcomes makes it possible for the teacher to guarantee the students' anonymity by allowing them to omit their names from their responses to affective instruments. Sometimes, however, it is desirable to identify individuals so that information derived from the answers can be used in conference with them for formative self-evaluation and guidance. When this is the case, then the student should be assured that his performance will not be criticized, let alone marked. This assurance can serve the same purpose as a guarantee of anonymity once the student is convinced that the results are in fact treated scrupulously in a confidential, unthreatening manner by school authorities. Such trust is the basis of any good guidance program in a school, and there is no reason teachers cannot treat affective information the way it is handled in a counselor-counselee relationship.

Once teachers realize that evaluation of affective outcomes need not either infringe upon a student's right to privacy or involve the assignment of a grade, then there are many techniques available for use in the formative or summative evaluation of a curriculum's affective objectives.

The interview schedule

The interview technique involves a face-to-face encounter of the interviewer, who asks carefully developed questions, and the respondent. The interview can be structured or unstructured in format.

In the structured interview, the wording and sequence of the questions are fixed. The interviewer is given little or no freedom to deviate from the fixed schedule except to clarify misunderstanding or ambiguities and to branch into other sections of the schedule when certain criteria are met. His principal job is to present the question to the respondent and record his answer. An example of a structured interview schedule and the directions given to the interviewer is provided by the following excerpt from a schedule developed by the National Opinion Research Center (Greeley & Rossi, 1966). After reading the directions to the respondent, the interviewer merely circles one of the codes, representing columns on an IBM card, to the right of each job.

71. I am going to read you a list of jobs. If a son of yours chose each job tell me whether you would feel *very pleased, somewhat pleased, somewhat disappointed,* or *very disappointed.*

(CIRCLE CODES IN FOLLOWING TABLE.)

	Very Pleased	*Somewhat Pleased*	*Somewhat Disappointed*	*Very Disappointed*	*Don't Know*
A. Business Executive	X	0	2	3	1
B. High School Teacher	5	6	8	9	7
C. Priest	X	0	2	3	1
D. Bank Teller	5	6	8	9	7
E. Author	X	0	2	3	1
F. Carpenter	5	6	8	9	7
G. Stock Broker	X	0	2	3	1
H. Furniture Mover	5	6	8	9	7

(Greeley & Rossi, 1966, p. 309, item 57.)

A classroom teacher who desires to use the structured interview approach does not always need a coding scheme as elaborate as the one illustrated above. The following questions are samples of structured interview items developed for a summative evaluation of affect toward an experimental course in Russian.[1] The respondents were culturally disadvantaged high school students who had long records of scholastic failure. The interviewer asked each question and then marked the alternative which most closely corresponded with the student's free answer.

72. How much do you like your Russian course?
    a) a lot
    b) indifferent
    c) not much
    d) don't know
73. Why?
    a) teacher
    b) subject matter
    c) fact that it's a special class
    d) friends are not in it
    e) get credit without work
    f) hardness or easiness
    g) ____________________
74. What is the most important thing you've learned in your Russian course so far?
    a) all teachers are not bad
    b) a good teacher can make a subject interesting

[1] This illustration is borrowed from items 1, 5, and 7 of an unpublished instrument developed by Dr. Peter W. Airasian, presently at Boston College, for the late Mr. Wayne Fisher, of the University of Chicago Laboratory School.

c) content response
d) I can do something well
e) a new respect for school
f) a new understanding of other school topics
g) a better understanding of current events
h) the relation between what goes on in school and out of school
i) ______________________________

75. What do other students in the course think of it?
a) like
b) dislike
c) indifferent
d) don't talk about it
e) afraid to say

76. What do students not in the class think of it?
a) a good idea
b) wish they had a course like it
c) don't ever say
d) dislike it
e) ______________________________

In the unstructured interview, a limited number of key questions about the topics of interest are constructed in order to maximize the analytic values of the responses, but within these limitations the interviewer listens and probes rather than leads. Here the approach is nondirective and the interviewer has almost unlimited freedom to explore subtle nuances, thereby clarifying a respondent's answers. This technique broadens and deepens the evaluative information by encouraging a more spontaneous and more immediately personal expression of attitudes on the part of the respondent. It enables him to indicate the whys and wherefores of the values he expresses and the attitudes he reflects.

In employing the unstructured interview to gather information about affective objectives, the teacher must be careful not to lead the respondent or influence him so that he gives what he considers to be the expected answer. Obviously the unstructured interview is more time-consuming to administer and process than is the structured interview. Despite this drawback, the unstructured instrument can give a teacher information impossible to gather in any other way.

Further, the unstructured technique has three additional uses: first, it can serve to suggest ideas for writing structured items; second, when used with a small sample in addition to a structured interview technique, it allows the investigator to check on the validity of the structured data; finally, it can add flesh and blood to the skeletal findings of the structured approach.

The open-ended question

The open-ended question calls for the respondent to answer by writing a statement which may vary in length. Raths, Harmin, and Simon (1966) list some open-ended questions which have been effective in getting at attitudes, beliefs, activities, and values:

77. With a gift of $100, I would . . .
78. If this next weekend were a three-day weekend, I would want to . . .
79. My best friends can be counted on to . . .
80. My bluest days are . . .
81. I can hardly wait to be able to . . .
82. My children won't have to . . . Because . . .
83. People can hurt my feelings the most by . . .
84. If I had a car of my own . . .
85. I've made up my mind to finally learn how to . . .
86. If I could get a free subscription to two magazines, I would select . . . Because . . .
87. Some people seem to want only to . . .
88. The night I stayed up later than ever before I . . .
89. If I could have seven wishes . . .
90. I believe . . .
91. Secretly I wish . . .
92. My advice to the world would be . . .

(Raths, Harmin, & Simon, 1966, pp. 137–138, items 1–16.)

The open-ended questionnaire has been widely used to measure attitude structure and socialization. Getzels and Walsh (1958) report on an interesting technique that can be used not only to measure socialization but also to reduce the tendency of respondents to indicate attitudes more favorable than their true beliefs. Their approach to the open-ended questionnaire involves the use of two instruments: the paired "direct" and the "projective" questionnaire. In the direct questionnaire each item includes a first-person pronoun; in the projective questionnaire the same items are phrased in the third person.

In responding to the direct instrument, the subject is fully aware of the self-revelatory and possibly evaluative nature of his responses. Because of this his response represents "the level of behavior at which the individual *permits* society to look at him" (Getzels & Walsh, 1958, p. 3). The projective questionnaire, in contrast, is devoid of personal reference, and thus affords a truer measure of respondents' beliefs. Several illustrative items may be drawn from Getzels and Walsh's monograph:

93. When I break a window while playing, I . . .	93a. When Alice breaks a window while playing, she . . .
94. Whenever they ask me to be in charge, I . . .	94a. Whenever they ask Freda to be in charge, she . . .
95. If the teacher caught me cheating on the test, I . . .	95a. If the teacher caught Bea cheating on the test, Bea . . .

(Getzels & Walsh, 1958, pp. 29–33, items 5, 23, 36; pp. 32–36, items 23, 13, 36.)

When used in the formative or summative evaluation of a curriculum that purports to change attitudes, the "projective" version will reduce the conscious and unconscious tendencies students have to give what they consider to be the socially acceptable response. Further, if both the direct and the projective versions are used, a student's responses can be classified as either positive or negative. The score is the number of negative responses. The proportion of negative responses on the projective version to positive responses on the direct instrument gives a discrepancy score between personal hypotheses and expressed reactions. This technique, coupled with assurances of confidentiality to the respondent, could help construct a truer picture of the curriculum's impact on attitudes.

The open-ended-question technique has two principal advantages from an evaluation point of view. First, it is an excellent device for making a formative evaluation of either the curriculum or the student. Student responses to open-ended questions can show the teacher areas of common concern, points of misunderstanding, and interests and attitudes on the part of the class which can then receive additional instructional emphasis while the curriculum is still fluid. When the student is aware of the teacher's objectives, realizes that he is free to answer such questions or not, and knows that he will not be graded on his opinions, then the questions serve to give the student valuable insights into his affective behavior. For formative student evaluation, Raths, Harmin, and Simon (1966) point out that the teacher can ask the student to clarify his response further, point out inconsistencies or assumptions that have been made, underline extreme statements, and ask the student such questions about his responses as "Have you done anything about this?" All these teacher actions give the student formative evaluative information about the present status, growth, or development of such affective characteristics as his interests, attitudes, and values.

The second value of the open-ended-question technique is similar to an advantage of the unstructured interview, described earlier: that the responses of the students become a rich source of alternative answers for a structured questionnaire. The open-ended-question technique allows the respondent freedom and spontaneity, but it is time-consuming and sometimes difficult to read; therefore, it is often desirable to construct a questionnaire which forces the respondent to choose among alternative replies. This in turn expedites and adds objectively to the processing of responses. The construction of meaningful and attractive alternative answers to items becomes easier when a teacher has first collected responses to open-ended questions.

The closed-item questionnaire

The questionnaire with fixed alternatives is similar to the structured interview described earlier except that the respondent completes it without the aid of an interviewer. The closed-item instrument takes several forms; it may be a rating scale, inventory, or index. The examples below illustrate the range of formats the closed-item questionnaire can assume as well as the wide varieties of behaviors to which it is applicable. Throughout the discussion the focus will remain on the item format and will not undertake to give an inclusive accounting of the several forms just mentioned.

Two examples of the format of items designed to evaluate a student's affect toward the study of mathematics are taken from the National Longitudinal Study of Mathematical Abilities (1964). Here the student is asked to choose the letter of the response that best fills the blank in the sentence.

96. I would like to teach English _____ than I would like to teach mathematics.
    [A.] a lot more
    [B.] a little more
    [C.] a little less
    [D.] a lot less

97. I like the problem "359 − 574 + 6840 − 999 − 46937 + 9748 + 87483 = ?" _____ than the problem "Jane is half as tall as Dick. Joe is half as tall as Jane. Mack is half as tall as Joe. Dick is 60 inches tall. How tall is Joe?"
    [A.] a lot more
    [B.] a little more
    [C.] a little less
    [D.] a lot less

(National Longitudinal Study of Mathematical Abilities, 1964, p. 25, item 12; p. 23, item 2.)

As Cronbach (1963) has pointed out, if these types of affective questions are asked in a context removed from the course in question, the validity of the responses is increased. Thus questionnaires designed to measure attitudes toward English are more trustworthy when administered by a neutral person (for instance, a guidance counselor or homeroom teacher) than when administered by the English teacher who wishes to have this kind of summative curriculum information.

In a questionnaire designed to evaluate changes in affect toward music, the following directions precede a list of fifty-one composers:

98. Please indicate your feeling about each [composer listed below] by circling the appropriate letter on the answer sheet in the following manner:

    ENCIRCLE: *A* if you enjoy *listening* to the music of the composer and do so *frequently*.
    B if you enjoy *listening* to the music but *do not do so frequently*.
    C if you *do not enjoy listening* to the music of the composer.
    D if you *are not acquainted* with the music of the composer *at all*.

    You are to encircle only *one* letter for each composer.

(Masia, 1965, p. 1, directions for items 28–78.)

A modification of the paired direct and projective technique of Getzels and Walsh also lends itself to the closed-item format, as is illustrated in the following item. The directions instruct the respondent to guess how the person described, an average person, would act in a difficult situation, and then how the respondent would act under the same circumstances.

A man is walking down a deserted street at 2:00 A.M. As he turns the corner he sees a hoodlum striking a woman about the head and trying to take her purse. She holds on to the purse tenaciously. The man knows that he should go to her aid. There is no one else to call for help in the area. The man could turn back around the corner and no one would know.

99. If a man goes to her aid the attacker might become frightened and run. The attacker does not seem armed.

Would the man try to help the woman?	Would you try to help the woman?
__a. Definitely	__a. Definitely
__b. Probably	__b. Probably
__c. Probably not	__c. Probably not
__d. Definitely not	__d. Definitely not

(The Bureau of Applied Social Research, undated, p. 1, item 1.)

The Health Interests Inventory 1.3 (1941), of the Cooperative Study in General Education, American Council on Education, is an example of how an affective inventory can be developed for formative and summative evaluation to identify areas in a health curriculum that need modifications. The directions and several illustrative items follow:

DIRECTIONS: Your school wants to determine the kinds of health problems which are of greatest interest to you. Your reaction to the questions below will aid us in defining such interests. Imagine that you were to seek the answer to each question. If the question interests you and you believe it should be dealt with in the school, blacken the space under "A" on the answer sheet corresponding to the number of the question; if the question interests you but you think it should not be dealt with in school, blacken the space under "U"; if the question holds little or no interest for you or if you are indifferent to the question, blacken the space under "D."

(A)—the question is *interesting* and *should be dealt with* in school
(U)—the question is *interesting*, but *should not be dealt with* in school
(D)—the question is *not interesting*

100. Do certain diseases of the skin result from beauty parlor or barber shop treatments?
101. Are pimples caused by poor digestion?
102. If the skin is dry and becomes itchy after bathing, what should be done?

(American Council on Education, 1941, p. 1, items 1–3.)

One could modify this type of inventory to make it applicable to any area of the curriculum, such as sex education, religion, or political science, simply by listing topics or problems and asking the student to rate them in the manner described above. This would give the teacher summative information covering the interest students hold for topics or problems which have been treated in class, or formative information on materials which are about to be covered.

Often teachers are interested in determining what impact, if any, an experimental course or extracurricular activity such as a film club is making on the student's leisure time. The Educational Testing Service's Background and Experience Questionnaire (Maier & Anderson, 1964), which deals with leisure-time activities, illustrates yet another kind of item. It can be developed to tap the leisure-time dimension of the student's life for formative or summative curriculum evaluation and for formative evaluation of the student. The following is an example of an item from that instrument:

How much time each week, on the average, have you spent watching each of the following kinds of TELEVISION programs during your junior and senior years? Do *not* include programs that were part of your school work. Do *not* include TV watching during school vacations.

103. Detective stories or mysteries
  A. Very little or none
  B. About 30 minutes a week
  C. Between 30 and 60 minutes a week
  D. Over 60 minutes a week

104. Movie features
  A. Very little or none
  B. Sometimes, but less than one a week
  C. About one a week
  D. Two or more a week

How often, on the average, have you read each of the following kinds of MAGAZINES?

105. Literary magazines such as *Atlantic Monthly*
  A. Rarely or never
  B. Occasionally*
  C. Regularly*
  **Name one* ____________

(Maier & Anderson, 1964, Appendix B, pp. 1–14, items 6, 16, 92.)

The San Diego County Inventory of Reading Attitude is illustrative of items teachers could develop for formative evaluation of the student's attitudes toward and interest in reading or for formative and summative information for curriculum modification.

Draw a circle around the word YES or NO, whichever shows your answer.

Yes No 106. Do you like to read before you go to bed?
Yes No 107. Do you think you are a poor reader?
Yes No 108. Are you interested in what other people read?
Yes No 109. Do you like to read when your mother and dad are reading?

Yes No 110. Is reading your favorite subject at school?

(San Diego County, undated, items 1–5.)

Often it is desirable to secure a measure of the intensity of a student's affect toward a phenomenon. Several response modes make this possible. One of the most common of these uses the categories "like," "indifferent," and "dislike." The Academic Interest Measures (AIM) developed by the Educational Testing Service (1963) employ this response mode. The AIM instrument consists of 192 activity items that ask the student how he feels about academic situations that are familiar to him. The respondent has to examine each statement and indicate, on a separate answer sheet, whether he would like to perform the activity or not or is indifferent to it.

There are twelve scales of sixteen items each that give a measure of a student's interest in biology, English, the fine arts, mathematics, the social sciences, secretarial training, the physical sciences, foreign languages, music, engineering, home economics, and executive training. The following are illustrative items:

111. To write stories (English)
112. To work with clay (Fine Arts)
113. To take part in a mathematics club (Mathematics)
114. To typewrite business letters (Secretarial)
115. To find out how dangerous bacteria may be kept out of water, milk and other foods (Biology)

(Educational Testing Service, 1963, pp. 2 and 5, items 2, 6, 16, 18, 82.)

Another kind of question that gauges the intensity of affective response asks the respondent to indicate whether he strongly agrees (SA), agrees (A), is undecided (?), disagrees (D), or strongly disagrees (SD) with the statement given. This is the format of the following items, designed to measure a general attitude toward school:

SA A ? D SD 116. Anyone can learn if he will study.

SA A ? D SD 117. School doesn't teach anything good.

SA A ? D SD 118. You must do your best in school.

SA A ? D SD 119. Good grades are the most important things in school.

SA A ? D SD 120. My friends think school is a waste of time.

Items of this type could be used at different points in time and at different grade levels to ascertain changes in a student's attitude toward school and learning. O'Hara (1958) describes a simple and speedy but highly valid format for measuring students' vocational self-concept in the areas of interests, general values, work values, and aptitudes. This method involves taking definitions of a particular trait or construct of interest to the investigator from either the test manual or the test itself, and asking the student to rate himself regarding the trait or construct on a nine-point scale. The following is an example of the self-concept scale corresponding with the artistic interest scale of the Kuder Preference Record. The student is directed to check the space that best describes the amount of his interest:

121. ARTISTIC INTEREST—Artistic interest means liking to do creative work with your hands—usually work that has "eye appeal," involving attractive design, colors and materials.

1	2	3	4	5
My interest ranks with the lowest group in this field	I have very much less interest than most people	I have much less interest than most people	I have less interest than most people	I have the same amount of interest as most people

6	7	8	9
I have a little more interest than most people	I have much more interest than most people	I have very much more interest than most people	My interest ranks with the highest group in this field

This form of item can encompass any concept, so that by changing the description from "artistic interest" to, say, "ability to think for oneself," a teacher can obtain an indication of the student's self-rating on many constructs. Using these scales as pre- and post-tests can give a teacher an indication of how his instruction is affecting the student's rating of himself on the pertinent trait.

Terwilliger (1966) offers an intriguing method designed to measure intensities or ordered "levels" of occupational interest. In this technique the item statements rather than the response mode are ordered in intensity. The respondent is directed to give a categorical "yes-no" response indicating his endorsement of various occupations for each level of intensity.

122. I would *seek out* an opportunity to be a(n) ______. (If there was a reasonable chance of getting into this work and succeeding, you would make a great effort to get such a job.)

123. I would gladly accept an opportunity to be a(n) ______. (You would be happy to accept a job offer in the occupation.)

124. I would *probably accept* an opportunity to be a(n) ______. (You would think seriously about an offer in the occupation, and would be quite likely to accept it.)

125. I would *find it enjoyable* if I were assigned to be a(n) ______. (You would find this type of work enjoyable if you were required to do it.)

126. I could *tolerate* it if I were assigned to be a(n) ______. (You could tolerate this type of work if you were required to do it.)

(Terwilliger, 1966, p. 6, items 1–5.)

Terwilliger's format could be modified for use in examining affective areas other than vocational interest. For example, one could ask about a student's willingness to elect certain courses by rephrasing Terwilliger's five questions to include the name of the appropriate course instead of an occupation.

Sometimes it is desirable to combine the advantages of the open-ended question and the closed-item format. This technique provides the evaluator with both quantitative and qualitative information while also giving data that allow for validity checks. The following example from the Independent Activities Questionnaire of the Educational Testing Service (1965) illustrates this combination.

127. During the last year have you read an entire book of either fiction or nonfiction other than for a classroom assignment? NO ☐ YES ☐
If "no" place an X in the "NO" box and [skip the next two questions]. If "yes" place an X in the "YES" box and go to [questions 128 and 129,] below.

128. Do you frequently discuss with family or friends ideas or impressions you have gained from books you have read? NO ☐ YES ☐
Describe most recent example: ______

129. Have you, on your own initiative, written out quotations, notes, or critiques of books that you have read? NO ☐ YES ☐
Describe most recent example: ______

(Educational Testing Service, 1965, items 23, 23a, 23b.)

The semantic differential technique

The semantic differential (SD) technique of Charles Osgood (Osgood, Suci, Tannenbaum, 1967) is a valuable and comprehensive research tool. One of its many uses, the only one we shall consider in this chapter, is the measuring of a generalized attitude. The form of the instrument involves a rating scale of bipolar adjective pairs related to a concept the attitudes toward which are of interest to the evaluator.

130. [Concept]

Polar term X __: __: __: __: __: __: __: Polar term Y
1 2 3 4 5 6 7

The scaled positions are defined as follows:
(1) extremely X
(2) quite X
(3) slightly X
(4) neither X nor Y; equally X and Y
(5) slightly Y
(6) quite Y
(7) extremely Y

The student checks the scale value along the adjective continuum corresponding with his attitude toward the concept in question. To measure generalized attitudes, Osgood recommends the use of adjectives he has labeled as Evaluative. Examples of such evaluative adjective pairs are "good–bad," "beautiful–ugly," "clean–dirty," "valuable–worthless," "beneficial–harmful," and "pleasant–unpleasant." A lengthy list of evaluative adjectives can be found in Osgood, Suci, and Tannenbaum's book *The Measurement of Meaning* (1967).

Almost any concept of interest could be used. For example, an English teacher might want to explore generalized attitudes toward drama, poetry, essay writing, or a Shakespearean play. Each concept is repeated separately with the same set of adjectives. The Social Studies Evaluation Program of the Education Development Center (1969) uses this technique to evaluate attitudes toward concepts contained in their social studies materials on Netsilik Eskimos. For example, attitudes toward the concept "Arctic" are assessed by the following semantic differential scales:

Arctic

(The Arctic is the area near the North Pole.)

131. ugly : __: __: __: __: __: beautiful
132. changing: __: __: __: __: __: changeless
133. windy : __: __: __: __: __: calm
134. strange : __: __: __: __: __: familiar
135. explored: __: __: __: __: __: unexplored
136. tame : __: __: __: __: __: wild
137. good : __: __: __: __: __: bad
138. deserted : __: __: __: __: __: inhabited
139. fierce : __: __: __: __: __: gentle
140. livable : __: __: __: __: __: not livable

(The Social Studies Evaluation Program, 1969, items 15–24.)

Using this instrument the evaluator can determine differences between concepts, between scales, or between individuals. For a more technical treatment of the analysis of SD data, the reader is referred to Osgood, Suci, and Tannenbaum's text.

Projective techniques

Getzels and Walsh's and Osgood's techniques are often considered to be semiprojective in that the purpose of the questions is less obvious to the respondent than it is in direct, first-person items. Projective techniques are designed to reveal information about a respondent's deeper levels of feelings, his covert reactions to a phenomenon, and for this reason they have long been used by clinical psychologists.

The present description concerns itself only with the use of projective techniques that are applicable to affective educational evaluation. One approach, sentence completion, has been dealt with in the discussion of paired direct and projective questionnaires. Another projective technique involves picture interpretation. This device is a modification of the well-known Thematic Apperception Test. The following instruction from the National Longitudinal Study of Mathematical Abilities battery, Form 121A (1962), precedes the presentation of four pictures, and constitutes a complete description of the nature and use of the technique:

141. The first section of this booklet contains four pictures. You are to look at a picture and think up a story about it. Try to think up as imaginative stories as possible. After each picture there is a blank page on which you can write your story. Write only one story on each sheet. You may use both sides of the page.

 In order to build a complete story, there are a set of

questions which you could use as guidelines in writing your story. These are the questions:

What do you think is going on?
Who are the people?
What happened in the past?
What are the people thinking?
Do any of them want anything?
What do they want?
What will happen afterward?
What will be done?

These questions are only a guide to help you write a story . . . a *complete* story with a beginning, a middle and an end. Let your imagination supply the details.

When requested to do so, you may turn the page and look at the first picture. You will have about twenty seconds to look at each picture. Then you will be asked to turn to the blank page following the picture and write your story. You will have only three minutes to write the story so you will have to work quickly. You will be warned when the time is almost up for each story. When the time is up, you will turn to the next picture.

There aren't any right or wrong kinds of stories. Any story is all right. You don't have to figure out exactly what is going on in the pictures. Just write the story that comes into your mind when you look at the picture. You don't have to worry much about spelling or grammar. Stories won't be graded. What we are interested in is how imaginative a story you can write.

(National Longitudinal Study of Mathematical Abilities, 1962, p. 2.)

Other forms the projective technique can take include story completion and essay writing, where the respondent is asked to write an essay on a value-laden topic such as "Civil Rights."

In analyzing projective data, the reader must interpret student responses according to a series of predetermined codes that help to ensure objectivity. These codes can be a function of a theory, a hypothesis, or previous knowledge. As with the unstructured interview, the recognition of nuances and subtleties depends to a large extent on the art of the interpreter.

Stone and his colleagues in their book *The General Inquirer* (1966) describe the application of computer technology to the content analysis of responses to thematic apperception tests, open-ended interviews, sentence-completion items, and essay questions. This technique has great possibilities for affective evaluation. The machine looks for repeated words, symbols, or themes in a text. Each word of a text is examined for possible relevance to a list of concepts of interest to the investigator. Presently there are at least fourteen dictionaries available to an investigator, although they are rather specialized. As the practice comes into wider use, a school system working in conjunction with university personnel and machinery may be able to develop its own dictionary specific to its own evaluation needs. In *Values and Teaching*, Raths, Harmin, and Simon (1966) describe key words and phrases indicative of interest, activities, aspirations, attitudes, and purposes. There is no reason to believe that lists like these could not eventually be automated for use with a program such as that discussed in *The General Inquirer*. Thus the machine might be instructed to retrieve and list all occurrences of the key phrases "I'm for . . . ," "I'm against . . . ," "If you ask me . . . ," and "In my opinion . . . ," suggested in *Values and Teaching*. The reader is urged to inspect the very useful key-word lists in that work.

Summary

Affective objectives can and should become integral goals of American education. The effectiveness of the schools in developing desired affective outcomes can and should be assessed. The real and imagined dangers associated with evaluating such instructional outcomes are reduced when the distinction between formative and summative evaluation of the pupil and the curriculum is observed. Assuring students either of anonymity or of freedom from grading or penalty for their responses can lead to valid evidence about the affective outcomes.

Thus the abuses often associated with affective evaluation can be overcome. Models of well-defined affective objectives and a variety of techniques to evaluate them are available to the teacher or school system willing to accept the obligation to assess previously neglected but important affective curriculum components.

REFERENCES

American Council on Education, Cooperative Study in General Education. *Health Interests Inventory 1.3.* Chicago: ACE, 1941.

Bureau of Applied Social Research, Columbia University. *Action in difficult situations.* New York: BASR, undated.

Cronbach, Lee J. Course improvement through evaluation. *Teachers College Record,* 64, No. 8, May 1963, 672–683.

The Social Studies Evaluation Program. *Netsilik Unit Test.* Cambridge, Mass.: EDC, Spring, 1969.

Educational Testing Service Experimental Comparative Prediction Batteries, High School and College Levels, Book C. Princeton, N.J.: ETS, 1963.

Educational Testing Service. *Independent Activities Questionnaire.* Princeton, N.J.: ETS, 1965.

Getzels, J. W., & Walsh, J. J. The method of paired direct and projective questionnaires in the study of attitude structure and socialization. *Psychological Monographs,* vol. 72, no. 1, whole, no. 454, 1958.

Greeley, A., & Rossi, P. *The education of Catholic Americans.* Chicago: Aldine, 1966.

Krathwohl, D. R., Bloom, B. S., & Masia, B. B. *Taxonomy of educational objectives: The classification of educational goals.* Handbook 2. *Affective domain.* New York: McKay, 1964.

Lewy, A. The empirical validity of major properties of a taxonomy of affective educational objectives. Unpublished doctoral dissertation, University of Chicago, 1966.

Maier, Milton H., and Anderson, Scarvia B. Growth study: I. Adolescent behavior and interests. Res. Bull. RDR-64-5, no. 6. Princeton, N.J.: ETS, 1964.

Masia, B. B. Questionnaire on music: Form III. Unpublished test, University of Chicago, 1965.

McMurrin, S. M. What tasks for the schools? *Saturday Review,* vol. L, no. 2, 1967, 40–43.

Metropolitan Achievement Tests: Directions for completing Individual Profile Chart, all batteries. New York: Harcourt, Brace, 1960.

National Longitudinal Study of Mathematical Abilities. *Ideas and preferences inventory, Form 121A.* Stanford, Calif.: NLSMA, 1962.

National Longitudinal Study of Mathematical Abilities. *12th grade battery.* Stanford, Calif.: NLSMA, 1964.

O'Hara, R. P. A cross-sectional study of growth in the relationship of self-ratings and test scores. Unpublished doctoral dissertation, Harvard University, 1958.

Osgood, C., Suci, G., & Tannenbaum, P. *The measurement of meaning.* Urbana, Ill.: University of Illinois Press, 1967.

Progressive Education Association. *Literature Questionnaire: The Novel, Test 3.22.* Chicago: PEA, 1940.

Raths, L., Harmin, M., & Simon, S. *Values and teaching: Working with values in the classroom.* Columbus: Merrill, 1966.

San Diego County. *San Diego County Inventory of Reading Attitude.* San Diego County, Calif.: SDC, undated.

Scriven, M. Student values as educational objectives. In *Proceedings of the 1965 Invitational Conference on Testing Problems.* Princeton, N.J.: Educational Testing Service, 1966. Pp. 33–49.

Smith, B. O. Teaching and testing values. In *Proceedings of the 1965 Invitational Conference on Testing Problems.* Princeton, N.J.: Educational Testing Service, 1966. Pp. 50–59.

Smith, E. R., & Tyler, R. W. *Appraising and recording student progress.* (Adventure in American Education Ser., Vol. 3) New York: Harper, 1942.

Stone, P. J., Dunphy, D. C., Smith, M. S., & Ogilvie, D. M., with associates. *The general inquirer.* Cambridge, Mass.: M.I.T. Press, 1966.

Terwilliger, J. S. Philosophical and psychometric problems in the measurement of interests. Paper presented at the Symposium on Interest Measurement, University of Minnesota, May 1966.

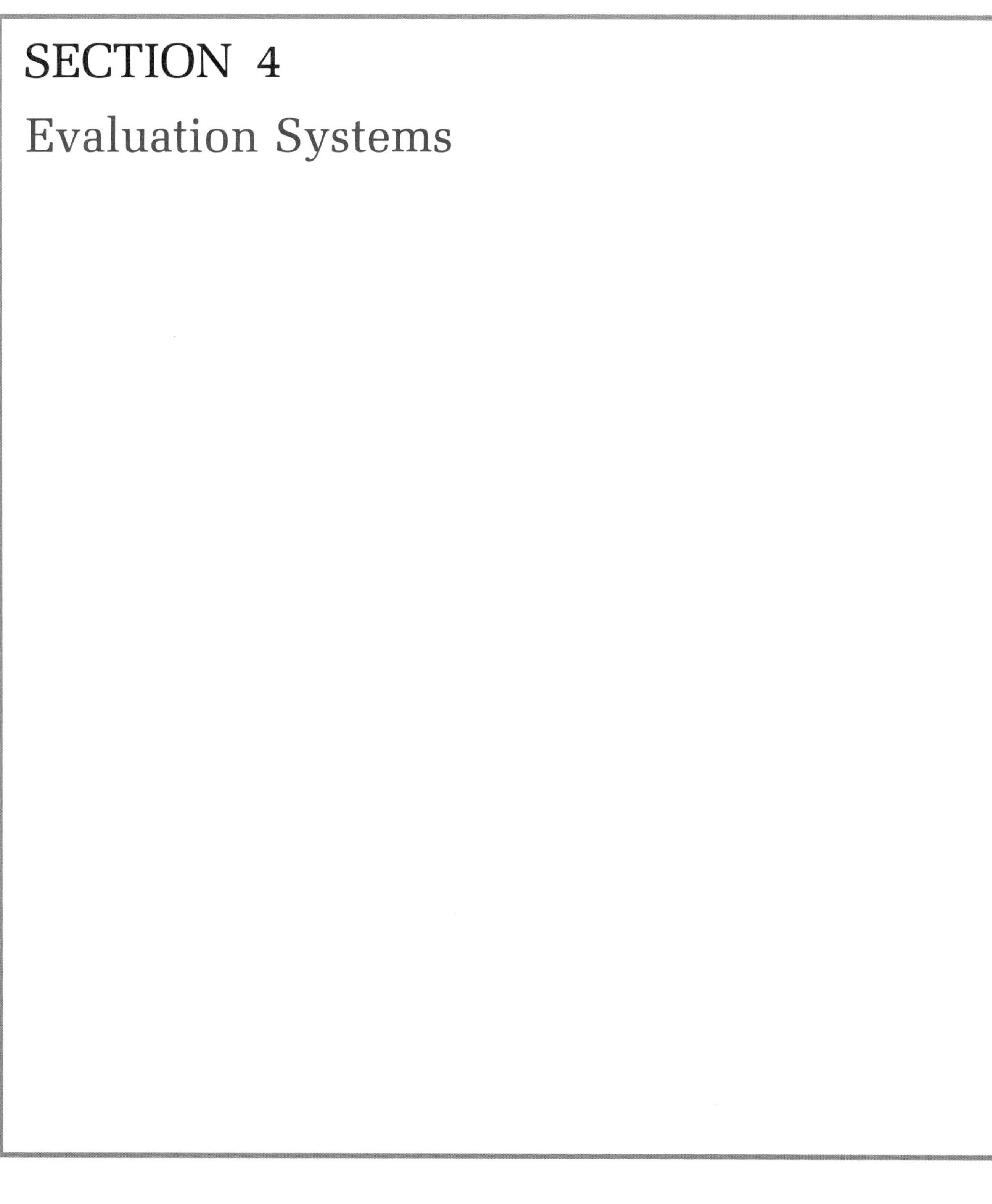

SECTION 4

Evaluation Systems

11

The Cooperative Development of Evaluation Systems

In every class during every lesson, teachers evaluate their students. They do this spontaneously without the intrusion of anything that would normally be called a test. Often the teacher's cue is a momentary facial expression, a tone of voice, a shift in posture; at other times, of course, he takes account of children's answers to questions. These cues, which Jackson (1968) has aptly called the "language of classroom behavior," continually tell the teacher how well he is communicating with the students. These spontaneous judgments fit neatly our definition of formative evaluation; they are assessments made while teaching is in progress for the purpose of guiding that teaching. Without them teaching could hardly be called teaching.

However, because this type of evaluation is unplanned, it is different from the systematic and quantitative types of evaluation—placement, formative, diagnostic, and summative—proposed in this book. This is not to suggest that spontaneous, informal evaluation is of little worth or that there is any basic contradiction between informal and formal evaluation. Our point throughout has simply been that informal evaluation should be supplemented by more systematic sorts of evidence gathering.

The busy teacher, however, responsible for the varied work of a large and varied class, can hardly be expected to have the time, energy, or expertise on his own to specify all the objectives and develop all the techniques and instruments necessary to evaluate adequately all aspects of student learning. The purpose of this chapter is to describe how the full range of techniques needed for a system of evaluation can be developed with only a minimum of demands on any individual teacher.

Cooperation in developing an evaluation system

While some evaluation instruments are commercially available (see the section on commercially issued tests in each of the Part II chapters), others will have to be locally constructed. It would be an illusion indeed to think that a satisfactory and complete range of evaluative techniques will ever be available readymade; there will always be local interpretations of commonly obtainable curricula as well as unique programs developed by an individual department, school, or school system. The argument of this book is that evaluation is an integral part of education; it follows that a department, school, or school system which has its own emphasis or program will need to undertake the task of developing its own evaluation system. That is, in addition to tests supplied by curriculum developers and other commercially published achievement and psychological tests, the local body will need instruments and techniques tailored to its special requirements.

But how is such a system to be developed? The answer is, through the cooperative effort of concerned teachers, administrators, and, where needed and available, outside consultants in evaluation and testing. If the evaluation system is to serve the needs of teachers, then they should have the central role in its development. This, however, assumes at least four things: first, an in-service training program which enhances the relevant skills of teachers; second, cooperation so that no one individual will have to carry too heavy a load; third, released time to work on the project; and finally, leadership to direct and coordinate the work.

The function of the leader is to convene the group; make provision for necessary in-service training; organize subgroups which will carry out specific tasks; arrange with the administration for proper released time, facilities, and budget; and generally guide the group.

A few school systems may be fortunate enough to have the services of an evaluation specialist, much as they have specialists in music, art, and guidance. Such a person would be an ideal leader to direct teachers in the development of an evaluation program. Other school systems may be able to release a teacher who already has or who can acquire expertise in evaluation. More likely the task of leadership will simply fall on a department head or interested teacher. In this case the leader's job would include, in addition to coordinating the activities, procuring consultant help from a local college or university when technical assistance is needed. Whoever the leader, it should be emphasized that his task is to coordinate the work of teachers, to work with them, and to make it possible for them to screen and develop all sorts of evaluation instruments.

The development of priorities

The realization of a complete evaluation system will take time. For example, evaluative techniques for all areas of the curriculum, especially in the elementary grades, cannot be attacked simultaneously. Furthermore, the development of the placement, formative, diagnostic, and summative components of an evaluation system need not be initiated at the same time. There is, of course, overlapping among these various components. The same instruments and items can often be used for different evaluative purposes. For example, a summative achievement test might also serve as a pre-entry placement test; the difference between a formative and summative item revolves more around the intent and time of its use than it does around form or substance. While taking advantage of any overlapping, cooperating teachers must nevertheless establish priorities among the various components of the system as well as among various content areas. Perhaps the first task of any group of teachers will be to establish such priorities. Once these are determined, then when necessary, in-service training can begin.

Acquiring the skills needed to specify objectives (see Chap. 2) will be among the first goals of the in-service training. Other chapters in Parts I and II, reflecting the priorities among placement, formative, diagnostic, and summative evaluations and among various content areas, could also serve as a basis for an in-service program.

At the completion of the in-service program, the task of cooperatively developing evaluation instruments can begin. The remainder of this chapter discusses the cooperative formation of item pools, which are useful in constructing various sorts of instruments, and the use of basic data-processing equipment (unit record equipment, test-scoring machines, and computers, which are rapidly becoming available in many school systems) to facilitate test scoring, test analysis, and record keeping.

The development of item pools

An item pool was described in Chap. 2 as a large number of items, each coded by behavioral aim, content, and approximate grade level, that can be used to assemble instruments to evaluate student outcomes. Such a pool can be thought of as a planned library consisting of test questions, checklist items, interview questions, and so forth that can be drawn on to build an evaluation instrument.

It is important to emphasize that an item pool is a planned library and not an amorphous collection. One cannot assemble an item pool simply by asking teachers to contribute old test questions or to write new ones. Such an unstructured procedure would only result in a hodgepodge of items, many unrelated to the objectives of the program for which the system is being evolved. Therefore, the first step in the creation of an item pool is the development by the teachers of a blueprint which outlines the specifications of the pool. Of course, once these specifications have been determined, teachers will find that many of their old test items and techniques do in fact fit various specifications and can be incorporated into the pool.

These specifications are nothing more or less than a clear delineation of the objectives of the course or program for which the evaluation system is being developed. It can take the form of a two-dimensional table, one axis containing subject matter, the other behaviors (see Chaps. 2 and 4 and each chapter in Part II) or, in the case of formative evaluation, the hierarchical structure of a unit or chapter in a textbook (see Chap. 6). For a desired balance of items in the pool, each cell in the table of specifications should be given a value weighting (see Chap. 4).

Once the table of specifications has been decided upon, each teacher in the group contributes a number of items to the pool designed to evaluate a particular aspect of the table. Instead of having every teacher build a separate and complete exam for a given unit of study, each teacher need only contribute items for a fraction of the total table of specifications. As it is often the case that a person is more adept at writing certain types of items than other kinds, this division of labor also utilizes the item-writing strengths and competences of each member of the group to maximum advantage. For example, persons more at home with a particular content area may take responsibility for items in that area; certain teachers may be more facile in developing items to test the higher mental processes (Chaps. 8 and 9), while others may work more effectively on knowledge items (Chap. 7); or some teachers may be more creative in developing affective than cognitive techniques (Chap. 10).

The contributed items, generally written on 3- by 5-inch file cards, must be screened. One screening method that eliminates long group discussions of each and every item is to have members of the group read the items independently and privately. The group can then meet to discuss those items judged to be in need of revision by two or more members. All individual suggestions for improvement can be passed on to the item writer for his consideration. Such individual and group screening can go a long way toward eliminating ambiguities, wrongly keyed answers, and other technical weaknesses. Further, these procedures help ensure that an item adequately measures the behavior and content in question.

Once the item has passed the screening process, it is ready to be coded for filing purposes. Like a library, an item pool must incorporate a coding system that permits the user to locate items easily. Since the purpose of the pool is to allow the teacher or department to assemble an instrument designed to measure particular objectives, the coding system must be readily relatable to the objectives. While coding systems will necessarily differ from one locality to another depending on specific needs, a code might include the following fields:

Field I: A number denoting the subject area. For example,
1.0. Algebra I
2.0. Geometry
3.0. Algebra II
4.0. General math

Field II: A letter denoting the intended taxonomic level of the item. For example,
A.0. Knowledge
B.0. Comprehension
C.0. Application
D.0. Analysis
E.0. Synthesis
F.0. Evaluation

Field III: A number denoting a content topic in the given subject the question deals with.

Field IV: A number denoting the textbook or curriculum guide for which the question is designed.

Field V: A number denoting the chapter within the textbook or curriculum guide for which the item is designed.

Field II could be further coded by specific behaviors under each major taxonomic category. For example, under Knowledge, A.1 might represent recall of specific facts, A.2 recognition of terminology, and so forth. Field III could likewise be subdivided as desired. (See Chap. 7 and relevant sections of Part II chapters.)

The following is an example of an item coded for the five fields just described (the asterisk indicates the correct answer):

Fields:	1	A.2	2.9	2	7	___	___	___	.79	.43
	I	II	III	IV	V	VI	VII	VIII	IX	X

Which of the following is an example of alternation?
a. 3/5 = 6/10 and −2/5 = −4/10
b. x/y = 2/3 and x/3 = 2/y
*c. x/y = 2/3 and 3/y = 2/x
d. 5/3 = 10/6 and 3/5 = 6/10

The empty fields can be used for additional code meanings as the necessity arises. For example, where the practice of departmental examinations is followed, it may be desirable to code an item to indicate that it is to be used only for quarterly and final examinations. Further, as each item is used, item analysis data can be computed (Chap. 4) and entered in a reserved field on the item file card; for example, the difficulty and discrimination indices for the above item have been entered in fields IX and X, respectively. Poorly constructed items not caught in the initial screening process can thus be detected and either corrected or dropped.

Of course, the pool should be constantly restocked and kept up to date as objectives are added, modified, or dropped. After a period of time, the pool will place at the disposal of teachers a large number of tried and proven items for each objective in the table of specifications. When a teacher wishes to build a formative or summative instrument to evaluate a unit of instruction, he can go to the file where the items are stored by predetermined code and choose those that fit the specifications of the instrument he wishes to assemble. Using the code he can arrange the items according to behavior, content, difficulty level, or type of test. The items are then refiled for further use.

The mathematics department of Thornridge High School in Dolton, Illinois, and the Middle School Project in Holliston, Massachusetts (1968), are excellent examples of how item pools can be formed by teachers who are given proper in-service training and leadership. Groups of instructors in each place are in the process of building up a large bank of items for purposes of systematic, formal evaluation.

The cooperative use by several school systems of extensive item pools is also possible. For example, the Institute for Education Research in Downers Grove, Illinois, working under the Title III project Evaluation for Individual Instruction, is developing a large item pool which will be available to school districts in the Chicago area. Teachers from participating school districts are formulating and coding the items with the assistance of the staff of the institute. Another example is the Computer Based Testing System (COMBAT) of the Metropolitan Area Testing

Program of the Portland, Oregon, public schools, which has a computerized item pool available to seventy school districts.

The use of data-processing equipment in the evaluation process

The tremendous labor-saving potential of a cooperatively built item pool can be increased through the use of basic data-processing equipment to reduce the burdensome clerical scoring and statistical work necessarily associated with systematic evaluation. Most school systems have on hand basic unit-record equipment, such as a keypunch, card sorter, card reproducer, printer, and collator, as part of their business, commercial, or vocational education programs. Some systems also have optical scanning test-scoring machines, like the IBM 1230 or the Digitek, as well as small computers, such as the IBM 1440 or IBM 1620. If a school system does not have either optical scanning equipment or a computer, it can often make use of such equipment found in nearby banks, factories, business offices, or colleges. Some systems, especially those located in metropolitan areas, may also have a formal arrangement with a nearby university computer center.

The filing, selection, and arrangement of items in an item pool

Once a large pool of items has been developed and coded, a desirable aid to teachers would be procedures for arranging and selecting items contained in the pool and for refiling them when they are finished with. Ordinary unit-record equipment found in most schools can provide the teacher with fast and efficient tools for the arrangement, selection, and refiling of items.

In developing its item pool, the mathematics department of Thornridge High School made use of the IBM keypunch and sorter to facilitate its filing. The actual item is written on the IBM card, but all of the coding is punched. By sorting the cards for various coding fields, the teacher can organize the item pool in various ways. For example, by sorting for behavior, he can organize the pool hierarchically according to taxonomic level. Further sorting by content field within each taxonomic level classifies the items by behavior and content. Once a teacher has selected items for a test, he can arrange the items in the test by difficulty level. When the item cards are in the desired order, they can then be turned over to a typist. Lyons Township High School in La Grange, Illinois, keypunches its test items, using one card for each line of the item and blank cards for proper spacing. Once a teacher has selected the desired items from the pool and arranged them, the cards are listed by an IBM printer on continuous IBM ditto masters. This avoids secretarial efforts, errors, and expenses.

Of course, it is not necessary to use data-processing equipment to arrange, select, and refile items. These are routine clerical chores that can be done by hand. However, there is a point—which must be determined in each situation—at which the savings in time and the increased accuracy in filing and maintaining order in the pool make the use of such machines a very desirable adjunct to the evaluation system.

The person who regularly operates such equipment could do the necessary board wiring and help develop regular routines for processing the item files. Any interested teacher can easily learn, with proper help and encouragement from the group leader and the person in charge of the equipment, both to operate unit-record machinery and to follow simple processing routines for arrangement, selection, and refiling.

Correcting multiple-choice examinations

Correcting multiple-choice examinations by hand is at best a slow, tedious, and boring task. While in some systems para-professionals can relieve teachers of this clerical function, the time lag between the administration of the test and the reporting of results is directly proportional to the number of questions and examinations. Further, hand-scoring does not provide item and test analysis data.

If a school system has mark-sensing equipment on its reproducing punches, students can record their answers to test items on mark-sensing cards. These cards can be processed through the reproducer to punch the students' responses and then through a card printer to obtain a rapid printout of the responses. If the cards are run through the sorter first, the answers can be ordered in various ways before the printing. This technique would be particularly useful for formative tests since patterns of item responses, the basis for formative decisions, could be inspected from the printout. As with unit-record equipment, easily learned routines can be set up for the use of these machines to expedite scoring.

If a school owns or has access to an optical scanning test-scoring machine, such as the IBM 1230 or the Optical Scanning Corporation's Digitek, the burdensome clerical work associated with test scoring can all but be eliminated and the reporting of test results greatly speeded up. Once again judgment must be exercised as to when it is desirable and more efficient to machine-score tests instead of correcting them manually. In the case of formative tests, it may be best to have students correct the tests themselves immediately and then later process them by machine for a more detailed analysis of response patterns. Quizzes given to small classes may be more efficiently and quickly scored by hand according to a simple answer key. Essay examinations will have to be hand-scored, at least for the immediate future. (See Chap. 4 for suggestions on scoring objectively.) However, there is little doubt that machines can score longer multiple-choice examinations administered to regular-sized classes more cheaply, quickly, and accurately than is possible manually.

The student records his responses with an ordinary number 2 pencil on a specially calibrated answer sheet costing approximately 2 cents. All that the teacher need do is bring the answer sheet along with the scoring key to the machine operator. The sheets can be scored rapidly, at the rate of twenty to thirty per minute, by the optical scanner. The machine will print a raw score for subtests and the total test on the side of each answer sheet. Perhaps the most important benefit associated with using such equipment is that it will also produce a computer card for each student containing his identification number and his responses to each question on the exam. These cards can be processed in various ways by the sorter, but more importantly, they can be used as input into a computer for test and item analysis.

Test and item analysis

Teachers cannot reasonably be expected to have the time or statistical training necessary to perform test and item analysis. Further, many are justifiably not interested in acquiring this skill. Generally, therefore, teachers do not perform technical analyses of their own tests. However, a formal evaluation system demands that the analyses be made. One solution is to utilize computers for this purpose. Small computers, such as the IBM 1620, which is available in many school systems, can handle such analyses. Moreover, prepackaged programs for test scoring and statistical analyses are available that teachers can very quickly learn how to operate.

The punched output from a test-scoring machine and another card describing the test (number of questions, options, examinations, and keyed answers) become the basic input into the computer.

The computer, depending on the program used, can produce various kinds of output:

1. A card for each student with a 0 or 1 for each question depending on whether it was answered incorrectly (0) or correctly (1). This card yields very valuable formative data.
2. A card containing each student's raw score for each subtest and the total test. Both this and the previous card become part of an information system maintained on each student for later evaluation.
3. An index of item difficulty and discrimination (see Chap. 4). These indices for each question are useful in updating each item in the item pool.
4. The Kuder-Richardson reliability index, formula number 20, for each subtest and the total test (see Chap. 4).
5. The standard error of measurement, an absolute index of test reliability.

1. Pass-fail for each item; raw scores on two subtests and total raw score; percent each raw score is of the possible total. This is produced on IBM cards.

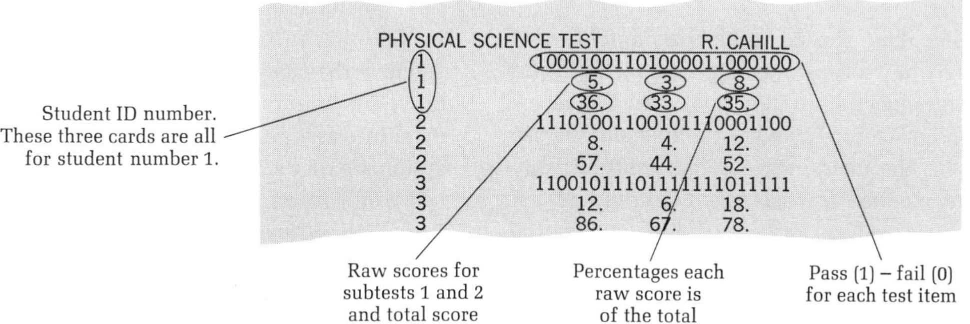

2. Printout of each student's performance.

Student identification

Class listing by ID number for total test

IDENT	NO. RIGHT	NO. WRONG	NO. OMITTED	RIGHTS AS PERCENT OF POSSIBLE	RIGHTS CORRECTED GUESSING
1	8	15	0	34	5
2	12	11	0	52	10
3	18	5	0	78	17
4	9	14	0	39	6
5	10	13	0	43	7
6	5	18	0	21	1
7	9	14	0	39	6
8	8	15	0	34	5
9	6	17	0	26	2
10	9	14	0	39	6
11	17	6	0		16
12	15				13
13	6				
14					

3. Item discrimination and difficulty indices.

ITEM NUMBERS	DISCRIMINATION INDEX	DIFFICULTY INDEX
1	.4343	.8965
2	.3382	.6896
3	.5480	.1379
4	.2433	.2758
5	.2090	.3793
6	.0781	.3448
7	.5063	.3793
8	.4632	

4. Reliability and standard error of measurement for the total test.

RELIABILITY	.67184
ST. ERROR MEAS.	2.05454

FIGURE 11-1 Sample computer output from an IBM 1620 test analysis program.

Figure 11-1 depicts the actual output produced with a 1620 test-scoring program that has utilized punched cards from the optical scanner as basic input.

In sum, then, the computer can quickly and accurately provide a group of teachers working on the development of an item pool with the necessary evidence for item and test refinement. Its use eliminates the uneasiness or discomfiture many teachers experience when asked to compute test statistics as well as the actual time-consuming computations. Further, it radically reduces the need to train teachers in statistical techniques, computations, and the use of statistical formulas. The machine alters the teacher's role from that of producer to that of consumer of test and item analysis data.

To be an intelligent consumer, however, teachers will need in-service training in the meaning, use, and limitations of the various statistics the machine generates. The leader of the group may be able to provide teachers with the necessary background in the interpretation of item and test data, or he may engage the services of an outside consultant from a local college or university for this purpose.

While many teachers might feel apprehensive over the thought of using a computer, the actual mechanics are very easily mastered, given proper guidance by the group leader and the operator in charge of the equipment. Teachers need not learn actually to operate the computer but merely how to set up the input in the form of a data deck, which is then left for the operator to process.

Affiliation with an outside computer center

Admittedly not all school systems have an optical scanner or a computer. Further, systems which have a small computer might find that their machine does not have enough memory capacity to perform the test scoring and analysis described above. This need not be a reason to forgo the time- and labor-saving assistance the computer can contribute to the development of an evaluation system. A school system without the necessary equipment should be able to affiliate with an outside computer center. Even school systems with adequate machinery for the requisite analyses find that an affiliation with a computer center can give their evaluation system additional flexibility. For example, the larger and more versatile machines as well as the skills of programmers and systems experts generally found in universities can result in an increased capability to process, store, and retrieve a large body of data on pupils.

The actual details and costs of affiliation with an outside computer center will vary from one place to another. In all cases, however, a representative of the school system will need to act as intermediary between the teachers developing the evaluation system and the computer center staff. If the center is used only for test scoring and analysis, this task might simply involve familiarizing teachers with the center's capabilities, routine, and procedures; checking to see that the data are properly set up; transporting and submitting the data for processing; and picking up the output. However, if the evaluation system becomes more sophisticated and computerized, the person acting as liaison will have the responsibility of transmitting the exact specifications for the system to the center staff.

The Middle School Project of Holliston, Massachusetts, funded under Title III of the ESEA, affords an example of how an affiliation with a university computer center (that of Boston College) can greatly extend the capabilities of a school's evaluation system. One of the goals of the Middle School Project is the individualization of instruction through proper placement and frequent formative evaluations. This in turn involves the processing, storage, and retrieval in usable form of a large body of data about a student's performance record. A systems programmer is working with the school to develop the computerized evaluation system pictured in Fig. 11-2.

Basic to the system depicted in the figure are the four disk storage files. The specifications of the kinds of information or units these files are to contain is the joint task of the teachers and

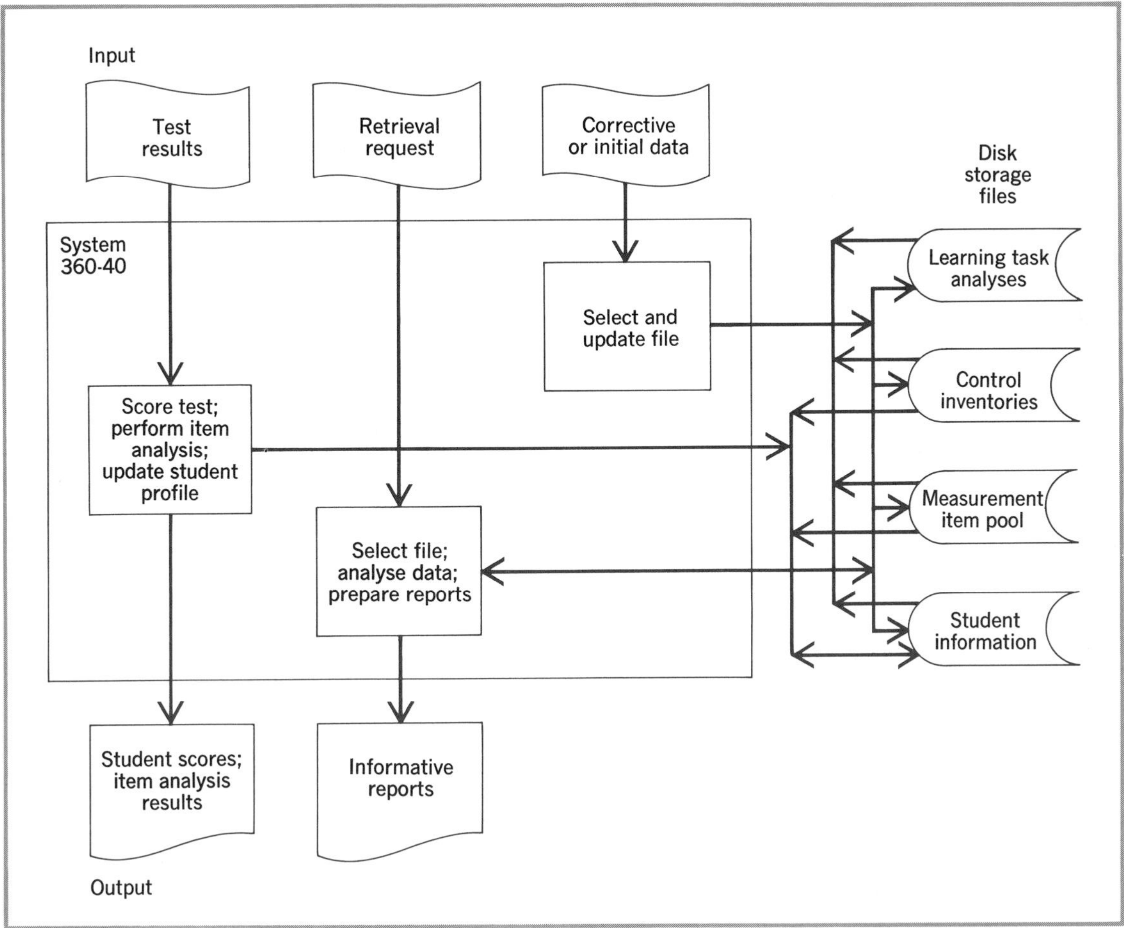

FIGURE 11-2 Flowchart of the projected computerized evaluation system for Holliston Middle School, Massachusetts, grades 5–8. (Middle School Project: A systems approach to middle school education. Application for Continuation Grant, November 30, 1968, Title III, ESEA Project No. 68-544, p. 24A.)

administrators who will use the system. Group cooperation in specifying objectives and in planning and developing items and techniques is therefore still at the heart of the system; the programmer's task is not to mastermind the specifications but instead to translate these cooperatively developed outputs into a machine-processable form. Furthermore, and most important, the machine does not evaluate; this is a human responsibility. The machine only facilitates the storage manipulation and retrieval of information at the request of teachers. The machine takes over the clerical but not the judgmental aspect of the evaluation system.

The first disk file in the system, *"Learning-task Analyses,"* will contain the results of analyses of instructional units in terms of tasks and skills. These analyses will be made in a manner similar to the procedures described in Chaps. 2 and 6. The file of knowledge and process "Control Inventories" will contain five subject-matter inventories. These inventories comprise knowledge and process objectives. Each objective is coded as to whether it is a summative or formative objective, as well as by behavior and content. The "Measurement Item Pool" file will contain an item bank developed by teachers working co-operatively, as described above, and coded to correspond with the data in the first two files. The final file, "Student Information," will contain a wide range of general data on students, recorded and maintained over a four-year period. All four files will be continually altered or updated as needs dictate.

This computerized evaluation system will eventually become one component of a complete computerized storage and retrieval system designed to service the requirements of the instructional and administrative systems. Because at every stage in its conception and implementation the system has had to conform with the specifications of concerned educators, any charge of Orwellian abuse can be anticipated and safeguards set.

Many schools will either not be ready for or not need a computerized evaluation system like the one being developed by Holliston. Such schools might want only to use the facilities of a computer center to perform test scoring and analyses. The Holliston example was offered merely to demonstrate the potential benefits of affiliation with a computer center. School systems desirous of taking advantage of the saving in time and labor afforded by the computer as they develop their own evaluation system should certainly investigate an affiliation with a computer center.

Summary

If a department or school is interested in developing the various components of an evaluation system, it cannot expect the busy teacher to do the job single-handed. The creation of such a system must be a cooperative effort organized and supervised by a leader who can serve as a resource person to groups of teachers working on various parts of the program. The cooperative development of an item pool for the system and the use of basic data-processing equipment in test scoring and analysis can greatly reduce the demands on any one person. Building an evaluation system is admittedly a slow and exacting job, but it is one which can be realized if teachers share the work and are given the proper help and time. The improvement in instruction and student learning that will result from the establishment of a carefully planned and cooperatively developed evaluation system makes it well worth the effort.

REFERENCES

Jackson, P. W. *Life in classrooms.* New York: Holt, Rinehart and Winston, 1968.

Middle School Project [Holliston, Mass.]: A systems approach to middle school education. Application for Continuation Grant, November 30, 1968, Title III, ESEA (Elementary and Secondary Education Act) Project No. 68-544.

12

Some Emerging Developments in Evaluation

As was suggested by the title of this book and delineated further in the Preface, the first eleven chapters deal with general and specific approaches to the evaluation of student learning. The focus is upon the progress of the individual student in terms of the goals of the classroom and upon the possibilities the individual teacher has for assessing such progress and using the results. Even where the whole school or the school system is discussed, as in Chap. 11 in its treatment of item pools and computer uses, it is as an aid to doing in a more complete or more efficient way the job just described. The eleven chapters constituting Part II of the book carry forward the same task, concerning themselves with application to specific content areas and levels.

The theories stated or reflected in these chapters have been supported in practice. The suggested procedures have been tried and found effective. The use of achievement tests for evaluating individual student outcomes is important for instruction and for student guidance. However, there are many other appropriate approaches to the evaluation of educational endeavors. Most of the serious attempts to develop other approaches have occurred in the last five years or so. Furthermore, descriptions of some of the methods and discussions of rationales have tended to appear in the "hidden literature" of ditto and mimeograph copies instead of in journals and books until just recently.

This chapter is intended to inform you of a few of the educational evaluation moves which are evolving in addition to the usual individual measurement approach. In the short space allotted for this purpose, you cannot be instructed in the use of these ideas for your particular area, but it is hoped that you can be encouraged to start inquiring into some approaches which will have much more prominence in the next several years.

The single most useful publication to date for information regarding new rationales and procedures in educational evaluation is the *AERA Monograph Series on Curriculum Evaluation*, published by Rand McNally & Co., Chicago. In the words of Robert E. Stake, Coordinating Editor:

> Acting upon this report [the report of a study committee appointed by 1964 AERA President Lee J. Cronbach] and upon his own perception of educational affairs, President Benjamin S. Bloom in 1965 commissioned an AERA Committee on Curriculum Evaluation to develop guidelines for quality control—model evaluation procedures—to accompany the development and revision of educational curricula. . . . This committee, like its predecessor, concluded that guidelines limited to contemporary testing and inquiry procedures were inadequate; that special observation, data-reduction, and decision-making techniques were needed; and that AERA should encourage writing and discussion of theory and rationales for such techniques.
>
> (Stake, 1967b, pp. 11–12)

The *Monograph Series* is a result of that conclusion. There are now five issues in the aperiodic series, with one to four articles in each. Several more are in preparation. The lengthy quotation was given above in order to suggest some of the urgency felt by leaders of the American Educational Research Association, America's largest professional organization in educational research—an urgency in seeking new approaches to assessing the worth of educational endeavors. To correct any misinterpretation of the acceptance by this group of achievement testing, which is the message of this book, we quote again from Stake in the same article:

> Most contemporary evaluations of instruction *begin and end with achievement testing*. . . . It is important to our concern here to emphasize that these tests have been developed to provide reliable discrimination among *individual students*. Discriminability among students is important for instruction and guidance. . . .
>
> (Stake, 1967b, p. 5; italics added)

There is no denying the essentiality of student tests for the uses suggested in this book. There is a need to look more broadly at evaluation of educational activities.

The remainder of this chapter treats only four current approaches or rationales, and there is no claim that these are the most important. There has been enough work on them, however, to indicate that persons charged with evaluating educational work would do well to consider them. It is hoped that such people, if they have not been aware of approaches other than that of individual testing, will become sufficiently interested to avail themselves of the current literature.

Evaluating objectives

Throughout the educational establishment we have become very familiar with the phrase "evaluating instructional objectives." For the most part only one meaning of this phrase has been discussed and studied very thoroughly. The phrase has at least two meanings. The one which has been studied most is that of collecting and judging evidence about learners in terms of the fit between stated objectives and actual outcomes of instruction. The other and obvious meaning which "evaluating instructional objectives" might have is that of collecting and analyzing evidence of the extent to which various groups value—see worth in—stated objectives.

Far too commonly the group developing a curriculum or the person teaching a course has been free to state whatever objectives it or he deemed desirable. It is true that there have always been some restraints. Gatekeepers for the school system dampen the chances of one's getting by with goals which appear to them antisocial. Local curriculum committees express more interest in some intended outcomes than in others. Much thought and time have gone into the selection or development of objectives for any national curriculum-development project. For example, expert biologists and experienced teachers spent considerable effort formulating and reformulating the goals of the Biological Sciences Curriculum Study (Grobman, 1969) at all three of the levels mentioned by Krathwohl (1965): program, curriculum, and instructional material. Local school system curriculum committees have devoted much hard labor to achieving a consensus on general and operational objectives. These comments are not intended to criticize either the methods used to arrive at goals or the goals themselves. They are intended to suggest that one of the many important aspects of educational evaluation is the *systematic description and valuing of objectives* by various appropriate groups.

Methodologies for collecting data and for analyzing them to determine the ordering of the values people give to various objectives have long been in existence. In general, such techniques have not been used as part of curriculum evaluation. Certainly, from the standpoint of judging the worth of a particular curriculum, course, or unit of instruction, it would be well to know the extent of alignment between the values ascribed to a set of objectives by subject experts and those ascribed by teachers. If the values attached to certain objectives by students differ much from those held by their teachers, then some sort of rethinking of the curriculum is suggested. For the sociopolitical roles of evaluation, it would be important to know how segments of the lay public value various objectives.

Taylor and Maguire (1966) developed a theoretical evaluation model one very important segment of which is the value ordering of objectives. In a later study Taylor (1966) investigated the abilities of certain groups to judge the importance of high school biology objectives in terms of curriculum development in biological science. This was followed by a study by Maguire (1967) attacking the problem of defining the value components of teachers' judgments of educational objectives. Maguire's study states,

> It has been noted earlier that in the new frontier of evaluation, the assessment of objectives at all levels of abstraction is as important an activity in a complete evaluation as the measurement of student outcomes. A potentially fruitful method of evaluating objectives is to delineate frames of reference within which judgments of worth should be made and then to suggest groups of judges who are qualified to make judgments within each framework. Thus, if as Taylor and Maguire suggested, one wished to determine the significance of an objective in terms of the public good, social philosophers would appear to be an appropriate group of judges. If one were concerned with assessing several sequential objectives in terms of the appropriateness to a particular age level one might elicit judgments from developmental psychologists. As an illustration of how one could use special groups to make assessments about objectives in terms of a particular framework of value, Taylor (1966), as one part of a larger study, asked groups of biological scientists, curriculum writers, and teachers to judge several high school biology objectives in terms of their importance to biological sciences curriculum development. The results of this portion of Taylor's study indicated that if one asks pertinent questions of appropriate judges a replicable assessment of an objective within a particular value-framework is possible.
>
> In the Taylor-Maguire model as in the Krathwohl classification, objectives were conceived of as being expressible at more than one level of abstraction. Taylor and Maguire suggested that judgments regarding the broadest objectives are most properly in the domain of those most concerned with the relationship between education and the broad directions of society. At more concrete levels, experts in pedagogy and subject-matter areas would seem to be an appropriate pool from which to draw judges. [pp. 14–15]

Maguire's study does offer a methodology which should be useful for determining the values ascribed to objectives by various segments of our society. A short description of his methods may be helpful.

In his study two samples of high school teachers were asked to make a series of judgments concerning two sets of fifteen educational objectives. The judgments consisted of rating the objectives on thirty "seven-point, bipolar, adjectival scales." The adjectives which made up the scales were descriptive of the value of educational objectives. For example, each person in the two samples was asked to make four hypothetical decisions concerning each of the fifteen objectives in a set. These decision tasks were to estimate the amount of time that should be devoted to the pursuit of the objective, to estimate the degree of commitment that the school should make to the objective, to estimate how far the respondent would commit himself to the pursuit of the objective, and to rank the fifteen objectives in order of importance.

In each sample a principal-components analysis was performed on the intercorrelations among scales, and the components were rotated to the varimax criterion. The resulting rotated components were called "value aspects." Six value aspects were isolated for each sample. Of these, four were found to be stable across different sets of teachers and objectives. They were described as "subject-matter value," "motivational qualities," "ease of implementation," and "statement properties."

Scores of the value aspects were calculated for each teacher's judgment of each objective. A linear model of decision-making behavior was postulated, relating the scores on the value aspects with the four decision-making tasks. It was found that the decisions could be accurately characterized by the linear combination of the value-aspect scores.

For each person a validity coefficient was calculated between each aspect and each decision. This resulted in a profile of validity coefficients for each teacher and each decision. A technique for grouping similar profiles was devised and carried out on the data for each decision-making situation within each sample. Essentially the technique resolves the observed validity-coefficient profiles into the weighted sum of component profiles. The weights were used to cluster individuals into homogeneous groups. Group membership was found to be quite constant over the four decision tasks, indicating that the judgmental policies remained relatively constant. Similarities were noted between the component profiles that were calculated for each sample.

The main point of this section is that there are two ways at least of looking at the evaluation of objectives. One of them concerns the matching of student performances to intended objectives. The other deals with obtaining descriptive data concerning values attached to objectives by various groups who are concerned with education. The latter meaning of the phrase "evaluating objectives" is an important one. With ever-growing areas of educational goals, and especially with the increase in socioeducational endeavors (for example, Head Start, Follow Through, and Triple-T), there will be a more urgent need to evaluate the goals themselves objectively.

Computer-aided Instruction and Formative Evaluation

We have noted in previous chapters that the term "formative evaluation" was originally defined by Scriven (1967). He states clearly, "As a matter of terminology, I think that novel terms are worthwhile here, to avoid inappropriate connotations, and I propose to use the terms 'formative' and 'summative' to qualify evaluation in these roles [p. 43]." "These roles" refers to the role of evaluation in improving a course (or curriculum, text, or other unit) while it is still fluid—being developed—and its role in finding the *worth* of a completed product (course, text, instructional package, and so forth).

Thus, throughout this book "formative" refers to evaluation of a student's learning *during* a course, when (presumably) changes can be made in the transactions of subsequent instruction on the basis of current attainment. "Summative" is used to designate student assessment at the *end* of a course or topic or unit, that is, when no subsequent changes in treatment *for that learning* will be made.

However, in this section "formative" is used more nearly with Scriven's original meaning. That is, the focus here is upon the alteration of a course or other unit during its development. The word is not restricted to the meaning of assessing individual student learning in the ongoing classroom. The "developer" may be a textbook author, a teacher in the classroom, or a committee or team of curriculum developers. The instrument for change in this case is *computer-assisted* or *computer-aided instruction* (CAI).

For the reader who is unfamiliar with CAI, it may be well to describe this instructional instrument briefly. The subsequent paragraphs are not intended to give the knowledge needed to use it in the development of instruction, but rather to provide enough background for an increased understanding of the later discussion of its application to formative evaluation.

Computer-aided instruction is the result of the convergence of two technologies: programmed-instruction technology and computer technology.

Although the former has been with us longer than the latter, they are both relatively new in their widespread use as instructional tools. As early as the 1930s, Sidney Pressey, of Ohio State University, developed some of the basic notions of what we know today as programmed instruction; but it was not until the 1950s, largely but not solely through the research work of B. F. Skinner at Harvard, that programmed instruction began to be used as a serious and pervasive educational technique. The reader who is unfamiliar with the technology is referred to the volume edited by Robert Glaser (1965).

Computer technology, as we know it at present, is only a couple of decades old. As almost every reader knows, computers are used today for such diverse tasks as solving complex structural problems in engineering, handling bank checks, and keeping track of sales and inventories. Early in the game, computers were used for processing the data from educational research—the statistical analyses. People in educational research were familiar with computers and their flexibility. These were in many cases the same people who were investigating the uses of programmed instruction. Therefore, it was not surprising that they and their counterparts in computer technology started adapting computers to the tasks of presenting information to the learner, asking him questions, recording and judging his responses, and presenting him with new or review information as needed.

That CAI will be available in the next four or five years to many schools for the special uses of formative evaluation as well as for instruction is supported by the following current facts. In the last few years CAI has grown in almost every way imaginable: in the subject areas and age levels involved, the complexity of the learning tasks being taught, the subtlety of the computer's "judgments of students' responses," and the usability and appropriateness of the hardware through which the learner receives information or with which he responds—the keyboard, the television screen or slide projector, the light pencil, and the audio system. In addition to this kind of growth, technology is making it possible to cut the costs per student hour vastly by greatly increasing the possible number of single stations which can be controlled by one computer as well as the number of individuals to whom a given instruction may be made available. Finally, the languages used to program computers for specific instructional episodes are being simplified so that virtually no training is needed to put a new program into the computer once the program is ready in the teacher's or author's regular language.

Although there are many different systems of CAI, the basic ingredients may be described briefly. A lesson to be taught is analyzed into the essential messages to the student. These messages may be delivered through words, graphs, pictures, or any combination. Some messages may be auditory. As materials are presented the student reacts to them by answering questions, working problems, identifying points on a graph or objects in a picture, giving examples, requesting more information or a chance to review messages presented previously, and so forth. Depending upon the student's response, the computer presents the next messages in the lesson, additional messages, ideas given earlier, a review of earlier messages, or additional "developing" questions. The interested reader might see the article by Bitzer and Easley (1964).

These operations can be part of any programmed instruction; in CAI, however, they are controlled by the computer. Therein lies the special application of CAI to formative evaluation, which is the main focus of this section. As stated previously, a computer can be used to analyze data very rapidly. Furthermore, the same computer which controls the instruction can be used to collect information concerning variables in the learners' responses, such as these:

Specific answers given to questions
Length of time between presentation of question and student response
Requests by the learner for review and the material reviewed
Requests for additional information or examples
Number of times the learner reviews an item or responds incorrectly after review

The reader can add to this list. The computer can store in its memory any "legal" move (response which is part of the program) which any student makes.

Add to the foregoing capability the fact that the computer can be requested to summarize such variables over students or subgroups of students. As a simple example, suppose a section of a lesson concerns the concept of the relation between volume and pressure in gases. Illustrations and definitions are presented, and then the student is asked to respond to some questions or apply the concept to a problem. Even though the students are progressing at different rates in reading the messages (words, pictures, graphs) and in responding to requests, the computer can keep track for each student of each of the sorts of variables listed above. It then can summarize across the students the numbers of correct or incorrect responses. Or if the teacher has subgrouped the students—for example by vocabulary level or previous grades in science—the computer can be requested to summarize each subgroup separately.

We now have a description of every move by each student and a summary for appropriate subgroups. The computer can then be commanded to show the relationships *between* moves by a given learner on different items. For instance, did he ask for review on the first problem but not on the second? Again, the computer can summarize such relations over subgroups.

All of the foregoing types of collection and analyses can be accomplished while the students are working on the lesson. The computer not only can accomplish them very rapidly but can, on request, display the results at a separate station for the author (that is, the administrator of the material).

There are at present some CAI systems in which the author can change materials in a lesson—the messages, the questions, and so forth—through the use of one of the student stations with a special control.

Imagine the situation in which an author has prepared a CAI lesson. He has several groups of students working at separate stations; for illustrative purposes we'll say that each group starts at a different time, one each half hour. The author himself is at a station designed to display student performance information and to allow him to change the program. As he gets information from the first group, he alters portions of the program for the second group. Again, he can alter material for the third group from results from the second. Admittedly this is a hypothetical case whose complexity is not necessary for useful formative evaluation. The mere collection of the group data would allow a classroom teacher or curriculum development team to revise lessons in a much better way than is customary today.

It is hoped that you recognize, from the brief description of general CAI procedures, that the formative evaluation ideas discussed in Chap. 6 may be embedded in good programs. Any experience and understanding you can acquire in the regular classroom with these operations and procedures connecting student evaluation and individualized instruction will be of great advantage as CAI facilities become more available, as they certainly will in the next several years.

Work along the lines just discussed has been reported by Easley (1968). The interested reader should also go to the many reports by centers which are using CAI, some of which are the Stanford Laboratory for Learning and Teaching, Stanford University; the Computer Assisted Instruction Center, State University of Florida, Tallahassee; the Computer-Based Educational Research Laboratory, University of Illinois, Urbana; and the Harvard Computing Center, Harvard University.

Perhaps general use of these methods in the near future will help develop part of the new evaluation technology suggested by Stake in the first issue of the *AERA Monograph Series on Curriculum Evaluation:*

> We need lesson-writing paradigms, including subroutines for helping an author maintain a pace, control reading difficulty, organize review exercises, discover inconsistencies, optimize redundancies, etc. Things like these, done today intuitively by authors and editors, should be done more explicitly with routine check on the quality of the materials written.
>
> (Stake, 1967b, p. 7)

We know comparatively little today about what kinds of student data can help authors and teachers improve the quality of instruction. This formative use of CAI can be an emerging development in evaluation.

Sampling tasks over students and summative evaluation

In Chap. 4 the discussion concerns summative evaluation, but most of the procedures and activities suggested have to do with discrimination among individuals by the usual psychometric considerations. Chapter 3 stresses mastery learning and teaching, as opposed to separating individuals psychometrically as though there were foreordained mastery levels, but it focuses on the evaluation of individual student learning—as it should, under the title of this book. At a number of different places in the book (notably Chaps. 7 to 9 and those in Part II), there are examples of "tasks" which are more like everyday tasks in life than are the usual academic test items. The emerging development in evaluation which is the focus of this short section combines parts of all of these ideas: summative evaluation, lifelike tasks, and mastery levels. However, its concern is with the broader curriculum, not the classroom course, and with evaluation across the group, not of individual learning.

As stated earlier in this chapter, there is a movement toward a technology of educational evaluation which encompasses more than the teacher, the classroom, and the differentiation of individual students. One of the important moves in this direction during the past five years is the formation of the Committee on Assessing the Progress of Education (previously called the National Assessment of Educational Progress; see Merwin, 1966; Tyler, 1966, 1967). This is an attempt to look at the results of education in several large, rather general geographic sections of the United States in terms of the percentages of learners capably performing certain meaningful tasks. The actual study is sampling students at a number of spaced grade levels and is using tasks representing comparatively few areas of learning. All respondents in the sample are school age.

Tyler suggests that part of the report on the national assessment might read as follows:

> For the sample of seventeen-year-old boys of higher socioeconomic status from rural and small town areas of the Midwest region, it was found that:
>
> 93% could read a typical newspaper paragraph like the following.
>
> 76% could write an acceptable letter ordering several items from a store like the following.
>
> 52% took a responsible part in working with other youth in playground and community activities like the following.
>
> 24% had occupational skills required for initial employment.
>
> (Tyler, 1967, p. 14)

Does not this look a good bit different from the usual report to the school board in terms of grade-equivalent averages and bar graphs of percentile scores? It does imply that the evaluator used a number of very similar or homogeneous tasks for each topic. It suggests that the sampling of students was appropriate. And it shows that the tasks reflected the behaviors alluded to in the report. These are difficult specifications to meet, but they are not impossible. A report which is meaningful to the school board and the public should be worth the effort!

The foregoing example refers to a nationwide evaluation of status. There is no reason that similar techniques could not be used with single school systems or even with single schools if the total grade enrollment is 75 to 100 (a figure of this order is needed for reliability of results). Those who execute such an evaluation and those to whom a report is directed would have to realize that they could not compare Johnny with Harry or give grades on the basis of the resulting data. Sampling two dozen tasks over seventy-five students would furnish reliable information on the group and perhaps also the school system but not useful comparisons among students. The tasks chosen should reflect the large goals of the school, the community, or the system but not necessarily the specific objectives of any given classroom. They probably should reflect an accretion of experience over several grade levels and subject areas.

The evaluation developments just described could never and should never substitute for the procedures and activities set forth in the other chapters of this book. They can, however, greatly increase the usefulness of educational evaluation in the coming years.

Other experts, their techniques, and educational evaluation

The previous sections of this chapter on emerging developments in educational evaluation have dealt with some specific techniques applied to problems of general concern: the valuing of objectives, evaluating for the improvement of materials, and the sampling of meaningful tasks in groups—not individuals. This final section treats a more general development: the use of a broad range of types of expertise in evaluating today's educational endeavors.

For several decades the expertise of educational evaluators has been grounded in educational measurement. Educational measurement in turn has been made up of techniques and methods from psychometrics backed by certain statistical methods borrowed from other areas of study. As any other expert must, the evaluator has had certain points of view and models which he has used in attacking problems which education has brought to him.

For the most part the problems brought to him by the school have concerned selecting and predicting; measuring outcomes in terms of individual differences for purposes of grading or certifying or career or academic guidance; and measuring differences so that the teacher might effectively treat individuals in the classroom. These were problems important to an education system which fed into society but was an institution somewhat apart from society. The evaluator has done relatively well with those problems in terms of his expertise—his methods. He uses these same techniques and methods and does quite well in evaluating student outcomes.

Education and the needs to be satisfied by the system have altered. Tyler (1967) speaks tellingly of some of the changes. Chapters 1 and 3 of this book make quite clear some of the new ways of looking at education, its purpose, and its conduct. During the past decade all of us have witnessed new relationships between the school and society. For example, such programs as Head Start and Follow Through have asked the school to tackle societal problems along with the traditional ones of education. Individual schools have become more concerned with community involvement. Increased educational costs in personnel and equipment are competing more than was previously the case with other objects of tax dollars, objects of real concern to the public.

These new perspectives and problems entail different techniques, methods, and models of problem solving from those of the educational measurement person, although his arsenal is still extremely necessary. These changes are resulting in a development in educational evaluation which calls for the techniques, models, and points of view of economists, sociologists, cultural anthropologists, and historians, among others. In many cases the person charged with evaluation in the school or even in the classroom will adopt some of the methods of these disciplines as well as those of educational measurement. In an ever-increasing number of instances, however, evaluation demands the expertise of several different types of specialists working together.

The reasons for these needed additions and the probable ill consequences if they are not provided are discussed in greater detail elsewhere (Glass, 1968; Hastings, 1969). The remainder of this section will give a few quite different examples of possible uses of several types of experts.

A large national program financed through the United States Office of Education is called Triple-T, the Trainers of Teacher Trainers. The idea of the program is about three years old, but the actual execution—in about forty university-school-community settings—has been in process only a little more than a year. The focus, far too simply put, is on the training at the doctoral level (in university departments of English, mathematics, history, and other disciplines) of people whose careers will consist in teaching the teachers of the schools. The intents of the program, however, also include strengthening ties between the faculties of colleges of education and of liberal arts; getting schools involved with both the concepts and the practices taught; and involving the community—especially the urban black community—in the relevance of the training and in locating societal needs.

Such a program demands evaluation. The moves of the usual educational evaluation professional (there are exceptions) would be to ask for a statement of objectives concerning the doctoral candidates, the ultimate teachers, and their students; to put these objectives in behavioral terms; to develop tests for these behaviors to give the tests to appropriate samples; and finally to report the results in terms of group and individual differences or gains. We would hope that one who has read *this* book would think of a few other things. For example, from Chap. 3 he would consider the place of mastery; from Chap. 10 he could draw some suggestions on affective outcomes; he might see in the present chapter the possibility of valuing the objectives or of sampling tasks over groups; and he surely would get valuable help for certain areas from Part II. However, this book was not intended to solve the problems of program evaluation.

Since Triple-T is such a new program, stating the learning objectives meaningfully would be very difficult—and probably foolhardy! The general goals possibly could be established, except that in an endeavor aimed at changing a social institution even large goals alter or shift their order as the program develops. Herein lies the need for a historian. Part of the description of the worth of given goals should concern itself with the effects on them of experience. The expert in historical methods is trained both formally and by unwritten practice to ascertain such changes, their sources, and the validity of documentary evidence. It is not merely that some historical techniques could be used to answer questions asked by others. More importantly the historian would come with his own special views of the possibilities.

For some of the intents of the national program—strengthening ties between education and liberal arts faculties and involving minority communities—an expert in sociology or cultural anthropology would be the appropriate person. Again, it is not only his tools the evaluator would need. His experience and training would allow him to ask questions about description and valuing which others would not pose and which would be important.

Accountants at the local-project and the national level would keep track of funds available and funds used. For evaluation purposes, however, an economist could plan descriptions of relationships between products and control of financing, between objectives and costs, which others would miss.

On the whole these specialists and perhaps others, working together with the evaluator trained in measurement, could produce a meaningful evaluation for those concerned—the teacher-training specialists, the Office of Education, the Congress, and the public.

One does not have to think in terms of a large national program to see the usefulness of increasing the range of types of expertise over those which educational evaluation has customarily brought to bear. In a local school system evaluation of the science curriculum or the reading program, it turns out that the public, the elected officials, and the teaching staff really have questions of quality which are not answered by gains in scores and results of criterion-based tests. There are public accounts in newspapers, board-meeting minutes, and faculty sessions which the historian could use to shed light on purposes, sources of change, and availability of resources. In most school systems there are subcultures which are affected by and have an affect upon the various programs. The expert in sociology could help shape the questions and locate appropriate data. Descriptions and judgments concerning cost benefits are important; the economist is best qualified in this domain.

In general there is a growing movement to think of educational evaluation in broader terms than those of educational measurement. This certainly does not mean that the indexing of learning lacks importance. It suggests rather that achievement results can have even greater importance than they have had if their descriptions and judgments are systematically related to relevant aspects of the total socioeconomic scene.

Summary

There is a developing technology which is broadening the base and the meaning of educational evaluation. The entire book is directed toward giving the reader new concepts and skills which will improve the ties between the evaluation of student learning and the instructional process. This chapter, however, is intended to make the reader aware of the broader context in which his new concepts and skills will have their rightful place. Although only four recent developments have been discussed, the reader who is disposed to go beyond these would do well to study some of the works cited in the *References* section.

REFERENCES

AERA Monograph Series on Curriculum Evaluation. Chicago: Rand McNally & Company, 1967, No. 1; 1968, No. 2; 1969, No. 3; 1970, Nos. 4, 5.

Atkin, J. M. Some evaluation problems in a course content improvement project. *Journal of Research in Science Teaching*, 1963, **1**, 129–132.

Bitzer, D. L., & Easley, J. A., Jr. *PLATO: A computer-controlled teaching system*. Urbana, Ill.: Computer-Based Educational Research Laboratory, University of Illinois, 1964.

Easley, J. A., Jr. *A project to develop and evaluate a computerized system for instructional response analysis*. (Final Rep., Contr. No. OE-6-10-184) Urbana, Ill.: Computer-Based Educational Research Laboratory, University of Illinois, 1968.

Gallagher, J. J. Teacher variation in concept presentation. *BSCS Newsletter*, 1967, No. 30, pp. 8–19.

Glaser, R. (Ed.) *Teaching machines and programmed learning*. Vol. 2. *Data and directions*. Washington, D.C.: National Education Association, 1965.

Glass, G. V. *Some observations on training educational researchers*. (Res. Pap. No. 22) Boulder, Colo.: Laboratory of Educational Research, University of Colorado, 1968.

Grobman, A. *The changing classroom: The role of the Biological Sciences Curriculum Study*. Garden City, N.Y.: Doubleday, 1969.

Grobman, H. Evaluation activities of curriculum projects. *AERA Monograph Series on Curriculum Evaluation*. Chicago: Rand McNally & Company, 1968, No. 2 (whole no.).

Hastings, J. T. The kith and kin of educational measurers. *Journal of Educational Measurement*, 1969, **6**, 127–130.

Krathwohl, D. R. Stating objectives appropriately for program, for curriculum, and for instructional materials development. *Journal of Teacher Education*, 1965, **12**, 83–92.

Maguire, T. O. Value components of teachers' judgments of educational objectives. Unpublished doctoral dissertation, University of Illinois at Urbana-Champaign, 1967.

Merwin, J. C. The progress of exploration toward a national assessment of educational progress. *Journal of Educational Measurement*, 1966, **3**, 5–10.

Scriven, M. The methodology of evaluation. *AERA Monograph Series on Curriculum Evaluation*. Chicago: Rand McNally & Company, 1967, No. 1, pp. 39–83.

Stake, R. E. The countenance of educational evaluation. *Teachers College Record*, 1967, **68**, 523–540. (a)

Stake, R. E. Toward a technology for the evaluation of educational programs. *AERA Monograph Series on Curriculum Evaluation*. Chicago: Rand McNally & Company, 1967, No. 1, pp. 1–12. (b)

Taylor, P. A. The mapping of concepts. Unpublished doctoral dissertation, University of Illinois at Urbana-Champaign, 1966.

Taylor, P. A., & Maguire, T. O. A theoretical evaluation model. *Manitoba Journal of Educational Research,* 1966, **1,** 12–17.

Tyler, R. W. The objectives and plans for a national assessment of educational progress. *Journal of Educational Measurement,* 1966, **3,** 1–4.

Tyler, R. W. Changing concepts of educational evaluation. *AERA Monograph Series on Curriculum Evaluation,* Chicago: Rand McNally & Company, 1967, No. 1, pp. 13–18.

APPENDIX

Condensed Version of the *Taxonomy of Educational Objectives**

Cognitive domain

Knowledge

1.00 Knowledge Knowledge, as defined here, involves the recall of specifics and universals, the recall of methods and processes, or the recall of a pattern, structure, or setting. For measurement purposes, the recall situation involves little more than bringing to mind the appropriate material. Although some alteration of the material may be required, this is a relatively minor part of the task. The knowledge objectives emphasize most the psychological processes of remembering. . . .

1.10 Knowledge of specifics The recall of specific and isolable bits of information. The emphasis is on symbols with concrete referents. This material, which is at a very low level of abstraction, may be thought of as the elements from which more complex and abstract forms of knowledge are built. . . .

1.20 Knowledge of ways and means of dealing with specifics Knowledge of the ways of organizing, studying, judging, and criticizing. This includes the methods of inquiry, the chronological sequences, and the standards of judgment within a field as well as the patterns of organization through which the areas of the fields themselves are determined and internally organized. . . .

1.30 Knowledge of the universals and abstractions in a field Knowledge of the major schemes and patterns by which phenomena and ideas are organized. These are the large structures, theories, and generalizations which dominate a subject field or which are quite generally used in studying phenomena or solving problems. These are at the highest levels of abstraction and complexity. . . .

* SOURCES: B. S. Bloom (Ed.). *Taxonomy of educational objectives: The classification of educational goals.* Handbook 1. *Cognitive domain.* New York: McKay, 1956. Pp. 201–207; D. R. Krathwohl, B. S. Bloom, & B. B. Masia. *Taxonomy of Educational objectives: The classification of educational goals.* Handbook 2. *Affective domain.* New York: McKay, 1964. Pp. 176–185.

Abilities and skills refer to organized modes of operation and generalized techniques for dealing with materials and problems. The materials and problems may be of such a nature that little or no specialized and technical information is required. Such information as is required can be assumed to be part of the individual's general fund of knowledge. Other problems may require specialized and technical information at a rather high level such that specific knowledge and skill in dealing with the problem and the materials are required. The abilities and skills objectives emphasize the mental processes of organizing and reorganizing material to achieve a particular purpose. The materials may be given or remembered.

2.00 Comprehension This represents the lowest level of understanding. It refers to a type of understanding or apprehension such that the individual knows what is being communicated and can make use of the material or idea being communicated without necessarily relating it to other material or seeing its fullest implications.

2.10 Translation Comprehension as evidenced by the care and accuracy with which the communication is paraphrased or rendered from one language or form of communication to another. Translation is judged on the basis of faithfulness and accuracy, that is, on the extent to which the material in the original communication is preserved although the form of the communication has been altered. . . .

2.20 Interpretation The explanation or summarization of a communication. Whereas translation involves an objective part-for-part rendering of a communication, interpretation involves a reordering, rearrangement, or a new view of the material. . . .

2.30 Extrapolation The extension of trends or tendencies beyond the given data to determine implications, consequences, corollaries, effects, etc., which are in accordance with the conditions described in the original communication. . . .

3.00 Application The use of abstractions in particular and concrete situations. The abstractions may be in the form of general ideas, rules of procedures, or generalized methods. The abstractions may also be technical principles, ideas, and theories which must be remembered and applied. . . .

4.00 Analysis The breakdown of a communication into its constituent elements or parts such that the relative hierarchy of ideas is made clear and/or the relations between the ideas expressed are made explicit. Such analyses are intended to clarify the communication, to indicate how the communication is organized, and [to show] the way in which it manages to convey its effects, as well as its basis and arrangement.

4.10 Analysis of elements Identification of the elements included in a communication. . . .

4.20 Analyses of relationships The connections and interactions between elements and parts of a communication. . . .

4.30 Analysis of organizational principles The organization, systematic arrangement, and structure which hold the communication together. This includes the "explicit" as well as "implicit" structure. It includes the bases, necessary arrangement, and the mechanics which make the communication a unit. . . .

5.00 Synthesis The putting together of elements and parts so as to form a whole. This involves the process of working with pieces, parts, elements, etc., and arranging and combining them in such a way as to constitute a pattern or structure not clearly there before.

5.10 Production of a unique communication The development of a communication in which the writer or speaker attempts to convey ideas, feelings, and/or experiences to others. . . .

5.20 Production of a plan or proposed set of operations The development of a plan of work or the proposal of a plan of operations. The plan should satisfy requirements of the task which may be given to the student or which he may develop for himself. . . .

5.30 Derivation of a set of abstract relations The development of a set of abstract relations either to classify or [to] explain particular data or phenomena, or the deduction of propositions and relations from a set of basic propositions or symbolic representations. . . .

6.00 Evaluation Judgments about the value of material and methods for given purposes. Quantitative and qualitative judgments about the extent to which material and methods satisfy criteria. Use of a standard of appraisal. The criteria may be those determined by the student or those which are given to him.

6.10 Judgments in terms of internal evidence Evaluation of the accuracy of a communication from such evidence as logical accuracy, consistency, and other internal criteria. . . .

6.20 Judgments in terms of external criteria Evaluation of material with reference to selected or remembered criteria. . . .

Affective domain

1.0 Receiving (attending) At this level we are concerned that the learner be sensitized to the existence of certain phenomena and stimuli; that is, that he be willing to receive or to attend to them. This is clearly the first and crucial step if the learner is to be properly oriented to learn what the teacher intends that he will. . . .

The category of *Receiving* has been divided into three subcategories to indicate three different levels of attending to phenomena. While the division points between the subcategories are arbitrary, the subcategories do represent a continuum. From an extremely passive position or role on the part of the learner, where the sole responsibility for the evocation of the behavior rests with the teacher—that is, the responsibility rests with him for "capturing" the student's attention —the continuum extends to a point at which the learner directs his attention, at least at a semiconscious level, toward the preferred stimuli.

1.1 Awareness *Awareness* is almost a cognitive behavior. But unlike *Knowledge*, the lowest level of the cognitive domain, we are not so much concerned with a memory of, or ability to recall, an item or fact as we are that, given appropriate opportunity, the learner will merely be conscious of something—that he take into account a situation, phenomenon, object, or state of affairs. Like *Knowledge* it does not imply an assessment of the qualities or nature of the stimulus, but unlike *Knowledge* it does not necessarily imply attention, phenomenon, object, or state of affairs. Like specific discrimination or recognition of the objective characteristics of the object, even though these characteristics must be deemed to have an effect. The individual may not be able to verbalize the aspects of the stimulus which cause the awareness.

1.2 Willingness to receive In this category we have come a step up the ladder but are still dealing with what appears to be cognitive behavior. At a minimum level, we are here describing the behavior of being willing to tolerate a given stimulus, not to avoid it. Like *Awareness*, it involves a neutrality or suspended judgment toward the stimulus. At this level of the continuum, the teacher is not concerned that the student seek it out, nor even, perhaps, that in an environment crowded with many other stimuli the learner will necessarily attend to the stimulus. Rather, at worst, given the opportunity to attend in a field with relatively few competing stimuli, the learner is not actively seeking to avoid it. At best, he is willing to take notice of the phenomenon and give it his attention.

1.3 Controlled or selected attention At a somewhat higher level we are concerned with a new phenomenon, the differentiation of a given stimulus into figure and ground at a conscious or perhaps semiconscious level—the differentiation of aspects of a stimulus which is perceived as clearly marked off from adjacent impressions. The perception is still without tension or assessment, and the student may not know the technical terms or symbols with which to describe it correctly or precisely to others. In some instances it may refer not so much to the selectivity of attention as to the control of attention, so that when certain stimuli are present they will be attended to. There is an element of the learner's controlling the attention here, so that the favored stimulus is selected and attended to despite competing and distracting stimuli.

2.0 Responding At this level we are concerned with responses which go beyond merely attending to the phenomenon. The student is sufficiently motivated that he is not just 1.2 *Willing to attend* [receive]; perhaps it is correct to say that he is actively attending. As a first stage in a "learning by doing" process the student is committing himself in some small measure to the phenomena involved. This is a very low level of commitment, and we would not say at this level that this was "a value of his" or that he had "such and such an attitude." These terms belong to the next higher level that we describe. But we could say that he is doing something with or about the phenomenon besides merely perceiving it, as would be true at the next level below this of 1.3 *Controlled or selected attention.*

This is the category that many teachers will find best describes their "interest" objectives. Most commonly we use the term to indicate the desire that a child become sufficiently involved in or committed to a subject, phenomenon, or activity that he will seek it out and gain satisfaction from working with it or engaging in it.

2.1 Acquiescence in responding We might use the word "obedience" or "compliance" to describe this behavior. As both of these terms indicate, there is a passiveness so far as the initiation of the behavior is concerned, and the stimulus calling for this behavior is not subtle. Compliance is perhaps a better term than obedience, since there is more of the element of reaction to a suggestion and less of the implication of resistance or yielding unwillingly. The student makes the response, but he has not fully accepted the necessity for doing so.

2.2 Willingness to respond The key to this level is in the term "willingness," with its implication of capacity for voluntary activity. There is the implication that the learner is sufficiently committed to exhibiting the behavior that he does so not just because of a fear of punishment, but "on his own" or voluntarily. It may help to note that the element of resistance or of yielding unwillingly, which is possibly present at the previous level, is here replaced with consent or proceeding from one's own choice.

2.3 Satisfaction in response The additional element in the step beyond the *Willingness to respond* level, the consent, the assent to responding, or the voluntary response, is that the behavior is accompanied by a feeling of satisfaction, an emotional response, generally of pleasure, zest, or enjoyment. The location of this category in the hierarchy has given us a great deal of difficulty. Just where in the process of internalization the attachment of an emotional response, kick, or thrill to a behavior occurs has been hard to determine. For that matter there is some uncertainty as to whether the level of internalization at which it occurs may not depend on the particular behavior. We have even questioned whether it should be a category. If our structure is to be a hierarchy, then each category should include the behavior in the next level below it. The emotional component appears gradually through the range of internalization categories. The attempt to specify a given position in the hierarchy as *the* one at which the emotional component is added is doomed to failure.

The category is arbitrarily placed at this point in the hierarchy where it seems to appear most frequently and where it is cited as or appears to be an important component of the objectives at this level on the continuum. The category's inclusion at this point serves the pragmatic purpose of reminding us of the presence of the emotional component and its value in the building of affective behaviors. But it should not be thought of as appearing and occurring at this one point in the continuum and thus destroying the hierarchy which we are attempting to build.

3.0 Valuing This is the only category headed by a term which is in common use in the expression of objectives by teachers. Further, it is employed in its usual sense: that a thing, phenomenon, or behavior has worth. This abstract concept of worth is in part a result of the individual's own valuing or assessment, but it is much more a social product that has been slowly internalized or accepted and has come to be used by the student as his own criterion of worth.

Behavior categorized at this level is sufficiently consistent and stable to have taken on the characteristics of a belief or an attitude. The learner displays this behavior with sufficient consistency in appropriate situations that he comes to be perceived as holding a value. At this level, we are not concerned with the relationships among values but rather with the internalization of a set of specified, ideal, values. Viewed from another standpoint, the objectives classified here are the prime stuff from which the conscience of the individual is developed into active control of behavior.

This category will be found appropriate for many objectives that use the term "attitude" (as well as, of course, "value").

An important element of behavior characterized by *Valuing* is that it is motivated, not by the desire to comply or obey, but by the individual's commitment to the underlying value guiding the behavior.

3.1 Acceptance of a value At this level we are concerned with the ascribing of worth to a phenomenon, behavior, object, etc. The term "belief," which is defined as "the emotional acceptance of a proposition or doctrine upon what one implicitly considers adequate ground" . . . describes quite well what may be thought of as the dominant characteristic here. Beliefs have varying degrees of certitude. At the lowest level of *Valuing* we are concerned with the lowest levels of certainty; that is, there is more of a readiness to reevaluate one's position than at the higher levels. It is a position that is somewhat tentative.

One of the distinguishing characteristics of this behavior is consistency of response to the class of objects, phenomena, etc. with which the belief or attitude is identified. It is consistent enough so that the person is perceived by others as holding the belief or value. At the level we are describing here, he is both sufficiently consistent that others can identify the value, and sufficiently committed that he is willing to be so identified.

3.2 Preference for a value The provision for this subdivision arose out of a feeling that there were objectives that expressed a level of internalization between the mere acceptance of a value and commitment or conviction in the usual connotation of deep involvement in an area. Behavior at this level implies not just the acceptance of a value to the point of being willing to be identified with it, but the individual is sufficiently committed to the value to pursue it, to seek it out, to want it.

3.3 Commitment Belief at this level involves a high degree of certainty. The ideas of "conviction" and "certainty beyond a shadow of a doubt" help to convey further the level of behavior intended. In some instances this may border on faith, in the sense of it being a firm emotional acceptance of a belief upon admittedly nonrational grounds. Loyalty to a position, group, or cause would also be classified here.

The person who displays behavior at this level is clearly perceived as holding the value. He acts to further the thing valued in some way, to extend the possibility of his developing it, to deepen his involvement with it and with the things representing it. He tries to convince others and seeks converts to his cause. There is a tension here which needs to be satisfied; action is the result of an aroused need or drive. There is a real motivation to act out the behavior.

4.0 Organization As the learner successively internalizes values, he encounters situations for which more than one value is relevant. Thus necessity arises for (a) the organization of the values into a system, (b) the determination of the interrelationships among them, and (c) the establishment of the dominant and pervasive ones. Such a system is built gradually, subject to change as new values are incorporated. This category is intended as the proper classification for objectives which describe the beginnings of the building of a value system. . . .

4.1 Conceptualization of a value In the previous category, 3.0 *Valuing*, we noted that consistency and stability are integral characteristics of the particular value or belief. At this level (4.1) the quality of abstraction or conceptualization is added. This permits the individual to see how the value relates to those that he already holds or to new ones that he is coming to hold.

Conceptualization will be abstract, and in this sense it will be symbolic. But the symbols need not be verbal symbols. Whether conceptualization first appears at this point on the affective continuum is a moot point. . . .

4.2 Organization of a value system Objectives properly classified here are those which require the learner to bring together a complex of values, possibly disparate values, and to bring these into an ordered relationship with one another. Ideally, the ordered relationship will be one which is harmonious and internally consistent. This is, of course, the goal of such objectives, which seek to have the student formulate a philosophy of life. In actuality, the integration may be something less than entirely harmonious. More likely the relationship is better described as a kind of dynamic equilibrium which is, in part, dependent upon those portions of the environment which are salient at any point in time. In many instances the organization of values may result in their synthesis into a new value or value complex of a higher order.

5.0 Characterization by a value or value complex At this level of internalization the values already have a place in the individual's value hierarchy, are organized into some kind of internally consistent system, have controlled the behavior of the individual for a sufficient time that he has adapted to behaving this way; and an evocation of the behavior no longer arouses emotion or affect except when the individual is threatened or challenged.

The individual acts consistently in accordance with the values he has internalized at this level, and our concern is to indicate two things: (a) the generalization of this control to so much of the individual's behavior that he is described and characterized as a person by these pervasive controlling tendencies, and (b) the integration of these beliefs, ideas, and attitudes into a total philosophy or world view. These two aspects constitute the subcategories.

5.1 Generalized set The generalized set is that which gives an internal consistency to the system of attitudes and values at any particular moment. It is selective responding at a very high level. It is sometimes spoken of as a determining tendency, an orientation toward phenomena, or a predisposition to act in a certain way. The generalized set is a response to highly generalized phenomena. It is a persistent and consistent response to a family of related situations or objects. It may often be an unconscious set which guides action without conscious forethought. The generalized set may be thought of as closely related to the idea of an attitude cluster, where the commonality is based on behavioral characteristics rather than the subject or object of the attitude. A generalized set is a basic orientation which enables the individual to reduce and order the complex world about him and to act consistently and effectively in it.

5.2 Characterization This, the peak of the internalization process, includes those objectives which are broadest with respect both to the phenomena covered and to the range of behavior which they comprise. Thus, here are found those objectives which concern one's view of the universe, one's philosophy of life, one's *Weltanschauung*—a value system having as its object the whole of what is known or knowable.

Objectives categorized here are more than generalized sets in the sense that they involve a greater inclusiveness and, within the group of attitudes, behaviors, beliefs, or ideas, an emphasis on internal consistency. Though this internal consistency may not always be exhibited behaviorally by the students toward whom the objective is directed, since we are categorizing teachers' objectives, this consistency feature will always be a component of *Characterization* objectives.

As the title of the category implies, these objectives are so encompassing that they tend to characterize the individual almost completely.

PART
2

13

Evaluation of Learning in

Preschool Education:

Socio-emotional, Perceptual-motor, and Cognitive Development

CONSTANCE K. KAMII

Curriculum Director
Ypsilanti Early Education Program
Ypsilanti Public Schools
Ypsilanti, Michigan

Constance K. Kamii received the Doctor of Philosophy degree in education and psychology and the Master of Arts degree in education from the University of Michigan, and the Bachelor of Arts degree in sociology from Pomona College. While she served as a diagnostician and counselor in the Ypsilanti Public Schools, her interests shifted from diagnosis and remediation to prevention of school problems. She served as Research Associate of the Perry Preschool Project in Ypsilanti. While working on this project, she became aware of the need for a curriculum based on a developmental theory and a theory of knowledge, and studied under Piaget, Inhelder, and Sinclair at the University of Geneva. She is currently directing the development of a preschool curriculum based on Piaget's theory.

Contents

13

Evaluation of Learning in

Preschool Education:[1]

Socio-emotional, Perceptual-motor, and Cognitive Development

Objectives of preschool education

Compared with the history of education for children over 6 years of age, the story of nursery school instruction is a short one. In the United States it began in the 1920s. Until the early 1960s the purpose of nursery schools was mainly to provide day care for working-class children and to foster the socio-emotional growth of middle-class children. By the middle of the 1960s, however, the focus had shifted to the lower lower class, or "disadvantaged." As the terms "nursery school" and "preschool" imply, the nursery school tends to be an extension of the home, whereas the preschool is a downward extension of the school to prevent the failure of lower-lower-class children in elementary school.

A brief historical review may clarify the difference between the objectives of the nursery school and those of preschools.

The first nursery schools in the 1920s were established for the most part in colleges and universities for research purposes. Their curriculum consisted primarily of habit training, for example, eating and napping, and the promotion of physical health (Sears & Dowley, 1963).

The Depression years of the 1930s introduced the first involvement of the federal government in nursery school education. The primary objective of these schools was to provide jobs for unemployed teachers. The curriculum continued to emphasize physical health and the "good" habits of dressing, washing, eating, and so forth, with surplus food made available from the farm program.

[1] Much of the content of this chapter is based on work done at the Ypsilanti Early Education Program, which is supported by a grant from the U.S. Office of Education (Title III, No. 67-042490, Elementary and Secondary Education Act of 1965). The opinions expressed herein, however, do not necessarily reflect the position or policy of the funding agency, and no official endorsement by the Office of Education should be inferred. The author wishes to express appreciation to the Social Science Research Council, which awarded a postdoctoral fellowship to her to study under Jean Piaget, Bärbel Inhelder, and Hermina Sinclair. This chapter could not have been written without a year of study at the University of Geneva on this fellowship. The author is also indebted to Benjamin Bloom, Hermina Sinclair, Louise Derman, Robert Peper, and Millie Almy, who contributed many valuable ideas to this chapter.

TABLE 13-1 TABLE OF SPECIFICATIONS FOR PRESCHOOL EDUCATION: SOCIO-EMOTIONAL, PERCEPTUAL-MOTOR, AND COGNITIVE OBJECTIVES

	OBJECTIVES																		
	Socio-emotional								*Perceptual-motor*		*Cognitive*								
													Logical knowledge					*Representation*	
	Dependence on the teacher	*Inner controls*	*Interaction: quantity*	*Interaction: quality*	*Comfort in school*	*Achievement motivation*	*Curiosity*	*Creativity*	*Gross motor coordination*	*Fine motor coordination*	*Physical knowledge*	*Social knowledge*	*Classification*	*Seriation*	*Number*	*Space*	*Time*	*Symbols*	*Language: signs*
CONTENT	*A*	*B*	*C*	*D*	*E*	*F*	*G*	*H*	*I*	*J*	*K*	*L*	*M*	N	*O*	*P*	Q	R	S
1. The self																			
2. Body parts																			
3. Members of the class																			
4. Members of the family																			
5. Community roles																			
6. Playground equipment																			
7. Foods																			
8. Clothes																			
9. Furniture																			
10. Houses and buildings																			
11. Tools																			
12. Kitchen utensils																			
13. Vehicles																			
14. Animals																			
15. Plants																			
16. Art materials (e.g., paint)																			
17. Toys (e.g., balls)																			
18. Colors																			
19. Sizes																			
20. Shapes																			

World War II brought about the allocation of federal funds for day-care centers for children of the many working mothers employed in war industries. Although the curriculum continued to center on child care, a new concern for children's emotional life came into being as a result of Freud's theory, the writings of Frank (1938), Gesell (1940, 1943), and Spock (1946), and the children's emotional problems stemming from the mother's employment and the father's absence (Stolz et al., 1954). Although nursery schools began as child-care centers, they thus gradually took on the function of providing preventive psychiatry.

The postwar years gave impetus to the cooperative nursery school. Although the nursery school had fostered children's socio-emotional growth ever since its beginning as part of providing good care for them, the cooperative nursery school placed a new conscious emphasis on socio-emotional development. This objective came to be articulated in the 1940s.

Cognitive development, too, was the concern of many nursery school educators ever since the 1920s (Isaacs, 1930; Johnson, 1928; Landreth, 1942). In the 1960s, two major forces contributed to a new emphasis on it. One was the civil rights movement and the massive federal funds which because of this movement became available to prevent school failures among lower-lower-class children. The other was the accumulation of knowledge that pointed to early childhood as the period when children are most susceptible to intervention (Bennett, Diamond, Kretch, & Rosenzweig, 1964; Bloom, 1964; Hunt, 1961; Kirk, 1958; Piaget, 1954; Skeels & Dye, 1939).

This brief historical review shows the evolution of the nursery school as beginning with general objectives that became more and more differentiated. This evolution took place as a result of the social and historical forces that emphasized different aspects of the child. In reality, it has never been possible to separate the physical care of the child from his socio-emotional development, or his socio-emotional development from his intellectual growth. The evolution of the nursery school is reflected in two editions of Read's *The Nursery School*. In the 1960 edition, only 13 of the 333 pages were devoted to a section entitled "Curriculum." However, such activities as painting, dramatic play, taking care of animals, and using playground equipment, which have cognitive as well as affective aspects, were included under "creative expression" and "building feelings of confidence and adequacy." In the 1966 edition of the same book, the author devoted an entire chapter to the child's intellectual development.

The above historical review shows the isolation of the nursery school from other educational institutions with regard to both objectives and institutional status. By the late 1960s, however, many preschools had become part of public schools in their objectives, although not in institutional status. This rapprochement can be seen in Hechinger (1966) and in Hess and Bear (1968).

The evolution of the objectives of preschools is summarized in Fig. 13-1. The present chapter will deal with the evaluation of preschool instruction in the broad sense, including the more traditional one of socio-emotional growth.

The various preschool programs in existence today differ considerably in their objectives and methods of instruction (Pines, 1966). However, it

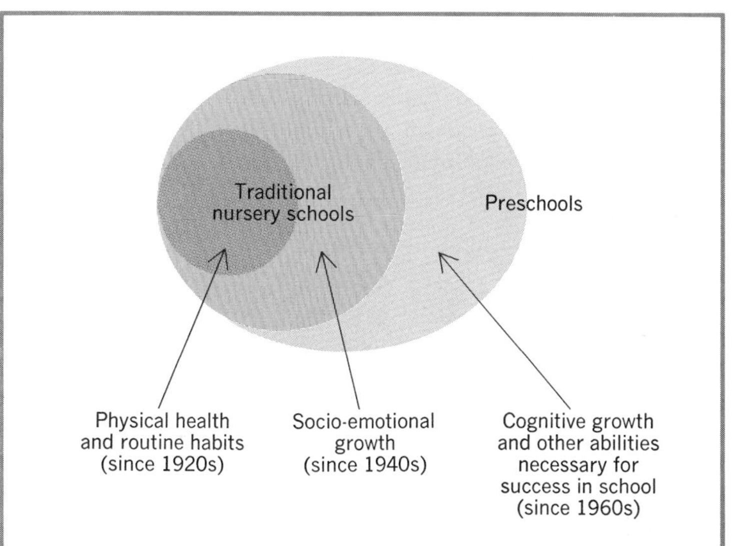

FIGURE 13-1 The evolution of nursery school and preschool objectives.

is possible to conceptualize the broad objectives of the field as a whole from such sources as Sears and Dowley (1963), Hechinger (1966), Hess and Bear (1968), and Almy (1964). Sears and Dowley review the field as it was before the 1960s. The books edited by Hechinger and by Hess and Bear reflect the focus of the 1960s, that is, how to use preschool education to help provide equal opportunity for lower-lower-class children. Almy points out that the thinking of young children differs qualitatively and fundamentally from that of adults, and that teaching in early childhood must take these differences into account. The objectives of preschool education can also be found in the specific program descriptions of Bereiter and Engelmann (1966); Gray, Klaus, Miller, and Forrester (1966); and Read (1960, 1966). The broad objectives of preschool education as gleaned from these sources and many others can be summarized as follows:

1. Socio-emotional development
2. Perceptual-motor development
3. Cognitive development
4. Language development

This chapter will deal with the first three of these four areas. The evaluation of language development is discussed in the next chapter by Courtney Cazden. Specific outcomes sought in the three areas and a few examples of the content which can be used appear in Table 13-1, Table of Specifications for Preschool Education: Socio-emotional, Perceptual-motor, and Cognitive Objectives.

Socio-emotional objectives (A–H)

Socio-emotional development is important not only in its own right but also for cognitive development. The various aspects of socio-emotional development that are stressed by various authors (Beller, 1968; Gray et al., 1966; Mumbauer, 1968; Piaget, 1963; Read, 1960, 1966; Sears & Dowley, 1963) are summarized below and discussed later in further detail.

1. In relation to the teacher
   a. Dependence on the teacher
   b. Inner controls
2. In relation to peers
   a. Interaction with other children
   b. Ability to get along with other children
3. In relation to schoolwork
   a. Comfort in school
   b. Achievement motivation and pride of mastery
   c. Curiosity
   d. Creativity

Dependence on the teacher (A) "Dependence" refers to the child's healthy seeking of emotional support from adults. The child who seeks the teacher's attention, help, and recognition as well as physical contact can be said to be emotionally dependent on him. "The fostering of identification with the teacher" is another way of stating this objective.

Dependence on the teacher appears to go hand in hand with the development of *Inner controls* (objective *B*), *Achievement motivation* (objective *F*), and the *Cognitive objectives* (*K–S*). In an investigation of the origins of inner controls, Kamii and Radin (1967) found that middle-class mothers interact with their 4-year-old children in ways that enhance dependence but that lower-lower-class mothers do not. Tracing the available threads of empirical and theoretical evidence, they concluded that the child's dependence on his parents is a prerequisite for his motivation to please them by behaving in accordance with their wishes. The cultivation of dependence on the teacher, therefore, appears to be a major part of compensatory education. The lower-lower-class child who develops a close emotional bond with his teacher is probably undergoing a delayed development of what normally occurs earlier in middle-class children. This emotional tie makes it possible for the teacher to reach the child and influence him to learn and become socialized.

In a comparison of lower-lower-class first-graders who entered school at ages 4, 5, and 6 (in nursery school, kindergarten, and first grade), Beller (1968) found that the child who is free to turn to the teacher for support has (1) a significantly higher IQ on both the Stanford-Binet and Peabody Picture Vocabulary Test and (2) more ability to initiate and complete activities on his own (an aspect of *Achievement motivation*). He also found that the earlier the child enters school, the more he develops healthy dependence on the teacher.

Inner controls (B) *Inner controls* refers to the child's ability to behave in accordance with the standards that are expected of him. In its minimal form, this ability can be contrasted with external controls, such as teachers, parents, and policemen, who will punish the child if he does not obey them. Inner controls thus refer first of all to the child's ability to obey the authority figures who are present without their having recourse to threats. The term also refers to the child's ability to behave well when authority figures are removed. In the most highly developed sense, therefore, inner controls can be equated with conscience.

Interaction with other children (C) Very young children begin by playing alone, and one of the objectives of preschool education is to develop in them a tendency to interact with other children (Read, 1966). Interpersonal interactions are desirable not only for intrinsic reasons but also for cognitive development. It is through the exchange of viewpoints that children develop their language and logic (Piaget, 1963).

Ability to get along with other children (D) It is probably desirable to increase the *amount* of children's interactions even if the *quality* may be too aggressive or too impulsive. However, once the children begin to interact with each other, the next instructional goal is to develop their ability to get along by sharing things, taking turns, and accepting other people's points of view. The child who is rejected by his peers because of his inability to get along is not likely to be happy in school, and his chances for success are seriously hampered.

Comfort in school (E) Coming to preschool is usually the child's very first venture outside the home, and some children remain insecure and constricted for a long time. The first concern of preschool education, therefore, is to enhance the child's comfort in school. Without security the child cannot learn very much.

Achievement motivation and pride of mastery (F) The desire to achieve is important to prepare the child to take part in a society that values individual accomplishments. The achievement motive refers to a tendency to (1) initiate activities, (2) persist in them until the task is completed, and (3) do the tasks well. The need to achieve does not necessarily imply the competitiveness to grit one's teeth to outdo others. It often refers to a capacity to *enjoy* learning and meeting challenges. The preschool years are a time when children naturally take enormous pride in their accomplishments.

In the study referred to earlier, Beller (1968) found that "autonomous achievement striving" correlated significantly both with IQ and with freedom to express dependence. These three variables clearly seem to make a package of "school readiness." In other words, dependence and independent achievement striving are not at opposite ends of the same continuum. Emotional dependence enables the child to internalize external expectations and to behave independently with pride of achievement.

A dimension which can be viewed as part of the achievement motive because of the internalized standards involved is reflectivity–impulsivity. "Reflectivity" refers to the child's taking time to think about his answer before responding to a question. "Impulsivity" is at the other end of the continuum, and reflects the shorter reaction time which is accompanied by many errors; impulsive children respond fast without reflecting critically on the correctness of the possible solutions. Impulsivity often stems from the fear of being wrong. In comparing "disadvantaged" and "advantaged" children, Mumbauer (1968)[2] found a significantly greater incidence of impulsivity among disadvantaged preschoolers than among

[2] Personal communications followed the publication of this newsletter.

middle- and upper-class children of the same age. She also found that impulsivity was related significantly to lower IQ on the Stanford-Binet. These findings suggest that reflectivity is an important aspect of achievement motivation.

Curiosity (G) For the child to grow cognitively, it is not enough for him to be comfortable, hard-working, and passive. One of the goals of preschool education is the fostering of curiosity, so that the child will reach out, experiment, and seek new knowledge rather than waiting for the teacher to feed it to him.

Creativity (H) *Creativity* is often found among the objectives of preschool education. A creative child has many ideas and comes up with many different things in a given situation. We need to educate children to tackle problems in many ways rather than teach them that there is only one correct answer to each question.

Perceptual-motor objectives (I, J)

Perceptual-motor abilities are those which enable the child to do with his muscles what he wants and intends to do. At 4 years of age many children cannot cut paper with scissors, for example, even if they intellectually know exactly what they want to do. The perceptual-motor objectives of preschool education are, therefore, to develop children's muscular coordination within the limits of their physical maturation. These objectives are stressed by Read (1960, 1966) and by Sears and Dowley (1963).

Perceptual-motor development is important for many reasons. First, the children's muscular development is essential for exercise and physical health. A child who moves awkwardly is likely to develop feelings of inferiority, and if he is preoccupied with his awkwardness, he is not free to concentrate on more intellectual tasks. There is also a body of evidence (Frostig, Maslow, Lefever, & Whittlesey, 1964; Kephart, 1960) which suggests that perceptual-motor disabilities may be associated with various learning problems.

Perceptual-motor objectives are usually divided into those involving gross muscle coordination and those involving fine muscle coordination.

Gross motor coordination (I) *Gross motor coordination* involves large movements of the major parts of the body. Some examples are the ability to climb the jungle gym, to walk on a balance board, to jump, and to throw and catch a large ball at the desired spot.

Fine motor coordination (J) *Fine motor coordination* in preschool education usually involves eye-hand coordination. Some examples are the ability to cut paper with scissors, to draw a line between two lines spaced a quarter of an inch apart, to fold paper, to paste, and to insert pegs in a pegboard.

A few comments must be made regarding some tasks which are usually called "perceptual" or "motor" in the literature but which are excluded from the *Perceptual-motor objectives* in this chapter. In the author's opinion, many of these tasks are cognitive and belong to the *Cognitive objectives*, below, because they involve the construction of the object, classification, seriation, and the structuring of space.

For example, in *Before First Grade* (Gray et al., 1966, pp. 21–22), "perception" is defined as follows:

> Perception may be thought of in simple terms as the recognition or identification of patterns of sensory stimulation. We perceive a pencil when a certain pattern of light waves gives us sensations of color as yellow, and of form as elongated with a single, pointed end. We perceive an apple through still other patterns of color and shape, as well as odor and taste. . . .

The development of this kind of "perception" is not considered under *Perceptual-motor objectives* in this chapter, as the author feels that the recognition of pencils, apples, and the like belongs to the cognitive realm of the construction of the object. The discrimination of colors, shapes, and sizes is likewise not included under *Perceptual-motor objectives* because it is felt that these are cognitive tasks involving classification, seriation, and the structuring of space.

Also excluded from this category of objectives are many abilities which are considered "perceptual" or "perceptual-motor" in the Developmental Test of Visual Perception (Frostig, 1963) and the Purdue Perceptual-motor Survey (Roach & Kephart, 1966). For example, the first subtest of the Developmental Test of Visual Perception is called Eye-motor Coordination. The first nine items of this subtest appear to be visual-motor coordination tasks, but the others require the connecting of two dots with a line, that is, the construction of the projective line (Piaget & Inhelder, 1967). "Imitation of body movement" and "angels-in-the snow," which appear in the Purdue Perceptual-motor Survey, likewise require much more than perceptual-motor coordination: they involve the reconstruction of sensory-motor knowledge of the body on the representational plane.

Cognitive objectives (K–S)

The importance of cognitive development has been stressed in many publications to which reference has already been made. As can be seen particularly in Hess and Bear (1968), many preschools are in existence primarily to foster children's cognitive development. However, these schools are operated without a theoretical framework that delineates the specific objectives of cognitive development. The only tightly organized set of objectives known to the author is that which is based on Piaget's theory of knowledge (Kamii & Radin, 1970; Sonquist, Kamii, & Derman, 1970). The cognitive objectives of the various preschool programs will be discussed below in relation to Piaget's framework, since it gives the most inclusive and organized set of objectives. This framework encompasses physical knowledge, social knowledge, logical knowledge, and representation.

Physical knowledge, social knowledge, and logical knowledge, according to Piaget, are structured from different sources of feedback. Physical knowledge is structured from feedback from objects; social knowledge is structured from feedback from people; and logical knowledge is structured from feedback from the cognitive structure that the child has already built. An example of physical knowledge is the child's dropping a glass and finding out that it breaks. An example of social knowledge is the child's finding out that when he breaks the glass, his mother gets angry. People are the only source of this kind of knowledge because anger comes from people, and rules about personal property and the money involved in replacing the glass are socially derived. As he drops many objects, the child finds out that *some* objects break and *others* do not. This kind of group that the child mentally makes is an example of logical knowledge. Unlike physical and social knowledge, which are built from feedback from external sources, logical knowledge is built from feedback from the cognitive structure that the child has already built. For example, the ability to judge whether or not there are more objects in the world than breakable objects, or more glass objects than breakable objects, cannot come from simple feedback from the external world. The child has to build a logical cognitive structure to become able to make this kind of judgment, and this structure can be built only from feedback from the structure that the child has already built.

Physical knowledge (K) According to Piaget, the child learns about the nature of matter by acting on objects and observing and systematizing the results of these actions. Stretching, folding, cutting, floating, hitting, tapping, squeezing, blowing, breaking, and dropping are examples of actions the child can perform on any object in his environment. By acting on things and observing how the objects react, the child gradually becomes able to predict the effects of these actions on particular objects.

The objectives of instruction in the teaching of physical knowledge are (1) to build the child's knowledge about the properties of all the objects in his environment and (2) to give him a repertoire of actions on objects to enable him to explore the properties of unfamiliar things.

Social knowledge (L) Social knowledge is derived from people and is most arbitrary from the child's point of view. It can be divided into knowledge of rules that apply to the child himself and knowledge that remains in the realm of information. An example of the former is "Tables are to sit at, not to sit on," and an example of the latter is "A doctor does certain things, and a fireman does certain other things." The instructional goal of preschools in social knowledge encompasses both the above two types. The first is closely related to the development of inner controls (objective *B*) in that the cognitive knowledge of social rules is a small part of the child's ability to behave in conformity with social expectations.

As can be seen in the Piaget-based framework (Kamii & Radin, 1970), logical knowledge is divided into logico-mathematical knowledge and spatio-temporal knowledge. The former is totally independent of all spatial and temporal considerations, and the latter is concerned strictly with space and time. Logico-mathematical knowledge is here further divided into classification, seriation, and numerical construction. They will now be discussed as objectives *M*, *N*, and *O*.

Logical knowledge: classification (M) The long-range objective of *Classification* is the ability to group objects together by coordinating their qualitative and quantitative aspects. This ability can be seen in class inclusion, which is attained at about 7 years of age. An example of class inclusion is the ability to see, if there are green and red wooden beads, that there are more wooden beads than red ones. The qualitative aspects in this situation are the color and material. The quantitative aspects are the notions of "some," "all," and "more."

Logical knowledge is structured very slowly and very gradually. Therefore, the function of preschool is to teach certain prerequisite abilities that will help the child to achieve class inclusion at about 7 years of age. Inhelder and Piaget (1964) have shown that many 4-year-olds tend to put together a blue square and a blue circle because they are both blue, and then add a red circle because they are circles. In order to maintain a consistent criterion, the child must develop not only the ability to abstract a similar attribute but also the mobility of thought that enables him to remember why he put the first and second objects together and to use the same criterion for the sixth and seventh objects.

When the child can select and apply one criterion consistently, the next objective for him is the ability to shift to another criterion. For example, after grouping geometric shapes by color (red versus blue), the child may shift to the criterion of shape (squares versus circles) when he is asked to group the objects in "a different way." The third objective for him is the ability to shift again. In this situation the third criterion may be size.

Logical knowledge: seriation (N) Whereas *classification* involves the grouping of objects without regard to how they are arranged within each group, *the establishment of relations* refers to the comparing and arranging of things according to a given dimension by coordinating transitive relationships. An example at the 7-year-old level is the seriation, or ordering, of ten sticks, all of different lengths, in a descending order without resorting to trial and error. By the time he is about 7, the child usually does not need to engage in trial and error because he can coordinate transitive relationships. In other words, he can *reason* that if D is shorter than C, C is shorter than B, and B is shorter than A, then D is the *shortest* of A, B, C, and D. D is at the same time the *longest* of D, E, F, G, H, I, and J if D is longer than E, E is longer than F, and so on. The child who cannot mentally coordinate these transitive relationships has to resort to external trial and error to order the ten sticks.

Logical knowledge in seriation too is structured very slowly. The objectives of preschool instruction should therefore include the teaching of prerequisites for seriation so that it will become possible a few years later. One of the objectives may be the ability to *find* "one that is bigger [or smaller] than this one" and "all those that are bigger [or smaller] than this one" with five or six objects that are identical except for size (for example, nesting cups of one color). Another objective may be the ability to *make* four balls, snakes, or other objects with clay, each one being bigger than the one that was made before. A third objective may be the ability to *order* by trial and error five or six objects all of different sizes.

Seriation involves transitive relationships which are found in many other qualities, such as different shades of the same color and hardness and softness. The 4-year-old needs to compare differences with a wide variety of content in order to construct eventually a logical system of transitive relationships. The above three objectives of preschool education must therefore be achieved not only with different sizes but also with shades of the same color, consistency of play dough, temperature differences, and so forth.

Logical knowledge: numerical construction (O) The instructional objective in this area might be the conservation of eight to ten objects with "provoked correspondence."[3] When given eight cups placed in a line, a 4- to 5-year-old child can be expected to put on the table "enough saucers for all the cups but not too many." When he spreads the saucers apart and pushes the cups close together, he is said to have conservation of number with provoked correspondence if he can tell whether or not there are still "enough saucers for all the cups but not too many."

Number is a complicated logical system involving the cognitive structures of classification and seriation. Therefore, the objective of teaching should not be the inductive learning of the "principle" that changing the spatial configuration does not change the number. Rather, the child should learn the logic involved in making quantitative comparisons of two groups of objects. He learns this logic by making collections, making gross comparisons between them ("a lot" versus "a little"), arranging and rearranging the objects in each collection, making an exact comparison by one-to-one correspondence, destroying this correspondence, and finding out whether or not the correspondence can be reestablished. Provoked correspondence helps the child maintain the correspondence logically when it is perceptually no longer present.

The structuring of space (P) Three directions of development can be discerned from Piaget's theory on the progressive structuring of space. One concerns the child's progressive structuring of space from a structure that has only topological characteristics to one that has euclidean characteristics as well.[4] Another involves the development of static space into more dynamic transformations. The third aspect is the reconstruction of sensory-motor space on a representational level.

The first instructional objective in the structuring of space may be the traditional ability to grasp the notions of "in-out," "over-under," "in front of–in back of," and so forth. These relationships are examples of topological space, out of which euclidean characteristics emerge. The preschool child should be able to handle these topological concepts not only concretely with his own body but also on the representational plane with toys, pictures, and words.

The second objective involving topological relationships concerns linear order: the ability to coordinate proximity relationships to copy the placement of objects (1) in exactly the same linear arrangement, (2) with objects of the copy squeezed closer together or spread farther apart than those of the model, and (3) in inverse order

[3] "Provoked correspondence" refers to the correspondence of two sets of objects which by their nature have a one-to-one relationship. For example, only one cup can go with a saucer, and this qualitative correspondence facilitates the establishment of the quantitative one-to-one correspondence. This provoked correspondence is thus easier than "spontaneous correspondence," which is exemplified by a set of pink cups to correspond with a set of blue cups.

[4] Topological space has such characteristics as openness and closure and separation and proximity, but not such euclidean characteristics as the projective line, angles, parallels, proportions, and number of elements. For a fuller explanation, see Piaget & Inhelder (1967).

(as in changing ABCD to DCBA). With clothes, for example, the child can be expected to arrange the objects on his clothes line in exactly the same way as the teacher's (a T-shirt, a pair of pants, a dress, and so on).

The third objective may relate to spatial transformation, such as the ability to cut a whole shape into many parts and put them back together, as shown in Fig. 13-2. Another example of spatial transformation is paper folding. A 4-year-old child can be expected to reproduce a model like the folded triangle shown in the same figure.

The last objective in the structuring of space may be the ability to reconstruct the sensory-motor knowledge of space on the representational plane. The perceptual task of *finding* another circle, square, or triangle is easy for a preschooler. However, the difficulty emerges when the same task is given at the representational level of copying the shapes (Piaget & Inhelder, 1967).

The structuring of time (Q) The instructional objectives for the structuring of time may concern the temporal ordering of three or four events. Temporal order is related closely to physical and social knowledge. For example, the child must be able to structure the sequence of getting milk out of the refrigerator, pouring it into a glass, knocking the full glass over, and having a puddle on the floor. Being able to order an undershirt, a dress shirt, a necktie, and a jacket in terms of what we put on first, next, next, and last is an example of temporal order related to social knowledge.

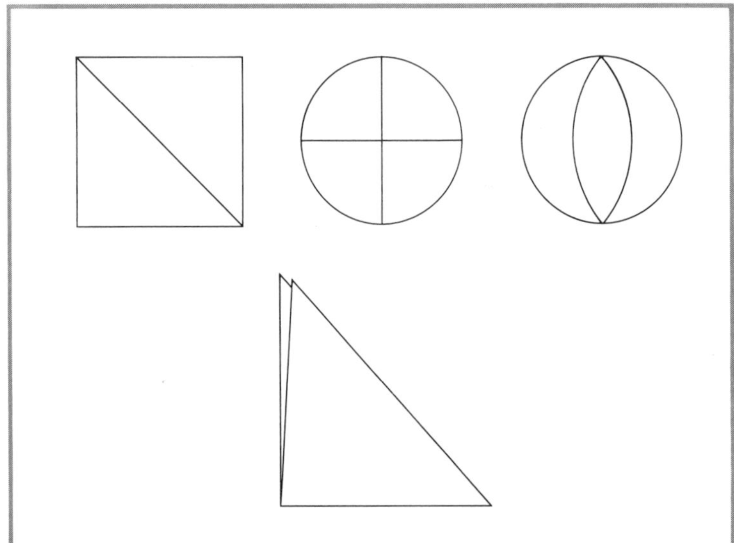

FIGURE 13-2 Examples of transformation by cutting and reassembling and by folding.

Representation at the symbol level (R) The three levels of representation delineated by Piaget are "indices," "symbols," and "signs."[5] As emphasized in Sonquist, Kamii, and Derman (1970), a major objective of preschool education is to strengthen children's mental image at the symbol level so as to make language meaningful. There are five types of symbols. Preschool instruction must strengthen the child's ability to symbolize in all of the following areas:

1. Imitation, or the use of the body to represent objects. An example might be the child's pretending to hold a telephone receiver.
2. Make-believe, or the use of objects to represent other objects. An example might be the child's holding a pencil to represent a telephone receiver.
3. Onomatopoeia, or the uttering of sounds such as "ring, ring" to represent an object.
4. Three-dimensional models, examples being the making of a model with clay or the use of toys.
5. Two-dimensional representations. Examples might be drawing pictures or recognizing objects in pictures.

A special area of representation is socio-dramatic play. It belongs largely to the symbol level of "imitation" and "make-believe" in the above conceptualization but also includes many other elements, among them temporal sequence, social knowledge, physical knowledge, classification, and language. Socio-dramatic play has a special place in the list of instructional objectives not

[5] The index differs from symbols and signs in that it is part of the object being represented. Symbols and signs are differentiated from the objects. Symbols differ from signs in that they bear a resemblance to the object being represented whereas signs do not resemble the object at all. For a fuller explanation, see Kamii and Radin (1970).

only because it integrates so many cognitive areas but also because it provides *the* bridge between sensory-motor intelligence and representational intelligence. While other symbols use media such as clay and paper, imitation allows the child to use his own body as a symbol. Thus imitation is the only form of representation in which the child uses himself both as a symbol and as a symbolizer.

The following list of instructional aims in socio-dramatic play is based on Smilansky (1968), with some modification.

1. Make-believe with regard to objects, or the use of toys and undefined objects as props in enacting a role
2. Imitative role play
3. Imitative role play involving specific situations[6]
4. Persistence, or making the play last longer
5. Interaction, or moving from parallel play to play in which the children interact with each other
6. Verbal communication, or moving from nonverbal interaction to more and more complex verbal interactions

Representation at the language level (S) One of the major objectives of preschool instruction is the development of language. Language involves the representation not only of individual objects but also of physical, social, and logical knowledge (objectives K to Q). In addition, language involves the child's making inferences to construct an entire system of grammatical rules. For example, "I don't have no shoes" and "Why I can't play outside?" are perfectly adequate sentences from the standpoint of representation and communication but inadequate from the standpoint of language. Moreover, the use of language for communication requires the ability to see things from viewpoints other than one's own. For example, saying, "Bring me my *zori*. They are a kind of sandal" requires the ability to anticipate that the listener does not know what "*zori*" means.

[6] A progressively greater use of language is involved in "imitative role play involving specific situations." For example, a child might say, "Let's pretend that I'm the Mommy, and let's pretend that I cut the bread with a knife and fed my baby and now I really must go to lie down because we're having guests this evening" (Smilansky, 1968, p. 24).

Because language thus has many aspects, it was listed on page 286 as the fourth major objective of preschool education. (The major objectives, it will be recalled, were said to be socio-emotional, perceptual-motor, cognitive, and language development.) Thus language development overlaps objective S, objectives K to Q, and the socio-emotional objectives. The evaluation of language development is discussed in the next chapter, by Cazden.

Content in relation to objectives

The preceding discussion has dealt with the objectives of preschool education without referring very much to the specific content. To teach physical, social, and logical knowledge as well as representation, the content can be literally anything that is found in the child's environment —glasses, spoons, pebbles, paint, and so forth. Those who emphasize "enrichment" believe in extending the child's knowledge of content, and therefore bring many novel things into the classroom and take children to farms, zoos, and museums.

Table 13-1, Table of Specifications for Preschool Education: Socio-emotional, Perceptual-motor, and Cognitive Objectives, presents examples of applicable content. The content can be conceptualized as consisting of the self, people in the immediate and distant environment, objects in the immediate and distant environment, and properties of things, for example, colors and sizes.

It can be seen from the table that "knowing" an object involves knowing it in a social sense, in a physical sense, in a logical sense, and in a representational sense. For example, a glass should be known socially (for instance, it is used to drink milk but not to drink soup) and physically (it breaks, it rolls, it is transparent, and so forth). Glasses should also be known logically. (They can be classified with certain objects, seriated according to size, and quantified so that there will be enough glasses for all the children in the class. They can also be known spatially in terms of "top-bottom," "in-out," and "round-straight" and through linear ordering. An example of knowing a glass in a temporal sense is the sequence of washing it, drying it, and putting it away.)

Table 13-1 represents a general way of looking at the objectives of preschool education. It is necessary to remember that the cells are not all equally important. For example, the self, body parts, playground equipment, and tools are important for perceptual-motor objectives, but community roles and plants are more suitable for other objectives.

In addition to cognitive objectives, teaching involves the constant weaving in of socio-emotional objectives. Thus, the teacher uses every teaching activity to enhance dependence, inner controls, peer interactions, comfort in school, achievement motivation, curiosity, and creativity (objectives *A* to *H*). Preschool education thus involves the use of many content variables to teach physical, social, and logical knowledge as well as to foster the child's socio-emotional and perceptual-motor development.

The objectives of various types of preschool programs

As described above in the historical review of preschool education, nursery schools evolved out of various social forces. As a result there are different types of preschool programs in existence today with varying views of the 4-year-old child and how he should be educated. The programs are so diverse and numerous that it is difficult to categorize them in ways that everyone could agree on. However, on the basis of the major recent publications (Bereiter & Engelmann, 1966; Deutsch, 1967; Gray et al., 1966; Hechinger, 1966; Hess & Bear, 1968; Kamii & Radin, 1970; Karnes, 1968; Karnes, Hodgins, & Teska, 1968; Montessori, 1967; Pines, 1966; Read, 1960, 1966; Sears & Dowley, 1963) and inferences from personal observations, the programs in existence will be grouped into three categories for the purposes of the present discussion. The three groups are the traditional nursery school, the cognitively oriented preschool, and the Piagetian cognitively oriented preschool. The objectives of the three types of programs will now be discussed with reference to Table 13-1 and illustrated graphically in Table 13-2, Tables of Specifications Showing the Stated Objectives of the Various Types of Preschool Programs.

The traditional nursery school

The traditional nursery school as represented by Read (1960, 1966) is concerned basically with the 4-year-old child as a socio-emotional being. Its stated objectives appear to be the following:

Objective	*Description*
B	The traditional nursery school discusses this objective not in terms of *Inner controls* but as the desire to foster socially desirable behavior in the child.
C and *D*	Learning to interact more with other children and to get along with them is of utmost importance in the traditional nursery school.
E–H	*Comfort in school, Achievement motivation and pride of mastery, Curiosity,* and *Creativity* are also of utmost importance. The traditional nursery school deemphasizes cognitive development. Its cognitive goals are usually subsumed under the socio-emotional objectives of mastery, curiosity, and creativity.
I and *J*	The development of perceptual-motor coordination has a prominent place in the nursery school.

In summary, the principal objectives of the nursery school are socio-emotional and perceptual-motor (objectives *B* to *J*).[7] It uses all the content enumerated in Table 13-1 to achieve its objectives. Therefore, we can say that the objectives of the traditional nursery school encompass the left half of Table 13-1, as can be seen in Table 13-2.

[7] The traditional nursery school does not consciously strive to develop emotional dependence on the teacher (objective *A*). Rather, it encourages independence (objective *F*). These two terms are not in opposition to each other. "Emotional dependence" refers to "identification," or an emotional bond, whereas "independence" refers to the child's behavior, for example, his ability to get dressed by himself. The omission of objective *A* from the list of nursery school objectives does not imply a total absence of incidental efforts in its direction.

Table 13-2 Tables of Specifications Showing the Stated Objectives of the Various Types of Preschool Programs

1. The traditional nursery school

Objectives

Content	Socio-Emotional	P.M.	Cognitive
	A B C D E F G H	I J	K L M N O P Q R S
1			
2			
3			
.			
.			
etc.			

2. The cognitively oriented preschool

(a) GRAY

Objectives

Content	Socio-Emotional	P.M.	Cognitive
	A B C D E F G H	I J	K L M N O P Q R S
1			
2			
3			
.			
.			
etc.			

(b) BEREITER-ENGELMANN

Objectives

Content	Socio-Emotional	P.M.	Cognitive
	A B C D E F G H	I J	K L M N O P Q R S
1			
2			
3			
.			
.			
etc.			

3. The Piagetian cognitively oriented preschool

Objectives

Content	Socio-Emotional	P.M.	Cognitive
	A B C D E F G H	I J	K L M N O P Q R S
1			
2			
3			
.			
.			
etc.			

[shaded box] Objectives included in the particular type of program

It must be pointed out, however, that in a less conscious and less systematic way, nursery schools engage in a great many cognitive activities. Growing plants, engaging in dramatic play, painting, listening to stories, singing, putting puzzles together, learning about sizes, and counting are examples of activities that are found in all nursery schools. However, these activities are not conducted deliberately for cognitive growth. The assumption of the traditional nursery school is that if the child's feelings of independence, mastery, and adequacy are developed, his cognitive growth will naturally follow.

The cognitively oriented preschool

The cognitively oriented preschool educator views the child as one who *can* learn cognitively and believes that preschool *will* make a difference in the child's ability to succeed in school. Just as psychiatry in the socio-emotional realm influenced the nursery school to make preventive efforts in the 1940s, theories of intelligence made an impact in the early 1960s in the cognitive domain. The cognitively oriented preschool, therefore, came into being to teach "school readiness" to prevent school failures among children of the lower-lower class.

Two major approaches are being tried to enhance school readiness. One is based essentially on a systematic use of traditional nursery school methods, while the other uses pattern drill in a unique way to develop the children's language. Deutsch (1967), Gray et al. (1966), Karnes et al. (1968), and Montessori (1967) are examples of those using the former approach. The latter approach was developed by Bereiter and Engelmann (1966). The objectives of the two will now be discussed.

The Early Training Project (DARCEE)[8] This project is selected as an example of the cognitively oriented preschool based on traditional methods, because its curriculum is widely available to the public and is well articulated with sample lessons (Gray et al., 1966). The two most important objectives of this program are the following:

Objective	*Description*
F	The fostering of achievement motivation is discussed under "attitude development." Delay of gratification, developing interest in school-type activities, and identification with achieving role models are also included under "attitude development."
K–S	The second set of objectives is called "aptitudes related to achievement." They consist of (1) the development of perception, (2) conceptual development, and (3) language development.

Perceptual-motor development (objectives *I* and *J*) is mentioned in passing because of its relevance to schoolwork (e.g., cutting with scissors, painting, coloring, using nails and hammers, etc.).

In spite of all its emphasis on group activities (e.g., dramatic play and field trips), there is no mention in this book of the development of peer relationships as an explicit objective of instruction. Peer relationships such as the control of aggression and learning to take turns are mentioned only in passing. The child's relationship with his teacher, too, is discussed incidentally only because of her importance as an achievement model. It can thus be said that, by and large, the explicit objectives of the cognitively oriented preschool are found on the right-hand side of Table 13-1, as can be seen in Table 13-2. The objectives of the traditional nursery school, in contrast, were found in the other half of Table 13-1. The two are very similar in content, however.

The Bereiter-Engelmann program As the term "the academically oriented preschool" suggests, the Bereiter-Engelmann preschool (Bereiter & Engelmann, 1966) is much more "academic," or verbal, than the Early Training Project. The objectives of this program are language development,

[8] The Early Training Project was an earlier program of DARCEE (Demonstration and Research Center for Early Education) under the direction of Dr. Susan Gray at the George Peabody College for Teachers. The author apologizes for singling out this program to compare the Piagetian preschool with all the other cognitively oriented preschools in America today. As stated in the text, this program was chosen as an example of the most clearly articulated published curriculum reflecting a psychology of education in the Anglo-Saxon tradition.

arithmetic, and reading. *Language development* (objective S) receives the greatest amount of attention and includes a set of words and sentence patterns that are given priority because of their wide logical use.

The Bereiter-Engelmann view of the 4-year-old disadvantaged child is that since he is already academically far behind his middle-class peers, he has to catch up by working extremely hard with a sense of urgency. They conceive of cultural deprivation as language deprivation and argue that words related to logic are particularly important for the child if he is to get along in school. Therefore, they give priority to words such as "or," "and," "not," "if-then," "on," "in," "under," "over," and "between." Also on the priority list are polar opposites (e.g., "big-little," "long-short," etc.) and names of things which belong to classes (e.g., tools, weapons, pieces of furniture, animals, and vehicles). The ability to name colors, to count, and to name vowels and consonants also receives priority.

As it can be seen in Table 13-2, objectives *A* to *J* have no part in the Bereiter-Engelmann program. For these authors, the teacher-pupil relationship is a by-product rather than an objective of preschool education. With regard to peer relationships, the two researchers feel that disadvantaged children already know how to play together; what they do not know is how to work together. Since all the instructional input comes from the teacher in this program, there is no room for curiosity and creativity. Perceptual-motor development likewise has no place in their list of objectives. While *Representation at the language level* (objective S) is greatly stressed, *Representation at the symbol level* (objective *R*) is conspicuously deemphasized. *Physical knowledge* (objective *K*), too, is left out of this program.

There is no list of content included in the Bereiter-Engelmann program. The author is under the impression that the range of content is not very different from what appears in Table 13-1.

A word of elaboration must be added regarding the cognitive objectives of the cognitively oriented preschool. The conceptualization of teaching in early childhood education is usually done in terms of (1) perceptual development, (2) conceptual development, and (3) language development, as if these were segments of a single continuum. There is an assumption in this analysis that perception is at the lowest, most concrete level, and that language is at the highest, most abstract and advanced level. The Bereiter-Engelmann program concentrates its efforts on the language level, whereas the DARCEE approach attempts to build cognition up from perception to language. Although the DARCEE and Bereiter approaches appear to differ in their objectives and theory of learning, they are both based on the same psychology of knowledge. This statement will be further clarified in the next section, on the Piagetian preschool.

The Piagetian cognitively oriented preschool

Piaget's theory is an epistemological one that says nothing about pedagogy. However, since it interprets the child's cognitive development from birth to adolescence, it gives a unique developmental perspective to early childhood education. It also gives the perspective of a broad theory of knowledge. Piaget's description of the structure and sources of knowledge suggests to the preschool educator the possibility of building a curriculum based on his framework. The framework makes it possible for the teacher to know what a 4-year-old has to master in order to progress to the level of a normal 7-year-old and eventually to that of an adolescent.

Piaget saw four major periods in the child's development of intelligence: the *sensory-motor period* (birth to 2 years of age), the *preoperational period* (2 to 7 years of age), the *period of concrete operations* (7 to 11 years of age), and the *period of formal operations* (after 11 or 12 years of age).[9] This developmental perspective can be translated into an educational program that prepares the child for concrete operations. Although operations are not possible in preschool, it is important for the child to build their prerequisites so that they will eventually become possible.

In addition to delineating the four major

[9] A fuller description of each period can be found in Flavell (1963).

periods, Piaget saw stages of development within each period. In most of the books cited in the bibliography, stages I and II refer to the two stages within the preoperational period and stage III refers to the period of concrete operations. Stage I is a completely illogical (or prelogical) stage in every area of logical knowledge. Stage II is a transitional stage, when the child's logic has become coherent up to a point. By the time the child has reached stage III, he has constructed a coherent system of logic. Examples of the three stages can be seen on pages 301 (with regard to classification), 318 (with regard to seriation), and 320 (with regard to number), and also in Table 13-3, page 299. On the basis of the children's chronological age, the objectives of preschool education can be set at the stage-II level of the preoperational period.

From Piaget's descriptive theory, some people draw the implication that development is a process of "unfolding," and that all the teacher can do is wait for this unfolding to take place. At the opposite extreme, others feel that whatever Piaget says a 4-year-old cannot do can be taught with explanations, repetitions, suggestions, and even operant conditioning. The Piaget-based preschool curriculum being developed in Ypsilanti, Michigan, works on the belief that the child should be helped to construct certain prerequisite abilities, but that these abilities should not be imposed by the teacher. The framework, objectives, and general methods of this developmental program can be found in Kamii and Radin (1970); Sonquist, Kamii, and Derman (1970); and Kamii (in press).

As can be seen in Table 13-2, the objectives of the Piagetian preschool program being developed in Ypsilanti include all those that are listed in Table 13-1. The delineation and organization of all the *Cognitive objectives* (*K* to *S*) in this table are based entirely on Piaget's framework.[10]

[10] Representation at the index level has been omitted from this framework because of the author's belief that it belongs more properly to formative evaluations in classification by touch alone and physical knowledge. An example of the former would be to ask the child to group all the balls together and all the blocks together by touch alone. An example of the latter would be to ask him whether or not there is any juice left in the can of fruit juice, and how he can find out about this bit of physical knowledge (by shaking or tilting the can).

The *Socio-emotional objectives* (*A* to *H*) of the Ypsilanti Early Education Program are derived indirectly from Piaget's theory. A point made by Piaget that is of importance to the socio-emotional objectives of preschool education is that social collaboration is essential for the child's intellectual and affective development (Piaget, 1963, 1967). "Operations" literally mean "co-operation," as logic is precisely a coordinated system of points of view, either in the sense of the points of view of different individuals or in the sense of the successive perceptions and intuitions of the same individual. With regard to affective development, Piaget says that social collaboration is important because both kinds of coordination give rise to a spirit of cooperation with adults and other children, and to personal autonomy. Beller (1968), Kamii and Radin (1967), and Read (1966) helped to conceptualize the socio-emotional objectives of preschool education more precisely.

The *Perceptual-motor objectives* (*I* and *J*) of the Ypsilanti Early Education Program are derived not from Piaget's theory but from the objectives of the traditional nursery school (Read, 1966) and the work of Frostig et al. (1963) and Kephart (1960).

The reader may ask, Why base a preschool program on Piaget's theory? There are two main reasons. One is that his theory enables the teacher to delineate and teach the broad basic abilities that are necessary for all the subjects that the child will have to cope with in elementary school. The other is that Piaget's theory encompasses all the activities that were developed by the traditional nursery school, and adds a great deal of depth and a developmental perspective to these activities. These two points will now be elaborated.

The compensatory preschool which bases its curriculum on traditional nursery school activities works on the belief that school readiness will naturally follow if the child is encouraged in an emotionally nurturing setting to climb, to sing, to draw, to engage in dramatic play, and so on. Modern preschool educators, on the other hand, believe that teaching must be structured with definite goals in mind if school readiness is to be

Table 13-3 Some Differences between a Piagetian and a Non-Piagetian Conceptualization of Cognitive Objectives

Cognitive areas in a Piagetian framework	*Cognitive objectives in a non-Piagetian framework*	*Insights given by Piaget's theory*
I. Physical knowledge	Cause-and-effect Growing plants and animals	Physical knowledge is built by structuring the results of actions on objects
II. Social knowledge	Cause-and-effect, in the sense of reward and punishment Community workers	Social knowledge is built by structuring the feedback from people
III. Logical knowledge A. Logico-mathematical operations 1. Classification	Colors Shapes Sizes Farm animals Clothing Foods Pieces of furniture Etc.	Classification is the coordination of qualitative and quantitative aspects of the objects being grouped --- Teaching goals should be set according to the following developmental stages: I: Graphic collections II: Nongraphic collections III: Classification
2. Seriation	Colors Sizes Qualities, e.g., soft-hard	Seriation is the coordination of transitive relationships --- Teaching goals should be set according to the following developmental stages: I: Uncoordinated small series of three or four II: Perceptual seriation III: Operational seriation
3. Number	Numbers Colors	Number is the synthesis of the structures of classification and seriation --- Teaching goals should be set according to the following developmental steps: I: Neither correspondence nor conservation II: Correspondence without conservation III: Both correspondence and conservation

(Continued on page 300.)

Table 13-3 Some Differences between a Piagetian and a Non-Piagetian Conceptualization of Cognitive Objectives (Continued)

Cognitive areas in a Piagetian framework	*Cognitive objectives in a non-Piagetian framework*	*Insights given by Piaget's theory*
B. Spatio-temporal operations 1. Spatial reasoning	Shapes Sizes Body scheme "Reading readiness" activities	Topological notions develop before euclidean ones The preoperational child's space is static Space is reconstructed on the representational plane several years after the structuring of the same organization on the sensory-motor level
2. Temporal reasoning	"Before-after"	Temporal sequence develops out of causal and means-ends relationships. These relationships require representation
IV. Representation	Deriving meaning from pictures and toys	Nonverbal representation at the "index" and "symbol" levels, particularly imitation, strengthens representation at the language level

achieved. The findings of recent research indicate that the latter philosophy is the more tenable of the two (Di Lorenzo & Salter, 1968; Karnes, 1968; Karnes et al., 1968). The question that many preschool educators are now asking is what kind of structure a preschool curriculum should have. One kind is the subject-matter structure; another is one that delineates broad areas cutting across and applying to all subjects. Piaget's theory is the only comprehensive one in existence that analyzes a 4-year-old's knowledge in terms of his past and his future, and I feel that the teaching of broad basic abilities is more fruitful than sequencing teaching goals by subject matter.

Classification is an example of a basic cognitive area that is necessary in all school subjects at the elementary, secondary, and college level. Piaget described how classification is rooted in infancy and develops into the ability to conduct scientific inquiry in adolescence. The baby finds out about "things that can (or cannot) go inside the mouth," "things that can (or cannot) be grasped with one hand," "things that make (or do not make) noises when they are shaken," etc. The baby also learns precursors of class inclusion by making a smaller container fit into a larger container and by experimenting with nesting cups. As a toddler, he continues to structure his intuitive knowledge into "nice people and mean people," "things that break and things that don't break," "things that can be moved and things that are too heavy to move," etc.

Later, when the child is about 4 years of age, he uses space as the principle of grouping things (stage I, the stage of graphic collections). Thus, when asked to put together things that go together, he will arrange objects into a spatial pattern with little regard to objective similarities among them. It is not until the next stage (stage II, the stage of nongraphic collections) that the child groups things according to their similarities and differences. At this time, he will group together "all the green wooden beads," "all the red wooden beads," and "all the red glass beads," but he cannot deal correctly with the quantitative aspect of classification. For instance, he will say that there are more green beads than wooden beads. When the child is about seven years of age (stage III, the stage of classification), however, he will be able to coordinate the quantitative and qualitative aspects of classification, and thus will say that there are more wooden beads than green ones. This coordination is called "class inclusion," which is the cognitive foundation for more and more inclusive hierarchical classes. Multiple classification, the shifting of criteria, and the ability to handle intersections of classes are also stage-III abilities.

The arithmetical operations of addition, subtraction, multiplication, and division, as well as elementary measurements of continuous quantities, are examples of *concrete* operations involving class inclusion with what is *real*. When the child reaches the period of *formal* operations at 11 or 12 years of age, class inclusion develops into the ability to grasp not only the *real* but also the *possible*. The quantification of probabilities and the hypothetico-deductive thinking of scientific inquiry involve class inclusion at the level of formal operations, requiring the coordination of what is hypothetical, or possible. Classes and relationships involve more or less complex groups of operations. A group of operations implies the existence of an invariant. In a way, the existence of an invariant is an observable symptom of the existence of a group of operations—hence, the importance attached to "conservation."

Conservation is rooted in infancy and is applicable to many school subjects.[11] The baby gradually constructs the object and attributes permanency to it. The permanence of the object later develops into the permanence of quantities, which begins to appear at around 5 to 6 years of age in the conservation of number. The conservation of length, area, substance, weight, and volume is subsequently attained during the period of concrete operations (7 to 11 years of age). This ability to conserve quantities in a gross way is the foundation for all precise measurements, which are necessary in mathematics, physics, and chemistry.

Although quantification at the level of concrete operations involves only the *real*, there are quantities which are found in the realm of the *possible*. An example is the concept of infinity in the numerical, spatial, and temporal sense. The child who does not have the conservation of real quantities cannot be expected to handle the hypothetical quantities which are constructed during the period of formal operations.

Reading and arithmetic also show the relevance of a Piaget-based preschool curriculum for the child's ability to cope with schoolwork. Reading, first of all, requires representation—i.e., the evocation of vivid mental images. From the mechanical point of view, it requires a well-structured space to discriminate letters (e.g., *p* versus *q*) and to conserve directions (e.g., left to right). The letters are grouped into words and sentences which require a classificatory scheme. Letters are also arranged linearly (e.g., "saw" versus "was"). A classificatory rule states when a capital letter is required at the beginning of a word, and when a period is required at its end. Most of the time, only an empty space is required between words. As far as content is concerned, the child must have not only the mental images of static, unrelated objects, but also the mobility of thought to coordinate the relationships among objects in space, time, and logic. For example, the passage "John went to the circus with his sister and father. There, he saw elephants and clowns"

[11] Conservation lies halfway between logico-mathematical and physical knowledge.

involves space,[12] time,[13] classification,[14] seriation,[15] number,[16] social knowledge,[17] and physical knowledge.[18]

In arithmetic, a typical problem may be "Mary went to the store with 15 cents and bought 5 cents worth of candy. How much did she have left?" In addition to number, this problem requires class inclusion to set up the equation. "Equal to" is a concept in seriation. Temporal sequence is involved in understanding that Mary left the house, bought candy, and then had some money left. Space, too, has to be coordinated with the problem, since Mary went from home (place A) to the store (place B). Social knowledge is involved in grasping what "store," "money," and "buying" mean. Representation is required to imagine the entire situation depicted in the problem.

The second reason given for basing a preschool curriculum on Piaget's theory is that it encompasses all the traditional nursery school activities and adds depth and insight to them. In the remainder of this section, the differences between the Piagetian preschool and other cognitively oriented preschools will be highlighted. The contrast will be shown by describing how the cognitively oriented preschool built upon the traditional nursery school, and how the Piagetian preschool further built upon the efforts of the cognitively oriented preschool.

To begin with objective K of Table 13-1 and proceed toward objective S, the cognitively oriented preschool adopted from the traditional nursery school the teaching of scientific facts and social roles (e.g., family roles and roles of community workers). Among the former are the growing of plants and animals and the teaching of cause-and-effect; e.g., that ice cubes melt when they are placed in a warm room (Gray et al., 1966, p. 26). Bereiter and Engelmann's objectives differ from those of other cognitively oriented preschools in that they exclude physical and social knowledge and concentrate on language which is relevant to logic.

The cognitively oriented preschool adopted from the nursery school the teaching of colors, shapes, sizes, and numbers. These objectives are usually found under the heading "perceptual discrimination," but the ultimate goal is to get children to verbalize the names of colors, shapes, sizes, and numbers. In spatial relationships, too, the cognitively oriented preschool attempts to achieve the same goal as the traditional nursery: i.e., to understand and verbalize the terms "in-out," "on-over-under," "in front of–in back of," etc. The teaching of classification is emphasized much more in the preschool than in the nursery school, but here, too, the goal is to teach the content and the words. Gray et al. (1966, pp. 25–27) mention the classes of dogs, animals, living things, fruit, vegetables, foods, clothes, and furniture. Bereiter and Engelmann (1966, pp. 49, 162) add to this list the classes of tools, weapons, wild animals, farm animals, plants, vehicles, letters, numbers, geometric shapes, things to read, toys, and buildings.

To the curriculum builder attempting to go beyond the work of the cognitively oriented preschool, Piaget's framework added the following insights:

1. It gave an organized structure to the unrelated mass of specific objectives and delineated the three major areas of knowledge as being structured from the feedback from objects (*Physical knowledge*), people (*Social knowledge*), and the internal consistency of the child's own logical system (*Logical knowledge*). The analysis of these processes enabled the curriculum builder to separate content variables (e.g., *Colors*) from process variables (e.g., *Classification* and *Seriation*).

[12] Some spatial concepts involved are place A (home) and place B (circus). The three people saw certain things at place B.

[13] An example of a temporal concept involved is that the three people saw the elephants during the interval spent at place B.

[14] Some classificatory schemes involved in this passage are "part of the family," "animals," "some people (clowns)," and "during a certain interval within an interval in the past."

[15] "Sister of," "brother of," and "father of" are concepts involving seriation.

[16] "Three people" is an example of numerical quantification. "*Some* elephants" and "*some* clowns" are examples of intensive, or logical, quantification.

[17] "Circus," "clowns," and "elephants at a circus" belong to the realm of social knowledge.

[18] The physical knowledge of the elephants' weight and their natural habitat is part of an appreciation of this passage.

2. It pointed out that intelligence is a structured *process* rather than a collection of facts. It thus enabled the curriculum maker to draw the implication that preschools should enhance the children's cognitive processes, and use content as a tool to build their cognitive structures.

3. It placed the cognition of the 4-year-old in a continuous developmental context, and at the same time showed the thinking of the preoperational child to be fundamentally different from that of an adult. In fact, the author knows of no other theory which gives such astonishing insights into the thinking of preschool children.

4. It clearly separated *Representation* from the three areas of knowledge, and showed that representation is a necessary but not a sufficient condition for knowledge.[19] The implication of this statement for education is that pictures and words may help the child when he has attained a certain cognitive level, but the teaching of words such as "red," "square," "big," and "four" does not at all ensure the child's ability to use these words logically. The concept of a preschool curriculum as proceeding linearly from perceptual development to cognitive development, and finally to language development, thus became completely inadequate.

Since the specific cognitive objectives of a Piagetian preschool have already been described (pages 289–293), the only thing that remains to be explained is how Piagetian objectives differ from those of other cognitively oriented preschools. An objective such as *Classification* in a Piagetian sense means something quite different from what the other cognitively oriented preschools mean by the same term.

In *Physical knowledge* (objective *K*), the Piagetian preschool attempts to teach not only specific facts about the nature of objects but also a repertoire of actions the child can perform on objects to explore their nature. No matter what the child wants the objects to do, objects will always react according to their own nature. For example, no matter how hard the child tries to push a piece of puzzle into a hole, the object will not change its shape. Lifting, shaking, squeezing, dropping, stretching, tearing, and folding are other examples of actions the Piagetian preschool teaches systematically to give to the children a repertoire of procedures which will help them find out about objects in their environment.

Piaget points out that people are the only source of *Social knowledge* (objective *L*) and that social knowledge tends to be arbitrary. This is the one area in which a Piagetian preschool does not differ very much from other cognitively oriented preschools.

In *Classification* (objective *M*), as has been stated, the cognitively oriented preschool relies heavily on language to teach specific content and words. It teaches, for example, that collies and beagles are both dogs, and that shirts, shorts, and socks are all items of clothing. In this way, the cognitively oriented preschool teaches specific content and uses language to impose socially determined classificatory schemes on the child. Piaget, on the other hand, pointed out that logical knowledge comes neither from people nor from language, but from the internal consistency of the system that the child himself has constructed. In classification, therefore, the Piagetian preschool attempts to develop the process of abstracting a criterion and using it consistently. In fact, in the Piagetian framework there is no right or wrong classification. There is only the criterion that the child himself chose, and his criterion is always correct as long as he applies it consistently to all the objects he puts together. In physical and social knowledge, objects and people determine the truth, but in logical knowledge the child determines it.

In order not to skip any intermediate stages that are necessary for a solid foundation in classification, the Piagetian preschool notes *how* the child goes about grouping objects. For example, if the child is at the stage of graphic collections,[20] he is not prematurely pushed into making nongraphic collections. If he can only make many small groups, more inclusive classes are not prematurely imposed.

[19] This is unfortunately a very complicated statement to explain, and the reader is referred to Furth (1969, 1970) for a clarification.

[20] The reader is referred to Inhelder & Piaget (1964) for an explanation of the preoperational stages of classification.

Piaget's *Seriation* (objective N) is much more than size discrimination and the "expanded polar concepts" that are taught in the cognitively oriented preschool. As it has already been said, the essence of seriation is the ability to coordinate many transitive relationships. Size discrimination is, therefore, only a rudimentary prerequisite for seriation, and the ability to verbalize "big," "bigger," and "biggest" is not the heart of seriation.

For the cognitively oriented preschool, the objective in *Number* (objective O) is the ability to count verbally and to abstract the same number from different pictures (e.g., a picture of four cherries is to be matched with a picture of four stars that are arranged differently spatially). In the Piagetian preschool, however, the objective is the strengthening of the child's logical structure of number to make it more powerful than his perception. The ability to establish the equivalence of two sets of objects by one-to-one correspondence is a logical process. The ability to conserve this equivalence when the spatial configuration is changed is also a logical process, underlying the child's ability to count meaningfully.

In the teaching of *Spatial concepts* (objective P), Piaget's theory puts the traditional objective of teaching terms such as "over" and "under" into a much larger context. According to his theory, space is progressively structured from the child's own body. Therefore, the important instructional objective is not to teach terms such as "over" and "under" but to structure space itself (1) from the self-to-object level to the object-to-object level, (2) from topological space to euclidean space, and (3) from the sensory-motor level to the representational level.[21]

In *Temporal relationships* (objective Q), the cognitively oriented preschool teaches words such as "before-after" and "first-next-last." But the Piagetian preschool attempts to teach children to reason in order to construct or reconstruct temporal sequence. This reasoning is done through causal relationships, means-ends relationships, and delayed imitation.

[21] The reader is referred to Piaget & Inhelder (1967) for an explanation of this statement.

Dramatic play, painting, modeling clay, and block building are activities that are used both in the traditional nursery school and the cognitively oriented preschool to teach creativity, imagination, and family roles. Piaget's theory showed that these activities involve not only imagination but also *Symbolization* (objective R). In dramatic play, according to him, the child uses his body both as symbol and as symbolizer. The Piagetian preschool, therefore, uses dramatic play, make-believe with objects, block building, painting, and clay modeling to teach representation as a foundation for the teaching of *Language* (objective S).

Table 13-3 summarizes some of the ways in which Piaget's theory encompasses all the non-Piagetian objectives and adds a structure, a developmental perspective, and depth to them. It can be seen in this table, for example, that the traditional goal of teaching colors appears next to *Classification* (sorting objects by color), *Seriation* (ordering colors according to darkness of shades), and *Numbers* (placing as many blue blocks as red ones). The traditional content of shapes appears next to *Classification* (sorting curvilinear and rectilinear shapes) and *The structuring of space* (progressive structuring from topological to euclidean shapes). Since a full discussion of the unique contributions of Piaget's theory is beyond the scope of this chapter, the reader is referred to the footnotes and References for more detailed sources.

Illustrations of summative evaluation

As it was shown in the preceding section, the various types of preschools have different views of the child and how he should be educated. The procedures for summative evaluation will, therefore, differ from program to program. This section will attempt to illustrate the type of evaluation procedures that might be used by each type of preschool to find out the extent to which it succeeded in reaching its own set of objectives. Ratings by the teacher are suggested as the most desirable procedure in the socio-emotional realm. In the perceptual-motor domain, parts of the Kephart and Frostig testing procedures, as well as other rating procedures, are recommended. Illustrations of summative evaluation in the cognitive areas are given first in ways that are suited for a regular cognitively oriented preschool. Procedures for a Piagetian preschool are then discussed.

For socio-emotional objectives (A–H)

For the evaluation of growth in the socio-emotional domain, I believe that ratings by the teacher are better suited than tests. Some of the reasons for this belief are the following: (1) At 4 and 5 years of age, children are much more honest in showing their true feelings, such as dependence, than when they are older. Therefore, it is not necessary to use complicated tests. (2) In the socio-emotional domain, what counts is not what a child *can do* on a given day on a test but what he actually *does* from day to day. The teacher is the only person in possession of this knowledge, and she is, therefore, the person best suited to evaluate the child's socio-emotional behavior. (3) A trained outside rater observing children for a number of days may be more objective than the teacher. However, such an outside observer is usually available only on research projects. Also, the teacher who interacts with children every day has more insight than an observer who remains outside these interactions.

To rate children on many dimensions, it is essential that the teacher be well trained to be thoroughly objective and have a clear understanding of each dimension. For example, *Dependence on the teacher* does not mean that we want to produce dependent children who will look at the teacher's face before making each move. Neither do we want to encourage healthy, autonomous children to become dependent. Similarly, there is a difference between spontaneity with inner controls, and the inner controls that produce constriction.

A rating form found to be useful is the Pupil Behavior Inventory (Vinter, Sarri, Vorwaller, & Schafer, 1966), which was developed for use by teachers rating pupils in a school setting. Since this inventory was developed for elementary and secondary school pupils, it is not ideally suited for preschool children. However, further work is in progress to discard irrelevant items and add others that rate children on *Curiosity* (objective *G*), *Creativity* (objective *H*), and reflectivity (part of objective *F*).

The Pupil Behavior Inventory consists of thirty-four items. Fourteen of the following dimensions are quoted from the inventory (Vinter et al., 1966, p. 18). The others were subsequently added on an experimental basis to evaluate children in all the socio-emotional aspects that were described in the first section of this chapter. Illustrative dimensions are given under each of the objectives.

Dependence on the teacher (A)

"Possessive of teacher"

"Seeks constant reassurance"

Trusts teacher

Initiates interaction with teacher

Appears concerned about teacher's opinions

Seeks teacher's approval

Uses teacher's behavior as a model

Inner controls (B)

"Disrupts classroom procedures"

"Resistant to teacher"

"Requires continuous supervision"

"Impulsive"

Follows directions

Interaction with other children (C)

"Withdrawn and uncommunicative"

Interacts with other children

Ability to get along with other children (D)

"Friendly and well received by other pupils"

"Aggressive toward peers"

"Teases or provokes students"

Shares things willingly

Is a leader

Comfort in school (E)

Appears comfortable and generally happy

Appears to have joyous experiences in school

Achievement motivation and pride of mastery (F)

"Motivated toward academic performance"

"Shows initiative"

"Completes assignments"

"Hesitant to try, or gives up easily"

Proud of what he makes

Takes time to reflect in making decisions

Can stay with one activity for some time

Short attention span

Brings his treasures to school

Curiosity (G)

Asks questions

Explores objects in his environment

Curious about environment

Asks information of teacher

Creativity (H)

Uses materials in a variety of ways

Shows flexibility

Using the preceding dimensions, the teacher rates the child on a 5-point scale (VF for "very frequently," F for "frequently," S for "sometimes," I for "infrequently," and VI for "very infrequently"). VF is the desirable direction for some items, such as "friendly and well received by other pupils." For other items, such as "aggressive toward peers," VI is the desirable direction.

These ratings can be converted into numbers for comprehension at a quick glance; a score of 5 always indicates the desirable rating. For example, the ratings on "friendly and well received by other pupils" are converted as follows:

VF—5
F—4
S—3
I—2
VI—1

The ratings on "aggressive toward peers" are converted as follows:

VF—1
F—2
S—3
I—4
VI—5

For perceptual-motor objectives (I, J)

Observation of individual children in standard test situations is recommended for evaluation in this realm rather than ratings based on memory. Unlike in the socio-emotional realm, where "performance" was more important than "competence,"[22] the teacher needs to rate the child on his "competence" in perceptual-motor coordination.

Gross motor coordination (I) Some examples of gross motor coordination have been said to be the ability to walk on a balance board, to jump, to climb the jungle gym, and to throw and catch a large ball. The first two of these examples are given below to illustrate procedures that might be used for evaluation.

1. Walking
   a. Material: Walking board
      "The walking board should be a section of two-by-four board measuring eight to twelve feet long and placed on brackets so that the board is at least six inches off the floor" (Roach & Kephart, 1966, p. 29).
   b. Instructions

I-1

1. The child walks on the four-inch flat surface of the board as he would walk on a fence rail. Be sure the child has plenty of room to use his arms in balancing without touching a wall, a chair, or other objects. Position the child on the floor at one end of

[22] "Competence" in this context refers to whether or not the child is able to do a given task. "Performance" refers to whether or not he does from day to day what he is able to do.

the board. Tell him, "Get up on the board and walk to the other end." When he has come to the far end of the board, say, "Now walk it backward." When he has walked across the board again, say, "Now walk it sidewise." When he has walked sidewise in one direction, say, "Now come back sidewise." Be sure he faces in the same direction as before so that in walking back he uses the opposite foot to lead. Many children will turn 180 degrees so that in the second sidewise task they use the same lead foot that they used in the first sidewise task.

(Roach & Kephart, 1966, p. 29.)

c. Criteria

The teacher checks off the descriptions that apply and makes additional comments.

Forward:

[__Walks easily with balance throughout]
- __Steps off board
- __Pauses frequently
- __Uses one side of body more consistently than other
- __Avoids balance
  - __Runs
  - __Long steps
  - __Feet crosswise of board
- __Maintains inflexible posture

Backward:

[__Walks easily with balance throughout]
- __Steps off board
- __Pauses frequently
- __Uses one side of body more consistently than other
- __Avoids balance
  - __Runs
  - __Long steps
  - __Feet crosswise of board
- __Twists body to see where he is going
- __Must look at feet
- __Maintains inflexible posture

Sidewise:

[__Walks easily with balance throughout]
- __Unable to shift weight from one foot to the other
- __Confusion or hesitation in shifting weight
- __Crosses one foot over the other
- __Steps off board
- __Performs more easily in one direction than the other
  - __Right lead
  - __Left lead

Comments:

____

____

____

(Roach & Kephart, 1966, pp. 72–73)

2. Jumping
   a. Instructions

I-2

2. *Both feet:* Say to the child, "Place both feet together. Jump one step forward."

   Right foot: Say to the child, "Stand on your right foot with your left foot off the floor. Jump one step forward without putting your left foot down."

   Left foot: Same as for right foot.

(Roach & Kephart, 1966, p. 33, tasks A–C.)

b. Criteria

Both feet:
- __Performs smoothly and easily
- __Cannot keep feet together
- __Uses one side of body only
- __Loses balance

One foot:

Right	Left	
__	__	Performs smoothly and easily
__	__	Performs better on one foot than the other
__	__	Cannot keep opposite foot off the floor
__	__	Loses balance

Comments:

____

____

____

(Adapted from Roach & Kephart, 1966, p. 73)

Fine motor coordination (J) The examples given as instructional goals in fine perceptual-motor coordination were the ability to cut paper with scissors, to draw a line between two lines spaced a quarter of an inch apart, to fold paper, to paste, and to insert pegs in a pegboard. The first two of these objectives are given below to illustrate evaluation procedures.

1. Cutting paper with scissors
   a. Instructions

J-2 and J-11

3. Give a piece of paper and a pair of scissors to the child and ask him to cut the paper (a) in any way he likes and (b) on a line that you have drawn on the paper.

   b. Criteria

   Cutting in any way the child likes:

   __Cuts easily without any trouble
   __Cuts with some slight difficulty
   __Cuts with considerable difficulty
   __Simply cannot cut and appears to be "all thumbs"

   Cutting on a line:

   (The following criteria refer not to the child's general ability to use scissors but to his specific ability to cut along a given line.)

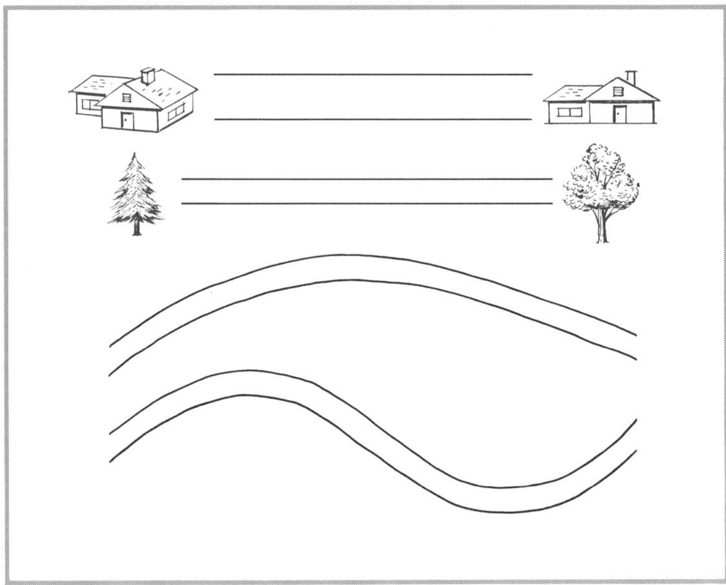

FIGURE 13-3 Illustrative procedures for evaluating eye-hand coordination. (M. Frostig. *Developmental Test of Visual Perception.* Palo Alto, Calif.: Consulting Psychologists Press, 1963. Pp. Ia, Ib; items 2, 3, 6, 7. By permission of Consulting Psychologists Press, Inc.)

   __Cuts easily and accurately on the line
   __Cuts easily but with a deviation within ¼ inch from the line
   __Cuts with some difficulty with a deviation of more than ¼ inch from the line.

   Comments:

   ____

   ____

   ____

2. Drawing a line between two lines spaced ¼ *inch* apart
   a. Material
      The drawings shown in Fig. 13-3
      Primary pencil
   b. Instructions

J-2 and J-16

4. For houses: "Here is a house [*point*] and here is a house [*point*]. When I tell you, you are to take your pencil and go from one house to the other house. Go down the middle of the road. Keep your pencil on the paper. Don't bump! Now go!"
5. For trees: "Now we go on the road with the trees [*point*] from one tree to the other tree [*trace*]. Take your pencil, stay in the middle of the road. Keep your pencil on the paper. Do not go back. Now go!"
6. For curved lines: "This is a road. Show with your pencil how you go from one end to the other [*point*] without bumping. Begin right here [*trace*] and stop at the end, here. (Have the children point to the beginning and end of line. . . .) . . . Now go ahead."

(Frostig, 1966, p. 11, items 2, 3, 6.)

   c. Criteria

   __Draws an unbroken line between the lines from one end to the other as shown in Fig. 13-4*a*.
   __Lifts pencil from paper but continues the line without a break as shown in Fig. 13-4*b*.
   __Lifts pencil from paper and makes a break, fork, or sharp angle as shown in Fig. 13-4*c*.
   __Touches the edge of the road as shown in Fig. 13-4*d*.
   __Makes a sketched, corrected, or broken line as shown in Fig. 13-4*e*.
   __Goes outside the edge of the road as shown in Fig. 13-4*f*.

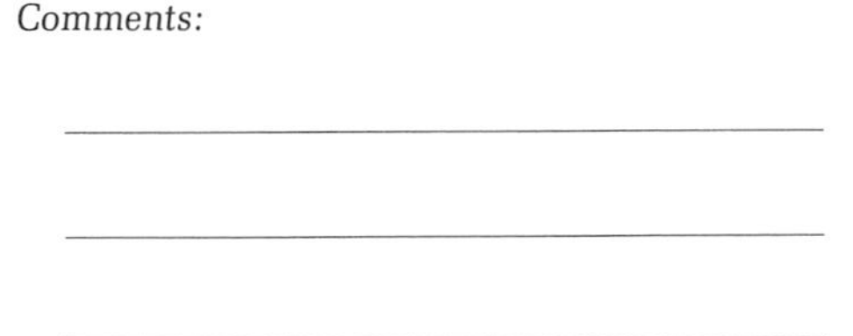

For cognitive objectives (K–S)

As it was pointed out in the preceding section, most cognitively oriented preschools view knowledge in basically the same way, although their curricula may differ in methods and specific content. It was said that although the Bereiter-Engelmann preschool may differ radically in many ways from those of Deutsch, Gray, and Karnes, the differences are negligible compared with the basic theory of knowledge that these programs share. It was explained that Piaget's theory differs fundamentally from the cognitively oriented preschools,[23] and the differences were enumerated. In the following discussion, therefore, procedures of summative evaluation for the two types of preschools will be illustrated.

Before going into specific evaluation procedures, a general remark must be made concerning two different ways of questioning the child to find out what he knows. One is the psychometric method, which uses standard items and procedures. The other is the exploratory, or clinical, method developed by Piaget and Inhelder. In the psychometric method, the tester follows prescribed steps without any deviation. Thus, if the child does not understand instructions such as, "Put together the things that go together," the examiner does not explain his instruction in any other way. The child's inability to understand the request is considered part of the score ("fail") that he receives on that item. In the exploratory method, on the other hand, the examiner follows the child's responses to find out how much help he needs to do the task. If the child does not understand a request to "put together the things that go together," the examiner changes the wording to anything else that the child might understand, such as "Put the same ones in a pile right here." If the child still has difficulty, the examiner gives additional help.

[23] For an elaboration of this statement, the reader is referred to Furth (1969, 1970), Gollin (1968), and Kohlberg (1968).

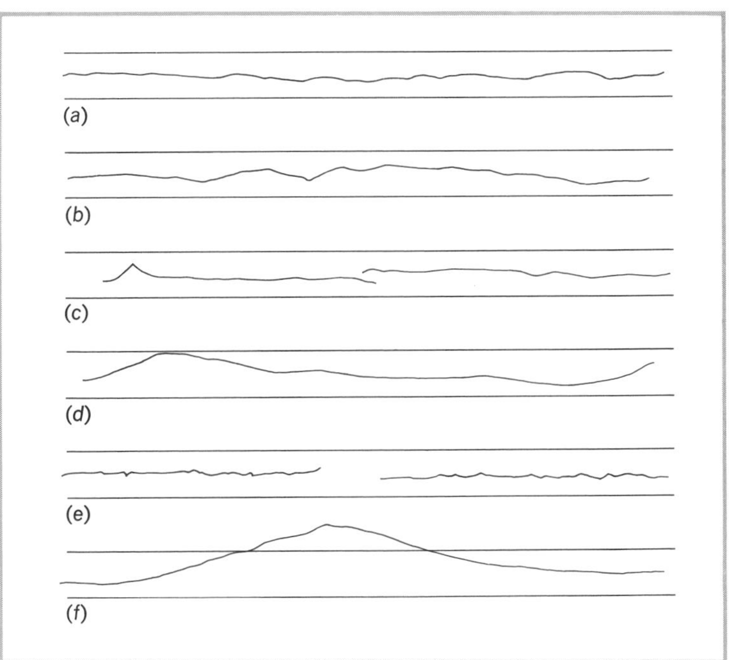

FIGURE 13-4 Scoring criteria for eye-hand coordination tasks. (M. Frostig. *Developmental Test of Visual Perception: Administration and Scoring Manual.* Palo Alto, Calif.: Consulting Psychologists Press, 1966. Pp. 18–19. By permission of Consulting Psychologists Press, Inc.)

The recording and scoring procedures of the two methods are also different. In the psychometric method, the tester is interested only in the answer; but in the Piagetian method, the examiner is interested not only in the final answer but also in the process the child goes through to arrive at it. For example, in classification the examiner notes whether the child picks up one object at a time or some or all of the objects at the same time. He also notes whether the child ends up with the objects carefully arranged or randomly placed. These procedural differences reveal important differences in children's developmental levels. To record these processes, it is desirable for the examiner to have another person to take down in a protocol the moment-to-moment process of interaction between the examiner and the child.

I feel that the use of the exploratory method should become part of the training of all teachers. The teachers who have used this method are helped enormously in their teaching, because through it they become acquainted with the fine points of young children's thinking. Although the following illustrations of evaluation procedures are too sketchy to convince prospective teachers of the importance of the exploratory method, it is hoped that they will serve to show the possibility of probing into children's thinking to evaluate the exact stage of their cognitive development. Illustrations of summative evaluation in the various cognitive areas will now be presented.

Physical knowledge (K)

1. In a preschool that is not Piagetian

   The objectives in the teaching of physical knowledge in a non-Piagetian curriculum tend to be to expose children to scientific objects (e.g., plants and pets) and to teach specific facts (e.g., the fact that rain comes from clouds). An evaluation procedure concerning these facts might be to ask the child a series of questions such as, "Where does rain come from?" and evaluate the correctness of his answers. An example of another procedure can be seen in the Test of Basic Information, which was developed by Moss for group administration. In this procedure the examiner shows to the child pictures such as the ones given in Fig. 13-5*a*, and asks him to find "the one that rain comes from." In the non-Piagetian evaluation procedure, the tendency is to look for the one correct answer to each question. Another example from Moss' Test of Basic Information is given in Fig. 13-5*b*, where the child is asked to find "the one that burns and melts" (Moss, 1967, items 5b, 6a).

   The above examples may not be representative of the content that a given preschool expects children to learn. However, they do serve to illustrate the principle of testing for specific scientific facts.

2. In a Piagetian preschool

   The objectives in a Piagetian preschool, as was said, are (a) to structure the child's knowledge of the properties of familiar objects, and (b) to give him a repertoire of actions he can perform to explore the physical nature of unfamiliar objects. Examples of evaluation procedures for both of these objectives will be given.

   a. To evaluate the child's physical knowledge of familiar objects

FIGURE 13-5 Pictures which can be used to evaluate physical knowledge. (M. H. Moss. Test of Basic Information. Unpublished test, George Washington University, 1967. Pp. 5–6, items 5b, 6a.)

Table 13-4 Evaluation Form for Physical Knowledge

	Objects				
Actions	*Block*	*Scissors*	*Chalk*	*Candle*	*Glass jar*
Dropping to see if it will break					
Rolling					
Floating					
Folding or bending					
Thumping					
Crumpling					
Stretching					

A useful procedure is to make a matrix like Table 13-4, with exploratory actions in the left-hand column and the familiar objects across the top. For evaluation, the teacher may choose a piece of chalk and take a protocol of what the child *says* as well as what he *does* in the following situations:

Spontaneous descriptions:

K-16

7. The teacher asks, "Tell me about this. . . . Show me what you can do with this. . . ." The child may say, "You can break it," or he may demonstrate writing with the chalk.

The criterion for evaluation is the variety of properties the child comes up with, either verbally or with actions.

Reactions to structured questions:

K-16

8. The teacher asks, "What will happen if you drop this?" "Can you bend it?" "Can you crumple it?" "Can you mix the crumbs with water?" "Can you eat it?" "Can you roll it?" "Can you stretch it?"

After each of these questions, the teacher asks the child to verify his answer. At the 4-year-old level, the criterion of evaluation is not the child's ability to *explain* phenomena but his ability to *predict* the result of his actions on objects.

Recapitulation:

K-16

9. The teacher asks, "Tell me [or show me] what we did with this, and what we found out about it."

The interest here is the evaluation of what the child learned during the session. Some children will add only one or two points to what they said spontaneously. Others will be able to recapitulate the entire sequence.

The overall criterion of evaluation is what the child knows about the objects. Some children can spontaneously describe many properties verbally. Others can show their knowledge only with actions, and some can describe the properties of objects only in response to structured questions. Some cannot make correct predictions but learn quickly from their own experience with objects.

b. To evaluate the child's repertoire of actions to explore unfamiliar objects.
Exploration:

K-15
10. The teacher gives the child a piece of coal on a white sheet of paper and asks him what it is. After ascertaining the child's degree of familiarity with the object, the teacher asks him to find out "what you can do with it so we can play a guessing game about what you can do with this."

The criterion of evaluation here is what the child *does* with the object—e.g., lifting it, pressing it, rubbing the paper with it, thumping it, smelling it, asking whether or not he can drop it on the floor, looking at his black fingers, etc.
Reactions to structured questions:

K-15
11. The teacher asks, "Can you make it flat like a pancake?" "Will it break if you drop it?" "Will it bounce if you drop it?" "Can you write on paper with it?" "Can you roll it?" "Can you stretch it?" "Will it float in water?" "Will it break if you hit it hard with a hammer?" "Can you burn it?"

The criterion of evaluation here is not the child's knowledge about the object per se but what he learned from his *process* of exploring the object. The child who explored the object in many ways and found out how the object reacted is able to answer most of the questions correctly.

Social knowledge (L) Social knowledge is the cognitive area in which there is probably the greatest similarity of content and objectives between the Piagetian and non-Piagetian preschools. Both schools teach (a) rules of conduct (e.g., you have to be quiet while others are talking), (b) family and community roles, and (c) certain social conventions (e.g., men do not wear skirts and high heels). The procedures for summative evaluation can, therefore, be similar in all three areas of social knowledge. The only difference might be found in the criteria used to evaluate the children's responses.

1. Rules of conduct

L-3, L-6
12. The teacher asks the child what he has to do when other people are talking, or what he must do when two people want to use the same swing at the same time.

2. Family and community roles. The Preschool Inventory includes the following examples:

L-5
13. What does a dentist do?
14. What does a policeman do?
15. What does a teacher do?
16. What does a father do?
17. What does a mother do?

(Caldwell, 1967, pp. 13–14, items 43–47. From *The Preschool Inventory*.)

The criteria of evaluation in this inventory follow the psychometric tradition of giving two points for certain answers, one point for other, supposedly lower-level, answers, and no points for certain other answers. For example, the scoring criteria for the question "What does a dentist do?" are the following:

2 points: "Fixes teeth," "Works on teeth," "Checks you—Q—your teeth, takes care of teeth," "Helps you—Q—fixes teeth."
1 point: "Drills teeth," "Looks at teeth," "Pulls teeth," "Helps you—Q—pulls teeth."
0 point: "Checks you," "Checks you—Q—looks at your throat," "Works in a hospital," etc.

(Caldwell, 1967, p. 13)

The notation "—Q—" indicates a question asked by the examiner. It can be seen from the Qs in the scoring criteria above that the only time the examiner can ask a probing question is when the child says, "Checks you" or "Helps you."

The Piagetian teacher would use different criteria. After the child's initial answer, she would ask a series of questions, such as, "Does he pull teeth?" "Does he put people in jail?" "Does he cook for

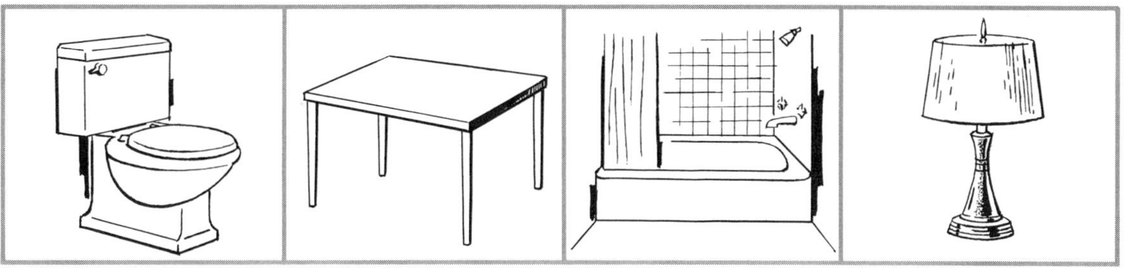

FIGURE 13-6 Pictures which can be used to evaluate social knowledge. (M. H. Moss. Test of Basic Information. Unpublished test, George Washington University, 1967. P. 9, item 9b.)

you?" "Does he look in your mouth?" The reason for this probing is, again, that the exploratory method goes beyond looking for the correct answer. To the Piagetian examiner, the answer "Drills teeth" is just as correct as "Fixes teeth." Negative statements (e.g., "A dentist does not put people in jail") are also an important part of the child's knowledge.

3. Social conventions

One item in the Test of Basic Information consists of the four pictures that appear in Fig. 13-6:

L-9

18. The teacher says, "Mark the one you find in the kitchen."

(Moss, 1967, p. 6, item 9b.)

Here, again, the examiner using the psychometric method looks for the one correct answer. The Piagetian examiner might give the same four pictures to the child and ask him to put together the ones that go together. The child may well put the lamp with the table ("because you put the lamp on the table") and the bathtub with the toilet ("because they are in the same room"). The child's social knowledge here would be considered entirely correct.

Logical knowledge: classification (M)

In a preschool that is not Piagetian. *Classification* in the non-Piagetian preschool, as was mentioned, differs fundamentally from that which is found in the Piagetian preschool. The objective in the former is the teaching of intensive properties of classes—e.g., the fact that an apple and a stop sign are both red. Programming is directed toward the teaching of conventional classificatory schemes—e.g., the fact that shirts, shorts, and socks are items of clothing.

To evaluate the child's ability to abstract common properties of objects, the teacher might show pictures such as those that appear in Fig. 13-7*a* and ask the child to find "the one without wheels" (Moss, 1967, p. 7, item 21a).

To evaluate the child's mastery of conventional class membership, the teacher might show pictures such as those appearing in Fig. 13-7*b* and ask the child to find "the one that does not belong."

The scoring criterion in these procedures is whether or not the child can give the one correct answer.

In a Piagetian preschool. In Piaget's conceptualization of logical knowledge, classification is based not on what other people say but on the internal consistency of the child's own logical system. Therefore, there is no right or wrong classification as long as the child is consistent. The instructional objectives are (a) the selection of a criterion and its consistent use and (b) the shifting of criteria.

An example of summative evaluation according to Piaget's notion of classification is given below.

1. Materials (geometric shapes cut out of paper)
   - 3 red circles, 25 millimeters in diameter
   - 3 blue circles, 25 mm in diameter
   - 2 red circles, 50 mm in diameter
   - 3 blue circles, 50 mm in diameter
   - 3 red squares, 25 mm × 25 mm
   - 3 blue squares, 25 mm × 25 mm

FIGURE 13-7 Pictures which can be used to evaluate classificatory ability. [(a) from M. H. Moss. Test of Basic Information. Unpublished test, George Washington University, 1967. P. 21, item 21a.]

3 red squares, 50 mm × 50 mm
2 blue squares, 50 mm × 50 mm
2 flat boxes, about 6 inches × 9 inches

2. Procedures
   a. Establishing the relevant perceptual discrimination and vocabulary

M-18, M-19, M-20

(Preliminary) The teacher places all the geometric figures randomly on the table and asks, "Tell me what you see." If the child does not spontaneously say, "red," "blue," "circle," "square," "big," and "little," the examiner picks up two pieces at a time for contrast. He might pick up a big and little red circle and ask the child, "Are these exactly the same? How are these not the same?"

   b. Free classification

M-18, M-19, M-20

19. The teacher gives one or more of the following instructions: "Put together all those that go together." "Put together all those that are alike." "Put together all those that are like each other." "Can you separate those that are not the same [different]?"

When the child has finished, the examiner asks for an explanation—e.g., "How did you know to put them together like this?"

   c. First dichotomy

M-18, M-19, M-20

20. The examiner mixes all the shapes, puts the two boxes in front of the child and says, "Now I want you to put them into two bunches, one bunch in this box, and another bunch in this box."

When the child has finished, the examiner asks for an explanation—e.g., "Can you explain to me why all these go together?"

   d. Second dichotomy

M-18, M-19, M-20

21. The shapes are again mixed, and the examiner says, "This time, I want you to make two bunches in another way. Put together the same ones in a different way." If the child starts to repeat his first dichotomy, the examiner says, "You've already done that. Can you find another way of putting them together?"

When the child has finished his second dichotomy, he is again asked for a justification.

e. Third dichotomy

M-18, M-19, M-20

22. The shapes are again mixed, and the procedure for the second dichotomy is repeated.

3. Criteria. These are explained in the following paragraphs.

In the Piagetian way of evaluating learning in classification, one of the criteria is the extent to which the child is still in the stage of graphic collections (stage I, when the child's only principle of uniting objects is their spatial arrangement). Evidence of this early stage can be found in two possible places: in the child's free classification and in his arrangement of shapes inside the box when he makes nongraphic collections. Graphic collections in free classification might look like Fig. 13-8*a*.[24] Remnants of graphic collections inside the box may look like Fig. 13-8*b*. When this kind of graphic remnant appears, the child can be said to be at the stage of nongraphic collections (stage II, when the child becomes capable of uniting objects on the basis of their similarity). However, he is not as advanced in stage II as the child who arranges the objects randomly.[25]

The second criterion of evaluation concerns the number of dichotomies the child can make. This criterion has to do with the child's ability to shift criteria when there are three possibilities open to him (division by color, by shape, and by size). In the Ypsilanti Early Education Program, half of the children can make two dichotomies at the end of the preschool year. The third dichotomy is found among the children who are more advanced in classification than the others.

The third criterion concerns the child's *process* of making dichotomies. Does he randomly pick

[24] For a fuller explanation, the reader is referred to Inhelder and Piaget (1964, Ch. 1).

[25] For a fuller explanation, the reader is referred to Inhelder and Piaget (1964, Ch. 2).

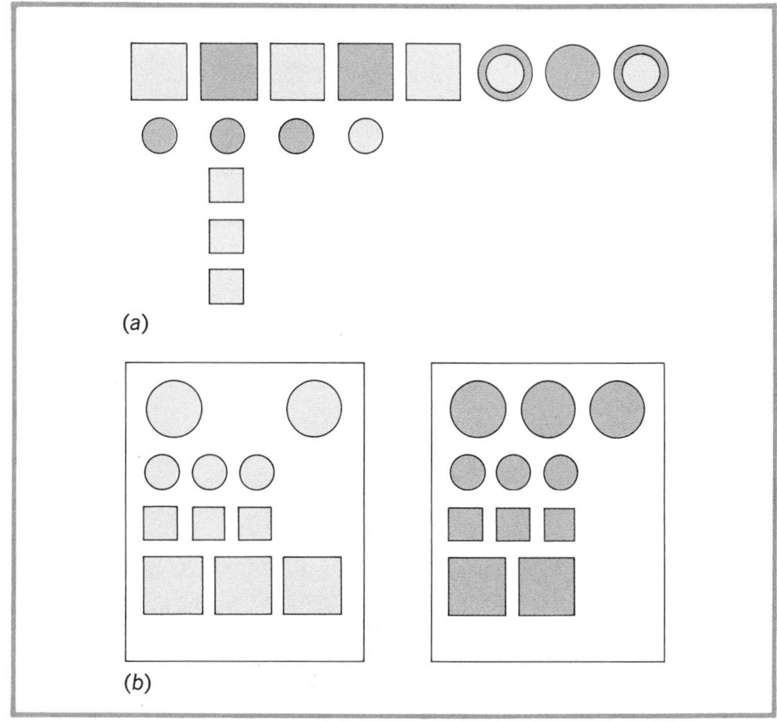

FIGURE 13-8 (*a*) A graphic collection and (*b*) graphic remnants.

up one object at a time and decide as he slowly goes along where to place each object? Or does he quickly select similar objects and pick up many at a time, as if he knew in advance exactly which ones to unite and which ones to separate? The latter process is, of course, at a higher level than the former, since it reveals the child's ability to anticipate how he will dichotomize the shapes.

The last criterion concerns the child's ability to justify verbally why he grouped the shapes as he did.

The form shown in Table 13-5 is helpful in summarizing the data that are gathered in the protocol.

Table 13-5 Evaluation Form for Classification

	Process	*Product*	*Justification*
Free classification			
First dichotomy			
Second dichotomy			
Third dichotomy			

Logical knowledge: seriation (N)

In a preschool that is not Piagetian. As has been pointed out, the non-Piagetian preschool does not teach seriation. The closest it comes to teaching seriation is the teaching of perceptual discrimination and the words that describe the differences involved in perceptual discrimination (e.g., "big-little," "big-bigger-biggest," "smooth-rough," "loud-soft"). Therefore, summative evaluation in seriation must remain in this context in a non-Piagetian preschool.

In the Preschool Inventory, for example, the child is given three boxes of different sizes and three cars, and is asked to put "one car in the middle-size box" or "three cars in the big box" (Caldwell, 1967, p. 10, items 22, 24). Later in the same inventory, the child is asked a series of questions such as

N-8, N-10, N-13, N-15, N-19, K, P, Q

23. "Which is *bigger*, a tree or a flower?"
24. "Which is *slower*, a car or a bicycle?"
25. "Which is *heavier*, a brick or a shoe?"

(Caldwell, p. 17, items 75–77.)

These questions require that the child know the words referring to the attribute in terms of which the objects are being compared. The first two questions use objects and words; later questions use words only.

The Test of Basic Information uses pictures and words. For example, it gives the pictures which appear in Fig. 13-9, and the child is asked to choose "the youngest tree," Fig. 13-9*a*, or "the heaviest one," Fig. 13-9*b* (Moss, 1967, p. 6, items 4a, 9a). Summative evaluation in these examples thus deals with the words that are associated with perceptual discrimination. As usual, the evaluator looks for the one answer that is considered correct.

In a Piagetian preschool. Seriation has already been described as the ability to coordinate transitive relationships in both directions (e.g., D is *at the same time shorter than* A, B, and C, and *longer than* E, F, G, H, I, and J). The general objective for preschool education is at the stage-II preoperational level. In the case of seriation, the stage-II level is perceptual, or empirical, seriation. The characteristics of this stage will be clarified in the following description of evaluation procedures.[26]

[26] For a fuller description, the reader is referred to Inhelder and Piaget (1964, Chs. 9, 10) and Piaget (1965, Ch. 5).

(a)

(b)

FIGURE 13-9 Pictures which can be used to evaluate perceptual discrimination and related vocabulary. (M. H. Moss. Test of Basic Information. Unpublished test, George Washington University, 1967. Pp. 4, 9; items 4a, 9a.)

1. Materials:
   10 dolls made with paper-towel tubes which are identical except for heights. (The heights range from 3 inches to 7½ inches, with intervals of ½ inch between the dolls. Painted facial features at the top of each paper tube, such as the eyes, the nose, and the mouth, are adequate for children to make believe that these are dolls.)
   10 sticks which are identical except for lengths. (The lengths range from 10.6 centimeters to 16 cm, with intervals of 0.6 cm between the sticks.)
2. Procedures:
   a. Establishing perceptual discrimination and the relevant vocabulary with the dolls

N-19

26. The teacher arranges all the dolls[27] from the tallest to the shortest as shown in Fig. 13-10*a* and asks, "Are these all alike?" "How are they different?" "Can you find two that are exactly the same?" She then asks, "Which one is the daddy?" "Which one is the mommy?" "Which one is the baby?" "Which ones are the brothers and sisters?"

   b. Seriation of ten dolls

N-19

27. The examiner mixes up all the dolls so that they will lie down on the table without being parallel to each other. He then asks the child to arrange the dolls as they were before, with "the daddy here, the mommy next to him, all the brothers and sisters, and finally the baby here."

   c. Seriation of five dolls (given only if the child cannot arrange ten dolls)

N-19

28. The teacher takes away the five biggest dolls and repeats the above procedure for "a smaller family."

If the child still cannot do the task, the examiner uses every other doll of the series so that there will be five dolls with intervals of 1 inch between them.

[27] It is important for the teacher not to demonstrate at this point how to seriate the dolls in the stage-III manner (by standing all of them up and systematically choosing the biggest one, the next biggest one, etc. . . .). Marking the heights on the inside of the tubes (e.g., 3, 3½, 4, 4½, etc.) enables the teacher to choose the dolls systematically without demonstrating how to do the task.

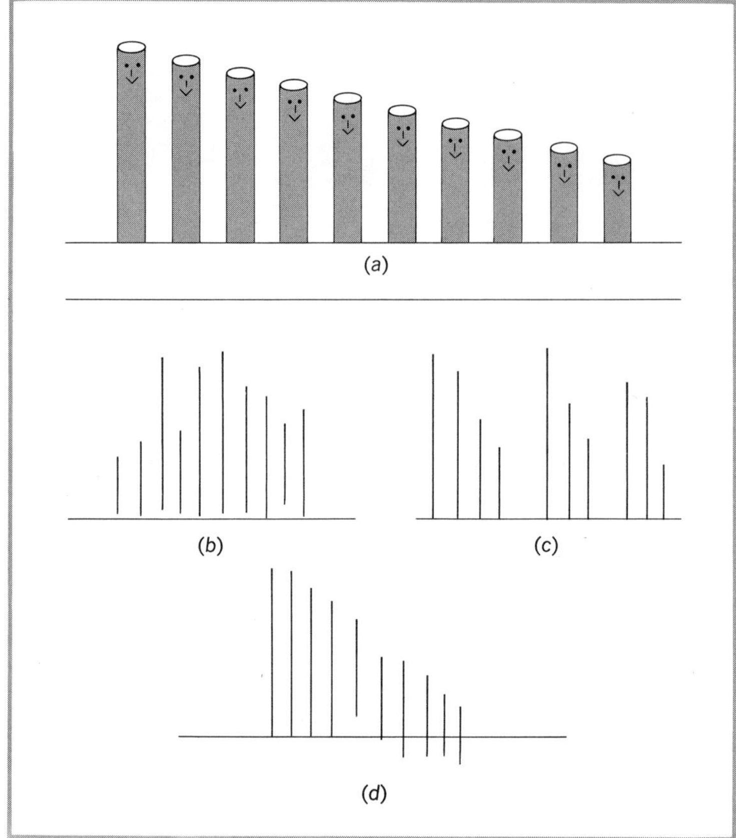

FIGURE 13-10 Materials used to evaluate seriation and illustrations of stage-I arrangements.

d. Seriation of ten sticks (given only if the child can arrange the ten dolls without any difficulty)

N-19

29. The examiner establishes perceptual discrimination as before by asking, "Can you find two that are exactly the same?" (without lining up the ends of all the sticks, since that would suggest to the child how to seriate the sticks at the stage-III level). The child is then asked to give the biggest stick to the daddy and "all the other sticks to the right persons."

3. Criteria. The above procedure shows that the order of difficulty of the tasks is as follows, and that a harder task should be given only if the child passes an easier one:

Seriation of five dolls with intervals of 1 inch between them

Seriation of five dolls with intervals of ½ inch between them

Seriation of 10 dolls

Seriation of 10 sticks

Within each of the above tasks can be found the following stages, which are illustrated in terms of the sticks:

Stage I: Making a random series as shown in Fig. 13-10*b*; making small series of 2, 3, or 4 sticks as shown in Fig. 13-10*c*; or respecting only one end of the sticks as shown in Fig. 13-10*d*.

Stage II: Perceptual seriation. Here, the child makes the correct seriated product by a process of trial and error. He engages in trial and error because he is guided by the perceptual configuration rather than by the logical relationships.

Stage III: Operational seriation. The child proceeds systematically by (1) lining up all the sticks at one end before arranging them on the table, and (2) selecting the sticks in sequence from the biggest to the smallest (or vice-versa) without any trial and error and without having to depend on the perceptual configuration of the series.

Most children can be expected to be very close to stage II by the end of the preschool year, which means that the perceptual seriation may not be quite perfect. The protocol, therefore, must show in detail the child's process, so that his cognitive level will be evident. Some children pick up any more-or-less big stick and intuitively give it to any more-or-less big doll. Others compare pairs of sticks and intuitively give each pair to the more-or-less big or little dolls. Others try to seriate all the sticks first before giving them to the ten dolls. These differences in the seriation of sticks can also be seen in the seriation of dolls.

Logical knowledge: numerical construction (O)

In a preschool that is not Piagetian. The objectives in the teaching of number in a non-Piagetian preschool are (1) the ability to count (usually to ten) and (2) the ability to abstract number from cards showing many objects that are arranged differently (e.g., four stars arranged vertically and four flowers in a bouquet). The ability to make judgments about "more" and "less" is sometimes a third objective.

The evaluation procedure for the first objective is as in the Binet (Terman & Merrill, 1960), where the child is given a dozen counting blocks and asked to give to the examiner three, ten, six, nine, etc., blocks.

For the second objective, the teacher might make pictures such as those in Fig. 13-11 and ask the child to match those that have the same number.

For the judgment of "more" and "less," the teacher might present the child with two sets of blocks (or buttons, or make-believe candy) and ask him, "Show me where there are more (or less)." The two sets to be compared can be changed from two and six objects to five and five or five and four.

In a Piagetian preschool. The objective in the teaching of number for the advanced pupils in the Piagetian preschool is conservation (with eight objects) with provoked correspondence. The following is an example of summative evaluation in number.

1. Materials. Two containers containing about fifteen tiny cups (½ to ¾ inch in diameter) and thirteen corresponding saucers, respectively. (There should not be exactly the same number of cups and saucers.)
2. Procedure
   a. Establishing the relevant vocabulary and the knowledge that one cup goes with one saucer

O-12

30. The teacher asks, "Do you know what these are?" "Can you show me how to use them?"

   b. Equivalence

O-12

31. The teacher puts 8 cups in a row in front of the child, spaced ¾ inch apart, and asks him to put out "*just* enough saucers for all the cups but not too many."

NOTE: It is important not to suggest to the child that he put a saucer in front of each cup. Such an instruction would give the answer away.

   c. The addition of one cup

O-12

32. The teacher says, "Watch what I'm going to do." She picks up a ninth cup, pushes the other eight cups closer together, and puts down the additional cup as shown in Fig. 13-12*a*. The row of cups now takes up exactly the same amount of space as the row of saucers, but there are nine cups for eight saucers. She then asks, "Do we have *just* enough saucers for all the cups?" If the child says, "No," he is asked what he should do to "make it right."

   d. Conservation

O-12

33. After the child re-establishes the equivalence of the two sets, the teacher asks him to watch carefully again because "I'm going to do something else." He bunches the cups close together and spreads the saucers apart as shown in Fig. 13-12*b*. The child is asked, "Now, do you think there are enough cups for all the saucers? Or are there more saucers, or more cups?" . . . "How do you know? Show me how you know."

FIGURE 13-11 Pictures which can be used to evaluate number concepts.

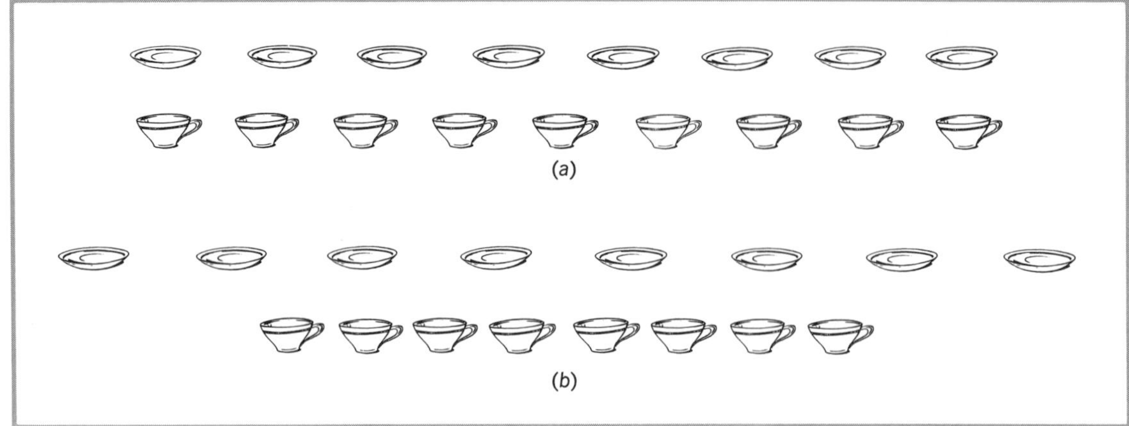

FIGURE 13-12 Two ways to evaluate the child's logical structure of number.

e. *Renversabilité* (given only to the child who cannot conserve, to find out how close he is to conserving)

O-12

34. The teacher asks, "Do you think we could put the cups and saucers back to the way they were before?" "If we put them back, do you think we could make it right so there will be enough cups for all the saucers? (Or will there be more saucers, or more cups?)"

The difference between conservation and *renversabilité* is clarified below, in the discussion of the scoring criteria.

3. Criteria. The developmental stages are as follows:

Stage I: *Neither equivalence nor conservation is possible.* The child tries to make the spatial frontiers come out the same, rather than using one-to-one correspondence.

Stage II: *Equivalence can be established, but not conservation.* The child uses one-to-one correspondence to establish the numerical equivalence of the two sets. However, when the spatial configuration is changed, he falls back on the space occupied as the basis for judgment. Therefore, he says that there are more saucers than cups.

Stage III: *Both equivalence and conservation are established.* The child has a logical structure which is by this time more powerful than the perceptual impression of the space occupied. Conservation becomes a *logical necessity*, which the child can explain by one of the following two arguments: (1) Identity: We did not add or take away anything from either set. All we did was move the objects. (2) Reversibility: We could return the objects back to the one-to-one spatial correspondence.

An intermediary stage just before stage III (*renversabilité*): Conversation is not achieved, but the child is close to it. He believes that if the objects are physically moved back to the original position, equivalence will be resumed, but not unless the objects are physically moved.

The difference between conservation and *renversabilité* is that the former is a compelling *logical necessity* to the child whose thought has become reversible. The latter is based on a consideration of *physically moving* the objects. The child who has reversibility of thought can conserve with the greatest of ease. The child who does not have this reversibility may or may not have renversabilité. If he has *renversabilité*, he is close to achieving conservation.

In general, the instructional goals have been set at the 5-year-old level of the Genevan norms. Success in class inclusion and seriation is usually not achieved before age 7½ or 8. On the other hand, the numerical construction involved in the situation described above is achieved earlier (by 50 percent of the 5-year-olds when eggs and egg cups are used).

The structuring of space (P)

In a preschool that is not Piagetian. The objective in non-Piagetian preschools puts the emphasis on terms such as "over-under," "in-out," and "in front of–in back of." The procedures for summative evaluation in this context might be the following:

1. Materials
   2 clay balls
   2 boxes about 3″ × 3″ × 3″
   3 blocks to make a stand on which to place the boxes sideways as shown in Fig. 13-13
2. Instructions

P-17

35. Put *this* ball *in* the box.
36. Put *this* ball (the second one) *on* the box.
37. Take the ball *out* of the box.
38. And put it *in front of* the box. [*Replace the ball after this so that it will not interfere with the question concerning "in back of."*]
39. Take the ball *off* the box.
40. And put it *in back of* the box.
41. Hold the ball *over* the box.
42. Hold your ball *over* the box like this [*demonstrate and have the child imitate from memory*].
43. Put the ball right *next to* the (this) box.
44. Put the ball *between* the boxes.
45. Put your ball *between* the boxes like this [demonstrate and have the child imitate from memory].
46. Put the ball *under* the box.
47. Hold the ball *above* the (this) box.

3. Criteria. When the examiner is in doubt as to whether or not the child knows exactly what he is doing, it is necessary to come back to the item in question after finishing the entire procedure. "Over" and "between" have been found to be difficult for many children. When a child cannot respond to the verbal instruction, it is desirable to determine whether or not he can do the same thing by delayed imitation of the examiner (items 42 and 45). The word "above" is sometimes easier than "over."

   NOTE: The two boxes are lying sideways without lids to lend themselves to the instruction involving "*in* the box" as well as that involving "*on* the box."

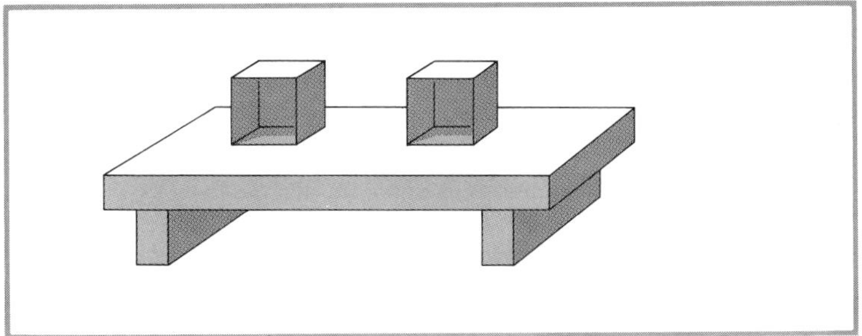

FIGURE 13-13 Equipment to evaluate the child's knowledge of terms in spatial relationships.

In a Piagetian preschool. The objectives in a Piagetian preschool put the emphasis on the structuring of space rather than on words that describe spatial relationships. The specific objectives might be (1) linear order, (2) transformations of geometric forms, and (3) the reconstruction of sensory-motor space on the representational level. The evaluation procedures for each objective are listed below:

1. Linear order
   a. Materials. Toy cars
      3 red cars
      3 light blue cars
      3 dark blue cars
      3 green cars
      3 white tow trucks
      3 turquoise cars
      3 purple cars
      3 yellow cars
      3 beige cars
      2 silver sportscars
      a red truck
      2 strips of paper (5 inches × 18 inches) to serve as "parking lots," and a shorter strip (5 inches × 12 inches)
   b. Procedure
      Straight copying:

P-13

48. The examiner puts down the longer strips of paper, one in front of the child and another at least 10 inches away from that one and parallel to it, and says, "We are going to build parking lots. First you watch how I park my cars." He places nine differ-

ent cars on his parking lot. The child is asked to park his cars to make his parking lot look just like the teacher's.

Copying with more space between objects (given only if the child can do straight copying):

P-13

49. The examiner puts the child's toys back into the box, and replaces his own long parking lot with the shorter one. He pushes his nine cars closer together to fit the length of the 12-inch strip. The child is asked to park his cars just like the teacher, but along a longer strip than the teacher's. The child has to fill up the entire length of his parking lot.

Copying in inverse order (given only if the child can do the above two tasks):

P-13

50. The examiner puts the child's cars back into the box and rearranges his own cars on the longer parking lot as before. The child is asked to park his cars again, but this time in inverse order (starting with I and H, and ending with B and A). This instruction is always hard for the child to understand, and the teacher demonstrates the procedure by placing the first two items for the child. The examiner puts his hands simultaneously on his own ninth item and the child's first item, and then on his own eighth item and the child's second item, explaining, "I want you to keep going this way, so you'll end up with the one that is the same as this one (his own first item)."

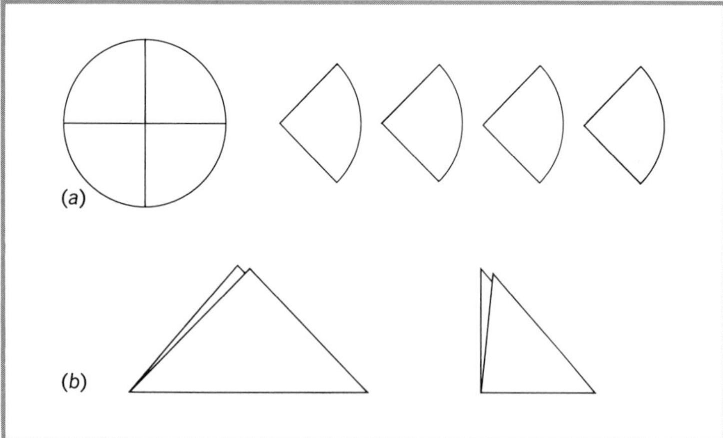

FIGURE 13-14 Illustrative procedures for evaluating transformation by (*a*) reassembling and (*b*) folding.

Straight copying with four objects (given only when the child cannot do the first item above—i.e., straight copying with nine objects): The procedure is the same as for item 48, above.

c. Criteria

The developmental criteria are as follows:

Stage 0: The child lines up any item, whether or not it appears in the examiner's model. The number of items may not be correct.

Stage I: The child picks out the correct items, but he can coordinate only two or three proximity relationships. Not even straight copying is possible, and the final product may look like ABDCFEGHI.

Stage II: Straight copying and copying with less (or more) space between the elements are possible, but not inverse order.

Stage III: All tasks including inverse order are possible.

Straight copying with four objects enables the teacher to see how close the child might be to attaining stage I.

2. Transformations of geometric forms
   a. Materials

      2 circles, cut out of construction paper, about 3½ inches in diameter

      Scissors

      2 squares about 6 inches by 6 inches
   b. Procedure

      For transformation by cutting and reassembling:

P-20

51. The teacher asks the child to ascertain that the two circles are exactly the same, then cuts one of them into four pieces and arranges the pieces on the table as shown in Fig. 13-14*a*. The child is asked to put the pieces back together to make them look like the model.

For transformation by folding:

P-20

52. The teacher shows to the child a square that has been folded diagonally twice (into four triangles) as

shown in Fig. 13-14*b*. He then asks the child to make his square look just like the model. (The examiner demonstrates the procedure if the child cannot do the task by himself.)

c. Criteria. The criteria are the correctness of the product and the process the child goes through. If the child arrives at the correct answer by trial and error, or if he needs a demonstration of the procedure, he is said to be at a lower level than if he quickly anticipates the necessary action by himself.

3. The reconstruction of sensory-motor space on the representational level
   a. Materials
      13 cards with the designs shown in Fig. 13-15
      13 sheets of paper, 8½ inches × 5½ inches
      primary pencil
      5 sticks, 3 inches long, that do not roll
      5 sticks, 1½ inches long, that do not roll
   b. Procedure
      Copying with the pencil:

P-20

53. The child is given one card and one sheet at a time and asked to draw "one just like this." He copies all thirteen designs, always with only one model visible at a time.

Copying with the sticks:

P-20

54. The child is shown the square, the rectangle, and the two crosses one at a time. He is asked to use the sticks to make a shape just like the model.

c. Criteria. Each drawing is evaluated separately first; then a global evaluation must be made. Developmentally, space is structured topologically first, and euclidean space develops out of a topological structure at the end of the following evolution:

Topological structure, which is characterized by the child's ability to use criteria of *contiguity*.

Projective structure, which is characterized by the appearance of the ability to construct a *projective line*.

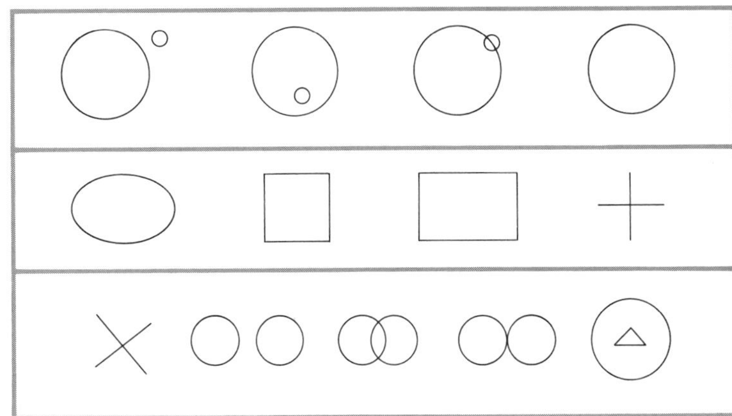

FIGURE 13-15 Designs used to evaluate the child's structuring of space at the representational level.

Affinity structure, which is characterized by the appearance of the ability to construct parallel lines.

Similitude structure, which is characterized by the appearance of *angles* and *proportions*.

Euclidean structure, which is characterized by the appearance of the child's ability to take into account the exact *length*.

The simplest way to explain the characteristics of structure is in terms of how a child's square evolves. Figure 13-16*a* shows how a child seems to reduce the square to a circle when his representational space is at a topological level. The only characteristic that is respected here is contiguity. The whole shape comes out as a whole without any mistake about whether it is an open or a closed shape. (An O is a closed shape, and a C is an open shape.) However, this shape has no straight line, no parallel, no angle, no proportion, and no reproduction of lengths.

Figure 13-16*b* shows the appearance of the straight line. This structure, however, does not have any parallels, and the angles are not yet defined. It is in Fig. 13-16*c* that parallels become structured, but the angles and proportions are not correct in this figure. Angles and proportions become structured later (Fig. 13-16*d*), and the exact lengths are the last thing to emerge (Fig. 13-16*e*).

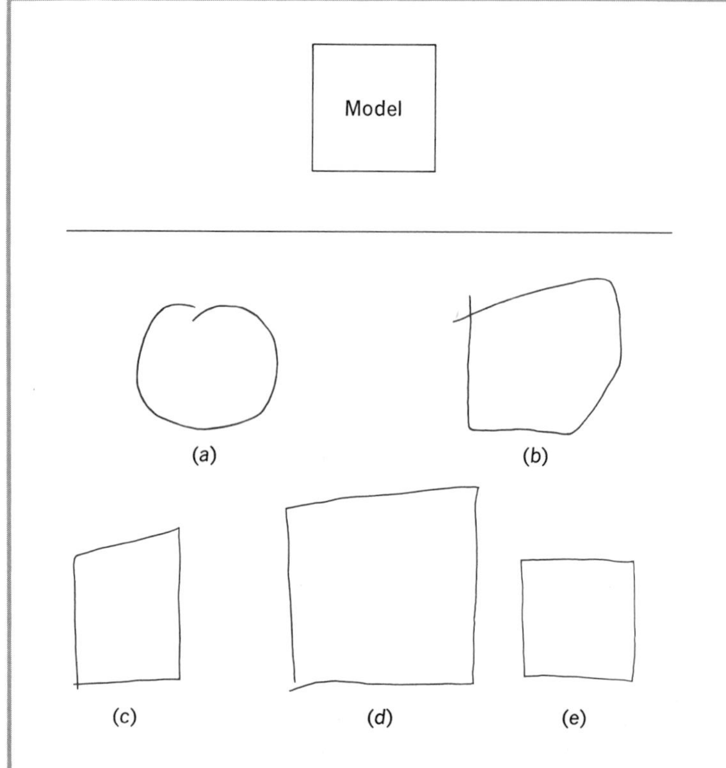

FIGURE 13-16 The progressive structuring of space as illustrated by the child's copying of a square.

This analysis illustrates the progressive structuring of space in Piaget's theory. The various characteristics, such as angles and proportions, do not emerge neatly at the same time across all the designs, but this procedure of evaluation gives to the teacher enough indication as to how far the child has progressed beyond the topological structure on the representational plane.

NOTE: The difference between sensory-motor space and representational space must be remembered. The 4-year-old child can *find* another square or rectangle (a sensory-motor task), but he cannot necessarily copy it (a representational task).

The structuring of time (Q) The Piagetian and non-Piagetian preschools do not conceptualize the teaching of temporal relationships very differently.[28] Both types of schools agree that time is very hard for children to deal with because it is intangible. Both schools would use sequence cards for summative evaluation. Below are three examples.

1. Material
   4 cards showing an apple:
      A whole apple
      The apple cut into 2 pieces (with a knife in the picture)
      A person cutting one of the halves into 2 pieces
      The apple cut into 4 pieces
   4 cards of a child painting at the easel, with his picture in view
      A clean sheet of paper
      One stroke on the paper
      The sheet half-covered with paint of two colors
      The entire sheet covered with paint of three colors
   4 cards of a boy getting dressed
      The boy in pajamas getting out of bed
      The boy fully dressed except for his bare feet
      The boy putting on a sock
      The boy (with both socks on) putting on his second shoe
2. Procedure

Q-7, Q-16, Q-8

55. The examiner gives to the child each series of four pictures in a mixed-up order, asking him to describe what he sees in each picture.
56. The examiner asks the child to arrange the pictures in such a way that they will tell a story.
57. The child is asked to explain what he just did.

3. Criteria
   a. The sequence must be considered correct as long as the child can justify what he did. However, the first two series describe irreversible processes which can be reconstructed from (1) causal relationships (i.e., one's action on the object causing a change in the object) and (2) spatial consideration (i.e., cutting an apple leaves spatial cues with which to reason; but the sequence of eating an apple and then painting at the easel leaves no spatial cues to help reconstruct the temporal

[28] This statement does not imply that Piaget's epistemology of time offers no new insights.

sequence). Therefore, the child who consistently makes up stories to fit the randomly arranged cards in the first two series (e.g., "He cut the apple . . . and got another one.") must be carefully examined.

The third series, on the other hand, can be arranged in either direction to represent either getting dressed or getting undressed.

b. The scoring may be done in terms of how many proximity relationships the child can coordinate. Piaget (1946) says that, as in linear ordering, the child first becomes able to coordinate the proximity relationship of only two elements at a time, and later becomes able to coordinate three or more elements as his thought becomes more mobile.

Representation at the symbol level (R)

In a preschool that is not Piagetian. By "representation" the non-Piagetian preschool means toys (three-dimensional representation), pictures (two-dimensional representation), and words. The procedure for summative evaluation in this framework would be similar to that of the Peabody Picture Vocabulary Test (Dunn, 1965). In this procedure, the child is shown four pictures and is given one word. His task is to point to the picture that best fits that word. By giving thirty or more similar questions, in the same manner, the examiner can evaluate both the child's vocabulary and his ability to interpret pictures.

In a Piagetian preschool. Piaget's theory of representation is fundamentally different from the Anglo-Saxon tradition (Furth, 1969, 1970). According to this theory, the bridge between the sensory-motor and the representational knowledge of an object is not pictures but imitation.[29] In a Piagetian preschool, therefore, summative evaluation in representation must begin with imitation and include other symbolic activities which are traditionally considered to be art, "creative," or "expressive" activities.

Representation includes imitation, make-believe, block building, making clay models, and drawing and painting, as well as copying seriated sticks and socio-dramatic play. Examples of evaluation procedures will now be given.

[29] The reader is referred to Piaget (1962) for a clarification of this statement.

1. Imitation
   a. Procedure

R-8, R-7, R-12, R-11

58. The teacher shows a hat, an apple, a cup, a hammer, etc., one at a time, and asks the child what the object is called. She then asks him to show what one does with the object.

It is often necessary to let children physically use the real objects, and then ask them again to imitate the action *without touching* the object.

b. Criteria. The protocol taker must note how exactly the child imitates the actions. With the hat, for example, some children barely put one hand on the head, while others act with elaborate accuracy. These differences often reflect the child's knowledge of the object.

Some children are not able to engage in imitation before touching and using the object first. This inability may reflect inhibition, but it often also reflects inability to externalize the mental image.

2. Make-believe
   a. Procedure

R-11 and R-12

59. With clay, the teacher makes something that looks like a short cigar. With the same piece of clay, she engages in the following imitative actions, one after another, as she asks, "Now, what is this? . . . And now what is it? . . ."

    Combing
    Smoking
    Brushing her teeth
    Eating (with a spoon)
    Drinking out of a straw
    Writing

The purpose of this exploration is to find out whether or not the child can impose different mental images on the same piece of clay as the teacher's imitative action changes.

b. Criteria. The child is to name each object. Some children will name only the *action*, rather than the *object*. Others may not be able to shift from the mental image of a comb to that of a cigarette. In make-believe, the child has to impose a mental image on an object to make believe that it is something else. Once the young child has decided that the piece of clay "is" a comb, it is often hard for him to shift to making believe that it "is" a cigarette.

3. Block building
   a. Procedure. Ratings of the child's daily performance seem better suited for this evaluation than putting the child in a test situation.
   b. Criteria. The following five-point scale can be refined into a seven-point scale:

1	2	3	4	5
Sensory-motor building	Representational building			

   Examples:
   1—Piling the blocks until they topple and repeating the same thing over and over.
   2—The same, simple, repetitious representation, such as the use of the cylindrical block only to set up a "gas station."
   3—Building a road so that the car can go around the block.
   4—Building a road and a bridge with a ramp, etc.
   5—Varied and elaborate buildings, such as a "castle" and a "hospital."

4. Making clay models
   a. Procedure

R

60. The teacher gives clay to the child and asks him to make as many things as he can. After the child indicates that he has finished, he is asked, "Tell me about it."

   b. Criteria. The teacher notes what the child says he made, and how much his product resembles the object. Some children will make no more than "snakes" and "pancakes." The important criterion here is not the child's technique but how many things he can make and see symbolically.

5. Drawing and painting. The following two activities may be desirable for evaluating the child's ability in two-dimensional representation: (a) drawing a person and (b) transforming a circle on the blackboard.
   a. Drawing a person: Procedure. The Goodenough-Harris Drawing Test (Harris, 1963) can be used.

R-1

61. The child is asked to draw the very best picture of a person that he can.

   Criteria. I know of no developmental norms stated in terms of the structuring of representational space. The establishment of such norms for preschool children awaits research. The best criteria at this time can be found in Harris's book.[30] It seems more meaningful to use raw scores than to use standard scores.
   b. Transforming a circle on the blackboard: Procedure

R-20

62. The teacher draws a circle on the blackboard (about 6 to 8 inches in diameter). Giving an eraser and a piece of chalk to the child, she asks him to draw something else in or around the circle to make it look like anything he wants it to become.

   Criteria. The teacher notes everything that the child draws and erases, as well as what he says—e.g., "Now it's a lollipop. . . . Now it's a face. . . . Now it's a flower. . . ." The teacher looks for the variety of ways in which the child can transform the original circle to symbolize many objects.

6. Seriated sticks. The preceding evaluation procedures dealt with single objects. Seriated sticks and sociodramatic play will deal with the representation of many related objects.
   a. Procedure

R-19

63. The teacher shows to the child a board on which five sticks have been glued as shown in Fig. 13-17*a*. She draws the bottom line at the base of the sticks, and asks the child to make a picture that looks just like the model.

   b. Criteria
   Stage O: Any number of sticks drawn in a variety of ways as shown in Fig. 13-17*b*.

[30] This test requires the drawing of three pictures: that of a man, a woman, and "yourself." Whether or not preschool children draw differently under the different instructions is not known.

Stage I: The dichotomous stage that can be seen in Fig. 13-17*c*.
Stage II: The trichotomous stage that can be seen in Fig. 13-17*d*.
Stage III: An accurate representation.

7. Socio-dramatic play. Ratings made by the teacher are recommended for summative evaluation in socio-dramatic play. For these ratings, the teacher can make a matrix evaluation form like Table 13-6, which is based, with some modification, on Smilansky's analysis (1968). The left-hand column of this matrix lists the various aspects of socio-dramatic play Smilansky analyzed, and the four other columns indicate the extent to which the child engages in each behavior.

Make-believe in Table 13-6 refers to how children use objects in their dramatic play. The first two rows involve toys, and the last two involve either "nothing" or a prop (e.g., a large carton to serve as a "car"). The use of "nothing" or a prop requires a much more active and vivid mental image than the use of toys. Playing with toys evolves from the mere sensory-motor "manipulation of the toy" to "using toys to enact roles." *Using props* requires a more powerful mental image than *Using nothing*, for in using a prop the child has to ignore the attributes of the prop itself—for example, to impose on the carton the image of a car.

Imitative play in this matrix refers to the child's behavior itself. In the first stage, he simply imitates actions (e.g., "driving" a car). In the second stage, he uses the imitative action as part of a role (e.g., the "daddy" driving a "car"). In the third stage, he puts the role in the context of a specific situation (e.g., the "daddy" driving a "car" to take his sick child to the hospital). At first, the child can persist only a few minutes in a given role, but he will gradually elaborate the role with consistency and continuity.

Make-believe and imitative play can take place without interactions with other roles. Smilansky refers to this parallel play as "dramatic" play, and states that it is interactions that make the difference between "dramatic" and "*socio*-dramatic" play. The interactions are at first nonverbal, but they become verbal particularly as the imitative play comes to involve specific situations. In order to share a common situation, the children must define it by communicating verbally with each other.

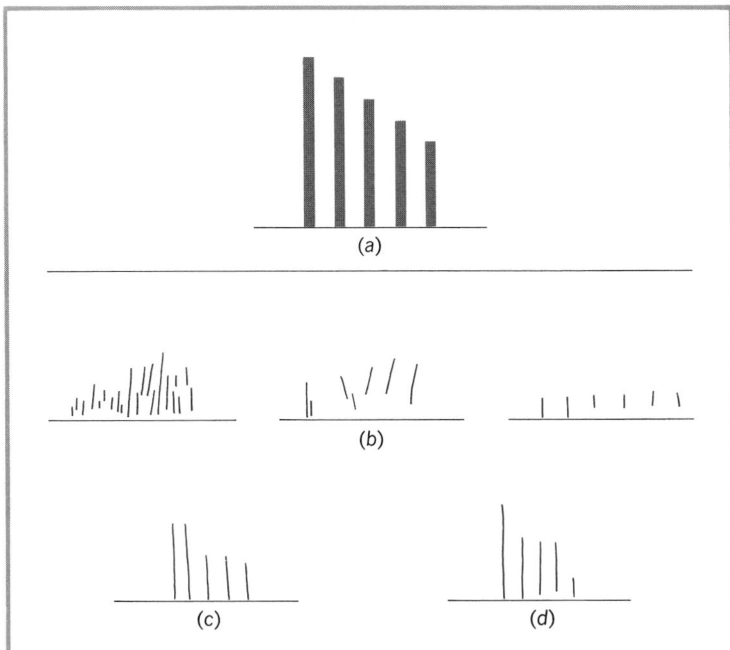

FIGURE 13-17 The child's representation of five seriated sticks.

There are other important observations to be made in socio-dramatic play, such as the variety of roles the child plays and whether he is a leader or a follower. All aspects of his representational knowledge, too, can be seen in socio-dramatic play. For example, confusions in temporal relationships are often evident (e.g., trying to accept an invitation before being invited to a birthday party). The child's ability in classification and seriation, too, can be seen when he puts away his "groceries." His social knowledge can be observed when he says, "Doctors don't wear a fireman's hat!" Statements like "Don't drop the eggs. They'll break," or "Put the milk back in the refrigerator. It will spoil," reflect his physical knowledge. Socio-dramatic play thus has a unique place in a Piagetian curriculum, because it involves all aspects of knowledge at the "symbol" and "sign" levels of representation.

Table 13-6 Evaluation Form for Socio-dramatic Play

Behavior	*Not at all*	*A little*	*Medium amount*	*A lot*	*Specify: roles, objects, situation, roles child interacts with*
1. Make-believe a. Manipulation of toys					
b. Using toys to enact roles					
c. Using "nothing" to enact roles					
d. Using props to enact roles					
2. Imitative play a. Actions					
b. Roles					
c. Situations					
3. Persistence within a role (specify approx. time)					
4. Interaction a. Nonverbal					
b. Verbal					

Comments:

The evaluation of the child's progress in language (objective S) is discussed in the next chapter by Cazden.

Problems of summative evaluation

The first problem in summative evaluation is specifying the objectives of instruction. This section will highlight some of the unresolved problems centering on the objectives of preschool education, the instruments of evaluation that can be found, and the norms that are available. This section will limit itself to summative evaluation within the context of the given set of objectives; the final section of this chapter will examine the objectives themselves in a larger context. The issue discussed in the final section will be summative evaluation of short-term gains versus summative evaluation which takes into account whether or not the pupils are building a solid foundation for development in the long run.

Reference has been made throughout this chapter to the fact that since preschool education is a new field emerging out of various social forces, there is no common core of agreement as to what its goals should be. The objectives tend to be stated either in broad terms (such as "school readiness") or in minute terms (such as "colors," "numbers to ten," "prepositions such as 'over' and 'under,'" "shapes," and "letters"). Some programs state their objectives as "perceptual, cognitive, and language development," without any further conceptualization of what to teach.

In preschool education, the lack of curriculum goals is accompanied by a lack of measurement techniques. Despite all the tests mentioned in this chapter and Cazden's, there is literally no achievement test in existence that comes anywhere near the level of achievement tests which are found in reading and arithmetic. Since the growth of measurement techniques usually follows the development of a curriculum, this state of affairs is not surprising.

In discussing curriculum evaluation, Scriven (1967, p. 59) delineates the three kinds of "matches" that must be present: (1) a match between the course goals and its content, (2) a match between the goals and the examination content, and (3) a match between the course content and the examination content. None of these types can be expected in the field of preschool education, where the course goals are nebulous, the course content is ill-defined, and the instrument of evaluation is unavailable. An overwhelming majority of preschools conceptualize their objective as "later success in school," leave the curriculum content up to the individual teachers, and use tests such as the Binet (Terman & Merrill, 1960), the Peabody Picture Vocabulary Test (Dunn, 1965), the Illinois Test of Psycholinguistic Abilities (Kirk, McCarthy, & Kirk, 1968), and the Developmental Test of Visual Perception (Frostig, 1963), none of which was intended for the evaluation of student learning in preschool. The Preschool Inventory (Caldwell, 1967), the Test of Basic Information (Moss, 1967), and the Basic Concept Inventory (Engelmann, 1967) represent efforts to match the examination content with the course content. In the first two, the match between goals and course content, and between goals and examination content, is not precisely stated.

Summative evaluation in the cognitively oriented preschools has taken two directions—toward the use of intelligence tests as achievement tests, and toward the construction of achievement tests. These two trends will now be discussed briefly.

The content of achievement tests is limited to given curriculum areas that are taught in school. Thus, a reading test attempts to measure the child's mastery of reading. Intelligence tests, on the other hand, avoid subjects that are systematically taught in school (e.g., reading). Intelligence tests were originally developed to assess the potential of the individual—particularly, to discover whether or not he was mentally defective if he showed academic difficulty in school. The child's potential was supposed to be inferable from his present abilities if the items on the test dealt with two kinds of content: (1) that which *all* children growing up in a culture are always taught as part of living in that culture and (2) that which *none* of the children are systematically taught. Both types of items were supposed to yield individual differences that were attributable to native intelligence. If all children are exposed to a given content, so ran the argument, the child who performs better on an item dealing with that content must have had more native ability. If none of the children are taught a given fact, the child who knows that fact must have picked it up with his superior native intelligence.

The distinction between intelligence and achievement tests has become impossible to maintain in recent years. The research cited in the first section of this chapter convinced educators that intelligence is not fixed at birth but is developed through the child's interaction with his environment; accordingly, they made more and more efforts to develop intelligence. During the same period, many leading theorists have come to regard the Binet more and more as an achievement test.

Many cognitively oriented preschools state their objective as the teaching of "readiness for school" and use the Binet as *the* instrument of evaluation. Many researchers who use the Binet in this way recognize the fact that they are leaving to chance the "match" between the course content and the examination content. However, they justify their practice by arguing that since the Binet predicts school success, preschools must raise the child's IQ. In the author's opinion, this argument is open to question and perpetuates the theoretical vacuum that puts pressure on the teacher to raise the child's IQ.

The danger of equating IQ with "intelligence" leads to another danger—the assumption of a positive linear correlation between increase in IQ and the degree of learning that the child accomplished in a preschool program. There is a tendency in both academic and legislative circles to assume that a 50-point mean IQ gain is necessarily better than a 30-point gain, and that a mean gain of 30 points is likewise better than a 10-point gain.[31]

The second direction in evaluation, it has been said, is toward the development of achievement tests. The Preschool Inventory (Caldwell, 1967), the Test of Basic Information (Moss, 1967), and the Basic Concept Inventory (Engelmann, 1967) have based their content on the relevant program of instruction. These efforts to increase the match between course content and examination content gave to the cognitively oriented preschools more appropriate means of evaluating learning.

The evaluation procedures proposed in the preceding section on the basis of Piaget's theory represent an initial effort to overcome some of the weaknesses of the existing achievement tests. Among these weaknesses is the fact that the tests were constructed in the psychometric tradition, which looks for the one correct answer to each question without regard to the child's process of thinking. The author believes that summative evaluation in preschool must examine the child's process of thinking, which makes the correct answer possible. Product-oriented, norm-based psychometric tests grew in the absence of a theory describing how young children think and develop. Now that cognition is better understood as a structured process, both teaching and the evaluation of instruction must examine cognitive processes in physical knowledge, social knowledge, logical knowledge, and representation.

The Piagetian procedures of summative evaluation presented in this chapter are being developed in the Ypsilanti Early Education Program as part of a project to develop a Piaget-based curriculum. The main drawback of these procedures is that no normative data are available. It is not yet evident to me what level of development can reasonably be expected of American 4-year-old children of various socioeconomic strata, and how preschools can improve children's development by building a solid foundation. In short, the work that remains to be done entails not only collecting normative data but also developing a curriculum. It is hoped that the procedures proposed in this chapter will serve at least to show the possibility of evaluating student learning in such a way that the teacher will gain insights into how to teach the child better, in ways that are natural to his development.

Illustrations of formative evaluation

"Formative evaluation" refers to diagnostic progress tests which are given once every two or three weeks to determine where the child is and what the next instructional goal should be for him. In this section, the teaching of numbers has been selected to illustrate how formative evaluation can be done in a cognitively oriented preschool that is not Piagetian, as well as in a Piagetian preschool.

[31] An article (Pine, 1968) on research projects attempting to develop intelligence in infancy says, for example, "Only seven years ago [J. McV.] Hunt was predicting that it might be possible to raise infant IQs 30 points by stimulation in very early childhood. Now with several years of experimentation behind him Hunt believes that the environment which infants encounter may vary IQs by as much as 50 to 70 points. 'This means,' he says, 'that infants with potential from a culturally deprived background might be elevated from the upper levels of mental retardation to do college work someday' [p. 15]."

In a preschool that is not Piagetian

It has been said earlier in this chapter that the objectives in the non-Piagetian preschool in the teaching of number are (1) the ability to count, (2) the ability to abstract number from pictures that have several objects arranged spatially differently, and (3) the ability to make judgments about "more" and "less."

Generally speaking, programming in this framework begins with the discrimination between 1 and 2, and builds up progressively to 3, 4, 5, etc. Six types of activities are listed in the left-hand column of Table 13-7. Formative evaluation should include all six, with the magnitude of the number increasing from one session to the next. To use this form, the teacher enters the date of the evaluation at the top of the column, and enters under that date the highest number the child could handle correctly in each of the six tasks. The first column of cells has been filled in as an example.

Saying the numbers refers to memorizing the number words in the correct sequence, in a manner similar to learning the days of the week. No objects are used in this task. The procedure here consists simply of asking the child how far he can count. At an advanced stage, the teacher might ask the child to count by starting at three, five, etc.

Counting objects refers to pairing words with objects. The procedure here would be to give to the child more pebbles, pegs, or plastic forks than he can count, and ask him to count them as far as he can go. His level of achievement for each session is the number he reaches before he makes his first mistake. The common mistakes are skipping a number, repeating a number, mixing up the sequence of number words, skipping an object, and counting the same object more than once.

The next three activities involve groups of objects. In *Making groups*, the teacher places about twenty counting blocks in front of the child and asks him to give her three, five, or any other number that is appropriate for him. In *Saying how many*, the teacher makes the groups and asks the child to *say* how many are in a group. *Making judgments about "more" and "less"* involves

Table 13-7 Formative Evaluation Form for the Teaching of Number in a Non-Piagetian Preschool

	10/4									
Saying the numbers	12									
Counting objects	5									
Making groups	4									
Saying how many	5									
Making judgments about "more" and "less"	2/5									
Picking out the card that has the same number	2									

FIGURE 13-18 Cards for the evaluation of number concepts.

comparing two groups. For example, the teacher makes a group of two checkers and one of five checkers and asks the child to *show* where there are more.

Picking out the card that has the same number is at the representational level—that is, groups are pictorially represented on cards. In this task, the child can be asked either to group all the cards that have the same number, or to pick out a card that has the same number as a given card. Figure 13-18 shows an example of the cards that can be made. This task can be said to be a classification game in which the important attribute is number. The objects themselves (e.g., cherries and flowers) and the spatial arrangement of the objects are the irrelevant attributes which must be ignored.

Formative evaluation in number in a non-Piagetian preschool would, then, consist of ascertaining the number that a child has mastered in each of the six tasks. In each task, the number that comes after that mastery level would be the next instructional goal.

In a Piagetian preschool

The appropriate goal in number for the end of the preschool year, as was noted, may be conservation with provoked correspondence. As can be seen in Table 13-8, the ultimate goal is conservation with objects that have a relationship of "spontaneous" correspondence. Since this level was not reached by most of the children in Geneva until 6 years of age, the goal for preschool education has been set at the stage of conservation with provoked correspondence.

The left-hand column of Table 13-8 lists the general sequence of development. The first distinction to be made in this column is between *provoked* and *spontaneous* correspondence. The former is easier than the latter. "Provoked correspondence" refers to the *qualitative* one-to-one relationship between objects that helps a child to establish the *quantitative* one-to-one correspondence—e.g., a set of bottles and their corresponding caps. With, for example, two sets of bottlecaps, on the other hand, there is no qualitative complementary relationship between the objects to support the quantitative one-to-one correspondence. This type of correspondence is called "spontaneous correspondence" by Piaget.[32]

The second broad distinction to be made in Table 13-8 is that between *spatial* and *temporal* correspondence. The former is one-to-one correspondence based on space, as shown below:

o o o o o o o o
o o o o o o o o

Temporal correspondence refers to one-to-one correspondence based on simultaneity and temporal sequence; e.g., each time a bead is dropped into one container, a bead is dropped into another container.

Although there could conceivably be "provoked temporal correspondence," this does not appear in Table 13-8. The reason for this omission is that provoked correspondence has a special function when the notion of "just enough" begins to appear. In this situation, spatial correspondence lends itself readily to the child's checking, for example, whether or not there are "just enough" bottlecaps for the bottles. Temporal correspondence appears to be an intermediary stage, when the establishment of spatial one-to-one correspondence is still too hard with objects that have a relationship of spontaneous correspondence.

[32] For a fuller explanation, the reader is referred to Piaget (1965, Chs. 3, 4).

Table 13-8 Formative Evaluation Form for the Teaching of Number in a Piagetian Preschool

Number / *Objects* / *Date*	4	4				
	cups saucers	*½-inch beads*				
	(10/4)	(10/4)				
Provoked spatial correspondence "A lot" and "a little"	+					
Equivalence	+					
Discrepancy of 1 or 2 Different space occupied	+					
Same space occupied	–					
Renversabilité						
Conservation						
Explanation of conservation						
Spontaneous temporal correspondence "A lot" and "a little"		+				
Equivalence		–				
Discrepancy of 1 or 2						
Renversabilité						
Conservation						
Explanation of conservation						
Spontaneous spatial correspondence "A lot" and "a little"						
Equivalence						
Discrepancy of 1 or 2 Different space occupied						
Same space occupied						
Renversabilité						
Conservation						
Explanation of conservation						

As can be seen in Table 13-8, there are at least six levels within each type of correspondence. The easiest level is gross comparisons between "a lot" and "a little," and the hardest task requires the explanation of conservation. The evaluation procedure for spatial correspondence at each level is given below.

Provoked spatial correspondence

"A lot" and "a little."

0-12

64. To test for the child's ability to make gross judgments between "a lot" and "a little," the teacher makes a group of 2 toy cups, for example, and a group of 8 saucers, and asks, "Show me where there's a lot." She changes the combination to 10 and 2, 3 and 9, etc., with a variety of objects. She can also ask the child to "put a lot here, and a little there." The terms "more" and "less" are harder for many 4-year-olds to understand than "a lot" and "a little."

Equivalence. The next level is the establishment of equivalence.

65. The teacher lines up 8 cups, for example, and asks the child to take out "enough saucers so there'll be *just* enough for all the cups."

The "+" or "–" to be entered here refers to whether or not the child placed the correct number of saucers at this point. Provoked correspondence enables the teacher to use such words as "just enough" rather than "the same number," which is hard for many children to understand.

Discrepancy of 1 or 2. This task should sometimes be given before the conservation task, and sometimes after it, to prevent children from memorizing the sequence of correct answers. It refers to adding or taking away one or two objects from one of the sets, after the establishment of their numerical equivalence.

66. Before introducing the discrepancy, the teacher says, "Watch what I'm going to do [*and adds a cup, for example, to the row of cups*]. Now, do we have *just* enough saucers for all the cups?"

The "+" or "–" to be entered refers to the child's answer to this question.

Discrepancy of 1 or 2 is easier when the two sets occupy different amounts of space. When the cup that the teacher adds sticks out of the space occupied by the two equivalent sets, as shown in Fig. 13-19*a*, the child can readily see that there are "more cups." However, when the additional cup is placed in the middle of the row, as shown in Fig. 13-19*b*, the task is much harder. In Table

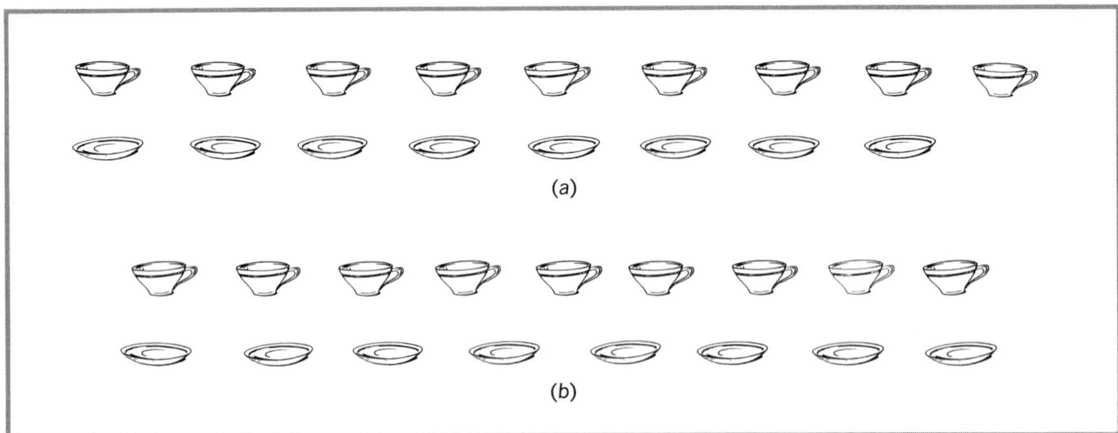

FIGURE 13-19 Two ways to arrange two sets that are not numerically equivalent.

13-8, therefore, *Different space occupied* is listed before *Same space occupied* under *Discrepancy of 1 or 2*. If the child answers correctly, he is asked what he should do "to make it right" (or, "to have enough saucers"). He can either add a saucer or take a cup away.

Conservation. Although *Renversabilité* appears before *Conservation* in Table 13-8, the conservation question is given first for reasons that will be clarified shortly. The conservation question is as follows:

67. After the child establishes the equivalence of the two sets, the teacher says, "Watch carefully what I'm going to do," and spreads the cups apart and pushes the saucers closer together in a way similar to the arrangement shown in Fig. 13-12*b*. She then asks, "Now do you think there are still enough saucers for all the cups?"

The "+" or "−" on *Conservation* refers to the correctness of the child's answer to this question. Strictly speaking, however, the child cannot be said to have conservation unless he can explain why he thinks the numerical equivalence has not changed (i.e., can answer the following question).

68. Whether or not the child answers the "conservation" question correctly, the teacher then asks, "How do you know? Show me."

The acceptable explanation of conservation is either identity ("You didn't add or take away anything") or reversibility ("We could move the things back to the way they were before"). The correctness of this answer is recorded next to *Explanation of conservation*.

The *Renversabilité* question is given only when the child is found to be unable to conserve.

Renversabilité.

69. The teacher asks, "Do you think we could put these cups and saucers back to the way they were before? Do you think there will then be enough saucers for all the cups?"

Children who have *renversabilité* think that the equivalence will be resumed when the objects are returned to their original position. Those who do not have *renversabilité* say, "I don't know," or "We will have to try and see."

The differences between *renversabilité* and conservation is that the former concerns *physically moving* the objects, rather than arriving at the conclusion by reversibility of *thought*, which makes conservation a *logical necessity*. The conservation question is asked before the *renversabilité* question because the latter sometimes suggests conservation to a child who otherwise would not be able to conserve,[33] and because the real question of interest at this point is whether or not the child can conserve. The *renversabilité* question is asked only if the child is unable to conserve, in order to find out how close he is to conservation.

To summarize the preceding procedures, a review of the three stages mentioned earlier in this chapter may be useful. In stage I, the child has neither equivalence nor conservation. In stage II, he can establish equivalence, but cannot conserve the equivalence. In stage III, both equivalence and conservation are achieved.

Temporal correspondence The procedures in temporal correspondence parallel those of spatial correspondence. (Formative evaluation in temporal correspondence is recommended for spontaneous correspondence only. For the reasons that were given in page 332, there is no point in doing a formative evaluation in provoked temporal correspondence.) Each task will now be described, and the reader is asked to refer to the procedures for spatial correspondence to clarify the details that are not repeated.

Equivalence.

O-17

70. The teacher gives a glass jar to the child and an identical jar to herself, and says, as she shows a box of beads to the child, "Each time *I* put a bead in, *you*

[33] The child is influenced by the *renversabilité* question when he is very close to achieving conservation. He is not so suggestible when he is at a lower level.

put one in. Ready? Let's begin." When she reaches the desired number, she says, "Now stop. Do you and I have exactly the same amount?"

To synchronize the dropping of the beads, she says, "Bing. . . bing. . . bing. . . bing. . ." The two beads must make a "bing" sound precisely at the same time. Otherwise, young children tend to believe that the two sets are not numerically the same.

Discrepancy of 1 or 2.

O-17

71. After stopping at the same time and thus establishing the equivalence of the two sets, the teacher says, "Now, watch carefully what I'm going to do," and adds 1 or 2 beads to her jar. She then asks, "Is it fair the way we gave ourselves the beads?" (Or, "Do we still have exactly the same amount?")

This procedure can be represented as follows:

Teacher: 1 + 1 + 1 + 1 + 1 + 1 + 1 + 1 + 1
Child: 1 + 1 + 1 + 1 + 1 + 1 + 1 + 1

Variations of the above task are the introduction of the discrepancy at the beginning or in the middle, as shown below:

C: 1 + 1 + 1 + 1 + 1 + 1 + 1 + 1 + 1
T: 1 + 1 + 1 + 1 + 1 + 1 + 1 + 1

or

T: 1 + 1 + 1 + 1 + 1 + 1 + 1 + 1 + 1
C: 1 + 1 + 1 + 1 + 1 + 1 + 1 + 1

Conservation.

O-17

72. The teacher pours the content of one of the jars into a container having different dimensions (such as a tiny vial or a very large jar), and asks, "If you took these and *I* took these, would we both have exactly the same amount?" Whether or not the child answers this question correctly, the teacher then asks, "How do you know?" [*Explanation of conservation.*]

If the child is found unable to conserve, the teacher asks the following question concerning *renversabilité.*

Renversabilité.

O-17

73. As in the case of spatial correspondence, the teacher asks, "Do you think we could put the beads back in this jar the way they were before? Would you and I have exactly the same amount then?"

Spontaneous spatial correspondence The procedure is exactly the same as that for provoked spatial correspondence (see pages 334–335) except for the objects used and some of the words that appear in the questions. The objects can be two sets of candy, counting blocks, or poker chips. The first question ("a lot" and "a little") is asked in the same way as in the case of provoked correspondence, but the wording of all the other questions has to be changed slightly. For the establishment of equivalence, the teacher says, "Take out *the same number*" (or "*the same amount*, so that you will have *exactly the same amount* as I do"), rather than saying, "Take out *just enough* [*saucers for all the cups*]." The questions concerning discrepancy of 1 or 2, conservation, and *renversabilité* are likewise asked with words that are appropriate to spontaneous correspondence.

Whether a given type of correspondence is easy or hard depends on the number of objects involved in the task. With a given set of objects, the preoperational child finds it easier to deal with four objects than with eight.[34] For formative

[34] Numbers up to about four are called "perceptual numbers" by Piaget because they can be judged perceptually rather than logically. Therefore, there is no such thing as the conservation of perceptual numbers. For diagnostic purposes, however, it is useful to see whether or not the child can "conserve" with 4 objects, since if there is no "conservation" with 4 objects, the teacher will not go on to a larger number.

evaluation, therefore, the teacher selects both the number and the kind of correspondence (provoked, spontaneous, spatial, or temporal) appropriate for the child at a given time. At the top of Table 13-8, she enters whatever number she considers suitable, the objects chosen, and the date of the formative evaluation. As usual, she takes notes about the child's process and enters on this form only the summary notations. A few pluses and minuses have been entered in Table 13-8 as an example. The notations indicate that on October 4, the teacher tried the number 4. In provoked correspondence, the child went as far as discrepancy of 1 or 2 with a difference in the space occupied. In spontaneous correspondence, the child could go only as far as "a lot" and "a little."

Linear ordering As described in Kamii and Radin (1970) and Sonquist, Kamii, and Derman (1970), linear order is part of what is taught in a Piagetian preschool for the construction of number. Formative evaluation for the teaching of number must, therefore, include linear ordering. The testing procedures have been described in the section dealing with structuring of space. For formative evaluation, the teacher selects the number of objects appropriate for each child—e.g., three objects for some children, eight for others.

It is important not to allow the child to copy the model by simple matching (which does not require the coordination of proximity relationships). The differences between the two tasks is shown in Fig. 13-20. Having a distance of at least 10 inches between the model and the copy is, therefore, necessary. Asking the child to space his objects wider apart is another way to prevent him from making the copy by simple matching.

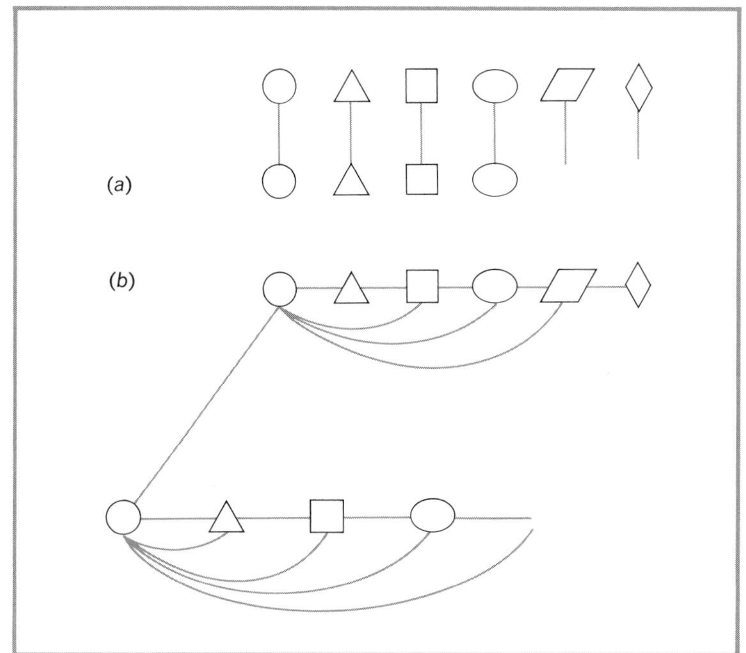

FIGURE 13-20 (*a*) Matching and (*b*) linear ordering.

Before concluding this section, a word of caution must be added about formative evaluation in relation to the teaching of number. Since number is constructed very gradually by a complex internal process, the teacher cannot and should not expect dramatic progress from one evaluation session to the next. The desirable interval between evaluation sessions might be one month, and this interval is recommended not for trying to produce a change each time, but for seeing a pattern of growth, changes in the child's reasoning process, and the permanency of his learning. As has been discussed, logico-mathematical structures are based on the internal consistency of the child's beliefs and cannot be taught by simple feedback from other people. To change the child's surface behavior (i.e., his verbal behavior) by operant conditioning would be easier and more visible than trying to change his logical structure. However, the Piagetian teacher must choose the slower, harder, and less dramatic of the two approaches and teach to develop the underlying cognitive structure rather than the surface behavior.

Problems of formative evaluation

The problems in the evaluation procedures just described stem from the fact that the precise sequence of development relative to Table 13-8 is not known. Since Piaget's research has been done in cross-sectional studies to investigate epistemological questions, his theory gives broad guidelines but not the detailed sequence of longitudinal development which would be helpful to the teacher. In the construction of number, Piaget first studied, among other things, equivalence and conservation with regard to spatial correspondence. In this initial research in the 1930s, he established the three basic stages that were first published in 1941 (Piaget, 1965). Many fine points remain to be clarified, among them the relationship between spatial correspondence and Piaget's later findings on temporal correspondence, the question of perceptual numbers, the variability in children's logic as a function of the objects used, and the effect of the distance between the two sets of objects at the time the conservation question is asked. Each of these problems will now be elaborated.

After the publication of the first volume on number in 1941, Piaget and Inhelder studied the child's attainment of equivalence by means of temporal correspondence, where the child himself performed the action of dropping beads into two jars. They found in this study that this temporal correspondence resulted in the child's establishment of equivalence slightly earlier than when correspondence was based on space (Inhelder & Piaget, 1963). I know of no publication which describes precisely how stages II and III of temporal correspondence fit longitudinally with stages II and III of provoked and spontaneous spatial correspondence. Another question that remains to be clarified concerns the difference between temporal correspondence in which the child drops the beads into *both* containers and the situation in which the child and the teacher drop beads into their respective jars. It may be that the first situation enables the child to establish equivalence much earlier than the second situation.

Piaget (1965, p. 70) states that at stage II, when conservation is impossible with eight objects, numbers up to three or four (perceptual numbers) do not cause the same difficulty. The reason for this difference is that with three or four objects the child can use perception to make the correct judgment. When the child has to deal with eight objects, however, perception is no longer adequate, and he needs to use logic to arrive at the correct conclusion. These statements about perceptual numbers introduce a question about how equivalence is first established with small numbers. It may be that spatial correspondence is more conducive to the establishment of the first small numbers than is temporal correspondence. This sequence would be the opposite of what was said in the preceding paragraph.

Piaget (1965, p. 53) also states that some objects having a high degree of complementarity provoke a slightly more advanced stage than other objects. He described how a few children who were not anywhere near stage III with glasses and bottles showed signs of approaching this stage when flowers and vases, and eggs and egg cups, were used. It would be highly desirable for the teacher to know how the particular objects used for formative evaluation affect the child's beliefs concerning equivalence and conservation.

Another factor Piaget (1965, p. 54) discusses concerns the distance between the two sets of objects at the time the conservation question is asked. He says that sometimes the child can remember the original equivalence only as long as the two sets of objects are in close proximity.

Each of the above questions has to be answered individually before their interrelationships can be better understood. A great deal of precise research, then, remains to be done. However, Table 13-8 can still be used as part of the teacher's effort to build a solid foundation for the child's construction of number. The reader is referred to Piaget (1965) for many other fruitful ideas which can be used in formative evaluation.

Standardized achievement tests

As has been pointed out, intelligence tests are widely used as achievement tests in preschool education. In the preschool section of a review of the literature of the past three years on educational and psychological testing, Deal and Wood (1968, p. 15) state, "The use of measures of intelligence as controls for program effectiveness is probably a result of the lack of available achievement measures." The overuse of the Binet has already been discussed; the Peabody Picture Vocabulary Test (Dunn, 1965), which also filled the vacuum of achievement tests, is discussed in the next chapter by Cazden.

The author is aware of only two achievement tests that are available to the public for the evaluation of learning in preschool: the Preschool Inventory and the Basic Concept Inventory. Two other tests, the Test of Basic Information (Moss, 1967) and the Preschool Academic Skills Test, are still being developed and are available only from their authors for experimental purposes.[35]

The Preschool Inventory is available from the Educational Testing Service, of Princeton.[36] It consists of eighty-five questions that yield four factor scores (Personal-social Responsiveness, Associative Vocabulary, Concept Activation—Numerical, and Concept Activation—Sensory) and a total score, which can be in either raw score or percentile. Personal-social Responsiveness includes such questions as "What is your first name?" and "When is your birthday?" Examples of Associative Vocabulary are "When do we eat breakfast?" and "What does a policeman do?" Concept Activation—Numerical includes questions such as "How many wheels does a car have?" and "How many eyes do you have?" Examples of Concept Activation—Sensory are the instructions to draw a line, a circle, a square, and a triangle, and questions such as "Which is bigger, a tree or a flower?" (Caldwell, 1967, pp. 8–18, items 1, 4, 34, 44, 48, 52, 67–70, 75).

The form of the eighty-five questions is heavily verbal, but the questions are sometimes presented along with objects. The form of the response is entirely verbal half the time and motoric half the time (e.g., pointing out where there are "more" checkers, showing which way a phonograph record goes, and obeying commands such as "Raise your hand").

The Basic Concept Inventory is available from the Follett Publishing Company, of Chicago. It is designed to evaluate the effects of the Bereiter-Engelmann program of instruction and consists of ninety items grouped into three parts: Basic Concepts, Statement Repetition and Comprehension, and Pattern Awareness. An example of Basic Concepts is the ability to find "the balls that are not big" when balls of two sizes and two colors are shown in a picture. An example of Statement Repetition and Comprehension is, "A boy is not walking when he is running. What is a boy not doing when he is running?" An example of Pattern Awareness is the repetition of "7-7-7, 4-4-4" (Engelmann, 1967, pp. 2–7, items 3*d*, 15*b*, 20*c*).

The Test of Basic Information (Moss, 1967) consists of fifty-four items yielding a total score which can be in the form of raw scores, standard scores, or percentile scores. The format of the testing procedure is to give a booklet of pictures to the child and present a set of verbal instructions, asking him to mark one of four pictures. Examples of this format can be seen in Figs. 13-5 and 13-9.

The Preschool Academic Skills Test (Provus, Kresh, & Green, 1968) uses pictures and consists of 105 items grouped into ten subtests: Verbal Labeling, Color Labeling, Classification, Functional Relationships, Visual Matching, Auditory Matching, Picture Arrangement, Symbol Series, Counting, and Verbal Concepts.

These achievement tests were constructed within the limitations of very practical considerations. The Preschool Inventory was developed to assess children's progress in Head Start programs, and therefore had to be administered by people not trained as psychologists, and machine scored. The other three tests, too, are intended for administration by teachers.

Practical considerations were among the factors which determined the type of achievement tests that came into being. Another factor was the psychometric tradition, which is characterized by looking for the one correct answer to each question and adding the total number of correct

[35] The Test of Basic Information was developed by Margaret Moss of George Washington University, Washington, D.C. The Preschool Academic Skills Test was developed by Esther Kresh of the Pittsburgh Public Schools and Bert F. Green of Carnegie-Mellon University.

[36] Educational Testing Service, Box 999, Princeton, New Jersey 08540.

answers. These practices reflect an additive view of knowledge and a philosophy of education that values the child's ability to give correct answers.

The preceding discussion describes the state of the art as I view it at the end of 1968. It is hoped that the situation will be different by the time this book is read. There are many valuable research projects in progress (an example is Melton et al., 1968), and the results of these efforts and many more will, it is hoped, soon become available. It seems always useful to remember in constructing or selecting an achievement test that the appropriateness of an achievement test depends on the objectives and instructional program of a particular preschool. The approach characterizing the achievement tests discussed in this section may be appropriate for the preschools in existence today. However, as will be pointed out in the next section, the development of achievement tests is inevitably related to theories of learning and cognitive development.

Concluding remarks

The foregoing discussion dealt only with the evaluation of pupil learning. Before concluding this chapter, we must examine pupil learning in the light of curriculum evaluation. How well a pupil mastered a curriculum content and how appropriate the curriculum[37] was for him are two interlocking questions that cannot be answered separately.

Scriven (1967) discusses two types of basically different approaches to curriculum evaluation: "intrinsic" evaluation and "payoff" evaluation. "Payoff" evaluation concerns the effects of a curriculum on the pupils and takes the form of pre- and posttest comparisons, usually with a control group. "Intrinsic" evaluation, on the other hand, involves an appraisal of the curriculum goals and content, as well as of the instrument used to measure payoff. Those who believe in payoff evaluation argue that what really counts is the effect of teaching on the students and that a curriculum can be defended only if it shows substantial payoff. Those who defend intrinsic evaluation consider other factors, which do not necessarily show up in the tests that are used to measure payoff.

Payoff evaluators rely mostly on standardized achievement tests to determine the effectiveness of a curriculum. However, these tests do not necessarily measure mastery. As is pointed out in Chap. 3 of this book, achievement tests are constructed psychometrically to detect the relative standing of students among each other rather than to assess their mastery of a subject. Psychometric data, such as percentiles and grade levels, are assumed to reflect the student's degree of mastery, but this assumption is not always tenable.

Payoff evaluation which uses IQs to measure "cognitive development" suffers from similar limitations. To quote Kohlberg (1968, p. 1052), "The Binet-Spearman approach has avoided defining basic cognitive achievements except in highly general terms. . . ." In the construction of an IQ test, an item is considered desirable if it elicits individual differences and correlates highly with the other items that involve cognition. Thus, "general intelligence" in a psychometric sense remains undefined, and it is hard to determine to what extent payoff in IQ is related to cognitive development. The following quotation from Kohlberg may illustrate this point:

> Our viewpoint suggests that the speeding up of cognitive-structural change is extremely difficult to achieve but is likely to have long range general effects, since invariant sequence implies that advance in one step of development may lead to advance in the next step. In contrast, specific learnings are more easily achieved but are unlikely to have long range developmental effects. As an example, it is relatively easy to teach culturally disadvantaged preschool children to discriminate and name animals, but it is difficult to "teach" them conservation. Naming and discriminating unfamiliar animals may lead to some temporary rise in the Stanford-Binet. . . . It is unlikely, however, in itself to lead to any future cognitive development which might lead to higher "general intelligence" some years later. By grade school, the children will have "spontaneously" picked up the

[37] "Curriculum" in this context refers inclusively to the goals, the sequence of units, and the teaching method of a course.

labels and discriminations involved in any case. In contrast, "teaching" the children conservation might lead to an accelerated general development of arithmetical and classificatory operations.

This quotation illustrates a difference between payoff evaluation and intrinsic evaluation: short-term payoff may or may not mean that the student mastered anything of lasting value in a preschool program. It must be recalled, above all, that the objectives of preschool education are not short-term gains.

Zimiles (1968) says of the use of the Binet for the evaluation of Head Start programs,

> This may be a defensible position for the evaluator to take as a first-level approach to the problem of evaluation if his main concern is simply to demonstrate that Head Start has some impact. It is probably even a necessary approach in a nation-wide evaluation that requires a standardized test. . . . But the evaluator must surely wonder . . . how sensitive a test which is so general can be and how much detailed information it can provide about what is actually happening to the cognitive structures of the participating children. Certainly, the crudity of the procedure should prevent him from regarding the results of his study as a definitive appraisal of the intellectual gains produced by Head Start. . . . But if the results of this evaluation cannot be definitive because of our limited knowledge, evaluation work should at least be geared to contribute the knowledge that is currently lacking [pp. 7–8].

This chapter was written in the spirit of the above quotation—in an attempt to contribute something new to our limited knowledge of the subject. Piaget's theory was selected because it is the only theory in existence that describes cognitive development continuously from birth to adolescence. His cognitive-developmental theory offers guidance to the curriculum developer about what to teach in preschool to enable the children to function more intelligently at ages 7, 10, and beyond. (A clarification of this statement can be found on pages 297–304.) Piaget's theory also deals with the precursors of a variety of school subjects, such as arithmetic, logic, geometry, physical knowledge, and representation, with a great deal of specificity and generality. His framework also suggests to the evaluator ways of sequencing the goals of teaching for both formative and summative evaluation.

Many of the objectives and procedures have been described in tentative terms in this chapter because they are based on the exploratory work of an experimental program which is struggling to develop a curriculum and a set of evaluation techniques. Formative and summative evaluation in preschool education lies at a frontier of knowledge, where an enormous amount of research waits to be done. It is the author's hope that many people will come to this frontier to contribute their talent and thoughtful work.

REFERENCES

Almy, M. Wishful thinking about children's thinking? In W. A. Fullagar, H. G. Lewis, & C. F. Cumbee (Eds.), *Readings for educational psychology.* New York: Crowell, 1964. Pp. 389–401.

Arthur, G. *Leiter International Performance Scale: Arthur adaptation.* Chicago: Stoelting, 1952.

Beller, E. K. Use of multiple criteria to evaluate effects of early educational intervention on subsequent school performance. Paper presented at the meeting of the American Educational Research Association, Chicago, February, 1968.

Bennett, E. L., Diamond, M. C., Kretch, D., & Rosenzweig, M. R. Chemical and anatomical plasticity of the brain. *Science,* 1964, **146,** 610–619.

Bereiter, C., & Engelmann, S. *Teaching disadvantaged children in the preschool.* Englewood Cliffs, N.J.: Prentice-Hall, 1966.

Bloom, B. S. *Stability and change in human characteristics.* New York: Wiley, 1964.

Bloom, B. S. (Ed.) *Taxonomy of educational objectives: The classification of educational goals.* Handbook 1. *Cognitive domain.* New York: McKay, 1956.

Caldwell, B. M. *Preschool inventory.* Princeton: Educational Testing Service, 1967.

Deal, T. N., & Wood, P. L. Testing the early educational and psychological development of children—Ages 3–6. *Review of Educational Research,* 1968, **38,** No. 1, 12–18.

Deutsch, M. Interim progress report to Ford Foundation. Institute for Developmental Studies, New York University, 1967.

Di Lorenzo, L. T., & Salter, R. An evaluation study of prekindergarten programs for educationally disadvantaged children: Followup and replication. *Exceptional Children,* 1968, **35,** 111–120.

Dunn, L. M. *Peabody Picture Vocabulary Test.* Minneapolis: American Guidance Service, 1965.

Engelmann, S. *The Basic Concept Inventory,* Pupil's Test and Scoring Booklet (Field Research Edition) Chicago: Follett, 1967.

Flavell, J. *The developmental psychology of Jean Piaget.* Princeton: Van Nostrand, 1963.

Frank, L. K. Fundamental needs of the child. *Mental Hygiene,* 1938, **22,** 353–379.

Frostig, M. *Developmental Test of Visual Perception.* Palo Alto, Calif.: Consulting Psychologists Press, 1963.

Frostig, M. *Developmental Test of Visual Perception: Administration and scoring manual.* Palo Alto, Calif.: Consulting Psychologists Press, 1966.

Frostig, M., Maslow, P., Lefever, D. W., & Whittlesey, J. R. B. *The Marianne Frostig Developmental Test of Visual Perception: 1963 standardization.* Palo Alto, Calif.: Consulting Psychologists Press, 1964.

Furth, H. G. *Piaget and knowledge.* Englewood Cliffs, N.J.: Prentice-Hall, 1969.

Furth, H. *Piaget for teachers.* Englewood Cliffs, N.J.: Prentice-Hall, 1970.

Gesell, A., et al. *The first five years of life.* New York: Harper, 1940.

Gesell, A., et al. *Infant and child in the culture of today.* New York: Harper, 1943.

Gollin, E. S. In R. S. Melton et al., *Cognitive growth in preschool children.* (Res. Memo. 68–13) Princeton: Educational Testing Service, 1968. Pp. 106–113.

Gray, S. W., Klaus, R. A., Miller, J. O., & Forrester, B. J. *Before first grade.* New York: Teachers College Press, 1966.

Harris, D. B. *Goodenough-Harris Drawing Test manual.* New York: Harcourt, Brace & World, 1963.

Hechinger, F. M. (Ed.) *Pre-school education today.* Garden City, N.Y.: Doubleday, 1966.

Hess, R. D., & Bear, R. M. (Eds.) *Early education.* Chicago: Aldine, 1968.

Hooper, F. H., & Marshall, W. H. The initial phase of a preschool curriculum development project. Final Report, August, 1968, West Virginia University, Contract No. OEC-3-7-062902-3070, U.S. Office of Education.

Hunt, J. McV. *Intelligence and experience.* New York: Ronald Press, 1961.

Inhelder, B., Bovet, M., Sinclair, H., & Smock, C. D. On cognitive development. *American Psychologist,* 1966, **21,** 160–164.

Inhelder, B., & Piaget, J. De l'itération des actions à la récurrence élémentaire. In P. Gréco, B. Inhelder, B. Matalon, & J. Piaget, *La formation des raisonnements récurrentiels.* (Études d'épistémologie génétique, 17) Paris: Presses universitaires de France, 1963. Pp. 47–120.

Inhelder, B., & Piaget, J. *The early growth of logic in the child.* New York: Harper & Row, 1964.

Isaacs, S. *Intellectual growth in children.* London: Routledge & Kegan Paul, 1930.

Johnson, H. *Children in the nursery school.* New York: John Day, 1928.

Kagan, J. Matching Familiar Figures Test. Unpublished test, Harvard University, 1965.

Kamii, C. An application of Piaget's theory to the conceptualization of a preschool curriculum. In R. K. Parker (Ed.), *Conceptualizations of preschool curricula.* Boston: Allyn & Bacon, in press.

Kamii, C., & Radin, N. L. Class differences in the socialization practices of Negro mothers. *Journal of Marriage and the Family,* 1967, **29,** 302–310.

Kamii, C., & Radin, N. L. A framework for a preschool curriculum based on Piaget's theory. In I. J. Athey & D. O. Rubadeau (Eds.), *Educational implications of Piaget's theory.* Waltham, Mass.: Ginn-Blaisdell, 1970, 89–100.

Karnes, M. A research program to determine the effects of various preschool intervention programs on the development of disadvantaged children and the strategic age for such intervention. Paper presented at the meeting of the American Educational Research Association, Chicago, February, 1968.

Karnes, M., Hodgins, A., & Teska, J. A. An evaluation of two preschool programs for disadvantaged children: A traditional and a highly structured experimental preschool. *Exceptional Children*, 1968, **34,** 667–676.

Kephart, N. C. *The slow learner in the classroom.* Columbus: Merrill, 1960.

Kirk, S. A. *Early education of the mentally retarded.* Urbana, Ill.: University of Illinois Press, 1958.

Kirk, S. A., McCarthy, J. J., & Kirk, W. D. *The Illinois Test of Psycholinguistic Abilities.* (Rev. ed.) Urbana, Ill.: University of Illinois Press, 1968.

Kohlberg, L. Early education: A cognitive-developmental view. *Child Development*, 1968, **39,** 1013–1062.

Landreth, C. *Education of the young child, a nursery school manual.* New York: Wiley, 1942.

Melton, R. S., et al. *Cognitive growth in preschool children.* (Res. Memo. 68-13) Princeton, N.J.: Educational Testing Service, 1968.

Montessori, M. *The Montessori method.* Cambridge, Mass.: Bentley, 1967.

Moss, M. H., Moss, J. W., & Gross, C. The development of a preschool group achievement test. Unpublished paper, George Washington University, undated.

Moss, M. H. Test of Basic Information. Unpublished test, George Washington University, 1967.

Mumbauer, C. Untitled article. *DARCEE Newsletter,* February, 1968 (Demonstration and Research Center for Early Education, George Peabody College for Teachers).

Piaget, J. *Le developpement de la notion de temps chez l'enfant.* Paris: Presses universitaires de France, 1946.

Piaget, J. *The construction of reality in the child.* New York: Basic, 1954.

Piaget, J. *Play, dreams and imitation in childhood.* New York: Norton, 1962.

Piaget, J. *Psychology of intelligence.* Paterson, N.J.: Littlefield, Adams, 1963.

Piaget, J. *The child's conception of number.* New York: Norton, 1965.

Piaget, J. *Six psychological studies.* New York: Random House, 1967.

Piaget, J., & Inhelder, B. *L'image mentale chez l'enfant.* Paris: Presses universitaires de France, 1966.

Piaget, J., & Inhelder, B. *The child's conception of space.* New York: Norton, 1967.

Piaget, J., Inhelder, B., & Szeminska, A. *The child's conception of geometry.* New York: Harper & Row, 1964.

Pine, P. Where education begins. *American Education,* 1968, **4,** no. 9, 15–19.

Pines, M. *Revolution in learning.* New York: Harper & Row, 1966.

Provus, M. M., Kresh, E., & Green, B. F. Manual for administering the Preschool Academic Skills Test. Unpublished text, Pittsburgh Public Schools, 1968.

Read, K. *The nursery school.* (3rd ed.) Philadelphia: Saunders, 1960.

Read, K. *The nursery school.* (4th ed.) Philadelphia: Saunders, 1966.

Roach, E. G., & Kephart, N. C. *The Purdue Perceptual-motor Survey.* Columbus: Merrill, 1966.

Scriven, M. The methodology of evaluation. *AERA Monograph Series on Curriculum Evaluation,* 1967, No. 1, pp. 39–83.

Sears, P. S., & Dowley, E. M. Research on teaching in the nursery school. In N. L. Gage (Ed.), *Handbook on research in teaching.* Chicago: Rand McNally, 1963. Pp. 814–864.

Skeels, H. M., & Dye, H. B. A study of the effects of differential stimulation on mentally retarded children. In *Proceedings of the American Association on Mental Deficiency.* 1939. Pp. 114–136.

Smilansky, S. *The effects of sociodramatic play on disadvantaged preschool children.* New York: Wiley, 1968.

Sonquist, H., Kamii, C., & Derman, L. A Piaget-derived preschool curriculum. In I. J. Athey & D. O. Rubadeau (Eds.), *Educational implications of Piaget's theory.* Waltham, Mass.: Ginn-Blaisdell, 1970, 101–114.

Spock, B. *Common sense book of baby and child care.* New York: Duell, Sloan & Pearce, 1946.

Stolz, L. M., et al. *Father relations of war-born children.* Stanford, Calif.: Stanford University Press, 1954.

Stott, L. H., & Ball, R. S. Infant and preschool mental tests: Review and evaluation. *Monographs of the Society for Research in Child Development*, 1965, **30,** serial no. 101.

Terman, L. M., & Merrill, M. A. *Stanford-Binet Intelligence Scale.* Boston: Houghton Mifflin, 1960.

Tuddenham, R. D. Psychometricizing Piaget's *méthode clinique.* Paper presented at the meeting of the American Educational Research Association, Chicago, February, 1968.

Vinter, R. D., Sarri, R. C., Vorwaller, D. J., & Schafer, W. E. *Pupil Behavior Inventory.* Ann Arbor, Mich.: Campus Publishers, 1966.

Wechsler, D. *Wechsler Preschool and Primary Scale of Intelligence.* New York: Psychological Corporation, 1963.

Zimiles, H. Problems of assessment of academic and intellectual variables. Paper presented at the meeting of the American Educational Research Association, Chicago, February, 1968.

14

Evaluation of Learning in

Preschool Education:

Early Language Development

COURTNEY B. CAZDEN

Harvard University
Cambridge, Massachusetts

Courtney B. Cazden, Associate Professor of Education, Harvard University, received the Bachelor of Arts degree from Radcliffe College with a major in philosophy, the Master of Education degree from the University of Illinois, and the Doctor of Education degree from Harvard University. She received her teacher training at the Bank Street College of Education and has taught in the primary grades of both private and public schools. Her primary research interest is the development of children's verbal abilities both in and out of school.

Contents

14

Evaluation of Learning in

Preschool Education:

Early Language Development[1]

Objectives in early language development

A historical perspective

Intensive educational focus on language development in early childhood education is a phenomenon of the past ten years. It is the result of two complementary and related pressures: the presence in preschools of children with greater need for help in language development, and the increasing attention by psychologists to the role of language in cognitive activity.

Concerning the place of language development as a specific educational objective, the ideas of two women important in the history of preschool education provide a contrast. From 1924 to 1927 Susan Isaacs taught children from professional and academic families in the Malting House School in Cambridge, England. "As the records show, our children were in general remarkable for their clarity and vividness of expression in words" (Isaacs, 1966, p. 40). In her school program she was more concerned with avoiding verbalism by keeping language closely related to the children's active exploration of objects and events than with promoting the use of language itself. Nothing we have learned about language development in the forty years since Isaacs wrote proves her wrong or misguided. In children from middle-class and professional families, language almost always develops with dramatic success.

From 1906 to 1908 Maria Montessori taught children from the slums of Rome in her Casa dei Bambini. She believed that there were two periods of special sensitivity for language. First, the "unfolding" or development of language takes place between the ages of 2 and 7. "In this period of life by the mysterious bond between the auditory channel and the motor channel of the spoken language it would seem that the auditory perceptions have the direct power of *provoking* the

[1] The preparation of this chapter was supported in part by Public Health Service Grant HD-02908 from the National Institute of Child Health and Development, Roger Brown, Principal Investigator. I am grateful to Mrs. Perry Grey for help as both research assistant and secretary, and to Dr. Constance Kamii for comments on an earlier draft.

TABLE 14-1 TABLE OF SPECIFICATIONS FOR PRESCHOOL EDUCATION: OBJECTIVES IN EARLY LANGUAGE DEVELOPMENT

	BEHAVIORS									
	Cognitive									*Affective*
	Understand and produce simple language forms	*Understand and produce elaborated language: describe*	*Understand and produce elaborated language: narrate*	*Understand and produce elaborated language: generalize, explain, and predict*	*Use language effectively for specific purposes to others: communication*	*Use language effectively for specific purposes to oneself: cognition*	*Operate on language: analyze*	*Operate on language: transform and translate*	*Operate on language: evaluate*	*Demonstrate the use of language frequently and with enjoyment*
CONTENT	*A*	*B*	*C*	*D*	*E*	*F*	*G*	*H*	*I*	*J*
1. Sounds	X							X	X	X
2. Words	X						X	X	X	X
3. Grammar	X						X	X	X	X
4. Objects		X		X						X
5. Events			X	X						X
6. Ideas				X						X
7. Reality: discussion					X					X
8. Fantasy: dramatic play					X					X
9. Thought						X				X

complicated movements of articulate speech which develop instinctively after such stimuli as if awakening from the slumber of heredity" (Montessori, 1965, p. 315). Later, according to Montessori, there is a second critical period during the elementary school years when a "superior language" develops which "no longer has its origin in the mechanism of language but in the intellectual development which makes use of the mechanical language. . . . This language will be enriched little by little by intellectual culture and perfected by the grammatical study of syntax" (p. 316).

In contrast to Isaacs, Montessori included in her school program deliberate instruction toward several language objectives. The first objective was "auricular education," to center the children's discriminative attention upon the "modulations of the sounds of the human voice" (Montessori, 1965, p. 203). The second was nomenclature, "to establish, by means of didactic materials, ideas which are very exact and clear, and to associate the proper word with these ideas" (p. 233). Examples of words she taught are names for colors and shapes and words for relative size, such as "narrow" and "long," "taller" and "thinner." The third was analysis of speech, "to establish exactly the movements necessary to a perfect articulation before the age of easy motor adaptations is passed" (p. 319). Since analysis by children of their own transient oral language is difficult, the children were taught graphic language before the age of 7 so that words in their written form could be analyzed into the component parts. Functional defects such as "dialectic accent" were also to be corrected in this way during the preschool period.

Montessori's insistence that there is a critical period for language development, and her advocacy of enriching language use before attempting metalinguistic analysis, have a contemporary ring—though her developmental separation of sounds and words from syntax does not. But her ideas on language and on preschool education in general were largely ignored in this country until the 1960s (Hunt, 1964).

Nursery schools (as educational institutions, not day-care centers) began in the United States in 1915 (Educational Testing Service, 1968, App. C). Nearly all of them were either private, philanthropic or university-laboratory schools, until the beginning of Head Start exactly fifty years later, and their pupils were from middle-class homes. While these children were not all as intellectually favored as the children at Isaacs' Malting House, it is not surprising that their language developed so naturally that other needs assumed greater educational priority.

During these fifty years, the National Society for the Study of Education published two yearbooks on preschool education. *The Twenty-eighth Yearbook* (Whipple, 1929) includes 143 reports on recent research in language development and suggests several methods of enriching the child's language environment. But detailed reports prepared by fourteen of the major university and philanthropic nursery schools failed to mention language once. This does not mean that nothing was being done about language. While helping children with creative expression, independent choices, sharing, maintaining their own rights, and being helpful, teachers in these schools were undoubtedly also fostering language development. It simply did not rate separate mention.

In the *Forty-sixth Yearbook*, Part II, Helen Dawe says that teachers should encourage children to talk and ask questions, emphasize the enjoyment of communication, and avoid stressing errors of grammar and pronunciation (Henry, 1947, pp. 193–208). Dawe (1942) has since become known as one of the first researchers to carry out an experimental program designed especially for language intervention.

In 1963–1964 an official pamphlet entitled *What Are Nursery Schools For?*, published jointly by the Association for Childhood Education and the National Association for the Education of Young Children, had the following to say about language:

> The nursery school teacher is alert to the child's vocabulary and verbal explanations—but is not dazzled

by them. . . . National anxiety for achievement is focused upon literacy. But literacy is more than words. It is language in context. . . . The good nursery school bubbles and boils with language. With the children's developing powers to see and hear and do comes talk, lots of it. With the desire and need to communicate come conversations that require words to express feelings and ideas. With many opportunities to investigate and observe materials and situations and people first hand come meanings and sensitivity to problems. . . . Verbal dexterity is not literacy. Words clearly linked to meaning and used for purposeful communication are.

(Law, 1963–1964, P. 6)

Day-care centers for lower-class children were widespread under the WPA during the 1930s, and under the War Emergency Child Care Commission during World War II (Educational Testing Service, 1968, App. C). But, because these schools were usually directed by child welfare specialists rather than educators, health and welfare objectives predominated. The Economic Opportunity Act of 1964, informally known as the "war on poverty," produced a sharp change. Having been preceded by pilot research programs, Head Start began in 1965, and its official policy manual requires that programs show evidence of plans for developing language skills (U.S. Office of Economic Opportunity, 1967, p. 36). Moreover, funds for research provided by the Economic Opportunity Act and funds concurrently appropriated through other government agencies enabled psychologists to start additional research and development projects in preschool education for lower-class children. The curricula of these projects will be discussed in the pages that follow. Influenced by the writings of fellow psychologists such as Bruner here and Vygotsky and Luria in the Soviet Union, and by new work in linguistics and psycholinguistics, the psychologists became convinced that language plays a critical role in human thought and therefore in educability, and that the child's early environment plays a critical role in the growth of language abilities. And they planned their education programs with these convictions in mind.

The range of current objectives

In current programs in early childhood education, the overall goal of facilitating language development has become differentiated into a wide range of more specific objectives. To assemble a picture of this range, twelve programs for which explicit descriptions are available were examined: Bank Street (Minuchin & Biber, 1968), Bereiter and Engelmann (1966, 1968, undated; Osborn, 1968), Blank (Blank & Solomon, 1968, 1969), Gray (Gray, Klaus, Miller, & Forrester, 1966; Klaus & Gray, 1968), Hodges, McCandless, and Spicker (1967), Kamii (Kamii & Radin, 1969; Sonquist, Kamii, & Derman, 1969), Moffett (1968a, 1968b), Nebraska (Nebraska Curriculum Development Center, 1966a, 1966b), New Nursery School (Meier, Nimnicht, & McAfee, 1968; Nimnicht, Meier, & McAfee, 1969), the Plowden Report (Central Advisory Council for Education, 1967), Smilansky (1968), and Weikart (1967).

These twelve programs form a mixed group in several ways. They differ in country of origin: the Plowden Report is from England; Smilansky works in Israel; the other ten programs were developed in the United States. They differ in source of ideas: Moffett and Nebraska were designed by people from the discipline of English; all the rest except the Plowden Report were designed by psychologists; the Plowden Report is based on multidisciplinary recommendations.[2] They differ in age of the children involved: the Plowden Report deals with education for children of 5 to 11 years; Moffett describes a curriculum for grades K to 6; the rest of the

[2] The division between programs designed by psychologists and those designed by people from English or linguistics is also a division between preschool programs and programs for kindergarten children and older. It is only in the preschool area that psychologists have had great influence. The important Anglo-American Conference on the Teaching of English (Dixon, 1967) held at Dartmouth in the summer of 1966 included James Moffett; Paul Olsen, from the Nebraska curriculum group; and David Mackay, whose literacy materials will be discussed on pages 379–380; but it included only two psychologists out of a roster of seventy, neither connected with any of the programs discussed in this chapter. It seems unfortunate that the several groups of experts are not collaborating more fully in planning programs for both younger and older children.

programs are designed for 4- to 5-year-olds, though six of them (Bank Street; Engelmann; a group at Educational Development Corporation in Cambridge, Mass., using the Plowden Report model; Miller from the Gray group; Glen Nimnicht from the New Nursery School group; and Weikart) are now adapting their preschool programs for use in public school primary classrooms in Follow Through programs around the country.

The twelve programs also differ in the objectives they select and the instructional techniques they use to attain those objectives. They will be categorized and discussed on these points in the following section. In the present section we have combined the objectives into a composite set shown in Table 14-1, Table of Specifications for Preschool Education: Objectives in Early Language Development. *Behaviors* are listed on the horizontal axis (*A* to *J*) and *Content* areas are listed on the vertical axis (1 to 9). An X at the intersection means that a behavior applies to that content in at least one of the language programs. For example, cell *E*-8 is *Use language in dramatic play*. The three sets of objectives *A*, *B* to *D*, and *E* and *F* are cumulative: the elementary language forms are included in more elaborated language which is then used for various communicative and cognitive purposes.

Cognitive objectives (A–I) Cognitive objectives in language are different from objectives in other areas of the school curriculum, at least in programs for young children. They are aimed not at "knowledge *that*" but at "knowledge *how to*." They are normally and naturally expressed in behavioral terms: for example, we want children to "speak in complete sentences" or "understand directions." With a few exceptions, which will be discussed below, the medium is indeed the message. The goal is the child's increasing ability to produce and comprehend the medium of oral language for a widening variety of purposes.

First is the ability to *Understand and produce simple language forms: Sounds* (*A*-1), *Words* (*A*-2), and basic *Grammar* (*A*-3). Learning the sounds (*A*-1) of English and learning to speak in complete simple sentences (*A*-3) are usually completed during the preschool years. An important controversy has arisen over the criterion for successful attainment of these two objectives. Should we be satisfied if the child is intelligible in the dialect of his home community, as long as he can understand the Standard English of the teacher, or should we try to teach the child to use the sounds and grammatical patterns of Standard English as well?

Unlike the learning of sounds and basic sentence patterns, the learning of vocabulary (*A*-2) is an open-ended objective which continues throughout formal education and beyond. Any educational program has to decide which words to teach if it is not to depend on the unpredictable results of incidental learning.

Simple sentences contain expressions of basic grammatical relations—actor and action, action and object, and modification. Virtually all educational programs want to help children conceive more differentiated relationships among objects, events, and ideas, and express them in more precise and elaborated language. In Moffett's words (1968b) these are levels of the referential (or I–it) relation. They differ from raw experience in degree of abstraction. Included here are the abilities to *Describe objects* and their spatial relationships (*B*-4), to *Narrate events* and their temporal sequence (*C*-5), and to *Explain objects, events*, and *ideas* in their logical and hierarchical relationships—whether in the real or the imagined world (*D*-4 to *D*-6). These abilities entail increasingly differentiated and varied use of adjectives and adverbs, prepositions and conjunctions, and phrases and clauses of all kinds. While sometimes the ability to use such forms may seem to be an end in itself, usually the objective is stated as the ability to organize experience and express that organization in explicit terms; it is not a matter of sentence-stretching (Dixon, 1967) for its own sake.

Experience can be organized and expressed for more than one purpose or function. There are also, in Moffett's words (1968b), levels of the rhetorical (or I–thou) relation. One level is *Communication with others in discussions* (*E*-7) or *in dramatic play* (*E*-8). The child expresses his own feelings, needs, and intentions and interprets similar expressions of others, whether real people or characters in stories; he asks for, gives, and understands increasingly complex statements about the world external to himself; and he makes and follows increasingly complex directions and plans for action. Another level is *Communication to oneself* (*F*-9). Facilitating the internalization of language for thought (*F*-9) may be an especially important objective in early childhood education, for two reasons. First, while variety in the forms and interpersonal functions of language may be an asset in a pluralistic society, covert language for thinking is essential for the educability of all children (John, 1967). Second—and this point is more specifically related to the early childhood years—the period from 5 to 7 years seems to be a critical period for the shift from associative to cognitive modes of processing information (White, 1965), or, in other words, from preoperational to operational thought (see discussion by Kamii in preceding chapter). Changes in the role of language are probably not the cause of this shift, but they seem to play some as yet undetermined role.

Metalinguistic ability to *Operate on language*, to manipulate it as an object of intellectual activity as well as its medium (*G* to *I*), is not easy to acquire. "Talking about language, using language about language is about as easy as burning wood in a wooden chulha [a wood-burning stove in India]" (Kelkar, 1969, p. 11). But this ability is important during early childhood education because of its relation to literacy.

Analysis (*G*) is well described as helping children to "conceptualize their awareness of language" (Dixon, 1967, p. 10), to bring to a conscious level aspects of language that the young child has been using for some time. For example, all children learn in some nonconscious way which sounds are alike and which are different; the speech of even a 4- or 5-year-old child would be impossible otherwise. Subsequent training in auditory discrimination and *Analysis of words* into component sounds (*G*-2) is training in the metalinguistic ability to reflect upon sounds in the words one speaks and hears and to make deliberate, conscious judgments of "same" and "different."

The same distinction between nonconscious use and conscious analysis applies to the decomposition of sentences into words (*G*-3). It is almost certainly not the case, as Bereiter and Engelmann (1966) assert, that the sentences of some lower-class children are like giant undifferentiated words (Labov et al., 1968, vol. 2, p. 342). Speech would be impossible if this were true. But conscious analysis of sentences into their component parts is needed when the child tries to write down even the simplest of sentences, and will be even more helpful when he confronts the "deliberate structuring of the web of meaning" (Vygotsky, 1962, p. 100) that more complex written composition requires.

In addition to such analysis of language forms, children are sometimes asked to *Transform and translate* words and sentences, as in defining and paraphrasing (*H*-2 and *H*-3). Such activities probably have considerable intellectual value, but it is important to remember that they too are metalinguistic activities. We know very little about "the conditions and the stages in which the children and young people become aware of language they have learnt to use; and the effects of such awareness or knowledge on their further learning and operating of language" (Dixon, 1967, p. 76).

Evaluation (*I*-1 to *I*-3), another metalinguistic objective, eventually becomes very important. Utterances are never good or bad in themselves. They can only be judged in relation to situation-specific criteria of intelligibility (which varies with familiarity between speaker and listener and the presence or absence of a shared context), grammaticality (which varies with the standard being invoked), accuracy or "fit to experience" (which varies with the task at hand), and social appropriateness (which varies with the characteristics of speaker, listener or listeners, and context). We know little about when and how such evaluations are made nonconsciously in early childhood, or about how helpful deliberate exploration of alternative forms of expression and deliberate choice can be to young children.

Note that even in the metalinguistic domain of operating on language, objectives for young children consist of "abilities to *do*," not "knowledge *about*." Examples of knowledge about language which could constitute objectives for older children would be familiarity with terms like "noun" and "verb," or knowledge of rules like "verbs agree in number with their subject." In the curricula listed above, at least, such knowledge is not sought in early childhood education. Letter names are taught, but as part of instruction in reading, not language, and so are not considered here. The only exceptions, so rare that they were omitted from Table 14-1, are brief topics in the Nebraska curriculum (Nebraska Curriculum Development Center, 1966b) contrasting human and animal communication and introducing the idea of languages other than English.

Affective objective (J) The division between *Cognitive* (*A* to *I*) and *Affective* (*J*) *objectives* is close in spirit to one meaning of the distinction in linguistics between competence and performance. "In the cognitive domain we are concerned that the student shall be able to do a task when requested. In the affective domain we are more concerned that he *does do* it when it is appropriate after he has learned that he *can* do it. Even though the whole school system rewards the student more on a *can do* than on a *does do* basis, it is the latter which every instructor seeks" Krathwohl, Bloom, & Masia, 1964, p. 60).

A teacher with only cognitive objectives would be satisfied if the child could, when prompted, demonstrate a certain ability—to interpret a negative statement, retell a story in correct order, or ask a series of productive questions in a game of Twenty Questions. By contrast, a teacher with both cognitive and affective objectives in mind would look for evidence that the child actually uses these abilities in the part of his life not directed by the teacher. Transfer to new situations can rightfully be considered simply a more stringent criterion of successful cognitive learning, but the criterion of frequent appropriate performance goes beyond that, into the affective domain. Here abilities must be linked to attitudes and values. Spontaneous questions depend not only on ability to ask questions but also on the desire to find out; using language for planning, by oneself or with others, depends not only on the ability to construct sentences but also on the belief that one can affect the environment with words. Hertzig, Birch, Thomas, and Mendez (1968) demonstrate that children who are initially equated on a measure of verbal ability (here the Stanford-Binet) still differ greatly in their disposition to make verbal responses.

Three representative programs

In order to select three programs for more detailed description, the twelve programs listed above have been categorized into three groups (A, B, and C) on the basis of several characteristics. This grouping is shown in Table 14-2.

Group A contains those programs in which the form of the children's intellectual activity has least structure imposed by the teacher. No caricature of permissive chaos is appropriate here, however; there may be strict rules governing social behavior and care of materials. But the children are freer than in groups B and C to select the stimuli they wish to respond to, and divergent responses to those stimuli are valued. These programs are the intellectual heirs of nursery education for middle-class children in this country and of Susan Isaacs' work in Great Britain. They assume that working-class children are more like their middle-class age mates than different from them, and so continue to focus on all aspects of the child's development. They have been influential in many Head Start programs because most Head Start teachers have been trained in this tradition.

At the other extreme are the programs in group C, in which instruction is carefully sequenced to meet the specific needs of lower-class children. Because these programs are by definition the most highly specified, their curricula can be more easily described and made widely available. For

Table 14-2 Categorization of oral language programs

	A	B	C
Characteristics	Children's activities are largely determined by their interests, with little or no imposition by the teacher of a predetermined sequence.		Children's activities are predetermined by the teacher's decision on optimal content and sequence.
	Divergent responses are encouraged.	Some middle ground, or a combination of characteristics of groups A and B.	Convergent responses are elicited.
	The teacher encourages the use of language in the context of the child's own play activities.		The teacher teaches language in situations designed for instructions in skills and subskills.
	The program is designed for both cognitive and affective goals and for all children.		The program is designed primarily for cognitive goals carefully selected to meet the needs of particular children.
Example selected for detailed description	English Infant School	Klaus and Gray Early Training Project	Bereiter-Engelmann program
Other programs in this category	Bank Street	Blank; Hodges; Kamii; Moffett; Nebraska; New Nursery School; Smilansky; Weikart	

this reason, among others, their influence will probably increase.

In between are the programs in group B, which share elements of A and C in varying degrees. All except Moffett's were designed, like those in group C, specifically for lower-class children. Moffett's program was designed (with support from the Carnegie Foundation) for general use.

Tables 14-3, 14-4, and 14-5 are Tables of Specifications showing detailed objectives of three programs: the English Infant School for 5- to 7-year-olds, recommended in the Plowden Report, as an example of group A; the Klaus and Gray Early Training Project for 4- to 5-year-olds as an example of group B; and the Bereiter-Engelmann program for 4-year-olds as an example of group C.

In each chart, the objectives given in Table 14-1 appear as column headings. Under these headings are listed the aims of each program in that area, stated—as much as possible—in the words of the program itself.

When one reads descriptions of the programs, it becomes clear that some objectives are truly shared by all programs, others are the same in name only, and still others appear in only one or two of the three groups. The ability to speak in complete sentences (*A*-3) is one objective shared by all; on this point, differences come from the means by which that objective is realized. Programs in group C include recitation lessons in which children are expected to respond in carefully specified ways, even repeat sentences after the teacher, whereas groups A and B rely on more natural conversational contexts.

An example of an objective which is more similar in name than in actual content is increasing knowledge of vocabulary (*A*-2), where the programs differ in degree of specificity. If emphasis is placed on the development of language in the context of experience selected by the child (group A), there is likely to be less focus on particular words preselected by the teacher. The goal is increased vocabulary in general; there is less attempt to make sure that particular words are learned. The more didactic programs, on the other hand, must make decisions on which words to teach.

One criterion for choice of words at the

TABLE 14-3 TABLE OF SPECIFICATIONS SHOWING OBJECTIVES OF THE ENGLISH INFANT SCHOOL

Cognitive domain				*Affective domain*
Use language				
A. Understand and produce simple language forms	*B–D. Understand and produce elaborated language*	*E, F. Use language effectively for specific purposes*	*G–I. Operate on language*	*J*
Show improved articulation, clarity, and fluency (clear communication the important criterion, not correctness) (*A*-1, *A*-3). Learn a rich vocabulary (*A*-2).	Give up phrases like "kind of" for more precise expression (*B*-4). Use language which is complex in structure, develops concepts of space, time, and contingency (*B–D*).	Plan, talk over, and explain experiences; ask increasingly penetrating questions; engage in dramatic play (*E*-7, *E*-8). Use language as a tool for categorization and generalization (*F*-9).		Show interest in the sound and meaning of words (*J*-1, *J*-2). Enjoy talking and listening in the context of warm relationships and vivid sensory and imaginative experience; gain greater confidence in speaking (*J*-7, *J*-8).

SOURCE: Central Advisory Council for Education, 1967.

TABLE 14-4 TABLE OF SPECIFICATIONS SHOWING OBJECTIVES OF THE KLAUS AND GRAY EARLY TRAINING PROJECT

Cognitive domain				*Affective domain*
Use language				
A. Understand and produce simple language forms	*B–D. Understand and produce elaborated language*	*E, F. Use language effectively for specific purposes*	*G–I. Operate on language*	*J*
Improve in pronunciation (especially of final consonants), vocabulary, and syntax; speak in complete sentences (*A*-1–*A*-3). Learn colors and numbers (*A*-2).	Describe sensory qualities of objects (*B*-4). Learn position concepts, action concepts, and simple time concepts (*B–C*).	Understand increasingly complex verbal directions (*E*-7). Request "turns" from peers (*E*-7). Relate our experiences; talk about stories; tell stories from pictures (*E*-7). Use puppets; participate in dramatization (*E*-8).		Realize that language can be used to attain goals (*J*-7).

SOURCE: Gray, Klaus, Miller, & Forrester, 1966; Klaus & Gray, 1968.

preschool level comes from a task analysis of requirements for coping successfully with the first-grade curriculum. If that curriculum assumes that children know names for colors and geometric shapes, these can be taught in preschool or kindergarten. If basal readers often deal with farm situations unfamiliar to urban children, the names of farm animals can be included. Some of the programs in group B choose vocabulary at least partly on this basis. Another criterion is selection of words for their presumed cognitive power. Here the objective shifts away from the inexhaustible set of nouns and verbs to a small set of logical connectives, comparatives, prepositions, and noun and verb inflections essential for elaborated language (*B* to *D*) and referred to hereafter as "relational" words. Group C and some group B programs concentrate their efforts here.

Another example of similarity more in name than in content is language for thinking (*F*-9). Some of the programs in groups A and B include statements about the importance of nonverbal antecedents of language and abstract thought. Bank Street, Kamii, and Smilansky stress the importance of dramatic play as a context for participating, at first nonverbally and then verbally, in a make-believe, "as-if," world. According to

Smilansky, this ability is a component of subsequent intellectual tasks in school:

> Problem solving in school subjects requires a great deal of make-believe (e.g. visualizing how Eskimos live; reading dramatic stories; imagining a story to write; solving verbal arithmetic problems): geography is make-believe, history is make-believe, literature is make-believe—all are conceptual constructions that the child has not directly experienced.
>
> (Smilansky, 1968, p. 12)

By contrast, dramatic play is not mentioned in group C, where learning to use language for thinking means understanding the implications of statements or using language silently as an aid to memory. For example, Bereiter and Engelmann's goals include the following:

> Ability to perform simple "if-then" deductions. The child is presented a diagram containing big squares and little squares. All the big squares are red, but

TABLE 14-5 TABLE OF SPECIFICATIONS SHOWING OBJECTIVES OF THE BEREITER-ENGELMANN PROGRAM

Cognitive domain				*Affective domain*
Use language				
A. Understand and produce simple language forms	*B–D. Understand and produce elaborated language*	*E, F. Use language effectively for specific purposes*	*G–I. Operate on language*	*J*
Speak in sentences made up of clearly pronounced, distinct words (*A*-1–*A*-3). Repeat sentences (*A*-3).	Master the use of structural words and inflections which are necessary for the expression and manipulation of logical relationships (*D*-4–*D*-6). Use language to acquire, process, and transmit information; perform operations on concepts: e.g., explain, describe, inquire, hypothesize, compare and deduce (*D*-4–D-6).	Carry on sustained dialogue with self or others, to accumulate and use information (*E*-7). Talk to oneself for planning and controlling behavior (*F*-9).	Recombine words, e.g., *green and red* to *red and green* (*G*-3, *H*-2). Transform sentences, e.g., imperatives to declaratives (*H*-3). Make and evaluate rhymes (*H*-1, *I*-1).	

SOURCE: Bereiter & Engelman, 1966, 1968, undated; Osborn, 1968.

the little squares are of various other colors. "If the square is big, what do you know about it?" "It's red."

Ability to use "not" in deductions. "If the square is little what do you know about it?" "It is *not* red."

Ability to use "or" in simple deductions. "If the square is little, then it is not red. What else do you know about it?" "It's blue or yellow."

(Adapted from Bereiter & Engelmann, 1966)

Some objectives do not appear in all programs even in name. The affective goal (*J*) does not appear in group C. Emphasis in these programs is on increasing intellectual competence, and the disposition to use language in real-life situations is considered more a result of instruction than its direct goal. Conversely, metalinguistic ability to operate on language, which is so important in group C, is not included in groups A and B.

Of course, programs may actually achieve more or less than they hope for. It is possible that group A programs have as much long-term effect on using language for logical thinking as do group C programs; it is also possible that group C programs have as much long-term effect on the child's belief in the ability of language to control his world as group A programs. These empirical questions are outside the scope of this chapter. Here, the stated objectives are taken at face value so that suggestions for evaluation can be made.

Groups A, B, and C were originally categorized on the basis of the degree to which structure is imposed on the children's activities by the teacher; but in general a continuum on this dimension corresponds with a continuum on the degree of specificity of curriculum content. In general, the programs in group C focus their instruction more narrowly on a smaller set of objectives which they believe to be critical to educability: not any and all words, but particular words with maximum intellectual content; not any and all functions of language, but language for seeking, processing, and transmitting information about the world. The correspondence of programs along these two continua is not perfect, however. The New Nursery School, which is called a "responsive environment," might be placed in group A because it encourages selection of activities by the child. But it is more like groups B and C in seeking, through the teacher's response to the child in the context of his ongoing activities, to focus the child's attention on certain aspects of the environment and thereby develop specific concepts of size, number, logical relationships, etc.—the same list as in the more structured programs. Similarly, Blank's program fits into group B as far as teacher-imposed structure is concerned, but the level of specificity of the content corresponds with group C.

Illustrations and discussion of evaluation procedures

Teachers can get feedback about the effects of their program on the language of their children in several ways. They may deliberately eavesdrop, as sensitive teachers have always done, as the children talk to one another while solving a puzzle or playing in the doll corner or on the playground. They may listen as the children respond in a teacher-directed situation such as listening to a story or talking during snacks. And they may set up structured situations for the specific purpose of assessing aspects of behavior which are not likely to display themselves spontaneously.

Observation of children in their normal school activities has its advantages. It is an unobtrusive form of measurement which does not take time from learning and teaching. And if children do display a desired behavior in their ongoing activities, the teacher can be sure that it has been learned well and incorporated into the child's repertoire. But not all behaviors appear spontaneously, even if they have been learned. For example, it is hard to find out whether children can understand passive sentences by listening to natural conversations, because passive sentences are rare, even in the talk of adults. Furthermore, even if certain behaviors are present, the natural situation is often not sufficiently controlled so that inferences about learning can be made. If the teacher says, "Please bring me the pencils from my desk," and the child correctly brings two pencils, one cannot conclude that the child attended to and understood the meaning of the plural *s*. He may have responded simply to the presence of two pencils on the desk and have seen no reason to leave one behind. For these reasons, structured situations are frequently necessary.

Sometimes these structured situations can be valuable for instruction as well. For instance, Language Lotto (Gotkin, 1966) can be used to assess a child's abilities to use certain prepositions, relational phrases like "part of," gerunds like "kicking," etc. But because it is a game which can be played again and again, it is also valuable for learning. The same combination of instruction and evaluation functions is characteristic of many of the activities suggested in the package of materials collectively titled *Let's Look at First Graders* (Educational Testing Service, 1965) from which some of the examples in the following pages are adapted:

> In addition to allowing a child to demonstrate his understanding and the teacher to observe it, many of these tasks also have *instructional* value in that they provide children with the kind of experience needed to *develop* their understanding. It is at this point that what is often called "assessment" or "measurement" blends wholly into what is really teaching.
>
> (From theory to classroom, p. 23)

Wherever possible, both observations and test situations will be described in the pages that follow. Hopefully, they will be useful to teachers in all varieties of programs in early childhood education. To the teachers in group A, these suggestions may guide their observations and inform their responses. To the teachers in group C, they may provide additional ways of finding out if instruction has been learned well enough for transfer beyond the situation in which it was taught.

Almost all the suggestions which follow require an observer to make notes or work individually with one child. Since preschools and a growing number of primary-grade classrooms are staffed with aides and volunteers in addition to the teacher, it should be possible to plan staff time for such evaluation.

The pronunciation and discrimination of speech sounds (A-1)

The intelligibility of children's pronunciation can be evaluated in their natural conversations. It is probably wise to listen to each child carefully in several situations, because everyone's articulation varies with situational demands. Normally, pronunciation is most accurate in careful speech —as when a child is asked to pronounce words in isolation or to repeat something that his listener did not hear. But there may also be children "whose articulation of individual sounds is acceptable, but whose speech disintegrates when they have to formulate complex ideas and the organizational load becomes too heavy" (De Hirsch, Jansky, & Langford, 1966, p. 20), as in telling a story or describing an experience in front of a group.

The trouble with natural conversations as a context for evaluation is that all the sound distinctions important in English are not likely to be spoken in any given period of time. Both to evaluate intelligibility more completely and to find out whether children attend to these sounds in the language they hear, test situations can be used.

To test pronunciation with young children, pictures are selected whose names contain the significant sounds (or "phonemes") and blends in various positions—e.g., "*m*an," "ha*mm*er," and "broo*m*." The teacher shows the pictures and asks the child to name the object. If the child does not know the name or uses a different name, the teacher can say the desired word and ask the child to repeat it.

To test discrimination of speech sounds, pairs of words are selected which differ in the smallest way possible. Such "minimal pairs" are the same except for one phoneme which varies in only one "distinctive feature." Examples are "peach-beach" (which differ only in the absence or presence of voicing in the initial consonant), and "cap-cat," which differ only in whether the final consonant is made with the lips or with the tip of the tongue. Again, pictures are used.

A-1

1. Here are two pictures. This is a picture of a *cat*. And this is a picture of a *cap*. Point to the *cap*. Now point to the *cat*.

The relation between order of presentation, order of request to the child, and left or right position should be varied (but not systematically alternated) so that the child cannot answer correctly by attention to clues other than sound.

Designing an entire test for these objectives requires specialized knowledge of speech sounds which few teachers have. Fortunately, speech therapists are experts in this area and should be consulted if at all possible. (See page 391 for suggestions of published tests.)

In real life, intelligibility must meet a shifting criterion. At any one time, an utterance is either understood or not understood by the listener; but identical pronunciation might be "intelligible" to one listener and not to another, depending on the listener's familiarity with the child and on how much information speaker and listener share. The Sapon Intelligibility Function Test (SIFT) has been designed with this fact about communication in mind:

> At first, the child is understandable to his mother and close family members only when they share the same environmental stimuli; later he is understood by his intimates without dependence on environmental cues; later he may be understood by strangers when the child and the stranger share a specific environment; still later he will be understood by any normal human being independent of environmental cues. . . .
>
> In accord with above analysis, a test instrument was designed and developed to yield both qualitative and quantitative measures of a child's "understandability." . . . The child is shown a series of forty large, drawn pictures and asked to name the objects portrayed. An audiotape recording of his responses is then played back to one of his parents, to parents of other children, and to non-parents. For the first twenty items, the judge must identify what he thinks the child said on the basis of acoustic properties alone. For each of the second twenty items, the judge is shown four pictures as he hears each response, one of which is the picture the child saw. He is asked to indicate the picture he thinks the child saw and what he thinks the child actually said.
>
> (Sapon, 1969, pp. 22–23)

The test can yield several scores for intelligibility with or without a shared environment and with a familiar adult or a stranger.

While this procedure in its exact form is probably more appropriate for research than for classroom use, the idea is usable. The teachers could record examples of a child's speech at the beginning and end of the school year and count the proportion of "morphemes" (meaningful units) that an adult unfamiliar with the child can hear. ("See big dog" = 3. "See the big dogs" = 5.) In that way, the teacher can make sure that his judgment of a child's growth in intelligibility is not simply a result of his increasing familiarity with the child's speech but reflects an objective change in the child.

If the concern of a particular program is not with intelligibility in general but with the comprehension and production of Standard English in particular, then a special set of sound distinctions become important. *Nonstandard Dialect* (National Council of Teachers of English, 1968), prepared for the New York City Board of Education by a committee which included the linguists Beryl Bailey and William Labov, provides a list of the most important pronunciation problems of speakers of nonstandard English in New York City. Ideally, this list should be verified or modified in each area of the country, but publication for national use was based on evidence that many of the same problems exist in other areas. Because the training of speech therapists is only now beginning to include training in differentiating social dialects from individual pathology, and because no published tests are available for this job, the most important pronunciation problems listed in *Nonstandard Dialect* are given here:

Simplification of consonant clusters at the ends of words:

- Where the final consonant is *t, d,* or *s, z*. These are not only the most common but also frequently carry important grammatical information. *T* and *d* form the past or past participle, as in *walked* or *listened*. *S* and *z* form plurals, possessives, and verb endings, as in *books, Mary's,* and *sees*.
- Where the final consonant is *s*: "le's go"; "tha's hot."

Where the final cluster ends in *k* or *p*: "desk" is "des'"; "wasp" becomes "was'".
Where the final cluster is *sts*, *sks*, or *sps*. These are the hardest clusters and are simplified in many ways.
Complete loss of some final consonants:
Final *l*: "She'll" becomes "she'"; "tall" becomes "ta'".
Final *d*: "Made" becomes "ma'"; "David" rhymes with "save it."
Pronunciation of *th*:
Substitution of *t* and *d* for the voiced and voiceless *th* at the beginning of words: "they" becomes "day"; "thin" becomes "tin."
Substitution of *v* and *f* for the voiced and voiceless *th* at the ends of words: "bathe" rhymes with "rave"; "Ruth" becomes "roof."

Progress in the child's ability to produce these Standard English sounds can be evaluated by listening to his spontaneous speech or asking him to pronounce particular words. Because in all dialects of English final consonants are more likely to be fully pronounced before a word beginning with a vowel than before a word beginning with another consonant, test sentences (as well as any instructional material) should be so constructed: "walked away" rather than "walked to town"; "ask a question" rather than "ask David." To test progress in discriminating pairs of words which are homonyms in nonstandard dialect—e.g., "desk-des'"—pictures can be used, as with "cap" and "cat" above, with a nonsense shape for the nonword (in this case, "des'"). Further suggestions for assessing production and comprehension of morphemes of tense, plurality, or possession will be given in the section below on *Basic grammar* (A-3).

Tests which require judgments of "same" or "different" about sounds, or identification of the position in a word where they appear, will be discussed in the section on metalinguistic objectives (G-1).

Words (A-2)

The speech sounds mentioned above, and the grammatical forms which are discussed later, can be evaluated with the aid of a finite list of items; this is not true of a child's vocabulary. Any evaluation of vocabulary, therefore, must be preceded by some decision about specific educational objectives. This applies for teachers in group A as well as those in groups B and C. The group A teacher can watch for growth in vocabulary in the context of a child's conversations during play, but he still has to decide which words he would be delighted to hear. He can watch the child develop from saying, "I want that," accompanied by pointing, to "I want that tricycle" to "I want that big, red tricycle" (Klaus & Gray, 1968, p. 18). And he can watch for decreasing frequency of the word "thing" used as a substitute for some unknown name. But beyond these general indications of progress, specification of words is required.

But there is an important difference between standardized vocabulary tests and the kind of evaluation described in this section. Standardized tests pick a small and supposedly representative set of the universe of words. When children are tested for their knowledge of these words, the result is a rank ordering of children, or an assignment of a mental-age equivalent, in terms of the number of words they know. The particular words used in the test are not important in themselves; they are merely indications of the general knowledge of words which they represent. Sometimes an item analysis of the answers to standardized vocabulary tests is used to make suggestions for instruction, but such analyses may be misleading. For example, John and Goldstein (1964) first noted that on the Peabody Picture Vocabulary Test gerunds like "running" are more frequently missed than nouns. This finding has since been repeated by others. But other words—like prepositions, which do not even appear on the test—are presumably even harder to learn and require even more deliberate instruction.

The vocabulary testing advocated here, on the other hand, is not testing of some set of words for their representative value, but testing of particular words which the program has decided to teach. In even the least didactic program, certain experiences are planned. For instance, if the group takes a trip to a farm in the fall and then returns to school to make applesauce and re-create the meaning of the trip in a variety of ways—discussion, dramatic play, block buildings, paintings, clay, etc.—the teacher should at some point evaluate, by observation or test, the children's learning of words used in the experience. In programs which include more structured teaching situations for some or all of the morning, the words tested will be those which have been explicitly taught—colors, conjunctions, etc.

Vocabulary testing takes two forms. To test *receptive* vocabulary, the teacher says the word in the presence of a set of pictures and asks the child to point to the appropriate picture.

To test *productive* vocabulary, the teacher points to a picture or part of a picture and asks the child for a name, probing further if the child says something but not the desired word. For example, the directions used by Lesser, Fifer, and Clark (1965) with 6-year-olds were as follows:

A-2

2. [Nouns:] Say: "What is this?"

   If child gives function or description of object:
   Say: "What is it called?"

   If child does not know name of object, or gives incorrect or unclear response:
   Say: "Tell me about it."

3. [Verbs:] Say: "Tell me in only one word what these people are doing."

   If child gives description:
   Say: "Tell me in only one word."

   If child does not know name of activity, or gives incorrect or unclear response:
   Say: "Tell me about it."

(Lesser et al., 1965, p. 94.)

The child's answers can then be scored on a 0–2 scale, rather than just right or wrong:

Mailman: 2—mailman, postman, letter carrier
1—man who carries letters
0—policeman

painting: 2—painting
1—working
0—fixing

Stern (1968d) has developed an Expressive Vocabulary Inventory which includes pronouns, prepositions, etc., as well as nouns and verbs.

Vocabulary tests as we have described them have two important limitations, one substantive and one procedural. The substantive problem is that usually the meaning of a word is treated in the tests as a single item of information which a child either does or does not know. But word meanings are changing, growing sets of component meanings (called "semantic features" by analogy with the distinctive features of speech sounds). For example, a child may understand that father is male but not be aware of the required generational relationship and so call a man in a picture with a woman the woman's father. Similarly, when a child asks his teacher to "draw a letter," the teacher can infer that the child knows that writing is making marks on paper with a pencil but does not yet know the distinction between drawings and letters or numbers. Vocabulary growth is just as much an enrichment of meanings for words previously used as it is the addition of new words to the child's mental dictionary.[3]

Evaluating this aspect of vocabulary growth is difficult, however, because construction of items can hardly be done until one hears a child express his partial understanding. Until then, it is uncertain what relevant contrasts should be presented. Teachers can listen for evidence of such immaturities, make a note of them for each child, and later check for more mature meaning. To test for "write":

A-2

4. Present two pictures of a child using a pencil: one is writing a name; one is drawing a picture. Say, "Point to the picture of the child who is writing."

[3] Many of the forms of cognitive development discussed in Kamii's chapter can be considered changes in word meanings as the child shifts from one developmental level to another. For instance, when a child says there are eight items here:

0 0 0 0 0 0 0 0 (set A)

and eight here:

00000000 (set B)

and then says there are "more" in set A, he is expressing a meaning of "more" that fits his cognitive level and that will change as development proceeds.

Let's Look at First Graders suggests three behavioral indications that children understand even more complex qualities of word meanings:

> He understands and is not confused by the fact that a single word can mean different things.
> *Examples:* Sheet—a piece of paper and something on a bed.
> Orange—a fruit and a color.
> He understands synonyms and can use different words to mean the same object or action without getting confused.
> *Examples:* boat and ship, car and automobile, start and begin, end and finish
> He understands that some words (and expressions) have a sense beyond their literal meaning.
> *Examples:* She is beside herself.
> His eyes are glued to the book.
> (Educational Testing Service, 1965, p. 15)

The procedural difficulty with vocabulary tests is that not all children have the same understanding of the conventions of pictorial representation. Sigel, Anderson, and Shapiro (1966) found that lower-class Negro preschool children had more trouble categorizing pictures of objects than categorizing the objects themselves, whereas for middle-class Negro children the level of representation made no difference. And when describing pictures in a communication experiment here at Harvard, middle-class 10-year-old white children said that black-and-white pictures in which coloring was shown by dots were "colored" or "shaded," while lower-class white children the same age said the pictures had "dots" or "dirt" or "stuff" in them.[4] To prevent this difference among children from interfering with valid vocabulary testing, three-dimensional objects can sometimes be substituted. Examples of test items using objects will be given in the next section. Objects also make it possible to ask the child to demonstrate his knowledge by active manipulation rather than by pointing.

Basic grammar (A-3)

The young child's ability to comprehend and produce simple sentences includes his knowledge of syntax or word order (which is usually correct even when some words are missing) and his knowledge of morphology or word endings such as plurals and past tense (which may still be missing). The child's knowledge of the important set of relational words—such as prepositions, conjunctions, and comparatives—could be discussed as vocabulary (*A*-2, above) or elaborated language (*B* to *D*, below); but because the same evaluation methods can be used for these words as for other aspects of grammar, they are included here. (Some are also included in Kamii's chapter; e.g., items like "over-under" for the structuring of space—her objective *P*).

The ability to speak in complete sentences can be assessed by direct observation, but only if the adult is a careful listener. Otherwise we may hear what we expect to hear—a full English sentence—even if some parts are in fact missing. In general, in children's speech the nouns and verbs and some adjectives appear first, and the rest of the sentence—inflections and function words—is added gradually. The following would be a natural progression of stages[5] from a telegraphic version to one kind of complete declarative sentence:

Stage 1. "Dog bark." (Noun and verb only.)
Stage 2. "Dog barking." (Earliest verb ending to appear.)
Stage 3. "The dog barking." (Article added to noun phrase.)
Stage 4. "The dog is barking." (Finally, auxiliary "is" added.)

Where transformations are required—for example, the changes in word order required in the formation of questions—the developmental stages along the way to mature speech will include forms which are not partial versions of the final behavior but rather unique childish constructions. For example, teachers of young children can listen for the following three stages

[4] This observation was made by Mrs. Kristine Rosenthal.

[5] In this chapter the term "stages" is used synonymously with "levels" to refer to successive points in a developmental sequence.

in asking questions (adapted from Klima & Bellugi, 1966):

Stage 1. "Why Mommy not come?"
(Question word simply added to beginning of immature sentence.)

Stage 2. "Can I go?"
"Why Pete is crying?"
(Correct inversion of auxiliary and subject in "yes-no" questions but not yet in *wh*- questions.)

Stage 3. "Where is she going?"
"Why I can't play outside?"
(Correct inversion on *wh*-affirmative questions, but not yet in *wh*-negative questions.)

Morphology consists of the rules for adding inflections to signify plurality, tense, comparison of adjectives and adverbs, etc. The careful listener will hear errors of both omission and commission: "two shoe" or "foots"; "Those Pamela boots"; "I goed to school"; "I want the more bigger one" (Cazden, 1968). Frequently the developmental progression is as follows:

Stage 1. "I went boom." (Superficially correct use of irregular past tense; probably learned as a single vocabulary item since regular past-tense endings are missing in the child's speech.)

Stage 2. "Where he goed?" (Temporary overgeneralization of the past-tense ending to verbs where it doesn't fit; dramatic evidence that the child has acquired a productive rule.)

Stage 3. "Daddy went to work." (Irregular past tense now used maturely along with correct regular endings.)

As with the evaluation of speech sounds (*A*-1), observation of the development of grammar is rarely sufficient because no child expresses more than a small part of his grammatical knowledge during any short period of time. Structured tests are therefore needed. One of the first systematic attempts to test for children's grammatical knowledge, and still one of the most successful, is Berko's (1958) test, in which she asked the children to generalize their knowledge of morphological rules to nonsense words. Her first item is shown in Fig. 14-1. Here are four more items appropriate for preschool children:

A-3

5. Progressive. Man balancing a ball on his nose. "This is a man who knows how to zib. What is he doing? He is ______."
6. Past tense. Man with a steaming pitcher on his head. "This is a man who knows how to spow. . . . He did the same thing yesterday. What did he do yesterday? Yesterday he ______."
7. Possessive. One animal wearing a hat. "This is a niz who owns a hat. Whose hat is it? It is the ______ hat."
8. Third person singular. Man shaking an object. "This is a man who knows how to naz. . . . He does it every day. . . . Every day he ______."

(Adapted from Berko, 1958, pp. 155–157, items 25, 3, 21, 15.)

Note that in Berko's test, by contrast with the vocabulary tests, the pictures play no intrinsic role. The test could be given without them if the child's attention and interest could be maintained. Homemade pictures can easily be used.

NOW THERE IS ANOTHER ONE.
THERE ARE TWO OF THEM.
THERE ARE TWO ______.

FIGURE 14-1 Test item for a plural morpheme. [J. Berko, The child's learning of English morphology. *Word*, 1958, **14**, p. 154. (Republished: In S. Saporta [Ed.] *Psycholinguistics*. New York: Holt, Rinehart and Winston, 1961. P. 361.) Figure 1. The plural allomorph in /-z/.]

Pictures can also be used to test children's knowledge of other aspects of grammar. For example, Fraser, Bellugi, and Brown (1963) designed a set of paired pictures to test children's comprehension and production of ten picturable grammatical forms. In each item, the only clue available to the child is a single grammatical contrast. For example, in item 11 nouns like "deer" and "sheep" must be used, so that the child can select the picture of one or two animals in response to "is" and "are" only.

A-3

9. Mass noun / Count noun.
   Some mog / A dap
10. Singular / Plural, marked by inflections.
    The kitten plays. / The kittens play.
11. Singular / Plural, marked by "is" and "are."
    The deer is running. / The deer are running.
12. Present progressive tense / Past tense.
    The paint is spilling. / The paint spilled.
13. Present progressive tense / Future tense.
    The baby is climbing. / The baby will climb.
14. Affirmative / Negative.
    The boy is sitting. / The boy is not sitting.
15. Singular / Plural, of 3rd-person possessive pronouns:
    Her dog / Their dog.
16. Subject / Object, in the active voice.
    The train bumps the car. / The car bumps the train.
17. Subject / Object, in the passive voice.
    The daddy is kissed by the mommy. / The mommy is kissed by the daddy.
18. Indirect object / Direct object.
    The girl shows the cat the dog. / The girl shows the dog the cat.

(Fraser et al., 1963, p. 127, items 1–10.)

Bussis expanded this idea into a twenty-item test (Melton ėt al., 1968). Lee (1969) has developed a similar twenty-item test for publication. Her item for testing the production and comprehension of passive sentences is shown in Fig. 14-2. As a variation of the original Fraser, Bellugi, and Brown test, Lee has added two decoy pictures to each pair of receptive items, thus reducing the probability that the child will point correctly by chance alone.

FIGURE 14-2 Test item for a passive sentence. (L. L. Lee. *Northwestern Syntax Screening Test.* Evanston, Ill.: Northwestern University Press, 1969. Item 19.)

To test comprehension, Lee's directions are as follows:

A-3

19. I'm going to tell you about these pictures. When I'm done, you show me the right picture. Look at all the pictures. Don't point until I tell you. *The cat is behind the chair. The cat is under the chair.* Show me *The cat is under the chair.* (Child points.) Now show me *The cat is behind the chair.* (Child points.)

(Lee, 1969, p. 2.)

To test production (for which different but comparable sentences are provided) the directions are as follows:

A-3

20. I will tell you about these pictures. When I am done, you copy me. Say just what I say. Don't talk until I tell you, though. Ready? Listen. *The baby is sleeping.* The baby is not sleeping.* Now, what's this picture? (Examiner points to asterisked picture, and child replies.) Now, what's this one? (Examiner points to unasterisked picture, and child replies.)

(Lee, 1969, p. 1.)

The advantages of asking children to manipulate objects rather than point to pictures were discussed earlier. Bellugi-Klima is developing an extended set of such manipulation tasks to test grammatical comprehension. Her suggestions for administration are as follows:

The objects for each problem should be set up on the table in such a way that they do not give cues to the solution of the problem (in terms of ordering or other such cues) and in such a way that the child has to make some changes or movement to demonstrate comprehension. If the problem has more than one part, it need not necessarily be given in any fixed order (mixing up orders of presentation would minimize the effects of "set").

The objects should be replaced in their original indeterminate position before asking another part of the problem.

The examiner [or teacher] should make sure at the onset of the problem that the child understands the words and action involved. For example, for the problem "The boy is washed by the girl" the examiner would identify the boy doll and the girl doll, and demonstrate how one washes the other, being careful not to give any cues to the problem. He might say for example, "This is how we wash," and then check the child's understanding of *boy*, *girl*, and *wash* before beginning.

(Bellugi-Klima, personal communication)

Adaptations of some of Bellugi-Klima's test items have been used successfully by the Harvard Preschool Project with children from 3 to 6 years. After that age most of these particular items become too easy. Here are seven of the items we used.[6]

A-3

21. Show me how	a. the boy washes *the girl.*
	b. the boy washes *himself.*
22. Point to	a. the daddy *of* the boy.
	b. the daddy's *boy.*
23. Make	a. the boy hit one of the girls.
	b. the girl *that* the boy hit run away.
24. Make this story:	a. *before* the girl put on her hat, she sat down.
25. Show me	a. what *can* he eat?
	b. what *can't* he eat?
26. Give	a. the *little* boy the *big* ball.
	b. the *big* boy the *little* ball.
27. Give me	a. a knife *and* a pencil.
	b. *either* a stick *or* a knife.
	c. something that is *neither* a stick *nor* a knife.

[6] This work was done by Eta Berner and Mrs. Mary M. Mokler.

Imaginative teachers who understand the purpose of these items can design their own to fit their children and their program. For instance a Montessori preschool teacher made up a test in which children manipulate large colored cardboard cutouts of geometric figures and a solid cube. Figure 14-3 shows several of her items (Bronson, 1969).

For children in the primary grades, such items (and vocabulary test items as well) can be placed on Ditto masters and directions for marking given orally by the teacher. *Let's Look at First Graders* (Educational Testing Service, 1965) includes similar items in its "Written Exercises."

A-3

28. Find the shoe that has a hole but *no* shoelaces.
    Put an X on the answer.
29. Find the apple *with* a stem but *without* a leaf.
    Put an X on the answer.
30. Find the jacket that has buttons *and* a pocket.
    Put an X on the answer.

(Educational Testing Service, 1965, *Written Exercises*, p. 42, items 9, 10, 11.)

Any teacher who tries to use such exercises with children below the first grade quickly realizes that successful completion of the test items requires many skills in addition to understanding of the test sentence. The child has to

Attend to a particular part of the page. Unless each page is a separate item, the child must learn to move down the page row by row. A cardboard marker which he can physically move down will help. So will an easily recognized symbol (a boat rather than a number) at the beginning of each row. But then this requires that he know where the row begins.

Make a recognizable mark (coloring or making a circle will be easier than an X for preschool children).

Keep up with a group pace, waiting when necessary and attending on demand.

These are all skills demanded in instructional as well as testing situations. Preschool and kindergarten teachers have to decide for themselves about the value of teaching them in their programs.

Grammatical knowledge can also be tested by oral completion items. For instance, if tag questions can be elicited from children 5 years or older, they will supply a great deal of information about the child's knowledge of pronouns and verbs. Slobin (1967)[7] includes a tag-question test developed by Bellugi-Klima.

> Children begin to produce tag questions (He is here, *isn't he*?) relatively late in their grammatical development. The tag question follows a statement, and generally asks for confirmation of the statement. The same purpose could be served by less elegant means: *He's here, right? You have some candies, huh?* or, *okay?* Children use the less elegant constructions for some time before they begin to produce tag questions. . . . Tag questions are particularly interesting because the shape of the tag is explicitly determined by the syntax of the statement it follows.
>
> (Slobin, 1967, p. 203)

Bellugi-Klima's directions are as follows:

A-3

31. Suppose I want to say something, and I'm not really sure about it. I might say: "The sun is shining today," and then, I might add: "isn't it?" We're going to play a game like that. I'll say something, and you add the last part, like this. I say: "That alligator can bite very hard," and you say . . .

(Slobin, 1967, p. 204.)

If the use of particular verb forms or pronouns has been emphasized, teachers can construct appropriate tag-question items to test for specific learnings. The following are only a few of many possible items:

A-3

32. Mother can do it, _____? (can't she?)
33. The bus is coming now, _____? (isn't it?)
34. The boy plays ball, _____? (doesn't he?)
35. Father won't go, _____? (will he?)
36. John and Bill play together, _____? (don't they?)
37. The girl pushed the boy, _____? (didn't she?)

Two cautions about constructing items to test children's production of any grammatical forms are in order. First, don't ask for constructions that are conversationally unnatural. For example, it is tempting to try to test a child's knowledge of verb

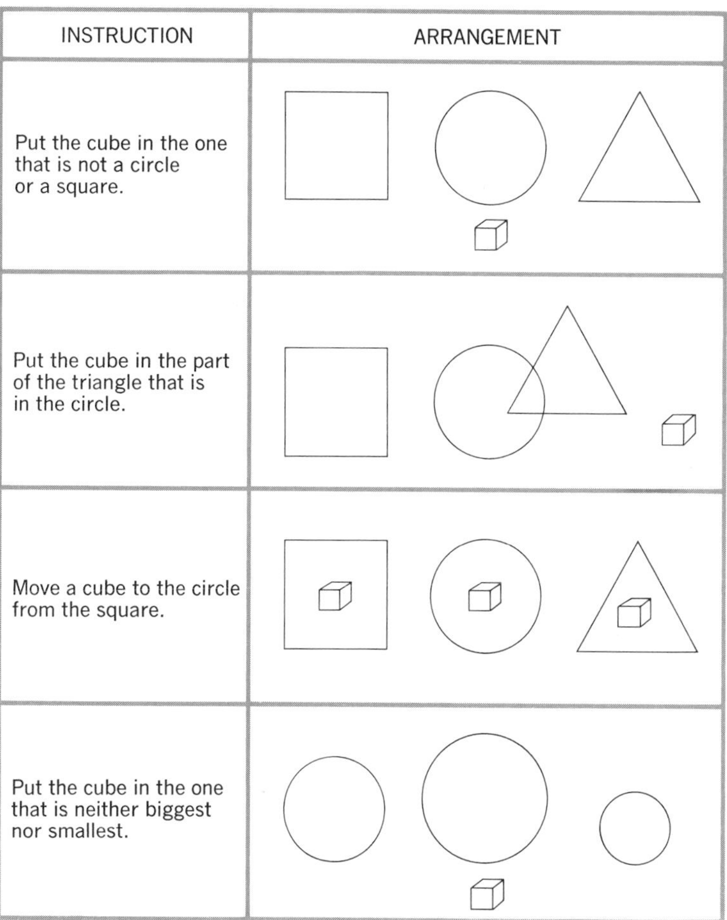

INSTRUCTION
ARRANGEMENT
Put the cube in the one that is not a circle or a square.
Put the cube in the part of the triangle that is in the circle.
Move a cube to the circle from the square.
Put the cube in the one that is neither biggest nor smallest.

FIGURE 14-3 Test items for a grammar comprehension test (*A*-3). (M. Bronson. Comprehension and production of function words. Unpublished term paper, Harvard University, Graduate School of Education, 1969. Items 2d, 3a, 6b, 10d.)

[7] This mimeographed manual was prepared for an interdisciplinary project directed by Dan Slobin (psychology), Susan Ervin-Tripp (speech), and John Gumperz (anthropology) as a guide to research workers studying the development of the child's communicative competence (not just grammatical development) in many diverse language communities (e.g. Samoa, Nigeria, Mexico, and Oakland, California). An excellent source of ideas and suggested procedures for research on children's language, it is available from the ASUC Bookstore, University of California at Berkeley.

tenses by saying: "Yesterday we walked to school. Today we . . ." and hope to elicit "walk." The trouble is that "walked" is entirely appropriate with "today" as well as with "yesterday." Similarly, it is tempting to say, "Today we are in school. Tomorrow we . . ." and hope to elicit "will be in school." But "are" is normal usage there as well. In constructing new completion items, teachers must be sure that what they hope to elicit is really the only possibility in normal, everyday speech. Second, don't insist on full sentences in answer to questions. When adults are asked, "Where do you live?" or, "What is the name of the book you're reading?" they rarely bother to answer in a complete sentence. Why should children?

As with pronunciation, the criterion for the child's ability to speak in complete simple sentences may be either clarity of communication or conformity to the rules of Standard English. If a program aims for the latter, then there are certain specific features of the child's grammar which need to be assessed. According to *Nonstandard Dialect* (National Council of Teachers of English, 1968) the following are among the important linguistic markers of speakers of nonstandard English:

Verb usage:

- Omission of forms of the verb "to be," especially in affirmative statements such as "He tired," or, "He running away."
- Different rules for subject-verb agreement, as in "They is coming."
- Omission of the regular third-person singular ending, as in "She know how."
- Use of a nonstandard form to signify intention, as in "I'm a hit you."
- Use of nonstandard forms for irregular verbs, as in "I seen it."

Noun inflections:

- Omission of plurals, especially with numbers, as in "Three book."
- Omission of possessive -s, as in "That my sister coat."

Irregular pronouns, as in "Them books."

Multiple negation, as "I ain't got no pencil."

Doubling of forms, as in "My sister she going."

These and other nonstandard forms are easy to spot in casual conversations. It is harder to determine whether they do in fact indicate the existence of a nonstandard dialect or whether they are lingering traces of immature speech. Some of the same features—omission of "be" and plural and possessive inflections, and use of irregular pronouns, multiple negations, and doubled forms—all appear in the speech of young speakers of Standard English as well as in the speech of older speakers of nonstandard English (though for entirely different reasons). This makes it difficult for teachers to decide when a deviant usage will be outgrown as development proceeds, and when it will last as a feature of the child's home language. The decision cannot be made by listening to the child alone; it can only be made on the basis of knowledge of the language community the child comes from and the way the child's family and neighborhood peers speak.

Whether or not the school is attempting to teach children to speak Standard English in school, teachers should be alert for any evidence of failures in comprehension that may be due to dialect differences, either in natural conversations or in the situations for testing grammatical situations described above. If a nonstandard dialect is spoken in the school community, it is all the more important to check on the child's ability to comprehend forms, such as plurals and possessives, which he may not produce himself.

A final method of evaluating children's knowledge of grammar is by an imitation test. The teacher says a sentence and asks the child to repeat it. Repetition on demand (as contrasted with spontaneous imitation) is, strictly speaking, a metalinguistic ability. It is simpler than those abilities listed in objectives *G* to *I*, since even 2-year-olds can do it, but it does involve conscious and deliberate attention to language as an object. It can be used to evaluate productive language because of the close relationship between the length and complexity of sentences children can repeat and those they spontaneously produce without a model (Brown & Fraser, 1964). Children assimilate what they hear to their own level of language development.

The directions are simple, with examples varied in simplicity and number to fit the age of the child. The following has been successful with 2-year-olds:

A-3

38. I'm going to say something and then you say what I say. Say, "Hello." [*Child repeats.*] Good. Now say "Peek-a-boo." [*Child repeats.*] Good. Now say "Red car." [*If child repeats this, continue with test items.*]

Imitation tests are designed for two different purposes. They can be designed to evaluate the child's knowledge of particular grammatical structures. The Fraser, Bellugi, and Brown (1963) sentences listed above for testing comprehension and production were also used as an imitation test. Osser, Wang, and Zaid (1969) have designed a related imitation test without the morphology items like the singular-plural contrast and with more items involving grammatical transformations. For example:

A-3

39. Reflexive: "The boy dries *himself* with a towel."
40. Conjunctive: "The boy *slides and another boy slides.*"
41. Relative clause: "The girl *who sits* is very fat."

(Osser, Wang, & Zaid, 1969, p. 1065.)

Teachers who have been trying to encourage the use of particular grammatical structures—for example, more complex modification (*B*-4)—can construct items accordingly. For this purpose, the child's responses are scored for the retention or omission of these particular structures.

Imitation tests can also yield a more global index of grammatical development and its growth over time. For this purpose, the child's responses are scored either in terms of number of correct sentences from a list graded on some criterion of length, complexity, or both, or in terms of the total number of morphemes retained from all the sentences on the list.

Sentence: "The boy is not sitting."
Imitation: "Boy not sitting."
Score: 4

Stern (1968b) has constructed an Echoic Response Inventory for Children with twenty sentences graded in length (as even the visual appearance of the list shows) and complexity. Three of her sentences are:

A-3

42. Dogs bark.
43. The young girl is sitting in the park.
44. If the ground is wet, the children won't be able to play in the park.

(Stern, 1968b, items 1, 11, 20.)

When imitation tests are used for evaluation, questions of dialect have to be considered. "Using standard English criterion for tests that ask 'How well has standard English been developed in this child' is excellent. However, using standard English as a criterion for tests that ask, 'How well has this child developed language' is absurd if the primary language that the child is developing is not that of standard English" (Baratz, 1969, p. 899).

Osser (1966, p. 3) takes dialect differences into account in scoring. He worked out a set of "functional equivalents" between Standard English and Negro nonstandard dialect:

"His sister hat" is scored as equivalent to "His sister's hat."
"Her washes herself" is scored as equivalent to "She washes herself."

Such a scoring system assumes that the child comprehends the test sentence as easily whether it is in his dialect or not, and then if necessary translates it into his own dialect (an example of objective *H*-3). Baratz has shown that children as young as third-graders can do just that. But since we don't yet know about comparable ability at preschool ages, nonstandard speakers may still be penalized even with these scoring dispensations.

An even better adjustment to dialect differences would be to construct a set of items in the child's dialect. The following are examples of adaptations of Baratz's sentences shortened for use with younger children:

A-3

45. That girl, she ain't go to school.
46. I ask Tom do he wanna go to the picture.
47. Henry live beside the ball park.
48. Patricia all the time be sitting in the front row.

Use elaborated language: description (B-4)

Elaborated language (behaviors *B* to *D*) takes many forms, including the precise expression of spatial relationships among *Objects* (content 4), temporal relationships among *Events* (5), and logical relationships among *Ideas* and concepts (6)—or *Description* (*B*), *Narration* (*C*), and *Explanation* (*D*). Suggestions for evaluation will be given for each in turn.

Children's ability to make increasingly precise descriptions can be assessed informally in many situations in the classroom: in the labels or captions which they give to their paintings, in stories dictated to an adult, in contributions to group discussions, and in discriminations between two or more objects.

For the youngest children, evidence of progress in providing captions for drawings starts from the base of an isolated label (even though the child is at a stage of speaking spontaneously in full sentences at the same time). Consider the growth in explicitness shown in the following captions.[8]

Single label: "Mommy" or "a house."
Labels joined by "and": "A boy and a dog."
Prepositional phrase: "The boy in the car."
Subject and predicate: "The boy is going into the house."
More complex sentence: "This is Grandmother, waving from her house."

[8] For these examples of children's captions and stories, I am grateful to the Department of Early Childhood Education of the Berkeley, California, public schools. Mrs. Mary Ann Kojan, Director.

In many situations, one can chart growth in the kinds of names—or nominalizations—which a child can construct. As long as children use pronouns—"I want that" or "See it over there"—precise description is impossible. One cannot talk about "a big red that." Furthermore, pronouns are interpretable only in a shared context. Their meaning must come from a referent previously stated by some party to the conversation or from a referent in the nonverbal context of the utterance. Therefore, one important feature of children's language is the relative frequency of pronouns and nouns in their speech (Hawkins, 1969).

Labels in English are not confined to nouns alone. We have rich and complex means for forming nominalizations, and teachers can listen for these to be used by their children. The following are examples of the possibilities:

Noun with preceding modifiers: "My friend's house" or "some big kids."
Noun modified by prepositional phrase: "My little brother opened his mouth to drink *some water from the rain.*"
Noun modified by a participial phrase and a relative clause: "Once upon a time at the Oakland International Airport *a dog named Cricket who rides a motorcycle* was on the airplane."

The kinds of modifications which children use can be evaluated in a situation where children are asked to tell the difference between two objects—for instance a short, thick piece of wood and a long, thin one at the workbench. Sinclair (Inhelder, Bovet, Sinclair, & Smock, 1966) found three differences in descriptions of such objects between children about 5 years old who understood the concept of conservation and children who did not (see Kamii's chapter for a discussion of conservation):

Conservers used relational terms such as *That one is shorter.*	Non-conservers said only *That is small and that is big.*
Conservers used more differentiated terms, like *wider, fatter, taller, thinner.*	Non-conservers were more restricted to the use of *big* and *little* for all differences in size.

Conservers used coordinated descriptions to talk about two dimensions: *That one is thinner and taller: that one is fatter and shorter.*	Non-conservers tended to mention only one of the dimensional differences: *That one is thin and that one is a bit big.*

Despite these differences, all children could comprehend the more differentiated language when given directions by the teacher. As is usually the case, children's comprehension of language forms precedes their ability to produce those forms. Whether or not language instruction helps children acquire the concept of conservation (in Sinclair's work it did not), teachers can listen for evidence that children can use language as Sinclair's conservers did as a legitimate sign of growth in the use of language itself.

Many of the aspects of elaborated language can be both taught and assessed while children play Language Lotto (Gotkin, 1966). There are six boxes in the entire set: *objects, actions, more actions, prepositions, compound sentences,* and *relationships.* Each set can be played at three levels, depending on the complexity of the child's task: he visually matches his card to the one held up by the teacher; he locates the correct picture from the teacher's verbal description; finally, he can himself supply the description. The following are examples of the statements the child has to understand or say:

B-4

49. *Prepositions:* The cookies are beside (next to) the plate.
50. *More actions:* The horse and the mouse are crawling under the fence.
51. *Compound sentences:* One girl has a doll and one girl has a hat.

(Gotkin, 1966.)

If a teacher or aide keeps track of which level of a particular box each child can play, evaluation of growth in elaborated language, at least with this particular content, can be relatively easy. Table 14-6 shows the checklist provided with the Language Lotto game.

Another kind of evaluation consists of eliciting

Table 14-6 Language Lotto Checklist

Name of child	*Game*	*Visual matching* *D = with difficulty* *E = easily*	*Finds the picture on the basis of verbal description* *D = with difficulty* *E = easily*	*Ability to verbalize correctly* *H = hesitantly* *F = fluently* *P = partially*

SOURCE: L. G. Gotkin. *Language Lotto*™. New York: Appleton-Century-Crofts, Division of Meredith Publishing Company. Copyright © 1966 by Meredith Publishing Company.

from the child a description of a picture and then scoring it on some objective scale. Watts's English Language Scale (Watts, 1944) could be adapted for such a purpose. Watts has designed six sets of pictures which require increasingly complex descriptions.

> The principle underlying the choice and the arrangement of the pictures is simple. As young children grow up and develop mentally they find themselves able to hold more and more images and ideas together in the mind at one time, and to speak of them in relation to one another more and more satisfactorily "at one go." Thus, children of the age of four will no doubt be able to say something intelligible about each of the first six pictures, but only those who have reached the age of eight or nine will be able, as a rule, to describe the last six in the manner required of them.
>
> (Watts, 1944, p. 287)

The following are examples of the descriptions required from the first four sets:

B-4

52. Stage 1 (4 to 5 years): A person or animal performing an action. "A girl lying down."
53. Stage 2 (5 to 6 years): Two people or objects joined by an action. "A boy riding on a donkey."
54. Stage 3 (6 to 7 years): Three people or objects joined by an action. "A girl lifting up a boy to put a letter in the letter box."
55. Stage 4 (7 to 8 years): Relation between two actions, whether or not the child uses "because." "A dog waiting for his master to throw a stick into the water."

(From Watts, 1944, pp. 288–294, items 6, 7, 16, 20.)

Comparable pictures—at least three or four at each stage—could be cut from magazines for such a test.

Use elaborated language: narration (C-5)

While *Descriptions* (*B*) require the expression of relationships between people and objects which are simultaneously present, *Narration* (*C*) requires the comparison of events, of which at least one and frequently both are no longer happening. The relationship is wholly conceptual, not perceptual, and is accordingly more difficult for young children. When a child asks *where* something is, the answer can often be given here and now in physical terms, by pointing or fetching. But if he asks *when* something will happen, the answer must be given in words alone, and frequently in words like "tomorrow" which are themselves relational words with a shifting referent.

It is therefore more difficult to elicit sentences that express temporal relationships than it is to elicit spatial relationships, because one cannot so easily present two events and ask the child to talk about them. One can stimulate discussion of past events, particularly if a sequence of things happened—as with a class trip or a classroom activity like cooking—and note what the children say. Beyond the elementary parts of simple sentences which are important for time reference, such as verb tenses, one could look for instances of the following, all of which appeared in the speech of two children by the time they were 5 years old:

Sentences that refer to more than one point in time:

"I'm gonna turn into a knight if you do that."
"I will show you what I got for Christmas."

Use of "before" and "after" in sentences which retain the order of events:

"I said that *after* my nap I could come outside."
"Now put him back on *before* he breaks again."

Use of "before" and "after" to reverse the actual order of events:

"And then sleep *after* I have lunch."
"And let me cover it *after* you finish that."

Use of words to express repetition, continuation or completion:

"Did I miss again?"
"You still there?"
"Robin's already married."

Use of time words to express ordering, sequence, or simultaneity:

"First you make the head. Then you make the eyes."
"Now green is gonna come out. Then pink one's gonna come out."
"When it's got a flat tire it needs to go to the station."

(Cromer, 1968)

It would be possible to use this list of five aspects of temporal reference as a checklist for evaluating each child's level of development; but even if such features of temporal reference are present in a child's linguistic competence, some of them (e.g., using "before" and "after" to reverse order) could easily go unnoticed without the aid of a tape recorder. For adequate evaluation, therefore, more structured situations are needed.

At first glance, the story-sequence cards which children order may seem useful for this purpose. But while they may be helpful in requiring a child to think about temporal order, they seem to discourage the expression of complex temporal relationships. Once the cards are arranged correctly from left to right, the only description likely is "*a* and then *b*, and then *c*, etc." Words, however, can do far more than simply repeat experience in another form. They allow us to transform experience, to talk about what came later before what came first, about the effect before the cause. We want to know how much children can take advantage of these possibilities which their language permits, and for this purpose a set of pictures which is restricted to a single linear sequence is too limited.

Another possibility is to tell a child a story which is rich in the forms of temporal reference suggested above and then ask the child to retell it. When a child retells a story, particularly one that is too long for immediate memory, he processes both content and expression through his own conceptual and linguistic system, simplifying and distorting as he does so. The features which are retained in the child's version are probably ones he has learned to handle—that is, they are features he can at least comprehend and probably produce as well—regardless of how infrequently they may appear in his spontaneous speech. A story-retelling task is like a longer, more complex version of a sentence-imitation test.

Vera John has used this technique with children from 4 to 7 years old. Her method is as follows:

> The child is told that after the story has been read, he will be asked to retell it. The child is then read a story while he looks at a sequence of pictures corresponding to parts of the text. Once the story is completed, the child is shown the illustrations and retells the story. Each picture is presented separately and in its proper sequence. (Young children are unable to retell the story without the sequential presentation of the illustrations as cues.) The examiner or teacher or aide, who is trained to avoid prompting, records the retold story.
>
> (John, Horner, & Berney, in press.)

This procedure, like the sequence cards, used a series of pictures, but here they are only hooks on which to hang a richer and more complex set of temporal relationships for the child to cope with. If expressions of temporal relationships such as Cromer has listed (above) are included in the story, the child's retold version can be scored for retention, distortion, or omission of those features.

Use elaborated language: explanation (D-4–D-6)

Of the many aspects of the expression of logical relationships among concepts and ideas, three will be discussed here: expressions of category membership; expressions of conditionality and causality with "if" and "because"; and use of connectors like "and," "or," and "not."

Growth in the child's ability to form categories and category systems—multiple classifications and hierarchical classifications—has been discussed in the preceding chapter. This ability usually develops before the child's ability to explain what he has done. We will mention here only one feature of the linguistic form such explanations take once they do appear. If a child is asked to form a group from an array of objects e.g., banana, peach, and potato) and then asked to explain the basis for his grouping, at least three choices are open. Let us assume that the child can find one way in which the particular set of objects are alike ("all food," or "all to eat"). He can say, "This is food and this is food and that is food too"; or, "Bananas and peaches and potatoes are all food"; or, "They are all food." Children who can say, "They are all food" or, "I can eat them" have learned to combine three separate ideas into one. As with the language of the conservers and nonconservers noted above, instruction in language for talking about categorization may or may not advance the child's thinking. But growth in the linguistic forms a child can use is important in itself.

Evaluation of children's ability to express ideas of conditionality and causality is difficult because the ideas and their linguistic expression may exist separately. Woodcock (undated)[9] reports examples of "pre-forms" in the speech of 2-year-olds in which the ideas expressed by "why," "because," and "if" are present even though the words themselves are missing.

Conditionality:

"Turn on dat, dat be hot."
"You eat your dinner, you have banana."

Causality:

"Janet don't need a coat on. Janet's too warm a coat."
"Don't sit on 'at radiator—very hot."
"I can't [come] now, I dus' dettin' dwessed."

Conversely, one may find the linguistic forms present with immature meaning. In this instance, production may precede true comprehension.

> In general, it is normal for children to master certain grammatical forms before they understand the logical ideas these forms represent. For instance, a child may use "because," "if," or "then" clauses long before he understands the notion of causal, conditional or temporal relationships. For this reason—because grammar generally *does precede* logic—the child's language can often be misleading as an indication of his actual level of logical understanding. On the other hand, the ability to use grammar *must precede*, if logical reasoning skills are to develop at all.
>
> [Educational Testing Service, *Let's Look at First Graders*, 1965, p. 14]

Any complete assessment, therefore, has to look for both the form and the conceptual content.

[9] Louise Woodcock was a nursery school teacher at the Bureau of Educational Experiments in New York City, a predecessor of the Bank Street College of Education.

Children's use of a variety of conjunctions necessary for elaborated description, narration, and explanation—including "if" and "because"—was first assessed by Piaget (1959). He presented children with sentences to complete, such as "That man fell off his bicycle because . . ." A student at Harvard, Anita Olds, tested 6-year-old children with this method. The following are some of her items, with examples of the children's responses. After each item, the first response shows evidence of mature integration of word and concept, while the second response does not:

D-5
56. The boy is taking a bath *even though* . . .
he's clean
because he's dirty

D-4
57. She is pretty *and* . . .
good
dirty

D-5
58. The car hit him *but* . . .
he's not dead
it is smashed

D-5
59. The kite will fly *if* . . .
it has string
it blows away

D-5
60. His mother spanked him and so . . .
he got mad
he wasn't good

D-5
61. I took my umbrella *because* . . .
it's raining
it blew away

(A. R. Olds, personal communication, 1968)

Use language for communication (E-7, E-8)

Ideally, children's language usage should be assessed in a wide variety of situations with different communicative demands. We will discuss here two components of successful communication (deciding what is most important to say and editing one's communication to fit the needs of the listener) and three specific uses of language for communicative purposes (understanding and giving directions, *E*-7; asking questions for information, *E*-7; and participating in dramatic play, *E*-8).

A two-person communication game can be used to evaluate a child's ability to select the most important ideas. Imagine a colored advertisement for overcoats from a Sunday newspaper supplement which shows two men standing side by side; both men are wearing overcoats, but one has his hat on while the other carries his hat and gloves in his hand. Two children, separated by an opaque screen, each have a copy of this picture. One child is designated the speaker and the other is the listener. (Later, with a different picture, the roles can be exchanged.) The teacher says to the speaker:

E-7

62. I'm going to point to one of the men in your picture. Then you see if you can tell _____ about that man so that he can guess which one you're talking about. Ok? This one. (Teacher points to one man.)

Does the child see that it is important to talk about the hat that only one man is wearing but not the overcoats that both are wearing?

Once the children have caught on to the game, pictures with three or four items can be used. But don't expect that children under 8 years will realize that even if there are several differences between items, the description of one may give sufficient information; the elimination of redundant information seems to be difficult even for 10-year-olds (Flavell et al., 1968). As with the Watts Scale, the spoken description in this communication game can be evaluated against a preset criterion: the description either does or does not adequately differentiate one picture from the other or others. In the communication game there is an additional functional criterion which the speaker himself can appreciate: was the listener able to guess correctly or not?

Young children frequently do not adjust their talk to the needs of their listener. To make such an adjustment requires an internal metalinguistic evaluation—conscious editing of one's expression of ideas to fit the particular communicative context of the moment. This is a very important ability and one which can be observed. For instance, when talking on a toy telephone, does a child point, gesture, and say "this" and "that," or does he take into consideration the difference between a telephone conversation and talking face to face? Does the child talk in school about people in his family as if the teacher and other children knew them well, or does he say, "Eric—he's my friend—came over last night"? The telephone situation involves understanding differences in perceptual perspectives and probably develops earlier than the understanding required by the second situation, which involves grasping differences in what people know. The kind of self-editing displayed when the child interpolates the explanation "he's my friend" is an especially important indication of developing communicative skill.

The child's ability to understand directions can be tested by giving him increasingly complex directions to follow:

> We start with "Put the book on the table," and many actions of this sort, then go on to, "Pick the book up off the chair and put it on the table," and even later to, "Put the book on the table and bring me the pencil that is on the desk."
>
> (Gray et al., 1966, p. 30)

Here complexity is created by lengthening the list of directions to be followed. Complexity can also be created by grammatical means. A word like "before" makes it possible to speak directions in one order which have to be carried out in the reverse order; "Before you bring me the pencil that is on the desk, put the book on the table." Note that there's no point in saying, "Before you put the book on the table, pick it up off the chair," because these two actions can be done in only one order. "Take X to ______ from ______" has the same reversed form.

Simple Simon is a favorite game which provides not only good practice for following directions but a context for assessment as well. Gotkin (undated) has worked out a sequence of increasingly complex levels of the game which assess the child's ability to respond selectively to verbal instructions:

Level 1: Teacher gives verbal direction and models correct action.
Level 2: Teacher gives verbal direction only.
Level 3: Teacher gives verbal direction and models incorrect action. Children must follow what they hear but not what they see.
Level 4: Teacher gives verbal directions without model, sometimes preceded by *Simon says* and sometimes not. The children must follow only some verbal directions and ignore others.
Level 5: Same as level 4, but teacher models action regardless of whether *Simon says* or not. Children must follow only some verbal directions and ignore visual model.
Level 6: Same as level 5, but sometimes teacher models a different action. Children must listen selectively in the presence of greater visual distraction.

(Adapted from Gotkin, undated, pp. 15–16)

A checklist could be used to keep track of individual children's ability to play increasingly demanding levels of this game.[10]

Children's ability to give directions as well as understand them can be evaluated when the child is placed in the role of the teacher—as in the Gray et al. practice session described above or in games like Language Lotto. Of course they will not give as complex directions as the adult will, but it is their clarity and explicitness that count. Note that in the Language Lotto situation one is evaluating how well the child has internalized a model; in the practice session he can be evaluated on his ability to formulate new directions that no one has given before.

Shifting from giving directions to asking questions, we know that children of preschool age can ask questions to get things that they want. But an important part of success in school is asking questions for information, and devising a good strategy for asking a series of questions when necessary.

Bereiter and Engelmann (1968, undated) use a variation of Simple Simon to provoke questions for information. After a series of familiar statements such as, "Touch your nose" and, "Touch your foot," the teacher says, "Touch your cranium." "Keep using different words, because the object is not to have the children learn the words, but to learn how to ask what they mean and then use the information to carry out the instructions" (Bereiter & Engelmann, undated, p. 19). Like many suggestions for evaluation, this one is useful both for instruction and for evaluating the responses of individual children.

Often a single question does not provide enough information to solve a particular problem. Can the child frame questions which gradually eliminate more and more possibilities until an answer is clear—that is, play the game of Twenty Questions? In his kindergarten program in Toronto, Bereiter has developed many versions of this game for instruction and assessment (Bereiter, Case, & Anderson, 1968). In one version the children stand around the teacher, eyes closed and one hand outstretched. The teacher pretends to put a paper clip into each child's hand but really puts it into only one child's. Hands down and eyes open, the children start asking questions. Mature questioning takes the form of constraint-type questions, not potshotting (Mosher & Hornsby, 1966): "Is it a girl?" or "Is she wearing red?" instead of "Is it Betty?" As each question is asked and answered, the children who are

[10] This game is used for the same purpose at the New Nursery School, where it is called "Leo the Lion" after the puppet who gives the directions, and in Basil Bernstein's Infant School language program in London, where it is called "O'Grady."

eliminated from further consideration step back and continue asking questions until the child holding the paper clip is identified. The rules of the game can specify either "yes-no" questions (as above), or *wh-* questions like "What color is his hair?" Score can be kept of how many questions are necessary for solution.

One important context for using language in many preschools is *Dramatic play* (E-8). Smilansky finds that speech during dramatic play has three functions: "It appears as imitation of adult speech, it is used for imaginative make-believe (Let's pretend), and it serves for the management of the play in forms of explanations, commands, discussion, and so on" (Smilansky, 1968, p. 27). She found that whereas middle-class children in Israel used speech for all three functions, working-class children talked mainly for managerial reasons. Her descriptions of the use of language for imitation and make-believe suggest what other teachers can listen for in their own children:

> The imitative element finds expression in both imitative actions and imitative speech. A little driver moves the wheel, signals with his hand, and makes movements of taking money and giving tickets like the real driver. He also tries to talk like him: *Please, watch your step!* A little mother undresses her doll, puts it down on a toy bed, and says, *Now darling, you must go to bed.*
>
> The make-believe element relies heavily on verbalization. Words take the place of reality. This appears in four forms.
>
> 1. Verbal declarations serve to change personal identity, to take on make-believe roles. (*I am the daddy, you will be the mommy, and the doll is our baby.*)
> 2. Identity of objects is changed by verbal declaration or action. (*I am drinking from the bottle,* when the child is drinking from his fist. The drinking movement is imitative, but pretending that the fist is a bottle is make-believe.)
> 3. Speech is substituted for *action.* (*Let's pretend I already returned from work, I cooked the food, and now I am setting the table,* when only the last activity is actually imitated.)
> 4. Language is used to describe *situations.* (*Let's pretend that the doctor is sick, so the nurse will do the operation,* or *Let's pretend that this is a hospital, and there are a lot of sick children in it.*)
>
> (Smilansky, 1968, pp. 7–8.)

A checklist could be designed so that teachers or aides eavesdropping on the doll corner, block area, or playground could keep a running account of each child's use of language in these ways.

Use language for cognition (F-9)

All the language discussed up to this point is language which is spoken aloud and which can therefore be assessed directly. But *Language for thinking* (F-9) is by nature language for oneself and silent. For a time between the ages of 4 and 7 years, young children do talk to themselves as they work at a puzzle or play with a doll. While it lasts, such overt speech for self-communication should be appreciated and observed. To the best of our knowledge, it becomes internalized into inner speech and continues as an accompaniment and directer of our activities.

Kohlberg, Yaeger, and Hjertholm (1968, pp. 707–708) suggest that the following types of self-communicative speech form a developmental sequence:

> *Level I. Presocial Self-stimulating Language*
>
> 1. *Word play and repetition.*—Repeating words or phrases for their own sake. . . . "A whats, a whats. Doodoodoo, round up in the sky."
>
> *Level II. Outward-directed Private Speech*
>
> 2. *Remarks addressed to nonhuman objects.*—For example, "Get back there," addressed to a piece of sticky paper clinging to the child's finger.
> 3. *Describing own activity.*— . . . Remarks about the self's activity which communicate no information to the listener not apparent from watching him, . . . [and which have] no task-solving relevance or planning function. . . .
>
> *Level III. Inward-directed or Self-guiding Private Speech*
>
> 4. *Questions answered by the self.*— . . . "Do you know why we wanted to do that? Because I need it to go a different way?"
> 5. *Self-guiding comments.*— . . . "The wheels go here. We need to start it all over again." . . . The difference between this category and 3, describing own activity, is that these comments are task or goal oriented. Speech precedes and controls activity rather than follows it. . . .

Level IV. External Manifestations of Inner Speech

6. *Inaudible muttering.*—Statements muttered in such a low voice that they are indecipherable to an auditor close by.

Level V. Silent Inner Speech or Thought

The teacher can keep a record of the types of self-communicative speech that she overhears. However, even if these types do form a developmental continuum (which has not yet been established), it will be difficult to assess the progress of a child's development. An increase in the frequency of type 5 (self-guiding comments) will be clear. But if the child is mumbling to himself as he works, is it poorly pronounced word play of type 1 or the nearly internalized speech of type 6?

To supplement direct observation, we can make indirect assessments of language for thinking by observing a child performing a task where we think inner speech should help and then inferring its presence or absence from the success of the child's efforts.[11] Two such opportunities are built into the Language Lotto game. In the simplest of the boxes, *objects*, one envelope has cards on which the matching objects are similar but not identical. For example, there are two different kinds of telephones, irons, etc. When the children are familiar with the game, it can be played without saying the names aloud. Then, presumably, if the child correctly and easily matches the two pictures of different telephones, he has said to himself the name that makes them equivalent. The last of the boxes, *relationships*, provides a similar but much more complex task, where the concept linking two pictures is a relationship like "goes on" or "part of" or "lives in."

The cards in the objects game can be used for another task which tests the child's ability to rehearse names as an aid to memory.

F-9

63. Lay out three cards. Point to two of them. Then pick up the cards and put them down again in a different arrangement. Ask the child to point to the same two cards in the same order.

[11] Whether language is necessary in such tasks is a controversial question. Hans Furth's (1966) research with deaf children suggests that some form of nonverbal representation can be used.

This task can be made more difficult by increasing the number of pictures in the total array, increasing the number of words in the list to be remembered, and using nonidentical cards so that when the cards are displayed the second time they are different examples of the same kind of object.

One further situation for examining a child's use of language as an aid to memory comes from Jensen and Rohwer's research on paired-associate learning. Rohwer (1966) found that when elementary school children are asked to learn to associate two nouns—e.g., "cow" and "train"—learning is aided if the child mentally joins the two words into a phrase or sentence. Particular verbal connections are more or less helpful, depending presumably on "the degree of semantic constraint exerted by the verbal context on the response [second] member of each pair" (Rohwer, 1966, p. 542). The following connections are increasingly helpful:

Conjunction: "The cow *and* the ball."
Preposition: "The cow *behind* the ball."
Verb: "The cow *chases* the ball."

(Note the similarity of these examples to the examples of increasing maturity of children's spontaneous captions for drawings, given above.) Children from 5 to 8 probably have a hard time with this task (Jensen & Rohwer, 1965), even when they are told to put the items together in a sentence, because they are most likely to use only conjunctions.

From this research, Gahagan and Gahagan (1968) constructed a test for evaluating Basil Bernstein's Infant School language program. They use eight cards with one object in color on each side. The procedure is in three stages.

Stage 1: On a practice item, the child is shown one card and asked to construct a sentence. The adult then suggests three model sentences, each containing a different verb—e.g., *likes*, *can see*, and *is eating*.

Stage 2: The child is asked to construct sentences for each of the eight pairs in turn.

Stage 3: The child's memory is tested. The adult shows the object on one side of a card, names it, and asks the child to name the object on the reverse side. Whether the child is correct or not, the adult then names the object. This procedure is repeated until the child has two errorless trials of all eight cards.

(Adapted from pp. 1124–5.)

Each child's responses can be scored in two ways: the number of different verbs he included in his sentences, and the number of trials he needed to reach the criterion. Gahagan and Gahagan found a significant negative correlation between the two: the children who used more varied verbs learned more quickly.

Operate on language: analysis (G-2, G-3)

At this point we shift from assessing the child's ability to use language itself to his "metalinguistic" ability—that is, his awareness of and ability to operate on language as an object of thought rather than its medium: to *Analyze* (*G*), perform some kind of *Translation* (*H*), and *Evaluate* (*I*). During early childhood education, children are expected to do this only at the level of the elementary language forms—*Sounds* (content 1), *Words* (2), and *Sentences* (3).

The *Analysis of words* (*G*-2) refers to the analysis of words into speech sounds or syllables, not the analysis of sounds into components such as distinctive features (only linguists do that). The usual auditory discrimination tasks and some reading readiness activities fit here. Correspondingly, *G*-3 refers to the *Analysis of sentences* into words.

G-2

64. Are the two words in each of the following pairs the same or different? pen-pin catch-cash
65. Is the *mm* sound at the beginning, middle, or end of these words? hammer Mother Jim
66. Do "run" and "water" start the same or not?
67. Do "run" and "sun" end the same (rhyme) or not?
68. How many syllables [*operationally defined by hand clapping*] in "look," "apple," "elephant"?
69. How many words are in the sentence "We are in school"? What is the first word? The last word?

Note that these test items assume a knowledge of specific concepts: "same-different" as applied to sounds and "beginning-middle-end" of a temporal sequence. It is important to teach and evaluate the child's understanding of these concepts before depending on that knowledge to evaluate his ability to analyze words into sounds.

These metalinguistic analytical abilities are important prerequisites of literacy. Ability to analyze words into sounds is required in reading and spelling, and can be assessed functionally in those tasks. Correspondingly, ability to analyze a sentence into words—to be aware of each part in its proper sequence—is required in written composition. The British linguist David Mackay (Mackay & Thompson, 1968) has constructed materials for children from 5 to 7 which separate the conceptual aspect of composition from the mechanical skill of handwriting. Each child has a "word folder" with a preselected store of words and some blanks for his personal collection. He also has a stand on which words from the folder can be set up as a text. Mackay and Thompson find (pp. 112–115) that in their awareness of words in a sentence, children go through several stages:

Stage 1: The child simply lists words with no apparent link—"dad" "boy" "girl"—and reads them as isolated words.

Stage 2: The child composes on his stand a telegraphic sentence—"children school"—but reads it as a complete sentence—"the children go to school." [I.e., when they are 5 or 6 years old, children may recapitulate at the metalinguistic level of awareness the development from telegraphic to complete sentence that they went through when they were 2 or 3 at the linguistic level of nonconscious production.]

Stage 3: The child realizes that words are missing from the stage 2 sentences and either adds them at the end—"mum home my is at"—or selects the missing words after the nouns and verbs but inserts them into their proper places.

Stage 4: The child produces partial sentences, sometimes with just a noun phrase—"my little teacher"—and sometimes with a noun phrase and then a statement about it—"my little teacher I love."

If these or comparable materials are used in the beginning literacy program, the teacher can keep track of the child's progress as he constructs sentences. As Mackay and Thompson point out, progress in this conceptual ability will not be revealed to the teacher if the child only copies from a model which she has written from his dictation, and it will be confounded with problems in handwriting, spelling, or both unless he has whole words in some form to work with.

Operate on language: transformation and translation (H-1–H-3)

The child can be asked to produce some kind of a *Transformation* at the level of *Sounds* (*H*-1):

H-1

70. Say a word that starts like "no."
71. Say a word that rhymes with "me."
72. Which hand-clapping pattern represents "Mother" and which represents "around" [*a loud clap followed by a soft one or vice versa*]?
73. Show me how you would clap "banana" and "holiday."

At the level of *Words* (*H*-2) children can be asked to give verbal definitions (translations) of words. Lesser et al. (1965) gave a verbal (as well as a picture) vocabulary test. For example, in the sample item the child is asked, "What is an apple?" Whatever he says, the adult gives a model answer: "Yes. It's something to eat, it has seeds, it's juicy, it grows on trees, and it's a fruit" (Lesser et al., 1965, p. 95). The child is then asked to define up to thirty more words (in two sessions of fifteen words each). The test is stopped after four consecutive failures. If the child does not give an adequate definition, the adult can probe: "Tell me more about ______" or, "Tell me what you mean" or "Take a guess" (Lesser et al., 1965, p. 95). The child's answer can be scored from 0 to 2, for example:

Stove: 2—concept of cooking, heating
1—association with food, but no idea of cooking; or description of a stove.
0—nothing relevant

At the level of sentences (*H*-3) the child can be asked to perform certain transformations. Stern (1968e) has constructed a Parallel Sentence Production Test in which children are asked to produce a sentence of the same grammatical form as the teacher's model sentence but with different semantic content.

H-3

74. There are two pictures—e.g., of a cat playing with a ball and a dog playing with a bone. The teacher points to the first and says a sentence, then points to the second and asks the child to tell about that picture.

(Adapted from Stern, 1968e.)

Other transformations may change form as well as meaning. For example, Bereiter and Engelmann (undated, pp. 22–24) suggest a series of tasks of increasing difficulty in which the child is asked to repeat a phrase in the reverse order:

First lists, then sentences.
First only two words, then three and more.
First with the perceptual support of pointing to actually present objects; then with perceptual support which has to be imagined—pointing to nonexistent objects in particular locations; then gestures are reduced until the child can reverse words alone.
Finally with sentences, at first where the child's reversal will be correct or amusing.

H-3

75. Teacher: "ball—chalk—marble." Child: "marble—chalk—ball."
76. Teacher: "Floor the touch." Child: "Touch the floor."
77. Teacher: "Lynn chews gum." Child: "Gum chews Lynn."
78. Teacher: "Look down here." Child: "Here down look."

(Adapted from Bereiter & Engelmann, undated, pp. 22–24.)

Operate on language: evaluation (I-1–I-3)

With young children, evaluation takes the form of selecting among alternatives according to simple criteria:

I-1

79. Which word rhymes with "Volkswagon": "Pontiac"—"Polkswagon"?

I-2

80. Which word means "not cold": "big"—"hot"?

I-3

81. Which of the following statements tell about that picture? [*Picture shows two boys climbing a tree and two girls watching from below.*]
    a. Cows are in the tree. (No)
    b. Four men are in a big car. (No)
    c. The girls are on the ground. (Yes)

(Adapted from Bereiter & Engelmann, undated, pp. 16–18, 27.)

A harder evaluation task is to decide which of the following questions can be answered by that same picture:

I-3

82. Where are the boys? (Yes)
83. What did they have for breakfast? (No)

The affective domain (J)

Ideally, we'd like children not only to have all the abilities described to this point, but to use them freely and with enjoyment. Successful attainment of oral language objectives constitutes an important achievement. But these objectives also constitute an increased aptitude for attaining further educational objectives, an increased ability to comprehend verbal instruction in other content areas. The oral language program will have this very powerful transfer value only if the children not only *can* use language more effectively but actually *do* so.

No test is appropriate here. The only possible kind of evaluation is to observe children and listen to what they say as they go about their regular activities. For example, when they first come to school in the morning, do they initiate conversations with other children? With adults? Do they often voluntarily participate in a small discussion group to listen to a story or talk over yesterday's visitor? On trips, do they ask more questions about what they see and hear? A checklist could be made up of such desired behavior, and a frequency check made with tally marks near the beginning and end of the school year.

Formative evaluation in two units

Somehow, the objectives of the oral language curriculum have to be turned into classroom experiences and these experiences then arranged in a sequence: at least this is true of the programs in group C and of some aspects of the programs in group B. In group A, by our definition, the sequence of each child's activities is under the control of the child to a much greater extent than it is under the control of the teacher. Presumably, though, the content of experiences selected by the child will contribute to the oral language objectives even though they were selected and structured for other reasons.

A sequence of experiences that can be separated out of the total oral language program because of some natural break in content can be called a "unit," regardless of the time needed for any one child to complete it. Because the structure of such a unit—the relations among its parts—reflects underlying beliefs about the nature of language and how it is learned, the structure may differ greatly from one program to another. Two units differing in structure as well as in content will be described here. The first focuses on the learning of what we have called "relational" words; the second is built around a particular piece of oral literature, *Millions of Cats.*

In one kind of structure, order is very important. Objective *A* must be taught before objective *B* because it is a component of objective *B*. So the temporal sequence of activities designed to attain these objectives is carefully controlled:

$$A \rightarrow B \rightarrow C \rightarrow D$$

The unit on relational words has this structure. A second kind of structure is nonlinear. Objectives are conceived as a nonordered set from which the teacher can pick and choose as occasions arise:

C
A *B*
D

The unit on *Millions of Cats* has this structure. Actual examples of formative evaluation will be given for the first unit only. Discussion of the second unit is included in order to raise questions about the sequencing of instruction for oral language objectives and implications of that sequence for evaluation.

A unit on relational words

As we mentioned earlier, most preschool oral language programs are meant to help children understand and use as many relational words as possible. The unit to be described here is a composite of lessons from the New Nursery School curriculum, Weikart, and Bereiter and Engelmann.

Table 14-7, Table of Specifications for a Unit on Relational Words, gives the set of objectives in this unit. Lines are used as in the charts in Chap. 6, Formative Evaluation, to indicate that a behavior at one level is necessary for another behavior at a more advanced level.

We will suggest one or two evaluation techniques at each of the four levels in Table 14-7. Other examples can be taken from the previous descriptions of evaluation techniques. And virtually any questioning procedure used for instruction can provide information for formative evaluation if the teacher (or an aide sitting in on a lesson in order to take notes) records the adequacy or inadequacy of each child's response and uses that information in planning further instruction.

In Table 14-7 the first level is simply the comprehension and production of the relational words—e.g., two pairs of prepositions: "in-out" and "over-under." Testing proceeds from understanding to production and from objects to pictures:

A-2

84. Understanding with objects: "Hold the ball under your foot." "Put the ball on the cup." [*Two paper cups, with rims around the bottom, one turned upside down; be sure not to associate one preposition invariably with a particular object, as "in" with "cup," or attention to the preposition itself will not be required.*]
85. Production with objects: The teacher demonstrates position of ball and asks, "Is the ball inside or outside the box?"

A-2

86. Repeat with pictures instead of objects.

The child may also be asked to construct appropriate positive and negative sentences with these prepositions:

A-2

87. Positive: The teacher demonstrates a spatial relationship and asks, "Where is the ball?"
88. Negative: The teacher asks, "Is the ball in the cup?" when it is in fact not.

In the Bereiter and Engelmann program, the children must answer in a complete sentence. Other teachers may establish different criteria for acceptable answers:

"The ball is in the cup."
"It is in the cup."
"In the cup."

At the second level, the use of relational words is expanded into more elaborated language. One possibility is the coordinated use of two dimensions, again both with objects and pictures.

TABLE 14-7 TABLE OF SPECIFICATIONS FOR A UNIT ON RELATIONAL WORDS

Cognitive domain				*Affective domain*
Use language				
A. Understand and produce simple language forms	*B–D. Understand and produce elaborated language*	*E, F. Use language effectively for specific purposes*	*G–I. Operate on language*	*J*
Understand and produce words of relative position or location (*A*-2) → "on" "in" "out" "under" "over" "between" "next to" "behind" "in front of" Answer question "Where is X?" in complete sentence (*A*-3).	Understand and produce sentences expressing a coordination of two or more spatial relationships (*B*-4): → "The ball is in the box under the chair."	Describe or give directions taking into account differences in visual perspective between speaker and listener (*E*-7, *E*-8).	Demonstrate understanding that some pairs of relational words are polar opposites (*H*-2) by answering the question: "What is the opposite of over?" or by naming a pair of opposites.	

B-4

89. Understanding: "Put the ball beside the book under the table."

90. Production: "Tell us two things about where this paper is [*between the books on the chair*].

Third, the elaborated descriptive statements can be put to specific communicative uses which involve still additional skills. One such use is to communicate a spatial position to another person who is viewing the scene from a different perspective. Figure 14-4 shows one possible test situation.

E-7

91. The children are standing on opposite sides of a table with a large box on it. Child B hides his eyes while the teacher points to spot X on the table. Child A is then asked to give B directions to put a small cube on that spot.

Immature response: "Put it behind the box." (True only for the speaker.)

Mature responses: "Put it in front of the box." (This reflects a switch to the listener's perspective but may confuse the listener if the problem of perspective is not made explicit.) "*Put it on the table next to your side of the box.*" (This would be even clearer.)

FIGURE 14-4 Test situation for considering the perspective of another person.

Finally, at the metalinguistic level, the child is expected to understand the concept of opposites, an abstract category name for pairs of relational terms:

H-2

92. Easier question: "What is the opposite of 'over'?"

93. Harder question: "Name one pair of opposites."

In formative evaluation, the teacher may not need to check the progress of all children at each step of the way. If she knows her children well from continuous checks on their progress in the past, recording the responses of a few representative children may be sufficient. Alternatively, if she does want to check on the progress of all the children, written exercises can be designed as suggested above.

A-2

Duplicated sheets have pictures of two trees: one with apples *on* it, one with apples *under* it. DIRECTIONS:

94. Put an X on the tree with the apples *under* it.

Or:

95. Color the apples *on* the tree yellow.

Either the teacher can give the directions to a group of children simultaneously, or she can use a Language Master tape recorder to give directions to children individually at different times of the day. The Language Master (produced by Bell & Howell) is shown in Fig. 14-5. It accepts cards with a strip of recording tape at the bottom. See Meier (1967) for further suggestions on using the Language Master for evaluation.

A unit on Millions of Cats

Of the programs discussed in this chapter, the Nebraska Curriculum is unique in being built around a core of literature. For grades 1 and 2 this means stories read aloud. Because it is unique, brief quotations from the rationale guiding the Nebraska Curriculum Development Center (1966b) will be given here:

> It is a basic premise of this curriculum that probably the best basis for building a child's competence in [oral and written] composition and his understanding of the nature and possibilities of his native language is an exposure to literature of superior quality over a relatively long period of time. . . .
>
> Since the child ordinarily enters school with a full intuitive grasp of the sound, morphology, and syntactic repertory of the language, he may appropriately be exposed to a language and literature program which will conform to and strengthen this grasp. Until the child has a good control of basic reading skills, this program must perforce be an oral one; even after the student controls the basic reading skills, however, a large part of the program may properly continue to be oral since such oral exposure to literature may quicken his ear to the "tunes" of language, sharpen his sense of syntax, and continue to widen his oral vocabulary [pp. xv, xxii].

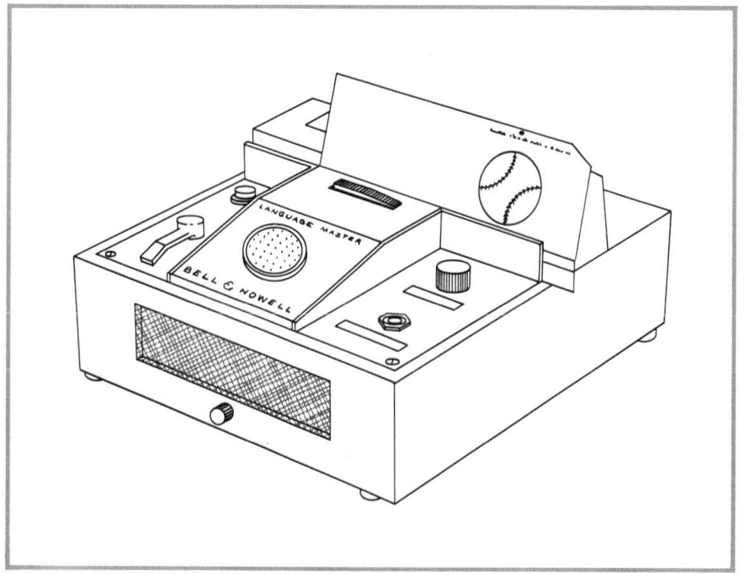

FIGURE 14-5 Bell & Howell Language Master®. (*Bell & Howell Company.*)

The suggested program for grade 1 consists of twelve units, each built around one, two, or three stories classified into nine groups, or "pseudogenres," such as folk tales, animal stories, etc. Within any one group, the stories suggested for one grade are to be taught before those assigned to the next grade because ". . . there is a definite progression from the first grade through the sixth grade units in the complexity of concepts presented. . . . But at any one level for the most part the order during any one year is left entirely to the teacher [p. x]."

The language activities suggested in each unit are called "language explorations" and, as the name implies, seem to be usable in any order. The only order required is that the story must be read aloud (and possibly reread) first. One of the animal-story units for grade 1 is based on Wanda Gag's story *Millions of Cats* (New York: Coward-McCann, 1938). The language explorations and extended activities of an oral language nature suggested for this unit are shown in Table 14-8, Table of Specifications for a Unit on *Millions of Cats*.

In formative evaluation of the unit on relational terms, the aim is to place a child in a curriculum sequence to determine what he already knows and where instruction should focus next. In the *Millions of Cats* unit there is no such sequence, and evaluation can only take the form of a "yes-no" answer to the question, Can the child do the task asked of him?—whether it be telling a story similar to the one read, or giving a word that starts like "cat." If the answer is no, the structure of the unit provides fewer guidelines for the teacher as she decides what to do next.

If the child is unable to achieve one of the objectives of this unit, the teacher has two alternatives. He can stick to the curriculum structure of the original unit and hope that the next time rhyming tasks (for example) appear in one of the units, the child will do better. In this case, the information he gets from formative evaluation is used only to guide the questions and responses he directs to individual children the next time that particular task appears in the curriculum; it is not used to sequence activities.

The other alternative is to mix the two kinds of curriculum structures and, when children are having difficulty, construct short sequential curricula for each of the *Millions of Cats* objectives and set out to teach them more in the fashion of the unit on relational words. In this case, information from formative evaluation is used to sequence future activities as in that unit.

TABLE 14-8 TABLE OF SPECIFICATIONS FOR A UNIT ON *MILLIONS OF CATS*

Cognitive domain				Affective domain
Use language				
A. Understand and produce simple language forms	*B–D. Understand and produce elaborated language*	*E, F. Use language effectively for specific purposes*	*G–I. Operate on language*	*J*
Words Understand words heard in the story (*A*-2) Action words like "trudged" Opposites like "homely" and "pretty" Synonyms like "thin" and "scraggy"	Understand *Millions of Cats* when read aloud (*B*-4, *C*-5)	Dramatize the story (*E*-8)	*Phonology* (*H*-1): 1. Construct phrases which match the intonation pattern of *Hundreds of cats, thousands of cats, millions and billions and trillions of cats.* 2. Produce words which start like "cat" 3. Produce words that rhyme with "cat," "man," "hill," etc. *Vocabulary* (*H*-2): 1. Construct metaphors: "The cat was as soft as ______." *Syntax* (*H*-3): 1. Transform a sentence from the story—e.g., "The old man walked a long, long time"—into other forms 2. Combine several small sentences into one more complex sentence *Structure larger than a sentence:* 1. Tell another story about some of the same characters (*H*-4) 2. Compare the plot of this story with others (*I*-5)	

SOURCE: Nebraska Curriculum Development Center, 1966a.

Discussion of this contrast in curriculum structure is included in the "Three Postscripts" at the end of this chapter.

Standardized achievement tests

We assume here that the aim of using standardized achievement tests is not to get some global measure of a child's standing which will have value for predicting later school success, but rather to find out whether a curriculum has been effective in improving the child's functioning in certain definite ways. It should be clear from all that has gone before in this chapter that the oral language objectives of programs for young children constitute a set of very diverse behaviors. Because these behaviors probably are affected differentially by particular preschool programs, it is extremely important to test achievement as specifically as possible—e.g., to deal specifically with pronunciation, vocabulary, or question-asking skill.

The most frequently used standardized achievement tests for evaluating the language objectives of preschool programs are the Stanford-Binet, the Peabody Picture Vocabulary Test, and the Illinois Test of Psycholinguistic Abilities. They will be discussed, along with others, under six headings. Table 14-9 gives some basic information on twelve tests in these six categories.

Table 14-9 Standardized Tests of Oral Language Skills

	Age range	*Group-individual*	*Time to administer (all untimed), minutes*	*Forms available*
Intelligence tests:				
WPPSI, three verbal subtests	4–6½ years	individual	less than 30	1
General language tests:				
ITPA	2½–9 years	individual	60–90	1
Cooperative Preschool Inventory	3–6 years	individual	15	1
Basic Concept Inventory	4–10 years	individual	20	1
Cooperative Primary Tests:				
Listening	grades 1–3	group	35 for this subtest	2 for grade 1; 2 for grades 2 and 3
Vocabulary tests:				
PPVT	2½–adult	individual	15	2
Primary Mental Abilities Test:				
Verbal Meaning subtest	K–grade 1	group	15 for this subtest	1
Language use tests:				
Torrance Tests of Creative Thinking:				
Thinking Creatively with Words	K-grade 3	individual	45	2
Speech sound tests:				
Goldman-Fristoe Test of Articulation	2 years and up	individual	10	1
Wepman Auditory Discrimination Test	5 to 8 years	individual	5–10	2
Reading readiness tests:				
Clymer-Barrett Prereading Battery	K–grade 1	group	30 for two speech sound subtests	2
Gates-MacGinitie Readiness Skills Test: two auditory subtests	K–grade 1	group	30 for two speech sound subtests	1

Intelligence tests

The Stanford-Binet (Terman & Merrill, 1960) must be rejected for our purposes because the only score is a global one which does not separate language from nonlanguage skills, much less permit differentiation within the language area itself. There is no question of the excellence of the Stanford-Binet for other purposes; it simply cannot function as a test of the achievement of particular language behaviors.

The Wechsler Preschool and Primary Scale of Intelligence (WPPSI) (Wechsler, 1963) is more useful. It yields separate verbal and performance scores. Furthermore, for each subtest within the verbal and nonverbal batteries "test age" equivalents are available from a sample of 1,200 children selected to be representative of all children in the United States according to the 1960 census. Of the six verbal subtests, three (vocabulary, similarities, and sentences) evaluate language achievement more purely than do the other three (information, arithmetic, and comprehension).

> Vocabulary: "What is a ______?" Or "What does ______ mean?" Scored: 2-1-0.
>
> Similarities: "In what way are a ______ and a ______ alike?" Or "You ride a train and you can also ride in a ______." Scored: 2-1-0.
>
> Sentence (supplementary): The child is asked to repeat a sentence 5 to 18 words long.
> Scored for omissions, transpositions, additions and substitutions.
>
> (Wechsler, 1963, Manual, pp. 50, 70–71, 83)

General language tests

The second widely used test for program evaluation is the Illinois Test of Psycholinguistic Abilities (ITPA) (Kirk, McCarthy, & Kirk, 1968). It consists of twelve subtests (formerly nine).

1. Grammatical closure (formerly "auditory vocal automatic"): A test of the child's knowledge of noun and verb inflections. "Here is a bed. Here are two ______." Similar to Berko's test of English morphology. The dialect the child speaks must be taken into account in interpreting scores.
2. Visual reception: The child is shown a picture (e.g., of a dog). It is removed, and he is shown a set of four photographs, one of which is a different dog, and asked to point to the similar picture. Because it is designed to be a test of visual decoding, not auditory memory, any tendency to say the name of the stimulus picture is to be stopped. With or without such a procedure, this subtest may still be a test of the use of language as an aid to memory.
3. Manual expression (formerly "motor encoding"): The child is shown a picture (e.g., of a hammer) and told, "Show me what you should do with this." No verbal response is required.
4. Auditory-vocal association: A kind of analogies test which taps children's knowledge of opposites. "A daddy is big; a baby is ______."
5. Visual-sequential memory (formerly "visual-motor sequential"): The examiner arranges a set of small geometric shapes in a certain order, leaves them before the child for five seconds, then mixes them up and asks the child to arrange them in the same order. As in item 2, language may be helpful in this supposedly motor subtest.
6. Verbal expression (formerly "vocal encoding"): The child is shown an object (e.g., a nail) and asked to describe it. His response is scored for the number of descriptions he gives—e.g., color, shape, use. This is the only subtest in which the child is asked to say more than one word, and even here one-word answers would be possible.
7. Auditory-sequential memory (formerly "auditory-vocal sequential"): The child is asked to repeat a series of numbers.
8. Visual-motor association: The child is shown a stimulus picture and then asked which of a set of four pictures goes with the first one (e.g., a dog and bones or a pillow and bed).
9. Auditory reception: The child is asked to say "yes" or "no" or nod or shake his head to questions such as "Do chairs eat?"
10. Visual closure (new): The child is shown a scene containing fourteen or fifteen partially concealed examples of a specified object (such as dogs) and asked to find as many as he can in thirty seconds.
11. Auditory closure (supplementary; new): A record plays words with a sound missing: "Who am I talking about? DA--Y. Who is that?"

12. Sound blending (supplementary; new): Sounds of words are spoken singly at half-second intervals—"D-OG"—and the child is asked to tell what the word is.

This test was originally designed for diagnosing language disabilities. Each subtest supposedly taps a particular psycholinguistic skill. It has been used for evaluating curricula because more appropriate tests have not been available. For such evaluation, however, a total ITPA score is no more useful than a Stanford-Binet score. But since language ages are given for each subtest, separate subtests may continue to be useful as tests of particular aspects of verbal behavior.

Two tests have recently been designed specifically for preschool program evaluation. One is the Cooperative Preschool Inventory (Caldwell, 1967). The eighty-five items constitute four subtests:

1. Items 1 to 26 test the child's personal-social responsiveness. The child is asked to give his name, age, and birth date, to name various parts of his body, and to carry out simple or complicated instructions such as raising his hand or placing an object in a verbally designated position.
2. Items 27 to 47 test the child's associative vocabulary. He is asked to tell and show how an object moves, when certain events happen, where to go for certain goods or services, and what certain people (such as teachers) do. The child is asked to provide verbal and gestural descriptions of the movement associated with certain objects (e.g., a phonograph record). He is also asked to identify seasons, to explain where certain objects might be found or what he might do in a given situation, and to describe the role that parents, teachers, or policemen perform in society.
3. Items 48 to 66 test the child's "numerical concept activation." Some questions involve simple counting exercises. Other questions require the child to demonstrate his understanding of positional relationships and of relative quantities by having him point out objects which are first, last, etc., in a series, and by asking him to judge whether one grouping of objects contains more or fewer pieces than another.
4. Items 67 to 85 test the child's "sensory concept activation." The child is asked to draw simple geometric figures, and then to associate these shapes with other objects. Questions involving objective comparisons of size, speed, or weight are also included. Finally, the child is asked to identify colors and to associate colors with certain objects.

As Kamii said in the previous chapter, this test primarily evaluates the child's knowledge of specific concepts. These concepts include some of those we have called relational words—more, fewer, first, last, etc.—but the subtest scores are a composite of such knowledge and intellectually less important concepts such as where to find a lion or how many wheels a rowboat has. For this reason, even the subtest scores are not really measures of language ability per se.

The Basic Concept Inventory (Engelmann, 1967) was designed to test the abilities taught in the Bereiter-Engelmann program. Despite the term "concept," it is entirely different in purpose and content from the Preschool Inventory:

> The Basic Concept Inventory is a broad checklist of basic concepts that are involved in new learning situations in the first grade. In a limited way, the Inventory reveals whether a child is familiar with those basic concepts (such as the concept *not*) used in explanations and instructions. It shows whether he is familiar with conventional statements and whether he can understand them. And it shows whether he can perceive the similarity of elements sequenced in a pattern—presumably an indication of whether he will be able to perceive other patterns when a teacher presents them in demonstrating a new concept.
>
> The Basic Concept Inventory is not, however, a complete checklist. It does not indicate whether a child knows colors, can list vehicles, or is able to count. Rather, the Inventory attempts to provide information about skills that are perhaps more basic, less likely to be taught, and less likely to be noticed and diagnosed by the teacher.
>
> (Engelmann, 1967, pp. 3–5)

The twenty-one items are divided into three parts:

1. Basic concepts (items 1–10): The child is asked to find the things in a picture which are described by the examiner. Different criteria for selection are required: plurals ("balls"); *not* ("white"); compound selection ("big and black"); full statements; and recognition of inadequate information.

2. Statement repetition and comprehension (items 11–18): The child is asked to repeat statements ("Puppies are baby dogs.") and then answer questions that are implied by these statements ("Are puppies baby dogs?").
3. Pattern awareness (items 19–21): The child is asked to repeat a sequence of hand motions, repeat a pattern of numbers (a digit repetition test in which the pattern aids memory if it is recognized), and blend the sounds in a word said very slowly.

Unlike any other published test for this age range, Engelmann's test is criterion-referenced (see Chap. 5). No norms are given. The assumption is that if the child has trouble with any item, the skill required in that item should be taught. "Since the skills tested are specific and relevant, we can see by examining a child's test performance precisely where his instruction has either failed or succeeded in teaching him what he should know" (Engelmann, 1967, p. 6).

Preschool educators may argue about the importance of the particular skills represented in Engelmann's test, but there can be no question of the importance of this first attempt to construct a criterion-referenced achievement test of language skills for preschool children.

The Cooperative Primary Tests for grades 1 to 3 (Educational Testing Service, 1967) includes a valuable listening subtest of fifty items which measure important skills in language comprehension. The items include words, sentences, and paragraphs (a paragraph is defined as at least two related sentences). For each item the child is asked to mark an X on the correct picture in a row of three.

I. Comprehension
   a. Identify an illustrative instance. "Mark the picture that goes best with *duck*." (Answer: a picture of a duck.)
   b. Identify an associated object or instance. "Mark the picture that goes best with *squirrel*." (Answer: a picture of an acorn.)

II. Recall: remember an element or elements; remember an element in order; or identify an omission. "Janet was supposed to erase the chalkboard and put all the books in stacks. She forgot part of her job." (Answer: a picture of books stacked and chalkboard not erased.)

III. Interpretation, evaluation, or inference. "The doctor found that Terry had a fever." (Answer: a picture of a doctor taking a boy's temperature.)

(Handbook, pp. 72–73, items 1, 2, 19, 34)

National norms are given in the form of percentile ranks, based on the scores of approximately 1,700 children in each of five groups: first grade, spring administration; second and third grades, spring administration; and second and third grades, fall administration. In addition, the percentage of children making each of the two wrong responses is given for each item, and teachers are encouraged to make an item analysis of their pupils' responses to determine which children need further instruction in each comprehension skill.

Vocabulary tests

The third widely used test is the Peabody Picture Vocabulary Test (PPVT) (Dunn, 1965). It can be used as an intelligence test, but it is recommended here simply as a test of vocabulary—probably the best individual vocabulary test available. The child is shown four pictures; the examiner says a word and asks the child to point to the correct picture. The 150 items are arranged in order of difficulty, and each child is asked only those items between his "basal" score (eight consecutive correct responses) and his ceiling (six failures out of eight consecutive responses). Mental-age equivalents are available, based on a sample of 4,012 white children in Nashville, Tennessee. The items are either nouns like "bed" or gerunds like "sitting."

The Verbal Meaning subtest of the Primary Mental Abilities Test (Thurstone, 1963) is also a picture vocabulary test. It is designed for group administration in kindergarten and grade 1. Each child has a booklet similar in format to reading-readiness tests. As he looks at a row of four pictures, the examiner says, "Put a mark on the ______"; or, "If you want to keep something cold, you put it in the ______"; or, "Mark the picture that goes with this story: Betty is hanging the doll's clothes on the clothesline." Mental-age equivalents are given for the subtest scores, but the manual does not give information about the sample of children on which the test was standardized.

Language use tests

Although the Torrance Tests of Creative Thinking (Torrance, 1966) may be basically intelligence tests (Wallach, 1968), the verbal batteries consist of seven tests of language skills not usually tapped, such as asking and hypothesizing.

1. The child is shown a picture and told to ask as many questions as he can about what's happening.
2. For the same picture, he is asked to guess possible causes of the action in the picture.
3. For the same picture, he is asked to guess the consequences of the action.
4. He is shown a picture of a toy and asked to suggest ways of improving it.
5. He is shown a picture of a container and asked to suggest unusual uses of it.
6. He is told to ask as many questions as he can about the object in item 5.
7. An improbable situation is described in words, and the child is asked to suggest its consequences.

The child's responses can be scored for fluency (the number of relevant responses); flexibility (the number of spontaneous shifts from one category of meaning to another); originality (the relative infrequency of the responses given); and elaboration (the detail and specificity of the responses). Comparison data are available for specific groups of children and adults, but so far, with the exception of one rural school in Wisconsin, all the comparisons are with children beyond the primary grades.

Speech-sound tests

Speech-sound tests are of two kinds: tests of production, or "articulation," and tests of reception, or "discrimination."

The Goldman-Fristoe Test of Articulation (Goldman & Fristoe, 1969) has two subtests:

1. Sounds-in-words: As the child names thirty-six pictures, the examiner obtains information on the child's pronunciation of the most important speech sounds in initial, medial, and final position.
2. Sounds-in-sentences: The examiner tells two stories. As the child retells the stories, the examiner records information about the child's pronunciation in sequential speech.

This is a new test currently being used in a large national survey of 30,000 children. Presumably, comparative information will be available when this survey is completed.

The classic test of speech-sound discrimination has been the Wepman Auditory Descrimination Test (Wepman, 1958). It consists of forty pairs of words, each a consonant-vowel-consonant sequence of sounds. The examiner teaches the child to say whether the two words are the same or different and then administers the test with the child's back turned so that he must judge by sound alone. In interpreting the results, a distinction must be made between the child's failure to make accurate judgments about sounds which he does in fact make himself and failure involving sounds which are not part of his own dialect. Social-class differences in Wepman scores are produced largely by the items which test discrimination of final sounds.

As we pointed out earlier, this test evaluates a metalinguistic skill of evaluating (rather than simply comprehending or producing) speech sounds. It is not suitable for children under 5. For children below that age, a test on which they demonstrate their knowledge by pointing to pictures is needed. No published standardized test is now available for this purpose. But copies of both the Stern (1968a) and the Pronovost tests (undated) can be obtained from the authors.

Reading-readiness tests

Reading-readiness tests deserve mention, because some of the subtests provide short standardized tests of specific language skills for which other standardized tests are not available.

The Clymer-Barrett Prereading Battery (Clymer & Barrett, 1968) has two subtests which test the child's ability to evaluate initial and final sounds as the same or different. In a row there are one picture and then three more.

ball / horn comb boy

The teacher pronounces the words, and the child is asked to mark the picture whose name begins with the same sound as the first name does.

The Gates-MacGinitie Readiness Skills Test (Gates & MacGinitie, 1968) has a subtest on auditory discrimination. Each item is a pair of pictures with similar sounding names: The teacher says both names—"money-monkey." Then she repeats one of the names and asks the child to make an X across that picture. In another subtest, the child is asked to make auditory blends. The teacher says the name of one of three pictures with a one-second pause between parts of the word: "RAB-BIT." The child puts an X on the correct picture.

Only two new reading-readiness tests are mentioned here. See the Appendix in Bond and Tinker (1967) for listings of other reading-readiness tests.

Three postscripts

At this point three postscripts are in order: on objectives, the sequencing of instruction, and evaluation.

Postscript on objectives

While we evaluate verbal behavior, we are almost always really interested in the intellectual development (or cognitive structure) that such behavior presumably expresses or indicates. In making an inference from behavior to cognitive structures we may be misled. For example:

> Recently, several kindergarten teachers, who had been introduced to Piaget's theory that children of five or six are likely to be in a transitional state between intuitive and operational thought, attempted to gather evidence about the kinds of thinking their children revealed. Coming from privileged homes, these youngsters were verbally facile, competent in managing most of their own affairs, and generally alert to their environment.
>
> At the beginning of the kindergarten year, all of one group of eighteen children were able to count, some of them to one thousand. Yet, the teacher discovered none of them had any stable notion of number beyond three. Asked to select four pebbles to match those held by the teacher, they scooped up as many as twelve. Only one child was ingenious enough to count off the number the teacher had with her own four fingers, and then apply the same four fingers to her pile of pebbles.
>
> (Almy, 1964, p. 396)

Concern for (and evaluation of) specific language objectives in early childhood education must be combined with concern for (and evaluation of) cognitive development, as described in Kamii's chapter. See Piaget (1968) for further discussion of this point of view on the relation between language and cognition; and see Glick (1968) on changes in superficial behavior versus changes in cognitive functioning.

Postscript on sequencing instruction

It is natural to assume that the more logically ordered unit on relational words is a more effective way to sequence the curriculum than the seemingly haphazard structure represented by *Millions of Cats*. But it is by no means certain that this is indeed so for all kinds of objectives.

Gagné, who developed the concept of learning hierarchies, now distinguishes between intellectual skills and verbalizable knowledge and reports research which suggests that "a learner may acquire certain intellectual skills from a presentation that is quite disorganized when viewed as a sequence of verbalizable knowledge"

(Gagné, 1968, p. 4). Oral language objectives are a mixture of intellectual skills (from the discrimination of speech sounds to the ability to shift to the listener's perspective) and verbalizable knowledge (word meanings), primarily the former.

The difference in structure between the two units also represents the controversy between part-task and whole-task instructional procedures.

> Educators who have been influenced by the programed-instruction movement take it as self-evident that the best way to teach a complex skill is to analyze it into component subskills and subconcepts, then teach each of these in turn. Cast in different language such an approach is a part-task method, to be contrasted with the whole-task method in which the student is required to perform the terminal behavior as best he can from the very beginning of training.
>
> (Anderson, 1968, p. 207)

In selecting among these two alternatives, one should note that all the oral language learning that takes place before the child goes to school (whether to preschool, kindergarten, or first grade) takes place on a whole-task basis. The child is surrounded by examples of mature speech behavior and is encouraged to participate as best he can from the very beginning. Somehow, if he is so surrounded and if he does have the chance to participate, each child takes from the environment what he needs to build his own language system. Whatever environmental assistance he gets during this process, it is clear that he never gets sequential tuition based on an analysis of component skills. When a richly supplied cafeteria is available from the beginning, no carefully prescribed diet is necessary. In the case of oral language objectives there is special justification, therefore, for the argument that the best way to continue instruction in school is on this whole-task basis. And as Anderson (1968) makes clear, the evidence for selection between these two instructional approaches is by no means conclusive in other content areas either.

It may be that the kind of structure in the unit on relational words represents the knowledge the effective teacher needs rather than a flowchart of teaching plans. This is what Resnick, herself also in the Gagné tradition, seems to suggest:

> A formal curriculum sequence has no necessary implications for the style of classroom organization. The sequence can be used, as in Bereiter and Engelmann's (1966) programs for the disadvantaged, in a manner that requires the participation of all children in all drills with little room for choice on the part of either child or teacher. However, it can be equally well used in a classroom whose organization is free and open as in the Montessori model or some modification of the progressive nursery school. In the latter situations, the child is free to move within the room, to choose his own activities within certain limitations, and to spend as long as he wishes at a given task. The curriculum sequence need not be evident to him as a constraint. However, the teacher can use the sequence to keep careful track of each child and how he is progressing through the hierarchy of skills.
>
> (Resnick, 1967, p. 14)

In other words, a careful understanding of learning hierarchies may be more important for planning evaluation than for sequencing instruction.

Postscript on evaluation

Of all aspects of human behavior, speech is probably the most susceptible to subtle situational influences. This is especially true of the influences inherent in any kind of testing situation. And it is especially true for subjects who are at any social disadvantage vis-à-vis the tester—e.g., child to adult, minority group member to majority group member, outsider to formal bureaucratic institution.

Hodges, McCandless, and Spicker report that "in the authors' observations of the administration of the ITPA, the subtests of Vocal and Motor Encoding are the most susceptible to examiner influence and are therefore more likely to show depressed scores for the shy, withdrawn child than for the more outgoing child" (Hodges et al., 1967, p. 86). More generally, Pasamanick and Knobloch (1955) and Resnick, Weld, and Lally

(1969) report evidence that the verbal expressiveness of lower-class Negro 2-year-olds is artificially depressed in testing situations. And a recent report on human deprivation prepared for the National Institute of Child Health and Development cautions that "a great deal of the testing of children's verbal abilities has taken place in the same environment as the school situation itself, and such tests therefore register the child's reaction to the social context primarily and only secondarily his actual verbal skills" (Birren & Hess, 1968, p. 135). While tests may seem a more valid evaluation procedure than observation, it is important to include in any complete evaluation plan observations of children in situations natural in their own culture.

REFERENCES

Almy, M. Wishful thinking about children's thinking? In W. A. Fullagar, H. G. Lewis, & C. F. Cumbee (Eds.), *Readings for educational psychology.* New York: Crowell, 1964. Pp. 389–401.

Anderson, R. C. Part-task versus whole-task procedures for teaching a problem-solving skill to first graders. *Journal of Educational Psychology,* 1968, **59,** 207–214.

Baratz, J. A bi-dialectal task for determining language proficiency in economically disadvantaged Negro children. *Child Development,* 1969, **40,** 889–901.

Bellugi-Klima, U. Evaluating the young child's language development. Unpublished paper available through National Laboratory on Early Childhood Education, Education Research Information Center (ERIC), Urbana, Illinois, 1968.

Bereiter, C., Case, R., & Anderson, V. Steps toward full intellectual functioning. *Journal of Research and Development in Education,* 1968, **1,** 70–79.

Bereiter, C., & Engelmann, S. *Teaching disadvantaged children in the preschool.* Englewood Cliffs, N.J.: Prentice-Hall, 1966.

Bereiter, C., & Engelmann, S. An academically oriented preschool for disadvantaged children: Results from the initial experimental group. In D. W. Brison & J. Hill (Eds.), *Psychology and early childhood education.* (Monogr. Ser. No. 4.) Toronto: Ontario Institute for Studies in Education, 1968. Pp. 17–36.

Bereiter, C., & Engelmann, S. *Language learning activities for the disadvantaged child.* New York: Anti-Defamation League, undated.

Berko, J. The child's learning of English morphology. *Word,* 1958, **14,** 150–177. [Republished: In S. Saporta (Ed.), *Psycholinguistics.* New York: Holt, Rinehart and Winston, 1961. Pp. 359–375.]

Birren, J. E., & Hess, R. Influence of biological, psychological and social deprivations upon learning and performance. In *Perspectives on human deprivation: Biological, psychological, and social.* Washington, D.C.: National Institute of Child Health and Development, 1968. Pp. 91–183.

Blank, M., & Solomon, F. A tutorial language program to develop abstract thinking in socially disadvantaged preschool children. *Child Development,* 1968, **39,** 379–389.

Blank, M., & Solomon, F. How shall the disadvantaged be taught? *Child Development,* 1969, **40,** 47–61.

Bond, G. L., & Tinker, M. A. *Reading difficulties: Their diagnosis and correction.* New York: Appleton-Century-Crofts, 1967.

Bronson, M. Comprehension and production of function words. Unpublished term paper, Harvard University, Graduate School of Education, 1969.

Brown, R., & Fraser, C. The acquisition of syntax. In U. Bellugi & R. Brown (Eds.), The acquisition of language. *Monographs of the Society for Research in Child Development,* 1964, **29**(1), 43–79.

Caldwell, B. M. *Preschool inventory.* Princeton, N.J.: Educational Testing Service, 1967.

Cazden, C. B. The acquisition of noun and verb inflections. *Child Development,* 1968, **39,** 433–448.

Central Advisory Council for Education. *Children and their primary schools.* (Plowden Rep.) Vol. 1. London: H. M. Stationery Office, 1967.

Clymer, T., & Barrett, T. C. *Clymer-Barrett Prereading Battery.* Princeton, N.J.: Personnel Press, 1968.

Cromer, R. F. The development of temporal reference during the acquisition of language. Unpublished doctoral dissertation, Harvard University, 1968.

Dawe, H. C. A study of the effect of an educational program upon language development and related mental functions in young children. *Journal of Experimental Education,* 1942, **11,** 200–209.

De Hirsch, K., Jansky, J. J., & Langford, W. S. *Predicting reading failure.* New York: Harper & Row, 1966.

Dixon, J. *Growth through English: A report based on the Dartmouth Seminar, 1966.* Reading, Eng.: National Association for the Teaching of English, 1967. (Also available from the National Council of Teachers of English, Champaign, Ill.)

Dunn, L. M. *Peabody Picture Vocabulary Test.* Minneapolis: American Guidance Service, 1965.

Educational Testing Service. Cooperative Primary Tests. Princeton, N.J.: ETS, 1967.

Educational Testing Service. Disadvantaged children and their first school experiences. Interim Report, OEO Contract No. 4206. Princeton, N.J.: ETS, 1968.

Educational Testing Service. *Let's look at first graders.* Princeton, N.J.: ETS, 1965.

Engelmann, S. *The Basic Concept Inventory.* Chicago: Follett, 1967.

Flavell, J. H., in collaboration with Botkin, P. T., Fry, C. L., Jr., Wright, J. W., and Jarvis, P. E. *The development of role-taking and communication skills in children.* New York: Wiley, 1968.

Fraser, C., Bellugi, U., & Brown, R. Control of grammar in imitation, comprehension and production. *Journal of Verbal Learning and Verbal Behavior,* 1963, **2,** 121–135.

Furth, H. *Thinking without language: Psychological implications of deafness.* New York: Free Press, 1966.

Gagné, R. M. Learning hierarchies. (Paper presented at the meeting of the American Psychological Association, Division 15, San Francisco, August 1968.) *Educational Psychologist,* 1968, **6**(1), 1–9.

Gahagan, G. A., & Gahagan, D. M. Paired-associate learning as a partial validation of a language development program. *Child Development,* 1968, **39,** 1119–1131.

Gates, A. I., & MacGinitie, W. H. *Gates-MacGinitie Readiness Skills Test.* New York: Teachers College Press, 1968.

Glick, J. Some problems in the evaluation of preschool intervention programs. In R. D. Hess & R. M. Bear (Eds.), *Early education.* Chicago: Aldine, 1968. Pp. 215–221.

Goldman, R., & Fristoe, M. *The Goldman-Fristoe Test of Articulation.* Circle Pines, Minn.: American Guidance Service, 1969.

Gotkin, L. G. *Language Lotto.* New York: Appleton-Century-Crofts, 1966.

Gotkin, L. G. Simon Says: A new look at an old game. Unpublished manuscript, Institute for Developmental Studies, New York University, undated.

Gray, S. W., Klaus, R. A., Miller, J. O., & Forrester, B. J. *Before first grade.* New York: Teachers College Press, 1966.

Hawkins, P. R. Social class, the nominal group and reference. *Language and Speech,* 1969, **12,** 125–135.

Henry, N. B. (Ed.) *Early childhood education: The forty-sixth yearbook of the National Society for the Study of Education.* Part II. Chicago: University of Chicago Press, 1947.

Hertzig, M. E., Birch, H. G., Thomas, A., & Mendez, O. A. Class and ethnic differences in the responsiveness of preschool children to cognitive demands. *Monographs of the Society for Research in Child Development,* 1968, **33** (1, Whole No. 117).

Hodges, W. L., McCandless, B. R., & Spicker, H. H. The development and evaluation of a diagnostically based curriculum for preschool psycho-socially deprived children. Final Report, Project No. 5-0350, U.S. Department of Health, Education, and Welfare, 1967.

Hunt, J. McV. Revisiting Montessori. (Intro.) In M. Montessori, *The Montessori method.* New York: Schocken, 1964. [Republished: In J. L. Frost (Ed.), *Early childhood education rediscovered.* New York: Holt, Rinehart and Winston, 1968. Pp. 102–127.]

Inhelder, B., Bovet, M., Sinclair, H., & Smock, C. D. On cognitive development. *American Psychologist,* 1966, **21,** 160–164.

Isaacs, S. *Intellectual growth in young children.* London: Routledge, 1930. (Republished: New York, Schocken, 1966.)

Jensen, A. R., & Rohwer, W. D., Jr. Syntactical mediation of serial and paired-associate learning as a function of age. *Child Development*, 1965, **36,** 601–608.

John, V. Communicative competence of low-income children: Assumptions and programs. Report to the Ford Foundation, Language Development Study Group, 1967.

John, V. P., & Goldstein, L. S. The social context of language acquisition. *Merrill-Palmer Quarterly*, 1964, **10,** 265–275.

John, V., Horner, V., & Berney, T. Story re-telling. In H. Levin (Ed.), *Basic studies in reading.* New York: Harper & Row, in press.

Kamii, C. K., & Radin, N. L. A framework for a preschool curriculum based on Piaget's theory. In I. J. Athey & D. O. Rubadeau (Eds.), *Educational implications of Piaget's theory: A book of readings.* Waltham, Mass.: Ginn-Blaisdell, 1970, 89–100.

Kelkar, A. R. Language: Linguistics: The applications. *Language Sciences*, 1969, No. 4, pp. 11–13.

Kirk, S. A., McCarthy, J. J., & Kirk, W. D. *The Illinois Test of Psycholinguistic Abilities.* (Rev. ed.) Urbana, Ill.: University of Illinois Press, 1968.

Klaus, R. A., & Gray, S. W. The early training project for disadvantaged children: A report after five years. *Monographs of the Society for Research in Child Development*, 1968, **33** (4, Whole No. 120).

Klima, E. S., & Bellugi, U. Syntactic regularities in the speech of children. In J. Lyons & R. J. Wales (Eds.), *Psycholinguistics papers.* Edinburgh: University Press, 1966. Pp. 183–208.

Kohlberg, L., Yaeger, J., & Hjertholm, E. The development of private speech: Four studies and a review of theory. *Child Development*, 1968, **39,** 691–736.

Krathwohl, D. R., Bloom, B. S., & Masia, B. B. *Taxonomy of educational objectives: The classification of educational goals.* Handbook 2. *Affective domain.* New York: McKay, 1964.

Labov, W., Cohen, P., Robins, C., & Lewis, J. A study of the non-standard English of Negro and Puerto Rican speakers in New York City. Vol. 1, Phonological and grammatical analysis; vol. 2, The use of language in the speech community. Final Report of Coop. Res. Proj. No. 3288, Columbia University, 1968. To be distributed through Education Research Information Center (ERIC), Urbana, Illinois.

Law, N. *What are nursery schools for?* Washington, D.C.: Association for Childhood Education International and National Association for the Education of Young Children, 1963–1964.

Lee, L. L. *Northwestern Syntax Screening Test.* Evanston, Ill.: Northwestern University Press, 1969.

Lesser, G. S., Fifer, G., & Clark, D. H. Mental abilities of children in different social and cultural groups. *Monographs of the Society for Research in Child Development*, 1965, **30** (4, Whole No. 102).

Mackay, D., & Thompson, B. *The initial teaching of reading and writing: Some notes toward a theory of literacy.* (Programme in Linguistics and English Teaching, Pap. No. 3) London: University College and Longmans, Green, 1968.

Meier, J. H. Innovations in assessing the disadvantaged child's potential. In J. Hellmuth (Ed.), *Disadvantaged child.* Vol. 1. Seattle: Special Child Publications, 1967. Pp. 173–199.

Meier, J. H., Nimnicht, G., & McAfee, O. An autotelic responsive environment nursery school for deprived children. In J. Hellmuth (Ed.), *Disadvantaged child.* Vol. 2. Seattle: Special Child Publications, 1968. Pp. 299–398.

Melton, R. S., et al. *Cognitive growth in preschool children.* (Res. Memo. 68-13) Princeton, N.J.: Educational Testing Service, 1968.

Minuchin, P., & Biber, B. A child development approach to language in the preschool disadvantaged child. In M. A. Brottman (Ed.), Language remediation for the disadvantaged preschool child. *Monographs of the Society for Research in Child Development*, 1968, **33**(8), 10–18.

Moffett, J. *An integrated curriculum in the language arts, K-12.* Boston: Houghton Mifflin, 1968. (a)

Moffett, J. *Teaching the universe of discourse.* Boston: Houghton Mifflin, 1968. (b)

Montessori, M. *The Montessori method.* (Frederick A. Stokes, 1912.) Reprinted Cambridge, Mass.: Robert Bentley, 1965.

Mosher, F. A., & Hornsby, J. R. On asking questions. In J. S. Bruner, R. R. Olver, & P. M. Greenfield (Eds.), *Studies in cognitive growth.* New York: Wiley, 1966. Pp. 86–102.

National Council of Teachers of English. *Nonstandard dialect.* Champaign, Ill.: NCTE, 1968.

Nebraska Curriculum Development Center. *A curriculum for English: Grade 1.* Lincoln, Nebr.: University of Nebraska Press, 1966. (a)

Nebraska Curriculum Development Center. *A curriculum for English: Language explorations for the elementary grades.* Lincoln, Nebr.: University of Nebraska Press, 1966. (b)

Nimnicht, G., Meier, J. H., & McAfee, O. The new nursery school. New York: General Learning, 1969.

Osborn, J. Teaching a teaching language to disadvantaged children. In M. A. Brottman (Ed.), Language remediation for the disadvantaged preschool child. *Monographs of the Society for Research in Child Development,* 1968, **33**(8), 36–48.

Osser, H. The syntactic structures of five-year-old culturally deprived children. Paper presented at the annual meeting of the Eastern Psychological Association, New York, April 1966.

Osser, H., Wang, M. D., & Zaid, F. The young child's ability to imitate and comprehend speech: A comparison of two subcultural groups. *Child Development,* 1969, **40,** 1063–1075.

Pasamanick, B., & Knobloch, H. Early language behavior in Negro children and the testing of intelligence. *Journal of Abnormal and Social Psychology,* 1955, **50,** 401–402.

Piaget, J. *Judgment and reasoning in the child.* Paterson, N.J.: Littlefield, Adams, 1959.

Piaget, J. *Six psychological studies.* New York: Random House, 1968.

Pronovost, W. *The Boston University Speech Sound Discrimination Picture Test.* Boston: Speech and Hearing Center, Boston University, undated.

Resnick, L. B. Design of an early learning curriculum. Working Paper No. 16, Learning R & D Center, University of Pittsburgh, 1967.

Resnick, M. B., Weld, G. L., & Lally, J. R. Verbalizations of environmentally deprived two-year-olds as a function of the presence of a tester in a standardized test situation. Paper presented at the meeting of the American Educational Research Association, Los Angeles, February 1969.

Rohwer, W. D., Jr. Constraint, syntax and meaning in paired-associate learning. *Journal of Verbal Learning and Verbal Behavior,* 1966, **5,** 541–547.

Sapon, S. Operant studies in the expansion and refinement of verbal behavior in disadvantaged children. Final Report of Contract no. OEO-2401. Rochester, New York: University of Rochester Bookstore. January 1969.

Sigel, I. E., Anderson, L. M., & Shapiro, H. Categorization behavior of lower- and middle-class Negro preschool children: Differences in dealing with representation of familiar objects. *Journal of Negro Education,* 1966, **35,** 218–229.

Slobin, D. I. (Ed.) *A field manual for cross-cultural study of the acquisition of communicative competence.* (2nd draft) Berkeley, Calif.: University of California, 1967.

Smilansky, S. *The effects of sociodramatic play on disadvantaged preschool children.* New York: Wiley, 1968.

Sonquist, H., Kamii, C., & Derman, L. A Piaget-derived preschool curriculum. In I. J. Athey & D. O. Rubadeau (Eds.), *Educational implications of Piaget's theory: A book of readings.* Waltham, Mass.: Ginn-Blaisdell, 1970.

Stern, C. Children's Auditory Discrimination Inventory. Unpublished test, University of California at Los Angeles, 1968. (a)

Stern, C. Echoic Response Inventory for Children. Unpublished test, University of California at Los Angeles, 1968. (b)

Stern, C. Evaluating language curricula for preschool children. In M. A. Brottman (Ed.), Language remediation for the disadvantaged preschool child. *Monographs of the Society for Research in Child Development,* 1968, **33**(8), 49–61. (c)

Stern, C. Expressive Vocabulary Inventory for Children. Unpublished test, University of California at Los Angeles, 1968. (d)

Stern, C. Parallel Sentence Production Test. Unpublished test, University of California at Los Angeles, 1968. (e)

Terman, L. M., & Merrill, M. A. *Stanford-Binet Intelligence Scale.* Boston: Houghton Mifflin, 1960.

Thurstone, T. G. *Primary Mental Abilities Test.* (Rev. ed.) Chicago: Science Research Associates, 1963.

Torrance, E. P. *Torrance Tests of Creative Thinking.* Princeton, N.J.: Personnel Press, 1966.

U.S. Office of Economic Opportunity. *Head Start child development programs: A manual of policies and instructions.* Washington, D.C.: USOEO, 1967.

Vygotsky, L. S. *Thought and language.* Cambridge, Mass.: M.I.T. Press, 1962.

Wallach, M. A. Review of *Torrance Tests of Creative Thinking. American Educational Research Journal*, 1968, **5,** 272–281.

Watts, A. R. *The language and mental development of children.* London: Harrap, 1944.

Wechsler, D. *Wechsler Preschool and Primary Scale of Intelligence.* New York: Psychological Corporation, 1963.

Weikart, D. P. (Ed.) *Preschool intervention: A preliminary report of the Perry Preschool Project.* Ann Arbor, Mich.: Campus Publications, 1967.

Wepman, J. *Auditory Discrimination Test.* Chicago: Language Research Associates, 1958.

Whipple, G. M. (Ed.) *Preschool and parent education: The Twenty-eighth yearbook of the National Society for the Study of Education.* Chicago: University of Chicago Press, 1929.

White, S. H. Evidence for a hierarchical arrangement of learning processes. *Advances in Child Development and Behavior*, 1965, **2,** 187–220.

Woodcock, L. P. *When children first say why, because, if.* New York: Bank Street Publications, undated.

15

Evaluation of Learning in

The Language Arts

WALTER J. MOORE

University of Illinois
Urbana, Illinois

LARRY D. KENNEDY

Illinois State University at Normal
Normal, Illinois

Walter J. Moore received the Bachelor of Arts degree from Hamilton College, the Master of Arts degree in Elementary Education from Syracuse University, and the Doctor of Philosophy degree in Educational Psychology from Syracuse University. In addition, he did graduate and postdoctoral work at Stanford University, Teachers College of Columbia University, and the University of Chicago. He has taught elementary and junior and senior high school in public schools in New York and Illinois, has held teaching and administrative posts at the Laboratory Schools of the University of Chicago, and is presently devoting time to the Washington School Project at the University of Illinois. In addition to acting as Coordinator of the University of Illinois' Interests in this experimental school project, he teaches language arts to undergraduates and graduate students at Illinois. His research interests are concerned with the evaluation of written composition of elementary school children. His most recent book, The Annotated Index to Elementary English, 1924–1967, *is currently undergoing revision.*

Larry Kennedy received the Bachelor of Science degree in Education from Ball State University, the Master of Arts degree in English from Ball State University, and the Doctor of Education degree in Elementary Education from the University of Illinois. He has taught elementary and junior and senior high school English, and has served as a language arts consultant to public schools in the State of Illinois. He is currently Assistant Professor of Education at Illinois State University. His primary interests in English education are concerned with the development of English education programs at the undergraduate level and with the development of in-service training programs for elementary and secondary school teachers.

Contents

15

Evaluation of Learning in The Language Arts

Objectives of instruction in the language arts

What is the situation in the language arts curriculum today and what purposes or goals are being sought in programs designed for grades K to 6? These are questions of grave importance, and they must be faced squarely and conscientiously. Clearly, the tasks confronting teachers who devise language arts programs today are many.

The responsibilities of the language arts teacher at the elementary school level are, admittedly, broad and diverse. And while it is true that such responsibilities require a wide range of teaching skills in a variety of subject areas, it is true also that there is a common thread of English skills which runs through the fabric of all subject areas. The National Council of Teachers of English (1968), in a statement entitled "The Workload of the Elementary School Teacher," notes that ". . . over half of the teaching time in the elementary school is related to one or another aspect of English. . . ." According to the article, English includes ". . . development of language skills (reading, writing, listening, and speaking), the study of literature, and the exploration of the nature of language [p. 224]."

While wording may differ slightly from one source to another, there appears to be essential agreement among English educators and elementary curriculum specialists on the general goals of English instruction. Tiedt and Tiedt (1967, p. 5), for example, state that the general aims for the elementary school English program should include the ability

1. To understand the English language and how it works
2. To communicate fluently and clearly in written and oral forms
3. To decode and encode English easily
4. To know and appreciate our literary heritage of prose and poetry

Programs in the elementary schools have not generally been identified as "English," however. Rather, the rubric "language arts" has been used.

TABLE 15-1 TABLE OF SPECIFICATIONS FOR THE LANGUAGE ARTS (K TO 6)

	BEHAVIORS																			
	Cognitive														*Affective*					
	A.0 Knowledge					*B.0 Comprehension*		*C.0 Analysis*			*D.0 Application*		*E.0 Evaluation*		*F.0 Attitudes*		*G.0 Reception*		*H.0 Participation*	
	Terminology	*Specific facts*	*Conventions*	*Classifications and categories*	*Criteria*	*Translation*	*Interpretation*	*Elements*	*Relationships*	*Organizational principles*	*Functional application*	*Expressive application*	*Objective evaluation*	*Subjective evaluation*	*Acceptance*	*Appreciation*	*Awareness*	*Selected attention*	*Willing participation*	*Enjoyment of participation*
CONTENT AND SKILLS	*A.1*	*A.2*	*A.3*	*A.4*	*A.5*	*B.1*	*B.2*	*C.1*	*C.2*	*C.3*	*D.1*	*D.2*	*E.1*	*E.2*	*F.1*	*F.2*	*G.1*	*G.2*	*H.1*	*H.2*
1.0 *Language*																				
1.1 Nature of language																				
1.2 History of language																				
1.3 Structure of language																				
1.31 Language sounds																				
1.32 Word forms																				
1.33 Word arrangement																				
1.4 Vocabulary																				
1.41 History of words																				
1.42 Word meanings																				
1.43 Dictionary making																				

1.5 Dialects																				
1.6 Usage																				
1.7 Spelling																				
2.0 *Language skills*																				
2.1 Listening																				
2.11 Basic listening skills																				
2.12 Listening activity																				
2.2 Speaking																				
2.21 Basic speaking skills																				
2.22 Speaking activity																				
2.3 Reading																				
2.31 Basic reading skills																				
2.32 Reading activity																				
2.4 Writing																				
2.41 Basic writing skills																				
2.42 Writing activity																				
3.0 *Literature*																				
3.1 Poetry																				
3.2 Prose																				

This term traditionally has implied that elementary school teachers are concerned with the development of language *skills*, as opposed to the more formal, content-centered approach of the secondary schools. In recent years, however, linguistics has offered insights into the nature of language which have led to the inclusion of a language content base within language skill instruction. It is quite probably more accurate to state that the content has always been in the elementary school language arts program, since skill development depends upon an underlying content base. But the important considerations for elementary school language arts programs are that the hitherto "submerged" language content has been raised to a level of respectability and that language content instruction as well as language skill development now go hand in hand in contemporary language arts programs.

Being responsible for teaching the language arts in today's elementary schools means, then, that a teacher is expected to advance pupils' skills in such areas as reading, speaking, writing, punctuation, capitalization, handwriting, and listening. In addition, considerably more time and effort should be devoted to developing a knowledge of the nature of language and literature. Such efforts should not, however, be considered as supplemental to an ongoing language arts program.

The interrelatedness of certain elements in the language arts complex is so close as to be confusing at times. For example, reading and listening have much in common. Training in one seems to support the other, but competence in one does not necessarily provide competence in the other. Some good readers are poor listeners, and some good listeners are poor readers. Speaking and reading are bound together also. Research has demonstrated the effects of oral language deprivation upon early school success in reading. And writing is profoundly affected by a child's listening, speaking, and reading skills. Although there is by no means universal agreement about the wisdom of combining such seemingly diverse skills as listening, speaking, reading, and writing into a communication structure, there is agreement that the ties binding these skills are stronger than the forces which would have them taught separately.

Goals for an area as broad and diverse as the language arts have not, of course, come forth full-bloom. They have developed, rather, as a result of considerable discussion and conflict over a period of years. In the past fifteen years in particular, attempts to identify goals for the language arts have been fraught with difficulties. Therefore, any statement of current goals should be examined against the recent background of shifting elementary curriculum emphases as well as the shifting emphases regarding the definition of English itself.

Curriculum trends in the language arts

Elementary Evaluative Criteria (Baker, 1954) described criteria designed to evaluate the program of a six- or eight-year educational curriculum. With regard to the language arts specifically, the report outlined the scope:

> The language arts include the instructional areas of reading, oral and written language, spelling, and handwriting. All of these areas direct instruction toward the development of communication skills, improvement of thinking abilities, and effective application as tool subjects essential for success in the whole elementary school program [p. 42].

It should be noted that listening was not included as a significant instructional area within the language arts in *Elementary Evaluative Criteria*. Considerably more emphasis was to be given to its role in later years. The work of Strickland (1962), Loban (1966), and others emphasized the significance of speech development in the elementary school child. Insights from linguistics also forwarded the idea that language is, first and foremost, speech, and that, as such, considerably more care and attention should be devoted to the development of linguistic fluency.

Elementary School Objectives (Kearney, 1953)

appeared in this same period of time. The report covered a wide variety of means by which man communicates. It emphasized the mechanical aspects and skills involved in reading, writing, composition, correct usage, spelling, punctuation, speaking, and listening.

The significance of *Elementary School Objectives* resided, however, in the identification of student behavioral patterns for the language arts: (1) knowledge and understanding, (2) skills and competences, (3) attitudes and interests, and (4) patterns of action. While the report did not specify the means by which these behavioral patterns were to be evaluated, it did set the stage for subsequent developments by removing the language arts from the limbo of quasi-behavioral objectives and terminology.

The period of the 1950s witnessed also the creation of the Commission on the English Curriculum of the National Council of Teachers of English. The commission's publications included *Language Arts for Today's Children* (National Council of Teachers of English, Commission on the English Curriculum, 1954). This book was significant because it gave official endorsement to a quartet of communication skills; that is, the commission recommended that the language arts curriculum at the elementary school level consist of listening, speaking, reading, and writing.

Definitional trends in the language arts

The Basic Issues Conference of 1959 (National Council of Teachers of English, 1959) succeeded in identifying issues confronting teachers of English, regardless of teaching level. The first issue discussed was "What is 'English'?" The report stated:

> We agree generally that English composition, language, and literature are within our province, but we are uncertain whether our boundaries should include world literature in translation, public speaking, journalism, listening, remedial reading, and general academic orientation. . . . [p. 7]

The significance of this statement resided in its attempt to redefine the boundaries of English instruction by suggesting a tripartite structure: (1) language, (2) composition, and (3) literature. And, because of the fundamental nature of this issue, it was followed by a question of paramount importance:

> Can basic programs in English be devised that are sequential and cumulative from the kindergarten through the graduate school? Can agreement be reached upon a body of knowledge and set of skills as standard at certain points in the curriculum, making due allowances for flexibility of planning, individual differences, and patterns of growth? [p. 7]

This question, in particular, summarizes the curriculum problems with which the language arts are faced today. As the report noted, ". . . unless we can find an answer to it, we must resign ourselves to an unhappy future in which the present curricular disorder persists and the whole liberal character of English continues to disintegrate and lose its character [p. 7]."

The impact of the Basic Issues Conference was felt in the circles of English education, and in 1961 the U.S. Office of Education established Project English, which in its three-year life was to have widespread influence upon English and language arts instruction at the elementary and secondary school levels. Project English funded many projects in basic and applied research, established curriculum centers and demonstration centers, and sponsored a wide assortment of conferences which focused upon research in English and the teaching of English.

Significantly, Project English stirred the thinking and the imagination of classroom teachers, as well as that of university professors. It gave notice that English was no longer to be the vague collection of skills, content, and social amenities it had once been. The range of English curriculum responsibilities was redefined, and the curriculum centers provided classroom teachers with outstanding units on a variety of grade levels.

In 1961, the National Council of Teachers of English issued *The National Interest and the*

Teaching of English (National Council of Teachers of English, Committee on National Interest, 1961). Three years later, the council published *The National Interest and the Continuing Education of Teachers of English* (1964). Both publications drew attention to the value of English instruction and clarified the goals of English education.

In 1965, the College Entrance Examination Board's Commission on English issued its report *Freedom and Discipline in English.* This document culminated five years of study, discussion, experimentation, and synthesis in which the commission agreed upon what it believed to be a consensus among teachers of English on the essential characteristics of English. The commission noted that "The scope of the English program [should] be defined as the study of language, literature, and composition, written and oral, and that such matters not clearly related to such study [should] be excluded from it [p. 13]."

Potentially, this statement aimed at "dropping" certain extraneous content such as social conduct and telephone manners from the English curriculum. The ultimate significance, however, lay in the statement of scope. The commission supported the findings of the Basic Issues Conference of 1959 and, in doing so, provided the base for the development of new programs in English.

Throughout the 1960s, insights from linguistics came into elementary and secondary school programs. While the debate over the ultimate value of such knowledge seems likely to be prolonged, linguistics did have a definite impact upon English instruction. Insights into the nature of grammar, the nature of language, language history, usage, dialect study, etc., served as revitalizing agents for language study at all levels. It should be noted, however, that considerable disagreement existed at both the university and the classroom level about the ultimate benefits of linguistics as it might be applied to classroom programs. Such concern was justified if linguistics offered only new dogmatic perspectives on language to replace an older and different dogmatism. Whatever the eventual outcome, linguistics in English instruction represented a major step in the attempts to redefine the discipline more rigorously and to revitalize the quality of English teaching.

During late August and early September of 1966, the Anglo-American Conference on the Teaching of English—or the Dartmouth Seminar (Dixon, 1967)—was convened because representatives from various organizations were aware that English as a school subject was facing a series of critical problems. This conference was one of many in the past fifteen years to recognize the urgent need for a different approach to the problems of teaching English as well as for a different approach to the very nature of the discipline.

In summary, then, it should be apparent that English teachers, regardless of the level of instruction, are confronted today with a situation that has been developing for years; and confronted as they are with multidimensional problems, it is urgent that they not regard these as being necessarily insurmountable. It is vital that they recognize the nature of these problems and that they seek help from the many sources which exist.

Curriculum development has to be regarded as the reeducation of the teacher, and as guidelines emerge and are identified, means for evaluating progress toward the selected goals must be examined. The chaotic state of the discipline of English does not render the evaluation any easier, and it is against this background that the teacher-evaluator must—as the editor of *Ends and Issues* (Frazier, 1966) has put it—endeavor to live with the incongruous, for as the need to impose order on ambiguity has been felt, many incongruities have emerged.

Specifications for the language arts: K to 6

The nature of the language arts program at the elementary school level is such that it is concerned with the learning of language and literary content and with the acquisition of language skills. The traditional elementary school emphasis upon the communicative function of language, for example, remains highly relevant for the young child because he must master the skills required to manipulate his language in an efficient and effective manner. Yet, it is true also that expanded insights into the form or the content of language in the past decade have led to the inclusion of significant content relative to the nature of language, the functioning of language, the history of language, and so forth. The problem of describing the content and skills which constitute the contemporary elementary school language arts program, then, is one of identifying the nature of content and of skills in the language arts and of understanding the nature of the relationship which exists between them.

Content in the elementary school language arts program consists of those facts, terms, conventions, etc., which make up the subject matter of English, that is, the broad body of knowledge which characterizes the particular nature of language and literature. The content of language in particular provides the base or the foundation for the teaching of the language skills.

Skills in the language arts refers to those interrelated processes of listening, speaking, reading, and writing which are designed to increase the pupil's control over all aspects of communication. As processes, the language skills represent the application of the content or the subject matter of English as the pupil engages in the transmission and the reception of communications through listening, speaking, reading, and writing. Content and skill in the elementary school language arts program are, then, inseparable.

The main problem confronting teachers of the language arts today centers about an identification of the components of an elementary school language arts program. The tripartite arrangement of language, literature, and composition is essentially a secondary school or a university structure. As such, it is not readily adaptable to the communication goals of the elementary school. Similarly, the arrangement of English into language and literature which grew out of the Dartmouth Seminar does not lend itself to the goals of the elementary school.

While each of these proposed structures has considerable merit, they must be adapted to the elementary school language arts program. Indeed, the ultimate value of the two structures for elementary school language arts programs might well reside in their redefinitions of the nature and scope of English and in the wealth of information which has been gathered about the form and function of language, composition, and literature.

Table 15-1, Table of Specifications for the Language Arts (K to 6), reflects the current state of the language arts at the elementary school level. The table is based upon an extensive collection of documents which describe the elementary school language arts program and which are taken from the writings of English scholars, English educators, elementary curriculum specialists, and various professional organizations such as the National Council of Teachers of English.[1] The table is also representative of those elements found in outstanding resource materials for the language arts.

The Table of Specifications suggests a model of language arts content, skills, and behaviors which should prove helpful to classroom teachers, curriculum developers, teachers of methods courses in the language arts at the university level, and specialists in the area of testing and evaluation. Thus, the table can assist those interested in the formation of appropriate instructional objectives for the language arts, and it can also point the direction toward evaluation of these instructional objectives. Its purpose is to define, at least in part, what is included in a contemporary language arts curriculum and what the curriculum is intended to accomplish.

Essentially, the Table of Specifications for the Language Arts should suggest what is to be learned within the curriculum, that is, what changes are expected to take place in students as a result of the language arts program. Until classroom teachers make such decisions on a local level, however, any discussion of materials, teaching procedures, instructional strategies, or evaluation techniques is decidedly premature.

[1] A list of the documents examined appears on page 443.

The Table of Specifications, then, should serve as a model of the outcomes of instruction for a language arts curriculum from which the classroom teacher can draw specific content, skill, and behavioral specifications which fit the needs of particular learners in local school situations. It should be noted that the table does not pretend to be all-inclusive, with regard either to content and skills or to cognitive and affective behaviors. Rather, the table reflects the language arts area in a general way. Further development of the content and skills or of the cognitive and affective behaviors should, of course, reflect the specific purposes of the user.

Through the use of a grid, the Table of Specifications shows the intersections of the content and skill elements with the behavioral elements of the language arts. The individual cells in the table, then, represent that relationship which exists between *specific content or skills* on the vertical axis and *specific behaviors* on the horizontal axis.

Instruction in literature, for example, is generally concerned more with affective behaviors than with cognitive behaviors. Teachers of the language arts are concerned with the development of *Attitudes*, such as *Acceptance* and *Appreciation* (*F*.1 and *F*.2). They are concerned also with the development of various *Receptive behaviors*, such as *Awareness* and *Selected attention* (*G*.1 and *G*.2). Finally, elementary school teachers want the pupils to become active participants in literature (*H*.1 and *H*.2). They encourage overt responses to poetry and to prose.

While it is true that elementary school teachers of the language arts do, indeed, deal with *Knowledge*, *Comprehension*, and *Analysis* (*A* to *C*) in the study of literature, such cognitive behaviors do not constitute the principal concerns of the language arts teacher. Rather, the development of cognitive behaviors in literature on a structured, in-depth level, is left for the secondary schools. At present, more emphasis is being given to the development of cognitive behaviors in literature at the elementary school level than in the past. Such emphasis should not, however, replace the primary concern—to develop affective behaviors at this introductory level.

It is conceivable that certain cells in the Table of Specifications will receive considerable attention. For example, elementary school teachers have traditionally sought to develop positive attitudinal, receptive, and participative behaviors throughout the language arts content. Conversely, it may be assumed that other cells will receive little or no attention; that is, it is conceivable that certain cognitive and affective behaviors may have little or no relationship to particular language arts content. Analysis of the elements of poetry and of other literary forms (3.1 and 3.2) may be deemed to be a significant behavior, but analysis of relationships or analysis of organizational principles in poetry or in prose may be identified as behaviors more suited to the secondary school English program.

The necessity for a Table of Specifications for the Language Arts seems obvious when one examines the total scope of the content, skills, and behaviors encompassed by the language arts. An effective, efficient program in the language arts cannot be left to chance. If such is the case, then reading might dominate the program to the detriment of listening, speaking, and writing as well as to the detriment of a study of language and literature. Similarly, it is conceivable that, in an effort to make the language arts more content-oriented with regard to language and literature, the classroom teacher might neglect language skill development. Any instructional program in the language arts should, then, be planned carefully with full attention given to all components of the curriculum.

Content of the language arts (1.0–3.0)

Language (1.0) *Language* may be defined as an arbitrary system of sounds which carry meaning and which are held in common by the members of a language community.

1.1. The *Nature of language* is concerned with an exploration of what a language is like, how language is produced, and how language works.

1.2. The *History of language* is concerned with the development of modern languages, particularly English. How did modern English come about? What is the history of modern English? What developments affected the growth of modern English?

1.3. The *Structure of language*, at least as far as English is concerned, centers about the study of

1.31. *Language sounds*, which deals with the sound system of a language. Specific concern at the elementary school level is directed toward an understanding of the sounds of the English language.

1.32. *Word forms*, which is the study of sound sequences that make up the basic grammatical elements of a language. This may include elements such as prefixes, suffixes, or those internal changes which modify a word's meaning.

1.33. *Word arrangement*, which is the study of the way that words are arranged to form phrases and sentences.

1.4. The study of *Vocabulary* centers about

1.41. The *History of words*, which is concerned with the development of words over a period of time.

1.42. *Word meanings*, which is concerned with a study of the meanings that words convey in communication.

1.43. *Dictionary usage*, which is concerned with the process by which words are found in the dictionary and with the process by which dictionaries are created.

1.5. *Dialect* study is concerned with regional and social aspects of language. Study involves such questions as How does language differ from one section of the country to another? How does language differ at different social levels?

1.6. *Usage* is concerned with the choices people make in the use of words and with the appropriateness of language in context.

1.7. *Spelling* is concerned with the act of composing words, either orally or in writing, according to accepted usage.

Language skills (2.0) *Language skills* includes the interrelated processes of listening, speaking, reading, and writing. While the interrelated nature of the language arts should be stressed, each communication skill contains two elements at the elementary school level, (1) the basic skills or mechanics of the area and (2) the activity context in which skills are taught.

2.1. *Listening* may be defined as the act of receiving oral language. While the term "auding" has gained some acceptance, "listening" is used throughout this chapter because of its general acceptance by classroom teachers and by language arts specialists.

2.11. *Basic listening skills* include auditory acuity and auditory discrimination.

2.12. *Listening activity* includes listening to stories and poetry, to reports and talks, and to conversations and discussions.

2.2. *Speaking* may be defined as the verbal transmission of communications. At the elementary school level, the primary emphasis is upon basic speech skills in functional situations and not upon formal public speaking.

2.21. *Basic speaking skills* includes articulation, enunciation, pronunciation, and voice.

2.22. *Speaking activity* includes speaking in conversation, reporting, story telling, dramatizing, etc.

2.3. *Reading* may be defined as the act of receiving meaning from the written word. It is understood, of course, that any definition of reading is subject to the criticisms of reading experts. The authors' intent, however, is simply to identify the *nature* of reading in a general way.

2.31. *Basic reading skills* include visual acuity, visual discrimination, left-to-right progression, etc.

2.32. *Reading activity* includes reading in which the pupil is involved in using a variety of materials such as poems, fiction, nonfiction, etc.

2.4. *Writing* may be defined as the act of transmitting communications through the written language.

2.41. *Basic writing skills* include penmanship, sentence structure, paragraph structure, capitalization, punctuation, sentence expansion, etc.

2.42. *Writing activity* includes the writing of letters, reports, summaries, poems, stories, essays, etc.

Some additional remarks about *Basic writing skills* (2.41) are in order. It should be understood that a study of the structure of the English language (the components of grammar) is incorporated as a subheading under *Language*, as content 1.3. The authors make a distinction, however, between that content and sentence expansion, or the application of the knowledge of the structure of English sentences when writing factual or creative compositions. Research has demonstrated that a study of grammar that is isolated from writing practice does not contribute appreciably to students' writing ability. Also implicit in the notion of sentence expansion in factual and creative writing is the belief that work with the grammar of English in a functional context will differ, qualitatively and quantitatively, from that study in the category of *Language*. That is, the application of grammar to students' writing will differ from the isolated, more formal presentations of grammar which are likely to be found in the *Language* category. Essentially, there should be concern on the part of educators that the content of *Language*, and, in particular, that content which deals with linguistic insights into language, not be presented in isolation from its relevance for listening, speaking, reading, and writing.

Finally, there may be concern over the placement of punctuation in the *Language skills* category and not in *Language*. While there are points of contact between spoken structural signals and written punctuation, considerable disagreements exist today. The authors believe that punctuation, in its current state in language arts instruction, should remain in the *Language skills* category. It is hoped, of course, that such aids to punctuation as might be found in spoken structural signals will be made relevant to punctuation in writing.

While the interrelatedness of the communication skills has been noted previously, the authors wish to stress once again that listening, speaking, reading, and writing do not exist in isolation. There is ample evidence today which demonstrates the necessity of giving careful consideration to a *total* language or to a program at the elementary school rather than to a program which emphasizes reading or writing in isolation from the other language skills.

Literature (3.0) With regard to *Literature*, Huck (1962, p. 307) notes:

> We have no literature program in the elementary school when we compare it with carefully planned developmental programs in reading, spelling and arithmetic. All our efforts are directed towards teaching children to read—no one seems to be concerned that they do read or what they read.

Fortunately, in the years since 1962, advances in the development of literature programs for elementary schools have been made.

Literature, at the elementary school level, may be defined as an extension and an enrichment of experience. The literature of the elementary school today is *not* adult literature which has been "watered down." Rather, it is literature which has been written particularly for the young reader.

3.1. *Poetry* may take many forms at the elementary level. Narrative poems, free verse, ballads, haiku, and so forth are all appropriate. Moreover, attention should be directed to matters of form, rhyming, etc.

3.2. *Prose* is a general subheading which is intended to include a wide range of fiction and nonfiction works of literature. Biography, essays, short stories, etc., provide the literary content. Attention should also be directed to certain literary techniques, such as plot, setting, etc.

The description of *Literature*, while brief in comparison with those of *Language* and *Language skills*, does not reflect upon its value. Rather, it reflects the "fluid" state of the subject. The authors could list individual pieces of poetry and of prose, but that would be of little value. The authors also could prepare an extensive listing of genres or of pseudo-genres for inclusion in prose and poetry. But it is felt that the study of literature should remain "fluid" according to the desires of the classroom teacher. The point of view of the authors, then, is that literature must remain an extension and an enrichment of experience, and, as such, its study should be left to the discretion of the individual teacher as that teacher can interpret the experiences of his pupils. For those who seek clarification of the common content knowledge concerning the category of *Literature*, reference should be made to the excellent publication *A Curriculum for English: Language Explorations for the Elementary Grades* (Nebraska Curriculum Development Center, 1966b). See also Chap. 20 of this book, which deals with literature, primarily at the secondary school level.

Language arts behaviors (A.0–H.0)

The horizontal axis in the Table of Specifications lists the cognitive and affective behaviors for the language arts. Each of the broad behavioral categories is divided into specific behaviors. These specific behaviors, in their relationship to the content of the language arts, provide the objectives or the specific goals of the language arts program. No attempts have been made to include every possible behavior. Such a task is not feasible within the limitations of this chapter. The authors believe, however, that those broad behavioral categories which are cited in the Table of Specifications include the major behavioral concerns of the language arts. This appraisal is based upon a careful and thoughtful review of the current state of the language arts as it is expressed in the professional literature.

Serious problems of terminology are encountered frequently in the language arts. For example, the literature in the field makes considerable use of the term "understanding." But what is "understanding" in the language arts? Can the term be applied universally, and can agreement be reached as to what constitutes "understanding"? It is common to find in language arts guides and textbooks the statement that the pupil should "understand" something or other. A few pages on, the guide might state that the pupil should "understand more fully." How does "more fully" differ from simple or plain "understanding"? Such is not an uncommon practice in the language arts. The tendency is great to add descriptive words to indicate what are really *levels* of comprehension. A similar predicament exists with "appreciation." How does "appreciate" differ from "appreciate more fully"?

Precision of terminology is, then, a serious problem in the language arts. Wherever possible, the authors have used those terms which are commonly accepted by classroom teachers and language arts specialists. But, in those instances where the terminology of the professionals does not lend itself to precise interpretation, the authors have borrowed certain terms from Bloom (1956) in an effort to identify more precisely those desirable cognitive and affective behaviors. The terms employed should serve to open a wider range of the literature on evaluation for the language arts teacher and for the elementary curriculum specialist. Much of the behavioral terminology employed in this chapter can be related to other chapters in this book which encompass a wide range of curricula at the elementary and the secondary school levels. The reader, then, is able to relate one field to another in terms of commonly specified terminology.

In order to convey to the reader what the authors mean by the behaviors cited in the Table of Specifications, the following information is presented. Again, not all possible behaviors have been exhausted, but major behavioral categories have been established, and specific behaviors are used to illustrate the scope of these categories.

Knowledge (A.0) *Knowledge* in the language arts is concerned with the acquisition of information about *Language*, *Language skills*, and *Literature*. This category does not include the *Application* of knowledge (*D*) to development of language skills. Rather, emphasis is placed upon the simple recall or recognition of information presented in class. This category is particularly significant for the language arts since there is considerable information to be learned. The range of information can be seen best through an examination of specific behaviors in the category.

A.1. *Knowledge of terminology* refers to the ability to recognize the meanings or the definitions of words and of those terms which are necessary for study in the language arts. Such terms may include "plot," "setting," "theme," "sentence," "comma," "period," "noun," "verb," "symbol," "articulation," "fable," "poem," and so forth.

A.2. *Knowledge of specific facts* may consist of the recall or the remembering of significant dates, events, persons, places, sources of information, and so forth. Specific facts in the language arts may include the names of poems and poets, knowledge about particular periods in the development of language, knowledge about writing, and knowledge about specific sources of information such as the dictionary, encyclopedia, atlas, etc. The range of potential facts in the language arts is, of course, quite great. Individuals must determine what is relevant and what is not.

A.3. *Knowledge of conventions* consists of knowing those rules and practices which are common to the language arts. Such behaviors include a knowledge of correct form and usage in oral and written communication, familiarity with the established conventions of literary works such as verse, plays, etc., and a knowledge of the conventions employed in marking words for pronunciation.

A.4. *Knowledge of classifications and categories* consists of knowing these broad classes, sets, or divisions of the subject field. For example, pupils should be familiar with a wide range of types of literature, be familiar with the types of speaking, know that words in the English language may be divided into classes, and so forth.

A.5. *Knowledge of criteria* implies the establishment of standards by which usage, dialect, oral composition, written composition, and literature may be judged.

Comprehension (B.0) *Comprehension* in the language arts includes those objectives, behaviors, or responses which are concerned solely with an understanding of the literal messages contained in communications.

B.1. *Translation* consists of such behaviors as having a person put the original communication into other terms or other types of communications. For example, this might include orally summarizing a written communication. The important consideration in the language arts is that pupils learn to move from one form of communication to another, that is, that they develop the ability to understand literal messages across communicative forms.

B.2. *Interpretation* involves an extension of the behavior of translation. In the language arts, this might include the ability to comprehend the significance of particular words in a poem in the light of the context of the poem. The significant aspect of interpretation as it is related to the language arts is that the pupil moves beyond literal translation of a literary work to the identification and the comprehension of the major ideas and their relationships.

Analysis (C.0) *Analysis* in the language arts consists of breaking down the broad fields of *Language, Language skills,* and *Literature* into their constituent elements.

C.1. *Analysis of elements* may consist of identifying the various structures which make a sentence—sounds, word forms, and syntactical patterns. In the area of oral and written composition, analysis of elements might include the ability to distinguish a spoken or written conclusion from statements which support it.

C.2. *Analysis of relationships* includes the ability to comprehend the interrelationships among ideas in oral and written composition, the ability to distinguish relevant from irrelevant statements, and the ability to comprehend the interrelationships among syntactical components.

C.3. *Analysis of organizational principles* includes the ability to infer the author's purpose and point of view from an examination of his work. It would include, for example, the ability to recognize the significance of word order to the English language.

Application (D.0) *Application* in the language arts refers to the production of both functional and expressive oral and written communications.

D.1. *Functional application* refers to the production of oral and written compositions which have as their primary purpose the dispensing of information. Functional speaking and writing are characterized by the intent to demonstrate knowledge of particular content in a formal, precise manner. While an element of originality or creativity may certainly appear in all such work, the primary purpose of the communication is not that of *Expressive application* (D.2). Reporting upon a book, writing science or other content reports, writing descriptive paragraphs, and oral demonstrations of apparatus are examples of this type of production.

D.2. *Expressive application* refers to the production of creative or expressive oral and written compositions. This behavior is limited to oral and written expression which is intended solely for the purpose of expressing original and creative thought, taste, views, etc. It would include the writing of original poems and stories, as well as the production of expressive oral communications where the intent is not the mechanical manipulation of form or content, but, rather, to be original in both form and content.

Evaluation (E.0) *Evaluation* in the language arts is generally twofold in that it emphasizes objective evaluation in terms of the mechanical appropriateness of the communication and subjective evaluation in terms of the expressive or creative effect of the communication.

E.1. *Objective evaluation* is concerned with the pupil's ability to evaluate language issues, language skills, and literature on the basis of the functional or mechanical appropriateness of the content of the communication. Critical reading, critical evaluation of the stories of other pupils, and self-evaluation of skills are all relevant for the language arts. The important consideration is that the criteria for evaluation are those which are relevant for the *content* of the communication. Thus, objective evaluation is not concerned with the personal or the expressive elements of the communications.

E.2. *Subjective evaluation* involves making judgments about the expressive views of oral and written compositions. Such evaluation is distinguishable from objective evaluation in that emphasis is placed upon an expressive or creative reaction to the communication, rather than upon the mechanical manipulation of form, syntax, or content. However, subjective evaluation should not function independently of objective evaluation. Both behaviors should be developed simultaneously because the distinction between the two is tenuous at best.

Attitudes (F.0) *Attitudes*, as a category, is concerned with predispositions or levels of interest in particular content.

F.1. *Acceptance* means only that a pupil is open and responsive to stimuli. Acceptance does not imply that a pupil appreciates. In the area of language, it means simply that he accepts a need for some level of standard usage; he accepts a need for writing from left-to-right, etc.

F.2. *Appreciation*, on the other hand, suggests not only that a pupil sees the need for a particular convention, but that he appreciates or values the necessity for it. This behavior represents an expansion or accepting by some sort of internalization of a value. Appreciation, in this sense, can also connote enjoyment. The pupil appreciates good books; he appreciates poetry, etc.

Reception (G.0) *Reception* refers to the full range of receptive behaviors in the language arts.

G.1. *Awareness* represents the first level of reception or of attending. The pupil pays attention to directions; he pays attention to what is said about margins, indentations, and so forth. But this behavior is more of a global attending to or reception of verbal stimuli.

G.2. *Selected attention* suggests the refinement of awareness behavior so that the reception of the pupil is now less global. Pupils listen to poetry and discriminate between "hard words" and "soft words." The pupil's receptive behaviors become more discriminating. He wants to listen. He wants to receive external stimuli.

Participation (H.0) *Participation* is a highly significant behavior in the language arts at the elementary school level. Learning in the language arts depends upon communication, and communication, in turn, depends upon participation.

H.1. Willing participation is similar to *Awareness* in that it is an initial level of participation. For example, the pupil participates in class discussions; he shares information; he completes assigned work. This behavior does not, however, suggest anything beyond what might be termed mandatory or obligatory participation.

H.2. Enjoyed participation operates at a higher level. Where in *H.1* the pupil participates willingly, such behavior occurs only in response to external stimuli. When the pupil enjoys participation, he voluntarily reads poetry and prose; he voluntarily shares information; and he voluntarily writes stories.

Illustration of the structure of selected language arts units

The purpose of this section is to demonstrate the relationship which exists between Table 15-1, the Table of Specifications, and the structure of two units in the language arts. The content of the two units will be described, and the structure of the units will be presented by means of separate tables of specifications. The tables of specifications for the units, then, illustrate only a small element of the Table of Specifications for the total language arts curriculum.

The preparation of tables of specifications which illustrate sample units *within the total language arts curriculum* is necessary if teachers are to avoid the pitfalls inherent in a curriculum as broad as the language arts. The state of the interrelatedness of the language arts is such that one content and skill area flows into another. Difficulties can occur when this happens if the teacher is unaware of the underlying content and skills. Units in the language arts have a structure, and it is only an understanding of that structure that keeps what is essentially a rigorous discipline from degenerating into a potpourri of social amenities, telephone conversations, etc. The determination of a structure of a unit serves to identify both the content and the behaviors and to give the teacher a clear look at what he is about. Without a table of specifications for a unit, it is easy to lose touch with what the interrelationships are and to view the unit as a mixture of this or that bit of content or skill. Further, a table of specifications for language arts units facilitates the development of testing items and evaluation procedures by illuminating the structure of the units.

A unit on fables *A Curriculum for English: Grade 1* is but one of several resource materials published by the Nebraska Curriculum Development Center (1966a). There are seventy units available at present. Table 15-2 shows the scope and sequence of the literature-centered program.

Table 15-3, Table of Specifications for a Unit on Fables, is adapted from *A Curriculum for English: Grade 1*. The unit is designed to serve as an introduction to the study of fables at some point in the primary grades.

This unit illustrates that section of Table 15-1, the Table of Specifications for the Language Arts, which is concerned with *Literature* (3.0). More specifically, this unit represents an expansion of the Table of Specifications in that "fables" would be identified as a pseudo-genre under *Prose* (3.2). The Table of Specifications for the Language Arts, then, can be expanded to include specific genres or pseudo-genres such as those found in Table 15-3.

The authors of the series stress the importance of following the sequence of fable presentation shown in Table 15-3 as well as the need to follow the sequences established for myths, folktales, historical fiction, biography, etc. The need for careful sequencing is occasioned by the progression in the complexity of the concepts which are presented in each genre. At the primary level, then, the fable unit serves to introduce the pupil to those devices and patterns which characterize the fable.

It should be noted that the attention of the unit to cognitive behaviors does not negate the significance of affective behaviors in the study of literature in particular or language arts in general. Rather, it is felt that the *structure* of a unit in language arts consists of the subject matter or the content which is to be learned. And it is that cognitive-content structure which the unit on fables and the subsequent unit on short-story writing attempts to show.

The literary content for the fable unit at the primary level is "The Dog and the Shadow" and "The Town Mouse and the Country Mouse." In Table 15-3 the appropriate content elements for each behavioral category are identified. This arrangement permits examination of the content, the behaviors, and the relations among these elements in the fable unit.

The teacher of young children does not, of course, teach such knowledge directly. Rather, through discussions, dramatizations, etc., the teacher should guide the pupils to an appropriate perception of the nature of fables. The presentation of such a unit at the primary level, then, is low-keyed and designed to revolve around the pupils' interest. The child at the primary level should not be required to know the precise terminology or the exacting conventions of the fable. Such knowledge might, however, be developed at the upper elementary grade levels in the continuing study of the fables mentioned in Table 15-3.

A unit on short-story writing Table 15-4, Table of Specifications for a Unit on Short-story Writing, shows the structure of a unit on writing at the upper grade level of the elementary school. A unit such as this demonstrates not only the interrelationships which exist among the behaviors, but also the interrelationships among the content areas of the unit.

The unit is concerned with the writing of short stories. Its objective is to have the pupils demonstrate a knowledge of the literary form of the short story through the production of original short stories. The unit includes the reading of various short stories which are appropriate for the grade level and a study of the form of the short story, the writing of short stories, and explorations into such elements of language as vocabulary, spelling, and usage.

The structure of this unit demonstrates the highly interrelated nature of the language arts at the elementary school level. The major purpose of the unit, the writing of short stories, demands attention to *Language* (1.0) as well as to *Literature* (3.0). The pupil does not write in isolation from other language skills, nor does he avoid the content which *Language* and *Literature* can provide. The strength of this unit lies in its "reading across" the artificial boundaries which separate English components at the secondary school level. Teachers of the language arts are aware that in any teaching art involving language, several areas of content and skills are being presented. Unfortunately, many teachers concentrate upon *only* one element of the total language arts program; related language areas are either neglected entirely or are not given significant consideration.

The Table of Specifications of this unit points out the content and the skill areas to be considered in the teaching of writing. In brief, the unit demonstrates the interrelatedness of the language arts at the elementary school level. Attention to such specifications, then, would tend to increase efficiency and effectiveness of instruction. Again, it should be pointed out that the primary emphasis in such a unit is upon *skill* development and not upon a *formal* content knowledge of terminology or exacting conventions.

Teaching procedures for a unit at the upper elementary level will differ from those at the primary level. Under certain circumstances, it is more efficient to teach the conventions of capitalization, punctuation, etc., in a direct manner. The fact that language usage is not logical precludes lengthy inductive discussions into questions of form. If the objective of a unit is such a discussion, then well and good. But when the primary aim is the production of written compositions, extended discussions of mechanics are not appropriate. In a consideration of short stories in literature, however, the teacher might well ask pupils to read a number of stories and then to induce those characteristics which identify them as particular literary forms.

The important consideration in unit teaching in the language arts lies in specifying the content and the behaviors of the unit. Without such a plan, learning is likely to be fragmented and chaotic, and evaluation is likely to suffer from the lack of clear purpose.

TABLE 15-2 Elementary School Units in the Literature-centered Program

Grade	*Folk*	*Fanciful*	*Animal*	*Adventure*
1	Little Red Hen Three Billy Goats Gruff The Gingerbread Boy	Little Black Sambo Peter Rabbit Where the Wild Things Are	Millions of Cats The Elephant's Child How the Rhinoceros Got His Skin Ferdinand	Little Tim and the Brave Sea Captai The Little Island
2	Little Red Riding Hood Story of the Three Pigs Story of the Three Bears	And to Think That I Saw It on Mulberry Street	Blaze and the Forest Fire How Whale Got His Throat The Beginning of the Armadillos The Cat That Walked by Himself	The 500 Hats of Bartholomew Cubbins The Bears on Heml Mountain
3	Sleeping Beauty Cinderella or the Little Glass Slipper Mother Holle	The Five Chinese Brothers Madeline Madeline's Rescue	The Blind Colt How the Camel Got His Hump How the Leopard Got His Spots The Sing-Song of Old Man Kangaroo	Winnie-the-Pooh Mr. Popper's Peng
4	Febold Feboldson	Charlotte's Web	Brighty of the Grand Canyon	Homer Price
5	Tall Tale America Rapunzel The Woodcutter's Child The Three Languages	The Snow Queen The Lion, the Witch, and the Wardrobe	King of the Wind	The Merry Adventu of Robin Hood Island of the Blue Dolphins
6	The Seven Voyages of Sinbad	Alice in Wonderland and Through the Looking Glass A Wrinkle in Time	Big Red	The Adventures of Tom Sawyer

Correlative units: "You Come Too"—Poetry of Robert Frost—Grade 6; *Poetry for the Elementary Grades; A Curriculum fc English: Language Explorations for Elementary Grades* (Nebraska Curriculum Development Center, 1966b).

Myth	*Fable*	*Other Lands and People*	*Historical Fiction*	*Biography*
Story of the First itterflies Story of the First oodpecker	The Dog and the Shadow The Town Mouse and the Country Mouse	A Pair of Red Clogs		They Were Strong and Good George Washington
Golden Touch	The Hare and the Tortoise The Ant and the Grasshopper	Crow Boy	Caroline and Her Kettle Named Maud	Ride on the Wind
lalus and Icarus e Narcissus	Chanticleer and the Fox The Musicians of Bremen	The Red Balloon	The Courage of Sarah Noble	Christopher Columbus and His Brothers
vatha's Fasting eus and the notaur hne eton and the ariot of the Sun	Jacobs: The Fables of Aesop	A Brother for the Orphelines	Little House on the Prairie The Matchlock Gun	Willa Leif the Lucky
s and Prosperine nta's Race n Labors of ercules	Bidpai Fables Jataka Tales	The Door in the Wall	Children of the Covered Wagon This Dear-Bought Land	Dr. George Washington Carver Scientist
Children of Odin Hobbit	The Wind in the Willows	Hans Brinker Secret of the Andes	The Book of King Arthur and His Noble Knights	Cartier Sails the St. Lawrence

TABLE 15-3 TABLE OF SPECIFICATIONS FOR A UNIT ON FABLES

	BEHAVIORS				
CONTENT AREA	*A.1 Terminology*	*A.3 Conventions*	*B.1 Translation*	*B.2 Interpretation*	*D.2 Expressive application*
3.0 Literature	Fable	Human actions presented by analogous animal actions			
	Theme		Translation of abstractions onto human level	Interpretation of thought or idea of fable	
	Style				Composition (oral or written) of descriptive words or phrases for words in fable

TABLE 15-4 TABLE OF SPECIFICATIONS FOR A UNIT ON SHORT-STORY WRITING

	BEHAVIORS				
CONTENT AREA	*A.1 Terminology*	*A.3 Conventions*	*B.1 Translation*	*B.2 Interpretation*	*D.2 Expressive application*
1.0 Language		Spelling Usage Vocabulary			
2.41 Basic writing skills		Punctuation Capitalization Sentence expansion Paragraph structure Handwriting			
2.42 Writing activity	Short story Theme Plot Setting Climax Protagonist Antagonist	Brevity Single effect Economy Originality Order of arrangement One prominent character			Writing of original short story
3.0 Literature	Short story Theme Plot Setting Climax Protagonist Antagonist	Brevity Single effect Economy Originality Order of arrangement One prominent character		Comprehension and interpretation of short stories	

Walter J. Moore and Larry D. Kennedy

Illustration of testing procedures

This section of the chapter is designed to illustrate specific test items which are appropriate for testing the major behaviors in the language arts at the elementary school level. Each behavior, cognitive and affective, will be considered. Attention will be directed to the illustration of test items which cover the content of the language arts program as it is identified along the vertical axis in the Table of Specifications. Further, the test items will illustrate different levels of complexity; that is, items will be selected which measure the same behaviors at a variety of levels of difficulty. Each individual behavioral category includes a brief discussion of the special problems of testing for that behavior and some notation of the particular features relevant to testing in that category.

Knowledge (A.0)

Testing for knowledge in the language arts includes a variety of behaviors to be evaluated. Since knowledge is concerned solely with the recall or the recognition of information, however, the techniques appropriate for assessing such information are relatively straightforward. Multiple choice, matching, true-false, and completion are appropriate formats for such assessment.

Knowledge of terminology (A.1)

A.1-3.2

1. Setting refers to
   a. the location of the story
   b. the main idea of the story
   c. the sequence of the story
   d. the theme of the story

Item 1 would be appropriate for middle to upper elementary pupils. The question is concerned with the terminology employed in literature. Additional questions of this type might test the knowledge of such terms as "plot," "theme," "mood," "character," and "genre."

There are several alternate procedures for testing for *Knowledge of terminology*. Item 1 could be placed in the following structure for pupils at the upper elementary level or for pupils who have already had experiences with short stories.

A.1-3.2

2. DIRECTIONS: Now that you have read the short story, draw a line under the sentence(s) which indicate the *setting* of the story.

In item 2, the pupil is asked to identify the term "setting" at an operational level. The item is also more complex than item 1 because in order to identify the term, the elements of the short story must also be analyzed. Item 2, then, calls for an analysis of elements (C.1-3.2) in addition to a knowledge of terminology.

A.1-1.42

3. Do you hang a ________ on your door at Christmas?
   wreck
   weather
   wreath
   whether

(*Metropolitan Achievement Tests:* 1959, p. 4, item 14.)

Question 3 is appropriate at the primary level. The pupil is asked to recognize which word belongs in the blank. Each word is similar to another, and the answer demands a precise knowledge of each word. Question 3 could also be delivered orally, in which case it would also test *Basic listening skills*, content 2.11. The teacher could then record the pupil's response on a separate sheet. Similar oral testing can be carried on in large and small groups. It is also possible to use tape recorders as a means of preserving pupil responses for future comparative purposes.

A.1-2.41

4. DIRECTIONS: Look at this sentence:
   Are men who travel in space brave?
   What is the name for this kind of sentence?

(Conlin & LeRoy, 1967, p. 21.)

Question 4 is appropriate at the primary level. The question may be administered in a pencil and paper test, or it may be given orally.

Question 5 demonstrates how a teacher of primary pupils might ask for a definition of a term. Notice the choices for response the teacher gives. He is willing to permit the pupils a great deal of latitude in their answers in order to encourage participation.

A.1-3.2

5. DIRECTIONS: Now I have finished reading one of the fables, and tomorrow I will read another. But first, who can tell me what a fable is? If you like, you may begin by telling me what some of the things were that went on in the story. Did anything surprise you? Did the story remind you of anything you have seen or heard before?

Knowledge of specific facts (A.2) *Knowledge of specific facts* represents a higher-level behavior in the general category of *Knowledge*. Item 6 is straightforward and assures a knowledge of such terms as "poet," "musician," and so forth. Thus, the question of specific fact depends upon prior knowledge of the terminology. Item 7 also demonstrates the notion of a hierarchy of behaviors. The pupil in the upper grades must know what historical fiction, biography, and other genres are before he can answer the question of fact. Teachers too frequently assume that knowledge of terms is present when they test for specific facts, although this may not be the case.

A.2-3.2

6. James Whitcomb Riley was
   a. a poet
   b. a musician
   c. a painter
   d. a teacher
7. *The Diary of Anne Frank* is
   a. historical fiction
   b. biography
   c. autobiography
   d. folktale

Knowledge of specific facts is highly relevant to the development of reading maturity. The following paragraph for primary pupils could be read to pupils or it could be in writing.

A.2-2.3

"When my brother Ted and I were sick, a man from the health department came to our house. He put a sign with the words MUMPS—KEEP OUT on our door. When the other boys saw that red sign, they knew they could not play with us. We had to stay at home until the man came back and took down the sign."

8. Who is telling this story?
   a. Ted's mother
   b. Ted's brother
   c. One of Ted's playmates
   d. A man from the health department
9. What was the matter with Ted?
   a. He did not want to play with the other boys.
   b. He did not like to go to school.
   c. He was angry with his sister.
   d. He was sick.

(*Iowa Tests of Basic Skills: Reading*, 1955, p. 8, items 1 and 2.)

Knowledge of conventions (A.3) The items on *Knowledge of conventions* demonstrate the range of conventions which teachers must consider in the language arts. Item 10 is concerned with knowing the conventions appropriate to the pronunciation of words.

A.3-1.31

10. The word *even* (ē′van) contains
   a. a short "e" sound
   b. a syllable that rhymes with geen
   c. a long "e" sound
   d. an initial vowel sound like that in seen

(*Stanford Achievement Test: Language*, 1964, p. 14, item 109.)

Item 10 could also be tested by having the pupil pronounce the word after he has been shown the word in context.

A.3-1.6

DIRECTIONS: Read each sentence below. Decide which, if either, of the two choices in each sentence is correct in standard written English. Look at the answer spaces at the right or on your answer sheet (if you have one). If the choice numbered 1 is correct, fill in the space under the 1. If the choice numbered 2 is correct, fill in the space under the 2. If neither choice 1 nor choice 2 is correct, fill in the space under the N. ("N" stands for "Neither.")

	1	2	N
11. Has the May queen been 1 choosed yet? / 2 chosen	☐	☐	☐
12. Why didn't you 1 brought / 2 brung your old clothes?	☐	☐	☐
13. Fred hurt 1 hisself / 2 himself playing hockey.	☐	☐	☐

(*Stanford Achievement Test: Language*, 1964, p. 10, items 4, 5, 6.)

Questions 11, 12, and 13 test a pupil's knowledge of usage conventions. The value of a testing format such as multiple choice lies in the ease of scoring and in the precision which can be achieved in questioning. No extraneous material is present in these questions. They are direct and to the point.

Questions 11, 12, and 13 do, however, evaluate usage conventions in isolation from practical communicative contexts. In order to measure knowledge of oral usage conventions, the teacher might tape-record personal conversations or group discussion and then listen to the tapes and record usage errors on a checklist or a rating scale. Such an evaluation would encompass both a knowledge of usage conventions (*A*.3-1.6) and a knowledge of usage conventions in a speaking activity (*A*.3-2.22).

______ ______

NAME DATE

	Usage errors	*Type*	*Frequency*
1.			
2.			
3.			

A checklist of this sort will provide the teacher with evidence of the pupil's usage in various speech activities. The checklist could also be used to evaluate pupil usage in writing (*A*.3-2.42) at an advanced grade level.

A.3-1.6

DIRECTIONS: Look at each of the sentences below. There are one or more circles above each sentence. The arrow on each of these circles points to a certain place in the sentence where a capital letter or some punctuation mark may be needed. If the arrow points to a letter which should be a capital letter, write the capital letter inside the circle. If the arrow points to a space where some punctuation mark is needed, write that mark inside the circle. If no capital letter or punctuation mark is needed, put a √ in the circle. (√) means all right as it is—no change needed.

14. Isnt your aunts house located on Cherry street
15. Tex and i both go to franklin school.
16. Thanksgiving is the last thursday in november

(*Metropolitan Achievement Tests*, 1959, p. 13, items 1–2, 5–7, 8–11.)

Items 14 to 16 are appropriate at the lower grade levels in the elementary school. Particular attention should be directed to the complexity of the directions. It is conceivable that the pupil could perform at a low level on such items because of an inability to read and comprehend the directions. Further, the efficacy of such a testing procedure must be questioned. Could not the testing of usage conventions be structured through writing activities (*A*.3-2.42)? Again, the value of the format employed in items 14 to 16 lies in their ease of composition and scoring. Ultimately, the teacher must be concerned with the issue of placing such test items in isolation or in the context of a language skill activity.

A.3-3.2

17. The outstanding stylistic characteristic of old folktales is
    a. repetition of words and situations
    b. repetition of rhyme
    c. the moral of the story
    d. the author's technique

Item 17 is concerned with a knowledge of the conventions of folktales in literature. This is also a fine example of the necessity for considering behaviors in a hierarchical manner. Item 17 assumes that the pupil knows such terms as "stylistic," "moral," "rhyme," "technique," and "folktale." It also assumes that the pupil who answers correctly knows certain terms and, in addition, specific facts about the characteristics of folktales.

Knowledge of classifications and categories (A.4) Item 18 is appropriate for an upper-grade class involved in the general study of literature. *The Seven Voyages of Sinbad* belongs to a class or genre or pseudo-genre. The pupil should be able to classify it accordingly. Again, this question assumes a knowledge of terminology and a knowledge of specific facts.

A.4-3.2

18. *The Seven Voyages of Sinbad* is an example of a
    a. folktale
    b. historical fiction
    c. myth
    d. biography

Knowledge of classifications can also be tested verbally. At the primary level, the teacher might be concerned with the ability of her pupils to classify the various parts of speech.

A.4-1.3

19. DIRECTIONS: I am going to read a list of words to you. I want you to tell me which word is not like the others in some way.

Group 1	Group 2	Group 3
boy	run	pretty
girl	jump	lovely
man	play	homely
woman	father	nice
swim	swing	slow

DIRECTIONS: Read each underlined word. Circle the other words in that line that go with it.

20. book	page	story	water	title
21. letter	game	address	envelope	greeting
22. song	music	sing	animal	words

(Adapted from Conlin & LeRoy, 1967, p. 77.)

Items 20 to 22 are of special interest. Assume that the pupil will know the initial term and that he will be able to identify other terms which belong in the same class or category. For example, the underlined word *book* should have *page, story,* and *title* as members of the subclass of the class of *book*. But a bright pupil might well identify *water* as being a member of the class *noun*. That is, the pupil might see all the words as being of the large class of nouns. Care should be taken, then, to write directions that are appropriate to the objective sought. Items 20 to 22, then, could suffer from a lack of sound directions. Such a situation makes precise behavioral identification difficult. It is not enough for the pupil to know only the term, he must be aware of the notion of classes or sets if he is to answer the question correctly.

Knowledge of criteria (A.5) It has been only in recent years that the notion of levels of appropriateness with regard to oral language has been of concern. Prior to certain linguistic insights into oral language and into regional and social dialects, something called "Standard English" was the model which pupils were to imitate in their daily speech. The current trend, however, is to recognize levels of usage as well as functional varieties of usage. Kenyon (1948) identifies two levels of usage, standard and substandard. His functional varieties of usage included colloquial, familiar, formal, scientific, and literary language. A knowledge of criteria, then, would include recognition of the standards by which levels and varieties of usage might be identified.

Knowledge of criteria suggests also that the pupil recognizes any standards or criteria which exist with regard to written composition and to literature. Such knowledge suggests that the pupil must recognize the ground rules which have been established and be prepared to apply those ground rules, at some future point, to the assessment of particular elements. But at this point it is important only for the pupil to know or to recognize the ground rules.

A.5-1.6

23. The statement "He unsheathed his dirk, and stealthily rose from his place behind his father" is characteristic of what variety of usage?
    __ a. colloquial
    __ b. literary
    __ c. scientific
    __ d. familiar

DIRECTIONS: This paragraph was in the minutes of a Camp Fire group. This part of the minutes tells of a hike.

1 It was Wednesday P.M. our Camp Fire group decided to go on a hike through Land park and take along a trail lunch. 2 At 3:30 we started first we started looking at kinds of trees. 3 I saw elm tree its leaves looked very interesting. 4 Next we saw a japanese red blossomed tree with the blossoms were very pretty.

A.5-2.41

24. Part 1 has more than one sentence in it. Which is the best way to change it?
   [A] It was in the P.M. of Wednesday. So a Camp Fire group decided to go, on a hike through Land park and, take along a trail lunch.
   [B] Wednesday afternoon our Camp Fire group decided to prepare a trail lunch and hike to Land park.
   [C] It was Wednesday afternoon when our Campfire group decided to hike through Land park and we take a trail lunch along.
   [D] Our Camp Fire group Wednesday P.M. decided on a hike through Land Park and a lunch to take along, to eat a trail lunch.

(Educational Testing Service, 1957b, p. 10, item 14.)

Questions such as 23 and 24 are especially appropriate for the language arts. Recent trends have emphasized the necessity for accepting different levels and varieties of usage. Acceptance does not, however, suggest approval. Such a notion simply says that levels and varieties of usage exist and that pupils should be knowledgeable of them. The objective of such a question as number 23 is to determine whether pupils can recognize the distinctions among colloquial, literary, scientific, and familiar varieties of usage. Question 24 is designed to measure the pupil's knowledge of established criteria for effective written communication. Such knowledge is also basic for producing written communications.

Comprehension (B.0)

Comprehension includes what is commonly termed "understanding" in the language arts. As it was defined earlier, comprehension includes both *Translation* and *Interpretation*. These two behaviors are of vital importance, since basic communication is involved. Pupils must be able to move from one form of communication to another; they must be able to comprehend what is said. Listening, speaking, reading, and writing demand that pupils be able to shift from encoding to decoding and back to encoding, and so forth.

Translation (B.1)

B.1-2.42

25. DIRECTIONS: I have read you one fable, and we read the other fable together. Yesterday we talked about what we all thought a fable was and what we thought about the town mouse and the country mouse. Today, I would like for you to read the story of "The Town Mouse and the Country Mouse" silently at your desks. When you finish, take a piece of paper and tell me the story in your own words. But this time, I want you to use names of people for the town mouse and the country mouse. You might call the town mouse "Max," and you might call the city mouse "Fred." Use whatever names you like.

This is a particularly difficult task for young children, and it is not intended for first-grade pupils, except in cases of special groups, etc. The problem for the pupils is to comprehend that fables, while using animals as characters, are, nonetheless, about people. Item 25, then, is a step in this direction. A great deal of personal guidance is necessary, and the teacher may wish to extend such an activity over a period of time. The important consideration, however, is that the pupils learn to "translate" fables to real-life people and situations. This can be done verbally at the primary level, and, in certain cases, it can be done through such a question as item 25.

Again, anecdotal comments or records would be appropriate for primary-level evaluation. A teacher might set up a checklist for evaluation.

Comments	*Yes*	*No*
1. Knows terms		
2. Knows conventions		
3. Knows criteria		
4. Translates characters		
5. Translates situations		

The checklist demonstrates the operation of such behaviors as knowledge of terminology and knowledge of conventions, in addition to the ability to translate from a reading of literature to a writing performance.

Interpretation (B.2)

B.2-2.32

DIRECTIONS: A number of short selections will be read aloud to you. After each selection, you will hear a group of questions or incomplete statements. Four suggested answers are given for each question or incomplete statement. You are to decide which one of these answers is best.

Selection

The moment a bolt of lightning strikes a power line carrying high voltage electricity, giant switches take the current off the line. Within a fraction of a second, the effect of the lightning passes and the switches automatically turn the current on again.

26. What will probably happen to the electric lights if a high-power line serving an area is struck by lightning?
    - __a. The lights will brighten
    - __b. The lights will flicker
    - __c. The lights will burn out
    - __d. Nothing will happen to the lights

(Educational Testing Service, 1957a, p. 5, item 0.)

B.2-1.42

DIRECTIONS: This story has three words left out. First, read the story and find the space with a number in it where a word or words have been left out. Then look at the group of words after the number below the story and find the word or words that belong to the story.

We saw a TV show about cowboys. They rode very fast on their horses and shot bad men with their guns. Mother said, "Real __27__ work hard taking care of __28__. They do not spend their time __29__ bad men."

27. horses	cowboys	men	people
28. grass	sheep	cattle	land
29. shooting	beating	shaking	soaring

(Adapted from Conlin & LeRoy, 1967, p. 75.)

Items 26 and 27 to 29 are all concerned with measuring the pupil's ability to interpret what he has read or heard. Item 26 is appropriate for middle or upper grade levels, and 27 to 29 are appropriate for lower-to-middle grade levels. Test items to measure interpretation behavior should be an extension and a refinement of translation behavior. Indeed, one poem, one story, or one oral presentation can serve as the content for the development and the testing of translation and interpretation behaviors.

Analysis (C.0)

Analysis in the language arts involves a complex of behaviors: *Analysis of elements*, *Analysis of relationships*, and *Analysis of organizational principles*. When a classroom teacher writes questions to measure these, he should be aware that he is measuring knowledge and comprehension behaviors as well. Analysis, then, suggests that pupils have moved from knowing to comprehending. The pupils know the terminology, the specific facts, the conventions, the classes or categories, the criteria relevant to folktales. The pupils also can translate folktales into other forms; they can interpret the purpose of the folktale. Now the pupils are ready to move into analyzing the elements, the relationships, and the organizational principles of folktales. The procedures with regard to other literary forms, English sentences, oral communications, etc., also follow this hierarchy of development.

Analysis of elements (C.1)

C.1-2.32

DIRECTIONS: Read the following passage and answer the questions which follow.

The lion cub is born with a deep-seated hunting instinct. One cub will stalk and pounce on another with the same eagerness and thrill exhibited by a kitten. During the year and a half of cubhood, this play develops into a hunting and killing technique. Skill comes through long practice, imitation of the old lions, and obedience to warning growls of the mother. Most of their prey consists of large and strong animals, well equipped for self-defense. A cub's first attempts to kill are made under the watchful care of the mother lioness.

The reason why most men killed by lions are mauled and die of blood poisoning or shock, rather than suddenly from the lion's customarily efficient attack, is that the man-killing is not a common subject in the training of lions. When once they learn how, they can be rather successful.

30. In which one of the following sentences does the writer gain emphasis by understatement?
    - 89-1 The lion cub is born with a deep-seated hunting instinct.
    - 89-2 During the year and a half of cubhood, this play develops into a hunting and killing technique.
    - 89-3 Most of their prey consists of large and strong animals, well equipped for self-defense.
    - 89-4 When once they learn how, they can be rather successful.
    - 89-5 A cub's first attempts to kill are made under the watchful care of the mother lioness.

(Educational Testing Service, Cooperative Test Division, 1948, p. 15, item 89.)

Question 30 is an example of a test item in which the pupil is asked to analyze a passage and then to identify a specific element within that passage. The content of the passage makes it appropriate for use with upper grades, but an abundance of similar passages are available or can be written for the lower and middle elementary grades.

Question 30 can also be adapted to a speaking-listening format. The teacher might read the passage aloud and then ask the pupils to respond. Such a question, then, would measure the listening behavior of the pupils (C.1-2.11).

At the primary level, pupils are asked frequently to identify phonic elements in particular sentences. Such a question is concerned with basic listening skills.

C.1-2.11

DIRECTIONS: I am going to read three words to you. I want you to listen for the sound of short o (ŏ) in the words, and then tell me which word or words has the short o sound.

31. dot
    door
    cot

The teacher might use such an item with the entire class, but evaluation of individual responses would be difficult. A better procedure would be to reserve such questions for small-group activities.

Analysis of relationships (C.2)

C.2-1.3

DIRECTIONS: Look at the following sentence diagram. Explain, in your own words, the relationships which exist among the elements of the sentence.

32.

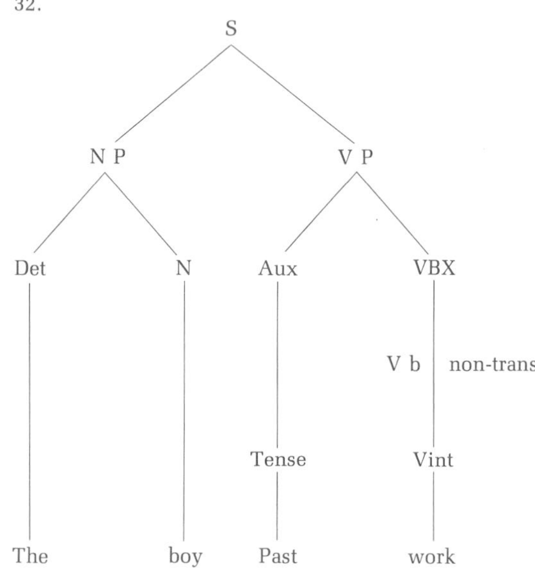

Item 32 is an interesting one. The major behavior being tested is that of analyzing relationships. But the question also demands the ability to analyze the various elements of the sentence, and it may well involve the ability to analyze organizational principles. The authors assume, however, that an analysis of organizational principles in item 32 would be concerned with the development of generalizations about the relationships. The item also involves translation because it asks the pupil to explain the relationships in his own words. Interpretation, then, would follow translation. And all these behaviors would be dependent upon knowledge of some type or another. Thus, item 32 illustrates, as have the other items, the range of cognitive behaviors. The important consideration for the teacher is that he recognize that such a question as item 32 actually measures a great many behaviors.

Analysis of organizational principles (C.3)

C.3-1.3

33. DIRECTIONS: Choose three of these sentences and make them grow by adding words at the beginning and at the end.
    a. Engines roared
    b. Sirens blew
    c. Firemen came
    d. Traffic stopped

(Adapted from Conlin & LeRoy, 1967, p. 77.)

Question 33 measures the pupil's ability to expand sentences and thereby tests his analytic skills.

Another technique to test such behavior would be to examine pupils' writing (C.3-2.42). The teacher might make the assignment to write descriptive paragraphs and then evaluate the structure of the sentences; that is, whether the sentences contain adjective, adverb, etc., and employ acceptable usage. A rating scale might look like this:

	Comments			
	Excellent	*Good*	*Fair*	*Poor*
1. Use of adjectives				
2. Use of adverbs				
3. Exclamatory sentences				
4. Question sentences				
5. Declarative sentences				

Application (*D*.0)

Application is viewed by the authors as the process of pulling knowledge, comprehension, and analytic skills together in the production of both functional and expressive oral and written compositions. It is in the application of knowledge, skills, and abilities that classroom teachers expect their pupils to pull everything together.

Functional application (D.1) It is frequently the case that teachers assign various types of factual or noncreative writing on some subject or area. The test item in such a situation might consist of no more than, "Today, you are going to write a business letter in class." Such a statement fails, however, to identify specifically what behaviors the teacher is looking for. The teacher should, rather, establish criteria by which the pupils know what is expected and by which he may evaluate their responses.

D.1-2.42

34. Today, you are going to write a business letter in class. As I read and evaluate your letters, I will be looking for certain things. These include
    a. spelling
    b. heading
    c. greeting
    d. indentation
    e. paragraphing
    f. penmanship
    g. brevity
    h. signature
    i. clarity of meaning

The format of such a test item will differ according to the demands of the subject. Procedures for testing for application are limitless.

Report writing also has a large place in the elementary school language arts program. In fact, functional writing for utilitarian purposes lends itself to the application of the mechanics of English better than expressive writing, since the primary evaluation emphasis in expressive writing should be upon the creative content of the composition. A tally sheet like that in Table 15-5 can be used to check the mechanics of English in report writing.

A tally sheet like this can provide the teacher with objective data on a pupil's performance in writing. The sheet has the advantage of permitting the teacher to look at the individual mechanics of English as they are expressed in a complete composition rather than in dated drill exercises.

Table 15-5 Tally Sheet for Evaluating Report Writing (D.1-2.42)

NAME ____________ ROOM ________ DATE ________

	Errors	*Misspelled words*	*Comments*
1. Sentences			
a. Fragments			
b. Comma faults			
c. Run-on sentences			
2. Verbs			
3. Pronouns			
4. Word division			
5. Punctuation			
a. Quotation marks			
b. Apostrophes			

SOURCE: Adapted from M. Dawson et al. *Guiding language learning*. New York: Harcourt, Brace & World, 1963, p. 305.

Expressive application (D.2)

DIRECTIONS: Think of some time in your own life when you were up against difficulty, something that stood in your way and had to be overcome. Tell it to the class. You will be evaluated on the basis of this rating sheet.

	Excellent	Good	Fair
D.2-2.11 35. Clarity of speech			
D.2-1.4 36. Use of descriptive words			
D.2-2.22 37. Organization of ideas			

Item 35 is a behavior which is related to pronunciation and enunciation. Item 36 is related to vocabulary development, and 37 to the sequential development of ideas. In general, then, the evaluation sheet tests several behaviors at one performance. It should be evident that the test is considerably more complex than one devoted to the recall of names, dates, places, etc. Such a test is aimed at higher-level behaviors and, consequently, it demands more thought and consideration on the part of the teacher.

It is not uncommon, of course, to hear a teacher say, "Write a composition for tomorrow on the subject of 'Safety in the School.'" The compositions are then written, read and evaluated by the teacher, and handed back to the pupils. But what has actually happened? What was the purpose of the assignment? What did the teacher hope to accomplish? Was he interested in the ability of his pupils to use standard punctuation, capitalization, and so forth? Was he interested in the organization of ideas, sentence structure, paragraph structure, vocabulary, spelling, originality? The point, of course, is that the teacher must have one or more objectives for the writing assignment. But he must know, specifically, what behaviors he is looking for, and he must know the criteria for evaluating these behaviors before he can do justice to the assignment.

Evaluation (E.0)

Evaluation in the elementary school language arts program is aimed at the development of critical and creative evaluative skills and abilities on the part of the pupil. Evaluation, as a cognitive behavior, suggests that the pupil learns to evaluate his own knowledge, skills, abilities, and factual and creative, oral and written, compositions on the basis of other than emotional criteria. Essentially, the pupil is asked to assess his own mental growth and development. This may be done by rating sheets of various types.

The questionnaire containing items 38 to 43 demonstrates the means by which a pupil may evaluate his oral expression in a critical manner. A separate column is included for evaluation by the teacher.

Objective evaluation (E.1)

E.1-2.22

DIRECTIONS: You are to listen to the tape recording of your report. As you listen to your presentation, look at the evaluation sheet. Play back your presentation a second time and fill out the evaluation sheet. I will go over it with you after you finish.

How Did I Speak?	Pupil Rating	Teacher Rating
38. Did I get and hold the attention of my listeners?		
39. Did I have a good opening sentence?		
40. Did I speak clearly and not too rapidly?		
41. Was I relaxed and at ease?		
42. Were my thoughts well organized?		
43. Did I summarize information so that listeners could recall main points?		

Evaluation code:

A. Much growth
B. Some growth
C. Little growth
D. No growth

(Adapted from Lamb, 1967, p. 341, items 1, 2, 3, 4, 10, 11.)

Subjective evaluation (E.2)

E.2-2.42

DIRECTIONS: Before you hand your composition in, go through the checklist. Answer the questions completely. The checklist should serve to guide you in the evaluation of your paper.

44. Do I try to write creatively?
45. Does the story have a good beginning?
46. Is the story interesting?
47. Are the details organized?
48. Are the words and phrases colorful?
49. Have I taken care of periods, commas, etc.?

(Adapted from Lamb, 1967, p. 350.)

Questions 44 to 49 might be used for evaluation by pupils other than the writers of the stories. If the objective of instruction is the development of subjective evaluation techniques, then each pupil might evaluate the paper of someone else and thereby gain insight into his own evaluation efforts. Obviously, an element of objective evaluation enters into any creative-evaluation assessment. Frequently, this cannot be helped, and no harm is done if the pupils realize both the distinction between subjective and objective evaluation as well as the points which join the two together.

E.2-2.42

DIRECTIONS: Now you are ready to write stories about your puppet. Follow these steps in telling your story.

a. Give your puppet a name.
b. Decide from this list of words how it will look:
   funny
   sad
   happy
   kind
c. Decide how you will dress your puppet.

50. Now, write a story about your puppet, using its name. Describe how it looks and what it is wearing.

(Adapted from Conlin & LeRoy, 1967, p. 76.)

Questions 44 to 49 and 50 demonstrate, at the upper and the lower elementary levels, the means by which written compositions may be evaluated. Questions 44 to 49 suggest the criteria to be used at a lower grade level in the evaluation of pupils' writing. The teacher would assess the pupils' ability to follow directions, select imaginative words, and so forth. The emphasis in this item, however, appears to be upon the content of the story, rather than upon any mechanics of writing.

Language arts instruction is not concerned solely with cognitive behaviors such as knowing, comprehending, analyzing, and applying. Indeed, considerable effort in the language arts is devoted to what has been traditionally called the formation of *Attitudes* (F.0). And it is here that the affective domain is encountered.

It is often the case in the affective domain that behaviors are tested in a somewhat cavalier fashion in the language arts. Subjective evaluation is almost exclusively used. But frequently there is more subjective evaluation than is necessary. This situation comes about when those concerned with the language arts are not informed about methods of testing other than directed and informal observations, logs, diaries, etc. Such a statement is not meant to deny the need for, and the value of, similar evaluational procedures. The authors feel, however, that subjective evaluation can become more systematic and more valuable if care is taken in the construction of attitude inventories, checklists, and rating scales. It is evidence of this type that rescues the teacher from statements such as "Yes, I think they all like the reading or the writing we have been doing."

Attitudes (F.0)

Attitudes toward language and communication are vital at the elementary school level. While there may be a wide range of possible attitudes, only *Acceptance* and *Appreciation* are identified in Table 15-1, Table of Specifications for the Language Arts (page 402). From a review of curriculum guides, these two attitudes seem highly significant. But a teacher cannot evaluate attitudes as he does knowledge or skills. Rather, attitudes, like other affective behaviors, can be evaluated through the use of checklists, rating scales, and attitude inventories.

Questions 51 to 55 and 56 to 60 are checklists designed to evaluate the attitude of accepting certain information which would be of value to the pupil in his work. The teacher might administer such a checklist to his entire class and then use the results to assess the attitude of acceptance of certain pupils or of all pupils. As it was defined previously, acceptance means that the pupil is open to outside stimuli. No internalized value is attached to the stimulus. The pupil merely accepts it at a conscious level.

Acceptance (F.1)

F.1-1.7

Questions About My Spelling Methods

	Always	Usually	Seldom	Never
51. Do I definitely center my attention upon the word?				
52. Do I try to visualize the word?				
53. Do I say the letters of the word to myself?				
54. Do I pronounce the word correctly and try to recall how each syllable appears?				
55. Do I compare the word with the correct written or printed copy?				

F.1-2.43

Questions About Writing

	Yes	No	Uncertain
56. Do you like to write stories in class?			
57. Do you feel that the teacher should grade the stories?			
58. Do you accept the need for certain conventions of writing?			
59. Do you feel that too much emphasis is placed upon mechanics of English?			
60. Do you like reading your stories aloud?			

(Adapted from Lamb, 1967, p. 342.)

Attitudes of acceptance can also be measured by direct observation and by the writing of anecdotal records. It is possible to evaluate a pupil's reaction to poetry or to discussions of the history of language by observing him and by being sensitive to his feelings. The following is a teacher's anecdotal record of a pupil's attitude of acceptance toward a study of the history of language (F.1-1.2).

September 12, 1970

Eddie is eight years old today. He seemed happy at the start of school, but he soon lapsed into silence when we began talking about the origins of the English language. Perhaps it is the content which does not interest him. He appears to be unwilling to accept the value of such study. I will try to interest him in a study of how language has changed.

This is a legitimate evaluation form. In fact, it is frequently the case that testing the various affective behaviors proceeds along the lines of direct observation and intuitive insight.

Appreciation (F.2)

F.2-2.42

DIRECTIONS: The purpose of this questionnaire is to discover what you really think about the writing you do in your leisure time. There are no "right" answers. Answer each question frankly.

	Yes	No
61. Do you sometimes create a character who is very much like you?		
62. Do you sometimes write about people you know?		
63. Do you write about things which have actually happened to you?		
64. Do you write about things which you would like to have happen to you?		

Please use the remainder of the space to add any comments you would like.

Questions 61 to 64 are a portion of a questionnaire which assesses whether a pupil appreciates or internalizes some activity, skill, content, etc. If a pupil were to answer the questions in the affirmative, this would indicate an attitudinal level beyond that of acceptance. The question assumes that the pupil does write independently of an assignment. Such an assumption indicates that the pupil already appreciates, at least to a degree, the value of written expression. If the teacher cannot assume that pupils write independently, then the directions to questions 61 to 64 might be altered by omitting "in your leisure time."

It should be emphasized to the pupils that there are no right or wrong answers to attitudinal items. Elementary school pupils are, when requested, brutally honest. This is the reaction any survey, questionnaire, or rating scale should elicit.

Teachers can determine whether or not a pupil appreciates or internalizes content by means of anecdotal records. The following example reports on a pupil's listening behavior (F.2-2.12).

October 12, 1967

John has shown considerable interest in listening to the stories on the record. Yesterday, he asked if he could remain in during recess and listen to additional stories. I asked him if he wanted to take a few of the records home, and he agreed happily.

Walter J. Moore and Larry D. Kennedy

Reception (G.0)

Reception suggests those behaviors concerned with the reception of stimuli. These may include listening, observing, sensing, feeling, etc. There may be several levels of receiving, but the two which seem to be important for the elementary school language arts are suggested here.

Awareness (G.1) *Awareness* can be measured by asking the pupil to respond to a number of statements. Content is presented in the statements, and the pupil reacts either positively or negatively. Often a teacher assumes that the pupil is conscious of particular phenomena. When he does this, he risks launching the pupil into more complex levels of awareness than the pupil is ready to handle.

Awareness can operate throughout the content area. A pupil can be aware of a teacher's voice. He can also be aware that certain knowledge exists without knowing the facts. After an extended discussion of the nature of language, for example, the teacher might measure conscious awareness of what was said in a manner similar to that in items 65 to 68.

G.1-1.1

DIRECTIONS: Read the following statements carefully. If you agree with the statement, put an A in the blank. If you disagree, put a D in the blank.

__65. Language changes constantly.

__66. All language usage is absolute.

__67. Change in language is normal.

__68. The written language is the primary form of language.

Questions 69 to 71 are concerned with whether the pupil is aware, at a noncognitive level, of such aspects of language structure as word order and structural relationships.

G.1-1.3

DIRECTIONS: Look at the following sentences on the board. What can you tell me about them?

69. The three ergs bogled in the poner.

70. Our emose was pummering his erstles.

71. She is the algest mooner in the whomper.

Selected attention (G.2) This behavior suggests that the pupil has moved beyond simple awareness to involvement with the stimuli. He wants to listen. He enjoys the rhythm of poetry. Test items for this behavior are generally of the interest-inventory type, although other types of test formats can be made appropriate.

G.2-3.2

DIRECTIONS: The purpose of these questions is to find out what you think about the reading we have been doing in class. Put a Y in the blank if your answer is "yes" to the question. If your answer is "no," put N in the blank. If you are undecided as to the answer, put U in the blank.

__72. Would you like to read more stories like *Homer Price and the Doughnut Machine*?

__73. Did you like the fables we read?

__74. Would you like to do more reading in the area of poetry?

__75. Do you think we should spend more time on any stories in particular? If so, which ones?

__76. Would you like to dramatize some of the stories we read?

Dawson et al. (1963, p. 405) suggest a means for testing for general receptiveness or, in our classification of behaviors, for attentiveness in listening (G.2.2.12). The following instructions are an adaptation.

> Have a teacher or supervisor observe the attention of the pupils as you teach. He should have a paper numbered down the left margin, there being as many numbers as there are minutes in the lesson. At the top, head three columns as follows: *Close attention*, *Partial attention*, and *No attention*. At one-minute intervals, the observer may note the number of pupils in each of the categories. Afterward, the percentage (per minute) in each category may be worked out.

Minutes	*Close attention*	*Partial attention*	*No attention*
1			
2			
3			
4			
5			
6			
7			
8			
9			
10			

The same procedure may, of course, be used to evaluate individual pupils as well.

There is a large measure of subjectivity in such an evaluation, however. For the past fifteen years there has been a determined effort on the part of some researchers in the field to convince all concerned that the term "listening" is not sufficiently precise to be of much help when one talks about the behaviors commonly blanketed under it. Caffrey (1955, p. 121) views "auding" as the process of hearing, listening to, recognizing, and interpreting and comprehending spoken language. Strickland (1962) has suggested different amounts of involvement in listening. No one level is necessarily better than any other, depending on the purpose involved. Thus, when one refers to listening, he may really be referring to (1) hearing sounds or words, (2) intermittent listening, (3) half listening, (4) listening passively with little or no observable response, or (5) narrow listening.

Certainly every teacher is at least aware of types or levels of listening. Test items which purport to measure listening, then, should be properly specified as to the type and the level of listening behavior to be evaluated. Subjective evaluations of listening, while certainly better than no evaluation at all, should be viewed in the context of their limitations.

Participation (H.0)

Participation is, of course, vital to language arts instruction. As defined by the authors, and in accordance with the views of English educators, participation means that the pupil is involved in overt participatory behaviors. Two behaviors are identified in this category: *Willing participation* (*H.*1) and *Enjoyment of participation* (*H.*2). The distinction between the two lies in the level of involvement. *Willing participation* indicates only that the pupil defers to teacher demands and that he participates only in response to external stimuli. *Enjoyment of participation*, on the other hand, suggests a strong affective component. The pupil wants to participate; he values participation for reasons which are important to him.

Willing participation (H.1)

H.1-2.42

Yes	No	
__	__	77. Would you be willing to serve as chairman of a committee?
__	__	78. Would you prefer to have a speaking part in the play?
__	__	79. Would you like to introduce guests to the room?
__	__	80. Would you like to be a member of the student council?
__	__	81. Would you rather share information than listen to others?

H.1-2.22

DIRECTIONS [to be administered orally and individually]: I am going to ask you some questions. I want you to tell me what you think about the questions. There are no right or wrong answers, and you may simply say "yes" or "no" if you wish. If you want to tell me more, that would be fine too.

82. Do you like to share your books, toys, and other things with the class during sharing time?
83. Do you like to lead the pledge to the flag?
84. Do you like to help collect the milk money?
85. Do you like to ask questions in class?
86. Do you like to answer questions in class?

Questions 77 to 81 and 82 to 86 are concerned with willing participation, and while they are identified as writing and speaking activities, respectively (2.42 and 2.22), the questionnaires measure a wide range of participatory behaviors. This is extremely necessary in an area such as the language arts, where participation of individuals cannot always be isolated according to particular content or activities. *Willing participation*, then, is more global than is *Enjoyment of participation*.

There is a qualitative difference between willing and enjoyed participation. At the elementary level, it is extremely difficult to discern this difference at times. Very often, surveys designed to get at *Willing participation* will "cross over" into *Enjoyment of participation* behaviors, since a quantitative boundary does not exist between the two. Objective measures, then, must be supported by direct observations of the pupils' likes and dislikes with regard to participation behaviors. Further, questions 87 to 91 are more specific than questions 82 to 86 in that they aim directly at enjoyment of reading.

Enjoyment of participation (H.2)

H.2-2.32

DIRECTIONS: The purpose of this questionnaire is to determine how you feel about the things we do in class. There are no right answers. Check the blank for "yes" if you agree with the statement. Check the blank for "no" if you disagree with the statement.

Yes No

__ __ 87. I like to read orally.

__ __ 88. I like to work on committees to discuss reading.

__ __ 89. I like to answer questions over my reading.

__ __ 90. I enjoy making reports of books.

__ __ 91. I enjoy reading certain parts of books orally.

Illustration of a set of interrelated evaluation items

Like other areas, the language arts present a variety of testing problems. But the major difficulty at all grade levels is that of recognizing the interrelationships of behaviors with respect to particular content areas of the language arts.

Teachers frequently design daily lessons in the language arts which have the potential for measuring several behaviors at one time. This may not be recognized initially, however, because the teacher is intent upon concentrating only upon one behavior. When the teacher does become aware of the interrelationships among the various behaviors, he may be literally overwhelmed with the complexity of the "simple" lesson. It is at this point that many language arts teachers determine that the task of sorting out and identifying specific behaviors for a particular lesson is too time-consuming and too difficult to be of value. Thus, integration of learning and of evaluation is lost when the task of identifying specific behaviors in the language arts is neglected. A simple reading passage should make the point clear.

At a given grade level, a teacher is concerned with whether his pupils have the ability to get at the central thought of the material they have been reading in encyclopedias. He develops a reading passage which is similar to that encountered in the reading of encyclopedias to determine whether his pupils can comprehend the central thought. (The italicizing serves some test items to be presented below.)

> Man has always been *interested* in his own past. Modern explorers have found the beginnings of civilization going back thousands of years. Explorers, called archaeologists, search for materials from which the story of man can be studied. The materials may be written records, pieces of art work, or old ruins.
>
> The explorers have developed *exact* methods of study. The methods *center* on dating what is found.
>
> The end of World War I marked the beginning of the period of growth in archaeology. In Egypt, an *exciting* discovery was made. A royal tomb from 1352 years before Christ was found. Finding the 18-year-old king, wrapped in gold and buried with a *huge* supply of gold objects, *awakened* the interest of the world.

The teacher then writes test questions designed to ascertain whether the pupil is able to get at the central thought in the passage, beginning with item 92 or 93.

B.2, Interpretation

92. This passage is mostly about
    a. modern explorers
    b. a royal tomb
    c. Egypt
    d. old records

93. Perhaps the best title for this passage would be
    a. *Uncovering Man's Past*
    b. *The Death of a King*
    c. *A New Interest in Art Works*
    d. *Do You Want To Be an Explorer?*

If the teacher stops at this point, however, he fails to examine the potential of the passage for the evaluation of further reading behaviors. The one rather simple passage provides a wealth of test items for both cognitive and affective behaviors.

The important consideration for language arts instruction is that learning and, subsequently, evaluation do not occur in isolation. One does not read for facts alone; nor does one read solely for purposes of vocabulary development. The various behaviors in language, language skills, and literature are inextricably linked together. And, while the teacher may well be aware of their individual nature or existence, testing situations should not consider these behaviors in isolation. Finally, the consideration of the interrelatedness of cognitive and affective behaviors stimulates thinking of learning and of evaluation in terms of a hierarchy of behaviors, with skill building upon skill toward the eventual comprehension and critical evaluation of the content or the material.

In addition to testing for the central thought of a passage, the teacher could also develop test items for determining how well pupils are able to respond to factual questions and how they can handle vocabulary, follow directions, and draw inferences. Some examples follow.

A.1, Knowledge of terminology

94. The word exact as underlined and used in this passage means about the same as
    a. precise
    b. difficult
    c. incorrect
    d. exaggerated

95. The word center as underlined and used in this passage means the opposite of
    a. concentrate
    b. focus
    c. converge
    d. disperse

96. The word exciting as underlined and used in this passage means
    a. thrilling
    b. meaningless
    c. disturbing
    d. interesting

97. The word huge as underlined and used in this passage means about the same as
    a. vast
    b. valuable
    c. valiant
    d. valid

98. The word awakened as underlined and used in this passage means about the same as
    a. aroused
    b. accused
    c. arraigned
    d. ascertained

99. The word interested as underlined and used in this passage means the opposite of
    a. negligent
    b. concerned
    c. fascinated
    d. engrossed

A.2, Knowledge of specific facts

100. Archaeologists do not search for
    a. new lands
    b. written records
    c. art work
    d. old ruins

101. The royal tomb contained
    a. gold objects
    b. much money
    c. many old ruins
    d. written records

102. According to this passage, an exciting archaeological discovery
    a. was made in Egypt
    b. is made frequently
    c. is worth much money
    d. means much hard work

103. According to this passage, man has always been interested in
   a. his own past
   b. exploring
   c. archaeology
   d. art work
104. The period of growth in archaeology
   a. began at the end of World War I
   b. followed an exciting discovery
   c. caused the development of exact methods of study
   d. marked the beginning of World War I
105. The 18-year-old king in this passage was
   a. wrapped in gold
   b. discovered during World War I
   c. interested in archaeology
   d. buried with many jewels

C.3, Analysis of organizational principles

106. From the information presented in this passage, it would seem that the study of archaeology is most nearly like the study of
   a. history
   b. geography
   c. law
   d. engineering
107. From the information presented in this passage, it is probably true that:
   a. Archaeology is a rather new study.
   b. Gold is a rather new metal.
   c. Archaeologists do most of their work in a library.
   d. Man became interested in his history after World War I.
108. From the information presented in this passage, it is probably true that:
   a. Pieces of art work are different for different periods in history.
   b. Old ruins are more important than works of art.
   c. Archaeologists are not very scientific.
   d. Ancient Egyptians lived to a very old age.

Special problems of testing in the language arts

There are major objectives in the language arts for which no test items have been written before. This is due, in part, to the confusion which has existed in the field for several years about what content should be measured. It has been only in the past few years, for example, that certain elements of language and of literature have been identified as belonging in elementary school language arts programs. The majority of schools have traditionally had extremely well-developed reading programs to the frequent exclusion of listening, speaking, and writing on an equally well-organized, structured level. Behaviors in these related language areas have not, then, been identified with a great deal of precision in relation to specific content, and as a result, they have frequently become secondary behaviors as they are related to general reading behaviors.

Literature, as an area apart from reading, is not given distinct consideration in the testing literature at the elementary school level. And, while it is true that reading skills are applied to literature, the fact remains that literature is possessed of a body of knowledge of its own. In the view of the authors, literature should not exist solely as the means for supplying material for use in the development of reading skills. Test makers, of course, have a great deal of difficulty in keeping pace with the shifting emphases and trends in language arts instruction. The fact remains, however, that standardized tests today have not kept pace with curricular reform in the language arts.

Such a situation is understandable when one considers the array of language arts programs in the schools today. An abundance of school systems have not yet felt the impact of increased knowledge about the nature of language and communication. Test makers are reluctant, therefore, to revise their instruments drastically. The authors have attempted to suggest test items and testing procedures which would be appropriate for the full range of content and behaviors as they are identified in the Table of Specifications.

Special testing problems exist in the early grades of the elementary school when young children are, as yet, unable to read and to write. While individuals may vary considerably, it seems to be only a matter of approximately two years from the time pupils enter kindergarten until they are able to respond to written directions and thereby handle paper and pencil tests. Pupils do, of course, take tests prior to the second grade. Such tests, however, depend upon careful verbal instructions and the use of pictures, drawings, etc., as response items.

Formative testing in the language arts

The use of summative evaluation in the elementary school language arts is not widespread. While achievement tests are certainly given at some time during the year and while there is more emphasis upon grading at the upper elementary level than at the primary level, the fact remains that the structure of the elementary school in terms of self-contained classrooms and the nature of early language learning are such that summative evaluation is not the dominant concern.

Formative evaluation, while not specifically identified as such, is the major type of evaluation employed in the language arts at the elementary school level. Indeed, in the area of language skill instruction, it is formative evaluation which serves to redirect instruction for individuals in listening, speaking, reading, and writing. It is formative evaluation which lets the pupil know what he has and has not learned about such skills. Further, it is particularly significant in language skill learning that the pupil comprehend the nature of his difficulties with the language skills; it is evaluation during the formation of learning which makes this possible.

Broadly conceived, formative testing in the language arts is diagnostic in nature. That is, the purpose of any diagnostic test is not to give a grade, but to adapt instruction to the needs of the individual and of the entire class as those needs are expressed in performance on diagnostic tests. The kind of test evidence most useful to the language arts teacher, then, is that evidence which supplies answers to the student as well as to the teacher about the "what" and the "why" of particular learning difficulties.

Formative evaluation, in the form of diagnostic tests, begins frequently in the kindergarten, but it is more often developed in the first grade. The principal purpose of diagnostic testing at this early level is to determine readiness for reading and for general school learning. The administration of such tests varies considerably, but they are usually given in the first four to six weeks of school. Such diagnostic evaluation enables the teacher to plan an appropriate program for the pupil. The pupil is told his strong points, and the areas of weakness are discussed, and plans are made with the pupil for the remediation of the difficulties. Personal conferences are held with individual pupils and the teacher generally makes such comments as these: "Susan, you did very well on your vowel sounds. I'm certain you won't have serious trouble with them. I do think, though, that we need to work more on your mastery of the single-consonant sounds. I'll sit down with you later in the morning and discuss these with you. Then, I have some special things for you to do that I think would help."

From the results of a diagnostic test, then, the teacher is able to redirect the learning experiences of her pupils. Such evaluation is not for the purpose of grading. It is designed specifically for the purpose of identifying difficulties in learning and determining the means by which to ameliorate the difficulties.

There is a wide variety of such tests available to the primary teacher today. Prior to the time the pupil is exposed to specific reading-readiness tests, tests of hearing, vision, color blindness, etc., may be administered. It is possible, for example, to test hearing ability quite well at an early level. This can be done through various mechanical aids which test loudness and pitch. Additionally, there are informal tests of hearing which are also useful. Kough and DeHaan (1955) describe such tests in *Identifying Children with Special Needs*. If individual pupils are found to have physiological difficulties, then the classroom teacher can make the appropriate adjustments.

There are factors, other than hearing, vision, and color blindness, which must be considered early in a child's school career. The regional or social dialect which a pupil brings to the classroom can, and often does, adversely affect his learning. Similarly, those pupils who already speak what could be termed a prestigious dialect might find "school language" to be dull or antiseptic. What is needed, then, are formative tests which measure the particular dialect of a pupil. Teachers are almost never unaware of dialects which differ from their own. They do need, however, to comprehend the effects of such dialectal differences upon listening, speaking, reading, and writing performances of their pupils.

The Botel Reading Inventory (Botel, 1962) is an excellent example of a diagnostic test which can be used in the formative evaluation of student learning. It should be stressed that the Botel test is not an achievement test; it is not concerned with evaluation at the end of a unit, course, or year's work. The Botel Reading Inventory is an informal test of word recognition and comprehension. As such, it is designed to be used by teachers to provide a basis for subsequent instruction in reading.

The Phonics Mastery Test of the Botel is designed to determine what sounds the pupils already know and to plan a phonics instruction program based on individual and class needs. The following item is taken from the Phonics Mastery Test.

A.3-1.31

DIRECTIONS: Now I shall read some other words. Listen carefully and write the first two letters of each word. (Note: Acceptable answers are in parentheses. Since this is a test on sounds, not on spelling, any indicated answer is correct.)

109. blithe (bl)	116. crass (cr)	122. scud (sc-sk)
110. clog (cl)	117. dredge (dr)	123. smear (sm)
111. flounce (fl)	118. frisk (fr)	124. snag (sn)
112. glum (gl)	119. gripe (gr)	125. spike (sp)
113. plush (pl)	120. prance (pr)	126. stint (st)
114. slink (sl)	121. trek (tr)	127. swap (sw)
115. bray (br)		

(Botel, 1962, p. 9, items 1–9.)

Pupils are not tested with grades in mind on such a test. Rather, the emphasis is upon evaluation as a guide to subsequent instruction.

The need in the language arts classroom today is for more formal and informal tests which evaluate learning during the process of learning. The Botel Reading Inventory is only one of a large number of tests appropriate for the elementary school. Care should be exercised in the selection of such tests, however. It is often the case that so-called diagnostic tests are actually achievement tests. The value of such tests for formative evaluation, then, is indeed negligible.

The unit on fables

In order to illustrate the possible uses of formative evaluation during the presentation of a unit of work, the following items are presented (some for the second time) with reference to the unit on fables discussed on pages 414–415. Table 15-3, Table of Specifications for a Unit of Fables, indicated that three terms are particularly relevant to the unit. These terms, "fable," "theme," and "style," are not, however, to be defined precisely by the pupils at this level. What the teacher is interested in knowing, in this case, is whether the pupil has learned to recognize the operational significance of such terms, and, if not, what difficulties he has encountered. Test items, then, should be geared toward an analysis of the cause of learning difficulties.

Knowledge of terminology (A.1)

A.1-3.2

128. DIRECTIONS: Now I have finished reading one of the fables, and tomorrow I will read another. But first, who can tell me what a fable is? If you like, you may begin by telling me what some of the things were that went on in the story. Did anything surprise you? Did the story remind you of anything you have seen or heard before?

The purpose of such a question is to determine (1) whether the pupils recognize, at an operational level, the term "fable" and (2) whether the lesson has been successful in terms of the teacher's objectives. At the primary level, children are quite willing to talk about what they hear or what they might eventually read. Through careful questioning, the teacher can evaluate the success of his teaching and can also restructure later lessons if necessary.

Anecdotal records can be used to record responses, and tape recorders, rating sheets, and checklists are appropriate for recording individual responses. Similar procedures could be used to evaluate responses to such terms as "theme" and "style." At this level, evaluation is almost always informal.

Translation (B.1)

B.1-3.2

129. DIRECTIONS: I have read you one fable, and we read the other fable together. Yesterday we talked about what we all thought a fable was and what we thought about the town mouse and the country mouse. Today, I would like for you to read the story of "The Town Mouse and the Country Mouse" silently at your desks. When you finish, take a piece of paper and tell me the story in your own words. But this time, I want you to use names of people for the town mouse and the country mouse. You might call the town mouse "Max," and you might call the city mouse "Fred." Use whatever names you like. I will come to your desks to help you get started.

As was stated previously, translation is a difficult task for young children. The problem for the pupils is to comprehend that fables are about people. Pupils should, then, learn to translate the fables to real-life people and situations.

Interpretation (B.2) The considerations for this behavior is that the pupil learn that there is a thought behind the fable and that he is able to interpret or to comprehend that thought. This should be done at an oral level, regardless of the individual grade level in the primary. Pupils gain much from such interaction as they attempt to "thrash out" their answers. A question might be stated:

B.2-3.2

130. DIRECTIONS: I read the fable to you in class, and then, we read it again together. We were all interested in what the town mouse and the country mouse had to say. What I want you to do today is to tell me what you thought the town mouse and the country mouse were trying to tell us. We know what they told each other. But, what do you think they were trying to say to you and to me?

Expressive application (D.2)

D.2-3.2

131. DIRECTIONS: I am going to write some words on the board which were in the fable we read and discussed. What I want you to do is to take each word and to add words to it to change its description or the way it looks. For example, here is the word "Dog." You might add some words to this and make it "A big brown fluffy dog," or "A little black shaggy dog." I want you to do the same thing with these other words. Try to use as many different words as you can to describe the words on the board. I will come around to answer whatever questions you have.

mouse
plank
brook
meat

This question calls for the pupils to use their imaginations to alter the words on the blackboard. Such an activity also calls into play the pupils' handwriting skills, spelling, and vocabulary. And it requires that the pupils produce unique descriptions within the appropriate range of their abilities.

The unit on short-story writing

The formative testing program for the unit on short-story writing (see page 415) is twofold. First, the teacher would test knowledge and comprehension of the short story as a literary genre. Second, the teacher would test the ability of the pupils to apply their knowledge and comprehension through the writing of expressive short stories. Formative testing emphasis here would be given to the demonstration of knowledge and comprehension of the form of the short story as well as to the mechanics of writing, usage, vocabulary, and spelling. An important testing consideration in such a unit is that the mechanics of writing, etc., should not be tested outside the context of the short story itself. There is little value in an isolated study of the mechanics of English. There is more value to a follow-up study of mechanics based upon the individual's ability to handle the mechanics in writing. Again, the main emphasis of the evaluation should be upon informing the pupil as to what he has learned and what he still needs to learn.

The test items which follow should help to illustrate the different levels of the structure of the short-story unit.

Knowledge of terminology (A.1)

A.1-3.2

132. Climax, as it is used in the short story, refers to
  a. the point where the complication ends and the resolution begins
  b. the technique of giving a reader a hint of what is to come
  c. the moment when opposing forces meet
  d. a series of related instances

There is, of course, always a question about how much technical terminology should be employed when teaching young children; and there are no clear-cut answers. The teacher should not assume initially, however, that the pupils are too young to understand terminology. Indeed, today's elementary school children are far better prepared to understand the technical nomenclature of a discipline than children in past years. It is possible, particularly at the intermediate level, to discuss and to write short stories without such knowledge. The assessment of the value of terminology is, then, a matter of personal assessment by the individual teacher.

Interpretation (B.2)

B.2-2.42, B.2-3.2

133. DIRECTIONS: Read carefully the short story which has been distributed. You are to demonstrate your understanding of the short story by writing a review of it. Be certain to pay attention in your review to theme, plot, setting, climax, and characterization.

In this item, the teacher asks the pupil to demonstrate his understanding of a new short story through the writing of a review of the story. The item requires that the pupil pay specific attention to the elements within a short story and that he deal with them in writing.

Expressive application (D.2)

D.2-2.42

DIRECTIONS: Your assignment is to write a short story. There will be no page limitations. I will evaluate you on the following points.

134. Appropriate short story conventions.
135. Appropriate use of mechanics of English, vocabulary, usage, and spelling.

This item would represent the "pulling together" of all the knowledge, skills, and abilities which make up the structure of this particular unit. It is in questions of *Application* that the elementary school teacher can witness the effects of the unit. If the short stories written by the pupils are not adequate in some way, then the objectives have not been met, and it is the responsibility of the teacher to restructure subsequent units of the same type to accomplish his objectives.

The preceding item also points up the difficulties which one encounters in the language arts in attempting to define what behavior is sought. Writing assignments such as this call for a host of behaviors. The teacher should take careful note of those initial behaviors which contribute to writing skills. The ability to produce functional and expressive written communications depends upon the mastery of previous elements. The great value of formative evaluation for the language arts lies in its attention to the total process of language growth and to its potential for demonstrating to the teacher the interrelatedness of behaviors in the language arts.

Standardized testing in the language arts

According to the 1965 edition of the *Mental Measurements Yearbook* (Buros, 1965), there are a number of standardized achievement tests which contain language subsections appropriate for the elementary grades. Caution should be exercised, however, in the use of those tests which do not show recent revisions. The authors do not wish to dismiss entirely those tests which were published prior to 1960, but the fact remains that English instruction at the elementary school level has been in a state of flux for more than a decade. Those tests which have not been revised significantly in recent years, then, do not reflect the curriculum changes of the past decade. Indeed, it is extremely doubtful whether any standardized test on the market today reflects those changes.

Of those tests reviewed in Buros, only four general achievement tests receive substantial attention. These are (1) the Science Research Associates Achievement Series: Language (Science Research Associates, 1957); (2) the Metropolitan Achievement Tests: Elem. Battery: Form B, Word Discrimination (1959); (3) the Stanford Achievement Test: Language (1953); and (4) the Iowa Every-pupil Tests of Basic Skills: Language (State University of Iowa, 1947). Additionally, attention is given to the California Language Test (Tiegs & Clark, 1957), a separate language skills test, and to the Sequential Tests of Educational Progress (STEP): Writing (Educational Testing Service, 1957b).

The four achievement tests are quite similar in their content and in the approach to the measurement of language skills. Considerable attention is given to (1) spelling, (2) word knowledge, (3) punctuation, (4) usage, (5) parts of speech, (6) reading, (7) sentence sense, and (8) word analysis. Individual subtests also include listening, handwriting, and a variety of vocabulary exercises.

Each of the achievement tests is concerned almost solely with language skills. And, in each of the tests, the more specific elements of English, such as punctuation, capitalization, etc., are tested with reasonable success. There is, however, a tendency in each of the tests toward excessive fragmentation of the language skills. The testing of one language skill in isolation from other related language skills seems questionable.

The language subtest of the Stanford Achievement Test: Primary II Battery, for example, has separate samples which deal with punctuation and capitalization. The two samples are in story and in letter form. The pupil is asked to supply the necessary capitalization for the story and the necessary punctuation for the letter. It seems obvious that the test makers were concerned with ease of scoring and with a format which did not present too many tasks for the pupil to perform at one time. But the fact remains that such fragmentation is highly artificial. In writing his own stories and letters, the pupil must put everything together; he cannot afford the luxury of being concerned solely with isolated skills.

The language subtests of the SRA Achievement Series, at least at the primary and the intermediate levels, measure knowledge of terms, facts, conventions, etc. In the sections of the subtests which deal with paragraph meaning, there is an extension of knowledge into comprehension and analysis behaviors at the upper elementary level. The fact remains, however, that language tests are weighted heavily to the recall or the recognition of terms, facts, and conventions.

While each of the four standardized tests received generally favorable reviews in Buros, there was concern expressed over the content or the skills which were being measured. Ample documentation has been made throughout this chapter with regard to the changing nature of language arts instruction at the elementary school level. It is highly questionable, therefore, whether current achievement tests reflect this changing character. What this criticism seems to suggest, then, is that existing tests measure only that small area which is concerned with certain mechanical manipulations of English conventions. And although subtests of reading comprehension, vocabulary, etc., may be of definite value, they represent only a fraction of the total area of the language arts.

The Writing Test of the Sequential Tests of Educational Progress presents a different approach to the measurement of language skills. The Writing Test is not, strictly speaking, a measure of language achievement. Rather, its intent is to measure the broad outcomes of general education apart from specific subject-matter concerns. The Writing Test includes categories of organization, conventions, critical thinking, effectiveness, and appropriateness. Pupils are expected to recognize errors in context and to select appropriate revisions. Thus, the procedures seem, on the surface at least, to be more relevant for the process of writing than do those achievement tests which consider language skills in isolation from any functional or creative context.

Serious doubts have been expressed, however, about the value of the Writing Test. The passages to be evaluated by the pupil have been criticized as being dull and ridden with errors. Allen (1965, p. 293) describes the test as "an attractive test of uncertain worth." Further, Black (1965, p. 542) notes that as a test of writing ability, STEP Writing is too much concerned with the measurement of conventions. Black criticizes STEP Writing further on the grounds that the pupil is concerned with making editorial revisions and not with the process of writing itself.

One of the special testing problems in English, however, is that of measuring writing in its entirety. It is extremely doubtful that any objective instrument, however conceived, can do more than evaluate isolated elements of the writing process.

The California Language Test does not differ substantially from the language subtests found in achievement batteries. Schutz (1965, p. 544) raises the issue of whether the California Language Test should be labeled a "language test," since it gives no consideration to dialectal differences, structural patterns, etc. This same criticism could, however, be applied to language subtests of achievement batteries.

Indeed, a major problem which falls upon those charged with the responsibility of selecting standardized language tests for the elementary school is that of determining whether the type of test items contained in such instruments are appropriate for contemporary language arts programs. There are, for example, no standardized tests for literature at the elementary school level reported in Buros. (The Stanford Achievement series Literature Test was dropped because of the wide diversity of literature curricula from school to school.) Similarly, as was noted previously, there are no standardized tests which incorporate linguistic findings of the past decade. The considerable interest in the nature of language, dialects, language history, etc., is not included in any standardized tests.

It may well be the case, as it was with the Literature Test of the Stanford Achievement series, that the wide diversity of language and literature curricula is such that it precludes the possibility of measurement by standardized instruments. The impact of the resource materials prepared under Project English may serve to point the direction to such evaluation in the near future.

The evaluation of oral compositions or of speaking presents another problem. At present, there are no standardized tests which measure speaking. While it is conceivable that tests to measure basic speech skills, such as pronunciation and enunciation, could be constructed, they would possess the same weaknesses as tests of English mechanics. Speaking is not concerned solely with such skills. Speaking is similar to writing in that mastery of particular skills is only one element of the larger communicative activity.

Considerable reservations must be made, therefore, with regard to the future testing for speaking and writing. The complexity of the factors involved in speaking and writing are such that only an extremely small sampling of ability can be measured. Perhaps the alternate value of such tests would be in their suggestions of what could and should be measured.

It may be true that English does not lend itself to measurement by objective standardized tests. If this is the case, teachers and curriculum personnel are left in the unenviable position of having a program in search of some means of standardized testing.

In summary, if the measurement of isolated language skills is felt to be significant, then existing standardized tests can be of limited value. However, if more than measurement of language mechanics is sought, then considerable effort must be made by those concerned with the teaching of the language arts and by those concerned with the construction of test instruments.

NOTE The documents reviewed for Table 15-1, Table of Specifications for the Language Arts (K to 6), include the following:

(1) Baker, J. F. *Elementary evaluative criteria.* Boston: Boston University, School of Education, 1954. (2) Board of Education of the City of New York. *Handbook for language arts: Pre-K, kindergarten, grades one and two.* (Curr. Bull. No. 8, 1965–66 Ser.) New York: BECNY, 1966. (3) College Entrance Examination Board, Commission on English. *Freedom and discipline in English.* New York: CEEB, 1965. (4) Dixon, J. *Growth through English: A report based on the Dartmouth Seminar, 1966.* Reading, Eng.: National Association for the Teaching of English, 1967. (5) Frazier, A. (Ed.) *Ends and issues, 1965–1966: Points of decision in the development of the English curriculum.* Champaign, Ill.: National Council of Teachers of English, 1966. (6) Kearney, N. C. *Elementary school objectives: A report for the Mid-Century Committee on Outcomes in Elementary Education.* New York: Russell Sage Foundation, 1953. (7) National Council of Teachers of English. The workload of the elementary school teacher: A statement of policy of the National Council of Teachers of English. *Elementary English,* 1968, **45,** 224–227. (8) National Council of Teachers of English, Commission on the English Curriculum. *Language arts for today's children.* New York: Appleton-Century-Crofts, 1954. (9) National Council of Teachers of English, Committee on National Interest. *The national interest and the teaching of English: A report on the status of the profession.* Champaign, Ill.: NCTE, 1961. (10) National Council of Teachers of English, Committee on National Interest. *The national interest and the continuing education of teachers of English: A report on the state of the profession.* Champaign, Ill.: NCTE, 1964. (11) Nebraska Curriculum Development Center. *A curriculum for English: Grade 1.* Lincoln, Nebr.: University of Nebraska Press, 1966. (12) Wisconsin Department of Public Instruction. *English language arts in Wisconsin: A growth curriculum in English language arts for the kindergarten through grade 12, 1968.* Madison, Wis.: WDPI, 1968.

REFERENCES

Allen, D. In O. K. Buros (Ed.) *The sixth mental measurements yearbook.* Highland Park, N.J.: Gryphon Press, 1965. Pp. 595–597.

Baker, J. F. *Elementary evaluative criteria.* Boston: Boston University, School of Education, 1954.

Black, H. In O. K. Buros (Ed.) *The sixth mental measurements yearbook.* Highland Park, N.J.: Gryphon Press, 1965. Pp. 592–594.

Bloom, B. S. (Ed.) *Taxonomy of educational objectives: The classification of educational goals.* Handbook 1. *Cognitive domain.* New York: McKay, 1956.

Board of Education of the City of New York. *Handbook for language arts: Pre-K, kindergarten, grades one and two.* (Curr. Bull. No. 8, 1965–66 Ser.) New York: BECNY, 1966.

Botel, M. *The Botel Reading Inventory.* Chicago: Follett, 1962.

Buros, O. K. (Ed.) *The sixth mental measurements yearbook.* Highland Park, N.J.: Gryphon Press, 1965.

Caffrey, J. Auding. *Review of Educational Research,* 1955, **25,** 121.

College Entrance Examination Board, Commission on English. *Freedom and discipline in English.* New York: CEEB, 1965.

Conlin, D. A., & LeRoy, A. R. *Our language today.* New York: American Book, 1967.

Dawson, M., et al. *Guiding language learning.* New York: Harcourt, Brace & World, 1963.

Dixon, J. *Growth through English: A report based on the Dartmouth Seminar, 1966.* Reading, Eng.: National Association for the Teaching of English, 1967.

Educational Testing Service. *Sequential Tests of Educational Progress: Reading.* Princeton, N.J.: ETS, 1957. (a)

Educational Testing Service. *Sequential Tests of Educational Progress: Writing.* Princeton, N.J.: ETS, 1957. (b)

Educational Testing Service, Cooperative Test Division. *Cooperative English Test: Reading Comprehension.* Princeton, N.J.: ETS, 1948.

Frazier, A. (Ed.) *Ends and issues, 1965–1966: Points of decision in the development of the English curriculum.* Champaign, Ill.: National Council of Teachers of English, 1966.

Huck, C. Planning the literature program for the elementary school. *Elementary English,* 1962, **39,** 307–313.

Iowa Tests of Basic Skills: Reading. Boston: Houghton Mifflin, 1955.

Kearney, N. C. *Elementary school objectives: A report for the Mid-Century Committee on Outcomes in Elementary Education.* New York: Russell Sage Foundation, 1953.

Kenyon, J. S. Cultural levels and functional varieties of English. *College English,* 1948, **10,** 31–36.

Kough, J., & DeHaan, R. *Identifying children with special needs.* Teacher's Guidance Handbook, Elem. School Ed., Vol. I. Chicago, Ill.: Science Research Associates, 1955.

Lamb, P. *Guiding children's language learning.* Dubuque, Iowa: Brown, 1967.

Loban, W. D. *The language of elementary school children.* Champaign, Ill.: National Council of Teachers of English, 1966.

McGinley, P. J's the jumping joy-walker. In P. McGinley, *All around the town.* Philadelphia: Lippincott, 1948.

Metropolitan Achievement Tests: Elem. Battery: Form B, Word Discrimination. New York: Harcourt, Brace, 1959.

National Council of Teachers of English. The basic issues in the teaching of English. *Elementary English,* 1959, **35,** 7, pp. 1–15.

National Council of Teachers of English. The workload of the elementary school teacher: A statement of policy of the National Council of Teachers of English. *Elementary English,* 1968, **45,** 224–227.

National Council of Teachers of English, Commission on the English Curriculum. *Language arts for today's children.* New York: Appleton-Century-Crofts, 1954.

National Council of Teachers of English, Committee on National Interest. *The national interest and the teaching of English: A report on the status of the profession.* Champaign, Ill.: NCTE, 1961.

National Council of Teachers of English, Committee on National Interest. *The national interest and the continuing education of teachers of English: A report on the state of the profession.* Champaign, Ill.: NCTE, 1964.

Nebraska Curriculum Development Center. *A curriculum for English: Grade* 1. Lincoln, Nebr.: University of Nebraska Press, 1966. (a)

Nebraska Curriculum Development Center. *A curriculum for English: Language explorations for the elementary grades.* Lincoln, Nebr.: University of Nebraska Press, 1966. (b)

Schutz, R. E. English. In O. K. Buros (Ed.), *The sixth mental measurements yearbook.* Highland Park, N.J.: Gryphon Press, 1965. Pp. 544–546.

Science Research Associates. *Science Research Associates Achievement Series: Language.* Chicago: SRA, 1957.

Stanford Achievement Test: Language. New York: Harcourt, Brace, 1964.

State University of Iowa. *Iowa Every-pupil Tests of Basic Skills: Language.* Iowa City: SUI, 1947.

Strickland, R. The language of elementary school children. *Bulletin of the School of Education, Indiana University,* 1962, **38**(4), 1–131.

Tiedt, I. M., & Tiedt, S. W. *Contemporary English in the elementary school.* Englewood Cliffs, N.J.: Prentice-Hall, 1967.

Tiegs, E. W., & Clark, W. W. *California Language Test.* Monterey, Calif.: California Test Bureau, 1957.

Wisconsin Department of Public Instruction. *English language arts in Wisconsin: A growth curriculum in English language arts for the kindergarten through grade 12, 1968.* Madison, Wis.: WDPI, 1968.

16

Evaluation of Learning in

Secondary School Social Studies

LISANIO R. ORLANDI

Lowell State College
Lowell, Massachusetts

Lisanio R. Orlandi received the Bachelor of Arts degree in Political Science and the Master of Education degree in Secondary School Social Studies from Boston University, and the Doctor of Philosophy degree in Educational Research from Boston College. He has taught in the public high schools in Massachusetts and has served as a research assistant in the Holliston, Massachusetts, public schools and as a lecturer at Boston College and Salem State College, Massachusetts. He is presently Assistant Professor of Education at Lowell State College in Massachusetts. He is interested in curriculum evaluation and in research into the creative development of children.

Contents

16

Evaluation of Learning in Secondary School Social Studies

Introduction

In the past seventy-five years the social studies curriculum has changed its emphasis with the major shifts in American thought. Social studies deals with the sensitive field of human behavior; presumably, it plays a large role in influencing the beliefs and attitudes of each upcoming generation. Powerful groups persuade or exert pressure upon curriculum policy makers to pursue an educational path to their liking. Such pressures may arise from national, state, or local organizations or from bands of individual citizens. The constant squeeze from liberals and conservatives in politics and education has bent and twisted social studies with the prevalent forces of the time.

Since the late nineteenth century these forces have wrought a number of major changes in the social studies curriculum. A very brief overview of some of the changes will be presented here.[1]

[1] Much of the historical interpretation of the social studies curriculum is drawn from Hunt & Metcalf (1968).

Historical overview of the social studies

High school social studies in the late nineteenth and early twentieth centuries comprised essentially history, government, and geography. Political and military history was taught in a chronological fashion as a series of facts to be memorized. Government machinery was also to be learned by heart. Both subjects were taught in such a way as to produce a "My country, right or wrong" type of patriotism. Geography lessons had very little to do with human beings acting in a physical environment.

As the twentieth century continued, the content of the social studies expanded. History, government, and geography were divided into an array of forms. John Dewey and the progressive movement encouraged the development of reflective thinking. However, the influence of Edward Thorndike, with its emphasis on memorization, proved to be more widespread, probably because it coincided with what teachers were accustomed to doing.

TABLE 16-1 TABLE OF SPECIFICATIONS FOR SELECTED SOCIAL STUDIES

	BEHAVIOR																
	Cognitive										*Affective*						
	Knowledge and comprehension			*Skills*								*Attitudes*					*Values*
	Knowl-edge	*Knowledge and compre-hension*			*Research*		*Critical thinking*			*Democratic group par-ticipation*		*Desirable intellectual behavior*		*Desirable social behavior*			*Desirable democratic behavior*
	Facts	*Concepts*	*Generalizations*	*Structures and models*	*Location of information*	*Interpretation of graphic and symbolic data*	*Identification of central issues and underlying assumptions*	*Evaluation of evidence and drawing of warranted conclusions*	*Formulation of reasonable hypotheses*	*Formal procedures*	*Informal procedures*	*Scientific approach to human behavior*	*Humanitarian outlook on the behavior of others*	*Awareness and interest*	*Acceptance of responsibility*	*Involvement*	*Basic democratic values*
CONTENT	*A*	*B*	*C*	*D*	*E*	*F*	*G*	*H*	*I*	*J*	*K*	*L*	*M*	*N*	*O*	*P*	*Q*
History																	
1.0 Historical focus							E	E	E	E	E	E	E		E	E	E
1.1 Location							E	E	E	E	E	E	E		E	E	E
1.2 Level of study							E	E	E	E	E	E	E		E	E	E
2.0 Analysis over time				I													
2.1 Time periods				I													
2.2 Sequence				I													
2.3 Continuity and change				I													
2.4 Relationships				I													
3.0 Topical emphases																	
3.1 Political																	
3.2 Social																	
3.3 Economic																	
3.4 Geographic																	
3.5 Intellectual																	

4.0 Method of inquiry				I													
4.1 Evidence				I													
4.2 Verification				I													
4.3 Imagination	E	E	E	I	E	E											
4.4 Probability				I		E											
4.5 Interdisciplinary contributions				I													
5.0 Historiography				I													
6.0 Historical issues and interpretations				E													
Political science																	
7.0 Governmental focus		E	E	E			E	E	E	E	E	E	E		E	E	E
7.1 Location		E	E	E			E	E	E	E	E	E	E		E	E	E
7.2 Level of study		E	E	E		E	E	E	E	E	E	E	E		E	E	E
8.0 Process of government																	
8.1 The governed																	
8.2 Authoritative officials																	
8.3 Political process																	
8.4 Structure of government																	
8.5 Policy making																	
8.6 Policy substance and application																	
9.0 International relations																	
9.1 National security																	
9.2 International organization																	
10.0 Factors affecting politics																	
10.1 National politics																	
10.2 International politics																	
11.0 Methods of inquiry				I	E												
11.1 Legal-institutional				I	E												
11.2 Behavioral				I	E												
12.0 Major political issues				E													
12.1 National				E													
12.2 International				E													

E = Empty cells

I = Improbable cells

With the tremendous Depression of the 1930s, the American social status quo was rattled, and reform became the order of the day. In social studies the progressives and their more radical brethren, the reconstructionists, embodied the dominant force of the era. Education for life and education for citizenship enjoyed an attentive audience under their philosophical impetus.

World War II ushered in a period of conservatism which was followed by the usual postwar reaction, personified in Senator Joseph McCarthy. In education, the progressive trend toward reflective thinking was smothered and memorization of facts again came into vogue. Teaching facts not only was less taxing upon the teacher but also was safer politically in a period which frowned upon the free conflict of ideas.

The fact-memorization era was sharply disrupted by the effectiveness of the Russian satellite program. High school physical science curricula were attacked and changed. In the wake of the upheaval, social studies was caught up in a transformation. The progressive influence was subjected to attacks from critics who, strangely enough, failed to see that the progressives had remodeled only the superstructure of American education and that the substructure had remained intact. Jerome Bruner laid emphasis upon the structure of a discipline as the content of a curriculum and the discovery approach as the process, and these became the crywords of the new education: concepts and theories were to be at the core of courses, and inductive teaching was to be the method for reaching them. The new terminology of education provided a new view of education only for those who were blind to certain strains of progressivism which had advocated fairly much the same educational direction over the previous several decades.

The prosperity of the mid-1960s and the wave of reform in social studies combined with liberal government purse strings to set conditions for the creation of numerous social studies curriculum project centers across the country to produce new social studies courses. Herein occurred a major difference between the progressives and the present-day reformers. The progressives expected each teacher and school to create courses and materials for their students. The task was a forbidding one. The new social studies projects create courses and materials for the teacher, who can then select the course which best fits his purposes. Already a deluge of these new materials has begun. The big problem for social studies education today is to select the program that will best suit its objectives. The overriding issue for social studies is in turn the recurring one of what its objectives are.

The vagueness of social studies objectives

Unfortunately, most objectives in social studies have been ill-defined. Many of them do not provide clear-cut guidelines for curriculum development and evaluation because of their general ambiguity. Why have they been so ambiguous? Several factors seem to be responsible.

First, social studies is concerned with topics on which people's attitudes are deep-seated and resistant to change. Yet many claim that the discipline is responsible for the development of attitudes conducive to democratic citizenship. An unequivocal statement of what constitutes democratic citizenship would probably encounter strong opposition because it would inevitably antagonize a sizable number of people. It is easier to get unanimous agreement when the definition of objectives is loose enough so that each individual can interpret it to suit himself. As a result, many of the objectives in social studies have been couched in cautious formulas to evade attack.

A second major reason is that educators disagree over the ultimate goals of social studies. Is the aim to create a democratic citizenry or to build reservoirs of information to be tapped when needed? Engle (1965a) views the conflict as extending over a pair of continua—the content continuum and the process continuum. He states:

> On the content continuum, we see the social studies varying at the extremes from the study of

> separate subjects, with no claim to any direct bearing on the broad problems of citizenship, to the direct study of broad areas and problems taken from the "life experience" of citizens. . . .
>
> On a second continuum, the "process" continuum, the extremes vary from those who see the central process in social studies instruction as the mastering of subject matter to those who see it as a problem-solving process [pp. 15–16].

A third reason for the vagueness of objectives in social studies is that they have not customarily been stated in behavioral, or operational, terms (see Chapter 2, the section on "Operationalism," pages 23–24). Probably the only way to overcome the semantic difficulty of ambiguous interpretation is by stating them behaviorally. Some of the new social studies projects have leaned toward this solution, and we are quite possibly on the threshold of an influx of definitions which will specify social studies objectives more concretely.

On the other hand, there is a fairly strong feeling among many educators in the field that a precise behavioral explication of objectives is impossible, deleterious, and unnecessary: impossible because the behaviorization of objectives would be complete only for lower levels of thinking and for trivial attitudes; deleterious because that incompleteness might channel instruction toward relatively insignificant objectives; unnecessary since other forms of structuring social studies objectives have been devised which are more suitable in that they do not close out aims which seem impossible to state behaviorally but are intuitively apparent.

Such arguments would certainly be apropos if the objectives were so poorly stated that learning would be impeded. However, a careful delineation of social studies objectives can avert these criticisms and serve to clarify the specific direction for instruction to take.

Structuring the social studies

Most social studies educators have not been comfortable with the unclear statement of objectives. Before the recent interest in behavioral definitions, several movements arose suggesting distinct approaches upon which to structure the social studies.

One movement proposed to identify basic social science generalizations as the foundation upon which to structure a social studies curriculum. Perhaps the finest statement of this approach is from the oft-quoted *Report to the California State Curriculum Commission* by the California State Central Committee on Social Studies (1961). The following are two of the eighteen generalizations which it presents (pp. 40–41) as a synthesis of the main ideas to be learned in an overall school social studies program:

1. Man's comprehension of the present and his wisdom in planning for the future depend upon his understanding of the events of the past and of the various forces and agencies in society that influence the present.
2. Change is a condition of human society; societies rise and fall; value systems improve or deteriorate; the tempo of change varies with cultures and periods of history.

As is apparent, these enunciations are indicative of less inclusive generalizations which would fall within their domain. If one peruses the generalizations from specific social science fields which precede the syntheses in the report, one can attach more meaning to the broader statements. Such summations have been helpful in bringing order to the social studies field, though some lists of generalizations are forbiddingly extensive, redundant, and disorganized, and thus provide more confusion than clarity.

Another approach to structuring the social studies has enjoyed some popularity recently. This movement has proposed that concepts be the keystones of the curriculum. Fenton (1967) has described how concepts have partially preempted the position previously held by generalizations. He sees the structure of the social studies as composed of two parts: the formation of hypotheses and the method of arriving at conclusions in a discipline. It is within the domain of hypothesis formation that concepts have come to serve a heuristic and thus a structural purpose. In Fenton's words:

> Lists of concepts form a more useful notion of structure than lists of generalizations. Let us suppose, for example, that a student knows four concepts from sociology—social class, status, role, and norms—and wants to analyze the society of Boston in 1750. These four concepts will help to guide his search for data. With them in mind, he will search for evidence about class structure: how many classes existed, and what characteristics distinguished members of one class from those of another. He will try to find out what roles members of each social class played in the society. He will ask himself which roles had high status and which ones ranked at the bottom of the prestige scale. Finally, he will seek evidence about which norms—patterns of behavior—were expected from everyone. The concepts are "imposed conceptions" which guide the search for data toward issues which sociologists have found useful for the analysis of society.
>
> (Fenton, 1967, p. 14)

A third approach to structuring the social studies has also gained some prominence. It assumes that each discipline in the field has an intrinsic structure which can furnish a frame of reference for learners. Certain concepts and generalizations are considered basic to each discipline, and the pattern of relationships among these elements provides the structure or framework. Gibson (1966) has constructed an excellent diagrammatic example of such an analysis of the political system, and it will be presented later, accompanied by key concepts and generalizations in political science (see Fig. 16-1 and page 464).

In brief, then, social studies has been groping for order and clarity. The vaguely stated objectives of past eras did not provide a sufficiently clear path to educators. Basic generalizations, basic concepts, and basic structures have been uncovered which give more direction in the murky field of social studies. Behavioral definitions have also inspired some interest and, it is hoped, may someday lead to relatively unambiguous specifications of the objectives in the field.

The goals of instruction in social studies

Traditional influences

Before beginning a comprehensive analysis of objectives in social studies, it is informative to examine the major intellectual strands which have influenced the development of these objectives.[2]

Three major intellectual traditions have made a mark on social studies. These can be labeled the liberal arts, the life adjustment, and the citizenship education schools of thought. Although there is considerable overlap among them, each tradition has its special emphasis.

The liberal arts outlook has a strong intellectual bent. The life adjustment tradition is associated with the impetus of a special form of progressive education in the social studies. This branch of progressive education is deeply concerned with the individual's socialization and his personal characteristics. Intellectualism is not decried by life adjustment educators, as some critics would have us believe; however, it does not receive so much attention as do the many practical, personal, and social questions facing the individual. The citizenship education tradition also traces its roots to the progressive education school. In contrast to the personalization of social studies implicit in the life adjustment philosophy, citizenship education tends to emphasize the individual's commitment, involvement, and action in society, primarily in political life. This emphasis receives its primary élan from the reconstructionist branch of progressive education, which exhorts the individual to participate in the reformation of society through rational discussion that leads to a consensus of dissent and pressure for change.

The traditions vary in their special emphases, therefore, though they share common bases. The liberal arts and life adjustment views are more clearly opposed to one another than is the

[2] Much of this philosophical presentation is drawn from Lewenstein (1963).

citizenship orientation to either. The citizenship educator borrows part of his thinking from both schools of thought and adds a strong element of political involvement to it. A detailed explanation of the positions of the three schools of thought is not possible here. Lewenstein (1963) provides an insightful presentation of the three traditions for the interested reader.

In the next section of this chapter a schema to classify the objectives of social studies instruction will be constructed. The problem of creating such a schema is exacerbated by the existence of the three philosophical traditions and their varied goals. The classification of the outcomes envisaged by the liberal arts tradition is relatively straightforward because these are essentially confined to cognitive and affective objectives conducive to intellectual enhancement. Cataloging the aims of the life adjustment tradition is relatively difficult because this tradition envisages few boundaries to the educational effects of social studies. The behaviors which it fosters stray into all aspects of an individual's existence, ranging from his consideration of others while driving a car, through his personal relationships with his parents and his activities as a Boy Scout, to his ability to read a sophisticated newspaper columnist, taking but a few examples. To put it another way, the life adjustment tradition so expunges course boundaries that clear-cut responsibility for certain educational results cannot be placed directly on any one area of the curriculum. Under such conditions virtually all problems can be construed as social studies problems and virtually all forms of behavioral outcomes can be striven for within the curriculum. Such an all-encompassing outlook is a major obstacle to selecting and classifying social studies goals. The citizenship education tradition, which to a degree synthesizes the others, is perplexed by the difficulty of choosing among the goals of the life adjustment school those which are essential to its purposes. Most of the intellectual goals can be absorbed into citizenship education, though their shape and emphasis may be considerably transformed in the process.

The approach espoused in this chapter is that social studies is primarily responsible for some fairly definite student outcomes and that certain other outcomes are primarily the concern of other parts of the school curriculum. This might seem to be a statement of the obvious, except that lists of social studies objectives have been infiltrated by an excess of aims which really ought to be considered as proper to other fields of study. Examples will be pointed out in the section on skills (pages 457–459).

Table of specifications for objectives in social studies

Treating only the essential objectives of the social studies, we can set up a table of specifications, that is, a two-dimensional matrix of behaviors and content. Traditionally, social studies behaviors have been divided into understandings, skills, and attitudes. Each of these divisions is appropriate for classification and may be improved slightly by substituting *Knowledge and comprehension* for "understanding" and by adding *Values* to the list of major behavioral headings. The four categories are actually intimately related to one another, but for purposes of analysis they will be treated separately.

The contents of the social studies are drawn from the social sciences. It is not possible here to categorize the essential aspects of each social science discipline. History and political science will be used as examples of how major course content can be classified in a table of specifications, shown in Table 16-1, Table of Specifications for Selected Social Studies. The table was constructed after perusal of statements of objectives in yearbooks and curriculum publications of the National Council for the Social Studies, curriculum outlines from across the country, major textbooks in the field, and books on historical method.[3]

[3] See *Note* on pages 495–496 for some of the materials which were examined.

Each of the behavioral and content dimensions of the matrix will be explained in the ensuing sections of this chapter under the appropriate headings. The reader will also note that the behaviors have each been labeled by capital letters and the content segments by numbers. Later, reference to various cells in the matrix will be made by presenting the letter and number of the cell. Also, certain cells have been identified as empty (E) or improbable (I), meaning that they either would not be expected or are highly unlikely to occur in a social studies curriculum.

Behaviors in social studies

Knowledge and comprehension (A–D) For purposes of the social studies, *Knowledge* involves the ability to recall or recognize, and *Comprehension* involves the ability to transform into other words. These powers assume several forms—*Knowledge of facts* and *Knowledge and comprehension of concepts, generalizations,* and *structures and models.*

The social studies, especially history, are notorious for their emphasis on specific *Facts* (*A*). Certain facts must be committed to memory in order to secure a base from which to operate. Various dates, names, constitutional provisions, legislative enactments, and the like serve as the raw material upon which the instruction is founded. The danger of fact-learning in the social studies is that it sometimes preempts the rightful place of the other objectives of instruction.

Concepts (*B*) derive from the act of categorizing. The sociological concept of social class which Fenton describes (see above, page 454) is such a categorization. Individuals within a society are grouped on various class levels according to distinguishing characteristics. As Fenton points out, once a concept has been learned, it acts as a stimulus to further analysis of social behavior. A concept is not a dead end; it is instrumental in further penetration. For this reason concepts are vital to social studies instruction.

A *Generalization* (*C*) deals with the relationship between two or more concepts. Some generalizations are more sweeping than others. The samples from the California report presented previously (page 453) are intended to be broad conclusions derived from less inclusive generalizations. Social studies, borrowing as it does from the social sciences, depends wholly on the progress of the social sciences for the breadth and certainty of its generalizations. Since the theoretical framework of the social sciences is not so firm as that of the natural sciences, social studies generalizations on the main have a much less definitive aura about them. Yet they are essential to the social studies because they bind concepts together and provide firm statements upon which to build theoretical structures or to revise previous generalizations.

In sum, then, facts are the minute building blocks of the social studies. Concepts are the tools by which meaning is attached to sets of facts. Generalizations are the conclusions which are derived by using concepts to analyze social situations, and may be further combined to produce more inclusive generalizations about human behavior. Generalizations may be somewhat tenuous because of the difficulties inherent in social science research; thus, like concepts, they act as a stimulus to further thought more often than they provide definitive theoretical statements.

A discipline's *Structure* (*D*) is erected from the concepts and generalizations in the discipline. It is a network of these concepts and generalizations. New concepts and new generalizations can be used to add to or alter the network so as to provide further elucidation of social problems. The structure is the grand design of the discipline into which new concepts and generalizations are placed so as to provide maximal theoretical insight.

A structure may also be on a less grandiose scale than that of the entire discipline. Within a discipline there may be certain elements whose net of relationships constitutes a substructure within the whole.

In addition to the structure and substructures, there is a related form of understanding, the *Model* (*D*). Models of man have long been and will continue to be proposed. In the words of Engle (1965b, p. 460), who summarizes the characteristics of models,

> The model . . . can be seen to include both descriptive and evaluative elements, that is, statements of what has been or is the case, statements of what is possible, and statements of what ought to be the case. The model will trace and even forecast lines of possible and desirable development, and it will suggest lines of attack on the persistent problems of society. The model will afford explanations and/or theories of why human beings behave as they do, and therefore it should enable us to predict with a fair degree of accuracy how human beings may be expected to behave in the future under a variety of conditions and circumstances.

Structures and models help the social scientist to aggregate what would otherwise be many fragmented facts, concepts, and generalizations.

Skills (E–K) The second major category in the social studies, *Skills*, contains a diverse range of behaviors. It belongs among the primary tasks of social studies to develop many of the skills; others command an equal or lesser role with regard to other subject areas. The skills to be dealt with in this chapter will be the essential ones in social studies, as already mentioned.

Many lists of social studies skills introduce two major categories which have been purposely excluded from our discussion because they are considered peripheral social studies objectives. The two categories are communications and personal skills and habits.

Communications skills would include reading, listening, writing, and speaking. Social studies may contribute to the development of each of these, but primary responsibility for them is certainly not in its purview.

Personal skills and habits, such as intelligent use of leisure time, worthy home membership, physical and mental health care, automobile safety, and intelligent purchase of consumer goods, constitute a mélange of behaviors so indirectly related to social studies instruction that their inclusion has been summarily dismissed.

Skills in the social studies can be broken down into three broad groups—research, critical thinking, and democratic group participation.

The first subcategory of skills, *Research* (*E* and *F*), deals with locating information and interpreting graphic and symbolic data. *Location of information* (*E*) centers on the use of research materials. The student must be able to find relevant treatments of a specific topic or problem. He must be able to use the library, including the card catalog; know the major library reference books with emphasis on social sciences; and be able to find appropriate information in books in the social sciences.

The location of information may go beyond the bibliographic skills in courses which expect students to use social science data-gathering techniques like sampling, interviewing, and constructing questionnaires. This type of research is currently limited to a minute portion of social studies courses, however, so that mentioning it here possibly provides more of a glimpse into the future than a portrayal of present conditions.

Once the student is able to locate information, he must be able to interpret its meaning. In social studies this interpretation occurs primarily in a reading situation. While reading is a generalized skill whose development per se is not a primary function of social studies courses, as we have said, they are responsible for the impartation of certain specific reading skills. This responsibility encompasses the ability to *Interpret graphic and symbolic data* (*F*), such as maps, graphs, tables, charts, time lines, and cartoons.

The second subcategory of skills, *Critical thinking* (*G–I*), is probably the central goal of social studies. Since the field as a whole deals with social issues of a controversial nature, it readily supplies problems requiring critical analysis. Critical thinking skills can be grouped in a number of ways, but one of the best classifications was produced by Dressel and Mayhew (1954, p. 1):

1. To identify central issues.
2. To recognize underlying assumptions.
3. To evaluate evidence or authority.
   a. To recognize stereotypes and cliches.

b. To recognize bias and emotional factors in a presentation.
c. To distinguish between verifiable and unverifiable data.
d. To distinguish between relevant and nonrelevant.
e. To distinguish between essential and incidental.
f. To recognize the adequacy of data.
g. To determine whether facts support a generalization.
h. To check consistency.
4. To draw warranted conclusions.

The four basic critical thinking skills in the list can actually be reduced to two closely related pairs: the *Identification of central issues and underlying assumptions* (G) and the *Evaluation of evidence and drawing of warranted conclusions* (H). Another component might be added to the list to make it more complete—the ability to *Formulate reasonable hypotheses* (I).

Each of the kinds of critical thinking is fundamental to the development of most of the other social studies objectives. For example, a student must be able to evaluate evidence before he can proceed to make generalizations. Comprehension is derived from a critical analysis of the substance of the social studies. Also, the formation of desirable attitudes is dependent on critical analysis, as will be pointed out later.

The third subcategory of skills, *Democratic group participation* (J and K), is linked to both the cognitive and affective domains of social studies objectives. It entails the ability to use the formal and informal processes of group decision making. *Formal, cognitive procedures* (J) might include the application of parliamentary rules, the mechanics of debate, and panel-discussion moderation—any formal group procedure appropriate to social studies classroom discussion. The *Informal, affective procedures* (K) are less easily specified but most inclusively might involve pervasive qualities of persuasiveness and effectiveness in producing reasonable group decisions. Persuasiveness stretches beyond the capacity to present a rational argument. It implies the subtle ability to sense the appropriate timing and manner for making statements within a group so that the group members are attracted to the speaker. Effectiveness involves the individual's ability to steer the group toward some reasonable solution or conclusion. To put it another way, persuasiveness is more a matter of style than of quality; the decision which the persuasive person leads the group to make may be quite unreasonable. By contrast, effectiveness relates to substance, to the objective merits of an argument. The effective speaker leads his fellow discussants to sound conclusions because of the clarity and reasonableness of his statements, whether he is presenting a single viewpoint or several.

The separate listing of the three major categories of skills in the social studies does not imply that these skills are unrelated. In fact, critical thinking and research skills are intimately interlocked. This is illustrated by Fenton (1967, pp. 16–17) in a succinct articulation of the procedures inherent in the solution of a social problem:

1. Recognizing a problem from data
2. Formulating hypotheses
   a. Asking analytical questions
   b. Stating hypotheses
   c. Remaining aware of the tentative nature of hypotheses
3. Recognizing the logical implications of hypotheses
4. Gathering data
   a. Deciding what data will be needed
   b. Selecting or rejecting sources
5. Analyzing, evaluating and interpreting data
   a. Selecting relevant data
   b. Evaluating sources
      (1) Determining the frame of reference of an author
      (2) Determining the accuracy of statements of fact
   c. Interpreting the data
6. Evaluating the hypothesis in the light of the data
   a. Modifying the hypothesis, if necessary
      (1) Rejecting a logical implication unsupported by data
      (2) Restating the hypothesis
   b. Stating a generalization

One can see that some aspect of the skill categories of critical thinking and research must be summoned to contend with every social problem.

Probably the most significant point which can be made about the skills is that there is substantial agreement among social studies educators that many of these skills ought to be developed in the social studies curriculum. There are strong differences of opinion about which skills deserve the most emphasis in the social studies, but most of them would be given serious consideration in a well-rounded social studies curriculum.

Attitudes and values (L–Q) The understandings and skills as well as the content of social studies curricula are viewed by many as instrumental to the development of *Attitudes* (*L–P*) and *Values* (*Q*) conducive to full democratic citizenship. They may go so far as to say that herein rests the essential nature of the social studies. It is an attempt to allow students to acquire profound, underlying democratic traits through rational, intellectual processes. Attitudinal change is the goal, but it must come primarily through rational rather than irrational means. In the family a child's basic traits are developed, but the child is not consciously aware of this development. In the social studies classroom his traits as a democratic citizen can be subjected to rational, logical analysis. The distinctive character of the social studies lies at least partly in their attempt to submit to conscious, rational, analytical techniques the mass of ideas about human behavior—some of them misconceptions and preconceptions—that we all have.

It is in this affective area involving the development of various attitudes and values that most of the argument over goals has erupted. The type of content and the types of knowledge, comprehension, and skills that are stressed in a curriculum are generally dependent upon the affective goals that are considered central. The question of which affective goals are desirable and ought to take precedence over others is muddled. One of the primary reasons for the confusion is that the affective goals of the social studies have not been carefully stated and categorized.

Most of the overall affective goals in the social studies can be subsumed under three basic headings—attitudes for *Desirable intellectual behavior* (*L* and *M*), attitudes for *Desirable social behavior* (*N–P*), and values for *Desirable democratic behavior* (*Q*). These divisions are not clear-cut and require clarification to serve a classificatory function.

Attitudes for desirable intellectual behavior are those which lead to the cultivation of an empirical, reasonable, and humane outlook. They would include two specific traits—a *Scientific approach to human behavior* and a *Humanitarian outlook on the behavior of others*.

A *Scientific approach to human behavior* (*L*) would encompass a spectrum of attitudes such as belief in the natural causation of personal and social behavior; the strong likelihood of multiple rather than single causes of social behavior; and objectivity, open-mindedness, relativism, skepticism, and precision in collecting and interpreting data.

A *Humanitarian outlook on the behavior of others* (*M*) includes two basic qualities—empathy and tolerance. Empathy is the capacity to undergo an emotional experience similar to that of someone else. One feels what it is like to be in someone else's position. For example, what was it like to be a Plains Indian chief in the post–Civil War period under the onslaught of the white man? An empathic view is often an essential part of social studies courses because a student who commences to participate in emotions comparable to those of other, sometimes very different people thus also commences to be more tolerant and more accepting of a wider range of individuals, their culture, and their ideas. Tolerance is a respect for the right of others to be different in their social behavior.

Attitudes for desirable social behavior can be divided into three overarching categories—*Awareness and interest*, *Acceptance of responsibility*, and *Involvement*.

Awareness (*N*) refers to the cognizance of social problems and of the social contributions of others. No individual, group, or nation stands alone or progresses without the aid of others. In the end each of us is strongly dependent on all of us for his security and well-being. A suburban white finds it hard to ignore the inner-city Negro. The wealthy white nation finds it hard to ignore the new black African state. The serious problems of other people, other groups, and other nations have a way of making themselves problems for all of us. If one recognizes this fact, he may begin to attack problems before they reach the crisis stage.

Interest (N) includes the manner and degree of attention to social problems which a person displays in his behavior. Does he read historical or political journal articles? Does he attend lectures or conferences or attend to appropriate radio or television programs? Does he discuss the issues with others? There are a number of ways in which an individual can show his interest in a specific social problem.

Acceptance of responsibility (O) includes a variety of desirable outcomes of social studies instruction, such as recognition of one's obligation to be well-informed on public issues before making decisions, cooperativeness in the solution of social problems, and willingness to act within the bounds of democratic procedure in attempting to promulgate some program of action.

Involvement (P) refers to a person's disposition to act on the basis of his convictions. Once a person has made a decision, he must commit himself to act on the basis of that decision. The more deeply an individual is committed, the more intent must be his action. If a person has used his critical judgment upon a well-researched social problem to arrive at some conclusion or solution, he must be prepared to involve himself in the furtherance of that position.

This activist commitment to positions on social problems leads us to the final behavior category of the social studies—desirable *Basic democratic values* (Q). A primary objective of social studies instruction is that students will assume a cluster of democratic values after a critical analysis of the arguments pro and con. These values are many, but some of the key elements are freedom of speech, press, and religion; the dignity, equality, and brotherhood of man; and the right of the majority to prevail and the minority to be respected.

Some of the truly desirable democratic values are paid lip-service in statements of American ideals but divide the individual and the nation in practice. Such value conflicts have been referred to as the "closed areas," the taboos, of American life. Generally, the affective significance of a social studies program is determined by the manner in which such closed areas are handled. If the values are broached to the student in a way that requires him to evaluate their worth, then the resultant value commitment is based on rational analysis fundamental to a democracy. However, the usual form of value discussion has been inculcation via preachment which is a form of authoritarian indoctrination subversive of a democratic system.

The three major affective divisions—*Attitudes for desirable intellectual* and *social behavior* and *Values for desirable democratic behavior*—encompass the essential affective goals of the social studies. Social studies courses vary in the locus of their affective development. Each discipline area in the social studies has developed its own set of affective objectives. Most of the objectives can be made interchangeable from one subject area to another through only minor changes in wording. Some disciplines, however, lend themselves more readily to the development of certain attitudinal objectives than do others. For example, the elimination of ethnocentrism can be attacked through any of the social sciences, but it is probably most readily attacked through anthropology or history. Similarly, political alienation is more directly attacked through political science than it is through the other social sciences. Nevertheless, all the social sciences can share essentially the same functions in attitude development. The function which they do serve is dependent on the manner in which they are shaped in school courses.

Content in social studies

Now that the behavioral objectives of social studies instruction have been examined through an analysis of knowledge and comprehension, skills, attitudes, and values, the source from which these behaviors are acquired calls for attention. Knowledge and comprehension, skills, attitudes, and values are learned through contact with social science content.

In recent years, social scientists have been concerned with analyzing the structure of their disciplines. Various structures have been proposed for the same discipline. Fields such as economics, political science, and sociology are far easier to structure than is history, because history is so broad in scope and eclectic in method. Yet, it is this very broadness and eclecticism of history that is uniquely striking. It is a subject area which can encompass all the other social science disciplines into its interpretation. Its proper treatment requires an interdisciplinary approach which has long been advocated for secondary school social studies.

History has often been the target of criticism of reform-minded educators. This is primarily attributable to the misuse of historical study that has been rampant in most classrooms. The drudgery of memorization of piles of worthless information has certainly stamped history as being dull and useless. This distortion of history into the memorization of a litany of names, dates, places, causes, events, and results is lamentable and to some degree has been discarded in many schools. History can and is being viewed more and more as a field in which the methodology, concepts, generalizations, and models of all the social sciences can be brought to bear. Since history is in many ways the most encompassing of the social science subjects and since it is the most deeply embedded in the curriculum, it will function as the major example of the content from which understandings in the social studies are derived.

Political science, which in one form or another also receives a great deal of attention in social studies curricula, will be used to exemplify the manner in which a less-encompassing discipline can be divided for analysis into its component parts. Comparable divisions of the other social science disciplines could be constructed, but spatial limitations require that such divisions be excluded. The division process will, in any case, be relatively clear to the reader once he has probed the following pages.

History courses (1.0–6.0) The field of history can be broken down in a number of ways. The breakdown listed in Table 16-1, Table of Specifications for Selected Social Studies, attempts to include the essential content areas of history in American secondary schools. The content breaks history down into six major categories: *Historical focus, Analysis over time, Topical emphases, Method of inquiry, Historiography*, and *Historical issues and interpretations.*

The first category, *Historical focus* (1.0), contains two major subcategories: *Location* and *Level of study.* Location refers to the part of the world under study—Europe, Asia, or Africa, for example. Level of study refers to the breadth of coverage—international, national, regional, cantonal, local, group, or individual. The first category, then, allows for the geographic placement and the type of grouping of individuals that can be studied in a history course.

The second and third categories classify history along its two prime axes. *Analysis over time* (2.0) can be viewed as the horizontal axis of history, and *Topical emphases* (3.0) as the vertical axis (Michaelis & Johnston, 1965). The key function of history is the long-range analysis of topics over periods of time. In history one can study very narrow topics or take a cross-topical outlook. One can focus on a very narrow period of time, or one can deal with a broad span of time. Further, one can deal with an individual or with all world civilizations. The scope of historical study is a matter of choice.

Analysis over time (2.0) contains four subcategories: *Time periods, Sequence, Continuity and change*, and *Relationships.*

Time divisions answer the historian's need for conceptualizing time by segmenting it into periods displaying special characteristics. All types of time classification can be used, again both broad and narrow. "Antiquity," "the Middle

Ages," "modern times," "the Dark Ages," "the Renaissance," "the Reformation," "the Enlightenment," "the Critical Period," "the age of Jackson," and "the progressive era," are all examples of conceptual time periods.

The historian is concerned with the sequence of events in time. Without knowledge of chronological sequence he would not be able to piece together the multitude of events that preceded or succeeded major points of interest.

The historian is not interested in sequence for its own sake. He is interested in causes and effects of change—the factors that provoked changes in the various aspects of man's life and the effects of these changes. Amidst all the change over time the historian is also concerned with elements which continue to remain relatively unchanged.

Finally, the historian is concerned with the relationships between various time periods. The relationship may be between different time periods in the same geographic area or between different geographic areas during the same or different time periods. For example, an analogy could be drawn between the internecine warfare and subsequent decline of the Greek city-states and the comparable warfare of modern European nation-states. Or the question of the demise of slavery in the United States, serfdom in Russia, and then slavery in Brazil within a short span of time may provoke analysis to uncover possible relationships underlying all three apparently separate events.

The analysis of man over time can be given an infinite number of *Topical emphases* (3.0), the most common and broadest of which are *Political, Social, Economic, Geographic, Intellectual,* and *Cultural*. Each topic of historical study can be narrowed still further. For example, political history can be subdivided into constitutional, diplomatic, and military history. The same sort of narrowing process can be applied to each of the succeeding topics. The broadest topic listed is cultural history, which, if we borrow the anthropologist's concept of culture, subsumes all the rest. It is an all-inclusive sort of history which, one might say, attempts to portray the "spirit of the time" by analyzing the characteristics of a people in all aspects of life, among them art, science, literature, and religion.

Within each of the topical emphases the historian may decide to study any number of aspects of a topic, such as the major individuals or groups involved or the major institutions, events, or movements. In any case, the historian analyzes topics over time.

How does the historian go about his tasks? What is his analytical technique? Historical analysis, or the *Method of inquiry* (4.0), is not easily defined. There are, however, several fairly well-established instruments of investigation—collection of *Evidence, Verification,* application of *Imagination,* assessment of *Probability,* and use of *Interdisciplinary contributions.*

Evidence refers to the variegated sources which historians examine to unearth facts. Barzun and Graff (1957) have provided a classification of historians' sources of evidence as a record drawn from written accounts, oral material, works of art, and relics; examples of these are biographies and diaries, ballads and folktales, portraits and films, and human remains and tools, respectively.

Evidence must be subjected to verification. The historian wants his information to be accurate. For this purpose he must combine objectivity with skepticism. He must accept nothing at face value in order not to be duped into accepting inaccurate evidence. He must be objective in the sense that he attempts to suppress his personal affinities for some concatenation of evidence that might distort the actual configuration. In the process of verifying evidence, the historian plays the role of an intellectual sleuth.

The historian must bring creative imagination to his work. He must be able to look anew at evidence that others have examined and derive a fresh interpretation. This knack for original interpretation is the key to historical insight.

The verification and imaginative interpretation of evidence must be accompanied by the probabilistic outlook of the true scientist. The evidence *may* be accurate and it *may* lead to some conclusion. One can never be absolutely certain of one's conclusions. Historians are very cautious people because they have no control over the welter of variables that have influenced their topic. They search for uniformities and present them as tentative generalizations about man. The historian is too cognizant of the uniqueness of each of the elements that he studies to produce cocksure generalizations.

A final aspect of the historian's method emanates from the sister disciplines of historical study, the other social sciences, which have all contributed to the historian's craft. Their concepts, generalizations, structures, and models have provided the historian with new perspectives. He asks new questions of his evidence with each new concept. He can look at history through the eyes of a psychologist, sociologist, or anthropologist, for example. The evidence of history continually takes on a new appearance with the steady increase in knowledge about human behavior provided by the other social sciences. This knowledge is an essential tool of the compleat historian.

Various social sciences have made another major contribution to the historical method through their techniques of gathering and analyzing data. Content analysis seems particularly close to the historian's art. Sampling is also a technique that would be beneficial to the historian, who sometimes has mounds of data that would take an interminable amount of time to analyze in toto. Statistical techniques of quantifying data also are quite applicable to the historian. A wealth of other techniques utilized in the allied social sciences could be included as applicable to the historian. Suffice it to say that such techniques are again part of the ominous demands made upon the individual who aspires to historical understanding.

The fifth content area, *Historiography* (5.0), refers to the systematic study of the assumptions and values upon which history has been written. Different historians have different assumptions and values which color their view of the past. The central concern of historiography is to determine the biases of professional historians. These biases can affect such matters as the types of problems that a historian chooses to study, the initial interpretation that he gives as the probable causes of the problems, the procedures he uses to investigate the problems, and the types of conclusions he draws. Historiography addresses itself to the investigation of these biases and to the classification of historians according to them.

The final category, *Historical issues and interpretations* (6.0), refers to the endless numbers of problems in history that have been and continue to be subjects of dispute. The fall of Rome, the Protestant Reformation, and the American Civil War, for example, are all subjects of controversial interpretation among historians. Such subjects are usually climactic points of historical inquiry and thus are very often the focal topics of historical study. The variety of evidence and the variety of interpretations offer boundless opportunity for analysis and reinterpretation.

It is apparent that the range of intellectual possibilities contained within the study of history would be difficult to match in any other discipline.

Political science courses (7.0-12.0) Political science in the schools can cover a tremendous range of content.[4] Again, an outline whereby all this content can be pigeonholed would provide some order for analytical purposes. The study of government can be either domestic or international. An outline, of course, would have to be sure to include both types of study.

The study of political science can be simplified into six categories—*Governmental focus*, the *Process of government*, *International relations*, *Factors affecting politics*, *Methods of inquiry*, and *Major political issues*. It is around these categories that the content of political science courses in the schools has been divided in Table 16-1.

Governmental focus (7.0) refers to the *Location* and *Level of study*. This category is the same as that of the historical outline and need not be further explained.

The *Process of government* (8.0) refers to the governed, the authoritative officials, the political process, the structure of government, policy making, and the substance and application of policy.

[4] Much of the content classification of political science in this chapter is drawn from Riddle & Cleary (1966).

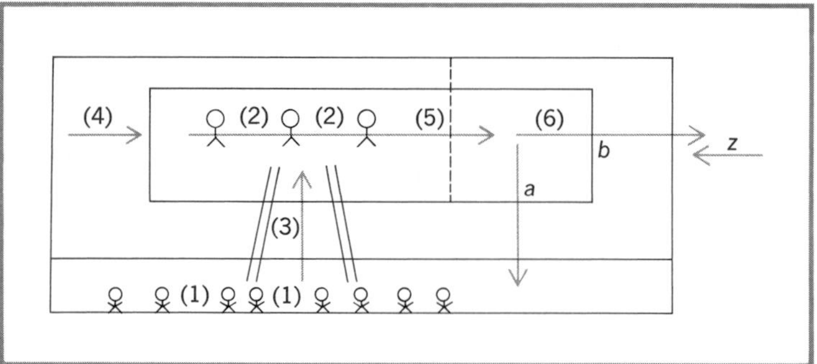

FIGURE 16-1. A polity. [J. S. Gibson. The process approach. In D. H. Riddle & R. E. Cleary (Eds.), *Political science in the social studies: Thirty-sixth yearbook of the National Council for the Social Studies.* Washington, D.C.: NCSS, 1966. P. 66.]

Gibson (1966, p. 66) has constructed a chart (see Fig. 16-1) showing each of these components, and below it he briefly explains them as follows:

1. Members of the national society, the people or the governed.
2. Authoritative officials who govern, and who may or may not be subjected to the same authoritative policy as the governed.
3. The political process or the procedure which elevates officials to their positions of authority and which helps to shape the formulation and application of official policy.
4. The structure of government, in which the officials make authoritative decisions and which, by its nature, is policy itself.
5. The shaping of authoritative policy, or policy-making.
6. The laws, rules, and regulations (authoritative policies) which serve to regulate people and institutions within the polity and which allocate things of value with a view to furthering the security and well-being of the polity (as determined by many variables), or official policy, and application thereof by officials. Policy is both domestic (*a*) and foreign (b), although the latter is under less control of authoritative officials than the former. The external arrow (z) is the impact and operation of the policy of an external polity upon the diagramed policy.

International relations (9.0) deal with politics among nations. International politics is characterized by a concern for national security. This concern for security motivates the participants to act in a number of ways, for example, set up diplomatic relations, make treaties, engage in war, make alliances, and spread propaganda. The nation-state system is essentially a very egotistical form of politics on an international basis. This relatively atomistic system is so explosive potentially that states have found it enticing to flirt with international organizations of various sorts. These organizations are caught in the tug-of-war between each state's refusal to divest itself of its national sovereignty and each state's desire for a peaceful approach to the settlement of international problems.

Both the process of government and the struggle for security and self-interest on the international level are influenced by a number of *Factors affecting politics* (10.0). These are the same sorts of variables that influence historical causation. The governed, for example, are influenced by historical, economic, geographic, ideological, religious, or educational factors. The list of factors that may influence national or international politics varies from state to state and era to era. It is a task of the political scientist to sort out and weigh the effects of these variables.

The *Methods* (11.0) which the political scientist uses to analyze the components of politics fall into the realm of two major strategies—the *Legal-institutional* approach and the *Behavioral* approach. The former, the traditional approach, is geared more to the analysis of the constitutional component of politics with a strong emphasis on political philosophy, economics, and law; the latter is more interdisciplinary, quantitative, and scientific. The two approaches represent the changing character of political science from the study of legislation, constitutions, formal governmental structures and offices, political philosophy, historical characteristics, etc., to the quantitative, multidisciplinary analysis of the political process hopefully culminating in a scientific theory of political behavior.

The two major methods of political science have their own techniques. Like the historian, the political scientist of either persuasion must approach his work with a certain cluster of scientific attitudes. The behavioral political scientist is more concerned with quantitative data and the techniques appropriate to collecting and analyzing them. The legal-institutional political scientist is more concerned with a personal interpretation of the factors that he selects to study. The two approaches to political science are not mutually exclusive by any means. The well-rounded political scientist is schooled in both approaches and complements the one with the other.

Major political issues (12.0) can be either *National* or *International* in form. The two types of issues often affect each other deeply. War, for example, can be spurred on because of domestic problems, or war can be a major spur to domestic change. The range of major political problems which may be studied is highly diverse, since most serious problems in a society become political problems sooner or later.

The six basic categories of political science attempt to subsume the content of political science courses in the secondary school. The field of political science has many subdivisions, all of which can be placed somewhere in these content categories which are purposely broad enough to subsume a variety of lesser course content.

Three social studies programs

The determination of program content and objectives

Education programs in the social studies vary in their emphases. Courses with the same title may differ considerably. For example, a course in world history may deal with the development of European civilization from prehistoric times to the present, or it may deal with the cultural development of the major civilizations across the globe. Any number of content choices have been selected not only for world history courses but for all social studies courses. The content of a social studies program is fairly easy to determine by an examination of the materials. For example, if the content of a course is essentially prescribed by a textbook, one can examine the table of contents and the reading itself to determine the basic content of the course.

More important, possibly, than the content emphases of various social studies programs has been the diversity of behavioral emphases. These are not so easily determined. Nevertheless, a thorough examination of such elements as objectives, reading materials, student activities, and test items can give an adequate indication of the primary emphases of an education program.

Three notes of caution must be mentioned concerning such an analysis. First, it is altogether possible to construct deceptive objectives that are not attained in the program because the activities and reading materials are inadequate. One might say that the intrinsic objectives of the program based on student activities and reading materials do not correspond to the extrinsic objectives of the course stated at the outset of the program. Second, the test items may not be adequate representatives of behavioral outcomes of the course. Third, the capability of the teacher may alter the substance of the program for better or worse.

Yet, an examination of the major behavioral and content components of a program ought to elucidate its essential characteristics so that a table of specifications that indicates these characteristics can be devised for purposes of comparison with other course programs or with the overall Table of Specifications for Selected Social Studies presented in Table 16-1 (pages 450–451). This, despite the fact that the caliber of teacher implementing the program may alter the inherent intent of the program. Such alteration is fortuitous and not a part of the basic design.

The three programs

Three course programs in junior and senior high school social studies will be briefly examined to elicit their intrinsic objectives in order to prepare a table of specifications demonstrative of these objectives. On the basis of each program's table of specifications, a clear picture of the program's emphases will emerge. If one compares each program's table of specifications with the overall table, one can easily evaluate the program in terms of what its intrinsic objectives are designed to accomplish and, very importantly, what these intrinsic objectives are not designed to accomplish.

The three programs have been selected because they represent three gradations of emphasis from the highly traditional—centering cognitively on knowledge and comprehension and affectively on avoidance of value conflict—to the very modern—centering cognitively on critical thinking and affectively on intimate, personal involvement. The programs are drawn from grades 7 to 12. One of the programs is based on a textbook analysis, another from an existing course, and another from a course in the pilot stage. The programs deal with American history and with government, two of the most prevalent subjects in the social studies.

An American history program First let us examine the American history program. In many classrooms the education program is dictated by the textbook and its intrinsic objectives determine the nature of student outcomes. *The Story of America* (Eibling, King, Harlow, & Finkelstein, 1969) is a standard example of the traditional form of United States history course on the junior high level. Chapter after chapter is strewn with facts, concepts, and generalizations to be committed to memory and activities designed to interest the child in a way that might more palatably allow him to sop up the flow of information. Some of the activities do require the student to engage in critical thinking, but more often they require the ability to cut, paste, sew, draw, paint, and perform, than they do critical thinking. The *Teacher's Manual* (Eibling, King, Harlow, & Finkelstein, undated) is equally concerned with the knowledge and comprehension of facts, concepts, and generalizations. Many of the "understandings" listed in the *Teacher's Manual* are nothing but facts inflated into sentence form.

In brief, the components of this textbook are the standard fare of political and economic history sprinkled with some social history and geography. As far as affective elements are concerned, the students are provided with an opportunity to become aware of the major cultural events of our history but not the trenchant problems of American life. The key question in terms of affective goals usually hinges upon the manner in which controversial issues are discussed. In this textbook, American values are moralized in a manner that averts any semblance of the existence of divisive issues in American life. In this respect, the text exerts a subtle, possibly unintended form of indoctrination which of itself is undesirable for democratic behavior.

If we now set up the Table of Specifications for the textbook, as in Table 16-2, we can see the major emphases of the course in a nutshell. This program and the two others to be discussed do contain other types of behavior and content, but they have been dealt with so lightly that they have been excluded from Tables 16-2, 16-3, and 16-4. Also, where the tables list an overall content heading, such as 1.0, *Historical focus*, it means that the program treats all subcategories shown in Table 16-1.

The reader will note that *Relationships* (2.4) over time and *Intellectual* (3.5) emphasis have been excluded as irrelevant to the content of this course. Also, the student is not exposed to historical methodology, historiography, or issues in the true sense of the word (4.0–6.0).

In the behavior axis of the table, one can see that in the cognitive area the key aspects of critical thinking are excluded and that in the affective area very little is done except to kindle some awareness and interest in the major events, people, and accomplishments in American history. In terms of its behavior components, the textbook excludes those behavior forms which challenge the student intellectually and emotionally.

A government program The second program to be examined is from a twelfth-grade course in government in Houston, Texas (Davis, 1965). This course appears to be a mixture of the traditional and the modern. The content with which it deals is essentially concerned with the process of government (8.0), with the usual major emphasis upon the structure of American government. As in most courses, the student is told about his civil rights and his obligations to be a well-informed voter. The course also deals with some of our standard problems in international relations (9.0), such as those with Latin America and with the Soviet Union and communism in general. The content is the usual fare of government courses.

The behaviors implicit in the course can be derived from the teaching suggestions and the student activities accompanying each unit. The teaching suggestions intimate that the primary role of teaching is explanation. The student activities range from asking the student to perform tasks requiring low-level cognitive forms of behavior such as knowledge and comprehension of generalizations (*C*) to fairly high-level tasks requiring critical thinking skills (*G* and *H*). For example, one low-level activity asks students to draw a diagram of the organization of the United Nations, whereas a high-level activity requires them to prepare a panel discussion to evaluate the merits and demerits of the welfare state as it is developing in the United States.

Formal group participation (*J*) is sometimes encouraged through debate or panel discussions. Informal participation (*K*) in terms of persuasiveness and effectiveness in steering toward group decision making is also mildly encouraged through a mock presidential election, a major activity. This activity and certain of the others attempt to interest the student to the point of involvement. However, most of the involvement asked of the student is dependent on superficial forms of political participation such as making a visit to the city hall and taking note of the various offices and facilities located there.

In terms of awareness of social problems (*N*), the student is alerted to the usual problems of labor relations, propaganda techniques, and the Communist conspiracy. It is doubtful that this course requires students to face up to any of the closed areas of the American value system.

As far as responsibility (*O*) is concerned, the student is more or less informed of his responsibilities and the dangers of irresponsibility, especially in voting, but little beyond this.

Finally, concerning values (*Q*), the course, though it does not actively indoctrinate, does not actively scrutinize the basic values of American life. Certain fairly heated issues such as labor and welfare problems are dealt with but most of the burning issues are left untouched.

Now that a brief description of the course has been presented, the Table of Specifications for the course can be set up, as shown in Table 16-3.

From the point of view of content the course deals with most of the content of political science, although primary emphasis is placed on the

TABLE 16-2 TABLE OF SPECIFICATIONS FOR AN AMERICAN HISTORY COURSE

	BEHAVIOR					
	Facts	*Concepts*	*Generalizations*	*Location of information*	*Interpretation of graphic and symbolic data*	*Awareness and interest*
CONTENT	A	B	C	E	F	N
1.0 Historical focus						
2.0 Analysis over time						
2.1 Time periods						
2.2 Sequence						
2.3 Continuity and change						
3.0 Topical emphases						
3.1 Political						
3.2 Social						
3.3 Economic						
3.4 Geographic						
3.6 Cultural						

TABLE 16-3 TABLE OF SPECIFICATIONS FOR A GOVERNMENT COURSE

	BEHAVIOR								
	Facts	*Concepts*	*Generalizations*	*Structures and models*	*Location of information*	*Identification of central issues and underlying assumptions*	*Evaluation of evidence and drawing of warranted conclusions*	*Formal procedures*	*Awareness and interest*
CONTENT	*A*	*B*	C	*D*	E	G	*H*	*J*	*N*
7.0 Governmental focus									
8.0 Process of government									
9.0 International relations									
10.0 Factors affecting politics									
11.0 Methods of inquiry									
11.1 Legal-institutional									
12.0 Major political issues									

process of government and the legal-institutional method of studying government (8.0 and 11.1).

From the point of view of behavior, this course does deal with higher levels of cognitive processes more often than did the previous program. There is some emphasis on critical analysis, especially in terms of evaluating evidence and drawing warranted conclusions (*H*). There is very little emphasis on hypothesis formulation (*I*) and apparently little on the interpretation of graphic and symbolic data (*F*). Formal procedures for group participation (*J*) also receive a good deal of emphasis, but the informal procedures (K) are generally left to chance rather than given purposeful practice.

In the affective area some issues of borderline value conflict (Q) are discussed, but essentially the divisive issues are circumvented. As a result, the affective component that is evoked is an awareness of some of America's problems but not with much incisiveness. The course does not orient itself sufficiently toward the critical analysis of controversial issues so that affective components of an intellectual bent have much opportunity to be developed.

In brief, one can see that this course is not so

rigidly oriented toward knowledge and comprehension as the previous one. It ventures into the critical analysis of some issues, but neither the analysis nor the issues permeate the course so as to shift its motif radically from a traditional stance.

An American government program The final program to be studied is from a course in American political behavior which was still in the pilot stage at the time of this writing (High School Curriculum Center in Government, 1968). The overall objectives of the course have been fairly explicitly drawn up (Mehlinger, 1967) and can serve as an indication of a high-powered course in terms of cognitive and affective goals.

Cognitively, the course is geared toward the student. Instead of focusing on the structure of government, the course emphasizes the individual's role in the government and why he acts as he does (8.1 and 8.3), political issues of continuing concern (12.0), the historical sources of American political values and beliefs (10.1), ways the individual can bring pressure to bear on the political system (8.5 and 10.1), and development of concepts that expand the political meaning of the individual's experience (C). Further, in order for the individual to attain this status of political sophistication, he has to be able to evaluate data so as to draw warranted conclusions (*H*) after constructing hypothetical, analytical questions (*I*) and carrying out investigations based on these questions (*E*). The course also develops fairly advanced social science techniques of interpretation and construction of symbolic and graphic data (*F*).

The course is basically affectively oriented in that it actively attempts to reach the individual's attitudinal structure. The basic affective purpose is to increase acceptance of democracy by nurturing students' political interest (*N*), effectiveness (*K*), toleration (*M*), acceptance of the legitimacy of specific majority decision-making rights (*Q*), and scientific disposition toward political behavior (*L*).

Before continuing a discussion of the course, let us construct a Table of Specifications, Table 16-4, to expose its characteristics at a glimpse.

As the reader can see, the content part of the matrix is complete except for the elimination of the international component. The method of political inquiry is noteworthy because the approach is geared toward a behavioral rather than a legal-institutional one, in line with the trend in political science.

In the behavioral component of the matrix one can see that almost the entire bloc of behaviors is represented. Whereas the first course dealt primarily with knowledge and comprehension and the second moved toward some elements of critical analysis and confrontation of issues, this course progresses to widespread hypothesizing, critical analysis, and grappling with political issues. There are courses which involve the individual more profoundly in political action and in the conflict of values, but this course will probably engage students in such behavior to a far greater degree than most. It requires the individual to analyze vital political issues in American life and thus provides the thrust to impel him attitudinally toward desirable intellectual and social behaviors. This same thrust ought to spur the individual's interest and evoke an awareness of social problems while placing him in a position to make responsible choices.

The only section of the behavior axis of Table 16-1 that has been excluded is *Formal procedures* (*J*). If the learning of formal group procedures is a part of the course, at present there is little indication of it. On the other hand, the course is designed with group discussion and decision making as built-in elements, so that the development of informal procedures of group participation seems unavoidable.

From Tables 16-2, 16-3, and 16-4 one can see the gradations from the traditional to the modern orientation of social studies courses. The behavior component of the course is the key element in determining its tenor. Knowledge and comprehension and interpretation of graphic and symbolic data are the prime ingredients of most social studies programs. The key to course differences usually depends on what other types of

TABLE 16-4 TABLE OF SPECIFICATIONS FOR AN AMERICAN GOVERNMENT COURSE

	BEHAVIOR															
	Facts	*Concepts*	*Generalizations*	*Structures and models*	*Location of information*	*Interpretation of graphic and symbolic data*	*Identification of central issues and underlying assumptions*	*Evaluation of evidence and drawing of warranted conclusions*	*Formulation of reasonable hypotheses*	*Informal procedures*	*Scientific approach to human behavior*	*Humanitarian outlook on the behavior of others*	*Awareness and interest*	*Acceptance of responsibility*	*Involvement*	*Basic democratic values*
CONTENT	*A*	*B*	*C*	*D*	*E*	*F*	*G*	*H*	*I*	*K*	*L*	*M*	*N*	*O*	*P*	*Q*
7.0 Governmental focus																
8.0 Process of government																
10.0 Factors affecting politics																
10.1 National politics																
11.0 Methods of inquiry																
11.2 Behavioral																
12.0 Major political issues																
12.1 National																

behavior are emphasized. Critical analysis of closed areas opens the affective sector of the matrix to students. Without critical analysis of such issues, most of the attitudinal and value goals are unattainable. The American history course averts questions of value and the concomitant critical analysis. The government course from Houston hedges in its handling of value issues and attempts to encourage critical analysis through the discussion of lukewarm social issues. The affective components of the course are thus kept at a low ebb. The pilot American government course delves into value issues and attempts to position the student intellectually and emotionally in a way that requires him to analyze and become involved in important social issues. The participatory aspect of the affective component of the Table of Specifications is thus sharply emphasized.

The behavior continuum portrayed in the three courses exemplifies the gamut of behavior that is expected of students in social studies courses.

Summative evaluation

The achievement of cognitive objectives may be evaluated through an objective or essay test or a combination of both. The construction of a test ought to be preceded by the careful statement of behavioral objectives and the preparation of a table of specifications. The table acts as a guide to the test developer to compose an equitable number of test items based on the emphasis devoted to each objective in the course once weights have been assigned to each cell in the matrix.

In social studies test construction it is generally far more difficult to create an item to evaluate the achievement of a specific type of behavior than it is to evaluate a specific segment of content. The following presentation of sample test items will be more concerned with the *Behavior* axis of Table 16-1 than the *Content* axis. It does not make much difference whether the content is history, political science, economics, or another subject. The items below will be drawn from history and political science to correspond with the content areas introduced earlier.

Each item will be preceded by the cell code identifying the specific behavior and content (many items pertain to more than one content) to which it is related on Table 16-1. Evaluation of each of the behavior components of the matrix will be exemplified by one or more items or approaches. Let us begin with *Knowledge and comprehension.*

Evaluation of knowledge and comprehension (A–D)

Facts (A)

A-3.1

1. Which of the following groups migrated in large numbers to Canada following the Revolutionary War?
   (1) Whigs
   (2) Copperheads
   (3) Quakers
   (4) Tories

(Anderson & Lindquist, 1957, p. 32, item 61.)

There are a number of ways in which an individual's knowledge of facts can be elicited. In the above situation students must have committed to memory a migration pattern pursued by a group of people as a result of a specific event. However, it is also possible that a student who had not memorized this fact might be able to deduce the appropriate answer based on his recognition of the term "Tories," referring to supporters of George III, and his knowledge that the British had lost the war. He might arrive at the selection of Tories after a successive elimination of each of the preceding responses based on a similar type of evaluation of each response.

DIRECTIONS: In the following questions the chronology of the history of the United States is broken up into four periods. Below each period are various descriptive statements, supposedly applicable to that period. For each item, *blacken*

answer space 1 if this statement correctly applies to the period named;
answer space 2 if it does *not* apply to that period, but to an *earlier one;*
answer space 3 if it does *not* apply to that period, but to a *later one;*
answer space 4 if it does not apply correctly to any period of American history.

Period: 1760–1815

A-3.1

2. The United States was established as an independent nation.
3. Representative institutions were first established in North America.

A-3.4

4. Most of the area between the Mississippi River and the Rocky Mountains was added to the United States.

(University of Chicago, College, 1945, p. 114, items 1, 6, 7.)

In item 1, the student is required to recognize which group was involved in an event that took place in a certain period. In items 2 to 4, the student is required to recognize whether an event took place in a certain period.

A-3.1

DIRECTIONS: For each of the following items, *blacken*

answer space A if it was in the *Articles of Confederation;*
answer space B if it was in the *Constitution* of 1787;
answer space C if it was in the *Bill of Rights* (Amendments I–X);
answer space D if it was in Amendments *XI–XXI;*
answer space E if it was in *two* or more of the above.

5. Protected life, liberty and property against governmental action without due process of law.
6. Provided for popular election of United States Senators.
7. Provided for a unicameral legislature.
8. Gave the treaty-making power to Congress.
9. Gave Congress power to borrow money.

(University of Chicago, College, 1948, p. 7, items 31–35.)

In items 5 to 9, the student is asked to determine in which document or documents a certain provision is located. Both sets of items, 2 to 4 and 5 to 9, are forms of a general item type in which the responses are keyed prior to introducing a group of stimuli based on the same group of responses. This approach allows for the testing of a wide sample of information very efficiently.

Concepts (B)

B-8.3

10. Which of these may be employed as a means of removing the President from office for cause?
    (1) Impeachment
    (2) Impressment
    (3) Injunction
    (4) Recall

(Anderson & Lindquist, 1957, p. 70, item 524.)

The term referred to in this item has a very definite constitutional meaning. Many of the terms in the social studies cannot be as unequivocally defined as can be the term "impeachment." There is no doubt as to the correct answer to the previous item because impeachment is a relatively clear-cut term. The distracters are, therefore, clearly incorrect. However, distracters for some of the more ambiguous concepts in the social studies could easily be made so attractive that the correct item response approaches being an arbitrary one. Concepts such as culture and id, for example, are rich in meaning but difficult to pin down. The more elusive the definition of the concept, the more likely it is that the distracters will be as reasonable as the correct response.

B-8.1

11. Political alienation is expressed by United States citizens in all of the following ways EXCEPT:
    a. their failure to vote in local elections,
    b. their attempts to impose their views on others through the use of force,
    c. their expression of views that differ from those of their political leaders,
    d. their attempts to organize armed resistance to government policies.

(Schultz, 1967, p. 13, item 2.)

In item 10, part of the definition of a concept was presented to the student and he was asked to choose the term which best fitted the definition. In item 11, the concept is stated in the stem and various behavioral expressions are presented from which the student is to choose the one appropriate to the concept. This type of conceptual testing requires the student to be able to identify the meaning of a concept in terms of its behavioral implications.

B-3.5

DIRECTIONS: Following in two columns, labeled X and Y, are words and phrases describing some important concepts found in William Graham Sumner's writings ("Challenge of Facts" and "Absurd Effort to Make the World Over"). For each item, *blacken*

answer space A if according to Sumner, X is *associated with* or *tends to encourage* Y;
answer space B if according to Sumner, X is *contrary to* or *works against* Y;
answer space C if neither "A" nor "B" is true.

	X	Y
12.	Competition	Progress
13.	Thirst for equality of rights	Progress
14.	Hereditary disadvantages	Failure in competition
15.	Social injustice	Misery and poverty
16.	The neutral but benevolent state	Protection of capital

(University of Chicago, College, 1948, p. 16, items 76–80.)

In this keyed item approach, some of the major concepts used by an individual author are placed in juxtaposition and the student is required to identify the form of the relationship existing between the concepts. This type of conceptual testing borders on testing for generalizations in that the student must be able to determine the direction of relationship, if any, between two concepts.

Generalizations (C)

C-2.3, C-3.3

17. The two most important issues during the second quarter of the nineteenth century were:
    1. Slavery and territorial expansion
    2. Territorial expansion and free silver
    3. Free silver and the tariff
    4. The tariff and federal support of internal improvement

(Anderson & Lindquist, 1957, p. 58, item 414.)

The social studies, especially history, devote much of their emphasis to general trends. Item 17 evaluates a student's knowledge of the prominent trend of a certain time period by requiring him to identify the major issues of that specific era.

C-3.3

DIRECTIONS: for each of the following items, *blacken*

answer space A if it best describes the *Progressive Movement;*

answer space B if it best describes the *New Deal;*

answer space C if it refers to *both* of the above;

answer space D if it refers to *neither* of the above.

18. Attempted to meet the farm problem by subsidizing farmers to reduce their output.
19. Sought to provide industry with government supervised methods of adopting codes of fair competition.
20. Succeeded in providing all with equal economic opportunity.

(University of Chicago, College, 1948, p. 9, items 242–244.)

In items 18 to 20, the student must be able to classify the descriptive generalization with the appropriate movement. Each movement has goals distinctive to itself or overlapping with those of other movements. This item type aids in determining whether the student comprehends the similarities, differences, and essentials of movements.

DIRECTIONS: Following are some predictions. For each item, *blacken*

answer space A if it is highly probable;

answer space B if it is highly improbable;

answer space C if neither of these judgments can be made.

C-2.3, C-3.1

21. State governments will take over most of the functions now exercised by the federal government within the next fifty years.

C-2.3, C-3.3

22. Productivity of labor will increase in the United States within the next thirty years.
23. The influence of the small stockholder on the management of corporations will increase after the war.

(University of Chicago, College, 1945, p. 118, items 22–24.)

Items 21 to 23 ask the student to predict the possible consequences of present trends. Instead of just identifying the existence of a trend in an era, the student is given the task of projecting present trends into the future and determining the probability of certain stated developments.

C-3.4

DIRECTIONS: For each of the following items, *blacken* the answer space corresponding to the number of the *one best* statement of connection between the two terms.

24. American frontier—Democracy
    1. The "rugged individualism" of the frontier destroys the equalitarian spirit on which democracy is based.
    2. On the frontier, the settlers took over the democratic institutions of the Indians.
    3. Democratic institutions and a democratic spirit developed out of the conditions of frontier life.
    4. American democracy developed in the cities along the Atlantic coast and reached from there to the frontier regions of the interior.

(University of Chicago, College, 1945, p. 115, item 69.)

In item 24, key concepts in American historical development are placed side by side and the student must select the generalization which best relates them. Unlike item 16, which simply asked for the direction of the relationship between two concepts, this item requires the student to select a valid historical generalization which can be made from their relationship.

Structures and models (D)

D-3.5

25. Jefferson's theory for the evolution of an ideal society included the belief that:
    1. The President should be elected for an indefinite term.
    2. The rights of the state should be strictly subordinated to those of the federal government.
    3. Laborers and mechanics should be the dominant class.
    4. Slavery should be gradually abolished.

(Anderson & Lindquist, 1957, p. 40, item 231.)

This item requires the individual to select a certain criterion for an ideal model of American society as envisaged by Jefferson. Much of political and social philosophy and much of the social sciences in general have been devoted to setting up criteria of effective operation.

D-3.5

26. What lessons from historical experience aided the Founding Fathers in building the Federal Constitution in 1787?
    1. Distrust of unlimited central authority.
    2. The need for effective union of the former colonies.
    3. The need for each state to make its own tariffs.
    4. The need for each state to keep its sovereignty.
    5. The need for an effective executive branch.
    6. The need for the central government to have an effective taxing power.
       a. 1, 2, 3, 4
       b. 3, 4, 5, 6
       c. 2 only
       d. 1, 2, 5, 6
       e. all of the above

(Crary, ed., 1951, Form Am, p. 6, item 90. Reproduced from Crary, American History Test, copyright 1951 by Harcourt, Brace & World, Inc. Reproduced by special permission.)

Item 26 requires the individual to be informed about a variety of problems characterizing a specific time period as envisaged by a group of individuals. In a way it is similar to the previous item except that it requires the individual to select the appropriate pattern of responses. It is not enough to be aware of individual criteria that influenced the decisions of the members of the Constitutional Convention but instead the congeries of experiences that influenced these decisions.

This item is interesting because of its technical design. It offers first a series of responses any one or more of which may be correct and is followed by five choices of cleverly contrived response combinations requiring the individual to choose from these combinations to display his knowledge of the model of decision-influencing factors which affected the Founding Fathers.

D-3.5

27. If the definition of what constitutes the "greatest good" were left to each system, which of the following would assert that the system was directed toward "the greatest good for the greatest number"? Defenders of
    a. the 19th-century liberal system.
    b. the socialist system in post-war England.

c. communism as currently practiced in the Soviet Union.
d. all of these systems.
e. none of these systems.

Whereas item 25 called for comprehension of an individual's model for general societal development and item 26 called for comprehension of a model held by a specific group of individuals, in a certain era, with a certain purpose in mind, item 27 requires the student to determine the general school of thought or practice to which some major philosophical assumption pertains. The item, then, tests for a more general criterion. This item also differs from the previous ones in that the criterion is placed in the stem, and particular individuals, groups, or schools of thought may be inserted as responses, one of which is most closely associated with the criterion.

Evaluation of skills (E–K)

The first set of social studies skills, *Research*, is divided into the *Location of information* (E) and the *Interpretation of graphic and symbolic data* (F). The location of information in terms of books and the proper usage of social studies reference works will be exemplified.

Location of information (E)

E-3.1

28. To locate the page in a text that gives information about Jackson's inauguration one should use the
    1. bibliography
    2. appendix
    3. index
    4. table of contents
    5. preface

(Morse & McCune, 1964, p. 44, item 29.)

Part A. Using Common References

DIRECTIONS: The degree to which a social studies library is useful to students is determined partly by the ability of students to obtain needed information. Below are two lists. One contains those books which could compose a Social Studies Reference Shelf. The other contains a list of questions which you might wish to have answered. Do *not* try to answer the questions. Indicate whether you could find the answers, by placing beside the *number* of the question the *letter* of the reference work in which you would be likely to find the answer most satisfactorily.

EXAMPLE: (F) 0. How many students are enrolled in American colleges and universities? The answer F refers to the *World Almanac*, a handbook of current information.

Reference Shelf

A. *Dictionary of American History*
B. An Atlas
C. *A Guide to the Study of The United States of America*
D. *Historical Statistics of the United States*
E. *Who's Who in America*
F. *The World Almanac*
G. *Readers' Guide to Periodical Literature*
H. Official State Government Handbook
I. *Dictionary of American Biography*
J. *Harvard Guide to American History*

E-3.4

29. How does North America compare in size with Africa?

E-8.2

30. Who is the chief justice of your state supreme court?

E-3.2

31. How many persons were killed by autos last year?

E-3.4

32. When was the Cumberland Road built?

E-8.2

33. Who is the official custodian of state law?

E-8.3

34. What was the political significance of the last Congressional election?

E-3.3

35. How much cotton was exported from the United States from 1950–1960?

(Morse & McCune, 1964, p. 43, items 1–7.)

The location of information is a relatively low-level skill. All of the previous items are primarily involved with remembering and an elementary form of application of knowledge. If the student knows the kind of information contained in the parts of a book or in different reference books, he can then relate the information he desires to the appropriate book or part of a book.

Interpretation of graphic and symbolic data (F) A major aspect of reading in the social studies is geared to the interpretation of maps, globes, graphs, tables, charts, and cartoons. The following are examples of test items based on graphs and tables.

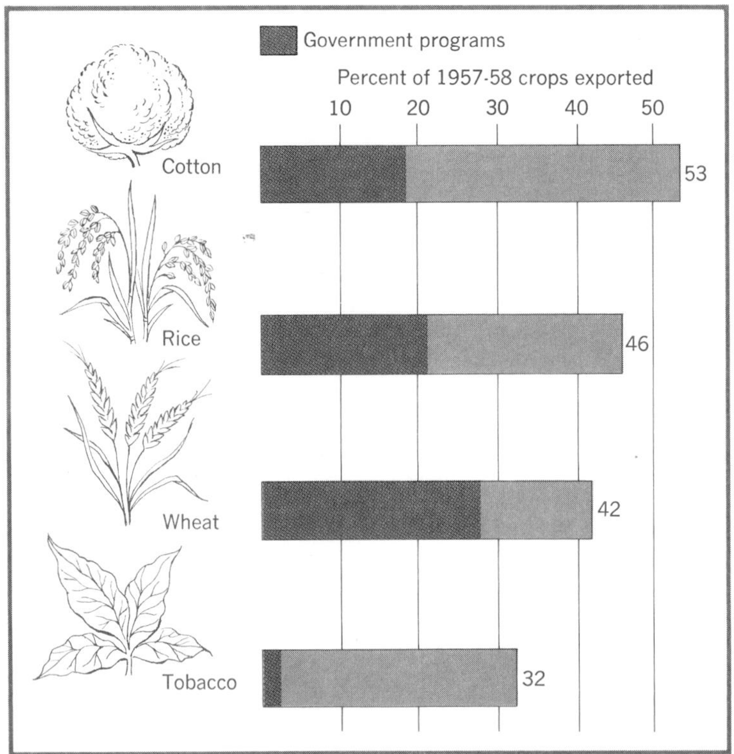

FIGURE 16-2. U.S. agriculture depends on exports. [U.S. Department of State, U.S. Department of Defense, & International Cooperation Administration. *Mutual security program, fiscal year 1960: A summary presentation.* Washington, D.C.: USDS, USDD, and ICA, March 1959. (Reprinted: In H. T. Morse & G. H. McCune. *Selected items for the testing of study skills and critical thinking.* [Bull. No. 15, 4th ed.] Washington, D.C.: National Council for the Social Sciences, 1964. P. 62.)]

DIRECTIONS: Use the following numbers to indicate your answer [to each of the questions concerning Fig. 16-2].

1. The statement is supported by the evidence given in the chart. . . .
3. Whether the statement is correct or incorrect cannot be determined by the evidence in the chart. . . .
5. The statement is contradicted by the evidence in the chart.

Questions on [Fig. 16-2]

F-10.0

36. The total farm economy of the United States depends upon exports.
37. Less than fifty percent of exports of agricultural products are government sponsored.
38. The American farmer would suffer great loss of income if government-sponsored programs were to be dropped.
39. Rice was the largest item in government-sponsored programs.
40. The United States consumes about two thirds of the tobacco produced.
41. The United States keeps for its own use over half of the rice and wheat grown.
42. The graph demonstrates that economic health in the United States depends upon the economic health of the countries that import our products.
43. Cotton exports would suffer least from the withdrawal of government-sponsored programs.

(Morse & McCune, 1964, pp. 62–63, items 33–40.)

The individual is required to examine the verifiability or the uncertainty of each statement relative to the accompanying graph. His ability to read the graph is estimated by his ability to determine the congruence of each conclusion with the evidence presented in the graph.

The next set of items requires the student to extrapolate from data presented in a table.

DIRECTIONS: This is a test of the ability to draw conclusions from statistical data. In making your decisions *consider only the evidence given in the table and any logical trends which may be reasonably inferred from the data,* even though you may be acquainted with other evidence which would indicate definitely that a statement is true or false.

ANSWER SYMBOLS: Use *numbers* only.

1. If the *evidence alone* is sufficient to make the statement *true;*
2. If the *evidence alone* is *sufficient* to indicate that the statement is probably *true;*
3. If the *evidence alone* is *not sufficient* to indicate any degree of *truth* or *falsity;*
4. If the *evidence alone* is sufficient to indicate the statement is probably *false;*
5. If the *evidence alone* is sufficient to make the statement *false* because it is contradicted by the data in the table [Table 16-5].

Questions on [*Table 16-5*]

F-3.3

44. Producing cotton has always been more time-consuming work than producing wheat or corn.
45. The increase in the yield per acre has been greater for wheat than corn.
46. Over the years the preparation of the soil for corn and the tending of the crop is more time-consuming than the harvesting of corn.
47. Between 1800 and 1860 labor-saving machinery was used to produce wheat and corn.
48. Over the years the harvesting of cotton has been more time-consuming than the harvesting of wheat.
49. More machinery is needed in the twentieth century for cotton to prepare the soil and tend the crop than for either wheat or corn.
50. Less cotton is raised in the twentieth century than in the nineteenth century.
51. More machinery is probably used in the production of wheat, corn, and cotton since World War II than in the period prior to the Civil War.

(Morse & McCune, 1964, p. 72, items 1–8.)

Table 16-5 Man-hours used to produce specified amounts of wheat, corn, and cotton: 1800–1950

Item	*1800*	*1840*	*1880*	*1900*	*1920*	*1940*	*1950*
Wheat							
Man-hours per acre	56	35	20	15	12.0	7.5	4.6
Before harvest	16	12	8	7	5.5	3.7	2.6
Harvest	40	23	12	8	6.5	3.8	2.0
Bushels per acre	15	15	13.2	13.9	13.8	15.9	16.6
Man-hours per 100 bushels	373	233	152	108	87	47	28
Corn							
Man-hours per acre	86	69	46	38	32	25	15.2
Before harvest	56	44	28	22	19	15	9.9
Harvest	30	25	18	16	13	10	5.3
Bushels per acre	25	25	25.6	25.9	28.4	30.3	39.0
Man-hours per 100 bushels	344	276	180	147	113	83	39
Cotton							
Man-hours per acre	185	135	119	112	90	98	74
Before harvest	135	90	67	62	55	46	33
Harvest	50	45	52	50	35	52	41
Pounds of lint—acre	147	147	179	191	160	245	283
Man-hours per bale†	601	439	318	280	269	191	126

SOURCE: *Historical Statistics of the United States.* In H. T. Morse & G. H. McCune. *Selected items for the testing of study skills and critical thinking.* (Bull. No. 15, 4th ed.) Washington, D.C.: National Council for the Social Studies, 1964. P. 71, Table B.

† Bale of cotton: 500 pounds gross weight, 480 pounds net weight of lint.

The last two groups of items are interesting because of the type of interpretation of student errors which can be derived from them. Student errors can be classified as overcautious, crude, and beyond the data. For example, in the extrapolation items, 44 to 51, the degree of an individual's overcaution is determined by counting the number of items marked 2 when the correct answer is 1; items marked 3 when the correct answer is 1, 2, 4, or 5; and items marked 4 when the correct answer is 5. The degree of crudeness is determined by counting the number of items marked 4 or 5 when the correct answer is 1 or 2 and the number of items marked 1 or 2 when the correct answer is 4 or 5. Going beyond the data is determined by counting the number of items marked 1 when the correct answer is 2; items marked 1, 2, 4, or 5 when the correct answer is 3; and items marked 5 when the correct answer is 4.

Identification of central issues and underlying assumptions (G) Critical thinking skills permeate the entire social studies program and thus are vital to the individual's processing of incoming and outgoing information. The critical comprehension of incoming information is handled through the identification of central issues and underlying assumptions. These are primarily analytical problems. The following items exemplify questions designed to tap these critical skills. Several of the multiple-choice items assume that the individual has read a pertinent passage before answering the item.

G-3.3 or G-10.0, G-6.0 or G-12.1

52. The general argument presented by the author assumes that
    1. agriculture is the fundamental American economic activity.
    2. the government should follow a strictly laissez-faire policy on foreign trade.
    3. general prosperity can be induced by assistance to certain industries.
    4. the national income is inequitably distributed.
53. The author evidently bases his statement *primarily* upon the assumption that Americans are strongly motivated by
    1. desire to maximize individual economic returns.
    2. willingness to place patriotism above profits.
    3. belief in the value of competition.
    4. concern for the general welfare.

(Dressel & Mayhew, 1954, p. 31, items 10, 9.)

In item 52 the student is faced with the problem of selecting the basic position of the passage and in item 53 with the problem of selecting the assumption upon which the author's position rests. Such answers seemingly involve little analysis. However, the more subtle an argument is, the more difficult it is to identify an author's position or his assumptions. In fact, so difficult does it become at times, that authoritative individuals often disagree concerning the correctness of a response. This is the danger of such analytical items—that competent individuals often disagree over the correctness of an answer because of the delicate nuances that differentiate the choices. Responses with eyelash differences often tend to produce items of fairly low discrimination which may turn out to be detrimental to the construction of an adequate measuring instrument.

G-9.0

54. In the light of your reading on foreign policy, describe three or four *principles* on which American foreign policy at the present might be based. (Suggested time, 20 minutes)

(University of Chicago, College, 1948, p. 26, essay II.)

Item 54 is an example of an essay question which requires the student to identify central principles derived from a wide variety of readings. To answer the question the student might have to reduce piles of information about foreign policy in a way that can be explained by a few key principles. The intellectual nature of this item would be completely transformed if key principles of American foreign policy had been presented to the student prior to the test rather than created by the student on his own.

Evaluation of evidence and drawing of warranted conclusions (H) The evaluation of evidence and the drawing of warranted conclusions can be tested in a number of ways. In the next item, the student is presented with the problem of determining in which of several aspects of an argument over the protective tariff the author is least rational.

H-3.3

55. Which of these paragraphs goes farthest in making an emotional appeal rather than a rational argument?
    1. b
    2. c
    3. d
    4. e

(Dressel & Mayhew, 1954, p. 32, item 13.)

Even without having read the statements preceding the item, one can visualize the evaluation problem inherent in such a choice, especially if the author is not bombastically emotional in any one of the paragraphs. The student is forced to weigh each paragraph against the other before making a decision.

Item 55 further underlines the potential disagreement that may arise if two or more choices are not far apart. The correct answer, then, turns out to be the almost arbitrary choice of the tester.

A second type of item concerning the evaluation of evidence and the drawing of warranted conclusions may deal with the determination of differences between two points of view, as follows:

H-3.3, H-3.4

56. Lloyd and Adams differ as to
    a. the desirability of a competitive economy.
    b. the importance of moral standards in economic relations.
    c. the danger of monopoly corruption of government.
    d. all of these.
    e. none of these.

(University of Chicago, College, 1948, p. 15, item 166.)

A third type of item in this category could require the student to determine the relationship between various elements, such as the maps in Fig. 16-3.

H-3.4 or H-10.0

57. Based on the maps which of the following factors seem to be most related?
    a. Major types of food and population
    b. Major types of food and rainfall
    c. Population and rainfall
    d. Population and religion

(Association of American Geographers, 1967, p. 6, item 20.)

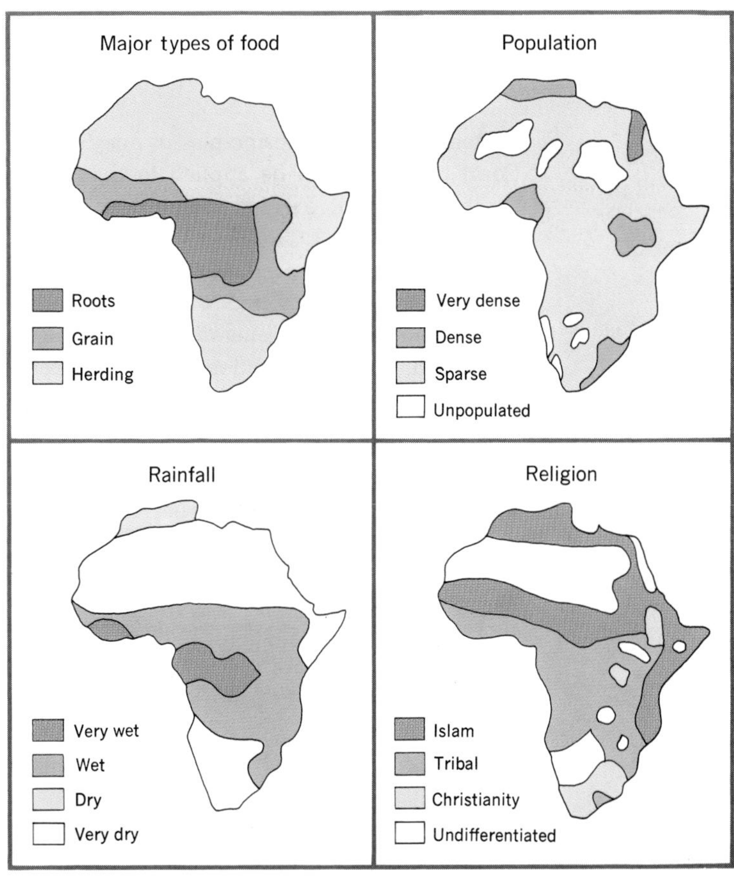

FIGURE 16-3. Maps of distribution of human and natural resources in Africa. (Association of American Geographers, High School Geography Project. *The Geography of Culture Change Test.* Washington, D.C.: AAG, 1967. P. 6.)

Item 57 asks the student to analyze four types of maps of Africa and to decide which of several pairs of variables are most related. He is presented with several conclusions and is forced to choose the best one.

A fourth type of item requires the student to make a reasonable inference on the basis of previously learned principles, as follows:

H-3.5

58. If the philosophy in the Allgeyer v. Louisiana case had been applied to the Slaughter House cases, the decision in the latter would have been
    a. sustained.
    b. reversed.
    c. partially sustained.
    d. undecided.
    e. based on the police power.

(University of Chicago, College, 1948, p. 17, item 88.)

In item 58, the basic principles of one Supreme Court decision must be applied to the facts of another case and a conclusion drawn on that basis.

A fifth type of item presents the student with what one writer has referred to as a subgeneralization and a substantive generalization. The former is limited in its application, and the latter is universal in its application.

H-3.2

DIRECTIONS: In each of the following items, you are given a fact followed by a conclusion. *Blacken*

answer space A if the fact is good evidence to *support* the conclusion;

answer space B if the fact is good evidence to *disprove* the conclusion;

answer space C if neither A nor B clearly applies.

59. FACT: The native tribes of Australia have a very complex social organization and a very simple technology.

    CONCLUSION: The complexity of non-material culture is not dependent upon high technological development.

(University of Chicago, College, 1945, p. 122, item 42.)

In item 59, the student is required to determine whether the subgeneralization, the "fact," supports, disproves, or neither supports nor disproves the substantive generalization, the conclusion.

A more complicated and more direct approach to testing the drawing of warranted conclusions requires the student to state the reason for his conclusion. Such an approach is exemplified in the following item, requiring lengthy directions. In the item, "D" and "J" are two individuals, Dick and John, whose ideas on labor have been presented throughout the test from which the item is drawn. Item 60 is the last one in the test, and the students ought to have a clear idea of the viewpoint of each speaker by this point.

Part F. How Convincing Are Some Statements?

H-10.0, H-12.1

60. The passage below is taken directly from the argument you read at the beginning of the test. Read this passage again looking for sentences that seem especially CONVINCING or UNCONVINCING. Identify each sentence which seems especially convincing or unconvincing to you by listing on your answer sheet the LAST WORD in the sentence plus the LINE in which the last word appears.

    After you have identified a sentence by listing its last word and line number, check on the answer sheet whether you think it is especially CONVINCING or UNCONVINCING and give your reason for checking one answer or the other.

    List only those sentences which strike you as being especially convincing or unconvincing. You probably will not have time to find sentences enough to complete the test. Continue working until your time is up.

Example

It has recently been reported that the sales of Ford cars increased 23% over the same period last year. Henry Ford II, president of the Ford Motor Company, explained this by stating that the Ford was the most economical and best styled car on the road. Mr. Ford also said that the Ford Company will begin to build two new assembly plants early next year.

Item

X. Last Word in Sentence (road) Line Number (9)
Convincing ( ) Unconvincing (x)

REASON: The president of the Ford Motor Company is likely to say that the cars his company makes are better than other cars simply because he wants to sell more cars.

D: Any labor expert will tell you that if the unions get weak, businessmen will grind the working man right down into the dust.

J: Let's face it. The working man is better off than he has ever been. He doesn't need a union leader to stand over his old enemy with a loaded gun when the enemy has been dead for 25 years. What the worker needs today is a law to take the gun away from the gangsters and union leaders who are robbing him.

D: Now the truth is out. You want to have Congress outlaw any kind of union that can deal effectively with business. That's just like you, always turning to the government when you want something. We all know that the working man is a long way from getting a fair break, and the union is the only way he can get it.

(Harvard University, 1959, p. 7, part F.)

The approach to testing for warranted conclusions exemplified in item 60 demonstrates a close relationship with reasonable hypothesis formation. The highly imaginative student might be able to produce many different and unusual reasons for his answer, all of which may be quite reasonable. This approach to testing conclusions can also be utilized to test hypothesis formation by asking students to make up as many reasons as they can think of for any position which they take on a given subject.

Formulation of reasonable hypotheses (I) An item which more explicitly requires the student to hypothesize is one which poses the student with the analysis of some problem and asks him to produce a series of hypotheses to test. In the following item, the student is asked to provide questions to guide research on a specific problem:

I-8.5

61. Suppose you wanted to investigate the way in which decisions are made in the government of a country you knew nothing about. Let's call it Authoritaria. How would you go about your investigation? In two or three paragraphs, describe the kinds of questions you would ask to guide your research and indicate why you think these questions would be useful.

(Schultz, 1967, p. 12, item 3.)

The number and kinds of questions which the student asks are partly dependent on his previous instruction and partly dependent on his imagination. This type of item evaluates the student's ability to produce reasonable social science hypotheses.

Formal procedures (J) Up to this point, pencil and paper tests have been the source of evaluative techniques. Effectiveness in democratic group participation and all types of attitudes are not easily evaluated validly or reliably. Pencil and paper techniques of evaluation tread uncertainly in some of these areas and require supplementary forms of evaluation to ascertain their conclusions.

Democratic group participation in Table 16-1 is divided into formal and informal procedures of participation. The formal procedures concern the general operations involved in such participation. Does the student know the formal procedure and is he able to use the formal techniques of debate, parliamentary procedure, panel discussion, and the like? The knowledge of such procedure can be easily tested through the same techniques presented earlier under the knowledge and comprehension section of testing. The application of this knowledge in an actual situation would probably be the best way of determining a student's competence in usage of the technique. His performance could be rated by an observer. For example, a student could be assigned as moderator of a panel discussion and could be evaluated by an observer on a five-point rating scale in terms of definite criteria. These might include whether the student elicits the opinions of all members of the group and whether he summarizes the differences among the group members concisely and accurately (*J*-6.0 or *J*-12.0).

Informal procedures (K) The informal group procedures are more difficult to evaluate. Two usable methods for such evaluation are the open-response and rating-scale techniques.

The open-response technique could be used in conjunction with a film, videotape, or aural tape. In order to determine a student's persuasiveness and ability to steer a group toward a decision, a film or tape of a panel discussion on some controversial issue in which the participants concluded in seemingly deeper dissent than when they began could be presented to the student. He could be asked that if he had been the moderator of the discussion and his goal was to attain a consensus, what strategy would he have devised for handling the discussion in a way that would promote a consensus. It is extremely difficult to set up suitable criteria to evaluate such strategies, since one that appears weak can be very effective when employed by certain individuals. The most effective paper plan may be completely botched by the individual who created it. The pencil and paper test of evaluation may be indicative of shrewd planning, but persuasiveness is a matter of implementation, and the poorest paper planner may unwittingly be the best actor.

Another way in which a film or tape could be used is in a form of student self-evaluation. A filmed or taped panel discussion led by an especially effective moderator could be stopped at decisive points. The student could then be asked to serve as moderator and to write down what he would have said, if anything, at each stopping point, whereupon the discussion would be continued, and the student would be allowed to compare his response with that of the moderator. In the same manner, a critique of an ineffective moderator could be handled through a student analysis of flaws at points immediately succeeding a moderator's remarks. The student's ability to discern such flaws would indicate his sensitivity to such pitfalls.

The essential difference between evaluation of formal group procedure and informal group procedure is in the criteria of the evaluation. The formal procedure involves the handling of the mechanical aspects of participation; the informal procedure involves the ability to manipulate others to arrive at a reasonable conclusion. The former approach is dependent on the implementation of a technique exclusive of the way in which the participants view the individual. The latter, on the other hand, is directly affected by the manner in which participants react to the way in which they are being handled. This can be either indirectly estimated through an outside observer or directly estimated through questioning the participants.

The rating scale can be a form of indirect or direct estimation of an individual's effectiveness in informal group procedures. If the rater is an outside observer, the estimation is indirect. If the rater is a participant, it is direct. The observer or participant might be asked to rate a student on whether his mind is closed to the opinions of others, or whether he is overtly manipulative to the point where he creates suspicion on the part of his fellow participants (*K*-6.0 or *K*-12.0). This type of rating can afford some indication of an individual's competence in informal group procedures.

Although the rating scale is an attractive device, it has two major deficiencies—the halo effect and differential response tendencies. The halo effect occurs when some aspect or aspects of an individual overshadow the rest of an individual's qualities and the individual's rating along other dimensions is strongly prejudiced by his rating on the protruding dimension or dimensions. Differential response tendency refers to the fact that observers with roughly the same view of an individual may produce discrepant ratings because of a personal tendency to place their answers on one part of a scale rather than on another.

All in all, through a combination of the open response and the observer and participant rating-scale techniques, an estimation of an individual's competence in informal group procedure can be determined. Probably the most important statement which can be made about evaluation of an individual's skills in democratic group participation is that evaluation through any one technique is dubious and credibility is enhanced through confirmation from diverse techniques.

Evaluation of attitudes (L–P)

Attitudes, which are of so much concern to the social studies, are exceptionally difficult to measure. One can either ask a person what his philosophy is or observe him in a situation in which he displays behavior demonstrative of a certain viewpoint. However, if he is asked his attitude toward some person or object, he may distort it either by prevaricating or by an inability to determine his actual position due to a lack of personal insight. Observation of behavior in lieu of personal questioning appears to be the solution to such intended and unintended distortion, except that observation has its shortcomings also. For example, if one wants to determine a person's attitude toward Jews, does he follow the person around until a situation occurs in which his behavior toward Jews registers some clear attitude? Obviously, such a procedure is infeasible. It is possible, however, to fabricate some situation in which an individual is asked to play a role that might elicit his attitude toward Jews, although the individual may guard his true feelings and simulate some others under these conditions. An individual who does not want to reveal himself can feign an attitudinal role of his choosing in the simulated situation.

Attitudinal evaluation is an uneasy trap. If you ask people how they feel about something, you cannot be sure whether to believe what they tell you. If you try to observe them in a real situation, you may find yourself waiting a long time before it arises. If you try to simulate the situation, you are faced with the problem of determining whether the behavior demonstrated under these conditions would be comparable to that in the real situation.

The first set of attitudes in social studies—*Desirable intellectual behavior*—is divided into *Scientific approach to human behavior* (*L*) and *Humanitarian outlook on the behavior of others* (*M*). The second set of attitudes—*Desirable social behavior*—is divided into *Awareness and interest* (*N*), *Acceptance of responsibility* (*O*), and *Involvement* (*P*). Techniques for evaluating these attitudes will be described in the following pages.

Scientific approach to human behavior (L) If one chooses to evaluate attitudes by asking a person directly, he can select either a closed or an open approach.

The closed-response approach to attitude estimation can be exemplified through the utilization of one of the several attitude scaling techniques which have been devised. Probably the easiest attitude scale to construct is of the Likert type. An individual is presented with a statement and is asked to take a position on it ranging from a level of agreement to a level of disagreement. The following item is an example of a Likert-type scale.

L-3.0 or L-10.0

62. It is possible to find universal principles of human behavior.
    a. strongly agree
    b. agree
    c. don't know
    d. disagree
    e. strongly disagree

In the above item, the individual is asked to select his position on a five-point scale ranging from strong agreement to strong disagreement. It is altogether possible that a student will pay lip service to the principle and in his actual behavior perform differently. A person can easily state one view and practice another.

Humanitarian outlook on the behavior of others (M) The open approach to attitude evaluation can be accomplished through some form of simulation, as in the role-playing technique. However, as already mentioned, simulated conditions allow for the simulation of attitudes, and the observer must be wary of his conclusions on the evaluation of student attitudes. An example of a role-playing situation which could be rated by an observer is the following item, intended to elicit the degree of humanitarianism or sensitivity of a student to the feelings of Negroes.

M-12.0

63. A student assumes the role of a Negro trying to rent an apartment in an all-white, lower-class, urban neighborhood. Another student assumes the role of landlord.

    The landlord-student demonstrates his attitude toward Negroes by the manner in which he deals with the student playing the Negro. Does he tell the Negro that he will not rent him the apartment? If so, does he do it threateningly, with regret, or how?

Another example of the open approach to evaluating humanitarian attitudes would be to present a student with the person or object concerning which an attitudinal estimation is desired in a way that encourages him to respond in a manner that will show his attitude. This could be accomplished by using sentence-completion techniques. For example, if one is interested in eliciting attitudes toward certain racial or ethnic groups, students could be asked to complete the following open-ended questions:

M-12.0

64. If I were a Negro I would . . .
65. If I were a Jew I would . . .
66. If I were an Italian I would . . .
67. Negroes always try to . . .
68. Jews always try to . . .
69. Italians always try to . . .

In the above items, the student may or may not indicate his attitude toward a specific group. The veracity and depth of his response depends upon his personal reaction to the stimulus.

In both the role-playing and sentence-completion techniques, the scoring of the response presents a major problem. Unless clear criteria for evaluating responses have been established, the scoring could be so subjective that it would result in a misleading interpretation of a student's attitudes.

Awareness and interest (N) Awareness and interest can be evaluated through either the open-response or the closed-response approach. The following sentence-completion item is intended to determine a student's awareness of social problems in the United States.

N-3.2, N-6.0, N-12.1

70. The major social problems facing the United States today are. . . .

One must be careful in passing judgment on an individual's awareness of social problems. It is possible that a student is quite conscious of certain problems but omits them from the list he constructs in answer to an incomplete sentence because he simply does not recall them at the time he is asked. If the student had been presented with a list of social problems from which he was asked to select the ones which he thought were most important, he might well select problems that he neglected to mention in a sentence-completion item. Nevertheless, item 70 requires the individual to list the social problems that are apparently uppermost in his mind.

Acceptance of responsibility (O) The attitude scale, role-playing technique, and sentence completion can be used to evaluate many attitudes. Discretion must be used in interpreting any of them. If possible, results from one technique ought to be confirmed by other evaluative evidence. Observational techniques used during regular classroom discussion can provide a rich source of evidence to confirm the results of other attitude evaluation instruments. The observational technique could take the form of a rating scale with a teacher or an outside observer doing the rating. For example, the teacher or an outside observer could rate an individual's performance during class discussion on a five-point scale—strongly favorable, favorable, neutral, unfavorable, strongly unfavorable—on whether a student is willing to try to cooperate with others in arriving at a solution to a social problem (O-3.2, O-12.0).

However, the rating-scale technique has often been misused because of the problems of the halo effect and differential response tendencies that were explained in the section on *Informal procedures* (K). Also, one must be aware that classroom discussion is often an inadequate indicator of attitudes for two reasons: first, many students remain relatively silent during discussions, and it is difficult to determine their attitudes; and second, those who do get involved often overstate their position during controversy. A verbal escalation of attitude position may occur during class discussion which exaggerates or distorts the real position of the student. However, if either observational information or results obtained by the role-playing or sentence-completion techniques is available, and it confirms the results of the attitude scales, then the conclusions drawn about a student's attitudes assume more validity.

Involvement (P) A second example of the closed approach to attitudinal evaluation is represented in the following item, which uses a Likert-type scale to determine a student's positive or negative interpretation of the role of political parties.

P-8.3

71. Political parties are run by politicians who are concerned with personal gain and power rather than the public good.
    1. Strongly agree
    2. Agree with reservation
    3. Tend to disagree
    4. Strongly disagree

(Massialas & Cox, 1966, p. 273, item 2.)

Here again, as in item 62, the examinee is asked to select his position on a multipoint scale. Through the response to items like this, one can judge whether a student is politically alienated. Political alienation may lead to such disillusionment with politics that the student may refuse even to vote.

Most attitude evaluation techniques are defective because a student can fake an attitude if he wishes. The most effective technique of attitudinal measurement is obviously one in which the testee is unaware that he is presenting evidence of his attitudinal position. Such instruments are difficult to devise. The reader is referred to Chap. 10 in this book for information on the construction of camouflaged techniques of attitudinal measurement. Another relatively effective technique of attitudinal evaluation is possible whenever one is interested in the attitudes of a group rather than of any specific individual. In the group situation it is possible to assure the students of complete anonymity. Such anonymity may reduce considerably distortion that occurs from outright lying.

The attitudinal items presented thus far are enough to demonstrate the technique of such evaluation, since the approach itself does not change when the attitude changes. Any attitude can be measured by either the open- or the closed-response approach. A combination of the two approaches is preferable to the use of one or the other because attitude evaluation can be so risky that evidence from two directions affords more credibility. There are other types of scales and methods for evaluating attitudes but, because of their complexity, they go beyond the scope of this chapter.

Evaluation of values (Q) Values are a special form of affective goal in the social studies. They are affective in their nature but cognitive in their development because they must be rationally attained to be democratic. It is not enough to find out what a student's values are. One must determine whether he holds these values because of a rational decision or whether they have been irrationally assumed. Does a person believe that Negroes are not intellectually inferior to whites because of an examination of the evidence or because some teacher whom he admired told him so? No matter how desirable the value may be, it is not desirable from the viewpoint of the social studies unless it has been attained through critical analysis. The individual himself must be the rational judge of the worth of a value.

The attainment of desirable democratic values can be evaluated by a form of essay question. For example, if one wanted to determine whether a person had rationally attained the belief in freedom of speech as a value in itself, one could ask the person to present reasons for belief in freedom of speech. It is altogether possible that a person could present "good" reasons for his belief in free speech without ever presenting his "real" reasons, which may have been the result of irrational inculcation. However, one has to make the cautious assumption that a well-reasoned argument for a position is indicative of critical analysis of the evidence and rational judgment.

Another approach to the evaluation of values is to present the students with a "value sheet." The students are required to take a position on some provocative statement that clarifies their stance. For example, the following value sheet on freedom forces the student to select, alter, or construct a position based on a rational understanding of the consequences of each position:

Q-12.0

Civil Liberties

72. Below are several paragraphs relating to one issue. Select the paragraph that comes closest to your own position and change the wording in it until it represents your thinking as exactly as possible. Or you may write a new position if none of the ones listed is close to the one you prefer. The idea is to get a statement about which you can say, "This is where I now stand."

    A useful way to decide between alternatives is to identify the *consequences* of each of the positions and then to decide which set of consequences it is that you prefer to come about. You may, of course, use other sources of information before committing yourself to a position.

    1. Freedom is basic to the existence of a democratic society. This does not mean license to do as one sees fit. Within the limitation of not interfering with someone else's freedom, it is desirable for the individual to pursue his own self-interest.
    2. In our society, everyone has freedom. One may do, think, and say that which he believes. We draw the line at a point, however. In the best interests of our society, we cannot permit anyone to hold doctrines or to preach anything that might undermine our society as it stands now. Erroneous beliefs, therefore, cannot be treated with the same tolerance as the normal and accepted doctrines, since their sole purpose is to destroy the very foundation of our society. Any dangerous opinions and beliefs must, therefore, be curbed.
    3. Many persons think of freedom as the right of suffrage, but this is only an illusion that one is free. He who thinks that his power of freedom comes from his vote has only to compare the power he has with that of the international financier, or a big businessman; voting provides freedom only in a flimsy parliamentarian sense. It is an illusion in which man is like the trained dog who thinks he learned the tricks by himself.
    4. The only true freedom that can ever exist comes about when we allow so-called truth and error to clash in the open market place of ideas. We cannot suppress any heresies nor can we censor thoughts, ideas, or practices; *nothing* is heretical. We must promote and encourage differences of opinion, and we must discourage uniformity of thinking. It is only this way that we can prevent a tyranny of the mind and body from ever imposing itself.
    5. True freedom is non-existent. Man acts out a plan that is set for him before he is five years old. His emotions reflect the society into which he is born. All his actions also reflect that society and are determined by it. Even his conception of freedom is one which has been drummed into him by the particular society. Convinced that he is free, it never occurs to him to question the fact that even in the ability to leave society, he is a slave to its laws.

(Raths, Harmin, & Simon, 1966, pp. 93–94, Value Sheet 5.)

In both approaches to the evaluation of values, the student is required to take a position and either construct or select a reasoned defense of the position. In both cases, the defense could be based on a rational argument summoned to support an irrationally acquired position. However, the stronger the argument, the more certain one can be that the position has been thoroughly examined, even if only to close up prejudicial loopholes. If the loopholes are gaping ones, the argument will crumble of its own, and the defender will be left with an ungrounded value in the face of a reasoned position.

It is in the area of values that the cognitive and affective elements of the social studies are most intimately bound. The affective value component is determined through a blend of cognitive and affective modes of evaluation. The student's values can be determined through techniques appropriate to attitudinal evaluation, and their basis through techniques appropriate to critical analysis.

Problems of testing in the social studies

The interpretive test

Most social studies achievement tests deal with knowledge and understanding of content and rarely test for critical thinking and research skills related to the content. A fertile approach to creating items to tap critical thinking skills is the interpretive test. This test is based upon a presentation of novel material to the student. Many of the items in this chapter calling for thought processes beyond knowledge and understanding have been of this type. The primary danger in the interpretive-test exercise is that it may turn out to be more of an aptitude than an achievement test. A student who has not studied but who has a high level of aptitude in the appropriate area can perform extremely well on such a test and vice versa for one who has studied a great deal but has a low level of aptitude. In order to circumvent such an awkward position, an instructor must be extremely careful in constructing the test. The social studies test must not swing to the extreme of being a test simply of higher-level thought processes completely disengaged from prior study of content. Both previously learned content and process are of utmost importance in an achievement test and can be built into an interpretive test. Probably the best way to include content in such a test is to include key facts, concepts, generalizations, structures, and models from the discipline involved in the introductory material. The test items based on this introductory material can require higher-level thinking processes.

It probably can be safely stated that in the social studies the best items are those which require prior knowledge of key understandings and deal with higher-level thinking processes. A test of understandings alone can reduce itself to a high-class memory test. A test of higher-level thinking processes can reduce itself to an aptitude test. It is no easy task to construct a test item based on both key understandings and high-level processes. The interpretive test is an excellent way of combining both, if carefully used. The interpretive test has its shortcomings, though. The longer the introductory interpretive material, the fewer the number of items that can be included in the test within a specific time period. The fewer the items in the test, the less reliable the test may be.

The essay test

Many social studies teachers have an aversion to objective tests because they claim that such tests do not require students to select and organize material to develop a uniform position. The criticism is well-taken, since in the real world individual citizens must select and organize ideas to take positions. The essay question is probably a more adaptable technique for such testing than is the multiple-choice question. The multiple-choice test in the social studies can do an excellent job in determining a student's performance in most cognitive areas except for those in which he must create hypotheses of his own or draw conclusions without being provided with several conclusions from which to choose. In these situations the teacher is advised to use the essay test, but in most other situations the objective test is feasible and advisable because the social studies essay test is extremely vulnerable to intra- and inter-scorer disagreement (Coffman & Kurfman, 1968). Objective-test scoring is not vulnerable to such disparity.

The essay test, when it is advisable, can be either quite general or quite specific. The general type of essay question may be of the following sort:

H-3.1

73. "The Vietnamese conflict is a direct extension of American foreign policy dating back to the early part of this century." Defend or disagree with this statement. Present evidence to support your position.

This free-wheeling essay question challenges the student to undertake an examination of American foreign policy in this century and to determine whether it supports or undermines the statement. The directions which a student may take in answering this question would be extremely difficult to foresee. The essays would probably have to be examined on an individual basis depending on the evidence selected to support or disprove the position. Such a scoring policy is open to a great deal of intra- and inter-scorer disagreement.

The more limited essay question has more foreseeable answers. The scoring is less subjective whenever certain types of responses can be considered as more appropriate than other types. The less individualistic the response suggested by the question, the more agreement that can be attained to judge the adequacy of the response. An example of a more limited essay question is the following:

G-3.1, H-3.1; G-3.2, H-3.2

74. Compare and contrast the political and economic development of Germany and the United States between World Wars I and II.

One can see that even though the answer requires the knowledge of a great deal of information and that the response can be extensive, the lines along which a response would follow are relatively well-definable. Intra- and inter-scorer disagreement will not be dispelled in the limited essay question, but they will be diminished.

The free-wheeling essay question can be challenging to students and worthwhile for a student to undertake as a wide-open attempt at analyzing history (especially as a term paper or project), but the tester must be aware of the difficulties in attempting to evaluate its results.

Attitude scales

Affective testing in the social studies is beset by certain problems. As pointed out heretofore, one must be especially cautious in interpreting the results of attitude scales in the schools. Students are aware of the biases of teachers and may bias their responses in a certain direction dependent upon the teachers' personalities rather than upon their personal convictions.

Also, attitudes are generally rock-ribbed and very difficult to change—except on a superficial level. A superficial change may occur in the attitudes of students based on some exhilarating experience, such as a motion picture. If the students' attitudes had been tested just before and just after a film, it is conceivable that an attitudinal change might be indicated on the basis of an administration of an attitude scale. However, such an attitudinal change may be short-lived. The change could easily vanish within a brief period of time. Such a caution concerning attitudinal measurement is also suggested at the end of a unit. It is conceivable that at the close of a unit an attitudinal instrument might indicate generally favorable attitudes toward the educationally desirable object. Such results must be hesitantly accepted since attitudinal testing a year or two later may indicate that an educationally undesirable, deep-lying attitude has resumed its former position. Further, even if the attitude scale seems to indicate important verbal changes on the part of students, teachers must be aware that such verbal change does not perforce imply that actual, personal behavior has changed. Students may say one thing and do another. Attitude scales are tenuous instruments that must be constructed even more carefully than cognitive achievement tests, and their results must be more carefully interpreted.

Formative evaluation units in American history and American government

Since a central theme of this book is formative evaluation, two schematic units of instruction and concomitant test items to demonstrate the formative evaluation of such units will be presented. Units from secondary school American history and American government have been chosen since they have already been dealt with as individual courses. Closely related units have been selected. The unit on American history will deal with democracy and the American Constitution. The unit on American government will deal with the American Congress. Both units are standard topics of such courses.

Construction of a formative social studies unit

Before formative test items can be drawn up, a structural unit—perhaps a chapter from the textbook for the course—must be analyzed into its behavior and content components. Six basic behavior categories may be used—*Knowledge of terms, Knowledge of facts, Knowledge of rules and principles, Knowledge of processes, Translation,* and *Application.*

Several of the categories correspond with the categories used up to this point in the chapter: the *Knowledge of facts* category is the same as presented earlier; *Knowledge of terms* may be considered as including *Knowledge of concepts;* and *Knowledge of rules and principles* corresponds with *Knowledge of generalizations. Translation* is a comprehension behavior; it is the ability to transform some communication into other words or symbols or the ability to recognize such a transformation. *Knowledge of processes* refers to knowledge of the methods or procedures by which some analysis is carried out. *Application* is the use of previously learned principles in new situations to arrive at a solution to a problem.

The analysis of a chapter or chapters as a structural unit is a time-consuming procedure. It requires a listing of each of the essential category areas. In the case of facts and terms the procedure is relatively straightforward in that essential new facts and terms are easily determined. Principles or generalizations in the social studies are not usually forthrightly stated and thus are not easily distinguished. Processes of analysis are not usually included in social studies units, although they are found in formative units on science and mathematics and may prove to be of use in the construction of some formative social studies units. Translation in the social studies is usually determined by the instructor. Reading material, however, can be conducive to or restrictive of translation depending primarily on the nature of the reading content. If the content includes overarching concepts and generalizations in addition to relatively narrow ones, the reader is forced to rearrange the formal verbal content into terminology meaningful to him. Finally, application of principles is often excluded from social studies texts because the principles are tenuous and thus difficult to apply, as will be pointed out later.

This entire procedure of specifying the essential components of the structural unit is somewhat subjective, especially as one passes from generalizations to translation. However, it is reasonable to expect that competent individuals can attain a high measure of agreement in classifying the components of a unit.

Once the classification has been completed, the interrelationships among the components in terms of their sequential development is determined. This too is a relatively difficult task because of the state of the social sciences, as will be pointed out later. The purpose of determining the sequential relationship between categories is to construct items to correspond to the categories so as to be able to designate the points at which a student who answers an item incorrectly is deficient in his understanding and requires remediation.

A formative American history unit and test items

The chapter on American history selected for analysis here is somewhat different from a traditional one dealing with the Constitution. It is drawn from a textbook with a social science orientation rather than from a standard history textbook. The chapter is entitled "Democracy and the American Constitution" from the book *Modern Society: An Introduction to Social Science* by John and Mavis Biesanz (1964). The chapter contains few of the political and economic details generally injected into such chapters. It is more concerned with the broader aspects of the Constitution in terms of the intellectual and political background influencing its construction and interpretation, and its implications for freedom and democratic government, especially concerning the role of the Supreme Court in these areas. The structural unit is presented in Table 16-6, Table of Specifications for a Unit on Democracy and the American Constitution, and in the following sample formative test items.

Terms

75. Which of the following is the *best* description of the Supreme Court's power of "judicial review"? The Supreme Court has the power to
    a. review the decisions of all state and federal court cases in the United States
    b. overrule a decision of a lower federal court once that decision is appealed to the Supreme Court
    c. pass judgment on legislation pending in Congress in order to advise legislators concerning its acceptability to the Court
    d. determine the constitutionality of a law in a case involving that law which is brought before it

Facts

76. Which of the following Supreme Court cases set the precedent for the Supreme Court's assumption of judicial review?
    a. Marbury v. Madison
    b. Baker v. Carr
    c. McCulloch v. Maryland
    d. Plessy v. Ferguson

Rules and principles

77. Judicial review is best described as an example of ______ in the American Constitution.
    a. federalism
    b. checks and balances
    c. states' rights
    d. democracy

Translation

78. In which of the following situations would the Supreme Court be exercising its power of judicial review?
    a. the impeachment trial of a President of the United States
    b. the judgment as to whether a person's rights had been violated by a federal wiretapping law
    c. the rejection of an appeal by a convicted criminal whose attorneys have uncovered new evidence
    d. the determination of a case in which a state is suing the newspaper of another state for slanderous remarks concerning its handling of civil liberties

Application

79. Which of the following state educational practices would the Court find most difficult to strike down as segregationist?
    a. state aid to private schools for Negroes
    b. rezoning of school districts along racial lines
    c. financial allotments to parents to contribute to a private school of their choice
    d. the maintenance of traditional neighborhood schools which coincide with racial boundaries

A formative American government unit and test items

The unit on Congress is also a standard one in courses dealing with American government. It is drawn from a competent book, *Official Makers of Public Policy: Congress and the President* by Louis W. Koenig (1965), and adheres to the traditional manner of studying the formal and informal structure and powers of Congress. Most of the attention in the unit centers around the diffusion of power in Congress primarily attributable to the

TABLE 16-6 TABLE OF SPECIFICATIONS FOR A UNIT ON DEMOCRACY AND THE AMERICAN CONSTITUTION

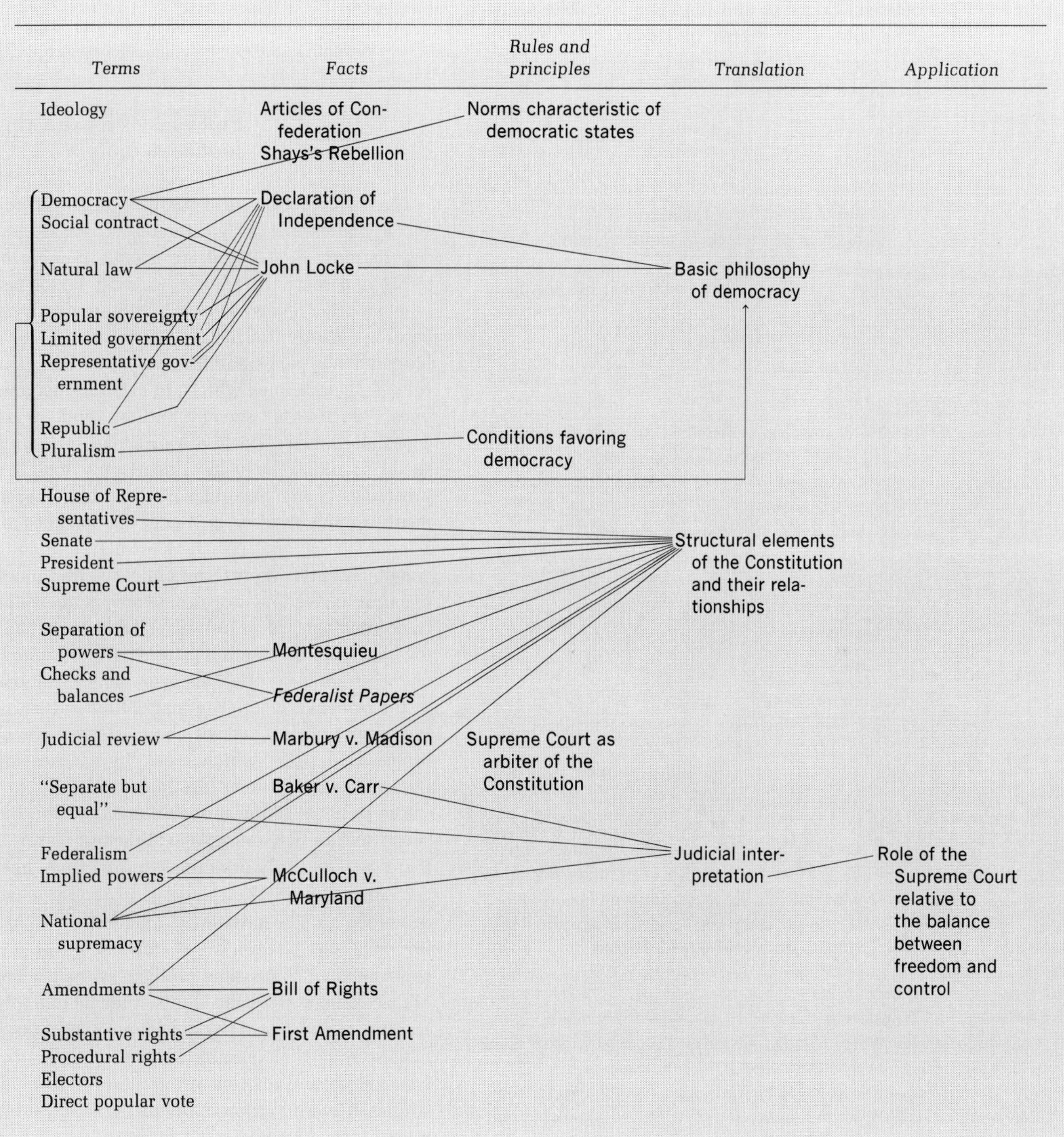

committee system. Attention is also geared toward the usual discussion of the difference in attitude, composition, and responsibility of Senate and House members and relations between Congress and the President. The structural unit is illustrated in Table 16-7, Table of Specifications for a Unit on Congress, and in the formative test items below.

Terms

80. The term "seniority" in Congress refers to the
   a. age of a member of Congress
   b. number of unbroken terms of service of a member of Congress
   c. total number of years a member has served in Congress
   d. influence wielded by a member of Congress

Facts

81. The chairman of a committee is usually the committee member of the majority party who has
   a. the longest number of unbroken years of service in Congress
   b. served the most years in Congress
   c. the most influence with the national party leadership
   d. the most support from the membership of the committee

Rules and principles

82. Committee chairmen have tended to come from rural areas because
   a. America has been primarily rural for most of its history until very recently
   b. farmers have held the balance of power in Congress in the business-labor conflict
   c. these areas have tended to be one-party areas with little chance of ousting incumbents
   d. the Constitution was devised in an agricultural era and was made to favor farmers

Translation

83. Which of the following would probably be selected as the chairman of his committee?
   a. a young man who has just been elected to his second term in office by an overwhelming majority
   b. a close friend of the President who has just entered Congress after having been encouraged to run by the President
   c. a very popular middle-aged man on the committee
   d. a fairly bland fellow who has just won his eleventh consecutive Congressional election

Problems of constructing formative units

The construction of structural units in the social studies is a fairly difficult task for at least two reasons. First, there are a large number of terms and facts introduced in most textbooks, whereas other levels of the structure are relatively bare, especially in history. This results in a lengthy list of terms and facts and little else. The rules and principles which do exist are tenuous ones, since the social studies, and again especially history, deal with problems for which social scientists have developed only tentative principles, if any. Second, social studies is not so neatly cumulative as is much mathematics or science. It is less clearly a structure than a conglomeration. Many terms and facts introduced in a unit have no relationship to one another. The basic elements of a unit usually do not hang together in a sequential pattern. The structural elements are more often discrete than continuous in their development. The instruction and learning of such a unit centers about isolated bits of information upon which weak hypotheses are imposed to string them together.

The problem of questionable principles in the social studies is a serious one to the test maker. If there are few sturdy principles to work from, how can one expect the student to apply such principles to new situations? The tester who has few principles to work from in the content area is confronted with the same problem as the teacher of that content area who wants students to apply learning to new situations but cannot expect them to do so since their learning has been composed of facts, terms, and dubious principles. But if social studies is ever to proceed, instruction and testing must proceed toward application of knowledge,

TABLE 16-7 TABLE OF SPECIFICATIONS FOR A UNIT ON CONGRESS

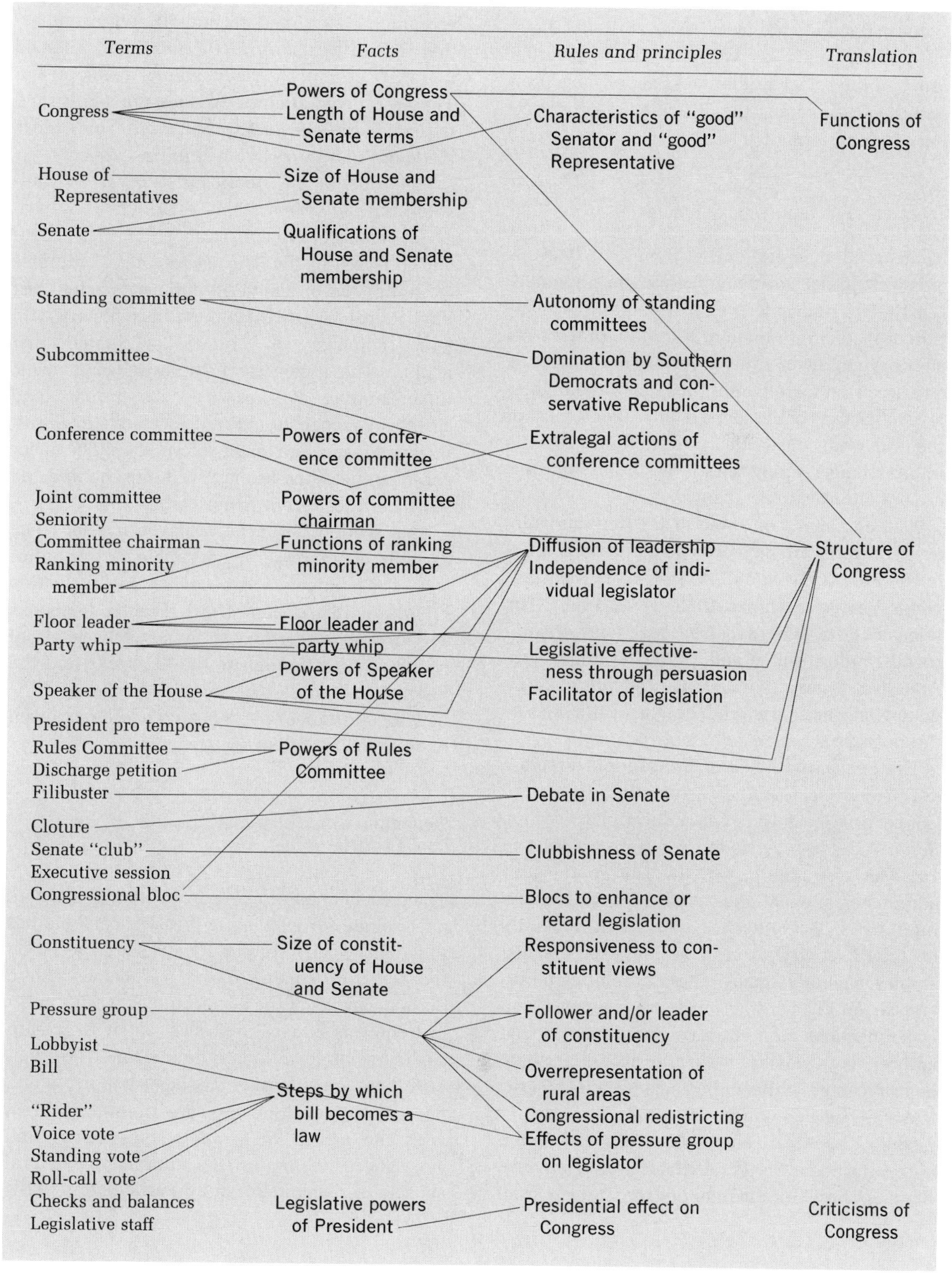

Terms	*Facts*	*Rules and principles*	*Translation*
Congress	Powers of Congress Length of House and Senate terms	Characteristics of "good" Senator and "good" Representative	Functions of Congress
House of Representatives	Size of House and Senate membership		
Senate	Qualifications of House and Senate membership		
Standing committee		Autonomy of standing committees	
Subcommittee		Domination by Southern Democrats and conservative Republicans	
Conference committee	Powers of conference committee	Extralegal actions of conference committees	
Joint committee	Powers of committee chairman		
Seniority			
Committee chairman	Functions of ranking minority member	Diffusion of leadership	Structure of Congress
Ranking minority member		Independence of individual legislator	
Floor leader	Floor leader and party whip		
Party whip		Legislative effectiveness through persuasion	
Speaker of the House	Powers of Speaker of the House	Facilitator of legislation	
President pro tempore			
Rules Committee	Powers of Rules Committee		
Discharge petition			
Filibuster		Debate in Senate	
Cloture			
Senate "club"		Clubbishness of Senate	
Executive session			
Congressional bloc		Blocs to enhance or retard legislation	
Constituency	Size of constituency of House and Senate	Responsiveness to constituent views	
Pressure group		Follower and/or leader of constituency	
Lobbyist			
Bill		Overrepresentation of rural areas	
"Rider"	Steps by which bill becomes a law	Congressional redistricting	
Voice vote		Effects of pressure group on legislator	
Standing vote			
Roll-call vote			
Checks and balances	Legislative powers of President	Presidential effect on Congress	Criticisms of Congress
Legislative staff			

which calls for very high levels of mental functioning, since the principles of social studies are not the airtight principles of physical science.

Formative tests are most easily and effectively created for units of well-integrated material. Much of the social studies lacks such integration and thus compounds the difficulty of constructing adequate formative tests.

Selected tests in the social studies

In this section several of the commercially available tests in the social studies will be presented. Most social studies tests simply demand recognition of factual information. Very few of the tests step beyond such a low level of understanding and, as a result, are poor indicators of the higher-level objectives of the social studies. Also, most of the tests were constructed prior to the large-scale reformation sweeping the social studies and thus are not attuned to the changes.

Brief comments on three of the commercially available tests will be presented based on reviews in the *Fourth, Fifth,* and *Sixth Mental Measurements Yearbook* (Buros, 1953, 1959, 1965). The selected tests offered below deal with general social studies skills and understandings, and American history. A more balanced presentation would have been preferred, but the available tests did not warrant such an exhibit.

The Sequential Tests of Educational Progress (STEP): Social Studies, available from the Cooperative Test Division, Educational Testing Service, has four levels ranging from grades 4 to 14. The test requires 90 to 100 minutes to administer, of which the actual student's test-taking time is 70 minutes. The test items generally deal with ability to read and interpret social studies materials—maps, charts, graphs, cartoons, and so on. The testee must use concepts and generalizations from history, geography, social anthropology, government, and economics that he has learned while at the same time using critical analysis techniques.

The Crary American History Test: Evaluation and Adjustment Series, available from Harcourt, Brace & World, Inc., is intended for students from grades 9 to 13. The test requires 50 minutes to administer, of which 40 minutes is actual test time. This test deals primarily with political and economic history and secondarily with intellectual and social history. Little attention is directed to literary, artistic, and educational development. The test does attempt to measure skills and understandings beyond factual recall. Some use is made of the interpretive test in this respect.

The Cooperative American History Test available from the Cooperative Test Division, Educational Testing Service, is intended for high school and college students. The test requires 45 minutes to administer, of which 40 minutes is actual test time. It deals primarily with political history with lesser emphasis on cultural and intellectual history. The items test for knowledge of facts, understanding of causes, effects, trends, and ability to recognize chronological relationships, interpret maps, and locate information. The major shortcoming of the test is that it must be updated to account for recent historical material.

This section has necessarily been brief since the bulk of commercially available social studies tests are relatively weak devices for evaluating high-level instruction. Until recently textbooks and instruction primarily tapped low levels of cognitive functioning. As the textbooks and the instruction change, the tests will change also. The new social studies will, if it succeeds, be followed by new social studies tests.

Evaluation of novel social studies patterns

The present chapter has been an attempt to set up a technique for evaluating present social studies programs. Social studies always seems to be on the brink of change that never comes about. Certain aspects of the social studies, such as critical analysis and value issues, augur to remain key elements for a long time to come. Nevertheless, there are at least two behaviors along which fairly new developments are unfolding. First, with the arrival of social studies games and simulation techniques, the informal procedural aspects of democratic group participation skills will probably play more of a role in the social studies than the incidental role they have played thus far. Second, with the sophisticated techniques of gathering, analyzing, and interpreting data that social scientists have devised, it seems as if some of the cruder techniques will filter down into the secondary schools.

Both the informal group procedures and the advanced social science methods of gathering, analyzing, and interpreting data will require special techniques of evaluation. The informal group procedures are essentially affective in nature, and evaluation of affective goals is still fairly gross. The specialized social science procedures are cognitive in nature, and many of the evaluation procedures discussed in this chapter will be applicable to their evaluation. The future of social studies evaluation will not be seriously affected by changes in cognitive elements, but the forthcoming changes in informal group procedures and the heralded emphasis on value commitment will strain the present evaluative techniques. More valid, reliable, and feasible modes of affective evaluation will be needed and, one hopes, will be forthcoming.

NOTE Sources for Table 16-1, Table of Specifications for Selected Social Studies, include the following:

(1) Aldrich, J. C., & Cottle, E. (Eds.) *Social studies for young adolescents: Programs for grades 7, 8, and 9.* (Curr. Ser. No. 6, 3d ed.) Washington, D.C.: National Council for the Social Studies, 1967. (2) Anderson, H. R. (Ed.) *Approaches to an understanding of world affairs: Twenty-fifth yearbook of the National Council for the Social Studies.* Washington, D.C.: NCSS, 1954. (3) Barzun, J., & Graff, H. F. *The modern researcher.* New York: Harcourt, Brace, 1957. (4) California State Central Committee on Social Studies. *Report to the California State Curriculum Commission.* Sacramento: California State Department of Education, 1961. (5) Cantor, N. F., & Schneider, R. I. *How to study history.* New York: Crowell, 1967. (6) Carpenter, H. McC. (Ed.) *Skills in social studies: Twenty-fourth yearbook of the National Council for the Social Studies.* Washington, D.C.: NCSS, 1953. (7) Carpenter, H. McC. (Ed.) *Skill development in social studies: Thirty-third yearbook of the National Council for the Social Studies.* Washington, D.C.: NCSS, 1963. (8) Cartwright, W. H., & Watson, R. L., Jr. (Eds.) *Interpreting and teaching American history: Thirty-first yearbook of the National Council for the Social Studies.* Washington, D.C.: NCSS, 1961. (9) Cleveland Heights Social Science Studies Program. *Innovator's kit.* Cleveland Heights, Ohio: Cleveland Heights–University Heights City School District, 1965. (10) Crary, R. W. (Ed.) *Education for democratic citizenship: Twenty-second yearbook of the National Council for the Social Studies.* Washington, D.C.: NCSS, 1951. (11) Cummings, H. H. (Ed.) *Science and the social studies: Twenty-seventh yearbook, National Council for the Social Studies.* Washington, D.C.: NCSS, 1956–1957. (12) Dressel, P. L., & Mayhew, L. B. *Critical thinking in social science: A handbook of suggestions for evaluation and teaching.* Dubuque, Iowa: Brown, 1954. (13) Ellsworth, R., & Sand, O. (Eds.) *Improving the social studies curriculum: Twenty-sixth yearbook of the National Council for the Social Studies.* Washington, D.C.: NCSS, 1955. (14) Engle, S. H. (Ed.) *New perspectives in world history: Thirty-fourth yearbook of the National Council for the Social Studies.* Washington, D.C.: NCSS, 1964. (15) Fenton, E. *The new social studies.* New York: Holt, Rinehart and Winston, 1967. (16) Gibson, J. S. *New frontiers in the social studies.* Vol. 1. *Goals for students, means for teachers.* New York: Citation Press, 1967. (17) Gross, R. E., Muessig, R. H., & Fersh, G. L. (Eds.) *The problems approach and the social studies.* (Curr. Ser. No. 9, rev. ed.) Washington, D.C.: National Council for the Social Studies, 1960. (18) Gross, R. E., &

Zeleny, L. D. *Educating citizens for democracy: Curriculum and instruction in social studies.* New York: Oxford University Press, 1958. (19) High, J. *Teaching secondary school social studies.* New York: Wiley, 1962. (20) Hunt, M. P., & Metcalf, L. E. *Teaching high school social studies: Problems in reflective thinking and social understanding.* (2d ed.) New York: Harper & Row, 1968. (21) Johnson, E. S. *Theory and practice of the social studies.* New York: Macmillan, 1956. (22) Lewenstein, M. R. *Teaching social studies in junior and senior high schools: An ends and means approach.* Chicago: Rand McNally, 1963. (23) Mahoney, J. J. *For us the living: An approach to civic education.* New York: Harper, 1945. (24) Massialas, B. G., & Cox, C. B. *Inquiry in social studies.* New York: McGraw-Hill, 1966. (25) Moreland, W. D. (Ed.) *Social studies in the senior high school: Programs for grades ten, eleven, and twelve.* (Curr. Ser. No. 7, rev. ed.) Washington, D.C.: National Council for the Social Studies, 1965. (26) National Council for the Social Studies. *A guide to contents in social studies.* Washington, D.C.: National Council for the Social Studies, 1958. (27) Oliver, D. W., & Shaver, J. P. *Teaching public issues in the high school.* Boston: Houghton Mifflin, 1966. (28) Patterson, F. (Ed.) *Citizenship and a free society: Education for the future. Thirtieth yearbook of the National Council for the Social Studies.* Washington, D.C.: NCSS, 1960. (29) Payne, J. C. (Ed.) *The teaching of contemporary affairs: Twenty-first yearbook of the National Council for the Social Studies.* Washington, D.C.: NCSS, 1950. (30) Quillen, I. J., & Hanna, L. A. *Education for social competence: The social studies in the secondary school.* Chicago: Scott, Foresman, 1961. (31) Riddle, D. H., & Cleary, R. E. (Eds.) *Political science in the social studies: Thirty-sixth yearbook of the National Council for the Social Studies.* Washington, D.C.: NCSS, 1966. (32) Stern, F. (Ed.) *The varieties of history: From Voltaire to the present.* Cleveland: World Publishing, 1956. (33) Thursfield, R. E. (Ed.) *The study and teaching of American history: Seventeenth yearbook of the National Council for the Social Studies.* Washington, D.C.: NCSS, 1946. (34) Tyler, R. W. The fact-finding study of the testing program of the United States Armed Forces Institute, 1952–1954. Report to the USAFI, University of Chicago, July 1954. (35) Wesley, E. B. *Teaching social studies in high schools.* (3d ed.) Boston: Heath, 1950. (36) West, E. *Developing skills in the social studies program.* Minneapolis: Project Social Studies Center, University of Minnesota, 1968. (37) West, E. (Ed.) *Improving the teaching of world history: Twentieth yearbook of the National Council for the Social Studies.* Washington, D.C.: NCSS, 1949.

REFERENCES

Aldrich, J. C., & Cottle, E. (Eds.) *Social studies for young adolescents: Programs for grades 7, 8, and 9.* (Curr. Ser. No. 6, 3d ed.) Washington, D.C.: National Council for the Social Studies, 1967.

Anderson, H. R. (Ed.) *Approaches to an understanding of world affairs: Twenty-fifth yearbook of the National Council for the Social Studies.* Washington, D.C.: NCSS, 1954.

Anderson, H. R., & Lindquist, C. F. *Selected test items in American history.* (Bull. No. 6, 4th ed., rev. by H. Stull) Washington, D.C.: National Council for the Social Studies, 1957.

Association of American Geographers, High School Geography Project. *The Geography of Culture Change Test.* Washington, D.C.: AAG, 1967.

Barzun, J., & Graff, H. F. *The modern researcher.* New York: Harcourt, Brace, 1957.

Beach, M. History of education. *Review of Educational Research,* 1969, **39,** 561–576.

Biesanz, J., & Biesanz, M. *Modern society: An introduction to social science.* Englewood Cliffs, N.J.: Prentice-Hall, 1964.

Buros, O. K. (Ed.) *The fourth mental measurements yearbook*. Highland Park, N.J.: Gryphon Press, 1953.

Buros, O. K. (Ed.) *The fifth mental measurements yearbook*. Highland Park, N.J.: Gryphon Press, 1959.

Buros, O. K. (Ed.) *The sixth mental measurements yearbook*. Highland Park, N.J.: Gryphon Press, 1965.

California State Central Committee on Social Studies. *Report to the California State Curriculum Commission*. Sacramento: California State Department of Education, 1961.

Cantor, N. F., & Schneider, R. I. *How to study history*. New York: Crowell, 1967.

Carpenter, H. McC. (Ed.) *Skills in social studies: Twenty-fourth yearbook of the National Council for the Social Studies*. Washington, D.C.: NCSS, 1953.

Carpenter, H. McC. (Ed.) *Skill development in social studies: Thirty-third yearbook of the National Council for the Social Studies*. Washington, D.C.: NCSS, 1963.

Cartwright, W. H., & Watson, R. L., Jr. (Eds.) *Interpreting and teaching American history: Thirty-first yearbook of the National Council for the Social Studies*. Washington, D.C.: NCSS, 1961.

Cleveland Heights Social Science Studies Program. *Innovator's kit*. Cleveland Heights, Ohio: Cleveland Heights–University Heights City School District, 1965.

Coffman, W. E., & Kurfman, D. A comparison of two methods of reading essay examinations. *American Educational Research Journal*, 1968, **5**, 99–107.

Crary, R. W. *Crary American History Test: Evaluation and adjustment series*. (Form Am) New York: Harcourt, Brace, 1951.

Crary, R. W. (Ed.) *Education for democratic citizenship: Twenty-second yearbook of the National Council for the Social Studies*. Washington, D.C.: NCSS, 1951.

Cummings, H. H. (Ed.) *Science and the social studies: Twenty-seventh yearbook of the National Council for the Social Studies*. Washington, D.C.: NCSS, 1956–1957.

Davis, C. M. *Course of study: Government*. (Houston Independent School District Curr. Bull. No. 65CBM19) Houston: HISD, 1965.

Dressel, P. L., & Mayhew, L. B. *Critical thinking in social science: A handbook of suggestions for evaluation and teaching*. Dubuque, Iowa: Brown, 1954.

Eibling, H. H., King, F. M., Harlow, J., & Finkelstein, M. *The story of America*. River Forest, Ill.: Laidlaw, 1969.

Eibling, H. H., King, F. M., Harlow, J., & Finkelstein, M. *Teacher's manual for use with The story of America*. River Forest, Ill. Laidlaw, undated.

Ellsworth, R., & Sand, O. (Eds.) *Improving the social studies curriculum: Twenty-sixth yearbook of the National Council for the Social Studies*. Washington, D.C.: NCSS, 1955.

Engle, S. H. Objectives of the social studies. In B. G. Massialas & F. R. Smith (Eds.), *New challenges in the social studies*. Belmont, Calif.: Wadsworth, 1965. Pp. 1–19. (a)

Engle, S. H. World history in the curriculum. *Social Education*, 1965, **29**, 459–463. (b)

Engle, S. H. (Ed.) *New perspectives in world history: Thirty-fourth yearbook of the National Council for the Social Studies*. Washington, D.C.: NCSS, 1964.

Fenton, E. *The new social studies*. New York: Holt, Rinehart and Winston, 1967.

Gibson, J. S. The process approach. In D. H. Riddle & R. E. Cleary (Eds.), *Political science in the social studies: Thirty-sixth yearbook of the National Council for the Social Studies*. Washington, D.C.: NCSS, 1966. Pp. 64–80.

Gibson, J. S. *New frontiers in the social studies*. Vol. 1. *Goals for students, means for teachers*. New York: Citation Press, 1967.

Gross, R. E., Muessig, R. H., & Fersh, G. L. (Eds.) *The problems approach and the social studies*. (Curr. Ser. No. 9, rev. ed.) Washington, D.C.: National Council for the Social Studies, 1960.

Gross, R. E., & Zeleny, L. D. *Educating citizens for democracy: Curriculum and instruction in social studies*. New York: Oxford University Press, 1958.

Harvard University, Graduate School of Education, Social Studies Research Project. *Harvard Social Issues Analysis Test*. (Form L-1) Cambridge, Mass.: HUGSE, 1959.

High, J. *Teaching secondary school social studies*. New York: Wiley, 1962.

High School Curriculum Center in Government. *American Political Behavior*. Book I; pilot version, rev. ed. Bloomington, Ind.: Indiana University Foundation, 1968.

Hunt, M. P., & Metcalf, L. E. *Teaching high school social studies: Problems in reflective thinking and social understanding.* (2d ed.) New York: Harper & Row, 1968.

Johnson, E. S. *Theory and practice of the social studies.* New York: Macmillan, 1956.

Koenig, L. W. *Official makers of public policy: Congress and the President.* Chicago: Scott, Foresman, 1965.

Lewenstein, M. R. *Teaching social studies in junior and senior high schools: An ends and means approach.* Chicago: Rand McNally, 1963.

Mahoney, J. J. *For us the living: An approach to civic education.* New York: Harper, 1945.

Massialas, B. G., & Cox, C. B. *Inquiry in social studies.* New York: McGraw-Hill, 1966.

Mehlinger, H. D. *The study of American political behavior.* (Occ. pap.) Bloomington, Ind.: High School Curriculum Center in Government, Indiana University, December 1967.

Michaelis, J. U., & Johnston, M. A. *The social sciences: Foundations of the social studies.* Boston: Allyn & Bacon, 1965.

Moreland, W. D. (Ed.) *Social studies in the senior high school: Programs for grades ten, eleven, and twelve.* (Curr. Ser. No. 7, rev. ed.) Washington, D.C.: National Council for the Social Studies, 1965.

Morse, H. T., & McCune, G. H. *Selected items for the testing of study skills and critical thinking.* (Bull. No. 15, 4th ed.) Washington, D.C.: National Council for the Social Studies, 1964.

National Council for the Social Studies. *A guide to contents in social studies.* Washington, D.C.: NCSS, 1958.

Oliver, D. W., & Shaver, J. P. *Teaching public issues in the high school.* Boston: Houghton Mifflin, 1966.

Patterson, F. (Ed.) *Citizenship and a free society: Education for the future. Thirtieth yearbook of the National Council for the Social Studies.* Washington, D.C.: NCSS, 1960.

Payne, J. C. (Ed.) *The teaching of contemporary affairs: Twenty-first yearbook of the National Council for the Social Studies.* Washington, D.C.: NCSS, 1950.

Quillen, I. J., & Hanna, L. A. *Education for social competence: The social studies in the secondary school.* Chicago: Scott, Foresman, 1961.

Raths, L. E., Harmin, M., & Simon, S. B. *Values and teaching: Working with values in the classroom.* Columbus: Merrill, 1966.

Riddle, D. H., & Cleary, R. E. (Eds.) *Political science in the social studies: Thirty-sixth yearbook of the National Council for the Social Studies.* Washington, D.C.: NCSS, 1966.

Schultz, M. *Tests for comparative political systems: An inquiry approach.* New York: Holt, Rinehart and Winston, 1967.

Stern, F. (Ed.) *The varieties of history: From Voltaire to the present.* Cleveland: World Publishing, 1956.

Thursfield, R. E. (Ed.) *The study and teaching of American history: Seventeenth yearbook of the National Council for the Social Studies.* Washington, D.C.: NCSS, 1946.

Tyler, R. W. The fact-finding study of the testing program of the United States Armed Forces Institute, 1952–1954. Report to the USAFI, University of Chicago, July 1954.

University of Chicago, College. *Sample questions: Comprehensive examinations.* Chicago: UCC, May 1945.

University of Chicago, College. *Sample questions from social science comprehensive examinations.* Chicago: UCC, April 1948.

Wesley, E. B. *Teaching social studies in high schools.* (3d ed.) Boston: Heath, 1950.

West, E. *Developing skills in the social studies program.* Minneapolis: Project Social Studies Center, University of Minnesota, 1968.

West, E. (Ed.) *Improving the teaching of world history: Twentieth yearbook of the National Council for the Social Studies.* Washington, D.C.: NCSS, 1949.

17

Evaluation of Learning in Art Education

BRENT G. WILSON

University of Iowa
Iowa City, Iowa

Brent G. Wilson received the Bachelor of Science degree in art education from Utah State University, the Master of Fine Arts degree in painting and sculpture from Cranbrook Academy of Art, and the Doctor of Philosophy degree in Art Education from The Ohio State University. He has taught elementary and junior and senior high school art, and has served as the art supervisor in the Salt Lake City, Utah, public schools and as a lecturer at the University of Utah. Currently, he is Associate Professor of Art and Education at the University of Iowa, and is a special consultant to National Assessment, with the responsibility for directing the development of art exercises for the assessment. His primary research interest is the study of the language used to describe and evaluate works of art. He is also an exhibiting sculptor working in cast bronze.

Contents

17

Evaluation of Learning in Art Education

Objectives of instruction in art education

Over the years art educators have written lists of objectives which have clarified their values and attempted to justify the importance of art education to those who have been concerned with the seemingly more practical and useful aspects of education. One of the first comprehensive lists of objectives was written in 1899 by a Committee of Ten on Drawing organized by the National Education Association (quoted in Klar, Winslow, & Kirby, 1933). In its report the committee listed the following as the primary aims of art education:

1. To offer a consistent development in the faculty of sight.
2. To develop an appreciation of the beautiful.
3. To acquire the ability to represent.
4. To develop the creative impulse.
5. To prepare pupils for manual industry is purely accidental.
6. The development of professional artists is in no sense the aim of art education in the public schools [p. 27].

Objectives 5 and 6 reflected the path art education had followed previously and from which it had begun to turn, and the first four aims were prophetic of what were to be the primary goals for art education during the major part of the decades to follow. As they were prophetic, they provide a frame of reference from which to view current objectives in art education and from which to review the events which led to today's objectives.

The training of professional artists

The traditional system of art education was to apprentice the aspiring artist to the workshop of an established master. In the workshop he would learn his craft by cleaning the master's brushes, grinding and mixing colors, and preparing canvases. At the same time, through observing and assisting his master, he acquired whatever instruction he could in drawing and painting, and he gained a knowledge of conventional themes and symbols and of methods of structuring works of art.

TABLE 17-1 TABLE OF SPECIFICATIONS FOR ART EDUCATION

	BEHAVIORS																							
	A.0 Perception			*B.0 Knowledge*								*C.0 Comprehension*		*D.0 Analysis*			*E.0 Evaluation*		*F.0 Appreciation*			*G.0 Production*	
	Within a work	*Between works*	*Among works*	*Terminology*	*Facts*	*Conventions*	*Trends and sequences*	*Classifications and categories*	*Criteria*	*Methodology*	*Theories*	*Translation*	*Interpretation*	*Elements*	*Relationships of parts*	*Relationship of parts to whole*	*Empirical*	*Systemic*	*Valuing*	*Empathizing*	*Feeling*	*Skill*	*Creativity*
CONTENT	*A.1*	*A.2*	*A.3*	*B.1*	*B.2*	*B.3*	*B.4*	*B.5*	*B.6*	*B.7*	*B.8*	*C.1*	*C.2*	*D.1*	*D.2*	*D.3*	*E.1*	*E.2*	*F.1*	*F.2*	*F.3*	*G.1*	*G.2*
1.0 Media, tools, and forming processes 1.1 Media 1.2 Tools 1.3 Processes 1.4 Techniques																							
2.0 Visual structure 2.1 Sensory qualities 2.2 Composition 2.3 Modal character																							
3.0 Subject matter 3.1 Objects, events, and themes 3.2 Symbols and allegories 3.3 Expressive content																							

4.0 Art form 4.1 Painting 4.2 Sculpture 4.3 Film 4.4 Happenings 4.5 Drawings 4.6 Prints 4.7 Collages 4.8 Architecture 4.9 Photographs 4.10 Pottery 4.11 Jewelry 4.12 Product design 4.13 Advertising design 4.14 Interior design 4.15 Weaving 4.16 Cartoons 4.17 Etc.																							
5.0 Cultural context 5.1 Artist 5.2 Date 5.3 Period 5.4 Location 5.5 Style 5.6 Use 5.7 Culture																							
6.0 Art theory and criticism 6.1 Art theories 6.2 Judgment standards																							

It was inconceivable that apprentice art training would benefit one who was not destined to be an artist. Such a preparation had only one purpose—the training of artists. Of course, art connoisseurship was important to those in a position to enjoy the luxury of art, but one became a connoisseur through experience with art and not through formal education.

The early art academies established in the United States were patterned after the European and were an extension of the apprentice system in that their central purpose was the training of professional artists.

Not until 1749 was it suggested—by Benjamin Franklin, in his *Proposed Hints for an Academy*—that art might be a useful subject for general inclusion in school programs. He wrote that "All should be taught a fair hand, and swift, as that is useful to all. And with it may be learned something of drawing by imitation of prints and some of the first principles of perspective" (quoted in De Francesco, 1958, p. 62). The purpose of art instruction was beginning to shift from training artists to conducting art activities which were considered practical and useful for all students, even if only for the sake of such things as penmanship. Two poles of a continuum are seen developing: one, the training of artists, and the other, art instruction for essentially nonaesthetic ends where art contributes to development in other areas. Since Franklin, many major art education goals have clustered around one or the other of these poles.

The first formal public school art programs in the United States followed Franklin's lead in making art instruction available to all students, but they retained the notion of training artists. In 1848 William Minife advocated art as a means of discovering art talent for use in industry. His idea was, "To get good designers we must take the proper means for educating, and if we should make drawing a branch of common school education, we should have an opportunity of selecting those who evidence superior talent for art . . ." (quoted in Whitford, 1929, p. 8). Minife went on to state that those who were not to continue in art would benefit from the instruction since they would gain an appreciation of art. In 1871 the legislature of the state of Massachusetts brought Walter Smith from England to establish drawing programs in the state which would lead to the same useful vocational skills to which Minife referred.

As evidenced by the goals written by the Committee of Ten on Drawing, by 1899 there was a strong reaction against the training of artists for service in industry. Despite this, an investigation of current high school art curriculum guides reveals that special courses in commercial art and advertising design are common. It is also found that general high school and even some junior high school art courses include units on advertising, fashion, interior, industrial, and architectural design. The objectives of these courses and units are strongly directed toward professional training in commercial art. For example, the New York City curriculum guide for art (Board of Education of the City of New York, 1961) lists this goal: "At this level the advertising art student should grow in power of self-expression, in the ability to understand, to analyze, and to solve the problems of the commercial artist with increased maturity [p. 168]." This goal reflects a major area of outcomes for current art instruction, and so, although the training of artists (particularly for service in industry) was questioned as early as 1899, it still remains an aim of art education. Although teachers in the field are often adamant in stating that training artists is not a central purpose of art instruction, still there are few who wish to do anything to thwart the budding artist, whether he is headed toward fine or commercial art. The objectives of commercial art classes in particular emphasize the training of the artist.

Studio production objectives

The 1899 objectives stated that "To acquire the ability to represent" was a major outcome of art instruction. At that time the production of school art meant drawing, and a particular type of drawing at that, where accurate delineation of type-form blocks was the steady diet. The blocks were three-dimensional cones, spheres, cubes, and cylinders. It was assumed that the representation of these forms would, among other things, assist students in the identification of the same shapes in natural objects.

The representation of geometric forms seems far removed from the pyrotechnic array of sculptures, collages, prints, batiks, paintings, and mobiles which characterize today's art classrooms. A small step was taken toward the current situation with the publication of Arthur Wesley Dow's book *Composition* in 1898 (see Logan, 1955, pp. 108–113). Dow had studied art in Paris in 1890 and 1891, and during this time had made an intensive study of the pictorial composition of paintings. On the basis of his study, Dow apparently believed that the primary objective of art education was to develop the student's ability to produce harmonious compositions. In his book instruction was based on the mastery of line, color, and notan. (*Notan* is a Japanese word describing the contrast of light and dark.) In a 1913 revision of *Composition*, the art principles of opposition, transition, subordination, repetition, and symmetry were included along with the elements.

Dow has had a lasting and monumental influence on art education. Texts of the 1960s still have sections devoted to design which are reminiscent of him. Although today's stated objectives of art education do not emphasize design, the space devoted to it in courses of study and the time allotted to it in many art classes belie any current deemphasis. Generations of public school art students have been trained to believe that making designs is the same as making art, which indeed is not the case. To be concerned only with formal and structural aspects is to ignore almost completely the deeper meanings of works of art. Design is only the dish upon which the meat of moods, feelings, symbols, and ideas is served, and starvation results from an empty dish. The overemphasis on design has been the source of at least a slight case of malnutrition in art education since Arthur Wesley Dow.

In 1908 Dow observed that young students liked to draw and paint independently, using subject matter of their own choosing. He concluded that free picture making might precede his more formal system of composition. Dow was stating what other art educators were beginning to realize—that young art students were capable of producing highly expressive works and that rigidly structured art lessons tended to stifle their expressiveness.

At the turn of the century a number of art teachers were beginning to take a close look at the free drawings of children, but it is a Viennese teacher, Franz Ciezek, who is considered the father of child art. Ciezek had a profound effect on the way in which the art of the young would be perceived and on the goals of art instruction. In 1885, while a student at the Academy of Fine Arts in Vienna, he lodged with a carpenter's family, and gave the children of the family art materials. He was astounded at the imaginativeness they showed in their work. Later he watched children drawing in chalk on a board fence opposite his room, and he was surprised to see that the children would actually fight for a place to draw. On a trip to Bohemia he noted that children's free drawings showed the same expressive character which he had previously observed, and he was even more surprised to recognize common characteristics in the children's drawings he had seen, even though the children could not usually have influenced one another. From his observations he concluded that all children unconsciously follow eternal laws of form, and he formulated the view that children should be allowed to develop in art in their own natural way without adult imposition.

In 1898 Ciezek opened his own juvenile art class. In it he taught no techniques, forced no formal standards on his students, and encouraged them to draw, paint, and print what they felt and what they had experienced. The works of art resulting from Ciezek's then radical methods were strikingly different from anything that had previously come from art instruction.

During the summer of 1908 the work of Ciezek's students came to the attention of art educators from the United States who were attending the Third International Drawing Conference held in London. Later, works of his students were exhibited in this country under the sponsorship of the International Red Cross. Ciezek and others who emphasized the child's expressive output as the major goal of art instruction had a marked influence on the nature of studio production. No longer did young students painstakingly render geometric forms and work from highly structured compositional exercises. Art teachers turned more and more to less restrictive methods of instruction where the student was encouraged to work from his own experiences. However, the notion of helping students produce unified compositions persisted. The older objective of unified compositions and the new emphasis on the expressive aspects of art are combined in this statement by Fredrik Nyquist (1929):

> In avoiding hackneyed representations the *"free expression" method* of teaching pictorial composition drawing has a distinct advantage. Since "free expression" drawing begins with the child's own experiences—his social experiences, play experiences, and emotional experiences—the themes for expression are practically unlimited in scope, and are apt to be more personal and direct in character [p. 94].

There are still art educators today who hold that one of the major goals of art instruction is the production of works of art in which the composition or structure is of primary concern. Wachowiak and Ramsay (1965), in outlining the standards by which elementary school students' works of art are to be evaluated, state:

> *There are some standards, however, based on aesthetic considerations that the teacher should use as criteria.* These involve design, composition, and basic art structure, ranging from simple and elementary guide posts in the primary grades to complex and subtle injunctions in the upper grades [p. 4].

In addition to the emphasis on achieving organized compositions, there are a multitude of subobjectives relating to media control, forming processes, and techniques which are consistently put forward. Indeed, many art teachers hold the acquisition of skill in these areas as the most important objectives of art education. It is also significant to note that much less emphasis has been placed on the production of totally integrated works of art where form and content are given equal consideration. Art education has generally concentrated on the form rather than the content. Although through the years studio production goals have consistently emphasized formal composition, the methods by which the goals might be achieved have varied markedly from rigidly structured drawing exercises to working from experience and imagination.

The development of creativity and other aspects of personality

The 1899 objective "To develop the creative impulse" gave emphasis to what was to become one of the objectives most often voiced for art education during much of the next half century. The production of works of art was still to be the central activity of art classes, but production was not to be an end in itself. It was to be merely the vehicle through which students were to become creative, expressive, well rounded, and well adjusted.

Viktor Lowenfeld was surely the most influential art educator in setting goals for art education in which the values relating to the process of making art far overshadowed the values of the end product. Lowenfeld was interested in facilitating students' creative and mental growth through art activities. He outlined six areas of growth—emotional, physical, perceptual, social, aesthetic, and creative—which were affected by art activities. Growth, according to Lowenfeld, occurred simultaneously in its different components and affected the child in his totality. He also believed that art teachers made the mistake of evaluating students' creative work from only one component—external aesthetic criteria of design quality, colors, shapes, and their relationships.

Lowenfeld maintained that an evaluation of only the design elements of children's works of art is unjust, not only to the creative product but also to the child, since he believed growth involves more than aesthetics. For him the final product is subordinated to the creative process.

The creative process is of paramount importance in the child's total growth. Aesthetic growth is only a portion of the total growth (Lowenfeld, 1959, pp. 48–49).

Lowenfeld established a series of principles which, if followed, he believed would assure the student's maximum growth in each of the major areas. He taught that a student's frame of reference must be extended through the teacher's assistance in reflecting upon and probing deeply into the student's experiences, and that art techniques cannot be taught or explained, but that each child must develop his own technical strategies for attacking his artistic tasks. He believed that the meaningfulness of the work to its creator must never be disturbed by "objective evaluations," that teachers should not impose their own subject matter and modes of expression on the child; that one child's creative work was never to be preferred over that of another; that students should never be allowed to copy any other work of art; and that the teacher must never work directly upon the child's creative productions. Each of Lowenfeld's principles emphasized the importance of the process of art as opposed to the final product. Anything that stood in the way of the child's free expression was thought to block creative growth and was to be systematically avoided.

When the first of five editions of Lowenfeld's *Creative and Mental Growth* was published in 1947, art teachers had been prepared for the objectives it contained through the earlier work of Ciezek and his followers and particularly through the work of a group of educators associated with the progressive education movement during the 1920s and 1930s. In each case the goal of creative expression was expounded above all others.

Two contrasting sets of objectives which have been advanced as the reason for having students produce works of art have been presented. One view holds the well-composed object as the central goal, while the other view places strong emphasis on the benefits derived from the process of making art. The views represent the thinking of influential art educators, and both views have had a marked influence on art educational practice. However, the process-oriented view has had its greatest impact in the elementary grades, and to a lesser degree in the junior high school. Much of the elementary school art instruction has been conducted by teachers with little specialized art training in self-contained classrooms. The goals of the process-oriented approach may have seemed more easily attainable, since the end product was deemphasized, and therefore it was not necessary to have a background in the studio aspects of art instruction. Most junior and senior high school art instructors have had strong studio backgrounds and, consequently, have emphasized the art product over the process. And surely, many art teachers have incorporated objectives from both positions into their programs.

Victor D'Amico is one art educator who has taken a stand which seems to fall between the two positions. In his book *Creative Teaching in Art* (1953), he states that "The art work of children is important to the teacher insofar as it tells him about the child and helps him to keep alive the child's imagination and also the will to express it. Experience, and not the product, is the precious aim of art education [p. 3]." However, the chapters of his book are titled "The Child as a Painter" and sculptor, potter, graphic artist, inventor, and designer craftsman. He places strong emphasis on media, forming process, design, and other aspects of the artist's craft. D'Amico's view is characterized when he notes that the child progresses from the subconscious use of art values in the elementary school to a conscious use of them in high school. He writes that these "aesthetic values are best learned through personal experience, rather than through general concepts; they should be discovered through activity, not dictated through principles. The art experience is more emotional than intellectual, especially at the lower age levels [p. 49]." D'Amico's goal for art education, which emphasizes the creative benefits of process, and his procedures, which center around the traditional aspects of visual structure, media, and technique, characterize quite accurately the twofold nature of objectives associated with creativity development.

Art appreciation and cultural knowledge objectives

Art appreciation objectives invariably have been stated in terms as general as they were in 1899 when the Committee of Ten on Drawing wrote as an objective, "To develop an appreciation of the beautiful." It is necessary, therefore, to look beyond the objectives to the procedures which have been followed in order to determine the meanings of the term "art appreciation" as used by art educators.

Helen Erickson seemed to hold that through particular art production activities students would automatically come to appreciate art, particularly that of their own making and that of their peers. In a chapter titled "Influences in the Cultivation of Art Appreciation" (1926), she outlined the methods used to develop art appreciation. The methods included making Gothic windows from cardboard; construction of a Renaissance portico; painting of stage backdrops to assist in celebrating harvest, spring, and Christmas festivals; and a series of activities such as producing puppet shows, illustrating poems, making costumes, constructing models of cities, and producing decorative maps. Art appreciation was assumed to follow naturally from an involvement in art and art-related social studies activities, and it should be emphasized that the appreciation to be developed was directed more toward the students' own productions than toward master works of art. Some art educators today still hold the same view of appreciation and make little effort to influence attitudes toward art other than that produced by their students.

In marked contrast to the view of art appreciation through art activities presented by Erickson was the picture study method of developing art appreciation. L. L. W. Wilson wrote in the introduction to her book *Picture Study in Elementary Schools* (1899) that the manual was "designed to aid teachers in imparting to children a true appreciation of, and love for, the paintings by the world's great masters [p. vii]." In the book each school of art (Italian, Spanish, Dutch, German, French, English, American, and Japanese) is represented with four or five famous examples. However, emphasis is placed on Italian Renaissance and French academic paintings, and the works included were chosen "with a view to the appropriateness of their subjects to the months of the school year [p. vii]." The methods suggested for presenting the reproductions to students center on pointing out the literal aspects of the painting's subject matter. For example, under the "method" for studying Gérôme's painting "A Leash of Hounds," these questions are listed for students: "Where is this? What desert? What are the dogs doing? The Arab? [p. 13]" The teacher is exhorted to precede the study of the picture with lessons on deserts.

Casey, in *Master Pieces in Art* (1915), continued the anecdotal methods of L. L. W. Wilson in introducing what were considered some of the most celebrated pictures in the world, but he also described each picture in terms of (1) the source of the subject, (2) the setting, (3) the arrangement, (4) the center of interest, (5) the supreme motive, (6) the light and shade, (7) the color, and (8) the history. Casey succeeded in moving from the narrow, literal picture study suggested by L. L. W. Wilson, but the rigid analysis of each work in terms of his categories contains the hidden assumption that all works must have such things as a center of interest or a supreme motive.

Art appreciation objectives of the picture-study variety were common until the 1930s when the appreciation-through-doing objectives took precedent. Currently art appreciation objectives from both schools of thought prevail in the field, with a shift back toward the picture-study approach taking place during the 1960s.

In studying works of art today the emphasis remains about the same as it has been through the years, with some attention being given to the anecdotal aspects which surround the work, a study of the artist's life, and some analysis of the work of art. It is surprising, however, that often an analytical study of the work of art receives the least attention, when it might be expected to receive the most. There is also a tendency to consider art appreciation as synonymous with the study of art history, in which students are acquainted with major artists, styles, and periods in the history of art. The objectives for such instruction usually center around the recognition, identification, and knowledge of major works of art, artists, and periods.

Taking a different approach to the study of art history, McFee (1961) has emphasized the importance of art as a means of cultural maintenance. She maintains that a sensitive appraisal of the artifacts of our culture—including such things as movies, television, cartoons, magazine "art," and the standard art forms—will assist in the continuation of the desirable aspects of our culture. She also recognizes the importance of gaining insights into our culture and other cultures through an appraisal of artifacts.

Cultural objectives notwithstanding, the theme running through most art appreciation objectives is still enjoyment of the work of art and art activities. However, the enjoyment is expected to be a discriminating one based on sensitive perception and evaluation. The goals for art appreciation seem most worthy; however, as in the past, it seems as if art appreciation practices are directed toward teaching students to like the "right" things rather than toward an open experience of a work of art in order to gain the pleasure and enrichment which the experience might provide. During the early 1900s French academic paintings were the dominant source of art appreciation materials. Today an assessment of the visual material used for art appreciation indicates a preponderance of French works from impressionism through cubism. The content of art appreciation today seems as outdated as were the French academic paintings used as late as the 1930s. If art appreciation is to be more than training students to like what is currently aesthetically safe and acceptable, a much broader selection of art to appreciate will have to be made.

Perceptual alteration as a goal for art education

The 1899 perceptual goal was "To offer a consistent development in the faculty of sight." Perceptual training is still a goal in art education. In *Education of Vision*, a book from a series of three dealing with artistic vision, Kepes (1965) states that a "key task of our own times is the education of vision—the developing of our neglected, atrophic sensibilities [p. iv]." These two statements, one made sixty-five years after the other, could perhaps not be considered analogous in their conception of perceptual training. Nevertheless, they do indicate that training in the faculty of vision has been and still is a major goal for art education.

Although visual training has been a longstanding goal, art educators have not been specific about what perceptual changes were to take place and how the changes were to be accomplished. McFee (1961), one art educator who has been quite definite in outlining the nature of perceptual change and the methods by which the change might be accomplished, has discussed some of the difficulty associated with visual training under the heading "A Controversial Question":

> The emphasis made on the need for perceptual training of children and students may cause some cries of "If you do this you will stifle creativity! Artists today do not copy nature." This criticism usually comes from people who are not aware of the complexity of the visual process. Visual training increases the wealth of material the children have to work with. If visual training becomes rigid and authoritarian it may inhibit creative activity, but if it is used to motivate visual curiosity and exploration it should widen the range of creative students. Much more effect of light and color, of form and line will become available for children to use. They will go beyond *cognitive* categorizing and see many more details and significant relations as they respond to their environment, both visually and cognitively [p. 63].

Guy Hubbard (1967) has reflected the view of many art educators in indicating the importance of visual training to everyday life as well as to the arts; he has expanded the concepts of perception to include the recalling of visual ideas and events:

> The utility of vision in everyday life is undeniable. Vision is also fundamental to the study of the visual arts whether one serves as a critic or as a producer of

> art. The person whose potential for thinking visually has been well developed is more likely to be prepared both for understanding and for creating works of art than a person whose visual abilities are untrained. The truly educated person has many visual resources to turn to for help. He has a large repertoire of things he has seen and he can recall many visual ideas and events. He can make fine visual comparisons, perceive in great detail, resolve visual problems. The poorly educated person, visually, cannot do these things nearly as well. His progress in art studies will be slower than that of the visually more mature student [p. 28].

Perhaps the primary difficulty of dealing with perceptual objectives is the problem of determining what behaviors will be taken as satisfactory evidence that an individual has learned to perceive in desired ways. For example, if one wishes to determine whether a student can recall in great detail what he has previously experienced, he might ask the student to describe or draw what he remembers; but describing and drawing are behaviors which, although relying on perception, also include other behaviors. Perhaps the student can perceive and recall vividly, but he cannot write or describe. Art educators are forced to make inferences about perceptual behaviors by assessing other more overt behaviors.

Visual training will surely remain as an important goal in art education. However, because of the difficulty in assessing the complex aspects of aesthetic visual perception, it might be more useful to concentrate on the more readily observable behaviors such as verbal analysis, production, and evaluation which are dependent upon perception as the objectives of art education.

The aesthetic experience as the central purpose of art education

Although related to a number of the 1899 objectives for art education, there is one objective which needs to be considered separately because of its importance today. The objective is concerned with increasing students' aesthetic experiencing abilities.

Lanier (1963) proposes the visual aesthetic experience as a key objective of art education. He regards the visual aesthetic experience as one in which there is a heightened response to the quality of a visual entity wherein the sequential parts of the experience are linked together and moving toward an anticipated consummation. He stated that "When one speaks of art education, major concepts of value must include the provision of visual aesthetic experience. Indeed, I would say that the more significant benefit that can be derived from art activities in school or out of school is the opportunity to partake of visual aesthetic experiences [p. 16]."

R. A. Smith (1968) has also proposed that humanities instruction might stress the idea of "aesthetic structure" and "aesthetic knowing." Smith argues that works of art embody various types of value—aesthetic, intellectual, moral, religious—and that a variety of explicit meanings is conveyed through dramatic feeling, tone, and sensuous imagery. Furthermore, he holds that aesthetic knowing is dependent upon a special kind of attention in order to explicate the work's aesthetic qualities and powers. He presents the method of the art critic as the means by which one might become aesthetically knowledgeable. As outlined, the method consists of (1) general knowledge of what the work of art has to offer and attention to aspects of works of art and (2) the making of critical statements, analyses, and interpretations. For Smith education in aesthetics would include the acquisition of the critical method of explicating the aesthetic nature of works of art as a most important objective.

This writer also maintains that the central purpose of art instruction is to assist students in achieving reasonably full aesthetic experiences with works of art and other visual phenomena which are capable of eliciting such experience. Aesthetic experience is defined as an open and active confrontation with an art object or event during which the individual performs a visual analysis of the multitude of qualities and aspects present in the situation. He attends to sensory qualities and their formal composition, media, technique, mood and feeling, literal and symbolic meanings, and also to the relationship of these aspects to his own feelings toward the situation. This active exploring and relating of aspects ends with a fusing of these aspects and with a determination of total character and significant meaning of the object or experience. The experience may also include an evaluation of aesthetic merit based on whether or not the aspects form a firmly integrated whole, whether the object or event has a uniquely vivid quality about it, whether the experience with the object or event leads to pleasureful feelings, or whether the object or event is well crafted, represents the time in which it was done, and seems to get at essences.

The aesthetic experience, as thus defined, is highly complex. It is obvious that young students could not experience art works in such a manner. But they can begin to learn of the aspects which an aesthetic work comprises, can learn to be open to experiences, can begin making limited aesthetic analyses and evaluations, and can certainly gain pleasure from their limited aesthetic experiencing.

If the aesthetic experience is the central goal of art education, how does it relate to the previously mentioned objectives of studio production, creativity, appreciation and cultural knowledge, and perception? The major factor in making a work of art is the relating of a great number of artistic aspects to form a unified whole. Knowing whether a unified whole has been achieved is dependent upon an aesthetic assessment. Appreciating art, the sensitive appraisal of works of art, is based on the aesthetic experience. The study of art history, which is essentially concerned with explaining why works of art look the way they do, is enhanced through careful aesthetic appraisal. Creativity is in part concerned with the production of the unique, and an aesthetic appraisal leads to a determination of uniqueness.

Art is the only subject commonly taught in the schools which has concern for developing the visual ability to experience aesthetically. The visual aesthetic experience is the unique domain of art education, and because it is basic to most other objectives in art education, a strong argument can be given for its consideration as the central objective of art education.

This section began with a brief statement of objectives for art education made in 1899. It now seems appropriate to end the section with a current set of objectives formulated by Barkan (1965) in the *Report of the Commission on Art Education*. Barkan's core of common goals includes

> *Sensitivity to visual relationships*
>
> The visual organization of shapes, positions, colors, tonal values, and textures;
>
> The use of materials to achieve particular qualities of visual organization.
>
> *Sensitivity to communications embodied in works of art*
>
> Emotional impact;
>
> Symbolic meanings;
>
> Meanings in particular qualities of visual organization.
>
> *Attitudes of adventure and discovery in processes of working and observing*
>
> Visual cues from the environment as sources for stimulation;
>
> The character of materials and tools as guidelines for action;
>
> Unforeseen possibilities that become apparent in any work in process;
>
> Elements of speculative play, uncertainty, struggle, and resolution as aspects of working process.
>
> *Insight into aesthetic qualities in works of art*
>
> Similarities and differences in works of art from a variety of traditions in our artistic heritage;
>
> Similarities and differences among the forms and characteristics of works of art in our own time;
>
> Similarities and differences in works of art produced by children and youth.
>
> *Insight into aesthetic qualities of visual experiences*
>
> The work of artists, craftsmen, designers, film makers, architects, and city planners, with the implications of their efforts for day-to-day experiences of people.
>
> *Skills for control and fluency*
>
> The nature of tools and materials, and ways to control the intended meanings for making works of art;
>
> Processes that encourage discovery, reconstruction, and refinement in work, observation, and analysis.
>
> [pp. 77–78]

512 Specifications for courses in art education

Brent G. Wilson

A single table of outcomes or objectives of art instruction appears as Table 17-1, Table of Specifications for Art Education (see pages 502–503). It is intended to present objectives for art instruction from the intermediate elementary grades through high school art classes, including the visual arts portion of high school humanities classes. The wide range of programs can be included in one table because similar content and behaviors characterize art instruction at each of these levels.

The unique nature of art and the unique ways in which learning in art takes place requires the curriculum worker in art education to deal with problems which are not encountered in sciences and mathematics, where units of instruction are essentially sequential. In art, and especially in the production of works of art, by far the most common art-classroom activity, it cannot always be shown that one unit of learning is prerequisite to another. The achievement of one skill, concept, or attitude is closely related to other skills, concepts, and attitudes, but the learning which takes place in art is usually concurrent rather than sequential. Before the components of the Table of Specifications are presented, the following discussion is given to illustrate some of the unique aspects of art learning and teaching.

The nonsequential nature of the presentation of units of art instruction stems from at least three factors: (1) the highly complex nature of artistic production which requires control of the vast number of qualities and aspects whose relationships comprise a work of art, (2) the fact that there is seldom a single solution to problems of artistic production, and (3) the fact that aesthetically successful works of art can be produced by students who possess only a limited ability to perceive, analyze, evaluate, and appreciate their own works of art.

When an artist produces a painting, he uses variables which may include the selection of (1) subject matter consisting of object, theme, symbol, and allegory; (2) composition and the nature of sensuous qualities such as colors, shapes, and lines; and (3) the medium and how it is to be controlled. Through the interrelationship of these and other variables the painting acquires meaning and style. An artist is considered successful if he is able to control artistic variables to achieve a coherent meaning and a unified style. Therefore, the artist trains himself to control artistic variables so that he might understand the consequences of the innumerable ways in which they might be related.

Such understanding and control seem highly complicated, as indeed they are. However, when a young student with little or no training in art is observed in an elementary school classroom at an easel producing a painting, he will likely use almost the same set of variables as the artist. He decides what subject matter to use, selects colors, produces lines and shapes to form a composition, and his painting may achieve meaning, expressive character, and perhaps even a style.

Since the student and the artist apparently perform many of the same operations in producing a painting and since they sometimes achieve amazingly similar results, it is reasonable to ask whether there are differences between the artist in his studio and the child working in art. The answer is obvious: there are important differences in the ways the two perform their tasks. The artist usually selects variables using his broad knowledge of the range of alternatives available. The student selects from a limited base, often having little awareness of what variables may be used in the production of his work. The artist is keenly aware of the consequences of his selections. The artist, through his training, usually has achieved a high degree of control over his variables so that he is able to visualize and recognize aesthetic ends and accomplish the operations needed to achieve them. The student may achieve brilliant results without realizing quite how and without having the necessary control to achieve them again, while the artist is keenly sensitive to the variables he selects and to how he controls them to produce a great number of desired ends. The student possesses much less sensitivity, awareness, and control. Even so, he might produce results which are highly admired by artists and other aesthetically aware individuals.

One of the reasons students with little training in art can produce such aesthetically admirable results is that work which is unique and unpredictable is currently valued highly. Students often achieve original results through happy accidents and through intuitive responses to subject matter and media stimuli. Obviously, strict sequential steps cannot be formulated for the achievement of these desirable open-ended results. Consequently, sequentially based teaching strategies are seldom found for the teaching of studio production. The student artist, on first try, might produce a highly complex painting having a vivid, expressive character, but he does not have to know about composition in order to structure his painting; his composition develops naturally. He does not need to know how to mix colors, since they mix accidentally on the paper. The shapes he uses are a consequence of the subject matter he selects. The successful student production of one work by means which have accidental and intuitive dimensions does not necessarily lead to subsequent successes, because the student lacks rational means of control.

The essential difference, then, between the artist and the student artist is that, although they both function intuitively, the artist, when he wishes to, is able to operate on a much more rational level than the child.

Studio instruction is often directed toward assisting students in perceiving, comprehending, analyzing, evaluating, and appreciating what they have already been able to produce, and toward assisting them in achieving a higher degree of rational control over their future productions in art.

It should be added that mastery over the control of artistic variables is not possible in art in the same sense that it is in a subject such as mathematics. The open-ended nature of artistic production, where the single correct response usually does not exist, makes it possible to achieve innumerable ends. Mastery in art might be viewed as a constantly increasing control over variables, but it is a partial mastery which is never complete in the sense that one has mastered addition or subtraction in mathematics.

Rational control over the variables which make up works of art involves concurrent consideration of the whole range of variables. It is virtually impossible to isolate these for pedagogical purposes. For example, even though during a phase of art instruction the teacher might wish to emphasize the subject-matter aspects of a work of art, when students incorporate subject matter into drawings or paintings, they must deal with composition, media, technique, and all the other variables which make up a work of art. Even though one aspect can be singled out for intensive study, the other variables remain as a part of the total consideration.

Because the variables of artistic production must receive concurrent consideration, it seems unreasonable to hold that design should be taught before media control, color before subject-matter considerations, and drawing before painting. They may be presented in any reasoned order or even in random order. The nature of learning in the studio portion of art instruction allows the teacher of art an amazing freedom in the structuring and sequencing of units (Barkan & Chapman, 1967).

Much of what has been said about how a student learns in the studio also applies to the perception, analysis, evaluation, and appreciation of works of art. The fuller varieties of aesthetic experience are those in which attention is directed to the interrelationships of aspects within works of art. As with studio production, the variables are dealt with concurrently; consequently, the same content is presented for all levels of art instruction.

Growth in art is seen as the acquiring of objectives arising from the more complex behaviors, that is, the relating of more aesthetic variables, whether the student is making a work of art or experiencing it in some other way.

The content of art education

The purpose of this section is to describe and illustrate the major aspects of content in art education. The criterion which guided the selection of these aspects was that, when the list was complete, there should be no major content of art programs which was not included. The six major content areas are *Media, tools, and forming processes* (1.0), *Visual structure* (2.0), *Subject matter* (3.0), *Art form* (4.0), *Cultural context* (5.0), and *Art theory and criticism* (6.0).[1]

Media, tools, and forming processes (1.0)

When an aesthetic object is to be formed, among the first considerations are of what it will be formed, by what methods, and using what tools. It is therefore appropriate that *Media, tools, and forming processes* be the first aspect of art contend entered on the Table of Specifications. The term *Media* (1.1) refers to the materials such as paint, clay, plaster, pencils, crayons, paper, canvas, and ink which form the physical work of art. *Tools* (1.2) are the equipment such as brushes, hammers, pens, cameras, and welders which are necessary to the forming process. Forming *Processes* (1.3) include such actions as painting, drawing, printing, carving, filming, constructing, spraying, coiling, and modeling. *Technique* (1.4) is considered to be a person's individual embellishment, or personal style employed in the forming process.

The importance with which acquisition of knowledge of and skill in the use of media is viewed is evident upon inspection of the literature in art education, particularly the popular periodicals.

Young students have little difficulty in learning basic control of paint, crayons, tempera, pencils, and clay, whereas advanced processes with these same media, such as the wheel throwing of clay, require substantial training.

Media and the ways in which they are formed are important factors affecting the final quality of a work of art. Sensitivity to the qualities of media and their forming processes is a requirement for skilled production, experiencing, and evaluation of works of art.

Visual structure (2.0) The second major category of the content of art is *Visual structure*. Three major aspects are included under visual structure: sensory qualities, composition, and modal character.

The *Sensory qualities* (2.1) are color, shape, line, and texture—the primary elements which make up works of art.

Composition (2.2), often referred to as "design," is the way in which the sensory qualities of a work of art are arranged and related to one another. Composition includes such aspects as value contrast, directional movement, tension, placement, size, location, pattern, balance, figure and ground, proximity, and closure. Composition is the carrier upon which aspects of feeling, meaning, and style ride. The importance of composition to the final success of a work of art has been emphasized by many critics and artists. John Ciardi (1959, p. 667) tells how W. H. Auden was once asked what advice he would give a young man who wished to become a poet. Auden replied that he would ask the young man why he wished to write poetry. If the answer was "Because I have something important to say," Auden would conclude that there was no hope for that young man as a poet. If, on the other hand, the answer was "Because I like to hang around words and overhear them talking to one another," then the young man was at least interested in a fundamental part of the poetic process. Paraphrasing Auden, if an aspiring sculptor says, "I like to push shapes around to watch them form one another," then it might be concluded that he has a basic understanding of what sculpture is about.

The collection of shapes, colors, lines, and textures, which in relationship to one another form the composition of a work of art, also performs another extremely valuable function in a work of art. This function is one of creating a mood or pervasive feeling of the work. When works of art are characterized as being sedate, warm, agitated, drab, turbulent, mellow, or garish, it is often the arrangement of sensory qualities to which the individual refers. *Modal character* (2.3), the third aspect of visual structure, might be likened to tone of voice. The same phrase can be spoken in many different ways, and each change in inflection, volume, and speed has the possibility of

[1] These categories are an adaptation and expansion of organizing centers of art instruction outlined by Barkan and Chapman in *Guidelines for Art Instruction through Television for the Elementary Schools* (1967).

expressing something different, however slightly. Taylor (1957) tells how in works of art the subject matter, theme, and symbols might be identical, yet, because of differences in the use of the sensory and compositional features of the work, the mood of the works might be entirely different.

Elementary school students are capable of becoming sensitively aware of the visual aspects of works of art (Wilson, 1966a), but it is usually not until junior high school that they are able to begin consciously controlling these aspects in order to alter the aesthetic character of their works of art (Harris, 1963; Lowenfeld, 1959).

Subject matter (3.0) *Subject matter* is concerned with the ideas, natural objects, events, themes, symbols, and allegories found in works of art. One level of meaning concerns Natural objects and events (3.1), which are usually viewed at face value with little or no attempt at reading any symbolic meaning into the subject matter. Lowenfeld (1959) has placed strong emphasis on careful selection and presentation of natural objects and events as the subject matter of students' art work. He further emphasizes the importance of students' using subject matter which has a close relationship to their immediate experiences, suggesting topics arising from their experiences of self, home, social life, nature, community, and industry. For specific subject matter, the student might portray himself yawning, laughing, thinking hard, sleeping, being angry, going upstairs; depict how he feels in the morning and on a rainy day; or show an evening at home, dancing at a party, and shoveling snow.

Lowenfeld's major concern is that art experiences be integrative—that they combine thinking, feeling, and perceiving into an inseparable whole. He holds that this integration can occur only if students use as the subject matter of their art those things which they have most thought about, felt, and perceived. For this reason the meaning of students' works of art is invariably at the level of natural objects and events. Even when a theme such as mother and child is suggested, it is the mother and child the student has experienced, and there is no attempt to relate the natural subject matter to the theme of mother and child in, for example, Christian art.

Emphasis on the literal aspects of meaning in works of art in and out of the art classroom helps to explain students' preoccupation with natural objects and events and lack of attention to symbolic and allegorical aspects both in the works they produce and in the way they experience the work of artists. *Symbols and allegories* (3.2) occupy a second level of understanding, and are used here to refer to meanings of objects, events, and aspects in works of art which go beyond natural, factual, and expressional interpretations. Symbols and allegories are of two main types: conventional symbols such as those in Christian art where the lily represents purity and the peacock immortality, and quasi-conventional symbols, those symbols which are used as conventional symbols but where there is no long-standing tradition which gives meaning. The hand holding the broken sword from which springs a flower in Picasso's painting "Guernica" could be considered a quasi-conventional symbol since it is indeed viewed as a symbol. The symbol has been interpreted in various ways (usually hope arising from destruction), yet, it is not grounded in conventional symbolism.

A third level of meaning in the visual arts, *Expressive content* (3.3; Taylor, 1957), has also been referred to as "intrinsic meaning" by Panofsky (1955). The expressive content of a work of art is determined by using the total work of art as a symbol. According to Panofsky it involves the ascertaining of underlying principles in a work of art which reveal "the basic attitude of a nation, period, class, religious or philosophical persuasion—all this unconsciously qualified by one personality and condensed into one work [p. 30]." Panofsky maintains that intrinsic meaning is more fully revealed when "idea," or subject matter, and "form" approach a state of equilibrium, where one does not outparade the other. Taylor states that expressive content arises from the unique fusion of subject matter and specific visual form, but he does not suggest that equilibrium between the two is necessary for a clear determination of meaning.

It is obvious that the determination of intrinsic meaning involves a highly complex set of operations which would generally be beyond the capabilities of most elementary and junior high school students. However, teaching to explicate the expressive content of works of art is often the major content of high school humanities programs.

Art form (4.0) *Art form* points out the distinctions among the different types of works within the visual arts. Works of art in their various forms embody basic elements of color, texture, line, and shape, but when these elements are combined in such different forms as buildings, paintings, films, and happenings they have different meanings, different functions, and different forming problems, and they are experienced in quite different ways. Barkan and Chapman (1967) state that

> An *art form* can be an effective organizing center for programs because it *draws attention to the contexts in which objects are seen to be within the province of art.* When a chair, a book, a painting, or a building is viewed as a work of art, then furniture design, typographical and book design, painting, and architecture are the respective art forms or contexts in which these objects are viewed as art. The qualities in all of these art forms—and others such as drawing, printmaking, sculpture, textiles, ceramics, theater and film, and the arts of commerce—result from the subjects, themes, or ideas embodied in them, the media and forming processes employed, and the styles or cultural idioms in which they are expressed. Indeed, the meanings inherent in any art form are the products of the intent, the handling of the medium, types of art structure, and the stylistic character which is evolved [p. 15].

Art form applies as much to the student's experiencing of works of art as to the making of works of art. Consequently, consideration of art form falls within the areas of art history, art criticism, and art appreciation as well as studio production.

Cultural context (5.0) *Cultural context* refers to factors which influenced the character of the work of art, including the *Artist* who created the work (5.1); the *Date, Period,* and *Location* from which the work of art came (5.2, 5.3, and 5.4); and the *Style,* or name given to works of art with similar characteristics (5.5). Each element of this aspect of content relates to the area of art history—to knowledge about why a work of art has the character it has, and how works of art, cultural factors, and factors of personality have influenced the character of subsequent works of art.

Barkan and Chapman (1967) urge that careful attention be given to this aspect of content in light of elementary students' limited sense of time and history. However, they state that "the extended horizons of intermediate level children and their interest in and grasp of relationships among past, present, and future demonstrate their ability to begin to perceive aspects of style and cultural idiom in works of art [p. 15]."

Art theory and criticism (6.0) Art theory (6.1), referred to as "aesthetics," is concerned with defining the nature of art. Weitz (1966) has said, "It is easier to teach art than to talk about its nature. Even so, teachers of art agree that it cannot be taught, or at least effectively taught, unless they can state truly its nature" (p. 49). By extending Weitz's view to the student it could also be said that students cannot learn art, at least effectively, unless they understand its nature. This view seems to underlie recent emphasis on art theory and criticism by Ecker and Eisner (1966) and R. A. Smith (1966).

Although Weitz maintains that art is an open concept for which it is impossible to name the "necessary and sufficient properties," he does believe that aestheticians who have attempted to define the nature of art are the greatest teachers of art. Through their theories are recommended "criteria or suggested properties that we should attend to if we are to get the most from paintings [p. 55]." Theories of art, then, serve as guides to direct the experiencing of works of art, and without them our experiences with art stand to be less rich and full.

Weitz has outlined what he considers to be the most important and influential theories of art. They are *imitationalism,* the doctrine that the defining properties of works of art are certain features that imitate the world outside art; *expressionism*, the doctrine that art imitates nothing but is a product of creative imagination; *emotionalism*, which defines a work of art as the embodiment in artistic media of an emotion or a collection of them; *formism*, which is the doctrine that works of art are essentially certain organizations of elements that produce a certain effect; and *organicism*, the doctrine that works of art are essentially unities.

The major theories of art listed by Weitz define, each in their own way, the nature of art. Each theory also provides within its structure the criteria, or *Judgment standards* (6.2), by which works of art are to be evaluated. Reasoned critical judgments of works of art usually are grounded in the standards which follow from the major theories of art, even though students who make aesthetic judgments might be unaware of the theory and, perhaps at least in part, unaware of the standards which they are applying. It seems reasonable to believe that if students in art learn to apply alternative standards of criticism to works of art, then their judgments would become more sensitive, more reasoned, and richer because the theories direct attention to different aspects of works of art. For this reason *Art theory and criticism* forms a major area of content in art education.

Art education behaviors

This section describes behaviors which, when related to the content of art education in Table 17-1, the Table of Specifications for Art Education, form the objectives or outcomes of art education. The behaviors presented in this section are classified under the headings *Perception, Knowledge, Comprehension, Analysis, Evaluation, Appreciation,* and *Production.* They are not necessarily presented in order since in art it is not always possible to determine which behaviors are most basic. For example, in the case of *Perception* and *Knowledge*, it is doubtful that meaningful aesthetic perception can occur without some knowledge of what there is to perceive in a given situation, and conversely, perception is necessary for the acquiring of much of the knowledge of art. However, in the case of the behaviors *Knowledge, Comprehension, Analysis, Evaluation,* and to a degree *Appreciation*, it seems that acquisition of the less complex behaviors in the order listed is often a necessary condition for the acquisition of the more complex behaviors.

Several of the behaviors have been taken almost directly or adapted from Handbooks 1 and 2 of the *Taxonomy of Educational Objectives* (Bloom, 1956; Krathwohl, Bloom, & Masia, 1964). In other instances the behaviors are adapted from sources within the literature of art education.

Perception (A.0) *Perception*, the process by which an individual transforms received sensory qualities into the world as he knows it, has been and still is the foundation for some of the most pervasive of art education objectives.

Clearly, the recognition of behaviors listed under *Knowledge* involves perception, but in art education, perception has a special meaning. Perception in art education refers to a refining of the senses, to the development of the ability to view objects and events in ways which go beyond customary perception and mere recognition. Art educators are taken by the idea that the world can be viewed in a variety of ways and that there is a customary mode of perception used in day-to-day existence which is usually passive and directed toward recognition of objects for use. A second mode of perception is less common and involves an individual's perceiving actively, broadly, openly, and from multiple points of view. This is considered to be the type of perception used by artists and art critics as they make and describe and evaluate works of art. What artists have said about their ways of perceiving has illuminated what might be called aesthetic perception. Matisse, when asked whether a tomato looked the same to him when he painted it as when he ate it, replied, "No, when I eat it I see it like [*sic*] everybody else" (quoted in Arnheim, 1960, p. 134). In a conversation with J. Gasquet, Cezanne also described the difference between the way an artist perceives and the way one customarily perceives:

> Sometimes I have accompanied a farmer behind his cart driving to the market to sell his potatoes. He had never seen Sainte Victoire [the mountain Cézanne painted so many times]. They know what has been planted there, along the road, how the weather is to be tomorrow, whether Sainte Victoire had his cloud cap on or not; they feel it like the animals do, like a dog who knows what this piece of bread is, only from their needs; but that the trees are green, and that this green is a tree, that this earth is red, and that this red rubble and boulders are hills, I really do not believe that most of them feel that, that they know it outside of their unconscious feeling for the useful.
>
> (Quoted in Schachtel, 1959, pp. 168–169)

Perception of the type of which Matisse and Cézanne speak is generally considered to be a necessary condition for the rational selection of artistic qualities and their arrangement to form works of art, and also a necessary condition for the sensitive experiencing and evaluation of works of art.

It can be argued that perception is not a behavior at all, since it cannot be observed directly. The assessment of perception requires the observation of other behaviors such as the selecting, grouping, and ranking of visual phenomena from which inferences are made about an individual's perception.

Clearly, visual perception involves observing, distinguishing, relating, selecting, judging, interpreting, analyzing, and synthesizing (Trismen, 1968). However, a distinction is made between behaviors involving perception which are assessable at the preverbal level through observation of how an individual orders, selects, relates, and groups visual aspects and works of art, and behaviors such as comprehension, analysis, and evaluation, which are generally assessed by observation of verbal behavior. In other words, those behaviors which are preverbal and preproduction in nature are considered useful for assessing perception, and the more complex behaviors such as production and analysis, while relying on perception but encompassing other behavioral aspects, are assessed through language or a work of art which has been produced.

Visual perception is possible in part because discriminations are made between and among qualities. In fact it is virtually impossible to perceive a single quality isolated from other qualities. Even when total darkness or blackness is perceived, that perception is based on recalling visually what nondarkness or nonblackness is like. The fact that we can speak of the single quality of redness as if we could perceive redness independently of other qualities must be attributed to the nature of language and not perception. Language permits the conceptual isolation of qualities, but such isolation simply does not exist in perception. Therefore, perception involves only the perception of relationships—of one color to another, of one object as differentiated from others, and of one expressive content as distinguished from other expressive contents.

It seems useful to categorize the types of relations one might perceive in art. For example, perception may be of the relationship between and among aspects such as color in a single work of art; between and among relationships of aspects such as composition and shapes of two works of art; or among relationships of aspects of three or more works of art. Thus, three useful categories of visual aesthetic perception are relations *Within a work* (*A*.1), relations *Between works* (*A*.2), and relations *Among works* (*A*.3).

Knowledge (B.0) *Knowledge* encompasses the behaviors of remembering, recalling, and recognizing those things which were present during an original learning situation, and in art education it is considered to be an almost entirely verbal behavior, since the visual aspects of recalling, remembering, and recognizing are dealt with under perceptual behavior. The knowledge behaviors which, when related to the content of art, form objectives for art education are knowledge of *Terminology, Facts, Conventions, Trends and sequences, Classifications and categories, Criteria, Methodology,* and *Theories.*

Knowledge of terminology in art (*B*.1) refers to the ability to remember definitions of the terms which distinguish art from other disciplines. Knowledge of these terms is basic to many aspects of further inquiry and production in art.

Examples of knowledge of terminology are recalling definitions of such terms as "color intensity and saturation," "concentric composition," "closure," "bas relief," "fresco," "pastel," "etching," and "mobile."

Knowledge of facts (*B*.2) involves remembering dates in art history, names of artists, works of art and their locations, and information regarding books, museums, collections, and other sources of information about art.

Knowledge of conventions (*B*.3) includes familiarity with the meaning of conventional signs, symbols, and allegories—knowing, for example, that in Christian art the wings on angels show that they are heavenly messengers, that the lily represents purity, and that the ape represents crassness or brutishness. Also included under knowledge of conventions is recall or recognition of the objects, themes, and events which artists traditionally have drawn upon for the subject matter of their works of art.

Knowledge of trends and sequences in art (*B*.4) refers to such things as the recalling of relationships among periods and movements in the history of art. It is knowing that impressionism preceded cubism and surrealism, and that the pop and minimal-art movements followed abstract expressionism.

Knowledge of classifications and categories (*B*.5) refers to recognizing the works of art of major styles, periods, and geographical regions. It also includes a familiarity with the different forms of the visual arts such as painting, prints, films, and architecture and what distinguishes these forms from one another.

Knowledge of criteria (*B*.6) refers primarily to the standards by which the aesthetic quality of works of art might be evaluated and to the standards by which the function of aesthetic objects such as pottery and architecture might be assessed.

Knowledge of methodology in art (*B*.7) refers to such things as being able to recall the procedure for coiling a clay pot, producing a contour drawing, printing a woodcut, and firing a kiln. In most cases knowledge of methodology is no end in itself, but it is merely a necessary intermediate step to have acquired before actually performing the process.

Knowledge of theories in art (*B*.8) refers to understanding philosophies of art such as organicism, emotionalism, and formism; and to the understanding of the theories which have guided artists in the production of their work. Examples of such theories are the color theory which guided the pointillist painters and the manifesto which guided the futurist painters and sculptors.

Comprehension (C.0) The two subcategories *Translation* and *Interpretation* found under the behavior *Comprehension* in the *Taxonomy of Educational Objectives* (Bloom, 1956) are the basis for only a few objectives in art education. Nevertheless, these behaviors do have a place in art. Comprehension in art generally refers to responses to works of art which indicate that an individual has an understanding of the literal, symbolic, or allegorical messages of works of art. The demonstration of such an understanding is generally the ability to describe these messages.

Translation (*C*.1) is dependent upon a knowledge of the objects, themes, events, symbols, and allegories which are found in works of art. It involves verbal descriptions of these visual subject-matter elements, usually as isolated bits of meaning. Occasionally, however, the meanings that these subject-matter aspects impart may be determined by the context in which they appear. The essential element of this behavior is that the individual is able to translate meanings from a visual to a verbal form.

Interpretation (*C*.2) involves dealing with a work of art as a configuration of meanings whose comprehension may require a recording of the ideas into a new configuration. To interpret a work of art the viewer must first translate the major subject-matter aspects to a verbal form. He then goes beyond a part-by-part rendering to comprehend the relationships between the various parts, and then he reorders, rearranges, and describes the meaning of the work's subject matter. Interpretation also includes the determining of which aspects are essential to the meaning and which are less essential or irrelevant. Whereas translation is generally concerned with an accounting of the obvious literal and conventional subject matter, interpretation involves a determination of the unconventional and less transparent aspects of subject matter in the context of the work.

Analysis (D.0) In art, *Analysis* usually refers to a dissection of the work of art into its constituent parts, a detection of the relationships among the parts, and a determination of the relationships of the parts to the whole. As with comprehension, analytical behavior is generally determined through an assessment of verbal descriptions. However, unlike comprehension, which is concerned almost entirely with understanding the meanings of the subject-matter aspects of works of art, analysis emphasizes the determination of *how* the work means by explicating the visual structure, unique character of the art form, media, style, and modal aspects, as well as the subject matter.

Although analysis may be an end in itself, it is more often used as a means for enhancing one's aesthetic experiences with a work of art and also as a prelude to an evaluation of the work. Three levels of analysis are considered: analysis of *Elements*, of *Relationships of parts*, and of the *Relationship of the parts to the whole*. The levels apply from the analysis of a single work to the analysis of a number of works of art.

Analysis of elements (*D*.1) is considered to be an item-by-item accounting of the aspects of a work of art. Some aspects are obvious and are easily recognized and classified, while others, such as subtle aspects of compositions, are often difficult to detect. Yet many aspects, although not easily recognized, are of primary importance in determining the nature of the work, and a reasonably full aesthetic experience is not possible until they are determined.

It was said earlier, but merits mentioning again, that it is only through the convention of language that parts of a visual structure can be isolated from one another. Although only relationships can be perceived, through language we can reduce qualities to individual, independent concepts. Analysis of elements does just that.

Analysis of the relationships of parts (*D*.2) involves the determining of some of the major connections among aspects of works of art. It includes such things as assessing how one color affects another; determining if objects stand out from their backgrounds; seeing if there are subtle, gradual, soft, sharp, or sudden contrasts of light and dark; and determining if the color of the objects in a painting correspond to the degree of naturalness with which the objects are drawn.

Analysis of the relationship of the parts to the whole (*D*.3) is the third level of analysis. It refers to reaching a conclusion about the expressive content of the work and explicating how the various aspects and their relationships fuse to form the expressive content. Determining expressive content requires a synthesizing as well as an explication of how the parts contribute to the whole.

Relating parts to the whole is a creative affair where the analyzer seeks out characters and relations which enrich his own aesthetic experience and the aesthetic experiences of others. Analysis of total character is analogous to the descriptive portion of art criticism and, although difficult to achieve, is one of the most important behaviors sought after in art education.

Evaluation (E.0) *Evaluation* in art education is primarily concerned with making reasoned critical judgments about the aesthetic quality and values of works of art. The making of such judgments is generally considered to depend upon an intimate knowledge of the field of art, sensitive perception, analysis, and the application of reliable aesthetic criteria. Although it is possible to apply reliable aesthetic criteria without being conscious of those being used, many would hold that there are distinct advantages to having a knowledge of the range of criteria which might be used in making a critical judgment, since knowing alternative criteria frees one to apply various standards rationally as they apply to the aesthetic situation.

There are numerous criteria for making judgments; however, only a few are considered adequate for the making of aesthetic evaluations. Pepper (1945) outlined four classes of criteria which he considers inadequate for aesthetic evaluations. They are criteria which owe their justification to authority, dogma, and supernatural revelation; criteria which appeal to common-sense ideas such as symmetry, neatness, simplicity, and intrinsic appeal; criteria from animistic sources and fundamentalist beliefs; and criteria derived from mystic sources. In short, he rejected anything which rested on an a priori claim of self-evidence, uncorroborated authority, and dogma.

Pepper holds that there are four adequate criteria, all based on theoretically sound world views, which form the basis for adequate judgment in art: the degree of internal relatedness and coherence within the work of art; the fusion and vividness of one's experiences with the work of art; the degree to which the work of art represents a norm, has been true to intrinsic demands of artistic media and forming processes, and reflects the expression of a culture; and the degree of aesthetic pleasure or pain generated within an individual by the work of art. These bases for criticism in the arts are broad, flexible, and widely applicable. They combine theoretical, formal, and empirical criteria in order to assess the essences, pleasures, fusions, and unities of works of art. As they are grounded in compatible world views, they are mutually compatible, and whether they are applied individually or together, they are the basis for systematic and comprehensive aesthetic evaluations and are termed in the Table of Specifications *Systemic evaluations* (*E*.2; P. Smith, 1966).

Of course there are criteria for evaluation of art in addition to systemic criteria. *Empirical evaluations* (*E*.1) are made on the basis of how well something serves the function for which it was intended. For example, a tea cup is evaluated on the basis not only of its aesthetic quality but also of how comfortably the handle fits one's fingers and how readily one can drink from it. Houses, such as some designed by Frank Lloyd Wright, can be judged to be of reasonably high aesthetic merit and also be judged to be unfunctional because of passageways which are too low to walk through without bending over and room layouts which ignore living patterns. A television commercial may be judged for its aesthetic quality but also on whether it sells what it advertises. Such evaluations are extra-aesthetic, yet they are important parts of evaluation of works of art which contain functional as well as aesthetic features.

Appreciation (F.0) It has been suggested that *Appreciation*, one of the most commonly voiced art education objectives, ceases to be listed as an objective because of the ambiguous way in which the term has been used in art education (Logan, 1955). However, appreciative behaviors persist as objectives for art education because there are concepts behind the term which are considered vitally important. Appreciation is considered to be a kind of connoisseurship—a sensitive appraisal, enjoyment, valuing, and feeling for what a work of art has to offer and for the contribution of the artist to society.

Connoisseurship implies that not every work of art will be appreciated, but only those works considered to have aesthetic merit which is determined through evaluation. Therefore, a sensitive aesthetic analysis and evaluation based on reasonable criteria is considered a prerequisite to the desirable forms of appreciation. It is well known, however, that aspects of appreciation such as enjoyment, feeling, and valuing occur with works of art considered to be aesthetically inferior. Jean Renoir, son of the French impressionist painter, tells how as a child he was given a present which touched him deeply. It was a very ugly plate, but he commented later, "I do not believe that children, even those grown in the midst of Renoir canvases, are easily shocked by ugliness" (quoted in Lark-Horovitz, Lewis, & Luca, 1967, p. 159).

Art appreciation has occasionally been taught through the presentation of a group of works of art which were considered by the teacher or some other authority as being worthy of appreciation. Most art teachers, however, are quite willing to accept whatever their students appreciate as long as the appreciation is based on prior aesthetic appraisal.

In addition to aspects of sensitive perception and evaluation dealt with in previous behaviors, art appreciation has the additional components *Valuing, Empathizing,* and *Feeling.*

Valuing (*F*.1) is considered to be high esteem for what has been judged to have aesthetic merit, the desire for aesthetic experiences, the cherishing of art objects, and respecting the role of art in society.

Empathizing (*F*.2) is a matter of indicating understanding, sympathy, and tolerance for the endeavors of those who work in the arts. Empathy could be directed toward artists, architects, art critics, art historians, and art teachers. In a sense it is to know what it would be like "to be in their shoes." Empathy does not necessarily imply approval, except, perhaps, an approval of the right of individuals to individuality.

Feeling (*F*.3), in terms of behavior in art education, refers to a "stirred up" or deeply sensed condition within the individual resulting from experiences with works of art or other phenomena capable of eliciting aesthetic response. Synonyms for feeling are pleasure, satisfaction, amusement, delight, thrill, ecstasy, bliss, disdain, revulsion, and tedium. The view is held that students ought to respond in active and passionate ways toward works of art which call out for such responses, but, as with each of the areas of appreciation, it is expected that the feelings be based on sensitive perception and evaluation.

Production (G.0) By far the most common group of objectives in art education concerns the making of works of art. *Production* refers to the putting together of artistic aspects to form a work of art. The highest level of production generally involves an ordering of formal aspects and subject-matter aspects into a whole which is firmly integrated, fused, and meaningful. At a lower level, production involves the manipulation of these same elements into a form which is less fused and integrated. Whether the final work is integrated or not, a work has been produced, and as any teacher of art knows, the achievement of a rationally controlled integrated work by the art student often results only after the production of a great number of unintegrated works.

For some art educators (Lowenfeld, 1959) the quality of the end product is of secondary concern, being overshadowed by the benefits to creativity, sensitivity, and personality development which accrue to the student during the *process* of producing a work of art. Other art educators agree with Wachowiak and Ramsay (1965) that the final product is of utmost importance and that the task of the art teacher is to direct the production of the student carefully in order to ensure the aesthetic quality of the works of art produced by the student.

Whether the process or the product is considered to be the objective of studio activities in art education, the student is involved in the production of works of art, and that production contains two major behavioral components considered important by art educators, *Skill* and *Creativity.*

Skill (*G*.1) refers primarily to the expertise with which the student controls art media and tools and his accuracy in depicting objects in a realistic manner. Another term for skill is craftsmanship—the technical skills of forming the physical materials of art in order to make the most of them.

There has been some attempt to discount the importance of skill in art education, but the role which skill has held traditionally and the continued emphasis on the technical aspects of art production in popular art educational periodicals indicate that it will continue to be regarded as a major objective in the field.

Creativity (*G*.2) has almost as many definitions as proponents. Nevertheless, Eisner (1966b) has gone far in specifying the meaning of creative behavior in the production of works of art. He has constructed a typology of creative behavior which is based on the various qualities and characteristics that historically have been considered creative in the visual arts. According to Eisner, analysis of children's art work, as well as that of adults, reveals that their qualities can be classified into a system of types. Some artists make their creative contribution through the treatment of form, and others through the selection and combination of subject matter; some through novel treatment of the conventional, and others through the creation of something utterly new. For Eisner the form and the subject matter of works of art constitute the loci within which creativity can be displayed. The four types of creative behavior are boundary pushing, inventing, boundary breaking, and aesthetic organizing. Boundary pushing is defined as the extension of ordinary subject matter and common forms through novel combinations or through novel elaboration. Inventing refers to the production of new subject matter or forms. Boundary breaking is defined as the production of new subject matter and utterly new forms through the creation of the completely new or through the revision of premises upon which the old subject matter or forms were developed. Aesthetic organizing refers to the ordering of specific forms so as to constitute a coherent, harmonious, and balanced whole.

The production of works of art need not contain the creativity dimension as evidenced by some highly prized art works which are direct copies of other works. However, at the present time an overwhelming majority of art educators maintain that the creative dimension is of paramount importance in the production of works of art.

Illustrations of the structure of selected art programs

This section relates the content and behaviors presented in Table 17-1, the Table of Specifications (pages 502–503), to the structure of units within specific art programs. This will be accomplished by describing the content of units of instruction from the programs and by presenting the structure of the units in a modified table of specifications.

Even the least complex art units generally contain objectives relating to several areas of content and behavior. In fact, one of the unique characteristics of art instruction is that several, and occasionally even most, of the aspects of content listed in the Table of Specifications are included in a single unit. For example, a unit may have the *Production* (G.0) of a tempera painting as the objective with *Media, tools, and forming processes* and *Art form* (1.0 and 4.0) the major content areas. The painting would have a composition and perhaps subject matter so that *Visual structure* and *Subject matter* (2.0 and 3.0) would be minor content areas. The teacher may use reproductions of paintings as examples illustrating problems in painting so that *Cultural context* (5.0) also becomes an aspect of content. In addition to the primary behavior, *Production*, it is conceivable that the behaviors *Analysis* and *Evaluation* (D.0 and E.0) might be directed toward the reproductions or toward the students' own works. Thus, a seemingly simple unit might contain objectives composed of several aspects of content and artistic behaviors. Conversely, other units may have objectives containing only one or two aspects of content and behavior.

An analysis of the structure of units within art programs explicates major and minor objectives as aspects of the programs which assist in achieving the objectives. Also indicated are isolated aspects which do not contribute to the acquisition of the objectives within the structure of a unit. Once the objectives have been identified it is possible to determine which (if any) of the objectives are prerequisite to the acquiring of more complex objectives within the unit. When the structure of the unit is revealed, the constructing and planning of testing items and evaluating strategies can proceed.

The structure of units from five art programs ranging from fourth- to twelfth-grade levels containing a range of art education objectives are illustrated.

A unit on drawing heads and hands[2] In a unit on drawing heads and hands in interesting positions, the primary objective is the production of drawings in which technique, expressive use of line, and careful placement of aspects within the composition convey particular moods. Before

[2] This unit is taken from *Major Art in the Academic High Schools* (Board of Education of the City of New York, 1961, p. 22).

TABLE 17-2 TABLE OF SPECIFICATIONS FOR A UNIT ON DRAWING HEADS AND HANDS IN INTERESTING POSITIONS

CONTENT	BEHAVIORS		
	B.2 Facts	*G.1 Skill*	*G.2 Creativity*
1.4 Technique	Rapid sketching intensifies the visual image	Ability to sketch rapidly in various ways	
2.1 Sensory qualities	Expressive use of line contributes to the character of drawings		
2.2 Composition 2.3 Modal character	Intensified image is gained through arrangement of images within boundaries of paper		
3.1 Objects	Heads and hands when represented in a variety of relationships convey moods		
4.5 Drawings			Production of drawings of heads and hands in which the mood is conveyed through sketching technique, expressive use of line, and placement of images

students begin their own drawings, several facts are presented which indicate how drawing technique, line quality, and composition contribute to the mood or feeling of drawings. The acquisition of this knowledge by the students does not ensure that they will consequently be able to produce drawings which use these factors successfully, but at least they are presented with some factors which they might attempt to use in their drawings. The major behavior of the unit is *Production* (*G*), and the major aspects of content are *Modal character*, *Objects*, and *Drawings* (2.3, 3.1, and 4.5). Acquisition of knowledge plays a minor role in the unit, and choice of media is left to the student. The unit's structure is shown in Table 17-2, Table of Specifications for a Unit on Drawing Heads and Hands in Interesting Positions.

A unit on space sculpture[3] In this unit for high school students, "space sculpture" is defined as a three-dimensional work of art in which negative space is a definite part of the design. The objective of the unit is the production of a space sculpture from an assortment of wood, wire, cardboard,

[3] The unit is taken from *ART Senior High*, the 1968 high school art guide for the Davenport, Iowa, Community Schools (1968, pp. 67–69).

string, and other materials. The sculpture is to show a concern for negative space as a part of the design. In addition to the production objective the students are to become familiar with the work of contemporary sculptors who utilize space in their pieces.

The unit contains only casual relationships between the knowledge and production components. The production of a space sculpture and knowledge about compositions of space sculptures could exist as separate elements. From the outline of the unit it is not clear whether the information about compositions of various space sculptures is to be presented before or after the students work on their own productions. If the information is presented before the students begin their own works, this knowledge may affect the outcome. However, the students could produce their own works without a knowledge of the compositions of other sculptures. Apparently there is to be no specific instruction in media and forming processes since the students are encouraged to develop their own methods. Therefore, skill and knowledge of forming processes are not considered prerequisite to the actual production of the students' works. There seems to be no necessary connection between the knowledge about space in sculptures and the production of the students' sculptures. The unit's structure is shown in Table 17-3, Table of Specifications for a Unit on Space Sculpture.

A unit for enhancing aesthetic experiencing[4] This unit has as its central purpose the transforming of experiences with drawings, paintings, sculptures, and other works of art into aesthetic experiences. Aesthetic experiences are defined as those which are loaded with significant

[4] The basic program was developed for high school use, but has also been adapted for use in junior high and elementary school art classes. It is part of the art curriculum of the University of Iowa Experimental School. The unit was developed by Hugh Stumbo (1968).

TABLE 17-3 TABLE OF SPECIFICATIONS FOR A UNIT ON SPACE SCULPTURE

	BEHAVIORS			
CONTENT	*B.1 Terminology*	*B.2 Facts*	*G.1 Skill*	*G.2 Creativity*
1.1 Media 1.2 Tools 1.3 Processes			Selecting, cutting, joining, and forming cardboard, wood, wire, and string using saw, glue, hammer and nails, and screws	
2.2 Composition	Negative space, positive space, direction of movement, planes, overlapping	Information about the composition of sculptures by Bertoia, Calder, de Rivera, Gabo, Gordon, and Goto		
4.2 Sculpture				Making a space sculpture which shows concern for negative spaces

detail, thus having an intensity and consistency of character. Aesthetic experiences are contrasted to more ordinary experiences in which various insignificant details do not fund into or fuse to form a unified whole containing a character which can be identified and described. The basic concept of the aesthetic experience corresponds closely with the concept presented by Dewey in *Art as Experience* (1934).

In behavioral terms, it is expected that the students will produce works of art in which it is obvious that they have manipulated the levels of meaning explicated during the program and that they will verbally analyze and evaluate their experiences with works of art (their own as well as the works of artists) in terms of the levels of meaning.

The program contains three basic characteristics. First, the study and analysis of works of art are the bases for each lesson. The works studied are those produced by the student and by the artists Franz Kline, Robert Motherwell, and Goya. Second, each work of art contains an element of social commentary such as violence, tragedy, or alienation. Third, the information necessary to the day-to-day work is prepared and arranged in such a way as to allow students to proceed as rapidly as the student and teacher deem appropriate. In addition to producing works of art the students read the writings of art critics on the works of the artist they are studying, read papers and articles commenting on current social events, and view films and videotapes having social content.

The unit begins with the presentation of a method for enhancing aesthetic experiences with works of art. The basic procedure for enriching these experiences consists of three steps: (1) observe the artifact, (2) describe that observation, and (3) observe the artifact again. The first step requires an openness to experience or a freedom from preconceptions which is similar to the methodological doubt of Descartes. The description which follows the open experiencing explicates relevant connections among details. The second observation of the artifact builds on the previous observation and explication. The basic process may be repeated over and over again to heighten the aesthetic experience. The most important aspect of this procedure is that the teacher uses the method to analyze the students' work. The students then use the method to explicate the work of artists as well as their own work.

The major concepts relating to levels of meaning in works of art include (1) *expressive meaning*, referring to the sensory elements of color, texture, line, shape, composition or structure, and the moods, feelings, and emotions suggested by the organization of basic elements; (2) *ordinary meaning*, referring to objects and events viewed literally rather than symbolically; (3) *allegorical meaning*, referring to the conjoining of expressive meaning and ordinary meaning aspects which are viewed symbolically; and (4) *significant meaning*, referring to the total quality of the work. In the program expressive meaning is illustrated through Franz Kline's painting "Two Horizontals" and Robert Motherwell's painting "Golden Fleece," ordinary meaning through Goya's print "Tampoco," and allegorical meaning through Goya's print "The Sleep of Reason." With the introduction of each new aspect of meaning the students receive instruction in studio production methods in order to produce their own works which contain particular meanings. After having their works analyzed by their instructor, the students in turn analyze and evaluate the artists' works and their own works. The structure of the unit is outlined in Table 17-4, Table of Specifications for a Unit on Aesthetic Experiencing.

A unit on drypoint etching[5] This unit for seventh- and eighth-grade students on drypoint etching on acetate is typical of many units in art which have production of a work of art as the central objective. The unit begins with an explanation of the procedures for (1) etching on acetate, (2) moistening paper, (3) inking the plate and rubbing off excess ink, and (4) printing the plate. The students follow these methods in producing their own prints. There is a direct relation between the acquisition of knowledge of *Methodology* (*B*.7) and the *Production* (*G*.0) of a print.

[5] The unit is taken from the plans of Jack Lerman, Haven Junior High School, Evanston, Illinois, as reproduced in Vincent Lanier's *Teaching Secondary Art* (1964, p. 149).

TABLE 17-4 TABLE OF SPECIFICATIONS FOR A UNIT ON AESTHETIC EXPERIENCING

	BEHAVIORS				
CONTENT	*B.1 Terminology*	*B.7 Methodology*	*D.2 Relationships of Parts*	*D.3 Relationship of Parts to Whole*	*G.2 Creativity*
1.1 Media 1.3 Processes		Tempera painting, watercolor painting, photocollage, transfer printing			
2.3 Modal character	Expressive meaning		Kline's "Two Horizontals," Motherwell's "Golden Fleece," student's watercolor and tempera paintings	Kline's "Two Horizontals," Motherwell's "Golden Fleece," student's watercolor and tempera paintings	
3.1 Objects 3.2 Symbols 3.3 Expressive content	Ordinary meaning, allegorical meaning, significant meaning		Goya's "Tampoco" and "Sleep of Reason" and student's photocollage and transfer print	Goya's "Tampoco" and "Sleep of Reason" and student's photocollage and transfer print	
4.1 Paintings 4.6 Prints 4.7 Collages					Tempera painting, watercolor painting, photocollage, transfer printing
6.1 Art theories	Aesthetic experience	Suspension of preconceptions (openness), observation, reflection, and observation			

TABLE 17-5 TABLE OF SPECIFICATIONS FOR A UNIT ON DRYPOINT ETCHING

CONTENT	BEHAVIORS *B.7 Methodology*	*G.0 Production*
1.1 Media 1.2 Tools 1.3 Processes	Etching acetate plate, moistening paper, inking plate, printing with etching press	
4.6 Prints		Completion of an acetate drypoint etching

The unit plan makes no mention of visual structure or subject matter, although the student might deal with both as he makes his print. The omission of these elements indicates the emphasis placed on *Media* and *Processes* (1.1 and 1.3). The unit's structure is presented in Table 17-5, Table of Specifications for a Unit on Drypoint Etching.

A unit on rules governing the proportion of human figures in Byzantine art[6] A unit for upper elementary grades on rules of proportion of human figures in Byzantine art has as its major objective

[6] The unit is part of the intermediate grade curriculum of the University of Iowa Experimental School (Wilson, 1966c).

TABLE 17-6 TABLE OF SPECIFICATIONS FOR A UNIT ON PROPOR

CONTENT	BEHAVIORS *B.1 Terminology*	*B.2 Facts*	*B.5 Classifications*
1.1 Media	Encaustic, egg tempera, mosaic	Byzantine artists worked in encaustic, egg tempera, mosaic, and goldleaf	
3.1 Objects	Natural proportion in human figures, unit of measure, ratio	Byzantine artists used the head as a unit of measure; adults are usually $7\frac{1}{2}$ to 8 heads high	
5.2 Date		The Byzantine era extended from A.D. 300 to 1400	
5.4 Location		The areas of Byzantine culture	
5.5 Style		Byzantine artists drew figures $8\frac{2}{3}$ heads high; heads contain three concentric circles	If figures are drawn $8\frac{2}{3}$ heads high and heads are drawn with three concentric circles, they are usually Byzantine or Byzantine-influenced
5.6 Use		Byzantines used art for learning religious concepts	
6.2 Judgment standards			

the ability to classify works of art according to whether Byzantine rules for drawing the human figure were followed (*B*.5). (Byzantine artists followed a strict set of rules which governed the height of their figures and the structure of heads.) To enable students to accomplish the desired objective, information is presented on natural proportion in human figures, units of measurement, and the rules followed by Byzantine artists. Other information which does not relate directly to the accomplishing of the major objectives is presented. For example, information is given on the media used by Byzantine artists (1.1), criteria for judging works of art (6.2), the uses to which Byzantine art was put (5.6), and other facts about the Byzantine civilization. The unit also contains assignments which require students to produce drawings and paintings following sets of rules governing proportion in human figures and to use media to gain qualities similar to those achieved by the Byzantine artists when they used goldleaf. These production activities are, however, of secondary importance and relate only indirectly to the achieving of the primary objective.

The structure of the unit shows a progression from knowledge of *Terminology*, *Facts*, and *Classifications* (*B*.1, *B*.2, and *B*.5) to *Analysis* (*D*.0) and *Production* (G.1 and G.2). This is outlined in Table 17-6, Table of Specifications for a Unit on Proportion in Byzantine Figures.

ION IN BYZANTINE FIGURES

BEHAVIORS			
B.6 Criteria	*D.0 Analysis*	*G.1 Skill*	*G.2 Creativity*
			Produce a tempera painting on a metallic surface
		Draw a human figure a specified number of heads high	
	Determine whether specific figures were drawn by Byzantine artists	Draw figures following a set of rules	
works are judged to be good by the way the parts go together and by whether the figures are drawn with natural proportion			

Illustrations of testing procedures in art education

Brent G. Wilson

This section illustrates procedures for testing and evaluating some of the major objectives of art instruction. The items will be presented behavior by behavior, beginning with *Perception* and ending with *Production*. Where possible, items dealing with a range of art content have been presented under each behavior. Because of space limitations there are, of course, many objectives for which no illustrative test items are presented. Indeed, in art education there are major objectives for which no test items have ever been written, even when the task of writing such items would seem easily accomplished. In some instances where no test items were located for important objectives, the author has taken the liberty of suggesting procedures which might be used to test those objectives.

EDUCATION THROUGH VISION

*Name:*____
Last First Middle

*Student identification number:*________________________ | 1 | 2 |

1 A B C D	2 A B C D	3 A B C D	4 A B C D	5 A B C D
6 A B C D	7 A B C D	8 A B C D	9 A B C D	10 A B C D
11 A B C D	12 A B C D	13 A B C D	14 A B C D	15 A B C D
16 A B C D	17 A B C D	18 A B C D	19 A B C D	20 A B C D
21 A B C D	22 A B C D	23 A B C D	24 A B C D	25 A B C D
26 A B C D	27 A B C D	28 A B C D	29 A B C D	30 A B C D

FIGURE 17-1 Education through Vision Test answer sheet. [D. A. Trismen. Evaluation of the Education through Vision curriculum, phase I. (Proj. No. 7-0049) Princeton, N.J.: U.S. Office of Education, Bureau of Research, 1968. P. 37.]

Testing for perception (A.0)

Even though perception traditionally has been the basis for many objectives in art education, there have been surprisingly few tests developed to measure perceptual achievement. Most of the tests in the aesthetic perceptual realm have been developed to measure innate aesthetic perceptual aptitudes. Of these instruments the Meier Art Tests (Meier, 1940, 1963) are perhaps the best known and most widely used. Meier's 1963 test, II: Aesthetic Perception, has its premise in the ability of artists to observe phenomena with greater adequacy than people lacking gifts or training in art. Meier held further that the aesthetically sensitive person will sense the aesthetic character of a completed work of art more readily. He constructed his test by selecting "masterpieces" which were reproduced along with systematic distortions of the same work of art. The examinee's task is to order the reproductions from best to poorest. The reproduction closest to the original is considered to be the most successfully organized, and the reproduction farthest from the original is considered the poorest. Meier's studies indicate that there are differences in scores among groups with differing amounts of art training, raising the question of whether his tests measure achievement or whether the scores on his test indicate that those with more aptitude sought more training. It is most important to note that Meier did not intend his tests to measure aesthetic perceptual achievement; yet his Art Judgment Test has been used as the criterion measure in experimental studies (Brandon, 1960). If Meier's tests actually measure aptitude, it is no wonder that findings of studies using his test as a criterion indicate no significant differences among treatments. The practice of using art aptitude tests as criterion measures in art is analogous to using IQ tests to measure achievement in mathematics.

Based on the empirical evidence presently available, it is impossible to determine just how amenable visual aesthetic perception is to alteration. Nevertheless, art teachers intuitively hold that the behavior is most malleable. One test which has attempted to measure visual aesthetic perceptual achievement is the Education through Vision End of Course Achievement Test (Trismen, 1968, pp. 47–50). The test contains a variety of perceptual questions dealing with such things as color, texture, composition, expressive content, symbolism, and visual inconsistencies. Although the test does not deal with such things as line, media, and forming processes, these and other aspects could easily be presented using the test format.

In the test four images are projected on a screen and the students are asked to make various types of discriminations among the sets of four images. Therefore, the items are considered to assess behavior A.3, *Perception of relations among works of art.*

The Education through Vision Test is important not only because it attempts to measure perceptual achievement, but also because of the techniques employed in the test. Two of the important testing techniques are that the examinees do not have to read the questions since they are read aloud via tape recorder and that to record their answer they are simply required to make an X on a square which corresponds with the visual images projected before them. Figure 17-1 illustrates the answer sheet.

As with most existing tests of visual perception, the instrument contains aspects of knowledge as well as perception. For example, before the examinee can answer the question in item 4 below correctly, he must know the meaning of the term "intense" as it applies to color. Each of the other test questions has a strong knowledge component along with the perceptual component.

Items 1, 2, and 3 are presented with the visual images which accompany the questions on the Education through Vision Test. Other test items from this source are presented without the accompanying visual images.

DIRECTIONS: Your answer sheet [Fig. 17-1] consists of thirty squares, each divided into four equal sections which are labeled A, B, C, and D. The number of the test question to which each square corresponds appears at the upper left hand corner of each square. For each of the questions on this test mark an "X" in the section of the appropriate square which corresponds to the best answer. [The directions and questions were tape recorded and the visual material was presented through 35mm colored slides. Each question was asked twice.]

A.3-2.3

1. Which of these groups of trademarks [in Fig. 17-2] most effectively conveys a feeling of strength and dependability?

FIGURE 17-2 Groups of trademarks used with the Education through Vision Test. [D. A. Trismen. Evaluation of the Education through Vision curriculum, phase I. (Proj. No. 7-0049) Princeton, N.J.: U.S. Office of Education, Bureau of Research, 1968.]

A.3-2.2

2. Which of these photographs [in Fig. 17-3] is an example of 45-degree sidelighting?

DIRECTIONS: Three of these panels [in Fig. 17-4] contain exact reproductions of original paintings. One panel contains a painting in which some prominent part of the original painting has been distorted or changed, resulting in a faulty picture composition.

3. Which of these panels contains a painting in which the composition has been altered?

(Trismen, 1968, pp. 48, 50, items 12, 15, 30.)

The following questions use essentially the same directions as given for the questions in items 1 and 2.

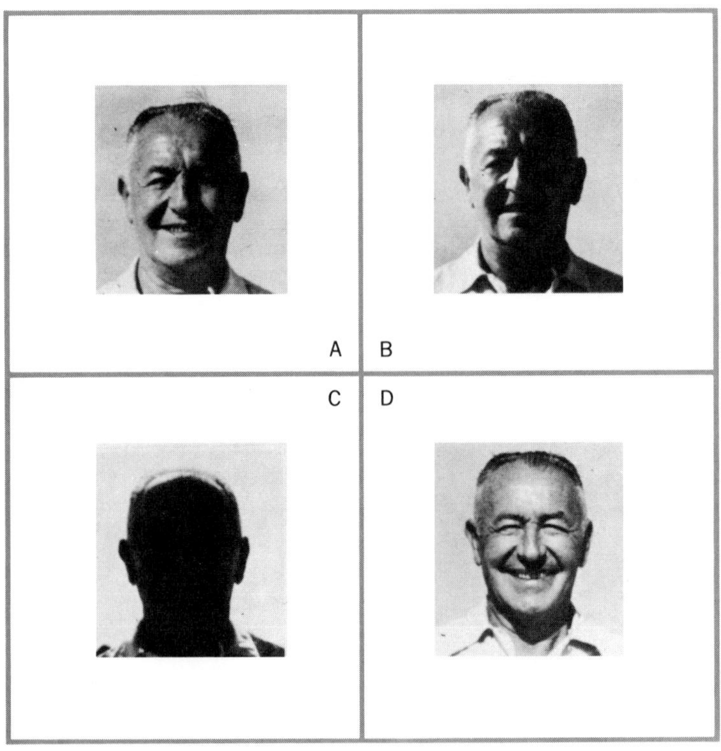

FIGURE 17-3 Photographs used with the Education through Vision Test answer sheet. [D. A. Trismen. Evaluation of the Education through Vision curriculum, phase I. (Proj. No. 7-0049) Princeton, N.J.: U.S. Office of Education, Bureau of Research, 1968.]

A.3-2.1

4. In each of these panels a different hue is superimposed on the same blue background. In what panel does the blue background seem most intense?
5. Which of these panels shows the three primary colors of pigment?
6. Which of these blocks seems to be illuminated by the light of the setting sun?

A.3-2.2

7. In each of these panels is a detail of a photograph. Which of the photographs was taken at a distance furthest from the subject being photographed?

A.3-1.4, A.3-2.1

8. Which of these details is NOT an example of paint applied to a surface to achieve a textural effect?

A.3-2.1, A.3-3.1

9. In which panel is there a clearly inconsistent color in the shadow field?

A.3-2.2, A.3-3.1

10. The figure to the right of each building represents an adult of average height. In which of these views is the observer about 45 feet above the ground?

A.3-2.1

11. Each of these four panels represents a statement about mixing equal proportions of two pigments. Which of these panels is an incorrect statement?
12. If you wanted to explain the form of a cube to a man who had never seen one, which of these drawings would best illustrate your explanation?

(Trismen, 1968, pp. 47–50, items 2, 8, 9, 13, 14, 16, 26–28.)

The two following questions on color had different directions.

DIRECTIONS: In the next question you will first be shown a color arrangement and then be shown a slide with four color arrangements. One of the four arrangements will be identical to the one you have just seen; you will be asked to identify this arrangement.

A.3-2.1, A.3-2.2

13. Which of these color arrangements is identical to the one you have just seen?

DIRECTIONS: In the next question you will first be shown a painting and then be shown a slide with four color designs. One of the color designs will use the same combinations of colors as the painting you have just seen. You will be asked to identify which of the color designs uses colors identical to those in the painting. Pay careful attention to the colors in each painting and to the color designs. You will see each slide only once.

14. Which of these designs uses the same combination of colors as the painting you have just seen?

(Trismen, 1968, pp. 47, 49, items 3, 19.)

The humanities section of the University of Chicago General Examination (University of Chicago Examiners' Office) contains questions with a strong perceptual component although knowledge of perspective is also required to answer the questions correctly. The test presents four reproductions of paintings by artists such as Jawlensky, Giotto, El Greco, and Perugino. The examinees are to read a series of statements and determine to which painting the statement most appropriately applies. The procedures used in the test are similar to those in the Education through Vision Test as the examinees are required to make perceptual discriminations among works of art.

The questions are written at an advanced level; however, the form followed would be most useful for less advanced students if the concepts were dealt with at a simpler level.

The questions are presented here without the accompanying visual material.

DIRECTIONS: The next items refer to the four pictures reproduced in the "Picture Supplement." *Blacken* the answer space corresponding to the letter of the picture to which each statement *best* applies (A for I; B for II; C for III; D for IV), and *blacken* the answer space E if the statement applies to *none*.

A.3-2.2

15. This composition makes use of symmetry and linear perspective.

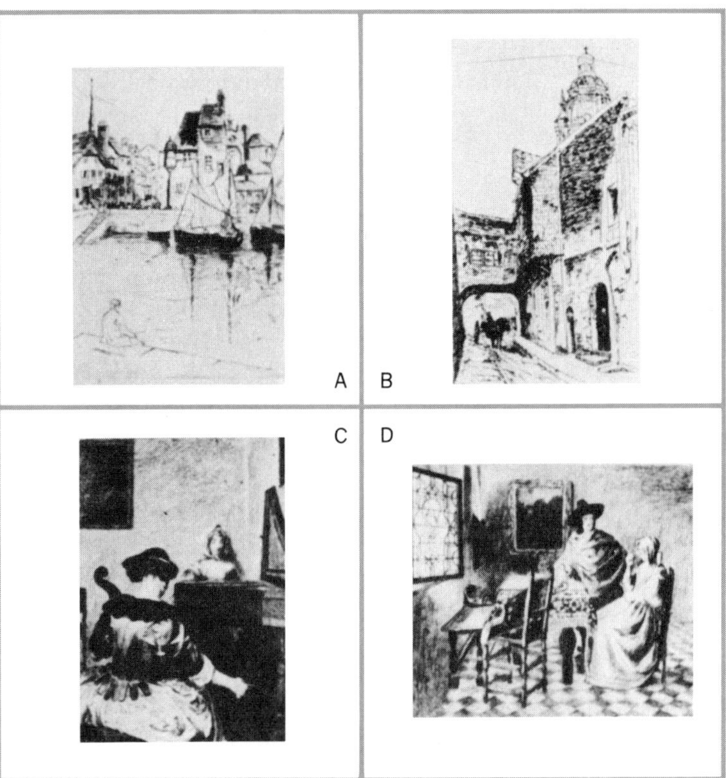

FIGURE 17-4 Painting reproductions used with the Education through Vision Test. [D. A. Trismen. Evaluation of the Education through Vision curriculum, phase I. (Proj. No. 7-0049) Princeton, N.J.: U.S. Office of Education, Bureau of Research, 1968.]

A.3-2.2, B.3-2.2

16. This composition betrays some ignorance of the laws of linear perspective.

A.3-2.1, A.3-2.2

17. The center of interest in this composition is placed near the bottom of the picture and is counterbalanced by a strong light and dark pattern in the upper part of the picture.

A.3-2.2, A.3-3.1

18. Distortion is used to accentuate the action and unify the design.

19. Architecture is the principal interest and the figures are subordinated to it.

(University of Chicago Examiners' Office.)

Dorthea Davis (1968) has developed a way of assessing the ability to perceive the compositional structure of a two-dimensional work of art. Her procedure is related to the diagrams art historians have used (Gardner, 1948) to indicate the formal compositions of paintings. The Davis instrument is intended for high school students, although it could be adapted for students of junior high school age and perhaps even for intermediate grade elementary school students if the works used contained fairly obvious compositional features. The questions in the instrument asked students to diagram such things as the light, middle, and dark value patterns; directional movements; planes; linear perspective lines; and volumes in reproductions of paintings. The test assesses category A.1, *Perception of relations within a single work of art.*

A.1-2.2

20. DIRECTIONS: Study the reproduction of Fra Filippo Lippi's "Madonna and Child" [Fig. 17-5*a*] and then in the box to the right make a line diagram showing the *two* major circular forms and the *two* major triangular forms of the painting's composition.

(Davis, 1968, item 4.)

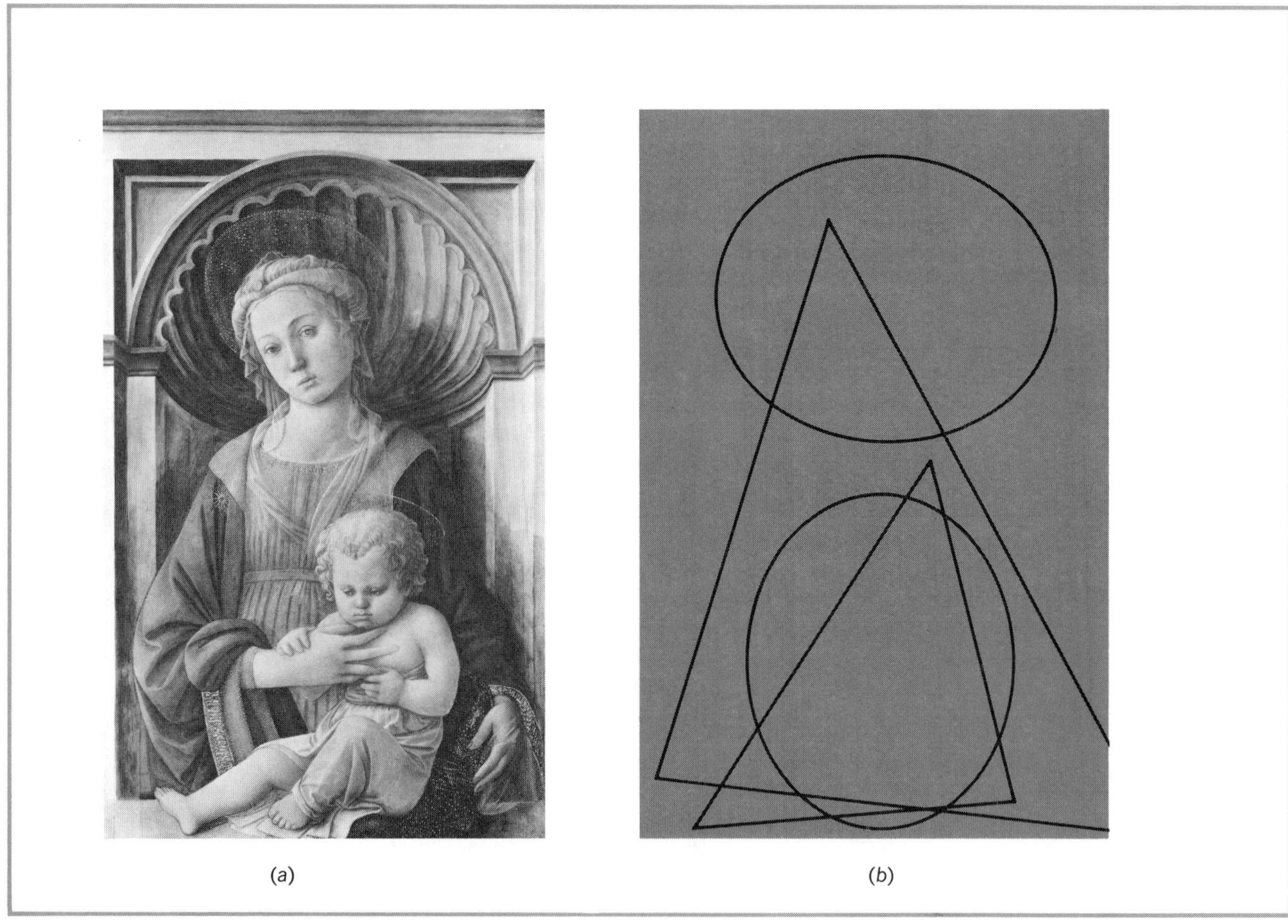

FIGURE 17-5 (*a*) Fra Filippo Lippi's "Madonna and Child" (National Gallery of Art, Washington, D.C., Samuel H. Kress Collection); (*b*) scoring guide for Lippi's composition.

The diagram is scored by giving a point for each shape which is diagramed correctly. The illustration in Fig. 17-5*b* shows a diagram which would receive four points.

A means of determining how successfully individuals remember the positions, colors, and shapes in relatively uncomplex paintings has been developed by Leonard Schoepp (1968). The procedure is to have examinees study a reproduction of a painting by Youngerman. After the painting has been observed it is removed and the examinee is given a group of shapes. The shapes correspond to those of the painting, but every shape of the painting has been reproduced in each color in the painting. The examinee's task is to select the shapes having the same colors as those in the painting and place them in the same relationship to one another as they were in the reproduction. Scoring of the exercise is based on (1) selection of correct colors, (2) placement of each shape in a face-up position, (3) placing the shapes in proper relationships to one another, and (4) positioning the shapes correctly. One point is given for each correct decision and placement. Correct positioning of shapes is scored on a scale with four points being given for placement within one-half inch, and one less point for each one-half inch of misplacement. The illustration in Fig. 17-6*a* shows the reproduction observed by the examinees, and Fig. 17-6*b* shows the parts which the examinee assembles.

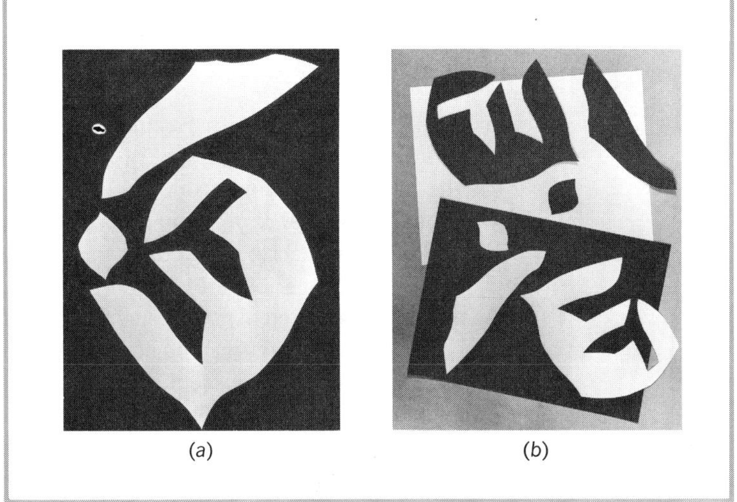

FIGURE 17-6 (*a*) Approximate composition of the Youngerman painting. (*b*) Components of the Schoepp test.

Most of the items testing perceptual behavior have dealt with aspects of visual structure, as indeed do most of the perceptual objectives in art education. The Davis and Schoepp procedures seem to point out a fruitful direction for perceptual assessment instruments because they measure perception of visual structure, yet they rely on only a minimum knowledge of terms and facts on the part of the examinee. They seem more clearly to be tests of visual perception than are the Education through Vision and University of Chicago tests.

Testing for knowledge (B.0)

Questions testing the ability to recall information are perhaps the most common assessment items in art. As with other subject-matter areas the techniques for testing knowledge follow established procedures. Knowledge of *Terminology, Facts, Criteria, Methodology,* and *Theories* lends itself to the customary multiple-choice, matching, and completion questions. The questions illustrating testing in these categories contain no unusual features and seem to require no detailed explanation. In the case of testing for methodology, although no such questions are given, it seems useful to ask questions such as "List the steps in preparing, cutting, and printing a woodcut"; "List the steps in making a copper repoussé"; or "List the procedures for centrifugal casting of silver jewelry."

It is surprising to note that in the case of knowledge of *Trends and sequences* and of *Classifications and categories*, few existing questions deal with the visual nature of art. Yet, for these categories the visual distinctions seem to be more important than the verbal distinctions which are called for on most test items. The items from the Salt Lake City Humanities Test (Salt Lake City Public Schools, 1966b, 1966c) indicate how questions based on visual qualities rather than verbal ones might be asked. The visual images are printed in the test booklet, but in classroom tests images could be displayed on tack boards or projected to serve the same purpose.

Also, when testing for trends and sequences and for classifications and categories, procedures which call for the examinee to rank or group works of art seem most useful. The examinee might be handed anywhere from two to almost any reasonable number of reproductions of works of art and be instructed to group them according to date, style, artist, period, art form, or meaning; or he might be instructed to rank them from oldest to most recent. Such tasks may be constructed to be extremely simple because of the wide differences between or among reproductions or they may be most difficult because of the subtle distinctions among the reproductions. Such procedures have the advantage of allowing the examinee to manipulate the actual reproductions in order to check visual relations. This seems to be a particular advantage in the case of young students. There is also the advantage of being able to include more items for ranking and grouping than is ordinarily possible on four- or five-part multiple-choice questions.

Questions on knowledge of Terminology (B.1)

B.1-2.2

21. Perspective refers to
    a. lightness-darkness.
    b. the color of objects.
    c. line drawings.
    d. two dimensions.
    e. the illusion of depth.

B.1-4.7

22. A collage is
    a. a type of abstract sculpture.
    b. an architect's plan.
    c. a silk screen print.
    d. a group of 2- or 3-dimensional objects applied to a surface.
    e. a large collection of art objects.

B.1-4.2

23. A bas relief is
    a. a type of lounge found in large art museums.
    b. a type of building.
    c. a Byzantine church.
    d. a type of sculpture in which the figures are raised slightly.
    e. a type of architecture in which steel and glass play an important part.

(Eisner, undated b, pp. 2, 3, items 11, 19, 20.)

Items 22 and 23 illustrate different levels of difficulty. The question in item 22 seems appropriate for intermediate grade elementary and junior high school students since it refers to an art form which is often produced by students in these grades, while item 23 refers to bas relief sculpture—information which might be studied in the visual arts portion of high school humanities courses.

Questions on knowledge of Facts (B.2)

B.2-4.2

24. An example of a 3-dimensional object is
    a. a painting.
    b. a sculpture.
    c. a lithograph.
    d. a drawing.
    e. an etching.

B.2-1.3

25. A mural painting that requires wet plaster for its surface is called a
    a. muricast.
    b. fresco.
    c. relief.
    d. lime plaster.
    e. siraglia.

B.2-5.1

26. Frank Lloyd Wright was
    a. a potter.
    b. an architect.
    c. a sculptor.
    d. a water colorist.
    e. an oil painter.

B.2-1.2, B.2-5.1

27. Michelangelo did numerous works in
    a. lithography.
    b. woodcut.
    c. mobiles.
    d. marble.
    e. pastel.

(Eisner, undated b, pp. 3, 4, 5, items 23, 25, 31, 39.)

B.2-4.8, B.2-5.5

28. The style of the main entrance of Chartres Cathedral is
    1. High Gothic
    2. Romanesque.
    3. Late Gothic.
    4. Classical.

(South, 1968, p. 93, item 11.)

Questions 24 to 27, from the Eisner test, are of a general nature. These and similar questions give a useful indication of the general level of art knowledge. The question on Chartres is much more specific, prepared for administration to high school humanities classes after they have viewed the film "Chartres Cathedral."

Questions on knowledge of Trends and sequences (B.4)

DIRECTIONS: Study the four pieces of sculpture [Fig. 17-7] and select the one correct answer for each of the following questions.

B.4-5.2

29. Which sculpture is the oldest?
    1. A
    2. B
    3. C
    4. D
30. Which sculpture was produced most recently?
    1. A
    2. B
    3. C
    4. D
31. Often a previous style of sculpture influences the style of sculpture produced at a later time. Which style of sculpture might possibly have influenced another style?
    1. A influenced C.
    2. B influenced C.
    3. B influenced D.
    4. D influenced B.
32. The ranking of the sculptures from oldest to newest is
    1. A, D, B, D.
    2. B, A, D, C.
    3. A, B, D, C.
    4. A, C, D, B.

(Salt Lake City Public Schools, 1966b, p. 3, items 2, 4, 7, 9.)

FIGURE 17-7 (*a*) "Portrait Panel of Hesy-ra" (Egyptian Museum, Cairo); (*b*) "Horsemen" from the West Frieze of the Parthenon (British Museum, London); (*c*) Jean Tinguely, "Narwa" (Museum of Modern Art, Stockholm); (*d*) Gianlorenzo Bernini, "The Ecstasy of St. Theresa" (Cornaro Chapel, Rome).

Questions on knowledge of Criteria (B.6)

B.6-6.2

33. If you looked at a work of art to decide whether it was good or not, what is the best reason you could give?
    a. The figures must be drawn in a natural way.
    b. The different parts of the art work must go together.
    c. The artist must always follow rules.
    d. The artist must not be messy.

(Wilson, 1966c, p. 2, item 16.)

The question illustrated above was written for fourth-grade students. A similar question for older students might be written:

B.6-6.2

34. Which of the following is the least adequate criterion for making aesthetic judgments?
    a. The manner in which the parts are related.
    b. The sensitivity with which the artist has used his materials.
    c. The pleasure one derives from viewing the work.
    d. The absence of a center of interest.

A question calling for knowledge of a particular basis for making aesthetic judgments might be written:

B.6-6.2

35. The organistic standard for making aesthetic judgments is based on
    a. the vividness and intensity of the work.
    b. the unity of the parts to form a whole.
    c. the presence of symmetrical forms.
    d. the degree to which the ideal is depicted.

Testing for comprehension (C.0)

There is often a narrow distinction between items which test knowledge and those which test comprehension. The items may be essentially the same for both behaviors except that the comprehension items call for more than a recall of previously presented material. Translation and interpretation are often tested by the presentation of an unfamiliar work of art.

Translating and interpreting the meanings of a work of art are acts which often results in different conclusions among individuals. Works of art have various levels of meaning, and at the symbolic and allegorical levels, there are often disagreements about meaning even among art historians and critics. Therefore, measuring comprehension of works of art may often be directed toward determining the meaning level at which an individual comprehends a work of art, as well as toward determining the correctness of the translation or interpretation.

Items on Translation of meanings of works of art (C.1) In art, translation is concerned mainly with the ability to translate isolated visual symbols of works of art into verbal terms. This item, an essay question, involves giving the meanings of conventional symbols in Christian art as well as recognizing that one of the elements, the buildings, most likely does not have a symbolic meaning. "The Annunciation" by the Master of the Barberini Panels from the National Gallery of Art is presented to the examinees along with these directions:

C.1-3.2

36. Numerous objects in this painting convey symbolic meanings which go beyond their natural meaning. Give the meaning of the (a) lily held by the angel, (b) descending dove, (c) buildings, (d) white rose in the vase, (e) wings on the angel, and (f) Virgin's blue mantle.

In the following item, two reproductions, (A) Thomas Eakins' "The Biglin Brothers Racing" and (B) Watteau's "Italian Comedians," are shown to the students, who are then tested on a list of words:

C.1-3.3

37. DIRECTIONS: Place an "A" in front of the words which best describe the ideas presented in painting A and a "B" in front of the words which best describe the ideas presented by painting B.
    __1. Physical
    __2. Artistic
    __3. Athletic
    __4. Open
    __5. Closed
    __6. Intellectual
    __7. Contained
    __8. Uncontained

Items on Interpretation of meanings of works of art (C.2) Most works of art require much more than a simple point-for-point translation of symbols from the visual to the verbal. The meaning of many works of art is highly dependent upon the interpretation of symbols within the context of the work. The following series of items were written about Vermeer's painting "A Lady Weighing Gold." Initially the painting appears to mean nothing more than the typical Dutch genre painting, a scene from everyday life; however, on closer inspection the painting appears to contain much more. The items attempt to assess not so much the correctness of an individual's interpretation of the painting as to assess the level of meaning at which the individual interprets works of art. It should be noted that interpretations dealing with the natural meaning as well as those dealing with the symbolic meaning could both be correct.

DIRECTIONS: Vermeer's painting, "A Lady Weighing Gold," contains objects with various meanings. Differing interpretations of these meanings are placed opposite one another. Mark an "X" in the blank which agrees most clearly with your own interpretation. An "X" nearest the statement indicates the strongest agreement, an "X" near the center indicates lesser agreement, and an "X" in the center blank indicates either an agreement or disagreement with both interpretations.

C.2-3.2

38. The woman stands for nothing but a woman.	__:__:__:__:__	The woman represents religious purity.
39. The scale is simply a weighing instrument.	__:__:__:__:__	The scale symbolizes a judgment.
40. The pearls are just jewelry.	__:__:__:__:__	The pearls represent worldly wealth.
41. The window allows light to enter the room.	__:__:__:__:__	The window signifies the entrance of a divine spirit.
42. There is little relation between the scales and the painting of the last judgment.	__:__:__:__:__	There is a strong relation between the scales and the painting of the last judgment.

(Messer, 1968, p. 3, item 6.)

Some of the aspects in the painting seem to have obvious symbolic connotations, such as the relation between the painting of the last judgment (a painting within the painting) and the scales, while other objects, such as the window, seem most reasonably interpreted as natural objects with no symbolic meaning. It is questionable whether any reasonable interpretation should be discounted, although in many paintings it is unusual for all aspects to have meaning at the same level. The items above give an indication of whether the individual is sensitive to different possible levels of meaning.

The most common means for assessing the ability to interpret the meaning of works of art is to ask essay questions. Such exercises may focus the interpretation by requiring the examinee to justify a given interpretation, or they may be open-ended where the examinee gives his own interpretation and justifies it on the basis of the data presented in the work.

An example of a focused question is:

C.2-3.2

43. Peter Bruegel's painting "The Cripples" has been said not only to depict deformed beggars but, seen in historic context, to have sharp social and political nuances. All the hats worn by the beggars are different. One wears a bishop's miter; another a soldier's red shako. What meaning might be attributed to the painting?

A more open item is:

C.2-3.2

44. Durer's engraving "Melencolia I" has long confounded scholars. Write your own speculations about the meaning of the work.

Interpretation of a work of art is usually a complex task and one which high school students can only begin to achieve. The task is less formidable when viewed from the point of view that there are numerous reasonable interpretations of works of art and that students can make reasoned inferences about the meaning of works of art.

Viewed in this light, high school students could deal with difficult questions such as the two presented above.

Testing for analysis (D.0)

Analysis in art is primarily concerned with the making of descriptive statements about aspects and relationships of aspects of works of art. Analysis, then, is essentially what an art critic does as he describes works of art in order to direct attention toward aspects that may otherwise remain unnoticed. Testing for analysis generally involves placing the examinee in a situation where he verbally explicates a work of art as an art critic would. Testing the ability to analyze works of art requires that the examinee be presented with unfamiliar material to eliminate the possibility of his merely recalling what he has previously learned.

Each item presented in this section calls for an open-ended verbal analysis requiring the examinee to describe rather than simply to select from multiple-choice answers, thus making the behavior similar to that performed by the art critic. However, some items, such as those illustrating analysis of elements, call for the examinee to give only short, directed, and easily evaluated answers. The more open a response is, the more difficult and time-consuming it is to score, since an analysis might move in numerous directions, thus making it difficult for the scorer to formulate predetermined evaluative criteria. It is possible to eliminate some of the scoring difficulties by specifying the aspects to be analyzed and by specifying the length of the response. However, in some cases there are advantages in allowing examinees freedom to analyze whatever they wish in the manner they choose, since by allowing this freedom, it is possible to determine the aspects to which the individual attends as well as how he deals with them.

FIGURE 17-8 Claude Monet's "Rouen Cathedral, West Façade, Sunlight" (National Gallery of Art, Washington, D.C., Chester Dale Collection).

Items on analysis of elements (D.1) The author has used the following technique to determine examinees' ability to dissect or break a work of art into its individual parts:

D.1-2.0

45. DIRECTIONS: Study the painting [in Fig. 17-8] titled "Rouen Cathedral, West Façade, Sunlight," by Monet. Make a list of the specific qualities, moods, parts, and things you see in the painting *in addition to a building and its parts, the sky, and people.* Make the list as long as you can.

The question directs attention toward a range of aspects, but particularly attempts to get at sensory qualities, modal character, and compositional aspects. Any descriptions except those relating to the subject matter of the work are acceptable.

Monet's "Rouen Cathedral" is a useful work for this purpose since once a building, the sky, and people are eliminated, only aspects of visual structure remain to be described. The item is scored by classifying the responses into categories used and the number of words within each category. It is also useful to note specificity and relevance of the responses.

Items on analysis of Relationships of parts (D.2) The item testing analysis of elements called for a simple listing of parts of a work of art. The more common procedure for assessing is to have the examinee discuss the ways in which aspects affect one another. The University of Chicago General Examination contains items in which examinees are asked to respond to a specific set of elements and compositional aspects.

D.2-2.1, D.2-2.2

46. DIRECTIONS: Describe the organization of *The Adoration of the Magi* in terms of balance, proportion, and representation—discussing the use of each of the elements: line, plane, volume, mass, texture, light and dark, and color. (20 minutes)

(University of Chicago Examiners' Office.)

The author has used items similar to those found in the University of Chicago General Examination, but has allowed the examinee complete freedom to determine which aspects he will analyze:

D.2-2.0, D.2-3.1, D.2-3.2

47. DIRECTIONS: Study the painting "Le Jour," by Georges Braque [Fig. 17-9]. Your task is to write about the parts, moods, qualities, and things you see in the painting and how they function in the painting. Please write about *anything* you see in the painting. You have fifteen minutes to complete the task.

Responses to analytical tasks such as the ones listed above may be evaluated by a systematic analysis of the language they contain (Wilson, 1966b). The procedure is to use each sentence in the response as a unit of analysis. The words within each sentence may be classified in many or a few categories, depending upon the information desired. Table 17-7 presents a set of categories for the classification of responses.

FIGURE 17-9 Georges Braque's "Le Jour" (National Gallery of Art, Washington, D.C., Chester Dale Collection).

A count of the number of times each category is used and the number of relational analyses made give an accurate profile of an individual's analytical ability. For example, the following excerpt from a description of Braque's "Le Jour" by an 11-year-old girl is presented along with a classification (in parentheses behind) using the categories listed in Table 17-7.

To me the painting (art form) expresses a mixed-up day (quasi-conventional meaning). The colors (color) are kind of dull (modal aspect) but they are bright (modal aspect) enough that the painting (art form) lets you know that there is hope of something cheerful (modal aspect) on a mixed-up day (quasi-conventional meaning).

The parts of the painting (art form) go together (relational analysis) quite well because they express mainly the same thing (quasi-conventional meaning).

Table 17-7 Categories for the analysis of descriptions of works of art

Category	*Terms indicating the category has been used*
Relational analysis	related, resembles, echoes, equal, associated, similar, connected, near, bearing on, affect, separate, together, around, alongside, juxtapose, below, parallel (indications that the individual has observed two or more aspects of the work functioning to produce an additional aspect, to affect some part of the work, or the entire work are classified as relational analysis)
Color	blue, green, light gray, bright red, dark maroon, etc.
Shape	squares, irregular forms, planes, circles, etc.
Line	outlines, marks, scratches, lines, etc.
Texture	smooth, rough, sleek, furry, bumpy, grainy, coarse, etc.
Composition	design, pattern, structure, composition, etc.
Modal aspect	mystical, sedate, gay, violent, stormy, tranquil, garish, discordant, vivid, bold, quiet (any term which characterizes the mood, feeling, or pervasive character of a portion of the total work)
Media and technique	oil paint, paper, bronze, painted, carved, thrown on, etc.
Literal meaning	man, house, tree, apple, king, arms, hair, child, etc.
Conventional and quasi-conventional meaning	symbolizes, means, represents, signifies, etc.
Art form	painting, drawing, print, etc.

The score for the excerpt is:

Quasi-conventional meaning	3
Modal aspect	3
Art form	3
Relational analysis	1
Color	1

In the procedure just illustrated a point is given each time a category is used. Another scoring procedure may be used where the primary aspect in each sentence is given a score of 3 and each secondary aspect is given a score of 1. When there are two or more primary aspects in the sentence each is given a score of 2. Using either scoring procedure it is possible to determine the types of relations an individual makes and also to what aspects of the art works he attends. A highly complex analysis of a work of art might attempt to indicate how each of the aspects of the work fuse or do not fuse together to produce a unified whole. Using the procedure it is also possible to determine what factors are not taken into account in the analysis of a work of art. Such information can form the basis for subsequent instruction.

There are many possible ways of classifying language describing works of art. For example, the categories color, texture, line, and shape could be combined into one category of sensory qualities, or other categories could be added classifying such things as metaphorical and analogical descriptions and characterizations of expressive content. By reducing the number of categories used for the analysis, it is possible to shorten the scoring time, since content analysis procedures are usually time-consuming to score. Such procedures are not generally practical for frequent testing; nevertheless, the procedure does provide useful information for comparisons of differences between beginning and end-of-course analytical abilities and for the evaluation of individual students' analytical abilities (Wilson, 1966b).

Thus far the analysis items have had as their purpose the assessment of the ability to analyze elements and relationships within a single work of art. Analysis can also be directed toward the relationships between or among works. Such analyses are particularly important in making art history comparisons. For example, Elsen has presented a Kwakiutl, a French Equatorial African, a New Ireland, and a Samurai mask with this question:

D.2-2.0, D.2-5.6

48. These masks served various magical functions. Knowing little or nothing of the cultures that produced them and the purposes they served, analyze how the heads have been transformed to perform extraordinary functions. Contrast the design of the same features in each work. How is each mask as a whole given intense expressiveness and visual coherence?

(Elsen, 1962, pp. 7, 9.)

A similar question was asked about a seated Buddha from Thailand and an enthroned Christ from Toulouse:

D.2-2.3, D.2-3.3, D.2-5.6

49. Establish the fundamental differences between the Christian and Buddhist approaches to the seated deities.

(Elsen, 1962, pp. 10, 12.)

Elsen's probing questions and unique ability for juxtaposing works of art containing striking similarities and differences make his questions useful models. Although his questions are written for college students, many of them could be used at the high school level. With some adaptation of language similar questions have been used at the elementary school level (Salt Lake City Public Schools, 1966a).

Other techniques used by Elsen are to show six drawings of the female figure by Picasso, ranging from a realistic rendering of the figure to a Cubist treatment, and to present this problem:

D.2-2.1, D.2-2.2, D.2-3.1

50. Within a short span of years in his career Picasso demonstrated his ability to transform the human body radically. Study drawing by drawing the changes that took place in the figure's reconstruction. Does the gradual loss of anatomical illusion accompany a loss in the quality of drawing? In the last two drawings, what decisions govern the placement of lines and shadings? Is there any vestige of the figure in the last work?

(Elsen, 1962, pp. 56, 58.)

Presenting two paintings, "The Gyp at Cards" by Caravaggio and "The Card Players" by Cézanne, he sets forth the following task:

D.2-3.3

51. Interpret the divergent attitudes toward a card game of Caravaggio and the nineteenth-century French painter Cézanne. By what means, psychological, physical, esthetic, did each artist individualize the card players? Of what importance is the setting to the formal organization of each painting?

(Elsen, 1962, pp. 26, 27.)

Items on Analysis of the relationship of parts to the whole (D.3) The following item, given without the accompanying reproduction, specifies which aspects of the painting are to be analyzed and also controls the length of the responses through space and time allotments. The relating of line, value, and objects to the overall idea of the work is highly complex, since determination of the overall idea requires the assessment of many other aspects of the work.

DIRECTIONS: Analyze Masaccio's *The Expulsion of Adam and Eve*, reproduced on this page, according to the following points, (1) line, (2) value, i.e., light and dark, and (3) choice of objects represented and their arrangement in the picture space. Comment briefly on each of the three points as to its appropriateness or lack of appropriateness to the idea which the artist was trying to express. (15 minutes)

D.3-2.1, D.3-2.2, D.3-3.1, D.3-3.3

52. Line [6 lines for writing]
53. Values [6 lines for writing]
54. Choice of objects, etc. [17 lines for writing]

(University of Chicago Examiners' Office.)

It is possible to test analysis of parts to the whole at a less complex level. For example, the following procedure has been used by the author. The procedure characterizes a quality of the whole work and asks the examinee to determine how specific parts contribute to the quality of the whole. The responses are scored by classifying the aspects analyzed into categories and also by determining specificity and relevance of the aspects to the quality of the whole. The item is presented without the accompanying visual material.

D.3-2.1, D.3-2.2, D.3-3.3

55. DIRECTIONS: Some have said that the painting "A Girl with a Watering Can" by Renoir has a very delicate feeling about it. Analyze the qualities and things in the painting which help it to present a delicate feeling, and then write how each of the aspects contribute to the feeling.

A related procedure may be followed which assesses whether the examinee is able to characterize the quality of the whole as affected by specific elements.

DIRECTIONS: Sometimes lines, colors, shapes, and textures help paintings to look in certain ways such as calm, warm, and solid. You will be shown a series of colored slides of paintings. As the slides are shown complete the sentence corresponding to the slide. Remember, don't judge the painting, just describe how one part affects how other parts look.

D.3-2.0, D.3-3.3

56. The lines make the painting look ______.
57. The colors make the painting look ______.
58. The arrangement of the lines and shapes gives the painting a ______ quality.
59. The placement of the figure in the center gives the painting a ______ character.

Testing for evaluation (E.0)

Evaluation, the second portion of the art critic's task, couples with the descriptive function, analysis, to make up the complete critical act. Evaluation in art, as with analysis, is almost always directed toward works of art, and evaluation generally follows a careful analysis. It is not uncommon to have single items which assess both analysis and evaluation. Some of the evaluation items reproduced in this section require that an analysis be conducted before the evaluation is performed. The evaluation items generally follow the same form as the analysis items inasmuch as they elicit verbal explications, but the explications are of the work's aesthetic worth or functional quality rather than its character.

Evaluation items, the same as analysis items, may be almost completely open-ended, or they may direct the examinee to assess specific features of works, or they may direct the examinee to apply a specific type of evaluative criterion.

Items testing Empirical evaluation (E.1) The following items call for judgments which are essentially empirical in nature inasmuch as they deal with such things as the suitability of a design to a specific medium or the relating of a building to a site. However, each of the items goes beyond a concern for the purely functional and calls for at least an element of systemic evaluation. The items are reproduced here without the intended accompanying visual material. It is, however, the form of the item which is important, and various works of art could be substituted for those with the items.

E.1-1.1, E.1-4.2

60. DIRECTIONS: For each of the next two items a slide will be projected showing a sketch for a work in free-standing sculpture to be considered in relation to the mediums suitable for its execution. *Blacken* the answer space corresponding to the letter of the best response.

    A—wood
    B—stone
    C—bronze
    D—terra cotta
    E—any of the above

DIRECTIONS: For each of the following items, *blacken* answer space

F.1-4.0

81. I stop to admire art work in magazines

82. When I go to the library, I look at art magazines

F.1-4.8

83. I stop to look at modern architecture

DIRECTIONS: The following are statements concerned with how you feel about your own art ability and art classes. Next to the appropriate letter on your answer sheet, blacken the space to indicate whether you

1. Strongly agree with the statement
2. Agree with the statement
3. Are uncertain about how you feel about the statement
4. Disagree with the statement
5. Strongly disagree with the statement

F.1-1.0, F.1-4.0

84. When I finish an art project, I usually do not like it

85. If I had a choice, I would take more art courses in school

F.1-1.4, F.1-4.1, F.1-4.5

86. I appreciate art, but I don't like to paint or draw myself.

F.1-1.0, F.1-4.0

87. I can never think of anything different to do in my art class

(Eisner, undated a, pp. 1–4, items 61, 64, 66, 69, 73, 76, 79, 80, 82, 88, 90, 92, 103, 104.)

DIRECTIONS: Read each statement carefully. Then indicate your reactions on the ANSWER SHEET by underlining one of the three letters after the number of the item. Underline

(A) If you feel that this statement is a fairly adequate expression of your general opinion.

(U) If you are uncertain whether you agree or disagree with the opinion expressed in this statement.

(D) If you disagree with the opinion expressed in the statement.

F.1-5.6

88. When a war is going on, no time or money should be spent on the arts, but all means and efforts should be concentrated on enterprises which directly contribute to the war effort.

89. The fine arts are a necessity for existence.

F.1-5.1

90. The artist is a person with special talents which set him off from the ordinary run of men and events.

F.1-4.0, F.1-6.2

91. Real works of art ought to depict only noble human emotions.

92. There is no way to decide once and for all what is a good work of art. Whatever I like is good art for me.

F.1-6.2

93. Different persons like different works of art. Personal preference is therefore no basis for deciding what is good and what is bad art.

F.1-5.6

94. Art is a powerful means to influence people.

F.1-5.6, F.3-5.6

95. Art can contribute nothing to society except a certain amount of pleasure for a few.

(Dunkel, 1947, pp. 312, 314, 315, items 1, 6, 31, 35, 36, 40, 51, 55.)

Items on Empathy for artists and what they do (F.2) The items below assess whether individuals have sympathy for and a willingness to accept what artists do, whether they are flexible enough to recognize new possibilities in art, and whether they demonstrate an openness toward new and unfamiliar works of art.

DIRECTIONS: The following statements are about artists and art works. On your answer sheet blacken the space which corresponds to a letter indicating that you

1. Strongly agree with the statement
2. Agree with the statement
3. Are uncertain about how you feel about the statement
4. Disagree with the statement
5. Strongly disagree with the statement.

F.2-5.1

96. People who become artists are usually the ones who could not succeed at other, more important tasks in life.
97. Artists should paint pictures the majority of people can understand.

F.2-5.1, F.2-4

98. It is good to have an appreciation of art, but it is not really very important.

F.2-5.6, F.2-5.7

99. Modern art is an important contribution to society.

F.2-5.1, F.2-5.6

100. An artist's contribution to society is not as important as that of a scientist.

(Eisner, undated a, p. 5, items 106–109, 118.)

The items below probe attitudes toward what Miró might have been trying to accomplish in his painting "Rosalie."

DIRECTIONS: Study the picture before you [Fig. 17-10] and then mark an "X" in the blank which most clearly expresses your opinion about the picture. The blank nearest the statement indicates you agree most strongly.

FIGURE 17-10 Joan Miró's "Rosalie" (University of Iowa Museum of Art).

The second and third blanks from the statement indicate that you still agree, but not as strongly. The center blank indicates that you have no opinion or that you don't know.

F.2-5.1

101. The painting should look more real.	__:__:__:__:__:__:__	The painting should not look more real.
102. The artist knew what he he was doing.	__:__:__:__:__:__:__	The artist did not know what he was doing.
103. An artist should make a painting like this.	__:__:__:__:__:__:__	An artist should not make a painting like this.
104. A painting like this should not be placed where the public can see it.	__:__:__:__:__:__:__	A painting like this should be placed where the public can see it.
105. The painting was easy for the artist to do.	__:__:__:__:__:__:__	The painting was difficult for the artist to do.

(Wilson, 1968, pp. 1–3, items 4, 20, 22, 32, 33.)

Items 106 to 109, from the Inventory of the Arts, use the same directions as given for items 88 to 95.

F.2-5.1

106. When artists have to struggle for a living or have many troubles, they become better artists, for the richer one's life and experience, the better one's works of art.

F.2-5.1, F.3-6.1

107. In appreciating art one undergoes the same experiences, the same emotions, which underlie the artist's creation.

F.2-5.1

108. Artists who defy tradition don't add anything to the main stream of art.
109. It is natural to identify oneself with the artist while looking at the work of art he has created.

(Dunkel, 1947, pp. 315, 319, items 50, 59, 64, 135.)

Items on Feelings about art (F.3) The following items from the Inventory of the Arts assess attitudes toward emotional experiences with works of art, and, more importantly, they assess the nature of emotional responses to specific works of art. The directions are again those given for items 88 to 95.

F.3-6.1

110. Only the emotional reaction counts. If a work of art leaves us cold (even if it is considered "great" by anybody else), it misses the point.
111. In appreciation the relation between the work of art and me is something very individual, strongly conditioned by *my* imagination and by the ideas aroused in *me* by the work of art.
112. When appreciating a work of art (music, literature), one should not "lose oneself" and live the life of the work of art. One should not be swayed by emotions but should preserve and make use of one's critical and rational abilities.
113. In looking at an art object one generally becomes deeply impressed by the mood the artist tried to convey.
114. Pleasure is the purpose of art.

(Dunkel, 1947, pp. 313–315, 317, items 14, 15, 41, 54, 92.)

While the items from the Inventory of the Arts assess general attitudes, the items below from the Wilson Art Inventory assess responses to a specific work, Miró's "Rosalie."

F.3-4.1

115.

The painting is boring.	__:__:__:__:__:__:__	The painting is interesting.

116.

I have an emotional reaction to the work.	__:__:__:__:__:__:__	I do not have an emotional reaction to the work.

117.

I get pleasure from viewing the painting.	__:__:__:__:__:__:__	I do not get pleasure from viewing the painting.

(Wilson, 1968, pp. 1, 3, items 1, 27, 29.)

This writer has also presented various works of art which seemed capable of eliciting emotional responses along with the following instructions:

F.3-4.0

118. Describe your reaction to the work, how it affects you, and how it makes you feel. It is not necessary to describe what you see in the work or whether you think the work is good or not. (10 minutes)

The criteria for assessing responses about feelings are to determine the sensitivity of the response and the degree of appropriateness of the response to the work. For example, if an individual described the happiness generated by one of De Kooning's expressionistic paintings of women, his degree of sensitivity and the appropriateness of the response might be questioned. It is realized, of course, that there is a wide range of feelings which might be considered appropriate for a given work.

A similar approach might be to present to the individual a selection of fifteen or twenty reproductions of art works and ask which of the works seems most capable of eliciting a range of specific feelings, such as excitement, impatience, content, solemnity, humor, and tedium.

Testing for production (G.0)

Although the production of works of art is the primary activity in most elementary and secondary school art classes, evaluation of students' productive abilities is seldom conducted in formal test situations. Evaluation of production is invariably conducted informally in the ongoing art classroom whether the evaluation is formative or summative. Consequently, there is a dearth of items available for the formal testing of production. This does not mean that such items cannot be produced, but they have not been developed because art teachers have not thought they needed them, since the works of art students are almost always immediately accessible to the teacher for evaluation at any stage of development.

A second factor which has hindered the development of specific instruments for the testing of studio production is the philosophy in art education that teachers ought to influence student production as little as possible and that a test requires some predetermined standard which would force students to produce in certain ways and thus negate teacher efforts to encourage student creativity.

Descriptive scales have been developed to assist teachers in evaluating student studio production during the formative and summative stages of production, and a few testing procedures have been developed to measure creative production in art. There are also procedures which could be used for formal testing of studio production in the areas of *Skill* and *Creativity*.

Items on Skill in the production of works of art (G.1) In many cases it seems that there would be distinct advantages in testing all the students in a class on a single variable of skill in art production. Using testing procedures, a teacher would be able to assess the source of students' individual problems and take remedial action to correct those problems. Skill test items would have the advantage of being a very quick means of gathering information based on tasks of a highly focused nature where only one or two variables are tested. This is in contrast to the usual studio assignment where a whole range of variables form the basis for evaluation.

It is often difficult to separate entirely the skill and creativity factors in the production of works of art. Nevertheless, production tasks can be developed in which only the skill factors are assessed. The following items are presented as possible means of evaluating skill in such activities as rendering objects and drawing in perspective.

G.1-1.4, G.1-3.1, G.1-4.5

119. DIRECTIONS: The model has been posed seated, with arms folded and legs crossed. Draw the model depicting as accurately as possible (1) the proportions of the model, (2) the attitude of the figure, and (3) the ways the parts are related to one another in the pose. Do not be concerned with such things as line quality, shading, and composition. Simply try to capture the essential character of the pose of the model, the proportions, and positions. (15 minutes)

In using such an item the instructor may wish to take several photographs of the model from different positions within the room for reference in scoring the drawings.

G.1-2.2, G.1-3.1, G.1-4.5

120. DIRECTIONS: Study the table filled with objects. At the end of one minute the table will be removed and you will be asked to draw the table and objects as accurately as possible. Your drawings will be scored on the basis of how accurately you are able to reproduce the character of the objects that are on the table, their positions in relation to one another, and whether you include all the objects. (10 minutes)

This item tests visual memory and the ability to do accurate reportage drawings. As with the first task it may be desirable to photograph the table for reference in scoring, or since the table can hold its "pose" longer than a model, the table with its objects can be saved for scoring. In scoring the item a point may be given for each object included, another point for accuracy in the depiction of the character of the object, and a point for each accurate placement of objects. Obviously the table setup may be as simple or as complex as desired.

The following procedure could be used to assess skill in using linear perspective.

G.1-2.2, G.1-3.1

121. DIRECTIONS: Do a drawing which contains six figures. At least one figure is to be in the foreground, another in the middle ground, and

another in the background. The relationship of the figures should reflect the rules of linear perspective. (10 minutes)

Other items similar to these might be developed to assess such things as the ability to mix colors in specific shades and tints.

Items on Creativity in the production of works of art (G.2) Many would hold that it is difficult if not impossible to assess the creative production of works of art through testing procedures, arguing that to be creative the individual must be allowed freedom to select practically all the variables which influence the quality of his work. But in the past works of art considered to be most creative were produced under circumstances where many aspects of the work were determined by the one who commissioned the work. It seems reasonable to maintain that since the making of a work of art requires mastery of factors of creativity which are subject to alteration in art classrooms, a more careful testing of some of those individual factors through methods such as the ones to be presented might bring about more effective art teaching through accurate pinpointing of students' creative achievements.

This type of procedure has been used to assess production achievement.[7]

G.2-1.1, G.2-1.4, G.2-2.2, G.2-2.3

122. DIRECTIONS: Using a full size of 14-inch by 20-inch paper plan a composition to be rendered in watercolor, tempera, or a combination of some other media. Select one of the following titles for your composition:

a. "Ocean Bathers"

b. "Metamorphosis"

c. "Building Site"

Write the name of the title you have selected in the upper right-hand corner of your composition. Your work will be judged for:

1. creation of a mood
2. the quality and originality of the composition
3. expressive handling of media.

[7] Similar procedures are found in the New York City Board of Education Teacher's License Examination (Gruber, 1962).

Items similar to the following might be used to assess more specific aspects of creative production.

G.2-2.2, G.2-3.1

123. DIRECTIONS: Artists have often rearranged elements from the way they appeared in nature to suit the purpose of the particular work of art they were producing. The photograph of a landscape before you is just as it appears in nature. Your task is to rearrange the landscape so that the composition forms a concentric pattern. (Medium: pencil on paper; time: one hour)

G.2-2.0, G.2-3.1

124. DIRECTIONS: Make a tempera painting of a single figure. The painting is to have a mood or feeling of turbulence. The feeling should result from the attitude of the figure, from the use of colors, textures, lines, and shapes, and from the composition of the painting. (One hour)

A variation of item 124 is to present a poem which contains a particular mood and ask students to produce a painting which contains essentially the same feeling.

Various scales have been developed to assess students' works of art. Some scales are used to make aesthetic judgments, and others are almost completely descriptive. Rouse (1968) developed one which, although called a descriptive scale, actually combines descriptive and evaluative elements. It contains categories such as shape, texture, detail, flatness, depth and nonsymbolism/symbolism which seem to be almost purely descriptive. But there are also categories such as nonunity/unity, amount of balance, noncraftsmanship/craftsmanship, and nonoriginality/originality which have a strong value component as these are the characteristics which are used to justify judgments of aesthetic goodness or the lack of it.

The way Rouse utilizes her categories is shown in Table 17-8.

Rouse developed her instrument to enable researchers to assess changes in artistic behavior over periods of time through the quantification

Table 17-8 Rouse's Descriptive Scales for Art Products

Shape: Non-variation/variation

In regard to shapes (two dimensional areas defined by contour), would you define the product as:

- ___ Shows *no* variation in shapes; shapes are all similar
- ___ Shapes are mainly similar, but some small variation is shown (approximately 75% to 25%)
- ___ Shows about 50% varied shapes, 50% similar shapes
- ___ Shapes are mainly varied, although some similarity is shown (approximately 75% to 25%)
- ___ Shapes are extremely varied; shows *no* similarity in shapes

Non-unity/unity

In regard to unity (shown by the object's possessing a sense of oneness; i.e.: all means and elements appear to be adapted to a single purpose or end), would you describe the product as:

- ___ Shows a complete lack of unity; is disorganized, chaotic
- ___ Shows only a small amount of unity, organization; is still mainly chaotic
- ___ Shows a moderate amount of unity, organization
- ___ Shows more unity, organization, than disunity, disorganization
- ___ Shows a high degree of unity, organization

Non-symbolism/symbolism

In regard to symbolism (forms which use suggestion to express ideas otherwise intangible), would you describe the product as:

- ___ Shows *no* symbolism
- ___ Shows only a small degree of symbolism
- ___ Shows a moderate amount of symbolism
- ___ Shows much symbolism, although some parts of composition may not be symbolic
- ___ Shows a high degree of symbolism; composition is completely symbolic

Non-originality/originality

In regard to originality (shown by inventiveness, uniqueness, non-imitativeness), would you describe the product as:

- ___ Shows complete lack of originality; is imitative, stereotyped
- ___ Shows mainly imitativeness or stereotype; although some small part may be somewhat out-of-the-ordinary
- ___ Shows moderate amount of originality
- ___ Shows a good deal of originality
- ___ Shows a high degree of originality

SOURCE: M. J. Rouse. *The development of a descriptive scale for art products.* [Bull. 44(1)] Bloomington, Ind.: Indiana University, School of Education, 1968. Pp. 31, 33, 34, 37.

of characteristics of works of art. Her instrument could be used as readily by teachers in formative and summative testing in art.

Formative evaluation in art education

Formative evaluation of the nonproduction aspects of art instruction

Art teachers have consistently and effectively used formative evaluation during studio teaching, but they have often ignored formative evaluation in other areas of art instruction. The assumption is often made that students understand the terminology teachers use, that they perceive the formal structure of works of art, and that they comprehend the meanings of art works, when often they do not. The absence of formative testing in the historical, critical, and appreciative aspects of art instruction has made instruction in these areas less effective than it might be.

To illustrate how formative evaluation might be used in art in areas other than studio production, items from the unit for enhancing aesthetic experience (Stumbo, 1968) are presented. The structure of the unit was discussed on pages 525–527, above.

Formative evaluation of Knowledge (B.0) As we saw, the key terms used in the unit are "expressive meaning," "ordinary meaning," "allegorical meaning," "significant meaning," and "aesthetic experience." Each of these terms is presented in the introduction of the unit, and it seems imperative that the students understand the meaning of each term before they proceed further in the unit. Although the unit does not contain specific formal test items at this point (knowledge of terms is assessed individually by the teacher), the following might be used:

B.1-3.2
125. The term "allegorical meaning," when applied to works of art, refers to ____________.

The free response, rather than a multiple-choice form of questioning, seems reasonable since there are only a few terms. A similar procedure could be used to assess knowledge of the method for enhancing aesthetic experiencing.

Formative evaluation of Analysis (D.0) To assess students' ability to analyze the expressive meaning of Kline's "Two Horizontals," they are first given a semantic differential scale to mark. The scale contains thirty sets of terms such as "violent 2 1 0 1 2 tranquil." Following the completion of the scale the students are given this task:

D.3-2.0
126. Now that you have completed the checklist go back over the list and circle the words that received scores of 2. Using the circled words as clues to the most outstanding features of your observation of his artifact, describe some of those features in the space provided below. Use complete descriptive sentences. They need not form a paragraph. [Students respond as directed.] Now that you have attempted to describe some of the most outstanding details of your observation of the Franz Kline painting, try to abstract from these separate descriptions one sentence which describes the character of this particular work of art.

(Stumbo, 1968, pp. 8–12.)

The students evaluate their analyses by comparing them with a videotaped critique of the same painting. They are given a checklist to assist in the comparison. The checklist is primarily concerned with the relationships between the black and white aspects of the painting and their effect on the expressive meaning of the painting.

Formative evaluation of production (G.0)

Formative evaluation, although not known by name, is used consistently by many art teachers. During the studio-production phase of art instruction (which takes up much of the art classroom time) art teachers often work with students on a one-to-one basis. They provide critiques of the students' work in progress, directing their evaluations toward the unique problems encountered by individual students. This type of formative evaluation occurs in the art classroom for two primary reasons: (1) the work of art, being visual, can at any stage of development be assessed almost immediately by a sensitive art teacher; and (2) formative evaluation on an individual, almost tutorial, basis is often necessary since even though students might be working on the same problem, any solution might be markedly different from others in the class, and individual solutions require individual evaluations. Continual formative evaluation of student productions is one of the unique features of art instruction; its uniqueness is that it is invariably informal. No test items are used, because they are not needed. Learning difficulties are noted and corrected as they occur, which is the primary purpose of formative evaluation.

Formative evaluation of studio production requires that the art teacher be adept at analyzing and evaluating student art products. Teachers also often attempt to bring students into the evaluation process by encouraging them to analyze and evaluate their own work.

Formative evaluation of a mural project Barkan (1960, pp. 260–264) has recorded an evaluation session in which a teacher and several fifth-grade girls evaluate together a partially completed mural on which they have been working for several days. They are displeased with their progress, and the teacher, Mrs. Hoyer, allows them to perform most of the evaluation. In fact, her role is similar to that of a nondirective therapist. She nominally guides the evaluation and gives positive reinforcement.

Nancy: We painted it too much.

Sandy: Well, you see these things (pointing with dissatisfaction to a section of the mural)—

Mrs. Hoyer: Wait a minute, Sandy. Let's all back up a little, so we can all see it.

Jolinda: It's too messy.

Mrs. Hoyer: Well, what don't you like about it?

Jolinda: The flowers are junky.

Kay: I don't like them.

Mrs. Hoyer: Well, now, let's slow down and find out what you mean.

Jolinda: It doesn't look right.

Kathy: We don't think that yellow is good. We don't think that brown—we don't think it looks like really a plant—we don't think there's that many plants at all.

Mrs. Hoyer: But the plants in the swamp are scrambled all together, aren't they?

Sandy: Did you see those chips of paint (pointing to a spot where some thick paint had chipped off)?

Jolinda: Look at it!

Mrs. Hoyer: Look at this part. Doesn't it look like the plants are coming right out of the water?

Kay: That's what we should try to do—more of that.

Nancy: No. They're all the same thing. They're too much the same color.

Mrs. Hoyer: Take a look at this part. Could this be a piece of old wood that had dropped off of a tree?

Nancy: But it isn't.

Mrs. Hoyer: Could it be?

Nancy: Yeah.

Jolinda: It's all scratchy.

Sandy: It was all mud. Then we put weeds, flowers. Then we put weeds, mud, weeds, flowers.

Mrs. Hoyer: Shouldn't some things be on top of other things?

Kay: But we have so much of everything.

Mrs. Hoyer: What do you think you should do?

Kathy: It's no good. We want to do a new one. Can't we start over again?

Nancy: There's so much paint on it already.

Mrs. Hoyer: There's one nice thing about this paint. You can paint right on top of it, and change the parts you don't like.

Sandy: But it's cracked too much.

Mrs. Hoyer: The few cracks don't hurt anything. Take a look at it right now. Pick out the parts that look good to you, because there are some parts that are really good.

Nancy: Some of those weeds.

Mrs. Hoyer: All right, now, is there another part that you like real well?

Kathy: Those weeds over there.

Mrs. Hoyer: All right. What other parts do you like?

Jolinda: If we're going to make our flowers, we should sketch one first.

Kathy: If everybody will start all over again, that'll make you feel better—get a nice clean sheet of paper and start over again. Now that this is all painted, you can't start over again.

Kay: We know our mistakes, and we know what we want it to be like.

Mrs. Hoyer: It will be a shame to lose all those nice weeds and swamp.

Kathy: We'll make a new swamp.

Mrs. Hoyer: What decision are you ready to reach?

Sandy: Well, we're gonna get our—um—and make it what we want it to be.

Mrs. Hoyer: With a new piece of paper?

Chorus: Yes.

Nancy: Paint it like you want it, because—

Mrs. Hoyer: You're going to paint on this some more?

Nancy: No. We're going to start over. We're going to plan a new one. Before, we didn't plan anything. We just painted.

Mrs. Hoyer: You think you need a little more planning. Well, that's good, but I hate to think of the time you've spent on this one, and now you're ready to give it up.

Jolinda: A new one will be better.

Mrs. Hoyer: Your idea of making a plan is a good one. Who's going to work on the plan?

Chorus: All of us.

Kay: Then we'll know what to do in the painting.

Kathy: We can draw with chalk on the old mural.

Mrs. Hoyer: That's a very good idea.

The students' major concern seemed to be for the manner in which they had rendered the subject matter and for what they considered to be their inadequate control of tempera paint. Their criticism of their work was much more severe than it appears Mrs. Hoyer's would have been; so severe that they believed a new start could be the only solution.

Of course, not all formative evaluation of student products is nondirective. The following excerpt of an evaluation of a high school student's tempera painting in progress (collected by the author) is typical of much formative evaluation in art education.

> Actually, I think you have a very good start. The use of reds in both the head and the guitar help pull together the opposing art styles, as does the repeat of brown and yellow in both sides of the painting. The pencil shading in the head is good and could be left as is. It forms a nice contrast with the paint. It would also be a good idea to leave charcoaling along the edge of the pitcher, and in the neck of the guitar, because it turns the charcoaling into an integrating force.
>
> There are a couple of things I want you to work on now. The area below the chin of the king's head is very unclear. Think about it for a while before doing anything else to it. How can you integrate this one part with the rest of the painting and define it at the same time?
>
> You have two different paint consistencies here too. The guitar's red is very strong and thick, but the red in the man's face is watery and lacking force. Try keeping all your paint the same consistency. If you want lighter red, mix white with the red instead of adding water.
>
> You should also start thinking about a background color. Do you want to leave it white? Try to be very consistent in your use of color—keep it strong as in the guitar. The washed-out brown is very weak.

In the excerpt the teacher has performed a critical evaluative act in which the primary criterion of judgment is the interrelatedness of parts of the work, their coherence in a unified whole. In art classroom tasks which require a high degree of skill, such as throwing pottery on the wheel or cutting a woodblock to make a print, teachers constantly observe students' performances of the various processes in order to detect problems which will impede their progress. Again, this is the most common type of formative evaluation.

The status of testing in art education

Buros (1961) lists ten tests in art. Of these only two could be considered achievement tests; one is a vocabulary test published in 1935, and the other one assesses college art programs. The remainder of the tests (most of which were published during the 1920s and 1930s) deal with some aspect of art aptitude. However, this information does not present an accurate picture of the status of testing in art. There is perhaps more activity in art testing currently than at any time since the 1930s. Many individuals are developing instruments, and this time the emphasis is on measuring achievement rather than aptitude.

It is tempting to speculate why there has been a dearth of achievement tests in art. There seem to be at least five reasons: (1) many art objectives are difficult to measure since they require procedures different from the customary multiple-choice items of many educational tests, (2) the content of art is so broad and may be approached in so many ways that there is little agreement on specific common objectives, (3) often art educational goals are not written with enough specification to direct the development of specific testing procedures, (4) until recently there has been little demand for test instruments (government-sponsored programs which require evaluation are increasing the demand for tests), and (5) art teachers have sometimes believed that art is too ethereal and pervaded with emotions and feelings to be measured satisfactorily. The unwillingness to measure, coupled with an abhorrence for specification and precision in the stating of objectives, has especially impeded the development of testing in art.

Corey (1967) has made a distinction between "teaching" and "instruction" which is useful in clarifying measurement problems in art education. Corey says that "teaching" is a term with so many interpretations that it has innumerable meanings. For example, in art it is sometimes said that there can be no teaching, that the teaching is that which one teaches himself, or that a teacher teaches only by example. As Corey states, "Not only is the word teaching an exceedingly inclusive generic term, but in part because it is an activity to which everyone has been a party, either as a teacher or as a pupil, the nature of the teaching process as well as the variables related to it are often described in a language that is poetic and metaphorical and even mystical [p. 6]."

In contrast to teaching, instruction is defined as a particular instance of teaching which has been formally organized so that a student's performance is precisely specified, directed, and measured. Instruction is characterized by specification of the behavior a student is to attain in art, a careful formulation of procedures which lead to the desired behaviors, and a means for assessing whether or not the desired behavior has been achieved.

In art education teaching is far more common than instruction. Often the teacher does not chart specific objectives. Quite to the contrary, he and his students take cues from the dynamics of the situation and follow a constantly changing course toward an unpredicted, but meaningful, conclusion. Formulating specific objectives, procedures, and measurement exercises is contrary to what the teacher might hope to accomplish through the fluid teaching structure. Such teaching must necessarily remain free from preformed objectives, and consequently the assessment strategies must also remain open to be formulated as they are needed.

Whereas the open-ended teaching is usually directed toward the studio-production aspects of art, there are other aspects of art education, particularly art history and criticism, where instruction is possible and desirable. Whenever art education can be formalized into instruction the task of evaluating and testing comes into much sharper focus, since instruction requires specification of objectives to the point that directives for testing are often clearly indicated.

Art teachers need to draw a sharper distinction between teaching where formal testing is not always possible nor desirable and instruction where carefully formulated formative and summative testing procedures are an integral part of the curriculum. Too often the assumption has been made that most art education, and consequently that most testing, should also be informal. Such an assumption impedes the effectiveness of some aspects of art education which seem to require formalization as instruction.

It would be unfortunate, indeed, if all the outcomes of particular art programs were completely specified before instruction began, since the very nature of art is to be open-ended with an element of the unexpected and unpredictable. Conversely, it would be just as unfortunate if no outcomes were specified prior to teaching and no testing was conducted. It is possible to achieve an amiable balance between art teaching and instruction, where teaching and instruction are conducted concurrently or alternately, and where the interplay between them enhances both.

This chapter has presented the view that most of the outcomes of art education are ultimately testable, but that art education still has some distance to travel before satisfactory measurement of the complex behaviors aesthetic analysis, evaluation, appreciation, and production is possible. Art educators, and especially their students, have much to gain through intensified testing activities.

REFERENCES

Arnheim, R. *Art and visual perception.* Berkeley, Calif.: University of California Press, 1960.

Barkan, M. *Through art to creativity.* Boston: Allyn & Bacon, 1960.

Barkan, M. Curriculum and the teaching of art. In J. J. Hausman (Ed.), *Report of the Commission on Art Education.* Washington, D.C.: National Art Education Association, 1965. Pp. 69–78.

Barkan, M., & Chapman, L. *Guidelines for art instruction through television for the elementary schools.* Bloomington, Ind.: National Center for School and College Television, 1967.

Bloom, B. S. (Ed.) *Taxonomy of educational objectives: The Classification of educational goals.* Handbook 1. *Cognitive domain.* New York: McKay, 1956.

Board of Education of the City of New York. *Major art in the academic high schools.* (Curr. Bull. No. 11, 1960–61 Ser.) New York: BECNY, 1961.

Brandon, C. M. The relative effectiveness of four different approaches in developing art appreciation. Unpublished doctoral dissertation, George Peabody College for Teachers, 1960.

Buros, O. K. *Tests in print.* Highland Park, N.J.: Gryphon Press, 1961.

Casey, W. C. *Master pieces in art.* Chicago: Flanagan, 1915.

Ciardi, J. *How does a poem mean?* Boston: Houghton Mifflin, 1959.

Corey, S. M. The nature of instruction. In P. C. Lange (Ed.), *Programed instruction: The sixty-sixth yearbook of the National Society for the Study of Education.* Bloomington, Ind.: NSSE, 1967. Pp. 5–27.

D'Amico, V. *Creative teaching in art.* Scranton: International Textbook, 1953.

Davenport Community Schools. *ART senior high.* Davenport, Iowa: DCS, 1968.

Davis, D. An exercise to test perception of unifying formal elements in paintings. Unpublished test, University of Iowa, 1968.

De Francesco, I. L. *Art education: Its means and ends.* New York: Harper, 1958.

Dewey, J. *Art as experience.* New York: Capricorn, 1934.

Dunkel, H. B. *General education in the humanities.* Washington, D.C.: American Council on Education, 1947.

Ecker, D. W., & Eisner, E. W. (Eds.) *Readings in art education.* Waltham, Mass.: Blaisdell, 1966.

Eisner, E. W. The development of information and attitude toward art at the secondary and college levels. *Studies in Art Education,* 1966, **8**(1), 43–58. (a)

Eisner, E. W. Typology of creativity in the visual arts. In D. W. Ecker & E. W. Eisner (Eds.), *Readings in art education.* Waltham, Mass.: Blaisdell, 1966. Pp. 323–335. (b)

Eisner, E. W. The Eisner Art Attitude Inventory. Unpublished test, University of Chicago, undated. (a)

Eisner, E. W. The Eisner Art Information Inventory. Unpublished test, University of Chicago, undated. (b)

Elsen, A. *Problem book to accompany Purposes of Art.* New York: Holt, Rinehart and Winston, 1962.

Erickson, H. Influences in the cultivation of art appreciation. In G. Hartman (Ed.), *Creative expression through art.* Washington, D.C.: Progressive Education Association, 1926. Pp. 179–183.

Gardner, H. *Art through the ages.* New York: Harcourt, Brace, 1948.

Gruber, E. C. (Ed.) *Teacher of fine arts: High school and junior high school.* New York: ARCO, 1962.

Harris, D. G. *Children's drawings as measures of intellectual maturity.* New York: Harcourt, Brace & World, 1963.

Hubbard, G. *Art in the high school.* Belmont, Calif.: Wadsworth, 1967.

Kaufman, I. *Art and education in contemporary culture.* New York: Macmillan, 1966.

Kepes, G. *Education of vision.* New York: Braziller, 1965.

Klar, W., Winslow, L. L., & Kirby, C. V. *Art education in principle and practice.* Springfield, Mass.: Bradley, 1933.

Krathwohl, D. R., Bloom, B. S., & Masia, B. B. *Taxonomy of educational objectives: The classification of educational goals.* Handbook 2. *Affective domain.* New York: McKay, 1964.

Lanier, V. Schismogenesis in contemporary art education. *Studies in Art Education,* 1963, **5**(1), 10–19.

Lanier, V. *Teaching secondary art.* Scranton: International Textbook, 1964.

Lark-Horovitz, B., Lewis, H., & Luca, M. *Understanding children's art for better teaching.* Columbus: Merrill, 1967.

Logan, F. M. *Growth of art in American schools.* New York: Harper, 1955.

Lowenfeld, V. *Creative and mental growth.* New York: Macmillan, 1959.

McFee, J. *Preparation for art.* Belmont, Calif.: Wadsworth, 1961.

Meier, N. C. *The Meier Art Tests: Part I. Art Judgment.* Iowa City: Bureau of Educational Research and Service, University of Iowa, 1940.

Meier, N. C. *The Meier Art Tests: Part II. Aesthetic Perception.* Iowa City: Bureau of Educational Research and Service, University of Iowa, 1963.

Messer, S. Test of the assessment of meaning in art. Unpublished test, 1st draft, University of Iowa, 1968.

Nyquist, F. *Art education in elementary schools.* Baltimore: Warwick and York, 1929.

Panofsky, E. *Meaning in the visual arts.* Garden City, N.Y.: Doubleday, 1955.

Pepper, S. *The basis of criticism in the arts.* Cambridge, Mass.: Harvard University Press, 1945.

Rouse, M. J. *The development of a descriptive scale for art products.* [Bull. 44, No. 1, January 1968] Bloomington, Ind.: Indiana University, School of Education, 1968.

Salt Lake City Public Schools. Experiencing art: Title I television programs for sixth graders. Unpublished teachers' guide, SLCPS, 1966. (a)

Salt Lake City Public Schools. Salt Lake City Humanities Test. Unpublished test, version 1, SLCPS, 1966. (b)

Salt Lake City Public Schools. Salt Lake City Humanities Test. Unpublished test, version 2, SLCPS, 1966. (c)

Schachtel, E. G. *Metamorphosis.* New York: Basic, 1959.

Schoepp, L. H. Untitled test kit. Unpublished kit, University of Iowa, 1968.

Smith, P. Verbal operations in classroom instruction. In D. W. Ecker (Ed.), *Improving the teaching of art appreciation.* (Final Rep. No. RF. 2006) Columbus: U.S. Office of Education, Bureau of Research, 1966. Pp. 107–143.

Smith, R. A. *Aesthetics and criticism in art education.* Chicago: Rand McNally, 1966.

Smith, R. A. Aesthetic education: A role for the humanities. *Teachers College Record,* 1968, **69,** 343–354.

South, J. An evaluation of a film's effect on high school students' knowledge of Chartres Cathedral. Unpublished master's dissertation, University of Iowa, 1968.

Stumbo, H. W. Untitled art curriculum. Unpublished manuscript, University of Iowa Experimental School, 1968.

Taylor, J. C. *Learning to look.* Chicago: University of Chicago Press, 1957.

Trismen, D. A. *Evaluation of the Education through Vision curriculum, phase I.* (Proj. No. 7-0049) Princeton, N.J.: U.S. Office of Education, Bureau of Research, 1968.

University of Chicago Examiners' Office. *University of Chicago General Examination,* Chicago: UCEO.

Wachowiak, F., & Ramsay, T. *Emphasis: Art.* Scranton: International Textbook, 1965.

Weitz, M. The nature of art. In D. W. Ecker & E. W. Eisner (Eds.), *Readings in art education.* Waltham, Mass.: Blaisdell, 1966. Pp. 49–56.

Whitford, W. G. *An introduction to art education.* New York: Appleton, 1929.

Wilson, B. G. The development and testing of an instrument to measure aspective perception of paintings. Unpublished doctoral dissertation, Ohio State University, 1966. (a)

Wilson, B. G. An experimental study designed to alter fifth and sixth grade students' perception of paintings. *Studies in Art Education,* 1966, **8**(1), 33–42. (b)

Wilson, B. G. The rules of Byzantine art. Unpublished intermediate grade art curriculum guide, University of Iowa Experimental School, 1966. (c)

Wilson, B. G. Wilson Art Inventory. Unpublished test, University of Iowa, 1968.

Wilson, L. L. W. *Picture study in elementary schools.* New York: Macmillan, 1899.

18

Evaluation of Learning in Science

LEOPOLD E. KLOPFER

Associate Professor of Education
and Research Associate, Learning Research and Development Center
University of Pittsburgh
Pittsburgh, Pennsylvania

Leopold E. Klopfer is currently on the faculty of the School of Education and on the senior staff of the Learning Research and Development Center (LRDC) at the University of Pittsburgh. This joint appointment reflects two facets of his interests in science education: the preparation and training of teachers in science, and the development and evaluation of science curriculum materials. In LRDC, he is director of the Individually Prescribed Instruction (IPI) Program in Science. Klopfer graduated from Cornell University with a bachelor's degree in chemistry and received his doctorate in science education at Harvard University. He served as chairman of the U.S. National Science Committee for the International Study of Educational Achievement. Among his publications are the History of Science Cases series and the Test On Understanding Science.

Contents

18

Evaluation of Learning in Science[1]

Objectives of science instruction

Introduction

The objectives of science instruction in today's American elementary and secondary schools present something of a paradox. Coexisting within the same state, the same city, the same district—sometimes even within the same school—are science programs and courses representing traditional objectives as well as programs and courses oriented toward the objectives of the science curriculum revision movement of the past decade. It is, therefore, not possible at present to state one set of objectives to which all teachers of science at each educational level would subscribe. The pronouncements of national groups are fairly unanimous on the ideal objectives of science education, it is true; but a realistic review of contemporary science instruction must take cognizance of the situation actually existing in schools. Here it becomes apparent that millions of children in both elementary schools and high schools are studying science in programs that seem to have been little affected by the curriculum revisions initiated in the late 1950s.

At that time, considerations of the changes in the nature, quantity, and status of science in the twentieth century evoked a massive reconsideration of the objectives of science education. This century has witnessed a new understanding of natural phenomena, as the concepts and theories of the traditional disciplines have changed and fields such as the space sciences, the earth sciences, and biochemistry have matured. In addition, an increasing accumulation of factual knowledge has resulted in what is appropriately called an "information crisis." Moreover, as applied science has come to hold a very important place in our world, our lives, and our political considerations, science has acquired great social significance. As a result, the principal pur-

[1] The author gratefully acknowledges the assistance of Miss Kit Kollenberg and Mrs. Susan Schacker, who compiled materials for illustrative test items, and Miss Pauline Walend, who ably and patiently typed and retyped the manuscript.

TABLE 18-1 TABLE OF SPECIFICATIONS FOR SCIENCE EDUCATION

	BEHAVIOR[a]																		
	A.0 Knowledge and comprehension											*B.0 Processes of scientific inquiry I: Observing and measuring*					*C.0 Processes of sc inquiry II: Seei problem and see ways to solve*		
	Knowledge of specific facts	*Knowledge of scientific terminology*	*Knowledge of concepts of science*	*Knowledge of conventions*	*Knowledge of trends and sequences*	*Knowledge of classifications, categories, and criteria*	*Knowledge of scientific techniques and procedures*	*Knowledge of scientific principles and laws*	*Knowledge of theories or major conceptual schemes*	*Identification of knowledge in a new context*	*Translation of knowledge from one symbolic form to another*	*Observation of objects and phenomena*	*Description of observations using appropriate language*	*Measurement of objects and changes*	*Selection of appropriate measuring instruments*	*Estimation of measurements and recognition of limits in accuracy*	*Recognition of a problem*	*Formulation of a working hypothesis*	*Selection of suitable tests of a hypothesis*
CONTENT	*A.1*	*A.2*	*A.3*	*A.4*	*A.5*	*A.6*	*A.7*	*A.8*	*A.9*	*A.10*	*A.11*	*B.1*	*B.2*	*B.3*	*B.4*	*B.5*	*C.1*	*C.2*	*C.3*
1.0 Biological sciences																			
1.1 Biology of the cell																			
1.11 Cell Structure and Function																			
1.12 Transport of Cellular Material																			
1.13 Cell Metabolism																			
1.14 Photosynthesis																			
1.15 Cell Responses																			
1.16 Concept of the Gene																			
1.2 Biology of the organism																			
1.21 Diversity of Life																			
1.22 Metabolism in Organisms																			
1.23 Regulation in Organisms																			
1.24 Coordination and Behavior																			
1.25 Reproduction and Development																			
1.26 Human Biology																			
1.3 Biology of populations																			
1.31 Natural Environment																			
1.32 Cycles in Nature																			
1.33 Natural Groups and Their Segregation																			
1.34 Population Genetics																			
1.35 Evolution																			
2.0 Physical sciences																			
2.1 Chemistry																			
2.11 Chemical Materials																			
2.12 Classification of Chemical Elements																			
2.13 Chemical Change																			
2.14 Chemical Laws																			
2.15 Energy Relationships and Equilibrium in Chemical Systems																			
2.16 Electrochemistry																			
2.17 Atomic and Molecular Structure																			
2.18 Introductory Organic Chemistry																			
2.19 Chemistry of Life Processes																			
2.110 Nuclear Chemistry																			
2.2 Physics																			
2.21 Kinematics																			
2.22 Dynamics																			
2.23 Energy and Its Conservation																			
2.24 Mechanical Advantage																			
2.25 Mechanics of Fluids																			
2.26 Heat and Kinetic Theory																			
2.27 Wave Phenomena																			
2.28 Sound																			
2.29 Light and Spectra																			
2.210 Static and Current Electricity																			
2.211 Magnetism and Electromagnetism																			
2.212 Electronics																			
2.213 Properties and Structure of Matter																			
2.214 Theoretical Physics																			
2.3 Earth and space sciences																			
2.31 Solar System																			
2.32 Stellar Systems																			
2.33 Meteorology																			
2.34 Physical Geology																			
2.35 Historical Geology																			
2.36 Geophysics and Geochemistry																			
2.37 Oceanography																			
3.0 General																			
3.1 Historical development																			
3.2 Nature and structure of science																			
3.3 Nature of scientific inquiry																			
3.4 Biographies of scientists																			
3.5 Measurement																			

[a] Some of the student behaviors are given here in abbreviated form. For complete wording, especially of behaviors *A.10*, *A.11*, *D.4*, *H.3*, and *I.1* to *I.3*, see pages 565–580.

BEHAVIOR[a]																											
D.0 Processes of scientific inquiry III: Interpreting data and formulating generalizations						*E.0 Processes of scientific inquiry IV: Building, testing, and revising a theoretical model*						*F.0 Application of scientific knowledge and methods*			*G.0 Manual skills*		*H.0 Attitudes and interests*						*I.0 Orientation*				
Processing of experimental data	*Presentation of data in the form of functional relationships*	*Interpretation of experimental data and observations*	*Extrapolation and interpolation*	*Evaluation of a hypothesis under test in the light of data obtained*	*Formulation of generalizations warranted by relationships found*	*Recognition of the need for a theoretical model*	*Formulation of a theoretical model to accommodate knowledge*	*Specification of relationships satisfied by a model*	*Deduction of new hypotheses from a theoretical model*	*Interpretation and evaluation of tests of a model*	*Formulation of a revised, refined, or extended model*	*Application to new problems in the same field of science*	*Application to new problems in a different field of science*	*Application to problems outside of science (including technology)*	*Development of skills in using common laboratory equipment*	*Performance of common laboratory techniques with care and safety*	*Manifestation of favorable attitudes toward science and scientists*	*Acceptance of scientific inquiry as a way of thought*	*Adoption of "scientific attitudes"*	*Enjoyment of science learning experiences*	*Development of interests in science and science-related activities*	*Development of interest in pursuing a career in science*	*Relationships among various types of statements in science*	*Recognition of the philosophical limitations and influence of scientific inquiry*	*Historical perspective: recognition of the background of science*	*Realization of the relationships among science, technology, and economics*	*Awareness of the social and moral implications of scientific inquiry and its results*
.1	*D.2*	*D.3*	*D.4*	*D.5*	*D.6*	*E.1*	*E.2*	*E.3*	*E.4*	*E.5*	*E.6*	*F.1*	*F.2*	*F.3*	*G.1*	*G.2*	*H.1*	*H.2*	*H.3*	*H.4*	*H.5*	*H.6*	*I.1*	*I.2*	*I.3*	*I.4*	*I.5*

pose of science education is to develop the students' "scientific literacy," a purpose that the traditional science curriculum has failed to fulfill effectively (California State Department of Education, 1967; Educational Research Council of Greater Cleveland, 1966; National Assessment of Education Progress, 1965a, 1965b; National Science Teachers Association, 1963, 1964).

Traditional science courses, concerned mostly with scientific knowledge, put forth a "rhetoric of conclusions" (Schwab, 1962, p. 24). In the traditional course, science is presented as a body of knowledge which is static and proven "true." The course is organized according to the subject areas of the discipline, and new scientific developments, when recognized, are incorporated in additional chapters of the text. The course has a very weak theoretical base, if it has any at all (Hurd, 1961; Marshall & Burkman, 1966). The philosophical nature of science might be stated, but it is not elaborated. All too often, little or no distinction is made between observation statements and interpretation statements; likewise, little distinction is made between "facts" and mental constructs, abstractions, or conceptual schemes. The "scientific method" is put forth, usually at the beginning of the course, but the methodology of science is generally neglected in presenting the subject matter (Brandwein, Watson, & Blackwood, 1958; National Society for the Study of Education, 1947). Finally, emphasis on technological aspects is frequently employed as a motivation to the material, and industrial applications are presented as "science," but neither the differences nor the complex relationship between science and its applications is made clear.

In the classroom teaching of the traditional course, lectures by the teacher and reading and recitation by the students are the predominant activities, since these instructional techniques are thought to be the most efficient in "covering" a great deal of text material. Student laboratory work, rare in the lower grades, is not really needed for the development of the course. In the laboratory exercises that students perform, procedures are prescribed and observations are anticipated; confirmation of already learned conclusions is sought.

The traditional science courses have been criticized because they tend to be outdated, organized in a "patchwork" manner, too massive, and too technical; and, further, because they do not involve the student in the real activities of science (Marshall & Burkman, 1966). The "information crisis" and the lack of understanding of the strategic role of science in today's world must be met, it is argued by modern educators, with a science curriculum that concentrates on "scientific literacy." The courses must include knowledge which has "survival value" and must seek to provide students with intellectual abilities and social values relevant to the scientific world of the future (Brandwein et al., 1958; Educational Research Council of Greater Cleveland, 1966; Hurd, 1961; National Science Teachers Association, 1963; National Society for the Study of Education, 1960). Rational, critical thought processes must be developed as students "learn to learn," and the complex relationship between science and society must be considered (Educational Research Council of Greater Cleveland, 1966). It is for these reasons that science educators choose to bring the "spirit of science" to the classroom (California State Department of Education, 1967; National Education Association, 1966).

The new science courses put emphasis on the nature and structure of science and on the processes of scientific inquiry. Goodlad, for example, discusses the

> . . . striking similarity in the aims and objectives of nearly all [new curriculum] projects. Objectives, as they are defined in various descriptive documents, stress the importance of understanding the structure of the discipline, the purposes and methods of the field, and the part that creative men and women played in developing the field. One of the major aims is that the students get to explore, invent, discover, as well as sense some of the feelings and satisfactions of research scholars, and develop some of the tools of inquiry appropriate to the field.
>
> (Goodlad, 1964, p. 54)

The new science courses strive to bring out the difference between observation and interpretation, between data and conceptual schemes.

"Facts" are no longer to be learned as ends in themselves, but are selectively presented elements in the development of concepts. The new science courses emphasize the notion that scientific conclusions have a history, are today tentative, and may be altered or rejected in the future. The roles of mathematics and of conceptual models in science are also stressed. Instead of having material arranged according to the subject areas of a discipline, new courses are organized around processes of scientific inquiry (particularly at the lower grade levels) and around unifying conceptual ideas (particularly in the specialized high school courses). Recent developments in the sciences are an integral part of the new courses, rather than simply material for extra chapters at the end of the text. Depth rather than breadth is favored, although the authors of the new courses realize that this approach might leave gaps in the amount of scientific knowledge which a student may acquire. Finally, the attention given to technological applications is minimal, and motivation is engendered instead by the posing of problems that scientists face. In this way, an appreciation of science as a human intellectual endeavor is sought (Goodlad, 1964; Lockard, 1967; Marshall & Burkman, 1966; National Science Foundation, 1966; National Science Teachers Association, 1964; Schwab & Brandwein, 1962).

Since it is understood that a change in materials alone does not automatically lead students to an improved understanding of science, the developers of the new courses advocate corresponding changes in teaching methods. Lectures, demonstrations, and films are frequently appropriate, but a more extensive use of class discussion is also encouraged (Brandwein et al., 1958; Lockard, 1967; Schwab, 1963). Further, laboratory experiences are woven into the fabric of the new courses, for it is hoped that by engaging in problem solving, students will obtain a grasp of the processes of science. The laboratory is usually used to introduce, explore, and suggest problems, rather than to confirm the treatment of a particular topic; for the developers of the new courses believe that discussions based on investigatory work carried out by the students themselves will provide illustrations of how problems in science are approached and handled, and that this teaching procedure will also serve to motivate greater participation by the students.

To summarize, the traditional science courses concentrate on the knowledge of scientific facts, laws, theories, and technological applications, while the newer courses put emphasis on the nature, structure, and unity of science and on the processes of scientific inquiry. The traditional programs attempt to cover a great number of topics, while modern programs prefer depth to breadth. The traditional courses are taught largely by the lecture and recitation method and seek confirmation in laboratory exercises which are not essential to the course, whereas the modern programs employ discovery investigations as the basis of course development. Clearly, the traditional and modern science programs show marked contrasts; both types of programs, with their contrasting objectives, are fully represented in science instruction in American schools today.

Table 18-1, Table of Specifications for Science Education, displays the range of instructional objectives encompassed by both traditional and modern science programs. No single program now in use in the schools seeks to attain all the objectives given in the chart, but any particular program can be characterized by the subset of these objectives which it does seek to attain. Later in this chapter, several representative science programs are characterized in this way, as well as by the range of subject-matter content which each includes. Before turning to these illustrations, however, it may be well to delineate and discuss the various instructional objectives and subject-matter areas presented in Table 18-1.

Student behaviors

The instructional objectives which the framers or teachers of a science course or program want to attain can be expressed in terms of behaviors that students are expected to exhibit. Such behaviors form the horizontal dimension of Table 18-1. While no scheme of categorization is perfect or will satisfy everyone, the scheme adopted here successfully accommodates the full range of student behaviors which may be sought as outcomes of science instruction in elementary and secondary schools. Some of the categories included in this scheme will be familiar to readers acquainted with the *Taxonomy of Educational Objectives*, Handbook 1 (Bloom, 1956; and see the Appendix to Part I of this book). A main focus of the scheme, however, is on categories of student behaviors related to carrying out the processes of scientific inquiry. This focus is justified, not only because the contemporary trend of science education is toward an emphasis on the processes of inquiry, but because science is meaningfully and significantly considered as a system of inquiry, rather than simply as structured knowledge. Our scheme of categories also incorporates other student behaviors uniquely associated with the learning of science—the student's skills in performing laboratory work, the student's attitudes toward science, and the student's orientation to the relationships of science to other aspects of culture and to the individual.

Knowledge and comprehension (A.0) This category refers to the knowledge and comprehension of science subject matter that the student obtains solely or almost exclusively from reading books, from listening to lectures, and from other secondary sources. These are all legitimate sources of scientific information, both for the student and for the working scientist, and there is no intention to imply here that knowledge and comprehension should not be acquired from secondary sources in the course of science instruction. These sources of knowledge are, however, differentiated from the student's acquisition of scientific information by empirical procedures (category *B*.0) and his formulation of concepts, generalizations, and theories through involvement in inquiry (categories *D*.0 and *E*.0). To the extent that any instructional program employs books, films, lectures, or other media to convey science subject matter (and virtually all existing programs do), there will be more or fewer entries in the *Knowledge and comprehension* category. The behaviors suggested by this category are, first, that the student has acquired the specified information and, second, that he can recall it when asked to do so (subcategories *A*.1 to *A*.9) and can demonstrate comprehension of the information by identifying it in a new context or by manipulating it (subcategories *A*.10 and *A*.11). The first nine subcategories are derived largely from the *Knowledge* classification in the cognitive domain of the *Taxonomy of Educational Objectives*, which provides an excellent framework for delineating the various types of science knowledge that a student may learn.

"A honeybee has six legs." "Limestone floats on mercury." "In the United States, the days are longer than the nights between 21 March and 23 September." These are illustrations of facts which a student in science might be expected to know, and they illustrate subcategory *A*.1, *Knowledge of specific facts*, in the *Knowledge and comprehension* category. Specific facts that students could learn are countless, and success in learning and recalling some facts is an expectation of almost all science programs and courses at every level of sophistication. As the level of sophistication increases, the facts to be learned tend to incorporate an increasing number of scientific terms, concepts, and conventions, but knowledge of these is itself often considered an objective of instruction. Subcategory *A*.2, *Knowledge of scientific terminology*, is concerned with correct definition and use of terms that have become established in the scientist's vocabulary. To illustrate: "The *head*, *thorax*, and *abdomen* are the three parts of the body of a honeybee." "Limestone is a *mineral*." "21 March is called the *vernal equinox*; 23 September, the *autumnal equinox*."

The next subcategory, *A*.3, *Knowledge of concepts of science*, is likewise concerned with definition and correct usage. Though there is no general agreement on what constitutes a "concept" in science, here the term "concepts of science" is taken to mean those abstractions of observed phenomena or relationships which scientists have found to be continually useful in investigating the natural world and for which they have agreed upon exact definitions. In this sense, "concepts of science" includes both fairly limited scientific ideas (such as density, chemical element, diffusion, symbiosis, and germination) and larger scientific ideas (such as cycle, system, force, equilibrium, and adaptation). The intent in subcategory *A*.3, however, is to stop short of those ideas which are represented by major conceptual schemes or theories (see subcategory *A*.9, below). For subcategory *A*.4, *Knowledge of conventions*, the focus is on the student's correct usage and interpretation of signs, symbols, abbreviations, and practices that have been adopted in a science discipline to represent certain entities and relationships. Some illustrations from physics are:

$\vec{v}$ ⊣⊢ $_{92}U^{238}$

From chemistry:

$Ag^{+} + Cl^{-} \rightleftharpoons AgCl$

From genetics:

Aa × AA

Knowledge of trends and sequences, subcategory *A*.5, refers to the student's ordering of phenomena in the correct sequence of their occurrence in nature or under experimental manipulation. "The life cycle of the honeybee proceeds through successive stages from birth to death." "The action of acidic ground water on limestone mountains over time tends to produce hollow caverns and leads to the formation of stalactites and stalagmites." "In the northern hemisphere, days become progressively longer than nights between the vernal equinox and the summer solstice." Subcategory *A*.6, *Knowledge of classifications, categories, and criteria*, refers to the student's ordering of objects and phenomena in accordance with the organizing structures established by scientists in a discipline, and his recognition of the characteristics or properties that determine the placement of an object or phenomenon in a particular category. "The honeybee is classified as an insect; its six legs and three-part body are criteria for placing it in this category." "Mercury is classified as a liquid; at ordinary temperatures, it flows readily and takes the shape of its container. In these properties, it is different from a solid, such as limestone, and from a gas, such as carbon dioxide." "Since mercury cannot be broken down into any simpler substances by ordinary chemical means, it is classified as a chemical element; and since limestone can be broken down, it is a chemical compound."

Knowledge of scientific techniques and procedures, subcategory *A*.7, should be distinguished from the student's actual performance of laboratory techniques (category *G*.0, *Manual skills*), and from his use of scientific techniques and procedures in inquiry (categories *B*.0 to *E*.0). Similarly, in subcategories *A*.8 and *A*.9, the intent is to focus on the knowledge of scientific principles, laws, and theories which the student has acquired, rather than on his formulation of these abstract ideas through inquiry (categories *D*.0 and *E*.0). Among the myriad procedures and techniques used by scientists, the student may be asked to recall and describe how the specific gravity of mercury can be determined, or how the growth and division of cells in a honeybee's body can be studied, or how the exact time of the vernal equinox is found. Also included in subcategory *A*.7 is knowledge of the general procedures employed by scientists in conducting inquiries, the processes of scientific inquiry. Subcategory *A*.8 includes the acquisition and recall by the student of a particular scientific principle or law, which is defined as a generalization derived and established by scientists on the basis of a large number of observations of phenomena. Archimedes' principle is a generalization of many observations relating to floating objects. Mendel's laws are generalizations of observations of inherited characteristics in many plants and animals. The student's knowledge of the most abstract formulations in science, its theories or major conceptual schemes, is placed in subcategory *A*.9, the last of our recall classifications. In this subcategory are found the significant organizing and explanatory ideas of every scientific field, such as the theory of evolution, the kinetic-molecular theory, the orbital model of the atom, and the general theory of relativity.

Beyond simply recalling something when prompted to do so, the student may demonstrate that he has acquired an item of knowledge in situations that do not probe directly for it. A successful demonstration of this sort is usually taken as evidence that the student has some comprehension of the item of knowledge in question. Under subcategory *A*.10, the student demonstrates that he can identify a fact, concept, procedure, classification scheme, criterion for classification, principle, or theory when it is presented in a new context—that is, one which differs from the context in which the original instruction was given. For example, a science student may have learned the concept of a cycle in the context of the stages in the lives of flowering plants from seed to seed; then when presented with information about water evaporating from lakes and oceans, condensing in clouds, falling to earth as rain, and eventually collecting in lakes and oceans, he identifies this closed series of stages as a cycle. Or a student who has learned the criteria for classifying organisms as insects when studying honeybees may identify these criteria in given information about grasshoppers and decide that they also are classified as insects. Another way for the student to demonstrate comprehension is by successful translation. Under subcategory *A*.11, the student demonstrates that he can translate a fact, term, concept, convention, trend, principle, or theory presented in one symbolic form to another symbolic form. For example, given a verbal description of the forces involved in the situation of a horse pulling a wagon over a rough road, the student translates this information into a vector diagram showing the interacting forces; or given the chemical equation for any reaction, the student translates it into a verbal statement about the reaction. Finally, it should be noted that demonstrations of the student's comprehension of knowledge, which are included here under category *A*.0, are not the same as demonstrations of application, category *F*.0, where the emphasis is on the student's utilization of his knowledge to solve new problems.

Processes of scientific inquiry I: Observing and measuring (B.0) This category and the following three focus on the behavior of the science student involved in inquiry. The ordering of these four categories is not arbitrary, but represents successively greater involvement in the processes scientists employ to investigate the natural world and to construct new ideas. Starting in category *B*.0 with *Observing and measuring*, which in any given instance may or may not be a prelude to the investigation of a problem (and which includes behaviors that might actually be presented as exercises in an instructional program), the student engaging in inquiry would move generally through the stages of categories *C*.0 to *E*.0. By formulating and reformulating a theoretical model in category *E*.0, the student at this stage may become involved in aspects of "fluid enquiry," in contrast to the more common "stable enquiry" of the preceding stages (see Schwab, 1962). A cautionary note, nevertheless, is in order. These four categories are offered as a taxonomy of student behaviors related to the processes of scientific inquiry; they are *not* meant to be a prescription for conducting inquiries. It is likely that many of the behaviors given in the subcategories could be observed at some time when an inquiry is proceeding, but it is not claimed that all the behaviors will be observed in the course of every inquiry or that they will always occur in the order in which the subcategories appear here.

In indicating the content and scope of the subcategories in this and the following three categories, illustrations will be drawn chiefly from inquiries relating to heat phenomena. These phenomena offer a fruitful area for inquiry by science students with varying degrees of sophistication, from the early elementary school grades right on through high school. Heat phenomena, moreover, are familiar to the student from his everyday experiences, which can provide initial observations and questions for investigation.

Representative examples of the *Observation of objects and phenomena*, subcategory *B*.1, would be a student watching an ice cube placed in a glass of water in a warm room or noting changes of the water in a beaker that is being heated on a hotplate. For either of these situations, several dozen discrete things can be observed in a few minutes, and the oral or written communication of these observables constitutes the next subcategory, *B*.2, *Description of observations using appropriate language*. The emphasis here is on the effectiveness of the communication of the observations rather than on the form of the language used—which could vary widely, depending upon the level of sophistication attained by the student, and still communicate accurately what he observed. "The outside of the glass got wet" is as appropriate a description for a young student of an observation of the ice-cube-in-water system as "moisture accumulated on the glass's outer surface" is for an older student.

When the student's observations go beyond being only qualitative and beyond simple counting and when he employs any instrument to make them, his behavior represents subcategory *B*.3, *Measurement of objects and changes*. In the ice-cube-in-water system, for example, the initial temperature of water might be measured with a thermometer and found to be 22°C. The temperature of the water being heated on the hotplate might change from 22°C to 24°C after one minute, to 27°C at the end of the second minute, to 30°C at the end of the third minute. To obtain the data he is seeking in any measurement, the student must select the appropriate measuring instrument (subcategory *B*.4)—"appropriate" in the sense that the instrument is capable of measuring the desired quantity and in that it is operative over the range of the quantity to be measured. A stopwatch is not the appropriate instrument for measuring the temperature of water in a beaker; a mercury-in-glass thermometer is not appropriate for measuring the temperature of a melt in a blast furnace. Finally, subcategory *B*.5 concerns the student's taking account of the calibration markings of a measuring instrument. He should recognize that accuracy in measuring a quantity with a particular instrument is limited by the smallest division shown on its scale, and, when he makes measurements with that instrument, he estimates the values of the next subdivision between the smallest division shown. If a thermometer is calibrated with 1-degree divisions, its limit of accuracy is whole numbers of degrees, but a student may estimate the temperature of a liquid with this thermometer to be, for example, 28.5°C. Also included under subcategory *B*.5 is the significant-figures convention that a more advanced science student is expected to use for indicating accuracy when he records and manipulates measurements.

Processes of scientific inquiry II: Seeing a problem and seeking ways to solve it (C.0) A beaker of water has been heated to 80°C on a hotplate. Leaving the thermometer in the water, the student removes the beaker from the hotplate and places it on his desk. After five minutes, the thermometer reads 72°C. Since the water has lost some heat without anything being done to it, the student recognizes that he has a problem. He wants to investigate heat phenomena in liquids, and this will be difficult if he has to contend with apparently spontaneous losses of heat from his liquid samples to the surrounding air. He must minimize such heat losses in order to carry out his investigation, and his problem is how to accomplish this. What materials should he use for the containers that hold his liquid samples? Is heat loss through the walls of a container the same for containers of all materials?

A student's *Recognition of a problem* (subcategory *C*.1) may pass through several stages, as the foregoing illustration suggests—from an awareness of the problem area to the identification of a specific problem that can be investigated experimentally. The last question in the preceding paragraph is a specific problem susceptible to experimental investigation, and it might quickly lead the student to the *Formulation of a working hypothesis* (subcategory *C*.2) that would give direction to the investigation. He might hypothesize, for example, that heat is lost more readily through the walls of containers made of some materials than through the walls of containers made of other materials. An alternative and equally plausible hypothesis might be that the amount of heat lost depends on the thickness of the walls of the container and not on the material of which the container is made. Whatever his hypothesis may be, the student next takes steps to determine whether or not it is correct.

The *Selection of suitable tests of a hypothesis*,

subcategory C.3, involves choosing a particular empirical approach or a series of experiments that logically can verify the hypothesis if it is correct. This subcategory is concerned with the question whether or not a proposed experiment constitutes a valid test of the hypothesis; it is not concerned with the manipulative details of an experiment or the construction and use of apparatus (except insofar as these might affect validity). These latter concerns are included under subcategory *C.4, Design of appropriate procedures for performing experimental tests.* To obtain a valid test of the hypothesis that the heat lost from a container depends on the thickness of its walls and not on the material of which the container is made, the student would have to employ a twofold experimental approach. First, he needs to measure heat losses in containers made of the same material but with different wall thicknesses. Second, he needs to measure heat losses in containers with exactly the same wall thickness but made of different materials. A suitable test of the alternative hypothesis, that heat is lost more readily through the walls of containers made of some materials than through the walls of containers made of other materials, is more straightforward. The student would simply have to measure heat losses in containers made of different materials.

Before performing his experiments, the student designs and devises appropriate procedures (subcategory C.4) for measuring heat losses in containers made of different materials. One procedure could be: (1) obtain or make containers of exactly the same size and shape but of different materials, e.g., metals, glass, ceramic, solid plastic, foam plastic, paper; (2) fill each container to the same level with boiling water; (3) stir the water with a thermometer and record the water temperature; (4) continue stirring and record the water temperature every 60 seconds for a period of 30 minutes. In this illustration the equipment and procedures used are quite simple, but this is not so in many experiments that students may carry out. A determination of the velocity of light or of other electromagnetic radiations calls for complex apparatus and an elaborate procedure.

Processes of scientific inquiry III: Interpreting data and formulating generalizations (D.0) Experimental data are obtained by the student in the form of recorded observations and measurements, and he must usually process these data to yield values for the quantities under study. Subcategory *D.1, Processing of experimental data,* is concerned with the student's behavior in manipulating, adjusting, and organizing his observations and measurements. In a typical calorimetry experiment to determine the amount of heat (in calories) gained by a sample of lead, the measurements recorded are the mass of the sample (in grams), its initial temperature (in degrees C), and its final temperature; processing of these data includes subtracting the initial from the final temperature and multiplying the difference by the mass of the sample to yield the number of calories gained. In volumetric experiments with gases, processing of recorded data includes adjusting the actual measurements of volume to STP by using the recorded measurements of atmospheric pressure and room temperature. Other aspects of data processing that fall under subcategory *D.*1 are organizing data in tables or in other readily readable formats and, for more advanced science students, carrying out an error analysis.

Subcategories *D.*2 and *D.*4 deal with the student's preparation of graphs and his use of graphs. In an experiment to measure the volume of a sample of air at different temperatures but under constant pressure, a student found that the volume of the sample was 18.7 cm^3 at a temperature of 100°C (or 373°K), 14.6 cm^3 at 20°C (or 293°K), 13.7 cm^3 at 0°C (or 273°K), and 11.6 cm^3 at −40°C (or 233°K). To make a presentation of these data in the form of a functional relationship, subcategory *D.2*, the student plots the data points on a sheet of graph paper with absolute temperature (in degrees K) on one axis and volume on the other axis. Since the points can be connected by a straight line, his graph shows the functional relationship between the two variables: volume of air is directly proportional to absolute temperature. Had the relationship not been linear, the curve of the graph would have shown a different shape. By plotting points for the observed values of variables on suitably ruled graph paper, a student can make a presentation of any functional relationship. Extrapolation, when warranted, of functional relationships beyond actual observations and interpolation between observed points, subcategory *D*.4, can also be made from a graph. In the experiment we've used as an example, observations were made at 20°C and at 0°C, but the volume of air at 10°C (or 283°K) was not measured. Interpolating on the graph of the relationship reveals that the volume of the sample of air at 283°K was 14.2 cm^3. Similarly, extrapolating above the highest observed temperature and below the lowest observed temperature shows that the volume of the sample of air would be 21.2 cm^3 at 425°K and 8.6 cm^3 at 173°K. Both the interpolation and the two extrapolations are warranted here because there are no intervening conditions that alter the functional relationship between temperature and volume of air. An extrapolation to 73°K would not be warranted, however, because the air would have changed from a gas to a liquid before that temperature was reached, and the temperature-volume relationship does not take into account this intervening condition.

Interpretation of experimental data and observations, subcategory *D*.3, is the first stage in the student's analysis of the results of his experiment. If the observations are qualitative, their interpretation involves collating them mentally and formulating a discrete concept of what the experimental results signify. If the data are presented in the form of a graph, their interpretation also includes formulating a conception of the trends or the functional relationship displayed and translating this information into an equivalent verbal or symbolic form. In an experiment where the volume of a sample of oxygen gas was measured under different external pressures and at constant temperature, a graph of the data obtained was prepared. Interpreting this graph, a student was able to state that the volume of oxygen is inversely proportional to the external pressure at constant temperature or, in symbols, $PV = k$ (at constant T). Besides interpreting data from his own experiments, the student may have occasion to interpret experimental findings obtained in inquiries of other persons, and such occasions are also included under subcategory *D*.3.

A further stage in the student's analysis of the results of an experiment falls under subcategory *D*.5, *Evaluation of a hypothesis under test in the light of the experimental data obtained.* A valid test of a hypothesis having been selected, designed, and carried out, data having been collected, organized, and interpreted, it is time to check whether or not the findings verify the hypothesis. The student now must answer the question, "Is the evidence consistent with the hypothesis?" If experimental data show that the temperature of water in metal containers drops more than water in plastic containers over the same period of time, this evidence is consistent with the hypothesis that heat is lost more readily through the walls of containers made of some materials than through the walls of containers made of other materials, and that hypothesis has been verified. Parenthetically, the behavior described in this subcategory is classified under *Analysis of relationships* (4.20) in the *Taxonomy of Educational Objectives* (Bloom, 1956).

In an inquiry into the changes in the volume of air at different temperatures, a student has found the relationship that, at constant pressure, the volume of a sample of air is directly proportional to its absolute temperature. Does this finding represent a general principle applicable to all samples of air? Is this an empirical law covering all gases, not only air? In the course of answering these questions, the student engages in behaviors included under subcategory *D*.6, *Formulation of appropriate generalizations (empirical laws or principles) that are warranted by the relationships found.* He considers the results of experiments with other samples of air and carries out or checks the reports of other similar inquiries using different gases. If his original finding is corroborated, he is justified in formulating an empirical generalization: at constant pressure, the volume of a gas is directly proportional to its absolute temperature. It should be noted that this stage in the student's analysis of the results of an experiment involves making comparisons with other results and deriving from all the evidence available an abstract relation covering a range of related phenomena. The outcome of the student's thinking, the generalization he formulates, is a synthesis (see subcategory 5.30, *Derivation of a set of abstract relations*, in Bloom, 1956). By virtue of the quite complex behaviors a student exhibits in this and the preceding two subcategories of category *D*.0, it is reasonable to infer that higher mental processes are operating.

Processes of scientific inquiry IV: Building, testing, and revising a theoretical model (E.0) As inquiry in any area of science proceeds, many observations and knowledge of many phenomena are accumulated, generalizing empirical laws and principles are formulated. When inquiries are carried out within the framework of an accepted conceptual structure, the investigator goes no further than the accumulation of knowledge or the formulation of principles. The investigator is engaging in "stable enquiry," as Schwab (1962) has termed it, and this type of inquiry characterizes most of the research of scientists and science students. There are some occasions, however, when the broad conceptual structure in an area of inquiry has not been established or when new findings call it into question, and it is then that an investigator can engage in "fluid enquiry." In this type of inquiry, the aim of research is not only to ascertain facts and to formulate principles, but to build a theoretical model that will satisfactorily interrelate and accommodate them. The science student, whose own conceptual structure is not yet fixed, can often engage in fluid inquiry, if care is taken not to implant existing scientific theories as dogmas in his mind, and he can have experiences in building and testing theoretical models. Key aspects of these experiences are included in the behaviors classified in category *E*.0.

Recognition of the need for a theoretical model to relate different phenomena and empirical laws or principles, subcategory *E*.1, refers to the student's acceptance of theory building as a legitimate part of scientific inquiry. This behavior is aptly illustrated by an example of its negation. During the nineteenth century many chemists refused to give serious consideration to the atomic theory or any other theoretical model of matter. They asserted that the only proper concern of the science of chemistry are macroscopic properties and changes that can be observed, and, eschewing speculative ideas, they based their science solely on various chemical laws and principles generalized from their laboratory experiences. Chemists today, on the other hand, like all scientists, recognize that empirical laws are not sufficient to organize and correlate all known phenomena, and they engage in the formulation of theoretical models, which serve three major functions in science. First, a theoretical model has a correlative function in that it ties together in a consistent, rational manner the various phenomena and generalizations in the area that it covers. Second, it has an explanatory function: a theoretical model is used to account for or explain the observations and generalizations in its area. Third, it has a heuristic function—to suggest new hypotheses, problems, and experiments that will give direction to further inquiries. When the science student is cognizant of these functions, he will be more apt to go beyond observations and empirical generalizations to the level of formulating and testing theoretical models.

Subcategory *E*.2, *Formulation of a theoretical model to accommodate known phenomena and principles*, identifies the first phase of the theory-building process. This phase, like the formulation of empirical generalizations (subcategory *D*.6), involves a synthesis of the student's knowledge to develop an abstract relationship; but the student is now operating at a higher level of abstraction. He tries to formulate a broad, general statement about the phenomena in an area of inquiry, and this statement will usually consist of a small set of postulates or assumptions about certain constituents or behaviors of nature. For example, after some time spent in investigating heat phenomena, the student might propose that the various observations and generalizations which were made can be explained by conceiving of heat as a fluid substance. This theoretical model of heat could be expressed in a set of postulates like the following:

1. Heat is a colorless, odorless, invisible fluid substance.
2. Heat fluid occupies space and has mass, like other substances, but it has a very small mass.
3. Heat fluid flows spontaneously from regions of high concentration to regions of low concentration (from hot objects to cooler objects).
4. Heat fluid is always associated with matter, and it increases disorder in the arrangement of particles of matter.
5. Heat fluid readily enters some gases, liquids, and solids, but it does not readily enter other gases, liquids, and solids.
6. When matter changes its state from solid to liquid or from liquid to gas, it absorbs heat fluid; and when matter changes its state from gas to liquid or from liquid to solid, it releases heat fluid.

If this theoretical model of heat has merit, the student can use it to account for or explain various heat phenomena. His specification of the phenomena and principles that he can explain in this way is the behavior classified as subcategory *E*.3.

The analyses which the student makes under this subcategory, *Specification of phenomena and principles that are satisfied or explained by a theoretical model,* are quite similar to the analyses he makes in evaluating hypotheses (subcategory *D*.5), but here he is operating across an additional level of abstraction. When he is evaluating hypotheses, the student analyzes the relationship between a hypothesis and observational evidence, but here under subcategory *E*.3 he analyzes the relationship between a theoretical model and both generalized evidence, expressed as empirical laws and principles, and discrete observations. The following are examples of some observations and empirical laws regarding heat that are satisfied by the theoretical model given above: "Metals are good conductors of heat but plastics are not" (explained by postulate 5). "When water at 60°C is added to water at 20°C, the resulting temperature of the water mixture is greater than 20°C" (explained by postulate 3). "The volume of a given quantity of any solid, liquid, or gas increases when it is heated" (explained by postulates 2, 3, and 4). "Additional heating is required to change water at 100°C to steam at 100°C" (explained by postulate 6). "At constant pressure, the volume of a gas is directly proportional to its absolute temperature" (explained by postulates 2 and 4). The greater the number of observations and principles that are encompassed by a theoretical model, the more successful it is in fulfilling its correlative and explanatory function. If the student can specify many phenomena that are satisfied by the theoretical model he has formulated, he will have increased confidence in its adequacy.

The heuristic function of a theoretical model is exemplified in the next subcategory of student behaviors, *E*.4, *Deduction of new hypotheses from a theoretical model,* to direct observations and experiments for testing it. This phase of theory building involves two identifiable mental operations. First, beginning with the statement of his theoretical model, the student reasons from it and in terms of it to certain deductions (hypotheses) that the model logically suggests or implies. This mental process is not unlike the logical derivation by deduction of new propositions from a given set of theorems in geometry. Once he has deduced a new hypothesis, the student then proposes a plan of experiments, observations, or both, which will test the hypothesis. This mental operation was discussed under subcategory *C*.3, *Selection of suitable tests of a hypothesis.* The significant difference between *E*.4 and *C*.3 is that here the proposed plan of inquiry serves not only to test the correctness of a hypothesis but also to test the adequacy of the theoretical model from which the student generated the hypothesis. To illustrate, postulate 2 of the theoretical model given above states that heat fluid, like other substances, has mass, though its mass is very small. From this and from postulate 3, which suggests that a hot object contains more heat fluid than a cold object, a student could deduce the hypothesis that an object has a greater mass when it is hot than when it is cold. Since, by postulate 2, the mass of heat fluid is very small, the comparison of the mass of the hot object with that of the cold object would have to be made over a large temperature difference, say 100°C or more, to test this hypothesis.

Another hypothesis a student might deduce from the theoretical model of heat fluid is suggested by postulate 5, that heat fluid readily enters some substances but does not readily enter some others. The student might deduce from this that a characteristic of different substances, say different metals, is their differing capacities to increase their temperature when the same amount of heat is available. The hypothesis is that each kind of metal, for example, has a "specific heat" which can be used to identify it. For either of these illustrative hypotheses, as well as for many others that could be deduced from the theoretical model, the student would next propose appropriate experiments and observations that would lead to a determination of whether or not the hypothesis is correct. Actually carrying out the proposed plan of inquiry is *not* a part of the behavior included under subcategory *E*.4; the indicated investigations may even be conducted by other persons. Such investigations would involve the processes of inquiry already described under subcategory *C*.4 and categories *B*.0 and *D*.0. Clearly, new cycles of inquiry have thus been stimulated by a theoretical model as it fulfills its heuristic function.

Like subcategory *E*.3, the student's behaviors included in subcategory *E*.5, *Interpretation and evaluation of the results of experiments to test a theoretical model,* involve analyses of relationships. In this subcategory, the student seeks to analyze the relationships between the empirical evidence obtained and the hypothesis tested *and* between the empirical evidence and the theoretical model from which the hypothesis was deduced. In addition, when these analyses are at hand, the student makes a judgment about the adequacy of the theoretical model itself. His judgment of the adequacy of the model is generally based both on evidence of consistency and precision throughout the theoretical structure and on the degree to which it satisfies scientists' criteria for a "good" model. Scientists commonly base their evaluation of a theoretical model on two kinds of criteria—analytical criteria related to how well the model fulfills its correlative, explanatory, and heuristic functions; and certain essentially aesthetic considerations about the model's parsimony, elegance, and persuasiveness. In the phase of theory building represented by subcategory *E*.5, the science student has opportunities to join with others in discussions and even arguments about the value of a theoretical model, since controversies among scientists are not unusual when competing models are being evaluated.

Suppose that a student has the results of a large number of experiments with many different metals which show that the "specific heat" of every metal tested differs from that of every other metal. These results confirm his hypothesis that each kind of metal has a "specific heat" which can be used to identify it, and this confirmation gives him some increased confidence in the theoretical model from which he deduced the hypothesis. Another student, however, has the results of many careful experiments repeatedly carried out to test his hypothesis that an object has a greater mass when it is hot than when it is cold. In none of the experiments was an increase detected in the mass of an object when its temperature was raised as much as 500°C. These results indicate that the student's hypothesis is not correct, and the failure to confirm it suggests that postulate 2 of the theoretical model, that heat fluid has mass, is not correct. The student might now reason that the entire theoretical model of heat as a fluid substance is thrown into question. If heat fluid has no mass, he would say, it is inconsistent to assume that heat is a substance, since no other substance without mass is known. But this case against the model is not decisive. As the first student, who has gained confidence in the model, could argue, the mass of heat fluid may be much smaller than originally anticipated, and it may actually be so small that the addition of heat fluid mass to the mass of an object in a temperature increase of only 500°C cannot be detected with the instruments used in the experiments. From this point on, a lively discussion evidently can proceed, as each student marshals evidence, reasoned arguments, and judgments in the process of interpreting the results of experiments and evaluating a theoretical model.

Through the accumulation of new observations, through the interpretation and reinterpretation of results of experiments, through discussions and debates, any theoretical model in science becomes modified and sometimes is overthrown.

The science student engaging in fluid inquiry will before long encounter a phase of theory building in which he finds it necessary to reformulate a theoretical model he has espoused. His behavior at this juncture is described by subcategory E.6, *Formulation of a revised, refined, or extended theoretical model*, when warranted by new observations or interpretations. Depending upon the nature and extent of the new observations or interpretations, the student's reformulation of his theoretical model may range from a minor modification to major surgery. The thought processes he employs here are not essentially different, of course, from those required for his original formulation of a theoretical model, subcategory E.2. The additional requisite under subcategory E.6, however, is that his reformulation take into account the wealth of new experiences and ideas developed in the intervening phases of theory building. Many observations and generalizations about heat were satisfactorily correlated and explained by the theoretical model above, and hypotheses deduced from it were confirmed by experiments. Other observations of heat phenomena and some derived hypotheses which were found to be incorrect suggested that the theoretical model was inadequate and should be modified or rejected. In confronting the task of reformulating his theoretical model of heat, the student must incorporate all this information in his thinking and devise a model that will obviate the defects of the original one without sacrificing its positive features. He may refine or extend the theoretical model by changing some of its postulates or by adding some, or he may revise his model entirely—for instance, by conceiving of heat as due to the motion of the particles of a substance. Whatever route his reformulation takes, he must ensure that his new model fulfills the correlative, explanatory, and heuristic functions and satisfies the criteria of parsimony, elegance, and persuasiveness expected of every acceptable theoretical model.

Application of scientific knowledge and methods (F.0) Both in his everyday life and in his schoolwork, the student confronts new problems that he must solve. He frequently can proceed toward a solution of a problem by calling upon his repertoire of scientific knowledge and inquiry skills. The student may have acquired the knowledge and skills which he can use in solving a particular problem either from secondary sources (category *A*.0) or through his participation in inquiry (categories *B*.0 to *E*.0). In either event, when he applies relevant scientific knowledge and methods to a new problem where the mode of solution is not specified, the student's behavior can be classified under category *F*.0, *Application*.

The behaviors involved when a student makes an application have been well described in the *Taxonomy of Educational Objectives* (Bloom, 1956, pp. 120–123), and this formulation is adopted here. The three subcategories of *F*.0 present a rough typology of problems to which the student may apply his scientific knowledge and inquiry skills, and their order suggests increasing remoteness from the learning situation in which he originally acquired the knowledge or skill. Subcategory *F*.1, *Application to new problems in the same field of science*, represents the most common situation in which students are called upon to make applications in the school context where their courses are organized by science fields. The following are a few illustrative problems, posed as questions to which the solutions call for the application of knowledge and skills from the same science field: "Why does this light bulb in this electrical circuit light up when I open this switch?" "How can you find out whether or not this rooster has a deficiency of male hormones?" "What can you do to speed up this chemical reaction?" "Will peeling off the bark of this birch tree cause it to die?" When the student uses a fact, concept, principle, theory, or method that he has learned in one science field to solve a problem in another field, his behavior is described under subcategory *F*.2, *Application to new problems in a different field of science*. "Why does water rise in the stem of this plant?" "How was this limestone cavern formed?" "How can nutriments pass through the wall of this frog's intestine?" "Why are there tides in the ocean?"

The last application subcategory, *F*.3, considers

the student applying his knowledge and inquiry skills to problems outside of science. Included in the designation "outside of science" are technological applications. Though the distinction between science and technology in some areas of investigation is sometimes obscure (e.g., in medical research or in nuclear energy research), it still seems desirable to distinguish problems of science, where the goal is the development of understanding, from problems of technology, where the motivation is the building, designing, or production of something directly useful. "How can large quantities of ammonia be cheaply made from nitrogen and hydrogen?" "What can be done to improve the quality of the corn produced on this farm?" "How can the spread of malaria in this region be checked?" "Will this bridge collapse if a 10-ton truck passes over it?" "Will this black coat keep me comfortably warm in Alaska in winter?" Under subcategory *F*.3, the applications of scientific knowledge and methods which a student can make outside of science extend virtually without limit. Not only his knowledge, but especially his skills in the processes of scientific inquiry, can be applied to almost every area of human endeavor.

Manual skills (G.0) The earlier discussions of categories *B*.0 and *C*.0 referred to such processes of scientific inquiry as making observations and measurements, selecting measuring instruments, and designing experimental procedures; and subcategory *A*.7 concerns the student's knowledge of scientific techniques and procedures. But nowhere so far in this categorization scheme has the focus been on the student's manipulative skills in performing laboratory tasks. To the author's knowledge, no comprehensive studies have yet been made of the manual skills involved in science laboratory work in schools. Still, students do laboratory work; moreover, they are usually expected to manipulate apparatus with some facility, to avoid hurting themselves and others, and not to damage the equipment.

The two subcategories of behaviors in category *G*.0 are practically self-explanatory. Lighting and regulating the flame of a Bunsen burner is a paradigm example of subcategory *G*.1, *Development of skills in using common laboratory equipment.* Other common equipment which the student should learn to manipulate includes the balance, microscope, and ruler, and chemical glassware. In subcategory *G*.1 the emphasis is on the manual and coordinating skills the student develops as he works with various tools of the scientist's trade, whereas subcategory *G*.2, *Performance of common laboratory techniques with care and safety,* is concerned with the student's carrying out of a sequence of manipulations toward a defined end. Examples are collecting a sample of a gas insoluble in water, preparing thin sections for microscopic examination, dissecting an animal specimen, finding the electrical resistance of a wire, and determining the hardness of a mineral specimen. A student's successful performance of these and other techniques calls for them to be done carefully, so that good results are obtained, and to be carried out with sufficient attention to safety to prevent injuring either the equipment or the experimenter.

Attitudes and interests (H.0) This category of behaviors ventures into the affective domain, the domain that includes "objectives which emphasize a feeling tone, an emotion, or a degree of acceptance or rejection." This characterization is taken from page 7 of the *Taxonomy of Educational Objectives*, Handbook 2, *Affective Domain* (Krathwohl, Bloom, & Masia, 1964), and it calls attention to classes of student behaviors which undoubtedly loom large among the desired outcomes of science instruction. Category *H*.0, however, does not pretend to be a complete taxonomy of the affective domain as it pertains to the student's learning in science. While it would be most desirable to have such a taxonomy, the present lack of reliable knowledge and the primitive level of discussions about the affective domain in science education make it unlikely that an affective-domain taxonomy for science can be constructed at this time. About the best that now seems possible is a categorization of aimed-for or hoped-for attitudes and interests that are frequently stated by science teachers and curriculum builders.

As the authors of the *Affective Domain* repeatedly point out, wide ranges of meaning are implied or intended when the affective terms "attitude" and "interest" are used in educational circles, and they propose that the more precise terminology of their taxonomy be substituted in discussions of students' affective behaviors. Again, because of the paucity of informed, analytical discussions of affective behaviors in science education until now, implementation of this proposal is hardly feasible at present. It is already amply clear, however, that a student's attitudes and interests are always associated with cognitive elements. The student's acquisition and understanding of some significant cognitive components that underlie or accompany general attitudes and interests in science are identified in category *I.0, Orientation*.

Probably every teacher of science hopes that his students will develop favorable attitudes toward science and scientists. Some teachers, but not all, consciously plan learning experiences that may promote the fulfillment of this hope, even though they realize that the development of attitudes is generally a long-term proposition. Whether the attitudes result from the efforts of a teacher or from other influences, behaviors which manifest favorable attitudes toward science and scientists are included under subcategory *H.1*. If a student denounces science as a sinister enterprise or refers to scientists as "eggheads" whom he prefers to ignore, he is hardly displaying favorable attitudes. More positive expressions of feelings and, when occasions arise, actions supportive of science and scientists are wanted. No one wishes to see the student affect a fawning awe of science or an uncritical reverence of scientists. Nonetheless, it is reasonable to see whether the student will speak, write, and act in ways which show that he places a positive value on the role of science in furthering man's understanding and that he gives due acknowledgment to scientists for their past and potential future contributions in this quest.

The next two subcategories, *H.2* and *H.3*, relate to the student's attitudes toward scientific inquiry. Subcategory *H.2* concerns his *Acceptance of scientific inquiry as a way of thought.* If a student accepts the processes of scientific inquiry as a valid way to conduct his thinking, his behavior in approaching a problem or novel situation will be sufficiently consistent for competent observers of his actions to describe him as "behaving just like a scientist." With reference to the terminology and classifications of the *Taxonomy of Educational Objectives,* Handbook 2, the student's acceptance of scientific inquiry as a way of thought is at least at the level of *Acceptance of a value* (3.1), thought his behavior also could be evidence of *Commitment* (3.3) or even an observable example of his *Generalized set* (5.1). It is entirely possible that a student could engage in the processes of scientific inquiry even though he viewed them merely as school exercises; that he could observe, measure, hypothesize, formulate generalizations, and devise and test theoretical models without any sense that these activities are personally valuable to him and without feeling that they might be valid guidelines for his own thinking. Such a student has not accepted scientific inquiry as his own way of thought. It is reasonable to conceive of scientific inquiry, fundamentally, as a state of mind. The student whose mind is attuned to inquiry is characterized by more than the mechanical performance of inquiry processes. His behaviors attest that he is personally convinced that scientific inquiry is a valuable operating mode, perhaps the only valid mode for him. Under subcategory *H.2* are included those behaviors which give evidence of the student's personal, cognitive-affective acceptance of scientific inquiry—with one exception: behaviors which show that the student has adopted any of the so-called "scientific attitudes" are assigned to subcategory *H.3*.

Over the years an idealized folklore about scientists' personal characteristics has been promulgated, which makes them appear both extremely virtuous and somewhat unreal. Scientists supposedly possess certain scientific attitudes, which include honesty, open-mindedness, self-criticism, willingness to suspend judgment, and commitment to accuracy. In actuality, the noble characteristics attributed to scientists are more a reflection of the nature of scientific inquiry and the internal social organization of science than of the personalities of scientists. What are generally known as "scientific attitudes" are better described as professional standards, to which adherence by practitioners of scientific inquiry is expected by the scientific community. Since a scientist's reported experiments and observations can almost always be checked or duplicated by other scientists, frauds and sloppy operators are rapidly detected. When carrying out inquiries, therefore, the scientist tries to be as accurate, honest, self-critical, and open-minded as he possibly can. If he is not, he will soon lose the respect of his colleagues and may be ostracized by his profession. Institutional pressures on the scientist, rather than virtuous personal attributes, account for the "scientific attitudes" that he displays in the conduct of inquiries. The science student conducting inquiries is usually expected to imitate the scientist at work; and it is hoped that the habits of thought the scientist then displays will become a part of the student's repertoire as well. If this has occurred, it will at some time be indicated in the student's actions and responses in novel situations, and these behaviors are included in subcategory *H.3*, *Adoption of "scientific attitudes"*—that is, habits of thought which ideally characterize scientists when they are engaged in inquiry.

Subcategory *H.4*, *Enjoyment of science learning experiences*, calls attention to an evidently desirable, but sadly not always evident, aspect of school science learning. There is strong psychological evidence that students learn better, learn more, and remember longer when they find pleasure in the learning experience. In science, the opportunities for the student to find pleasure in learning are enormous. The sight, sound, and smell of phenomena; the uncovering of a new relationship, generalization, or explanation; the spark of discussions of conflicting ideas—these are all potential sources of involvement and enjoyment. The student who enjoys his learning experiences in science will express his feelings, either in words or in other ways. Assign these expressions to subcategory *H.4*.

The student's interests are the focus of the last two subcategories in category *H.0*. Under subcategory *H.5*, *Development of interests in science and science-related activities*, there are two main aspects. First are the student's interests in activities that he can carry out himself. A general criterion for a student's interest in a science or science-related activity is that he does it voluntarily and without regard to the requirements of a science course. A few examples are doing chemical experiments, collecting butterflies, building a "ham" radio receiver, and experimenting with hybrid flowers. The second aspect of the student's interests in science activities concerns the attention he gives to the ongoing events in science and in the societal interactions of science. Here the student generally participates vicariously, although on occasions when a science-related issue is brought to public notice, he may be able to demonstrate his interest through concrete action. Some examples of behavior which show that the student has interests in science activities in this second sense are reading about new developments in solid-state physics, watching a television program on cancer research, or circulating a petition for preservation of a wildlife refuge.

While subcategory *H.5* deals with the student's more or less transitory interests in particular science activities and with the interests of the scientifically literate person, subcategory *H.6* concerns vocational interests. It is true that, in comparison with the total population at any school level, only a small proportion of students evince the inclination and aptitude for scientific or science-related careers. For the student who does, however, *Development of his interest in pursuing a career in science or science-related work* (subcategory *H.6*) is a legitimate and worthy part of his learning in science. If this interest is developed by a student, his behavior in relevant situations—e.g., responding to a survey on vocational interests—will show a commitment in the direction of careers or jobs in which science is involved.

Orientation (I.0) The intention of the newer science courses and programs to develop the student's appreciation of science as a human intellectual endeavor was noted in the introductory pages of this chapter. The new programs also tend to concentrate on fostering "scientific literacy," and several direct the student's attention to the complex relationships between science and society. Taken together, these aspects of the new science program seem to call for competencies and understandings that enlarge the student's perspective of the world and help him to orient himself in it.

Category *I.0*, *Orientation*, has five subcategories, and the reader should note that a key term in four of these is "recognition," "realization," or "awareness." What is implied and intended by these terms is a certain sensitivity on the student's part to the *relationships* between science and other large areas of human endeavor and other ways of thought. Relationships are emphasized because these are the primary focus of the student's orientation, which enables him to perceive the enterprise of science and his study of science in a more meaningful manner. Unfortunately, space limitations preclude a discussion of these relationships here. The reader should refer to selected writings in the considerable body of literature on "scientific literacy" for explorations of the relationships indicated in the subcategories of category *I.0*. (For a bibliography of 100 referents to scientific literacy, see Pella, O'Hearn, & Gale, 1967.)

Subcategories *I.1* and *I.2* concern the student's orientation toward some significant philosophical aspects of science. His awareness of the logical status of statements he and scientists make is the concern of subcategory *I.1*, *Relationships among and distinctions between various types of statements in science* (for example, observation, interpretation, law, theory). Our earlier discussion of the processes of scientific inquiry, categories *B.0* to *E.0*, referred to these distinctions and relationships. They are entered again in this subcategory under *Orientation* to emphasize that the student should be aware of them whenever he is engaged in inquiry and when he steps back to view science in a larger perspective. This latter behavior would be a part of the student's orientation indicated by subcategory *I.2*, *Recognition of the limitations of scientific explanation and of the influence of scientific inquiry on general philosophy*. While relatively few students will wish to delve very deeply into such recondite matters, almost every student can acquire some awareness of the relationship between the kind of thinking which he practices in his science courses and alternative ways of construing the world. (For the reader interested in discussion of these matters, books such as those by Nagel, 1961; Nash, 1963; and Walker, 1963, will be useful.)

Subcategory *I.3* suggests an orientation of the student to the evolutionary character of science. Every scientific idea has a history. The history of a particular idea and the circumstances in which it is developed determine, in large measure, what the present content of the idea is and what it may become. This perspective can become a part of the orientation of any student who traces the historical development of one or more scientific ideas. The student's recognition that the past, present, and future development of science is a product of its own history and a reflection of the general culture of its time gives him a historical perspective on the scientific enterprise. (For further discussion, see Conant, 1951; Klopfer, 1969.)

The two final *Orientation* subcategories concern the relationships between science and the larger culture in which it flourishes. These relationships, referred to by some writers as the "external social aspects" of science, are reciprocal. The more obvious influence of science on society is seen in the changes in man's daily life brought about by technological applications of scientific principles and ideas. Refrigerators, television, nuclear bombs, antibiotics, and birth-control pills are but a few examples. More subtle, and probably more fundamental, is the influence of scientific ideas on human values and man's perception of the world. The ideas of heliocentrism, the geological time scale, and evolution have greatly altered man's outlook; ideas from physiology, biochemistry, and genetics, applied to producing "the pill," performing organ transplants, and altering human heredity, raise new questions of morality. Reciprocally, society influences science and scientific inquiry. The financial support that is available from public and private agencies often determines which research problems scientists investigate. The state of technological development and the industrial capacity of a nation affect the quantity and quality of equipment and supplies available to support scientific research projects. The quality of a nation's educational system and the encouragement it gives to scientific study determine the number and the competence of scientists who emerge from it. A society's general intellectual climate, its attitudes toward inquiry, and the value it places on scientific work are reflected both in the number of persons who choose science as a career and in the amount of scientific inquiry the society supports.

The science student's orientation to the interactions between science and culture are summarized in subcategory I.4, *Realization of the relationships among scientific progress, technical achievement, and economic development,* and subcategory I.5, *Awareness of the social and moral implications of scientific inquiry,* and its results for the individual, community, nation, and the world. Relating these two subcategories to category H.0, *Attitudes and interests,* it is noteworthy that the perspectives on the relations between science and culture which the student gains here complements, and provides some essential cognitive elements for, his personal view of the relation between himself and science.

Content

The vertical dimension of Table 18-1 presents the range of content included in elementary and secondary school science programs. Though there are many possible ways of categorizing the subject matter of science, the advantages of the scheme adopted here are that it encompasses virtually all the content of school science instruction, both in traditional and modern courses, and that it reflects the divisions and subdivisions of the subject that are commonly accepted by contemporary science teachers and educators. Most current practice separates the biological sciences from the physical sciences, even though the interconnections between them are recognized, and this bifurcation provides the first two categories for our content scheme. Category 3.0, called *General,* includes those aspects of the content of science instruction which pertain to all the natural sciences.

Biological sciences (1.0) The three subcategories of category 1.0 correspond with three levels of biological organization—the cellular level, the organism level, and the population level. These subcategories offer a convenient way of arranging the biological content of instruction, and they have been selected without prejudice to any side in the current debate over which of these or other levels of organization should have priority in children's science education. The fact is that all three levels are represented in the biological science children now study in schools. Biological phenomena at the molecular level are also studied in some courses; these have been placed, for the most part, in content area 2.19 in this categorization scheme, under the physical sciences.

Each of the subcategories has been divided further into a number of content areas. As will become evident, these content areas serve as reference points for the structures of science programs and for the illustrative test items in the next two sections of this chapter. In the following listing, specific topics and ideas included in each content area of the three subcategories are identified.

1.1 *Biology of the cell*
- 1.11 *Cell structure and function*
  Organisms are made of cells; the cell as the unit of structure and function.
- 1.12 *Transport of cellular material*
  Diffusion and osmosis; osmoregulation, permeability, membrane phenomena.
- 1.13 *Cell metabolism*
  Basic ideas of metabolism and respiration; intracellular metabolism.
- 1.14 *Photosynthesis*
  Organismic, cellular, and biochemical aspects of photosynthesis.

1.15 *Cell responses*
Regulation of cell response and cell behavior.

1.16 *Concept of the gene*
The idea of an inheritable unit; gene and gene action; deoxyribonucleic acid (DNA).

1.2 *Biology of the organism*

1.21 *Diversity of life*
Variety of life; classification of plants and animals, taxonomic relationships between plants and animals; the diversity of plant and animal forms and its implications.

1.22 *Metabolism in organisms*
Ideas of breathing, digestion, etc.; plant and animal physiology; metabolism in organisms and the structural adaptations involved.

1.23 *Regulation in organisms*
Regulation of temperature and water balance; homeostasis at the level of the multicellular organism.

1.24 *Coordination and behavior*
Plant and animal reactions to external stimuli; plant and animal coordination and responses, behavior; nervous and hormonal regulation.

1.25 *Reproduction and development*
Ideas of reproduction, life histories; animal reproduction and development, metamorphosis; plant reproduction and development.

1.26 *Human biology*
Man as a living organism; man in his physical and social environment.

1.3 *Biology of populations*

1.31 *Natural environment*
Interrelationships between plants and animals in their environment; energy relationships in ecosystems.

1.32 *Cycles in nature*
Food chains and food relationships; predators and scavengers; food cycles, pyramid of numbers.

1.33 *Natural groups and their segregation*
Concept of natural groups; speciation, modern taxonomy.

1.34 *Population genetics*

1.35 *Evolution*
Basic ideas of evolution; variation, competition, adaptation, natural selection.

Physical sciences (2.0) This category is divided into three subcategories which correspond to the physical-science courses most commonly offered in secondary schools—chemistry, physics, and earth and space sciences. The content areas under each subcategory include all topics taken up in traditional and modern versions of these courses. Since the physical-science content of elementary and junior high school science is, in general, arranged to be propaedeutic for the courses offered in high school, the same content areas also satisfactorily serve for this educational level. The specific topics and ideas included in each content area are indicated in the following list.

2.1 *Chemistry*

2.11 *Chemical materials*
Recognition and uses of chemical materials; division of chemical materials into heterogeneous and homogeneous substances; compounds, mixtures; purification and separation of chemical materials; extraction processes from raw materials.

2.12 *Classification of chemical elements*
Metals versus nonmetals; periodic table; periodic system.

2.13 *Chemical change*
Definition of chemical change; oxidation and reduction; laboratory preparation of common elements and compounds; industrial processes.

2.14 *Chemical laws*
Conservation of mass; laws of chemical combination, stoichiometry.

2.15 *Energy relationships and equilibrium in chemical systems*
Exothermal and endothermal reactions; energy relationships, chemical equilibrium, chemical kinetics.

2.16 *Electrochemistry*
Electrolysis and ionization; ionic equations, redox reactions.

2.17 *Atomic and molecular structure*
Elements and compounds, atoms, molecules; chemical bonding and chemical structure, modern atomic theories.

2.18 *Introductory organic chemistry*
Hydrocarbons, polymerization and polymers, esterification, natural and synthetic processes.

2.19 *Chemistry of life processes*

Chemistry of respiration and nutrition; biochemical reactions, enzymes.

2.110 *Nuclear chemistry*
Nuclear reactions, radioactivity, isotopes.

2.2 *Physics*

2.21 *Kinematics*
Motion, velocity, acceleration; vectors; time and timing.

2.22 *Dynamics*
Force, inertia, mass, weight, gravitation, momentum, friction; Newton's laws; law of moments, equilibrium.

2.23 *Energy and its conservation*
Forms of energy, work, transformations of energy; mechanical energy, potential energy, kinetic energy; conservation of energy.

2.24 *Mechanical advantage*
Lever, pulley, and inclined plane, combinations of simple machines, types of levers; mechanical advantage and efficiency.

2.25 *Mechanics of fluids*
Pressure, flotation; hydrostatics, hydrodynamics, fluid flow.

2.26 *Heat and kinetic theory*
Expansion and contraction, thermometers, transfer of heat; change of state, latent heats; specific heat, expansion coefficients; gas laws; elementary kinetic theory, thermodynamics.

2.27 *Wave phenomena*
Reflection, refraction, interference, diffraction, polarization; longitudinal waves, transverse waves.

2.28 *Sound*
Properties of sound; instruments; mechanical vibration, acoustics.

2.29 *Light and spectra*
Mirrors and lenses; geometrical optics, optical instruments, photometry; colors; spectra; electromagnetic spectrum.

2.210 *Static and current electricity*
Static electricity, electrostatics; current electricity, circuits, units, meters; Ohm's law; direct current, electrolysis; alternating current.

2.211 *Magnetism and electromagnetism*
Magnets and compasses; terrestrial magnetism, electromagnetism; electromagnetic induction, transformers.

2.212 *Electronics*
Vacuum tubes in circuits; thermionics, photoemission, semiconductors.

2.213 *Properties and structure of matter*
Properties of matter; solids, liquids, gases; structure of molecular systems; nuclear physics, structure of matter.

2.214 *Theoretical physics*
Relativity, wave mechanics.

2.3 *Earth and space sciences*

2.31 *Solar system*
Earth and moon in relation to the sun, direction, seasons; solar system, explanation of apparent solar motions; planetary motion, Kepler's laws, Newton's explanation.

2.32 *Stellar systems*
Appearances of the sky at night, constellations; stars and galaxies, stellar distances and sizes; cosmology.

2.33 *Meteorology*
Weather phenomena; weather maps and their interpretation, forecasting; climate.

2.34 *Physical geology*
Earth's crust, stratigraphy; rocks and minerals, material resources, soil studies, petrology; earth forms, deposition, erosion, weathering.

2.35 *Historical geology*
Long-term processes, uniformitanism; fossils and fossilization; palaeontology; geological time scale and major periods.

2.36 *Geophysics and geochemistry*

2.37 *Oceanography*

General (3.0) The third content category differs from the preceding two in that, instead of making subdivisions of the subject matter of science, it is concerned with those broad aspects of science and science instruction that are pertinent to all the natural sciences. These general aspects have become increasingly important as a result of the recent and continuing science curriculum reforms, and it is anticipated that they will be even more emphasized in the content of newly developing programs. A future listing of the content of elementary and secondary school science curricula would probably include several more "cross-cutting ideas" (see Van Deventer, 1966) than are included in the general aspects of science category here. Content headings such as "systems," "equilibrium," "randomness in nature," and "change and variation" have already been proposed, and science instruction will be more frequently organized under broad concepts like these as the movement for unified science education expands (see Klopfer, 1966; Showalter, 1964). For the present, five subcategories have been identified under the *General* category, and each of these is described below.

3.1 *Historical development*
Consideration of the historical background and development through time of observations, concepts, theories, and methods in science; the relevance of new data and new instruments to scientific progress; the interrelationships between scientific development and the general state and advance of society.

3.2 *Nature and structure of science*
The relationship between empiricism and rationalism; the differences between observation and interpretation, and between data and conceptualization; the philosophical status of statements of scientific observation, law, and theory; the tentative quality of scientific data, concepts, and theories.

3.3 *Nature of scientific inquiry*
Multiplicity of approaches in formulating a question, proposing hypotheses, deciding on appropriate procedures, gathering and interpreting relevant data, formulating laws and principles, interpolating, extrapolating, theorizing, validating, predicting.

3.4 *Biographies of scientists*
Presentations of scientists as human beings who engage in scientific work as a profession; recognition that scientists are people with diverse educational backgrounds, families, personal problems, and interest in fields of human endeavor outside the sciences.

3.5 *Measurement*
Basic forms of measurement encountered in science, such as number, length, mass, and time; simple combinations of the basic measurements, such as volume, density, speed, growth rate; the practical and theoretical aspects of units, standards, scaling, and errors of measurement.

Structures of science programs and units

The categories and subcategories of student behavior and content described in the preceding section can be used to characterize any science program or unit. The process is simple. Analyses of the instructional materials are made to determine which student behaviors they seek to promote with regard to each science content area included in the program or unit. An X or some other mark is entered on a copy of the master Table of Specifications, Table 18-1, at each behavior-content intersection that the analyses have identified. The result of this process is a specifications grid of all the instructional objectives that are sought for all the science content that is taken up. Since a particular program or unit takes up only a limited range of content, a simplified table may next be prepared by deleting all the horizontal rows where there is no X entered. The simplified specifications grid, which is used in the illustrations in this section, shows the same information as the larger display, takes up less space, and is easier to read.

Besides characterizing a science program or unit, the table of specifications reveals its structure. With respect to each included content area, the grid shows where expected knowledge objectives lead to comprehension or application behaviors, and it shows where knowledge objectives exist largely in isolation. The specifications grid identifies those content areas where development of the student's skills in different processes of scientific inquiry is aimed for. It shows where there are objectives in the attitude, manual skills, and orientation categories, and their relation, if any, to objectives in other categories. When the structure of a program or unit has been made explicit, planning for an effective evaluation of the student's attainment of the objectives can proceed.

Two high school chemistry programs

To illustrate the function of a specifications grid in revealing the structure of a science program, Table 18-2, Table of Specifications for *Modern Chemistry*, has been prepared for a widely used high school chemistry program. The entries in the table are based on analyses of the textbook by Metcalfe, Williams, and Castka (1966b) and the accompanying laboratory guide (1966a) and teacher's edition (1966c). The grid shows that for

TABLE 18-2 TABLE OF SPECIFICATIONS FOR *MODERN CHEMIST*

	BEHAVIOR																		
	A.0 Knowledge and comprehension											*B.0 Observing and measuring*					*C.0 Seeing a proble[m] and seeking ways to solve it*		
CONTENT	*A.1*	*A.2*	*A.3*	*A.4*	*A.5*	*A.6*	*A.7*	*A.8*	*A.9*	*A.10*	*A.11*	*B.1*	*B.2*	*B.3*	*B.4*	*B.5*	*C.1*	*C.2*	*C.3*
2.11	X	X	X	X	X	X	X			X		X	X	X					
2.12	X	X	X		X	X	X			X	X								
2.13	X	X	X	X	X	X	X	X		X		X	X	X					
2.14		X	X	X			X	X		X	X	X	X	X					
2.15	X	X	X	X	X		X	X	X	X	X	X	X	X					
2.16	X	X	X	X	X	X		X	X	X	X	X	X	X					
2.17	X	X	X	X		X	X		X	X	X	X	X						
2.18	X	X	X	X	X	X				X		X	X						
2.19	X	X		X			X												
2.110	X	X	X	X	X		X		X	X									
2.23	X	X	X		X		X		X	X									
2.26	X	X	X		X		X	X	X	X	X	X	X	X					
2.210	X	X	X							X									
2.211		X	X		X														
2.214	X	X	X		X	X	X			X		X	X	X					
3.1	X																		
3.2	X																		
3.3	X																		
3.4	X																		
3.5	X	X	X		X	X				X	X	X	X	X	X	X			

* Metcalfe, Williams, & Castka, 1966a, 1966b, 1966c.

nearly every content area, application of knowledge and methods (*F*.1) is among the desired objectives. The entries under *Observing and measuring* (*B*.1 to *B*.3) for most content areas reflect the laboratory activities of the program. The absence of entries in category *C*.0 and the paucity of entries in category *D*.0 indicate that inquiries into chemical problems are not highly stressed in this program. Except for topics in atomic and molecular structure (2.17), the building and testing of theoretical models by the student (*E*.0) is also not stressed. Orientation to the relationships existing between scientific progress and technical achievement (*I*.4) appears as an objective in relation to five content areas—chemical materials (2.11), chemical change (2.13), electrochemistry (2.16), organic chemistry (2.18), and nuclear chemistry (2.110)—and orientation to the historical development of science (*I*.3) has four entries on the grid. *Attitudes and interests* (category *H*.0) are apparently not important objectives with respect to

BEHAVIOR

D.0 Interpreting data and formulating generalizations					E.0 Building, testing, and revising a theoretical model						F.0 Application of scientific knowledge and methods			G.0 Manual skills		H.0 Attitudes and interests						I.0 Orientation				
D.2	D.3	D.4	D.5	D.6	E.1	E.2	E.3	E.4	E.5	E.6	F.1	F.2	F.3	G.1	G.2	H.1	H.2	H.3	H.4	H.5	H.6	I.1	I.2	I.3	I.4	I.5
											X			X	X										X	
	X										X													X		
											X			X	X										X	
	X										X															
	X														X											
											X				X										X	
					X		X				X															
													X												X	
											X													X	X	
											X															
	X										X			X	X											
											X															
	X										X			X	X									X		
																				X				X		
																X							X			
																		X				X				
																X					X					
														X				X				X				

any particular content area, but there are some entries of objectives in this category with respect to some of the general aspects of science (3.1 to 3.5).

The high school chemistry course whose specifications grid is shown in Table 18-2 represents a traditional science program, in the sense that the term "traditional" was used in the discussion at the beginning of this chapter. It should be instructive to compare the structure of this chemistry program with that of another chemistry program, representing the "modern" trend. Table 18-3, Table of Specifications for *Chemistry: An Experimental Science*, provides some of the data. This is a specifications grid based on analyses of a textbook prepared by the Chemical Education Material Study (CHEMS, 1963b), and the accompanying laboratory guide (1963c) and teachers' guide (1963d). Immediately apparent on this grid are the considerable number of entries under categories C.0, D.0, and E.0. Faithful to its title, this program does treat chemistry as an experimental science and stresses the carrying out of inquiries

TABLE 18-3 TABLE OF SPECIFICATIONS FOR *CHEMISTRY: AN*

	BEHAVIOR																		
	A.0 Knowledge and comprehension											*B.0 Observing and measuring*					*C.0 Seeing a problem and seeking ways to solve it*		
CONTENT	A.1	A.2	A.3	A.4	A.5	A.6	A.7	A.8	A.9	A.10	A.11	B.1	B.2	B.3	B.4	B.5	C.1	C.2	C.3
2.11	X	X	X	X	X	X	X			X		X	X	X					
2.12	X	X	X		X	X	X			X	X	X	X						
2.13	X	X	X	X	X	X	X	X		X		X	X	X					
2.14		X	X	X			X	X		X	X	X	X	X		X			X
2.15	X	X	X	X	X		X	X	X	X	X	X	X	X		X			
2.16		X	X	X	X		X	X		X	X	X	X	X	X	X			X
2.17	X	X	X	X		X	X		X	X	X	X	X	X		X			X
2.18	X	X	X	X	X	X				X		X	X						
2.19		X	X		X							X	X						
2.110	X	X	X	X	X		X		X	X		X	X	X					
2.23	X	X	X		X		X		X	X		X	X						
2.26		X	X		X		X	X	X	X	X	X	X	X					
2.210		X	X		X					X									
2.211		X	X		X					X									
2.214	X	X	X		X	X	X			X		X	X	X					
3.1	X																		
3.2	X																		
3.3	X				X		X												
3.4	X																		
3.5	X	X				X	X			X	X	X	X	X	X	X			

* Chemical Education Material Study, 1963b, 1963c, 1963d.

and the building and testing of theoretical models as explicit objectives in many content areas. Other characteristics of the structure of the program may also be noted in the specifications grid. For nearly every content area included, applications of knowledge and skills (*F*.1) are among the objectives sought, just as they were in the first program considered. In the *Orientation* category, however, there are some differences. Note, for example, that there are no entries under subcategory *I*.4 in Table 18-3. On the other hand, there are ten entries here under subcategory *I*.1, so that orientation to the distinction between various types of statements in science is an explicit objective in relation to many content areas; and orientation to the historical development of science (*I*.3) has the same number of entries on this grid. In regard to attitudes and interests (category *H*.0), the objectives of the two programs appear to be quite similar, with the grids in Tables 18-2 and 18-3 both showing no entries at any specific content area and six and eight entries respectively for the general aspects of science (3.1 to 3.5).

The similarities and differences in the struc-

RIMENTAL SCIENCE*

BEHAVIOR																											
D.0 Interpreting data and formulating generalizations						*E.0 Building, testing, and revising a theoretical model*						*F.0 Application of scientific knowledge and methods*			*G.0 Manual skills*		*H.0 Attitudes and interests*						*I.0 Orientation*				
1	D.2	D.3	D.4	D.5	D.6	E.1	E.2	E.3	E.4	E.5	E.6	F.1	F.2	F.3	G.1	G.2	H.1	H.2	H.3	H.4	H.5	H.6	I.1	I.2	I.3	I.4	I.5
		X				X		X		X		X			X	X											
		X				X		X				X			X								X		X		
		X						X		X		X			X	X									X		
	X	X	X	X	X	X	X	X		X		X				X							X		X		
	X	X	X	X	X	X		X		X		X				X							X		X		
	X	X		X	X	X		X		X		X				X									X		
	X	X	X	X	X	X		X				X		X	X	X							X	X	X		
		X				X		X															X				
		X																									
		X						X				X											X		X		X
												X															
		X	X		X							X			X	X							X				
												X			X	X							X		X		
																					X				X		
																	X							X			
																	X	X	X				X	X			
																	X					X			X		
	X	X	X									X			X	X			X				X				

tures of the two chemistry programs considered suggest that there would be corresponding similarities and differences in evaluating the student's attainment of objectives in the two programs. In both programs, testing the student only for recall of knowledge would not be sufficient, and measurement of his comprehension and his ability to apply knowledge would also have to be incorporated. By contrast, assessment of the student's inquiry skills, as defined by the entries in categories C.0, D.0, and E.0 of the Tables of Specifications, is not a significant part of the evaluation plan for the first program, but it is an essential component of an adequate evaluation of the second.

An elementary school science unit

"The Fall of a Tree," a unit in Book 4 of *Concepts in Science*, by Brandwein, Cooper, Blackwood, and Hone (1966a), will be used to illustrate the use of a specifications grid to reveal the structure of a single unit. The entries in Table 18-4,

TABLE 18-4 TABLE OF SPECIFICATIONS FOR "THE FALL OF

	BEHAVIOR																			
	A.0 Knowledge and comprehension											B.0 Observing and measuring					C.0 Seeing a problem and seeking ways to solve it			
CONTENT	A.1	A.2	A.3	A.4	A.5	A.6	A.7	A.8	A.9	A.10	A.11	B.1	B.2	B.3	B.4	B.5	C.1	C.2	C.3	C
1.11	X	X			X		X													
1.14	X	X	X			X														
1.21			X																	
1.22	X	X	X									X	X							
1.25	X	X	X		X		X			X		X	X	X						
1.31	X	X	X		X			X		X		X	X	X					X	
1.32	X		X									X	X							
2.11	X	X					X					X	X							
2.17	X	X							X		X									
2.19	X											X	X						X	
2.23	X	X	X									X	X							
3.1	X																			
3.3	X						X													

* Brandwein, Cooper, Blackwood, & Hone, 1966a, 1966b, pp. T-76–T-97.

Table of Specifications for "The Fall of a Tree," are derived from analyses of the unit's presentation in the student's textbook and of the corresponding commentary in the teacher's edition (Brandwein, Cooper, Blackwood, & Hone, 1966b). The grid shows that the subject-matter content of this unit is wide-ranging, but the major thrust is in the content area on natural environment (1.31). Indeed, the major concept developed in the unit, as stated in the teacher's edition, is, "Living things capture matter from the environment and return it to the environment [p. T-76]."

The objectives in content area 1.31 include not only knowledge but also comprehension and application. Moreover, there is an emphasis here on inquiry skills, as the student is expected to observe and measure, formulate and test hypotheses, and interpret and evaluate results of experiments. A similar emphasis on these skills may be seen in other content areas, notably in regard to the chemistry of the principal plant nutrients (2.19) and the development of plants (1.25). For a few content areas, such as 1.14 and 1.21, the objective of knowledge of facts or concepts stands quite alone, with neither a direct extension into comprehension or application nor necessary direct observation by the student, but these are exceptions to the general trend of the structure of the unit. The development of interests in science activities (*H*.5) is included in the desired behaviors in two content areas. Some attention is given also to *Orientation* subcategories *I*.1 and *I*.3, an unusual but salutary feature in a science unit for the early elementary school grades.

Another illustration of a specifications grid for a single science unit, using a somewhat different format, is presented in Table 18-5, page 590.

BEHAVIOR																											
	D.0 Interpreting data and formulating generalizations					E.0 Building, testing, and revising a theoretical model						F.0 Application of scientific knowledge and methods			G.0 Manual skills		H.0 Attitudes and interests						I.0 Orientation				
1	D.2	D.3	D.4	D.5	D.6	E.1	E.2	E.3	E.4	E.5	E.6	F.1	F.2	F.3	G.1	G.2	H.1	H.2	H.3	H.4	H.5	H.6	I.1	I.2	I.3	I.4	I.5
												X															
																					X						
		X																									
		X																					X		X		
		X		X								X	X	X							X						
		X																									
		X		X																							
		X											X														

The preparation of a specifications grid in any format is a facilitating step, as the reader undoubtedly realizes by now, in the design or selection of suitable evaluation procedures. A sampling of procedures for evaluation in science education constitutes the next section.

Selected evaluation procedures in science education

Having formulated the objectives of a science course or program in terms of behaviors and content, the science teacher or educator must also attend to the difficult task of assessing the extent to which students attain these objectives in their study of science. In science teaching today, the most common practice is to make this assessment after the students have completed a course or a unit of study. In other words, the evaluation of the student's attainment of objectives is summative. While summative evaluation is not appropriate for assessing certain desired behaviors in science, notably some behaviors under the *Processes of scientific inquiry* subcategories that must be observed as they happen, it is by far the most popular form of evaluation and testing in elementary and secondary school science classes. Formative evaluation as a systematic procedure has only recently been introduced into science teaching (see the section beginning on page 627).

This section discusses evaluation procedures and presents illustrative test items for assessing the behaviors shown in the master Table of Specifications for Science Education (Table 18-1). Among all evaluation procedures that have been devised, the most highly refined techniques are presently found in the paper and pencil examina-

Table 18-5 ***Portion*** **of the Table of Specifications for Chapters 4 and 5 of** ***Modern Biology*** **(Otto & Towle, 1965)**

A.2 Knowledge of terminology	*A.1 Knowledge of specific facts*	*A.6 Knowledge of classifications and categories*	*A.7 Knowledge of methodology*	*A.8 Knowledge of principles and generalizations*	*A.11 Translation*
Permeable		Capacity of various substances to penetrate membrane allows grouping according to rate, degree		Movement of materials is dependent upon their size, membrane, surrounding conditions, water solubility of material	
Differentially permeable	Numerous spaces between various molecules composing membrane				
Passive transport					
Active transport				Principle of active transport	
Diffusion Diffusion pressure	Diffusion is affected by 1. molecular concentration 2. temperature 3. pressure			Laws of diffusion	Interpretation of diagrams
Osmosis Turgor Turgor pressure	Water diffuses through differentially permeable membrane into a cell to build up pressure			Sufficient internal water supply in cell environment enables turgor pressure to be maintained	
Contractile vacuole	Eliminate water through cell membrane as fast as it diffuses into cell			Cell walls in plants withstand turgor pressure. Animals, with no cell wall, require water-eliminating system	Interpretation of diagrams

tion. Science students more frequently encounter written examination questions, both of the subjective and objective type, than any other form of evaluation. Students have become accustomed to responding to written tests and test items, and at the same time science teachers have become accustomed to using pencil and paper tests as the principal means of assessing their students' attainment of instructional objectives. For these reasons, pencil and paper testing receives the greatest emphasis in this section.

In the following subsections, attention is given in turn to each of the categories of behaviors, from *Knowledge and comprehension* to *Orientation*. For every subcategory of behaviors, one or more illustrative test items are presented whenever these could be found in a diligent search of the science testing literature. The reader should note the references for these illustrative items: taken together, these works constitute a respectable bibliography of published science tests and sources of science test items.

Testing for knowledge and comprehension (A.0)

Knowledge and comprehension of science content are most often measured in most published science tests; consequently, there was no dearth of test items which could serve as illustrations in this category. To keep this subsection within bounds, only two items were selected to illustrate each behavior subcategory. The two items were generally selected to represent either quite elementary science content and more advanced content, or science content from two different content categories. The behavior subcategory and the content area are indicated for each item; for their descriptions, the reader should refer to Table 18-1 and the opening section of the chapter.

Testing for knowledge is primarily a matter of finding out if the student can recall something he has learned. Test items designed to accomplish this are best kept simple and straightforward, and these characteristics generally apply to illustrative items 1 to 18. Hence further discussion of these items seems unnecessary, except for a few comments which follow certain items below. A slightly greater complexity may be introduced in items which test for comprehension, which is illustrated in items 8, 10, and 19 to 22.

A.1-2.34

1. The chenical element that is most abundant in the earth's crust is
   a. hydrogen　　c. potassium
   b. calcium　　d. oxygen

(Adapted from Borman & Sanders, 1964.)

A.1-1.22

2. Desert animals conserve the most water when they excrete nitrogenous waste as
   a. urea　　c. ammonia
   b. uric acid　　d. nucleic acid

(Adapted from Biological Sciences Curriculum Study, 1965b.)

A.2-1.25

3. Carrots take two years to grow before they blossom and produce seed. Thus the carrot plant is a
   a. perennial　　c. biennial
   b. annual　　d. spore

(Adapted from Borman & Sanders, 1964.)

A.2-3.5

4. If you were told that an animal measured one micron in length, you would know that the animal had a length of
   a. 1/1000 of a millimeter
   b. 1/1000 of a meter
   c. 1,000 times a millimeter
   d. 1/1000 of a centimeter
   e. 1,000 times a meter

A.3-2.13

5. An example of a chemical change would be
   a. ice melting
   b. making oxygen from water
   c. condensation of water vapor
   d. sugar dissolving in tea

(Adapted from Cross & Sanders, 1964.)

A.3-1.34

6. In a certain genus there are two species. Species I reproduces by fission, and species II reproduces by gametes. If the environment changes, the chance of survival probably would be
   a. greater for species I than for species II
   b. greater for species II than for species I
   c. unchanged for both species I and II
   d. about zero for both species I and II

(Adapted from Biological Sciences Curriculum Study, 1965b.)

Items 5 and 6 both illustrate the testing for behavior A.3, *Knowledge of concepts of science*, but item 6 is considerably more sophisticated than 5. Item 5 represents the type of item which simply attempts to test the student's knowledge of the definition of a concept. The student is asked to show that he knows the definition of chemical change by selecting an example of this concept. Item 6 calls on the student to display his knowledge of the concepts of asexual reproduction and sexual reproduction, with their respective survival advantages. To answer the item correctly, he must also know the scientific terms "fission" and "gametes," and he must know that these are examples, respectively, of the asexual and sexual reproductive modes. This item has been included to illustrate that testing for knowledge of concepts need not be limited to selecting from a list the best definition or example of a concept.

A.4-2.211

7. The poles of a bar magnet are usually called
   a. anode and cathode
   b. paramagnetic and dimagnetic
   c. strong and weak
   d. north and south
   e. equal and opposite

A.4-2.21, A.10-2.21, A.11-2.21

8. The arrows show the direction of the velocity and acceleration vectors for a car at five separate instants of time. The car travels chiefly toward the east, but changes direction at times.

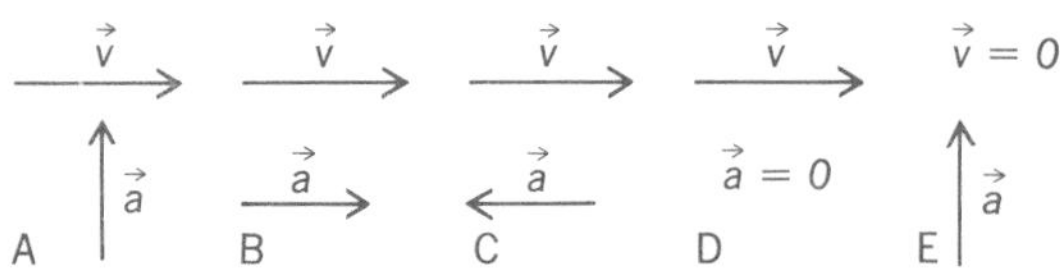

(1) Which diagram represents the car at an instant while turning a corner?
   a. Diagram A
   b. Diagram B
   c. Diagram C
   d. Diagram D
   e. Diagram E

(2) Which diagram represents a decrease in the speed of the car? [Same alternatives as in question (1).]

(3) Which diagram represents the car starting from rest? [Same alternatives as in question (1).]

(4) Which diagram represents the car increasing the magnitude of its velocity? [Same alternatives as in question (1).]

(Adapted from Rutherford et al., 1966a.)

The series of questions under item 8 involves not only behavior A.4, *Knowledge of conventions*, but comprehension behaviors as well. The eliciting of student behaviors under several subcategories will be found in many of the illustrative test items presented in this section, and item 8 is merely the first. In this instance, the student's knowledge of the vector conventions is crucial for his successful response to the questions. If he knows the conventions, he can then identify the velocity and acceleration concepts in each described situation in the questions (A.10) and translate these from the verbal to the corresponding symbolic form (A.11).

A.5-1.25

9. Which of the following lists gives the stages in the life history of the housefly in their correct order?
   a. pupa, larva, egg, adult
   b. egg, larva, pupa, adult
   c. larva, egg, pupa, adult
   d. egg, larva, adult, pupa
   e. pupa, egg, larva, adult

(Adapted from Hedges, 1966. p. 36.)

A.5-2.210, A.11-2.210

10. Questions 1–3 relate to the following diagram and information:

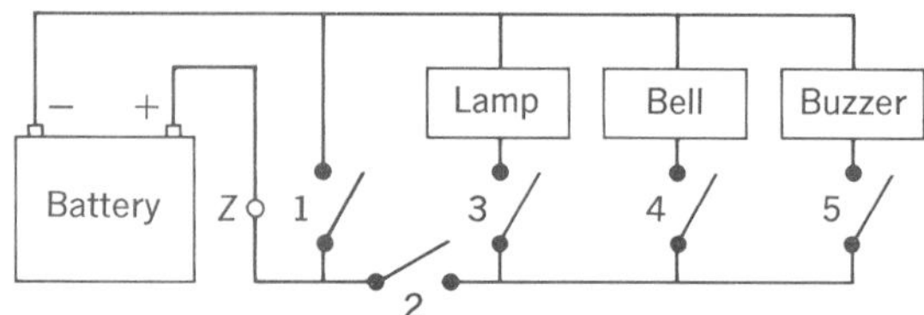

The diagram above shows an electric circuit which contains a battery, several switches, a lamp, a bell, and a buzzer.

(1) In the diagram as it appears above, the current will

a. ring the bell
b. sound the buzzer
c. light the lamp
d. heat the wires
e. not flow

(2) Closing which of the following switches will cause the lamp to light?

a. 1 only
b. 2 only
c. 1 and 3
d. 2 and 3
e. 3 and 4

(3) A fuse is often included in a circuit to prevent the wires from overheating. In the circuit shown above, where is the best place to put the fuse?

a. At Point Z
b. Between Switch 1 and Switch 2
c. Between Switch 2 and Switch 3
d. Between Switch 3 and Switch 4
e. Between Switch 4 and Switch 5

(Educational Testing Service, 1962b, p. 11, items 57–59.)

Though some translation from the diagrammatic to the verbal form is involved in item 10, this behavior is probably not the principal factor contributing to the student's success with the questions. The key to answering the questions is knowing the sequence of points through which a current must pass in an electric circuit.

A.6-1.21

11. Which of the following would show the *most* diversity in structure?
    a. five classes of vertebrates
    b. five species of reptiles adapted for life in seas, deserts, tropical forests, temperate forests, and ponds
    c. five orders of mammals adapted for digging, gliding, jumping, plant feeding, and predation
    d. five genera of moths that feed on the nectar of tulips, daffodils, peas, honeysuckles, and orchids

(Adapted from Biological Sciences Curriculum Study, 1965b.)

A.6-2.12

12. Helium, neon, argon, and krypton are in the same family of elements. This means that they
    a. have similar chemical properties
    b. were discovered in the same year
    c. were discovered by the same person
    d. can be decomposed into similar substances
    e. have the same melting and boiling points

(Educational Testing Service, 1962a, p. 17, sec. 4, item 35.)

A.7-2.11

13. How can you tell whether or not a substance contains starch?
    a. Boiling it will make it soft.
    b. Adding iodine will produce a blue color.
    c. Putting it in alcohol will make it green.
    d. Lime water will become cloudy when mixed with it.

(Adapted from Boyer & Gordon, 1959.)

A.7-3.3

14. If a botanist wants to determine the factors that contribute to the growth of a certain plant, which of the following things will he be *least likely* to do?
    a. formulate a hypothesis based on what he thinks the factors are
    b. write a mathematical equation of the growth curve
    c. think about the factors that contribute to the growth of other plants
    d. look the subject up in the library

(Adapted from Cooley & Klopfer, 1961.)

The inclusion of item 14 here should serve as a reminder that subcategory *A.7, Knowledge of scientific techniques and procedures,* also includes the student's knowledge of the processes of scientific inquiry.

A.8-1.35

15. Specialization is an evolutionary process whereby organisms in a species
    a. tend to produce varied offspring
    b. gain the ability to adjust to changes in the environment
    c. develop body parts which perform definite and different functions
    d. regress to an ancestral form

(Adapted from Educational Testing Service, 1948.)

A.8-2.210, A.3-2.10; A.8-2.26, A.3-2.26

16. Use the following key to answer questions (1) to (7).

KEY:

A. The statement is true if the condition applies.
B. The statement is true regardless of the condition.
C. The statement is false if the condition applies.
D. The statement is false regardless of the condition.
E. Impossible to determine without more data.

	Statement	Condition
(1)	The force of attraction or repulsion between two charges is inversely proportional to the square of their distances	if the charges are quantitatively the same
(2)	The direction of the flow of electrons through a conductor is irreversible even	if the charges on the terminals are reversed
(3)	Two charged particles repel each other	if the particles approach closely enough
(4)	A negatively charged particle repels a positively charged particle	if the negative particle has the larger charge
(5)	Two charged objects repel each other	if both attract similarly charged objects
(6)	At constant volume the absolute temperature and pressure of a gas are directly proportional	if the temperature is expressed in degrees Centigrade
(7)	At constant temperature the absolute pressure and volume of a gas are inversely proportional	if the pressure is expressed in millimeters of mercury and the volume is expressed in cubic centimeters

(Adapted from Nelson, 1967, p. 7.)

Items 15 and 16, which test for behavior under subcategory A.8, *Knowledge of scientific principles and laws,* are a representative pair very much like items 5 and 6, where the first item simply calls for a definition and the second tests for knowledge at a more sophisticated level. In item 16, the student is required to have a fair degree of precision in his knowledge of the principles and laws, or concept for question (3), that are cited. This item also happens to be the first illustration in this presentation of the key list form for test items.

A.9-1.35

17. Natural selection, as described in Darwin's scheme of evolution, assumed
    a. a stable nonchanging population of organisms
    b. changes from generation to generation based upon mutation
    c. environmental stimuli that resulted in changes of body structure in successive generations of offspring
    d. differential survival value of random differences in offspring

(Adapted from Biological Sciences Curriculum Study, 1965b.)

A.9-2.213

18. The tremendous amount of energy released in a nuclear fission reactor results from
    a. an exothermic chemical reaction
    b. the combustion of subdivided atoms
    c. the disappearance of a quantity of mass
    d. a bombardment of gamma rays
    e. high-energy neutrons proceeding in all directions

(Adapted from Hedges, 1966, p. 47.)

A.10-2.23

19. Some situations are described below in which one form of energy is transformed to another form of energy. In which situation is kinetic energy transformed into thermal energy?
    a. Some people were climbing a mountain when a rock close to them dislodged and rolled down the mountainside.
    b. The sun's rays were shining on a piece of glass so that the glass became quite warm.
    c. A person was rocking in a rocking chair, and the gliders were continually rubbing against the floor.

(Adapted from American Association for the Advancement of Science, 1966c, p. GT-81.)

A.10-1.24

20. A lizard placed before three plates, one at a temperature of 50°C, one at a temperature of 37°C, and one at a temperature of 15°C, consistently moves to the 37°C plate.
    (1) This behavior is an example of
        a. a response to a stimulus
        b. reasoning
        c. reflex arc
        d. anthropomorphism

(2) Many eggs from these lizards were hatched under laboratory conditions. The young lizards consistently moved to the 37°C plate. This behavior can best be called

a. social c. learned
b. innate d. intelligent

(Biological Sciences Curriculum Study, 1965b.)

A.11-1.16

21. What genetic process is illustrated in the following diagram?

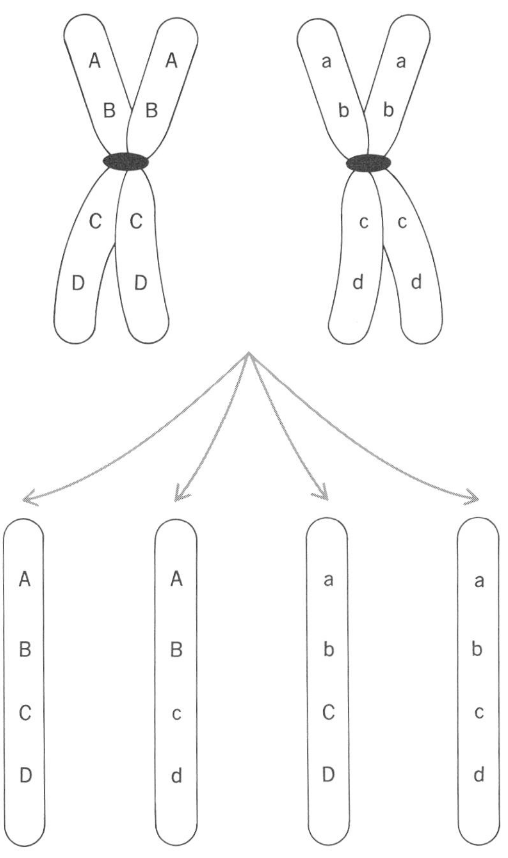

a. nondisjunction c. crossing-over
b. sex linkage d. natural selection

(Adapted from Biological Sciences Curriculum Study, 1965b.)

A.11-2.27

22. (1) Which of the wave patterns [at the top of next column] has the *longest* wave length?

a. graph (*a*) d. graph (*d*)
b. graph (*b*) e. graph (*e*)
c. graph (*c*)

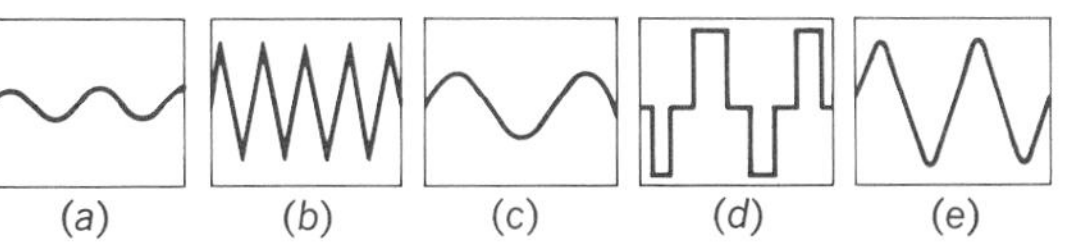

(2) Which of the above wave patterns has the greatest amplitude? [Same alternatives as in question (1).]

(3) If all the waves shown have the same speed, which pattern has the *highest* frequency? [Same alternatives as in question (1).]

(Adapted from Rutherford et al., 1966a.)

Items 19 to 22 illustrate testing for comprehension, and they are quite pure examples of subcategories *A*.10 and *A*.11. Items 19 and 20 call on the student to identify a concept in a new context (*A*.10); 19 is intended for elementary school students and 20 for high school students. In items 21 and 22, the student must translate a concept presented in one symbolic form to another symbolic form; from a diagrammatic presentation into words in item 21, from a graph into words in item 22. In all these illustrations, it is assumed that the student already knows the applicable scientific terminology. Additional illustrations of the identification and translation subcategories were given in items 8 and 10, and the student will need to use these behaviors many times again as a part of responding successfully to numerous succeeding items which have been placed under other subcategories to illustrate other behaviors of interest—e.g., items 32, 36, 43, 48, 50, 60, and 81.

Evaluation of observing and measuring: Processes of scientific inquiry I (B.0)

Without doubt, the best way to assess the student's skill in using the processes of observing and measuring is to observe his behavior when he is actively engaged in inquiry in the laboratory or field. Paper and pencil test items generally can pick up only a part, usually the dead part, of the behaviors specified in the subcategories of category *B*.0. This stricture applies particularly to subcategories *B*.1 and *B*.3, where it is hard to conceive of any after-the-fact written exercise that could adequately substitute for the living activity of the moments when a student makes observations and measurements.

In observing a student's behavior, the teacher will find it helpful to keep some sort of record of what he sees or hears and to have some guidelines for the particular aspects of behavior that he is looking for. The form of the teacher's record may be quite informal and may consist simply of anecdotal notes about the student's performance. A set of notes taken over a period of time, and kept in a notebook with a page for each student or on index cards, provides an appropriate record for assessing the student's observing and measuring skills. Alternatively, a more systematic record may be devised in the form of a checklist consisting of descriptions of aspects of the student's observing and measuring behaviors that the teacher considers important. Some descriptions for such a checklist might include: "notices many properties of observed objects, phenomena, or systems"; "discriminates details in making observations"; "identifies similarities and differences in comparing two or more objects or phenomena"; "records observations systematically in notebook"; "uses appropriate measuring instruments to quantify observations"; "uses proper procedures for handling, positioning, or operating measuring instruments to minimize observational errors"; "reads instruments accurately"; "checks and rechecks observations."

For evaluating behavior subcategory *B*.2, *Description of observations using appropriate language*, the obvious method of choice is to obtain samples of the student's descriptions of his observations. These may be oral descriptions given by the student with the teacher assessing them on the spot for accuracy, thoroughness, and comprehensibility. More commonly, however, the teacher would ask for written descriptions so that he can make his assessment more at leisure and more carefully. The student may be asked to submit just a written description of observations, though usually this will be a part of a report on an investigation or a laboratory report. Practices differ widely among science teachers with regard to prescribing a form and format for laboratory reports, but no teacher has yet omitted a description or record of observations from his expectations. Whatever the format of the laboratory report may be, it provides an excellent means for evaluating the student's skill in describing observations and also in other processes of scientific inquiry, notably those assigned to behavior subcategories *B*.5, *C*.4, *D*.1 to *D*.5, and *E*.5.

The following seven items illustrate certain aspects of observing and measuring which *can* be probed into by means of paper and pencil tests.

B.1-2.31

23. It is very difficult to take accurate photographs of the stars from the surface of the Earth, mainly because
    a. the stars move too fast
    b. the Earth moves too fast
    c. the Moon gets in the way
    d. the Earth's atmosphere creates distortions
    e. the Sun is too close and gets in the way

(Adapted from Educational Testing Service, 1962b, p. 3, item 10.)

B.1-2.11

24. Imagine that you're playing an observing game, where you earn five points for making the best possible observation of different things. You have a sample of a single unknown substance in a closed metal box with a small hole in the lid. By sniffing at the hole, you can smell a musty odor in the box, and the odor is still there when you sniff again one hour later. Which of the following sentences gives the best observation you could make about the substance?
    a. It's either a liquid or a gas, but not a solid.
    b. It's either a liquid or something that readily becomes a liquid.
    c. It's either a solid or a liquid, but not a gas.
    d. It's either a gas or something that readily gives off a gas.

Items 23 and 24 do not pretend to evaluate the student's observational skills. They illustrate a class of test items which ask about the conditions necessary for making a certain observation or about what the limits of a particular observation are. They probe the student's knowledge of specified observations. Item 24 is somewhat more complex and comes close to testing for the interpretation of an observation (subcategory *D*.3).

B.3-2.25

25. If you were rising in a balloon, which of the following measurements would be most useful to you in determining your altitude?
    a. The air pressure at your altitude
    b. The air temperature at your altitude
    c. The relative humidity at your altitude
    d. The absolute humidity at your altitude
    e. The electrical charge put on the balloon by the atmosphere

(Educational Testing Service, 1962a, p. 8, sec. 2, item 42.

B.3-2.35

26. Geological time is most accurately measured by the
    a. size of fossils
    b. thicknesses of sedimentary layers
    c. rate of radioactive decay of uranium
    d. rate of salt accumulation in the ocean

(Adapted from Biological Sciences Curriculum Study, 1965b.)

The class of items illustrated in 25 and 26 requires the student to specify what quantity or quantities should be measured to find out some fact, change, or property of interest. They are simple items which ask for knowledge about certain measurements. Another example of the same class would be: "What would you measure to decide whether or not a person is anemic?" Probing much further into *how* the measurements are made would place items like these under subcategory *A*.7, *Knowledge of scientific techniques and procedures*.

B.4-3.5

27. [Photographs of five measuring instruments omitted.]
    (1) Which piece of equipment would be used for measuring volume?
        a. graduated beaker
        b. ruler
        c. equal arm balance
        d. thermometer
        e. spring scale
    (2) Which piece of equipment would be used for measuring mass? [Same alternatives as in question (1).]

(Adapted from American Association for the Advancement of Science, 1966b, pp. GT-7–GT-8.)

Subcategory *B*.4, *Selection of appropriate measuring instruments*, is the only behavior in category *B*.0 for which paper and pencil testing offers a really good venue. The question asked of the student is straightforward: "Which instrument should be used to measure quantity X?" A more difficult form of the question would be: "Which instrument is used to measure quantity X in range Y?" Though the illustrative item asks this question at an elementary level, analogous items for higher levels and for any content area can be readily devised.

B.5-3.5

28. [Drawing of an irregular figure omitted.] Estimate without the use of any instruments, the area of this figure and give the possible error of your estimate —for example, 40 ± 5 cm^2.

(Slightly adapted from Nedelsky, p. 347, item L1.1–2. From SCIENCE TEACHING AND TESTING by Leo Nedelsky, 1965b, © 1965 by Harcourt, Brace & World, Inc., and adapted and reproduced with their permission.)

B.5-3.5

29. A crucible with a precipitate in it has a mass of 24.201 grams. The empty crucible has a mass of 24.100 grams. The mass of the precipitate should be reported to how many significant figures?
    a. one
    b. two
    c. three
    d. four
    e. five

(Adapted from Educational Testing Service, 1963a, pt. II, item 1.

In addition to the items given, estimation of measurement (*B*.5) may be simulated on a paper and pencil test by presenting a drawing of the scale of a ruler or other instrument and asking the student to state the reading at an indicated point. Much to be preferred to this simulation, however, is an observation of the student actually estimating the reading on a real instrument in the laboratory. Item 29 illustrates testing for the correct use of the significant-figures convention, which is also included under subcategory *B*.5.

Evaluation of seeing a problem and seeking ways to solve it: Processes of scientific inquiry II (*C*.0)

As for category *B*.0, critical observations of inquiry in action provide the best means of assessing the student's behaviors under category *C*.0. If it is not feasible to make these observations, in either an informal or a systematic way, the teacher must realize that his evaluation of the inquiry processes here is necessarily based on second-best data. He is then not really assessing the student's performance in inquiry, but only probing into aspects of the inquiry processes that can be set up in more or less cleverly contrived descriptions of inquiry situations.

The descriptive story of inquiry does provide a mechanism for testing the conceptual components of most of the behaviors in category *C*.0. The story situation presented may be realistic or imaginary; and the student may be asked questions which require him to construct an appropriate response, or the questions may provide several alternative responses from which he is to choose. In the former testing form, such questions may be asked as: "What hypotheses can you suggest to account for these observations? Select one of your hypotheses and describe how you could find out whether or not it is correct. What kind of samples and what controls will be needed to test this hypothesis? How will the experiments for testing this hypothesis be carried out?" The latter form of questioning is illustrated in the items given below. Two additional points may be noted in these illustrations. Since the descriptive story usually begins with a problem already presented, it is difficult to test for behavior subcategory *C*.1, *Recognition of a problem*, by this mechanism. (An exception to this is displayed in item 34.) Also note that the descriptive story makes it possible to ask successive questions which carry through several behavior subcategories of category *C*.0 and even into category *D*.0.

C.2-1.26, C.3-1.26

30. A missionary reported that the root of a plant much like the Rauwolfia plant had been used by an African witch doctor to cure him of a serious illness.
    (1) What is the most reasonable hypothesis that can be made on the basis of this report?
        a. The plant is useless since witch doctors are not trained physicians.
        b. The plant is useless because the missionary cannot judge how effective the plant was in curing his illness.
        c. The plant may have been helpful since the missionary recovered after the witch doctor's treatment.
        d. The plant was helpful because recent medical reports show that reserpine, a drug effective in lowering blood pressure, is extracted from Rauwolfia.
    (2) Which of the following tests would be most appropriate in a preliminary investigation of the medicinal properties of this plant?
        a. Administer portions of the plant to a group of human beings, with appropriate controls, and record the effects.
        b. Select two groups of rats as experimental and control groups to test the effects of the plant.
        c. Send purified samples of the drug to hundreds of physicians throughout the world to assure an adequate sample.
        d. Cross the plant with Rauwolfia to determine how closely these two plants are related.

(Biological Sciences Curriculum Study, 1965a.)

C.2-1.22, C.3-1.22, D.5-1.22

31. Suppose the following experiment is done for the purpose of showing that a plant growing in a bell jar decreases the amount of carbon dioxide, CO_2, and increases the amount of oxygen, O_2, in the bell jar.

    A plant and a burning candle are placed beneath a bell jar as shown. The candle burns one minute and then goes out. Three days later the candle is ignited by means of the electrical apparatus and burns one minute before going out.
    (1) Which of the following questions is answered by the experiment?

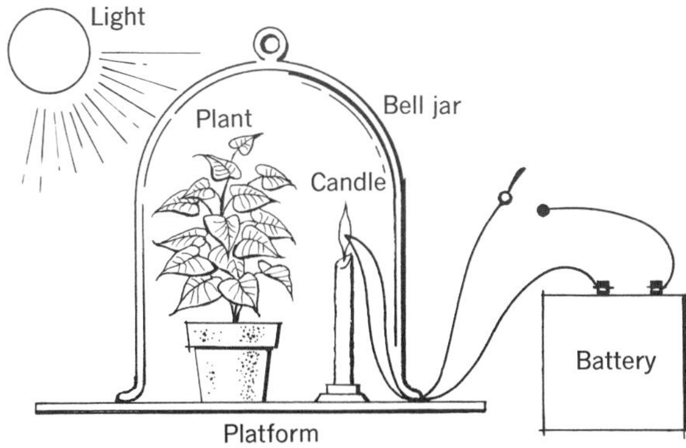

a. Do all parts of a plant take up CO_2 and give off O_2?
b. Do plants require light to take up CO_2 and give off O_2?
c. Do plants and burning candles have the same effect on air?
d. Is the amount of CO_2 taken up by a plant greater than the amount of O_2 given off?

(2) Before any conclusions could be drawn from this experiment, the experiment should be repeated with which one of the following changes?
a. Use a larger bell jar.
b. Omit the candle.
c. Omit the plant.
d. Ignite the candle with a concentrated beam of light.

(3) Suppose it is definitely shown that a plant growing in a bell jar decreases the carbon dioxide, CO_2, and increases the oxygen, O_2, present. How is this finding related to the observation that plants restore the ability of air to support the burning of a candle?
a. It adds information which contradicts the observation.
b. It adds information which fits with the observation.
c. It adds nothing to the observation.
d. It and the observation cannot both be correct.

(Adapted from Biological Sciences Curriculum Study, 1965a.)

C.4-2.21

32. Suppose you are given two balls and you are told one is hollow and one is solid, but you cannot tell which is which merely by looking at them. If you wanted to decide which of the two balls was hollow and which was solid, which of the procedures pictured below would you use?

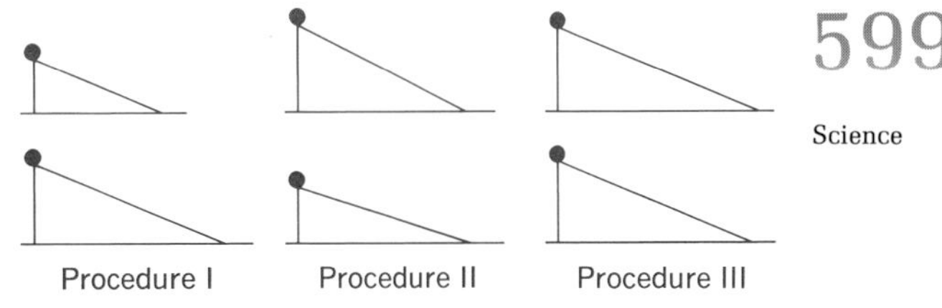

a. procedure I
b. procedure II
c. procedure III

(Adapted from American Association for the Advancement of Science, 1966a, p. GT-23.)

C.4-2.26

33. Questions (1)–(3) refer to the following experiment:

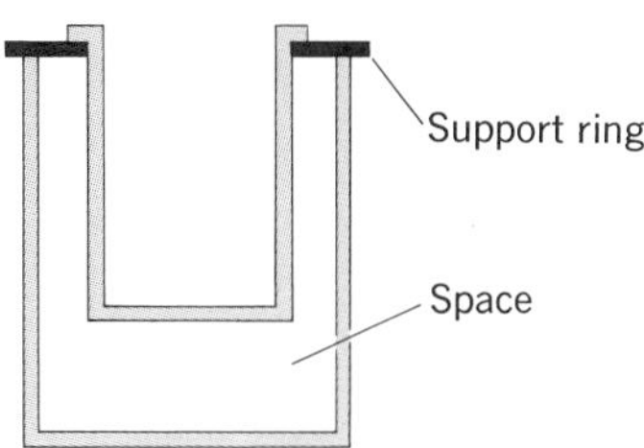

A student, desiring to do some experiments to determine the specific heat of various substances, constructed his own calorimeter. He used two tin cans, nested one inside the other, as shown in the diagram above. The hot sample will be dropped into water held in the inner can.

(1) Of the following, the best material to use for the support ring is
a. smooth aluminum.
b. dull, black steel.
c. rough copper.
d. heavy cardboard.
e. the same material as the can.

(2) The space between the inner and outer cans should be filled with
a. air.
b. ice.
c. water.
d. a liquid of high density.
e. a liquid of low density.

(3) Which of the following would have to be known to obtain accurate results with this apparatus?
I. The specific heat of the inner can
II. The specific gravity of the inner can
III. The mass of the inner can

a. I only
b. II only
c. III only
d. I and II
e. I and III

(Educational Testing Service, 1963b, p. 16, items 23–25. Copyright © 1963 by Educational Testing Service. All rights reserved.)

Items 32 and 33, the first quite simple and the second calling for a considerable fund of background knowledge, illustrate testing in the same behavior subcategory, C.4, *Design of appropriate procedures for performing experimental tests*. Note that the focus here is quite different from the questions asked in items 30 and 31, which deal with the ideational aspects of hypothesis formulation and testing.

C.1-2.11, C.3-2.11, C.4-2.11, D.3-2.11, D.5-2.11;
C.1-2.13, C.3-2.13, C.4-2.13, D.3-2.13, D.5-2.13

34. While Xano and Flo were wandering along a beach one day, Xano found a grayish-white rock. "Look, Flo, I've found a piece of limestone," said Xano, holding up the rock. "I know this is limestone because I found several limestone rocks on the beach last year and they looked just like this rock."
   (1) Xano's last statement shows that he believed, quite correctly, that
      a. limestone is so stable that it cannot be broken down by ordinary chemical means
      b. limestone would have the same appearance now as it had last year
      c. in its natural state, limestone would usually be found on a beach
      d. the appearance of limestone would change as it is described in different chemical terms

   Flo smiled at her hasty friend. "I'm not so sure you're right, Xano," she argued. "This rock doesn't have to be limestone simply because it looks like some limestone you found here last year."
   (2) Which of the following is the best reason in support of Flo's argument?
      a. The chemical properties of limestone might have changed since last year.
      b. Any limestone rocks on the beach since last year would have been dissolved by seawater.
      c. The physical characteristics of minerals seldom change, even over long periods of time.
      d. Different minerals often have similar physical characteristics.
   (3) "I'll prove to you that this rock is limestone," Xano said angrily. He took the rock home and placed a piece of it in a beaker. When Xano poured acid on the piece of rock, there was a good deal of bubbling. "There!" Xano shouted. "This test proves it's limestone." But Flo said she did not agree. Flo was right, because
      a. many different tests for limestone are needed for different rock samples
      b. limestone does not bubble when acid is poured on it
      c. many different substances bubble when acid is poured on them
      d. the proper test for limestone is to add a limited amount of water to the rock and observe whether it becomes hot and smokes
   (4) Xano next heated a piece of the rock in a kiln for several hours. He then took some of the substance that was left after heating and dissolved it in water. When Xano breathed into this solution through a tube, the liquid turned cloudy. Xano exclaimed, "At last! This test proves that the rock is limestone." But again, Flo patiently pointed out that Xano was forgetting something in his reasoning. What was it?
      a. An experiment can reveal only one property of a substance.
      b. Different substances can have similar properties.
      c. Different properties can only be found in similar substances.
      d. The materials of the physical world cannot change.

(Adapted from Klopfer, 1964a, pp. 33–35. © 1964, Science Research Associates, Inc. Reprinted by permission of the publisher.)

The eight successive questions in this rather lengthy illustration (only partly reprinted here) indicate the considerable range of behaviors it is possible to sample by use of the descriptive story. In all eight questions, the five categories of behavior listed at the head of the illustration are sampled, several of them more than once. Not included in the listing is the knowledge of chemical facts, terminology, concepts, and procedures that it is assumed the student confronting these questions possesses. Since this story is designed to be part of a test following a unit where the relevant chemical knowledge is studied, making that assumption is justified.

C.3-3.3, C.3-1.22, C.3-1.23, C.3-1.26, C.3-1.31

35. For items (1) to (6), choose from the KEY the type or design of experiment that is BEST illustrated in each of the statements.

KEY:

A. All things believed to be necessary for the event to take place are brought together to see if the event occurs as expected.
B. Something that is believed to be necessary is taken away or left out to see if the event fails to occur.
C. One or more of the things believed to be necessary are *strengthened* to see if the event occurs differently.
D. One or more of the things believed to be necessary are *weakened* to see if the event occurs differently.
E. The event is observed in as many different cases as possible and all accompanying conditions are recorded carefully.

(1) To see if seeds hold more stored food than is taken up by the seedling before the seedling becomes self-supporting, various amounts of the seed leaves were cut away from bean seeds before they were planted.

(2) To see if willow twigs which sprout roots when left standing in water give off a "rooting" hormone, several willow twigs were placed upside-down in water in which right-side-up willow twigs had sprouted roots.

(3) To see if light is necessary for green plants to carry on photosynthesis, a leaf was removed from a plant before sunrise and then the leaf was tested with iodine solution for the presence or absence of starch.

(4) While seeking the cause or causes of lung cancer, an investigator set out to see if men who smoked cigars had lung cancer less often than did men who smoked pipes and if men who smoke cigarettes have lung cancer more often than do men who smoke either cigars or pipes.

(5) To see if the kinds and numbers of tiny plants and animals which live in streams change as the stream becomes increasingly polluted, the living things in samples of water from a stream near the edges of a growing city were observed carefully week by week for a year.

(6) While seeking the cause or causes of skin acne (pimples), an investigator gave several young volunteers nothing to eat for several days except chocolate candy.

(Adapted from Woodburn et al., 1967.)

This interesting item is somewhat of a variant of behavior subcategory C.3, *Selection of suitable tests of a hypothesis*, in that it asks the student to think about the *type* of test of a hypothesis which an investigator has selected. As a whole, the item calls attention to different methodologies for testing hypotheses, which is an idea related to content subcategory 3.3, *Nature of scientific inquiry.* Though content areas are also listed for this item, the student actually needs very little content knowledge to respond to the several questions.

Evaluation of interpreting data and formulating generalizations: Processes of scientific inquiry III (D.0)

In evaluating the student's behaviors under category *D.0*, the teacher would most frequently look to a written report of an investigation or laboratory experiment. Such a report provides the means for capturing some evidence of the student's performance and thinking as he moves from the raw observations and data to an evaluation of the hypothesis tested in his inquiry. In the section of the lab report devoted to the processing of experimental data (*D.*1), the student displays the computations he made to reduce the data to a form suitable for interpretation, and he may also be asked to make an analysis of the errors in measurements and in observing that are inherent in the experiment. When numerical data are obtained, the student's lab report will usually present these in tables, graphs, or both (*D.*2), and when necessary he will make extrapolations beyond or interpolations between observed points on a graph (*D.*4). Finally, as part of his lab report, the student gives his interpretation of the data and observations (*D.*3), and he states his evaluation of the hypothesis under test (*D*.5), a statement to which the label "conclusion" is commonly affixed.

When a lab report represents the culmination of a series of inquiries, the student may justifiably include in it his formulation of an empirical law or principle (*D*.6). Such generalizations will not be found in most lab reports, however, and other means of evaluating his performance in this subcategory are needed. Either by observing the student in a discussion or by asking him to respond to an essay question, the teacher can assess the student's ability to synthesize empirical findings from diverse sources.

For most of the *D*.0 subcategories of student behavior, paper and pencil test items also are available. These items generally consist of a series of questions about a real or imaginary experiment, and thus simulate the situation that a student faces in preparing a lab report. In the greatest number of the following illustrations (items 39 to 45), the main concern is with interpretation of observations (*D*.3), and these items test for this behavior at various levels of complexity. Evaluation of a hypothesis being tested (*D*.5) is a main concern of a second group of illustrations, items 46 to 50. Testing for behaviors under subcategories *D*.1, *D*.2, and *D*.4 is presented in the first three of the following illustrations.

D.1-2.22

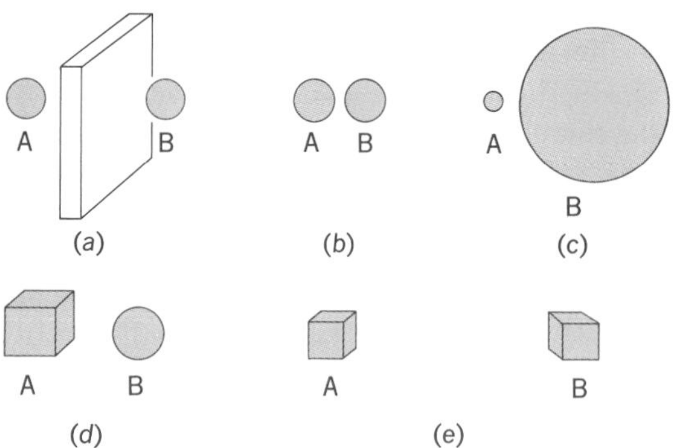

36. In which of the situations shown above would you expect to get the poorest result from the use of

$$F_{\text{grav}} = G\frac{m_A m_B}{R^2}$$

to find the gravitational force between objects *A* and *B*?

(Adapted from Rutherford et al., 1966a.)

This item requires the student to make a qualitative, or perhaps semiquantitative, assessment of the errors involved in alternative ways of performing an experiment to measure the gravitational force between two objects, and it represents an ingenious way of getting the student to think about errors inherent in an experiment. Error analysis is included under behavior subcategory *D*.1.

D.2-1.26, D.4-1.26

37. Questions (1) to (3) relate to the following table which gives the heights and weights of 6 boys.

Boy	*Height (cm)*	*Weight (kg)*
1	120	35
2	135	40
3	150	45
4	165	60
5	180	80
6	195	85

(1) Which of the following is the best reason for presenting the above data in a table?
  a. It requires no interpretation.
  b. It is an effective way of showing relationships.
  c. It has fewer mistakes than a descriptive paragraph.
  d. It points up the reason tall boys weigh more.

(2) Which of graphs (*a*), (*b*), (*c*), and (*d*) correctly expresses the data in the table?

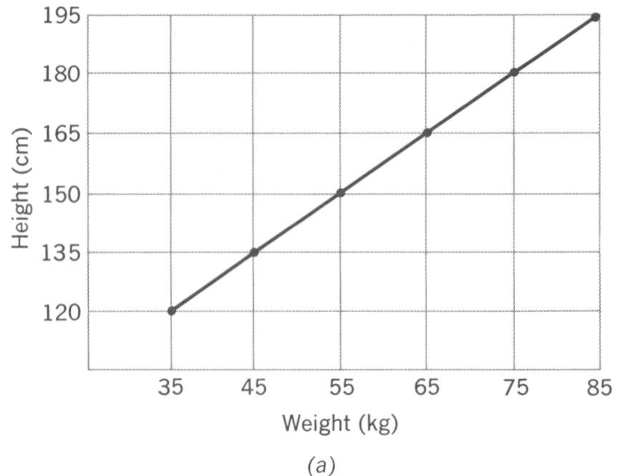

(*a*)

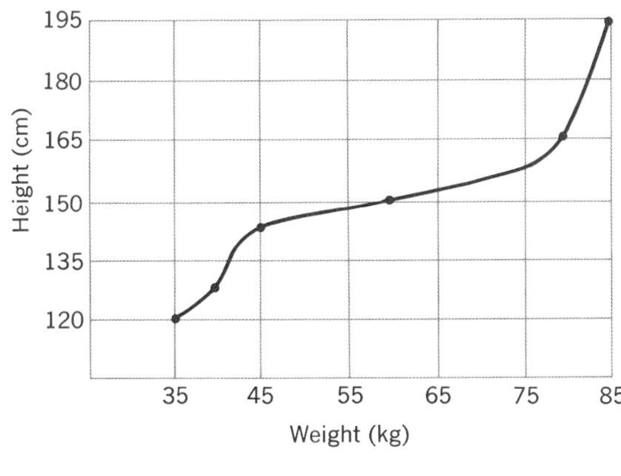

(*b*)

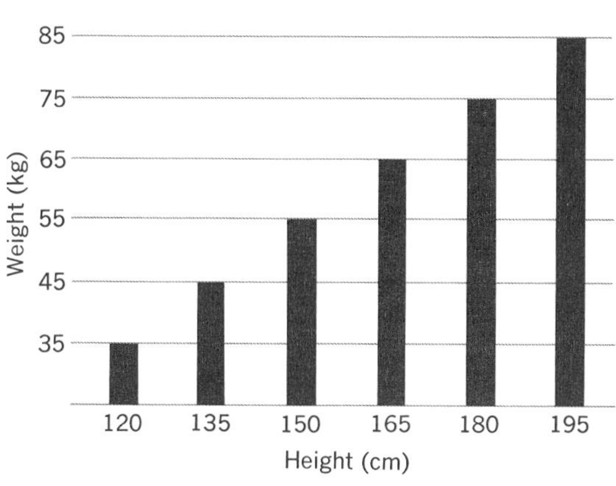

(*c*)

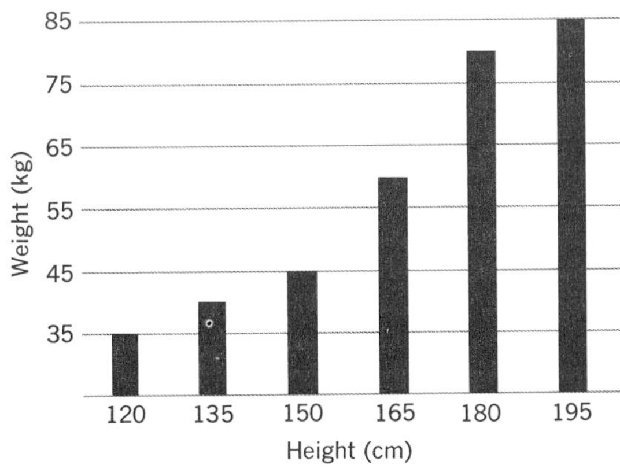

(*d*)

(3) On the basis of the data given, it could be reasonably predicted that the weight of a boy 160 cm tall would be most nearly

a. 45 kg
b. 55 kg
c. 65 kg
d. 75 kg

(Adapted from Biological Sciences Curriculum Study, 1965a.)

D.2-2.29, F.1-2.29

38. Questions (1) to (4) relate to a pair of optical experiments. Each question is to be answered with one of the five graphs below. The horizontal axis of the graph represents the object distance. A graph may be used once, more than once, or not at all.

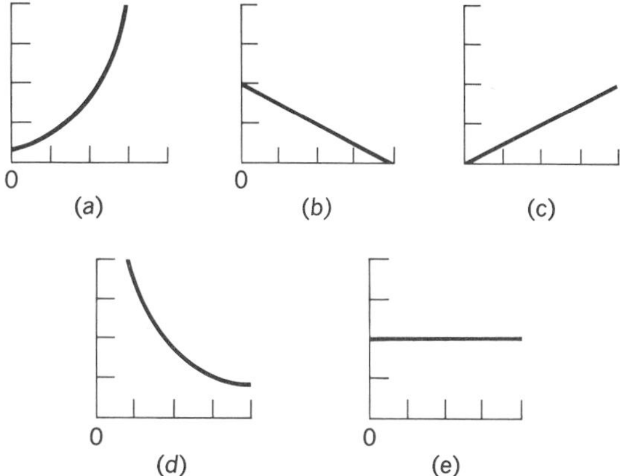

An object is placed at the principal focus of a converging lens and moved slowly away from the lens.

(1) Which graph could represent the location of the image as the object moves away?

(2) Which graph could represent the product of the object distance times the image distance as the object moves away?

(3) Which graph could represent the height of the image as the object moves away?

(4) The object is now placed at the principal focus of a parabolic mirror and moved away from the mirror. As the object moves away, which graph could represent the following ratio?

$$\frac{\text{object size}}{\text{image size}}$$

(Adapted from Physical Science Study Committee, 1963b.)

Items 37 and 38 both test for correct presentations of data in the form of functional relationships.

(Strictly speaking, height is being compared with mass, not weight, in item 37.) To pick the correct graphs in item 38, the student must have a good grasp both of the experimental situations described in the questions and of the optical principles involved in each; hence, behavior F.1 (*Application*) is also listed. In question (3) of item 37, the student must interpolate between observed points (*D*.4). Once a table or graph of observed points is presented, interpolation and extrapolation questions are not difficult to construct. Additional illustrations may be found in items 45 and 50 below.

D.3-2.11

39. Two tubes containing liquids at the same temperature were turned upside-down at the same time. An air bubble began to rise in each tube. After ten seconds the two tubes looked like this:

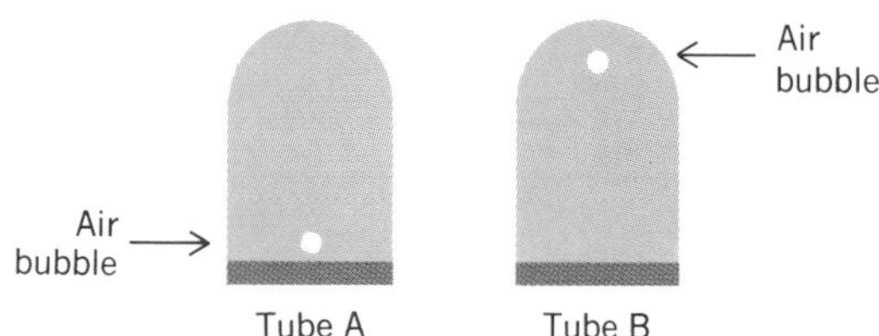

Which of the following statements is correct?

a. The liquid in tube A is the same as the liquid in tube B.
b. The liquid in tube A is different from the liquid in tube B.
c. It is impossible to tell whether the liquids in A and B are the same or different.

(Adapted from American Association for the Advancement of Science, 1966c, p. GT-19.)

D.3-2.22

40. An experiment is performed in which a compressed spring projects a ball along a rough horizontal surface. The relationship between the distance (*c*) the spring is compressed, the distance (*s*) the ball rolls, and the time (*t*) during which the ball is in motion is tabulated below.

c (cm)	0.50	1.00	2.00	4.00
t (sec)	0.25	0.50	1.00	2.00
s (cm)	5.0	20	180	320

What is the relationship between the compression (*c*) and the distance (*s*) (*k* is a constant)?

a. $s = kc$
b. $s = kc^2$
c. $s^2 = kc$
d. $s = \frac{k}{c}$
e. $s = \frac{k}{c^2}$

(Nedelsky, 1965a.)

D.3-2.26, A.10-2.26

41. The table below gives the approximate melting points of a few common elements.

Element	*Melting point in degrees Centigrade*
Aluminum	660
Chlorine	−102
Iron	1535
Lead	327
Mercury	−39

Suppose that samples of all these elements are heated in an oven to a temperature of 1555°C. If the temperature of the oven is then lowered, which of the samples would solidify first?

a. Aluminum
b. Chlorine
c. Iron
d. Lead
e. Mercury

(Educational Testing Service, 1962a, p. 12, sec. 3, item 5.

D.3-2.210, A.10-2.210

42. By convention, the charge acquired by a glass rod which has been rubbed with a cloth is called positive (+). A student possessing five charged objects (I, II, III, IV, V) performs some experiments and records the following data.

I repels glass charged with a cloth but attracts IV.
II attracts V but repels III.
IV repels II.
The force between I and II is 1 unit when they are 4 cm apart.
The force between II and III is 8 units when they are 1 cm apart.

(1) Which of the following can the student correctly conclude regarding the signs of the charges on the objects?

a. I, V positive; II, III, IV negative
b. I, II positive; III, IV, V negative
c. II, III positive; I, IV, V negative
d. I, III, V positive; II, IV negative
e. none of the above

(2) What will be the force between objects I and II when they are 1 cm apart?

a. ¼ unit
b. 4 units
c. 8 units
d. 16 units
e. none of the above

(3) What is the ratio of the charge on I to the charge on III?

a. 4:1
b. 2:1
c. 1:1
d. 1:2
e. none of the above

(Adapted from Chemical Bond Approach Project, 1966, Chs. 1–4, items 14, 15, 16. Adapted by permission from TESTS FOR CHEMICAL SYSTEMS by Chemical Bond Approach Project. Copyright © 1966 by Earlham College Press, Inc. Published by Webster Division, McGraw-Hill Book Company.)

D.3-2.26, A.11-2.26, F.1-2.26

43. The graph below represents the temperature curve for a 78-g sample of benzene (C_6H_6). A constant source of heat is used which supplied 7.0×10^2 cal/min to the C_6H_6 sample. The pressure is constant at 1 atmosphere.

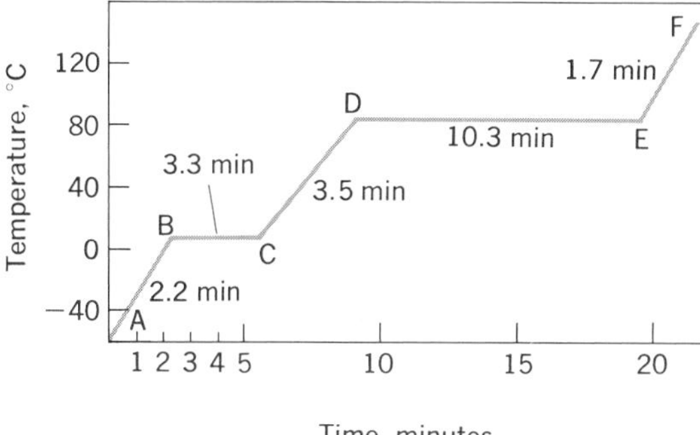

(1) The portion of the graph between D and E represents the time the substance is

a. being warmed as a solid
b. being warmed as a liquid
c. being warmed as a gas
d. changing from solid to liquid at its melting temperature
e. changing from liquid to gas at its boiling temperature

(2) In which portion of the curve do the molecules have the highest average kinetic energy? In the region from

a. A to B
b. B to C
c. C to D
d. D to E
e. E to F

(3) The heat required to change the 78-g sample of benzene from the solid to liquid state without changing its temperature can be determined approximately by making which one of the following calculations?

a. 2.2 min × 700 cal/min
b. 3.3 min × 700 cal/min
c. 3.5 min × 700 cal/min
d. 10.3 min × 700 cal/min
e. 1.7 min × 700 cal/min

(Adapted from Chemical Education Material Study, 1963a, items 16, 17, 19.)

D.3-3.5

44. Here is a picture of a box with the top and front removed. A grid has been drawn on the bottom,

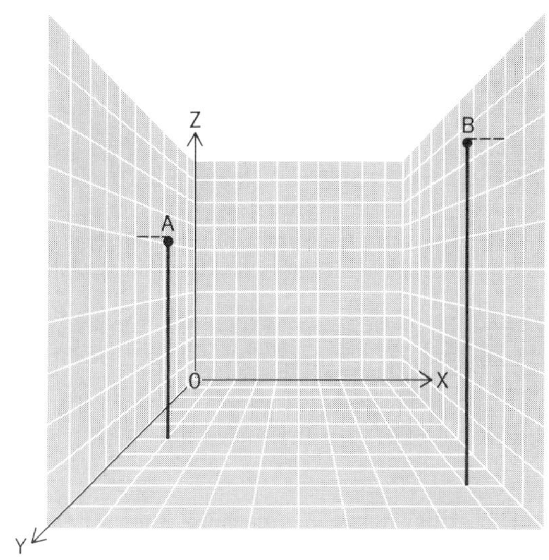

back, and sides of the box. The width of the box is the *X*-coordinate. The depth of the box is the *Y*-coordinate. The height of the box is the *Z*-coordinate. The point at which the three coordinates come together is labeled with an O. All measurements are to be made from this point.

(1) The three coordinates of A are

a. 5, 6, 1
b. 1, 5, 6
c. 0, 1, 5
d. 1, 6, 5

(2) The three coordinates of B are

a. 8, 9, 8
b. 8, 8, 9
c. 0, 8, 9
d. 9, 8, 8

(Adapted from American Association for the Adavancement of Science, 1966b, pp. GT-26, GT-28.)

D.3-3.5, D.4-3.5

45. Questions (1) and (2) relate to the calibration of an instrument. When five known quantities are measured, these scale readings are observed on the instrument.

Known quantities (Q)	*Scale readings (S)*
0.00 units	0.00
1.00	0.50
2.00	2.00
4.00	8.00
6.00	18.00

(1) Which of the formulas below correctly expresses the observed relationship between the known quantities (Q) and the scale readings (S)? (k is a constant.)

I. $S \propto Q$ III. $S = kQ^2$

II. $S \propto Q^2$ IV. $S = \frac{k}{Q^2}$

a. I only
b. II only
c. II and III only
d. I and IV only
e. II, III, and IV only

(2) If a known quantity of 5.00 units were measured with the instrument, what would the scale reading be?

a. 10.0 d. 15.0
b. 12.5 e. 16.5
c. 13.0

(Adapted from Physical Science Study Committee, 1963a.)

Constructing items to measure the student's ability to interpret experimental data and observations is a reasonably popular sport among test makers, as the number and variety of illustrations for subcategory *D*.3 bear witness. These illustrations also show that different interpretation of data items may call on the student to bring more or less knowledge to the situations presented and to respond in various ways. The student's response may be an interpretation in the form of a simple qualitative statement, as in item 39, or it may be a simple quantitative statement, as in item 44. When he is called on to express his interpretation in the form of an algebraic function or equation, as in item 40 and in question (1) of item 45, the student must also bring some of his mathematical knowledge to bear on the selection of his response. Still more complex items may combine testing for interpretation of data with testing for identification in the given data of relevant concepts or principles (subcategory *A*.10), as is done in items 41 and 42. By adding additional questions based on the given data or observations, quite sophisticated items can be built, as is illustrated in item 43, where testing for interpretation of data presented in a graph is combined with questions that involve a translation to another symbolic form (subcategory *A*.11) and application of the data to the solution of a further problem (*F*.1). Interpretation items may also be extended by including questions that ask for an evaluation of the hypothesis being tested (*D*.5). This is illustrated in items 34 and 50.

D.5-1.22

46. Suppose an inference is made that a change in weight of a cut portion of fruit or vegetable can be explained by a change in moisture content. Which of the following statements about the two situations pictured below is the best?
a. Situation (*a*) supports the inference.
b. Situation (*b*) supports the inference.
c. Both situations support the inference.
d. Neither situation supports the inference.

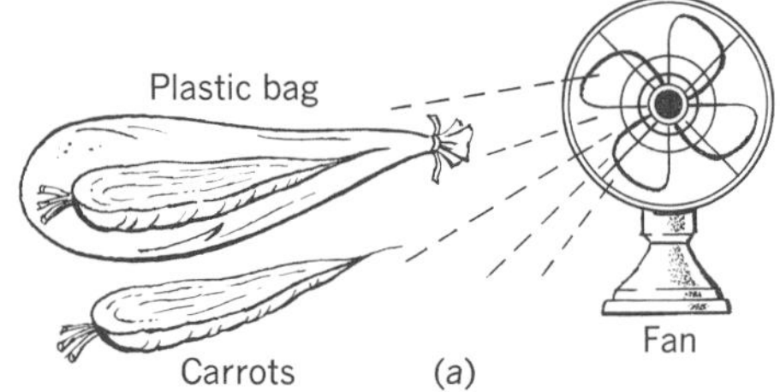

(*a*)

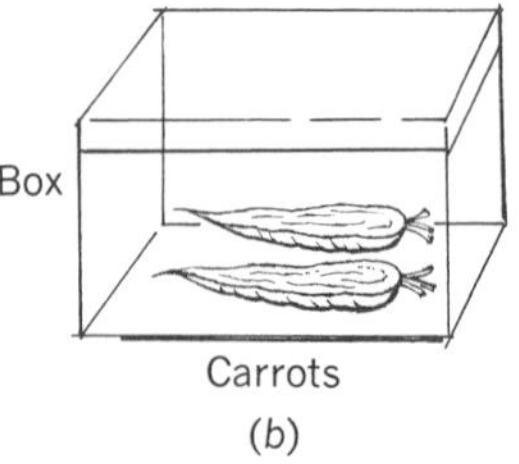

(*b*)

(Adapted from American Association for the Advancement of Science, 1966a, p. GT-22.)

D.5-1.24

47. HYPOTHESIS: Young birds can learn to migrate south in the autumn by accompanying their parents.

Each of the following items states observational or experimental facts. For items (1) and (2) mark space
A—if the fact or facts tend to support the hypothesis
B—if the fact or facts tend to refute the hypothesis
C—if the fact or facts are irrelevant to the hypothesis

(1) In making the trip from northern Canada to the Argentine, adult golden plovers fly in groups due south from Labrador, above the Atlantic Ocean, 1,000 miles from the eastern coast of North America, thence over Brazil to the Argentine. The young golden plovers fly in groups by way of the Mississippi Valley and over the Gulf of Mexico, thence over Bolivia and Peru to the Argentine. On their return trip the old and young alike take the Mississippi Valley route.

(2) Cowbirds build no nests of their own but lay their eggs in the nests of some thirty species of other birds; here the eggs are incubated, hatched, and the young reared by these foster parents. When the first migratory trip is completed, the young cowbirds are found in the South neither among their true parents nor scattered among the thirty different destinations of their foster parents, but instead in one locality occupied predominantly by their own kind.

(3) In the light of the facts given in items (1) and (2), what is the status of the hypothesis at this point?
a. It is established as probably true.
b. It is refuted as probably false.
c. It remains as much unsettled as at the outset.

(Adapted from Nelson, 1967, p. 9.)

D.5-2.18

48. The molecular formula for an organic compound is found to be $C_4H_8O_2$. The following properties of the compound were experimentally determined:

I. 0.1 mole of sodium metal reacts with 0.1 mole of the compound to liberate 0.05 mole of $H_2(g)$.
II. The compound reacts with an alcohol to form an ester.
III. The functional group in the compound is not easily oxidized.

Five hypothesized structures of the compound $C_4H_8O_2$ are shown in structural formulas a. to e. On the basis of the above information, which is the most likely structural formula for the compound?

```
a.      H   H
        |   |      O
    H—C—C—C//       H
        |   |   \    /
        H   H    O—C—H
                      \
                       H

b.      H   H   H
        |   |   |     O
    H—C—C—C—C//
        |   |   |    \
        H   H   H     O—H

c.      H
        |       O—H
        |      /
    H—C—C—H
        |   |
    H—C   C—H
      / \ / \
     H   O   H

d.      H   H   H
        |   |   |     O
    H—C—C—C—C//
        |   |   |    \
        H   OH  H     H

e.      H   H       H
        |   |       |
    H—C—C=C—C—H
        |       |   |
        OH      H   OH
```

(Adapted from Chemical Education Material Study, 1963a.)

D.5-1.26, A.10-1.26, D.5-1.22, A.10-1.22, D.5-1.24, A.10-1.24

49. Each of the items [below] presents a brief description of an experiment followed by a conclusion drawn from the experiment. Use the most applicable statement of the key to evaluate the conclusion.

KEY

A. The conclusion does not answer the problem prompting the experiment.
B. The conclusion is not in agreement with the facts of the experiment.
C. There are not enough facts revealed by the experiment to make the conclusion valid even though the conclusion is in agreement with biological science.
D. Due to the lack of proper controls or other poor experimental technique, the observations from the experiment prompted a conclusion in disagreement with accepted biological science.
E. The conclusion is tentatively justified.

(1) A student hypothesized that the accumulation of carbon dioxide in the lungs affects the rate of

breathing. He breathed into an instrument that eliminated exhaled carbon dioxide and also controlled the oxygen content of the inspired air. These observations were recorded.

		Percentage composition of air in instrument	
Time	*Breathing rate*	*Oxygen*	*Carbon dioxide*
0	16	60	.03
5	15	50	.03
10	17	40	.03
15	18	30	.03
20	18	20	.03
25	18	15	.03

Conclusion—An increase in the carbon dioxide concentration of inspired air will increase the breathing rate.

(2) To answer the question, How do we learn?, a group of students obtained ten pens of identical white rats. They were divided into two groups of five pens and treated identically except that one group was given training in finding food hidden in a maze. This training involved practice in which the rats received an electrical shock each time they made the wrong turn. At the conclusion of the experiment a trained rat could find the hidden food in one minute but it required five minutes for an equally hungry but untrained rat.

Conclusion—We learn by the satisfaction of a successful trial and the dissatisfaction of an unsuccessful error.

(Dressel & Nelson, 1956, p. 30, items 170, 171. Copyright © by Educational Testing Service.)

D.3-1.23, D.4-1.23, D.5-1.23

50. INSTRUCTIONS: This portion of the test was designed to measure your ability to interpret data. Following the data you will find a number of statements and hypotheses. You are to assume that the data as presented are correct. Evaluate each statement or hypothesis according to the following key.

KEY

A. Correct: The data alone are sufficient to show that the statement or hypothesis is correct.
B. Probably correct: The data indicate that the statement or hypothesis may be correct, that it is logical on the basis of the data but the data are not sufficient to say that it is definitely correct.
C. Insufficient evidence: There are no data to indicate whether or not the statement or hypothesis is correct.
D. Probably incorrect: The data indicate that the statement or hypothesis is probably incorrect, that is, it is not logical on the basis of the data but the data are not sufficient to say that it is definitely wrong.
E. Incorrect: The data alone are sufficient to show that the statement or hypothesis is incorrect.

Questions (1) to (8) refer to the following graph. Use the key above to answer the items. The lizard is considered to be cold-blooded, the others warm-blooded.

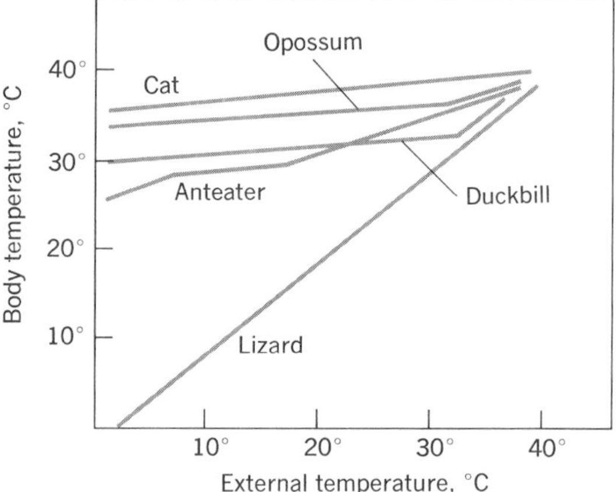

(1) When the external temperature is 50°C, the temperature of the lizard is also 50°C.
(2) At an external temperature of 50°C, the temperature of the cat is 50°C.
(3) When the external temperature is 50°C, the temperature of the anteater would be higher than the temperature of the cat.
(4) The temperature of a mouse would be about halfway between that of the cat and the anteater.
(5) At no time during the experiment did any of the animals have the same body temperature.
(6) There is a close correlation between the body temperature of the lizard and that of the external environment.
(7) At 20 degrees below 0°C, the lizard would be frozen.
(8) If the temperature of other cold-blooded animals were plotted, it would resemble that of the lizard.

(Adapted from Burmester, 1951.)

In asking the student to evaluate hypotheses in the light of experimental data obtained, the test item may require him to bring varying amounts of knowledge into his judgment. In items 46 and 47, the amount of additional knowledge needed is minimal. The question asked in both these illustrations is essentially "Given certain experimental results or observations, what is the status of the hypothesis being tested?" Note also that both items offer the possibility that the reported experiments or observations are irrelevant to the hypothesis. This same possibility is suggested by alternative A in item 49 and by alternative C in item 50. The experimental results reported in item 48 are hardly sufficient in themselves to allow the student to make a judgment, and he must bring to bear his knowledge of the chemical reactions for which only the outcomes are given. This item is also interesting because it requires the student to successively evaluate five hypotheses, the five possible structures of the organic compound $C_4H_8O_2$, in the light of the experimental results reported. In item 49, knowledge of biological principles and concepts is explicitly called for in two of the five alternative responses of the key list, and the student's analysis task is a rather complicated one. For each question in this illustration, he first has to evaluate the status of the stated hypothesis following the experiment which is described; then, using the alternatives in the key list, he evaluates the stated conclusion—i.e., the stated evaluation of the hypothesis. A similar complicated task is involved in questions (4) and (8) of item 50. This item tests the student not only on evaluating hypotheses, but also on interpreting experimental data and on extrapolation.

Evaluation of building, testing, and revising a theoretical model: Processes of scientific inquiry IV (E.0)

In science instruction the analyses, syntheses, and deliberations by students that are described in category *E*.0 normally take place in the context of group discussions. The trick, therefore, in evaluating a student's behavior under *E*.0 is to capture samples of the thinking he displays in these discussions. To accomplish this, the teacher may observe and take notes on the kinds of comments contributed to the discussion by each student, but this is difficult to do if he is simultaneously involved in following the arguments of the discussion as leader or participant. A preferable procedure is to record the discussion on audiotape or videotape and to make a content analysis afterward of what each student said. The content-analysis scheme need not be elaborate. It can consist merely of categorizing each of the student's remarks under the six headings of behaviors *E*.1 to *E*.6 and judging the quality of the reasoning displayed in the remark. A code number for the quality of the reasoning (e.g., 3 = insightful, 2 = reasonable, 1 = doubtful or poor) can then be entered next to the student's name under the behavioral heading on a checklist. The particular advantage of using a tape recording is that it does capture samples of the student's behaviors which, by playing back the tape or portions of it, can be assessed or reassessed at any time.

A procedure like the foregoing is necessary for making adequate evaluations in category *E*.0 since, as in categories *B*.0 and *C*.0, only some aspects of the included behaviors can be caught successfully on paper and pencil tests. The illustrative test items in the following group cover each of the *E*.0 subcategories and indicate both the possibilities and the limitations of testing by this means for the student's ability to build, test, and revise a theoretical model.

E.1-3.2

51. A scientific *theory* should
    a. provide the final answer to scientific questions
    b. supply directions for making useful things
    c. tie together and explain many natural events
    d. suggest good rules for carrying out experiments

(Adapted from Carrier, Geis, Klopfer, & Shoresman, 1966.)

This item relates the student's recognition of the need for a theoretical model (behavior *E*.1) to his understanding of the nature and structure of science, rather than to a particular problem in a science content area. Written at the level and in the language of the elementary school student, the item calls for the correct selection of the functions of a theoretical model in science.

E.2-2.26

52. The kinetic theory of gases includes the postulate that gases are composed of particles. Listed below are *some* of the properties of *a* particle gas model.
    I. A particle is made up of a single atom or a combination of the same or different atoms, so that particles of different gases may have different masses.
    II. The particles must be perfectly elastic and must be in continuous random motion.
    III. Equal volumes of different gases compared at the same temperature and pressure contain equal numbers of particles.

    In questions (1) to (3) choose *one or more* of the properties *needed* in the model to account for the experimentally determined behavior of gases mentioned in each question.

    (1) For a given gas, the pressure-volume product is a constant ($PV =$ constant) when the amount of gas and temperature are constant.
        a. I
        b. II
        c. III
        d. II and III
        e. I and III
    (2) Some gases have color while others do not. [Same alternatives as in question (1).]
    (3) Equal volumes of hydrogen gas and chlorine gas, compared at the same temperature and pressure, have different weights but react with each other in a volume ratio of 1 to 1 to form hydrogen chloride. [Same alternatives as in question (1).]

(Adapted from Chemical Education Material Study, 1963a, items 24, 25, 26.)

In responding to the questions in item 52, the student must select certain postulates (called "properties" in the item) that are needed in a theoretical model to account for known facts and an empirical law. This task is one component part, though not the whole, of the behavior of formulating a theoretical model (*E*.2).

E.3-2.31

53. (1) Which one of the following observations can be explained by a simple geocentric model with uniform motion about the center of circular orbits?
        a. The sun moves slower in the summer and faster in the winter.
        b. The moon shows phases in the period of one month.
        c. The planets vary in speed at different points in their orbits.
        d. The size and duration of Mars' retrograde motion is not the same at successive recurrences.
        e. The planets move with different speeds against the stars at different points of their orbits.
    (2) Given are three observations about the solar system:
        1. Each day the sun rises in the east and sets in the west.
        2. During the night the stars appear to move about the North Celestial Pole.
        3. Eclipses of the sun occur at regular intervals.

        Which of the above observations cannot be represented by a model of the solar system in which the sun revolves around the earth?
        a. 1 and 2 only
        b. 2 and 3 only
        c. 1 and 3 only
        d. 1, 2, and 3
        e. none of the above

(Adapted from Rutherford et al., 1966a.)

The two questions of this item provide good tests of behavior *E*.3, *Specification of phenomena and principles that are satisfied or explained by a theoretical model*. Note that the two questions illustrate complementary ways of setting the task. Question (1) asks for an analysis of phenomena that *can* be explained by a given model, while question (2) asks for an analysis of phenomena that *cannot* be explained.

E.4-2.17, F.1-2.17

54. Questions (1) to (4) relate to the following information about an imaginary place called Flatland.

In Flatland there are only two dimensions, and all molecules are planar. Electrons can be considered to be negative charge discs. A charge disc may be one or two, but not more than two, electrons. For example, a molecule of planar He, an inert substance, is represented by a nucleus at the center of a two-electron charge disc. The most stable arrangement for the later elements of the second period is an equilateral triangular arrangement of charge discs around the central small charge disc. This arrangement is shown in the following diagram.

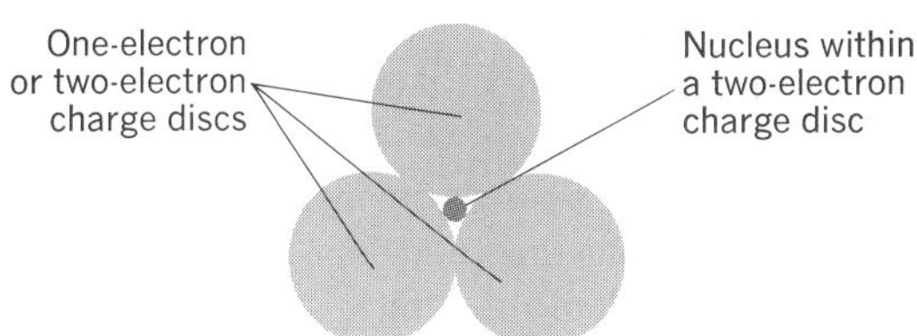

(1) The atomic number of Flatland's first inert substance is 2. The atomic number of the second inert substance would be
 a. 4
 b. 8
 c. 10
 d. 18
 e. an odd number

(2) It can be logically predicted that in Flatland the element with atomic number 3 would
 a. tend to form sheet-like polymers
 b. be a nonconductor of electricity
 c. be highly reactive when brought in contact with the element of atomic number 8
 d. not react with the element of atomic number 1
 e. not have diatomic molecules

(3) Element X has an atomic number of 5, and element Z has an atomic number of 7. The formula for the compound of these two elements would be
 a. X_3Z
 b. XZ_3
 c. XZ
 d. X_2Z_3
 e. X_3Z_2

(4) The *least* stable diatomic molecule in the second period of the Flatland periodic table would be formed from two atoms of the element with atomic number
 a. 3 d. 6
 b. 4 e. 7
 c. 5

(Adapted from Chemical Bond Approach Project, 1966, items 10, 11, 15, 16. Adapted by permission from TESTS FOR CHEMICAL SYSTEMS by Chemical Bond Approach Project. Copyright © 1966 by Earlham College Press, Inc. Published by Webster Division, McGraw-Hill Book Company.)

The use of an imaginary theoretical model is illustrated in item 54, and the same could be done in testing for other *E*.0 behaviors (see item 57). When answering the several questions in this item, a part of the student's task is to make logical deductions from the theoretical model presented. In most of the questions, he must then apply to these deductions his knowledge of chemical bonding and atomic structure. The deductions might be thought of as hypotheses about Flatland's chemical elements, but, since we are not in Flatland, these hypotheses unfortunately cannot be checked out. The task set in this item, therefore, is somewhat different from behavior *E*.4, *Deduction of new hypotheses from a theoretical model,* to direct observations and experiments for testing it, although the task is certainly a part of that behavior.

E.5-1.16

55. In a certain organism, long body (L) is dominant to short body (l) and striped body (S) is dominant to speckled body (s).

A cross between a LlSs male and a llss female produces F_1 progeny as follows:

	Males	*Females*
Long, striped body	50%	50%
Short, speckled body	50%	50%

(1) The percentage of F_1 phenotypes is explained by which of the following postulates of genetic theory?
 a. Nondisjunction of adjacent chromosomes
 b. Crossing-over of genes L and S
 c. Sex linkage of gene L to s
 d. Linkage of genes on the same pair of chromosomes

(2) If Mendel had obtained these results, which of the postulates in his theoretical model of the genes would he have had to reject?

a. There are determiners for hereditary traits.
b. Hereditary determiners sort independently of one another.
c. Hereditary determiners do not influence one another.
d. The hereditary determiners can be either dominant or recessive.

(Adapted from Biological Sciences Curriculum Study, 1965b.)

E.5-2.29

56. Two theories are used at the present time to explain the nature of light and other electromagnetic radiation. The first of these theories is the wave theory which proposes that all electromagnetic radiation consists of waves whose period and frequency coincide with the period and frequency of the source which gives rise to the waves. The second of the theories is the corpuscular or quantum theory of radiation which proposes that all electromagnetic radiation consists of corpuscles or packets of energy, the energy content of any one packet being dependent upon the energy difference between two stationary energy states of an atom or molecule. Items [(1)–(4)] are experimental observations of electromagnetic radiation phenomena and are to be evaluated in accordance with the following key.

KEY

A. The observation supports or can best be explained by the wave theory of radiation.
B. The observation supports or can best be explained by the corpuscular theory of radiation.
C. The observation can be explained equally well by either theory.
D. The observation cannot be explained by either theory.

(1) When radiation passes through an aperture or past the edge of an obstacle, it always spreads to some extent into the region which is not directly exposed to the oncoming radiation.

(2) When a beam of light is incident on certain materials, such as cesium, electrons may be ejected from the material, the maximum speed of the ejected electrons being independent of the intensity of the incident light.

(3) When light from a single source is split into two beams by passing the light through two slits and then allowed to fall on a screen, a symmetrical pattern of evenly spaced light and dark bands or fringes may be observed.

(4) The velocity of light (and other electromagnetic radiation) in a vacuum has been accurately determined to be 2.99776×10^{10} centimeters per second.

(Dressel & Nelson, 1956, p. 662, items 425–428. Copyright © 1956 by Educational Testing Service.)

Both of these illustrations satisfactorily test for the analytical thinking involved in behavior subcategory *E*.5. Note that the format of the items is not very different from that of some of the illustrations which test for behavior *D*.5 (items 46 to 50), but here the student's reasoning must be carried across an additional level of abstraction, from the results of experiments to their implications for a theoretical model. Item 55 tests for the implications of results of an experimental cross between two genotypes for a theoretical model of the genetics, and the student must have some knowledge of the postulates of the model to answer the questions. Item 56, however, seems to demand less specific background knowledge of the student, though having more knowledge will help him, and it manages to catch more of the actual situation where this kind of analysis generally occurs in science—a controversy over two competing theoretical models.

E.6-2.213

57. A crystalline solid may be thought of as a group of spheres in three dimensions, each sphere connected to its neighbors by a stiff spring. The spheres are vibrating in various directions. A number of facts about crystalline solids are given below. Before each fact write the letter of the response that best states the applicability of the model as an explanation of the fact. Note that only one response should be given for each fact.

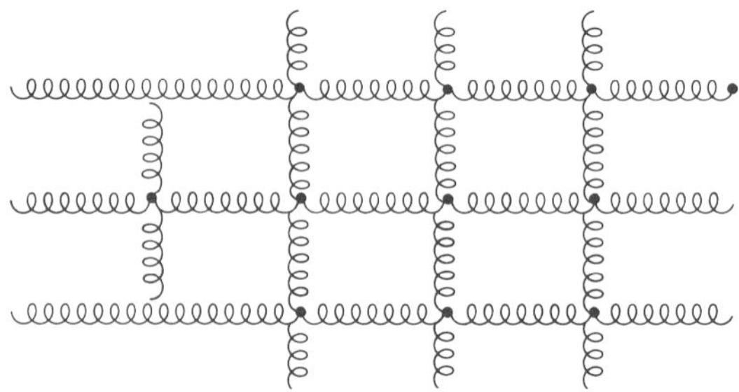

RESPONSES

A. The fact is explained by the model given above.
B. The fact can be explained by modifying the model as follows: the amplitude of vibration of the spheres depends upon the temperature.
C. The fact can be explained by modifying the model as follows: there are irregularities in the arrangement of the spheres.
D. The fact can be explained by modifying the model as follows: the elasticity of the springs is different for different solids.
E. The fact cannot be explained on the basis of the model, even by changing it as above.

FACTS

Solids contract on cooling.
Solids may be compressed slightly.
Solids do not diffuse through one another.
Solids conduct heat.
Some solids are harder than others.
The speed of sound through steel is greater than its speed through lead.

(Nedelsky, 1965b, p. 269, item 2.12-7. From SCIENCE TEACHING AND TESTING by Leo Nedelsky, © 1965 by Harcourt, Brace & World, Inc., and reproduced with their permission.)

For each observation (fact) presented in this item, the student must decide whether or not the given theoretical model of a solid explains the observation and, if it does not, select an appropriate revision of the model from the key list. The reasoning involved in this task probably closely resembles that involved in the student's formulation of a revised, refined, or extended theoretical model (E.6). Nevertheless, as is also true of a number of other illustrative test items for the E.0 subcategories, the task of responding to cleverly constructed questions seems to be lacking in the vitality and immediacy of confrontation that can be observed in the student's behavior when he formulates, evaluates, debates, reformulates theoretical models as he engages in fluid inquiry.

Testing for application of scientific knowledge and methods (F.0)

As the student learns science in any instructional program, he is continually asked to apply concepts, principles, and methods taught in one situation to new situations or examples. Exercises that must be solved by applying a concept, principle, or method help to promote the student's learning of that concept, principle, or method, but they can also be used to assess how well it was learned. Many science teachers feel that a student has not really learned a concept, principle, or method unless he can apply it successfully to the solution of a new problem. Partly for this reason, problem exercises abound at the ends of chapters in science textbooks. Test makers, too, have included many application items in published science tests.

In compiling the following group of illustrative items, only a few application items were selected from the sizable existing pool to show various forms and techniques of testing in category F.0. One caution about items placed in this category must be borne in mind, however: no item can be definitely categorized as *Application* for a particular student unless we know his learning history. If the situation or problem presented in the item is not new to him—if he encountered the same situation before in the original instruction or elsewhere—then he need not make any application in responding to the item; he must only recall the answer. The same item may be testing for application for one student while it may simply be testing for knowledge for another student with a different learning history. Thus, each illustrative item here can be placed under *Application* only with the proviso that the situation presented actually is a new one to the student confronting it.

F.1-2.31

58. A space probe that missed its target went into orbit around the sun at a mean distance 9 times as great as the earth's orbit. What is the period of revolution of the probe?
    a. 3 years
    b. 9 years
    c. 27 years
    d. 54 years
    e. 81 years

(Adapted from Rutherford et al., 1966a.)

F.1-1.35

59. These diagrams represent examples of tree trunks from four different forest environments.

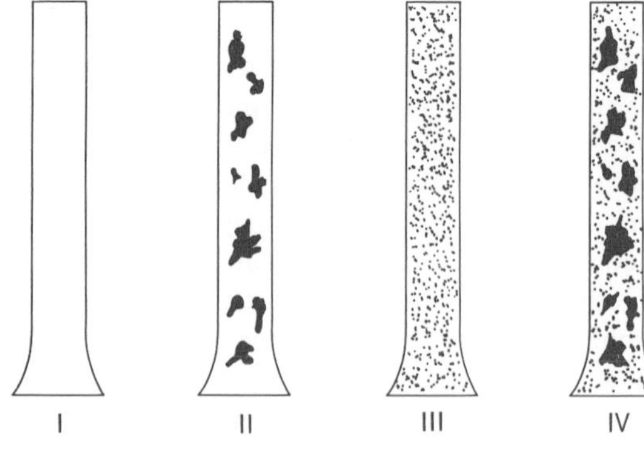

1,000 white and 1,000 black moths were released in a forest environment near a large city. Three weeks later, 778 white moths and 135 black moths were recaptured.

(1) The experimental forest most likely was composed of trees whose trunks closely resembled
- a. I
- b. II
- c. III
- d. IV

(2) If 100 years later the experiment were repeated and 950 black and 55 white moths were recovered, then the most probable reason for these data would be that the
- a. number of moth predators had decreased
- b. number of moth predators had increased
- c. percentage of soot in the air had increased
- d. rate of evolutionary change had decreased

(Adapted from Biological Sciences Curriculum Study, 1965b.)

F.1-1.16

60. Items (1) to (4) are based on the following situation, which involves the inheritance of baldness, a sex-influenced trait.

A young female circus acrobat who hangs by her hair as part of her act is wondering whether she should change her profession, if necessary, before it becomes too late. Her problem is this: Her mother is bald, but her father has a normal head of hair. Her older brother is rapidly losing his hair and will soon be bald.

Let B represent the gene for baldness and b the gene for nonbaldness. In the heterozygous condition B is dominant in males, but b is dominant in females. A heterozygous man will be bald, but a heterozygous woman will not be bald.

(1) Which of the following matings represents the parents of the young female circus acrobat?
- a. BbXX × BbXY
- b. bbXX × BBXY
- c. BbXX × bbXY
- d. BBXX × bbXY
- e. BBXX × BbXY

(2) The genotype of the older brother of the young female circus acrobat is represented by
- a. BbXY
- b. bbXY
- c. BbXX
- d. BBXY
- e. BBXX

(3) The genotype of the young female circus acrobat is represented by
- a. BbXY
- b. BBXY
- c. bbXX
- d. BBXX
- e. BbXX

(4) On the basis of the data, which of the following suggestions to the young female circus acrobat would be most justifiable?
- a. You need not change your profession—according to the genetic evidence there is no likelihood at all that you will become bald.
- b. The chances are 1 in 4 that you will become bald.
- c. The chances are 3 in 4 that you will become bald.
- d. There is a 50 percent chance that you will become bald.
- e. Change your profession—according to the genetic evidence, you are almost certain to become bald.

(Adapted from Nelson, 1967, p. 17.)

F.1-2.17, A.10-2.17

61. (1) Glubbium is a semiconductor. Therefore, as its temperature is increased, its electrical conductivity
- a. increases
- b. decreases
- c. remains the same
- d. immediately goes to zero
- e. immediately goes to infinity

(2) The behavior of semiconductors referred to in question (1) is explained by which of the following statements?
- a. It becomes harder to make a good contact between the sample and the wires from the measuring device.
- b. Electrons pick up energy and overcome the forces which hold them when they are at lower temperatures.

c. Nuclei vibrate faster and collide with more electrons, scattering them away from the original direction of motion.
d. The electrons move much faster and therefore are not influenced by the vibrating nuclei.
e. None of the above.

(3) As glubbium is in group IV of the periodic table, one might expect that the addition of small quantities of gribbium (group V) to a very pure sample of glubbium would make the electrical conductivity of the sample
a. decrease
b. increase
c. stay the same
d. immediately go to zero
e. immediately go to infinity

(Adapted from Chemical Bond Approach Project, 1966, Chs. 8, 9, items 28, 29, 30. Adapted by permission from TESTS FOR CHEMICAL SYSTEMS by Chemical Bond Approach Project. Copyright © 1966 by Earlham College Press, Inc. Published by Webster Division, McGraw-Hill Book Company.)

F.1-2.13, A.10-2.213

62. To calculate how alpha particles scatter as they pass through gold foil, we can assume, with Rutherford, that the alpha particles and gold nuclei act as charged points. Some of the following questions deal with the differences between the scattering of alpha particles from idealized point nuclei and the scattering from actual atoms, which include the electronic cloud around the nucleus.

(1) Two individual alpha particles with the same energy are observed to be scattered through different angles. Considering only scattering by nuclei, the particle with the larger scattering angle
a. came closer to a nucleus than did the other
b. did not get as close to a nucleus as did the other
c. may have passed either closer to or farther from a nucleus than did the other
d. was certainly scattered by more than one nucleus
e. must have been scattered by an impurity atom instead of gold

(2) If an alpha particle of 10^7 ev passes through the electron clouds of 10^5 atoms before it comes to rest, the average energy loss per atom passed is
a. 1 ev
b. 10 ev
c. 10^2 ev
d. 10^3 ev
e. 5×10^4 ev

(3) The smallest distance that the alpha particle described in question (2) would travel (as measured along its path through the gold) before coming to rest would be approximately
a. 10 meters
b. 10^{-1} meters
c. 10^{-3} meters
d. 10^{-5} meters
e. 10^{-7} meters

(4) It is found that the number of *high-energy* alpha particles with kinetic energy more than 2×10^7 ev scattered through angles of approximately 180° is somewhat different from that predicted by the Rutherford theory. The reason is that
a. the nucleus is not a point but has a finite but small size
b. the nucleus has electrons about it
c. Coulomb's law does not hold near the nucleus
d. the alpha particle loses less energy to the gold atom than to the point nucleus of the model
e. the nucleus plus its electrons is neutral

(Adapted from Physical Science Study Committee, 1959.)

Item 58 represents a very common form of application item, where the student must apply a principle or concept to the solution of a numerical problem. Items in this form may be viewed as typical end-of-chapter problem exercises that have been relocated on tests. The test item asks only for the correct answer to the problem, not for any of the steps leading to the solution. In item 58, if the student chooses the correct answer, it is inferred that he has correctly applied Kepler's third law in solving the problem. This type of inference frequently must be made in items which test for application. Items 59, 60, and 61 illustrate the form of application item where a hypothetical or fictional situation is presented and the student must apply a principle or concept in answering the questions based on the situation. These three items represent different content areas and levels of complexity, and, as item 60 particularly well testifies, the variety of situations that can be invented for this form of application testing is limited only by the ingenuity of the test maker. Item 62 deals with a real situation that is likely to be familiar to the student, but novel questions that he is not likely to have considered before are asked about it. Again, to answer the question the student must apply pertinent principles, concepts, or both. In both items 61 and 62, the student is also asked to identify the principle or concept which he applied in answering a question (see question (2) in item 61 and question (4) in item 62). The inclusion of questions such as these in testing for application serves to obtain a more complete record of the application process.

F.2-2.26, F.2-2.33

63. Temperatures change more slowly and less extensively along the seashore and near large lakes than in areas far from water. These more moderate temperature changes are mainly due to the fact that
    a. water is warmer than soil.
    b. water is colder than soil.
    c. water warms and cools more slowly than soil.
    d. water warms and cools more rapidly than soil.
    e. winds are generally stronger in areas far from water.

(Educational Testing Service, 1962b, p. 3, item 11.)

F.2-2.25, F.2-1.22

64. The inhabitants of the Andes, situated at an altitude of over 13,000 feet, have almost twice as many red corpuscles in their blood as do the people living in the valleys. Which of the following best accounts for this phenomena?
    a. The high air pressure in the Andes forces more red corpuscles into the blood.
    b. Inhabitants of the Andes breathe more slowly.
    c. The low air pressure of the Andes requires more surface area (more red corpuscles) to maintain the needed oxygen supply to body cells.
    d. The inhabitants of the Andes work harder and therefore need more red corpuscles to furnish oxygen to body cells.
    e. The low air pressure in the Andes speeds the blood circulation so that more red corpuscles are needed.

(Educational Testing Service, 1962a, p. 4, pt. 1, sec. 1, item 11.)

As far as the forms of questions and techniques are concerned, there is nothing unique about testing for application in a different field of science (*F*.2) as compared with testing for application in the same field of science (*F*.1). Item 63 is similar to item 59, question (2); item 64 is very much like item 61, question (2). Providing further illustrations for subcategory *F*.2 would be redundant. Nevertheless, it is worth noting that it is not very common to find items on published science tests which can justly be placed in *F*.2. Partly this is because the boundaries of science fields are not well-defined; where, for example, is the boundary line between chemistry and physics? A more practical reason is that published science tests reflect the content of current science courses. The content of most high school science courses focuses on a single field, and applications are made predominantly within that field—a situation unlikely to change very much until unified or integrated science courses become more widespread.

F.3-2.24

65. The advantage gained when a man lifts one end of an automobile with a jack is that
    a. the work done by the jack in lifting the car is greater than the work done by the man
    b. the force exerted by the jack is greater than the force exerted by the man
    c. the efficiency of the man's muscles is increased by using the jack
    d. the energy input of the man is greater than the energy output of the jack

F.3-1.26

66. A sailor, adrift in the ocean on a raft, ran out of a supply of fresh water. He became terribly thirsty but was afraid to drink the sea water because he had heard it could cause death. What biological principle would make the sailor's drinking of sea water disastrous? Select from the five possibilities listed below:
    a. There are many microorganisms in sea water, some of which would cause death.
    b. The various salts that sea water contains would tend to erode the stomach.
    c. When the salt water reached the sailor's intestines, the natural salt already in his blood cells would leave to mingle with the intestinal salts.
    d. The salt water would travel to and through the kidneys so rapidly that it would overburden

them, thus producing death from kidney malfunction.

e. Some of the water content of the blood would leave the blood to join the sea water in the intestines.

(Adapted from Hedges, 1966, p. 68.)

F.3-2.14, F.3-2.25

67. A utility company changed its gas for domestic use from water gas (about 50 percent by volume hydrogen, H_2, and 50 percent carbon monoxide, CO) to coke-oven gas (about 30 percent hydrogen and 70 percent methane, CH_4) without altering burners or pressure. A suit was filed against the utility by a man who claimed that he was made ill by carbon monoxide escaping unburned from a lighted cookstove.

The main parts of a typical gas burner on a cookstove are shown in the accompanying diagram.

Under proper conditions, hydrogen is known to burn to H_2O, carbon monoxide to CO_2, and methane to H_2O and CO_2.

$$2H_2 + O_2 \rightarrow 2H_2O$$
$$2CO + O_2 \rightarrow 2CO_2$$
$$CH_4 + 2O_2 \rightarrow CO_2 + 2H_2O$$

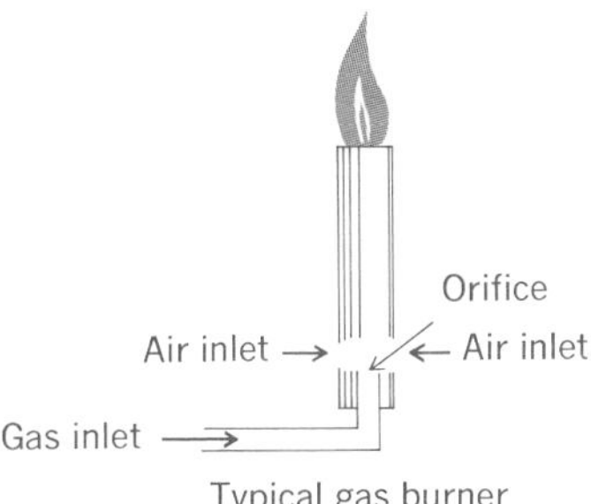

Typical gas burner

If oxygen is limited, carbon monoxide may be formed from methane.

$$2CH_4 + 3O_2 \rightarrow 2CO + 4H_2O$$

(1) Which of the following should be most useful in investigating the possibility of CO formation due to oxygen deficiency?
  a. the law that gases combine in fixed ratios by volume
  b. the table of atomic weights
  c. the laws relating pressure, volume, and temperature of gases
  d. the laws of chemical equilibrium
  e. the law of definite proportions by weight

(2) The complainant's attorney held that the utility company should have increased the gas pressure in the mains. What would probably have been the result?
  a. It would have allowed a more complete combustion.
  b. The combustion would have been more complete, but a large waste of gas would have resulted.
  c. I would have rectified the condition but would have produced a flame of a lower temperature.
  d. It would have made the combustion even less complete.

(Slightly adapted from Nedelsky, 1965b, pp. 282–283, item 2.22-1. From SCIENCE TEACHING AND TESTING by Leo Nedelsky, © 1965 by Harcourt, Brace & World, Inc., and adapted and reproduced with their permission.)

The techniques of testing for application in subcategory *F*.3 are not different from those in *F*.1 and *F*.2, but items 65 to 67 deal with problems outside of science to which the student is asked to apply scientific concepts, principles, and methods. Item 65 deals with a simple technological application of a scientific concept, and it stands for the class of technological application items, which may reach considerable complexity. Items 66 and 67 represent the class of items in which the student applies science concepts, principles, or both, to examples of practical problems in life. Unfortunately, application items of this class are not so abundant in the science testing literature as they well might be.

Evaluation of manual skills (G.0)

Little that is not intuitively obvious can be said about evaluating the student's behavior in category *G*.0. To evaluate manual skills, some form of observation must be made of the student manipulating laboratory equipment and materials. These observations may be made informally by the teacher while the student is carrying out an investigation, or they may be made in connection with an organized performance test.

Though the development of performance tests and of specific criteria for judging performance is a generally neglected area in science education, some good work on performance tests in physics has been accomplished (see Kruglag & Wall, 1959). The techniques are readily adaptable to other science fields. One approach to evaluation in subcategory *G*.2, *Performance of common laboratory techniques with care and safety*, is to set up a number of simple exercises around the laboratory (say twenty) and have the student move from one to another at two- or three-minute intervals. Some suitable exercises for this kind of performance test are given in the illustration below. In this situation, the student's skill in carrying out the techniques can be observed by the teacher and his success with the techniques is indicated in the results he reports.

G.2-2.11, G.2-2.13, G.2-2.29, G.2-3.5

68. (1) Take a little of each of the liquids A, B, C into each of three test-tubes. Blow the air from your lungs into each liquid in turn, through a drinking-straw. State what happens.
(A = water; B = lime-water; C = water + 2 drops neutral litmus solution)
(2) Make a saturated solution of ammonium chloride in a test-tube and note the lowest temperature reached.
(3) Find the focal length of the convex lens, D, by reading the distance from the white screen at which a distant object produces a sharply defined image on the screen.
(4) (Half-meter rule pivoted at mid-point.) Using the 50-g mass provided, find the mass of the object E.

(Science Masters Association, 1957, pp. 98–99.)

Testing for attitudes and interests (H.0)

The kinds of items presented above for testing categories *A*.0 to *F*.0 are quite familiar in educational circles. Science teachers have designed and administered countless tests made up of items like those illustrated, and science students regularly confront and respond to these tests. When it comes to measuring attitudes and interests, however, these types of tests so commonly found in education will no longer serve. Testing techniques and instruments must be utilized which are less familiar in education and more closely identified with fields like social psychology and sociology. Though the background and literature of the several techniques cannot be discussed here, this subsection provides illustrations of their application to testing in science under category *H*.0, *Attitudes and interests*.

Illustrative test items in this subsection represent five different techniques. (1) Several different formats for using Likert-type items to measure attitudes and interests are shown in items 69, 71, 73, and 77. (A basic reference for this technique is Likert, 1932.) (2) An attitude scale using the method of equal-appearing intervals is illustrated in item 70 (see Thurstone & Chave, 1929). (3) The semantic differential technique is illustrated in items 72 and 74 (see Geis, 1968). (4) Two formats for using a forced-choice questionnaire are shown in items 73 and 76. (5) An activities inventory is illustrated in item 75 (see Reed, 1959). While it is possible in principle to use these techniques to measure attitudes and interests concerning any science content area or combination of areas, almost all instruments which have been constructed either treat all science fields together without differentiation or deal with content at the subcategory level in our classification scheme. This is indicated in the content designations of the illustrations. No illustrations are given below for behavior subcategories *H*.2 and *H*.3, but the illustrated techniques and modifications of these techniques can also be used to measure the student's acceptance of scientific inquiry as a way of thought and his adoption of the so-called scientific attitudes.

H.1-1.0, H.1-2.0, H.1-3.4

69. INSTRUCTIONS: Please give your reactions to the following list of statements regarding science, scientists, and scientific careers. Work rapidly. Record your first impression—the feeling that comes to mind as you read the item.
Draw a circle around AA if you completely agree with the item.
Draw a circle around A if you are in partial agreement.
Draw a circle around N if you are neutral.

Draw a circle around D if you partially disagree.
Draw a circle around DD if you totally disagree.

AA A N D DD (1) The development of new ideas is the scientist's greatest source of satisfaction.

AA A N D DD (2) Scientific investigations are undertaken as a means of achieving economic gains.

AA A N D DD (3) Modern science is too complicated for the average citizen to understand and appreciate.

AA A N D DD (4) Scientists possess too much power in our society.

AA A N D DD (5) Scientists are an "odd" lot.

AA A N D DD (6) Scientists are communistic.

AA A N D DD (7) Science and its inventions have caused more harm than good.

AA A N D DD (8) Scientists are essentially magicians, making two blades of grass where one grew before.

(Allen, 1959, pp. 48–51, items 4, 16, 23, 24, 37, 57, 76, 84. Reprinted with the permission of the publisher from Hugh Allen, Jr.'s *Attitudes of Certain High School Seniors toward Science and Scientific Careers*. New York: Teachers College Press, copyright 1959.)

H.1-1.0, H.1-2.0

70. INSTRUCTIONS: Read each statement below carefully. If you *agree* with the statement, place a check on the line in front of the statement number.

__ (1) Science is unrelated to life experiences.
__ (2) Science seems to be "over my head."
__ (3) I am always interested in learning more about science.
__ (4) Science is very important in this scientific age in which we live.
__ (5) Science is interesting, but not as important as other subjects.

(Dutton & Stephens, 1963, p. 40, items 2, 6, 10, 15, 17.)

H.1-1.0, I.4-1.0, I.5-1.0; H.1-2.0, I.4-2.0, I.5-2.0; H.1-3.1, I.4-3.1, I.5-3.1

71. INSTRUCTIONS: Below is a list of some opinions regarding the place, worth, and value of the physical sciences and physical scientists in the modern world. The physical sciences include such areas as chemistry, physics, biology, biochemistry, etc. Circle

5 if you strongly agree with the statement as written
4 if you moderately agree with the statement as written
3 if you are neutral or indifferent to the statement as written
2 if you moderately disagree with the statement as written
1 if you strongly disagree with the statement written

5 4 3 2 1 (1) The progress of mankind is the progress of science.

5 4 3 2 1 (2) Science is just one establishment of the society in which we live, no more and no less important than any other establishment.

5 4 3 2 1 (3) Science more than any other field of inquiry can lead the way to a better future world.

5 4 3 2 1 (4) The scientist's responsibility to maintain society and its order is greater than his responsibility to chart unknown paths, paths which might produce unknown societal consequences.

5 4 3 2 1 (5) Science, by constantly improving man's life, has created social problems which outweigh the value of the scientific advances themselves.

(Airasian, 1967, items 1, 2, 5, 11, 18.)

H.1-2.2, H.5-2.2

72. DIRECTIONS: In this study, we want to find out how you describe different things. There are no "right" or "wrong" answers. On each page in this booklet you will find a heading printed like this:

CHEMISTRY

The rest of the page contains pairs of words that you will use to describe your image of the heading at the top of the page. Each pair of words will be on a scale which looks like this:

Quick □ □ □ □ □ Slow

You are to make a check in the box which best represents how you feel that word pair describes the heading at the top of the page. For example, you might check the "QUICK–SLOW" scale this way for "CHEMISTRY."

If you feel that "CHEMISTRY" is very closely connected with "QUICK," check the scale like this:

Quick ☑ □ □ □ □ Slow

If you feel that "CHEMISTRY" is only somewhat connected with "QUICK," check the scale like this:

Quick □ ☑ □ □ □ Slow

If you feel that "CHEMISTRY" is equally connected with "QUICK" and "SLOW," or *not connected with either*, check the scale like this:

Quick □ □ ☑ □ □ Slow

If you feel that "CHEMISTRY" is somewhat connected with "SLOW" or very closely connected with "SLOW," you would check one of the two boxes next to "SLOW" just as above.

Look at the heading at the top of the page; get an impression of it in your mind, and then work down the page checking the scales as *quickly* as you can. We are interested in your first impressions, so work rapidly and do not go back and change any marks. *Be sure to check every scale* and only make one check on each scale.

PLEASE DO NOT TURN THE PAGE UNTIL TOLD TO DO SO.

PHYSICS

Safe	□	□	□	□	□	Dangerous
Uninvolved	□	□	□	□	□	Involved
Enjoyable	□	□	□	□	□	Unenjoyable
Threatening	□	□	□	□	□	Comforting
Refreshing	□	□	□	□	□	Weary
Solemn	□	□	□	□	□	Cheerful
Organized	□	□	□	□	□	Messy
Unproductive	□	□	□	□	□	Productive
Complex	□	□	□	□	□	Simple
Important	□	□	□	□	□	Unimportant
Interesting	□	□	□	□	□	Dull
Gloomy	□	□	□	□	□	Joyful
Worthless	□	□	□	□	□	Worthwhile
Risky	□	□	□	□	□	Sure
Boring	□	□	□	□	□	Exciting

(Rutherford et al., 1966c.)

The common theme in all the illustrations shown as items 69 to 72 is the measurement of one aspect of the student's behavior under subcategory *H.1, Manifestation of favorable attitudes toward science and scientists.* In items 69 and 71, the student's attitude may be inferred from responses indicating the degree of his agreement with favorable and unfavorable statements about science and scientists. These two illustrations not only show two different formats for presenting Likert-type items, but also represent two different levels of sophistication in the statements that the student is asked to rate. Since statements with any desired level of sophistication can be constructed, this measurement technique can be adapted for use with both young and older students in science. Item 70 illustrates another approach to attitude measurement, with an instrument where the respondent simply checks those statements with which he agrees. Each statement has a scale value determined by means of a jury rating procedure; the more favorable or positive a statement is, the higher is its scale value. An attitude score is obtained by summing the scale values of all the checked statements. Instruments of this type also can be constructed with statements at different levels of sophistication, so that the technique has good potential for use with students of different ages and different degrees of experience in science.

A very versatile technique for investigating the student's image of science, scientists, or any concept is the semantic differential, illustrated in item 72. In responding to a semantic differential instrument, the student rates a given concept on a series of bipolar adjectival scales, each of which may be thought to represent a component of the image of the concept for the student. The kind of information that can be obtained from a semantic differential instrument depends upon particular scales which are selected for inclusion. If, for example, the test maker elects to include scales consisting of words having evaluative connotations (e.g., good–bad, important–unimportant), the instrument will provide a measure of the student's attitude toward the concept. When analyzing the responses on a semantic differential instrument, the scale ratings may be treated individually, but it is customary to combine the ratings on several scales which belong to a common factor or cluster, as determined by factor analysis or another appropriate procedure. In illustrative item 72 the concept PHYSICS was rated on fifteen scales, but factor analysis of student responses revealed four principal common factors (see Geis, 1968, Table A.3.8). The factor labeled *Interest* included the scales "interesting-dull," "boring-exciting," "refreshing-weary," "enjoyable-unenjoyable," "gloomy-joyful"; the *Importance* factor included the scales "important-unimportant," "unproductive-productive," "worthless-worthwhile"; the *Danger* factor included the scales "safe-dangerous," "risky-sure," "threatening-comforting"; and the *Difficulty* factor included the scales "uninvolved-involved," "complex-simple," "organized-messy." These factors provide a description of the student's image of physics, and they may be used to assess changes in that image during a science course. Using the semantic differential technique, similar assessments of changes may be made, not only of the student's image of physics, but of any concept pertaining to science or science instruction.

H.4-1.0, H.4-2.0

73. DIRECTIONS: Each sentence below has a blank space in the middle. Following each sentence are *five* ways you can fill the blank. After you read the sentence carefully, choose the *one* answer which is MOST like the way you really FEEL. Choose ONLY ONE answer for each sentence. Remember, there are no right or wrong answers to any of these sentences. When you have decided which answer is most like the way you feel, CIRCLE the letter *in front of* your choice.

(1) I like reading about a great writer ______ reading about scientific discoveries.
  a. a lot more than
  b. a little more than
  c. just as much as
  d. a little less than
  e. a lot less than

(2) I like talking about problems in science ______ talking about problems in social studies. [Same alternatives as in question (1).]

(3) I like writing answers to social studies questions ______ writing answers to science questions. [Same alternatives as in question (1).]

DIRECTIONS: Listed below are some statements. We would like to know how you FEEL about them. Read *each* statement carefully and then decide how you feel about it—that is, whether you (A) agree with it a lot, (B) agree with it a little bit, (C) don't know how you feel about it, (D) disagree with it a little bit, or (E) disagree with it a lot. CIRCLE the letter in front of the answer *which is most like the way you feel.* Remember, there are no right or wrong answers to these questions. We just want to know how you feel about them.

(4) The subject I *like most* is science.
  A. I agree a lot.
  B. I agree a little bit.
  C. I don't know.
  D. I disagree a little bit.
  E. I disagree a lot.

(5) I enjoy doing science experiments. [Same alternatives as in question (4).]

(6) There is so much hard work in science that it takes the fun out of it. [Same alternatives as in question (4).]

(7) I worry when my teacher says that she is going to ask me questions to find out how much I know about science. [Same alternatives as in question (4).]

(Shoresman, 1965, items 1, 6, 7, 33, 28, 34, 37.)

H.4-3.3, H.4-3.5

74. [Typical directions for a semantic differential instrument were given in item 72.]

DOING SCIENCE EXPERIMENTS

Dull	A	B	C	D	E	Exciting
Bad	A	B	C	D	E	Good
Unenjoyable	A	B	C	D	E	Enjoyable
Boring	A	B	C	D	E	Interesting

MAKING MEASUREMENTS

Dull	A	B	C	D	E	Exciting
Bad	A	B	C	D	E	Good
Unenjoyable	A	B	C	D	E	Enjoyable
Boring	A	B	C	D	E	Interesting

(Klopfer, 1964b.)

Items 73 and 74 illustrate several ways of asking the student about his enjoyment of science learning experiences, subcategory *H.4*. The first part of item 73 is very direct and makes use of forced-choice questions. Question (1), for example, is simply a verbal reworking of "How much do you like reading about a great writer compared with reading about scientific discoveries?"—to which the student must respond with one of five choices. Note that the introductory directions are designed to persuade the student to answer the questions honestly. The second part of item 73 consists of Likert-type items, presented in a simplified format for elementary school students. On the actual instrument, the five alternative responses are repeated after each statement, and there are many more statements concerning different experiences of the child in science class. Item 74 reproduces portions of two pages from a semantic differential instrument designed for fifth-grade students. In this instrument, concepts were rated on fifteen bipolar adjectival scales, and the concepts DOING SCIENCE EXPERIMENTS and MAKING MEASUREMENTS represented two of the students' current learning activities. Factor analyses of the responses revealed several common factors, and one of these included the four scales excerpted in the illustration. This factor was interpreted as a "personal enjoyment" factor, since it could be differentiated from another factor which included scales containing impersonal evaluative adjectives, such as important-unimportant. For these fifth-grade students, then, a measure of their enjoyment of certain science learning activities was obtained, and any changes in this factor over time could be assessed. The semantic differential technique may also be used with other groups of science students, with other concepts, and with appropriately selected scales to question the students about their enjoyment of any science learning experience.

H.5-1.0, H.5-2.0, H.5-3.0

75. DIRECTIONS:

1. There are no right or wrong answers. An answer is right if it is right for you.
2. Indicate how often you have done the things mentioned in the statements *voluntarily, because you were interested,* during the past school year.
3. Blacken the appropriate space on the answer sheet to show how often you have done each thing. Mark your answers as follows:

Things I Have Done this Year Because I Am Interested	*I Have Done This Thing*				
	Never	*Seldom*	*Occasionally*	*Frequently*	*Often*
(0) Gone fishing.	1	2	3	4	5

If, for example, you have done this frequently, blacken space 4 on the answer sheet; if you have done this seldom, blacken space 2.

(1) Read newspaper articles concerning scientific things, because I like to.	1	2	3	4	5
(2) Tried to find out about the lives of scientists.	1	2	3	4	5
(3) Talked with adults about science, because I am interested.	1	2	3	4	5
(4) Did extra problems in my school science work.	1	2	3	4	5
(5) Thought about problems like how the earth, the sun, the stars, or life came to be.	1	2	3	4	5
(6) Tried to find out about the history of scientific discoveries.	1	2	3	4	5
(7) Investigated how electric motors and appliances work, because I am interested.	1	2	3	4	5
(8) Visited the zoo, because I like to.	1	2	3	4	5

(Rutherford et al., 1966b, items 1, 13, 15, 21, 34, 51, 54, 66.)

H.5-1.0, H.5-2.0

76. INSTRUCTIONS: Below is a list of physical science and science related activities. Rate these on a scale from 3 to 1 [as follows:]

3 if you would like to attempt such an activity

2 if you are indifferent about attempting such an activity

1 if you would not like to attempt such an activity

You are to assume that you have ample time to attempt any activity which may interest you.

3 2 1 (1) discuss in a chemistry class the nature of chemical bonding
3 2 1 (2) include some science books in your general reading program
3 2 1 (3) discuss with a friend how the present image of science can be improved
3 2 1 (4) join a science club
3 2 1 (5) perform an experiment using a bomb calorimeter
3 2 1 (6) lead a field trip seeking to collect various leaf specimens
3 2 1 (7) operate a U.V. Spectrophotometer

(Airasian, 1967, items 21, 22, 25, 27, 32, 33, 40.)

If a student is interested in science and science-related activities, he will ordinarily manifest this interest by doing something. To obtain a measure of manifest interest, a student activities inventory may be used. The inventory illustrated in item 75 includes activities of many types, from thinking about profound scientific questions to tinkering with motors and radios, and it provides for the computation of a total interest score and part scores for each type of activity. When the inventory is administered in a science course as a pretest and again as a posttest, increases in the student's scores would indicate that he has developed his interests in science and science-related activities (behavior subcategory *H*.5) during the time he was taking the course. Another approach to measuring science interests is to ask the student to tell what activities he would like to carry out, regardless of whether he has done or will be able to do so. The measurement of expressed interest, using the forced-choice question technique, is illustrated in item 76.

H.6-3.4

77. [Same instructions as for illustrative item 69.]

AA A N D DD (1) For me, training for a career in science is not worth the time and effort required.

AA A N D DD (2) Girls have very little mechanical aptitude, and therefore should not consider scientific careers.

AA A N D DD (3) I don't have the intelligence for a successful scientific career.

AA A N D DD (4) There is much self-satisfaction to be received from work as a scientist.

AA A N D DD (5) A scientist's life is full of adventure.

AA A N D DD (6) Scientific work is monotonous.

(Allen, 1959, pp. 49–52, items 31, 34, 46, 66, 67, 86. Reprinted with the permission of the publisher from Hugh Allen, Jr.'s *Attitudes of Certain High School Seniors toward Science and Scientific Careers*. New York: Teachers College Press, copyright 1959.)

The student's responses to Likert-type items in this illustration indicate his interest in pursuing a career in science (*H*.6). Direct questions designed to have the student express his interest are also appropriate for testing in this subcategory. In addition, pertinent information can be obtained by having the student complete a standardized vocational preference instrument, such as the Strong Vocational Interests Blank.

Testing for orientation (I.0)

At the elementary and secondary school level, testing in the *Orientation* category generally deals only with the student's knowledge and comprehension of the relationships between science and other areas of human endeavor and other modes of thought. The behaviors which are tested, therefore, are not very different from those exhibited in responding to test questions under category *A*.0. Though the many relationships which are included in the *Orientation* category can be subjected to detailed analysis and can be applied, in some instances, to the solution of new problems, the ability of the science student to deal with the relationships in these ways is rarely explored on tests below the college level. This treatment of *Orientation* in testing makes some sense, since it is in accord with the overall intent of category *I*.0, the development in the student of sensitivity to the included relationships. On this view, penetration of these relationships beyond the stage of knowledge and comprehension is probably not necessary.

Illustrations of testing for each of the *Orientation* subcategories are given in the items below. In practice, this testing takes two forms: (1) questions concerning an aspect of an *Orientation* subcategory with respect to a specific science content area; (2) questions with respect to science as a whole, or with respect to an aspect of science which is classified under content category 3.0, *General*, or both. In practice also, even though the *Orientation* subcategories are concerned with cognitive matters, with relationships the student should know and comprehend, questions about them are sometimes combined on testing instruments with the measurement of attitudes (e.g., items 82 and 88).

I.1-1.24

78. The following key is to be used for the succeeding paragraph. Certain parts of the paragraph are italicized, and each italicized item is a question. Choose the proper response from the key and blacken the appropriate space on the answer sheet.

KEY:

A. A major problem (stated or implied).
B. Hypothesis (possible solution to problem).
C. Result of experimentation.
D. Initial observation (not experimental).
E. Conclusion (probable solution to problem).

(1) *How a homing pigeon navigates over territory it has never seen before is not fully understood.* (2) *Do air currents stimulate the pigeon in some way?* (3) *Are pigeons equipped with some sort of magnetic compasses; that is, are they sensitive to the earth's magnetism?* A scientist tested the latter by fastening small magnets to the wings of well-trained pigeons. (4) *Most of these birds never got home.* (5) *Others, carrying equal wing weights of nonmagnetic copper, made the home roost without trouble,* (6) *indicating that the earth's magnetism is a factor in pigeon navigation.* However, a magnetic compass could not, by itself, bring the pigeon back to his roost, because many places on the earth's surface have identical magnetic conditions. The scientist attempted (7) *to determine the other guiding factor.* (8) *It might be the sun or stars,* but pigeons navigate under clouds. . . . (9) *Just where the birds' instruments for navigation are located is still unknown;* but the scientist found that (10) *birds have a mysterious organ in their eyes, at the end of the optic nerve.* (11) *This organ may contain the nerve fibers that pick up vibrations of magnetism and the sense that measures the earth's turning.*

(Adapted from Burmester, 1951.)

I.1-2.26

79. Items (1)–(6) refer to the kinetic-molecular theory. After each item number on the answer sheet, blacken space
A—if the item refers to observational or experimental evidence which supports the theory.
B—if the item refers to an hypothesis or an assumption concerning the theory which was formulated long before there was experimental evidence to test it, or has not as yet been entirely proven to be true experimentally.
C—if the item refers to something which has nothing to do with the theory.
(1) The volume of a gas increases with an increase in temperature when the pressure remains constant.
(2) A gas always exerts pressure no matter how much it expands.
(3) Most gases are colorless.
(4) Gases are composed of small particles called molecules which are relatively far apart and in rapid motion.
(5) Gases diffuse readily.
(6) Molecules on colliding lose no energy.

(Dressel & Nelson, 1956, p. 569, items 42–46, 48. Copyright © 1956 by Educational Testing Service.)

I.1-3.2

80. (1) When a scientist completes a new scientific theory, we know that he has
a. created one of the laws of nature
b. helped bring mankind closer to the truth
c. discovered new ways of experimenting
d. developed new ideas and understandings
(2) When we say that a scientist has formed a hypothesis about an experiment, we mean that he has
a. indicated which measurements were made
b. designed equipment needed for the experiment
c. described how the experiment turned out
d. made a careful guess about what will happen
(3) A scientific *law* describes

a. rules which scientists must obey
b. rules which connect events in nature
c. rules for doing good experiments
d. good guesses about how things happen

(Adapted from Carrier et al., 1966.)

The first two illustrations in this group are quite straightforward tests of behavior subcategory *I*.1, *Distinction between various types of statements in science*. Item 78 tests for this behavior with respect to a specific content area of the biological sciences, but it gives so much information that the student needs no additional knowledge in the content area to answer the questions. In item 79, which tests for the same behavior with respect to a content area of the physical sciences, the student must have some knowledge about the experimental evidence for the kinetic-molecular theory to be able to respond correctly to some of the questions. Item 80 tests for behavior *I*.1 with respect to science in general and asks the student to select the best characterizations of a hypothesis, empirical law, and theoretical model. The wording of these characterizations and of the questions has been adapted to the language level of the elementary school student.

I.2-2.15, I.2-2.17, I.2-210, I.2-2.29

81. (1) Before each question below, write S if it is a question that can be answered fully by using the methods of empirical science: either by using established theories and facts or by performing new experiments. Write N if it is *not* such a question. (2) In the space below each question, briefly defend your judgment.

Is the orderliness of nature real or is it in man's mind only?

Why is heat given off when a violent chemical reaction takes place?

Can we know the true nature of matter?

Why are there only two kinds of electric charge, positive and negative?

Can the standard of living in the South be raised by subsidizing industry in the South?

Can dogs distinguish between green and blue?

Has philosophy influenced the development of science?

(Nedelsky, 1965b, p. 286, item 2.23-3. From SCIENCE TEACHING AND TESTING by Leo Nedelsky, © 1965 by Harcourt, Brace & World, Inc., and reproduced with their permission.)

I.2-3.2, H.1-3.2; I.2-3.3, H.1-3.3

82. DIRECTIONS: Circle letter A if you generally AGREE with the statement; circle letter D if you generally DISAGREE.

(1) Classification schemes are inherent in the materials classified, rather than imposed on nature by the scientist. A D
(2) Scientists assume a real world exists outside of the mind. A D
(3) Scientists assume nature is likely to change suddenly. A D
(4) Those people who carry on the practice of science assume if a change in factor A leads to a change in factor B, then factor A is a cause of factor B. A D
(5) The essential test of a scientific theory is its use in predicting future events. A D
(6) Science is essentially statistical in nature and deals in terms of probabilities. A D
(7) Although a scientific hypothesis may have to be changed on the basis of new data, a physical law is pertinent. A D

(Welch, 1966, items 61, 104, 109, 71, 8, 125, 14.)

With respect to several content areas of chemistry and physics and to science as a whole, the series of questions in item 81 offer a nearly perfect match to the title statement of behavior subcategory *I*.2, *Recognition of the limitations of scientific explanation and of the influence of scientific inquiry on general philosophy*. (No, the title of *I*.2 was *not* written after item 81 was found.) Item 82 probes for the student's knowledge about a number of components of subcategory *I*.2 and uses an attitude-testing format. Most of the excerpted questions are actually true-false items, but some may reflect the student's attitude toward science, or at least his opinion about a debatable issue, for example, question (5). The inventory also contains other agree-disagree statements, not reproduced here, which are essentially measures of attitude.

I.3-1.31, I.3-3.3

83. In 1929, Dr. Fleming discovered that a mold called *Penicillium notatum* could stop the growth of bacteria in a culture dish. However, it remained for other scientists to develop the present uses of

penicillin. The best evaluation of Dr. Fleming's discovery is that he

a. was a good scientist but a poor humanitarian
b. achieved a remarkable scientific advance even though he did not find uses for penicillin
c. should receive minor credit for his work since he found no practical uses for penicillin
d. did not use the scientific methods properly or he would have done further research

(Adapted from Biological Sciences Curriculum Study, 1965a.)

I.3-2.31, I.3-3.1

84. (1) Which of the following was an important factor that worked against the acceptance of Copernicus's heliocentric solar system hypothesis in the sixteenth century?
    a. When Venus was observed through a telescope, phases were seen.
    b. Stellar parallax had never been observed.
    c. The calendar failed to keep pace with the seasons.
    d. Galileo observed four satellites moving around Jupiter.
    e. Venus had never been observed more than 48° from the sun.

(2) Newton's Law of Universal Gravitation was distinctive in the history of science because it was the first
    a. explanation of the cause of gravity
    b. demonstration that the same equations can be used to describe motion on the earth and in the heavens
    c. accurate mathematical description of the planetary orbits
    d. use of algebra to describe physical phenomena

(Adapted from Rutherford et al., 1966a.)

I.3-3.2, I.3-3.4

85. (1) Of the following, which is the best statement about scientific knowledge?
    a. Scientific knowledge is a systematic collection of facts.
    b. Data and ideas from the past contribute to today's scientific knowledge.
    c. Each generation starts anew to build up its own scientific knowledge.
    d. Statements are not accepted as scientific knowledge unless they are absolutely true.

(2) In the past, many important scientific discoveries were made by men who were clergymen, statesmen, or businessmen, and who worked on science as amateurs. This is no longer true today because
    a. men in other professions are less interested in science today than they used to be
    b. scientific research today requires many years of preparation, usually study beyond college
    c. important discoveries cannot be made today without expensive equipment which only scientists possess
    d. only professional scientists have the abilities needed to make important discoveries

(Adapted from Cooley & Klopfer, 1961.)

Testing for components of the student's historical perspective on science (*I.3*) is the common focus of this group of items. All three illustrations are drawn from tests designed for secondary school students, and all of the questions probe a salient characteristic of the historical development of science. This emphasis, rather than the recall of names and dates, is the proper one when testing for historical perspective.

I.4-2.34

86. When new highways are completed, plants and shrubs are generally planted on the slopes along the roads. This is done mainly because the plants
    a. aid in preventing soil erosion.
    b. utilize carbon dioxide from the exhaust of automobiles.
    c. provide hiding places for wild animals.
    d. add moisture to the atmosphere.
    e. aid in regulating temperatures.

(Educational Testing Service, 1962a, p. 3, pt. 1, sec. 1, item 2.)

I.4-3.1, I.5-3.1; I.4-1.31, I.5-1.31; I.4-2.11, I.5-2.11

87. The following questions are designed to test this objective, "The student will show understanding of the symbiotic evolution of the scientific enterprise and the living standards of man."

(1) When given a list of 10 scientific breakthroughs, he will be able to identify 5 that have changed world events and list at least one way in which each of the 5 selected has changed world events.

(2) He can cite 5 specific instances where tradition has been of value and 5 other instances where tradition has been a factor limiting progress.
(3) He speaks for and in defense of such issues as conservation of natural resources, control of air and water pollution, promotion of better education.
(4) He can arrange at least 3 flow charts that explain the chain of events from raw materials to finished product.

(Eiss & Harbeck, 1969, p. 33.)

I.4-1.0, I.5-1.0, H.1-1.0; I.4-2.0, I.5-2.0, H.1-2.0; I.4-3.1, I.5-3.1, H.1-3.1

88. [Same instructions as for item 69.]

AA A N D DD (1) Science and technology are essential to the development of present-day cultures.

AA A N D DD (2) Decisive economic, political, and social processes are greatly influenced by science.

AA A N D DD (3) Scientific activity is greatly influenced by culture.

AA A N D DD (4) Scientific concepts and discoveries often bring about new sociological problems.

AA A N D DD (5) The social environment of the United States is hostile to the development of scientific talent.

AA A N D DD (6) Public interest in science is essential to the maintenance of scientific research.

(Allen, 1959, pp. 48–51, items 6, 25, 43, 72, 77, 80. Reprinted with the permission of the publisher from Hugh Allen, Jr.'s *Attitudes of Certain High School Seniors toward Science and Scientific Careers*. New York: Teachers College Press, copyright 1959.)

By presenting a situation which relates economic considerations to scientific knowledge, item 86 illustrates how one component of *Orientation*, subcategory *I*.4, can be tested with respect to a specific content area. The item itself is not a direct test of *I*.4, but it represents the many possible items which present analogous situations depicting the interactions of knowledge in a science content area with technological applications, economic factors, or both. The student's selection of the correct response to these items depends, at least partially, on his realization of the existing relationships among science, technology, and economics. While the student's response to one test item doesn't provide much evidence about his awareness of these relationships, his responses to many items of the same kind do. Another approach for obtaining evidence of the student's awareness of these relationships and of the relationships indicated in subcategory *I*.5 is suggested by item 87. The four activities proposed here are ones which a scientifically literate student would be likely to perform but a student lacking this orientation probably would not. Each activity in item 87 is really a separate behavioral test, under either *I*.4 or *I*.5. Item 88 illustrates testing for both of these *Orientation* subcategories with respect to science taken as a whole. The statements which the student is asked to rate here reflect many aspects of the relationships between science and culture. If the student is aware of these matters, he will agree with the correct statements and disagree with the incorrect ones. The format of the instrument, as well as the circumstances of its construction, indicates that it was designed to measure attitudes, and so it does, but at the same time it is testing for the student's knowledge and comprehension of the relationships under *Orientation* subcategories *I*.4 and *I*.5. The reader will recall that the combining on one instrument of testing for *Orientation* and testing for *Attitudes* was previously noted in items 71 and 82.

Formative evaluation

Formative evaluation has received little systematic attention in science teaching to date. While many science teachers sometimes employ short tests or quizzes to help students gage their learning progress, the standard procedure in science classrooms is to administer tests as the culminating activity of a unit of study, of a group of related units, or of an entire course, and to use the test results as the principal basis for assigning grades. Most science teachers are aware that tests and test items can be used to diagnose a student's learning difficulties, but only a small minority have set up effective procedures that give each student access to this information about himself and that prescribe appropriate actions to be followed in light of the diagnosis. "Going over a test" usually means simply finding out what the correct answers are or how particular problems should be worked; the crucial element of suggesting how the student can best proceed to attain mastery of the material is too often lacking. In short, formative evaluation is presently quite an undeveloped art in the teaching of science.

This situation is not without irony, since the technical means for practicing formative evaluation in science are readily available. As the illustrations in the preceding section testify, teachers and testers have displayed considerable skill and ingenuity in devising test items for assessing a broad range of student behaviors in all science content areas. Items from this well-endowed pool could be employed in constructing formative evaluation tests just as easily as they are now being compiled into tests used exclusively for summative evaluation. The essential difference between summative and formative evaluation does not lie in the structure or contents of the tests, but rather is a difference in how the tests are used to promote the student's progress in learning science. In summative evaluation, the student takes an achievement test at the end of a small or large unit of study and seldom has an opportunity to study the material in that unit further. Summative evaluation is an "after the fact" affair. In formative evaluation, the student takes diagnostic tests at several points in the course of his study, and, on the basis of test results, he obtains some guidance as to how he should proceed next. Formative evaluation is an ingredient of an ongoing learning process.

Although there is now a marked imbalance in favor of summative evaluation in science teaching, several promising approaches to developing formative evaluation are currently under way. One of these is a part of the Mastery Learning Project, under the direction of Professor Bloom, at the University of Chicago. This approach is based on principles set forth elsewhere in this book (see Chap. 6), and an illustration of this approach for science teaching will be given here. The subject of the illustration selected happens to be biology, but the same techniques can be applied to any science course.

High school biology

Formative evaluation tests were constructed by teachers taking part in the University of Chicago project on the basis of detailed analyses of the subject-matter content and teaching objectives of *Modern Biology*, by Otto and Towle (1965), a textbook widely used in high school biology courses. The biology course was divided into units, consisting of one or two chapters of the text, and a formative test for each unit was developed. The categories of teaching objectives for the analyses of the units were drawn from the *Taxonomy of Educational Objectives* (Bloom, 1956), and these are listed below. For each category, the code of the corresponding student behavior, as shown in the master Table of Specifications for Science Education (Table 18-1), is given in parentheses.

Knowledge of terminology (A.2)
Knowledge of specific facts (A.1)
Knowledge of classifications and categories (A.6)
Knowledge of methodology (A.7)
Knowledge of principles and generalizations (A.8)
Translation (A.11)
Application (F.1)

These teaching objective categories were used to define one dimension of each unit's table of specifications, similar to the grids presented on pages 584–589, and the subject-matter content formed the second dimension. To illustrate, a small section of the grid for the unit on two chapters in the textbook (titled "The Structural Basis of Life" and "The Cell and Its Environment") is shown in Table 18-5, Portion of the

Table of Specifications for Chapters 4 and 5 of *Modern Biology*. (See page 590.)

Thorough examination of the specifications grid for each unit led to the drawing up of the content hierarchy of the unit. This displayed all the elements of subject matter taken up in the unit, the teaching objective for each subject-matter element, and the logical and pedagogical connections existing between these elements. The content hierarchy serves the important function of identifying the key points in the unit for which test items should be included in the formative evaluation test. The content hierarchy also defines the particular teaching objective for each subject-matter element that should be assessed by the test items. For example, the content hierarchy for the unit on the two chapters of *Modern Biology* showed that the student was expected only to have the factual knowledge that certain named structures are parts of the cell; no translation or application of this knowledge was expected here. On the other hand, the content hierarchy also showed the student was expected to apply his knowledge about homeostasis to the analysis of new situations or examples not previously discussed; simply knowing the definition of the term "homeostasis" was not the desired teaching objective for this subject-matter element. Test items that corresponded to these expectations shown in the content hierarchy, as well as other items that matched the definitions of teaching objectives for other subject-matter elements, were designed for the unit's formative evaluation test.

Several items from this formative test are reproduced below as illustrative item 89. The original numbers of the sample items on the test are shown in parentheses. Item (8) tests for knowledge of the parts of a cell. Items (1), (22), and (23) test for several levels of teaching objectives in respect to the concept of homeostasis. Other items test for specific teaching objectives in respect to other subject-matter elements. The reader may note that these items are technically no different from the illustrative test items presented on pages 591–617. The design of items for formative testing demands no new or unusual skills in test item construction.

A.2-1.11, A.2-1.12, A.2-1.23, A.8-1.12, A.8-1.23, F.1-1.23

89. (1) Homeostasis is the
    a. means by which organisms obtain their nutrients
    b. balance organisms maintain by making self-regulating adjustments to changing conditions
    c. means by which organisms control molecular traffic in the cells
    d. means by which organisms transport water
    e. balance organisms maintain between the water and other materials in the cell

(2) Variation in the rate and degree of penetration is a property of
    a. a plasma membrane
    b. a differentially permeable membrane
    c. a cell membrane
    d. all of the above
    e. none of the above

(8) The main parts of the cell are the
    a. cell wall, nucleus, and chromosomes
    b. cell wall, cytoplasm, and chromosomes
    c. cell wall, nucleus, and cytoplasm
    d. cell wall, chromosomes, and ribosomes
    e. chromosomes, nucleus, and cytoplasm

(16) Movement of materials through the cell membrane is dependent upon
    a. the size of the materials, the composition of the membrane, and the concentration of the materials
    b. the temperature and the pressure of the surrounding environment
    c. the degree of solubility of the material in water and the electrical charge of the membrane
    d. a and b
    e. a, b, and c

(17) The laws of diffusion state that
    a. molecules move from an area of their greater concentration to an area of their lesser concentration
    b. diffusion occurs more rapidly at low temperatures
    c. diffusion continues until an equilibrium has been reached
    d. a and b
    e. a and c

(22) The principle of homeostasis applies to
    a. cells, colonial organisms, and muscle tissues
    b. snakes, plants, and people

c. water molecules and ions
d. a and b
e. none of the above

(23) The adjustment which a person must undergo when he receives a heart transplant is an example of
a. absorption
b. circulation
c. homeostasis
d. synthesis
e. osmosis

When a formative evaluation test is constructed, a rather useful accompanying diagram is also usually prepared. This diagram displays the hierarchy of the items on the test. The structural diagram for the formative test of the unit on Chapters 4 and 5 of *Modern Biology* is shown in Table 18-6. The diagram identifies the subject-matter element and teaching objective for each test item, and the reader may wish to locate on it the place of each of the sample items given above. If a formative evaluation test has been well designed, the structural diagram will reflect as closely as possible the content hierarchy of its unit. When this condition is fulfilled, the structural diagram can serve as a useful tool for diagnosing a student's difficulty in mastering the content of the unit. For example, with reference to the diagram in Table 18-6, if a student fails

Table 18-6 Structural diagram for a formative test on Chapters 4 and 5 of *Modern Biology* (Otto & Towle, 1965)

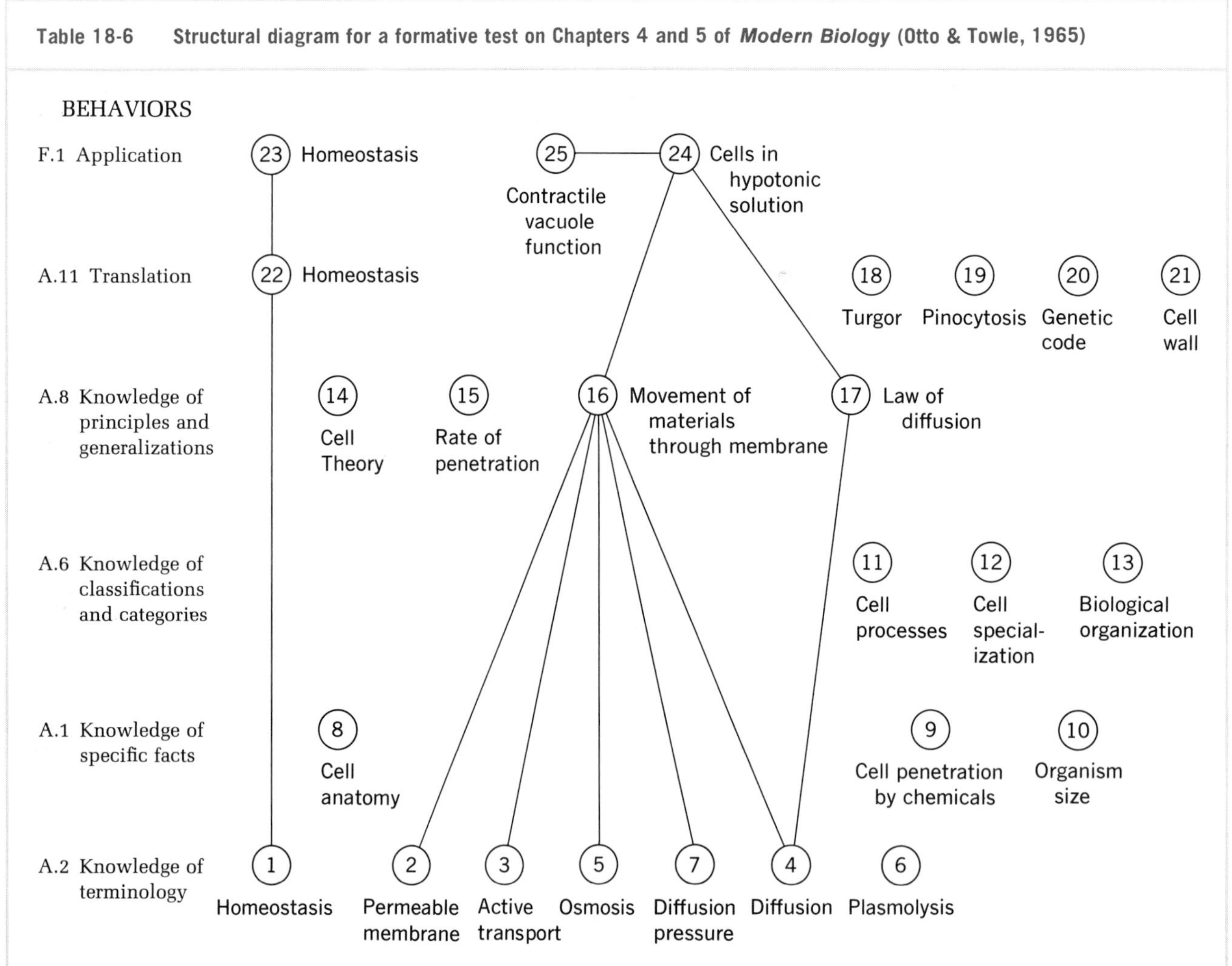

item 17, which tests for knowledge of the laws of diffusion, it is quite informative to look at his performance on item 4, which tests whether or not he knows the meaning of the term "diffusion." Similarly, a student's failure on items which involve translation as the teaching objective, such as numbers 18 to 22, may indicate that he has not learned the meanings of the pertinent terms well enough to use them. The diagram showing the hierarchy of test items can be placed in the hands of the students, and, with a little instruction, they can easily make these kinds of diagnoses of their individual learning needs.

The student is also entitled to other assistance in choosing appropriate remedial action in consideration of his performance on a formative test. One way of helping him is to suggest alternative learning resources for study of the ideas or facts which were tested by items he answered incorrectly on the test. A form which may be used to accomplish this (and which also serves as the test answer sheet) is illustrated in Fig. 18-1. The alternative learning resources entered in this example are, again, for the unit based on Chapters 4 and 5 of *Modern Biology*, but references are also given now to other biology textbooks which treat the same subject-matter topics in a different fashion. Other alternative learning resources may also be suggested to the student. These include appropriate audiovisual materials or programmed learning sequences, discussions with other students about the content of the unit, and individual tutoring. Whatever alternative learning resource may be suitable for a particular student's situation, the diagnosis afforded by his performance on the formative test has enabled him to focus his study on those aspects of the unit where he needs to concentrate as he proceeds toward mastery.

Elementary science

Another approach to formative evaluation in science is represented in the Individually Prescribed Instruction (IPI) Program currently being developed at the Learning Research and Development Center at the University of Pittsburgh. Since the intent of the IPI Program is to provide each student with an individualized sequence of learning experiences appropriate to his needs and capacities, formative evaluation plays a major role in its design and operation. Science teaching in the IPI Program begins when the student is in kindergarten or first grade and continues throughout the elementary school years. When completed, the IPI Science program will offer science learning experiences up to about the ninth-grade level. Illustrations from the earliest series of units in IPI Science will be given here, since they demonstrate how formative evaluation can be made operational even with very young children.

Level A of IPI Science presently consists of thirteen short units, each of which contains two to four lessons. Study in any unit is prescribed for a student on the basis of whether or not he has attained mastery of the content of that unit. The student's mastery of a particular unit's content may derive from any of his experiences, not only his study in IPI Science. For this reason, careful assessments of the student's knowledge and understanding are required continually in order that prescriptions appropriate for him can be made. Formative evaluation tests provide these assessments.

Underlying the construction of all formative tests used in IPI Science are the statements of objectives prepared for every lesson. Each objective specifies the science subject-matter content dealt with in the lesson, and it specifies the behavior that the student is expected to exhibit with respect to that content. In an IPI Science objective, "science subject-matter content" must be interpreted broadly enough to include a particular object or piece of apparatus that is used in the lesson, as may be seen in some of the following examples of objectives for several A-Level lessons (Learning Research and Development Center, 1969c, pp. 2–3):

> Given one sound at a time, the student identifies the object or event which makes that sound.

*Name*____________________________

*Date*____________ *Test Number*__4__

CIRCLE your answer for each question. When you score this test, put an R beside each correct answer. Leave your incorrect answers blank.

Alternative learning resources: This test has been designed to inform you of your learning difficulties. It will not count as part of your final grade. Below is a list of learning materials which will explain the ideas you still need to learn. For each item you did not get right, read across to find where the correct answer or idea is explained.

						Right (R)	*Modern Biology* by Otto and Towle	BSCS Green Version; *High School Biology*	BSCS Yellow Version; *Biological Science: An Inquiry Into Life*	
1.	A	B	C	D	E		70		6, 351	
2.	A	B	C	D	E		71-72	385	123-124	
3.	A	B	C	D	E		73	387-388	421-422	
4.	A	B	C	D	E		73	384-385	103	
5.	A	B	C	D	E		75	386-387		
6.	A	B	C	D	E		76			
7.	A	B	C	D	E		74			
8.	A	B	C	D	E		57	379-381	123, 136, 124	
9.	A	B	C	D	E		77		125	
10.	A	B	C	D	E		56	401		
11.	A	B	C	D	E		57			
12.	A	B	C	D	E		65	406-407	154	
13.	A	B	C	D	E		65-68	406-407	154-155	
14.	A	B	C	D	E		56	378-379	63-64	
15.	A	B	C	D	E		72		350	
16.	A	B	C	D	E		74, 76, 77-79	387-388	124-126	
17.	A	B	C	D	E		73	384-385	124	
18.	A	B	C	D	E		75			
19.	A	B	C	D	E		79		125-126	
20.	A	B	C	D	E		57-58	379-380	136	
21.	A	B	C	D	E		55	382	53	
22.	A	B	C	D	E		70-71		6-7, 351	
23.	A	B	C	D	E		70-71		6-7	
24.	A	B	C	D	E		76		125, 350-351	
25.	A	B	C	D	E		76		350-351	

FIGURE 18-1 Answer sheet and alternative learning resources form for a formative test on Chapters 4 and 5 of *Modern Biology* (Otto & Towle, 1965).

Given different objects, the student makes two or more different sorts of these objects on the basis of properties chosen by the student, but not more than one sort should be made on the basis of color, size, [or] shape. The student states the criterion for each sort.

Given several objects that differ in length and width, the student orders them by length, [and] then uses one of the given objects as an arbitrary unit of length to measure the length and width of an object.

Given four pictures of a continuous event, the student orders them into correct time sequence.

Using a color-coded thermometer, the student measures the change in temperature of an object over a period of time.

Before a kindergarten or first-grade child begins his study in IPI Science, his ability to carry out certain tasks necessary for success in the early A-Level lessons is assessed by means of an Inventory of Prerequisite Skills (Learning Research and Development Center, 1969b). This formative test is designed to measure how well the student can follow directions, how well he can recognize and write twelve letters of the alphabet, how well he can recognize and write the numerals 1 through 9, and how well he can identify colors. The Inventory of Prerequisite Skills is group-administered, and a response booklet is provided for each student. After the student's booklet is scored, the teacher advises him in a conference about his readiness to begin IPI Science. If he has not attained mastery of some of the prerequisite skills, the student is prescribed appropriate exercises to develop the unmastered skills.

Decisions about what the student should study in the A-Level of IPI Science are made largely on the basis of his performance on a placement test. There are three of these formative tests in A-Level, and each test, covering several of the thirteen units, is designed to indicate in which units the student has attained mastery through his previous experiences and which units should be prescribed. If the student passes the placement test items corresponding to any unit, he is credited with mastery of that unit; if the student fails the placement test items for a unit, this unit becomes a part of his prescribed instruction.

A portion of the script for the second A-Level Placement Test is reproduced below. The script contains the text of the magnetic tape recording to which the student listens as he takes the test individually, and describes the materials which the student is instructed to manipulate. When a placement test is prescribed for him, the student takes the kit of materials and the magnetic tape cartridge to a booth equipped with a small tape recorder, inserts the tape cartridge in the machine, and, using the attached headset, begins to listen to the taped instructions. The tape recorder is designed to stop automatically at preset points, marked "Tape stop" in the script, where the student is asked to manipulate materials or to write a response in the placement test workbook. After carrying out the indicated instruction, the student simply presses a button on the machine to restart the tape.

B.1-3.5, B.3-3.5, G.1-3.5

90. MATERIALS: One primary ruler (markings at inches only) in box

(1) Hello! Today you will work with your booklet and with more objects in the science box. I will tell you what to do; then you do the best work you can. Do not worry if you don't know how to do everything. Just try to do your best. (Slight pause.) Look at page one of your booklet. There are pictures of pieces of wood. The pieces are in three sets: Set A, Set B, and Set C. Find the set that is in order by length. (Slight pause.) Put an X on the set that is ordered by length. (Tape stop.)

(2) Turn to page 2. (Pause.) There are pictures of three sets of objects on this page: Set D, Set E, and Set F. Look at the sets, and find the set that is in order by length. (Slight pause.) Put an X on the set that is ordered by length. (Tape stop.)

(3) Turn to page 3. (Pause.) Look in your box and find the stick with numbers on it. This stick is called a ruler. You will use the ruler to measure some pictures of objects. (Slight pause.) Look at the picture of the box on page 3. Use the ruler to measure the *length* of the box. (Slight pause.) On line L write the number that tells how *long* the box is. (Tape stop.)

(4) Now measure the width of the box. (Slight pause.) On line W, write the number that tells how *wide* the box is. (Tape stop.)

(5) Turn to page 4. (Pause.) There is a picture of a stick on page 4. Use the ruler to measure the *length* of the stick. (Slight pause.) On line L, write the number that tells how *long* the stick is. (Tape stop.)

(6) Measure the *width* of the stick. (Slight pause.) On line W write the number that tells how *wide* the stick is. (Tape stop.)

(Learning Research and Development Center, 1969d, pp. 6–8.)

To illustrate how the placement test data are used, suppose that the student does not answer most of the above items correctly. In this case, his prescriptions in the A-Level will include study in the corresponding unit called "Inching Along." After he has completed his work in all units preceding "Inching Along," the student is prescribed his first lesson in this unit. This may be a small-group lesson or an individual taped lesson.

The individual taped lessons in the "Inching Along" unit, like most of the taped lessons in A-Level, consists of an instructional section and a formative testing section. The latter section is referred to as a "curriculum-embedded test" (CET); its purpose is to assess the extent of the student's mastery of the objective of the lesson. A part of the script for the CET in one lesson of the "Inching Along" unit is reprinted below as illustrative item 91 (the original step numbers are shown in parentheses). Like the placement test, this lesson is presented on magnetic tape, and the student uses a kit of materials and a workbook for recording responses as he works through the instruction and the CET.

Lesson Inching Along 3

B.3-3.5, G.1-3.5

91. BEHAVIORAL OBJECTIVE: Measures the length and width of objects with a measuring stick with two-inch color-coded calibrations. . . .
    - (24) Now find the red shape in your lesson kit. (Tape stop.)
    - (25) Measure the length of the red shape. Go ahead and measure the length of the red shape. Remember, the length is the long side of the shape. (Tape stop.)
    - (26) Turn to page 5. To the end of what measuring unit does the length go? (Slight pause.) Find the crayon that matches the color of that measuring unit. (Tape stop.)
    - (27) Find the letter L on page 5. Color the box beside the L the same color as the unit that measured the length of the shape. (Tape stop.)
    - (28) How many units long is the length of the shape? (Slight pause.) Write your answer on the line under the letter L. (Tape stop.)
    - (29) Measure the width of the shape. (Tape stop.)
    - (30) To the end of what measuring unit does the width go? (Slight pause.) Find the matching crayon. (Slight pause.) Color the box beside the letter W. (Tape stop.)
    - (31) How many units wide is the shape? (Slight pause.) Write your answer on the line under the W. (Tape stop.)
    - (32) Put away the red shape and take out the green shape. Remember, take out the green shape. (Tape stop.)
    - (33) Measure the length of the green shape. (Tape stop.)
    - (34) Turn to page 6. (Slight pause.) How many units long is the length of the green shape? (Slight pause.) Write your answer on the line beside the letter L.

(Learning Research and Development Center, 1969a, Lesson 3, pp. 5–7.)

Responses written in the lesson workbook are scored by the teacher or teacher's aide and are used to diagnose difficulties the student might have encountered in the lesson. Where appropriate, the teacher may prescribe some supplementary instruction or experience directed to the same objective. Among the alternatives available to the student in IPI Science if the scoring of his CET shows that he has not mastered a particular objective, are tutoring in that objective by the teacher, repeating a previously studied lesson in which instruction toward the objective is given, working on an alternative lesson or activity that builds toward the objective, small-group discussions led by the teacher, and peer tutoring. Through any or all of these means, the student can take effective steps to complete his mastery of all objectives of the unit. When he has demonstrated this mastery, he moves on to the IPI Science learning task next indicated for him by the formative placement test.

Again, the reader should note that, except for the feature of presenting test items on magnetic tape, which was not previously encountered, there is nothing unusual about the formative tests used in IPI Science. It is the use of the tests for diagnosis and prescription that justifies the appellation of "formative evaluation" for this illustration.

A small library on testing and evaluation in science

While the reader of these pages hopefully will obtain some insight into evaluation and testing in science, as well as some practical help, the discussions and illustrations presented in this chapter do not purport to be an exhaustive treatment of this large subject. The science teacher, curriculum developer, or educational researcher seriously concerned about test construction and evaluation in science will wish to turn to other publications for ideas and potentially usable materials. This section suggests a small, select group of references which should be readily at hand.

The arrangement of these references is designed to assist the teacher or graduate student who doesn't have much money to spend in building a personal library on testing and evaluation in science. The first four books, which can be acquired for about $15, form a basic collection. From among the remaining references, beginning with Dressel and Nelson, selections for a personal library may be made on the basis of individual needs and interests. School science departments and curriculum centers, whose budgets are invariably limited, should also find this listing helpful in setting priorities for acquisition of relevant materials.

Bloom, B. S. (Ed.) *Taxonomy of educational objectives: The classification of educational goals.* Handbook 1. *Cognitive domain.* New York: McKay, 1956.

Krathwohl, D. R., Bloom, B. S., & Masia, B. B. *Taxonomy of educational objectives: The classification of educational goals.* Handbook 2. *Affective domain.* New York: McKay, 1964.

These two paperbound books offer a classification of educational goals in the two indicated domains. Frequent references to the *Taxonomy* were made in the first part of this chapter and, although a different classification for student behaviors was adopted here, there are naturally many points in common. (The major categories in the cognitive and affective domains of the *Taxonomy* are outlined in the Appendix to Part I of the present book.) Each major category in both domains has a number of subcategories, and these are discussed in detail and illustrated with representative educational objectives and test items. A good deal of work in testing has been based on the *Taxonomy,* especially its cognitive domain, and it has helped to improve the precision of communication among educators concerned with evaluation.

Nedelsky, L. *Science teaching and testing.* New York: Harcourt, Brace & World, 1965.

There are two parts in this incisive book of 360 pages: Part I, Theory and Method, occupies about two-thirds of the text; Part II, Sample Exercises with Comments, occupying the remaining third, complements and amplifies the discussions in the first part. Nedelsky classifies the objectives of physical science teaching under three major student abilities —knowledge, verbal and mathematical; understanding, verbal and mathematical; and ability to learn— and under three corresponding laboratory abilities —laboratory knowledge, laboratory understanding, and ability to learn from experiment or observation. Generally lively discussions with few holds barred explain the objectives placed under each major ability; and numerous sample test items, most of them using physics or chemistry content, illustrate each objective. Other features of the book include two chapters on the theory of testing, a chapter on writing and judging test exercises, and critical reviews of a sample of science tests.

Hedges, W. D. *Testing and evaluation for the sciences.* Belmont, Calif.: Wadsworth, 1966.

Intended as a practical guide for the practicing secondary school science teacher, this 250-page paperbound book offers a wealth of suggestions for constructing and using science achievement tests. Several sample test items are given for every subcategory in the cognitive domain in the *Taxonomy of Educational Objectives.* Chapter-length discussions, including many illustrations, are devoted to five major types of test items—essay, multiple-choice, true-false, matching, completion. Included in the appendix are a lengthy (but not complete) list of science tests in print and a directory of test publishers.

Dressel, P. L., & Nelson, C. H. *Questions and problems in Science: Test items folio no. 1.* Princeton, N.J.: Educational Testing Service, 1956.

True to its title, this book is essentially a large collection of test items in the biological and physical sciences. The several thousand items are grouped according to their subject-matter content, and, using the subcategory numbers of the cognitive domain of the *Taxonomy of Educational Objectives,* the objective being tested is indicated for each item. The items were designed primarily for use in introductory college science courses in the mid-1950s, but many are suitable, with perhaps some changes, for today's high school courses. Altogether, this book offers a fairly expensive way (about $30) to acquire a pool of interesting test items.

Lindvall, C. M. *Measuring pupil achievement and aptitude.* New York: Harcourt, Brace & World, 1967.

Addressed to the beginning teacher and the tyro to educational testing, this paperbound book provides an exemplary brief introduction to the basic principles of testing and evaluation. Testing is treated as part of a planned process of evaluation, and consistency between specified objectives and their evaluation is emphasized. Various kinds of achievement and aptitude tests are described and illustrated, two chapters are devoted to basic statistical methods for deriving test scores and for appraising tests, and there are numerous helpful suggestions for fuller treatments of every topic discussed.

Furst, E. J. *Constructing evaluation instruments.* New York: McKay, 1958.

This is decidedly a "how to do it" book, and it gives careful attention to the practical problems of building all types of evaluation instruments. Noteworthy are the discussions of instruments for measuring opinions, attitudes, and interests which are included, in addition to the treatments of various forms and formats of cognitive tests.

Smith, E. R., & Tyler, R. W. *Appraising and recording student progress.* (Adventure in American Education Ser., Vol. 3) New York: Harper, 1942.

Though this venerable work is more than a quarter of a century old, it is recommended especially for its penetrating discussions in two chapters—"Aspects of Thinking" and "Evaluation of Interests." The illustrations presented from tests on interpretation of data, application of principles of science, application of principles of logical reasoning, and the nature of proof are very suggestive and particularly suitable for use in formative evaluation.

Nelson, C. H. *Improving objective tests in science.* Washington, D.C.: National Science Teachers Association, 1967.

This small pamphlet offers the reader ready access to Dr. Nelson's thinking and many years' effort on behalf of improving the quality of science tests. The first part of the pamphlet reviews the educational objectives that are considered in making tests and gives guideposts for preparation of tests. In the second part, numerous illustrations are presented to demonstrate the relationships between grouped questions directed toward solving and understanding problems, and a section is devoted to selecting and preparing reading passages for testing situations.

Walbesser, H. H. Curriculum evaluation by means of behavioral objectives. *Journal of Research in Science Teaching,* 1963, **1,** 296–301.

Walbesser, H. H. *An evaluation model and its application: Second report.* (AAAS misc. pub. 68-4) Washington, D.C.: American Association for the Advancement of Science, 1968.

As director of the evaluation work for Science—A Process Approach, the elementary school science program sponsored by the AAAS, Walbesser has developed a system for assessing student achievement individually by means of competency measures. The first reference describes the theoretical model for the system, and the second is an interim report on some of the results obtained. This work represents the first substantial systematic effort which has been made to assess the science student's attainment of process skills.

Another resource needed by someone actively involved in evaluation of science learning is a collection of published science tests. References to many of these tests are incorporated in the source notes for the illustrative test items on pages 591–627 of this chapter. The catalogs of the major test publishers provide many additional references to tests in virtually all science subjects at various educational levels. However, the best single source of information about published science tests is the following.

Buros, O. K. (Ed.) *The sixth mental measurements yearbook.* Highland Park, N.J.: Gryphon Press, 1965.

This massive volume and its five predecessors contain full descriptions of practically all achievement, aptitude, interest, and personality tests that have been regularly published (up to 1965). Included also are critical test reviews especially prepared for the *Yearbook* by authorities in the pertinent fields and references to other reviews of the tests. A comprehensive indexing system makes it easy to locate the descriptions and reviews of available tests in any science subject. (Because of its size, scope, and cost, this general reference work would not necessarily be found in the personal library of a teacher or educator interested only in testing and evaluation in science.)

Information about science tests which have not been published or which have been prepared primarily for use in research studies can be obtained through (1) articles in the periodical publications of science education, among them the *Journal of Research in Science Teaching, School Science and Mathematics, Science Education,* and *The Science Teacher;* or (2) abstracts and bibliographies prepared by the Science Education Information and Analysis Center, located at the Ohio State University, Columbus, Ohio.

Some problems of evaluation in science

As education plunges into the decade of the 1970s, probably the most serious problem of evaluation in science is the disparity between the methods and techniques which are available to the science teacher and what generally happens in the science classroom. This chapter has presented illustrations of many means of evaluating a broad range of student behaviors, but it is undeniable that the overwhelming majority of tests foisted on science students today rarely ask for behaviors other than those in category A.0, *Knowledge and comprehension.* There isn't space here to delve into the complex of reasons and circumstances which has produced this disparate situation, nor is this the place to castigate anyone for its existence. Those readers familiar with the organizational demands of schools, the inertia imposed by traditional forms of operation, the time pressures on science teachers, typical attitudes nurtured in students by years of school experiences, and other realities of the present scene could readily explain the sizable gap between existing possibilities for evaluation in science and actual practice. It would be folly to suggest that this gap can be narrowed either very easily or very quickly, and exactly how to obtain more widespread application in science teaching of already available techniques of testing and evaluation is far from clear. In optimistic moments, this writer hopes that perhaps this chapter, within the context of this book, may make a modest contribution to that end.

Turning to another problem, a lacuna in existing evaluation techniques was noted previously, with regard to the science student's performance in *Manual skills* (category G.0). How much emphasis is to be placed on the development of manual skills in any particular science program is still a debatable question, of course, and individual science teachers probably will continue to differ in the attention they give to the students' proper manipulation of equipment and carrying out of laboratory techniques. Nevertheless, research into this area, a part of the psychomotor domain of educational objectives, is woefully lacking, and there are presently no well-justified, generally agreed-upon criteria for judging a student's performance in science laboratory skills. The main problem, however, is not confined to making judgments about performance in these manual skills. In numerous science evaluation situations when observations of a student's performance are called for, there is a substantial degree of uncertainty in deciding how well he has done and how to guide him to do better. Many of the student behaviors included under the four *Processes of scientific inquiry* categories offer cases in point. The problem, then, is to find ways of developing much more detailed and precise specifications than have heretofore been attempted of the behaviors that the student is to attain. These specifications would also delineate the prerequisite behaviors leading to the desired criterion behaviors, so that the student who has not attained mastery may be given soundly based guidance. Clearly, quite a massive expenditure of energy and ingenuity will be needed to acquire behavioral descriptions having the necessary specificity. Without them, however, most observations of the student's performance in science laboratory and inquiry skills are likely to remain relatively rudimentary.

Allied to the development of more complete behavioral specifications of student performance is the problem of developing more widespread interest in and commitment to formative evaluation. As long as evaluation is viewed primarily as an after-the-fact, summative enterprise, there is very little inclination to construct the detailed specifications of performance that are needed for adequate diagnosis and guidance of the student's science learning. On the other hand, when a commitment has been made to formative evaluation, the need for careful specifications of the behavioral components of performance becomes apparent. The problem of gaining greater commitment to formative evaluation is largely a problem of communicating the idea to more science teachers and educators. Most teachers who learn about an operational system of formative evaluation respond positively and want to adapt it for their classes. This is not altogether unexpected. Formative evaluation is, after all, a natural complement to good teaching. As was pointed out, only a few promising beginnings have thus far been made in developing formative evaluation in science teaching. Nevertheless, as the word spreads among science teachers, it is reasonable to expect that many more innovative approaches to formative evaluation will be spawned, tried, and adopted in many different science programs. A responsibility rests with those who have devised successfully innovations in formative evaluation to share their experiences and procedures with the science education community as expeditiously as possible, so that the benefits of formative evaluation may be realized by larger numbers of science students.

In the coming years, increasing attention will undoubtedly be given in science programs at all educational levels to the student behaviors placed at the right side of Table 18-1, that is, *Attitudes and interests* (category *H*.0) and *Orientation* (category *I*.0). Concurrently with the construction of instructional materials which promote these behaviors, more effective means of evaluating their attainment must be developed. This problem, the last problem of evaluation in science to be noted here, is an urgent one. In comparison with the techniques already at hand for testing and evaluating in the cognitive domain, the means of evaluation in the affective domain and in scientific literacy are flaccid and unsophisticated. Significant improvements are unlikely to come until more detailed specifications than are presently extant of desired student behaviors under both these categories have been compiled. Assiduous analyses are just as necessary here as in the specifications of the components of performance in inquiry and laboratory skills, and the task is no easier. Even when it has been done, however, the problem will not be completely solved. Already existing examples of the measurement of attitudes, interests, and aspects of scientific literacy demonstrate that the methods and techniques appropriate here are generally quite different from the measures of cognitive achievement to which science students and educators have become accustomed. Still more unusual methods, techniques, approaches, and forms can be anticipated to implement evaluation in the affective domain and in scientific literacy when schools give them more attention, but the new approaches and instruments have yet to be devised. Some imaginative means of assessment needs must follow or accompany the comprehensive specifications of the student's affective and scientifically literate behaviors. Mounting and adequately manning the dual thrust necessary for the resolution of this evaluation problem is a matter of high priority, for the affective side of learning and the development of scientific literacy will occupy a central portion of the stage in science education in the 1970s and beyond.

Airasian, P. Physical Sciences Questionnaire. Unpublished test, University of Chicago, 1967. (Available from the author, Boston College, Chestnut Hill, Mass. 02167)

Allen, H., Jr. *Attitudes of certain high school seniors toward science and scientific careers.* New York: Teachers College Press, 1959.

American Association for the Advancement of Science. *Science—A process approach. Competency measures, part five.* (AAAS misc. pub. 66-23) Washington, D.C.: AAAS, 1966. (a)

American Association for the Advancement of Science. *Science—A process approach. Competency measures, part six.* (AAAS misc. pub. 66-26) Washington, D.C.: AAAS, 1966. (b)

American Association for the Advancement of Science. *Science—A process approach. Competency measures, part seven.* (AAAS misc. pub. 66-29) Washington, D.C.: AAAS, 1966. (c)

Biological Sciences Curriculum Study. *BSCS Processes of Science Test, Form A.* Boulder, Colo.: University of Colorado, 1965. (a)

Biological Sciences Curriculum Study. *Final Examination, Form J.* (Rev.) Boulder, Colo.: University of Colorado, 1965. (b)

Bloom, B. S. (Ed.) *Taxonomy of educational objectives: The classification of educational goals.* Handbook 1. *Cognitive domain.* New York: McKay, 1956.

Borman, I. M., & Sanders, M. W. *Borman-Sanders Elementary Science Test, grades 5–8.* Emporia, Kans.: Kansas State Teachers College, 1964.

Boyer, P. A., & Gordon, H. C. *General Science Objective Test.* Chicago: Lyons & Carnahan, 1959.

Brandwein, P. F., Cooper, E. K., Blackwood, P. E., & Hone, E. B. *Concepts in science: Book 4.* New York: Harcourt, Brace & World, 1966. (a)

Brandwein, P. F., Cooper, E. K., Blackwood, P. E., & Hone, E. B. *Concepts in science: Book 4, teacher's edition.* New York: Harcourt, Brace & World, 1966. (b)

Brandwein, P. F., Watson, F. G., & Blackwood, P. E. *Teaching high school science: A book of methods.* New York: Harcourt, Brace, 1958.

Burmester, M. A. *A test of aspects of scientific thinking.* East Lansing, Mich.: Michigan State University, 1951. (Also available from the author, Department of Natural Science, Michigan State University)

California State Department of Education. *Report of the State Advisory Committee on Science Education.* Sacramento: CSDE, 1967.

Carrier, E. O., Geis, F., Klopfer, L. E., & Shoresman, P. B. *Test On Understanding Science, Form Ew.* Urbana, Ill.: Authors, 1966. (Available from P. B. Shoresman, School of Education, University of Illinois, Urbana, Ill.)

Chemical Bond Approach Project, Earlham College. *Tests for chemical systems.* New York: McGraw-Hill, 1966.

Chemical Education Material Study (CHEMS). *CHEM Study achievement tests.* Berkeley, Calif.: University of California, 1963. (a)

Chemical Education Material Study (CHEMS). *Chemistry: An experimental science.* San Francisco: Freeman, 1963. (b)

Chemical Education Material Study (CHEMS). *Chemistry: An experimental science, laboratory manual.* San Francisco: Freeman, 1963. (c)

Chemical Education Material Study (CHEMS). *Chemistry: An experimental science, teachers' guide.* San Francisco: Freeman, 1963. 2 vols. (d)

Conant, J. B. *Science and common sense.* New Haven, Conn.: Yale University Press, 1951.

Cooley, W. W., & Klopfer, L. E. *Test On Understanding Science, Form W.* Princeton, N.J.: Educational Testing Service, 1961.

Cross, D., & Sanders, M. W. *Emporia General Science Test.* Emporia, Kans.: Kansas State Teachers College, 1964.

Dressel, P. L., & Nelson, C. H. *Questions and problems in science: Test items folio no. 1.* Princeton, N.J.: Educational Testing Service, 1956.

Dutton, W. H., & Stephens, L. Measuring attitudes toward science. *School Science and Mathematics,* 1963, **63,** 43–49.

Educational Research Council of Greater Cleveland. *Sequential programs in science for a restructured curriculum, grades 7–12*. Cleveland: ERCGC, 1966.

Educational Testing Service. *Cooperative Biology Test, Form Y*. Princeton, N.J.: ETS, 1948.

Educational Testing Service. *Cooperative Science Tests, Advanced General Science, Form B*. Princeton, N.J.: ETS, 1962. (a)

Educational Testing Service. *Cooperative Science Tests, General Science, Form B*. Princeton, N.J.: ETS, 1962. (b)

Educational Testing Service. *Cooperative Science Tests, Chemistry, Form B*. Princeton, N.J.: ETS, 1963. (a)

Educational Testing Service. *Cooperative Science Tests, Physics, Form B*. Princeton, N.J.: ETS, 1963. (b)

Eiss, A. F., & Harbeck, M. B. *Behavioral objectives in the affective domain*. Washington, D.C.: National Science Teachers Association, 1969.

Geis, F., Jr. The semantic differential technique as a means of evaluating changes in affect. Unpublished doctoral dissertation, Harvard University, 1968.

Goodlad, J. I. *School curricular reform in the United States*. New York: Fund for the Advancement of Education, 1964.

Hedges, W. D. *Testing and evaluation for the sciences*. Belmont, Calif.: Wadsworth, 1966.

Hurd, P. D. *Biological education in American secondary schools, 1890–1960*. (BSCS Bull. No. 1) Washington, D.C.: American Institute of Biological Sciences, 1961.

Hurd, P. D. (Ed.) *The new school science*. Washington, D.C.: American Association for the Advancement of Science, 1963.

Klopfer, L. E. *The chemistry of fixed air: Teacher's guide*. Chicago: Science Research Associates, 1964. (a)

Klopfer, L. E. *Word Association Study, Form Ez*. Urbana, Ill.: Elementary-school Science Project, University of Illinois, February 1964. (b)

Klopfer, L. E. Integrated Science for the secondary school: Progress, process, and prospects. *Science Teacher*, 1966, **33**(8), 27–31.

Klopfer, L. E. The teaching of science and the history of science. *Journal of Research in Science Teaching*, 1969, **6**, 87–95.

Krathwohl, D. R., Bloom, B. S., & Masia, B. B. *Taxonomy of educational objectives: The classification of educational goals*. Handbook 2. *Affective domain*. New York: McKay, 1964.

Kruglag, H., & Wall, C. N. *Laboratory performance tests for general physics*. Kalamazoo, Mich.: Western Michigan University, 1959.

Learning Research and Development Center, University of Pittsburgh. Individually Prescribed Instruction Program: Science, Level A, Inching Along unit. Unpublished lesson, University of Pittsburgh, 1969. (a)

Learning Research and Development Center, University of Pittsburgh. Individually Prescribed Instruction Program: Science, Level A, Inventory of Prerequisite Skills. Unpublished test, University of Pittsburgh, 1969. (b)

Learning Research and Development Center, University of Pittsburgh. Individually Prescribed Instruction Program: Science, Level A objectives. Unpublished manuscript, University of Pittsburgh, 1969. (c)

Learning Research and Development Center, University of Pittsburgh. Individually Prescribed Instruction Program: Science, Level A Placement Test, Part II. Unpublished test, University of Pittsburgh, 1969. (d)

Likert, R. A technique for the measurement of attitudes. *Archives of Psychology*, 1932, No. 140(Whole No.).

Lockard, J. D. *Report of the International Clearinghouse on Science and Mathematics Curriculum Developments, 1967*. Washington, D.C.: American Association for the Advancement of Science, 1967.

Marshall, J. S., & Burkman, E. *Current trends in science education*. New York: Center for Applied Research in Education, 1966.

Metcalfe, H. C., Williams, J. E., & Castka, J. F. *Laboratory experiments in chemistry*. New York: Holt, Rinehart and Winston, 1966. (a)

Metcalfe, H. C., Williams, J. E., & Castka, J. F. *Modern chemistry*. New York: Holt, Rinehart and Winston, 1966. (b)

Metcalfe, H. C., Williams, J. E., & Castka, J. F. *Teacher's guide to the Modern chemistry program*. New York: Holt, Rinehart and Winston, 1966. (c)

Nagel, E. *The structure of science*. London: Routledge & Kegan Paul, 1961.

Nash, L. K. *The nature of the natural sciences.* Boston: Little, Brown, 1963.

National Assessment of Education Progress. *Objectives of science education.* (ETS vers.) Princeton, N.J.: Educational Testing Service, 1965. (a)

National Assessment of Education Progress. *Objectives of science education.* (SRA vers.) Chicago: Science Research Associates, 1965. (b)

National Education Association, Educational Policies Commission. *Education and the spirit of science.* Washington, D.C.: NEA, 1966.

National Science Foundation. *Course and curriculum improvement projects.* (NSF 66-22) Washington, D.C.: NSF, 1966.

National Science Teachers Association. *Position statement on curriculum.* Washington, D.C.: NSTA, 1963.

National Science Teachers Association. *Theory into action in science curriculum development.* Washington, D.C.: NSTA, 1964.

National Society for the Study of Education. *46th yearbook.* Part I. *Science education in American schools.* Chicago: University of Chicago Press, 1947.

National Society for the Study of Education. *59th yearbook.* Part I. *Rethinking science education.* Chicago: University of Chicago Press, 1960.

Nedelsky, L. Physics item pool. Unpublished manuscript prepared for the American Association of Physics Teachers, Committee on Testing, Chicago, 1965. (a)

Nedelsky, L. *Science teaching and testing.* New York: Harcourt, Brace & World, 1965. (b)

Nelson, C. H. *Improving objective tests in science.* Washington, D.C.: National Science Teachers Association, 1967.

Otto, J. H., & Towle, A. *Modern biology.* New York: Holt, Rinehart and Winston, 1965.

Pella, M. O., O'Hearn, G. T., & Gale, C. W. Referents to scientific literacy. *Journal of Research in Science Teaching,* 1967, **4,** 199–208.

Physical Science Study Committee, Educational Services. *Tests of the Physical Science Study Committee, Test 9: The Atom.* Princeton, N.J.: Educational Testing Service, Cooperative Test Division, 1959.

Physical Science Study Committee, Educational Services. *Tests of the Physical Science Study Committee, Series N, Test 1: Space, Time, and Motion.* Princeton, N.J.: Educational Testing Service, Cooperative Test Division, 1963. (a)

Physical Science Study Committee, Educational Services. *Tests of the Physical Science Study Committee, Series N, Test 3: The Behavior of Light.* Princeton, N.J.: Educational Testing Service, Cooperative Test Division, 1963. (b)

Reed, H. B. Pupils' interest in science. Unpublished doctoral dissertation, Harvard University, 1959.

Rutherford, F. J., et al. *Harvard Project Physics unit tests.* Cambridge, Mass.: Harvard Project Physics, 1966. (a)

Rutherford, F. J., et al. *Pupil Activity Inventory.* Cambridge, Mass.: Harvard Project Physics, 1966. (b)

Rutherford, F. J., et al. *Semantic Differential Test.* Cambridge, Mass.: Harvard Project Physics, 1966. (c)

Schwab, J. J. The teaching of science as enquiry. In J. J. Schwab & P. F. Brandwein, *The teaching of science.* Cambridge, Mass.: Harvard University Press, 1962. Pp. 1–103.

Schwab, J. J. (Ed.) *Biology teachers' handbook.* New York: Wiley, 1963.

Schwab, J. J., & Brandwein, P. F. *The teaching of science.* Cambridge, Mass.: Harvard University Press, 1962.

Science Masters Association. *Secondary modern science teaching: Part II.* London: Murray, 1957.

Shoresman, P. B. *Interests and Ideas, Form AV.* Urbana, Ill.: Elementary-school Science Project, University of Illinois, November 1965.

Showalter, V. L. Unified science: Alternative to tradition. *Science Teacher,* 1964, **31**(1), 24–28.

Thurstone, L. L., & Chave, E. J. *The measurement of attitude.* Chicago: University of Chicago Press, 1929.

Van Deventer, W. C. *The development of junior high school science activities.* (Michigan Science Curriculum Committee, Junior High School Project) Lansing, Mich.: State Department of Education, 1966.

Walker, M. *The nature of scientific thought.* Englewood Cliffs, N.J.: Prentice-Hall, 1963.

Welch, W. W. *Welch Science Process Inventory, Form D.* Cambridge, Mass.: Author, 1966. (Available from the author, 330 Burton Hall, University of Minnesota, Minneapolis, Minn. 55455)

Woodburn, J. H., et al. *The Methods and Procedures of Science: An Examination.* Rockville, Md.: Authors, 1967. (Available from the senior author, Charles W. Woodward High School, Rockville, Md.)

19

Evaluation of Learning in

Secondary School Mathematics

JAMES W. WILSON

University of Georgia
Athens, Georgia

James W. Wilson is Chairman of the Department of Mathematics Education at the University of Georgia. He received the B.S.Ed. degree from Kansas State Teachers College and graduate degrees from KSTC, Notre Dame, and Stanford. He was a member of the headquarters staff of the School Mathematics Study Group, with the Research and Test Development Section and, as project coordinator, the Research and Analysis Section. He has taught mathematics in Kansas in public secondary schools and has been on college faculties in Kansas, Vermont, and Georgia. His professional affiliations include NCTM, MAA, AERA, NCME, the Psychometric Society, and Phi Delta Kappa; and he is on the editorial board of the Journal for Research in Mathematics Education *and a contributor to the sixty-ninth yearbook of the National Society for the Study of Education. His interests include undergraduate teacher training, graduate-study direction, and research on secondary school mathematics education.*

Contents

19

Evaluation of Learning in Secondary School Mathematics

The task of this chapter is to discuss and illustrate testing for purposes of summative and formative evaluation of classroom learning in secondary school mathematics. The discussion will involve the contemporary mathematics curriculum for the seventh to twelfth grades. It is hoped that the materials presented here illustrate at least in part some of the general principles of evaluation given in Chaps. 1 to 6; show some of the wide latitude of interpretation and applicability of the general principles; exhibit both similarities to and differences from testing procedures in other subjects; and provide prototype materials to enable teachers and curriculum workers to produce better mathematics testing for evaluation.

Evaluation in mathematics learning does not first occur in grade 7. But the present chapter necessarily had to be limited, and the split between elementary and secondary school was a logical one. The illustrations given here could quite easily be extended to the elementary grades, since the mathematics curriculum is sequential from kindergarten on up.

The goals of instruction in secondary school mathematics

This section will describe in a general way the outcomes of contemporary mathematics instruction. This is best done by some sort of organizational framework, model, or table of specifications. A table of specifications following the guidelines provided in Chaps. 1 to 6, will be constructed by describing two dimensions—a content dimension and a behavior or objectives dimension. No specific school, curriculum, or teacher is being described here. Therefore, the table of specifications may not be a prescriptive one for some of us concerned with the evaluation of mathematics learning. That is good. What is to be learned from this section is how one would go about specifying a model for identifying goals of instruction in mathematics. If the table of specifications provided here is not satisfactory for an individual reader, he can modify it for the particular curriculum or classroom where evaluation is being done or start from the principles

TABLE 19-1 TABLE OF SPECIFICATIONS FOR SECONDARY

	Cognitive								
	A.0 Computation			*B.0 Comprehension*					
	Knowledge of specific facts	*Knowledge of terminology*	*Ability to carry out algorithms*	*Knowledge of concepts*	*Knowledge of principles, rules, and generalizations*	*Knowledge of mathematical structure*	*Ability to transform problem elements from one mode to another*	*Ability to follow a line of reasoning*	*Ability to read and interpret a problem*
CONTENT	*A.1*	*A.2*	*A.3*	*B.1*	*B.2*	*B.3*	*B.4*	*B.5*	*B.6*
1.0 Number systems									
1.1 Whole numbers									
1.2 Integers									
1.3 Rational numbers									
1.4 Real numbers									
1.5 Complex numbers									
1.6 Finite number systems									
1.7 Matrices and determinants									
1.8 Probability									
1.9 Numeration systems									
2.0 Algebra									
2.1 Algebraic expressions									
2.2 Algebraic sentences and their solutions									
2.3 Relations and functions									
3.0 Geometry									
3.1 Measurement									
3.2 Geometric phenomena									
3.3 Formal reasoning									
3.4 Coördinate systems and graphs									

* The Table of Specifications is placed here to introduce the chapter and for ease of reference. Its development and description are given on pages 653 ff.

BEHAVIORS

									Affective							
C.0 Application				D.0 Analysis					E.0 Interests and attitudes					F.0 Appreciation		
Ability to solve routine problems	*Ability to make comparisons*	*Ability to analyze data*	*Ability to recognize patterns, isomorphisms, and symmetries*	*Ability to solve nonroutine problems*	*Ability to discover relationships*	*Ability to construct proofs*	*Ability to criticize proofs*	*Ability to formulate and validate generalizations*	*Attitude*	*Interest*	*Motivation*	*Anxiety*	*Self-concept*	*Extrinsic*	*Intrinsic*	*Operational*
C.1	C.2	C.3	C.4	D.1	D.2	D.3	D.4	D.5	E.1	E.2	E.3	E.4	E.5	F.1	F.2	F.3

of Chap. 1 and build a better one. The process of building the table of specifications may be more important than the table of specifications itself.

The goals of instruction that are identified in this section are a composite of the instruction in mathematics in the United States at this time. They represent an impression of what *is* rather than what *should be* or what *has been*. Of necessity, the secondary mathematics curriculum will change; it is hoped that the reader will be able to adapt the table of specifications to changes in the goals of mathematics instruction and in the mathematics content of the curriculum. Table 19-1 is the Table of Specifications for Secondary School Mathematics. It is really the end product of this section, rather than the beginning. Therefore, let us develop the table of specifications by starting from a simpler model of mathematics achievement.

A model for mathematics achievement

A model may serve a number of purposes and uses. It can, for example, provide a unifying theme for considering three different types of problems: problems of mathematics curriculum, instruction, and evaluation. But the mathematics achievement of students is at the heart of all of the concerns which the model may serve. Although measures of mathematics achievement—all cognitive outcomes—are emphasized, there is no intent to disregard affective outcomes such as attitude, appreciation, interest, and anxiety. (A separate model could be developed for such outcomes in a mathematics program.) But the first concern of evaluation in mathematics learning has been, and will continue to be, cognitive outcomes or achievement. The affective outcomes are supportive and important, but still secondary to, or at most of equal importance with, achievement.

Mathematics achievement has many facets. That is, mathematics achievement is not a unitary trait and, therefore, a strategy that ensures consideration of many *different measures* of mathematics achievement is necessary. A strategy that has been used to some extent in a variety of contexts is to stratify the outcomes of mathematics instruction in two ways: first, by types of mathematics content, and second, by levels of behavior.

One such double classification scheme was developed by the staff and consultants of the School Mathematics Study Group (SMSG) in its National Longitudinal Study of Mathematical Abilities (NLSMA). This model is described in several of the NLSMA reports (Romberg & Wilson, 1969; Carry & Weaver, 1969; Carry, 1970; McLeod & Kilpatrick, 1969, 1970; Kilpatrick & McLeod, 1970; Wilson, 1970). The development of the model and its most complete description are given in NLSMA Report No. 7 (Romberg & Wilson, 1969, Ch. 3). An adaptation of this NLSMA model will be useful here to introduce some vocabulary and to provide a starting point for building a table of specifications appropriate for the task of evaluating mathematics learning in the classroom.[1]

The essential idea of the model is that measures of mathematics achievement, or test items, can be classified in two ways: (1) by categories of mathematical content, and (2) by levels of behavior. The levels of behavior reflect the cognitive complexity of a task (*not* simply the difficulty of a task). In Table 19-2, Model for Mathematics Achievement,[2] the categories of mathematical content are *Number systems*, *Algebra*, and *Geometry*. The levels of behavior are *Computation*, *Comprehension*, *Application*, and *Analysis*.

Although the levels of behavior have to do specifically with mathematics, this dimension of the NLSMA model was developed by careful study of the *Taxonomy of Educational Objectives: Cognitive Domain* (Bloom, 1956; see the Appendix to Part I) and by use of the *Taxonomy* to work with item writing and test development in NLSMA.

[1] The following description very closely resembles that given in the various NLSMA reports. It has been modified slightly, however, to better suit the purposes of this chapter.

[2] This model will be expanded and developed in the following discussion into the Table of Specifications given in Table 19-1. A thorough description of the specific subcategories in Table 19-1 is then presented (see pages 653 ff.).

TABLE 19-2 MODEL FOR MATHEMATICS ACHIEVEMENT

	A.0 Computation	B.0 Comprehension	C.0 Application	D.0 Analysis
1.0 Number systems				
2.0 Algebra				
3.0 Geometry				

The model presented requires explicit specification of the terms along each dimension. The categories of the mathematics content might be described as follows. The content *Number systems* (1.0) includes items concerned with the nature and properties of whole numbers, integers, the rational numbers, the real numbers, and the complex numbers and with the techniques and properties of the arithmetic operations. *Algebra* items (2.0) involve open sentences, algebraic expressions, factoring, the solution of equations and inequalities, systems of equations, algebraic and transcendental functions, the graphing of functions and solution sets, the theory of equations, and trigonometry. *Geometry* (3.0) is tested with items on linear and angular measurement, area, and volume; points, lines, planes; polygons and circles; solids; congruence and similarity; construction; graphs and coordinate geometry; formal proofs; and spatial visualization.

The model in Table 19-2 contains four levels of behavior. *Computation* items (*A*.0) are designed to require recall of basic facts and terminology or the manipulation of problem elements according to rules the students presumably have learned. Emphasis is upon knowing and performing operations and not upon deciding which operations are appropriate. *Comprehension* (*B*.0) relates either to recall of concepts and generalizations or to transformation of problem elements from one mode to another. The emphasis is upon demonstrating understanding of concepts and their relationships, not upon using concepts to produce a solution. *Application* items (*C*.0) require recall of relevant knowledge, selection of appropriate operations, and performance of the operations. They require the student to use concepts in a specific context and in a way he has presumably practiced. *Analysis* items (*D*.0) require a nonroutine application of concepts. They may require the detection of relationships, the finding of patterns, and the organization and use of concepts and operations in a nonpracticed context.

The second dimension, levels of behavior, is both hierarchical and ordered. It is ordered in the sense that analysis is more cognitively complex than application, which is in turn more cognitively complex than comprehension, and the computation level includes those items which are the least cognitively complex. It is hierarchical in that, for example, an item at the application level may require both comprehension level skills (selection of appropriate operations) and computation level skills (performance of an operation).

As this chapter goes on, the model in Table 19-2 will be expanded in two ways. First, each of the categories in each dimension will be divided into finer subcategories. Second, components for the affective domain will be included. The expanded model will be the Table of Specifications given in Table 19-1.

The model, even in this simplistic form, emphasizes the complexity of outcomes in mathematics learning. Take any mathematics topic, such as whole numbers: there are outcomes for each of the cognitive levels; there are affective outcomes as well. It is not enough that the student learn to manipulate whole numbers. Rather, he must also understand something about the system of whole numbers and algorithms for their manipulation; he should be able to use whole numbers and whole number concepts in solving problems; and he should be able to use whole numbers in unfamiliar situations, to apply them in the solution of problems he has not encountered previously, or to generate new algorithms for using whole numbers in solving classes of problems. Further, it is essential that the student derive some satisfaction, enjoyment, and appreciation of whole numbers, their use, and their structure.

Mathematics teachers often state their goals of instruction to include all cognitive levels. They want their students to be able to solve problems creatively, etc. But then their instruction, their testing, and their grading tend to emphasize the lower behavior levels, such as computation and comprehension. It might be enlightening for the reader to try an experiment. Take your file of mathematics tests for a course you have taught recently. In Table 19-2, mark down the percentage of test items you think *should be* in each of the cells, considering the course and the expectations you had for it. Then take the file and tally the number of items you think best fits into each cell. It is a reasonable prediction that your tallies will exceed your prediction at the lower cognitive levels and that the reverse will be true for the higher cognitive levels.

Often, it is assumed that performance at one cognitive level requires *mastery* of related content at lower levels. There is no evidence to support this assumption. The level of mastery of computational skills, for example, does not have to be highly honed in order to study applications. There is some logic to claiming that performance at all cognitive levels should be expected for all students. Pity the student who has never been allowed any interesting and challenging mathematics because he is a "slow learner" and hence is never expected or offered anything more than routine computation. (And pity the student who is given too much challenge and never led to success by thoughtful and well-organized instruction.)

The goals of mathematics instruction in the secondary schools of this country vary, because there are a multiplicity of outcomes expected from mathematics instruction for any given set of students; because there are college preparatory, vocational, and terminal programs of mathematics instruction; because regions, states, schools, or teachers may stress different sets of outcomes; and because mathematics is so universal.

Mathematics is sequential. The secondary school curriculum builds upon the elementary curriculum and extends into the college curriculum, or a terminal course. This sequential nature of mathematics, together with the underlying structure of the subject, frequently leads mathematics teachers to think of the goals of instruction only in terms of content. Quite often the operation of a mathematics class is to "cover the material in the textbook." This, obviously, is either a poor practice or an inadequate description of what the teacher is doing. The goals of instruction must ultimately be in terms of what students are expected to *do*.

There is an aspect of mathematics instruction, however, that is central to the goals of mathematics instruction but does not lend itself to description of content or of levels of behavior. It is embedded in a simple but subtle question—"What is mathematics?"—and in a companion question, blunt but also subtle—"Why study mathematics?" These questions have a philosophical ring; they cannot be dismissed with a simple answer. The teacher, in his approach to instruction, is answering these two questions each day in his classroom (even though he may never have reflected on them explicitly), and he may be giving horrible answers.

In part, mathematics is a tool useful in the other sciences and an aspect of intelligent communication for most people. But beyond that, mathematics involves a process, a way of being, which can be learned; in fact, "Doing mathematical thinking" can be given as an answer to "What is mathematics?"—an answer which emphasizes that mathematics is, in part, a process.

A useful heuristic for the teacher is to seriously consider the above two questions from time to time and even generate class discussions of them. Mathematics is a dynamic, elegant field of human creation. Avital and Shettleworth (1968) claim "the most important part of the learning experience is actual contact with living mathematics [p. 2]"; by "living mathematics" they were describing the process through which mathematics is developed.

Similar models and useful references

Brief mention can be made of several mathematics projects that have used a matrix similar to the model. Wood (1968) has discussed the similarities and differences of several of the levels of the behavior dimension. His Item Banking Project in England uses the following levels of behavior:

A. Knowledge and information: recall of definitions, notations, concepts.
B. Techniques and skill: computation, manipulation of symbols.
C. Comprehension: capacity to understand problems, to translate symbolic forms, to follow and extend reasoning.
D. Application: of appropriate concepts in unfamiliar mathematical situations.
E. Inventiveness: reasoning creatively in mathematics.

(p. 89)

Wood uses a combination of the *Taxonomy* (Bloom, 1956) and the model reported in *The International Study of Achievement in Mathematics* (Husén, 1967) to arrive at his categories. Levels A, B, and E are the same for the two projects. The International Study's categories C and D are

C. Translation of data into symbols or schema or vice versa.
D. Comprehension: capacity to analyze problems to follow reasoning.

(Husén, 1967, vol. I, p. 94)

The International Study of Educational Achievement (IEA) planning committee arrived at these categories after considerable investigation in the twelve participating countries.

A report of a preliminary study for the IEA from the United States (Manheim et al., 1961, p. 5) utilizes these classifications of content and behavior.

Content

A. Arithmetic
B. Algebra
C. Geometry
   - C_1 Plane Geometry
   - C_2 Solid Geometry
   - C_3 Analytical Geometry
D. Trigonometry
E. Miscellaneous
   - E_1 Probability and statistics
   - E_2 Calculus
F. General

Behavior

1. Ability to remember or recall definitions, notations
2. Operations and concepts
3. Ability to interpret symbolic data
4. Ability to put data into symbols
5. Ability to follow proofs
6. Ability to construct proofs
7. Ability to apply concepts to mathematical problems
8. Ability to apply concepts to non-mathematical problems
9. Ability to analyze problems and determine the operations which may be applied
10. Ability to invent mathematical generalizations

These classifications are similar to those presented in Table 19-2. The limited work in the schools in probability and statistics could easily be included with number systems and algebra. Trigonometry in recent years has become integrated with algebra, which builds into calculus. For the behavior levels, 1 and 2 above are for the most part computation; 3 and 4 and part of 1 are comprehension; 5, 7, 8, and 9 are application; and 6 and 10 are analysis.

This report contains a large number of illustrative items for the various objectives of mathematics learning as defined by content and behavior components. In addition, tables are presented which describe the extent to which objectives are (or are supposed to be) emphasized in the United States. Finer classifications of content are used for these tables.

An interesting—and controversial—current project is the National Assessment of Educational Progress. This project is directed by the Committee on Assessing the Progress in Education (CAPE).[3] Mathematics is one of ten areas which will be given national assessment on a three-year cycle. The development of suitable mathematics items used a content-by-levels-of-behavior scheme. The original categories for both dimensions were almost the same as in the IEA preliminary study (Manheim et al., 1961). The cognitive levels were later reorganized as follows:

1. Recall and/or recognize definitions, facts, and symbols
2. Perform mathematical manipulations
3. Understand mathematical concepts and processes
4. Solve mathematical problems—social, technical, and academic
5. Use mathematics and mathematical reasoning to analyze problem situations, define problems, formulate hypotheses
6. Appreciate and use mathematics

(Committee on Assessing the Progress of Education, 1969, p. 6)

Level 6 is notable in this scheme in that it is, in part, a noncognitive category. Level 1 is a separate knowledge category. Except for this separation of knowledge-level behaviors, the cognitive levels are very much like the ones given in Table 19-2. The definitions given for the cognitive levels of computation and comprehension in the model subsume the behavior from the knowledge level. Too much of our testing consists only of recall of definition, facts, and symbolism.

The Statewide Mathematics Advisory Committee (SMAC) in California has taken the cognitive levels given in the model and used them in conjunction with the content organization presented in its Strands Report (Statewide Mathematics Advisory Committee, 1967, 1968) in a massive item-writing project to prepare for a statewide assessment of mathematics achievement. The SMAC content categories are whole numbers, rational numbers, real numbers, number line and number plane, mathematical sentences, geometry, measurement, probability and statistics, functions and graphs, and logical thinking. This content classification is more appropriate for the SMAC assessment activities than would be the classification given with Table 19-2, because SMAC is describing the content of grades 1 to 8, the SMAC content categories are prescriptive rather than descriptive of the content in those grades in the mid-1970s, and the content classification is tied to a policy statement, the Strands Report, that will shape the mathematics curriculum development and evaluation in California.

The IEA preliminary report (Manheim et al., 1961) is similar in its organization to the present chapter. That is, a content-by-behavior matrix is presented, and then representative items are provided to demonstrate and discuss the resulting model of achievement. For reference, some other statements of evaluation of classroom learning in mathematics should be noted.

Avital and Shettleworth (1968) provide an extremely useful statement addressed to the teacher. A taxonomy of objectives in mathematics learning is presented, and representative items are given, along with some discussion. The reader will find this inexpensive pamphlet by Avital and Shettleworth a useful supplement to the present chapter.

The *Twenty-sixth Yearbook* of the National Council of Teachers of Mathematics (NCTM, 1961) deals with the evaluation of mathematics learning. This book too is a useful reference for teachers, but it lacks an organizational framework for discussing achievement or evaluation. The chapter by Corcoran and Gibb (1961) is very good for its information and suggestions on appraising attitudes.

Finally, the NLSMA reports are good sources of well-constructed items. Reports Nos. 1, 2,

[3] This group has now been renamed the National Assessment of Educational Progress (NAEP): A project of the Education Commission of the States.

and 3 contain the test batteries used over the five years of the study for grades 4 to 8, 7 to 11, and 10 to 12 respectively (Wilson, Cahen, & Begle, 1968a, 1968b, 1968c). NLSMA Report No. 7 (Romberg & Wilson, 1969) provides the rationale and background for all test batteries in the study and a discussion of the model for mathematical achievement, in its various levels of specificity, which was used in the NLSMA.

An expanded model of outcomes for secondary school mathematics

Each of the classifications of content and of behaviors cited above was designed to serve the purpose of a particular project. The level of detail and the comprehensiveness of the classification scheme were determined by the needs of the project.

In this chapter, a comprehensive examination of the outcomes of mathematics instruction in the secondary school is attempted. Therefore, the classification schemes need to be given in more detail than in Table 19-2. Also, the behavior classification must be extended to include the noncognitive outcomes.

This writer has worked with the classification schemes of the NLSMA, the Strands project, and the National Assessment. Table 19-1, Table of Specifications for Secondary School Mathematics (pages 646–647), represents an expanded model of mathematics achievement which incorporates these classification schemes and the others cited above. The details of the classification schemes for both the content dimension and the behavior dimension will be given in the sections which follow. In part, the expanded model is derived from the NLSMA model (Table 19-2), which in turn has its origins in several other schemes of classification. But the expanded model is also derived from a point of view about mathematics and experience with a wide range of mathematics textbooks that belongs with the writer.

The coding scheme is consistent with those in other chapters. A cell is identified by giving its *column* identification first and then its *row* identification.[4] Therefore, cell *B*.4-2.1 in the expanded model can be identified as *Ability to transform problem elements from one mode to another in algebraic expressions.*

The code identifying the behavior level and content category will be given through the rest of the chapter in conjunction with each topic or illustrative test item.

Content

The content of instruction in mathematics has been separated into three broad categories: *Number systems, Algebra,* and *Geometry.* We should not lose sight, however, of some of the general unifying themes of secondary school mathematics which spread across any classification. Examples of unifying themes are the use of set language and set notation, the structure of mathematical systems (a structure tied to content, rather than a psychological structure), and the processes of mathematics (for example, the concern with patterns, forms, and relationships).

An additional comment, parenthetical to the discussion of content but quite important, must be made in distinguishing between course names and the content categories given here. Traditionally, the college preparatory course for the ninth grade has been a first course in algebra, and the usual course for the tenth grade has been plane geometry. Grades 7 and 8 typically have had a combination of arithmetic, prealgebra, and pregeometry. Such a description would also fit the contemporary college preparatory sequence. But this is not the content classification we want to use in the model shown in Table 19-1. In the model, we want to identify number-systems concepts found in grades 7 to 12. Similarly, for algebra and geometry, there are concepts at each grade level. It is true that a first course in algebra for grade 9 will deal primarily with algebra con-

[4] This means of identifying cells in the matrix, which is the opposite of the practice in mathematics (where the row identification of a matrix is given first and the column identification second), has been used here to be consistent with other chapters. Mathematics readers please bear with us.

tent. There is, however, a good deal of number-systems content in an algebra course, and usually a little geometry.

Number systems (1.0) The study of number systems in the secondary school emphasizes developing the structure of the various number systems to facilitate computation, comprehension, and application.

The content of number systems can be divided into the following subcategories: *Whole numbers*, *Integers*, *Rational numbers*, *Real numbers*, *Complex numbers*, *Finite number systems*, *Matrices and determinants*, elementary *Probability*, and *Numeration systems*. The first five of these subcategories are pedagogically related in two very important ways: each successive set of numbers includes the previous ones as proper subsets, and each set of numbers satisfies a set of properties—in part, the so-called "structure of mathematics." The set of properties is enlarged for each successive set of numbers in our list.

The *Whole numbers* (1.1) are the set

$$W = \{0, 1, 2, 3, \ldots\}$$

The binary operations of addition and multiplication are usually presented for this set of numbers, and then a set of basic properties hold. If a, b, c are members[5] of W, then we have, for all a, b, c, in W,

1. Closure for addition: $a + b \in W$
2. Closure for multiplication: $a \cdot b \in W$
3. Associative property for addition: $(a + b) + c = a + (b + c)$
4. Associative property for multiplication: $(a \cdot b) \cdot c = a \cdot (b \cdot c)$
5. Commutative property for addition: $a + b = b + a$
6. Commutative property for multiplication: $a \cdot b = b \cdot a$
7. Distributive property: $a \cdot (b + c) = a \cdot b + a \cdot c$
8. Identity for addition: $a + 0 = a$
9. Identity for multiplication: $a \cdot 1 = a$

[5] We use the symbol "ϵ" to mean "is a member of the set."

The set W, under the operations of addition and multiplication together with these properties, comprises a *system* of whole numbers. Usually, secondary school discussion of number systems begins with set W. Sometimes, however, the set

$$N = \{1, 2, 3, \ldots\}$$

is considered first. This is the set of natural numbers. If the properties given above are discussed with regard to the set of natural numbers, property 8, the identity for addition, does not hold.

The properties as stated here lack much of the rigor, abstractness, and qualification which are important to more advanced, formal treatments of number systems or algebraic structures. But the goal is to use mathematical structure as a pedagogical device; the introduction of rigor at an early level is not desirable. Unfortunately, it is all too easy in secondary school mathematics instruction to seize upon the mathematical structure as an end, overwhelm the students with formalism and rigor, and replace routine drill on number combinations with drill in mathematical syntax.

The sets of numbers, such as W and N, are usually developed in the elementary school out of concrete experiences provided for the students. The properties can be discussed (discovered) and developed in an informal way as well. Just as the number concepts are abstractions from the student's experiences, so are the various properties abstractions about the whole set of number concepts. Formalism and rigor should be a late stage in the study of number systems.

The essential pedagogical theme in stressing the mathematical structure of number systems is that of "expanding" the set of elements and the set of properties. Both the motivation and accomplishment of this expansion can be done in an intuitive and meaningful way at the several levels of mathematical maturity at which students study number systems concepts: in elementary grades, in seventh grade, during an algebra course, or as part of an advanced mathematics course in the upper grades. Let us follow through this expansion.

The set of *Integers* (1.2), I,

$$I = \{. \ . \ . \ , -3, -2, -1, 0, 1, 2, 3, \ . \ . \ .\}$$

contains set W, the whole numbers, as a proper subset. All the properties that hold for set W can be shown to hold for set I. But in addition there is a property that holds for set I but does not hold for W:

10. Inverse property for addition: $a + (-a) = 0$

That is, for every element in I, there is another element in the set which when added to the first element gives 0. Again, such an extension need not be done in a formal way, but rather can come out of concrete experience and intuitive development of number concepts.

The system of *Rational numbers* (1.3), S,

$$S = \left\{\frac{a}{b} \,\middle|\, a \in I, b \in I, b \neq 0\right\}$$

requires a more careful development to carry through the theme of expansion of the number system. But a rational number can be designated by a *pair* of integers. Further rules for the addition and multiplication of these pairs can be generated and are typically expressed as follows:

If

$$\frac{a}{b} \in S, \quad \frac{c}{d} \in S$$

then

$$\frac{a}{b} + \frac{c}{d} = \frac{ad + bc}{bd}$$

and

$$\frac{a}{b} \cdot \frac{c}{d} = \frac{a \cdot c}{b \cdot d}$$

This provides a means for operations with rational numbers in terms of the operations with integers. Further, it is easily shown that when $b = 1$, a/b is equal to an integer. Therefore, a subset of set S has all of the values in set I. The previous set of properties, 1 to 10, can be shown to hold for set S, and one further property holds:

11. Inverse property for multiplication: For all rational numbers $a \neq 0$ there exists an inverse a^{-1} such that

$$a \cdot a^{-1} = 1$$

Or, since

$$a^{-1} = \frac{1}{a}$$

then

$$a \cdot \frac{1}{a} = 1$$

At some appropriate time the development can be continued to generate the set of *Real numbers* (1.4), R, and further, the generation of the set of *Complex numbers* (1.5), C (this is usually reserved for eleventh or twelfth grade)

The study of *Finite number systems* (1.6) in the secondary school has as its objective the illustration and understanding of number-systems properties and number systems; this is attained by providing some nontrivial contexts other than those in which arithmetic exercises and drill have been done by the student. The simplest of these is the set B of two elements

$$B = \{0,1\}$$

where addition (+) and multiplication (·) are defined as follows:

+	0	1
0	0	1
1	1	0

·	0	1
0	0	0
1	0	1

This corresponds to even and odd numbers

+	even	odd
even	even	odd
odd	odd	even

	even	odd
even	even	even
odd	even	odd

Matrices and determinants (1.7) are generally encountered at the eleventh or twelfth grade and represent a rather advanced "number systems" topic. Similarly, *Probability* concepts (1.8) are usually found only in an advanced course, if at all, in the secondary school. Some of the recent texts, however, are introducing probability concepts as early as seventh grade. Indeed, the language of probability is becoming more and more a part of our culture (e.g., in weather reports). Probability concepts can be expected to form part of the whole range of secondary school content in the future.

Concepts of *Numeration systems* (1.9) and elementary number-theory problems are found in most present seventh- and eighth-grade mathematics. Our aim is to understand the place-value, base 10 numeration system. In the past, mathematics curricula have included the study of other numeration systems, such as the Roman numerals, which are not place-value systems. This study is minimized in present mathematics curricula.

The study of place-value numeration systems in bases other than 10 has been incorporated into seventh- and eighth-grade classes over the past ten years. The primary reason for including such topics is to aid in understanding place value, exponentiation, and notation. The development of computational facility in base 5, base 2, or base 12 numeration is a misplaced emphasis. Similarly, extensive practice in changing from one number base to another is a dubious undertaking. But these are the emphases which have been stressed in the name of the "new mathematics." It has not been established, in fact, that any study of other number bases will lead to better understanding of base 10 numeration than would the same amount of effort expended on study of base 10. Therefore, it is even more likely that a heavy emphasis on the practice of computation in number bases other than 10 is misplaced effort.

The study of numeration other than base 10 is an acceptable objective in its own right; the hypothesis that such study will enhance the understanding of general principles of place-value numeration also has merit. But these reasons for teaching such numerations call for the development of concepts rather than for emphasis on computational facility.

Elementary topics in number theory, such as the study of factors and primes, are very important in seventh- and eighth-grade mathematics. Such topics generalize to algebra at the later grade levels. In addition, there is a wealth of problem material of interest to students after a very limited introduction to elementary concepts in number theory. For example, seventh-grade students study the properties of even and odd numbers.

Exponential notation is encountered throughout the secondary school mathematics curriculum. The study ranges from basic concepts during the study of factors and primes, through laws of exponentiation, to utilization in algebra, to noninteger exponents, and eventually, to the introduction to logarithms.

Also a part of the study of numeration systems for rational numbers are the various topics of decimal notation. For the most part, this is the province of the elementary school, but it does receive attention in grades 7 to 9, for some curricula.

Scientific notation has not been included in mathematics curricula to the extent that experts in science believe necessary. Certainly the use of scientific notation—that is, writing numbers as the product of a power of 10 and a decimal fraction with one digit to the left of the decimal—is becoming more a part of our cultural discourse, required for both mathematical literacy and the language of the scientist.

Algebra (2.0) As was stated previously, we want to consider the algebra content across grades 7 to 12, rather than a specific course. Certainly many algebra topics are closely related to topics we have included under number systems and will include under geometry. The dividing line between content areas is not important. Algebraic concepts are incorporated into all grade levels and probably include 40 to 60 percent of the total content in the secondary school.

The algebra content of secondary school mathematics programs seems to divide conveniently into three broad areas: *Algebraic expressions* (2.1), *Algebraic sentences and their solutions*

(2.2), and *Relations and functions* (2.3). We will describe each briefly.

Many of the basic concepts and tools in algebra would be included under the heading of *Algebraic expressions* (2.1). To begin with, there is an area of algebra content which is best described as vocabulary and symbolism. For example, the terms "variable," "domain," "open sentence," "truth set," "absolute value," "factor," "polynomial," and "function" have rather explicit meaning in algebraic content. There are conventions in the use of symbols such as parentheses for grouping, =, <, >, ≤, ≥, and | |, which are extensions of the use of the same symbols in number-systems content.

A second category under algebraic expressions would deal with algebraic representation. Here we are concerned with the algebra material which leads a student to familiarity with and mastery of the use of symbols to represent general form or pattern. This is the heart of the algebraic technique. It involves material on the use of a variable to represent an unspecified quantity; and it can involve the practice of representing quantitative phrases symbolically. For instance, "the sum of three times the number and five" might be represented concisely by "$3x + 5$." Or, we may be interested in the expression of a statement. For instance, "$0 < x < 10$" expresses the fact that we are interested in a number between 0 and 10. Algebraic representation can also be used to express a theorem, such as "If a and b represent the length of the legs of a right triangle and c the length of the hypotenuse, then $a^2 + b^2 = c^2$." On the other hand, an entire theory may be elegantly expressed with algebraic representation. The equation $E = mc^2$, which expresses the theory of relativity, is a well-known example.

Mathematical structure, which was discussed under number systems, is also very much the province of algebra. Students in algebra study the properties of groups, integral domains, and fields, although such algebraic structures may not be identified by name. Within this context, identities—that is, statements which are true for all replacements of the variable—are studied, and the proof of algebraic identities sometimes serves as the student's first introduction to mathematical proof. In this way, and through the study of proofs in geometry, the student is led indirectly to understand the principles of logic. Very seldom is an explicit unit on logic a part of the secondary school curriculum.

Factoring is a basic skill in algebra. For the most part, we are concerned with the factoring of a polynomial into the product of two or more polynomials or the product of a monomial and polynomials. Particular emphasis is given to the problem of factoring a trinomial into the product of two binomials.

There is, if you will, an arithmetic of algebraic expressions. In other words, algebraic expressions can be added, subtracted, multiplied, and divided. This set of manipulations of algebraic expressions—this arithmetic of algebraic expressions—we will call "rational operations." Rational operations may include the simplification of rational expressions, which may be encountered in grade 8, and a range of topics up through the so-called "synthetic division," which may be encountered in an eleventh- or twelfth-grade course.

Finally, forming the last category under algebraic expressions, there is a good deal of algebra content dealing with powers and roots.

The content for *Algebraic sentences and their solutions* (2.2) can be described more concisely than the content for algebraic expressions. Essentially, we identify six categories of algebraic sentences: *linear, quadratic, simultaneous, polynomial, logarithmic* and *exponential*, and *literal* or *formula*. Within each of these categories we identify the subtopics: equations and inequalities. It should be emphasized that for each of these types of algebraic sentences, we are interested in a whole range of behaviors, from manipulative exercises to complex problem solving. Except for literal equations and formulas, the categories of algebraic sentences are listed approximately in the order in which they are usually encountered in the curriculum. That is, simple linear sentences and their solutions are encountered in seventh grade, developed during eighth grade, and more or less mastered during ninth grade. Quadratic sentences, on the other hand, will generally not be encountered until the ninth grade, and then will be heavily emphasized in the eleventh-grade course. The study of simultaneous sentences is generally limited to linear sentences, and will be found late in the ninth-grade course and throughout the typical eleventh-grade course. Polynomial (higher-order) sentences will generally be studied in the eleventh and twelfth grades, as will logarithmic and exponential sentences.

In the present secondary school mathematics program, *Relations and functions* (2.3) are for the most part the province of eleventh- and twelfth-grade mathematics. It is expected that the notion of a function will be utilized as a unifying theme in some of the future mathematics curricula. Indeed, it can be argued that the notion of a function is an underlying theme of present curricula, but its explicit study does not occur until late in the ninth grade. Even then the emphasis is upon functions of continuous sets, such as polynomial or rational functions. In the eleventh and twelfth grades, considerable attention is given to the circular functions, exponential functions, and logarithmic functions. To a lesser extent, the functions of discrete sets, such as sequences, series, recursive functions, mathematical induction, or limits, are introduced in the secondary school curriculum. They are rarely studied in any depth. Similarly, the algebra of functions, or even the basic concepts, are studied very little in secondary school curricula.

Geometry (3.0) Again, it must be emphasized that we are discussing a content area that is incorporated throughout the secondary school curriculum from seventh grade through twelfth grade, rather than a specific course. We will divide the geometry content of the secondary school mathematics curriculum into the following categories: *Measurement* (3.1), *Geometric phenomena* (3.2), *Formal reasoning* (3.3), and *Coordinate systems and graphs* (3.4).

Most of the study of *Measurement* (3.1) in the secondary school mathematics curriculum builds upon the basic concepts developed in the elementary school in dealing with length along a line, length along an arc, angle, area, volume, time, money, and other measures. The secondary school mathematics curriculum goes into more depth in all these basic concepts and also includes two additional topics: error and approximation.

Basic *Geometric phenomena* (3.2) are studied intuitively in grades 7 and 8 and more formally in grade 10. The first category under the geometric phenomena would be the basic configurations. This would include definitions, some simple postulates or axioms, and some properties of points and lines.

The next subcategory of geometric phenomena would be the study of perpendiculars and parallels. For the most part, in the secondary school mathematics curriculum this topic is concerned with perpendicular and parallel lines; but the world around us is three-dimensional, and some informal study of 3-space is included.

Similarity and congruence are geometric phenomena of sufficient interest to warrant a separate category. Indeed, these two concepts occupy a substantial portion of the formal geometry course in grade 10.

Finally, topics dealing with construction and the locus of point sets are included in both the junior high school and the senior high school grades. Representative problems of great historical interest in the study of geometry are to be found in construction and locus problems.

When we talk of *Formal reasoning* (3.3) in the study of geometry, we are usually concerned with the study of proofs. It is well to keep in mind that a mathematical proof with its tight deductive presentation is the means by which a mathematician presents his work to other mathematicians. It does not represent the means by which he arrived at his result. The construction of a proof is very much like any other problem-solving activity: the one constructing the proof generates hypotheses and tests them, carries out plausible reasoning, and behaves in an inductive manner to construct a deductive argument.

The subcategory of *Coordinate systems and graphs* (3.4) includes the study of cartesian and polar coordinate systems, coordinate geometry, analytical geometry, vectors, and statistical graphs.

Sequential aspects As we have surveyed the content of the mathematics curriculum of the secondary schools, comments have been given on the grade placement of many topics. There is a sequential nature to the mathematics curriculum. A given topic may be presented at increasing levels of sophistication as successive grade levels. For instance, linear equations progress from

Table 19-3 Approximate Grade Placement of Mathematics Topics

	Grade						
Topic	*K–3*	*4–6*	*7–8*	*9*	*10*	*11–12*	
Number systems	Concept of zero and whole numbers. Place value. Counting. Addition and subtraction up to 3 place numbers.	Numeration systems. Nature, properties, and techniques of the operations on integers. Factors, primes, and exponents.	Nature, properties, and techniques of the operations on rationals. Introduction to negative integers. Decimal system. Factors, primes, and exponents.	Operations on negative numbers.		Irrational numbers. Real number system. Complex numbers.	
Algebra			Solutions of open sentences. Introduction to algebra.	Solutions of equations. Polynomials and factoring. Algebraic expressions.		Polynomials and factoring. Equations, systems of equations. Polynomial functions. Transcendental functions.	Transcendental functions. Algebra of trigonometry. Theory of equations.
Geometry	Awareness and definitions of common shapes.	Sets of points. Sides and relationships of triangle.	Informal plane geometry (coordinates, similarity and congruence).		Characteristics of lines, triangles, solid figures, other polygons, etc. Congruence and similarity. Loci and constructions.	Analytical geometry of quadratics. Graphs of functions.	Analytical geometry.
Measurement	Awareness of common systems.	Linear and angular measurement. Area.	Linear and angular measurement. Area. Volume. Metric systems.		Measurement as a system. Proofs involving measurements. Area, perimeter, etc.		
Application	Application of measurement. Simple arithmetic operations.	Application of measurement. Application of area. Problems involving more than one operation.	Application of measurement. Application of rational numbers. Area. Volume.	Application of algebra to solution of problems.	Application of loci.	Application of logarithms and trigonometry.	Introduction to calculus. (Tangent to a curve.) Probability and statistics. Functions.
Analysis, Logic, Statistics, etc.		Introduction to sets.	Sets. Graphs and measures of central tendency.		Proof (deductive).	Mathematical induction.	

SOURCE: Adapted from T. A. Romberg & J. Kilpatrick. Preliminary study on evaluation in mathematics education. In T. A. Romberg & J. W. Wilson, *The development of tests.* (NLSMA Report No. 7) Stanford, Calif.: School Mathematics Study Group, 1969. P. 285.

simple equations with integer coefficients, at eighth grade, to involved and complicated equations with real coefficients or to systems of linear equations, at the higher grades. On the other hand, some topics logically precede others. For example, the study of whole numbers naturally precedes the study of rational numbers.

To summarize and illustrate the approximate grade placement of various topics in the mathematics curriculum, Table 19-3 has been included. This table, taken from Romberg and Kilpatrick (1969), uses a slightly different content stratification, but the correspondence to the one presented in this chapter is obvious. Romberg and Kilpatrick include the sequence from kindergarten through sixth grade as well as from the secondary school.

Behaviors

Computation (A.0) The computation level represents the least complex behaviors which we expect from students as outcomes of instruction in mathematics. The computation level should be described so as to include exercises of simple recall and exercises of routine manipulation. The level represents primarily those outcomes which require of the student no decision making or complex memory.

The first subcategory is the *Knowledge of specific facts* (*A*.1). This could include objectives where the student is expected to reproduce or recognize material in almost exactly the same form as it was presented in the course of study. It could also include fundamental units of knowledge that a student can be reasonably assumed to know because he has been exposed to them over a long period of time. An example of the latter case would be the basic number facts: presumably, students in secondary school have been exposed to the number facts all through the elementary grades; items explicitly designed to measure number facts might not correspond to an explicit part of the course of study. On the other hand, to say that the student is expected to know that the measure of a right angle is 90° is an example of an outcome which assumes that material has been covered in the course of study.

A second subcategory under computation is *Knowledge of terminology* (*A*.2). For instance, for an appropriate course of study, students should be able to recognize an acute, an obtuse, or a right angle; in an algebra course they should know what is meant by the instruction "simplify the expression."

Obviously, knowledge of specific facts and knowledge of terminology are required as part of any more complex level of behavior. Measuring a more complex behavior, therefore, involves the indirect assessment of behaviors dealing with knowledge of specific facts or knowledge of terminology. There are objectives in the secondary school mathematics curriculum, however, for which we will want to assess these very elementary behaviors.

A most important subcategory of the computation level is the *Ability to carry out algorithms* (*A*.3). Restated, this is the ability to manipulate elements of a stimulus according to some learned rules. The student is not expected to select the algorithm; such selection involves a certain level of choosing and decision making which appropriately belongs at a more complex level of behavior. The algorithms are not limited to arithmetic: for instance, bisecting a line segment might be a computation behavior in geometry, and solving a simple linear equation might be a computation behavior in ninth-grade algebra.

Comprehension (B.0) Comprehension is designed to be a more complex set of behaviors than computation, although the dividing line between the categories is artificial and vague and computation-level behaviors are sometimes assumed or incorporated within comprehension-level behaviors.

Knowledge of concepts (*B*.1) is included as comprehension-level behavior because a concept is an abstraction, and an abstraction theoretically requires some implicit decision making in using a concept or in saying whether an object is an instance of a concept. In some sense, the knowledge of a concept is more complex than the knowledge of a specific fact.

Similar reasoning applies to the *Knowledge of principles, rules, and generalizations* (B.2); hence, such behaviors are included under comprehension. Such knowledge behaviors assume a correspondence with a course of study. Whether an item measures knowledge of a principle, rule, or generalization depends upon the material the student has studied. If he must *generate* a principle, rule, or generalization, or *use* a principle, rule, or generalization in order to answer a question, then the behavior is at a higher level than comprehension.

Knowledge of mathematical structure (B.3) is also a comprehension-level behavior. We are now talking about the properties of number systems and of algebraic structures, as discussed above in the description of content.

One central comprehension-level behavior is the *Ability to transform problem elements from one mode to another* (B.4). This can mean translation from a verbal description to a pictorial representation, or translation from a verbal representation to a symbolic form, or vice versa in each case.

Another comprehension-level behavior is the *Ability to follow a line of reasoning* (B.5). This might be restated as the "ability to read or listen to a mathematical argument." It is the ability to receive communication about mathematics.

Finally, the *Ability to read and interpret a mathematics problem* (B.6) is also a comprehension-level behavior. This is far less than the ability to solve a problem, but it is certainly a necessary first step. In the reading of mathematics material and problems, there appear to be skills involved that go beyond normal verbal skills and general reading ability.

Application (C.0) The application-level behaviors involve a sequence of responses from the student; this characteristic distinguishes them from computation-level or comprehension-level behaviors. On the other hand, the application-level behaviors are to be closely related to the course of study: they deal with activities that are routine in the sense that items like these application-level items (not identical to them) would have been studied. The transfer to new situations is minimal. Four categories of applications are identified.

The *Ability to solve routine problems* (C.1), in its most limited case, involves selecting and carrying out an algorithm. If the problem is stated verbally, the behavior of solving is preceded by the behavior of formulating the problem in symbolic terms. The sequence can be more complicated, for the problem may involve selecting a principle or rule, using the principle in selecting an algorithm or making several calculations. If it cannot be expected that the student will recognize the problem as similar to those he has studied in the course of instruction, then higher-order problem solving is required and the item would be at the analysis level.

The *Ability to make comparisons* (C.2) is an application-level behavior because the student is expected to recall relevant information (concepts, rules, mathematical structure, terminology), discover a relationship, and formulate a decision. When a student is making comparisons, he is in a sense generating an algorithm and then following the algorithm to make a decision. This generation is of a routine nature and therefore belongs at the application level rather than at the analysis level. An important part of this ability is the behavior of choosing from among available alternatives.

The *Ability to analyze data* (C.3) is the third applications category. This is a well-practiced part of the mathematics curriculum. It involves reading and interpreting information, manipulating that information, and making decisions or drawing conclusions as a result. The behavior is the ability to separate a problem into its component parts, to distinguish relevant from irrelevant information, and to establish a connection with subproblems which have already been solved.

The *Ability to recognize patterns, isomorphisms, and symmetries* (C.4) may involve recalling relevant information, transforming problem elements, manipulating these elements in a sequence, and recognizing a relationship. It is a sequence of behaviors and hence belongs rightfully at the application level. If the student is asked to formulate or generate new patterns, isomorphisms, or symmetries, then the behavior belongs at the analysis level. It is assumed that similar patterns, isomorphisms, or symmetries have been studied by the student and that recognition is possible; otherwise, a higher-level behavior is implied.

Analysis (D.0) This behavior level is the highest of the cognitive categories—comprising the most complex behaviors. It includes most behaviors described in the *Taxonomy* (Bloom, 1956) as analysis, synthesis, or evaluation. It includes what Avital and Shettleworth (1968) have called "open search." Here we will include nonroutine problem solving, discovery experiences, and creative behavior as it relates to mathematics. It differs from application-level or comprehension-level behaviors in that it involves a degree of transfer to a context in which there has been no practice. In order to respond satisfactorily to test items at this level, there must be a greater reliance on heuristic behavior. Many of the "ultimate" objectives of mathematics instruction are at the analysis level. Five categories of analysis-level behavior are identified.

The *Ability to solve nonroutine problems* (*D*.1) requires the student to exhibit transfer of previous mathematics learning to a new context. Perhaps some word other than "nonroutine" would be more descriptive; the objective is to develop the ability to solve problems unlike those which have been solved previously. Such problem solving may involve separating a problem into parts and exploring what can be learned about each part. It may involve reorganizing the problem elements in a new way in order to determine a solution. In all cases, the student is given a problem situation for which an algorithmic solution is not available to him. Perhaps a heuristic approach is required—such as establishing a plan and carrying it out, or repeatedly comparing the given situation and the goal to determine differences, which are in turn eliminated one at a time to gradually bring about a solution.

Another analysis-level category is the *Ability to discover relationships* (*D*.2). To discover requires the restructuring of problem elements in a new way to formulate a relationship. This ability differs from the last category of the applications level in that the student must discover (formulate) a new relationship rather than recognize a familiar relationship in new data.

The *Ability to construct proofs* (*D*.3) is an essential analysis-level behavior. The language of proof is the language by which the mathematician presents his work to his colleagues. Here, we are interested in the ability to construct proofs as opposed to the ability to reproduce proofs (application level) or recall proofs (computation level). Thus, when the proof of the theorem that $\sqrt{2}$ is irrational has been developed in class and then the item "Prove $\sqrt{3}$ is irrational" is assigned, most likely the proof will correspond exactly to the proof dealing with $\sqrt{2}$ and therefore will exhibit application-level behavior.

The *Ability to criticize proofs* (*D*.4) is an analysis-level behavior. Perhaps this could be stated a little more generally as the "ability to criticize any mathematical argument."

Finally, the *Ability to formulate and validate generalizations* (*D*.5) is included as an analysis-level behavior category. It is similar to some previous analysis categories; stated another way, it is the ability to discover a relationship and to construct a proof to substantiate the discovery.

Interests and attitudes (E.0) We now begin expanding the model of mathematics achievement given in Table 19-2 by adding on some noncognitive types of behavior. The first of these categories, called *Interests and attitudes* for lack of a better title, will in fact include the affective categories *Attitude* (*E*.1), *Interest* (*E*.2), *Motivation* (*E*.3), *Anxiety* (*E*.4), and *Self-concept* (*E*.5).

Any affective construct has an object associated with it. One does not just have an attitude; rather, one has an attitude *toward* something. The "something" here is mathematics or the various pieces of mathematics. Therefore, we are interested in attitudes toward mathematics, interests in mathematics, motivation to study mathematics, and so forth.

An affect, whether it be an attitude, an interest, a motivation, an anxiety, or a self-concept, tends to have three components. The first of these is the object—mathematics in this case. The second is a feeling, an emotion. This emotion has a direction, or valence, and, it is assumed, some strength—otherwise it could not be measured. The third component is a tendency to act on the object according to the valence and strength of the feeling.

The affective outcomes are important objectives of mathematics instruction. That is, we want students to develop or maintain a strong positive feeling toward mathematics. But all these affective outcomes are complex. They present measurement problems much more difficult than those presented by cognitive outcomes. Nevertheless, attention must be paid to them in the evaluation of our instruction. The reader is guided once again to the chapter by Corcoran and Gibb (1961) for a discussion of the testing of these outcomes. Aiken (1969) has presented a comprehensive review of recent research on attitudes toward mathematics.

Appreciation (F.0) The appreciation of mathematics is one of our often-stated objectives—hence, it is added here as a sixth behavior category. Three categories of appreciation are distinguished.

First, *Extrinsic appreciation* (F.1) deals with the usefulness of mathematics. We can justify and appreciate mathematics because of its social utility. It is necessary for ordinary communication and the conduct of business.

Intrinsic appreciation (F.2), on the other hand, is an appreciation of mathematics that is derived from its structure, its power, and its beauty. Mathematics is an art; to understand this is to have some intrinsic appreciation of mathematics. We do mathematics because it is fun; we enjoy it—we have, then, some intrinsic appreciation of mathematics.

There is an *Operational appreciation* (F.3) of mathematics, however, that overlaps each of the other two, yet is distinct. This is the appreciation of mathematics that comes from communicating mathematics to others, where the mathematics is the object of the communication (as opposed to the means). The most obvious type of operational appreciation is the desire to teach mathematics to others.

Two contemporary secondary school mathematics courses

In this section, we are concerned with the description of two contemporary mathematics courses. An attempt has been made to relate the courses to the expanded model. There was a vast change in the objectives of mathematics instruction in the 1960s. To some extent, this may be explained in terms of new content; but the greatest portion of the changes have occurred in the shift of expected behaviors. It is a shift from an emphasis on computation and application to an emphasis on comprehension and analysis, the inclusion of some noncognitive outcomes, and the exploration of developing intrinsic appreciation rather than extrinsic appreciation.

Seventh-grade mathematics

The contemporary seventh-grade mathematics course is to a large extent concerned with outcomes in the following shaded cells of Table 19-1:

	BEHAVIORS					
CONTENT	*A.0*	*B.0*	*C.0*	*D.0*	*E.0*	*F.0*
1.0						
2.0						
3.0						

This is not to say that outcomes in the unshaded regions are ignored. But the objectives of a contemporary seventh-grade mathematics course are primarily in the content areas of number systems and geometry.

Two cells in the model, *B*.0-1.0 and *C*.0-1.0, have been heavily shaded. Probably 50 to 60 percent of the objectives of mathematics instruction in seventh grade can be classified under the headings of comprehension and application of number systems. Typically, a contemporary seventh-grade course will include the study of whole numbers (1.1), numeration (1.9), rational numbers (1.3), factoring and primes (1.1), perhaps the integers (1.2), and occasionally some probability (1.8). The emphasis will tend to be not on computation but rather on conceptual development (*B*.0) and problem-solving activities (*C*.0 and *D*.0).

Geometry in the seventh grade is generally at an introductory and intuitive level (*A*.0 and *B*.0). Measurement may include a good deal of application-level behavior (*C*.0). But the study of nonmetric geometry, parallels, triangles, and circles for the most part is first encountered at this point in the curriculum, and the outcomes emphasized tend to be at the computation and comprehension levels (*A*.0 and *B*.0).

The first course in algebra

The content of the first course in algebra twenty or thirty years ago was not greatly different from the contemporary first course. Students worked with variables, simplified algebraic expressions, solved algebraic sentences, worked with radicals, made graphs, and struggled with quadratic polynomials, as students do now. The changes in mathematics programs during the 1950s and 1960s were not with the basic content. Rather, there were emphases on precision of language, reorganization of content to correspond with mathematical structures, and the inclusion of work with inequalities. Most important, there was a shift of objectives from the algorithmic and routine application to the heuristic and creative. Topics in proof were incorporated. It became fashionable to enjoy mathematics as an activity in itself rather than as a tool.

The contemporary algebra course emphasizes objectives in the following shaded cells of the model:

	BEHAVIORS					
CONTENT	*A*.0	*B*.0	*C*.0	*D*.0	*E*.0	*F*.0
1.0						
2.0						
3.0						

The number-systems content in the contemporary algebra course includes concepts about the system of real numbers (1.4). The geometry material deals primarily with the graphs of equations (3.4) to solve problems or to find the solutions to equations.

Summative evaluation

This section is devoted to providing sample items which measure outcomes of mathematics instruction in each of the behavior levels of the expanded model shown in Table 19-1. In each case, items are provided from several content and possible grade-level categories.

In order to illustrate that an item is appropriate for measuring a particular level of behavior, assumptions often need to be made about the background of a student. In some cases, but not always, such assumptions are discussed along with the item.

It is clear that for a particular student, the response to an item may not illustrate the level of behavior indicated here. For instance, if the student has been provided with the proof that $\sqrt{2}$ is an irrational number, then the item "Prove $\sqrt{3}$ is irrational" may elicit application-level behavior (*C*.0) rather than analysis-level behavior (*D*.0). If a student has already solved a problem, then he may only have to recall the solution (*A*.0) rather than develop it. Providing the solution to a problem may be an analysis- or application-level behavior the first time a student encounters the problem; on subsequent encounters with the same problem, the behavior may be at the computation level (recall of specific facts—the previous solution).

Another problem in determining the level of behavior at which to place an item is that the way a student solves a problem may determine the level of behavior. That is, for certain items some students may respond with analysis-level behavior while other students respond with routine, algorithmic application-level behavior. For example, consider the following problem: "Find the sum of the integers from 1 to 25." This problem can be solved by simply adding $1 + 2 + 3 + 4 + 5 + \cdots + 25$ in a straightforward application of addition algorithms. On the other hand, analysis-level behavior may be used to solve this problem, as the often-cited anecdote about Gauss and his solution illustrates. The story is that young Gauss was given a similar problem by his teacher in order to keep him occupied, but he was through in a very short time. Upon examination of his work, the teacher found that he had solved the problem in an insightful way, with only a small amount of calculation. Observe that if the sum is written *twice*, in the following way,

$$\begin{array}{l} 1 + \ 2 + \ 3 + \ 4 + \cdots + 24 + 25 \\ 25 + 24 + 23 + 22 + \cdots + \ 2 + \ 1 \end{array}$$

then adding corresponding terms in every case gives 26. There are 25 of these, and therefore *two* of the sums gives $25 \cdot 26$, or 650. Therefore, the sum is 325. Clearly, young Gauss was engaged in analysis-level behavior in finding this solution.

The examples given in this section are meant to illustrate the level at which it is judged *most* students, or the "average" student, would be expected to respond for a particular grade level. It should not be necessary to keep repeating hedging phrases such as "would normally be expected" or "on the average."

Many of these items have been taken from textbooks, tests, or other publications. The source is cited with the item in such cases, and complete documentation can be found in the References section at the end of the chapter.

The computation-level behaviors include knowledge of specific facts, knowledge of terminology, and the ability to carry out algorithms. Sample items for each of these categories are readily available in multiple-choice and other formats. Each of the subcategories of computation-level behavior is examined separately.

Knowledge of specific facts (A.1) Often we want to test at the end of the unit to see if the specific facts covered in this instruction have been learned. Items for this purpose assume the material has been presented in the same way as in the item.

A.1-1.1

1. Which of the following is not a whole number?
   a. 0 c. $1/2$
   b. 3 d. 4

A.1-1.3

2. The multiplication inverse of 5 is
   a. -5 d. 5
   b. $-\frac{1}{5}$ e. [Don't know]
   c. $\frac{1}{5}$

(Lankton, 1965, p. 3. Reproduced from Lankton First-year Algebra Test, copyright 1965 by Harcourt, Brace and World, Inc. Reproduced by special permission of the publisher.)

3. State the addition algorithm for rational numbers a/b and c/d.

$$\frac{a}{b} + \frac{c}{d} = \underline{\hspace{3em}}$$

A.1-1.4

4. Which of the following operations is not defined for the real numbers?
   a. $3 + 0$ d. $\frac{3}{0}$
   b. 3×0 e. $0 - 3$
   c. $\frac{0}{3}$

A.1-2.2, A.1-3.4

5. Write an example of two equations for parallel lines.

Item 5 would be knowledge of a specific fact in an eleventh-grade algebra course where the topics of graphing, slope, and intercept had been taught. On the other hand, if the item was an exercise given very early in the study of graphs of linear equations, it could well be considered an analysis-level item. Note that the item may be placed in the content categories under *Algebraic sentences* (2.2) or *Coordinate systems* (3.4).

A.1-3.1

6. The formula for the circumference of a circle with a radius r is

   a. $C = \pi r^2$ c. $C = \pi r$

   b. $C = 2\pi r$ d. $C = 2\pi$

(Romberg & Kilpatrick, 1969, p. 289.)

7. Which is longest?

   a. 35 inches c. 1 yard

   b. $3\frac{1}{2}$ feet d. 1 meter

A.1-3.4

8. The *slope* of a horizontal line is

Item 7 might be considered an extremely simple applications item, since although the students might go through a sequence of behaviors to translate all lengths to inches and then make comparison, it is more likely that most of the relationships are known as specific facts without translation.

Knowledge of terminology (A.2) There is a great deal of terminology in the study of mathematics. The danger exists, in fact, that we may become so immersed in terminology that our tests are too full of items measuring knowledge of it.

A.2-1.0

9. The set with no elements is called the ________ set.

10. Identify the properties which are illustrated by the following:

   (1) $a + b = b + a$ (4) $a \cdot (b + c) = a \cdot b + a \cdot c$

   (2) $a + 0 = a$ (5) $a \cdot 1 = a$

   (3) $a + (b + c) = (a + b) + c$ (6) $a \cdot b = b \cdot a$

The following item measures knowledge of the factorial symbol and hence is included under knowledge of terminology.

A.2-1.1

11. 5! equals

   a. $5 \times 5 \times 5 \times 5 \times 5$ d. $5 + 4 + 3 + 2 + 1$

   b. $\sqrt[5]{5}$ e. $\frac{5 \times 4}{2}$

   c. $5 \times 4 \times 3 \times 2 \times 1$

A.2-1.3

12. Write five names of the coordinate of the point associated with $\frac{2}{3}$.

A.2-1.4

13. The absolute value of any number is written as

   a. $\sqrt{k}$ d. k

   b. $|k|$ e. [Don't know]

   c. $-k$

(Lankton, 1965, p. 4. Reproduced from Lankton First-year College Test, copyright 1965 by Harcourt, Brace and World, Inc. Reproduced by special permission of the publisher.)

A.2-2.1

14. Write an example of

   (1) a trinomial

   (2) a binomial

   (3) a monomial

   (4) a polynomial that is none of the above

A.2-3.2

15. A polygon has

   a. exactly three sides d. more than three sides

   b. exactly five sides e. three or more sides

   c. fewer than five sides

(Wilson et al., 1968e, p. 292.)

16. Draw an example of an isosceles triangle.

17. A segment joining one vertex of a triangle and the midpoint of the opposite side is called
    a. a median
    b. an angle bisector
    c. an altitude
    d. a perpendicular bisector
    e. a diagonal
18. A polygon which is both equilateral and equiangular is called
    a. complex
    b. scalene
    c. regular
    d. asymmetric
    e. spherical
19. In which of the following figures are angles x and y adjacent?

a.
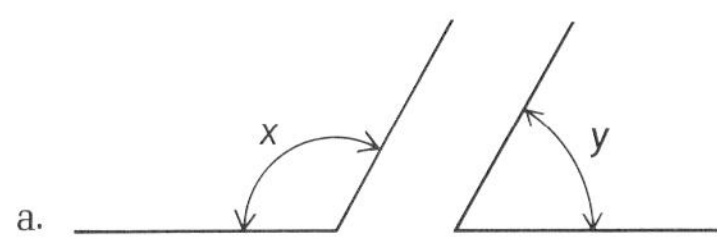

b.
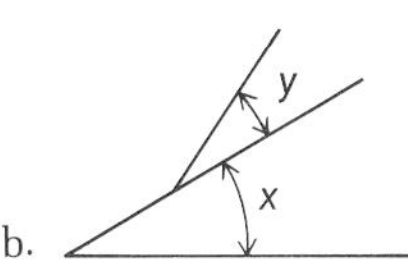

d.
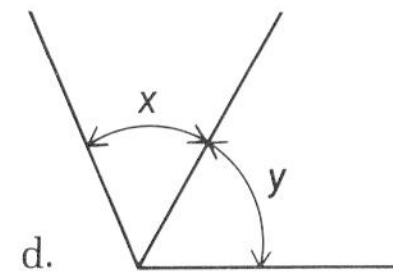

c.
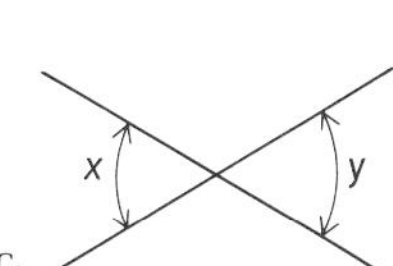

e.
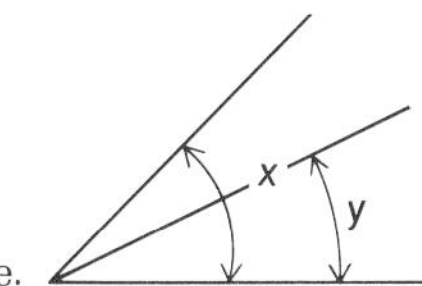

(Wilson et al., 1968e, pp. 292, 295, 293.)

A.2-3.3

20. An axiom is
    a. a proof
    b. a corollary
    c. an undefined term
    d. a proposition to be proved
    e. an assumption

The example items which have been given for computation subcategories *A*.1 and *A*.2 require no discussion. Let us go on to the third subcategory, for which sample items are also plentiful.

Ability to carry out algorithms (A.3) These items should have in common the expectation that students will be required to perform routine manipulations of the elements in the problem in a manner they have previously learned. The items should require essentially no decision making. Items for numerical calculation, such as follow below, are obviously in this subcategory.

A.3-1.1

21. Which of the following is a prime number?
    a. 6
    b. 11
    c. 15
    d. 39
    e. 51

Although a student could use a search strategy to answer item 21, the typical exposure to primes and factors in seventh grade and eighth grade would probably induce a manipulative response to this item.

A.3-1.2

22. $6-(-3)=$ __________.

Item 22, merely representative of many routine exercises, does explicitly ask a question about a particularly troublesome type of calculation when the student is first introduced to directed numbers.

A.3-1.3

23. Divide 10.342 by 2.61.
24. $93.6 \div 3 =$
    a. 3.12 b. 31.2 c. 312 d. 280.8
25. $\frac{2}{3} \div \frac{1}{6} =$
    a. $\frac{1}{9}$ b. $\frac{1}{4}$ c. 4 d. 6
26. Subtract: $3^{1}/_{4} - {}^{1}/_{3}$
    a. ${}^{3}/_{4}$ b. $2^{1}/_{12}$ c. $2^{11}/_{12}$ d. $3^{1}/_{12}$ e. $3^{1}/_{7}$

(Wilson et al., 1968b, p. 3.)

27. Convert to a *percent:* ${}^{1}/_{20}$.
    a. 5% b. 10% c. 20% d. 40%
28. Express the following as fractions in lowest terms:
    ${}^{3}/_{15}$ ${}^{25}/_{45}$
    ${}^{10}/_{12}$ ${}^{24}/_{39}$
29. What is the least common denominator of ${}^{1}/_{105}$ and ${}^{1}/_{70}$?

A.3-1.4

30. Find $\sqrt{324}$.

A.3-1.9

31. Multiply (1.3×10^6) by (1.1×10^4).

The last item would be a computation-level item for students exposed to the study of scientific notation or for eleventh-grade algebra students.

So far, all the example items in this subcategory have come from the number-systems content. More items are readily available in exercise sets from almost any seventh- or eighth-grade mathematics textbook, from the NLSMA reports, and from published tests on arithmetic computation. It will be more fruitful now to provide additional examples from the other content areas.

32. If $x + 2 = y$, what is the value of $|x - y| + |y - x|$?
    a. -4 b. 0 c. 2 d. 4
    e. It cannot be determined from the information given.

(Adapted from College Entrance Examination Board, 1970, p. 53.)

33. $\frac{a-b}{a+b} - \frac{b}{a+b}$ equals
    a. $\frac{1}{b}$
    b. $\frac{a-1}{a}$
    c. $\frac{a}{2(a+b)}$
    d. $\frac{a-2b}{a+b}$
    e. $\frac{a-2b}{a(a+b)}$

(Lankton, 1965, p. 3. Reproduced from Lankton First-year Algebra Test, copyright 1950 by Harcourt, Brace and World, Inc. Reproduced by permission of the publisher.)

A.3-2.2

34. Multiply the following:
    $(x + 2)(x + 3)$ $(x - 6)(x + 4)$
    $(2x + 3)(x + 1)$ $(x - 3)(x - 2)$

35. If $\frac{1}{8}x = 12$, then x equals
    a. $\frac{2}{3}$ b. $\frac{3}{2}$ c. 96 d. 20 e. [Don't know]

(Lankton, 1965, p. 3. Reproduced from Lankton First-year Algebra Test, copyright 1965 by Harcourt, Brace and World, Inc. Reproduced by special permission of the publisher.)

Item 36 would most likely be a computation-level item for the eleventh-grade algebra student.

A.3-2.2

36. Solve the following set of equations and check your result in both equations.
    $x^2 - 3xy + 8y^2 = 9$ $x - 2y = 3$

37. Solve the equation $x + \frac{1}{x} = x - \frac{1}{x}$
    a. 0
    b. 1
    c. 0 and 1
    d. -1
    e. The equation has no solution.

(Wilson et al., 1968f, p. 185.)

38. Solve $\frac{7}{n} - \frac{5}{n} = \frac{1}{4}$.

39. Solve $x^2 - 7x + 12 = 0$.

40. If $x^2 + kx + 6 = (x + 2)(x + 3)$ for all x, then k equals
    a. -1
    b. 1
    c. 3
    d. 5
    e. 6

41. If $F = \frac{GmM}{d^2}$, then m equals
    a. $\frac{Fd^2}{GM}$
    b. Fd^2GM
    c. $\frac{F + d^2}{GM}$
    d. $\frac{FGM}{d^2}$
    e. $Fd^2 - GM$

(Wilson et al., 1968f, p. 32.)

A.3-2.3

42. Find the positive value of $\sin\left(\arctan \frac{2}{\sqrt{5}}\right)$.

(University of the State of New York, 1960.)

Item 42 would be a computation item for eleventh- or twelfth-grade students who had studied the circular functions and their inverses. Likewise, item 43 assumes exposure to circular functions.

A.3-2.3

43. In triangle ABC, $a = 5$, $b = 7$ and $c = 8$. The cosine of angle C is

a. $\frac{1}{7}$ b. $\frac{2}{7}$ c. $\frac{1}{10}$ d. $\frac{7}{8}$

(University of the State of New York, 1960.)

A.3-3.1

44. The circumference of a circle is 8π inches. What is the area of the circle?
    a. 8π sq in.
    b. 16π sq in.
    c. 32π sq in.
    d. 64π sq in.
    e. 256π sq in.

A.3-3.2

45. Find by construction the center of the circle below.

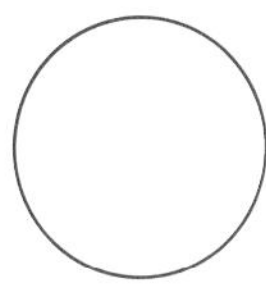

(University of the State of New York, 1960.)

46. In bisecting a line segment, you
    a. also construct a perpendicular to the line segment
    b. use a pencil, protractor, and straightedge
    c. need an accurate ruler for measuring
    d. [do] none of these

(Romberg & Kilpatrick, 1969, p. 289.)

47. Construct a triangle ABC on segment AB such that $\triangle ABC$ is similar to $\triangle PQR$.

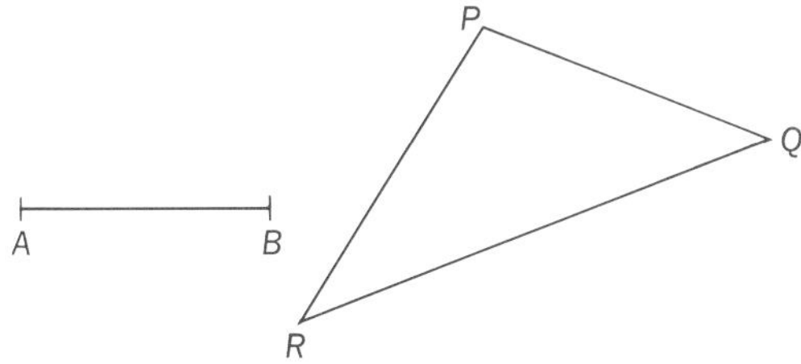

48. Inscribe a regular hexagon in a circle by construction.

A.3-3.4

49. The graph of the equation $y = mx + b$ is shown by l_1 in the figure. Write an appropriate equation for l_2.

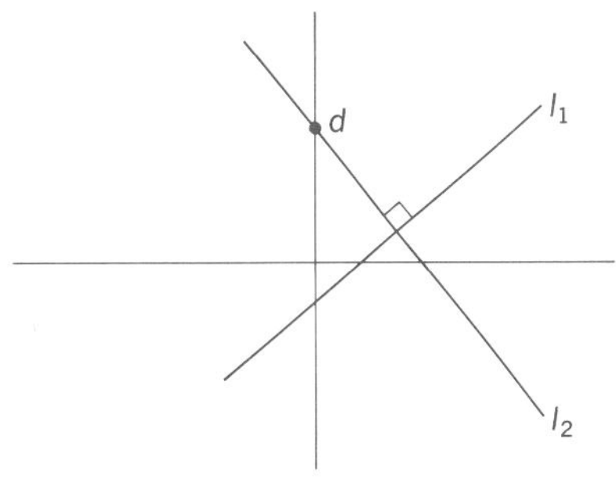

(Romberg & Kilpatrick, 1969, p. 297.)

Questions for comprehension (B.0)

The same pattern will be followed here as was used in the preceding section. Sample items from each of the subcategories of *Comprehension* will be provided.

Knowledge of concepts (B.1) The distinction between knowledge of a concept and knowledge of a specific fact is not sharply defined. In a sense, a concept is made up of a set of attributes, and each of these attributes is a specific fact. Therefore, one may look upon a concept as a *set* of related specific facts; but this subtle distinction is not particularly helpful. If will suffice to observe that a concept is intended to be a more cognitively complex thing than a specific fact. The exact location of the dividing line between them is not as relevant as the recognition of extremes in levels of complexity.

B.1-1.1

50. In what way does the set of whole numbers differ from the set of natural numbers?
51. Write the prime factors of 120.

B.1-1.3

52. If the following rational numbers are arranged in order of their closeness to 1, then the order would be
    a. $\frac{3}{4}, \frac{3}{2}, \frac{1}{3}, \frac{7}{8}, \frac{4}{3}$
    b. $\frac{1}{3}, \frac{3}{4}, \frac{7}{8}, \frac{4}{3}, \frac{3}{2}$
    c. $\frac{3}{2}, \frac{4}{3}, \frac{7}{8}, \frac{3}{4}, \frac{1}{3}$
    d. $\frac{7}{8}, \frac{3}{4}, \frac{4}{3}, \frac{3}{2}, \frac{1}{3}$
    e. $\frac{3}{2}, \frac{1}{3}, \frac{3}{4}, \frac{7}{8}, \frac{4}{3}$

(Wilson et al., 1968f, p. 206.)

B.1-1.5

53. Given the complex number $5 + 3i$, its conjugate is
   a. $-5 + 3i$ c. $5 - 3i$
   b. $3 + 5i$ d. $3 - 5i$

B.1-2.1

54. If $f(x) = 2x + 1$ and $g(x) = 3x - 1$, then $f(g(x)) =$
   a. $6x - 1$
   b. $6x + 2$
   c. $x - 2$
   d. $5x$
   e. $6x^2 + x - 1$

(Adapted from College Entrance Examination Board, 1970, p. 54.)

B.1-2.2, B.1-3.4

55. Which of the following is an equation of the straight line through the points $(0, -2)$ and $(3,4)$?
   a. $y = -2x + 2$ d. $y = x - 2$
   b. $y = \frac{1}{2}x - 2$ e. $y = 2x - 2$
   c. $y = \frac{2}{3}x - 2$

B.1-2.2

56. Any formula may be expressed in the form of
   a. a binomial d. a distribution
   b. an equation e. a percent
   c. a radical

(Adapted from Orshansky, 1948, p. 6.)

B.1-2.3

57. *The volume of a gas increases as the pressure decreases.* In this connection the idea of "function" in mathematics may be best illustrated by the statement,
   a. "The volume of a gas is a function of the gas."
   b. "The volume of a gas is a function of the increase in volume."
   c. "The volume of a gas is a function of the pressure of a gas."
   d. "The volume of a gas increases as the function of the pressure."
   e. "The volume of a gas is an independent function."

(Adapted from Orshansky, 1950a, p. 4.)

B.1-3.2

58. Suppose A and B are two acute angles of $p°$ and $q°$, respectively. A and B are complementary angles if and only if
   a. $p - q = 0$ d. $0 < p + q < 90$
   b. $p + q = 90$ e. $90 < p + q < 180$
   c. $p + q = 180$

59. How many endpoints does a ray have?
   a. None d. Three
   b. One e. Infinitely many
   c. Two

60. A matchbox is a model of a
   a. pyramid d. rhomboid
   b. tetrahedron e. parallelepiped
   c. dodecahedron

(Wilson et al., 1968e, pp. 294, 296.)

61. If two angles are complementary, then both are
   a. acute d. congruent
   b. obtuse e. similar
   c. right

62. Which of the following *cannot* be a plane figure?
   a. circle d. trapezoid
   b. quadrilateral e. pentagon
   c. tetrahedron

Item 63 deals with geometric phenomena (3.2) rather than measurement (3.1), because it is the concept of an obtuse angle that is being assessed.

B.1-3.2

63. Which of the following is the measure of an obtuse angle?
   a. 45° d. 180°
   b. 90° e. 225°
   c. 135°

64. What is the locus of points in a plane at a given distance from a given point?
   a. A line
   b. Two parallel lines
   c. Two perpendicular lines
   d. A circle
   e. Two points

(Wilson et al., 1968e, p. 300.)

Knowledge of principles, rules, and generalizations (B.2) These items pertain to relationships among concepts and problem elements which the student can be expected to know as a result of his course of study. The same items might well measure analysis-level behaviors if the item represented the student's first contact with the principle, rule, or generalization.

B.2-1.3

65. If the numerator and denominator of a fraction each are multiplied by the same number
    a. the fraction will become smaller.
    b. the fraction will remain the same in value.
    c. the fraction will become larger.
    d. the result will depend on whether the number is greater than 1 or less than 1.

(Thorpe, Lefever, & Naslund, 1955, p. 16. From *SRA Achievement Series, Arithmetic, Grades 6–9, Form A.* Copyright 1955 by Science Research Associates, Inc. Reproduced by permission of the publisher.)

66. If three fractions have denominators that are relatively prime, the least common denominator is equal to the
    a. largest denominator
    b. smallest denominator
    c. product of all three denominators
    d. largest factor common to the three denominators
    e. sum of all three denominators.

67. If the numerator and denominator of a fraction are equal, the value of the fraction
    a. is always greater than 1
    b. is always less than 1
    c. is always equal to 1
    d. depends on the size of the numerator.

68. If the decimal point in a number is moved *three places to the right*, we are
    a. dividing the number by 1000
    b. dividing the number by 100
    c. multiplying the number by 3
    d. multiplying the number by 1000.

(Thorpe, Lefever, & Naslund, 1955, p. 16. From *SRA Achievement Series, Arithmetic, Grades 6–9, Form A.* Copyright 1955 by Science Research Associates, Inc. Reproduced by permission of the publisher.)

B.2-3.2

69. DIRECTIONS: For each of the following statements, fill the blank with
    A if the triangles are similar but not necessarily congruent
    B if the triangles are congruent but not necessarily similar
    C if the triangles are congruent and similar
    D if the triangles are not necessarily congruent or similar

    ____(1) The angles of one triangle are congruent, respectively, to the angles of another triangle.
    ____(2) Two angles of one triangle are congruent, respectively, to two angles of another triangle.
    ____(3) One angle of one triangle is congruent to one angle of another triangle.
    ____(4) Three sides of one triangle are congruent, respectively, to three sides of another triangle.

70. If the intersection of two different planes is not empty, then the intersection is
    a. a point
    b. two different points
    c. a line
    d. two different lines
    e. a plane

71. The sum of the angles of a triangle
    a. is between 90° and 180°
    b. is 180°
    c. is between 180° and 360°
    d. is 360°
    e. depends on the sizes of the angles

72. An exterior angle of a triangle equals the
    a. sum of the interior angles
    b. sum of the nonadjacent interior angles
    c. sum of the exterior angles
    d. difference of the nonadjacent interior angles
    e. difference of the nonadjacent exterior angles

(Wilson et al., 1968e, pp. 292, 293, 298.)

B.2-3.4

73. A line k is perpendicular to the line whose equation is $2x + 2y + 3 = 0$. What is the slope of line k?

(University of the State of New York, 1960.)

Knowledge of mathematical structure (B.3)

The behaviors to be measured by items in this category are distinct from knowledge of terminology (*A*.2). Too often, items dealing only with the terminology of modern mathematics have been used to measure the knowledge of mathematical structure (see Romberg, 1968). It is this mathematical structure which is proposed as a unifying theme in the secondary school mathematics program; knowledge of this structure must, therefore, be assessed.

Let us begin the sample items for this category with items designed for use in the upper elementary grades. There is no harm in persons interested in secondary school mathematics taking an occasional glance into the elementary program. The following set of items are from the NLSMA fourth- and sixth-grade batteries.

B.3-1.1

74. WHICH IS THE MISSING NUMBER?

$24 + 76 = 76 + \square$

a. 24
b. 34
c. 52
d. 100
e. None of these

$6 \times 15 = \square \times 6$

a. 9
b. 15
c. 90
d. 540
e. None of these

$(108 \div 12) \times \square = 108$

a. 1
b. 9
c. 10
d. 12
e. None of these

$(70 + 30) + 50 = 70 + (\square + 50)$

a. 20
b. 30
c. 50
d. 70
e. None of these

$(64 \times \square) \div 16 = 64$

a. 0
b. 4
c. 16
d. 64
e. None of these

$3 \times 26 = (3 \times \square) + (3 \times 6)$

a. 2
b. 6
c. 20
d. 26
e. None of these

(Wilson et al., 1968d, p. 93.)

The six questions above make up a short NLSMA test scale titled "Whole Number Structure." Students *might* respond by solving the equations, but more likely they will respond on the basis of properties from mathematical structure.

The next item is for eleventh-grade algebra students.

B.3-1.1, B.3-2.1

75. If $(N + 68)^2 = 654{,}481$, then $(N + 58)(N + 78) = (?)$.

a. 654,381
b. 654,471
c. 654,481
d. 654,581
e. 654,524

(Wilson et al., 1968f, p. 202.)

The response to item 75 will be based on a knowledge of the structure or form. On the other hand, students at lower grade levels would probably respond to this question by attempting to solve the equation.

B.3-1.1

76. For what number n does $47 \times 52 = (47 \times n) + (47 \times 2)$?

a. 2
b. 50
c. 52
d. 2350
e. 2444

(Wilson et al., 1968e, p. 251.)

B.3-1.4

77. If $a \cdot b = 0$, then

a. a must be zero
b. b must be zero
c. either a or b must be zero
d. both a and b must be zero
e. all the choices above are correct

B.3-2.1

78. If $P = M + N$, then which of the following will be true?

I. $N = P - M$
II. $P - N = M$
III. $N + M = P$

a. I only
b. III only
c. I and II only
d. II and III only
e. I, II and III

79. If the number b is between a and c, then

a. $2b$ is between $2c$ and $2a$
b. $2c$ is between $2a$ and $2b$
c. $2a$ is between $2b$ and $2c$
d. all of the above
e. none of the above

B.3-2.2

80. What number can you use for *both* frames to make this sentence *false*?

$25 + \diamond = \diamond + 30 - 5$

a. 0
b. 5
c. 25
d. No number
e. Every number

(Wilson, 1968e, pp. 251, 252.)

Ability to transform problem elements from one mode to another (B.4) This is probably the most easily identified ability at the comprehension level. The student is asked to translate, but the ability to translate does not include carrying out an algorithm after the translation. Therefore, transforming a verbal statement into an equation calls for this ability, but solving the problem would be an application-level accomplishment even though it requires only carrying out an algorithm after the translation.

B.4-1.3

81. $\frac{1}{8}$ percent of x =

a. .000125x
b. .00125x
c. .0125x
d. .125x
e. 1.25x

82. According to one plan for traveling to Mars, the round trip would take nearly three earth years, including a stay on Mars of 449 earth days. If 34,000,000 miles is taken as the distance between Mars and earth, which of the following can be used to determine the average speed of travel in miles per hour?

a. $\frac{(3 \times 365 - 449) \times 12}{34{,}000{,}000}$

b. $\frac{34{,}000{,}000}{(3 \times 365 - 449) \times 24}$

c. $\frac{2 \times 34{,}000{,}000}{(3 \times 365 - 449) \times 24}$

d. $\frac{34{,}000{,}000 \times 24}{2 \times (3 \times 365 - 449)}$

(Adapted from Educational Testing Service, 1957a, p. 6.)

B.4-1.3, B.4-2.2

83. Write an equation that could be used to solve the following problem. State what the letter or letters represent. (Solution of the equation is not required.)

A tailor paid $144 for material for some suits. The following season he sent the same amount of money for the same material but was informed that, because of an increase in cost of $1 per yard, he would receive 2 yards less. How many yards of material were in the first order?

B.4-1.4

84. Suppose that an operation $\triangle$ on any numbers a and b is defined by $a \triangle b = a + (a \times b)$. Then $5 \triangle 2$ equals

a. 10
b. 12
c. 15
d. 20
e. 35

(Wilson et al., 1968e, p. 251.)

B.4-1.9

85. In Circleland, people write:

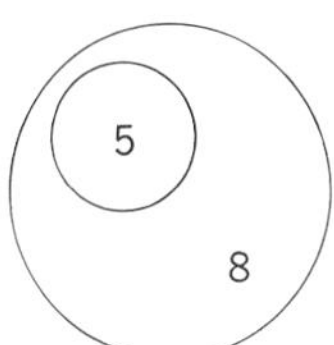

when they mean 58, and they write:

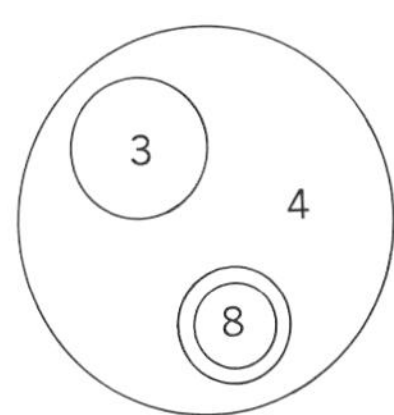

when they mean 834. What number do you think they mean when they write the following?

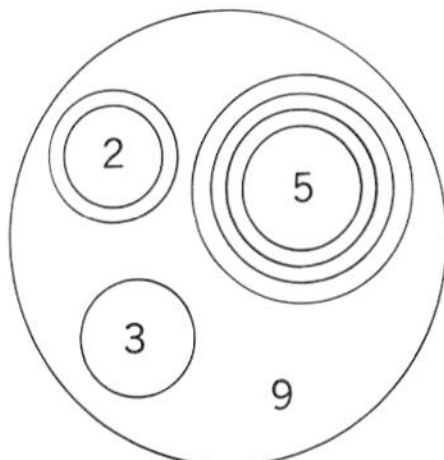

a. 2359 b. 5239 c. 9325 d. 50239 e. 55239

(Wilson et al., 1968f, p. 201.)

86. A new system of number notation uses the following symbols:

△ stands for zero　　□ stands for five

◇ stands for eight　　○ stands for two

Which is the correct answer to the example below?

□△○
− ○◇△

a. □△○　　d. ○○◇
b. ○△○　　e. ○○○
c. □○○

(Wilson et al., 1968a, p. 121.)

B.4-2.2

87. The price of pork increased 10 percent last month. If pork now sells for 66 cents a pound, which of the given equations would it be correct to use in finding the price P before the increase?

a. $P - 0.10 = 66$　　d. $P - 0.1P = 66$
b. $P + 0.1 = 66$　　e. none of these
c. $P + 0.1P = 66$

88. During the summer a student worked n weeks at k dollars a week. His expenses for the summer were p dollars. His savings, in dollars, were

a. $n + k + p$　　d. $n + k - p$
b. $np - k$　　e. none of these
c. $np \div k$

B.4-2.2, B.4-3.1

89. Write an equation that could be used to solve the following problem. State what the letter or letters represent. (Solution of the equation is not required.)

The perimeter of a rectangle is 102 inches. If one diagonal of the rectangle is 39 inches, find the length and width of the rectangle.

B.4-3.2

90. A circle whose radius is r is inscribed in a square. Express the area of the square in terms of r.

(University of the State of New York, 1960.)

91. A straight line l cuts a circle with center at P in two different points M and N. The distance from M to N is equal to the radius of the circle. You are to choose the one figure [at top of next column] that fits this description.

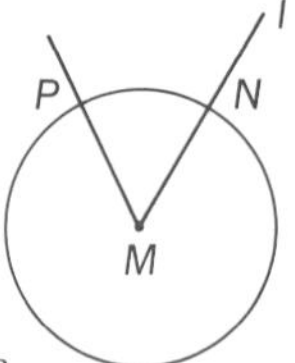

a.

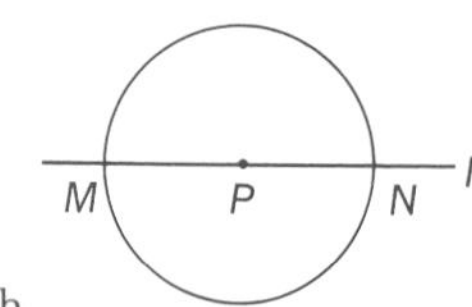

b.

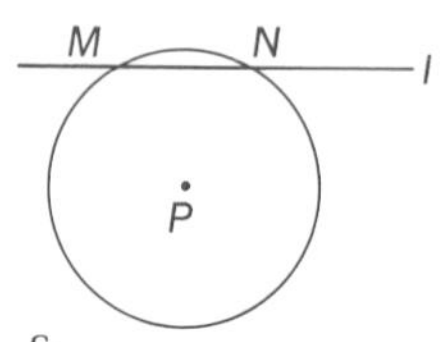

c.

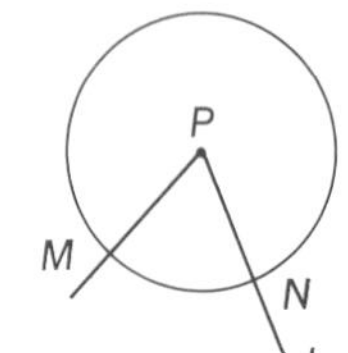

d.

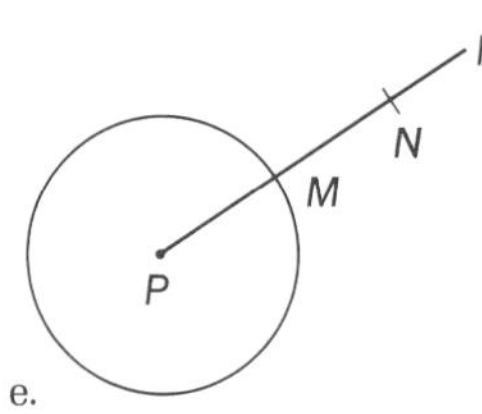

e.

(Wilson et al., 1968d, p. 168.)

Ability to follow a line of reasoning (B.5) Much of mathematics is presented in a deductive format: it is the language of a mathematician communicating his work to others. For this reason, the ability to follow a line of reasoning is, in part, the ability to read mathematical presentations. It is perhaps this aspect of reading mathematics that distinguishes it from general reading ability.

The following item, which might well be appropriate to measures about indirect proof, does not fit any of the content categories. Consequently, only the behavior level is identified.

B.5

92. Mrs. Adams purchased a set of knives, forks, and spoons advertised as a stainless steel product. After using the set for several months, she found that the set was beginning to rust. She thereupon decided that the set was not stainless steel and returned it for refund.

In this example of indirect proof, identify (1) the statement to be proved, (2) the supposition made, (3) the conclusion resulting from the supposition, and (4) the known fact contradictory to (3).

(Romberg & Kilpatrick, 1969, p. 296.)

Items such as this, which clearly belong in the domain of mathematics instruction, help to point out that no classification scheme will be completely satisfactory.

B.5-2.2

93. Given the following pair of equations:

$$x^2 + xy + y^2 = 25$$
$$xy \quad = 0$$

Which of the following arguments is correct?

a. If we substitute $xy = 0$ into the first equation, this equation becomes: $x^2 + y^2 = 25$. Hence the given pair of equations reduces to a single equation in two unknowns. Therefore, there are infinitely many solutions.
b. If we divide the second equation by x, we obtain $y = 0$, and if we divide it by y, we obtain $x = 0$. Substituting these values into the first equation yields $0 = 25$, which is impossible! Therefore the equations are inconsistent, i.e., there are no solutions.
c. Since $xy = 0$, it follows that either $x = 0$ or $y = 0$. Substituting first $x = 0$ into the first equation yields $y = \pm 5$, and then substituting $y = 0$ into this same equation yields $x = \pm 5$. Consequently, there are exactly four solutions.
d. If the second equation is divided by x, it yields $y = 0$. Since $y = 0$, we may not divide the second equation by y. Instead, we substitute $y = 0$ into the first equation to obtain $x = \pm 5$. Hence, there are only two solutions.
e. Adding the two equations yields $x^2 + 2xy + y^2 = 25$. Since the left member is a square, we may take the square root of both sides to obtain $x + y = 5$. Solving this simultaneously with $xy = 0$ yields two solutions.

(Adapted from Wilson et al., 1968f, p. 194.)

Items 94 and 95 are appropriate for a tenth-grade geometry student.

B.5-3.2

94. Given: $\triangle ABC$ and $\triangle ABD$ with common base AB: $\angle 1 = \angle 2$ and $\angle CAB = \angle ABC$. $\angle CAD$ can be proved equal to $\angle DBC$ by a direct application of which of the following axioms?
   a. If equals are divided by equals, the results are equal.
   b. If equals are subtracted from equals, the results are equal.
   c. The whole is greater than any of its parts.
   d. If equals are added to equals, the results are equal.
   e. Doubles of equals are equal.

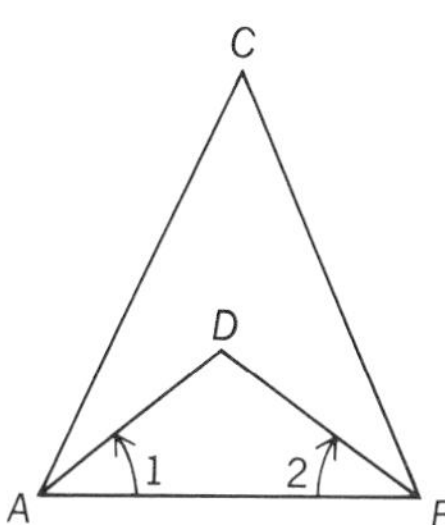

95. Below are listed the statements in part of a proof that the diagonals of a regular pentagon are greater than the sides of the pentagon (refer to the figure below).

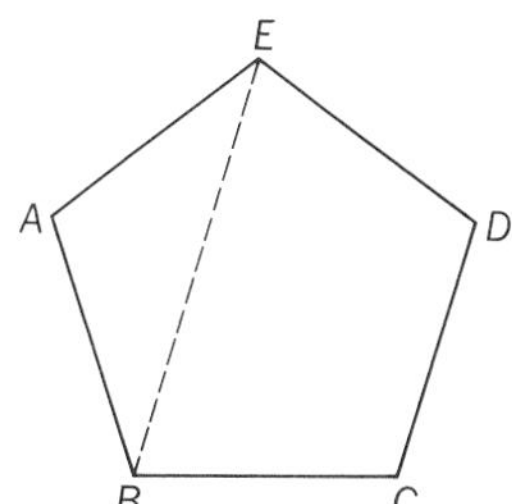

Statements

1. $ABCDE$ is a regular pentagon
2. $\angle AED > \angle AEB$
3. $\angle AED = \angle A$
4. $\angle A > \angle AEB$
5. $EB > AB$
6. $AB = BC = CD = DE = EA$
7. $EB > BC$, $EB > CD$, $EB > DE$, etc.

The statement in step 6 is result of, or depends upon, the statement in step

a. 1.
b. 2.
c. 3.
d. 4.
e. 5.

(Adapted from Orshansky, 1950b, pp. 6, 7.)

Ability to read and interpret a problem (B.6) Items to measure this ability may be adapted from items to measure other categories. For example, the item below is an example of an application-level item about which questions which assess the ability to read and interpret a problem have been asked.

B.6-1.3

96. Mrs. Brown bought a table at a sale. The price tag stated that the original price was $60. The tables were selling at a 20% discount. What was the amount of the discount? (Answer the questions below; do not solve.)
    A. What is the *rate* in the problem?
    B. What is the base?
    C. What are you asked to find?

Some questions, on the other hand, measure the ability more directly.

B.6-1.1

97. What whole numbers make the following sentence true?

    $5 < N + 3 < 10$

B.6-3.4

98. The solution of the pair of simultaneous equations represented by lines AA′ and BB′ on the graph below is
    a. (4,0) b. (3,4) c. (3,1) d. (1,3) e. (0,4)

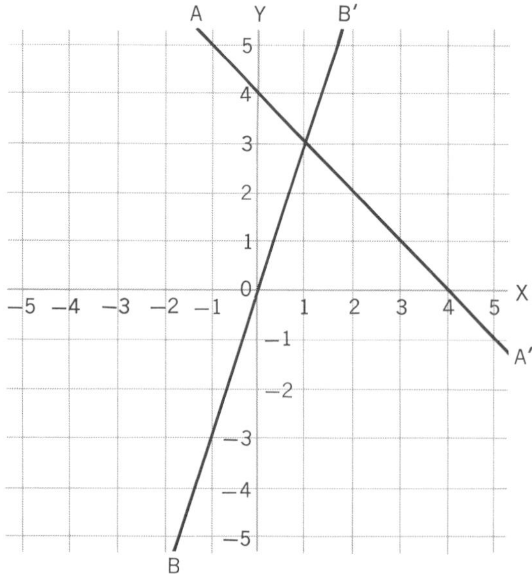

(Adapted from Orshansky, 1950b, p. 3.)

Questions for application (C.0)

Application-level behaviors involve a sequence of responses by the student. Routine problem-solving and decision-making activities are in the category. The content of application-level behaviors would be expected as a part of the course of instruction: that is, an item placed at the application level should be familiar to the student because it is similar to material he has encountered during instruction.

Exercises which require the student to choose an algorithm *and* carry it out would be at the application level. The difficulty of such exercises might be quite low. It should be remembered that the behavior classification of a task is based on its cognitive complexity rather than its level of difficulty.

Ability to solve routine problems (C.1) Routine problems are those similar to problems which have been encountered during the course of instruction. Essentially, the student is asked to perform a sequence of comprehension-level behaviors and carry out an algorithm to arrive at a solution. For this ability the primary concern is solving the routine problem. Checking the result and searching for a better (more elegant) solution are very desirable behaviors that are probably of a higher level.

C.1-1.1

99. Which of the following numbers, expressed in base-7 numeration, is both prime and odd?
    a. 11 b. 12 c. 13 d. 14

C.1-1.3

100. A class of 24 pupils decided to impose a book-loss insurance fee based on the average book price of $2.40 and the rate of loss in the previous year of 9 books lost per 24 pupils. What fee should each pupil be charged in order to cover the total expected loss for the current year?
    a. $0.24
    b. $0.30
    c. $0.72
    d. $0.80
    e. $0.90

(Romberg & Kilpatrick, 1969, p. 291.)

101. Miss Roland bought a fur coat priced at \$500. The state sales tax was 2%, and the Federal luxury tax on the coat was 15%. What was her total bill?
a. \$576.50 c. \$586.50
b. \$585.00 d. None of these

(Adapted from State University of Iowa, 1949.)

C.1-2.1

102. The tens digit of a two-digit number is twice the units digit. If the units digit is represented by x, the number can be represented by
a. 3x b. 12x c. 21x d. 30x

(University of the State of New York, 1960.)

At first glance item 102 appears to be one of representation and translation (B.4). It does, however, require the student to select and carry out an addition algorithm in order to obtain a solution.

C.1-2.3

103. Given $\log_b 2 = 0.693$ and $\log_b 3 = 1.099$, find $\log_b 12$.

(University of the State of New York, 1960.)

C.1-3.1

104. Two sides and the included angle of a parallelogram are 12 inches, 20 inches, and 120° respectively. Find the length of the longer diagonal.

105. A room is 40 feet long, 32 feet wide, and 11 feet high.
(1) Find the number of square feet in its floor area.
(2) If its window area is 25 percent of its floor area, find the number of square feet in its window area.
(3) Find the number of cubic feet of space in this room.

106. Webbing, 2 feet 8 inches long, is needed to make one belt for students on the safety patrol. If Lincoln School has 15 members on the safety patrol, how many yards of webbing are needed?

(Romberg & Kilpatrick, 1969, p. 290.)

C.1-3.2

107. A piece of wire 36 inches long is bent into the form of a right triangle. If one of the legs is 12 inches long, find the length of the other leg.

(University of the State of New York, 1960.)

108. In the figure [below], O is the center of the circle and YO is perpendicular to OZ. If the area of the circle is 16π, then the area of $\triangle YOZ =$

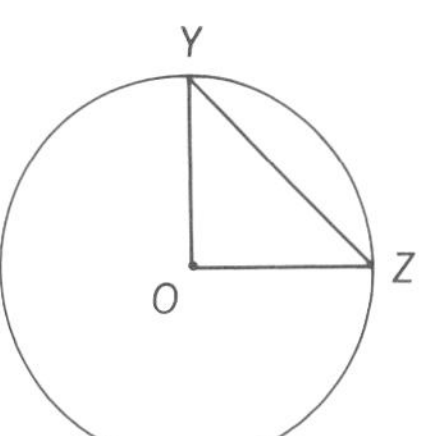

a. 8
b. 9
c. 10
d. 12
e. 16

(Romberg & Kilpatrick, 1969, p. 294.)

109. In the circle shown below, chord AC and diameter BD intersect at E. Arc $AB = 68°$ and angle $BAC = 64°$. Find the number of degrees in arc AD, arc BC, angle BEC, and angle ABC.

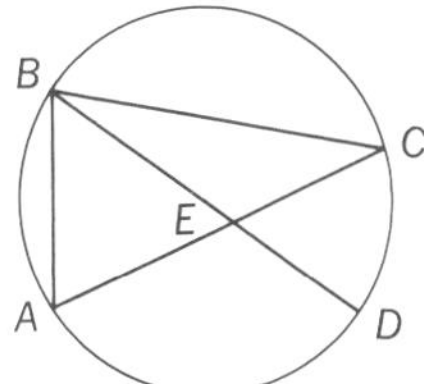

(University of the State of New York, 1960.)

Ability to make comparisons (C.2) **The items in this application-level behavior should require the student to determine a relationship between two sets of information and to formulate a decision. Calculation may be involved, and recall of relevant knowledge is almost always needed. The exercise may, however, also elicit reasoning and logical thinking.**

C.2-1.0

110. The following annual salaries were received by a group of ten employees:

\$4,000	\$6,000	\$12,500	\$5,000	\$7,000
\$5,500	\$4,500	\$5,000	\$6,500	\$6,000

How many salaries are greater than the mean?

(Romberg & Kilpatrick, 1969, p. 290.)

C.2-1.1

111. The difference in the circumference between the larger and smaller of two balls is 3 inches. Which of the following is the best estimate of the difference in their diameters?
  a. slightly less than 1 inch
  b. exactly 1 inch
  c. slightly more than 1 inch
  d. slightly more than 9 inches

C.2-1.3

112. Two different savings plans are available to you. At the bank, your savings will earn 5 percent compounded quarterly. The savings and loan Association pays 5.25 percent compounded annually. Where should you place your money to earn the maximum interest?

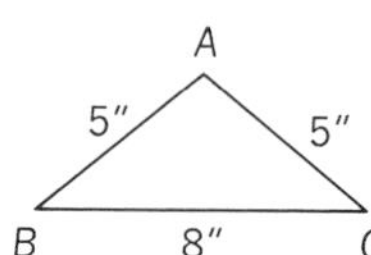

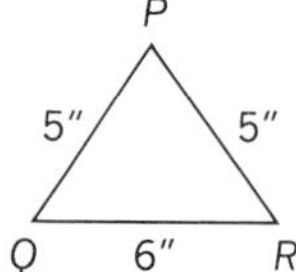

113. Compare the areas of the two triangles.
  a. *ABC* has the larger area.
  b. *PQR* has the larger area.
  c. The areas are the same.

C.2-1.8

114. Ten objects are numbered from 1 through 10 and distributed into bags. If it is known that 1, 4, and 7 are in the same bag, the pair 2 and 10 are in the same bag, and similarly for the pairs 3 and 6, 1 and 5, 3 and 8, 7 and 9, 2 and 6, what is the largest number of bags which can contain at least one object?
  a. 1 b. 2 c. 3 d. 4 e. 5

(Wilson et al., 1968f, p. 201.)

Ability to analyze data (C.3) This behavior requires that the student take a set of information in an exercise and make a sequence of decisions. He may be required to distinguish relevant from irrelevant information, to assess what additional information is required, to determine what related problems may be examined to help with solution of the present exercise, or to separate the exercise into component parts. While solution of the problem may be required, or may result from the analysis of data, the behavior of interest in this category is primarily a sequence of decision making.

C.3-1.0

115. The graph in the diagram [below] shows the population of a suburban town at intervals of 5 years from 1945 through 1955. How much more did the population increase between 1950 and 1955 than it did between 1945 and 1950?
  a. 500 b. 1,000 c. 1,500

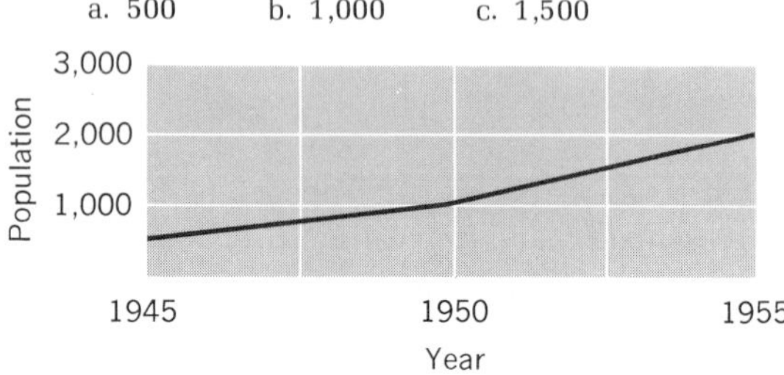

(University of the State of New York, 1960.)

C.3-1.2

116. Five spelling tests are to be given to John's class. Each test has a value of 25 points. John's average for the first four tests is 15. What is the lowest score he can get on the fifth test to have an average of at least 16?
  a. 15 b. 16 c. 17 d. 20 e. 25

(Wilson et al., 1968c, p. 48.)

C.3-1.3

117. Part of a problem reads, "How much interest compounded quarterly does a bank pay on $300 kept in a savings account for one year?" What, if any, additional information must be known in order to solve the problem?
  a. No additional information
  b. When the money will be withdrawn
  c. The purpose of the savings
  d. The age of the person whose money it is
  e. The interest rate

(Adapted from Orshansky, 1948, p. 13.)

118. Harriet wanted 6 pairs of socks. Store *X* sold them at 2 pairs for $1.25; the same brand sold in store *Y* at 3 pairs for $1.98. To be economical, what should Harriet do?
  a. Buy the socks at Store *X*.
  b. Buy the socks at Store *Y*.

c. Buy the socks at either store; it makes no difference.

d. It cannot be determined from the facts given.

(Adapted from Educational Testing Service, 1957b, p. 6.)

C.3-2.3

119. On the same set of axes, sketch the graphs of $y = \sin x$ and $y = \cos \frac{1}{2}x$ as x varies from 0 to 2π radians. Determine from the graphs the quadrant in which $\sin x - \cos \frac{1}{2}x$ is always positive.

C.3-3.1

120. A rectangle has length 313 inches and width 211 inches. Its area is 313×211 square inches. (Do not do any multiplication.) If a new rectangle is twice as long and twice as wide, its area is $(2 \times 313) \times (2 \times 211)$ square inches. What does this say about the areas of the two rectangles?

(Romberg & Kilpatrick, 1969, p. 289.)

121. T is the set of all triangles XYZ with the following properties: $XY > XZ$ and the radian measure of $\angle Y$ is $\frac{\pi}{3}$. Which of the following is the set of all numbers p such that p is the radian measure of $\angle X$ for some $\triangle XYZ$ in T?

a. $\left\{p \middle| 0 < p < \frac{\pi}{6}\right\}$
b. $\left\{p \middle| 0 < p < \frac{\pi}{3}\right\}$
c. $\left\{p \middle| \frac{\pi}{6} < p < \frac{\pi}{3}\right\}$
d. $\left\{p \middle| \frac{\pi}{3} < p < \frac{\pi}{2}\right\}$
e. $\left\{p \middle| \frac{\pi}{3} < p < \frac{2\pi}{3}\right\}$

(Adapted from College Entrance Examination Board, 1970, p. 55.)

Ability to recognize patterns, isomorphisms, and symmetries (C.4) The behavior required at this level again calls for a sequence: recall of information, transformation of problem elements, manipulation of data, and recognition of a relationship. The student is asked to find something familiar in a set of data, in given information, or in a problem context.

C.4-1.1

122. In an election, 356 people vote to choose one of five candidates. The candidate with most votes is the winner. What is the smallest number of votes the winner could receive?

a. 179
b. 178
c. 89
d. 72
e. 71

C.4-1.3

123. The amount of weight a board of a certain width, depth, and material can support at its midpoint is inversely proportional to the distance between its supports. If the distance between the supports is made three times as great, the weight which can be supported is

a. decreased by 3
b. multiplied by 3
c. increased by 3
d. divided by 3
e. unchanged

(Adapted from Blyth, 1953, p. 5. Reproduced from Blyth Second-year Algebra Test, copyright 1953 by Harcourt, Brace and World, Inc. Reproduced by special permission of the publisher.)

C.4-1.4

124. If x and y are two distinct real numbers and $xz = yz$, then $z =$

a. $\frac{1}{x - y}$
b. $x - y$
c. 0
d. 1
e. $\frac{x}{y}$

(Romberg & Kilpatrick, 1969, p. 292.)

Item 125, for able twelfth-graders, would be an application-level item since they will usually have been exposed to number patterns in their courses. It could be placed at the analysis level to measure the ability to discover relationships (*D*.2) for students at lower grade levels.

C.4-1.9

125. The last digit in 4^{10} is

a. 0
b. 2
c. 4
d. 6
e. 8

(Wilson et al., 1968f, p. 273.)

C.4-3.2

126. Mr. Smith wanted to reduce the area of the drive-way (below) without changing its 20-foot width

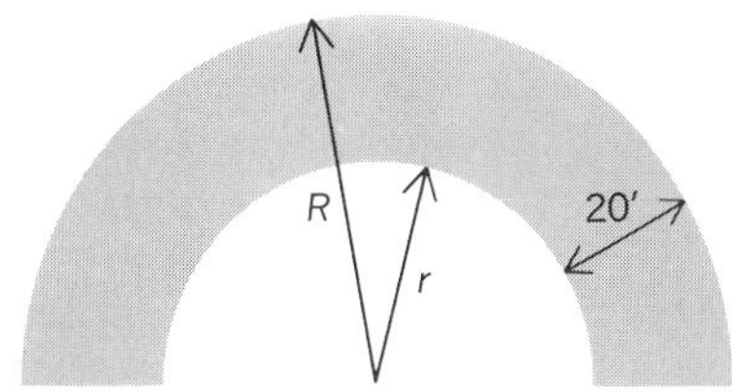

or its semicircular shape. He could do this by

a. reducing only the outer radius R
b. increasing only the inner radius r
c. reducing the outer radius R and increasing the inner radius r by the same amount
d. reducing both radii by the same amount

(Adapted from Educational Testing Service, 1957a, p. 4.)

Questions for analysis (D.0)

The analysis-level behaviors are essentially those where we ask the student to go beyond what he has done during previous instruction. It is this level of behavior that is "doing mathematics." The problems in this category are sometimes called "nonroutine," but this does not mean such problems are unusual to mathematics instruction. Indeed, many of our most important objectives in mathematics instruction are at the analysis level.

A source of problems, mostly of the analysis level, which is available at low cost to all teachers, are *The Contest Problem Book* (Salkind, 1961) and *The MAA Problem Book II* (Salkind, 1967). These books contain problems, with solutions, from the annual high school mathematics contests of the Mathematical Association of America from 1950 through 1965. (Questions from these two books have not been included in this chapter, because the books are readily available.)

Ability to solve nonroutine problems (D.1) The exercises below show some of the variety of test items which can be placed in this category. The discussion in the application-level section on the ability to solve routine problems (C.1), along with the heading above, fairly well specifies this category: problem solving in mathematics in nonpracticed contexts.

D.1-1.3

127. Two ferry boats start from the same dock on the shore of a bay at noon one day. One travels at $4^1/_2$ miles per hour, and the other at 4 miles per hour. They travel back and forth continuously. [Assume no time is lost in slowing down, unloading, and reloading.] The next time they are together in the same dock is at noon the next day, when they meet at their starting point. How wide is the bay?

a. 2 miles
b. 3 miles
c. 4 miles
d. 6 miles
e. 8 miles

(Wilson et al., 1968f, p. 276.)

128. What is the largest rational number which is the sum of two rational numbers each having a numerator of 1 and a whole number for its denominator?

Item 128 might be an analysis item in the junior high grades. On the other hand, the following item could be an analysis item for secondary level grades. Note that the correct response to question (3) is "no solution."

D.1-2.2

129. Given set $p = r^2 - t^2$, where p is a *prime* number, find t if

(1) $r = 7$ (2) $r = 157$ (3) $r = 58$

130. Which of the following values of x satisfies the equation $ax^2 + bx + c = 0$ when $a + b + c = 0$?

a. $\frac{b}{a}$
b. $\frac{c}{a}$
c. $\frac{a+c}{b}$
d. $\frac{-b}{a}$
e. $\frac{-c}{a}$

131. Find the one equation below which can be satisfied by both (19,−27) and (19,27).

a. $7x + 3y = 52$
b. $|7x + 3y|^2 = 2{,}704$
c. $x^2 = y^2 + 367$
d. $7x^2 - 3y^3 = 61{,}576$
e. $7x + 3y^4 = 1{,}594{,}456$

132. Find the *largest* value of x which satisfies the equation $2(8^x) + 4(8^{-x}) - 9 = 0$

a. $\frac{-1}{3}$
b. $\frac{1}{2}$
c. $\frac{2}{3}$
d. $\frac{3}{2}$
e. 4

(Wilson et al., 1968f, p. 190.)

133. If $2a + 2b + 5c = 9$, and if $c = 1$, then $a + b + c =$

a. 2 d. 5
b. 3 e. 8
c. $4^1/_2$

(Romberg & Kilpatrick, 1969, p. 292.)

134. If a, b, c, d are four distinct numbers, and if
$d + a = d$
$a \cdot d = a$
$b + c = a$
$a(a + d) = d$
$b - c = d$
then d equals

a. −1 d. 2
b. 0 e. 3
c. 1

(Wilson et al., 1968f, p. 276.)

D.1-3.2

135. The figure [below] shows a building whose roof forms part of a right circular cylindrical surface.

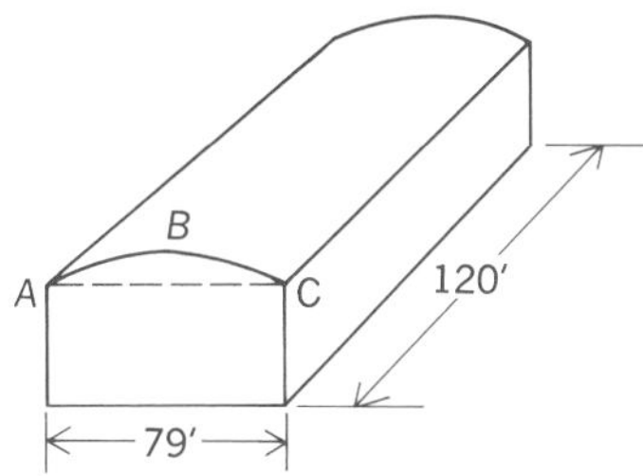

Arc $ABC = 60°$, the distance from A to C is 79 feet, and the building is 120 feet long. If the roof costs $2.72 per square yard, find the cost of the roof to the *nearest ten* dollars.

(University of the State of New York, 1960.)

136. In the figure below CE and DF are perpendicular to AF, and BE and CF are perpendicular to AD.

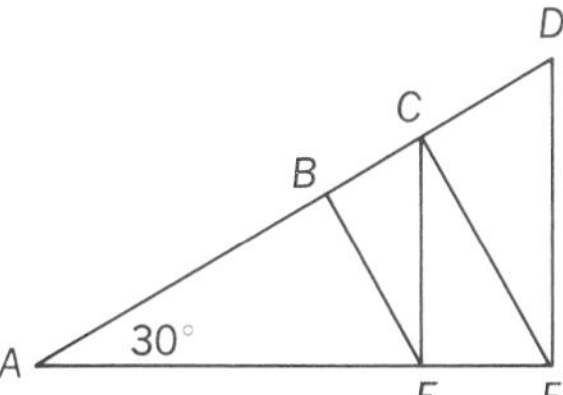

If $AD = 8$, then AB equals

a. 4 d. 5.5
b. 4.5 e. none of these
c. 5

(Adapted from University of Chicago, 1952.)

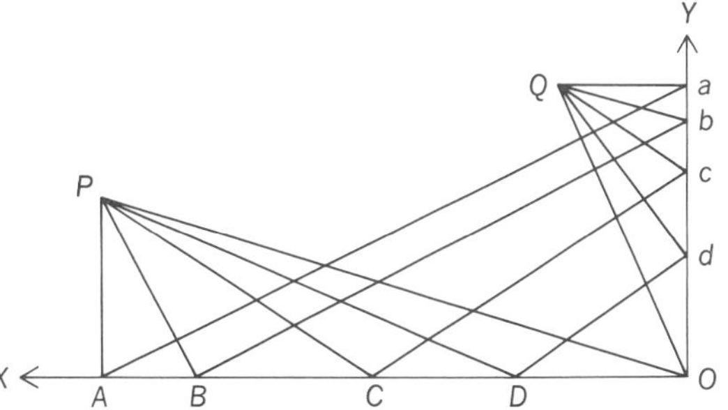

137. In the figure above what is the shortest path from P to Q which touches both line XO and line OY?

a. $PAaQ$ d. $PDdQ$
b. $PBbQ$ e. POQ
c. $PCcQ$

(Adapted from Wilson et al., 1968f, p. 181.)

Ability to discover relationships (D.2) The exercises at this level should demand that the student restructure the elements in the problem and formulate a relationship—which may in turn be used to solve a problem.

The first two items, of relatively low difficulty, might be appropriate for the seventh grade.

D.2-3.1

138. In the figure above, T, L, and P are three towns on a road. Notice that L is twice as far from T as it is from P. There is another town on this road which is also twice as far from T as it is from P. How many miles is this town from L?

a. 3 d. 15
b. 9 e. 18
c. 12

(Adapted from Romberg & Kilpatrick, 1969, p. 295.)

139. The length of a diagonal of a square is $x + y$. Find its area.

Item 139 is best solved by discovering the relationship between the length of a side and the length of a diagonal in a square. The solution follows easily.

140. A barn is 60 feet long and 30 feet wide. A chain 55 feet long is attached to the barn at the middle of one of its longer sides. Another chain 55 feet long is attached to the barn at one of its corners. Either chain may be used to tether a cow for grazing.
   (1) Which chain gives the tethered cow the greater area of land over which to graze?
   (2) How much difference is there between the areas of the two regions? (Use 3.14 as an approximation of π).

141. In a circular race track the diameter of the inside lane is 100 feet and the diameter of the outside lane is 108 feet. Write a set of instructions telling how to determine the "head start" a boy running in the outside lane should have so that he will run the same distance as a boy running the inside lane for a race of one lap.

(Adapted from Romberg & Kilpatrick, 1969, p. 289.)

D.2-3.2

142. Suppose that, after an Earth satellite is launched, two persons, one standing on the Earth's equator and the other in a balloon 5 miles directly overhead from the first, each use a telescope to watch it. The satellite will be traveling in a circular orbit 400 miles out in space from the Earth's equator. While the satellite is traveling overhead, the man on the Earth, as compared with the man in the balloon, must turn his telescope
   a. more rapidly
   b. less rapidly
   c. at the same rate
   d. more or less rapidly, depending on whether or not the satellite moved opposite to the direction of rotation of the Earth

143. Determine the number of lines obtained by joining n distinct points in the plane, no three of which are collinear.

144. Find the number of diagonals in a convex polygon
   (1) with 5 sides
   (2) with 25 sides
   (3) with n sides

D.2-3.4

145. For what value of m will the graphs of the following equations intersect at the origin?

$$3x - 5y = 2$$
$$6x - my = 0$$

(Adapted from Romberg & Kilpatrick, 1969, p. 297.)

Ability to construct proofs (D.3) The language of proof is the language for presenting mathematics to a fellow mathematician. Traditionally, proof was restricted for the most part to the tenth-grade geometry course. The recent changes in mathematics curricula have brought about the introduction of proof throughout mathematics content.

D.3-1.1

146. Show that $\square + \square = 2 \cdot \square$.

It would be necessary to assume a set of postulates from which the above item would follow. In other words, the context of the problem would need to be meaningful. Items such as the one above are found in seventh grade or lower grades.

D.3-1.2

147. Show that $-(-a) = a$.

148. Given the properties of the integers, definition of the set of rational numbers, and definition of addition and multiplication of rational numbers, show that the rational numbers form a number system.

149. Prove that for every positive integer n,

$$\frac{n^5}{5} + \frac{n^3}{3} + \frac{7n}{15}$$

is an integer.

150. Prove

$$\sum_{k=1}^{n} k = \frac{n(n-1)}{2}$$

by induction.

151. Prove by induction that

$$\sum_{k=1}^{n} k^3 = \frac{n^2(n+1)^2}{4}$$

D.3-1.3

152. Show that

$$\frac{\frac{a}{b}}{\frac{c}{d}} = \frac{a}{b} \times \frac{d}{c}$$

for rational numbers $\frac{a}{b}$ and $\frac{c}{d} \neq 0$.

D.3-1.4

153. Prove that $a \cdot 0 = 0$ for all real numbers.

D.3-2.3

154. Prove the identity:

$$\cot \theta \frac{\cos 2\theta}{\sin \theta \cos \theta} = \tan \theta$$

155. Show that the expression

$$\frac{\sin 3x + \sin x}{\cos 3x + \cos x}$$

may be reduced to the form $\tan 2x$.

(University of the State of New York, 1960.)

156. Suppose that $f(x)$ is a function with a continuous derivative for $0 \leqslant x \leqslant 1$ and such that $f'(x) \geqslant m > 0$ for $0 \leqslant x \leqslant 1$. Prove that $f(1) \geqslant f(0) + m$.

(University of Chicago, 1952.)

D.3-3.2

157. In the diagram below, B is the midpoint of major arc AC. Chords BD and AC intersect at E. Chords AD and AB are drawn.
PROVE: $BD \times BE = (AB)^2$.

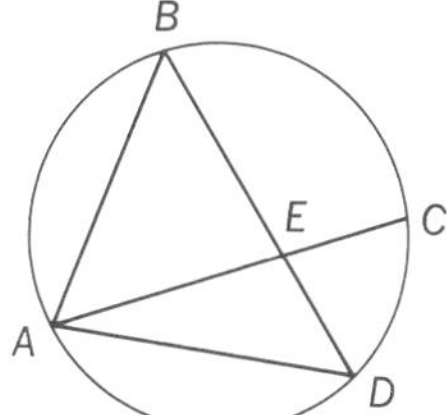

158. Line segments AB and CD are both equal and parallel. They are oblique to plane M and meet it at points A and C. Parallel lines are drawn from B and D to meet plane M at points R and S, respectively.
PROVE: $AR = CS$.

159. Prove by the methods of analytic geometry that the three altitudes of a triangle meet in a point.

(Adapted from University of the State of New York, 1960.)

The ability to construct proofs ($D.3$) is difficult to assess with multiple-choice items. Two reasonably good attempts are illustrated by items 160 and 161.

D.3-3.3

160. For each of the following proofs, select the arrow diagram below it which best represents the pattern of reasoning. A diagram like $(3) \longrightarrow (5)$ means that statement (3) of the proof is needed to deduce statement (5). A diagram like $\begin{matrix}(2)\\(3)\end{matrix}\!\!\gt\!\!\rightarrow (5)$ means that *both* statement (2) and statement (3) are needed to deduce statement (5) and that *neither* statement (2) nor statement (3) alone is sufficient. In each case, study the proof, then select one diagram.
GIVEN: For $\triangle QPS$ [below],

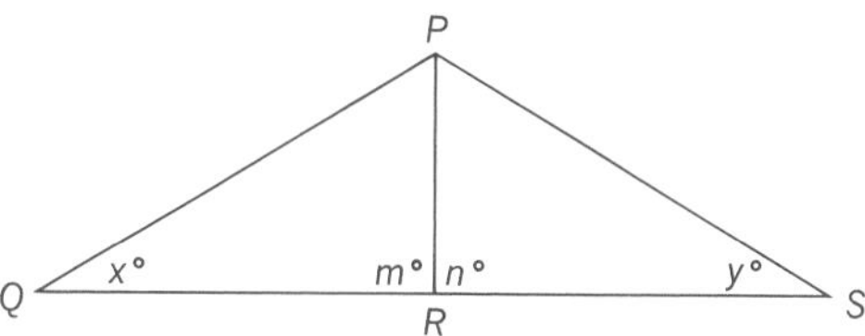

$QR = RS$, and $m = n$

PROVE: $x = y$

STATEMENTS IN PROOF: (Reasons omitted.)
(1) $QR = RS$ and $PR = PR$
(2) $m = n$
(3) $\triangle PRQ \cong \triangle PRS$
(4) $x = y$

a. $(1) \rightarrow \begin{matrix}(2)\\(3)\end{matrix}\!\!\gt\!\!\rightarrow (4)$

b. $(1) \longrightarrow (2) \longrightarrow (3) \longrightarrow (4)$

c. $(1) \longrightarrow (3) \longrightarrow (4)$

d. $\begin{matrix}(1)\\(2)\end{matrix}\!\!\gt\!\!\rightarrow (3) \longrightarrow (4)$

e. $\begin{matrix}(1)\\(2) \longrightarrow (3)\end{matrix}\!\!\gt\!\!\rightarrow (4)$

(Wilson et al., 1968e, pp. 352–353.)

161. GIVEN: Each of triangles PQR and PTS [next page] is isosceles, and each has vertex P; $\triangle PQR \sim \triangle PTS$, with $\overline{QR}$ corresponding to $\overline{TS}$.
PROVE: $QT = RS$

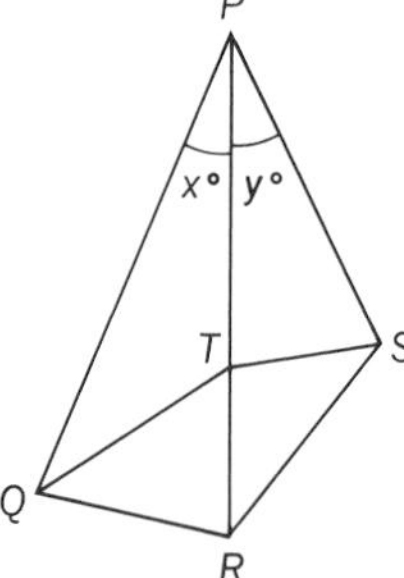

STATEMENTS IN PROOF: (Reasons omitted.)
(1) $\triangle PQR$ and $\triangle PTS$ are isosceles with vertex P
(2) $\triangle PQR \sim \triangle PTS$, with $\overline{QR}$ corresponding to $\overline{TS}$
(3) $PQ = PR$ and $PT = PS$
(4) $x = y$
(5) $\triangle PTQ \cong \triangle PSR$
(6) $QT = RS$

a. (1)⟶(3) and (2)⟶(4), both ⟶(5)⟶(6)
b. (1) and (2) ⟶(3)⟶(4)⟶(5)⟶(6)
c. (1) and (3) ⟶(4)⟶(5)⟶(6)
d. (2) and (3) ⟶(4); (1) and (4) ⟶(5)⟶(6)
e. (1)⟶(2)⟶(4); (3) and (4) ⟶(5)⟶(6)

Ability to criticize proofs (D.4) The ability to criticize proofs is a logical counterpart of the ability to construct them. The former may be a more complex behavior than the latter. Avital and Shettleworth (1968) provide several sample items in this category in their appendix. Multiple-choice items to assess this behavior are generally difficult to write; items 163 and 164 are examples.

D.4-1.0
162. Let us attempt to prove the following remarkable proposition: *Any two numbers are equal.*

Call the two numbers a and b; call their sum c. Thus, we have the equation

(1) $a + b = c$

From (1) we obtain the equations:

(2) $c - b = a$

and

(3) $c - a = b$

Multiply each side of (2) by $-b$, and multiply each side of (3) by $-a$, to get

(4) $b^2 - bc = -ab$

and

(5) $a^2 - ac = -ab$

From (4) and (5) we have

(6) $b^2 - bc = a^2 - ac$

Add $c^2/4$ to each side of (6) to get

(7) $b^2 - bc + \frac{c^2}{4} = a^2 - ac + \frac{c^2}{4}$

Take the square root of each side of (7) to get

(8) $b - \frac{c}{2} = a - \frac{c}{2}$

Then add $c/2$ to each side of (8) to get, finally: $b = a$.

WHAT'S WRONG?

(Romberg & Kilpatrick, 1969, p. 295.)

D.4-1.4
163. The following is a "proof" that any two real numbers are equal to each other. Which step of the proof is *incorrect?*

(1) Let $c = \frac{a + b}{2}$, and $a \neq b$
(2) $2c = a + b$
(3) $2c(a - b) = (a + b)(a - b)$
(4) $2ac - 2bc = a^2 - b^2$
(5) $b^2 - 2bc + c^2 = a^2 - 2ac + c^2$
(6) $b^2 - 2bc + c^2 = a^2 - 2ac + c^2$
(7) $(b - c)^2 = (a - c)^2$
(8) $b - c = a - c$
(9) $b = a$

a. from (2) to (3)
b. from (4) to (5)
c. from (5) to (6)
d. from (7) to (8)
e. from (8) to (9)

(Wilson et al., 1968f, p. 202.)

D.4-2.3

164. Consider the following argument

A. If y is not even, then $y = f(x)$.

B. Only if x is odd is y even.

C. If $y = f(x)$, then $y = x^2 + x + 1$.

Suppose that $x = n + 3$;

CONCLUSION: A sufficient condition that $y = 31$ is that $n = 2$.

(1) Is the conclusion valid?

(2) If it is not valid, rewrite it to make it valid.

(Adapted from Romberg & Kilpatrick, 1969, p. 298.)

Ability to formulate and validate generalizations (D.5) While this category is similar to the previous analysis categories, it is probably more complex in that the student is asked to formulate *and* to validate a relationship. That is, he may be required to discover and to prove a mathematical statement. He may be asked to produce an algorithm and to show that it works.

D.5-1.1

165. Without actually making the calculations, write out in detail a step-by-step procedure for determining

(1) whether 12,087 is a prime number

(2) the largest prime less than 5,000

D.5-1.2

166. Observe the following table.

Row	*Item*	*Sum*
1	1	
2	1 + 3	
3	1 + 3 + 5	
4		
5		
.		
.		
.		
n		

(1) Write the 4th and 5th rows.

(2) Find the sums for each row.

(3) Generalize for the nth row.

(4) Prove your generalization by mathematical induction.

(Romberg & Kilpatrick, 1969, pp. 297, 298.)

D.5-1.3, D.5-2.3

167. Find

$$\sum_{k=1}^{n} k^2 \text{ as a function of } n.$$

D.5-3.2

168. On your paper draw three triangles: one with three acute angles, one with one right angle, and one with one obtuse angle. Using straightedge and compasses, bisect each angle of each triangle.

What relationship do you observe between the three angle bisectors of each triangle? Do you think this would be true for every triangle? Why?

(Romberg & Kilpatrick, 1969, p. 296.)

Questions for interests and attitudes (E.0)

Questions designed to measure outcomes in the affective domain are deceptively difficult for the classroom teacher or the mathematician to write, use, or interpret. In part, this is due to the extreme complexity of these noncognitive outcomes; in part, it is because the social psychology and measurement experts need to provide more assistance to classroom teachers. But primarily, the difficulty comes from the failure of mathematics educators to conduct research and development activities in this area. Consequently, our teacher-training and curriculum-development activities hardly ever deal with outcomes in the affective domain except to note that such outcomes are *very* important. What little has been done is generally without a conceptual or a theoretical framework.

Attitude (E.1) There can be several kinds of attitude toward mathematics. One should take care to describe his measure of attitude just as he would carefully describe a measure of achievement. For instance, one can try to ascertain how well a student likes mathematics and how important he considers it in relation to other school subjects, using items like the following.

E.1-1.0–E.1-3.0

169. I like story books ________ than mathematics books.
    a. a lot more c. a little less
    b. a little more d. a lot less
170. I like doing mathematics ________ than doing anything else. [Same alternatives as in item 169.]
171. I like writing answers to social studies questions ________ than doing words problems in mathematics. [Same alternatives as in item 169.]
172. I like mathematics books ________ than social studies books. [Same alternatives as in item 169.]
173. I like subtracting fractions ________ than reading a story about Brazil. [Same alternatives as in item 169.]
174. I would like to teach English ________ than I would like to teach mathematics. [Same alternatives as in item 169.]

(Wilson et al., 1968f, p. 215.)

Or a measure of attitude toward mathematics can be designed to assess the pleasure or boredom a student experiences with regard to mathematics. The following items are examples:

E.1-1.0–E.1-3.0

175. The subject I enjoy least is mathematics.
    a. strongly agree
    b. agree
    c. don't know
    d. disagree
    e. strongly disagree
176. I cannot understand how some students think mathematics is fun.
    a. strongly agree
    b. agree
    c. mildly agree
    d. mildly disagree
    e. disagree
    f. strongly disagree
177. Mathematics is boring. [Same alternatives as in item 175.]
178. Mathematics is fun. [Same alternatives as in item 175.]

(Wilson et al., 1968f, pp. 217–218.)

The last two items are direct and to the point. Such items have the danger, however, that the responses they elicit from the student are based more on what he thinks the teacher wants than on what he himself feels.

Another attitude measure may assess the ease or difficulty which a student associates with mathematics performance; here are some examples:

E.1-1.0–E.1-3.0

179. Mathematics is so hard to understand that I do not like it as well as other subjects.
    a. strongly agree
    b. agree
    c. don't know
    d. disagree
    e. strongly disagree
180. To do well in mathematics, you have to be smarter than you have to be to do well in reading. [Same alternatives as in item 179.]
181. Most students work very hard to do well in mathematics. [Same alternatives as in item 179.]
182. Mathematics is more of a game than it is hard work. [Same alternatives as in item 179.]
183. No matter how hard I try, I cannot understand mathematics. [Same alternatives as in item 179.]
184. Mathematics is a subject which is more difficult to understand than any other subject. [Same alternatives as in item 179.]
185. There is so much hard work in mathematics that it takes the fun out of it. [Same alternatives as in item 179.]
186. I would like mathematics better if it were not made so hard in class. [Same alternatives as in item 179.]
187. Mathematics is easier for me than my other subjects. [Same alternatives as in item 179.]

(Wilson et al., 1968f, pp. 216–219.)

The point that is so often missed by teachers is that there are many attitudes toward mathematics. Items similar to the ones given here could easily be written to assess attitudes toward algebra or geometry.

E.1-1.0, E.1-2.0

188. I like the problem "$359 - 574 + 6840 - 999 - 46937 + 9748 + 97483 = ?$" ________ than the

problem "Jane is half as tall as Dick. Joe is half as tall as Jane. Mark is half as tall as Joe. Dick is 60 inches tall. How tall is Joe?"
a. a lot more
b. a little more
c. a little less
d. a lot less

E.1-1.0–E.1-3.0

189. My parents think mathematics is not very practical.
a. strongly agree
b. agree
c. don't know
d. disagree
e. strongly disagree

190. Most mathematics is too concerned with ideas to be really useful. [Same alternatives as in item 189.]

(Wilson, 1968f, pp. 218, 223.)

These sample items all come from the NLSMA test batteries. The development of these batteries is discussed by Romberg and Wilson (1969, Chap. 13).

Interest (E.2) Items to assess interest in mathematics give the student an opportunity to express a preference for mathematics activities over other choices. Another word for this level of behavior might be "preference." The expression of interest in mathematics may have a rather low level of feeling or emotion associated with it.

E.2

191. I would like to learn to program a computer
a. not at all
b. just a little
c. quite well
d. expertly

E.2-1.0–E.2-3.0

192. I would like to be a mathematician.
a. strongly disagree
b. disagree
c. don't know
d. agree
e. strongly agree

193. I would like to study mathematics
a. no more
b. one more year
c. two more years
d. three more years

194. Outside of school, I would like to use mathematics:
a. every chance I get
b. often
c. sometimes
d. hardly ever
e. never

195. I use mathematics outside of school in my games, reading, hobbies, or when watching TV
a. very often
b. quite often
c. sometimes
d. hardly ever
e. never

(Wilson et al., 1968e, p. 217.)

196. I would like to study about the life of Gauss
a. not at all
b. a little
c. a lot

197. I would like to use mathematics in my science courses
a. strongly disagree
b. disagree
c. don't know
d. agree
e. strongly agree

Motivation (E.3) Items to measure this level deal with a strong emotional component that is a drive or force within the individual causing him to act favorably toward mathematics. "Desire" might be another word for the behavior. Some test items are given below; this is a behavior, however, that might also be measured indirectly or by observation. For instance, the number of mathematics books checked out of the library by a student during a term could indicate his level of motivation. A student's enthusiasm can be observed in the classroom; we can also observe the persistence with which he pursues a problem or the thoroughness with which he does his assignments. Motivation is measured by action rather than intention.

E.3-1.0–E.3-3.0

198. Do you check the solution to a mathematics problem?
a. never
b. sometimes
c. almost always

199. What is the most time you have ever spent working an interesting mathematics problem?
a. about thirty minutes or less
b. about one hour
c. up to four hours
d. off and on for several days

200. How many unassigned problems have you solved this term?

a. none
b. one to five
c. six to fifteen
d. more than fifteen

201. Do you complete your mathematics assignments?
a. almost never
b. usually
c. always

Anxiety (E.4) Each of us is acquainted with someone who expresses a fear of mathematics, a feeling of apprehension. Such behavior might be called "anxiety." A feeling of apprehension could possibly spur a student into working hard and hence improve his performance. In this case, there would be a facilitating anxiety. On the other hand, the apprehension could be so intense that normal reasoning powers were inhibited; in this case, the anxiety would be a debilitating anxiety. The discussion could be extended by observing that the object of anxiety might be more general than mathematics (for instance, the student may be apprehensive about school, about pressures from his peer group, or about social contacts); but for the most part the mathematics teacher will be interested particularly in anxiety about mathematics.

The following items are taken from scales developed for the NLSMA test batteries to measure anxiety regarding mathematics tests. Information on the development of the scales for facilitating anxiety and debilitating anxiety is given in NLSMA Report No. 7 (Romberg & Wilson, 1969, pages 154–155). The scales were used in grades 5 to 11.

The first three items are from a scale for facilitating anxiety.

E.4-1.0–E.4-3.0

202. I work best on mathematics tests that are important.
a. always
b. usually
c. sometimes
d. hardly ever
e. never

203. I keep my mathematics grades up mainly by doing well on the big tests rather than on homework and quizzes. [Same alternatives as in item 202.]

204. Whether or not I an nervous before taking a mathematics test, once I start I seem to forget my nervousness.
a. I always forget my nervousness
b. I usually forget my nervousness
c. I sometimes forget my nervousness
d. I rarely forget my nervousness
e. I never forget my nervousness

(Wilson et al., 1968f, p. 220.)

The following four items are from a scale for debilitating anxiety.

E.4-1.0–E.4-3.0

205. Nervousness while taking a mathematics test keeps me from doing well.
a. always
b. often
c. sometimes
d. rarely
e. never

206. When I have been doing poorly in mathematics, my fear of a bad grade keeps me from doing my best.
a. never
b. hardly ever
c. sometimes
d. usually
e. always

207. When I am poorly prepared for a mathematics test, I get upset and do even less well than I expected. [Same alternatives as in item 206.]

208. The more important the mathematics test, the less well I seem to do. [Same alternatives as in item 206, but in reverse order.]

(Wilson et al., 1968f, pp. 220–221.)

Self-concept (E.5) A child's estimation of himself both as a person and as a student of mathematics can have implications for his mathematics performance. A theoretical formulation of this construct can be found in the work of Coopersmith (1959). The scales from which the following items are taken are described in Romberg and Wilson (1969). NLSMA self-concept scales were used in grades 5 to 12.

The first NLSMA self-concept scale is an *ideal* self-concept scale. It measures how a student wishes he were in relation to mathematics.

E.5-1.0–E.5-3.0

209. I wish it were easier for me to talk in front of my mathematics class.
a. strongly agree
b. agree
c. mildly agree
d. mildly disagree
e. disagree
f. strongly disagree

210. I wish I were proud of my mathematics homework. [Same alternatives as in item 209.]
211. I wish I were trying harder in mathematics. [Same alternatives as in item 209.]
212. I would like to be called on in mathematics class more often. [Same alternatives as in item 209.]
213. I wish I could do better in mathematics. [Same alternatives as in item 209.]
214. I wish I felt less upset in mathematics class. [Same alternatives as in item 209.]
215. I wish my mathematics teacher did not make me feel that I am doing poorly. [Same alternatives as in item 209.]
216. I wish I were not so discouraged with my mathematics schoolwork. [Same alternatives as in item 209.]

(Wilson et al., 1968f, pp. 216, 220.)

The second NLSMA self-concept scale is an actual self-concept scale. It is designed to measure how a student sees himself in relation to mathematics.

E.5-1.0–E.5-3.0

217. I find it hard to talk in front of my mathematics class. [Same alternatives as in item 209.]
218. I am very proud of my mathematics schoolwork. [Same alternatives as in item 209.]
219. I try to do the very best work in mathematics that I can. [Same alternatives as in item 209.]
220. I like to be called on in mathematics class. [Same alternatives as in item 209.]
221. I think I am not doing very well in mathematics class. [Same alternatives as in item 209.]
222. I feel upset in mathematics class. [Same alternatives as in item 209.]
223. My math teacher makes me feel that I am doing poorly. [Same alternatives as in item 209.]
224. I am discouraged with my mathematics schoolwork. [Same alternatives as in item 209.]

(Wilson et al., 1968f, pp. 227–228.)

Although only NLSMA items have been presented here, they are sufficient to call attention to the idea of self-concept with regard to mathematics. The NLSMA scales are probably the only published scales of self-concept toward mathematics, but many general attitude tests will include similar items.

Questions for appreciation (F.0)

This category is both cognitive and affective in its makeup. In one sense, it represents the most subtle and most complex combination of mathematics content and behaviors related to mathematics achievement.

Most questions of appreciation are open-ended. They ask the student to produce an organized response about mathematics or a piece of mathematics. An earlier section of this chapter discussed the importance of the following appreciation items.

F.0-1.0–F.0-1.3

225. Why study mathematics?
226. What is mathematics?

These items, and similar ones for specific mathematics topics, are general questions of appreciation—they cannot be identified as extrinsic, intrinsic, or operational until after a response has been constructed. The questions can be restated slightly to elicit either an essay response or a brief answer.

Extrinsic appreciation (F.1) Test items for this category deal with the usefulness of mathematics.

F.1-1.0–F.1-3.0

227. In what ways have you used mathematics this week?
228. How does a farmer use mathematics in his work?

F.1-2.0

229. How can algebra be useful to a homemaker?

Intrinsic appreciation (F.2) Mathematics can be appreciated and enjoyed just because it is mathematics. The following questions explore this kind of appreciation.

F.2-1.0–F.2-3.0

230. What do you enjoy most about mathematics?
231. What do you think the poet meant who said, "Euclid alone has looked on beauty bare"?

The "scoring" of such items is a judgment of the source of enjoyment the student receives from mathematics.

F.2-3.0

232. Why is geometry appropriate for students who plan to go to college?

The item above may elicit responses showing extrinsic appreciation as well as intrinsic appreciation; but even so, judgment about the intrinsic appreciation of geometry can be made. An item with a slightly different point of view follows:

233. A friend of yours who is taking algebra has asked you some questions about the geometry course you are taking. Write a letter to him in which you explain why geometry is a deductive system and what it means to prove a theorem.

Operational appreciation (F.3) The final appreciation category concerns the various activities involved in communicating mathematics content to other persons through various media.

F.3-3.2

234. Explain to the class how to construct a circle through any three given noncollinear points.

Verbalizing the instructions is a more complex behavior than the understanding of the procedure or the ability to do the construction.

F.3-2.0, F.3-3.0

235. Write five mathematics test items for measuring the ability to follow a line of reasoning.

F.3-1.3

236. Make up a test for seventh-graders to measure the ability to do computation with fractions.

F.3-1.4

237. Write a letter to a friend in the ninth grade explaining how to obtain the square root of any number less than 5,000.
238. Write an efficient computer program to calculate the mean and standard deviation for any set of data.

The operational appreciation of mathematics is actualized by the communication of mathematics context. Other "test items" might involve having one student tutor another student on a particular piece of mathematics or perhaps present a mathematics item to the class (e.g., explaining a homework problem).

Formative evaluation in mathematics learning

The concepts of the formative evaluation of classroom learning were presented in Chap. 6. A brief section is appropriate here to demonstrate the application of those concepts of formative evaluation to a mathematics context.

The model in Table 19-1, Table of Specifications for Secondary School Mathematics (pages 646–647), can apply to the formative evaluation problem as well as summative evaluation, for the essential difference is in the amount of material to be covered by the unit. Formative evaluation requires a more microscopic and diagnostic analysis of the content. The information obtained from formative evaluation is used to feed back into the learning system in order to determine subsequent activities for the learner. The analysis of error responses by students is also appropriate and useful for formative evaluation.

The material given below is adapted from the Mastery Learning Project at the University of Chicago,[6] which took as a unit of material for instruction Chapter 1 of the SMSG *First Course in Algebra* (School Mathematics Study Group, 1961). This is a modern mathematics textbook typically for ninth-grade students, and Chapter

[6] The Mastery Learning Project is directed by Professor Benjamin S. Bloom. The material from which this section was adapted was prepared by Mario Feliciano Crespo and Efrain Serrano Vazquez.

1 serves as a review or introduction to some noncomputational aspects of arithmetic.

As a unit, Chapter 1 is a rather brief, concise set of material. The first task, following the general guidelines for formative evaluation of classroom learning, is to analyze the unit carefully in terms of content and levels of behavior. Once this has been completed, a set of test items can be written for each of the topics or ideas in the chapter. The following is a list of topics from Chapter 1 of the SMSG algebra text with notations of the cell codes indicating level of behavior and content.

1. Notion of a set	A.2-1.0
2. Notion of a subset	A.2-1.0
3. Elements of a set	A.2-1.0
4. Identification of natural numbers	A.2-1.1
5. Identification of whole numbers	A.2-1.1
6. Notion of the null set	B.1-1.0
7. Notion of a finite set	B.1-1.0
8. Notation for infinite set	A.2-1.0
9. Identification of rational numbers	A.2-1.3
10. Number line terminology	A.2-1.4
11. Notion of a graph	A.2-1.0
12. Notion of a successor of a number	B.1-1.1
13. Correspondence of number line points and numbers	B.1-1.4
14. Specification of sets	A.3-1.0
15. Addition on the number line	A.3-1.1
16. Multiplication on the number line	A.3-1.1
17. Translations from descriptions of a set to specification of a set	B.4-1.1
18. Graph of a set	B.4-1.1
19. Specification of a set from its graph	B.4-1.1

In general, this list of topics follows the presentation in the chapter and can be organized in a treelike diagram. The levels of behavior required in an introductory chapter are not very complex—there are really no application or analysis behaviors expected in this chapter. The treelike diagram in Fig. 19-1 is proposed to indicate the

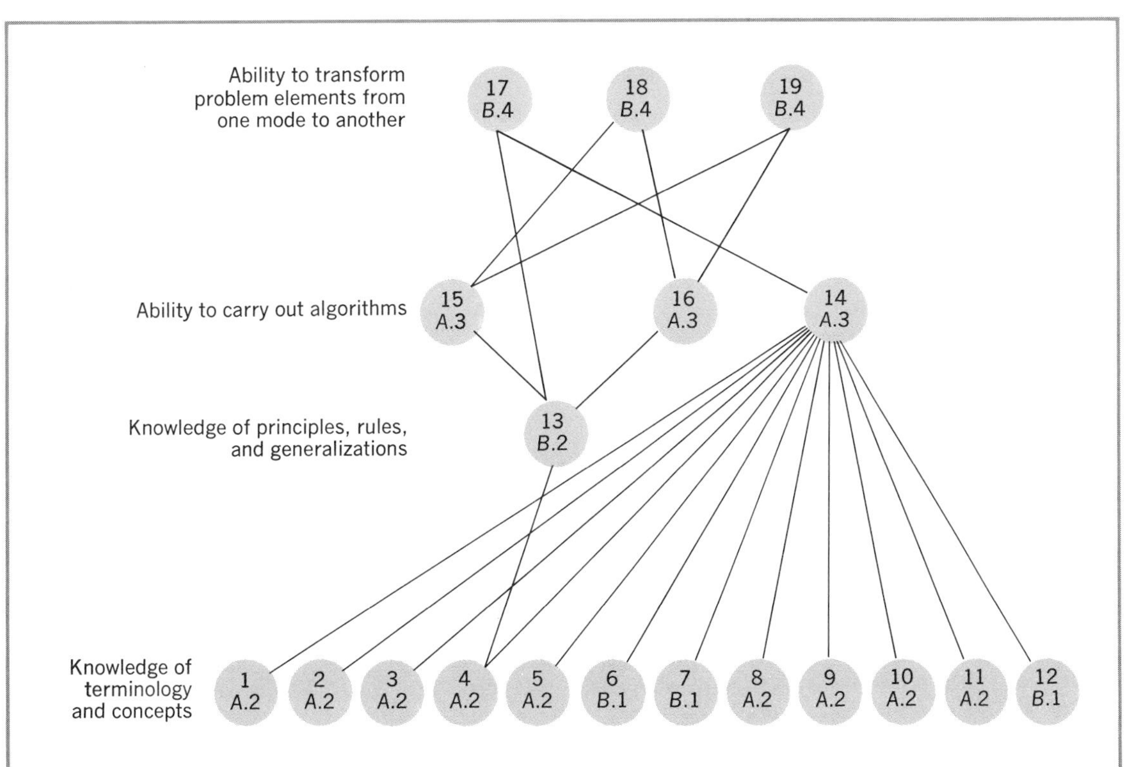

FIGURE 19-1 Learning hierarchy for formative evaluation of a unit from *First Course in Algebra* (School Mathematics Study Group, 1961, Ch. 1).

learning hierarchy; it will be useful in interpreting formative evaluation data and in prescribing alternative learning experiences for students who miss questions at particular levels in the diagram.

Items were prepared by the Mastery Learning Project staff for each of these nineteen topics and placed in a test in the numbered order indicated in the list. The test is reproduced here, with slight editing of items 5, 6, 13, and 15, and with the addition of the pertinent cell codes from Table 19-1.

Formative Evaluation for
Chapter 1, SMSG First Course in Algebra

Mastery Learning Project, University of Chicago

Test Authors: Mario Feliciano Crespo, Puerto Rico Public Schools; Efrain Serrano Vazquez, Puerto Rico Public Schools

This formative evaluation is intended to give you information about how well you have learned the subject matter presented in one section of your textbook. Each question is designed to test an important idea from this part of your course.
Put your name on the answer sheet.
Answer each question in this test by putting a circle around the appropriate letter on the answer sheet.

A.2-1.0

1. A set is a(n)
   a. operation symbol
   b. collection of elements
   c. group of people
   d. one-to-one correspondence
2. Which of the following sets is a subset of $A = \{0,1,2,3,4,5,6,7\}$
   a. $\{1,5,7,9\}$ c. $\{0,1,2,3, . . .\}$
   b. $\{0,2,4,6, . . .\}$ d. $\{0\}$
3. All members of a set are called
   a. infinite d. subsets
   b. finite e. numbers
   c. elements

A.2-1.1

4. The numbers which we use to count are called
   a. rational d. fractions
   b. real e. natural
   c. literal
5. The number 30 is a ________ number
   a. fraction c. whole
   b. decimal d. negative

B.1-1.0

6. A set which contains no elements is called
   a. improper c. null
   b. infinite d. numeral
7. Which of the following is a finite set?
   a. all natural numbers less than 100
   b. all real numbers less than 100
   c. natural numbers greater than 100
   d. none of the above

A.2-1.0

8. The set $A = \{1,2,3, . . .\}$ is
   a. infinite d. proper
   b. finite e. improper
   c. null

A.2-1.3

9. The fraction 3/4 is a ________ number
   a. whole d. finite
   b. natural e. rational
   c. decimal

A.2-1.4

10. The number which is paired with a point on the number line is the
    a. graph d. coordinate
    b. set e. subset
    c. element

A.2-1.0

11. The representation of a set on the number line is called its
    a. graph c. image
    b. picture d. none of the above

B.1-1.1

12. In the set $A = \{7,4,5,3,8,2\}$ which element is not a successor of any element of the set?
    a. 3 c. 8
    b. 5 d. 7

B.2-1.4

13. Each point on the number line corresponds to

a. an integer
b. a positive integer
c. a negative integer
d. a number
e. a rational number

A.3-1.0

14. A set can be specified by
    a. listing its subsets
    b. listing its elements
    c. counting its members
    d. none of the above

A.3-1.1

15. Consider the following diagram:

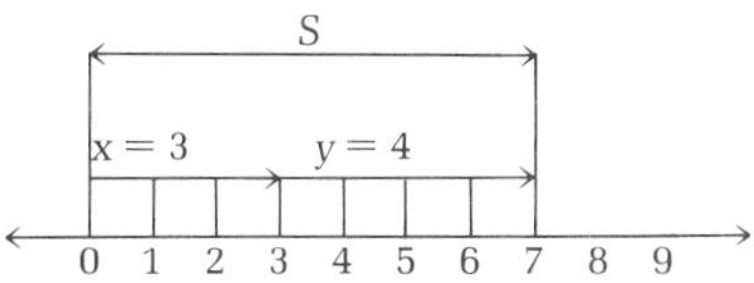

Which is the best description for the length of S?
    a. 4 + 3
    b. 3 + 4
    c. 4 × 3
    d. 3 × 4
    e. y + x

16. Consider the following diagram:

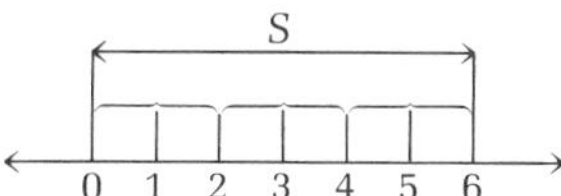

Which is the best description of the length of S?
    a. 2 × 3
    b. 3 × 2
    c. 3 + 2
    d. 2 + 3

B.4-1.1

17. The set of whole numbers between 2 and 10 can be written
    a. {2,3,4,5,6,7,8,9}
    b. {3,4,5,6,7,8,9,10}
    c. {2,3,4, . . . 10}
    d. {1,2,3, . . . 10}
    e. {3,4,5,6,7,8,9}

18. Which of the following graphs represents the set B = {1,2,3}

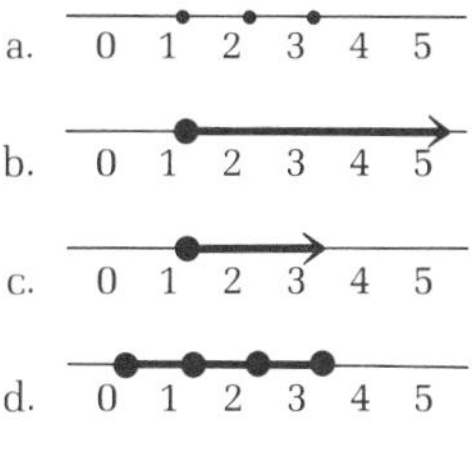

19. The graph 0 1 2 3 4 represents the set of
    a. natural numbers greater than 3
    b. natural numbers equal to or greater than 3
    c. rational numbers equal to or greater than 3
    d. all numbers equal to or greater than 3
    e. all numbers greater than 3

This particular example was chosen only to illustrate how the principles of formative evaluation could apply to a unit of mathematics and how the model for mathematics achievement in Table 19-1 could be adapted to the problem of formative evaluation. Needless to say, the analysis of content in this level of detail and the preparation of test items is a time-consuming task. But the goal is an improved learning experience for all students, and that is worth the effort.

Summary

Testing in secondary school mathematics for the summative or formative evaluation of classroom learning has been examined in this chapter. A model, Table 19-1, has been proposed as an organizational framework to identify outcomes of instruction according to a detailed classification diagramming content by levels of behavior.

The broad categories for the levels of behavior are computation, comprehension, application, and analysis. While these categories can be traced and related to the *Taxonomy* (Bloom, 1956), the description and subcategories presented with the model are more appropriate to instruction in mathematics. Therefore, the model, along with the extensive set of example items for each of the categories, should help make the following point of view operational for mathematics teachers, mathematics curriculum specialists, or test developers: *Mathematics learning is a many-component task. It should be measured or evaluated over a broad range of criteria. The evaluation of mathematics learning in terms of a single measure leads to incomplete or even erroneous information.* This point of view is central to the organization of this chapter.

The use of standardized tests in the evaluation of classroom learning is of limited value. They are inappropriate for formative evaluation. For summative evaluation, standardized tests tend to concentrate on one level of behavior (and hence limit the range of outcomes to be considered) or combine scores across levels of behavior or content (and hence limit the information that may be available in the test.)

The use of standardized mathematics tests is further complicated by the revolution that has taken place in mathematics curricula over the past fifteen years, for which there has yet to be a corresponding revolution in mathematics tests. Some tests which have been developed to measure modern mathematics have been judged to concentrate on terminology (Romberg, 1968).

These comments are not extended as a claim that all available standardized mathematics tests are bad. Rather, they are a call for caution in the use and interpretation of such tests (as indeed the test developers themselves sometimes call for caution). Standardized mathematics tests can be extremely useful for counseling, for evaluation of programs, and even for the evaluation of learning.

One of the important aspects of the revolution in mathematics curricula has been the involvement of the scholar in program development. Yet there has been no corresponding involvement of the scholar—the mathematician—in evaluation activities. During curriculum development activities, evaluation specialists have had little impact. There are several reasons for this: means of communication among the scholar, the writer, and the evaluator have been limited; a framework or model has been needed to encompass the ideas and contribution of each; evaluation is a much more difficult and time-consuming task than curriculum writing; and the evaluator, with his outdated tools and concepts of evaluation, has had little to contribute. While these points are made with reference to curriculum development and evaluation, they carry over into the evaluation of mathematics learning. The concepts of evaluation expressed and illustrated in this book should help the mathematician become as involved in the problems of evaluation as he has been involved in curriculum writing. The development of mathematics education as an academic discipline has been and will continue to be an important link from the scholar to the classroom teacher.

This chapter has been produced in the hope that it will enable classroom teachers, mathematicians, mathematics educators, and evaluation specialists to work together for the production of better tests, better testing programs, and hence better evaluation of classroom learning. For, surely, the problems of evaluation require the talents and cooperation of all these specialists.

REFERENCES

Aiken, L. R., Jr. Attitudes toward mathematics. In J. W. Wilson & L. R. Carry (Eds.), *Reviews of recent research in mathematics education.* (SMSG Studies in Mathematics, Vol. 19) Stanford, Calif.: School Mathematics Study Group, 1969. Pp. 1–49.

Avital, S. M., & Shettleworth, S. J. *Objectives for mathematics learning.* (Bull. No. 3) Toronto, Ontario, Can.: Ontario Institute for Studies in Education, 1968.

Begle, E. G., & Wilson, J. W. Evaluation of mathematics programs. In E. G. Begle (Ed.), *Mathematics education: Sixty-ninth yearbook of the National Society for the Study of Education.* Part I. Chicago: University of Chicago Press, 1970.

Bloom, B. S. (Ed.) *Taxonomy of educational objectives: The classification of educational goals.* Handbook 1. *Cognitive domain.* New York: McKay, 1956.

Blyth, M. I. *Blyth Second-year Algebra Test.* (Evaluation and Adjustment Ser.) New York: Harcourt, Brace & World, 1953.

Carry, L. R. *Patterns of mathematics achievement in grades 7 and 8: X-Population.* (NLSMA Report No. 11), J. W. Wilson, L. S. Cahen, & E. G. Begle (Eds.). Stanford, Calif.: School Mathematics Study Group, 1970.

Carry, L. R., & Weaver, J. F. *Patterns of mathematics achievement in grades 4, 5, and 6: X-Population.* (NLSMA Report No. 10), J. W. Wilson, L. S. Cahen, & E. G. Begle (Eds.). Stanford, Calif.: School Mathematics Study Group, 1969.

College Entrance Examination Board. *Mathematics: A description of the College Board achievement tests.* New York: CEEB, 1970.

Committee on Assessing the Progress of Education. Objectives for national assessment. *CAPE Newsletter,* 1969, **2**(4), 6.

Coopersmith, S. A method for determining types of self-esteem. *Journal of Abnormal and Social Psychology,* 1959, **59,** 87–94.

Corcoran, M., & Gibb, E. G. Appraising attitudes in the learning of mathematics. In National Council of Teachers of Mathematics, *Evaluation in mathematics: Twenty-sixth yearbook.* Washington, D.C.: NCTM, 1961. Pp. 105–122.

Educational Testing Service, Cooperative Test Division. *Sequential Tests of Educational Progress, Form 2A.* Princeton, N.J.: ETS, 1957. (a)

Educational Testing Service, Cooperative Test Division. *Sequential Tests of Educational Progress, Form 3A.* Princeton, N.J.: ETS, 1957. (b)

Husén, T. (Ed.) *International study of achievement in mathematics: A comparison of twelve countries.* New York: Wiley, 1967, 2 vols.

Lankton, R. S. *Lankton First-year Algebra Test, Form Am.* New York: Harcourt, Brace & World, 1950.

Lankton, R. S. *Lankton First-year Algebra Test, Form F.* New York: Harcourt, Brace and World, 1965.

Kilpatrick, J., & McLeod, G. K. *Patterns of mathematics achievement in grade 9: Y-Population.* (NLSMA Report No. 13), J. W. Wilson, L. S. Cahen, & E. G. Begle (eds.). Stanford, Calif.: School Mathematics Study Group, 1970. (a)

Kilpatrick, J., & McLeod, G. K. *Patterns of mathematics achievement in grade 11: Y-Population.* (NLSMA Report No. 15), J. W. Wilson, L. S. Cahen, & E. G. Begle (Eds.). Stanford, Calif.: School Mathematics Study Group, 1970. (b)

Manheim, J., et al. Report of the U.S.A. on the mathematics section of the Cross-national Project on the Evaluation of Achievement. Unpublished manuscript, University of Chicago, June 1, 1961.

McLeod, G. K., & Kilpatrick, J. *Patterns of mathematics achievement in grades 7 and 8: Y-Population.* (NLSMA Report No. 12), J. W. Wilson, L. S. Cahen, & E. G. Begle (Eds.). Stanford, Calif.: School Mathematics Study Group, 1969.

McLeod, G. K., & Kilpatrick, J. *Patterns of mathematics achievement in grade 10: Y-Population.* (NLSMA Report No. 14), J. W. Wilson, L. S. Cahen, & E. G. Begle (Eds.). Stanford, Calif.: School Mathematics Study Group, 1970.

National Council of Teachers of Mathematics. *Evaluation in mathematics: Twenty-sixth yearbook.* Washington, D.C.: NCTM, 1961.

Orshansky, B. *Cooperative Mathematics Test for Grades 7, 8, and 9, Form Y.* Princeton, N.J.: Educational Testing Service, Cooperative Test Division, 1948.

Orshansky, B. *Cooperative Intermediate Algebra Test: Quadratics and Beyond, Form Z.* Princeton, N.J.: Educational Testing Service, Cooperative Test Division, 1950. (a)

Orshansky, B. *Cooperative Intermediate Algebra Test: Quadratics and Beyond, Form Z.* Princeton, N.J. Educational Testing Service, Cooperative Test Division, 1950.(a)

Orshansky, B. *Cooperative Plane Geometry Test, Form Z.* Princeton, N.J.: Educational Testing Service, Cooperative Test Division, 1950. (b)

Romberg, T. A. Contemporary mathematics test series. *Journal of Educational Measurement,* 1968, **5,** 349–351.

Romberg, T. A., & Kilpatrick, J. Preliminary study on evaluation in mathematics education. In T. A. Romberg & J. W. Wilson, *The development of tests* (NLSMA Report No. 7), J. W. Wilson, L. S. Cahen, & E. G. Begle (Eds.). Stanford, Calif.: School Mathematics Study Group, 1969. Pp. 281–298.

Romberg, T. A., & Wilson, J. W. *The development of tests* (NLSMA Report No. 7), J. W. Wilson, L. S. Cahen, & E. G. Begle (Eds.). Stanford, Calif.: School Mathematics Study Group, 1969.

Salkind, C. T. *The contest problem book: Annual high school contests of the MAA, 1950–1960.* (SMSG New Mathematics Library, No. 5) New York: Random House, 1961.

Salkind, C. T. *The MAA problem book II: Annual high school contests of the MAA, 1961–1965.* (SMSG New Mathematics Library, No. 17) New York: Random House, 1967.

School Mathematics Study Group. *First course in algebra: Units 9 and 10.* New Haven, Conn.: Yale University Press, 1961.

Shah, S. A. *Principles of the teaching of mathematics.* London: Longmans, Green, 1966.

State University of Iowa, Bureau of Educational Research and Service. *Iowa Every-pupil Tests of Basic Skills, grades 5–9.* Iowa City: SUI, 1949.

Statewide Mathematics Advisory Committee. The Strands Report, '67–'68, part 1. *Bulletin of the California Mathematics Council,* 1967, **25**(1), 1–11.

Statewide Mathematics Advisory Committee. Reprint of the Strands Report, '67–'68, part 2. *Bulletin of the California Mathematics Council,* 1968.

Thorpe, L. P., Lefever, D. W., & Naslund, D. W. (Eds.) *SRA Achievement Series: Arithmetic, Grades 6–9, Form A.* Chicago: Science Research Associates, 1955.

University of Chicago, Board of Examinations. *Comprehensive examinations in mathematics.* Chicago: 1952.

University of the State of New York, Board of Regents. *Regents high school examination.* Albany: SUNY, 1960.

Wilson, J. W. *Patterns of mathematics achievement in grade 10: Z-Population.* (NLSMA Report No. 16), J. W. Wilson, L. S. Cahen, & E. G. Begle (Eds.). Stanford, Calif.: School Mathematics Study Group, 1970.

Wilson, J. W., Cahen, L. S., & Begle, E. G. (Eds.) *Description and statistical properties of X-Population scales.* (NLSMA Report No. 4) Stanford, Calif.: School Mathematics Study Group, 1968. (a)

Wilson, J. W., Cahen, L. S., & Begle, E. G. (Eds.) *Description and statistical properties of Y-Population scales.* (NLSMA Report No. 5) Stanford, Calif.: School Mathematics Study Group, 1968. (b)

Wilson, J. W., Cahen, L. S., & Begle, E. G. (Eds.) *Description and statistical properties of Z-Population scales.* (NLSMA Report No. 6) Stanford, Calif.: School Mathematics Study Group, 1968. (c)

Wilson, J. W., Cahen, L. S., & Begle, E. G. (Eds.) *X-Population test batteries.* (NLSMA Report No. 1) Stanford, Calif.: School Mathematics Study Group, 1968. (d)

Wilson, J. W., Cahen, L. S., & Begle, E. G. (Eds.) *Y-Population test batteries.* (NLSMA Report No. 2) Stanford, Calif.: School Mathematics Study Group, 1968. (e)

Wilson, J. W., Cahen, L. S., & Begle, E. G. (Eds.) *Z-Population test batteries.* (NLSMA Report No. 3) Stanford, Calif.: School Mathematics Study Group, 1968. (f)

Wood, R. Objectives in the teaching of mathematics. *Educational Research,* 1968, **10,** 83–98.

20

Evaluation of learning in Literature

ALAN C. PURVES

University of Illinois
Urbana, Illinois

Alan C. Purves received a bachelor's degree from Harvard College and a master's and doctorate in English from Columbia University. He has taught at Columbia and Barnard colleges and served as an examiner in the humanities for the Educational Testing Service. He is currently Professor of English at the University of Illinois, Urbana campus. He is the editor of The Selected Essays of Theodore Spencer *and the author, with Victoria Rippere, of* Elements of Writing about a Literary Work; *he has also written some fifteen articles and reviews on English literature, criticism, and curriculum. He is chairman of the International Literature Committee of the International Association for the Evaluation of Educational Achievement (IEA).*

Contents

20

Evaluation of learning in Literature

The goals of instruction in literature

Introduction

The goals of literature instruction in the schools of the United States are often confounded with general goals in English; these in turn are confounded with goals that refer to the deportment of the educated man. If one looks at the aims of instruction in English, one is likely to see a statement like "Learn to appreciate the values of precise literary expression" immediately followed by "Learn to use the card catalog independently" or "Learn to be neat and accurate in one's work." English teachers have often complained that they have to do "everything else," and their complaint is justified—but in one sense their subject matter, literature, is "everything else." It treats of all human experience: even the person who is not neat and accurate, or the person who cannot use the card catalog can be the subject of a novel or a play. If the teacher reads and talks about these phenomena, and his students write about them, no wonder he becomes the Pooh-bah of the schools.

If we look at literature teaching in this century, we see that it has gone through four stages. The first might be said to be the use of literature for literacy, oratory, and moral training: students read texts for practice in reading and declamation and read only texts that were uplifting. The second stage was literature as history, or the use of literature to implant the cultural heritage. This view of literature came to the schools from universities, but there was a counterthrust from the advocates of progressive education to use literature for "life adjustment" or as a socializing force. In the 1930s these two theories alternated, but at the same time there began a movement, started by the "new critics," to use literature as a means of training the critical faculties of the students and of instilling a habit of scientific criticism. In the 1960s this last view has been dominant, although it is modified by the second and the third. There is, as we shall see from the reports of a recent conference of British and

TABLE 20-1 TABLE OF SPECIFICATIONS FOR CONTENT AND BEHAVIORS IN LITERATURE

		BEHAVIOR																			
		Knowledge	Application						Response	Expressed Response									Participation		
		Know	Apply knowledge of specific literary texts	Apply biographical information	Apply literary, cultural, social, political, and intellectual history	Apply literary terms	Apply critical systems	Apply cultural information	Respond	Re-create	Express one's engagement with	Analyze the parts	Analyze the relationships, the organization, or the whole	Express one's interpretation	Express one's evaluation	Express a pattern of preference	Express a pattern of response	Express a variety of responses	Be willing to respond	Take satisfaction in responding	Accept the importance
CONTENT		A	B	C	D	E	F	G	H	I	J	K	L	M	N	O	P	Q	R	S	T
Literary works	1 Epic and narrative poetry (precontemporary)[a]	1	1	1	1	2	0	0	1	0	1	2	2	2	1	0	0	0	0	0	1
	2 Epic and narrative poetry (contemporary)	0	0	0	0	0	0	0	0	0	0	0	0	0	0	0	0	0	0	0	0
	3 Lyric poetry (precontemporary)	1	1	1	1	2	0	0	1	1	1	2	2	3	1	0	0	0	0	0	0

	6 Poetic drama (contemporary)	0	0	0	0	0	—	0	0	0	0	0	0	0	0	—	—	—	—	—	0
	7 Prose drama (precontemporary)	0	0	0	0	1	0	0	0	1	0	1	1	1	0	0	0	0	0	0	1
	8 Prose drama (contemporary)	1	0	0	1	1	0	0	1	1	1	1	1	2	1	0	0	0	0	0	1
	9 Novel (precontemporary)	1	1	1	1	1	0	0	1	0	1	2	2	3	1	0	0	0	0	0	1
	10 Novel (contemporary)	1	0	0	0	1	0	0	1	0	1	0	0	2	0	0	0	0	0	0	0
	11 Short fiction (precontemporary)	1	0	1	1	1	0	0	1	0	1	1	1	2	0	0	0	0	0	0	1
	12 Short fiction (contemporary)	1	0	1	1	1	0	0	1	0	1	1	1	2	1	0	0	0	0	0	1
	13 Nonfiction prose (precontemporary)	1	0	0	0	0	0	0	1	0	1	0	0	1	0	0	0	0	0	0	0
	14 Nonfiction prose (contemporary)	0	0	0	0	0	0	0	1	0	1	0	0	1	0	0	—	0	0	0	0
	15 Belles lettres (precontemporary)	1	0	1	0	0	0	0	0	0	1	0	0	1	0	0	0	0	0	0	1
	16 Belles lettres (contemporary)	0	0	0	0	0	0	0	0	0	0	0	0	1	0	0	0	0	0	0	0
	17 Any literary work	2	1	1	2	3	1	0	3	1	3	3	3	3*	3	1	0	2	3	3	1
	18 Movies and television	1	0	—	—	—	—	—	—	—	0	—	—	0	0	—	0	0	0	0	0
	19 Other mass media	1	1	—	—	—	—	—	—	—	0	—	—	0	0	—	—	0	0	0	0
Contextual information	20 Biography of authors	1	0	—	—	—	—	—	—	—	—	—	—	—	—	—	—	—	—	—	—
	21 Literary, cultural, social, political, and intellectual history	2	1	—	—	—	—	—	—	—	—	—	—	—	—	—	—	—	—	—	0
Literary theory	22 Literary terms	2	0	—	—	—	—	—	—	—	—	—	—	—	—	—	—	—	—	—	0
	23 Critical systems	0	—	—	—	—	—	—	—	—	—	—	—	—	—	—	—	—	—	—	—
Cultural information	24 Cultural information and folklore	2	—	—	—	—	—	—	0	—	0	0	0	0	—	—	—	0	—	—	0

The figures in the cells represent the emphasis in all the curriculum statements taken as a whole.

3*...extremely heavily emphasized
3.....heavily emphasized
2.....major emphasis
1.....minor emphasis
0.....mentioned but not emphasized
–.....not mentioned

[a] The division between precontemporary and contemporary literature is now the First World War (c. 1915).

American teachers of English, an attempt to find an eclectic unity that will resolve the conflict.

The series of goals that seems particularly to pertain to the study of literature in the secondary school of today may be summarized by the four objectives outlined by the College Entrance Examination Board's Committee of Review for the Examinations in English in 1965:

1. To read broadly in English, American, and world literature;
2. To understand in depth those literary works which are covered in class;
3. To respond to literature both affectively and evaluatively;
4. To use critical skill in reading unfamiliar texts.

(Purves, 1968, p. 16)

Another objective of most curricula is that the student like literature, gain satisfaction from it, or want to read more or better books—such an attitudinal objective may of course be given some other formulation. To this might be added the broad goal of gaining insight into the human situation. However important this last goal may be to the study of literature, it seems to belong to literature less peculiarly than do the other five; it is also referred to in the social sciences, and, further (as I shall observe in greater detail later), seems to partake of the nature more of a precondition than of a goal. At this point one can simply affirm that an understanding of human nature is something we both bring to and take from a work of literature (see Rosenblatt, 1968, *passim*).

To see the relative power of these goals, let us look at two recent statements about the curriculum. In *Freedom and Discipline in English* (College Entrance Examination Board, 1965), the Commission on English of the College Entrance Examination Board states that the content of the curriculum in literature "consists mainly of American and English literature. . . . Along with major and minor classics it will certainly include a selection of more recent books [p. 47]." The commission would organize this literature in three ways: by historical pattern, by literary theme, and by genre or type (pp. 51–54). Students are to learn "how to think, talk, and write about what they read. . . . This is criticism, and this criticism, this process of coming to understand and evaluate, goes on as long as whatever we read continues to touch our interests and experience [pp. 54–55]." For the commission, two kinds of criticism are important: close reading and comparison. Close reading includes questions of form, questions of rhetoric, questions of meaning, and questions of value, both personal and objective (pp. 58 ff.). Comparative criticism entails both the intellectual comparison of one work with another and the semiconscious comparison of a work with the reader's other experiences (p. 66). The commission's whole statement of goals in literary education emphasizes the objectives of understanding in depth, responding to literature, and reading critically, and thus represents an academic view of the curriculum—which is natural for a group concerned primarily with college-bound students. It is subject-centered, and except for the last objective mentioned, it is highly intellectual, as befits its clientele.

A set of goals directed at the student in general education may be derived from the report of the Anglo-American Seminar on the Teaching of English, popularly known as the Dartmouth Seminar (see Muller, 1967). The central goal of education is "to get the child actively 'involved' or 'engaged' in a work of literature," and the principal aim is that students acquire not merely an ability to read well but a lasting desire to read books (Muller, 1967, p. 79). The participants in the seminar were less concerned than were the members of the Commission on English that the students read classics, but they agreed with the commission that the history of literature is unimportant (pp. 79–80). Although they expressed concern for raising the students' level of taste, they were opposed to teaching about literature and to the teaching of critical formulas or methodologies. The individual response to the individual work is all-important. Although this response may be enhanced by a close reading of the text and by class discussion, it should remain the student's response and never conform to the teacher's preconception of what the response should be.

If the Dartmouth Seminar represents a powerful new trend in the curriculum, as I think it does, it is a trend away from the historical treatment of literature, which degenerated into biography and history, away from "critical" analysis of literature, which degenerated into critical formalism and rigidity, toward a treatment of the student as audience and as an active participant in the literary transaction between writer and reader. It seeks to give the student confidence in his response, his judgment, and his taste. It pays attention to the affective side of the literary work and of the student. It can degenerate into a psychologism that might neglect the work of literature or into a sentimentalism about literature and about the student—whether it will or not remains to be seen.

When one scrutinizes the individual objectives as they are stated in these documents, one sees that they need a great deal of definition before they can be turned into the specifications for some sort of summative evaluation—be it a year-end test or a national examination. To take the goal of broad reading, how broad is "broad"? Does "broad" entail reading both high and low art? What does "depth" mean? What is "response"? What is "critical skill"? If one is concerned with any sort of test involving more than one class, one must realize that there are few works which every student ought to have read. One must realize that to some teachers "depth" means factual recall, to others an ability to create a coherent interpretation. "Response" is a term that encompasses a variety of behaviors, not all of which are equally applauded by all teachers. And "critical skill" is as unclear a term as all the others: does it refer to analytical, interpretive, classificatory, or evaluative criticism? What the examiner needs is some way of dealing with this plethora of conflicts.

One method of handling the problem is to create a grid with content on one axis and behaviors on the other, and determine from the grid those cells (or content-behavior intersections) which seem to be emphasized in a particular class, school, or curriculum. Such a grid does not imply that the curriculum is seen as behaviorally oriented, but simply that there are observable behaviors which should result from the curriculum, be it experiential, logical, or behavioral in emphasis. Such a grid was devised in 1967 for a report (Dill & Purves with Weiss & Foshay, 1967) submitted to the International Literature Project of the International Association for the Evaluation of Educational Attainment (IEA), of which Table 20-1, Table of Specifications for Content and Behaviors in Literature, is a slight modification. In this report, which sought to describe the American goals of education so that they could be compared with those of other countries to form the specifications for a cross-national study of achievement in literature, a number of documents describing the literature curricula in the secondary schools were examined,[1] first to identify general and specific statements of aims, second to classify these statements as to content and behavior, and third to tally the importance of each of the cells as it was indicated in the various documents.

Those terms used in Table 20-1 which may be unfamiliar are fully defined in the following section. I will here simply call attention to the distinction between "response" and "expressed response": the former is the private, inarticulate, affective, cognitive, psychomotor response to a work of literature which precedes any expression of that response. The figures in the cells were obtained by scanning each document to see the importance given to each content item and each behavior (the scale was 1 to 3). For each document a product was derived for each cell, and the products were added and then reduced to a four-point scale: 0 means mentioned but with virtually no emphasis; 1, minor emphasis; 2, major emphasis; and 3, great emphasis. A dash indicates that the cell is not mentioned at all, and an asterisk indicates a disproportionately great emphasis. For a fuller discussion of the figures, see pages 715–716.

[1] See *Note* on page 762 for a listing of some of these sources.

The content of instruction in literature falls into four general categories: literary works, contextual information (about the author and the work), literary theory and terminology, and cultural information (mythology, folklore, and common symbols).

Literary works (1–19) Literary works may be subclassified by genres, which is the usual classification in anthologies and critical works, even those which prefer to organize literature by theme or chronology. For the secondary school, the most common subclassifications are epic and narrative poetry, lyric poetry, poetic drama, prose drama, the novel, the short story, long nonfiction prose, and belles lettres (1 to 16). These classifications are based on length, structure, fictionality, form, and rhythm, or some combination of these five. Further subdivisions —biography, satire, romance, and the like—are possible but these receive so little separate attention in the literature about the field as to be superfluous.

Across these subclassifications cuts another dimension which has received increasing emphasis in recent writings about the subject matter of teaching: chronology. Most of the curriculum guides refer to something called "our literary heritage," by which they mean works written before World War I; accordingly, they emphasize those works to the exclusion of contemporary literature. In the past decade, however, teachers and writers on the curriculum have urged that the balance be shifted. Jerry L. Walker (1968) has written, "I agree . . . that the study of English should give students greater insight into themselves and the world around them. To do that, we will have to force more of our study on today's culture, today's writers, today's literature, and today's youth [p. 634]." Walker's position is an extreme one, but he is supported by the report of James R. Squire and Roger Applebee (1966) and by the reports of the Dartmouth Seminar. The degree to which contemporaneity is espoused varies according to genre, as Table 20-1 shows: poetic drama, for example, is not a contemporary phenomenon; the short story is. With the novel, poetry, and nonfiction, the curriculum statements taken as a whole show a clear balance between the past and the present.

In addition to these genres (divided chronologically), three other categories appear under the general heading of literary works. Two of them, movies and television (18) and other mass media (newspapers, radio, magazines; 19), appear "subliterary" to some curriculum builders; yet they are given increasing attention in the schools simply because of their persistence in our culture.

> Nevertheless most participants [in the Dartmouth Seminar] chose not to treat the mass media simply as the enemy. . . . More maintained that the English teacher should try to make the best of them as new art forms and could hope to do so because of the wide range of their offerings, which included reputable works along with all the trash. Those who were repelled by the mass media could agree that the teacher should help youngsters to be less passive in their choices, to reflect on them, and to develop more discriminating tastes in the source of entertainment they were sure to feed on anyway.
>
> (Muller, 1967, p. 138)

The third category, *Any literary work* (17), is included for two reasons. The first is that more often than not, curriculum statements refer to "works of literature" without any distinction as to genre or chronology. The second is that many statements refer to abilities and behaviors that are transferable from one work to another. "Critical reading of literature," for instance, is an objective in itself and is not segmented into "critical reading of poetry" or "critical reading of *Macbeth*." Most of the national tests in literary analysis and interpretation derive their rationales from this content classification, so that the tests can be free of any one curriculum structure or any one book. Further, this classification rests on an assumption which, as we shall see, is pivotal in the teaching and testing of literary ability: that literary works are bound together by certain linguistic, rhetorical, and referential (that is, having to do with objects portrayed by words) phenomena which, when combined by an artist, produce a unique literary product. Uniqueness, however, is a function of the combination of phenomena, not of the presence or absence of any one phenomenon. All literary works use words, spoken or written, in a pattern based on our grammatical and lexical expectations. All literary works employ some measure of connotation or some affective valence to words or combinations of words, and they create some sort of structure; that is, they all use some metaphorical language that has an effect on an audience and that somehow limits and patterns the experiences they portray. All, finally, deal in some measure with the human experience, if only because they use words, which are human utterances with human significances. Whether a literary work deals with a crime of passion or with the expansion of the universe, it does so by means of language which we assume to be the expression of a speaker or writer—therefore, a human expression.

These three dimensions of literature—language, rhetoric, and content—exist in every literary work. The ability to deal with each of these in some fashion points to the ability to deal with all of them as they may be combined in a particular literary work. Table 20-1 does not break down literary works into their components, because curricula usually do not treat those components separately, insisting that what is important is the unity and integrity of the whole work. Whether they would be more successful in achieving their goals were they to forgo the study of works in favor of a study of components is a question to which we shall return later.

Contextual information (20, 21) The second large category of content is *Contextual information,* which may be subdivided into two parts: the biography of authors (20) and literary, cultural, social, political, and intellectual history (21). At the secondary school level, there is very little need to break this second division into its parts, for they remain undifferentiated in high school curricula and even in most undergraduate curricula. As Table 20-1 shows, at the secondary school level the history of literature is less important for itself than as a background to be applied to the works. Some new curricula, like that of the Oregon Curriculum Study Center (1965), tend to do away with it altogether, but it does persist to a greater or lesser degree in most schools, primarily because of the habitual yoking of American history and American literature in the schools. This yoking tends to perpetuate the historical view, as does the idea that study of literature is a form of acculturation and that acculturation necessarily implies cultural history.

Literary theory (22, 23) *Literary theory,* the third large category, includes two subcategories: literary terms (22) and critical systems (23). The first comprises the technical vocabulary of literary study and the concepts that lie behind that vocabulary, whether they be concepts about parts of works (like metrics and imagery), or concepts about whole works (like sonnet, rhyme scheme, tone, or mood). The various statements disagree somewhat as to whether terminology has any great value as long as concepts are mastered by the student. Many maintain that a concept is made more easily understood if a specific term is used. The same argument applies to the critical system: Is using it enough or should one realize that it is a system which can be discussed abstractly? A system might be a theory of genres or critical methodology—like that of Brooks and Warren (1960) or the Freudians—or of archetypes and themes. Critical systems do inform some curricula: that of the Nebraska Curriculum Development Center (1965) is based on an elaborate theory of genres combined with an adaptation of some of the categories of Northrop Frye (1957) and is the most critically consistent of any of the systems proclaimed by the various program English curriculum centers. Like the less systematic curricula, however, the Nebraska program is not greatly concerned that the student master the abstract theory of the genres; it is, rather, concerned that his teacher master it so that the student might operate within the framework of the system. A critical system is, therefore, less an object of study in and of itself than a principle which may inform the structure, sequence, and techniques in a course of instruction.

Cultural information (24) The final division of content is *Cultural information*, what someone has called "the central metaphors of a culture upon which literature bases itself." It includes, of course, mythology—Greek, Roman, Norse, American, and British—the Bible, and the major archetypes of which the myths are manifestations. These would include the quest, the scapegoat, the seasons of the year, and various psychological fantasies such as regression, aggression, and castration. In addition to these myths as they might be conceived of generally, as archetypes, or specifically, as incidents in, say, the corpus of Greek mythology, there are also figures which have acquired a penumbra of association to the extent that their names alone conjure up worlds of meaning—such figures as Cassandra or Goliath, or—from a more modern context—Charlie Brown.

These four general categories, then, literary works, contextual information, literary theory, and cultural information, seem to be the major categories of the content of the study of literature. One might argue that there are only two—literary works and everything else. But the "everything else" seems to exist in three distinct groups: that which surrounds the production of a work, that which might be thought of as the tool kit of the critic-reader, and that which is the stuff from which literature is made and which connects one literary work to another in a way stronger than such other connectives as chronology, geography, and history.

One other item of content might be mentioned here, for it has become increasingly important since the Dartmouth conference: the reader's self—his responses, his personal associations, his psychology as a reader. This was seldom mentioned in earlier curriculum statements, but it figures prominently in *Response to Literature* (Squire, 1968), one of the pamphlets resulting from the seminar. This report reaffirms the claim made by Louise Rosenblatt in *Literature as Exploration* (1968) that the individual reader's experience of the work of literature is of paramount importance and that some of the reader-student's attention should be devoted to that experience. This experience would include personal associations, the nature and degree of the reader's identification with a character or situation, and the residuum of ideas and emotions that remain in the reader. It is seldom mentioned as an item of content for the student to contemplate, yet it is in many ways the basis of all talk about a literary work, as *Response to Literature* indicates: "In a significant sense, works of art exist as perceived, or as a constantly growing and developing body of perceptions" (Squire, 1968, p. 23). It is awareness of this fact toward which many teachers would lead their students, and they would do so by asking their students to consider their own responses and to seek the causes of those responses in the work and in themselves. Despite its importance to the teaching of English, however, response as content has not really entered the literature curricula of this country.

Behaviors in literature (A–T)

The behaviors described in literature curricula may be grouped under the headings *Knowledge*, *Application*, *Response*, *Expressed response*, and *Participation*. As one can see, they do not fall neatly into the taxonomical domains of the cognitive and the affective. One reason for this is that the central behavior, *Respond to* (*H*), is at once cognitive, affective, perceptual, and psychomotor; a second is that much of critical analysis involves an admixture of feeling and attitude. Literature seeks to shape feelings and attitudes, and so the reader is led into biases of which he becomes cognizant only if he is a particularly keen analyst, and even then he is often analyzing his attitude rather than the phenomenon represented by the printed words on paper. Although separation of the various aspects of response is difficult, the primary behaviors can be classified, and they are here stated in terms somewhat different from those of the *Taxonomy of Educational Objectives* (see the Appendix to

Part I of this book), to which connections may readily be drawn.

Knowledge (A) The first behavior is to *Know* (*A*) which consists of recognition and recall. "Recall" is the demonstration of knowledge of specific facts, generalizations, and theories. Recall does not necessarily imply any understanding or application of what it is that has been recalled, although of course it underlies any kind of application and is a highly useful tool of the critical reader, who is often asked to match his past reading or bits of it with the words in the text confronting him. It is this kind of recall which permits one to take pleasure in so highly allusive a work as *Finnegans Wake*. "Recognition" refers primarily to the ability to identify specific instances of a given phenomenon when one is told what to look for. For example, if someone is told what a metaphor is and then asked to pick out the metaphors in a poem, he is recognizing. If he is asked to say which of a group of sonnets is by Shakespeare, he is being asked to recognize a Shakespearean sonnet. Recognition differs from the next series of behaviors, application, in that recognition is the matching of one given with another, while application requires one to decide which concept or percept he already possesses goes with a new phenomenon. If the individual is assumed to have the notion of a metaphor, he is being asked to apply his knowledge when he is asked to name the literary device in the lines

> All the world's a stage;
> And all the men and women merely players. . . .

If he is asked what the metaphor or comparison in the line is, he is being asked to recognize a literary device.

Application (B–G) Application consists of six specific types, all of which demand that the student match some concept that he has already acquired with the phenomenon that he is considering. It is a classificatory process, and usually that which is to be classified is a work or a part of a work. In fact, the object of each of these six behaviors—indeed, of all the behaviors other than to recognize and to recall—is usually a literary work. At the university level, there may be some application to or analysis or evaluation of a critical system or of some contextual information, but this attention to the ways by which the scholarly mind operates is not part of general education even though it may inform a curriculum. Most literary study in general education is, in this sense, practical rather than theoretical.

The first type of application is to *Apply knowledge of specific literary texts* (*B*). This is the process of comparing and contrasting texts, of saying that Whitman's "When Lilacs Last in the Dooryard Bloomed" is like Shelley's "Adonais." The point of comparison may be simple or complex, indeed may even reach to the creation of a network connecting each work of literature to every other, as has been done by Northrop Frye.

The second type of application, *Apply biographical information* (C), asks the individual to relate his knowledge about the author to a literary work or part of one. The third type, to *Apply literary, cultural, social, political, and intellectual history* (*D*), includes nearly all the nonbiographical and noncritical information that might be brought to bear on a given text. Obviously these two behaviors comprise the greater part of historical criticism, particularly as it is taught in the university. It is an extrinsic approach to the work, seeking to shed light on the work by using all available information about the world up to the creation of the work. Recently, literary history has moved in a different direction, particularly in the work of the phenomenological critics; Georges Poulet (1959) in France and Hillis Miller (1965) in this country are two notable examples. They seek to apply the knowledge of a work to the context of its creation, to induce a "spirit of the author" and a "spirit of the age" from an examination of a central work in an author's corpus. In the schools, this kind of application occurs most frequently in humanities courses, although as we shall see, it does underlie part of the Carnegie Institute of Technology curriculum in American literature.

The fourth and fifth types of application are to *Apply literary terms* (*E*) and *Apply critical sys-*

tems (*F*). The first of these, which I have already briefly described, is the classification by type of a work or part of a work. The types might be devices (personification, metaphor, dialogue), genres or forms (sonnet, *Bildungsroman*, play), or modes (comedy, tragedy, satire, romance). This behavior usually precedes a literary analysis of the operation of any one of these devices or forms, but it need not necessarily do so. One could perform the analysis without the term. Suppose a student were to say, "In this story the doctor says the girl is like a heifer. Calling her this is like what he does later on when he calls her a cat. He thinks of her as an animal." He would seem to have successfully analyzed the metaphoric structure of a work without ever applying the term "metaphor." If on a test the student were to show he did not know what a metaphor or an image was, one would have difficulty asserting that he was applying literary terminology.

Applying critical systems is somewhat like applying historical knowledge in that it demands that mastery of a complex series of concepts precede their application to a particular phenomenon. If a student were asked to apply Aristotle's theory of tragedy or Bergson's theory of comedy to a particular play, he would have to have the whole theory at his command. What would emerge might not be a sustained piece of criticism but simply a classification of the work according to the critical system, something like "Macbeth is an Aristotelian tragic hero, combining, as he does, nobility and the tragic flaw of *hubris*."

The final classificatory behavior is *Apply cultural information* (*G*), which would include identifying the allusions to mythology that might be in a work, identifying the archetypes that one saw in a work, and relating the work to traditional stories and themes. This kind of classification might generally be thought of as "archetypal." When a person goes beyond identifying the archetype and discusses the meaning of the work in terms of that archetype, he is interpreting the work. The application of cultural information would consist in saying, for example, that *Huckleberry Finn* is a quest and showing in what ways it resembles certain other quest stories. If one were to go on to say that it was a quest for values in a valueless society, he would have moved beyond classification to interpretation.

Response (H) The next series of behaviors are those often summarized by the phrase *Respond to* (*H*), and may be divided into covert and overt behaviors or into response and articulation of response. "Response" refers to all those perceptual, cognitive, affective, and psychomotor behaviors that occur when someone reads, hears, or watches a performance of a literary work. "Response is not passive but implies active involvement; . . . it includes not only immediate response but later effects; . . . overt response (verbal, etc.) may indicate very little of the inner response" (Squire, 1968, p. 11).

Response begins the moment one first confronts the work and ends—well, in some cases, it ends only when the individual dies. It includes reading, thinking, feeling, and acting in some relation to the stimulus of the literary work. It manifests itself in a variety of ways: throwing a book down in disgust or boredom, being quiet or boisterous after a theatrical performance, not getting up for a beer during a television show, imagining oneself a part of a story, saying nothing, or writing a critical essay or a poem. As a behavior to be cultivated, it is considered by many curriculum writers the most important of all they mention, because without an active and deep response—whatever form it may take—no one will pursue literature save for some trivial reason—grades, for instance. Horace said that the twin purposes of literature were *dulce et utile*, and response attaches itself to both purposes and is the way by which the pleasure and utility derived from a work are internalized. As Norman Holland has shown in *The Dynamics of Literary Response* (1968, *passim*), response consists of both intellection and introjection—the process of relating one's unconscious to the central fantasy of the work, of subsuming oneself within the work.

Quite obviously, therefore, response has a primary place as an educational objective, but it—or at least part of it, Holland's introjection—is unteachable. One gains in the capacity to respond, one somehow comes to respond to more "literary" works and to respond to them more deeply and more pleasurably, but the direct inculcation of response seems impossible. Direct measurement of response seems impossible too, simply because response is neural and psychological (its psychological aspect has to do with both conscious and unconscious processes). Some indirect means of measurement do exist, but they are only partial indices. One of these is counting the number of candy wrappers left on the floor of a theater: if there are few, the response has been greater and more positive than if there are many. But one can add little to that observation.

Expressed response (I–Q) If response cannot be wholly and directly measured or taught, its articulation can be. Articulation of response takes two major forms: re-creation (*I*) of the work in some oral, dramatic, or artistic form (dancing a poem, drawing the illustrations to a story, acting out a play) and talking or writing about the response (*J* to *Q*). It is the second, the expressed response, which receives greater pedagogical emphasis in the secondary school, because it seems more closely allied to cognition and therefore more amenable to teaching. The re-creative response is somewhat suspect in English classes because it strikes many teachers as being too close to play and too far from learning. It is play, of course, but, as the various proponents of oral interpretation and creative and re-creative dramatics have observed, it follows upon a great deal of intellection about the work. (It is curious that the re-creative response is coming to the curriculum in literature just as it seems to be leaving the curriculum in music.) The re-creative response appears in very few school curricula; only in the reports of the Dartmouth Seminar does it receive any prominence at all.

The expressed response, on the other hand, remains, and probably will remain, central to the teaching of literature in the secondary school —whether it should or not is another question. In an earlier study, *The Elements of Writing About a Literary Work* (1968), I have sought to classify the expressed response. I shall not repeat that classification at great length here, but shall simply define the four major categories of expressed response—engagement, perception, interpretation, and evaluation (*J* to *O*)—since they appear as distinct goals in most curriculum guides.

In performing the operation *Express one's engagement* (*J*), the student describes the effect the work has on him as an individual. He describes his reaction to the work, whether it be boredom or exhilaration; he describes the way the form or the content of the work makes him feel; and he talks about the characters or events of the work as if they were real people and real events. The reader of the work identifies with the work itself, or seeks to, and describes the degree of his success in identifying with it. In a sense, the person who describes his engagement is describing the rapt state of belief in a work, a state that many authors consider the goal of their art. It is this artistic goal that succeeded when a member of a rustic audience at a melodrama stood up and shot the actor who was playing the villain.

Engagement is, of course, a goal in the curriculum toward which teachers may be ambivalent. For if a teacher wants his students to become enraptured by a work, he also wants them to cultivate some sort of distance from it, both so that they may examine it dispassionately and —even more—so that they may treat the work as a fiction and accept its fictionality. Readers want to identify with the characters in a work; they want to feel like Rhett Butler and Scarlett O'Hara, to have vicarious experiences of passion and heroism. But they must also be able to accept the fact that *Gone with the Wind* is fantasy; and they must learn both to accept the fantasy and to identify with it in a work lacking verisimilitude like *The Fellowship of the Ring*. This acceptance of fantasy is particularly important to the understanding of metaphor, since a literalist may not be able to read lines comparing ships with plows or the dawn with a person. As Walter Ong has argued (1962, pp. 49–68), the reader must believe *in* the writer; this is much more important than believing *that* something is true or possible. In fact, "belief in" leads to "belief that." Engagement, then, involves an identification with the work, a fusion of subject and object, and a degree of distance from the work—so that the reader is capable of accepting the fantasy in the work without feeling threatened by that fantasy. It is of this that Aristotle speaks when he says we fear for Oedipus while realizing that what is happening is a representation of an action.

Quite obviously, there is a cognitive discrimination involved in engagement, the discrimination between the work of art and one's experience of that work, or between fact and event.[2] At its simplest level, it manifests itself in the child's realization that "it's just a story." That realization comes after a period during which the child is absorbed in the story and participates in it fully. At the later stage, he is able to separate cause from effect, to say that he was scared because he was "right in the room when the scorpion crept up on the little child," or that he was sad after hearing the poem because it talked about death and used long "o" sounds. Still later, he may come to discriminate between the mood of the work and the mood that the work evokes in him. I remember reading Wordsworth's "Resolution and Independence" when I was desperately in love and projecting myself on the speaker of the poem—although I thought I was interpreting the poem—so that I said that he was talking about being in love. Now I read his concern as more general and dealing more with matters aesthetic, and I suspect that my present reading is more in accord with the facts of the text. Similar confusion can be observed in those students who read contemporary political or social allegories into Shakespeare or Sophocles. Every interpretation of a literary text is, to a certain extent, an interpretation based on the experiences and habits of mind of the interpreter; that is why interpretations of literary works have varied over the years. But if the reader totally fails to disengage himself from the text, if he fails to recognize its objective existence, he can live in a fantasy world in which all literature is an allegory of himself. A similar fantasy world is that obverse one in which one never leaves the literary work he reads. Engagement is a good thing, but an excess of engagement can lead to a complete disassociation from reality. Bruno Bettelheim writes of the "TV child,"

> Children who have been taught, or conditioned to listen passively most of the day to the warm verbal communications coming from the TV screen, to the deep emotional appeal of the so-called TV personality, are often unable to respond to real persons because they arouse so much less feeling than the skilled actor. Worse, they lose the ability to learn from reality because life experiences are more complicated than those they see on the screen, and there is no one who comes in at the end to explain it all.
>
> (Bettelheim, 1960, p. 50)

The child has lost the ability to discriminate between art and life, or is in jeopardy of doing so.

The expression of perception, the second category of the expressed response, comprises a number of cognitive behaviors, particularly classification, which I have described earlier, and analysis. Analysis may be divided into two major educational objectives: *Analyze the parts* (*K*) and *Analyze the relationships, the organization, or the whole* (*L*).

The analysis of parts would include linguistic analysis of the phonemic features (rhythm, meter, alliteration, and rhyme, for instance), of the lexical features (diction, etymology, connotation, and ambiguity), or of the syntactic features (grammar, sentence type, sentence length, or sentence transformations). Each of these kinds of analysis indicates both objectivity and training on the part of the student. He must be able to see the words as linguistic phenomena separate from his experience of what they convey, and he must have some training in the use of analytic tools and terminology, the last to classify the phenomena he is analyzing.

In addition to the linguistic, there are two other main kinds of analysis of parts: the analysis of literary devices and the analysis of content. The former would include the description of metaphors, images, and other literary or rhe-

[2] I am indebted to Professor Henry W. Sams of The Pennsylvania State University for pointing out the importance of this ability.

torical devices such as paradox, irony, foreshadowing, dialogue, and narration. Beyond the description of a metaphor, simply saying that there is a comparison, there might be some description of the exact points of comparison. Analysis of "When the evening is spread out against the sky/Like a patient etherised upon a table"[3] might include a discussion of whether the comparison is primarily visual (the darkness of evening lies flat on the horizon like a patient), or kinetic (the darkness is absolutely motionless and seemingly dead). It might include discussing the comparison of what is normally considered beautiful with the grotesque. To go beyond this discussion—to relate the metaphor to Prufrock himself—would be a different kind of analysis, that of relationships.

Analysis of content, the third aspect of the analysis of parts, involves perceiving and discussing the traditional triad of literary content: action, character, and setting. To these might be added theme. Such analysis would include a discussion of character relationships, what happens, who the narrator is, when and where the work takes place, and, as in the case of an essay like Swift's "Modest Proposal," what the subject of the work is (the ways of handling the Irish problem).

As one might suspect, to *Analyze the relationships, the organization, or the whole* primarily involves the relationships in and between language, literary devices, and content. The most usual facet of this kind of analysis is one that shows the interrelationship of content and form. A student might well point out a relationship between rhyme as a linguistic characteristic and content in

> The great Duke of Wellington
> Reduced himself to a skellington[4]

and say that the three-syllable rhyme combined with the fabricated "skellington" helps to show that the author is treating the Duke less than seriously. He might go on to summarize this relationship as it concerns the tone, mood, or attitude expressed in the couplet. Such summary statements, together with statements about the structure of the work (e.g., that *Huckleberry Finn* is a series of related episodes framed by the comic and romantic scenes with Tom Sawyer), or about image patterns (the blood images in *Macbeth*), or about the relation of one part of a work to the whole (Friar Laurence's soliloquy on flowers—II.iii.1–30—and its relationship to the conflict in *Romeo and Juliet*), are only some of the kinds of analysis of relationships that might occur in a discussion about literature. I have already covered the analysis of relationships between works in the discussion of application both of one literary work to another and of literary terminology and critical systems to a work. Quite obviously these behaviors are among the higher cognitive behaviors required of a literary student, for the analysis of relationships seems but a short step away from synthetic statement about the work. One might go so far as to say that the synthetic statement—that Friar Laurence's speech, for instance, is an epitome of the structure and theme of the play—is simply the result of analysis and not a higher order of behavior. But it is a somewhat different order of behavior, for it requires the individual to do more than simply note relationships—he must summarize them and put them under some sort of verbal umbrella. For the purposes of our treatment of curricula, however, summary of analysis is placed under its own umbrella, analysis of relationships. Other umbrellas are engagement ("I like it"), interpretation ("it means"), classification ("it is"), and evaluation ("it's good").

To *Express one's interpretation* (*M*) is the behavior of ascribing meaning or significance to a literary work or to its parts. One can interpret a character, say what his psychological state is; one can interpret a metaphor, say that Prufrock's comparison of an evening and an anesthetized patient is a metaphor of passivity; one can make certain inferences about the motivation of characters, say why Huck rejects the world of the

[3] "The Love Song of J. Alfred Prufrock," ll. 2–3. The quotations of T. S. Eliot in this chapter are taken from *Complete Poems, 1909–1935* (London: Faber & Faber, 1936).

[4] E. C. Bentley, "The Duke of Wellington," from *Clerihews Complete* (London: T. Werner Laurie, 1951).

town and lights out for the territory or why Tarzan rejects society. In each of the works cited, some indication of motive or implication exists, but the reader must base his inference on both his reading and his knowledge of human nature.

Similarly, any summary statement about the significance of a work depends on both the ability to perceive the work and the ability to make certain kinds of generalizations. Conrad's *Heart of Darkness*, for example, is the story of a riverboat captain in the Belgian Congo who becomes involved in the search for an ivory trader who has "gone native." He finds the trader dying; hears him utter, "The horror!"; returns to Brussels; and at the end of the book lies to the trader's fiancée about those last words. Such is the story. Commentators have said that it is a story about man's journey into his unconscious, about the horrors of civilization, about the brutality of natural man, about the evils of Belgian colonialism, about man's depravity when he departs from the redemptive force of religion, and about a journey into hell. They have also held that it is a story about art, about a storyteller who creates a seemingly simple yet finally impenetrable narrative. They have argued about whether it is symbolic or not and about whether or not Joseph Conrad is pointing a moral. In every case, the commentators have been interpreting the work, showing what they think it means. This process is one of matching the events described in the work and the words used to describe those events to some context outside the work—to some conceptual system: psychology, sociology, politics, history, ethics, theology, aesthetics, or anthropology (the archetypal reading). Interpreters assert that what the work actually depicts reflects a particular universe or that the work contains a series of symbols (the river or the jungle) that represent certain abstractions (life, error, natural man). Their interpretations state that the work is either a direct or an indirect means of communication, and may go on to assert that the communication shows the bias of the writer toward his subject, that he is urging us to take a similar position or to take some action. The validity of an interpretation depends on both the amount of evidence the interpreter has adduced from within the work and the rhetoric of his argument.

The last category of the expressed response as it deals with an individual work is *Express one's evaluation* (N)—that is, take up the question of the worth of the work. In literature, evaluation takes one of three general forms: evaluation based on effect, evaluation of technique, and evaluation of the vision of the artist. The first asks how successful the work has been in moving the reader; the second asks how well constructed the work is or whether it accords with its genre or form; and the third asks how significant it is, whether or not it conforms to some moral criterion, or whether it proves useful in some way. The second criterion would seem to be the aesthetic one, the first that of *dulce*, and the third that of *utile*. In a sense, evaluation is a higher order of behavior than engagement, perception, or interpretation, since it rests on one of these three; the individual takes emotion, form, or meaning, conceptualizes it, and establishes it as a criterion by which to judge the work or his experience of the work. His logic in deriving an affective evaluation runs as follows: I am excited or moved by some stories I read or hear; I like this experience; those works that provide this experience are good works. The reader then matches his reading of a new work to the concept which has become a criterion. Similar criterion concepts might be derived from a classification, an analysis, or an interpretation of literature. If the criterion concept derives from an analysis of those works or parts of works which give the individual reader pleasure—if, that is, he begins with himself and his experience in deriving the concepts—the more valid those concepts will be for him. Of course, many students are handed criteria by their teachers and asked to subscribe to those criteria for the duration of instruction.

From evaluation, and particularly from this last aspect of it—giving of criteria to students—comes the next behavior of expressed response: *Express a pattern of preference* (O). This behavior, unlike the previously mentioned responses, need not be verbally expressed; indeed, all that is necessary is that the individual read certain kinds of poems or stories or novels in preference to certain other kinds. This objective is most frequently described by the word "taste," and the elevation of taste in the classroom is one of the more controversial objectives in the teaching of literature. The controversy arises from the fact that although we all want children to like what we like (or have been taught to like), at the same time we protest that ours is a democratic society and that everyone is free to like whatever he wants to. Many curriculum guides simply set as a goal, "Read a variety of works," hoping that the taste thus stimulated will be catholic. Others set "Read works of literary merit" or "Learn to prefer works of literary merit," but they are not any more specific than that and never define "literary merit"—on the assumption, I suppose, that everyone knows what that is. As Herbert Muller observed in the passage from *The Uses of English* that I quoted on page 704, even the members of the Dartmouth Seminar were of mixed minds as to whether or not a specific taste was to be inculcated, although they did talk of "reputable works" in a vague way. Some of the participants in the seminar and several writers since then, notably Jerry L. Walker (1968), have attacked traditional literature as irrelevant to today's youth and have urged the teacher to abandon as doomed any attempt to develop in his students a taste for Milton, Wordsworth, or even Shakespeare. They go so far as to urge English teachers to teach an appreciation of "youth culture" or "pop culture" and to forget about taste. But even such an approach supports a particular taste, for it reinforces the taste of the students—or what it assumes to be their taste. These critics and those they criticize see the English class as a means of conditioning to affect the reading habits of the students. In sum, the modification or reinforcement of taste is a paramount goal—covertly rather than overtly taught—but there is no clarity as to the direction of the goal, whether it should be up or down.

The next behavior is almost as conflict-ridden: *Express a pattern of response* (*P*). It implies that there is a preferred manner of discourse about a literary work, which may approach a critical system but usually does not. A course of instruction may set as a goal that students always seek to find the meaning of a work, that they talk or write only about that which is capable of empirical verification, that they eschew seeking a moral or talking about their personal reactions. On a more positive note, the Curriculum in English, Grades 7–12, of the Oregon Curriculum Study Center (1965) urges that students learn to look at "subject," "form," and "point of view" in every work they read, and that they learn to describe these in greater depth and with greater detail as they proceed through the curriculum (pp. 4–6). This curriculum gives priority to analysis of parts, analysis of relationships, and interpretation of a literary work. Many of the other program English curriculum centers set as their goal patterns of expressed response not unlike that of Oregon. But this kind of pattern has been coming under increasing attack, particularly from those curriculum makers who have been influenced by John Dewey. For them, teaching a pattern of response comes dangerously close to teaching criticism, which they believe becomes a stumbling block to the reader of literature. They are opposed to the idea set forth by Northrop Frye that one does not teach literature, for literature cannot be taught, but rather teaches criticism, an ordered mode of discourse and of knowledge about literature. Ranged against this position is the Committee on Response to Literature of the Dartmouth Seminar, which states in its report:

> Response is a word that reminds the teacher that the experience of art is a thing of our making, an activity in which we are our own interpretive artist. The dryness of schematic analysis of imagery, symbols, myth, structural relations, *et al.* should be avoided passionately at school and often at college. *It is literature, not literary criticism*, which is the subject.
>
> (Squire, 1968, p. 26)

The adherents to this view would rather cultivate whatever response the individual has than inculcate a pattern of response which may be alien. The pattern they seek is not one preestablished by critical theorizing but the fullest expansion of whatever pattern the individual seems to possess at one time.

The behavior which seems to approximate this objective is *Express a variety of responses* (Q), but actually that behavior differs from the converse of *Express a pattern of response* in that it refers not to a single mode of response but to the acquisition of a repertoire of response patterns. What is desired under this heading is that an individual see *Winnie the Pooh* as a delightful children's book and as a work of literary art that can be analyzed and interpreted. The individual should preserve a naïve response and at the same time develop a set of analytical tools (if they are what is desired), so that he can read a mystery story with one kind of response and *Hamlet* with another. In Norman Holland's terms, the behavior demands a variable proportion of introjective and intellective capacities, dependent upon the demands of the situation. Introjection is, of course, unteachable, as I observed, but this behavior demands that the intellective never dominate the introjective to the point where a person can no longer say, "I enjoyed it." One may read a mystery story quite passively on vacation, but quite actively if one is writing a thesis on the art of detective fiction. The development of this kind of repertoire of response patterns would seem to ensure a catholicity of taste and the achievement of the specifically attitudinal behaviors.

Participation (R–T) The three behaviors grouped under the heading *Participation* seem peculiarly affective, although response, the expression of response, and taste all have their affective dimensions. The first is to *Be willing to respond* (R), which asks that the individual take some active role in becoming part of the literary audience. Such a behavior consists of an interest in literature, which derives from a positive attitude toward it. It may take the tangible form of joining a book club or theater club, or it may simply involve taking a book from the shelf or turning to a dramatic show on television, rather than going to a basketball game or painting the porch furniture.

The second, to *Take satisfaction in responding* (S), would follow from the first, or rather would be the condition upon which the first is founded. It demands that the individual participate as an audience because he finds it rewarding or pleasurable, not because it affects his income or his status in the community. Many people do participate in the cultural life of the community simply because they think it will advance them socially or "improve their minds"; a few participate because they think it's fun. This behavior is an increasingly important goal to the curriculum makers, because they see that the social or moral impetus toward culture has not had an invigorating effect on our cultural life. It is increasingly important, too, because social and moral appeals have little effect on the culturally disadvantaged; for them it is more important to enjoy than to be uplifted. If they do enjoy, perhaps they will be uplifted. The curriculum makers, therefore, are just beginning to seek to present literature as a pleasurable activity, not simply a vehicle for improving the intellect. Their emphasis is increasingly on *dulce*, not *utile*.

The final affective behavior is *Accept the importance* (T) of a literary work, a behavior which might be termed an intellectual attitude. It is the behavior which underlies the curriculum goal of recognizing the importance of a free literature in a free society, of seeing that literature is both a source of pleasure and a source of knowledge. In its most obvious form, the behavior manifests itself in opposition to censorship, financial or moral support of literary endeavors, and provision of various literary activities for one's children. As a measurable goal, it will probably be latent in the schoolchild and manifest in the adult when he is a parent, voter, or school-board member. Some of the attitudes can, of course, be measured in the school years, but whether they have become ingrained or not remains debatable until some opportunity for action occurs.

The current emphases in literature teaching

Such, then, are the major categories of the content of literature instruction and the behaviors sought through that instruction. Table 20-1 shows the emphases on these behaviors in the major curriculum statements up to 1967 (see the *Note* on pages 764–766).

Certain aspects of this grid are worthy of note. The first is that although all the genres are mentioned in the various documents, two stand out as being of primary importance—poetic drama and the novel. An obvious explanation of this is that the one author mentioned by all curriculum writers is Shakespeare. Novels are the next most frequently mentioned, simply because they are longish works and form a fairly large bulk of the curriculum. More striking than these two facts is the fact that contemporary literature (except for the short story) receives considerably less attention than does the literature that one might call classical. Such a condition may be explained, I think, by the fact that most curricula derive from the objective that students be exposed to their literary heritage. Usually the heritage suffers a time lag of about a hundred years, although the gap seems to be lessening. Certainly the impact of F. R. Leavis, of the Dartmouth Seminar, and of those who demand a curriculum relevant to the culturally disadvantaged (who, as far as the high culture of literature is concerned, make up 75 percent of the school population) will tend to make the gap disappear. The reports of the Dartmouth Seminar would seem to reverse the trend of the older curricula and place at least equal emphasis on contemporary and precontemporary literature.

The primacy of the literary heritage also accounts for the minimal emphasis on the mass media and for a strong emphasis on the recall of historical information. Literary history as such seems to be on the decline, however, and literary terminology in the ascendant, as the advocates of critical reading gain supporters. The newer trends in the curriculum, notably those espoused at the Dartmouth Seminar, would seem to denigrate the learning of such terminology as a goal and would seek instead to use whatever general knowledge might be available to the student. Both the recall and the application of literary terminology would be given minor emphasis as a result of the seminar.

When one examines the behaviors, one notes certain anomalies. The first is that although the recall of cultural information is stressed, its application is hardly mentioned. This is not true of the other kinds of contextual information, all of which are seen as useful to the reading of literary works. Only one curriculum, that of the Nebraska Curriculum Development Center (which was not included in the original tabulation), stresses the application of cultural information; in fact it would seem to make this central to the expression of response. It is also one of the few of the new curricula that gives importance to the re-creation of literature.

The second anomaly is that of all the modes of expressed response, interpretation is by far the most important, receiving a third again as much emphasis as its nearest competitor, engagement, and twice as much as evaluation; yet at the same time there is virtually no mention of inculcating a pattern of response. This might be explained by the fact that although the curriculum writers are deeply concerned that students learn how to derive meaning from works of literature, they are careful not to announce that they want this to be the only acceptable mode of response. The curricula are in a sense denying that they seek to inculcate what they are actually seeking to inculcate. I might add that the documents of the Dartmouth Seminar do not place as much importance on interpretation as do the earlier curricula; they mention engagement and evaluation more frequently.

The final anomaly is the comparative lack of emphasis on the affective goals, particularly that of accepting the importance of literature. In part this may be explained by the fact that these goals are more often stated as assumptions or hopes rather than as educational objectives. To a certain extent the kind of commitment they describe is unteachable and not readily measurable. A second partial explanation may be that these goals are not seen as consonant with the prevailing informal educational philosophy that school is a time for work and the intellect, and that it is not particularly important to see literature as pleasurable. The professional study of literature, be it philological, historical, or critical, is thought of—to use the phrase of Matthew Arnold and R. P. Blackmur—as a "job of work." This conception has permeated the American school, which sees literature as a serious enterprise from which we gain wisdom and skill in critical thinking. Joy in bookville is only now beginning to reenter the curriculum, and with it a concern for the other affective goals of interest and intellectual acceptance. Thirty years ago it was taken for granted that people read for pleasure or escape; now, thanks to the strong competition of the mass media and other possibilities for leisure time, we must purposefully set out to hook people on books.

Three high school English programs

Despite the diversity of the English programs in the secondary school, there are two courses which permeate the curriculum for the college-bound student and one which is beginning to become recognized as having merit for the academically disadvantaged student. Each of these courses reaches toward some of the educational objectives I have cited. The first of these is a course in American literature, usually given in the eleventh grade. The second is an introduction to literature, usually formulated as an introduction to the literary genres. The third is a broad reading program.

In treating each of these courses, I shall take one unit as an example in order to reduce the risk of redundancy. One can do this in literature and still exemplify the aims of a whole semester or year, because the objectives of each unit epitomize those of the course. The behaviors remain the same, and while the content might shift, there is usually a repetition of what goes on from unit to unit. Each unit seeks to build on the skills mastered in the preceding unit, to deepen and strengthen them, so that the objective of a unit is both the mastery of the work at hand and the mastery of the skills of reading and responding to that work so that one is able to read and respond to the next work. The works of literature themselves, the contextual information, even the literary terms, do not exist in a hierarchy that precludes the interchanging of works, terms, or history. Occasionally there is an order within a unit so that the student can master the progression of an idea, a genre, or a stylistic device, and he need not necessarily have studied the earlier unit in order to make this progression. The curriculum builder's plan may have a sequence to it, of course, but seldom is this sequence developmental.

In this section, I shall describe the three courses in terms of their objectives and organization, using as examples the American literature curriculum produced by the Curriculum Study Center in English, Carnegie Institute of Technology, now Carnegie-Mellon University (Steinberg, Slack, Cottrell, & Josephs, undated); the volume *Types of Literature* (Bennett, Evans, and Gordon, 1967) for the introduction to the genres; and the volume *Hooked on Books* (Fader & Shaevitz, 1966) to illustrate a reading program for the disadvantaged.

Thematic curriculum

The writers of the Carnegie curriculum define literature as "mankind's record, expressed in verbal art forms, of what it is like to be alive" (Steinberg et al., p. 3). In this eleventh-grade course, they are particularly concerned with the modification of the universal concerns of literature that are imposed by particular cultural patterns, in this case the American. About half the emphasis of the curriculum is on these modifications, about one quarter on the universal concerns (the focus of the tenth grade), and about one quarter on literary art forms (the focus of the twelfth grade).

> The eleventh-grade course consists of American literature which demonstrates how universal concerns are modified by the American cultural pattern from Puritan times to the present. The approach to the American literature chosen is roughly historical, but looks nothing like the traditional survey. Rather, the course focuses on important aspects of the American character as they are revealed in our literature—such aspects as American Puritanism, the American desire to get ahead in the world, American optimism, and the American social conscience [p. 3].

There are six units: the American Puritan Attitude, the American Desire for Success, American Idealism, the American Darker Spirit, the American Social Conscience, and the Modern American Quest for Identity (pp. 6–7). An important point about this program is that it is inductive—it moves from the text to the concept so that the student is forced to define the concept using the various texts as the means of definition.

In terms of Table 20-1, the two main objectives would be the interpretation of texts (primarily of novels, plays, and lyric poems), both contemporary and precontemporary, and the application of the knowledge of those texts to literary, cultural, political, and social history (as well as the application of history to the texts). Important as a first step is recall. The most important objective of expressed response is interpretation.

Taking one unit as an example and indicating its major points of emphasis, we can see how these objectives are made operational. In the unit on the American Desire for Success, the students read Franklin's *Autobiography*, *The Rise of Silas Lapham*, *All My Sons*, and *The Great Gatsby*. The indicated points of emphasis are:

1. Franklin's moral attitudes
2. Franklin's concept of success
3. Franklin's advice concerning the road to success: morality, industry, frugality, moderation
4. The development of character (for *The Rise of Silas Lapham*, *All My Sons*, and *The Great Gatsby*)
5. Social classes in the United States: contrast between the old rich and the new rich
6. The development of the narrative: techniques of realism
7. How each character in *Silas Lapham* represents one strength of the American character
8. Howell's balanced view of the American man's desire for success
9. Comparison of heroines
10. Views of success held by Howells, Franklin, and the American Puritans
11. The relationship of the individual to society: moral and social obligations
12. Miller's criticism of American materialism and the American man's desire for success
13. Arthur Miller as a playwright
14. Comparisons: characters and writers
15. The society of the twenties
16. Final delineation of character
17. The degree to which Keller and Gatsby show qualities of the tragic hero
18. Criticism of American materialism in the novel
19. Universal concerns in *The Great Gatsby*, *All My Sons*, and *The Rise of Silas Lapham* (as they are modified by the American culture)

Of these nineteen points, ten are concerned with the major theme of the unit, five are devoted to character analysis, two to the art of the writer, and the rest to analysis of parts of the works. The ten are primarily interpretive—dealing with one work. Only two deal with the application of more than one work to intellectual and social history. The points dealing with character would seem to involve both analysis and interpretation; one deals with the application of a critical system (Aristotle's) to the work. It is difficult to tell whether the two points dealing with the craft of the writer are analytical or evaluative, but from the class questions it would seem they deal with the analysis of the structure of the literary work.

From these points, one can gain, I think, a sense of the unit and the course as a whole (see Table 20-2, Table of Specifications Showing the Emphasis of the Carnegie Curriculum).

Genre curriculum

A second typical course of study is the generic one as it is exemplified in the tenth-grade volume,

TABLE 20-2 TABLE OF SPECIFICATIONS SHOWING THE EMPHASIS OF THE CARNEGIE CURRICULUM

	A	B	C	D	E	F	G	H	I	J	K	L	M	N	O	P	Q	R	S	T
1	—	—																		
2	—																			
3	—																			
4	—																			
5	—																			
6	—																			
7	—																			
8	1	3		2	1	0					1	2	3							
9	1	3		2	1	0					1	2	3							
10	1	3		2	1	0					1	2	3							
11	—																			
12	—																			
13	1	3		2	1	0					1	2	3							
14	—																			
15	—																			
16	—																			
17	—																			
18	—																			
19	—																			
20	1	1																		
21	2	3																		
22	2																			
23	1																			
24	—																			

Types of Literature, of the series published by Ginn and Company (Bennett et al., 1967). The general aims of the whole Ginn program are "to enable the student to read with increasing understanding the various forms of literature, . . . to bring the student to enjoy reading and develop taste in his choice of books, . . . to acquaint the student with the cultural heritage, . . . [and] to help the student to develop his values and to understand more about himself" (Evans, 1967, p. 1). The genres covered in the volume are the short story, drama, the essay, biography, the novel, poetry—both lyric and narrative—and poetic drama. The emphasis of the course is on the first of the general goals, and, in particular, on literary techniques in each of the genres and on the orderly structure in a work of literature (Bennett et al., 1967, p. 5). There is some emphasis on meaning and almost none on evaluation in the study questions following each work. The primary goals of the course would seem to be, in order of importance,

1. To apply literary terms (*E*)
2. To analyze the parts (*K*)
3. To analyze the relationships, the organization, and the whole (*L*)
4. To express one's interpretation (*M*)
5. To apply knowledge of specific literary texts (*B*)

The other general goals are of lesser importance in this particular year of the series (see Table 20-3, Table of Specifications Showing the Emphasis of the Ginn Program).

To take one of the units as an example, let us examine the unit on poetry. The student is urged to ask three main questions about each poem: "*What is the experience being described? How is the poem put together? What does the experience mean?*" (Bennett et al., 1967, p. 470.) He is asked to pay attention to images, figurative language, rhythm, and sound. These four are, in fact, the major technical differentiating characteristics of poetry. Further, he is asked to apply the following terms to a literary work: concrete terms, abstract terms, image, simile, personification, metaphor, symbol, fable, couplet, iambic foot, free verse, masculine rhyme, feminine rhyme, end rhyme, internal rhyme, alliteration, onomatopoeia, euphony, cacophony, diction, narrative poetry, lyric poetry, dramatic poetry, idyll, and allegory. There is also a note on the technical terms of meter, but these seem less important than those listed above.

In both these courses, the objectives of the unit approximate the objectives of the whole curriculum. The first emphasizes interpretation, the analysis leading to it, and the cultural inferences following from it. The second emphasizes the analysis of literary structure and the application of literary terminology. Neither of them is particularly concerned with the other aspects of the expressed response—engagement or evaluation—or with attitudes, probably because both are curricula for the academically talented. As Daniel Fader has written, "Attitude only follows performance when children are performance-oriented, and even with such children the attitude may not be the one that educators intend to foster" (Fader & Shaevitz, 1966, p. 13).

Attitudinal curriculum

In contrast to the other two, Fader's own program, the English in Every Classroom program developed for boys in a reformatory, set as its main goal changing the attitudes of the students so that they would want to read and write. The literature part of the program sought to saturate the students with newspapers, magazines, and paperback books. Beyond that, the approach to the literature was social: the works were to be "of immediate interest and particular relevance to the student's situation" (Fader & Shaevitz, 1966, p. 67). What discussion there was centered on engagement and interpretation.

One sample unit is included in the volume, a unit on *West Side Story*, which emphasizes twenty points. Although the points are somewhat repetitive, I shall reproduce them mainly to show their contrast with the points of emphasis of the other two curricula:

TABLE 20-3 TABLE OF SPECIFICATIONS SHOWING THE EMPHASIS OF THE GINN PROGRAM

	A	*B*	*C*	*D*	*E*	*F*	*G*	*H*	*I*	*J*	*K*	*L*	*M*	*N*	*O*	*P*	*Q*	*R*	*S*	*T*
1	1	0			3						3	3	2			2				
2	1	0			3						3	3	2			2				
3	1	0			3						3	3	2			2				
4	1	0			3						3	3	2			2				
5	1	0			3						3	3	2			2				
6	1	0			3						3	3	2			2				
7	1	0			3						3	3	2			2				
8	1	0			3						3	3	2			2				
9	1	0			3						3	3	2			2				
10	1	0			3						3	3	2			2				
11	1	0			3						3	3	2			2				
12	1	0			3						3	3	2			2				
13	1	0			3						3	3	2			2				
14	1	0			3						3	3	2			2				
15	1	0			3						3	3	2			2				
16	1	0			3						3	3	2			2				
17																				
18																				
19																				
20																				
21																				
22	3																			
23	2																			
24																				

1. To show how fear and dissatisfaction with oneself and one's way of living cause:
   A. Some people to try to change the status quo;
   B. Other people to fight tooth and nail to maintain it.
2. To show that fear and dissatisfaction cause:
   A. Some people to group together in order to protect their interests;
   B. Other people to come together to try to better their lives.
3. To show how fear and dissatisfaction cause:
   A. Some people to "go along" even though they don't really approve;
   B. Other people to try to break away.
4. To show how the same motivations of fear and dissatisfactions were the conditions that created the two gangs.
5. To show how failure to recognize and understand their similarities caused them only to see their differences.
6. To show how hatred is a result of dissatisfaction, fear, frustration, lack of love, failure to recognize similarities, and relentless concentration on differences.
7. To show how two individuals were temporarily able to overcome their personal fears and group frustrations to love each other.
8. To show how the gang's collective hatred caused them to destroy the individual love of Tony and Maria.
9. To show how common hatred led to a common tragedy.
10. To show how hate, instead of solving problems, only creates more hatred, more problems, and finally leads to tragedy.
11. To show the close relationship between ignorance and prejudice, and ignorance and fear.
12. To encourage investigation of one's own attitudes toward other people.
13. To encourage empathy or "putting yourself in the other person's shoes."
14. To show how the needs for acceptance, status, and recognition are traits basic to all human beings.
15. To show how friendship can be abused and used selfishly.
16. To show how vengeance only makes things worse in the long run.
17. To show how good intentions, if not thought-out carefully, can lead to tragedy for everyone.
18. To encourage personal comparison of one's own feelings with story book characters.
19. To show that literature, music, art, plays, and movies are expressions of situations that usually are true to life.
20. To encourage oral, written, graphic, and dramatic expression.

(Fader & Shaevitz, 1966, pp. 80–81)

To some observers, the first eleven points might seem to smack of the now-discarded school of message-hunting and moralism, as might points 15, 16, and 17, because they seem to speak less of objective analysis than of internalizing the thoughts that the work might arouse. This is interpretation of a sort, but not the kind of interpretation that is encouraged in the other two curricula; it is really the talk that emerges from engagement. There is a certain ingenuousness in the list, for it buries its two key objectives (numbers 13 and 18) in the middle of a long list of morals. But if these two objectives are met, the interpretation will be, not the moral derived from a fable, but a judgment of the characters and situations as if they were real people. Many of the discussion questions begin "If you had been X, what would you have done?" and thus encourage the students to identify themselves with the characters and situations and to consider them as real experiences, not as fictions. The program as a whole seems to encourage a high degree of transfer between real and fictional experiences. The interpretation, therefore, is less objective than most moral interpretations, more personal, and perhaps more relevant to the students.

The final activities of the unit include reenactment of the story, writing and talking about the student's engagement—the parts of the story that interested the students and how they felt when they finished it—and writing about some of the characters (Fader & Shaevitz, 1966, pp. 92–93). These activities are related to the goals of engagement and interpretation, and the evaluation of the program deals primarily with the student's attitudes toward literature, not with his knowledge or abilities. The program's objectives, questions, and evaluation seem about as different from those of the Carnegie curriculum and the Ginn series as could be (Table 20-4).

TABLE 20-4 TABLE OF SPECIFICATIONS SHOWING THE EMPHASIS OF THE "HOOKED ON BOOKS" PROGRAM

	A	*B*	*C*	*D*	*E*	*F*	*G*	*H*	*I*	*J*	*K*	*L*	*M*	*N*	*O*	*P*	*Q*	*R*	*S*	*T*
1																				
2																				
3																				
4																				
5																				
6																				
7																				
8								3	1	3	1	1	3	1		1	2	3	3	3
9																				
10								3	1	3	1	1	3	1		1	2	3	3	3
11																				
12								3	1	3	1	1	3	1		1	2	3	3	3
13																				
14								3	1	3	1	1	3	1		1	2	3	3	3
15																				
16																				
17								3	1	3	1	1	3	1		1	2	3	3	3
18																				
19																				
20																				
21																				
22																				
23																				
24																				

Yet there is one connecting link—interpretation, the relating of the work to some one of the frameworks which we use to order the universe. The Carnegie and Ginn programs, however, view interpretation as a verifiable statement about work; the Ginn *Teachers' Handbook*, in fact, includes an essay by Laurence Perrine on "The Nature of Proof in the Interpretation of Poetry" (Evans, pp. 254–262), which asserts that interpretations can be right or wrong (many critics have insisted that there are no absolutes, or that if there are, they exist in heaven). For *Hooked on Books*, however, interpretation is seen as relative and personal to each reader. Witness the following assignment: "Give oral reports on parts of the story that especially interested you. For example, some of these parts might be: prejudice, love, hate, revenge, dissatisfaction, status, hope, acceptance, kindness. If you choose one of these, you could tell what these words mean to you and use various characters from the story to support your ideas" (Fader & Shaevitz, p. 93). To a certain extent, the assignment is one in "bibliotherapy," for the assumption behind it is that meaning is personal, not objective, that one gets out of literature a meaning that is useful and appropriate to him.

This idea and the curriculum around it are aimed at the culturally disadvantaged; the authors consider it necessary that cognition be made relevant to the students, and see motivation as a necessary first step toward learning. A program that aims at changing attitudes and arousing the capacity for involvement, then, can hardly be compared to a program which seeks to increase certain analytic and interpretive skills. The latter can establish norms and demand that students meet those norms (whether the norms are valid or not is another question). The former, however, does not ask for specific or normative behaviors, but simply for some change in behavior—from a negative to a positive attitude. This change can be described, of course, but the student cannot be held accountable if no change occurs—only the program can be held accountable. The more traditional curricula have been ignoring the affective and attitudinal goals of literary instruction, so that they have been content with what is "normable." Whether their ignoring of these goals results from the fact that the goals have no norms and are not easy to assess is hard to determine (I suspect that teachers too often teach what is easily tested). It is certainly apparent, however, that as cultural disadvantage increases, schools will have to pay more attention to both measurement of and instruction toward these goals as they have been set forth in *Hooked on Books* and the Dartmouth Seminar.

Summative evaluation

As the preceding section has, I trust, indicated, each curriculum or unit has its own goals, related to and based upon the content and behaviors described in the opening section of this chapter. If one devises his goals behaviorally, as each of these curriculum writers has done—that is, if one is quite specific about ascertaining the content he is dealing with and the behaviors he is seeking to modify, strengthen, or inculcate—one is in a fine position to devise the means of evaluating the success of his course or unit. By determining the degree of emphasis he assigns to each cell he has chosen, he can determine the proportion of the evaluation that should be devoted to each. Such a set of specifications should precede the actual test construction, for with specifications one is able to see how a particular set of questions might be pointed.

In discussing the types of evaluation one might use, I shall deal with each of the behaviors in turn and illustrate them with sample questions that will deal with various parts of the content of literature.[5] My reasons for proceeding in this

[5] Unless otherwise noted, the sample items were written by the author for this text or adapted by him from item types in tests that he worked on while a member of the Test Development Staff of the Educational Testing Service. Many of the items have parallels on such tests of the College Entrance Examination Board as the Literature Achievement Test, the Advanced Placement Test (English), and the College Level Program humanities test. Many have parallels in such a test as the Graduate Record Examination, Advanced Test, Literature in English. Still others have parallels in the items devised for the National Assessment in Literature. The reader should not expect that these items or items like them will necessarily be found in those tests, because programs and test formats change. The author is grateful to his former colleagues at the Educational Testing Service for their cooperation.

manner are two: first, a question calling for recall of a poem is so similar to one calling for recall of a play that repetition would prove boring; second, it is more profitable to explore the behaviors thoroughly, as we have seen, and we will turn to questions of content when we come to the problem of test construction.

Questions of knowledge (A)

Questions seeking to measure this behavior are usually questions of recall and recognition, and as such may be quite easily cast in a multiple-choice or short-answer frame.

A-3 Know a precontemporary lyric poem

1. "Old Ironsides" was
   a. A nickname given to Andrew Jackson
   b. A poem about a battleship
   c. A short story about Abraham Lincoln
   d. A patriotic song by Julia Ward Howe

(Davis, Roahan, & Schrammel, 1938, p. 2, item 4.)

A-20 Biographical information

2. Ill health caused him to take up his residence in the Samoan Islands, where at his death in 1894 he was buried as a native chieftain.
   a. Matthew Arnold
   b. Joseph Conrad . . .
   g. Robert Louis Stevenson

(Progressive Education Association, 1937, p. 4, item 41.)

A-21 Literary history

3. Which of the following works was composed first?
   a. *The Faerie Queen*
   b. *Hamlet*
   c. *Beowulf*
   d. *Le Morte d'Arthur*
   e. *Ivanhoe*

A-22 Literary terminology

4. A lyric poem having a uniform length of fourteen iambic pentameter lines.
   a. Autobiography c. Ballad . . .
   b. Allegory g. Sonnet

(Progressive Education Association, 1937, p. 5, item 72.)

A-23 Critical systems

5 In the Preface to *Lyrical Ballads* (1800), Wordsworth said that poetry
   a. "should not mean but be"
   b. "does not paint the streaks of a tulip"
   c. "is the spontaneous overflow of powerful feelings"
   d. "approaches the condition of music"
   e. "is as a fading coal in the mind of the poet"

A-24 Cultural information

6. In Greek mythology, Hera was
   a. a muse
   b. the goddess of love
   c. the wife of Zeus
   d. the girl who helped Theseus slay the minotaur
   e. the sea nymph who was Achilles's mother

Writing a knowledge question is a fairly straightforward process; its one danger is in making up the distracters. There always lurks the urge to create a distracter which is close to the right answer. In item 3, on literary history, the correct answer is of course *Beowulf*, but someone could substitute *Paradise Lost* for *Beowulf* and the King James Version for *Le Morte d'Arthur*. This would narrow the range excessively for all but the specialized student. The other danger is that the phrasing of the question might lead to a poor choice. The item on critical systems calls for a recall of the exact words that Wordsworth used, and so it is safe to employ a distracter like *a* or *e*. If item 5 asked to which of the statements Wordsworth adhered, there would be a defense for choosing either of those two distracters, even though one is by MacLeish and the other by Shelley.

Items calling for identification of works offer some of the same pitfalls to the test maker as those testing knowledge about works. These items are of course extremely useful for checking on whether students have sorted out the various works they have read. The most usual form is to give a passage and ask students to identify it:

A-5 Precontemporary poetic drama

7. "Howl! Howl! Howl! O, you are men of stones!
Had I your tongue and eyes, I'd use them so

That heaven's vault should crack. She's gone forever! . . .
Cordelia! Cordelia, stay a little. Ha!"
a. *The Merchant of Venice*—William Shakespeare
b. *King Lear*—William Shakespeare
c. *The Tempest*—William Shakespeare

(Center & Durost, 1952, p. 4, item 39.)

One might argue that by including the last line, which gives the name "Cordelia," the authors of the test have actually asked a question of recall, since the item really is asking which of the plays contains a character named Cordelia. In a sense the criticism is just, and it would be a better item if the last line were omitted. The passage or excerpt chosen must be representative of the work and must be full enough to contain clear indications that it is from that work and no other. A line like "What early tongue so sweet saluteth me?" given by itself contains nothing in it to indicate definitely that it is from *Romeo and Juliet;* lines like the following, on the other hand, are defensible in that they are complete, representative, and important to the play:

Come bitter conduct, come unsavoury guide!
Thou desperate pilot, now at once run on
The dashing rocks thy sea-sick weary bark,
Here's to my love! O true Apothecary!
Thy drugs are quick. Thus with a kiss I die.

(v. iii.116–120)[6]

The "what early tongue" excerpt is one which has often been used in tests of recognition; it is just the sort of question that a teacher uses to "catch them up"—obscure, because it calls for a minute knowledge of the text; trivial, because answering it correctly or incorrectly has nothing to do with understanding the play. The second passage is more reasonable, because it is full enough to have context clues, comes from a climactic scene in the play, and contributes to the climax by recalling earlier events and commenting on them somewhat ruefully. A better quotation for a national examination might be from the balcony scene or from Mercutio's "Queen Mab" speech, as those are the scenes that people who have read the play remember, and a national test is designed simply to distinguish those who have read the play from those who have not. A unit or course test can demand somewhat finer knowledge, but it must avoid minutiae.

[6] For Shakespearean quotations in this chapter, *The Complete Works of Shakespeare*, edited by Hardin Craig (Chicago: Scott, Foresman, 1951), was used.

Another kind of recognition item is the recognition of cultural figures and themes. Like the recognition of literary passages, the item would be based on figures that had been read about or studied, and the most useful form of the item would be one which checked to see if the figure could be recognized in another context:

A-24 Know cultural information

8. Which of the following names would most appropriately be placed in the blank in the following sentence? "______-like, he warned the directors of the company that the stock would decline, and heedlessly they kept on buying."
   a. Judas
   b. Cassandra
   c. Electra
   d. Lot

If one is to write items like this, one must be careful to make sure that the context one sets up clearly supports the correct option and no other. A Biblical name like Samson, which on the face of it seems far-fetched, would actually not be a good distracter, for Samson did prophesy, or at least warn, and went unheeded.

Questions of application (B–G)

Application questions may take two forms, the objective question and the essay, both of which ask the student to match two pieces of knowledge that he has and to determine their significant relationships. The latter is a particularly useful question for a summative test that seeks to find out how many pieces of information the student can bring together. The essay question for this type of evaluation would most probably be categorized under the behavior *Apply knowledge of specific texts,* and the content might be another work, contextual information, literary terminology or theory, or cultural information. When these are applied to a particular literary work, an objective measure would seem to be most appropriate.

Apply knowledge of specific literary texts (B)

B-3 Apply knowledge of a specific literary work to a lyric poem

9. Choose two of the poems you have read in this unit that deal with similar themes, and write an essay in which you compare the attitudes that the authors show toward their subjects and the means by which they make their attitudes apparent. In your answer, define the attitude of each, and show by what techniques of language, imagery, or metaphor, that attitude is made apparent. Then compare and contrast both the attitudes and the techniques in the two poems.

B-20 Apply knowledge of specific literary works to the biography of authors

10. Choosing one of the poets you have read, show the extent to which his poems reflect his life. You may wish to show how his images are related to the area from which he comes, how his themes are related to his personal philosophy, or how certain of his poems reflect some of his personal struggles. You may, if you wish, show that his poetry is unrelated to his life, that there is no common strand to hold them together.

B-21 Apply knowledge of specific literary works to literary, cultural, political, social, and intellectual history

11. Trace the changes in the attitudes towards success in American culture as those attitudes are represented by Franklin, Howells, Miller, and Fitzgerald. In your discussion, define the attitudes expressed by Franklin and show how each succeeding author criticizes, supports, or modifies Franklin's attitudes.

B-22 Apply knowledge of specific literary works to literary terms

12. "In many novels and plays, minor characters contribute significantly to the work. They often figure crucially in the plot or as commentators on the action or the main characters." Choose two minor characters, one from each of two different novels you have read this year, and show how each functions in the work in which he appears.

B-24 Apply knowledge of specific literary works to cultural information

13. Write an essay in which you show how two authors have treated one of the following legends. In your essay compare the authors as to the use of specific incidents from the legend they have selected, their point of view in telling the legend, their attitude toward the characters in the legend, and their interpretation of the significance of the legend. You should select one of the following: Electra, the fall of Troy, Job, the wanderings of Ulysses, Antigone, or Samson and Delilah.

Each of these questions asks the student to match two or more works that he is presumed to have read with some central concept—thematic, biographical, historical, critical, theoretical, or cultural. He is being asked to compare the two works in terms of their relationship to that concept. Such a comparison may lead the student to a statement of value, either because he discovers it or because he thinks the teacher wants him to make one. Teachers may want to criticize the value that has been derived, but they should remember that such a statement of value is extraneous to the problem posed by the question, and should not be held against the student or in his favor. The judging of the essay must be in terms of the question, and such questions as these allow students to add values or interpretations that may not be those of the marker of the paper. If, however, they are consistent, they should not be counted against the student. In the readings of the Advanced Placement Examination in English, the chief reader and the group leaders often caution the readers that the papers they will be reading come from students who have been in schools all over the world, and that they have often been taught particular interpretations of a work. The reader must forgo his own interpretation of the work in question and judge the papers on the consistency of the interpretations they set forth and on the way in which these interpretations were brought to bear on the problem at hand. I remember one reader who became convinced that he was the only one who really understood *Hamlet* and that no one who had a different understanding of the play should pass. He had the good sense, fortunately, never to read a paper on *Hamlet*.

As one might notice, the questions I have cited, adapted from examinations like the Advanced Placement Examination, give complete and detailed specifications for what the student is to do. Some might object that this method hampers the student's imagination too much; they would rather see a question like

14. Choose two novels and compare them in terms of their being representative of the age in which they were written.

It may be that this question will stimulate the imaginative student to write a brilliant "off-beat" answer, but the imaginations of ordinary mortals will be stimulated only to ask what the devil is meant by "representative"—is the question to be answered in terms of subject matter, attitude, theme, style, or all four? Should the student choose works from the same period or from different periods of literary history? The student has so many questions that he may spend half the examination period settling on his topic and not write enough to allow one to judge the quality of his work.

A second objection to this type of unstructured question is that it places too much of a premium on the compositional aspect of the solution. It is perfectly valid to present a student with an essay topic like "Write two paragraphs on the word 'green'" (I dislike the topic, but it *is* valid), if one is going to evaluate the answer on its rhetoric and imaginativeness. This sort of question has little place in an examination of literary knowledge, however, where the problem is the literary one of applying one's knowledge of specific works to a historical or critical crux. For this reason, it is advisable to make the rhetorical choices for the student so that he does not have to worry about them. If the question calls for a discussion of more than one work, the more able student will make a true comparison of the two, but the less able will tend to discuss each separately. If it is to be a discussion of one work, the more able students will tend to discuss style and to bring other knowledge to bear on the problem; the less able will catalog without synthesis. Synthesizing, which marks the better student, will tend to appear whether or not the question is structured, and a greater amount of structure in the question will enable the weaker students to display what they know. For these reasons, a preferable form of the question would be:

15. No matter how timeless, a work of literature is first of all representative of the age in which it was written. It reflects the ideas, attitudes, and customs that prevailed during the author's lifetime.

    Choose two novels written in different countries or at different times and show how they are or are not representative of the age in which they were written, with respect to *one* of the following: women, war, marriage, education, the good life, success. In your essay, show first what the belief or attitude of the time was and then how the work you have chosen reflects, attacks, or criticizes that belief.

The question is still a bit cumbersome, for it asks the student to do a great number of things before he starts writing. He has to choose the topic; he has to choose the works; and he has to decide upon the relationship of the works to the topic. Further, unless he has had a chance to study intellectual and cultural history, he may be led to think that a particular novel is criticizing a generally held attitude, when, in fact, its target is local. It would be better to have the tester make more of the choice for the student and offer him a question like:

16. Choose two novels written in different periods of literary history and compare the attitudes expressed by their authors toward marriage. In your essay show that each author appears to think a good marriage is; how it is related to love, duty, honor, or money; and how he makes his attitude apparent to the reader. Finally, compare the two works as to both the author's attitude and the techniques by which that attitude is made apparent.

This seems a far cry from the first formulation of the question, perhaps, but it is now a question that can be managed by many students, and it retains the intellectual integrity that item 15 had.

The general rule for the writer of the essay question is, therefore, to do what he advises his students to do: narrow the topic. He will point his students in the direction he wants them to go, in terms that they can comprehend; he is not putting them in the desert without a compass. It may be that a teacher will want to give an assignment or a test that forces the student to do his own narrowing, particularly as a first assignment to see what sort of focus a class might have, or as an invitation to the class to consider the part of the course that they found most fruitful or relevant. These types of assignments, however, differ from the general purposes of summative evaluation, which will be best served by specific questions.

The application of contextual information, literary theory, and cultural information to a specific literary work can be measured by multiple-choice or essay questions, but more efficiently by the former, in the sense that multiple-choice questions can determine whether or not students have acquired a number of discrete facts and concepts and can apply them to specific situations. The essay question allows them to bring these discrete facts together into some sort of synthesis. The framing of this sort of question, I hope I have shown, is best done if one asks the student to apply the works to the context, rather than the context to the works. The former operation allows the inductive process to operate more naturally than would the latter. To determine whether a student does bring his knowledge of extrinsic materials to bear on a text, one would have him write an analytic essay on the text and then determine whether or not he did use his outside knowledge. To determine whether he *can* do so, one would ask questions like those that follow.

C-3 Apply biographical information (C)

C-3 Apply biographical information to a poem

17. William Blake's "Songs of Experience" reflect all of the following except Blake's
    a. training as an engraver
    b. study of the writing of Emmanuel Swedenborg
    c. marriage to a butcher's daughter
    d. acquaintance with Tom Paine

In this question the problem for the student is to determine which of four true statements about Blake's life is least relevant to the poems in "Songs of Experience." From reading the poems he would know that they are engraved and illustrated, that they reflect Tom Paine's libertarianism, that they use some Swedenborgian terminology, but that they do not have much to do with the background of Catherine Blake. To be sure, the student could have been told all this in a lecture and thus for him the item would be one of knowledge, but the student who has read the poems thoroughly and who knows the facts about Blake's life could match the two for himself.

The following items exhibit a similar demand on the student, who must determine in item 18 which of five men who could have influenced Joyce did in fact exert an apparent influence, in item 19 which set of critical terms is most peculiar to a group of critics, in item 20 which aspect of *Macbeth* is most germane to Aristotle's *Poetics*, in item 21 which legend is most nearly in accord with a definition of tragedy, and in item 22 which most nearly approximates a modern story.

Apply literary, cultural, social, political, and intellectual history (D)

D-20 Apply intellectual history to biographical information

18. Which of the following asserted the most clear influence on the writing of James Joyce?
    a. Charles Darwin
    b. Karl Marx
    c. Sir James Jeans
    d. Sigmund Freud
    e. Benedetto Croce

Apply literary terms (E)

E-23 Apply literary terms to critical systems

19. The "new criticism" is most often associated with which of the following terms?
    a. tragedy and comedy
    b. myth and symbol
    c. pity and fear
    d. paradox and ambiguity

Apply critical systems (F)

F-5 Apply critical systems to a poetic drama

20. Which of the following reasons would Aristotle have given for calling *Macbeth* a tragedy?
    a. It deals with a Scots royal legend.
    b. The leading character becomes a king.
    c. The action is serious and important.
    d. There are few changes of setting.

F-24 Apply critical systems to cultural information

21. Which of the following legends would Aristotle see as best suited for a tragedy?
    a. Rip Van Winkle
    b. Pocahontas
    c. Daniel Boone
    d. John Brown
    e. Joe Magarac

Apply cultural information (G)

G-17 Apply cultural information to any work of literature

The company had tried to set a price for its computers with the other electronics companies, but the government had found out about it. Now someone would have to stand trial, but who would it be? The president gathered together the sales staff and had them draw lots. All were nervous.

22. This story is a retelling of the old theme of the
    a. Golden Fleece
    b. scapegoat
    c. labyrinth
    d. fall of Adam

Most of the items in this sampling have been composed for this chapter. They are imitations of items that can be found in tests like the College Level Program humanities test, the Graduate Record Examination, and other tests of general or specialized information. As the reader may have observed, the items are listed as measuring the application of one kind of knowledge to another, and it is perfectly possible to claim that a question dealing with the application of literary terms to biographical information is the same as one dealing with the application of biographical information to literary terms. Virtually all of the items are reversible in this sense, as is the following pair of items calling for the application of cultural information to cultural information.

G-24 Apply cultural information to cultural information and folklore

23. Which of the following legendary figures is closest to the type of the cowboy hero?
    a. a Myrmidon
    b. a Knight of the Round Table
    c. the prodigal son
    d. a leprechaun

24. Which of the following is the modern counterpart of a Knight of the Round Table?
    a. a cowboy hero
    b. a baseball umpire
    c. a jazz musician
    d. a mad scientist

Only a casuist would argue that the two items call for different abilities; an item writer would argue that they were the same and that in this particular instance item 23 is easier to write and better. There are great resemblances between a cowboy hero like Shane and a knight of Arthurian romance: the superiority of friendship to love, the code of honor, and the convention of being kind to one's animal are but a few. The distracters in item 24 are not particularly attractive even to the person who knows little about the Arthurian knight, and other figures from modern folklore like the baseball player and the private eye have too many similarities to the knight (although not as many as the cowboy); it is easier, then, to make up the distracters for the first item than it is for the second. The test maker learns that with this type of matching question, it is easier to put the more general figure in the question and have the more specific figures in the options. There are dangers of course, but they can be overcome by careful scrutiny of each question and each option.

Questions of expressed response (I–Q)

We have already noted that response to a work of literature is private, highly complex, and unmeasurable except in indirect ways. Besides those unobtrusive and not very reliable measures of looking at what the student does when he reads or attends to literature, we must content ourselves with looking at either the re-creative or the expressed response. The re-creative response (*I*)—declamation, recitation, acting, mime—is extremely important, but the judgment of its merits is difficult and based on the holistic impression of the audience. One may fault a student for being unexpressive or overdramatic, for thumping out a rhythm or exhibiting a tin ear, but between these extremes the criteria for judgment must be accumulated over several years of watching and listening, and the teacher must beware of being overly sure of his judgment. The expressed response, on the other hand, is much more susceptible to evaluation and measurement.

Engagement (J) The expressed response has its affective and its cognitive sides, and we shall deal with them in order, starting with the expression of engagement. This behavior involves accepting a work or being willing to read it; liking or disliking the work (that is, deriving or not deriving some sort of passive pleasure from it); having some emotional reaction to its language, its style, or its content (a reaction which indicates a more active involvement); identifying oneself with the work or projecting oneself into it; incorporating the work into one's conscious or unconscious mind (that is, introjecting the work); and transferring the experience of that work into other experiences (this reaction may be said to be a manifestation of introjection). As one can see, these six aspects of engagement form a progression toward a complete fusion between the work and the reader, and it may be that they do in fact form a continuum similar to that established in *Taxonomy of Educational Objectives: Affective Domain* (see the Appendix to Part I of this book). It seems possible that one could set up a measure and a scale to indicate depth of engagement, but the problems involved would be immense—particularly the problems of text selection. Obviously a person might go further along the scale with one work than with another. I will accept Arnold Bennett's novels, but I do not like them, and find myself stultified by them; on the other hand, I become engrossed in *The Hound of the Baskervilles*, and I have found myself transferring the experience of reading *1984* to my thinking about current social issues.

The problem of text selection for measuring engagement can be solved in two ways. The simplest is to do away with any text at all and simply ask the student to refer to his favorite book or books in answering the questions you put to him. One might then analyze the selections that a class or group makes to see if certain kinds of books elicit certain kinds of responses. The second, and more frustrating, solution is to select a battery of passages representing certain types of content or style. One could, for instance, choose four basic myths or fantasies and present each of them in a narrative, a dramatic, and a lyric mode to see which mode of which myth the group enters most deeply into. The problem with such a technique lies in the fact that each text might have some special aspect—locale, diction, characterization—that would set it apart from the other passages in a way that the tester could not predict; this would make any generalization about the results invalid. The same problem, needless to say, lurks in every preference measure, where no one can definitely assert that the work preferred by students is preferred because it belongs in a certain class (it might be preferred, for instance, because the title or first line is catchy for some irrelevant reason). Despite the appeal of preselecting texts to measure engagement or preference, the difficulties in generalizing seem to make the textless method the more practicable. In a classroom, of course, a teacher can simply use all the texts the class has read in the year or the semester, and not attempt to generalize about those texts. If the class responded most deeply to *The Red Badge of Courage*, for example, it might be dangerous to generalize—to say that they did so because it was a war novel, or a short novel, or a symbolic work, or a book about maturation. None of these facts or any combination of them might have been the reason.

Most of the questions themselves can be cast in some sort of multiple-choice or short-answer form. Some might object that these will lead a student, but if a student is assured that he is to give his opinion, and that no best answer exists, he will be reasonably honest. Further, most of the questions can be provided with a range of answers that closely approximates the full range of possible responses. Questions dealing with acceptance lend themselves particularly to an objective form, since what the examiner is interested in is a yes-or-no answer to "Might you read *X*?" or an indication of those aspects of a literary work that might hinder acceptance. To find out what hinders acceptance, one might devise a questionnaire to determine what preconceptions about literature a student holds and asking what he likes or dislikes about literature in general.

Preconception might be measured by means of questions like the following:

J-3 Express one's engagement in a precontemporary lyric line

Read the line below and answer the questions that follow it as honestly as you can.

"And the tree is my seat, that once lent me a shade."

25. This line (is) (is not) poetic. Cross out the one that does not apply.
26. What makes it poetic?
    a. its sound
    b. its words
    c. what it says
27. What keeps it from being poetic?
    a. its sound
    b. its words
    c. what it says

J-17 Express one's engagement in any literary work

28. What do you think a play should be about?
29. Is there anything plays should not be about?
30. Should plays use any special kind of language?

Below are listed a number of dislikes which many people feel toward fiction or toward certain aspects of it. Read the statements and record your reaction to them by blackening

answer space A—if the statement expresses a dislike which you too feel ["agree"]

answer space U—if you are uncertain either of your opinion or the meaning of the statement

answer space D—if you do not share this dislike ["disagree"]

31. I dislike fiction in which the characters are sick or deformed.
32. I dislike fiction which ignores the great moral and social questions of society.

(American Council on Education, 1942, pp. 8, items 159, 161.)

Each of these seeks to determine whether the student has acquired any generalized preconceptions about what literature *should* be that would preclude his reading and enjoying works which had to him unattractive or unliterary characteristics.

Except for transfer, the measurement of other levels of engagement should focus on the student's reading of a particular book or books. Here one is working not in the open world of predilection and preconception, but in the specific world of the individual's confrontation with a work. That confrontation may, of course, result from a predilection or a preconception, but now the teacher is concerned with what happens to preconceptions and because of them. The first level, liking or disliking, can best be measured using the direct question, "Did you like it?" This question should be followed by questions like "What parts did you particularly like? What parts did you particularly dislike? Did you like the way it was written? Did you like what it was about?" Each of these in turn should be followed by "Why?" or "explain."

Having examined whether or not the student likes the work, one can go further and find out about his emotional experience. Here the important questions are (1) whether the emotional experience was stimulated by the events in the work, by the way it was written, or by some personal association; (2) whether the emotional experience corresponds with the mood or tone of the work; and (3) whether or not there were some fluctuations or changes in the emotional experience. The first question is important because it can tell the teacher whether the student has reached the point of being aware of the impact of language and style and is thus susceptible to literature of more subtle character than *Mad* or *True Confessions*. The second and third questions help the teacher to see whether the effect seen by critical consensus, so that he can see whether the time spent in talk about the work affected the emotional perceptions of the students or not. If, after two weeks' discussion of *Romeo and Juliet*, the class thinks the play silly and not sad, the teacher should seek to determine where his presentation went wrong. It is usually useless to cajole or persuade the class to be sad; perhaps one should simply present the play differently next time, emphasizing the conflict and not the architecture of the Globe Theatre and the difficulties of Elizabethan English. These aspects of engagement can also be measured by some sort of yes-no questioning, with subquestions to allow the students to dilate upon their answers. Whether the reader's reaction corresponds to the mood of the work can also be measured by a series of questions like the Logasa-Wright test of reader participation (Logasa & McCoy-Wright, undated b). An early version of this test had a clear set of five options —pleasure, agreeableness, indifference, disagreeableness, and pain (these five were expanded to nine)—from among which the student had to choose his reaction. These terms were set against passages like

33. A bevy of boys
    In naked beauty—
    The chill clung to the water;
    Venturesome,
    Shivering,
    Shy with wonderment
    Huddled into themselves
    Like street sparrows
    On snowy mornings

(Logasa & McCoy-Wright, undated a, p. 3, item 6.)

I have seen no key for this version, so I cannot tell whether there is a desired option. I would assume, however, that the intended mood is approximately one of mild disagreeableness. If a student chose "pleasure," the teacher would have to have him explain why. This particular passage was dropped from the final version of the test, perhaps because the mood of the passage alternates between pleasure and pain as one shifts from the boys to the spectator's view of them. A passage in a test like the Logasa-Wright test should have a mood clearly on one side or the other of the line dividing pleasure from pain, although the mood may approach that line closely. A passage of shifting moods will not work. Thus, if the passage is one with a painful mood, the student who chooses "pleasure" will probably be reacting to the artistry with which the mood is expressed, not the mood itself.

Although the authors of the test called it a measure of participation, it would be so only if the scale were unipolar rather than bipolar.[7] One participates or one does not. One identifies with the characters or situations or one does not. A participation scale for the passage quoted above might be like the following:

J-4 Express one's engagement in a contemporary lyric poem

34. Which of the following comes closest to describing the way you felt as you read the poem?
    __ I felt I was one of the boys.
    __ I felt like the boys.
    __ I understood how the boys felt.
    __ I did not feel one way or another about the boys.

[7] See the summary of studies of response to literature in Squire (1964, pp. 3–7).

This scale moves from complete identification to apathy; a scale moving from apathy to antipathy might also be feasible—possibly with respect to these boys and certainly with respect to a villain in a story episode—but if antipathy was expressed, this too would be a sign of projection into the work. If there are antagonists in an episode, therefore, one should give the student the choice of identifying with either of them and not assume that everyone is going to hiss the villain. There is some question whether acceptance or rejection of the philosophy of a work—Candide's "Let us cultivate our gardens," for instance—is identification in the participatory sense we have been discussing; to me it is. One can enter into the beliefs of Thoreau as fully as one can enter into his personality. One can say, "We really *do* lead lives of quiet desperation," just as one can say, "I really felt as if I were living at Walden" (in fact, it is probably easier to say the former).

With respect to a longer work, the degree of identification is matched in importance by the object of identification. Does one identify with Lear, Kent, or Cordelia, or with all three? Does one sympathize with them, suffer with them, or remain detached from and critical of them? These questions can be asked in a questionnaire about the play: "Did you identify with any of the characters? Who? Did you ever feel you were part of the play? When? Did you find yourself agreeing with any of the thoughts of the author? When?" Questions like these can, of course, be changed into a series of specific questions for each character and each scene.

The question I cited above about whether a person agrees with the author brings up one aspect of identification that deserves special treatment. Many people who read a story identify to such an extent that they make moral judgments about the characters as if those characters were people the reader had actually met, or they take the characters out of the fictional world and project a future for them. Some will say of a girl in a story, "When she grows up she will never get a husband if she keeps on acting that way." They will call people good or bad, nice or nasty—in fact, treat them as if they had stepped out of the book and into their own lives. This is a common form of identification, and it can be discovered by the tester by means of questions like "Do you think any of the people in the story are particularly good or bad, nice or nasty? Who? Do you feel as if you really know any of the people in the story?"

All of these are direct measures of identification, the kind one might ask if one were specifically hunting for some statement about identification. One could, of course, simply ask the students to talk or write about the work and then record the proportion of their statements that deal with identification, as has Squire (1964). This method is particularly useful if one wants to determine how great a part identification plays in the total pattern of expressed response, and this kind of measure is, as we shall see, particularly useful as a measurement of patterns of response. Whichever way one seeks to determine type and degree of identification, such a measure is important to summative and formative evaluation, because, as Squire says,

> . . . readers who become strongly involved emotionally in a story tend, either while reading, or more frequently at the end of reading a selection, to analyze the elements in a story which give rise to their involvement. Involved readers are more likely to make statements which might be coded as literary judgements than are readers who are not so involved. They thus tend to be superior readers in that they open themselves to a maximum of facets, accommodate imaginatively the widest possible number of avenues to the literary experience.
>
> (Squire, 1964, pp. 22–23)

The two deepest levels of involvement—incorporation, or introjection, and transfer—are best measured simultaneously, for it would seem that if there is some sort of transfer, there will have been incorporation. If there seems to be no indication of transfer, there may or may not have been introjection, but it would seem impossible to discover this except by some sort of testimonial like "Gee, I can't get that story out of my mind," or "I feel as if I'm still watching that movie, and

I saw it two days ago." Remembering the work indicates incorporation, but a memory may be only briefly held or it may be only of having read or seen the work, or only of those details of the work the student felt he must remember for a test. The deeper sort of incorporation of which we are speaking would be a long-term or semi-permanent matter. The level at which it chiefly manifests itself is the comparison of an experience encountered in art with experiences in one's life. It is the inverse of that form of identification in which the reader brings his experiences to the work, for now the reader uses literary experiences as analogues of nonliterary ones. A person might meet someone and say, "Why, he's just like Androcles, the way he makes you think he's henpecked." He might visit Hannibal, Missouri, because of having read *Tom Sawyer*. He might find himself pursuing the bureaucratic round in getting a building permit and feel he is reenacting Kafka's *The Castle*. He might be faced with a moral decision, remember how Wordsworth solved the same problem, and adopt a similar solution. This aspect of transfer can be measured readily by means of a questionnaire with questions like "Have you ever gone out of your way to visit a place that you read about in a story? Where? What story?" An alternative would be to present a situation as if in a newspaper account and ask the students if it reminded them of anything they had encountered before. Some might make literary connections, some not. If it is assumed that all the students had been exposed to the literary analogues, those who mentioned them might be supposed to have transferred them—but this would, I think, be a risky presumption.

The deeper aspects of transfer present almost insurmountable problems of measurement and I shall mention them only briefly to offer a challenge to those who would create some sort of a test. A test is important, for it would seek to determine the cumulative effect of literary study. Two claims for the study of literature have often been made: one, that it provides the student with a tolerance for ambiguity; two, that it provides aesthetic distance. The first claim is that having encountered a variety of human experiences vicariously, having witnessed various forms of love, duplicity, or conflicts between the head and the heart and between appearance and reality as they appear in literary works—by virtue of these multitudinous and multifarious experiences—a person is enabled to bring this sum total of experience to bear on whatever new experience he might confront. Such a thesis underlies Louise Rosenblatt's *Literature as Exploration* (1968). The problem in measuring this growing sophistication—tolerance for ambiguity and tentativeness in judging new experiences—is that although one can assert that such qualities exist, they may not exist as a result of literature. Even when it is probable that literature is a great part of the cause, it would seem nearly impossible to say what part. Certainly, however, such a measurement could follow along the lines suggested in the *Taxonomy of Educational Objectives: Affective Domain* for behavior 5.1, *Generalized set* (Krathwohl, Bloom, & Masia, 1964, pp. 168 ff.), for it is a generalized set with which we are dealing. Having made such a measurement at the end of a course in literature, one could make some tentative assertion about the effect of the course—but the assertion would have to remain tentative.

The second and related dimension of transfer is what we call "aesthetic distance from" or "aesthetic structuring of" an experience and is the technical term for the ability to distinguish between a work and one's experience of it. This behavior derives from a thorough experiencing and understanding of literary structures, of the *how* of a literary work more than the *what*. One builds up a repertoire of perceptions when dealing with literary works; one is able to see that a work is tragic or comic, to see how it is organized, to see its symbolic import, and to see that it might be judged beautiful or good on various grounds. Obviously this is not a transfer of a particular work or of the experience of a particular work as the other two sorts of transfer are, but a transfer of a mode of perception. As such, it might not be considered part of engagement, but I include it here because it seems to me the culmination of one sort of engagement with a literary work, the intellective. All this is done, as I have observed, with some repression of the emotional effect of the work, and it is this repression which involves the separation of perceiver from object that we call "aesthetic distance." The intellective apprehension is aesthetic structuring. If literary training seeks to enhance the ability to achieve distance by structuring, one of the manifestations of that ability will appear in the response to a new work of literature: this would fall under the behavior *Express a pattern of response* (P). A second manifestation would occur in the response to a nonliterary event: this, in effect, is transfer—not of the works, however, but of the mode of engagement with them. The possible manifestations are numerous: calling a situation ironic or comic; saying that a particular advertisement is symbolic of our whole culture; looking at a political campaign and comparing it to a five-act tragedy or a farce; taking the American transportation system and analyzing it as a medium (as Marshall McLuhan has done). It may be simple or elaborate, as simple or elaborate as the articulation of a response to a novel or a lyric.

One way to measure distancing and structuring would be to construct a situation or present a photograph, ask the student to write or talk about it, and analyze the response to ascertain the degree to which the two phenomena occur. Here again, however, the results might be unsure, in this case because of the nature of the stimulus. It might be that one photograph would produce a literary response because it had no personal associations for the student; another might have such strong associations that some sort of blocking might occur. The same problem, of course, exists with literary works themselves, but one can get around this by using a variety of works. With a variety of photographs, say three or four, and a corresponding number of essays or tapes, one could get an index of distancing; but the problem of time would seem to preclude this kind of measure for the classroom teacher. Further, the same questions of source occur with distancing as with tolerance for ambiguity.

It would seem, therefore, that the most reliable and valid measure of transfer would be the one that sought to find out what specific analogues one has incorporated from literature—whether he sees literary characters in the people he meets, whether he sees literary situations in the situations he encounters, whether he derives a part of his working morality from literature, and whether the comparison of literary and nonliterary events is a commonplace with him. In each case, the questions can be direct and specific, and the information is not clouded by the possibility that the incorporation of literature is really something we might call general maturation.

I have spent so much time discussing the measurement of engagement not simply because it raises so many problems for the tester but because, despite these problems, it is an exceedingly important behavior for the teacher to measure. Its importance to the curriculum we have observed in the statements of the Dartmouth Seminar and the Fader curriculum reported in *Hooked on Books*. It is important, too, because, as Squire observed, engagement seems to touch off the desire to analyze and interpret works of literature. Given its importance as a base of the literary response, then, it must be measured so that the teacher can see how firmly he has built that base.

Analysis (K, L) Questions which deal with analysis ask the student to make certain kinds of discriminations, to examine a literary structure and note relationships which the untrained eye might miss or to make explicit that which he has observed, and to make certain generalizations. The discriminations, which lie at the basis of literary analysis, fall into a number of categories which enable the tester to classify his questions. These categories are related to the language, the literary structure, and the content of literature, and they range from comprehension of the surface meaning of a text to a highly complex form of inferential reasoning. I shall try to define these abilities and illustrate them mainly as they might be tested in questions dealing with a single text; for the sake of continuity and clarity, I shall generally confine myself to questions dealing with one text, John Keats's "On First Looking into Chapman's Homer,"[8]

Much have I traveled in the realms of gold,
And many goodly states and kingdoms seen;
Round many western islands have I been
Which bards in fealty to Apollo hold.
Oft of one wide expanse had I been told
That deep-browed Homer ruled as his demesne;
Yet did I never breathe its pure serene
Till I heard Chapman speak out loud and bold;
Then felt I like some watcher of the skies
When a new planet swims into his ken;
Or like stout Cortez when with eagle eyes
He stared at the Pacific—and all his men
Looked at each other with a wild surmise—
Silent, upon a peak in Darien.

The ability to comprehend the mother tongue. This is the most basic constitutent, comprehending as it does the possession of a lexicon and a grammar. We tend to assume that this ability has been achieved by most students by the time they complete elementary education, although we realize that works of literature may contain unfamiliar words and unfamiliar grammatical constructions like the absolute or the appositive, and we must always check to make sure that our students' lexica and grammar are sufficient to the work they are to comprehend. This is particularly important when they are being asked to read precontemporary literature or dialect literature.

With Keats's poem, it might be useful to find out whether students know the meaning of "demesne" or "in fealty" or whether they can determine that meaning from context.

K-3 Analyze a precontemporary lyric poem (diction)

35. Which of the following best expresses the sense of line 4?
    a. Which poets own in submission to Apollo
    b. Which poets use to make fun of Apollo
    c. Which poets try to keep from Apollo
    d. Which poets chained to Apollo cling to

Literary Analysis and the Teaching of English at the University of Illinois for their assistance in deriving these categories.

The ability to recognize puns or verbal ambiguities. This ability is a further dimension of lexical growth, comprising as it does the knowledge that certain words have more than one denotation and that denotation depends on context. The student should be able to see, for instance, that the italicized words in the following passages are puns:

"Did you *take* a shower this morning?" "Why, is there one missing?"

"No, 'tis not so deep as a well, nor so wide as a church-door; but 'tis enough, 'twill serve: ask for me to-morrow, and you shall find me a *grave* man."

(*Romeo and Juliet*, III.i.99–101)

He should also be aware of ambiguities in reference of pronoun and in modification that may occur in literature, as in this highly complex reference:

"And the tree is my seat, *that* once lent me a shade" (Cowper, "The Poplar Field").

There are no major ambiguities in Keats's poem, and I must use another example here:

K-17 Analyze a work of literature (puns)

You are going to hear someone read a number of sentences or lines from poems. The voice will say each one twice. The sentences or lines that you will hear are written on the sheet in front of you. Some of the sentences contain a *pun*, which is a word that has two meanings at the same time and makes the sentence mean two different things at the same time. Here is an example:

"What has four wheels and flies?"

"A garbage truck."

In this joke, "flies" means to go in the air like an airplane and it also means a little insect—so that the question is about some strange sort of aircraft and it is about a truck or wagon that has flies around it. "Flies" is a pun. On the sheet in front of you, draw a line under "flies" to indicate that you know it is a pun. After you listen to each of the sentences or lines, decide whether or not it contains a pun; if it does, draw a line under the word or words you think are puns. If you think there is no pun, write the word "none" after the passage.

36. "I thought that was a fly on your nose, but it's not."

The ability to comprehend the connotative value in words. The other important aspect of the lexicon to literature is the implications of words that occur in literature. An awareness of these implications betokens an awareness of the aspect of literature called "diction" or "poetic diction." One comes to realize the penumbra of associations around a world like "vial" and its difference from that around a word like "glass" or "chalice." One also comes to realize that connotation in literature is a matter of the individual word set in a verbal context, so that the author can manipulate connotation simply by setting up a verbal context that limits the connotations of an individual word. Thus the connotations around "gander" in these two nursery rhymes are different:

Goosey goosey gander,
Whither dost thou wander?

Grey goose and grey gander
Waft your wings together.

The difference is partly one of denotation—the first gander is walking and the second is flying—but the different actions of the two ganders have different implications and associations: the first of awkwardness, the second of grace. The ability to comprehend connotations would imply the ability to see that there may be incongruities in connotation, as in these lines from Wordsworth's "Reverie of Poor Susan":

'Tis a note of enchantment; what ails her? She sees
A mountain ascending, a vision of trees;

in which the connotations of the words "ails" and "trees" are not consonant with the connotations of "enchantment," "ascending," and "vision."

K-3 Analyze a precontemporary lyric poem (connotation)

37. Which of the following words in lines 1 and 2 most clearly intimates that the traveling is a profitable and important occupation for the speaker?
    a. realms
    b. gold
    c. goodly
    d. kingdoms

It is the word "gold," of course, which sets tone of the passage and of the whole metaphor of the journey; "realms" could be changed to "lands," "goodly" to "comely," and "kingdoms" to "countries" without greatly modifying the tone; but if "gold" were replaced, the sense of the richness and beauty of the lands would disappear.

The ability to discriminate among rhythms. Sensitivity to rhythms may be an ability of the eye or of the ear. The eye, for example, would be able to discriminate between haiku, with seventeen syllables, and a limerick, with some thirty. The ear would be able to distinguish between the rhythm of

If to her share some female errors fall,
Look on her face, and you'll forget 'em all.
(Pope, *The Rape of the Lock*, II.17–18)

and that of

And up he rises like a vapor,
Supported high on wings of paper:
(Swift, *The Progress of Poetry*, ll. 43–44)

It would also include the ability to distinguish between bisyllabic and trisyllabic meters, between rhymed and unrhymed verse, and between the presence or absence of alliteration, assonance, or consonance. At a more basic level, it would be an ability to distinguish between verse and prose. With prose, the discrimination among rhythms becomes problematical, because the principle of regular repetition does not obtain. Certain kinds of discrimination are possible, however, such as that between long and short sentences, between prose that uses parallelism and that which does not, and between prose that employs devices of sound in some pattern and prose that does not. Whether this ability necessarily entails the acquisition of nomenclature—iambic, slant rhyme, caesura, balance, assonance, and the like—is moot, but one may well argue that at a more sophisticated level of discrimination the student is helped by knowing such terms.

K-3 Analyze a precontemporary lyric poem (rhythm)

38. The normal rhythm of this poem consists of an unaccented syllable followed by an accented syllable. At times, however, this rhythm is reversed and the accented syllable comes first. This happens most frequently
    a. at the beginning of a line
    b. in the middle of a line
    c. at the end of a line
    d. at no particular point in the line

The ability to decode abnormal syntax. Decoding entails matching a newly encountered group of words against one of the common syntactic patterns—a kernel sentence, say, or one of the transformations. The abnormality of literary syntax usually consists of some sort of ellipsis, some sort of inversion, some sort of interpolation, or some sort of substitution. A simple form of ellipsis might be

The lion sleeps with open eyes
That none may take him by surprise[9]

in which "so" or "in order" is to be inserted before "that" to make the relationship between clauses apparent. A more complex form of ellipsis occurs in lines like

The winter evening settles down
With smell of steaks in passageways.
Six o'clock.
The burnt-out ends of smoky days.
(T. S. Eliot, "Preludes," ll. 1–4)

Here the whole predicate (or the subject and verb to which this might be a complement) needs to be supplied in line 4. The second type of distortion is inversion, which ranges from the fairly simple subject-verb reversal of

Into the valley of Death
Rode the six hundred

to the more complex Miltonic inversion of

Him the Almighty Power
Hurled headlong flaming from the ethereal sky
With hideous ruin and combustion down
To bottomless perdition, there to dwell
In adamantine chains and penal fire,
Who durst defy the Omnipotent to arms.
(*Paradise Lost*, I,44–49)

Interpolation, which is the placement of a lengthy modifier or appositive between two elements of the sentence, occurs in the passage from *Paradise Lost* above and in the opening stanza of Bryant's "Lines to a Waterfowl":

Whither, midst falling dew,
While glow the heavens with the last steps of day,
Far, through their rosy depths dost thou pursue
Thy solitary way?

The last main syntactic abnormality occurs when a writer substitutes one function word for another, a common practice of a poet like Dylan Thomas:

And once below a time I lordly had the trees and
leaves. . . .[10]

Each of these syntactic distortions requires the reader to match the word pattern he observes against his everyday syntax so that he may decode the passage.

K-3 Analyze the parts of a precontemporary lyric poem (syntax)

39. The adjective "Silent" (line 14) modifies
    a. "I" (line 9)
    b. "watcher" (line 9)
    c. "He" (line 12)
    d. "Men" (line 12)

[9] X. J. Kennedy, "Faces from a Bestiary," ll. 1–2, from *Nude Descending a Stairway* (New York: Doubleday, 1961); quoted in *New Poets of England and America*, edited by Donald Hall and Robert Pack (Cleveland: World Publishing, 1962, p. 251).

[10] "Fern Hill," l. 7, from *Collected Poems of Dylan Thomas* (New York: New Directions, 1957).

The ability to comprehend metaphorical language. Some would argue that this is the primary literary ability, since literature is essentially metaphoric and hypothetical. Literature posits a hypothetical universe and operates by a series of analogies in order to make its effect or meaning more apparent. A girl is compared to a flower to emphasize her beauty or fragility. A world in which pigs can talk and build houses is hypothesized in order to make a more trenchant comment on the value of industry. An imaginary narrator who invites us to call him Ishmael is posited in order that we may think about his tale of whaling in a number of ways and compare the hunt to various moral problems. Each of these hypotheses rests on the principle that meaning in literature is derived from a consideration of the relationship between things—roses and girls, pigs and people, whalers and Ishmael. Comprehending these analogies involves perceiving the relationship that is established (what is being compared to what and in what ways) and the effect or meaning of the relationship itself (what such a comparison tells us about how we are to think or feel about the object of our attention). With the following two metaphors, for instance, the reader must observe that the frost is being compared to a ghost in its color in order to see that it is not sparkling and fresh but about to disappear dully. He must also see that the sun is compared to a human eye and that the day is therefore given a humanity that is bereft of something ("desolate"):

> I leant upon a coppice gate
> When Frost was specter-gray,
> And Winter's dregs made desolate
> The weakening eye of day.
>
> (Thomas Hardy, "The Darkling Thrush," ll. 1–4)

The reader might also see a third and submerged metaphor comparing winter with something which (like coffee) can leave a residue and thus seem less than attractive. Each of the metaphors supports a sense of dreariness that might come from a jaundiced pen, but the ability to make that last inference is less the ability to comprehend the metaphors themselves than to make inferences about attitude and possibly motivation. Ability to comprehend a metaphor quite obviously depends on linguistic ability—knowing the words—and experience of the referents of the words involved. In this case, one must know what a dreg is and one must have had some contact with dregs in order to understand the metaphor. This dual experience underlies the knowledge of language, of course, but it is of particular importance in metaphor. To understand that "The ship plows the seas" compares a ship and the act of plowing is not particularly meaningful unless one has seen the motion of a plow through earth. It has some meaning, to be sure, but the sense of power that one gains from having watched a plow turn over earth is lost to the person who has had no experience of this. To use I. A. Richards's terms, one can comprehend the vehicle but is less than master of the tenor. For this reason, it is not as easy for the tester to ascertain a difficult metaphor as it is to ascertain difficult syntax or a difficult problem in human motivation or mood.

Under metaphor I would include personification, metonymy, imagery (which establishes, by its repeated references to a milieu, a submerged metaphor), and symbol. In the case of imagery and symbol, the student must be able to match words to a concept or make a word-referent analogy with only one side of the equation. The ability to comprehend one-sided analogies must be accompanied, it would seem, by a habit of mind which drives one to seek these analogies. A person must, in fact, hunt for symbols or patterns of images, because they do not make themselves verbally apparent. The much-attacked symbol hunter is simply a person who by training or habit has come to consider that everything exists in a world of analogies, much like the way the medieval allegorist thought; his sins are sins of excess. The more ordinary person will not associate an image with an event or thought as readily; he would not associate the moon in Coleridge's "Ancient Mariner" with the mariner's punishment and redemption and then hypothesize a causal relationship unless someone had trained him to do so. How this ability is developed I am not sure, but I suspect it is transferred from the process of learning the language and from constant exposure to metaphor.

Only a short step from the process of divining symbols is the process of allegorizing or mythologizing an action or series of actions and relating it to a parallel action or an abstraction. One says of Stephen Daedalus and Leopold Bloom that they are "parallel to" Telemachus and Odysseus (this relationship is almost explicit by virtue of the book's title); or one may say that they are symbols of the father and the son as psychological types, and then proceed to draw parallels between the types and the characters. In such a case the individual person or event is considered as the type he represents, and that type is considered for its abstract qualities—as *a son*, to *son*, to *sonness*. If the anthropologists are correct, this ability seems virtually instinctive, and in some people it is habitual.

K-3 Analyze the parts of a precontemporary lyric poem (literary devices)

40. In the first six lines, there is a comparison of travel with
    a. business
    b. reading
    c. chivalry
    d. astronomy

The ability to draw inferences about human behavior. When we read a description of a girl hiding her face when she sees a strange man, we guess that she is shy. When we hear a person say, "I'm going to fix your wagon," we assume that he is angry and seeking revenge. Human actions and human language have a consistency about them that enable the observer to relate one observation to previous similar observations and thus to establish a cause, a motive, or a meaning. It is this quality of our actions and language that enables us to live in societies and to communicate with one another. When a person sees another run away from something, he might assume that the other was frightened. Later, he may learn that running away can have various causes—anger, spite, jealousy, mischievousness, and that there are different kinds of running which betray each of these causes. The observer has learned, quite simply, to make finer and finer discriminations, similar to the finer discriminations among language, and the finely discriminating person is the one who can tolerate ambiguity. Some of these discriminations result from meeting experience vicariously through literature, some from meeting experience directly. In either case, one comes to the point at which one can read about Henry in *The Red Badge of Courage* and know from his actions, his talk, and the talk of the narrator what a complex individual he is, that he is dreamer, boy, coward, hero, man, and more. In a drama there is usually less evidence than in a novel; one must tell from a speech that begins, "If it were done when 'tis done, then 'twere well/It were done quickly," that the speaker wants to get something unpleasant over with.

K-3 Analyze the parts of a precontemporary lyric poem (content)

41. The speaker of the poem is primarily describing his
    a. feelings
    b. plans
    c. thoughts
    d. childhood experiences

The ability to discriminate among tones and moods. Similar to the preceding ability in many respects, this one is more specific in that it refers not to motivation but to the emotions and attitudes. One early learns that a laugh indicates happiness; tears, sadness. Later, one learns that there are different kinds of laughter and tears, not all of them unequivocally happy or sad. One learns to distinguish between the moods of verbal descriptions as well; for example, between the mood of

> Once again
> Do I behold these steep and lofty cliffs,
> That on a wild secluded scene impress
> Thoughts of more deep seclusion

and the mood of

> The sounding cataract
> Haunted me like a passion: the tall rock,
> The mountain, and the deep and gloomy wood,
> Their colors and their forms, were then to me
> An appetite. . . .
>
> (Wordsworth, "Lines Composed a Few Miles above Tintern Abbey," ll. 4–7, 76–80)

He can do these things because he has developed a sense of the normal emotional associations of words and combinations of words so that he can match "steep," "lofty," "cliffs," "wild," "secluded," "impress" and "thoughts" against "cataract," "haunted," "passion," "tall rock," "deep and gloomy wood," and "appetite," and derive a mood of awed thoughtfulness from the one and a mood of morbid excitement from the other. Further, he can distinguish the ironic from the straightforward—he can tell that Swift didn't really want us to eat those babies because he is able to match the usual association of cannibalism against the idea of benevolent despotism that the narrator of "A Modest Proposal" implies in his language and infer that the two can only exist in some antagonistic relationship. This ability, then, is associated with the ability to discriminate among connotations and among motives, but it goes further in that it can see these words and actions as symbolic of attitudes.

L-3 Analyze the whole of a precontemporary lyric poem (mood)

42. The mood of the speaker is best described as
    a. wistfully joyous
    b. apprehensive and excited
    c. sardonically amused
    d. awed and exhilarated

The ability to recognize relationships between parts and part-whole relationships. This ability is related to the critical dictum that a work of literature is an organic whole and that therefore a necessary and important connection exists between language and content, beginnings and ends, parts and parts, and parts and the whole. The student need not have the theory at his command, but he should see that in Keats's "On First Looking into Chapman's Homer," for example, there is a relationship between the "realms" of line 1 and the "demesne" of line 6, between the image of the traveler and Cortez the explorer, between the placement of "silent" in the last line and the sense of awe that the whole sestet conveys. The ability to note relationships is quite obviously a matter of training and proceeds from an ability to note figure-ground relationships either visually, orally, or tactilely. Here, however, the student is dealing in words—or, in drama, with actions and sounds. As the student becomes more able, he can see more subtle relationships or relationships between more disparate things. He could, for example, see the relationship between Cortez and the astronomer, or between the phonemes in "silent" and the phonemic structure of the whole poem (see Hymes, 1958). Beyond this noting of simple relationships there is the noting of complex relationships that we call "structure" or "plot" or "architectonic" relationships. Whether this ability follows from the ability to perceive one-to-one relationships is a subject of psychological debate, but I would suspect that it does not. Some people can perceive the structure of a whole without necessarily noting or noticing all the part-to-part relationships. A final aspect of this ability is that of distinguishing between the more or less important relationships, between those which contribute to the sense of the whole and those which do not. To take another example from the Keats sonnet, the relationship between the traveler and Cortez is more important to the structure of the poem than the relationship between the consonants in "deep-browed Homer ruled as his demesne," because it encompasses a greater part of the whole poem (whereas the other only connects the sounds of a line). Even less important is the relationship between the rhyme words ("gold," "hold," "told," "bold"), although in another poem that relationship might be important. The criterion would seem to be the contribution that the parts or the relationships make to one's sense of the whole.

L-3 Analyze the relationships in a precontemporary lyric poem (relationship between parts)

43. Which of the following best describes the relationship between the first eight lines and the last six lines?
    a. The first eight lines explain the condition of the speaker; the last six give his reaction.
    b. The first eight lines present a problem facing the speaker; the last six lines present his solution.
    c. The first eight lines give the situation of the speaker; the last six lines a symbolic interpretation of the situation.
    d. The first eight lines present the dilemma in which the speaker finds himself; the last six his prayer for deliverance.

L-3 Analyze the relationships in a precontemporary lyric poem (relationship between form and content)

44. The mood of the speaker is made most apparent by
    a. the single-syllable rhymes
    b. the lack of caesuras in twelve of the lines
    c. the contrast between the lonely astronomer and the band of explorers led by Cortez
    d. the two images of vast vision—in the sky and over the ocean

The ability to discriminate among genres and types is the ability to differentiate gestalts. Seen in its simplest form, this is the ability to tell verse from prose; in more refined forms it is the ability to distinguish ballads from sonnets, biographies from autobiographies, short stories from novellas, and pastoral elegies from dirges. The basis of distinction may derive from language, structure, subject matter, tone, or a combination of the four. Obviously this ability depends on exposure to and acquaintance with the various forms and some sense of the basis for differentiation, yet we can suppose it possible for an untutored person, who can say verse is not prose, to say also that a Shakespearean sonnet is not a Petrarchan sonnet without being able to annotate rhymes and without a definition of either form. What is requisite is an ability to see that things very nearly similar are not entirely similar and to see that some differences are more important than others. The latter is obvious from, say, the fact that "Barbara Allen" and "Get Up and Bar the Door" have a similarity in form and a difference in subject matter, so that they can be said to be different species of the same genus. As this ability becomes more highly developed, one is able to perceive a whole series of interlocking relationships like those set forth by Northop Frye in *Anatomy of Criticism*.

L-3 Analyze the organization of a precontemporary lyric poem (genre)

45. In its use of the sonnet form, this poem is most similar to which of the following?
    a. "That time of year thou mayst in me behold," Shakespeare
    b. "England in 1819," Shelley
    c. "Evening on Calais Beach," Wordsworth
    d. "Shakespeare," Arnold

It should be noted that this question presupposes the student's familiarity with the texts and is thus close to a question of application. A better and truer analytic question would be one that reproduced the texts of the four poems and asked the student to choose the one most resembling Keats's.

Another kind of question that draws on this ability to recognize the whole structure of a work as well as to see the relationship between parts and the whole is one that asks the student to pick out the missing line of a poem or a prose passage.

L-3 Analyze the organization of a precontemporary lyric poem

Whenas in silks my Julia goes,
Then, then, methinks, how sweetly flows
The liquefaction of her clothes!
Next, when I cast mine eyes and see
. . . .
—O how that glittering taketh me!

46. Which of the following is best placed in the line marked by points?
    a. How she runs up and kisses me
    b. That brave vibration each way free
    c. Her slip and bruise her dainty knee
    d. Vibrations freeing themselves towards me

Interpretation (M) Questions of interpretation draw on these analytic abilities but go further, for they ask the student to make inferences about the text and come up with some sort of summary statement, as in this question:

M-3 Express one's interpretation of a precontemporary lyric poem

47. Which of the following is the best interpretation of lines 1 to 4?
    a. I have traveled a great deal in search of the gold that has been sung about by ancient poets.
    b. I have read a good deal of great literature, particularly the classic poets.
    c. I have read a great deal of travel literature, particularly in verse by American travelers.
    d. I have dreamed of being an immortal poet like the ancient bards who were led by Apollo.

This question of interpretation shows the limit of the multiple-choice form. If one were to take a text like this,

Legal

"No Trespassing" it said; but I
Not asking anybody's pardon,
Climbed the fence and saw the garden,
And knew not whether to laugh or cry.
Would you learn what sight I saw?
Then must you also break the law.[11]

one might be tempted to ask a question like

M-4 Express one's interpretation of a precontemporary lyric poem

48. Which of the following is the best interpretation of the poem?
    a. In order to gain experience, one must break the taboos of society.
    b. In order to gain insight into oneself, each person must rely on his own experience.
    c. Men are tempted by the forbidden and seek to tempt others.
    d. Every man must make his own journey for spiritual awareness.

[11] From Theodore Spencer, *An Acre in the Seed* (Cambridge, Mass.: Harvard University Press, 1948).

I have stacked the cards against this item; each one of the answers is defensible. I lean to the first answer, but I can see arguments for each of the others. One could take the question and turn it into a negatively phrased item, "Which of the following interpretations is least valid?" The problem with this kind of question is that the best answer would have to be as far-fetched as "Each man must make his own choice between the laws of society and the laws of nature," and even that has a faint ring of plausibility. The poem deals with the idea that each man must do something for himself, and with the idea that what he must do is forbidden, dangerous, and mystifying. This could refer to a psychological, social, moral, or theological event; it could, possibly, refer to the creation of art. All options which contain some specification of the general ingredients of an interpretation are more or less defensible in terms of the text. Any option which does not have those ingredients is obviously less defensible, but to put that option in as the answer makes the problem one of reading the item carefully to notice that one of the options differs from the other three. The item can be answered by anyone, whether or not he has read the poem. Questions of interpretation are best as short-answer or essay questions; a good essay question on "Legal" would be: "Write an essay in which you define the central situation of the poem, the attitude of the speaker, and the possible ramifications of the situation and the speaker's attitude. In your answer, consider whether the poem might be interpreted morally, religiously, psychologically, or socially." Such an essay question would allow the teacher to see whether the students are capable of defining the situation and tone in the poem and relating the poem to various ways man has devised of ordering his universe: these processes constitute interpretation. In grading the answer, the teacher must beware of marking down a student for offering, for instance, a religious interpretation to a poem the teacher sees as psychological. The teacher's view is probably the more astute, but there may be sufficient textual support for the student's. The basis of judgment, therefore, should be the way the student handles the problem of interpretation, rather than the correctness of his interpretation itself. It should concern itself with whether the student has accounted for all of the lines in the text, whether he has rendered a consistent interpretation, and whether he has used the statement, the imagery, and the tone of the poem to support his interpretation. In our example, if he simply took the word "garden" and wove an allegory about Adam and Eve and the speaker's being the snake, he would not have taken enough of the poem into consideration.

Evaluation (N) More closely related to engagement than is either analysis or interpretation is the behavior *Express one's evaluation* (N) of a literary work; for evaluation is, as we have noted, abstracting some quality of the literary experience or the literary work and making it a criterion of value. Evaluation can be measured in two ways: the normative and the descriptive. The former is predicated on some standard of judgment which the teacher believes he has inculcated and is an attempt to determine whether the student can apply that criterion. A criterion might be one of affect, technique, or meaning, and it can be measured by means of a simple multiple-choice format, usually one which asks the student to pick the better of two or the best of three or more works or versions of works. One can use a general criterion like "literary merit" as in the Carroll Prose Appreciation Test (see below), but the phrase is so vague that the test comes to be one of preference.

N-17 Express one's evaluation of any literary work

I. "Hello, my girlie. Let's sit down here and hearken to those fellows playing music. It's quiet enough. Then we'll both go home. What say to that, my girl?"

II. "The moon presents a nice picture as its rich glorious rays come down on this wonderful big bank. Let us rest down here and listen to the precious music, which sounds most sweet in the peaceful quiet of the soft, stilly night. Is not this scene nearly perfect, Jessica? Come here, gentle musicians, and let your sweetest divine music charm us. The angelic moon shines in most precious glory. Let us stay and listen to the heavenly melodies, most sweet, most immortal of harmonies."

III. "How sweet the moonlight sits upon this bank. Here will we sit and let the sound of music creep in our ears. Soft stillness and the night become the touches of sweet harmony. Sit, Jessica. Such harmony is in immortal souls. Come ho! and wake Diana with a hymn. With sweetest touches pierce your mistress' ear, and draw her home with music."

49. In the . . . three paragraphs
    a. paragraph II shows the best choice of words
    b. paragraph I shows the best choice of words
    c. paragraph III shows the best choice of words

50. In the . . . three paragraphs
    a. paragraph III is most convincing
    b. paragraph II is most convincing
    c. paragraph I is most convincing

51. In the . . . three paragraphs
    a. paragraph II is spoiled by too much exaggeration
    b. paragraph III is spoiled by too much exaggeration
    c. paragraph I is spoiled by too much exaggeration

(Speer & Smith, 1937, p. 3, items 1, 2, 3.)

As with any comparative question, the selections have to be distinct enough so that a choice can be made. Although the Shakespeare passage does stand out in this threesome, and, taken by itself, has the best choice of words, it is not necessarily the most convincing or the best written of the three. Those judgments depend on the context of the passages. Students who might think selection I was taken from a Damon Runyon story might well say its diction is the best. Even II could be convincing if attributed to one of the characters in *Peyton Place*. The third question is the only one that is beyond this quite serious cavil, for exaggeration is a readily discernible characteristic and the second passage is clearly distinct from the other two in this respect. The dangers in the first two questions might be summed up as being those of the "Guess what I am thinking" variety of question, an all too frequent phenomenon in literature testing.

The descriptive measure avoids this danger and the parallel danger of instilling in the student the notion that there is a single criterion by which a literary work should be judged. This test would seek to ascertain what criterion or criteria a student uses, with the hope that as he progresses he will use objective as well as visceral criteria. One form of this test might be the following:

N-17 Express one's evaluation of a poem

52. Which of the following come closest to what you think about this poem? Make one, two, or three choices, but no more than three. Put a circle around the letter of the choice or choices you have made.
    a. It is a good poem because it makes me see the world differently.
    b. It is a good poem because it makes me feel good.
    c. It is a good poem because it is about one thing and doesn't use any extra words.
    d. It is a good poem because it asks an important question.
    e. It is a good poem because the words are right for what it is talking about.
    f. It is a poor poem because it does not rhyme.
    g. It is a poor poem because it does not teach a lesson.
    h. It is a poor poem because it does not make sense.
    i. It is a poor poem because it does not hang together.
    j. It is a poor poem because it uses simple words.
    k. It is a poor poem because it deals with an unimportant subject.
    l. It is a poor poem because it does not make me feel anything.

One would need to repeat this sort of question with several passages to see whether the student uses one criterion consistently or not.

A pattern of preference (O) The behavior *Express a pattern of preference* (*O*) refers to taste, and there have been a variety of taste tests, which fall into one of three usual forms. The first form takes style as the main distinguishing factor of the selections among which the student must choose. Usually style is considered high, middle, and low, or classical, contemporary, and debased (or some similar designation), and the student is asked to indicate his preference from among the three. A good example of such a test is that by Herbert A. Carroll (1932a), which is somewhat dated in its selections but still serves as a prototype. The following is taken from the *Examiner's Manual:*

O-17 Express a pattern of preference for any literary work

[The passages] were taken from four sources: first choices from books generally regarded as of excellent quality; second choices from books generally regarded as of poor quality; third choices, from the less literary magazines; fourth choices, from mutilations. A sample set (No. III in the senior test) follows:

53. *An Interior*

A

"I went with the little maid into a gorgeously decorated bed-room, all of cream color and light blue that blended prettily. The bed was a great wide affair of beautifully carved and ornamented wood, painted creamy white with blue and gold trimmings. There was a wonderful bureau and a dressing table to match, and in one corner of the room a mirror that went from floor to ceiling. I had to hold my breath."

B

"Lollie had never seen such a pretty room, and it made her gasp to see how pretty the furniture was, as well as how pretty the rugs were, and the curtains at the window and the pictures on the wall, but what she really liked best was that furniture, for it looked comfortable as well as pretty, and she knew it must have cost hundreds and hundreds of dollars. She wished she could live and die in that one room, it was so pretty."

C

"An air of Sabbath had descended on the room. The sun shone brightly through the window, spreading a golden lustre over the white walls; only along the north wall, where the bed stood, a half shadow lingered . . . the table had been spread with a white cover; upon it lay the open hymn book, with the page turned down. Beside the hymn book stood a bowl of water; beside that lay a piece of white cloth. . . . Kjersti was tending the stove, piling the wood in diligently. . . . Sorine sat in the corner crooning over a tiny bundle; out of the bundle at intervals came faint wheezy chirrups, like the sounds that rise from a nest of young birds."

D

"Major Prime had the west sitting room. It was lined with low bookcases, full of old, old books. There was a fireplace, a winged chair, a broad couch, a big desk of dark seasoned mahogany, and over the mantle a steel engraving of Robert E. Lee. The low windows at the back looked out upon the wooded green of the ascending hill; at the front was a porch which gave a view of the valley."

(Carroll, 1932b, pp. 3–4.)

The student is asked to rank these passages in terms of their literary merit—which would make the test one of evaluation except that Carroll does not define the term; the student, then, seems to be thrown back on preference. Carroll's test has a norm of good taste, which some might challenge. His "good" passage, C, is from Rolvaag's *Giants in the Earth*; D is presumably from a "less good" book and A from a "less literary" magazine. Even the mutilation—B—has its merits, and this fact gives rise to one of the major problems of such a test—its discouraging results. More often than not a class, even a class of graduate students, will prefer what their instructor considers the inferior selection. If this happens, and if a developed taste is a primary objective for the course, should the instructor fail his students? Few have done so.

Perhaps, however, if the instructor adopted a descriptive measure which gave him a broader range of selections to present to the students and thus an opportunity to describe their taste more accurately, he would be more successful. One way of doing this is to present the students with a number of passages—prose, poetry, and drama, classical and contemporary or elegiac, adulatory, and ironic, for example—and ask the students to rank the passages in order of preference. The taste of individuals and the group could then be charted. As we have observed about engagement, however, there are great problems in text selection, so great that any generalization about taste is risky.

One way to avoid risk is to eschew texts and use titles or descriptions of books. Such a method has been used many times, with varying degrees of success. Two researchers, P. Saarinen and A. Lehtovaara, in the volume *School Age Reading Interests: A Methodological Approach*, report on their attempt to determine the best method of presenting such a list (Saarinen & Lehtovaara, 1964; see Purves, 1967). They presented the students with excerpts, descriptions of categories (spy stories, books about art, etc.), and titles accompanied by a brief description, and in each case asked them to rate each item on the list. Titles with brief descriptions proved the most reliable. After having made up one's list of categories, one need only look for a representative title for each category, or (better, because there is less chance of an ambiguous title) write a description of a typical work in the category ("A girl recounts her adventures with animals while working on a farm"). The student can be asked either to rank the selections or to rate each one on a scale. In either case, the result will be a profile of the student's preferences.

The book list does not account for style and structure, just as a test like Carroll's does not account for variations in content. A person might want to read a novel by D. H. Lawrence about that girl on the farm, but not one by Louisa May Alcott. Similarly, a person might prefer the first of Carroll's passages simply because he suspects a seduction and sees this as the thoughts of the dumb-but-innocent victim. Carroll's term "literary merit" is vague. It is impossible to separate form and content in selecting passages for a preference test, just as impossible as it is for analysis and other aspects of response (although people do make such a separation when they talk or write about a work). It is also impossible to assert categorically that Johnny prefers westerns to lyric poetry or the middle style to the classical style on the basis of either form of the test.

The best measure of taste is one which allows the individual to compile his own list of favorites and give his own criteria for selection. One might simply ask the student to list his ten favorite books or to describe what he thinks the ideal book should be. One could, then, classify these titles and these criteria and thus describe the taste of the student. The problem of classification remains thorny unless the student gives some brief explanation of his preference ("It's a good story"; "It's gotta lotta action"; "It makes you cry"). With such a measure we have both an index to taste and a criterion for engagement or evaluation. Another way of checking preference is simply to note the works the student takes out of the library or chooses for his free-reading assignment. This unobtrusive measure is probably the most reliable index despite the fact that it does not catch the student's home reading or paperback buying, if any takes place.

Patterns and varieties of responses (P, Q) The two behaviors *Express a pattern of response* (*P*) and *Express a variety of responses* (*Q*) can be measured in similar ways. Both of them require the tester to present the student with a work, or preferably several works, and see whether he responds consistently or not. To measure the second behavior, it would in addition be desirable to retest over a period of time to see whether the response pattern changes as the student learns more and grows up. The best way of measuring either of these behaviors is to ask the student to read and discuss (in writing or orally) a work presented to him, and to give him no further instructions. The tester then proceeds to use some form of content analysis: informal, like that of I. A. Richards in *Practical Criticism* (1930); or more formal, like that of Squire or myself (see Squire, 1964; Purves with Rippere, 1968). Whichever method one chooses, one should provide a variety of works in one genre (as Squire and Richards preferred) or in several genres. Such a procedure will ensure that the response is not simply the result of a particular confrontation with a particular work. In one test of this sort, a group of us used a short story by Kafka that was patently allegorical; it produced, as might be expected, nothing but symbolic interpretations.

An objective measurement of response preference (*P*) is as feasible as a free-response measurement, although it limits the student somewhat and forces him to choose from the options presented to him. In a small study using high school freshmen and seniors, Dean A. W. Foshay of Teachers College, Columbia University, demonstrated a sufficiently high correlation between what the students wrote and their choices on a preferential objective test to assert that the latter was a possible substitute for a free essay. The form that was used served as the prototype for the International Educational Attainment test of response preference. It consists of two questions appended to a short story.

P-17 Express a pattern of response to any literary work

54. If you were to write an essay on ______, which of the following topics would you choose?
    a. How good a story ______ is
    b. What the author of ______ wanted to tell us when he wrote the story
    c. How ______ is put together
    d. How reading ______ affected me
55. Below are twenty questions which people have asked about ______. Some of them you may think are more important than others. Read through the questions and put an X in front of the nine questions that you think are important to your understanding of ______. When you have done that, look at the nine questions you have chosen and put a 1 next to the one that you think is most important, a 2 next to the one you think is next most important, and so on until you have rated five of the nine questions.
    a. Is this a proper subject for a story?
    b. How does ______ make me feel?
    c. Are any of the characters in ______ like people I know?
    d. Has the writer used words differently from the way people usually use them?
    e. What tricks that authors use are in this story?
    f. What happens in ______?
    g. Does the way it is told fit what ______ is about?
    h. How does the story develop?
    i. What does the author think about the people he is writing about in ______?
    j. What type of story is ______? Is it like any other story I know?
    k. When was ______ written? What is the background of the story?
    l. Is there one part of ______ that explains the whole story?

m. Is there anything in ______ that has a hidden meaning?
n. How can we explain the way people behave in ______?
o. What does ______ tell me about the way people are?
p. What does ______ tell us about people in general?
q. Does ______ teach us a lesson?
r. Is ______ effective in making me feel the way I am supposed to?
s. Is ______ well-written?
t. Does ______ have something important to say?

The four options in item 54 correspond with the four categories: engagement, perception (or analysis), interpretation, and evaluation. In item 55 these four are broken down into twenty subcategories. From the ratings they give, one may infer what the students' preferred responses are, and these may then be checked against the aims of instruction in the class or the school, whether those are to instill a single pattern of expressed response or a variety of responses.

Another way of measuring these two behaviors is that developed by the Carnegie curriculum project. Here the student is given a passage or a story followed by a series of multiple-choice questions on parts of the passage and on the whole passage. Each of the four choices can be placed in one of five categories—entertainment, facts, the craft of the writer, the theme, or the principles (Steinberg, Slack, & Forehand, undated, pp. 58 ff.). A total score for each of the four responses can then be determined. The Carnegie test would, of course, have to be repeated with another story or poem to measure the expression of a variety of responses.

Questions of participation (R–T)

Interest in responding (R) An observation of preference would also measure a student's willingness to respond to literature or his interest in it (*R*). There are two other types of measurement of interest: that which seeks to determine the relative weight of an interest in literature among a diversity of competing interests, and that which seeks to determine depth of interest. The first is adequately represented by the activity inventory of Project Talent, in which the student is asked to rate each of some eighty activities on a five-point scale: "I would like this very much," "I would like this fairly well," "Indifferent" or "don't know much about it," "I would dislike this a little," and "I would dislike this very much." Among the activities are reading, watching TV, literature, and poetry (University of Pittsburgh, 1960b, p. 3). One might, of course, refine "reading" more for an inventory specifically aimed at literary interests, and one would seek to clear up the ambiguity created by the juxtaposition of an activity like "reading" and an entity like "literature."

The inventory of depth of interest would seek to find out how often a student reads, whether he belongs to a book club, whether he rereads books or reads series of books, and so forth. Such a measurement could be made by means of a multiple-choice format with four options, two indicating low interest and two indicating high interest ("never," "rarely," "fairly often," "frequently," or some numerical equivalent):

R-18 Be willing to respond to television

56. How much time each week, on the average, have you spent watching each of the following kinds of television programs?
    Detective stories or mysteries
    a. Very little or none
    b. About 30 minutes a week
    c. Between 30 and 60 minutes a week
    d. Over 60 minutes a week

(Educational Testing Service, 1965, p. 2, item 6.)

Other questions might be phrased thus:

R-17 Be willing to respond to any literary work

57. How often in the past year have you gone out of the way to read another book by the author of a book you have read?

__ never
__ seldom
__ occasionally
__ several times

This question reaches the outer limit of how far back one can expect a person to remember his reading. Item 57 is somewhat more felicitous in its phrasing, since it asks for an approximation and does not force the student to ponder how much he watched in the past week or month. In the second item, the lack of specificity in the options eases the burden on his memory somewhat, but perhaps not enough.

An interest or activity inventory should include a variety of literary activities and a variety of media so as to give each student the opportunity to make a positive response. Interest in literature is not merely indicated by the number of books read: some deeply interested people read seldom but go to the theater a great deal; others might read literary quarterlies rather than books. Each student should, therefore, be given a chance to display his interest.

Satisfaction in responding (S) One might suppose that interest in or willingness to respond to literature implies the behavior *Take satisfaction in responding* (S), but this is not necessarily the case. A teacher should attempt to determine the motivation for an interest in literature and should therefore seek to determine his students' attitudes toward literature in general. One way of doing so would be to imitate the tests used in the English in Every Classroom program. Two of these tests deal with this behavior; one is the Behavior Rating Form, which gives fifty-one statements like "Books are things I like to have around" and "I hate books," and asks the students to mark after each one "like me" or "not like me" (Fader & Shaevitz, 1966, p. 109). The second is a Literary Attitude Scale based on the semantic differential (Osgood, Suci, & Tannenbaum, 1957), which asks the students to rate books, teachers, writing, sports, and sixteen other items on five scales, "good–bad," "weak–strong," "interesting–dull," "small–big," and "important–unimportant," with a range for each scale like the following:

S-17 Take satisfaction in responding to any literary work

58. BOOKS ARE

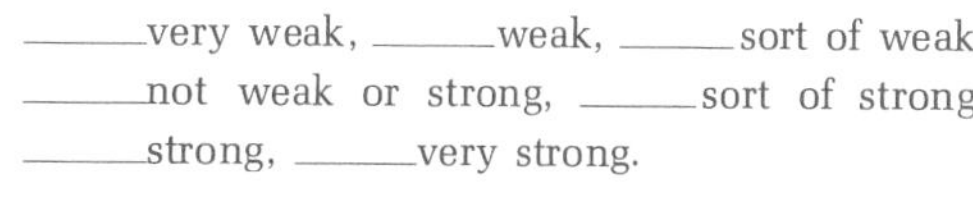
____very weak, ____weak, ____sort of weak, ____not weak or strong, ____sort of strong, ____strong, ____very strong.

(Fader & Shaevitz, 1966, p. 112.)

This measurement indicates a general attitude toward literature and is thus an index of acceptance (*T*) as well as of satisfaction. Indeed, it can be charged that the semantic differential measures not emotional attitude but an intellectual set. To label books "very strong" is not necessarily to like them. Fader's first test clearly gives an index of satisfaction, but not as clear or as probing an index as the following:

Read each statement carefully. Then

(A) If you feel you *do* get satisfaction from your general reading of fiction, blacken answer space A ["agree"].

(U) If you are *uncertain* as to your general attitude, or if the statement seems *unclear* or *meaningless*, blacken answer space U.

(D) If you feel you *do not* get this satisfaction, blacken answer space D ["disagree"].

59. Finding rest and relaxation after a hard day's work.

60. Passing the time when there is nothing else better to do.

There are 150 statements like these two, and these are classified under the following headings: relaxation and pastime, escape, associational values, information about intimate personal relations, socio-civic information, philosophy of life and religion, miscellaneous information, technical-critical, and self-development. Such a questionnaire can be scored both for the total number of positive responses and for the types of satisfaction an individual or a class most commonly takes in reading fiction. Similar questionnaires could, of course, be developed for other genres.

One problem with this type of questionnaire, as with any attitude or interest questionnaire, is that a student can seek to please the teacher by offering the approved answers rather than his real attitudes. The advantage of a 150-item questionnaire is that by its very length and complexity, it prevents a test-wise student from outguessing the teacher. A similar advantage seems to be enjoyed by the semantic differential test. I suspect that for most teachers a set of direct questions anonymously answered will give some information, but they should beware of being overjoyed by positive answers on any attitude or interest questionnaire.[12]

General attitudes (T) The same would hold true for a test of the last behavior, *Accept the importance* (*T*) of a literary work. Tests of this behavior fall into three divisions: a test of personal importance like that using the semantic differential; a test of attitudes toward censorship or other abridgment of the rights of authors and readers; and a test of stereotyped thinking about literature and the people who make it. Each of these tests indicates how highly a student prizes literature; whether he approves it, whether he thinks it is an important and viable cultural force, and whether he thinks it worth preserving against the forces that would curb it.

The first sort of test we have already looked at; the second sort would contain items like these:

T-17 Accept the importance of any literary work

61. Most poetry seems like a meaningless jumble of words.
    1. Strongly agree
    2. Agree
    3. Disagree
    4. Strongly disagree

62. Literature has no useful or practical ideas.
    1. Strongly agree
    2. Agree
    3. Disagree
    4. Strongly disagree

(American Council on Education, undated, p. 4, items 16, 20.)

Other types of statements might be "Poets dress differently from other people," "People in the theater are immoral," and "Literature tells us more about the past than history books do," for a test like this should contain a fairly large number of statements and should balance negative against positive statements. From such a test a teacher can derive a general index of positive or negative attitudes toward literature and an indication as to whether or not a student thinks in clichés about literature and writers.

The third kind of measure deals with censorship. This again can be cast in the multiple-choice opinion form, presenting a statement and asking the student the extent to which he agrees or disagrees with it. Censorship should not be treated in a blanket fashion, however, but should be divided into degrees of censorship—by national government, by local government, by recommendation of one of these groups, and none at all—and into objects of censorship—sex, religion, patriotism, racism, and the like. In this way one can determine what the students' prejudices are and how deeply they are held. There is today an obvious trend away from belief in government control with regard to sexy literature, but a trend toward the belief that racist and intolerant literature should be censored. It is important to note how strong these trends are in a class or a school and then to consider whether and how they should be dealt with.

All these attitudes and interests can, of course, be garnered through some sort of question asking for the student's free response, but the experience of attitude and opinion pollsters is so great, and the techniques they have developed are so useful, that more of these should be used in the schools and in the classroom. These measurements are increasingly important because they permit us to know the state of literature in the schools—

[12] Since this chapter was written, a new volume describing the "Hooked on Books" curriculum has appeared (Fader & McNeill, 1968). Although the program has remained the same, the evaluation of the program has become more sophisticated. The semantic differential, however, remains the core of the evaluation program. Readers are referred to this newer description of the evaluation.

whether it is taken seriously by the students, whether its impact is great, whether the artist is respected, whether the student is caught up in works of art. If the results are negative, one can foresee a dwindling of the importance of the humanities and of the culture that English teachers and humanists have cherished and sought to preserve. Surely they are worth preserving, and if the students do not think so, something is radically wrong with the state of literary education. There is a growth of interest in writers and writing, a growth of a sense of the power of the word, but the words and the writing are not those in the anthologies or the curricula. It would seem necessary, therefore, to measure the gap between the curriculum and the students so that we can plan bridges to span it.

Problems in Testing Literature

Having examined the various behaviors involved in the study of literature, we come now to the matter of test construction. If we look at the general group of behaviors, we see that they define three main types of test: literary acquaintance, literary analysis and interpretation, and attitudes toward literature and the literary response.

Acquaintance tests

A test of literary acquaintance might be used to find out how much knowledge the student has acquired and whether he can apply that knowledge to other knowledge that he has accumulated or to some new concept. Such a test might be given at the beginning of a year to find out where the students are or at the end to find out how much they have mastered. For tests given at the end of the year, essay questions, such as those we have described in the section on application, are particularly appropriate, for they enable the student to bring together much of what he has learned.

For a general test of acquaintance, one using many short-answer or multiple-choice questions, the main difficulty is selecting material to be tested, particularly literary works. There is not too much of a problem about the literary terms one might ask a group to understand. There is a common stock, one not unlike that listed in the Ginn series, *Types of Literature* (Bennett et al., 1967). There are a few critical systems one might expect a college-preparatory senior class to know: Aristotle's definition of tragedy, something of the system of genres, something of the new critical method. The amount of biographical and contextual information would depend on the particular course, as would the actual works themselves.

In a classroom year-end test—not to mention a multiclassroom, local, regional, or national examination—one can never be fully sure that everyone has had an opportunity to read everything in the syllabus—if there is a syllabus. Even in a single class, this condition might obtain if the program included, as many now do, an individual reading program. At a larger level, we know from a survey conducted by Scarvia Anderson that in 1963 *Macbeth* was taught to more than 90 percent of the students, *Julius Caesar* to more than 80 percent, and *Silas Marner* to more than 50 percent; but beyond those, fewer than one-third of the school population could be expected to have read any one book (Anderson, 1964, p. 5). If this is true of full-length works, one can probably expect even less unanimity about short stories and lyric poems. To give the students a chance to show what they know, the tester must include questions dealing with some fifty to seventy-five titles, and he must not be surprised if even then the score achieved by any one student is not particularly high. At the college and graduate levels, of course, one can expect more uniformity, simply because the courses tend to be history of literature courses with a more standardized canon.

Tests of analysis and interpretation

The second type of summative examination is examination of the expressed response, usually referred to as a test of literary analysis and interpretation. This type of examination asks the student to treat a familiar or—more usually—an unfamiliar text, and to see whether he has mastered the classificatory, analytic, or interpretive skills that the course or the curriculum has sought to engender. These tests do not usually call for the student to express his engagement or his evaluation (unless that be by some preestablished criterion) because of the lack of a norm by which to judge the student. How deeply involved should a person be? Should he find a particular work good or bad? What criterion should he have by which to judge a work? One could, of course, determine how deep his engagement is, whether or not he thinks a work good, and what criterion he uses to evaluate what he reads. Having done this, one would know a great deal more about the student and be able to describe his critical style, but this is not the same as measuring his critical acumen. Although I believe critical style to be as important as critical acumen, I do realize that our entire concept of course evaluation must change before a descriptive measure replaces the normative.

According to the traditional notions of achievement, then, a summative measure of mastery of a literary work will deal with the classificatory and analytic skills. One set of specifications for an examination of this sort is that for the Literature Achievement Test of the College Entrance Examination Board:

> It was decided that the test questions should seek to measure a student's ability: (1) to paraphrase parts of the work or summarize the whole work; (2) to comprehend the structure of the text; (3) to comprehend language and style; (4) to comprehend rhetorical and literary devices; (5) to comprehend the ways by which structure and language and rhetorical and literary devices enhance and even create the meaning and form of a work; (6) to classify a text by genre, tradition, or period; (7) to understand allusions to common figures or symbols in mythology, literature, and folklore; and (8) to deal with such general aspects of literary study as theme, history and the writer's art. . . . In the hour-long test, there will be from 6 to 12 passages varying in length, genre, form, and historical period.
>
> (Purves, 1968, p. 18)

The first seven of these abilities cover most of the behaviors of classification, analysis of parts, and analysis of relationships. There is some coverage of the expression of interpretation, but, as we have seen, this is necessarily restricted in a multiple-choice examination. The seven abilities are those which are susceptible to objective questions. The eighth is a broad specification for essay questions.

Text-centered tests In such tests, the organizing principle is not so much the behavior as the text. One takes a text presumably unfamiliar to the students and asks a series of specific questions about it, which might cover a range of behaviors. This kind of organization is critically sound, as it does not assume that one short question suffices for a poem; and it is economical for the tester because the student who undertakes a fair amount of difficult reading must therefore answer several questions. Quite obviously one text is not enough to measure mastery of the comprehension and analysis of literary texts, although one might suffice for a unit test. For a year-end test there should be enough texts to let the examiner make sure the student has mastered literary analysis. One text may evoke no response or may evoke a psychologically blocked response; further, no one short text provides a sufficient array of problems in language, human behavior, and literary structure at similar degrees of complexity to warrant a teacher's saying, "He mastered this text; therefore, he can master any."

One may define a "difficult" text as one that uses recherché, ambiguous, or highly connotative language; complex rhythms, syntactic structures, or human motivations; subtle moods and tones; tenuous analogies or complex symbols; intricate relationships among its parts; a form that partakes of a mixture of types; a multitude of archetypes; and a matter or manner that involves the reader to such an extent that he finds it difficult to become objective about it. Few works combine all these attributes, of course, but the teacher must not delude himself that the difficulty of a literary work depends on one attribute alone, and, moreover, that a student who cannot seem to master one dimension of difficulty is literarily stupid. Just as the literary work will have varying proportions of difficulty along these twelve dimensions, so too will a student have varying degrees of ability in the twelve kinds of discrimination. Further, we cannot assert that because a student has a high proficiency in one kind he will have a correspondingly high proficiency in another. One exception to what I have just said would be that the comprehension of the mother tongue would seem to precede and predict the capability to handle puns, although not necessarily an ability to do so. There may exist a similar relationship between the ability to discriminate between denotation and connotation and among connotations and the ability to discriminate among tones and moods, but these seem the only necessary relationships.

For these reasons, therefore, a test should contain passages of poetry and prose which are diverse in style, period, and theme, in order to ensure a variety of dictions, literary devices and structures, and types of human experience. One need not expect to have the questions cover all the facets of each passage or lead to a full analysis of each, but there should be such a set of questions on one or two of the passages. One reason for this is psychological: it is good to give the student a sense that he has accomplished something through the questions—that he has, in effect, programmed himself through to an understanding of the passage.

What sorts of texts should be used? For a short series of questions covering a single point, almost any text will do. Take "Legal," for example:

"No Trespassing" it said; but I
Not asking anybody's pardon,
Climbed the fence and saw the garden,
And knew not whether to laugh or cry.
Would you learn what sight I saw?
Then you must also break the law.

One might ask a question about the tone of the speaker, or about the division of the poem at line 4. There might be a question about the allusion which the poem makes, but it is only a faint allusion to the Garden of Eden. Beyond that there are few worthwhile questions one could ask about the poem, despite its quality. In a sense it is "oversimple" in that its statement is direct and it depends on its capability to summon up associations for its effects. The moral, social, religious, and psychological ramifications lurk outside the text and cannot be used as correct or incorrect answers in a test on the poem, simply because one person might see one set of ramifications, another person another set.

A text, then, should have some problem of statement, some complexity of language and of form, in order for the questions to be worthwhile. It cannot rely, as "Legal" does, on one kind of complexity. Similarly, a poem which presents a powerful emotion directly is also a poor choice for a long series of questions, because the reader seems to be offered no option but to assent or not to assent to the emotion. He may not be able to analyze the parts or the structure of the work, if he cannot accept the emotion of a poem like "Break, Break, Break":

Break, break, break,
On thy cold gray stones, O Sea!
And I would that my tongue could utter
The thoughts that arise in me.

O well for the fisherman's boy,
That he shouts with his sister play!
O well for the sailor lad,
That he sings in his boat on the bay!

And the stately ships go on
To their haven under the hill;
But O, for the touch of a vanished hand,
And the sound of a voice that is still!

Break, break, break,
At the foot of thy crags, O Sea!
But the tender grace of a day that is dead
Will never come back to me.

(Tennyson)

In a sense, the problem with testing this poem is that the emotion is so direct that if one responds to it correctly one will be speechless.

The selection that one chooses should raise questions of both what and how, statement and structure. There should be questions about the diction and the attitude, and questions about what the imagery tells us of the subject, tone, and point of view. As James Britton has said,

"The test seeks to find out if the student is able to read a poem, re-creating for himself the structure that embodies the experience in the poem" (Britton with Purves, 1967, p. 4). What is true for a poem is equally true for a passage of prose. There, the problem is also one of finding a passage that is self-contained or needs only the briefest of introductions. A second problem is choosing a passage about which the students can answer questions without having recourse to a knowledge of the whole work. This problem often occurs in a question about an excerpt from a novel, for the tester sees as foreshadowing what the student only sees as enigmatic. In the opening of "The Short Happy Life of Francis Macomber," Macomber orders a lemon squash, his shrewish wife a gimlet. It is only after one has read the whole story that one sees the portentousness of the two drinks. The student who was given the opening paragraphs and asked to indicate how the drinks indicated the characters of the people involved would probably be able to say that she drank and he was a teetotaler—which is not particularly true nor particularly important to the character relationships in the story. It is his softness and her shrewishness that the drinks portend.

When one turns to the sets of questions themselves, one is given a number of options. The one most often taken by test makers is to ask a number of questions about what is called "the plain-sense meaning" of the work. Too often, however, this train of questioning turns into a test of reading comprehension, with questions like "What does the phrase ______ mean?" Such questions can be important, but they should not be the staple of a test. An alternative to this is to ask a series of questions calling for the application of literary terms, like "Metonymy is found in which line?" and "Which line contains alliteration?" Both types of questions have their place, but they should not be the only kind of question asked; there should also be an attempt to move the student to some sort of summary statement.

In the unpublished memorandum for the IEA, James Britton has written:

> The intention of the questions is to set up a process as like as possible to the process a reader would actually carry out in reading a poem of his own volition. In other words, a reading situation, and not a test situation; a desire to get to grips with an experience and not a desire to get "the right answer" and a high score.
>
> Assuming the process of comprehension to be a process of *penetration*, we may conceive of a reader sometimes setting off on false trails, but, if he is a good reader, discarding them in favour of a trail that gets somewhere; and even, in a sense, of *arrival* —of coming to a position in which his view of things in the poem has most in common with what one must presume is the poet's own view. Arrived here, he may easily answer questions which to a reader who has not arrived will be puzzling if not meaningless.
>
> Each *set* of questions . . . seeks to pose some problem of central meaning—the meaning of a part of the poem or an aspect of the meaning of the whole poem. Often the final question in the set is the one that elicits this point of "central meaning" and the earlier questions in the set lead up to it—are the "trail," the suggested route. A reader ought therefore to be *better* able to tackle the final question by virtue of the help the earlier questions have given him, the way his attention has been focused by them. . . . Sets of questions are best thought of as "trails" or "routes": this helps examiners to insure that every question is going somewhere; it may for other purposes be valuable to know whether a student can recognize internal rhyme when he sees it or know the meaning of the word "ample"; but unless the answers to such questions lead on to an understanding of something central to the meaning of the particular poem concerned, they will have no place in these tests.
>
> (Britton with Purves, 1967, pp. 7–8)

One of the best ways to ensure that this sort of questioning takes place is to write the final question first, and then ascertain what questions will best lead the student to that final question. The virtue of such a set of questions is that they give the student a sense that he has come to some mastery of the text, and even the student who gets them wrong will realize that his time has not been wasted. Such questions may also have their usefulness in formative tests, although, as we shall see, their usefulness is limited by the fact that one can never be sure where the student went wrong.

To return to our example, Keats's "On First Looking into Chapman's Homer," one might have, in addition to some of the items we have described earlier, an item asking about Chapman or what Homer wrote. We might ask a question about Keats's education, particularly having to do with the fact that he knew no Greek—which might be inferred from the text. But such questions of knowledge or the application of extrinsic information—like naming the alliterative spots in the text—seem relatively trivial when compared with questions like those on structure and language. To answer those questions correctly is to indicate that one can read the poem, not merely reel off bits of information, and can handle the syntactic and rhetorical problems that the shifting, allusive, linguistic structure we call a poem presents to the reader. I do not think the questions of recall and application are so trivial as to be worthless, but they seem to measure literary acquaintance more than literary understanding. In a sense, this prejudice of mine represents a thorough grounding in the new criticism. Simultaneously, I have absorbed a great deal of information about Keats and a disdain for using that information in criticizing his poetry. So, too, with the terminology of much literary criticism. Now I decry the use of both the information and the terminology, and yet—and yet I use both to validate my unhistorical and "naïve" reading of the poems. These bits of information are important to my understanding of the text; they make that understanding come much easier, but they seem not to be part of the logic by which I come to understand the poem. Knowing about Keats's education enables me to know why Keats wrote the poem, but I do not think it helps me to understand or appreciate his excitement. Perhaps it does help me, however; perhaps every bit of information that I have acquired enables me to deal with the poem in a more comprehensive way than I could have without that information—I shall never know. At any rate, there does seem to be some truth to the proposition that knowledge about literature better enables one to comprehend a literary text; but the exact connection remains unclear, and until it is clarified, questions about those matters which seem external to the text will be viewed with suspicion by those who believe that an active reader of literature can respond intelligently with a minimum of information beyond that offered by the words of the text themselves.

A well-designed set of items dealing with the passage would, therefore, concentrate on the analytic and interpretive questions, and would attempt to follow the process of reading the text. The final point at which such a set would aim might be the summary of the mood of the speaker of the poem, and how that mood is effected. It would seem reasonable, then, to have three spurts of questions, one dealing with the octave, one with the sestet, and one with the poem as a whole. They might include questions like these (which I shall phrase as short-answer rather than multiple-choice):

Questions on the octave

K-3

63. What kind of a land would be a realm of gold?

D-3

64. Why do bards owe fealty to Apollo?

K-3

65. In lines 1 to 8, to what is travel being compared?
66. Restate lines 1 to 4, showing what they mean in terms of the implied comparison.

M-3

67. Chapman was the translator of Homer's poetry. What is the poet saying about Homer and Chapman in lines 5 to 8?

K-3

68. What is the poet's attitude toward literature as it is made apparent in lines 1 to 8? What words in those lines make that attitude apparent?

Questions on the sestet

K-3

69. In lines 9 to 14, what aspect of himself is the poet describing?
70. What sense do the two comparisons of lines 9 to 14 emphasize?

71. What do the watcher of the skies and Cortez have in common?
72. A contrast is established between Cortez and his men. What is that contrast?
73. What word does "silent" (line 14) modify?
74. Summarize the mood described in lines 9 to 14.

Questions on the poem as a whole
L-3
75. What is the relationship between the implied comparison of lines 1 to 8 and the comparisons of lines 9 to 14?
76. What is the relationship between the attitude described in lines 1 to 8 and the mood established in lines 9 to 14?

These fourteen short questions seek to break down into its constituents the answer to a possible essay question on the text:

L-3 Analyze the whole of a precontemporary lyric poem
77. Describe the way in which the structure of the poem reinforces the speaker's mood as it is presented in lines 9 to 14. In your essay show how the attitude in the first part of the poem is related to the mood at the end of the poem.

This question is a slightly more structured version of "Write an analysis of the poem."

Items 63 to 76 are all capable of being transformed into multiple-choice questions in that they all have better and poorer answers. The best answer to item 74 might be phrased, "The mood is one of excitement and awe at discovery by one who knows and respects what he is looking for." A false answer might be one that described the mood as a naïve surprise at finding the unimagined. That mood would be applicable to Cortez's men, not to Cortez or to the speaker of the poem. A poor distracter would be one that described the mood as the reverence of a worshiper. That would seem to be a justifiable definition of the mood, although not as accurate as the awe of a connoisseur. A multiple-choice question in literary analysis can be subtle and complex in that it can deal with mood and intricate relationships, but it cannot deal in nuances of mood.

Behavior-centered tests There is an alternative to using the text as the shaping force in a test of analysis and interpretation: using the behaviors. The abilities to discriminate among ambiguities of language, denotations and connotations, rhythms, syntactic abnormalities, genres, tones, motives, and behaviors, and to comprehend metaphor, all exist on continua. There are, that is to say, easy and hard discriminations, and one can see that the pun in

"Why is a hinge like a pretty girl?"
"Because both are something to *adore*."

is probably easier to "get" than that in

Of Man's first disobedience and the *fruit*
Of that forbidden tree . . .
(Milton, *Paradise Lost*, I. 1–2)

in which both "fruit" and "of" have a second meaning. The basis of difficulty would depend on the frequency of both meanings in the language and on whether or not one of the meanings depends on outside knowledge (in the case of the lines from Milton, knowledge of Genesis). Given these bases, one could construct a pun test; on comparable bases, one could construct tests of metaphor, diction, syntax, rhythm, genre, tone, behavior, connotation, and part-whole relationships. This last might very well use the type of item that asks the student to supply a missing line in a poem or a prose passage, as does item 46 (page 742). Such a series of tests could give a firm index of the student's ability in literary analysis, firmer than one based on a text; it would tell the teacher the specific areas of the student's strengths and weaknesses. With such knowledge a teacher could better choose the sorts of texts or the sorts of abilities that he should concentrate on. Such a series of tests would, therefore, serve both a judgmental and a descriptive function, and the descriptive function is perhaps the most important and the safest in literature testing, for it does not run the risk of establishing a norm that may disappear when the critical winds change.

Attitude tests

We come now to the third kind of summative evaluation, the evaluation of attitudes and interests. Within this rough grouping come measures of engagement, evaluation, patterns of preference for works of literature and of responses, willingness to respond, satisfaction in response, and acceptance of the importance of literature (*J* and *N* to *T*). Most of these behaviors are not usually measured in the classroom or the school except in connection with some research program, because the success or failure of the student does not depend on his performance in these behaviors. Yet they are important and should be treated seriously by teachers, for the success or failure of the teacher is at stake. In a real sense, the mastery of information about literature and the mastery of critical acumen are worthless if the student does not enjoy literature, if he does not develop his taste, and if he develops no desire to read another book. Literature study is one of the few parts of the required school curriculum which deliberately seeks to create in students the desire to participate in a leisure activity. Literature is disinterested in the sense that it has little practical purpose—it doesn't help one get ahead, except as a literature teacher—but its importance to the curriculum is twofold: it embodies the traditions of the culture, and it presents experience vicariously and artistically. Mastering it, therefore, implies acculturization and maturity, but nothing more demonstrably practical than those.

The only practical argument for the study of literature is that since literature may be defined as the manipulation of language to provoke a response, the study of it enables one to better master his language and avoid the misuses of language that men of ill-will have perpetrated. But this justification of the study of literature as a form of propaganda analysis pales beside the assertion that literature produces a high form of aesthetic pleasure and that studying it enables one to move from sensual pleasure to the pleasures of the imagination and the intellect. Studying literature enables one to contemplate experiences he would not come into direct contact with and to contemplate experience which has been ordered so as to produce a pleasurable response. The study of literature, then, enables one to strike a balance between intellection and introjection.

For this reason, therefore, the behaviors that we call "attitudinal" are extremely important to the curriculum, and their measurement is important for both the student and the curriculum. If the student is reading better but enjoying it less, he may become a disdainful nonreader, and this would be the result of an imbalance in his course of study. The problems of measuring attitudes, however, are what have led teachers to remain clear of them, for the measurement is too often inaccurate, difficult to interpret, and misunderstood. The problem of inaccuracy arises because many of the measures are questionnaires and people are known to answer them less than truthfully. The problems of interpretation arise from the same source and from the fact that one must separate wanted from gratuitous information—people who answer questionnaires often run on and on after they have answered a question. It is misunderstanding which presents the most serious problem. Much attitude measurement is necessarily descriptive: it seeks to find out what an attitude is. One can determine, for instance, what books an individual prefers, how deeply engrossed in a work of literature he finds himself, how strongly he dislikes poetry or censorship. Having determined these attitudes or preferences, one may evaluate them—saying, for example, that the fact that 90 percent of a population prefers *Batman* to *Beowulf* represents a deplorable anticultural bias. Someone else, however, might claim that such a preference is to be applauded because the two works are remarkably similar in their underlying fantasies and in some of their trappings, and that the preference shows how ready the students are to read *Beowulf*, provided the teacher makes the proper connection. This type of argument about value is perfectly respectable, but a problem arises when someone predetermines what a good response to a question of attitude is and claims that there is a "right" response. Attitudes are the result of a commingling of personal and societal values, and while we can say now that it is bad to approve of censorship, we must realize that in another era or another culture censorship may be approved. We must also realize that tastes change and that the premises on which they are based also change. Thirty years ago, few might have challenged the teaching of *Silas Marner*; now it is widely deplored. Fifty years ago, the "good work" was the work that moved the reader; today it is the work that displays ambiguity, paradox, and structural perfection.

Too often, however, we tend to think of these values as fixed, and so we tend to make a normative test out of what should be a descriptive one. The Logasa-Wright Tests for the Appreciation of Literature (Logasa & McCoy-Wright, undated a) include an excellent measure of "reader participation," which asks the student to give his reaction to various passages by checking one of nine adjectives (cheerfulness, amusement, delight, exaltation, horror, terror, pity, discomfort, and indifference). The only problem with the measure is that the authors have given a correct answer for each passage: for instance,

> But words are things, and a small drop of ink,
> Falling like dew upon a thought, produces
> That which makes thousands, perhaps millions,
> think,

is supposed to evoke indifference. I, for one, think that I participate fairly fully in literature, and I am torn between amusement and horror at the metaphor and a degree of delight at the thought. But I am not indifferent.

The authors have another test in which they ask the student to say whether a metaphor is true, far-fetched, or mixed. In their directions, they consider a comparison of a bird to a blossom "true" and one of birds to pennies "far-fetched" —they do not say why it is far-fetched, and I think I could argue that it is a more effective metaphor than the one they call true. Similarly, they have a test calling for a student to say whether he thinks an expression trite or not. In this case, their argument for a norm is stronger but still not ironclad, because triteness is determined by context. Each of these measures could give the teacher a great deal of information about the student's predilections and responses, but such information cannot be placed on a scale of good to bad. The authors of the tests are, in fact, asking the students to agree with their taste and their response; in doing so, they are neglecting the fact that tastes and responses change (even their taste probably changed a year after the test was devised) and that the affective and evaluative aspects of a response are to a certain extent unique. At one time, we were all expected to weep at the death of Little Nell; now we are expected to be amused or bored. The stock market of literature fluctuates almost as much as the New York Stock Exchange. There are some blue chips, and there are some highly speculative classics like Poe and Kipling. Further, although there may be a critical consensus, there is far from critical unanimity about value and even about the appropriate response to a particular work. One established critic, for example, reads *Billy Budd* as satire.

All this is not to say that there should be no summative evaluation of response and attitude —quite the contrary. There should be more summative evaluation in these areas, but it should be descriptive rather than prescriptive, so that the evaluator may say, "This is the kind of student our curriculum has produced." If the school does not like his looks, it can only examine the curriculum to see what might have produced this student. Of course, some attitudes must be modified: a prospective book burner should be stopped; a prospective man of letters encouraged. An intelligent person who only reads *Mad* might be led to Swift and other satirists. A person who wants to read but has no idea what to read should be directed.

Units of learning and formative evaluation in literature

As we have already noted in the discussion of the three curricula (Sec. II), what is achieved in a semester's or a year's work in literature is simply what was achieved in a unit or in a lesson on a poem writ large. As far as behavior is concerned, it makes little difference whether the content is one text of two lines or an 800-page anthology; the student is expected to know it, to apply his knowledge of other texts or other external information to it, to respond to it and to articulate that response, and to like it and accept its value as literature. All of these behaviors exist virtually simultaneously in that all of them are expected from the first time literature is given serious attention to the defense of a doctoral thesis. One may well ask why literature is given so much attention if this is true. The answer is that there is a lot of it and that response to it, particularly the analytic response, involves a long process of moving from grosser to finer discriminations. Therefore the course of literature is the repetition, deepening, and strengthening of each of these behaviors.

It is for this reason that the content of literature curricula can be so various. The sequence of units, be it based on chronology, theme, genre, or rhetorical or literary device, has a logic to the curriculum planner which may well be in accord with critical theory but which may be irrelevant, or nearly so, to the developing abilities of the child. The sequence of difficulty is the only one that is pedagogically meaningful, and that sequence, as we have observed, is beclouded. The work that deals in a complex mood—Burns's "My love is like a red, red rose"—is simple in rhythm, diction, and syntax. Some of E. E. Cummings's complex verbal structures, like "in just spring," are quite simple in mood. For this reason a sequence of difficulty is hard to create.

What does distinguish the unit from the course is size. In a unit like that from the Carnegie curriculum (Steinberg et al., undated), the students treat one theme and five works. In the course, there are several themes and perhaps fifty or sixty works. Usually, when one has completed the first unit, he simply turns to the next and makes a fresh start. There may be some transition, and there is accumulation, but it is not a sequential accumulation. The same may be said for a generic curriculum or even a response-centered curriculum like that of *Hooked on Books* (Fader & Shaevitz, 1966); one "does" poetry or one "does" *West Side Story*—however one defines "does"—and then moves on. This lack of continuity is not necessarily bad; it does not disturb the students or their teachers too much, because both see each encounter with a literary work as a unique event, calling on various abilities connected with response and on the sum total of past experiences with literary and nonliterary events. There is, therefore, a behavioral continuity, although not a sequence of behaviors.

Knowledge accumulates, to be sure; but the accumulation is less than systematic, and it becomes systematic only when one is called upon to systematize it in applying it to a newly encountered work or to some new generalization—critical, thematic, or personal. One might never before have thought of "the good marriage," and then be forced to bring together one's reading and think about what was said there about the good marriage—similarly, perhaps, with American materialism, or with a newly presented sonnet. For this reason, the best kinds of summative evaluation are those which ask the student to apply his reading to a concept or to a new work which he must analyze and interpret. A third major kind of summative evaluation is that which asks him to describe and consider his attitudes and preferences.

Given the microcosmic nature of the unit in literature, one might well ask whether formative evaluation is different from summative evaluation. Let us look again at the unit on the American Desire for Success in the Carnegie curriculum. The points covered in that unit are character analysis, the interpretation of four works and their application to the concept of success, and the narrative and dramatic techniques used by the authors. Analysis, application, and interpretation are the dominant behaviors, and they are repeated from work to work—particularly the analysis of character and the application of the works to the theme. The other units in the series may place less emphasis on character analysis and more on plot analysis and discussion of mood and language, but the application of the work to the theme remains paramount. The problem of the unit is simply the problem of the lessons in a larger framework, and the problem of the course repeats the unit pattern on a still larger scale.

As far as evaluation of knowledge, application, and analysis goes, there is little difference between the evaluation of a unit and the evaluation of the course. The only thing that differs is that the unit test is concerned with what has been read (four works); a course test might be concerned with what has not been read—that is, some new work or some new blending of concepts. Similarly, a unit test might concentrate on the analytic abilities related to the genre under study, a course test on several genres. A course test might well include some attitudinal material, and attitudes would probably not be measured during the course of the several units. A response preference will probably not show much difference during the course of a year, although it may show a great difference between the beginning and end of the year. The same is true of taste and attitudes: Fader and Shaevitz do not appear to think their curriculum will have its effect in a week or a month; they do expect it to have one at the end of a year.

One other difference between formative and summative evaluation has to do with acquaintance. One expects the knowledge of the details of a work to be fresh at the end of a unit, but hardly so at the end of a year. One is tempted, therefore, to test for such knowledge in unit tests, and to test only for that knowledge. That temptation is one that should be strongly resisted, as I hope these pages have proved; so, too, should the temptation to stress knowledge in summative evaluation when the other behaviors seem to be more important to the curriculum and to the teacher. One can, nevertheless, use a test of knowledge in a unit test to see how well the work is remembered and whether the salient points of the novel are well enough known so that they can be brought back in a final examination. In a unit test, as in a final test, however, the trivial and the nasty should be avoided.

One particularly valuable kind of measure for formative evaluation is the questionnaire concerning engagement. If it is found that the students are rather negative, that they have not entered into the works they have just been studying, that their response is correct but apathetic, the teacher is in a good position to change his strategy. He could not do so at the end of the year. This kind of evaluation, like many of the other kinds that we have discussed, is particularly appropriate for diagnosis of one's class at the beginning of the year, and its results can form the basis for the whole year's work.

In general, therefore, formative evaluation is a microcosm of summative evaluation in that it deals with a single work or a small group of works and usually with a smaller segment of the spectrum of behaviors. I would hope, of course, that during the course of the year all the behaviors and all of the content would be touched upon. In this way, the teacher can be sure that he is not limiting himself to a narrow part of the domain of literature or to a limited set of behaviors. All of them are, as I hope I have shown, necessary and integral to mastery of literature, and their neglect may be perilous for the student.

There remains but one point to make about evaluation in literature, and that is whether it should exist at all. It does exist under the current reward system in education, but it has been attacked as inimical to the teaching of literature, particularly as regards the response to literature. Such an attack was leveled by members of the Dartmouth Seminar (see Muller, 1967) and has been repeated in the *Times Literary Supplement*. There, W. W. Robson (1968, p. 774) points to the major criticism of examining in literature: "I think of a candidate whose sincere response to a poem is blankness: it 'leaves him cold.' Is he to say nothing? Surely he ought to say nothing. Yet if he does, he will fail the examination." This criticism is the most frequently posed.

Another, nearly as frequent, is that examinations concentrate on the examinable, that in most cases the examinable is factual information about works and authors—that is, the minutiae—and that concentration on minutiae makes literature trivial.

Both these criticisms are valid, given the nature of most tests in literature. The examination of factual knowledge is the staple of much literature examining; and knowledge, as we have seen, is only one of twenty behaviors and far from the most significant, both in the various curricula and in the national conception of the domain of literature. Certainly it should be relegated to a minor position and not dominate national tests, textbook tests, or teacher-made tests. Such a redress of balance is, I think, in the offing.

Robson's criticism can also be seen as valid given much of the testing of the expressed response. Many tests ask the student to "Analyze and interpret *X*," a question which is roughly comparable to throwing a child into ten feet of water to see whether he can do the butterfly stroke. Such questions have their place if one is seeking to find out which student can do what, but not to find out if all can measure up to some standard. A set of questions like those Britton describes seems to have a stronger assurance of determining how far a student can go, and it gives each student more of a chance to put down a part of his response and not feel threatened into denying what he thinks the poem means in favor of some predigested interpretation or analysis. If these questions are repeated with several texts, the sensitive but reticent student will not fail the examination. Such testing is quite clearly a test of certain limited perceptual abilities and makes no higher claim, so that the student can remain apathetic in a part of his response, or silent out of awe, and still make the basic perceptual statements.

Both criticisms of literature tests can be further countered, I trust, by the whole of this discussion. For both summative and formative evaluation, the teacher should include as many of the behaviors as possible; and when he is dealing with the attitudinal behaviors and even with the perceptual abilities, he should disabuse himself of the notion that there is a God-given norm, that a student should have such and such a preference, that he should be able to analyze such and such a verbal structure. Instead, the teacher should seek to find out where the student is, what his attitudes are, what his abilities are. Having done so, he can devise a teaching strategy to make the student aware of these attitudes and abilities and see whether the former might be modified or at least discussed and whether the latter can be strengthened. In this way, beginning with a knowledge of where the student is, the teacher can lead him to a mastery of all the behaviors involved in the study of literature.

The state of current tests in literature

According to the 1965 edition of Buros's *Mental Measurements Yearbook*, there are approximately a score of literature test programs in print.[13] Some of these programs, like the Objective Tests in English of the Perfection Form Company, consist of some fifty or more separate tests—one each on a novel, play, or long poem. Of the tests in print, if indeed they are now in print, almost half antedate the Second World War. Whether a teacher should consider using these tests in the classroom at all is a problem, because some are imaginative in format and item type but hopelessly dated as to content—either the works of which they demand knowledge are no longer in the schools or the passages of which they demand analysis are remote from the types of literature usually treated in the classroom today. A teacher should beware of tests published even fifteen years ago and should examine them to determine their relevance to the literature and to the objectives of teaching literature that obtain in the classroom today.

Of the tests purporting to deal with books standard in the schools—tests of great books, for instance—most deal with recall of specific

[13] Since 1965 a number of tests in literature have appeared. Most of these tests are measures of literary analysis and interpretation. The comments made here apply, in general, to the newer tests.

instances and contain questions like "Huck and Jim spent the night on Jackson's Island. True or false?" Tests dominated by questions like this are of little real use to the teacher because they do not accord with the current curriculum objectives, as we have seen. They tell the teacher only whether a student has read the work, not whether he has read it with understanding—a teacher usually needs only a two-minute quiz to find out the former. Those questions on tests of great works that purport to deal with analysis and interpretation are usually susceptible to criticism on the grounds of triviality or ambiguity. Whether Huck Finn is "good" or not cannot be answered with a simple yes or no. The final criticism of these tests is that their simplicity tends to give the students the impression that mastery of literature is simply the mastery of facts, a misapprehension which this chapter has sought to dispel.

The tests of literary acquaintance fall under the same general criticism. Too often they deal with knowledge only, not with the application of knowledge. Furthermore, these are the tests which the publishers have not revised, so that they ask for information which students can no longer be expected to possess. One exception is the Graduate Record Examination in Literature in English, but that test is not germane to high school examining.

Only one test of preference or attitudes seems to be in print and commercially available: the Riggs Poetry Judgment Test, originally published in 1942. It suffers from the same strengths and weaknesses as the Carroll Prose Appreciation Test, which I discussed earlier (pages 745 and following). The weaknesses are somewhat compounded by the fact that the "inferior" version is described as a parody of the "better," or original, version, though at times these parodies seem an improvement on the original. Like the Carroll test, this test represents a standard of taste which is somewhat distant from the standards by which students and teachers operate today, and so the effectiveness of the measure is somewhat dissipated.

There is only one test of literary analysis and interpretation in print and commercially available, the Literature Test in the Iowa Tests of Educational Development series. This, like the literature tests in the College Entrance Examination Board Achievement and College Level Program series, presents the student with unfamiliar passages and asks him to analyze and interpret them. These tests might strike the untrained observer as being tests of reading comprehension, but if one compares them with tests of reading, one sees that the passages in the literature tests are more allusive and imaginative and that the questions deal with matters of style as well as with matters of content. The Iowa Tests appear somewhat closer to reading comprehension than do the College Board Tests and such out-of-print tests as the United States Armed Forces Institute Tests of General Educational Development, because the questions are not in sequence from the factual to the critical. They are, however, satisfactory and useful tests.

It is in the area of analysis and interpretation, then, that the teacher is most sure of acquiring a commercial test of quality. Tests of acquaintance and attitude of a caliber sufficient to improve on the teacher's own tests are simply not available, and the teacher would do better to construct his own tests, arduous as that task might seem. To the end of creating better tests of his own, I trust this chapter will have served the teacher in some degree.

NOTE The documents analyzed for the construction of Table 20-1, Table of Specifications for Content and Behaviors in Literature, are the following:

(1) Bennett, R., Evans, V., & Gordon, E. J. *Types of literature.* Boston: Ginn, 1967. (2) Burton, D. L. *Literature study in the high schools.* (Rev. ed.) New York: Holt, Rinehart and Winston,

1964. (3) College Entrance Examination Board, Advanced Placement Committees. *Advanced placement program: 1966–68 course descriptions.* New York: CEEB, 1966. (4) College Entrance Examination Board, Commission on English. *Freedom and Discipline in English.* New York: CEEB, 1965. (5) Craig, G. A., Rice, F. M., & Gordon, E. J. *English literature.* Boston: Ginn, 1964. (6) Diederich, P. B. (Ed.) Objectives for reading. Chicago: University of Chicago, 1965. (7) Educational Testing Service, Curriculum Studies Division. *National assessment—Phase 1.* Princeton, N.J.: ETS, 1966. (8) Eller, W., Reeves, R., & Gordon, E. J. *The study of literature.* Boston: Ginn, 1964. (9) Eller, W., Welch, B. Y., & Gordon, E. J. *Introduction to literature.* Boston: Ginn, 1964. (10) Fowler, M. E. *Teaching language, composition, and literature.* New York: McGraw-Hill, 1965. (11) Frazier, A. (Ed.) *Ends and issues, 1965–1966: Points of decision in the development of the English curriculum.* Champaign, Ill.: National Council of Teachers of English, 1966. (12) French, W., and associates. *Behavioral goals of general education in high school.* New York: Russell Sage Foundation, 1957. (13) Frye, N. (Ed.) *Design for learning.* Toronto: University of Toronto Press, 1962. (14) Fuller, E., & Kinnick, B. J. *Adventures in American literature.* New York: Harcourt, Brace & World, 1963. (15) Genauer, E., Hume, P., Barr, D., & Fadiman, C. *Schools and the fine arts: What should be taught in art, music, and literature?* Washington, D.C.: Council for Basic Education, 1966. (16) Gordon, E. J. (Ed.) *Writing and literature in the secondary school.* New York: Holt, Rinehart and Winston, 1965. (17) Gordon, E. J., & Noyes, E. S. (Eds.) *Essays on the teaching of English: Reports of the Yale Conferences on the Teaching of English.* New York: Appleton-Century-Crofts, 1960. (18) Hook, J. N. *The teaching of high school English.* (3d ed.) New York: Ronald Press, 1959. (19) Kitzhaber, A. R., Correll, R. M., & Roberts, P. *Education for college.* New York: Ronald Press, 1961. (20) Loban, W., & Olmstead, R. *Adventures in appreciation.* New York: Harcourt, Brace & World, 1963. (21) Loban, W., Ryan, M., & Squire, J. R. *Teaching language and literature.* New York: Harcourt, Brace & World, 1961. (22) Lodge, E., & Braymer, M. *Adventures in reading.* New York: Harcourt, Brace & World, 1963. (23) National Council of Teachers of English, Commission on the English Curriculum. *The English language arts in the secondary school.* (Curr. Ser. No. 3) Champaign, Ill.: NCTE, 1956. (24) New York State Department of Education. *Syllabus in English for secondary schools, grades 7 through 12.* Albany: NYSDE, 1960. (25) Nieman, E., & O'Daly, E. *Adventures for readers: Book 2.* New York: Harcourt, Brace & World, 1963. (26) O'Daly, E., & Nieman, E. *Adventures for readers: Book 1.* New York: Harcourt, Brace & World, 1963. (27) Porter, A. J., Terrie, H. C., Jr., & Gordon, E. J. *American literature.* Boston: Ginn, 1964. (28) Priestley, J. B., & Spear, J. *Adventures in English literature.* New York: Harcourt, Brace & World, 1963. (29) Rosenblatt, L. M. Literature: A performing art. *Teachers College Record,* 1967, **68,** 307–315. (30) Squire, J. R., & Applebee, R. K. A study of English programs in selected high schools which consistently educate outstanding students in English. Cooperative Research Project No. 1994, University of Illinois, 1966. (31) Stone, G. W. (Ed.) *Issues, problems, and approaches in the teaching of English.* New York: Holt, Rinehart and Winston, 1961. (32) Tyler, R. W. The fact-finding study of the testing program of the United States Armed Forces Institute, 1952–1954. Report to the USAFI, University of Chicago, July 1954. (33) White, E., Wofford, J., & Gordon, E. J. *Understanding literature.* Boston: Ginn, 1964.

A supplementary list of documents examined but not analyzed includes the following:

(1) Chicago Public Schools. *Essential English in the secondary school: Literature, composition, language.* Chicago: Chicago Board of Education, 1964. (2) Chicago Public Schools. *Teaching guide for the language arts.* (Grades 7–8) Chicago: Board of Education, 1958. (3) Cleveland Public Schools. *An English program for the academically talented and the basic*

course of study in English for the college board. (Grades 9–12) Cleveland: Cleveland Board of Education, 1962. (4) Cleveland Public Schools. *English/College bound.* (Senior high school) Cleveland: Cleveland Board of Education, 1966. (5) *English Journal,* 1965–1969, **54–58.** (Consulted on attention given to mass media.) (6) Reid, V. M. (Ed.) *Children's literature: Old and new.* Champaign, Ill.: National Council of Teachers of English, Committee on Children's Literature: Old and New, 1964. (7) Seattle Public Schools. *Guide posts to English literature.* (Elementary–senior high school) Seattle: Seattle Board of Education, 1962. (8) Seattle Public Schools. *English language arts for the superior student.* Seattle: Seattle Board of Education, 1964. (9) Stafford, W. E. *Friends to this ground: A statement for readers, teachers, and writers of literature.* (Statement of the Commission on Literature, National Council of Teachers of English) Champaign, Ill.: National Council of Teachers of English, 1967.

REFERENCES

American Council on Education, Cooperative Study of General Education. *Inventory H-B2: Satisfactions Found in Reading Fiction.* Washington, D.C.: ACE, 1942.

American Council on Education, Cooperative Study of General Education. *Inventory of Humanities Attitudes.* Washington, D.C.: ACE, undated.

Anderson, S. *Between the Grimms and The Group.* Princeton, N.J.: Educational Testing Service, 1964.

Bennett, R. A., Evans, V., & Gordon, E. J. *Types of literature.* Boston: Ginn, 1967.

Bettelheim, B. *The informed heart: Autonomy in a mass age.* Glencoe, Ill.: Free Press, 1960.

Bloom, B. S. (Ed.) *Cross-national Study of Educational Attainment: Stage I of the I.E.A. investigation in six subject areas.* (Final Rep., Proj. No. 6-2527, Grant No. HEW-OEG-3-6-062527-2226) Vol. 2. *Instruments and materials.* Bklt. 3. *Mother Tongue Tests.* Hamburg, Ger.: International Association for the Evaluation of Educational Attainment (IEA), 1969.

Britton, J. N., with Purves, A. C. Guidelines for the measure of understanding of lyric poetry to be prepared by the National Committees, International Literature Project. Report No. IEA/LIT/6, International Association for the Evaluation of Educational Achievement, Hamburg, Ger., 1967.

Brooks, C., & Warren, R. P. *Understanding poetry.* (3d ed.) New York: Holt, Rinehart and Winston, 1960.

Buros, O. K. (Ed.) *The sixth mental measurements yearbook.* Highland Park, N.J.: Gryphon Press, 1965.

Carroll, H. A. *Prose Application Test.* Minneapolis: Educational Test Bureau, 1932. (a)

Carroll, H. A. *Prose Appreciation Test: Examiner's manual.* Minneapolis: Educational Test Bureau, 1932. (b)

Center, S., & Durost, W. *Center-Durost Literature Acquaintance Test.* Chicago: World Book, 1952.

College Entrance Examination Board, Commission on English. *Freedom and discipline in English.* New York: CEEB, 1965.

Davis, V. A., Roahan, R. L., & Schrammel, H. E. *Tests in literary appreciation.* Emporia, Kans.: Bureau of Educational Measurement, Kansas State Teachers College, 1938.

Dill, N. L., & Purves, A. C., with Weiss, J., & Foshay, A. W. The teaching of literature: Report of the United States National Committee, International Literature Project. Unpublished report, Teachers College, Columbia University, 1967. Available through NCTE ERIC, ED 039 399.

Educational Testing Service, Cooperative Test Division. *Background and Experience Questionnaire.* Princeton, N.J.: ETS, 1965.

Evans, V. *Teachers' handbook and key: Types of literature.* Boston: Ginn, 1967.

Fader, D. N., & McNeill, E. *Hooked on books:* Program and proof. New York: Berkley, 1968.

Fader, D. N., & Shaevitz, M. H. *Hooked on books.* New York: Berkley, 1966.

Frye, N. *Anatomy of criticism.* Princeton, N.J.: Princeton University Press, 1957.

Holland, N. *The dynamics of literary response.* New York: Oxford University Press, 1968.

Hymes, D. Phonological aspects of style: Some English sonnets. In T. Sebeok (Ed.), *Style in language.* Bloomington, Ind.: Indiana University Press, 1958. Pp. 118–129.

Krathwohl, D. R., Bloom, B. S., & Masia, B. B. *Taxonomy of educational objectives: The classification of educational goals.* Handbook 2. *Affective domain.* New York: McKay, 1964.

Lindquist, E. F. (Ed.) *The Iowa Tests of Educational Development: Test 7, Interpretation of Literary Materials.* Chicago: Science Research Associates, 1952.

Logasa, H., & McCoy-Wright, M. *Tests for the appreciation of literature.* (Prelim. prtg.) undated. (a)

Logasa, H., & McCoy-Wright, M. *Tests for the appreciation of literature.* Bloomington, Ill.: Public School Publishers, undated. (b)

Miller, J. H. *The disappearance of God.* New York: Schocken, 1965.

Muller, H. J. *The uses of English.* New York: Holt, Rinehart and Winston, 1967.

Nebraska Curriculum Development Center. *A curriculum for English: 12C.* Teacher Packet I. *Fable: The musicians of Bremen and Chanticleer and the fox.* II. *Satiric fable: The wind in the willows.* Lincoln, Nebr.: University of Nebraska Press, 1965.

Ong, W. J., S.J. Voice as a summons for belief. In W. J. Ong, S.J. *The barbarian within, and other fugitive essays and studies.* New York: Macmillan, 1962. Pp. 49–68.

Oregon Curriculum Study Center, University of Oregon. *A curriculum in English, grades 7–12.* (Doc. 10A) Eugene, Oreg.: University of Oregon, 1965.

Osgood, E. C., Suci, G. J., & Tannenbaum, P. *The measurement of meaning.* Urbana, Ill.: University of Illinois Press, 1957.

Poulet, G. *The interior distance.* Baltimore: Johns Hopkins Press, 1959.

Progressive Education Association, Evaluation in the Eight-year Study. *Literary Information Test.* Chicago: PEA, 1937.

Progressive Education Association, Evaluation in the Eight-year Study. *Questionnaire on Voluntary Reading.* Chicago: PEA, 1940.

Purves, A. Review of P. Saarinen & A. Lehtovaara, *School age reading interests: A methodological approach. International Journal of Education,* 1967, **13**(1), 107–111.

Purves, A. C. Designing the Board's new Literature Achievement Test. *College Board Review,* Spring 1968, No. 67, pp. 16–20.

Purves, A. C., with Rippere, V. *The elements of writing about a literary work.* Champaign, Ill.: National Council of Teachers of English, 1968.

Richards, I. A. *Practical criticism.* New York: Harcourt, Brace & World, 1930.

Robson, W. W. The future of English studies. *Times Literary Supplement* (London), July 25, 1968, pp. 774–775.

Rosenblatt, L. *Literature as exploration.* (Rev. ed.) New York: Noble & Noble, 1968.

Saarinen, P., & Lehtovaara, A. *School age reading interests: A methodological approach.* Helsinki: Suomalainen Tiedeakatemia, 1964.

Speer, R. K., & Smith, S. *National Achievement Tests: Literature Test.* Rockville Centre, N.Y.: Acorn, 1937.

Squire, J. R. *The responses of adolescents while reading four short stories.* Champaign, Ill.: National Council of Teachers of English, 1964.

Squire, J. R. (Ed.) *Response to literature.* Champaign, Ill.: National Council of Teachers of English, 1968.

Squire, J. R., & Applebee, R. K. *A study of English programs in selected high schools which consistently educate outstanding students in English.* Cooperative Research Project No. 1994, University of Illinois, 1966.

Steinberg, E., Slack, R. C., Cottrell, B. W., & Josephs, L. *A senior high school curriculum in English for able college-bound students.* Vol. 2. *The eleventh grade.* Pittsburgh: Curriculum Study Center in English, Carnegie Institute of Technology, undated.

Steinberg, E., Slack, R., & Forehand, G. *An evaluative study of a senior high school curriculum in English for able college-bound students.* Vol. 4. *Evaluation.* Pittsburgh: Curriculum Study Center in English, Carnegie Institute of Technology, undated.

University of Pittsburgh, Project Talent. *A national inventory of aptitudes and abilities.* Pittsburgh: University of Pittsburgh, 1960. (a)

University of Pittsburgh, Project Talent. *A national inventory of aptitudes and abilities: Test booklet B.* Pittsburgh: University of Pittsburgh, 1960. (b)

Walker, J. L. Bach, Rembrandt, Milton and those other cats. *English Journal,* 1968, **57,** 631–635.

21

Evaluation of Learning in Writing

JOSEPH J. FOLEY

Assistant Professor of English
Boston State College
Boston, Massachusetts

Joseph J. Foley, Assistant Professor of English at Boston State College, is a Ph.D. candidate at Boston College. He received his B.A. degree from Holy Cross College and his M.A.T. degree from Boston College, and has done graduate work in English at Columbia University. Before his present teaching at the undergraduate and graduate levels, he taught English in senior high school. As research associate at the Computation Center, Massachusetts Institute of Technology, his research was in heuristic programs for the machine processing of natural language. His special interest in that field is in computational stylistics.

Contents

21

Evaluation of Learning in Writing

Objectives of instruction in writing

Conditions and problems peculiar to the field of writing

The major objectives in the field of writing involve the identity of the recipients of the instructional product to an extent not required in other subject fields. In the natural and social sciences, objectives may serve their purpose well enough, while forgetful or even ignorant of the kinds of people who will use the product—the chemical or economic analysis, for example. For objectives in composition, the matter of the identity of those who receive the communication is intrinsically important, and automatically relevant; readership is, therefore, a matter which should be, but seldom is, a focus of attention when objectives are formulated.

A very common, and seemingly unexceptionable, objective for instruction in composition states: "The student will write a clear and effective essay on an assigned topic." It is difficult at first glance to suppose that the statement would give pause to any student or teacher. But "clear" to whom? "Effective" upon what audience? The student prose that is perfectly clear to a classmate may be unintelligible to an instructor who is one or two generations removed.

While objectives for courses in writing suffer most when they fail to consider readership, two other problems continue to impede successful formulation of these objectives.

The first of these two difficulties arises from the prevalent belief that the objectives are obvious because everyone knows why writing is taught. Accordingly, concerning the precise goals of writing instruction, there is almost unbroken silence in academic departments, in texts, and in published research. Faculty rooms resound with one or another version of the universal plaint, "These students just can't write!" But no explicit aim supplies help in the pause that follows. Among the texts, a "programmed" text in composition would seem, more than any other kind of book, to promise explicit treatment of objec-

TABLE 21-1 TABLE OF SPECIFICATIONS FOR WRITING

			BEHAVIOR																	
			Cognitive													*Affective*				
			Recall and Recognition				*Understanding*			*Criticism*				*Production*		*Interest*		*Appreciation*		
			Terms	*Trends*	*Classifications*	*Methods*	*Interpretation*	*Paraphrase*	*Application*	*Analysis of elements*	*Analysis of relationships*	*Analysis of organizational principles*	*Judgment*	*Composing a draft*	*Composing a final copy*	*Willingness*	*Satisfaction*	*Acceptance of a value*	*Preference for a value*	*Commitment*
CONTENT			A	B	C	D	E	F	G	H	I	J	K	L	M	N	O	P	Q	R
1.0 Ideas	Relevance	1.1																		
	Logic	1.2																		
	Subordination	1.3																		
2.0 Organization	Emphasis	2.1																		
	Transition	2.2																		
	Paragraph structure	2.3																		
	Theme structure	2.4																		
3.0 Style	Tone	3.1																		
	Originality	3.2																		
4.0 Mechanics	Spelling	4.1																		
	Punctuation	4.2																		
	Syntax	4.3																		
5.0 Choice of words	Fluency	5.1																		
	Range	5.2																		
	Connotation–Denotation	5.3																		
	Concrete–Abstract	5.4																		
	Literal–Figurative	5.5																		
	Level of usage	5.6																		

NOTE: The crosshatched cells are empty cells. (For example, cell *F*-4.2 shows that the behavior *Paraphrase* is inapplicable to the content *Punctuation*.)

tives, since so much of what is known about the value of objectives comes from work with programmed materials. That promise is denied, however, by a pioneer programmed text for writing (Ferster, 1965). The inattention to concise objectives extends also throughout the published research on the subject. Representative of this characteristic in the research is the centrally important study by Godshalk, Swineford, and Coffman (1966), which, despite its many excellences, has no mention of or reference to the instructional objectives behind the writing skills measured in the study.

The second problem facing the formulator of goals inheres in the disarming assertion that "Writing is writing." Although it is clear enough that there is a kind of skill which, when developed, is relatively constant and transcends subject matter, more of the truth is served when the phrase is turned to say, "Writing is *writing about*." The shaping power of the medium itself is well described by McLuhan (1954, p. 7): "The very form of any medium of communication is as important as anything that it conveys. . . ." Attention to the number and variety of the opportunities both lost and gained by the choice of writing as communicative medium is of earliest importance to the preparation of goals.

This second problem threatening the successful formulation of objectives is further illustrated by the very common cry that "Something must be done about this writing." What appears important in the cry is the finding of the "something"; the seductive assumption is that everyone knows what is meant by the word "writing."

Trends in the focus of objectives

The trend in the nature of the goals has been from focus upon the student to focus upon the document which he produces. The former emphasis is discernible in a broad objective stated by the Commission on the English Curriculum of the National Council of Teachers of English (NCTE; 1952): "The language arts classroom, above all others, . . . should furnish a normal social situation in which freedom to pursue one's own purposes and opportunity to plan and to work together with others fosters the processes and skills of dynamic expression [pp. 41–42]." A whole generation of graduate students has meanwhile been schooled in the so-called New Criticism, with its intense and exclusive concentration upon "the black marks on the white paper." Matters of structure, tension, paradox, ambiguity, and the like are raised and resolved through exclusive recourse to the document itself. Only secondary attention is paid to artist and audience—thought to be a dangerous shift of attention at that, as suggested by the phrases "intentional fallacy" (artist) and "affective fallacy" (audience). An excellent indication of the New Critics' preoccupation with the text itself is found in the definition of "tone" given by Brooks and Warren (1949): "'Tone' may be defined as the reflection *in the writing itself* of the author's attitude toward his audience and toward his material" (p. 479; italics supplied). The italicized phrase documents the insistence upon *formal* analysis that characterizes so much of modern criticism. Every specimen of student writing is, of course, open to inspection for quality of tone. As the most recent generation of graduate students of English moved around to the lonely side of the lectern, they brought a well-trained disposition to concentrate on the structural elements which they found—or found wanting—in student writing. When the young instructors describe their goals for writing classes, they characteristically consider the formal properties of the composition. Brooks and Warren (1949) raise the question in the first sentence of chapter 1 of their book: "Where should the study of writing begin [p. 11]?" Their answer, on the same page, is that the study "should . . . be first concerned with general [formal] problems of organization."

The contrasting foci of two objectives may more clearly demonstrate the shift of attention. Smith (1941, p. 107) quotes the following objective from the New York State Syllabus in English for Secondary Schools, 1935: "To develop power to express thoughts in clear-cut, forceful English." The goal is vague and has reference primarily to change in the writer. The trend toward transfer of focus to the writing itself has resulted in the formulation of objectives in terms like the following from Lazarus and Knudson (1967, p. 69): "To be able to develop paragraphs through the use of examples, comparison-contrast, cause-effect, time flow (from then to now, or now to then) and space-flow (from here to there, or there to here)."

The trend from objectives which focus on the writer to those which focus on the writing may also be described as a trend from expression to communication. The terms are bothersome. The word "expression" has, in fact, been used when "communication" is the intended meaning: in the objective from the New York State Syllabus, quoted above, the behavior sought is obviously communication, but the verb is "express." In the introduction to the 1958 edition of his important text *The Logic and Rhetoric of Exposition*, Harold Martin writes (p. 5): "To the process of communicating what is known [the book gives] the title 'Expression.'"

The song in solitude is expression, and it is no less valuable when identified as such. The word "expression" and its various forms can serve to describe those goals which primarily concern change in the writer; the term "communication" properly includes goals which focus upon the writing itself.

Examples from national commissions

The precise formulation of operational goals for writing is as difficult as it is rare. The goals to be found do offer the broad guidelines necessary for later and more specific development; that the vague objectives, however, are seldom so developed is a circumstance by no means peculiar to the field of writing. The following statements from *The English Language Arts in the Secondary School* of the National Council of Teachers of English, are representative of much of the available material on goals:

> [The adolescent] must develop for himself powers of expression commensurate with the requirements of an enlarged and interrelated world. . . .
>
> If one is to plan a useful program . . . he must examine carefully the purposes for which adolescents write and the forms which their written expression habitually takes. . . . Personal Writing gives young people a chance to express their feelings, to share their emotions. . . . It also involves such social communications as invitations and replies, letters of condolence or congratulation, and notes of thanks for gifts or favors received. . . . A second type of writing . . . involves the clarification and expression of ideas and the gathering, organization and presentation of information for some specific purpose. . . . A third and important purpose for writing is doing business by mail. . . . Finally, service writing of various kinds is used constantly throughout high school years—posting written notices of meetings, keeping minutes, thanking a speaker for an assembly talk, or congratulating a fellow student upon his success in dramatics or sports.

[National Council of Teachers of English, Commission on the English Curriculum, 1956, pp. 10, 297–298]

The passage first prompts a reaction which anticipates some remarks on the Table of Specifications to be presented below (page 774). The comments there describe some hazards attendant upon efforts to conjoin behaviors and content for courses in writing; the hazards involve chiefly the overlap in the content of writing instruction. Concerning the passage quoted, the attempt to specify the content of a program by listing the purposes of writing has resulted in the repetition of goals in the "personal" and "service" categories. The confusion results from a failure to attend to those components of writing which are *common* to the purposes listed.

A later passage from the same NCTE publication will serve to recapitulate these pages on objectives by affording opportunity to refine a broad goal into terms more useful, because they are more precise. In that volume, the chapter on instruction in composition devotes several pages to a section titled "The Importance of Words."

Therein the reader is advised (p. 336) that "young people should be led through their writing to a greater awareness of words—the wealth of words available and the power that comes from the use of the exact word. . . ." (Compare: "To develop a sensitivity toward word meanings and to appreciate the connotations of words"—Certner & Bromberg, 1963, p. 4.) Not an operational goal, not specific—but clearly one which moves in that direction. The same page adds: "Older students should learn to use such reference sources as Roget's *Thesaurus* to aid them in finding the exact word to express what they have to say." This is closer still to the degree of specificity which characterizes a usefully stated objective. And the direction is still toward the center of importance; Hazlitt has warned, "There may be ten synonyms, yet only one that exactly answers to the idea we have in our minds." A desirable formulation might finally state the goal thus: "Given a sentence containing one underlined word, the student will describe the shift in connotation that occurs when synonyms from a thesaurus are substituted for the underlined word." The student behavior called forth by the objective is, at the most elementary level, the recall or recognition of the meanings of words. The goal has now, however, arrived at the heart of the matter, by inviting the growth of the habit which makes all the difference, namely, the habit of *choosing* words. Mark Twain has said it: "The difference between the *almost right* word and the right word is really a large matter—'tis the difference between the lightning bug and the lightning."

The content and behaviors of instruction in writing

Content of instruction as independent of differences in writers, readers, and purposes

The readers in a factorial study of writing (Diederich, French, and Carlton, 1961) included English teachers, social scientists, natural scientists, writers, lawyers, and businessmen. The variety in the occupational fields promised some insight into common dimensions among the criteria of writing ability; the readers were instructed to sort papers in order of merit and to use their own judgment about what constitutes writing ability. Five factors emerged as common concerns of the disparate groups of readers; they were, in the terms used by Diederich and his fellow authors: ideas, form, flavor, mechanics, and wording.

If these factors are trustworthy references to whatever there is in writing that transcends differences in writer, reader, purpose, and subject (two topics were used in the experiment), then they might be expected to emerge from, and apply to, other studies of writing. That they are so to be trusted is apparent from the similarities found in other such lists of criteria. Pamphlets on the evaluation of student writing, prepared by a number of state affiliates, are distributed by the NCTE. Terms similar to those listed by Diederich, French, and Carlton (ideas, form, flavor, mechanics, and wording) are seen in the following sampling of components to be judged, among the materials from the state affiliates: "content, organization, style—mechanics" (California Association of Teachers of English, 1960, p. 13); "content, organization, sentence structure, diction, grammar—punctuation—spelling" (Indiana Council of Teachers of English, 1960, p. 3); "content, form, mechanics" (Association of English Teachers of Western Pennsylvania, undated b, p. 4).

Fostvedt (1965) surveyed literature from "nine sources of national importance [p. 108]" to discover what criteria were emphasized in the evaluation of English composition. On the basis of frequency of mention in the literature, five criteria were identified: coherence and logic, development of ideas, diction, emphasis, and organization through sentence structure and paragraphing.

The categories are of proven value in two quite different kinds of research. Page (1969) reports the latest findings in computer grading of essays (Project Essay Grade, at the University of Connecticut) and lists "five traits believed important in essays . . . ideas or content, organization, style, mechanics, creativity [pp. 5, 6]." Klare (1963), surveying research on readability formulas, notes that "formulas measure only one aspect of writing—style. Perhaps certain formulas, especially those concerned with abstractness of *words* or analysis of *ideas*, approach a measure of content. . . . Formulas do not touch on *organization, word order, format,* or *imagery* in writing . . ." (p. 24; italics supplied).

The five traits listed along the vertical axis of Table 21-1, Table of Specifications for Writing, represent an abstraction and adaptation of factors common to the foregoing sources and uses. The table presents the factors as content for instruction in writing. (Several of the labels for the subdivisions appear also in the study by Diederich, French, and Carlton.) The terms listed across the horizontal axis identify the cognitive and affective behaviors desired of the student for this content; they will be discussed shortly. References to the cells in the table—the intersections of content and behavior—will identify a behavior column first, and then a content row or set of rows; for example, *F*-1.1 or *F*-1.0.

The necessity of overlap in content

Perhaps the most cogent inquiry which Table 21-1 invites is one that investigates the degree of separability of the entries along the *Content* axis. For example, one might claim that the content labeled *Organization* (2.0) is always a function of the concepts in the rows labeled *Ideas* (1.0). Thus Stalnaker (1951, pp. 507–508) writes that "abilities to organize, to write clearly, etc., cannot at this time be measured independently of the topic in which the writing centers." Carroll addresses the same point (1966, p. 411, italics in the original): "We have not yet been able [by 1961] to measure the reasoning and organizational aspects of good expository and creative writing independently of writing itself, *perhaps because the two are inextricably bound together.*"

Similarly, there is something attractive about the argument that the rows labeled *Mechanics* (4.0) also refer to matters inseparable from *Ideas.* Here the reasoning would hold, for example, that a communication is identifiable as a business letter mainly because the *mechanical* conventions contribute so much to what is conveyed by the writing. The point is reflected in a statement by McLuhan (1954): "It is only common sense to realize that the general situation created by a communicative channel and its audience is a large part of that in which and by which they commune [p. 10]." To continue the example of the business letter—the businessman communicates the necessity of order and expedition in his enterprise as much by the mechanical *form* of the letters as by their semantic content.

In an essay whose power has won renewed respect twenty years after its appearance, Schorer (1948) begins a paragraph with a deceptively simple observation, "One should correct Buffon ['*le style est l'homme*'] and say that style is the subject" [p. 27]. Again the effect is the coalescence of two of the rows of content in the Table of Specifications.

One row remains to be mentioned in this context of overlap—that labeled *Choice of words* (5.0). The obvious relationship between word choice and style need not be insisted upon; their relationship is etymologically apparent: the stylus used on wax tablets had one end broad and flat, and "to turn the stylus" (style) was to scratch one word in favor of another.

It will appear circular to worry the idea that factors which emerge from an analysis of ratings of themes display tendencies to overlap when they are construed as content categories for courses in writing. In the factorial study referred to above (Diederich et al., 1961), the factors were clusters of readers; and the reader who attends chiefly to diction, for example, will nevertheless favor other elements of writing, also.

What is important is that the categories are definable, that some readers did choose without special direction to pay much attention to certain of the factors, and that accordingly when course work emphasizes the factors it concentrates on measurable characteristics of writing. In the evaluation of writing, the "unmeasurable" has a most subversive allure.

Although admittedly his remark concerns "creative writing," Archibald MacLeish (1960, p. 91) avers that in a writing course "not only is there no subject, there is no content either. Or, more precisely, the content is the work produced by students in the course." The present chapter suggests a different point of view. For when the term of the writer in residence is over and he has departed, the school recognizes that certain rather bothersome questions remain: what is the nature of the differences in "the work produced by the students" and what is the comparative efficacy of methods of improving that work?

In the presence of the foregoing reservations about the Table of Specifications, two considerations offer some comfort. First, the experiment which identified these categories for the *Content* axis was mathematically and conceptually rigorous; and second, the common sense of an instructional approach which isolates such a component as mechanics (punctuation, spelling, verb and pronoun concord, and the like) accords well with very widely accepted notions of what writing is about.

The subdivisions of the categories of content

The interaction among the five categories of content will be further observed in the following brief inspection of the subdivisions in each category. *Relevance* (1.1) refers primarily to internal patterns in the writing; as used here, the term is not meant to invoke such notions as "connection with," "application to," "importance for," present reality—notions suggested by the current usage of the term in a phrase like "writing on topics that are relevant." The interaction of emphasis, transition, syntax, and fluency (2.1, 2.2, 4.3, and 5.1) with those internal patterns referred to as *Relevance* will seem as necessary as it is obvious. *Within* the category of ideas, the interdependence of relevance, logic, and subordination will appear quite natural, also. The term *Logic* (1.2) is meant to apply generally to the accuracy, consistency, and completeness with which the writing presents "the way things are."

Subordination (1.3) in a paper refers to the evidence of discrimination—the evidence that not all ideas weigh the same.

The primary concern in *Emphasis* (2.1) is the distribution of the ideas in the writing. Like tone, fluency, and level of usage (3.1, 5.1, and 5.6), this subdivision involves a property that is particularly dependent on the linear mode in which writing operates: "emphatic" tends to mean "well timed."

Transition (2.2) is discussed usually at the same time as coherence. The traits are closely allied; but because transition suggests elements more clearly defined in a paper—more precisely locatable—the term offers some advantage. The elements of transition customarily include pronouns, repeated words, and so-called transitional words like "so," "such," and "then." *Paragraph structure* (2.3) and *Theme structure* (2.4) present no esoteric concepts. They serve the teacher most significantly, perhaps, when they focus attention on a practice as misleading as it is widespread, namely, the practice of assigning "paragraphs" as writing exercises. By definition, a paragraph is part of a larger unit of discourse; its most important element is the white space in the indentation. When assignments repeatedly call for paragraphs without concurrent work on the structure of the larger unit to which they contribute, the concept "paragraph" is undermined.

The definition on which these pages rely identifies *Tone* (3.1) as the reflection, in the writing itself, of the writer's attitude toward subject and audience. The particular merit of the definition is the exclusion of all sources except the writing, in the investigation of the writer's attitude. *Originality* (3.2) refers to that attribute which equates style and the man. The difficulty of reducing the attribute to sets and sequences of elements must not obscure the strength of this attribute—in studies of disputed authorship, for example. The term includes less novelty than the term "creativity." It ensures that the instruction provides for effects that are not under the conscious control of the writer—though no less his own for their being so located below the threshold of awareness.

Of the subdivisions of mechanics, only *Syntax* (4.3) need be remarked upon. The term is meant to include that set of conventions, exclusive of *Spelling* (4.1) and *Punctuation* (4.2), to which the term "grammar" is most often—and quite loosely—applied. Syntax subsumes, for example, matters of agreement in form between subject and verb, pronoun and antecedent, modifier and element modified; matters of sequence in tense and mood; matters of conjugation and case. Again the interactive effect is present: an immediately relevant subdivision is that of *Level of usage* (5.6).

Fluency (5.1) in writing refers to the *rate* at which the available vocabulary is "used up"; *Range* (5.2) involves the *size* of the available vocabulary. The three distinctions which follow in Table 21-1 comprehend much of the study of diction. *Connotation–denotation* (5.3) represents the spectrum from subjective to objective meanings. Although a single word may denote one thing and connote another, the distinction is used chiefly to describe differences *among* the denotations and connotations of groups of words. (Examples: molar, global, holistic; smart, clever, bright, crafty.) *Concrete–abstract* (5.4) offers polarities within which various degrees of abstraction are available to the purposes of the writer. Like the other two sets of distinctions, concrete–abstract enables the writer to gain effects both by controlled movement within the polarities and by unmoving concentration at one or the other end of the spectrum or at one point between. (Examples: animal, quadruped, dog, hound, cur, mongrel.) *Literal–figurative* (5.5) comprises a range of opportunities to say one thing in terms of another. Unlike concrete–abstract, this distinction often accommodates the same word at both ends of the spectrum. (Examples: jewel, lemon, light.)

The last subdivision, *Level of usage* (5.6), involves assumptions and decisions about the appropriateness of the written words to the forum in which they communicate. At times an instructor will require that the student imagine a particular forum, and perhaps even adopt a writing "voice" that is different from his own. Time, place, audience, and topic are variables which determine the appropriateness of such levels of word usage as formal, informal, and colloquial. This subdivision interacts with *Syntax* (4.3), as already noted, and with *Tone* (3.1) as well.

The behaviors in the table of specifications (A–R)

The columns in Table 21-1 follow in general a left-to-right increase in complexity, in both cognitive (*A* to *M*) and affective (*N* to *R*) behaviors. Columns *A* to *D*, *Recall and recognition*, correspond with *Knowledge* in the *Taxonomy of Educational Objectives* (Bloom, 1956; see the Appendix to Part I of this book).

Columns *A* to *D* specify the kinds of knowledge outcomes which a course in writing might pursue. A knowledge of trends in topics for school writing in cell *B*-1.0 might serve to keep the writer alert to the fact that he is not the first student to look into the immediate past, and the immediate surroundings, for his subject matter. This same behavior is involved when the student recognizes the changing nature of the topics generally considered appropriate in school—the trend away from "safe" topics toward ever more sensitive issues.

Moving across these same columns, the table shows that the instruction might aim at knowledge of the *Terms* (*A*-2.0), *Trends* (*B*-2.0), *Classifications* (*C*-2.0), and *Methods* (*D*-2.0) of the *Organization* of a piece of writing. Here would be discussed such terms as "form," "structure," "unity," "coherence," "tagmeme"; such trends as that from the beginning-middle-end modules to the stream-of-consciousness; such classifications as temporal, spatial, comparison-contrast, deductive-inductive, general-specific; and such methodology as outlining, partitioning, reordering, editing, and abstracting. Cells *A*-3.0, *B*-3.0, *C*-3.0, and *D*-3.0 in similar fashion specify the knowledge of stylistic terms, trends, classifications, and methodology which a course might include among its objectives.

Columns *E* and *F* include activity which Table 21-1 labels *Understanding* and the *Taxonomy* calls *Comprehension*. *Interpretation* and *Paraphrase* are similar activities, the latter almost invariably shorter than the document worked on, whereas many interpretations are longer than the text interpreted. The instruction, in a test, to "state in your own words" the content of a communication is a frequently encountered example of a paraphrase. When the activity goes beyond restatement to a reordering of a text and a relating of it to the background experience of the student, then interpretation is exercised. In these matters interpretation is like analysis; the emphasis in analysis, however, is on the formal properties of the communication, and not, as in interpretation, on the semantic content.

Application (*G*) is so labeled in the *Taxonomy*. It usually involves applying in a new context a rule, or method, or principle. The student's management of the conventions governing the punctuation and paragraphing of dialogue (*G*-2.3, *G*-4.2, and *G*-4.3) during a workbook exercise new to him is an *Application* behavior.

Criticism, in columns *H* to *K*, includes analytic and judgmental activities which correspond to the fourth and sixth levels of the *Taxonomy*, namely, *Analysis* and *Evaluation*. The behaviors include the student's *Analysis* and *Judgment* of his own writing and of that done by others. The analytic work ordinarily involves distinguishing in a paragraph, for example, those structural *Elements* (column *H*) which carry the topic of the paragraph and those which support, clarify, qualify, or otherwise interact with the topic. The analysis proceeds usually to an examination of the nature of the *Relationships* (column *I*) among the elements—whether they are in fact supportive or clarifying and, if so, whether by repetition, or repetition with modification, or whatever. The *Analysis of organizational principles* (column *J*) attends globally to the communication, for the purpose of identifying the structural properties that unify the paragraph, or text of whatever kind; here a writer's satiric intent, for example, might be seen to have governed the choice of elements in a paragraph (*H*-2.3 and *H*-3.1) and the operation of the relationships among those elements (*I*-2.3 and *I*-3.1). *Judgment*, in column *K*, invokes criteria which attend to such internal evidence as consistency and proportion, and such external evidence as the accuracy and efficacy of the document. To criticize is to engage in both analytic and judgmental activity. The criticism which offers judgment without analysis is incompetent; that which presents analysis without judgment is incomplete.

Columns *L* and *M* represent two kinds of *Production*. The composing of a first draft focuses on the "what" of writing; for work on final copy the emphasis shifts to the "how." The former activity concentrates heavily on the *Ideas* row in Table 21-1; preparation of final copy shifts emphasis to the other four content rows, reserving the very last stage of composition for whatever conscious work on *Mechanics* may be required.

The behaviors in columns *N* through *R* correspond with *Responding* and *Valuing* in the *Taxonomy of Educational Objectives, Handbook 2, Affective Domain* (Krathwohl, Bloom, & Masia, 1964; again, see the Appendix to Part I). *Willingness* and *Satisfaction* (columns *N* and *O*) characterize the desirable kind of interest with which Table 21-1 is concerned. The interest is not forced, nor is it fed with much reward beyond the activity itself. When the behavior thus voluntarily entered upon is accompanied by pleasurable emotional response, it assumes the self-reinforcing characteristic that identifies

Satisfaction (column *O*). The willingness and satisfaction may be overt or covert, and a consequently wide range of instructional and evaluative methods will be appropriate for the activities described by the *Interest* columns.

The three columns labeled *Appreciation* concern behaviors which the affective *Taxonomy* discusses under the term *Valuing*. From a willingness to be known as one who values writing (column *P*) to a pattern of choice of writing in the presence of other media (column *Q*) to a campaign to encourage others to write (column *R*), the values represent hierarchical stages of internalization. An example of relevant activities might be seen in the several ways a student involves himself with a letter to the editor. His publication of his name on more than one such letter can be interpreted as *Acceptance of a value*; a choice of such means of communication in the presence of other means that were equally or more accessible can be interpreted as *Preference for a value*; and his public encouragement of such letters can be seen as *Commitment*. The occasional use of cognitive behaviors as evidence of affective outcomes is found in the relationship between *Judgment* (column *K*) and *Appreciation* (columns *P* to *R*). Smith and Tyler (1942) state the relationships thus: "Appreciation manifests itself in a conscious effort on the part of the individual to evaluate the thing appreciated in terms of such standards of merit as he himself, at the moment, tends to subscribe to [p. 249]." Attempts by the student to criticize his own writing objectively and his requests for the judgments of others constitute pertinent evidence of the values described in the last columns of the Table of Specifications.

Courses of instruction represented by the table

There is no single course known and employed nationally which will serve to illustrate how the cells are worked out in practice. Even the most popular courses tend to be known only within the regions and systems where they were developed. The professional journals from time to time print descriptions of successful courses, as would be expected; occasionally, also, an effective course is elaborated into a composition text. The situation contrasts with that in the sciences, where nationally known courses or programs might well illustrate the cells in a relevant table of specifications.

In a general sense the work of the NCTE Commission on the English Curriculum will be seen to have been represented by the content and behaviors under discussion here. In *The English Language Arts in the Secondary School* (1956) the broad outlines of a course appear in the ninth chapter, titled "Meeting Youth's Needs through Writing." Early attention is given the affective outcomes: "The first business of the teacher of writing is to create in the classroom an atmosphere in which sharing personal experiences comes naturally . . . [p. 299]." The relevant portions of Table 21-1 include, under behaviors, the willingness-to-respond and satisfaction-in-response subdivisions of *Interest*; *Ideas* is the appropriate category of content (cells *N*-1.0; *O*-1.0). Reserving first attention for "Personal Writing," the chapter supplies what the table specifies as knowledge of trends in ideas (*B*-1.0): "Writing of this [personal] kind forms a continuous thread in the writing program from the seventh grade through the twelfth [p. 298]." The columns which concern application, analysis, and composing of drafts and final copy (*G* to *J*, *L*, and *M*) represent that part of instruction which the same chapter describes in a subdivision on the requisite orderliness in thinking: "Examination of one's own thinking, breaking an idea into its parts, and expanding each in turn logically and completely are extremely important activities . . . [p. 317]." The cells for recall and recognition of the methodology of organization (*D*-2.0) specify an objective clearly involved in the statement that "no better basis for outlining has been found than the question, 'What does the reader need to know, and in what order should I proceed so that he will follow my thinking? [p. 325].'"

A similarly important source of general descriptions of course work is *Freedom and Discipline in English,* a report of the Commission on English of the College Entrance Examination Board (CEEB; 1965). Again, the early emphasis is on the affective outcomes:

> In the early grades, and early in every grade—the teacher must try to reach the student's inmost interests and real thoughts. . . . The assignments must be difficult enough to make the student reach higher than he thought he could and stimulating enough to make him want to write. . . . Any method of making a writer feel that what he has written and how he has written it are worth serious attention is a good method [pp. 90, 92, 102].

The pages on instruction in composition adopt among other organizational devices three conventional divisions of rhetorical theory—invention, style, and organization. Under the last of these, in a passage which relates to the cells for analysis of organizational elements and relationships (*H*-2.0 and *I*-2.0), the report states (p. 104), "In most cases, once the sense of the essay is clear, the first question that should be put about it is, 'How is the essay organized; what is the order of its parts?' . . . It is from such analytical study of structures they [the students] are likely to learn most for their own compositional purposes. . . ."

Inspection of the work of the two commissions just described yields only the most generalized plans for courses. The CEEB report, for example, arranges some of its recommendations around the "romance-precision-generalization" model of education offered by Whitehead (1929). Whitehead describes a rhythmic cycle in education, in which the first stage, romance, consists of the freedom to wonder, to explore, to experiment, to discover; the stage of precision involves the order and discipline necessary for exact knowledge of details and mastery of principles; the third stage, generalization, returns freedom to the cycle—the freedom to apply in practice the principles acquired in the preceding stage. When the writers of the CEEB report apply the model to composition, they identify an emphasis on expression as the stage of romance, concentration on the discipline of form as the stage of precision, and the development of style as the stage of generalization. "They are the stages of every cycle of instruction in composition," states the report (p. 91).

Within such "macro" designs, however, very divergent approaches are possible. What is not to be found is a nationally known course whose teaching strategies are implemented by a suitable and tested array of tactics. That a very different situation obtains is dramatically documented in the report of the Dartmouth Study of Student Writing (Kitzhaber, 1963). The study surveyed freshman English courses in a representative cross section of four-year colleges and universities:

> The only constant in all varieties of the course [Kitzhaber reports], is some provision for supervised practice in writing, but, ironically, most of the confusion in freshman English stems from differing notions of how writing ought to be taught. The most diverse content may be dumped into the course on the grounds that it will help the student learn to write better. . . . What goes by the name of freshman composition on one campus may bear little resemblance to a course by the same name on another. . . . The second semester is likely to be either a totally different course from the first . . . or a mere repetition of the first semester distinguished only by the requirement of a long paper [pp. 10–13].

Instructional strategies and units

> *If you want to learn to write, then read*

Among the many and disparate approaches to the teaching of writing in secondary and higher education, three broad groupings may be discerned. The tripartition may be indicated thus: If you want to learn to write, then read/write/think. The first of these subsumes the manifold courses which require the use of one or more of the hundreds of books of readings. The nature of the approach is reflected by the titles of three popular texts: *Writing Themes about Literature* (Roberts, 1962); *A Reading Approach to College Writing* (Cox & Foote, 1961); and *Writing about Reading* (Howard, 1966). The principle behind the approach would not seriously be distorted if it were described by this simplistic maxim: If in writing you want to have good taste, then taste good things. Kitzhaber (1963) comes to the heart of the danger of this strategy when he observes, "The books of readings [are] used presumably for analysis and imitation but actually [serve] more often than not merely as springboards for discussions of things in general . . . [p. 16]."

Units for the reading approach Differences in units of instruction follow the general nature of the differences in the three major approaches to the organization of composition courses. All teachers of writing combine all three: the strategies obviously involve overlapping instructional activities. When, for example, reading, writing, and thinking coalesce in an exercise requiring the annotating of a text, they are separable only for convenience of discussion. In general practice, nevertheless, the focus of units of learning differs quite discernibly across approaches.

The characteristics of a unit in the reading approach to writing may be identified in any one of the scores of texts developed for this focus in course work. Three of these were cited above. Another such text is *Prose Models: An Inductive Approach to Writing* (Levin, 1964). The seventeen brief selections assembled under the title "Diction," for example, may constitute a unit of learning in the content area *Choice of words* in the Table of Specifications. The prose models are grouped under such labels as "connotation," "faulty diction," "imagery," and "clichés." The kinds of student behaviors sought in the unit may be recognized in the questions and assignments that accompany each selection. Recognition of denotations (*A*-5.3) is at the base of the activity called for in this assignment (p. 138): "Use the synonym listings in your dictionary to determine the exact difference in meaning between the following and write ten sentences using any ten of the italicized words in their precise dictionary meanings: a. *essential* and necessary; b. *perturbed* and agitated; c. *inculcate* and infuse. . . ." Paraphrasing (*F*-1.0) is added to recognition in the behaviors required in another question (p. 128): "Write a sentence-for-sentence paraphrase . . . of the passage, eliminating the figurative language." Interpretation is the behavior sought on p. 127: "What do 'eye' and 'heart' represent in the sentence 'The sun illuminates only the eye of the man, but shines into the eye and the heart of the child'?" The assigned essays which follow the selections involve, of course, the composing behaviors listed in the Table of Specifications, and they also include analysis, interpretation, and judgment.

The problems associated with the reading approach to writing are numerous. Matters of length, selectivity, and arrangement of models offer many challenges to those who prepare and those who use the texts; the matter of apparatus in a text is complicated by the large number of possible combinations of headnotes, footnotes, questions, discussions, assignments, suggested topics, explication, and lists of supplementary readings. More important than any of the preceding matters, however, is the unresolved question of the actual method whereby reading influences writing behavior. It is apparent that the imitation which comprises the heart of this approach is accomplished in great part without the writer's conscious effort; that the mode of influence is chiefly unconscious seems especially true of imitations of style. The most compelling arguments for the unconscious influence of style are found among the writings on plagiarism; of these, the extensive work by Poe includes, at the end of one study, the observation that "What the poet intensely admires becomes . . . in very fact, although only partially, a portion of his own intellect."

Table 21-2, Table of Specifications for the Reading Approach to Instruction in Writing, identifies those sections of Table 21-1 which constitute the usual province of the reading approach.

The teaching illustrated in Table 21-2 concentrates on the written ideas of others, rather than on ideas originating in the student's own productions. Accordingly, the columns for recall and recognition, interpretation, paraphrase, criticism, and interest appear as belonging to this first strategy.

In Table 21-2 there *is* provision made, of course, for the application and production behaviors; these are elicited, however, not as original *actions* on the part of the student but as *reactions* to the readings. That is, the writing consists chiefly of a response to the thinking preserved in the selections, rather than a record of ideas generated by the student himself. Because the burden of instruction thus rests on a collection of ideas not original to the student, the wary instructor-evaluator will ensure that the student become aware of the principle of selectivity which governed the assembling of the readings. The student must be sensitized to the significance of the choice of a particular genre, period, or rhetorical mode, for example, as a principle controlling the selection of readings. The reading approach invites the question, What principle of selectivity governs the work both of the editor of the readings and of the instructor who uses them? (It is well to recognize, in this connection, that ten selections can be read in 3,628,800 different sequences, that each sequence can have a cumulative instructional effect, and that there will inevitably be differences among these effects.)

When the teacher evaluates the main concerns identified in Table 21-2, he will look in the assigned readings for topics for test exercises. Even overworked "compare and contrast" items can provoke insights, if the teacher carefully controls both choice of subject and the basis for the comparison and contrast. He will utilize the following kinds of questions, which are characteristic of evaluation in the reading approach; the questions have numerous technical flaws, but are offered to help define the particular emphasis this first strategy adopts:

Compare and contrast (characters, plots, themes, arguments, intentions, effects, etc.) in selections X and Y (*I*-1.0 to *I*-3.0; *I*-5.0).

Choose from passages A, B, C, and D the most consistent interpretation of selection X (*E*-1.0 and *K*-1.0).

For the blank spaces in the following description, choose from the accompanying list those words which reveal particular characteristics of fictional character X (*J*-1.0, *J*-5.0).

Choose from passages A, B, C, and D that which most closely approaches the style of writer X (*H*-3.0 and *K*-3.0).

Label the level of usage which predominates in selection X (*C*-5.6).

Restore the order of the sentences which are out of sequence in passage X (*I*-1.0).

If you want to learn to write, then write

In the second major division of current instruction, the attention focuses on writing and rewriting. The "theme-a-day" courses at Yale and Harvard included in-class work on the student writings, and criticism by the students of their own work. The nature of the work of one instructor in such a course is remembered, in detail and with respect, by Diederich (1965, pp. 38–39):

> I had one of the original "theme-a-day" courses at Harvard, taught at that time by Professor Hurlbut. So far as I can remember, he practically never said anything bad about our papers. About two or three times in an average paper we did something that was worthy of praise. We usually knew it, and his comment invariably indicated that he knew it, too. The space between these high points in our papers was filled with the usual student bilge, which he never

TABLE 21-2 TABLE OF SPECIFICATIONS FOR THE WRITING READING APPROACH TO INSTRUCTION IN

			BEHAVIOR											
			Cognitive										*Affective*	
			Recall and Recognition				*Understanding*		*Criticism*				*Interest*	
			Terms	*Trends*	*Classifications*	*Methods*	*Interpretation*	*Paraphrase*	*Analysis of elements*	*Analysis of relationships*	*Analysis of organizational principles*	*Judgment*	*Willingness*	*Satisfaction*
CONTENT			*A*	*B*	*C*	*D*	*E*	*F*	*H*	*I*	*J*	*K*	*N*	*O*
1.0 Ideas	Relevance	1.1												
	Logic	1.2												
	Subordination	1.3												
2.0 Organization	Emphasis	2.1												
	Transition	2.2												
	Paragraph structure	2.3												
	Theme structure	2.4												
3.0 Style	Tone	3.1												
	Originality	3.2												
4.0 Mechanics	Spelling	4.1												
	Punctuation	4.2												
	Syntax	4.3												
5.0 Choice of words	Fluency	5.1												
	Range	5.2												
	Connotation–Denotation	5.3												
	Concrete–Abstract	5.4												
	Literal–Figurative	5.5												
	Level of usage	5.6												

NOTE: The crosshatched cells are empty cells.

> honored with a comment. Whenever he said nothing, we knew that the verdict was "undistinguished" but that he was too much of a gentleman to say so.
>
> About all Professor Hurlbut ever did in class was to read papers that he regarded as unusually good, without telling us who had written them. We sat there gasping, wishing that we had written them ourselves. He seldom stopped to say what was good about these papers. We either knew it, or his voice told us. In rare cases he might ask, "Now what was particularly good about that?"
>
> I cannot remember a single instance in which he ever asked what was bad about a paper. For him to express dispraise was as rare as for him to lose his temper—which was almost inconceivable.

The reminiscence serves as a valuable reminder that the role of the constant reader is essential to success in this second strategy. Much writing means much reading. In the "Have them write" approach the range and number of demands and challenges which the teacher faces are too seldom recognized.

The rewriting done in this second major grouping of courses varies in emphasis from the student's private revision of his work to in-class concentration on reproductions of student writings. Various methods of reproduction are endorsed: Hayakawa (1965) recommends the use of dittoing machines; Peterson (1965) has elaborated the use of the overhead projector into a complete course. Whatever the mode of reproduction—even the reading aloud of themes by the instructor—the main thrust of the whole of this second strategy is the process of revision.

Units for the writing approach A reference earlier to "theme-a-day" courses identified the major thrust of the writing approach to writing. Mizener (1960) refers briefly to a course requiring daily themes at Yale, as taught by Professor Nangle. Nangle is quoted as saying, "[The students] all start out . . . being fine writers. But about the third or fourth week they begin to get desperate and write on 'Shaving in the Morning.' That's when they really begin to write [p. 178]." Courses of the kind referred to here are rare, and the exorbitant demand on the instructor's time is the obvious reason.

The units of learning in the writing approach are organized to afford frequent written exercises, the work usually being unified around a topic or pattern within a mode of discourse—around process analysis, for example, within the expository mode. In recent years the emphasis has shifted from volume of output to "pattern practice" (Lefevre & Lefevre, 1965; Whitten, 1966).

Several elaborate units of learning, explicitly attentive to learning theory, have been developed by Rippey (1967). The units, "maps for English composition," consist of "a strategy and an exemplar which was to serve as a model for student writing. . . . The goal of each lesson was limited to a single aspect of writing behavior at a time . . . [pp. 403, 405]." The "strategy" referred to is a script for a programmed lesson, or a set of detailed instructions for a "dialectical" lesson. Although the model paragraphs are literary, the burden of the instruction falls not on critical reading, but upon the patterning of student writings after the model.

Table 21-3, Table of Specifications for the Writing Approach to Instruction in Writing, indicates what cells are the characteristic concern of the writing approach.

The abilities to interpret, paraphrase, analyze, and judge are played down, the latter two critical energies being invested in the self-criticism necessary for good rewriting. What reading is done is likely to concentrate on a study of literature "in the making"—on a study of the stages of growth of a manuscript; the attention is on the writing *process*. As in the first approach, there is a concern for affective outcomes, to the end that the ease which much practice brings might become the basis on which the student develops the desired degree of interest and appreciation. Intensive work on the two levels of composing (columns *L* and *M*) forms the main thrust of the writing approach to the teaching of writing.

For testing, Table 21-3 suggests to the teacher

TABLE 21-3 TABLE OF SPECIFICATIONS FOR THE WRITING APPROACH TO INSTRUCTION IN WRITING

			BEHAVIOR											
			Cognitive							*Affective*				
			Recall and Recognition					*Pro-duc-tion*		*Interest*		*Apprecia-tion*		
			Terms	*Trends*	*Classifications*	*Methods*	*Application*	*Composing a draft*	*Composing a final copy*	*Willingness*	*Satisfaction*	*Acceptance of a value*	*Preference for a value*	*Commitment*
CONTENT			*A*	*B*	*C*	*D*	*G*	*L*	*M*	*N*	*O*	*P*	*Q*	*R*
1.0 Ideas	Relevance	1.1												
	Logic	1.2												
	Subordination	1.3												
2.0 Organization	Emphasis	2.1												
	Transition	2.2												
	Paragraph structure	2.3												
	Theme structure	2.4												
3.0 Style	Tone	3.1												
	Originality	3.2												
4.0 Mechanics	Spelling	4.1												
	Punctuation	4.2												
	Syntax	4.3												
5.0 Choice of words	Fluency	5.1												
	Range	5.2												
	Connotation–Denotation	5.3												
	Concrete–Abstract	5.4												
	Literal–Figurative	5.5												
	Level of usage	5.6												

NOTE: The crosshatched cells are empty cells.

different techniques from those suggested by Table 21-2. The writing approach will be tested by exercises which involve revision, often the student's revision of his own work. The teacher willingly risks the ruin of an inspired first draft. (His justification of the risk is not so much a probability statement as an "improbability" statement.) He is willing also, on occasion, to reward plans in place of performance. A student's response which accurately describes priorities in the needed revision of a test passage, without actually revising the passage, would be appropriate in the evaluation of this second major strategy.

The evaluator in the writing approach sets such exercises as these:

Write different opening paragraphs for three papers on topic X. Address a different audience in each (incomplete) paper. After each paragraph, identify the audience, and explain how differences in the audiences have caused differences in the writing (*L*-2.4, *L*-3.1, *L*-5.0).

Choose from sentences A, B, C, and D the one which makes the diction of the first sentence more consistent with the formal diction of the rest of passage X (*G*-5.6).

Revise the accompanying copy of the most recent paper submitted in class. Explain the reasons for the changes made (*M*-1.0 to *M*-5.0).

Identify the earliest draft among passages A, B, C, and D, and state the reasons for the choice (*G*-1.0 to *G*-5.0).

Identify, on the basis of recent instruction, which parts of passage X would receive attention before other parts in the process of revision (*L*-1.0, *L*-2.0). Explain the reasons for the priorities assigned.

If you want to learn to write, then think

The third group of courses carries the label "rhetorical." Although the term must include a glut of perdurable courses imprisoned in the exposition-description-narration-argument complex (EDNA), the label more importantly must include the "New Rhetoric." In *New Trends in the Teaching of English in Secondary Schools* (Evans & Walker, 1966), the contrast is developed thus (pp. 53–54):

> While traditional rhetoric was concerned with skill in expressing preconceived arguments and points of view, the new rhetoric is concerned with the exploration of ideas. While traditional rhetoric was based on established patterns of discourse, the new rhetoric is based on the assumption that organization grows out of the subject being treated. The new rhetoric, in short, is based on the notion that the basic process of composition is discovery, not recovery.

Evidence in various sources supports the validity of the seemingly naïve doctrine that good writing is the result of "having something to say." In a popular and very reputable text for teaching high school English (Hook, 1965), the chapter on the teaching of writing is titled, "Composition Is Thinking." Harold Martin, in an essay reprinted in Gordon and Noyes (1960), addresses the doctrine directly, under the title, "Writing and Thinking." Much of the current and relevant emphasis on the thinking necessary during "prewriting" (see Evans & Walker, 1966, pp. 55–56) is traceable to an influential paper by Rohman (1965) titled "Pre-writing: The Stage of Discovery in the Writing Process."

All "rhetorical" approaches, whatever their particular persuasion, unite in an insistence upon the primacy and efficacy of thoughtful inquiry.

Units for the "thinking" approach In the "thinking" or "rhetorical" approach, the units of instruction emphasize the art of discovery. The business of the class meeting characteristically centers on the process of thought. In an exemplary account of such a class, Martin (1960) prints not only the rationale for a dialectical unit, but an illustrative student-teacher dialogue (p. 164). "'Johnson, what do you make of that statement?' 'It's nonsense—superstition.' 'The two are the same, nonsense and superstition?'" And so on. Martin states (p. 166) that the purpose of the in-class work is not to arrive at a definition, but "to make definition seem important, to make it become not the process of 'looking up the word in the dictionary' but that of thinking the matter through."

In the units of instruction in the "rhetorical" approach some care is necessary to avoid the presumption that having something to say guarantees the ability to say it. That such a presumption can threaten the approach is made evident in remarks by Robert Frost (1968): "Somebody says we don't need to show . . . [people] how to think; bye and bye they will think. We will give them the forms of sentences and, if they have any ideas, then they will know how to write them. But that is preposterous. *All there is to writing is having ideas. To learn to write is to learn to have ideas*" (pp. 42–43; italics added). Behind the dangers that are thus apparent, there remains a saving truth for the thinking units: if the student does in fact originate an idea, he will earn some perspective, at least, on writing; an original idea impetrates an audience, and if writing is the only communicative channel open, the thought will somehow be made to move across.

Table 21-4, Table of Specifications for the Thinking Approach to Instruction in Writing, defines the areas of concentration in this third approach.

Table 21-4 assigns emphasis to the cognitive behaviors and accepts whatever progress is made in the affective domain as a welcome by-product of thought. More specifically, the emphasis is on prewriting behaviors. The traditional approach has been through more or less elaborate training in logic; and random inspection will reveal as common to most rhetorical texts discussions of such matters as induction, deduction, and analogy. More recently, as noted above by Evans and Walker, there has been a shift in focus toward modes of discovery; that is, a shift toward training in heuristics. Accordingly, the instruction emphasized in Table 21-4 is designed to equip the student with a variety of "probes," "tools," or "strategies" of discovery; and the goal is that the student will achieve novelty and versatility in his attack upon a given topic for writing. The goal also includes the ability to generate topics. The matter of novelty illustrates why recognition, though an ability of lower order, is included in the thinking approach. Given the apparently hopeless topic "My Summer Vacation," the student must first *recognize* it as trite, and then *recognize* the consequent demand for novelty, before the topic may successfully be addressed.

The evaluation appropriate for this third major approach will include concern for both the inquiry and the results. It is not enough that the student be equipped with versatile and innovative techniques of inquiry; the techniques must be effective. The evaluator rewards the student's *fluent* use of a variety of modes of discovery. The thinking approach invites creativity, but is not concerned exclusively with that concept. The asking and answering of an inclusive array of questions already known to be relevant to a topic is, for example, of evaluative interest in this third strategy.

The following are test exercises representative of the thinking approach:

Write a series of short papers on topic X. Explain how differences in techniques of reasoning have caused differences in the form and content of the papers (*M*-1.0 to *M*-5.0).

Identify in list X those topics which have been much used and those which are new (*B*-1.0).

Write as complete as possible a list of questions which may be asked in preparation for writing a paper on topic X (*G*-1.0 and *G*-3.2).

Match passages A, B, C, and D with the reasoning technique in list X which was employed in the composing of the passages (*I*-1.0).

An inspection of Tables 21-2, 21-3, and 21-4 reveals that a number of the cells are common to the three major strategies. One such common set is that block of cells at the intersection of columns *A* to *D* and the set of rows 1.0. The learning which

TABLE 21-4 TABLE OF SPECIFICATIONS FOR THE THINKING APPROACH TO INSTRUCTION IN WRITING

			BEHAVIOR												
			Recall and Recognition				*Under-stand-ing*			*Criticism*				*Pro-duc-tion*	
			Terms	*Trends*	*Classifications*	*Methods*	*Interpretation*	*Paraphrase*	*Application*	*Analysis of elements*	*Analysis of relationships*	*Analysis of organizational principles*	*Judgment*	*Composing a draft*	*Composing a final copy*
CONTENT			*A*	*B*	*C*	*D*	*E*	*F*	*G*	*H*	*I*	*J*	*K*	*L*	*M*
1.0 Ideas	Relevance	1.1													
	Logic	1.2													
	Subordination	1.3													
2.0 Organization	Emphasis	2.1													
	Transition	2.2													
	Paragraph structure	2.3													
	Theme structure	2.4													
3.0 Style	Tone	3.1													
	Originality	3.2													
4.0 Mechanics	Spelling	4.1													
	Punctuation	4.2													
	Syntax	4.3													
5.0 Choice of words	Fluency	5.1													
	Range	5.2													
	Connotation–Denotation	5.3													
	Concrete–Abstract	5.4													
	Literal–Figurative	5.5													
	Level of usage	5.6													

NOTE: The crosshatched cells are empty cells.

these common cells isolate will nevertheless involve differences in the three approaches. In the reading approach, the terms recalled are literary —character names, authors, titles, and so forth; in the writing approach the technical terms—like "recast," "fair copy," "insert"—are recalled; in the thinking approach the terms recalled are intellective—"premise," "syllogism," "fallacy," and so forth. The content of what is recalled is, of course, not unique in each approach, but the differences relate to the difference in emphasis seen also in the kinds of questions characteristic of each approach.

Evaluation of the learning represented by cells in the table of specifications

Recall and recognition (*A–D*)

The pages that immediately follow present a variety of methods for evaluating the learning described in Table 21-1, the overall Table of Specifications for Writing. Throughout the examples in this section, the emphasis is on the identification of a technique in evaluation. There may very well be differences of opinion on the substantive matters raised in an item; but the techniques need not be thought damaged by whatever disagreement on their content the examples may provoke. It will be convenient, in discussing the table, to move across the behaviors axis, that is, across the top of Table 21-1.

The process of evaluating the learning described by cell *A*-1.1 brings into focus one of the most important differences between direct and indirect methods of evaluating writing. The essence of this difference is that the writer, in the direct method, knows what he intends to say and to what extent his composition satisfies the intention. In an indirect method, one in which the respondent must work with writing that is supplied him, the matter of intention is at one remove. One must, and usually can, argue back to what was intended, but the condition of knowledge is seen to be fundamentally different. (It may be that good writing comes sometime after the writer accepts as inevitable a discrepancy between competence and performance.)

In the first cell, *A*-1.1, the learning includes a recognition of the terms that carry the ideas which relate to the main import of the writing. The student will often, during instruction, "recognize" relevance on the basis of relationships known to him as writer but unstated in the writing. The familiar "*That's* what I meant to say" is a clear indication, during discussion of student writing, of unrealized intent. Later, in evaluation, an item which requires the student to identify terms relevant to the main theme of his composition will measure achievement in cell *A*-1.1; what must be remembered is the likelihood of differences in performance on items based on the respondent's own writing and items based on writing not done by the respondent. To test the latter kind of performance, the teacher may find use for the following kind of item; it is based on a close reading by Ray and Ray (1968) of a paragraph from *Walden:*

A-1.1

1. One formulation of the main point of this paragraph might state that Thoreau intended to make the abstraction *life* concrete. Draw circles and squares around those terms that are relevant to the main point:

   [S1] I went to the woods because I wished to live deliberately, to front only the essential facts of life, and see if I could not learn what it had to teach, and not, when I came to die, discover that I had not lived. [S2] I did not wish to live what was not life, living is so dear; nor did I wish to practice resignation, unless it was quite necessary. [S3] I wanted to live deep and suck out all the marrow of life, to live so sturdily and Spartan-like as to put to rout all that was not life, to cut a broad swath and shave close, to drive life into a corner, and reduce it to its lowest terms, and if it proved to be mean, why then to get the whole and genuine meanness of it, and publish its meanness to the world; or if it were sublime, to know it by experience, and be able to give a true account of it in my next excursion. [S4] For most men, it appears to me, are in a strange uncertainty about it, whether it is of the devil or of God, and have *somewhat hastily* concluded that it is the chief end of man to "glorify God and enjoy him forever."

(Ray and Ray, 1968, p. 3. The directions have been added.)

The pattern of terms shown here is as presented by Ray and Ray. During further analysis, they would accept "to front . . . sturdily . . . Spartan-like . . . to put to rout . . ." as parts of the same pattern. Obviously the concept of a set of relevant terms must include other patterns in the Thoreau paragraph; the authors, in similar "close readings," identify a number of these, including the dominance of "I" in the first half of the passage, and "it" in the second half. In choosing a passage for evaluation of this cell, the teacher would be guided by these "additive" characteristics of the sample item. Having accepted, for example, the number of terms shown by Ray and Ray, he would reserve time after the test for adding terms and phrases in the manner just described.

Important at this early stage in the work with Table 21-1 is the matter of the precise nature of the mental behavior which the item is intended to elicit. The activity involved in identifying the main point of a paragraph involves behavior of a higher order than recognition. Hence, for evaluation of the goal described by the first cell, the main point is supplied, as in the example. The objective in *A*-1.1 is not trivial, however, nor always merely prerequisite to such a higher-order activity as analysis; it concerns a worthy precaution against irrelevance—a fault too easily introduced by a beginning writer's sedulous pursuit of parallelism, rhythm, euphony, and other such components of style.

Evaluation appropriate for the same group of behaviors, *A* to *D*, with other categories of content, is illustrated in the next series of examples. The first concerns cell *A*-5.3, one of the most frequently evaluated learning outcomes in the table. The content and behavior comprise an almost unitary event: the *Recall and recognition of terms* (*A*) amounts to much the same thing that the phrase *Denotation—connotation* (5.3) signifies. The cell describes learning measured by what is usually referred to as a vocabulary test. The most familiar form requires the choice of that word, among several options, which most closely approximates the meaning of the word in the stem. The variations are many and predictable; they include changes in the stem (from word, to phrase, to sentence) and changes in the nature of the choices (to choice of antonym, for example). The competence tested is often referred to as a "recognition" vocabulary. An item type that seeks a measure of *active* vocabulary offers somewhat more complexity. The examinee being given the following item is instructed to indicate which of the letters listed is the first letter of a word which completes the sentence. The number 4 indicates the number of letters in the correct response.

A-5.3

2. An apple that has a sharp, pungent, but not disagreeably sour or bitter, taste is said to be 4
   (1) R
   (2) S
   (3) T
   (4) U
   (5) V

(Ebel, 1951, p. 199.)

In modifications of this format the teacher may wish to accept two or more words of the length he specifies, and develop a unit on their differences in connotation.

For recall or recognition of literal and figurative terms the examiner might adopt the following simplified format:

A-5.5

3. Choose five of the following words. For each write two sentences, one illustrating the literal use of the word, the other its nonliteral use:

astronomical	Cassandra	foggy
antidote	collosus	Rubicon
ballast	doldrums	oasis

(College Entrance Examination Board, Commission on English, 1963, p. 3.)

Spelling, in cell *A*-4.1, is tested in a variety of question formats and is ordinarily a recall and recognition behavior. The basic format presents a misspelled word in a group of words and requires that the misspelled word be identified. However, when space is provided for entering the correct spelling, the behavior may involve more than recall; it may involve the *Application* (G) of rules for prefixes, suffixes, plurals, and so forth. One variation of the format for spelling raises a special problem and must accordingly be used with an awareness of the relative "trade-off" values when the format is adopted:

A-4.1, A-4.2, A-5.6

DIRECTIONS. Read each three-line sentence and decide whether there are errors in *usage, spelling, punctuation*, or *capitalization* in any of the three parts. . . . If no error, mark 0 on the answer sheet.

4. When all the marks were
added together, his standing
was forth in the class.
5. If he don't learn to be more polite,
I'm afraid that he will find himself
without any friends when he needs them

(Educational Testing Service, 1960, p. 5.)

The problem is that this type of item requires the examinee to check the spelling of hundreds of words, while scanning also for other mechanical errors. The loss in efficiency is traded off for inclusiveness, but the loss can be significant; many of the words which inevitably become suspect will contribute nothing to the discovery of important spelling problems, while consuming time available for the test period.

Column *B* describes recall and recognition of trends, and when the behavior is exercised on the same matter as that presented in the last example—literal and figurative usage—the teacher might present a list which includes words like "foil," "crestfallen," "salary," "eliminate," "window," and "front." To evaluate cell *B*-5.5 he would ask for the original meaning of those words in the list whose figurative meaning has worn away.

In column *C* the teacher often addresses this same matter of diction. Cell C-5.5 can be tested by matching classifications of figures of speech with terms from a test paragraph; a question which elicits such classifications as "formal," "informal," "colloquial," and "slang" will test cell C-5.6.

Column *D* involves recall and recognition of methods. The following item evaluates the learning described by the joining of the recall behavior and the content called *Paragraph structure*.

D-2.3

6. It has been several times truly remarked that bills of rights are, in their origin, reservations of powers not surrendered to the government. Such was MAGNA CHARTA, obtained by the barons, sword in hand, from King John. Such was the *Petition of Right*, assented to by Charles I. Such, also, was the *Declaration of Right* presented by the Lords and Commons to the Prince of Orange in 1688, and afterwards thrown into the form of an act of parliament called the *Bill of Rights*. It is evident, therefore, that, according to their original meaning, bills of rights have no application to constitutions founded upon the power of the people and executed by their immediate representatives and servants. Here in strictness, the people surrender nothing; and, as they retain everything, they have no need of particular reservations. "WE, THE PEOPLE of the United States, to secure blessings of liberty to ourselves and our posterity, do ordain and establish this Constitution for the United States of America." Here is a better recognition of popular rights than volumes of those aphorisms which make the principal figure in several of our State bills of rights, and which would sound much better in a treatise of ethics than in a constitution of government.

In [item 6] Hamilton supports his view of the original meaning of bill of rights by
(1) an appeal to authority
(2) analogy
(3) an inductive argument
(4) a deductive argument

(Palmer & Diederich, 1955, pp. 184–185, 188.)

In choosing or constructing items of this kind, the teacher would ordinarily include among multiple choices such standard methods of organization as appear in choices 1, 2, and 3.

The teacher of writing would predictably find a special interest in the "cloze" procedure developed by Taylor (1953, 1956). Although the method is primarily a measure of readability, a subject to be discussed later, mention of the method here offers an early opportunity to notice that the behaviors are ordinarily evaluated not serially, but severally. Composite exercises test a number of the behaviors at one time. In the cloze method, randomly chosen words in a document are replaced by blanks of standard size. Recall of level of usage, *A*-5.6, is one of the cells tested when the student attempts to replace the blanks with the original words. But the behavior required is very close to interpolation, an activity which Table 21-1 would categorize as *Understanding*. Of the two subdivisions, cloze procedures would apply primarily to measures of interpretation.

Understanding (*E*, *F*)

The second major category of behaviors is *Understanding*. Of the two subdivisions in this category, the instructional and evaluation practice in the field invests significantly less time in *Paraphrase* (*F*) than in *Interpretation* (*E*). Behavior *F* is elicited in direct measures of writing by the presentation of a passage and the instruction to "State the meaning in your own words." An indirect measure of the ability to paraphrase is seen in the following item:

F-1.0

In the West, the old people efface themselves and prefer to live alone in some hotel with a restaurant on the ground floor, out of consideration for their children and an entirely unselfish desire not to interfere in their home life. But the old people have a right to interfere and if the interference is unpleasant, it is nevertheless natural, for all life, particularly the domestic life, is a lesson in restraint. Parents interfere with their children anyway when they are young, and the logic of non-interference is already seen in the results of the Behaviorists, who think that all children should be taken away from their parents. If one cannot tolerate one's own parents when they are old and comparatively helpless, parents who have done so much for us, whom else can one tolerate in the home? One has to learn self-restraint anyway, or even marriage will go on the rocks. And how can the personal service and devotion and adoration of loving children ever be replaced by the best hotel waiters?

(Lin Yutang)

7. Which argument is *not* used to justify interference by parents in the lives of their children?
   (1) Some interference is unavoidable.
   (2) Parents have to interfere during the children's youth.
   (3) Interference by parents is not unpleasant.
   (4) Though the interference of parents may be unpleasant, it is not unnatural.
8. Which of the following is Lin Yutang's opinion concerning parents' living with their children?
   (1) It is disadvantageous for both.
   (2) Though disadvantageous for children, it is advantageous for parents.
   (3) Though disadvantageous for parents, it is advantageous for children.
   (4) There are advantages to be derived by both parents and children.

(Palmer & Diederich, 1955, pp. 158–159, 164.)

Each of the choices paraphrases the paragraph; the combination of options in item 7 amounts to a paraphrase, also. The use of "none of the above" would require the student to work out the set of multiple choices as a paraphrase.

To illustrate how column *E* might be evaluated, cell *E*-3.1 can be isolated. Here the learning involves the interpretation of tone, defined earlier in the words of Brooks and Warren (1949, p. 479) as "the reflection in the writing itself of the author's attitude toward his audience and toward his material." (The attitude mentioned bears no relationship to the affective outcomes in columns *N* to *R* in the table.) Tone is complex; such matters as diction, structure, rhythm, mood, and imagery cooperate in tonal effects. The following series of items represents increasing effectiveness in the evaluation of *E*-3.1. In the first item, which uses a quotation from Thackeray, the approach is quite direct:

E-3.1

There were audacious young freethinkers, who adored nobody or nothing except perhaps Robespierre and the Koran, and panted for the day when the pale name of priest should shrink and dwindle away before the indignation of an enlightened world.

9. DIRECTIONS. From the evidence of this passage, how do you think the author feels toward the "young freethinkers"?

(College Entrance Examination Board, Commission on English, 1968, p. 290.)

Item 9 offers no criteria for the "evidence"; that fact itself, however, may serve to remind the respondent that such evidence tends to be coextensive with the document. The student must account for the influence of "audacious . . . adored . . . panted . . . pale . . . shrink" among other elements in his assessment of how "the author feels."

The second example offers somewhat more direction. The "description" mentioned in the item consists of two paragraphs by T. E. Lawrence; it need not be reproduced, since the nature of the questions about it is of chief interest here.

E-3.1

10. In the following description we get an impression of Judda . . . What is the author's attitude toward this [Arabian] city? Does he loath it? Admire it? Feel affection for it? Is his writing florid? Studiedly dry?

(Brooks & Warren, 1958, p. 362.)

Again the lack of criteria serves notice that impressionistic accounts of tone are as inconclusive as they are unsatisfying; but again the invitation is to a reliance on the writing itself. In preparing items for evaluating *E*-3.1, the teacher may wish to imitate the marking of a passage illustrated above in item 1, from Ray and Ray. Diagrams similar to the one they imposed upon the Thoreau paragraph will help avoid subjectivity by requiring the student to focus on provable patterns within the work.

An elaborate but very effective item for use with this cell demonstrates the change in tone that is forced by change of audience:

E-3.1

Two or three days and nights went by; I reckon I might say they swum by, they slid along so quiet and smooth and lovely. Here is the way we put in the time. It was a monstrous big river down there—sometimes a mile and half wide; we run nights, and laid up and hid daytimes; soon as night was most gone we stopped navigating and tied up—nearly always in the dead water under a towhead; and then cut young cottonwoods and willows, and hid the raft with them. Then we set out the lines. Next we slid into the river and had a swim, so as to freshen up and cool off; then we set down on the sandy bottom where the water was about knee-deep, and watched the daylight come. Not a sound anywheres—perfectly still—just like the whole world was asleep, only sometimes the bullfrogs a-cluttering, maybe. The first thing you see, looking away over the water, was a kind of dull line—that was the woods on t'other side; you couldn't make nothing else out; then a pale place in the sky; then more paleness spreading around; then the river softened up away off, and warn't black any more, but gray; you could see little dark spots drifting along ever so far away—trading-scows, and such things; and long black streaks—rafts; sometimes you could hear a sweep screaking; or jumbled-up voices, it was so still, and sounds come so far; and by and by you could see a streak on the water which you know by the look of the streak that there's a snag there in a swift current which breaks on it and makes that streak look that way; and you see the mist curl up off of the water and the east reddens up, and the river, and you make out a log cabin in the edge of the woods, aways on the bank on t'other side of the river, being a woodyard, likely, and piled by them cheats so you can throw a dog through it anywheres; then the nice breeze springs up, and comes fanning you from over there, so cool and fresh and sweet to smell on account of the woods and the flowers; but sometimes not that way, because they've left dead fish laying around, gars and such, and they do get pretty rank; and next you've got the full day, and everything smiling in the sun, and the song-birds just going it!

(Mark Twain, *Huckleberry Finn*)

I still keep in mind a certain wonderful sunset which I witnessed when steamboating was new to me. A broad expanse of the river was turned to blood; in the middle distance the red hue brightened into gold, through which a solitary log came floating, black and conspicuous; in one place a long, slanting mark lay sparkling upon the water, in another the surface was broken by boiling, tumbling rings, that were as many-tinted as an opal; where the ruddy flush was faintest, was a smooth spot that was covered with graceful circles and radiating lines, ever so delicately traced; the shore on our left was densely wooded, and the somber shadow that fell from this forest was broken in one place by a long, ruffled trail that shone like silver and high above the forest wall a clean-stemmed dead tree waved a single leafy bough that glowed like a flame in the unobstructed splendor that was flowing from the sun. There were graceful curves, reflected images, woody heights, soft distances; and over the whole scene, far and near, the dissolving lights drifted steadily, enriching it, every passing moment, with new marvels of coloring.

(Mark Twain, *Life on the Mississippi*)

Questions on excerpt from Huckleberry Finn

11. What kind of person do you think the speaker in the excerpt is? . . .
12. What is the relationship between Huck and the author? . . .
13. What does Huck's level of usage tell you about him? . . .
14. How would you describe Huck's voice in this paragraph?

Questions on excerpt from Life on the Mississippi

The aim is to show that the author's purpose is very likely not only to describe a sunset but also to please, perhaps even to impress, his *Atlantic Monthly* audience. [Footnote here documents the fact of serial publication of parts of the novel.] It is to show the speaker as therefore more pretentious than Huck in diction, imagery, and sentence structure . . . .

15. How much does the first sentence tell you about the speaker? . . .
16. What characteristics of the speaker's language in the rest of the passage reveal him as different from Huck? . . .
17. What have you learned from these two passages about the effect of an author's audience on the choices in his writing?

(College Entrance Examination Board, Commission on English, 1968, pp. 331–333.)

Not all the questions that follow the excerpts are reproduced in items 11 to 17; several were selected on the basis of their relevance to the interpretation of tone. They satisfy the major concerns of cell *E*-3.1, and offer the comfort of focus upon a major literary craftsman. For younger students, the choice of models will be governed by the need for appropriately shorter passages.

Because tone *inheres*, the otherwise useful practice of modifying a selection to make it yield more items in a test is to be avoided. Ebel (1951, pp. 241–249) describes the "interpretive test exercise," which consists of "questions calling for various interpretations [p. 241]." He advocates the rewriting of a passage for the purpose of increasing the yield of items per line in the selection. Although the interpretive exercise has every sign of utility for the cell now being considered, it is clear that one step in its preparation—the modification of a passage—is almost certain to destroy some of the tonal attributes which the exercise seeks to uncover.

Application (G)

The intersection of the behavior labeled *Application* and the content labeled *Mechanics* (G-4.0) constitutes another very frequently tested main cell in the table. The standard approach to evaluation of this ability presents material new to the student and requires the application of relevant conventions and rules. Here is an example.

A-4.0, G-4.0

DIRECTIONS: Below are several paragraphs in which certain parts are underlined and numbered. These numbers correspond to the number of the item on the answer sheet. For each part which is underlined and numbered, decide which one of the following choices is correct:

C There is an error in CAPITALIZATION.
G There is an error in GRAMMAR.
P There is an error in PUNCTUATION.
S There is an error in SPELLING.
NE There is no error.

Then, on your separate answer sheet, fill in the space which has the same letter as the answer you have chosen.

SAMPLES: There was three puppies in the box
A
Its a great day for the Yankees
B

Charlie

Charlie always hated school: So him and another boy
[18] [19]
desided to play hookey. Eccept for certian feelings of
[20] [21] [22]
guilt, they had a wonderful time. Even their parents didn't know they weren't going to school. They did this for two or three months. But when they went back to school the shock came. Charlie wasn't going to gradu-
[23]
ate because he was going to fail english. The next year,
[24]
he refused to go back to school because he would of had to have the same teacher. And this he would not
[25]
do. But the year after that, this teacher took a leave of absence. He went to graduate school at the university
[26]
of Missouri. Charlie went back to high school and
[27]
really studied this time. Years later, Charlie and this teacher became close friends.

(*Stanford Achievement Test*, 1965, p. 2.)

The most readily and safely predictable reaction to such a set of items is to find fault. Two reasons may explain much of the reaction: first, every native speaker is an expert on his language, in a number of important ways, and no pronouncement is likely to go unchallenged; second, more than two centuries of instruction in prescriptive grammar have developed among educated people a querulous predisposition to challenge the keyed response, when command of grammatical rules is at issue. It is probably true, on the other hand, that if a test of language ability were developed containing items with which no one could find fault, the test would measure nothing that could interest anyone.

The exercise presented above is composite. Although the cells represent separable units of learning, the usual practice is to combine columns and rows for efficient evaluative techniques. The foregoing exercise combines columns *A* and *G* with rows 4.1, 4.2, and 4.3.

It will be remembered that the novelty of the situation is what ranks the behavior as *Application* and not simple *Recall*. One might protest that the mental activity involved at point 24 in the exercise—that is, at english—cannot be more than recall of the word as the respondent has seen it spelled; because there is a conventional lower-case use of the word, however, the respondent must go beyond the word to the context, and when the context is new, such behavior is, by definition, *Application*. At points 20, 21, and 22 ("desided . . . eccept . . . certian") the exercise measures recall—specifically, cell *A*-4.1—there being no such forms as those given.

Another approach to the composite exercise is found in the Writing Test in the series of Sequential Tests of Educational Progress (STEP):

G-4.0

28. Georgeville, Texas
29. January 6, 1956

30. Dear Betty;
31. I was sick too. 32. And I know how you feel.
33. It's not much fun to have nothing to do is it . . .
34. Yours truly,
35. Sandra

How should 30 be punctuated:

a. Dear Betty; (as it is now)
b. Dear Betty,
c. Dear Betty:
d. Dear Betty

(Educational Testing Service, 1957, p. 2.)

A slightly different format also supplies marks of punctuation and capital letters:

G-4.0

36. Lindbergh flew alone across the atlantic ocean.
A B

A. [o] [O]
B. [.] [,] [NP] [DK]
NP—no punctuation
DK—don't know

(Durost et al., 1962, p. 12.)

The learning described by cell *G*-4.3 concerns application of matters of syntax, for which a previous (composite) format is serviceable, but less challenging than the type which follows:

G-4.3, I-1.0, L-1.0, L-4.0

37. In the following question you are given a complete sentence to be rephrased according to the directions which follow it. You should rephrase the sentence mentally to save time, although you may make notes in your test book if you wish.

Below the sentence and its directions are listed words or phrases that may occur in your revised sentence. When you have thought out a good sentence, find in the choices A to E the word or entire phrase that is included in your revised sentence. The word or phrase you choose should be the most accurate and most nearly complete of all the choices given.

Although the directions may require you to change the relationship between parts of the sentence or to make slight changes in meaning in other ways, make only those changes that the directions require; that is, keep the meaning the same, or as nearly the same as the directions permit. If you think that more than one good sentence can be made according to the directions, select the sentence that is most exact, effective, and natural in phrasing and construction.

SENTENCE: John, shy as he was of girls, still managed to marry one of the most desirable of them.

DIRECTIONS: Substitute *John's shyness* for *John, shy*.

Your rewritten sentence will contain which of the following?

a. him being married to
b. himself married to
c. him from marrying
d. was himself married to
e. him to have married

(Educational Testing Service, 1963, p. 16.)

The *Educational Testing Service* booklet (1963) explains, "This type of question is designed, therefore, to assess the student's mastery of variety in sentence structure, his ability to make a change within a sentence so that it says what he intends to say more smoothly, concisely, and effectively than the original version may [p. 17]." The format elicits application, criticism, and production, and the requisite exercise of these higher-order mental behaviors is well worth the price in item writing difficulty which this technique exacts.

An illustration drawn from another content area will indicate that the instructor's main effort in assessing application is in supplying new and appropriate exercises in which the rules, principles, etc., may be applied. Cell *G*-2.2 concerns the application behaviors in the matter of transition. If the instruction included work on transitional devices, and no work on Emerson, the following item would measure application of transition:

G-2.2

38. In the following paragraph underline transitional words once, repeated words and synonyms twice, and pronouns three times.

A foolish consistency is the hobgoblin of little minds, adored by little statesmen and philosophers and divines. With consistency a great soul has simply nothing to do. He may as well concern himself with his shadow on the wall. Speak what you think now in hard words, and to-morrow speak what to-morrow thinks in hard words again, though it contradict everything you said to-day. —"Ah, so you shall be sure to be misunderstood." —Is it so bad, then, to be misunderstood? Pythagoras was misunderstood, and Socrates, and Jesus, and Luther, and Copernicus, and Galileo, and Newton, and every pure and wise spirit that ever took flesh. To be great is to be misunderstood.

(Ralph Waldo Emerson, "Self-Reliance")

(Watkins & Martin, 1961, p. 292. Underscoring by Watkins and Martin omitted here.)

As noted earlier, in the discussion of cell *A*-1.1 following item 1, the teacher will seek a passage which permits both a satisfactory collection of evidence and an opportunity to elaborate the evidence. Not all the students will accomplish all the underlining called for in the sample item. The format therefore lends itself to instructional use after the test.

Criticism (H–K)

The *Analysis* and *Judgment* involved in columns *H* to *K* constitute the *Criticism* and self-criticism sought in writing courses and units. The units of material for analysis vary in length from sentences to essays. An example of very brief materials for analysis is found in the familiar format of the "analogy" item. Cells *I*-1.2 and *I*-5.0 concern analysis of relationships among words and ideas, and may be tested as in items 39 and 40. The directions require the examinee to choose the words which make the sentence "true and sensible."

I-5.4

39. ______ is to night as breakfast is to ______
    a. supper — corner
    b. gentle — morning
    c. door — corner
    d. flow — enjoy
    e. supper — morning
40. ______ is to one as second is to ______
    a. two — middle
    b. first — fire
    c. queen — hill
    d. first — two
    e. rain — fire

(Bennett, Seashore, & Wesman, 1961, p. 3.)

In a comment on items of this type, the test manual (Bennett, Seashore, & Wesman, 1966, p. 6) states: "[They are] aimed at the evaluation of the student's ability to abstract or generalize and to think constructively, rather than at simple fluency or vocabulary recognition." The item type is usually associated with tests of intelligence, and may in the stem leave blank either one or two of the parts of the analogy; it is, however, satisfactorily useful in cell *I*-5.4.

Longer exercises in criticism illustrate the way in which efficient techniques combine several columns and rows in one exercise. Returning again to the Thoreau paragraph on page 788, one recognizes that the exercise there described becomes analytic when the instructions require the student to identify the main point of the paragraph and the elements, relationships, and organizing principles which cooperate to make that point. The cells thereby combined are *A*-1.0, *H*-2.3, *I*-2.3, and *J*-2.3.

In the next example, the questions following the paragraph, which is by Walter Lippmann, have been chosen from a set of about twenty questions provided in the original source. They were chosen to indicate how the items test the several kinds of analyses for all content categories except *Mechanics*.

This is the creative principle of freedom of speech, not that it is a system for the tolerating of error, but that it is a system for finding the truth. It may not produce the truth, or the whole truth all the time, or often, or in some cases ever. But if the truth can be found, there is no other system which will normally and habitually find so much truth. Until we have thoroughly understood this principle, we shall not know why we must value our liberty, or how we can protect and develop it.

H-1.1, H-5.3

41. Explain the implications of the word "creative" in the first sentence.

I-2.3, J-2.3

42. Discuss the development of this idea through the remainder of the paragraph.

H-3.0, I-5.2

43. Explain Lippmann's repetition of certain words and phrases in this paragraph.

J-1.1, J-3.1

44. How does Lippmann decide what words and phrases to repeat?

(Burtness, Ober, & Seat, 1962, pp. 154–155.)

Judgment, in column K, is evaluated by requiring the student to provide sets of criteria, justify their appropriateness, and apply them to a communication. The criteria will fall into two general groups, one for the internal, the other for the external evidences of the value of the communication. The appropriateness of the criteria is a function of the thoroughness of the activity in the other three columns under *Criticism*. Reporting the results of the application of the criteria completes the judgment. In the following item the paragraphs are as presented in the source, while the questions are modifications of, and additions to, the questions in the source:

K-1.0–K-5.0

Paragraph 1

His days were rich in formal experience. Wearing overalls and an old sweater (the accepted uniform of the private seminary), he sallied forth at morn accompanied by a nurse or a parent and walked (or was pulled) two blocks to a corner where the school bus made a flag stop. This flashy vehicle was as punctual as death: seeing us waiting at the cold curb, it would sweep to a halt, open its mouth, suck the boy in, and spring away with an angry growl. It was a good deal like a train picking up a bag of mail. At school the scholar was worked on for six or seven hours by half a dozen teachers and a nurse, and was revived on orange juice in midmorning. In a cinder court he played games supervised by an athletic instructor, and in a cafeteria he ate lunch worked out by a dietitian.

Paragraph 2

His days followed a set routine. He wore overalls and an old sweater, as everyone else did in his school. In the morning, a parent or nurse walked the two blocks with him to the corner where he met the school bus. The bus was always on time. During the six or seven hours of the school day, he had six teachers. The school also employed a nurse and a dietitian. Games were supervised. The children ate in the cafeteria. Orange juice was served during the morning session.

45. Explain which of the two paragraphs is the better. Include in your answer
    (1) the basis on which you make your choice
    (2) the reason for use of that basis
    (3) the most complete evidence you can gather to illustrate the basis of your choice of paragraph.

(College Entrance Examination Board, Commission on English, 1963, pp. 1, 2.)

Following the presentation of this item, the Commission on English prints sample answers to part of a question which required the student to "explain why paragraph 1 is more effective and interesting than paragraph 2." One of the sample responses follows (the student's punctuation has been preserved):

Paragraph 1 is more effective than paragraph 2 because it does not simply tell what happened each day in school, but rather takes a certain viewpoint. It uses vivid, slightly exaggerated verbs and comparisons to leave an impression on the reader. Games were "supervised", lunch "worked out", scholars "worked on." These give the idea of a rigid little army of controlled boys. The impression of the dread and overwork of the school is conveyed by the student being "revived on orange juice in mid-morning". Saying that orange juice was "served" completely lacks the message that it *had* to be served if the students were to get through the day. Saying that "days followed a set routine" fails to show how mechanically and rigidly this routine was repeated day after day. Thus these slightly distorted, but true-to-the-boy's-viewpoint, verbs completely change the reader's attitude, towards and impressions of the boy and his school.

(College Entrance Examination Board, Commission on English, 1963, p. 19.)

In the response the major basis for the choice was certain attributes of tone found in paragraph 1 and found wanting in paragraph 2. The response does not become explicit about this basis of choice, nor about the appropriateness of this basis. Internal evidence is adduced in support of generalizations about the verbs and about the "impression of dread." The phrases "leave an impression on the reader," and "completely change the reader's attitude" invoke external evidence. Little more than an awareness of these differences in criteria for evidence need be added to the sample answer to make it succeed with the added questions listed above. The teacher would accordingly introduce a requirement in the question that the criteria be discussed briefly in the response.

Production (L, M)

Columns *L* and *M*, under *Production*, are evaluated in a direct fashion when the student prepares draft and final copies of a piece of writing. The columns differ in some emphases, as suggested in an earlier page. Work on a draft (column *L*) is sporadic, out of sequence, future directed; preparation of final copy (column *M*) is steady, sequential, and past oriented, hopeful of preservation or recovery of whatever inspiration and success the composing enjoyed.

As will later be noted (see page 802), it is advisable to have the papers to be evaluated address the same topic, with recourse, if possible, to the same materials. An example of an exercise useful in formative evaluation follows:

I-1.0 to I-5.0, L-1.0 to L-5.0, M-1.0 to M-5.0

46. Write two descriptions of a single stationary object located out of doors (a building, statue, tree, lamppost, gate, or fountain, for instance): the first should be a description of the object as it appears in one kind of weather or at one time of day; the second a description as it appears in quite different weather or at a different time of day. Write the first draft of each description while you are observing the object.
Suggestions:
(1) Describe only what you see.
(2) Indicate the time of day or the weather by statement or by details.
(3) Do not write about so large an area as a woods, garden, or beach; keep to a single object.
(4) Use detail to individualize your description.

TO THE TEACHER. On the day the papers are due, have students write in class and attach to their two descriptions the answers to the following questions:

47. Are the differences between your two descriptions in any way the result of a difference in your feeling about the object at the two different times?
48. Are they in any way the result of a difference in purpose?
49. Were your feeling and purpose in each case related?

(College Entrance Examination Board, Commission on English, 1968, p. 326.)

In using this approach, the teacher may consider adding the requirement that the first drafts, also, be attached to the final copy.

The current fashion of using a brief text as point of departure is seen in a question from the same source:

E-1.0, I-1.0, L-1.0 to L-5.0, M-1.0 to M-5.0

"I believe in aristocracy . . . not an aristocracy of power, based upon rank and influence, but an aristocracy of the sensitive, the considerate and the plucky." Note *plucky* means brave.

50. From your reading select a character who in some ways seems fitted for membership in this kind of aristocracy. In a carefully planned composition show the extent to which this description does and does not apply to the character you have chosen. Be certain to identify the character, the work, and the author.

(College Entrance Examination Board, Commission on English, 1968, pp. 2–3.)

In this technique, much care must be taken to avoid complicating the evaluation of the writing by introducing the effect of variability in the student's reading powers. The text must be brief; the extreme in the other direction was reached by the pages of reading required in the General Composition Test (College Entrance Examination Board, 1955), no longer in use.

Interest and appreciation (N–R)

The cells in columns *N* to *R* concern behaviors in the affective domain. The close relationship between the constructs *Interest* and *Appreciation*, and the difficulty of distinguishing them in particular cases, were given early attention by Smith and Tyler (1942, pp. 245, 313). They drew the distinction in these terms: "Interests emphasize 'liking' an activity, while appreciations include 'liking' but emphasize 'insight' into the activity: understanding it, realizing its true values, distinguishing the better from the worse, and the like [p. 245]." The continuum of internalization in Handbook 2 of the *Taxonomy of Educational Objectives* (Krathwohl et al., 1964) offers assistance in distinguishing interests and appreciation by describing interest as present at lower levels of the affective *Taxonomy* than *Appreciation*.

The learning described by these columns, like that leading to most affective outcomes, is most often evaluated through inferences from student behavior.

An early technique for evaluating appreciation is found in Smith and Tyler (1942, pp. 248–252). The technique involves first the construction of a list of overt acts and verbal responses which would reveal whether certain types of internal behavior were present or absent. The list which follows was developed for the evaluation of appreciation of literature; its value as a model is seen when it is modified by substituting the idea of "writing" for "reading" at each point, as done in brackets. The desired behaviors are indicated before each set of observable acts or verbal responses:

1. Satisfaction in the thing appreciated. . . .
   He [completes a draft] without stopping, or with a minimum of interruption.
   He [writes] for considerable periods of time.
2. Desire for more of the thing appreciated. . . .
   He [commences writing] similar things as soon after [writing] the first as possible. . . .
3. Desire to know more about the thing appreciated. . . .
   He asks other people for information or sources of information about [the field of writing].
   He attends literary meetings devoted to reviews, criticisms, discussions, etc. . . .
4. Desire to express one's self creatively. . . .
   He produces, or at least undertakes to produce, a creative product more or less after the manner of the thing appreciated.
   He writes critical appreciations. . . .
7. Desire to evaluate the thing appreciated. . . .
   He points out, both orally and in writing, the elements which in his opinion make it good [writing].
   He explains how certain unacceptable elements (if any) could be improved. . . .

(Smith & Tyler, 1942, pp. 251–252)

In later steps the entries in the list are recast in the form of questions, and the questionnaire is administered as a self-report. When the teacher's observations of these behaviors are added, the necessary assumptions about student capability at self-report, and student honesty, may be somewhat relaxed.

It is possible to develop questionnaires, indexes, inventories, rating scales, and the like, after the models in Handbook 2 of the *Taxonomy* or after the many models available in Shaw and Wright (1967). Self-report techniques offer simple instruments for evaluation. The teacher might develop a series of similar questions from such entries as Do you like writing? Do you work on writing assignments before assignments in other courses? Do you write regularly for any purpose other than completing assigned school work? Like all such reports, the usefulness of the questionnaire depends on honesty in the responses. The teacher, therefore, stresses that the questionnaire has no influence on grades and that it can be answered anonymously.

The teacher may wish to consider the further expedient of having such an instrument administered to the students during a class in another course.

Data on interest and appreciation can be gathered also by use of the semantic differential. The procedure in its simplest form presents a concept like "writing" and a series of adjective pairs:

N-1.0 to N-5.0, O-1.0 to O-5.0, P-1.0 to P-5.0, Q-1.1, Q-1.2, Q-3.0, Q-5.0

51. *Writing*

good	_ _ _ _ _ _ _	bad
pleasant	_ _ _ _ _ _ _	unpleasant
simple	_ _ _ _ _ _ _	complicated
important	_ _ _ _ _ _ _	unimportant
attractive	_ _ _ _ _ _ _	unattractive

The student marks on each seven-point scale that point which describes his feelings toward the concept of writing. Because writing is always *writing about*, the teacher will be drawn toward experimentation with such concepts as "Writing about Self" and "Writing about My Community" for work with this technique. Detailed instructions for the use of the semantic differential are found in Osgood and Tannenbaum (1957).

Very little evaluative material has been developed for the affective outcomes of instruction in the field of writing. The evaluation depends most often upon the ingenuity of the teacher in structuring situations for the unobtrusive gathering of evaluative data. Simple observation can transform journals, workbooks, and notebooks into eloquent witnesses—if the evaluator is sensitive and cautious about ways in which the act of observing affects what is observed.

It is characteristic of the evaluation in these last columns that the quantity of the most significant data is very small. The compelling evidence has usually a value very disproportionate to size of the signal: the unasked-for paper, the amendments on fair copy, the revision added to the revision that was required—these slender things are the measure of progress in this domain.

Special problems in testing

The dilemma of audience

The usual practice in the teaching of writing involves papers that are assigned and completed without explicit attention, by teacher or student, to the matter of readership. That the instructor serves usually as sole and special reader is a matter of first importance. But because his role is so obvious, its importance is seldom appreciated. Each assigned paper becomes instead a hurdle to be passed, a part of a quota which the English teachers of the school set and meet with more or less devotion. The themes are assigned, written, submitted, read, "corrected," graded, returned—and burned. A part of the total practice succeeds in delaying the last step by requiring that a revision be returned. What is lost in current practice is the communicative function of the act of writing. It is well for student and teacher to be concerned in a paper with the kind of structural quality which is independent of the identity of the reader. The desirable next step nevertheless remains to be taken: the paper should—sometime, somewhere—reach into at least one reader who is a member of the set of readers addressed by the paper.

When the dilemma of audience remains unresolved, the writing test exercises an ability of little consequence. The product *might* have worked with certain readers, but one cannot be sure. The fact that the tested ability satisfied, or failed to satisfy, the instructor is an almost meaningless circumstance in view of the peculiar constraints associated with his role as reader, among which three are quite powerful: (1) the atypical circumstance of his reading a score of other papers at the same time, on the same topic; (2) the requirement that he identify himself with the kind of reader the paper addresses while preserving his identity as evaluator; and (3) the fact of his changing perceptions of the student's ability. This latter consideration will be returned to in a discussion of formative evaluation.

The salutary attempts at resolution of this problem assign priority to the practice of addressing the same point to different audiences. One example of the fundamental changes that result is seen in the selections from Mark Twain (pages 792–793). The strategy begins with an understanding of the nature and causes of the differences in the treatment of the same idea for different audiences; then "practice" audiences are identified, and the writing attempts to reflect their several needs and interests.

A further example of the practical results of a change in audience is developed by Brooks, Purser, and Warren (1964, pp. 1–8). Their sequence of sample writings demonstrates how the telling of an incident varies with readership (and, of course, with the tellers themselves). The incident—"A man murders a girl with whom he is in love"—is narrated, with consequent differences, for readers of the autopsy surgeon, a newspaper reporter, and a "sob sister." Although the material was developed for the special purpose of examining a fourth, and poetic, treatment of the story, the shaping influence of readership is demonstrated clearly by the exercise.

When the teacher puts these ideas into practice, he may find very helpful an approach described by Elbow (1968). The program involves the distribution of copies of all papers, to the end that "Every member of the class will judge all the papers [p. 117]." The program encourages the student to develop rather than accept the criteria of good reasoning and style by requiring that he concentrate first on the criterion of *effect*. The hypothesis is "The student's best language skills are brought out and developed when writing is considered as words on paper designed to produce a specific effect in a specific reader [p. 119]." In this approach, the important matter of choice of topic requires unusual care. Because all students will judge, all should agree on a topic worth writing about. The teacher will of necessity continue to play the role of member of the target audience, but he should find that a program like the one mentioned here moves the dilemma of audience more than one step toward resolution.

The mode of response

A second special testing problem involves the intuitive appeal of the idea that the best way to evaluate writing ability is to have the student write. A very considerable amount of data amassed by CEEB studies supplies evidence, however, that "a verbal aptitude test could predict English grades or ratings on writing ability better than a test which actually required the students to write" (French, 1966, p. 587). The same writer offers an inclusive statement of the sources of error in the scores on a test requiring actual writing (p. 588):

1. Student Error. A student can do well one day and poorly another day on the very same task. This is, of course, true of both composition and objective tests, but can be greatly aggravated for the composition test, because the student may guess sometimes correctly and sometimes incorrectly about what style of writing or what kind of content his particular examiner will want to find.
2. Test Error. A test calls for a sample of the student's behavior. A long objective test calls for many small samples or items; the items that happen to favor one group of students are usually balanced by items that are especially difficult for the same group. The composition test is almost like a one-item test. Some students may happen to enjoy the topic assigned, while others may find it difficult and unstimulating; this results in error.
3. Scale Error. The reader of a composition can be an easy marker or a tough marker. Therein hangs much of a student's fate. To get all readers for an examination to grade papers on the same scale is no easy matter. It may be largely a matter of administrative persuasion.
4. Reader Disagreement. Even if readers could be persuaded to use the same scale, that is, to give the same proportion of A's, B's, C's, etc., their grades would still not look alike, because there is disagreement on what kind of writing is best.

Given this account of the hazards of reliability and validity in a test of writing, the teacher might hesitate where before he plunged—"have the students write." Yet the appeal of that plunge is compelling. Its attraction is felt another way in a now commonplace encounter: a famous writer begins his remarks to students with a challenge uttered usually in the form of three questions—"All of you here want to learn to write? Then why are you here? Why don't you go home and write?"

The very natural predisposition to judge as best the obvious (direct) measure of writing ability is even more understandable in the light of the extensive support rallied for this view by the composition textbooks. "You can learn to write only by writing . . ." (Moore, 1965, p. 3); "The only way a person learns to write is by writing . . ." (Norman & Sawin, 1962, p. x); "*The only way to learn to write is to write*" (Wykoff & Shaw, 1962, p. 24). A corresponding —and apparently groundless—distrust awaits the use of indirect measures. To take one example, it is difficult to adjust to the appropriateness of the phrase "Writing Exercise" as the title for the multiple-choice tests found throughout the excellent text by Palmer and Diederich (1955).

That behaviors other than writing itself are legitimate and valuable as measures of writing ability is a concept justified by experience throughout the field of psychological testing. Many of the most useful tests involve behaviors which have at face value very little to do with the ability being measured. For this problem, the obvious plan of attack happens to be the best: the values of direct and indirect measures of writing ability are sooner realized when a program makes a point of employing both modes of response.

Reliability of raters

The third and fourth sources of error listed by French in the preceding section are elements of the notorious problem of the reliability of raters. The notoriety received early impetus in the classic work of Starch and Elliott (1912). Two decades later the Commission on English of the CEEB listed eleven factors adversely affecting the reliability of raters, and prefaced the list with the disarming statement that "the Commission freely admits that the Board's readers sometimes make mistakes in the appraisal of separate answer books in English" (1931, p. 98). A review of the research on rater reliability two decades later led Huddleston (1954) to conclude that the problem was so pronounced that a test of verbal ability would accurately accomplish what tests of writing purported—but failed—to do. In recent years the prohibitive cost of developing, administering, and scoring tests involving actual writing has forced greater reliance on objective tests and has shifted attention to problems of validity. The College Board still includes twenty minutes of writing in the English Composition Test, but the time itself raises the issue of validity.

Meckel (1963, p. 988) lists a number of procedures suggested by Diederich for increasing reliability. The suggestions include having all students write on the same topic and on a common set of materials; removing the names from the papers; training the readers in marking practices; using two sets of readers; and averaging the grades of two samples of writing obtained from each student at different sessions. As is so often true of efforts to increase reliability, these steps introduce costs which must be weighed. In mass testing the cost is monetarily quite definable; for classroom work, the cost of adding readers includes the loss of that formative advantage the teacher earns by getting to know the cumulative work of each student.

To the steps outlined above may be added a suggestion prompted by the findings of Coffman and Kurfman (1968), namely, that the readers employ a global, or holistic, method in assigning scores, rather than an analytic one. The latter suggestion takes into account an important whole-part phenomenon expressed in a seminal study by Eley (1953, p. 3); the idea, namely, that "an essay [is] in some way a whole which [can] not be defined by a simple addition of its parts. . . ." The analytic method of scoring may fragment effects that remain intact in global reading. Nyberg (1968) touches this same point in a factorial study of the reliability of essay grading: "The variable 'general impression' had a very high loading, but it was not clear whether this score was awarded on the basis of an unconscious *totalling* of the subscores, or whether, in reading an essay, a marker quickly formed a general impression, then made the subscores fit his impression" (p. 3; italics supplied). What seems more and more clear is that studies of reliability have too much labored the preparation and the product in essay evaluation. In preservice sessions the training in marking schemes and criteria is serious and often intense; the postservice analysis of the ratings is sophisticated beyond comfort; but the careful and complete study of the *grading act itself* remains long overdue.

For very practical advice on the problem of reliability, the teacher will find he is nowhere better served than in the essay from which the following passage is taken:

> I recommend the following as a standard method of computing the reliability of grades or ratings on test papers. Have two papers written on topics requiring the same mode of writing, preferably on different days. Have paper 1 rated by Judges A and B; have paper 2 rated by judges C and D. Then correlate the sum of the two ratings on the first paper with the sum of the two ratings on the second paper. This procedure takes into account both variations in judges and variations in students from one paper to another. With ordinary grading procedures, the best you can expect is that the correlation between the two sums will be about .5. This is the reliability of one paper, graded in the usual fashion by two judges. To find out how many such papers you need from each student to work up to a reliability of .9, use this formula:
>
> $$\frac{(\text{The reliability you want}) \times (1 - \text{the reliability you got})}{(\text{The reliability you got}) \times (1 - \text{the reliability you want})}$$
>
> If you want .9 and got .5 on the first trial, this becomes:
>
> $$\frac{.9 \times (1 - .5)}{.5 \times (1 - .9)} = \frac{.9 \times .5}{.5 \times .1} = \frac{.45}{.05} = 9 \text{ (papers)}$$
>
> Thus, you will need nine such papers, each graded in this fashion by two judges, to work up to a reliability of .9.
>
> (Diederich, 1964, p. 60)

The conditions of testing

A third special testing problem concerns the disparity between the conditions of writing done in tests and those attendant upon most other writing. Writing tests are timed and taken by students in public groups. The applicant for college admission had sixty minutes in which to produce the document known as the "writing sample." The ability being sampled, however, is one which is most often exercised in a manner far different from that employed in a test—different in time, different because more private, and different especially in the number of lines discarded. Although there is wisdom, sometimes, in letting an inspired first draft stand, the most probable condition among student writers is best described by the maxim that there is no such thing as good writing; there is only good rewriting. Seldom in education do the products themselves more convincingly support the "preparation-incubation-illumination-elaboration" model of creativity than in writing. The appearance—the very existence—of preliminary drafts serves to distinguish almost all other writing from that done during a test.

Because of the prohibitive number of variables involved in outside writing, the research that attempts to discover and improve measures of writing ability is mainly restricted to data from tests and other in-school writing. In an interesting experiment on the effects of different correction techniques (marginal, terminal, and both) on papers written outside of class, the investigators employed in-class writing as pretest and post-test measures. The design forced the predictable disclaimer: "We are, of course, not able to determine what effect, if any, the different correction techniques have upon outside-of-class writing" (Stiff, 1967, p. 60).

The constraints on the physical conditions of testing admit little hope that conditions will improve beyond present levels. The effort therefore turns to the nature of the test behaviors themselves. Questions which seek polished writing ignore the realities of the test; emphasis on the power to prepare writing is more justifiable. An item, for example, which requires the composing of an introductory paragraph or passage makes use, in a sense, of time beyond that available in the test; for an appropriate criterion would be the proportion maintained between what was written and the projected form of the document, were time available for its completion. An outline of the complete document would assist the application of this criterion. Tests requiring the production of concluding paragraphs and introductory and concluding paragraphs are among the variations of this technique which readily suggest themselves.

Handwriting

A discussion of special problems in the testing of writing would be incomplete without reference to handwriting—a problem different in kind from those already mentioned. At present, and for some time to come, measures that do involve production of student writing are and will be handwritten by the student. Essay questions in other disciplines are, of course, handwritten also. But the problem peculiar to the matter of writing ability involves the interaction of legibility and that factor sometimes termed "flavor," or "style." The latter dimension relates to the question of how the student says what he has to say. Style operates in a cumulative fashion upon the reader; handwriting which causes annoyance or partial illegibility is also cumulative in its effect. The destructive interaction of these effects constitutes a problem peculiar to the measurement of writing.

Chase (1968) investigated the following problem: "What is the effect of quality of handwriting, spelling accuracy, and use of a scoring key on scores given essay test items?" Two of his findings are relevant to the present discussion: first, that quality of handwriting significantly influences scores on essay tests; and second, that although on the first of two items readers score papers handwritten well about the same as those handwritten poorly, the scores on the second item reflect the positive halo of good handwriting and the negative halo of poor handwriting (p. 318).

The study leads to two practical suggestions: first, that only one paper from a student be read at a time, when the sets of papers include more than one from each student; and second, that where possible the papers written in good and poor hands be interspersed in the reading. The suggestion by Johnson (1962) is relevant and useful; namely, that before accepting a set of papers, the instructor quickly inspect the entire set and reject those which do not appear superficially acceptable. One of the preparatory handbooks for students planning to sit for CEEB tests of writing (Shostak, 1964) puts the matter gently and clearly (p. 73): "The reader will be inclined more favorably to a paper that is easier to read than he will be toward one that requires much time to decipher."

Minimal care will prompt the student to have one other person read all papers handwritten out of school, before such papers are submitted for evaluation. Time reserved in class for improving legibility is well spent. While the profession awaits the accessibility of optical scanners for cursive script, the instructional emphasis will probably profit most from an insistence on *le brouillon*—the rough-draft habit which requires copying over, and invites some second thoughts.

Formative evaluation

The range of benefits and challenges

Few components of curriculum offer so clear an illustration of formative evaluation as a set of student writings submitted during a school term. Even the least structured sequence of composition offers the essential feedback loop, and the mere return of the work done has instructional and evaluative significance. Dressel (1961, p. 209) observes, "Often the most important use which can be made of a writing assignment is in further teaching." The Commission on English of the CEEB (1965) describes the ideal form of such evaluation (p. 99): "In the course of a year the comments [on graded themes] should make as coherent a progress as the classroom teaching, directing each writer to examine and correct his worst faults one by one, so that at the end of the year he can look back on measurable improvement."

Standard practice returns the writings with at least some record of a reaction; and among the benefits this kind of evaluation invites, some are as subtle as they are challenging. A college experiment described by Hodgkinson, Walter, and Coover (1968) concerned the now familiar notion of tape-recording the criticism of themes. One student's comments on the system, however, are valuable here as evidence of the formidable range of challenges open to formative evaluation (p. 10; italics added):

> *I like to think that a teacher recalls all my past work as he views each paper.* If he congratulated me on my correction of previous errors, I am not only encouraged, but *pleased* that he remembered.
>
> The type of comments I find most useful are those which deal with any personal problems I may have in my style of writing. . . .
>
> *I try to correct my mistakes to a degree determined by my teacher's interest.*

The challenges include opportunities in the affective domain, as indicated by the second and third passages italicized. That similar expectations would seem only reasonable to each student is a circumstance easily lost sight of by the teacher of large classes.

If some of the opportunities and benefits of formative evaluation in writing are subtle, some of the problems are no less so. Chief among these is a characteristic of readership which receives little attention in the literature; earlier this difficulty was referred to as one that involved "change in the reader." Put briefly, the problem is this: the continuous feedback of evaluation through papers submitted during a term implies a *constant* reader; the assumption is that the instructor serves exactly this function. But the teacher who reads the first papers in a term is not the teacher who reads the last: he has changed. T. S. Eliot (1932, p. 87) writes, "Some one said 'The dead writers are remote from us because we *know* so much more than they did.' Precisely, and they are that which we know." Over a school term, knowledge changes the teacher of writing. And the students, and their writings, are that which he comes to know.

The nice discriminations required of the formative evaluator of student writing are evidenced in the matter of mechanics. A student's papers may, through feedback, move from many faults in convention to few or none. The price, however, may be a similar reduction in another content row—that for ideas. The handling of the conventions in good writing is, of course, well below the threshold of awareness. The need to determine the degree of conscious work on mechanics that will reduce error, but not impede the flow of ideas, is another of the guarantees that the writing instructor is always adequately challenged.

In the following quotation from a volume sponsored by the National Council of Teachers of English (NCTE), Gorrell (1965, p. 111) has touched not only upon the requisite framework of formative evaluation, but upon two of the areas of content that appear in Table 21-1, Table of Specifications for Writing:

> The course [freshman English] should be organized to give the student some sense of accomplishment, of progression. Too often the course is mainly a series of writing assignments, differing little in the kind of task they impose or in difficulty, with readings and discussion of usage scattered among them. Learning composition, of course, does not have any obvious natural order. It may begin with a study of diction and go on toward a study of organization of large units of composition, or it may work in reverse direction with equal logic. Since the student is writing as he learns, he is actually studying all topics at once. But a kind of order can be imposed, even though it may be mainly arbitrary, as a pedagogical device, a way of helping students to see some sense in what they are doing.

In a comprehensive survey of research in written composition published by the NCTE (Braddock, Lloyd-Jones, & Schoer, 1963), the matter of the particular form of the feedback is given clear, if reluctant, summary (pp. 36–37): "In short, research has so far given no clear indication of the most efficacious way to mark papers except for the qualified endorsement by Buxton [1958] of thorough marking, a sentence or two of constructive comment at the end, and a grade, and that endorsement does not necessarily hold good for younger people." One decade later, in an experiment designed as "a logical extension of the Buxton study," Stiff (1967) finds the matter still unresolved. Braddock, Lloyd-Jones, and Schoer are not insensitive to the vagueness of their term "most efficacious"; they are quick to emphasize that the research might well specify "*what kinds of writing* following *what kinds of instruction* to *what kinds of students* [pp. 34–35]."

Resolution of this problem begins by asking which of the three (read/write/think) strategies describes the writing instruction. If the approach is through reading, the formative evaluator will—and should—react first to opportunities to make the best use of the next reading to be done; feedback in the writing approach concentrates first on the implications in present writing for the next paper to be prepared; the thinking approach pursues first the evidence of student interest in a particular idea, or range of ideas.

Perhaps the most helpful practice in scoring papers is to inform the students not only of the criteria, but of the distribution of emphasis among the criteria. If five readers marked student papers and each reader was particularly responsive to a different content area in Table 21-1, the average of their scores on each paper would constitute a most valuable score. The teacher cannot reproduce this ideal by reading each paper five times. He can, however, make it clear that in a particular set of papers he intends to concentrate his attention on one of the five categories of content. By turning to another category with a new set of papers, he should eventually be able to reveal both the strengths and weaknesses of each student, across all content categories.

Within each strategy the best formative evaluation preserves the flexibility required by the three variables mentioned above by Braddock and coauthors (kind of writing, kind of instruction, kind of student). Throughout formative evaluation, the particular decisions and practices might profit much by attention to a theoretical model like Whitehead's romance-precision-generalization cycle, referred to on page 779. The practical effect of this model on formative evaluation would be the concentration, in marking early papers, on arousal or furtherance of student interest; at midsemester, the feedback would emphasize matters of conventions and other mechanical aids to precision; near the end of the course the comments return close attention to the affective domain, especially to the development of student interest in new forms and channels for his writing.

Standardized tests

A score on the College Entrance Examination Board Achievement Test in English Composition (ECT) represents, for hundreds of thousands of secondary school students each year, a summative evaluation of their writing ability. That the ECT predicts well their English grades in the first year of college does not disturb a view of the test as an end-of-treatment measure. The fact that this instrument has also a formative role is quite clear. Repeatedly, in discussions of the CEEB examinations, the fear is voiced that the nature of the tests will have curricular effects on the lower grades. Noyes touches this issue in considering the comparative effects of the ECT and the Writing Sample (1963, p. 10): "If the schools know that a theme is likely to become a part of the regular ECT, will not the effect on their teaching of composition be as great as, or greater than, that of the Writing Sample?"

The ECT (which has only objective items in some forms, and includes a twenty-minute essay in others) dominates the commercial measures of writing ability; but the honor is a diminished thing. No early resolution appears likely for the validity of problems of objective tests or the reliability problems of tests involving actual writing. But no reason exists why direct and indirect measures cannot be used in concert. Diederich (1966, p. 435) offers a carefully detailed scheme to answer the question, How much growth in writing ability comes about in each year of your program? The scheme is clear and complete. What must be guarded against is an inadequate sample of each student's writing. Braddock et al. (1963, p. 45) recommend that for such (summative) purposes, a minimum of three papers be obtained from each student.

The set of items 30 to 35 on page 794 reproduces items from the second of the two major tests of writing—the Sequential Tests of Educational Progress: Writing (Educational Testing Service, 1957). In print also is the Writing Skills Test, a multiple-choice instrument designed for grades 9 to 12 (Thomas, 1961).

The problem yet to be resolved by current indirect and direct measures commercially available is the discrepancy between the circumstances of a test and those that attend writing whenever else it is done.

Trends in the evaluation of writing

Lay readers

An NCTE study (1961) reported the findings of survey work in California on the matter of writing frequency, and the consequent expenditures of teachers' time. In an average 50.8-hour work week the secondary school teacher spends a total of 28.5 hours working on compositions. The average time per paper, for 150 papers, was 11.4 minutes, including the time spent checking the student's revision of his work. It is clear that the schools are likely to attain something less than the full range of evaluative opportunities.

Sauer (1962) and Logan (1964) report success with programs wherein readers not professionally prepared as teachers of English assist in the reading of student papers. Sauer describes a program of "contract correcting" which, though begun in 1957 as an emergency response to the conditions outlined by the NCTE study above, continued in operation for about eight years. Logan endorses the Diederich Plan, which was the basis of a project involving lay readers in Detroit. Whether they be referred to as lay readers or teacher aides, the trend in the evaluation of writing is toward increasing involvement of readers not professionally prepared as teachers of English. The most important implication of the trend is the necessity that it be reflected in the formulation of course objectives. The kind of attention given to mechanics, for example, will be governed to some extent by the usually high effectiveness lay readers have in evaluating that category of content. The teacher will adjust the emphasis which his objectives place on the kinds of outcomes which depend heavily for their assessment on his professional preparation and experience.

Machine applications

Three trends in the machine processing of natural language hold out promise of combining the benefits of direct and indirect measures of writing ability. For each trend, the past difficulty of converting natural language to a form readable by machine offers with each passing year progressively less difficulty.

The first is the development of techniques in content analysis. Chief among the powerful techniques in the field is the set of programs known as The General Inquirer (Stone, Dunphy, Smith, & Ogilvie, 1966). By developing or adapting the basic "dictionary" with which documents are to be analyzed, the investigator controls the nature of the quantitative output that describes the documents under study. Perhaps more exciting than the statistical sophistication acquired, however, are the opportunities to discover deep-level structures and patterns that are hidden by the limitations of human processing speeds (Rippey, 1966; Page, 1966).

The second trend in automated analysis develops statistical information on word counts, word frequencies, and the like, without concern for semantic issues. A simple—but far from trivial—example is the type-token ratio. How many different words (types) did the student employ in writing the total number of words (tokens) in his latest paper? In his first paper? The questions seem hopelessly ordinary, until one tries to recall when and where the concept of the number of different words in a paper was last encountered. There is no shortage of attention given, for example, to the matter of fluency; the number of new words per total in successive segments of a particular length (the "decremental type-token ratio") offers an unambiguous definition of fluency. It needs little imagination to appreciate the variety of quantitative language complexities that will yield to the heuristic use of machines in this second of the trends.

The third trend involves machine procedures for the application of readability formulas. The somewhat cumbersome computations required in the past have discouraged the use of readability formulas in the evaluation of writing. Klare (1969) reports progress in programming the syllable, word, and sentence counts needed for calculating the level of readability. The teacher of writing will welcome what the formulas provide: an objective index of the stylistic difficulty of a student paper. He will see the index, however, as an evaluative device useful in combination with other devices, and not as an independent criterion.

Perhaps it is time to insist that the measurement of writing ability be pursued more often in a context that includes measures of the environment *and* measures of the intended audience's ability to read. Measuring writer, and not reader too, comes rather too close to the enigma spoken by Yeats: "Who can tell the dancer from the dance?" An evaluation of writing ability tells something about the writing, something about the writer, and something, always, about the evaluator.

REFERENCES

Ashburn, R. R. An experiment in the essay-type question. *Journal of Experimental Education*, 1938, **7**, 1–3.

Association of English Teachers of Western Pennsylvania. *Suggestions for evaluating junior high school writing*. Champaign, Ill.: National Council of Teachers of English, undated. (a)

Association of English Teachers of Western Pennsylvania. *Suggestions for evaluating senior high school writing*. Champaign, Ill.: National Council of Teachers of English, undated. (b)

Bennett, G. K., Seashore, H. G., & Wesman, A. G. *Differential Aptitude Tests*. New York: Psychological Corporation, 1961.

Bennett, G. K., Seashore, H. G., & Wesman, A. G. *Manual for the Differential Aptitude Tests*. (4th ed.) New York: Psychological Corporation, 1966.

Bhushan, V., & Ginther, J. Discriminating between a good and a poor essay. *Behavioral Science*, 1968, **13**, 417–423.

Bloom, B. S. (Ed.) *Taxonomy of educational objectives: The classification of educational goals*. Handbook 1. *Cognitive domain*. New York: McKay, 1956.

Braddock, R., Lloyd-Jones, R., & Schoer, L. *Research in written composition*. Champaign, Ill.: National Council of Teachers of English, 1963.

Brooks, C., Purser, J. T., & Warren, R. P. *An approach to literature*. New York: Appleton-Century-Crofts, 1964.

Brooks, C., & Warren, R. P. *Modern rhetoric*. New York: Harcourt, Brace, 1949.

Brooks, C., & Warren, R. P. *Modern rhetoric.* (2nd ed.) New York: Harcourt, Brace, 1958.

Burtness, P. S., Ober, W. W., & Seat, W. R., Jr. *The close reading of factual prose.* Evanston, Ill.: Row, Peterson, 1962.

Burton, D. L., & Arnold, L. Effects of frequency of writing and intensity of teacher evaluation upon high school students' performance in written composition. Report on Cooperative Research Project No. 1523, Florida State University, 1963, sponsored by the Cooperative Research Program, U. S. Office of Education.

Buxton, E. W. An experiment to test the effects of writing frequency and guided practice upon students' skill in written expression. Unpublished doctoral dissertation, Stanford University, 1958.

California Association of Teachers of English. *A scale for evaluation of high school student essays.* Champaign, Ill.: National Council of Teachers of English, 1960.

Carroll, J. B. Factors of verbal achievement. In A. Anastasi (Ed.), *Testing problems in perspective: Twenty-fifth anniversary volume of topical readings from the Invitational Conference on Testing Problems.* Washington, D.C.: American Council on Education, 1966. Pp. 406–413.

Carruthers, R. B. *Building better English tests: A guide for teachers of English in the secondary schools.* Champaign, Ill.: National Council of Teachers of English, 1963.

Certner, S. *Tested topics and techniques for improving writing.* New York: Teachers Practical Press, 1964.

Certner, S., & Bromberg, M. *Getting your students to write more effectively.* New York: Teachers Practical Press, 1963.

Chase, C. I. The impact of some obvious variables on essay test scores. *Journal of Educational Measurement,* 1968, **5,** 315–318.

Coffman, W. E., & Kurfman, D. A comparison of two methods of reading essay examinations. *American Educational Research Journal,* 1968, **5,** 99–107.

College Entrance Examination Board. *General Composition Test.* Princeton, N.J.: CEEB, 1955.

College Entrance Examination Board, Commission on English. *Examining the examination in English: A report to the College Entrance Examination Board.* Cambridge, Mass.: Harvard University Press, 1931.

College Entrance Examination Board, Commission on English. *End-of-year examinations in English for college-bound students.* Princeton, N.J.: CEEB, 1963.

College Entrance Examination Board, Commission on English. *Freedom and discipline in English.* New York: CEEB, 1965.

College Entrance Examination Board, Commission on English. *12,000 students and their English teachers.* Princeton, N.J.: CEEB, 1968.

Cox, M. H., & Foote, D. N. *A reading approach to college writing.* San Francisco: Chandler, 1961.

Derrick, C. Tests of writing. *English Journal,* 1964, **53,** 496–499.

Diederich, P. Problems and possibilities of research in the teaching of composition. In D. H. Russell, E. J. Farrell, & M. J. Early (Eds.), *Research design and the teaching of English: Proceedings of the San Francisco Conference on Research Design and the Teaching of English.* Champaign, Ill.: National Council of Teachers of English, 1964. Pp. 52–73.

Diederich, P. B. In praise of praise. In Sister M. Judine (Ed.), *A guide for evaluating student composition.* Champaign, Ill.: National Council of Teachers of English, 1965. Pp. 38–40.

Diederich, P. B. How to measure growth in writing ability. *English Journal,* 1966, **55,** 435–449.

Diederich, P. B., French, J. W., & Carlton, S. T. *Factors in judgments of writing ability.* (Res. Bull. RB-61-15) Princeton, N.J.: Educational Testing Service, 1961.

Dressel, P. L. *Evaluation in higher education.* Boston: Houghton Mifflin, 1961.

Dressel, P. L., & Mayhew, L. B. *Handbook for theme analysis.* Dubuque, Iowa: Brown, 1954.

Durost, W. N., et al. *Metropolitan Achievement Test.* New York: Harcourt, Brace & World, 1962.

Ebel, R. L. Writing the test item. In E. F. Lindquist (Ed.), *Educational measurement.* Washington, D.C.: American Council on Education, 1951. Pp. 185–249.

Educational Testing Service. *Cooperative Sequential Tests of Educational Progress: Writing.* Princeton, N.J.: ETS, 1957.

Educational Testing Service. *Cooperative English Test.* Princeton, N.J.: ETS, 1960.

Educational Testing Service. *Multiple-choice questions: A close look.* Princeton, N.J.: ETS, 1963.

Elbow, P. A method for teaching writing. *College English*, 1968, **30,** 115–125.

Eley, E. G. An analysis of writing competence. Unpublished doctoral dissertation, University of Chicago, 1953.

Eliot, T. S. *Selected essays: 1917–1932*. New York: Harcourt, Brace, 1932.

Evans, W. H., & Cardone, M. J. *Specialized courses in methods of teaching English*. Champaign, Ill.: National Council of Teachers of English, 1964.

Evans, W. H., & Walker, J. L. *New trends in the teaching of English in secondary schools*. Chicago: Rand McNally, 1966.

Ferster, M. B. *Programmed college composition*. New York: Appleton-Century-Crofts, 1965.

Finlayson, D. S. The reliability of marking of essays. *British Journal of Educational Psychology*, 1951, **21,** 126–134.

Follman, J. C., & Anderson, J. A. An investigation of the reliability of five procedures for grading English themes. *Research in the Teaching of English*, 1967, **1,** 190–200.

Fostvedt, D. R. Criteria for the evaluation of high-school English composition. *Journal of Educational Research*, 1965, **59,** 108–110.

Frazier, A. (Ed.) *Ends and issues, 1965–1966: Points of decision in the development of the English curriculum*. Champaign, Ill.: National Council of Teachers of English, 1966.

French, J. W. Schools of thought in judging excellence of English themes. In A. Anastasi (Ed.), *Testing problems in perspective: Twenty-fifth anniversary volume of topical readings from the Invitational Conference on Testing Problems*. Washington, D.C.: American Council on Education, 1966. Pp. 587–596.

Frost, R. Education by poetry. In H. Cox & E. C. Lathem (Eds.), *Selected prose of Robert Frost*. New York: Collier Books, 1968. Pp. 33–46.

Gage, N. L. (Ed.) *Handbook of research on teaching*. Chicago: Rand McNally, 1963.

Gerber, J. C. (Ed.) *The college teaching of English*. New York: Appleton-Century-Crofts, 1965.

Godshalk, F. I., Swineford, F., & Coffman, W. E. *The measurement of writing ability*. New York: College Entrance Examination Board, 1966.

Gorrell, R. M. Freshman composition. In J. C. Gerber (Ed.), *The college teaching of English*. New York: Appleton-Century-Crofts, 1965. Pp. 91–114.

Goyer, R. S. A test to measure the ability to organize ideas. *Journal of Educational Measurement*, 1967, **4,** 63–64.

Guth, H. P. *English today and tomorrow*. Englewood Cliffs, N.J.: Prentice-Hall, 1964.

Hayakawa, S. I. Linguistic science and teaching composition. In Sister M. Judine (Ed.), *A guide for evaluating student composition*. Champaign, Ill.: National Council of Teachers of English, 1965. Pp. 1–5.

Hodgkinson, H., Walter, W., & Coover, R. Board corrects freshman themes on tape. *CEA Critic*, 1968, **31**(1), 10–11.

Hogan, R. F. (Ed.) *The English language in the school program*. Champaign, Ill.: National Council of Teachers of English, 1966.

Hook, J. N. *The teaching of high school English*. New York: Ronald Press, 1965.

Howard, D. F. *Writing about reading*. Boston: Little, Brown, 1966.

Huddleston, E. Measurement of writing ability at the college entrance level: Objective vs. subjective techniques. *Journal of Experimental Education*, 1954, **22,** 165–213.

Indiana Council of Teachers of English. Standards for written English in grade 12. *Indiana English Leaflet*, 1960, **3**(1, whole no.).

Indiana Council of Teachers of English. Standards for written English in grade 9. *Indiana English Leaflet*, 1962, **4**(4). (Offprint)

Jewett, A., & Bish, C. E. (Eds.) *Improving English composition*. Washington, D.C.: National Education Association, 1965.

Johnson, E. W. Avoiding martyrdom in teaching writing. *English Journal*, 1962, **51,** 399–402.

Judine, Sister M. (Ed.) *A gude for evaluating student composition*. Champaign, Ill.: National Council of Teachers of English, 1965.

Kitzhaber, A. R. *Themes, theories, and therapy: The teaching of writing in college*. New York: McGraw-Hill, 1963.

Klare, G. R. *The measurement of readability.* Ames, Iowa: Iowa State University Press, 1963.

Klare, G. R. Words, sentences, and readability. Technical Report No. B.1.1, Project CREATES, Computer-Aided Instruction Laboratory, Harvard University, May, 1969.

Klein, S. P., & Hart, F. H. Chance and systematic factors affecting essay grades. *Journal of Educational Measurement,* 1968, **5,** 197–206.

Krathwohl, D. R., Bloom, B. S., & Masia, B. B. *Taxonomy of educational objectives: The classification of educational goals.* Handbook 2. *Affective domain.* New York: McKay, 1964.

Lazarus, A., & Knudson, R. *Selected objectives for the English language arts: Grades 7–12.* Boston: Houghton Mifflin, 1967.

Lefevre, H. E., & Lefevre, C. A. *Writing by patterns,* New York: Knopf, 1965.

Levin, G. H. *Prose models: An inductive approach to writing.* New York: Harcourt, Brace & World, 1964.

Logan, E. The Diederich Plan revisited. *English Journal,* 1964, **53,** 484–487.

Lorge, I. Estimating structure in prose. In A. Anastasi (Ed.), *Testing problems in perspective: Twenty-fifth anniversary volume of topical readings from the Invitational Conference on Testing Problems.* Washington, D.C.: American Council on Education, 1966. Pp. 597–606.

MacLeish, A. On the teaching of writing. In J. Fischer & R. B. Silvers (Eds.), *Writing in America.* New Brunswick, N.J.: Rutgers University Press, 1960. Pp. 88–94.

Madaus, G. F., & Rippey, R. M. Zeroing in on the STEP Writing test: What does it tell a teacher? *Journal of Educational Measurement,* 1966, **3,** 19–25.

Mager, R. F. *Preparing instructional objectives.* Palo Alto, Calif.: Fearon, 1962.

Marshall, J. C. Composition errors and essay grades re-examined. *American Educational Research Journal,* 1967, **4,** 375–385.

Martin, H. C. *The logic and rhetoric of exposition.* New York: Rinehart, 1958.

Martin, H. C. Writing and thinking. In E. J. Gordon & E. S. Noyes (Eds.), *Essays on the teaching of English: Reports on the Yale Conferences on the Teaching of English.* New York: Appleton-Century-Crofts, 1960. Pp. 161–174.

McCrimmon, J. M. *Writing with a purpose.* Boston: Houghton Mifflin, 1963.

McLuhan, M. Sight, sound and the fury. *Commonweal,* 1954, **60**(1), 7–11.

Meckel, H. C. Research on teaching composition and literature. In N. L. Gage (Ed.), *Handbook of research on teaching.* Chicago: Rand McNally, 1963. Pp. 966–1066.

Mizener, A. The craft of composition. In E. J. Gordon & E. S. Noyes (Eds.), *Essays on the teaching of English: Reports of the Yale Conferences on the Teaching of English.* New York: Appleton-Century-Crofts, 1960. Pp. 175–187.

Moore, R. H. *Effective writing.* (3d ed.) New York: Holt, Rinehart and Winston, 1965.

Myers, A., McConville, C. B., & Coffman, W. E. Simpler structure in the grading of essay tests. *Educational and Psychological Measurement,* 1966, **26,** 41–54.

National Council of Teachers of English, Commission on the English Curriculum. *The English language arts.* Champaign, Ill.: NCTE, 1952.

National Council of Teachers of English, Commission on the English Curriculum. *The English language arts in the secondary school.* New York: Appleton-Century-Crofts, 1956.

National Council of Teachers of English, Committee on National Interest. *The national interest and the teaching of English: A report on the state of the profession.* Champaign, Ill.: NCTE, 1961.

National Council of Teachers of English, Committee on National Interest. *The national interest and the continuing education of teachers of English: A report on the state of the profession.* Champaign, Ill.: NCTE, 1964.

Norman, A., & Sawin, L. *Written words: A literary introduction to English composition.* New York: Random House, 1962.

Noyes, E. S. Essay and objective tests in English. *College Board Review,* 1963, **49,** 7–10.

Nyberg, V. R. *The reliability of essay grading.* (Paper presented at the Sixth Canadian Conference on Educational Research) Ottawa: Canadian Council for Research in Education, 1968.

Orgel, J. R. *Writing the composition.* Cambridge, Mass.: Educators Publishing Service, 1962.

Osgood, G., & Tannenbaum, P. *The measurement of meaning.* Urbana, Ill.: University of Illinois Press, 1957.

Page, E. Statistical and linguistic strategies in the computer grading of essays. Paper presented at the meeting of the American Educational Research Association, Los Angeles, February, 1969.

Page, E. B. Grading essays by computer. *Phi Delta Kappan,* 1966, **47,** 238–243.

Palmer, O. Sense or nonsense? The objective testing of English composition. *English Journal,* 1961, **50,** 314–320.

Palmer, O. E., & Diederich, P. B. *Critical thinking in reading and writing.* New York: Holt, 1955.

Peterson, R. S. A magic lantern for English. In Sister M. Judine (Ed.), *A guide for evaluating student composition.* Champaign, Ill.: National Council of Teachers of English, 1965. Pp. 61–63.

Pilgrim, G. H. *Learning and teaching practices in English.* New York: Center for Applied Research in Education, 1966.

Pilliner, A. E. G. Examinations. In H. J. Butcher & H. B. Pont (Eds.), *Educational research in Britain.* New York: American Elsevier, 1968. Pp. 167–184.

Porter, D. The behavior repertoire of writing. In *Linguistics, composing and verbal learning: Papers from the 1962 Conference on College Composition and Communication.* Champaign, Ill.: National Council of Teachers of English, 1962. Pp. 14–17.

Ray, R. J., & Ray, A. *The art of reading: A handbook on writing.* Waltham, Mass.: Blaisdell, 1968.

Rippey, R. The analysis of written language about problems and pressures. Paper presented at the meeting of the American Psychological Association, New York, 1966.

Rippey, R. Maps for English composition. *School Review,* 1967, **75,** 401–413.

Robbins, P. *Incentives to composition: An approach to writing through subject stimulus.* Cambridge, Mass.: Harvard University Press, 1936.

Roberts, E. V. *Writing themes about literature.* Englewood Cliffs, N.J.: Prentice-Hall, 1962.

Rohman, D. G. Pre-writing: The stage of discovery in the writing process. *College Composition and Communication,* 1965, **16,** 106–112.

Rohman, D. G., & Wlecke, A. O. *Pre-writing: The construction and application of models for concept formation in writing.* (Report on Coop. Res. Proj. No. 2174, sponsored by the Cooperative Research Program, U.S. Office of Education) East Lansing, Mich.: Michigan State University Press, 1964.

Sauer, E. H. Co-operative correction of paragraphs. In E. J. Gordon & E. S. Noyes (Eds.), *Essays on the teaching of English: Reports of the Yale Conferences on the Teaching of English.* New York: Appleton-Century-Crofts, 1960. Pp. 138–149.

Sauer, E. H. *Contract correcting: The use of lay readers in the high school composition program.* School and University Program for Research and Development; distributed by Harvard University Press, Cambridge, Mass., 1962.

Schorer, M. Technique as discovery. In W. V. O'Connor (Ed.), *Forms of modern fiction: Essays collected in honor of Joseph Warren Beach.* Minneapolis: University of Minnesota Press, 1948. Pp. 9–29.

Shaw, M. E., & Wright, J. M. *Scales for the measurement of attitudes.* New York: McGraw-Hill, 1967.

Shostak, J. *How to prepare for College Board Achievement Tests: English Composition, the Writing Sample.* Woodbury, N.Y.: Barron's Educational Series, 1964.

Smith, D. V. *Evaluating instruction in secondary school English.* Chicago: National Council of Teachers of English, 1941.

Smith, E. R., & Tyler, R. W. *Appraising and recording student progress.* (Adventure in American Education Ser., Vol. 3) New York: Harper, 1942.

Stalnaker, J. M. The essay type of examination. In E. F. Lindquist (Ed.), *Educational measurement.* Washington, D.C.: American Council on Education, 1951. Pp. 495–530.

Stanford Achievement Test, High School Basic Battery. New York: Harcourt, Brace & World, 1965.

Starch, D., & Elliott, E. C. Reliability of grading high school work in English. *School Review,* 1912, **20,** 442–457.

Steeves, F. L. *The subjects in the curriculum: Selected readings.* New York: Odyssey Press, 1968.

Stiff, R. The effect upon student composition of particular correction techniques. *Research in the Teaching of English,* 1967, **1,** 54–75.

Stone, G. W., Jr. (Ed.) *Issues, problems, and approaches in the teaching of English.* New York: Holt, Rinehart and Winston, 1964.

Stone, P. J., Dunphy, D. C., Smith, M. S., & Ogilvie, D. M., with associates. *The General Inquirer*. Cambridge, Mass.: M.I.T. Press, 1966.

Stryker, D. (Ed.) *Method in the teaching of English: Selected addresses delivered at the Fifth Conference on English Education, University of Georgia, 1967*. Champaign, Ill.: National Council of Teachers of English, 1967.

Sutton, J. T., & Allen, E. D. The effect of practice and evaluation on improvement in written composition. Report on Cooperative Research Project No. 1993, Stetson University, 1964, sponsored by the Cooperative Research Program, U.S. Office of Education.

Taylor, W. L. Cloze procedure: A new tool for measuring readability. *Journalism Quarterly*, 1953, **30**, 415–433.

Taylor, W. L. Recent developments in the use of "cloze procedure." *Journalism Quarterly*, 1956, **33**, 42–48.

Thomas, E. S. *Evaluating student themes*. Madison, Wis.: University of Wisconsin Press, 1966.

Ward, W. S. (Ed.) *Principles and standards in composition for Kentucky high schools and colleges*. Frankfort, Ky.: Kentucky State Department of Education, 1956.

Watkins, F. C., & Martin, E. T. *Practical English handbook*. Boston: Houghton Mifflin, 1961.

West, W. W. Written composition. *Review of Educational Research*, 1967, **37**, 159–167.

Whitehead, A. N. *The aims of education*. New York: Macmillan, 1929.

Whitten, M. E. *Creative pattern practice: A new approach to writing*. New York: Harcourt, Brace & World, 1966.

Wolf, M. H. Effect of writing frequency upon proficiency in a college freshman English course. Report on Cooperative Research Project No. 2846, University of Massachusetts, 1966, sponsored by the Cooperative Research Program, U.S. Office of Education.

Wykoff, G. S., & Shaw, H. *The Harper handbook of college composition*. New York: Harper, 1962.

22

Evaluation of Learning in

A Second Language

REBECCA M. VALETTE

Boston College
Chestnut Hill, Massachusetts

*Rebecca M. Valette received the Bachelor of Arts degree from Mount Holyoke College and the Doctor of Philosophy degree in French from the University of Colorado. For two years she held the position of Examiner in Foreign Languages at the University of South Florida. She has taught at both the university and the elementary school level in this country and has taught English as a second language in France. She is presently Associate Professor of Romance Languages and Director of the Language Laboratory at Boston College. She is a member of the Massachusetts Advisory Committee on Foreign Languages and is editor of the "Testing Section" of the Annual ACTFL Bibliography (American Council on the Teaching of Foreign Languages). She has published widely in the areas of literature (*Arthur de Gobineau and the Short Story*, University of North Carolina Press) and foreign language testing and methodology, and has brought out several French readers. She and her husband are currently developing a junior–senior high French program.*

Contents

22

Evaluation of Learning in A Second Language

Introduction

Second-language learning is a cumulative process which combines cognitive behaviors and new psychomotor skills. Gradually, the student acquires a second system of communication. He comes to realize that the new language is not simply a "code" by which he can express his own ideas, but an integral part of a culture different from his own; in fact, he will find that some distinctions he makes in English cannot be made in the new language, and that other ways of viewing experience are not only possible but necessary if he intends to communicate in that language. For example, if the student wants to express in English his affection for another person, he must decide whether to use "like" or "love," but in French both ends of the like–love continuum and the vague middle ground are contained in the one word *aimer*. On the other hand, if the student wants to talk about something he "knows" in a language such as French, Spanish, or German, to use the correct verb he must decide whether what he "knows" is something he is acquainted with (*connaître, conocer, kennen*) or some fact he has learned and is sure of (*savoir, saber, wissen*).

At advanced levels of second-language instruction, the student can use the new system of communication as a means of broadening his knowledge and appreciation of literature, humanities, history, and geography. The reading knowledge of a second language has long been considered a research tool in almost all fields of intellectual endeavor.

In this chapter we shall focus on the acquisition of a second language and the role of testing in this learning process.

The objectives of second-language instruction

The objectives of second-language instruction are entering a period of stabilization. Over the past two decades, emphasis in modern languages has been placed on the spoken language and the development of proper speech habits. Now a balance is being sought between the spoken

TABLE 22-1 TABLE OF SPECIFICATIONS FOR SECOND LANGUAGE INSTRUCTION

	BEHAVIORS																
	Cognitive and psychomotor skills										*Affective domain*						
	Knowledge and perception				*Manipulation*		*Understanding and production*				*Participation*						
	Knowledge of elements	*Ability to differentiate and discriminate among elements*	*Knowledge of rules and patterns*	*Ability to differentiate and discriminate among rules and patterns*	*Ability to reproduce elements and patterns*	*Ability to manipulate elements and patterns*	*Ability to grasp explicit (surface) meaning of utterances or patterns G.1 paraphrase G.2 English equivalents*	*Ability to produce utterances or patterns conveying the desired explicit meaning*	*Ability to analyze utterances or patterns in terms of implicit (deep) meaning*	*Ability to analyze utterances or patterns conveying the desired implicit meaning*	*Greater awareness of the phenomenon*	*Increased tolerance of differences*	*Demonstrated interest in the phenomenon*	*Satisfaction derived from achievement*	*Continuing desire to improve competence and increase understanding*	*Active promotion of cross-cultural understanding*	
CONTENT	*A*	*B*	*C*	*D*	*E*	*F*	*G*	*H*	*I*	*J*	*K*	*L*	*M*	*N*	*O*	*P*	
1.0 Spoken language 1.1 Vocabulary 1.2 Grammar 1.3 Phonology																■	Language
2.0 Written language 2.1 Vocabulary 2.2 Grammar 2.3 Spelling																■	Language
3.0 Kinesics (or body language)									▨	▨						■	Language
4.0 Way-of-life culture 4.1 Society 4.2 Culture									▨	▨							Culture
5.0 Civilization		■			■	■	▨	■	▨	■						■	Culture
6.0 Arts		▨		▨	■	■	▨	■	▨	■						■	Culture
7.0 Literature		■		■	■	■		■		■						■	*Literature*
8.0 Communication 8.1 Face-to-face 8.2 Telephone 8.3 Message	■	■	■	■	■	■					■	■	■	■	■	■	Communication

■ empty cells ▨ improbable cells

language and the written language, culture and civilization (including history and the arts), cognitive processes, and acquisition of habits. A brief history of teaching aims will provide a sense of perspective.

Historical perspective

At the turn of the century modern languages, under the influence of Latin instruction, were usually presented through a grammar–translation approach. The student learned a set of rules of grammar and a list of vocabulary items and then was expected to translate from the foreign language to English and from English to the foreign language. Speaking was not stressed. The Committee of Twelve, which investigated the state of the foreign-language profession at the turn of the century, said in their 1900 report, "In our general scheme of secondary education the ability to converse in French and German should be regarded as of subordinate importance" (quoted in Newmark, 1948, p. 191).

In the late 1920s the Modern Foreign Language Study took up the ambitious project of evaluating the status of language teaching; the results were summarized by Algernon Coleman (1931) in volume 12 of the reports. The study recommended that classroom efforts during the first two years be centered primarily on the development of reading skill and that all types of class exercises converge toward the goal of bringing the student to read the foreign language as easily as he might read English. Although this conclusion received a certain amount of opposition, the principal objective of subsequent courses was almost exclusively the development of the student's ability to read the foreign language. In textbooks built on the reading approach, the lesson would begin with a reading selection followed by a vocabulary list and grammar exercises. Graded readers were widely used to develop reading comprehension and to foster vocabulary building. Translation as a skill was deemphasized; it was used primarily as a check on comprehension.

It should be noted that both the grammar–translation approach and the reading approach were designed to develop students' ability to read a second language, although the former involved intensive study of a small amount of material, whereas the latter entailed extensive practice in reading. In neither approach, however, was the spoken language entirely forgotten. Correct pronunciation was recommended; teachers who spoke the foreign language fluently often conducted their classes in that language rather than in English; and there were even some school systems, such as Greater Cleveland under the leadership of De Sauzé, where the spoken language was given primacy. But by 1940, reading was widely accepted as the main objective which might be attained in a two-year course of instruction.

When the United States entered World War II, it was discovered that very few Americans could speak a second language well enough to make themselves understood. Linguists and methodologists collaborated with the Army Specialized Training Program (ASTP) to develop intensive courses in spoken Japanese, spoken French, and so on. The success of this war effort, the commitment of many teachers and linguists, and the availability of more versatile recording equipment, records, and tapes brought about a gradual change in emphasis in postwar language instruction. The primacy of the spoken language over the written language was proclaimed, and courses were created to cultivate oral language skills. The launching of the sputniks and the subsequent interest by the government in promoting instruction of the traditionally taught foreign languages as well as Russian, Chinese, and other "critical" languages culminated in the National Defense Education Act of 1958. The audiolingual approach gained widespread acceptance as funds became available for disseminating new materials, installing language laboratory facilities, retraining teachers in oral skills and dialogue-and-drill methods, and setting up a variety of research projects in the area of language learning and linguistics. Standard tests were developed in the four skills: listening, speaking, reading, and writing. Translation was "out" as far as standard tests were concerned, with the exception of proficiency tests for teachers.

It was the intention of the proponents of the

audiolingual programs that the student come to regard a text in French, for example, as the written representation of a language with which he had become familiar rather than an English message in disguise. For students studying a foreign literature, a knowledge of the spoken language would provide the necessary foundation for an appreciation of literary texts: the student would approach the literary works of a second language much the same as he approached works written in English—with an awareness of how the author uses the components of everyday speech to create specific literary effects. The validity of these long-range goals has been accepted by language teachers: the problem has been one of means, and the question has been whether the audiolingual approach elicits the desired behaviors from students.

Now the theoretical underpinnings of the audiolingual approach are being questioned (see Bolinger, 1968; Rivers, 1964) and the tenets of behavioral psychology and structural linguistics are being challenged by those who emphasize the "creative" aspect of language and the views of the generative (or transformational) linguists. To oversimplify the situation, we might say that the grammar–translation method and the reading method—which for Carroll (1965) are based on the cognitive code-learning theory—concentrated uniquely on the cognitive domain of the *Taxonomy of Educational Objectives* (see the Appendix to Part I of this book), whereas the audiolingual habit theory in its original form ignored the cognitive domain to stress habit formation and behaviors in the psychomotor domain. It might be stated that the success of either approach was a function of how effectively the teacher managed to weave in elements from the slighted domain.

It appears that the language programs of the coming decade will incorporate features of both the cognitive code-learning approach and the audiolingual habit-formation approach and will focus on the development of communicative competence (see Jakobovits, 1968). Communicative competence in our native English allows us to grasp the underlying meanings of what people around us say ("It's not *what* he said, it's *how* he said it!"). It implies the existence of a "state of expectancy" for certain forms, words, expressions, etc., and explains why we can get the gist of a conversation even if noise drowns out part of it.

In the classical languages, the current linguistic aim is the development of the reading skill. This shift from a grammar–translation approach to a reading approach becomes most evident if we compare the new Latin programs with older texts. Certain new materials have now adopted an audiolingual or a pattern-practice approach at the elementary stages of instruction: the oral skills are introduced in order to bring the student more effectively to the level where he can read a classical text with direct comprehension.

"Culture," when mentioned in connection with foreign-language instruction before World War II, referred to formal culture: knowledge and appreciation of the outstanding social, scientific, and especially artistic accomplishments of the country (or countries) in question. The ultimate goal of language study was reading and enjoyment of the literature which the culture in question has produced. This goal still exists in some current language programs. However, over the past decade the language teacher has begun to focus on "deep" culture: the multitude of elements constituting the way of life of the people who use the foreign language. The Sapir-Whorf hypothesis of linguistic relativity, which postulates the close interdependence of a person's language and his concept of reality, has influenced the development of new teaching materials. A people's culture, for example, is partially mirrored in their dialogues and gestures. Again, the creative use of visual aids helps the student realize that his idea of a "house" is not identical with the Spaniard's image of a *casa*. The American's concept of "lunch" cannot be effectively superimposed on the French *déjeuner*; the German *Gemütlichkeit* has no exact English equivalent. Current programs aim to develop the student's awareness of cultural differences and of the role language plays in the expression of culture.

MLA statement of objectives

The present position of the profession in regard to the value of second-language instruction has been formulated in the following statement, made in 1956 by the Steering Committee of the Foreign Language Program of the Modern Language Association:

> The study of a foreign language, skillfully taught under proper conditions, provides a *new experience*, progressively enlarging the pupil's horizon through the introduction to a new medium of communication and a new culture pattern, and progressively adding to his sense of pleasurable achievement. This experience involves:
>
> 1. The acquisition of a set of *skills*, which can become real mastery for professional use when practiced long enough. The international contacts and responsibilities of the United States make the possession of these skills by more and more Americans a matter of national urgency. These skills include:
>
> *a*. The increasing ability to *understand* a foreign language when spoken, making possible greater profit and enjoyment in such steadily expanding activities as foreign travel, business abroad, foreign language movies and broadcasts.
>
> *b*. The increasing ability to *speak* a foreign language in direct communication with people of another culture, either for business or pleasure.
>
> *c*. The ability to *read* the foreign language with progressively greater ease and enjoyment, making possible the broadening effects of direct acquaintance with the recorded thoughts of another people, or making possible study for vocational or professional (e.g., scientific or journalistic) purposes.
>
> 2. A new understanding of *language*, progressively revealing to the pupil the *structure* of language and giving him a new perspective on English, as well as an increased vocabulary and greater effectiveness in expression.
>
> 3. A gradually expanding and deepening knowledge of a foreign country—its geography, history, social organization, literature, and culture—and, as a consequence, a better perspective on American culture and a more enlightened Americanism through adjustment to the concept of differences between cultures.
>
> Progress in any one of these experiences is relative to the emphasis given it in the instructional program and to the interests and aptitude of the learner. Language *skills*, like all practical skills, may never be perfected and may be forgotten later, yet the enlarging and enriching results of the *cultural experience* endure throughout life ["FL Program Policy," 1956, no. 4, pt. 2, xiii].

A table of specifications for second-language instruction

The objectives in second-language instruction and their interrelationships will become clearer if we reduce them to a two-dimensional chart. Table 22-1, Table of Specifications for Second-language Instruction, presents the course content on the vertical axis and the outcomes or behaviors on the horizontal axis. We shall first describe these classifications and then show how various courses emphasize certain aspects of the table and skip over others. (See also Valette, 1969, for a similar version of this table.)

Content of instruction

Language (1.0–3.0) The primary content area in foreign languages is, as would be expected, the language itself. Language is a communication system which functions on three interrelated bands:

The audiolingual band (or *Spoken language*; content 1.0)
The graphic-material band (or *Written language*; content 2.0)
The visual-gestural band (body language, or *Kinesics*; content 3.0)

In addition to these three bands, there is the area of paralanguage which includes features such as tone of voice, choice of dialect, style of handwriting, and types of print.

In most language programs being used in American schools, the emphasis falls on spoken and written language. Students are expected to learn the "correct" pronunciation and spelling, the "accepted" vocabulary and grammar. In some languages, such as Spanish, the "fit" between the spoken language and the written language (that is, the correspondence between how the language sounds and how the words are spelled) is very close. In other languages, such as French (and

English), the fit is much looser.[1] In the commonly taught Western languages, the written language is transcribed by means of an alphabet which contains letters for consonant and vowel sounds; consequently, the spoken vocabulary and grammar are very similar to the written vocabulary and grammar.

Whereas writing has a conservative effect on language (one form is considered correct), more flexibility exists with respect to the spoken language, which is in a state of gradual evolution. This brings up certain questions—Should the student be taught the formal pronunciation? The usual pronunciation of educated natives? The rapid speech variations in common use? Dialect or slang?[2] The trend now is to teach actively the pronunciation educated persons use in conversation, and to teach the student to recognize and understand the formal pronunciation and the rapid speech variations.

Kinesics, or body language, is rarely incorporated into classroom instruction in a planned manner. If the teacher is a native of the foreign country, and if he has not shed his foreign personality for an American one, then his gestures and manners will provide the student with an accurate kinesic model. This band of communication is just beginning to receive serious study (see Green, 1968; Hall, 1959), and at this time the only carryover into the classroom is the teaching of a few externals, such as how the French shake hands.

Culture (4.0–6.0) "Culture" is a broad term which has received many interpretations. *Way-of-life culture* (4.0) includes two main aspects: "society," or social structure and institutions, and "culture," or the value system and attitudes of the people. It is this type of "culture" which is receiving the greatest attention from curriculum builders and language teachers. This culture is closely related to all three communication bands—spoken language, written language, and kinesics—for a language is a product of a culture, and cultural views and values are in part determined or suggested by language.

Civilization culture (5.0) refers to the history, the geography, the scientific achievements, and the worldwide contributions of the country in question. Such topics have been presented in foreign-language classes over the decades, but they are usually taught at the level of simple knowledge. The *Arts* (6.0) are part of the civilization of a nation, but they are sometimes treated separately (in Table 22-1 they are granted independent status). Here, too, most programs aim at making the student familiar with the great works of art (painting, music, architecture, sculpture, and so forth) of the foreign country, but the objectives rarely progress beyond the level of knowledge.

Literature (7.0) Literature is an artistic product of the foreign culture and conveys its message by means of language. Within the context of foreign-language instruction, the term "literature" is capable of triggering violent polemics. Since literature is an art, is it necessarily a more serious academic discipline than language? Should the aim of learning a second language be to enable the student to read the literature of that language? Should literary works be abridged and presented early in the students' instruction? Or should the teaching of literature be delayed until the student can handle the language easily?

The current practice seems to be to introduce brief literary selections (especially twentieth-century poetry and short stories) as early as possible and in limited quantity, to allow the student to hear and to read artistic samplings of the foreign language as a supplement to the diet of dialogues and drills. Students may learn the titles of great works and the names of well-known authors. Only much later in their instruction (fifth-year high school classes or college classes for majors)

[1] Note the English verb "have," with its three common pronunciations: /hæv/ in "I have your book"; /hæf/ in "I have to go"; and /Ωv/ in "I would have come earlier." Similarly, in French the word *dix* (meaning "ten") is pronounced /dis/ when the number occurs in isolation, /diz/ before a noun beginning with a vowel sound, as in *dix amis*, and /di/ before a noun beginning with a consonant sound, as in *dix garçons*.

[2] Notice the English verb "going." In formal pronunciation one says "going to"; in conversation among educated persons, "goin' to"; in rapid speech, "gonna"; in dialect, "gwine" (or "gwine ter").

do the students begin to analyze literary texts and to read for deeper meaning.[3]

Communication (8.0) In Table 22-1, *Communication* forms a "global" category—that is, a general category, combining language, culture, and occasionally literary references. Face-to-face communication (8.1) involves the give and take of continuous two-way exchanges. The speaker not only formulates what he is saying, but his ear is monitoring what he has just said, within the context of other voices or background noises, and his eyes are picking up the reactions of those around him. The telephone conversation (8.2) is similar, but the visual contact is missing. The message (8.3) may be written, recorded, taped, or videotaped: here the student plays only the role of receiver.

The student simultaneously operates on three levels of meaning (see Jakobovits, 1970): linguistic meaning (or explicit meaning), implicit meaning, and implicative meaning. Note, for example, the question: "Do you have a match?" At the linguistic level of meaning, we understand that the speaker is asking one or several persons if they have a box of matches, a book of matches, or perhaps (if they are playing Old Maid) a matched set of cards. The implicit meaning is derived from the context within which the question was asked: is the speaker holding a pack of cigarettes or a hand of cards? The implicative meaning of the question in the former case is, "May I please have a light?" In other cases, the implicative meaning may be carried in the tone of voice: a disgusted "thanks" from a waiter who finds the tip too small doesn't really mean "thank you" at all.

Effective communication does not require the possession of a near-native accent (content 1.3.); we all know that Maurice Chevalier, for example, communicates with American audiences in spite of (perhaps even because of) his heavy French accent. It is possible to communicate with a rather small vocabulary and limited grammar *if* you have a sympathetic audience who will answer your questions when the conversation ranges over topics you do not understand. On the other hand, it is possible to possess a large vocabulary, much knowledge of grammar, and a near-native accent, and still fail to communicate effectively—perhaps because of hesitancy to speak or fear of making errors.

In recent years teachers have concentrated on getting the student to produce "correct" or "acceptable" sentences in the second language; creativity was discouraged because errors might creep into the language. Now more and more attention is being focused on the communicative aspect of language learning.

Behaviors in second-language learning

Knowledge and perception (A–D) The behavioral objectives in second-language learning cross all three domains of the taxonomy: cognitive, psychomotor, and affective. The presence of the affective component is typical of all subject-matter areas of the curriculum. Languages differ from other academic subjects, however, because of the heavy psychomotor component present in the early stages of learning.

As we examine the *Knowledge and perception* objectives, we become immediately aware of the parallel existence of the cognitive and psychomotor components. The knowledge of elements and patterns (*A* and *C*) requires thinking and recall on the part of the student. Differentiation and discrimination among patterns and elements (*D* and *B*) is done by means of the eye or ear and requires acting more than thinking. The knowledge of elements (*A*) includes knowledge of vocabulary, of gestures, of cultural terms, names of artists, names of literary works, main characters, and plot lines. The knowledge of rules and patterns (*C*) includes grammar, sound-symbol relationships, cultural themes, historical trends, artistic conventions, and literary genres.

However, in certain content areas knowledge cannot exist in isolation. In the realm of spoken language, it is not enough to know that certain

[3] For a broader analysis of literature objectives, see Purves, "Evaluation of Learning in Literature," Chap. 20 of this book.

new sounds (or phonemes) exist in French; one must be able to identify them upon hearing them. In the area of written language, one must learn to distinguish the characters of a new alphabet or writing system (Russian, Arabic, or Hebrew, for instance). One learns to notice those gestures which bear meaning, and which of the road signs, for example, means "one way." The degree to which perception is developed within the language classroom with respect to the arts is probably rather limited. After learning to differentiate among individual elements (*B*), the student must learn to recognize these elements in new patterns and configurations (*D*): he must learn to "read" groups of letters and to perceive patterns of stress and intonation (suprasegmental phonemes) as well as the sounds themselves.

Manipulation (drill; E, F) The ability to reproduce and to manipulate elements and patterns is principally part of the psychomotor domain. In spoken language, the student repeats dialogue sentences, memorizes them, and then builds on them with pattern drills, directed dialogues, and other manipulative exercises: these various activities may be termed "vocalizing." Of themselves they do not constitute communication or speaking, but they help the student internalize appropriate language patterns. In written language, the student of Russian, for example, learns to copy Cyrillic script, write sentences from memory, and fill workbook pages with writing exercises. Learning gestures or stances, or the proper way to hold a knife and fork, usually begins with imitation and then continues with trying these gestures out in new contexts. The aim of manipulation drills is to render new actions habitual.

Understanding and production (G–J) In the area of spoken and written language, these behaviors are loosely called "the four skills": listening comprehension, speaking, reading comprehension, and writing. Objectives *G* to *J* represent a hierarchy which becomes more evident if we compare these behaviors with the classifications of the cognitive domain of the taxonomy. Behavior *G*, the *Ability to grasp the explicit meaning of utterances or patterns*, may be equated with *Comprehension* (see Appendix). *H*, the *Ability to produce utterances or patterns conveying the desired explicit meaning*, is equivalent to *Application*. Objective *I*, the *Ability to analyze utterances or patterns in terms of implicit and implicative meaning*, would be classified as *Analysis*. Objective *J*, the *Ability to produce utterances or patterns conveying the desired implicit or implicative meanings*, is at the level of *Synthesis*. If we turn to the four skills, listening comprehension and reading comprehension fall under *G* when the emphasis is on direct meaning (as is typically the case in beginning, intermediate, and even some advanced language courses); they fall under *I* when the students are expected to derive the deeper or fuller meaning of the text or recording. The skills of speaking and writing, the productive skills, come under behavior *H* when the student tries to convey direct meaning and under *J* when the student wants to express deeper levels of meaning.

These higher behaviors may be applied to kinesics and culture, but in the context of the American classroom this application is rather rare. Unless new instructional programs are developed which stress these areas, most teachers will continue to introduce smatterings of culture and kinesics at the levels of knowledge and manipulation. The abilities of comprehension and analysis are utilized in the study of literature at the advanced level, but in this chapter, we shall treat literature goals only cursorily.

In the global category of communicative competence, behaviors *G*, *H*, *I*, and *J* become intertwined. In face-to-face communication, the student is aware of direct linguistic meaning as well as implicit and implicative meaning. He is simultaneously producing and receiving, speaking and listening. In content category 8.3, *Message*, the student is either preparing or receiving the message, and communication proceeds in only one direction.

Participation (K–P) The participation objectives, *K* to *P*, fall in the affective domain. Language teachers do, it would seem, almost unanimously accept all these behavioral objectives as desirable. Everyone assumes that the experience of learning a second language (even if the language is later forgotten through disuse) is rewarding and stimulating, that it contains many benefits in the affective area. Whether this is actually the case remains for research teams of the future to discover.

Objective *K* states that the student will be more aware of language, of the distinction between written and spoken language, and of the differences between languages. He will become aware of other ways of acting, other ways of looking at the activities of everyday existence, other values, other countries, other contributions to the arts and sciences.

Behavior *L* posits an increase in tolerance. The student will accept the fact that other people may speak other languages, and that this is not a sign of inferiority or superiority. He will be open to differences in manners, in dress, in world view, in philosophy of life.

Objective *M* states that the student will become more interested in language and culture, in social studies, literature, and the arts. In part, this interest may go together with the sense of satisfaction (*N*) that the student derives from mastering certain aspects of a new language or from learning about another culture. From the academic point of view, the teacher wants to transmit to students (who will perhaps become future teachers) the love of learning and the desire to improve one's competence in the new language, perhaps to spend some time abroad, to learn more about foreign cultures and American culture (*O*).

P reflects a "national interest" goal: if students study another language, derive satisfaction from that experience, and realize that cross-cultural understanding is a difficult but necessary goal, they will each contribute in some way to the achievement of that goal.

These participation aims could be classified in the affective domain of the taxonomy as follows: *Receiving* (*K* and *L*), *Responding* (*M* and *N*), and *Valuing* (*O* and *P*).

The objectives of current language programs

The current language programs are often grouped in three categories: traditional, audiolingual (or functional skills), and modified audiolingual. The dichotomy between "traditional" and "audiolingual" parallels the differences between the cognitive code-learning theory and audiolingual habit-formation theory. The modified audiolingual approach represents a compromise position.

In recent years, two substantial research projects have studied the relative effectiveness of these types of programs. A University of Colorado study (Scherer & Wertheimer, 1964) found that after one year of German instruction, students taught by the traditional approach were superior in reading, writing, and translation; students taught by the audiolingual approach were superior in listening and speaking. After two years of instruction, the differences in listening, reading, and German-to-English translation had disappeared. However, the "traditional students" maintained their superiority in writing and in English-to-German translation, while the "audiolingual students" performed better in the speaking test. The "Pennsylvania Project" reported by Smith and Berger (1968) found that after one year of instruction at the high school level, classes in French and German taught by the traditional approach performed significantly better than classes which stressed functional skills (the audiolingual approach) and classes using the modified audiolingual approach on the MLA Coop Reading Test (MLA Cooperative Foreign Language Tests) and on the reading-aloud section (Critical Sounds) of the MLA Coop Speaking Test. On the remaining sections of the MLA Coop Speaking Test and on the MLA Coop Listening and Writing Tests, there were no significant differences among the groups. It would appear that the better performance on the reading test is a function of vocabulary load, since the traditional approach taught about 1,400 to 1,500 vocabulary items, whereas the functional skills and the modified audiolingual approaches presented only 500 to 600 vocabulary items. After two years of instruction (Smith & Baranyi, 1968), there were no significant differences in listening, speaking, and writing (as measured by the MLA Coop Tests). The traditional classes performed significantly better than the functional skills classes in reading, but there were no significant differences between the performances of the traditional classes and the modified audiolingual classes on the MLA Coop Reading Test. Both of these studies—one with college students and the other with high school students—lead us to conclude that whatever differences exist after one year among classes taught by different methods tend to disappear after two years of instruction. However, language teachers must carefully scrutinize the content of the MLA Coop Tests to see which types of behaviors are actually being measured by the battery.

If we turn our attention back to Table 22-1, we note that the traditional program (and the word "traditional" is a blanket term with many interpretations) emphasizes content areas 2.0, 5.0, and 7.0 and gives less attention to areas 1.0, 4.0, and 6.0. The behavioral objectives are cognitive in nature: *A*, *C*, *G* (especially *G*.2), and to a lesser extent *H*. An example of a traditional program is Dale and Dale (1956). Direct Method texts, such as the Alliance française (Paris) course by Mauger (1953), employ a cognitive approach which uses the foreign language as the medium of communication; because of their emphasis on cognitive aims, these courses are generally grouped with the "traditional" texts even though the spoken language (content area 1.0) is stressed from the outset.

The audiolingual program stresses content areas 1.0 and 4.0, giving less emphasis to 2.0, 3.0, 5.0, 6.0, and 7.0. Communication (8.0) is the long-range goal. At the beginning level, the psychomotor behaviors are taught, and often the cognitive objectives receive little attention. *B*, *D*, *E*, and *F* are gradually supplemented by *G* and *H*. The three major audiolingual programs are Harcourt, Brace & World: the *A-LM* series (1961) in French, German, Spanish, Italian, and Russian; the Holt, Rinehart and Winston series (1962) in French, Spanish, and German; and the McGraw-Hill series (1961) in French and Spanish.

The modified audiolingual programs combine features of both the traditional and the audiolingual programs. Content areas 1.0, 2.0, and 4.0 are complemented with the addition of 3.0, 5.0, 6.0, and (later) 7.0. Communication (8.0) remains the long-range aim. Behaviors *A* to *H* are all incorporated in the elementary and intermediate levels. The modified programs are of two sorts, depending on the orientation of the original material. In the early 1960s appeared the revisions of traditional texts (such as O'Brien, Lafrance, et al., 1965) complete with tapes, pattern drills, and optional dialogues. In subsequent years the second editions of the audiolingual series mentioned above have appeared: these texts contain vocabulary exercises and explanations of grammar.

The audiovisual programs are built around filmstrips or movies—e.g., Chilton: *Voix et Images;* Encyclopaedia Britannica Educational Corporation: *Je Parle Français* and *El Español por el Mundo*. These programs are similar in their emphasis to the audiolingual programs, although they too are currently undergoing modification.

The "new" Latin programs—e.g., Waldo Sweet's programmed Latin (*Artes Latinae*, Encyclopaedia Britannica Educational Corporation) and Ashley & Lashbrook, *Living Latin* (1967) —have incorporated the findings of structural linguistics and introduce certain psychomotor objectives in addition to the traditional cognitive objectives. Familiarity with spoken Latin is intended to help the students learn to read texts for direct comprehension (a shift from behavioral objective *G*.2 to *G*.1).

Summative evaluation

Given the wide range of instructional objectives in second-language learning, a broad variety of testing procedures and item types have been developed to measure students' progress toward the various goals and to evaluate proficiency in the content areas of language, culture, literature, and communication. I have prepared a testing handbook for modern language teachers in which many item types are described in detail (Valette, 1967). In this section we shall simply indicate the more common testing techniques for evaluating the major cells in the Table 22-1, Table of Specifications for Secondary-language Instruction. In referring to the cells of Table 22-1, we shall give the letter of the objective and the number of the content. For example, *A*-1.1 is *Knowledge of elements of spoken language vocabulary*, or, more simply, knowledge of the spoken vocabulary.

We shall give the following examples largely in French. Each illustration is accompanied by an English translation so that teachers of languages other than French will be able to construct similar items in the language with which they are concerned. In multiple-choice items, the desired response is circled.

Knowledge and perception (A–D)

Questions of knowledge and perception evaluate the simplest behaviors in the cognitive and psychomotor domains. These questions constitute the bulk of the items on both standard and homemade classroom tests.

Knowledge of elements (A) In the area of spoken and written language, the elements to be learned are vocabulary (content words), grammatical function words (such as "the," "and," and "for"), the pronunciation of specific letters or letter combinations, and the spelling of specific sounds. The testing of these elements must include the passive or receptive skills of recognition (that is, listening and reading) and the active or productive skills of recall (that is, speaking and writing). Since the current trend in foreign-language testing prohibits the use of English in such items, pictures or other visual aids are often employed. Note the following examples, which can be used to test either speaking or writing:

A-1.1, A-2.1

(*a*)

(*b*)

(*c*)

1. *Voilà un chien.*

[There is a dog.]

2. *Qu'est-ce que c'est?*
   (Response: *C'est un chien.*)

[What is that? (Response: It's a dog.)]

When the stimulus is recorded on tape or read aloud by the teacher, item 1 tests vocabulary through listening; when the stimulus is printed in the student test book, the item tests vocabulary through reading. Similarly, the student may either speak or write his answer to item 2; if the answer is to be spoken, the stimulus question is usually recorded on the master tape. In item 2 the scorer may listen only for the word *chien* (the content word), or he may insist that the student say *le chien* or *un chien* (using the correct function word, in this case the definite or indefinite article, with the content word).

At more advanced levels of language learning, knowledge of vocabulary is evaluated predominantly by means of the reading skill. The current trend is to test vocabulary in meaningful context.

A-2.1

3. *Le brouillard était si épais qu'on* ______ *plus rien.*
   (a.) *ne voyait*
   b. *n'entendait*
   c. *ne sentait*

[The fog was so thick that we could no longer ______ anything. (a) see, (b) hear, (c) smell]

4. *"Ô là là, que je suis épuisé!" disait Jean à son frère. . . .*
   Dans ce passage, Jean dit qu'il est très
   a. *content*
   (b.) *fatigué*
   c. *fort*

["Boy, am I exhausted!" said John to his brother. . . . In this passage, John says that he is very (a) happy, (b) tired, (c) strong.]

The above items illustrate two typical means by which vocabulary knowledge is evaluated. The discrete item (3) is usually called a "vocabulary" item. The passage item (4) is often called a "reading comprehension" item, because the difficult word is embedded in a longer narration. The example, however, is obviously a vocabulary item, for the student can select the correct answer only if he knows the meaning of the word *épuisé*.

Knowledge items in the area of culture may be worded either in English or in the foreign language. Knowledge items in literature usually appear in the foreign language.

A-4.1

5. In France the system of *allocations familiales* pays mothers according to
   (a.) the number of children they have
   b. the amount of medical care required by the children
   c. the school expenses incurred by the children (books, transportation)

Knowledge of rules and patterns (C) In present second-language materials, rules play a minor role. If the formulation of a rule helps the student assimilate a pattern, then such a rule is mentioned. The audiolingual textbooks contain very few rules, and those are descriptive rather than prescriptive. Test items in the foreign language, therefore, never ask for formulations of rules. Knowledge of rules is evaluated indirectly by having the student recognize or produce language samples which contain the appropriate patterns. These rules and patterns cover derivations of words, morphological forms (conjugations, declensions, etc.), syntax (word order), and patterns of pronunciation and spelling.

C-1.1, C-1.2, C-2.1, C-2.2

6. *Dites (écrivez) les adjectifs qui correspondent aux adverbes suivants: heureusement; vraiment; énormément.*
   (Responses: *heureux; vrai; énorme*)

[Say (write) the adjectives which correspond with the following adverbs: happily, really or truly, enormously. (Responses: happy; real or true; enormous)]

C-2.1

7. *Le cerisier est un arbre qui donne des* ______. (Response: *cerises*)

[The cherry tree is a tree which bears ______. (Response: cherries)]

C-2.2

8. *Répondez aux questions suivantes. Employez le même verbe.*
   (1) *Allez-vous au cinéma? Oui, nous* ______ *au cinéma.*
   (Response: *allons*)
   (2) *Allez-vous au théâtre? Oui, je* ______ *au théâtre.*
   (Response: *vais*)

[Answer the following questions. Use the same verb. (1) Are you going to the movies? Yes, we ______ to the movies. (Response: are going) (2) Are you going to the theater? Yes, I ______ to the theater. (Response: (am going)]

C-1.3, C-2.3

9. Which of the following words are pronounced the same?
   a. *seau*
   b. *saute*
   c. *sot*

(Answer sheet: a, b (a, c) b, c a, b, c)

Item 6 tests the knowledge of rules governing the formation of adverbs, and 7 tests knowledge of the formation of the names of fruit trees. The student does not apply the rule (that is, he is not asked to develop the adverb form or the name of the tree); he demonstrates his awareness of the pattern by providing the root word (*heureux*, *cerise*), which is already part of his vocabulary. The student's ability to provide the appropriate adverb or tree name is an example of behavior F, *Ability to manipulate elements and patterns*. Item 8 is the modern version of the verb paradigm: the student does not write out the conjugation of *aller* in the present tense (this being considered an "artificial" exercise) but provides the appropriate forms in the context of the sentence. Item 9 tests knowledge of pronunciation and spelling rules. Items of this type were common thirty years ago; currently, they have been replaced by items testing the student's actual ability to produce the sounds (behaviors *E* and *F*).

C-3.0

10. When two French friends meet each other on the street, they say hello and s_____ h_____.
    (Response: shake hands)

C-4.0

11. Describe how the French celebrate the Feast of the Three Kings (*la fête des Rois*) on January 6.
12. State three of the main themes of French culture and give an example of each.[4]

C-7.0

13. *Les sonnets de Baudelaire sont divisés en deux _____ suivis de deux _____.*
    (Response: *quatrains, tercets*)

[Baudelaire's sonnets are divided into two _____ followed by _____.]

Differentiation and discrimination of elements and patterns (B, D) The goals of differentiation and discrimination belong to the lowest category of the psychomotor domain which we have called *Perception* (see Valette, 1969). The student can differentiate elements and patterns when he can point out whether a pair is similar or different. When he is also able to identify each sound, for example, and tell which is which, he demonstrates his ability to discriminate among elements. This differentiation and discrimination are done aurally in the case of sounds and visually in the case of written forms and gestures. The area of culture may introduce new visual and aural discriminations, such as noticing the little ribbons Frenchmen may wear in their lapel (Légion d'honneur, etc.) or whistling at a performance (indicating displeasure).

B-1.3

14. Indicate whether the two sentences you hear are the same or different. Tape:
    a. *Il vient manger.*
    b. *Il vient de manger.*

[(a) He is coming to eat. (b) He has just eaten.]

[4] Nostrand (1968) gives twelve main themes of French culture.

The only difference in pronunciation is the presence of /d/: the first sentence is pronounced /ilvjɛ̃mɑ̃ʒe/ and the second /ilvjɛ̃dmɑ̃ʒe/.

B-1.3

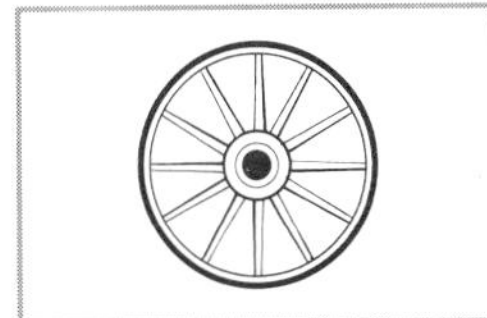

15. Select the appropriate picture. Tape:
    Voilà la roue.

Roue means "wheel" and is pronounced /ru/; the distracter is *rue*, /ry/, meaning "street."

D-1.2

16. Mark A if the subject and verb are in the singular; mark B if the subject and verb are in the plural; mark C if the subject and verb could be either singular or plural. Tape:
    (1) *Il vient ce soir.* (Answer sheet: Ⓐ B C)
    (2) *Il(s) parle(nt) français.* (Answer sheet: A B Ⓒ)
    (3) *Elles sortent demain.* (Answer sheet: A Ⓑ C)

[(1) He is coming tonight. (2) He speaks (they speak) French. (3) They are going out tomorrow.]

There are many presentations possible for same/different items like item 14; see Lado (1961), Valette (1967), and Brière (1967). Items 15 and 16 evaluate the student's ability to discriminate among sounds. It is assumed that the vocabulary (in the item, *roue* and *rue*) or the grammar (here, the verb forms) is familiar to him and that his choice of the correct answer depends on his ability to hear the significant differences in the pronunciation.

Visual discrimination items (cells *B*-2 and *D*-2) are effective when testing a language using a different alphabet or writing system, such as Russian, Arabic, or Chinese. Students indicate whether two characters or sentences are the same or different, or they point out changes of meaning which are caused by (seemingly) slight changes in writing.

Perception items in the content areas of *Kinesics* and *Culture* are built around visual stimuli. A series of videotaped clips could show different people meeting each other, and the student would identify those which were typical of the target culture (*D*-3). The student might see a series of slides showing different French uniforms (police, firemen, mailmen, etc.) which he would identify (*C*-4, if slides were shown slowly; *D*-4, if slides were shown quickly). Or the student might be shown views of different church windows or portals which he would identify as Roman or Gothic in style (*C*-6 or *D*-6).

Manipulation of elements and patterns (E, F)

The manipulation of elements and patterns refers to classroom activities such as learning dialogues and pattern drill activity. The aim of these drills is to instill in the student correct habits in the written skills. Since both spoken and written drills are of the stimulus-response variety, they lend themselves easily to testing.

E-1.0

17. Recitation of a learned dialogue (scored for fluency and pronunciation).

E-2.0

18. Copying a passage printed in Cyrillic uppercase (scored for accuracy in writing in Cyrillic script and ease in copying).

F-1.0, F-2.0

19. Following the model. (The model is given, but there are no explicit instructions.)
    Model: *Il va à l'école.*
    (Response: *Ils vont à l'école.*)
    Item: *Il vient chez moi.*
    (Response: *Ils viennent chez moi.*)

[Model: He goes to school. (Response: They go to school.) Item: He is coming to my house. (Response: They are coming to my house.)]

20. Following instructions.
    Place the following sentences in the negative.
    Stimulus: *Il va à l'école.*
    (Response: *Il ne va pas à l'école.*)

[Stimulus: He goes to school. (Response: He doesn't go to school.)]

E-3.0, F-3.0

21. Imitating gestures (scored for naturalness and appropriateness).
    (1) Sit down at the table the way a French child would.
    (Response: hands in fists, with thumbs up; both fists on the table.)
    (2) Show how you would eat a piece of meat.
    (Response: Fork is always held in left hand, both for cutting and for eating.)

F-4.0

22. Setting the table.
    The teacher sets out the needed props: dishes, glasses, silverware. The students are given directions (in the target language): Set the table the French way. First, put out the plates and glasses. Then the silverware.
    Response: The correct place setting looks like this (from the American point of view, fork and spoon are "upside-down"):

Items 17 to 20 and the many variations described in Valette (1967) have become commonplace in the language classroom; types 18 and 19 are also found on commercial language tests. Items 21 and 22 are examples of how culture and kinesics (linked to culture) might be tested; at present, these areas are not stressed in the curriculum.

Understanding and conveying explicit (surface) meaning (G, H)

The four language skills—listening comprehension, speaking, reading comprehension, and writing—fall under this heading, for within the context of high school language programs the teacher wants primarily to develop the student's ability to grasp and convey *direct* meaning. (The matter of grasping and conveying implicit meanings is commonly postponed to the college level.) Item types testing the language skills have been more carefully refined than those evaluating similar goals with respect to kinesics and culture.

G-1.0

23. Following directions.
    Students are given a street map on which they trace the route described on tape; they may also be asked to label buildings and topographical features.
24. Sentence comprehension.

(*a*)

(*b*)

(*c*)

(*d*)

Students are shown four pictures and given an A-B-C-D answer sheet. Tape:

(1) *La soupe est bonne.*
(2) *Où est le menu?*
(3) *J'aime cette piscine.*
(4) *La neige est belle aujourd'hui.*
(Responses: (1)A, (2)A, (3)C, (4)D)

[(1) The soup is good. (2) Where is the menu? (3) I do like this swimming pool. (4) The snow is lovely today.]

G-2.0

25. Passage comprehension.[5]
    Une fois ses études terminées, mon frère décida de s'installer dans une région d'Afrique où la santé précaire des habitants lui garantissait une clientèle inépuisable. Il partit quelques jours après Pâques. En voyant son avion décoller, je me rendis compte que je ne le reverrais pas de si tôt.
    (1) *Mon frère est*
        a. *explorateur*
        b. *commerçant*
        ⓒ *médecin*
    (2) *Il est probable que mon frère avait l'intention de rester en Afrique*
        a. *quelques jours*
        b. *une semaine*
        ⓒ *des années*

[Once he had finished his studies, my brother decided to settle in a region of Africa where the delicate health of the inhabitants would guarantee him an inexhaustible number of patients. He left several days after Easter. As I watched his airplane take off, I realized that I would not see him again soon. (1) My brother is (a) an explorer, (b) a trader, (c) a doctor. (2) My brother probably had the intention of staying in Africa (a) several days, (b) one week, (c) some years.]

G.2-1.0, G.2-2.0

26. English equivalent.
    The student furnishes the English equivalent of spoken or printed sentences.

H-2.0

27. Dehydrated sentences.
    homme/aller/èglise
    (Response: *L'homme va à l'église.*)

[man/to go/church (Response: The man goes to church.)]

[5] Passage items do not necessarily measure general comprehension. Frequently a passage item tests knowledge of a single word; e.g.,
(3) *Mon frère est parti*
    a. *au printemps*
    b. *en automne*
    c. *en hiver*
[My brother left (a) in spring, (b) in fall, (c) in winter.]
In this example, the student can select the correct answer if he knows that *Pâques* is the French word for Easter. To answer the item he does not have to understand the rest of the passage.

H-1.0

28. Lightning translation.
    The teacher says a sentence in English, and the student responds with the French equivalent. (Scored on fluency and accuracy.)

H-2.0

29. Sentence completion.
    Voyez-vous (cet) homme? (Il) est professeur de
    [*ce*] [*C'*]
    musique.
    (Responses: *cet*, *Il*)

[Do you see that man? He is a music teacher.]

G-3.0

30. Film clips.
    Scene 1: Two men are driving in a car. As another car begins to pass them, a truck comes over the hill.
    Scene 2: The man next to the driver is making the following gesture: his right arm is extended and the hand is rapidly and loosely shaking up and down from the wrist.
    We know that
    a. the truck collided with the passing car
    b. the passing car had plenty of time to slow down and get back into its own lane
    c. the accident was avoided, but it was a close call

G-4.0

31. Matching street signs.
    The student is given a page of American highway signs and a page of European highway signs, and must match the equivalent signs.

The above sample items are by no means exhaustive (for other item types, see Valette, 1967). Items 23 and 24 test listening comprehension. They are called "pure" items (rather than "hybrid" items) because they require the student to use only one skill—listening comprehension. A "hybrid" item requires two or more skills; e.g., an item with a taped stimulus and printed responses. Item 25 is a series of pure reading-comprehension questions. Teachers have mixed opinions about the use of English (items 26 and 28); while it is generally accepted that word-for-word translations lead to fractured English or French (or whatever the target language may be), the use of idiomatic equivalents has often been found effective in evaluating comprehension and in eliciting specific sentences. It is entirely possible to create effective second-language tests without having recourse to English at all, except in the instructions. Dehydrated sentences (item 27) often have more than one correct response. Item 29 tests the student's ability to apply his knowledge of elements and patterns of language in a specific context. In the multiple-choice format, the options may be increased to three and four (such items generally test out to be statistically difficult). In the classroom test, the student may be asked to fill in the blanks, provided the context is precise enough to enable him to find the correct completion.

Understanding and conveying implicit (deep) meaning (I, J)

Most of the items in this area are still experimental, for only recently have the implicit and implicative meanings of utterances and cultural patterns been receiving much attention. It must be remembered that these types of behaviors are usually achieved only by advanced students, and that many advanced students develop these behaviors on their own after years of experience with the language and culture.

I-2.0, I-4.0

32. Give a literal translation and a meaningful English equivalent:
    Tu veux que je te fasse le grand jeu? ou préfères-tu le marc de café?
    (Literal response: Do you want me to make the big play for you, or do you prefer coffee grounds?)

[Do you want me to use the crystal ball, or do you prefer tea leaves?]

(Adapted from Belasco, 1967, p. 86.)

I-1.0, I-2.0

33. Transformation testing drill.
    Transform the following sentences so that the infinitive appears as a finite verb in a dependent rela-

tive and/or subordinate clause, depending on the function of its subject.
(1) *Je vois venir mon père.*
(2) *Elle emmène boire le chien.*
(Responses: (1) *Je vois mon père qui vient*, or *Je vois que mon père vient.* (2) *Elle emmène le chien qui boit.*)

This type of item is often almost impossible to translate. A similar item in English would require the student to transform the following sentences, which look similar with respect to surface structure: "John is eager to please" and "John is easy to please." Response: One can say, "To please John is easy," but not "To please John is eager." Similarly, one can say, "John is eager; he likes to please," but not "John is easy; he likes to please" (see Belasco, 1967).

J-1.0
34. Acting out situations.
Tell a friend you are going to a meeting. Express yourself so as to convey the idea of
(1) obligation
(2) permission
(3) irony
(Responses: (1) *Je dois aller à ce meeting.* [I have to go to the meeting.] (2) *Est-ce que je peux aller à ce meeting?* [Am I allowed to go to the meeting?] (3) *Quel plaisir! J'ai un meeting ce soir.* [How delightful. I have a meeting tonight!])

(Adapted from Jakobovits, 1970.)

J-2.0
35. Paraphrase.
Rewrite the following sentence to make it more intense: *La lumière était trop forte.* ["The light was too bright."]
(Response: *La lumière m'aveuglait.* [It was a blinding light.])

Items such as number 32 may carry a heavy cultural load. In order to understand the test sentence, the student must know that in France the fortune teller refers to the movement of the hands above the crystal ball rather than the act of looking into it; furthermore, fortunes are read in coffee grounds rather than tea leaves. Item 33 tests the student's familiarity with the deep structure of the language. Items of this type have grown out of the application of certain findings of transformational linguistics to language teaching: has the student developed a "sentence recognizer" in the Chomskyan sense, so that he can distinguish between possible (correct) sentences and impossible (incorrect) sentences? Items 34 and 35 evaluate the student's ability to vary shades of meaning by means of tone of voice, choice of words, and other transformations. Many suggestions for developing items along these lines are to be found in Jakobovits (1970).

Communication: overall proficiency (G-8.0–J-8.0)

The global category of *Communication* (8.0) combines behaviors *G, H, I,* and *J* with the content areas of language and culture. Items in this category evaluate the student's ability to use the second language in a way similar to that in which he uses his native English. Subcategories 8.1 and 8.2 refer to live communication; items 36 and 37 may be used to test either form.

G-8.1–J-8.1, G-8.2–J-8.2
36. Person-to-person interview. The student is interviewed by the examiner or by a skilled interviewer.

The student is evaluated on several scales:

1. The student asked for clarification
   1—never
   2—rarely
   3—about half the time
   4—frequently
2. The student used grammatical constructions which were correct
   1—always
   2—usually
   3—about half the time
   4—rarely

3. The student's pronunciation was
   1—near-native
   2—easy to understand, some accent
   3—rather difficult to understand
   4—incomprehensible

G-8.1–J-8.1, G-8.2–J-8.2

37. Search for information. The student is told to find out specific information (when and where the train leaves, what Mr. X thinks of American tourists, etc.) from a native speaker who is instructed to act as if he understands no English.

The student is evaluated on his ability to return with accurate information; a secondary score might represent the native speaker's impression as to how much clarification the student required:

1. The student understood my rapid response immediately.
2. The student asked me to speak more slowly and then he understood.
3. The student asked me to slow down and then also asked me to clarify some terms.
4. The student had difficulty understanding and asked me to write down the information.

Items like 36 and 37 must be administered individually. Consequently, they are practical only in situations where a small number of candidates are to be examined.

Indirect measures of the communication skill exist, but the techniques remain to be refined and the results must be validated. Here are several examples.

G-8.3–J-8.3

38. Delivery rate. The student speaks on a topic, and his speech is recorded.

The student's score is the rate of syllables per minute. Marty (1968) states that students of French should reach 150 syllables per minute for free speech and 200 syllables per minute for directed expression.

G-8.3–J-8.3

39. Complexity of written sentences. The student writes on a topic such as the following:
    Mon oncle qui habite Paris est venu nous voir et nous sommes allés à la plage.

[My uncle who lives in Paris came to see us, and we went to the beach.]

The student's sentences are broken into minimal terminable units, or T-units. The T-unit is defined as the shortest sentence within a longer utterance. Then the average length of the T-unit is calculated. (See Jakobovits, 1970, pp. 27–31.) Score: The above sentence contains two T-units—*Mon oncle qui habite Paris est venu nous voir* and *Nous sommes allés à la plage.* The first sentence contains 9 words, the second 6; the average length is 7.5 words.

G-8.3–J-8.3

40. Dictation. The student hears a passage which he writes down in the second language. (Score is the count of the number of words containing errors.)
41. Dictation under distorting conditions. The student writes down a series of sentences, but the recording contains a certain level of white noise. (Score is the count of the number of words containing errors; see Spolsky, Siguard, Sako, Walker, & Aterburn, 1968.)
42. Reading speed. The student is given a long reading passage in the target language. He is told that he will occasionally come across an extraneous word which he should draw a line through. The test is speeded. The English translation of an example would read thus:
    Usually there is no need to put anything ~~toy~~ on a baby's feet until he has learned to walk. Of course, if it is cold ~~crib~~ outside, then shoes are needed.

The score on item 42 represents the amount of reading covered as measured by the last inappropriate word which has been crossed out.

G-8.3–J-8.3

43. "Cloze" techniques. The student is given a passage to read for comprehension. Every *n*th word has been left out.

The student's proficiency is measured by how many blanks he can fill in. Credit is given only if student furnishes the exact word of the original.

Items 38 through 43 promise to become increasingly useful once their validity has been well established. If any one of these techniques provides scores which correlate highly with measures of overall proficiency, then it will be possible to construct brief and relatively objective tests which replace the "four-skills" batteries or the interview test. One potential difficulty is the effect of previous training: Valette (1964) noted that the dictation scores (for items like 40) correlated highly with comprehensive test scores *only* when the students did not have much practice with dictation. Dictation practice improved dictation test scores but did not have a comparable effect of improving general proficiency. Similarly, if a student knows that his composition will be scored on sentence (or T-unit) length, he will try to write longer sentences. If his speech sample is uniquely on rate of delivery, he will try to speak faster. The resulting longer sentences and faster delivery will not necessarily be indications of greater overall proficiency.

The technique of introducing sound distortion (item 41) or the elimination of words (item 43) is perhaps more valid from a linguistic point of view. All languages have a certain redundancy, and a student's comprehension increases as he becomes aware of these redundant elements. The Defense Language Institute in Monterey encourages the development of selective listening by increasing the level of background noise in its instructional tapes—e.g., Russian conversation forms the background of the Hungarian language tapes.

Participation (K–P)

Measures of interest and attitude have not been widely used in the area of second-language instruction. The following items suggest forms such tests might assume.

K-5.0–K-7.0

44. Match the following names with the role for which these persons are best known:

(1) Gauguin	a. painter
(2) Pasteur	b. novelist
(3) Curie	c. scientist
(4) Victor Hugo	
(5) Stendhal	
(6) Monet	
(7) Toulouse-Lautrec	

(Responses: (1)A, (2)C, (3)C, (4)B, (5)B, (6)A, (7)A)

This is not a cognitive test of material learned in class but a general measure of awareness; students who become receptive to French art and civilization will gradually associate the names of great Frenchmen with the activity through which they achieved fame.

M-4.0

45. Interest inventory.

Would you like to do any of the following activities? Answer Y (yes), N (no), or I (indifferent).

(1) Exchange letters with a French student.
(2) Listen to French-Canadian radio broadcasts.
(3) Study French place names in the United States.
(4) Go to French movies.

N-1.0, N-2, N-4

46. Interest inventory.

Below is a list of several activities. Write S if you *do* get satisfaction from performing the activity. Write U if you are *uncertain* about your reaction to performing the activity. Write D if you *do not* get satisfaction from performing the activity. Write X if you have *never* performed the activity.

(1) To pick out French words in articles and advertisements and try to figure out what they mean.
(2) To compare French and English words to see how they are similar and where they differ.
(3) To mimic a French accent when speaking English.
(4) To read newspaper stories which have to do with France.
(5) To listen to French records.

O-2.0, O-4.0

47. Pen pals. Students who indicate interest are given the name and address of a French pen pal. [If a student writes frequently, collects information to send his pen pal, and rereads the letters received several times, he is exhibiting a continuing desire to improve his French and to learn more about France.]

P-4.0

48. UNESCO or international club.
The student is active in a UNESCO group or international club. He often shows foreign students around and invites them to his house to meet more American students. [Activities of this type are an indication that the student values cross-cultural understanding.]

Items 44, 45, and 46 are indirect measures of the student's willingness to attend to and to learn about a second language and the people who speak that language. Inventories (items 45 and 46) are difficult to develop and use because test-wise students try to give the response they feel the teachers are looking for. With respect to a foreign culture, test developers must determine whether they wish to measure the student's integrative attitude toward the culture (i.e., his tendency to focus on the good points of the culture and to give the foreigners the "benefit of the doubt") or whether they are concerned with the student's manipulative or instrumental attitude (i.e., a detached appraisal of both the foreign culture and his own).

Special problems in testing second-language learning

The general problems in second-language testing fall into three areas: the relationship between methodology and evaluation, the testing of culture, and the practicality and reliability of scorers. The question of the validity of the content is discussed later, in the section devoted to commercial tests.

The conflict between methodology and evaluation

Two tenets of the audiolingual approach, that is, second-language learning is basically a matter of habit formation and that English should consequently be banned from the classroom as much as possible, have had a pronounced effect on language tests. Since testing is viewed as an adjunct to learning, it is held that a test itself should promote no "wrong" learning. Consequently, language test items include no wrong forms, only inappropriate ones, for proper habits can be formed only through constant confrontation with correct forms. Of course, one might postulate that inappropriate forms are incorrect in certain contexts, but it is probably a benefit to elementary students to see only words and structures common to the language they are studying. (Tests for teacher candidates do include wrong forms, for since the teacher will have to correct student's compositions, such items become a valid measure of proficiency.) Furthermore, the ban on translation as an educational objective in the first years of language instruction has brought with it a ban on translation as a means of testing other objectives. Gradually, however, English is being viewed in its proper perspective, and the use of English "equivalents" is acquiring more widespread acceptance. Future language tests will probably use English as a means of testing other objectives.

To what extent should language tests reflect the theories and techniques of current methodologies? It would seem appropriate for standard achievement tests to remain neutral in the polemics of methodology and reflect any and all aspects of the subject matter: the second language. The existence of a complete battery of unbiased measurement instruments would also provide a yardstick against which the performance of various approaches and methods might objectively be compared.

Problems in testing culture

The major problem in testing culture arises from the lack of agreement as to what constitutes "culture" and what the objectives of foreign-language instruction should be in this regard. Within the cognitive domain, language teachers have not been able to determine how much knowledge the student should acquire in sociology, anthropology, geography, arts and sciences, history, etc. Should emphasis be placed on the contents of a woman's handbag or the contents of the Louvre? It is sometimes felt that as specific knowledge about a foreign culture is a valid instructional aim, the real emphasis in a language course should be on the cultivation of affective objectives: an attitude toward the foreign culture under study and other cultures in general. Seelye (1970) has taken a first step in defining cultural aims of instruction. Until teachers can establish their objectives with respect to the teaching of culture, it will be difficult to develop valid tests in this area.

Problems of practicality

Paper and pencil tests of written language proficiency have existed for centuries. The problem of practicality arises with the measurement of proficiency in listening and speaking; of the two skills, listening is by far the easier to test. If the listening skill is to be evaluated in isolation—that is, without introducing the skills of reading or writing—then the question must either be of the multiple-choice type or present the student with a task to accomplish (an action to perform, a map to draw, a picture to color, or the like). In keeping with current trends in language teaching, the student is usually not asked to furnish an English equivalent or summary of what he has heard.

The first problem in listening tests is the possibility of cheating. In the typical classroom, it is relatively easy for the student to glance at his neighbor's paper; if the test is administered in a language laboratory, however, the baffles between the booths significantly reduce this problem. Moreover, if the test is recorded in advance and played over a console, the teacher may move around the laboratory to proctor the examination. More serious is the matter of arm and hand movements during listening tests in which both the questions and the answer options are presented on tape. Consider the following item: "When I leave my friend's house to go home, I say (a) goodbye; (b) hello; (c) may I please?" If the students who recognize (a) as the correct response begin marking their papers before (b) and (c) have been read, the others in the class will be aware of the movement. This problem can be alleviated by having students wait until the end of the item before marking their answer sheets.

The second problem is preparation. Good completion items are difficult to write. The teacher, therefore, should always allow time for a colleague to go over the questions and point out ambiguities in the distracters. Then, there is the additional time involved in preparing a recording of such items, especially since conversation items are more effective when recorded by two different voices. If the options are pictures, rather than spoken responses, the recording time is greatly reduced, but this creates a new problem: finding three or four pictures each for ten to twenty items. Here the practical solution would be to select four appropriate pictures from a magazine and to prepare twenty sentences which would each correspond to one or another of the selected pictures. If the laboratory possesses an opaque projector, the pictures can be thrown on a screen at the front of the lab, so that no reproduction is needed. Items testing the recognition of structure can be readily prepared in a similar way: the teacher records twenty sentences containing, for example, verbs in the present, the imperfect and the conditional. An overhead transparency projected on the screen indicates to the student that A = present, B = imperfect, and C = conditional. Such tests provide valid measures of diverse aspects of the listening comprehension skill and lend themselves to rather rapid preparation and fast scoring.

It is the speaking tests which present the thorniest problem to the language teacher. Forty years ago it was felt that the development of standard speaking tests was an unattainable objective. Since the Second World War, however, the availability of recording equipment and the establishment of reliable scoring techniques have made such tests a reality. All students hear the same recorded stimulus over their headsets and record their responses on individual tapes. These student tapes are then evaluated against a clearly defined criterion: for example, in sentence 1 the scorer listens only for the production of the sound /e/, whereas in sentence 30 he pays attention only to the word order. The individual teacher can prepare speaking tests on the model of the standard tests, adapting the content to the specific unit or units under instruction, and develop quite a reliable scoring system. If the school language laboratory contains recording facilities, the speaking test may be administered to the class as a group in a matter of ten to fifteen minutes. Thus in theory the problems have been solved.

But in practice, however, the problems have just begun. If the laboratory is an older installation, the student tapes will have recorded both the stimulus on the master tape and the student's response. For a ten-minute test, then, the teacher will have a ten-minute tape for each student. If teacher A has four sections to which he has administered speaking tests during a given week, he will find himself with about 120 tapes to correct. The listening time itself is 1,200 minutes, or twenty hours; to this must be added the additional time involved in placing each tape on the machine, starting it, rewinding it at the end of the test, and placing it in its box. For 120 tapes, this would add about four additional hours of scoring time. (If cartridges are used, this manipulation time would be cut to about half an hour.) In laboratories where student assistants are available, all the student tapes could be spliced together on one reel, but this is a rather time-consuming enterprise.

Fortunately, many laboratories have a switch at the console which permits the teacher to start and stop all recording decks at will. With such a system the teacher plays the stimulus on the master tape and then starts the student decks only to record the responses. For a ten-minute test, therefore, each student produces a three- or four-minute tape. Correcting 120 four-minute tapes entails eight hours of playing time plus the manipulation of the individual tapes or cartridges. For the busy classroom teacher, ten hours of correction time is already a frightful proposition, and to this must be added the frustration caused by the occasional tape which was not properly recorded and cannot be scored. It is not surprising, therefore, that most language teachers try to avoid formal speaking tests and that those who undertake the project do so only once a semester.

Language teachers recognize, however, that if the development of the speaking skill is a major objective of the course, means must be instituted to measure students' performance in that area. The following four techniques are widely used, either singly or in combination:

1. Classroom grading: the teacher regularly scores recitations of prepared dialogues, oral drills and other oral activities.
2. Laboratory grading: The teacher monitors students' performances in the laboratory and assigns two or three scores per student per laboratory session (see Stack, 1966).
3. Interview tests: While the rest of the class is engaged in some self-directed activity (usually written exercises) the teacher calls each student individually for a brief test which may include reading aloud, questions and answers, and so on; given the size of the average class, such testing often takes two or three days.
4. Tape-recorder test: While the rest of the class is otherwise occupied, individual students are called up to the teacher's desk to record their names and a brief one-minute speech sample (prepared passage or dialogue, a selection to be read aloud, selected drills); the teacher later corrects the continuous thirty-minute tape.

In scoring quizzes of types 1 and 2, the teacher listens for one or two features per sentence. On subsequent days, other features are evaluated. Although performance on one day does not provide a reliable estimate of a student's ability, the cumulative average of such scores over the quarter or the semester does furnish results in which the teacher may have confidence. It should be added that although the teacher will be hearing different utterances from each student, he should nonetheless be evaluating each sentence for identical features. For tests of types 3 and 4, the teacher would prepare a set of mimeographed scoring sheets; then as each student comes in, or as the teacher listens to each recording, he enters the student's name at the top of the sheet and scores the various features marked on the sheet. After having listened to all the tests, the teacher adds up the score for each student.

Formative evaluation

Formative evaluation has a critical role to play in the teaching and learning of a second language.

The role of formative evaluation

The creative application of formative evaluation techniques may lead the way to resolving two pressing problems in the area of foreign languages: the high attrition rate in foreign-language enrollments and the problem of the underachiever.

The cumulative nature of second-language learning In the first few years of instruction, learning a second language is a cumulative process. The material presented in one unit becomes the foundation of the following unit: the vocabulary and structures contained in the first-year course are basic to the second-year course. The student who fails to master the material in one lesson will have difficulty with the next lesson, and unless help is forthcoming that student will soon drop out of the language course altogether. In languages there is no hope that the new unit will offer the student a "second chance" (as would be the case in English literature, for example, where a student who had difficulty with poetry might still expect to do better with short stories). Mastery is the requisite for success. Formative evaluation will provide a means of regulating which students are ready to proceed from one lesson to the next.

In the case of foreign languages it might even be postulated that a grade of A or B should be required of students going into a subsequent year of study. Pimsleur, Sundland, and McIntyre (1966) found that of all the subjects in the secondary school curriculum, foreign languages was the most sequential. In their study of students in a midwestern city, they found that of all the students who received an A, B, or C in their first year of French or Spanish, close to 60 percent received a *lower* grade the second year. This means that over half the students who earned a C the first year received a D or E the next year. One third of the first-year D students failed the second-year course. Almost no student improved his grade the second year. It is evident that students must learn for mastery if they are to learn at all.

The underachiever and language aptitude The underachiever is the student whose grades in foreign languages are one or more points below his general grade-point average. In their study on underachievement, Pimsleur et al. (1966) noted that the underachiever often had difficulty with the auditory aspect of language learning. (This auditory factor is measured in all three of the available language aptitude tests: the Carroll-Sapon Modern Language Aptitude Test, or MLAT; the Pimsleur Language Aptitude Battery; and the Carroll-Sapon Elementary Modern Language Aptitude Test, or EMLAT.) Another factor in language learning, a factor which the above tests also measure, is grammatical sensitivity.

Let us assume that a school system has decided to implement the learning for mastery strategy described in Chap. 3. Language aptitude tests might be administered for diagnostic purposes to all beginning language students; students who will probably need more help with the listening and speaking skills may be grouped in one class, while students who will probably have difficulty with grammar would be placed in another section. However, homogeneous grouping is not of itself sufficient to guarantee mastery. Frequent formative evaluation will let both the teachers and the students know when the material of a given unit has been assimilated by the class. The creative use of formative tests will be an important factor in reducing to zero the correlation between scores on language aptitude tests and measures of achievement.

Practical considerations The first practical consideration is the definition of "mastery level." Bloom suggests accuracy scores of 80 to 85 percent. With respect to foreign languages, this level must be determined empirically. Given the tight construction and sequential nature of elementary language programs, it is conceivable that the minimum acceptable passing score will have to be set at 90 percent rather than 80 percent. The student who has failed to master one-fifth (20 percent) of the material in one lesson will probably have serious difficulty mastering the next lesson, and it would perhaps be wiser to help him learn the material in the first lesson before letting him go on.

The second practical consideration is one of class management. Let us imagine that the teacher has presented lesson 1, given a formative test, and discovered that two-thirds of the students have passed at a 90-percent accuracy level and that one-third have scored lower. It is possible to let those who have passed move to lesson 2 and to keep those who failed on lesson 1 until they are ready to continue. But if the teacher splits up the class after each mastery test, he will soon have many groups working at different levels. In a subject where speaking and listening practice and actual oral communication are essential to the course, as they are in foreign-language courses, the existence of several groups, each on a different lesson, makes the attainment of the aural-oral objectives rather difficult. A solution I have suggested (Valette, 1968a) is the development of teaching materials based on a core program which all students will master. Those who assimilate the material in a given lesson ahead of the others will do individualized work in reading and listening comprehension. At any given time, however, all students will be working on the same lesson so that all can participate in oral work and conversation practice. Thus, each student will be working at his own level and yet the class as a whole can enjoy the experience of using the language teacher as a means of communication.

Tables of specifications for formative evaluation

In Chap. 6 a general model for a unit specifications table was presented (see pages 120 to 123). This model contains six behaviors:

Knowledge of terms
Knowledge of facts
Knowledge of rules and principles
Skill in using processes and procedures
Ability to make translations
Ability to make applications

In considering these categories, the language teacher would not readily see how they might be applied to language learning. Some teachers might notice the words "rules" and "translations" and feel such a table represented a return to the methods and procedures of forty years ago. We have found it advisable to label these behaviors with terms that the language teacher will readily understand. These appear as the column headings in Table 22-2, Table of Specifications for Formative Evaluation in Second-language Instruction.

It is often necessary to prepare the table for a unit in two parts: one for the spoken language and one for the written. In foreign languages in the elementary school (FLES) programs, only the spoken language is taught at first, so the teacher would have no need for the written-language section. In some audiolingual programs, students are learning one lesson aurally and are learning to write material from a previous lesson: here the

TABLE 22-2 TABLE SPECIFICATION FOR FORMATIVE EVALUATION IN SECOND-LANGUAGE INSTRUCTION

	A *Knowledge of vocabulary and phonology*	B *Knowledge of morphology*	C *Knowledge of syntax and phonological patterns*	D *Skill in manipulating dialogues and drills*	E *Listening and reading comprehension*	F *Speaking and writing abilities*
1.0 Spoken language						
2.0 Written language						

double table is a necessity. In other programs, students are introduced to spoken and written forms in the same unit; here the double table is helpful in showing the teacher which items are tested with respect to the written language and which are tested by means of the spoken language.

The following brief explanations will help clarify the behaviors mentioned in Table 22-2.

Knowledge of vocabulary and phonology (A) This category includes knowledge of individual words and idioms, including aspects of words such as the gender of nouns and the principal parts of verbs. Knowledge of phonology includes knowing the sounds of the foreign language. Also included in this category are two psychomotor behaviors: the ability to differentiate between English sounds and those of the foreign language, and the ability to discriminate among the phonemes (i.e., those sounds which bear meaning) of the new language.

Knowledge of morphology (B) This category includes knowledge of the declensions of nouns, the forms of adjectives, and the conjugations of verbs. It also includes knowledge of function words.

Knowledge of syntax and phonological patterns (C) This category includes knowledge of word order and sentence structure, as well as patterns of intonation, stress, rhythm, etc. Also included here is knowledge of the morphophonemic (or Sandhi) variations, such as liaison patterns, etc.

Skill in manipulating dialogues and drills (D) This category includes classroom activities typical of audiolingual programs and many of the modified audiolingual programs—recitation of dialogues, acting out of directed dialogues, and the manipulation of a variety of pattern drills. (Often the assimilation of these skills precedes the actual presentation of vocabulary, morphology, and syntax; in most programs, actually, only a minimum of grammar is described in the text.) The simplest of these skills is the memorization of a dialogue: the teacher must realize that the student has not "learned" or mastered the material in the dialogue until he can manipulate the new words and forms fluently in drills and free exercises.

Listening and reading comprehension (E) The ability to understand what is written or said, at the surface level of meaning, is essential to the communication process. In this level of behavior, the student understands passages which are recombinations of learned vocabulary, morphology, and syntax. Occasionally he can infer the meanings of unfamiliar words either from the context or from their resemblance to known words (English or foreign). Many teachers fail to develop behaviors in this category and limit their objectives to the lower categories. If language learning is to constitute a meaningful experience for the student, however, he must experience the satisfaction of understanding material he has never heard or read before. Note that the term "comprehension" is preferred to "translation." Translation into English is one type of comprehension check, but many teachers prefer using other means of checking whether the student has understood the passage he has heard or read. Furthermore, the term "translation" is ambiguous. Translation into English is a comprehension check and consequently a behavior in category *E*; translation into the foreign language is an example of application, category *F*, for here English is a stimulus and the student must apply previous knowledge to formulate his response.

Speaking and writing abilities (F) Whereas listening and reading represent passive behaviors on the part of the student, speaking and writing allow him to express his own ideas actively in the foreign language. At the early levels this activity takes the form of guided speaking or guided writing; some programs limit the use of the language to drills and dialogues and do not attempt to reach this level of behavior until the second or third year of instruction. (Newer programs will encourage the student to speak and write much earlier, because psychologists feel that the frustration built up by the denial of experimentation with the second language is more harmful to motivation than the possibility of creating bad "language habits" by making mistakes; see Rivers, 1964). Speaking and writing in this category are not to be confused with the directed speaking and writing drills which constitute category *D*. Indirect methods of evaluating speaking and writing ability, however, often resemble drills in form in that they require the student to apply his knowledge and skills in a new context, such as filling in blanks or transforming sentences *without* the guide of a model.

Kinesics and culture play a limited role in current language programs. At present, most "cultural" material takes the form of knowledge of facts (category *A*), and kinesics appears in conjunction with dialogues and drills (category *D*).

The Table of Specifications for Formative Evaluation in Second-language Instruction is most applicable to the first three or four levels of learning. As such it includes only a portion of the cells of Table 22-1. The relationship between Table 22-2 and the general Table of Specifications for Objectives in Second-language Instruction may be seen below:

Categories *A*, *B*, and *C* (knowledge of vocabulary, morphology, and syntax): cells *A*-1.0 to *D*-1.0 and *A*-2.0 to *D*-2.0
Category *D* (skill in manipulating drills): cells *E*-1.0, *F*-1.0, *E*-2.0, and *F*-2.0
Category *E* (listening and reading comprehension): cells *G*-1.0 and *G*-2.0
Category *F* (speaking and writing): cells *H*-1.0 and *H*-2.0

Sample units of learning

The unit of learning, with regard to a second language, coincides with the unit or chapter of the textbook. It is, of course, possible to envisage a unit on French geography or on the Spanish Golden Age, but such "units" are supplementary and must be worked around or fitted into the basic language lesson. For the language teacher, then, the unit of learning is defined by the textbook or program utilized in his school system. The specific objectives of the unit, however, are determined by the individual teacher: will he stress the learning of dialogues and the manipulation of pattern drills, or will he aim for the ability to understand and produce original speech? Will he stress the spoken language or the written language? Will he stress accurate pronunciation, or will he place more emphasis on fluency of expression? Will he stress knowledge of vocabulary and grammar or the abilities to speak and write? What kind of balance will he achieve?

The FLES unit In the first year of language instruction at the elementary school level, the students come into contact only with the spoken language. The course, whether presented by television, on film, or by a live teacher, does provide an instructor's manual; but the student text, if one exists, contains simply pictures and other visual representations.

As a sample unit, let us consider unit 5 of the McGraw-Hill series "Let's Speak French." In the teacher's text, the objectives for the unit are listed as follows:

1. To increase the student's vocabulary
2. To teach the singular and third-person-plural form of the verbs in *-er* (*dessiner, regarder, parler, fumer*) [to draw, to look at, to speak, to smoke]
3. To teach the personal pronouns *ils, elles* [they]
4. To teach understanding of the imperative singular of verbs in *-er*
5. To teach understanding of the interrogative expression *qu'est-ce que . . . ?* [what . . . ?]

(Okin & Schmitt, 1966, p. 65)

The unit as it is described in the teacher's guide contains a cognitive component and a psychomotor (or skills) component. In the cognitive domain, the student is taught to recognize and understand certain vocabulary items and certain structural forms when he hears them in context. Although he is not expected to know how certain structural phenomena work, he is to use these structures (in this case, certain verb forms in the present and the subject pronouns *ils* and *elles*) accurately in controlled speaking drills. The content of this unit is schematically presented in Table 22-3, Table of Specifications for a FLES Unit.

The teacher of the FLES course is working within rigorously defined constraints. Only the foreign language is to be used in the classroom, and the choice of vocabulary and structure is strictly limited. At the same time, the objectives are also restricted, for the aim of the FLES course is to bring the student into contact only with material he can thoroughly master. The solidity of the student's language foundation, rather than its breadth, determines the effectiveness of the FLES course. It is essential, therefore, that the students master the material in each unit at a high level of accuracy.

In the FLES course, the teacher assesses the student's performance at each step in the unit. In teaching vocabulary, the teacher first checks whether the student can understand the new words in a minimal context; for example, behavior *A*: *Voilà le salon!* [There is the living room]; *Voici la famille*! [Here is the family]. Then the new words are presented in longer sentences; e.g., behavior *B*: *La famille est dans le salon* [The family is in the living room]. Similarly, the new grammatical forms are first introduced in a minimal context—e.g., behavior *B*: *Je fume* [I am smoking], *Il fume* [He is smoking]—and then in longer sentences; e.g., behavior *E*: *Papa fume sa pipe* [Daddy is smoking his pipe]. In presenting drills (behavior *D*), the teacher first insists on the correct imitation of isolated sentences before having the students memorize and perform a dialogue. Students also practice using the new words and new forms by doing simple question-answer drills—e.g., Teacher: *Qu'est-ce que c'est?* [*pointing to a picture*]; Student: *C'est le salon* [What is this? It's the living room]. When the students demonstrate mastery of the new material in the unit, the teacher reintroduces vocabulary and forms from previous units into drills (behavior *D*) and into longer listening-comprehension segments (behavior *E*).

The teaching-learning process in the FLES program may be thought of as comprising four steps:

1. Presenting new material (vocabulary and morphology) in minimal context: behaviors *A* and *B*; in later lessons this includes the presentation of syntax: behavior *C*
2. Drilling material in minimal context (repetition and simple questions and answers): behavior *D*
3. Presenting the new material in the extended context of other material in the unit and drilling the material in longer sentences: behaviors *E* and *D*
4. Presenting the new material in the context of the present unit plus all previous units and drilling the material in this broad context: behaviors *E* and *D*

At this level, students usually do not freely express their own ideas but use the language only within the context prescribed by the teacher. Behavior *F* (speaking and writing) is introduced in the later years of the FLES sequence.

The secondary school unit: level 1 Elementary and intermediate language courses at the secondary school level are similar to those of the FLES program in their sequential presentation of linguistic material for mastery. The units are more intensive in presentation and broader in scope and include a larger vocabulary and more grammar. Moreover, most secondary school courses introduce the written language together with the spoken language.

As a sample unit, we have selected lesson 11 of the revised edition of *French 1*, by O'Brien, Lafrance, Brachfeld, and Churchill (1965). This is a middle-of-the-road text which combines features of the audiolingual approach and the cognitive code-learning (or traditional) approach. English is used sparingly to reinforce comprehension and to summarize grammatical points. The lesson includes the following material:

Reading: *Ma Journée* [My Day]
Grammar: Reflexive verbs; *n'est-ce pas?* [Isn't it? aren't we? etc.]; irregular verb: *vouloir* [to want]
Dialogue: *Question de goûts* [A Question of Taste]
Cultural reading: *L'écolier français* [The French Schoolboy]
Punctuation marks in French
Phonology: some final consonants, /e/ and /ɛ/; unstable e

(O'Brien et al., 1965, xi.)

TABLE 22-3 TABLE OF SPECIFICATIONS FOR A FLES UNIT

	A Knowledge of vocabulary	B Knowledge of morphology	C Knowledge of syntax and phonological patterns	D Skill in manipulating dialogues and drills	E Listening comprehension	F Speaking ability
1.0 Spoken language		ils, elles		( )		
	dessiner regarder parler fumer	present tense (1, 2, 3 sing., 3 plural)		( )		
		imperative sing.		( )		
	qu'est-ce que. . .			( )		
	la famille le salon la pipe la télévision la fille le chat le garçon le chien le téléphone le drapeau la photo			( )		

The core of the lesson consists of the first reading (where new vocabulary is introduced) and the grammar section. Mastery of this core is a requisite for continuing to lesson 12. Most teachers will expand this core to include the knowledge of French punctuation marks (for these terms will be used in future dictation exercises) and the practical mastery of the elements of pronunciation. The dialogue may be used for listening comprehension or may be memorized and presented by the students; any new vocabulary occurring in this dialogue is not, however, considered part of the core material. The cultural reading is optional. (One possible utilization of the lesson content is the following: The teacher presents the reading, the grammar, and the punctuation marks as core material. The pronunciation section is drilled by the class, but "knowledge" of the content is not required. After the first formative test is given, those receiving passing scores work on the dialogue and the cultural reading passage; those who fail to demonstrate mastery focus their attention on the core vocabulary and grammar.)

The structural breakdown of the basic lesson material is presented in Table 22-4, Table of Specifications for a Secondary School Unit in Second-language Instruction.

In this program, listening, speaking, reading, and writing receive equal stress after the first ten lessons. Consequently, the specifications table for lesson 11 is in two parts: the teacher must test behaviors by means of both the spoken language and the written language. This dual testing is particularly important in French, where the "fit" between the way the language is written and the way it is spoken is not always tight (e.g., the irregular verb *vouloir* has four spoken forms and five written forms in the present indicative). The teaching-learning process in the secondary program comprises the same four steps as those for the FLES program, but the presentation takes place by means of both the spoken and the printed word. The reentry of previously learned material (step 4) is selective, however, and the teacher must prepare such materials himself; perhaps with lesson 11 he will bring in all the vocabulary of lessons 5, 8, and 10. Many teachers will want to add a fifth step, as follows:

5. Encouraging the student to use the vocabulary and structures he has mastered in order to express his own ideas: behavior *F*

Illustrative testing procedures

Many of the item types described with respect to summative evaluation may also be used for formative evaluation. Often the teacher will use informal techniques to evaluate the students' progress as the teaching of the unit progresses. Before having the students pronounce a new word or phrase, the teacher first makes certain that they understand the meaning of that word or sentence (behaviors *A* and *B*). In the teaching of a second-language unit, the teacher might consider giving several formative tests which would correspond to the steps described above. Here we shall present a sequence of items testing a group of vocabulary items across the various behaviors shown in Table 22-3.

The FLES unit

A-1.0 Knowledge of vocabulary

49. The teacher prepares pictures of a telephone, a flag, a television set, a pipe, a living room, a girl, a boy, a dog, a cat. He points to each of the pictures in turn.
    The teacher asks: "Qu'est-ce que c'est?" [What is this?]
    The student replies: "C'est un téléphone." "C'est un drapeau." Etc. [It's a telephone. It's a flag. Etc.]

B-1.0 Knowledge of morphology

50. The teacher uses the same pictures as in the above item, and again points to them in turn.
    The teacher asks: "Qu'est-ce que tu dessines?" [What are you drawing?]
    The student replies: "Je dessine un chat." "Je dessine un chien." Etc. [I am drawing a cat. I am drawing a dog. Etc.]

C-1.0 Knowledge of syntax and phonological patterns

51. The teacher asks: "Robert, demande à Christine si elle dessine." [Robert, ask Christine if she is drawing.]
    Robert answers: "Christine, est-ce que tu dessines?" [Christine, are you drawing?]

TABLE 22-4 TABLE OF SPECIFICATIONS FOR A SECONDARY SCHOOL UNIT IN SECOND-LANGUAGE INSTRUCTION

	A *Knowledge of vocabulary and phonology*	B *Knowledge of morphology*	C *Knowledge of syntax and phonological patterns*	D *Skill in manipulating dialogues and drills*	E *Listening and reading comprehension*	F *Speaking and writing abilities*
2.0 Written language	s'amuser se coucher se laver se lever s'habiller	( )	( )	( )		
	le matin le soir l'après-midi la journée		time of day ( )	( )		
	à quelle heure?		(time (hours))	( )		
	n'est-ce pas?			( )		
	vouloir	(pres. tense)	( )			
	les céréales le goûter le jus de fruit l'oeuf le pain grillé le petit déjeuner les cours d'anglais les devoirs l'histoire les mathématiques le film le journal la télévision la vedette			( )		
	après dehors quand quelquefois souvent					
1.0 Spoken language	/e/ /ɛ/ /ə/			( )		
	final consonants			( )		
	punctuation marks				( )	
4.0 Culture	(School day in France)					

D-1.0 Skill in manipulating dialogues and drills

52. The teacher says: "Marie dessine un chat. Pierre. Chien." [Marie is drawing a cat. Pierre. Dog.]
A student answers: "Pierre dessine un chien." [Pierre is drawing a dog.]
The teacher says: "Monique. Drapeau." [Monica. Flag.]
Another student answers: "Monique dessine un drapeau." [Monica is drawing a flag.]

E-1.0 Listening comprehension

53. The teacher prepares a set of ten numbered pictures. Then the teacher reads ten sentences. Students mark whether sentence 1 describes picture 1 correctly.
(1) "Marie dessine un garçon." [Marie is drawing a boy.]
(2) "La fille regarde la télévision." [The girl is watching television.]

F-1.0 Speaking ability (optional)

54. The teacher prepares a picture showing a family in the living room. He asks general questions to elicit responses, and from those responses throws out more questions to the students. (Often the suggested response is contained in the question, especially for the slower students.) For the first question, he points to the picture as a whole.
The teacher asks: "Qu'est-ce que c'est?" [What is this?]
A student answers: "C'est un salon." [It's a living room.]
The teacher asks: "Qui est dans le salon?" [Who is in the living room?]
Another student answers: "La famille est dans le salon." [The family is in the living room.]
The teacher asks: "Est-ce que les enfants dessinent? ou est-ce qu'ils regardent la télévision?" [Are the children drawing, or are they watching television?]
A third student answers: "Les enfants regardent la télévision." [The children are watching television.]

At the FLES level, much of the testing takes the form of group testing. A game presentation (such as a spelldown) may be used in evaluating the three knowledge behaviors and the skill in handling drills. Dialogues, if assigned, may be acted out by individual groups; the teacher grades students on their pronunciation and fluency. The listening-comprehension objective lends itself to a more formal pencil and paper test. Often the speaking objective (behavior *F*) is not formally evaluated, but is introduced as a game or a reward for having mastered the material: at this point the students can use their imagination (within the limitations of their vocabulary) in answering the questions.

The secondary school unit The secondary unit contains a series of oral-aural items similar to those suggested for the FLES unit. With junior high and high school students, all the knowledge items need not be picture-oriented. The student's "state of expectancy" with respect to listening might be tested with an item like the following one:

B-1.0 Knowledge of morphology

55. You will hear a series of sentences. Some will contain words you do not know. Listen carefully, however, and decide whether the verb in the sentence is reflexive or not. If the verb is reflexive, mark "R"; if the verb is not reflexive, mark "NR."

EXAMPLE: "Ils se regardent," [They are looking at each other.]
(Response: Reflexive.)
Je préfère le football. [I prefer football.]
(Response: Not reflexive.)
Elle me comprend. [She understands me.]
(Response: Not reflexive.)

(1) Pierre s'habille. [Pierre is getting dressed.]
(2) Je lave la chemise. [I am washing the shirt.]
(3) Il se lave le matin. [He washes in the morning.]
(Responses: (1) R, (2) NR, (3) R.)

The following items constitute a testing series to ascertain whether the student has mastered the new vocabulary and structure (by means of reading and writing) across the six behaviors specified in Table 22-4.

B-2.0 Knowledge of vocabulary

56. Matching.

Sentences	Line drawings
(1) Je m'amuse.	a. A person going downstairs.
(2) Je me couche.	b. A person reading.
(3) Je me lave.	c. A person getting into bed.

(4) Je lis. d. A person getting up.
(5) Je me lève. e. A person laughing and having a good time.
(6) Je descends. f. A person washing up.
g. A person eating breakfast.
h. A person playing cards.

(Responses: (1) e, (2) c, (3) f, (4) b, (5) d, (6) a)

B-2.0 Knowledge of morphology

57. *Completion*
   (1) Elle ______ couche. [She is going to bed.]
   (2) Vous ______ lavez. [You are washing up.]
   (3) Je ______ lève. [I am getting up.]
   (4) Nous ______ amusons. [We are having fun.]
   (5) Ils ______ habillent. [They are getting dressed.]

(Responses: (1) se, (2) vous, (3) me, (4) nous, (5) s')

C-2.0 Knowledge of syntax and phonological patterns

58. Change the following sentences to the interrogative form:
   (1) Tu t'habilles. [You are getting dressed.]
   (2) Vous vous amusez. [You are having fun.]
   (3) Elles se couchent. [They are going to bed.]
   (4) Je me lave. [I am getting washed.]

(Responses: (1) T'habilles-tu? (2) Vous amusez-vous? (3) Se couchent-elles? (4) Est-ce que je me lave?)

D-2.0 Skill in manipulating dialogues and drills

59. Answer the following questions:
   (1) A quelle heure te couches-tu? (3 h.) [When do you go to bed?]
   (2) A quelle heure descends-tu? (8 h.) [When do you go downstairs?]
   (3) A quelle heure te lèves-tu? (7 h.) [When do you get up?]
   (4) A quelle heure te laves-tu? (5 h.) [When do you wash up?]

(Responses: (1) Je me couche à trois heures. (2) Je descends à huit heures. (3) Je me lève à sept heures. (4) Je me lave à cinq heures.)

E-2.0 Reading comprehension

60. The teacher prepares a reading text recombining the material in the lesson, or the teacher selects a text at the appropriate level from another book, glossing unknown vocabulary items. Comprehension may be checked by multiple-choice completion questions, true-false statements, pictures, etc. See item 25, above.

F-2.0 Writing ability

61. Lightning translation: The teacher dictates ten sentences in English which incorporate the vocabulary and structure of the lesson. After reading the first sentence, the teacher waits for all students to write down the French equivalent. At the end of the test, the ten sentences are reread rather quickly and the papers are collected.

There is a lack of agreement among language teachers with respect to the role of English in the teaching and testing of foreign languages. If a teacher wishes to minimize reference to English writing samples may be elicited by means of pictures, dehydrated sentences, and the like.

Commercial tests in foreign languages

Commercial language tests are of three types: nonstandardized tests which accompany teaching materials, secure tests whose forms change with each administration and whose results are used for selection purposes, and standardized tests which are available for local administration.

Tests which accompany teaching materials

Over half of the commercial second-language materials contain testing programs which the schools may or may not buy. Some of these programs test proficiency across the four language skills; others emphasize reading comprehension. If the teacher proposes to use the commercial tests which are marketed by the publisher, he should carefully analyze the content of those tests to determine whether they measure the behaviors and objectives he has set for his class.

Secure competitive tests

In the category of secure and constantly evolving tests, we include the College Entrance Examination Board Achievement Tests, the New York State Regents Examinations, the Advanced Placement Examinations, and (at a higher level) the Graduate Record Examinations. The most influential of these examinations are the College Board tests: in the new composite test, students take a forty-minute achievement test on the written language (knowledge of vocabulary, application of grammar, reading comprehension) consisting of multiple-choice questions followed by a twenty-minute listening-comprehension test.

Commercial standard tests

There are four series of commercial standard tests intended for local administration. None of the tests contains English except in the instructions.

1. The MLA Proficiency Tests for Teachers and Advanced Students (Educational Testing Service, 1961) exist for five languages (French, German, Italian, Russian, and Spanish) and consist of seven subtests grouped in two batteries: Battery A, Listening, Speaking, Reading, and Writing; Battery B, Culture and Civilization, Applied Linguistics, and Professional Preparation. Although one form of this battery is still secure, the first two forms are now available for purchase as forms HA and HB of the MLA Cooperative Foreign Language Tests. The scores on these tests are required in some states for teacher certification. Battery B contains English.
2. The Common Concepts Foreign Language Test (California Test Bureau, 1962) exists in two forms for four languages (English, French, German, and Spanish). It is a level-1 listening-comprehension test consisting of eighty statements for each of which the student must select the most appropriate among four pictures.
3. The MLA Cooperative Foreign Language Tests (Educational Testing Service, 1963) exist for five languages (French, German, Italian, Russian, and Spanish), with two forms at each of two levels (approximately levels 2 and 4) in the four skills of listening, speaking, reading, and writing.
4. The Pimsleur Language Proficiency Tests (Harcourt, Brace & World, 1967) exist in French, German, and Spanish, with one form at each of two levels (the end of level 1 and the end of level 2) in the four skills of listening, speaking, reading, and writing.

Problems with respect to commercial tests

Language itself is such a complex phenomenon, and second-language learning entails such a variety of factors, that the matter of test validity—specifically, content validity—becomes a crucial problem. Language tests have existed for centuries and have all measured some feature of second-language acquisition, but the real question to be asked concerning both the older tests and the newer tests, both the standard tests and the classroom tests, is, What does this test actually measure?

Use of the language or knowledge about the language The current modern-language tests evaluate the student's ability to use the language and to apply his knowledge of the language in producing acceptable sentences and paragraphs. Only the Latin tests regularly include items "about" the language (e.g., "Which of the above sentences contains an ablative absolute?"). This problem of emphasis is one over which the teachers of classical languages have not yet come to agreement.

The vocabulary bias Knowledge of vocabulary is obviously an important component in second-language learning. Without a rudimentary vocabulary, no student is able to acquire the structure of the language. It is highly questionable, however, whether the size of a student's vocabulary may be directly equated with his second-language proficiency. But since size of vocabulary is relatively easy to measure, and since vocabulary items generally perform very well statistically, the current standard tests contain an excessively high proportion of items which the candidate can answer correctly only if he knows the meaning of one or two key words. Knowledge of structure and more general comprehension of structure is measured in a much smaller percentage of the items. Consequently, the current language tests present a heavy vocabulary bias, which favors those students taking courses in which vocabulary acquisition is stressed. Although the extent of this vocabulary bias remains to be established, the validity of current standard tests as overall measures of language proficiency must be verified.

The logic bias The ability to think logically and draw accurate inferences constitutes one of the components of "reading comprehension" and "listening comprehension." However, the presence of inference questions in elementary language tests raises the following question: Did the student select the wrong answer because he misunderstood the passage or because he drew the wrong conclusion even though he grasped the manifest content of the passage? In an inference item the student may be presented with a recorded conversation and then be asked to identify the people who are speaking. At the elementary level it would seem that the teacher would need to know, first, whether the student understood the remarks which were exchanged in the conversation, and, second, whether the student could identify the speakers. It is possible that standard tests with a high percentage of inference items discriminate against those junior high school students who have difficulty drawing such inferences even in their native language.

Conclusion

As we look at the field of second-language testing, we see several areas open to further experimentation and investigation.

Criterion-referenced language tests For almost ten years language teachers have stated the need for a measurement instrument whereby the present common college-entrance requirement of two years of high school foreign language could be expressed in terms of a specific level of proficiency. In French, for example, such a test might be built on *Le Français fondamental, premier degré.*[6] A general battery of criterion-referenced tests for beginning and intermediate students should also be developed: such tests would be rather similar to formative classroom tests in that they would perform a diagnostic function, but the item content would stress only knowledge of vocabulary, morphology, and structure. A subsequent set of related tests might measure levels of comprehension; e.g., given a group of students who have mastered 500 vocabulary items and specific grammatical structures, how many can understand conversations based on this content when the speakers talk rapidly? When the speakers talk at normal speed? When the speakers enunciate carefully? A tentative model for a criterion-referenced battery of foreign-language tests is described in Valette (1968b).

Communicative competence We must develop tests which go beyond the surface structure of the language or the surface meaning of a text and delve into deep structure and implicit meaning. Such tests are needed to assess the proficiency of more advanced students. At the lower levels we must develop scoring systems which allow us to distinguish between errors which impair communication ("serious" errors) and errors which do not ("minor" errors).

Overall proficiency We must investigate the reliability and validity of indirect measures of overall language proficiency, such as those illustrated in items 38 to 43. Such tests would be especially useful in placing advanced students and in evaluating the capabilities of students who want to study abroad. (Such tests are also being developed by universities who need to determine whether foreign students possess a command of English sufficient to allow them to profit from study in the United States.)

Vocabulary The role of vocabulary in language proficiency must be investigated. The items appearing in current commercial tests must be studied to determine the extent of their vocabulary bias. This is essential if we continue to use these tests in research projects designed to evaluate the relative merits of different methods

[6] This is a listing of basic grammatical patterns and a core vocabulary of about 1,300 words established by the French Ministry of Education.

of instruction, different language laboratory systems, etc.

Culture Members of the profession must determine what should be the cultural goals of foreign-language instruction. Only then can appropriate teaching materials and tests be developed.

Affective aims Language teachers have long spoken of the great variety of affective benefits of foreign-language instruction. The existence or nonexistence of these benefits remains to be empirically established; but before this can be done, we must design appropriate tests in the affective domain.

Formative evaluation Techniques of formative evaluation must be developed in foreign languages, and such formative tests must be incorporated into the language courses of the future. These courses must also provide sufficient materials to allow the faster students to increase their levels of listening and reading comprehension and simultaneously to provide the slower students with varied presentations of core material. The emphasis in forthcoming language programs must be placed on mastery learning, for only in this way can we hope to reduce the problems of underachievement and attrition now facing teachers of foreign languages.

REFERENCES

Banathy, B., et al. *The Common Concepts Foreign Language Test.* Monterey, Calif.: California Test Bureau, 1962.

Belasco, S. The plateau; or the case for comprehension: the "concept" approach. *Modern Language Journal,* 1967, **51,** 82–88.

Bolinger, D. The theorist and the language teacher. *Foreign Language Annals,* 1968, **2,** 30–41.

Brière, E. J. Phonological testing reconsidered. *Language Learning,* 1967, **17,** 163–171.

Carroll, J. B. The contributions of psychological theory and educational research to the teaching of foreign languages. *Modern Language Journal,* 1965, **49,** 273–281.

Carroll, J. B., & Sapon, S. *Modern Language Aptitude Test.* New York: Psychological Corporation, 1958, 1959.

Carroll, J. B., & Sapon, S. *Elementary Modern Language Aptitude Test.* New York: Psychological Corporation, 1967.

Coleman, A. *The teaching of modern foreign languages in the United States.* New York: Macmillan, 1931.

Dale, J. B., & Dale, M. L. *Cours élémentaire de Français,* 2d ed. Boston: D. C. Heath, 1956.

FL program policy. *PMLA,* September, 1956, **71,** no. 4, pt. 2, xiii.

Green, J. R. *A gesture inventory for the teaching of Spanish.* Philadelphia: Chilton, 1968.

Hall, E. T. *The silent language.* Garden City, N.Y.: Doubleday, 1959.

Jakobovits, L. A. *Foreign language learning, a psycholinguistic analysis of the issues.* Rowley, Mass.: Newbury House, 1970.

Lado, R. *Language testing.* New York: McGraw-Hill, 1961.

Marty, F. *Teaching French.* Roanoke, Va.: Audio-Visual Publications, 1968.

Mauger, G. *Langue et Civilisation Françaises.* Paris: Hachette, 1953.

Modern Language Association. *The MLA Proficiency Tests for Teachers and Advanced Students.* Princeton: ETS, 1961.

Modern Language Association. *The MLA Cooperative Foreign Language Tests.* Princeton: ETS, 1963.

Newmark, M. *Twentieth century modern language teaching.* New York: Philosophical Library, 1948.

Nostrand, H. L. Levels of sociocultural understanding for language classes. In H. N. Seelye (Ed.), *A handbook on Latin America for teachers*. Springfield, Ill.: Office of the Superintendent of Public Instruction, 1968, Chapter 4, pp. 19–24.

Okin, J. P.-D., & Schmitt, C. J. *Let's speak French 1: Teacher's guide*. St. Louis: McGraw-Hill, 1966.

O'Brien, K., Lafrance, M., Brachfeld, G., & Churchill, G. *French 1*. Boston: Ginn, 1965.

Pimsleur, P. *Pimsleur Language Aptitude Battery*. New York: Harcourt, Brace & World, 1966.

Pimsleur, P., Sundland, D. M., & McIntyre, R. D. *Underachievement in foreign language learning*. New York: Modern Language Association, 1966.

Rivers, W. *The psychologist and the foreign language teacher*. Chicago: University of Chicago Press, 1964.

Scherer, G. A. C., & Wertheimer, M. *A psycholinguistic experiment in foreign-language teaching*. New York: McGraw-Hill, 1964.

Seelye, H. N. Performance objectives for teaching cultural concepts. *Foreign Language Annals*, 1970, **3**, 566–578.

Smith, P. D., Jr., & Baranyi, H. A. *A comparison study of the effectiveness of the traditional and audiolingual approaches to foreign language instruction utilizing laboratory equipment*. (Final Rep., Proj. No. 7-0133) Washington, D.C.: U.S. Department of Health, Education, and Welfare, Office of Education, Bureau of Research, October, 1968.

Smith, P. D., Jr., & Berger, E. *An assessment of three foreign language teaching strategies utilizing three language laboratory systems*. (Final Rep., Proj. No. 5-0683) Washington, D.C.: U.S. Department of Health, Education, and Welfare, Office of Education, Bureau of Research, January, 1968.

Spolsky, B., Siguard, B., Sako, M., Walker, E., & Aterburn, C. Preliminary studies in the development of techniques for testing overall second language proficiency. In J. A. Upshur & J. Fata (Eds.), Problems in foreign language testing. *Language Learning*, 1968 (Spec. Iss. No. 3), 79–102.

Stack, E. M. *The language laboratory and modern language teaching*. (Rev. ed.) New York: Oxford University Press, 1966.

Valette, R. M. The use of the dictée in the French language classroom. *Modern Language Journal*, 1964, **48**, 431–434.

Valette, R. M. *Modern language testing*. New York: Harcourt, Brace & World, 1967.

Valette, R. M. Testing and motivation. In S. Newell (Ed.), *Dimension: Languages 1968. Proceedings of the Fourth Southern Conference on Language Teaching*. Spartanburg, S.C.: Converse College, 1968. Pp. 65–69. (a)

Valette, R. M. Evaluating oral and written communication: Suggestions for an integrated testing program. In J. A. Upshur & J. Fata (Eds.), Problems in foreign language testing. *Language Learning*, 1968 (Spec. Iss. No. 3), 111–120. (b)

Valette, R. M. *Directions in foreign language testing*. New York: ERIC Clearinghouse on the Teaching of Foreign Languages and of English in Higher Education and the Modern Language Association (1969).

23

Evaluation of Learning in

Industrial Education

THOMAS S. BALDWIN

University of Illinois
Urbana, Illinois

Thomas S. Baldwin received the Bachelor of Science and Master of Arts degrees in Psychology from the University of South Carolina, and the Doctor of Philosophy degree in Industrial Psychology and Measurement from The Ohio State University. He has worked for the federal government and private industry in the areas of test development and validation. He taught industrial education and psychological measurement at North Carolina State University and currently is Associate Professor of Vocational and Technical Education at the University of Illinois. His major research interest is in methodological problems in test development, and he has been actively engaged in research in this area under the sponsorship of the U.S. Office of Education for several years.

Contents

23

Evaluation of Learning in Industrial Education[1]

Objectives

Traditional objectives

It is rather difficult to give a comprehensive list of objectives for industrial education at a general level. Unlike most of the academic disciplines, such as mathematics education, science education, and language education, industrial education is oriented toward bridging the gap between man and his work. Since industrial education is occupation-oriented rather than discipline-oriented, any consideration of this field covers a far more heterogeneous group of educational programs than is found in the discipline-oriented fields.[2]

[1] The breadth of subject matter covered by industrial education precludes any one individual's becoming knowledgeable in all content areas. In writing about the field in general, it is imperative that one rely on the technical expertise of others. The author would like to express his appreciation to Bruce H. Kemelgor, Emory E. Wiseman, and Robert C. Harris for their assistance on the technical subject matter contained in this chapter.

[2] Moreover, although this chapter is titled Evaluation of Learning in Industrial Education, the problems of educational measurement which are discussed are much broader. Since other areas of vocational education encounter essentially the same types of measurement problems as does industrial education, the techniques of assessment discussed herein have applicability to vocational education in general.

Traditionally, industrial education has encompassed education that prepares individuals for employment in the areas of industrial arts, trades, and technologies. With the rapid changes in our technological society, new areas are constantly being added to the responsibility of industrial education.

Further complicating the problem of listing a single set of objectives for all industrial education is the fact that industrial education engages in the preparation of individuals for employment at a wide range of skill levels. One might think, therefore, of the areas encompassed by industrial education in two dimensions, one dimension of which represents the particular occupational area while the other represents the level of training. For example, a student might prepare to earn a living in the field of electronics at the high school level or by undertaking a course of study in a two-year post high school technical institute.

While it is fair to say, then, that the objectives of a broad field of industrial education include the preparation of man to begin and progress in a productive work experience, a meaningful interpretation of the purview of industrial education can be had by examining the coverage of occupations and the changing philosophy that has

TABLE 23-1 TABLE OF GENERAL SPECIFICATIONS FOR OBJECTIVES IN INDUSTRIAL EDUCATION

Explicit ■
Implicit ▨

	BEHAVIORS																		
	Cognitive				Perceptual					Psychomotor					Affective				
	Knowledge	Understanding	Application of knowledge	Application of understanding	Sensation	Figure perception	Symbol perception	Perception of meaning	Perception of performance	Perception	Set	Guided response	Mechanism	Complex response	Receiving	Responding	Valuing	Organization	Value complex
CONTENT	A	B	C	D	E	F	G	H	I	J	K	L	M	N	O	P	Q	R	S
Trade education																			
Auto mechanic	■	■	■	■	■	■	■	■	■	■	■	■	■					▨	▨
Machine shop	■	■	■	■	■	■	■	■	■	■	■	■	■					▨	▨
Welding	■	■	■		■	■	■	■		■	■	■	■					▨	▨
Radio-television repair	■	■	■	■	■	■	■	■		■	■	■	■					▨	▨
Etc.																			
Technical education																			
Electronics	■	■	■	■														▨	▨
Data processing	■	■	■	■														▨	▨
Mechanical technology	■	■	■	■														▨	▨
Etc.																			
General education in industrial arts	■	■	■		■	■	■			■	■	■			■	■	■		

accompanied the increased coverage over relatively recent times.

Until recently much if not most of industrial training was provided outside the system of public educational institutions. A major responsibility for preparing individuals to enter the labor market was assumed by proprietary schools offering training in such areas as business, cosmetology, and the trades. There is presently a trend for large corporations to get into the education "business," often by merging with proprietary schools offering industrial training.

Another major source of industrial training has been the military. In fact, the large number of highly trained workers available to the labor market after World War II did much to focus attention on the need for providing industrial education on a much broader scale than had been true traditionally. Present-day manpower requirements and the demands of a highly technological armed forces often introduce new occupations to society.

While the military and proprietary schools still account for much of the industrial training available in our society, perhaps the best single index to the national sentiment regarding the field of industrial education can be obtained by reviewing some key legislation. The first federal legislation bearing directly on vocational education was the Smith-Hughes Act of 1917, which provided $7 million to the states for vocational education. These funds were allocated to support training in vocational agriculture, trades and industries, and home economics education. In 1946 Congress passed the George-Barden Act, which authorized an additional $29 million to be spent on vocational education. With minor alterations, this act provided for the additional funds to be spent in much the same way as the Smith-Hughes Act. Both acts were essentially aimed at the preparation of individuals for entry into work on the farm or farm home or into a trade or industrial job. The appropriations under these acts and the restrictions regarding expenditures under them remained essentially unchanged until 1957. Programs funded under these acts were to be of less than college level and terminal in nature. Both acts were heavily weighted toward rural areas with major emphasis given to vocational agriculture and home economics. Funds were authorized only for operational, as contrasted with capital, expenditures. The philosophy was that such training should have immediate benefit for the student, and general education to accompany this vocational training was excluded from reimbursement under this act.

Because of the apparent technological superiority of the Russians, as reflected in the 1957 launching of the sputniks, Congress passed in 1958 the National Defense Education Act. With this "external" motivation the United States came to recognize the serious shortage of technical manpower and the inadequacy of existing facilities for training such manpower. Title VIII of the act attempted to alleviate the situation by providing funds for training in occupations necessary for national defense. While this section of the act, entitled Area Vocational Education, was eventually placed in the statutes of Title III as the George-Barden Act, and therefore subject to the restrictions of the earlier act, it does provide recognition of the broader implications of vocational education.

Two further acts, the Area Redevelopment Act of 1961 and Manpower Development and Training Act of 1962, are relevant to vocational education. While both of these acts might be considered remedial in the sense that they are designed to retrain individuals who have inadequate skill levels, they do provide implicit recognition of the importance of vocational education in preparing individuals for the world of work.

A major redirection in vocational education came with the recommendation of a panel of consultants on vocational education appointed by the Secretary of Health, Education, and Welfare at the direction of President John F. Kennedy. Most of the recommendations of this panel were incorporated in the Vocational Education Act of 1963. This act provided for a substantially broader interpretation of vocational education. The 1963 act provided funds for making vocational training or retraining available to all persons 14 years old or older. Vocational education was also viewed in the act as being much broader than the traditional fields of vocational agriculture, home economics, etc. Interpretation of this act supported the basic and general education necessary for, or prerequisite to, vocational training.

A major change reflected in the 1963 act was that vocational education was to be offered to meet the needs of people rather than the needs of the labor market as had been true of all previous legislation. Under the 1963 act, funds were provided for training persons in the secondary schools, persons who wanted to continue vocational education beyond the high school, employed persons wanting further training for advancement or upgrading, and persons having special handicaps which prevented them from succeeding in the regular programs designed to produce given skill levels. The earlier philosophy of providing vocational education to meet labor shortages in specific occupations was abandoned.

The most current thinking regarding the directions which vocational education should take in the future is reflected in the report of the Advisory Council on Vocational Education, established under the provision of the Vocational Education Act of 1963 (U. S. Senate, 1968). This report makes a number of specific recommendations for the improvement of vocational education in the future. While most of these recommendations have to do with the implementation of programs in vocational education, they are based upon careful analyses by the council of the overall objectives of providing vocational education which will serve as "the bridge between man and his work." A review of the characteristics of an adequate vocational education program provides considerable insight into the most current thinking of national leaders in the field.

It is the opinion of this council (pp. 50–52) that preparation for the world of work should begin with a general orientation provided by the elementary schools. At the junior high school level "economic orientation and occupational preparation should reach a more sophisticated stage with study by all students of the economic and industrial system by which goods and services are produced and distributed." In high school, occupational preparation should be more specific, though still not limited to a single occupation. It is the belief of the council that each student at the high school level, perhaps with the exception of college-bound students, should be provided with at least an entry-level job skill by the time he completes the secondary level. The traditional dichotomy between vocational and general education is considered to be false and should be done away with. The council's position is that "vocational preparation should be used to make general education concrete and understandable; general education should point up the vocational implications of all education."

A goal to be set for the near future would provide some formal post secondary occupational training for everyone. The increasing demands for more sophisticated skills in our society suggest that a twelve-year educational program will be inadequate in the near future. Furthermore, the public school system should provide education for those who want part-time or, in some cases, full-time educational opportunities to advance the level of their occupational skill. The vastly increased breadth of vocational education in relatively recent time is attested to by the council's opinion that ". . . any occupation which contributes to the good of society is a fit subject for vocational education." Furthermore, the council strongly recommends that occupational preparation be conducted where possible in conjunction with industry. Such an arrangement minimizes the need for expensive equipment required in much of occupational education and provides an opportunity for the student to achieve many of the affective educational objectives of occupational education which are most difficult to provide in the classroom.

Guidance and placement services, as well as follow-up studies of students and their progress in the world of work, are considered essential for successful occupational education. Remedial programs are recognized as necessary, although presumably they would be minimized with an effective occupational program in the public school system. The council again gives emphasis to the needs of those requiring special help.

Curriculum trends

Since the mid-1950s, much emphasis in education has been placed on curriculum research and experimentation. Projects of national significance in mathematics, sciences, foreign languages, social studies, and English have been initiated since that time. Unfortunately, the field of industrial education has not received the federal and foundation support necessary for the larger-scale experimentation characterizing these other fields. In summarizing the support provided by the federal government through the National Defense Education Act for curriculum research, Inlow (1966, p. 136) concludes that ". . . the fine and applied arts, along with the classical languages, are being almost totally neglected."

Fortunately, some of the lag that has existed in industrial education curriculum development has been corrected as a result of the Vocational Education Act of 1963. It is reasonable to expect that the 1968 amendments to this act will result in further advances in the state of the art in industrial education curricula. Two projects, both dealing with industrial education curricula, currently enjoy the sort of national prominence that has been attained by curriculum projects in other fields.

The American Industry Project at Stout State University purportedly introduces a new discipline into the secondary school system (Face & Flug, 1966). While this project does claim to be a new curriculum area, it addresses itself to two traditional objectives of industrial arts—to develop an understanding of industry and to develop problem-solving ability related to industry. Rather than teaching about specific materials and processes related to industry, the Stout State plan is organized around concepts associated with industry. These include communications, transportation, public interest, finance, physical facilities, research, purchasing, industrial relations, marketing, management, production, materials, processes, and energy. Three levels of courses dealing with these concepts are proposed by the American Industry program. Levels one and two deal with the development of an increasing depth of understanding of the concepts mentioned above and with an increasing ability to recognize and solve complex industrial problems. Level three of American Industry concentrates on developing the interests, knowledge, and problem-solving ability of the student in one or more related concepts. Pilot projects to evaluate this approach to teaching this curriculum area are currently in progress in several states. It is anticipated that curriculum materials developed within the project will be available to the education community within the next year.

The second project of national significance is clearly identified as an industrial arts project. This project is being conducted at The Ohio State University and is titled the Industrial Arts Curriculum Project (IACP). It was initiated in 1965 and is projected to run through 1971. The objective of the IACP is to identify a body of knowledge which is referred to as industrial technology and which is important to the study of industry. Objectives of the program include teaching this knowledge, field testing and revision, and the preparation of teachers. The knowledge is organized around two courses, the World of Construction and the World of Manufacturing. While the IACP, like the American Industry Project, concentrates on teaching more abstract concepts about industry, it differs from the American Industry Project in its emphasis on psychomotor objectives. The philosophy of the IACP is that the most efficient learning can take place by having the student involved in both cognitive and psychomotor aspects of the subject-matter content. While the project is not designed to teach technical skills, it holds to the philosophy that learning of concepts is enhanced by the combined cognitive-psychomotor approach to learning.

Curriculum materials developed in this project are currently being field tested, and it is anticipated that they will be available to industrial arts educators at the end of the four-year evaluation period, which is to include three revisions of test material. The initial field evaluation began in the 1967–1968 academic year.

A number of additional programs in curriculum development for industrial education are being conducted (Bushnell, 1968; Olson, 1966; Turnquist, 1965). While many of these programs unquestionably have a contribution to make to curriculum development in industrial education, they do not currently represent efforts recognized as being of national significance; therefore, they will not be reviewed here.

Behavioral objectives

From this brief historical account it can be seen then that vocational education has traditionally been tied to specific programs and that the objectives of the overall field have seldom been stated in behavioral terms. This program orientation, which is a direct outgrowth of federal funds provided for conducting vocational education, has caused educators to pay less attention to behavioral objectives of vocational education than they might have. The difficulty inherent in doing this for a field with such diverse subject-matter content undoubtedly accounts for the lack of attention to overall behavioral objectives for vocational education.

With the changing emphasis in federal legislation in recent years, the need for a way of conceptualizing the objectives of vocational education in behavioral terms becomes increasingly apparent. At the most general level, conceptualization provides the educator with a means of focusing his attention on the noncognitive domains of behavior for which objectives are seldom stated explicitly. Such a system also provides a means by which an overview of programs of entirely different subject-matter content might be compared and analyzed with respect to the domains in which they purport to modify behavior.

Educational objectives have typically been envisioned as falling into three domains: the cognitive, the affective, and the psychomotor. An extensive analysis of cognitive objectives was published in 1956 (Bloom, 1956). In 1964, a committee headed by Krathwohl published their analysis of objectives in the affective domain (Krathwohl, Bloom, & Masia, 1964). Summaries of these works appear in the Appendix to Part I of this book. While both committees recognized the importance of psychomotor objectives, neither undertook work on this domain. In 1966, Simpson (1966) published a preliminary taxonomy for the psychomotor domain, and this remains the only published work covering it.

According to the original concept of the authors who developed the taxonomy for the cognitive domain, these three domains should be sufficient for explaining all educational objectives. Moore (1967), at Educational Testing Service, felt that an additional domain was necessary to supplement the other three, and in 1967 she published a taxonomy for the perceptual domain. While she fully recognized, as did authors of the other taxonomies, that there were interrelationships and a degree of duplication in the several domains, she felt that a perceptual taxonomy was necessary in order to give a complete picture of educational objectives. While this author will not attempt to resolve questions of overlap and duplication, he does feel that the concept of perceptual objectives is an important one, particularly for vocational education.

One possible way to conceptualize objectives of vocational education at the broadest level is given in Table 23-1, Table of General Specifications for Objectives in Industrial Education. It can be seen that this table incorporates objectives at the most general level in each of the four domains discussed above. Selected programs in each of the major divisions of industrial education[3] have been included for illustration of

[3] It should be noted that considerable controversy exists over the definition of terms such as "industrial arts," "trades and industries," and "practical arts." The author has selected the categories of *Trades education*, *Technical education*, and *General education in industrial arts* as providing reasonably distinct areas, fully recognizing that some will object to the inclusion of industrial arts under the heading of industrial education. Nevertheless, it is a meaningful categorization for illustrating problems of educational measurement.

relative emphasis placed on each of the four domains. No attempt is made here to provide an exhaustive list of educational programs in the entire field of industrial education. Rather, the purpose is to provide the instructor with a means of focusing his attention on the domains within which specific educational programs intend to bring about behavioral changes. After viewing the broad objectives of a particular program in industrial education, it should be possible to orient oneself to more specific objectives in each of the domains and design test instruments to measure these objectives. Most of the remainder of this chapter is devoted to the measurement of specific objectives.

The instructor will, of course, need to become familiar with the details of the several taxonomies as a guide to constructing adequate test instruments. It is this author's contention that the several taxonomies best serve the purpose of providing a conceptual framework within which the test designer can function. The operational definition of each of the detailed categories in the several domains is considered to be of less importance at this point than providing a broad view of the domains in which particular educational programs purport to operate. The authors of each of the taxonomies have proposed that their system is *one* way of categorizing educational objectives. The individual instructor may well find that strict adherence to each of these four systems when constructing test items is difficult, if not impossible. He should, therefore, consider modifications of the particular taxonomy with which he is working in order to best meet his needs for constructing measurement instruments. The most important facts to be kept in mind are that educational objectives do fall in different domains and that assessment of all behaviors intended to be taught in a particular educational program is essential. It should also be kept in mind that behavioral changes which were not intended sometimes occur, and the teacher is in a position to determine these through observation of students. For example, it might be quite important for a teacher to assess the extent to which an unintended negative attitude has resulted from classroom experiences.

The main reason for providing a means of conceptualizing educational objectives in the four domains can be illustrated by borrowing the concept of criterion deficiency (Brogden & Taylor, 1950). This concept, originally developed in the context of measuring job performance in industrial situations, refers to the failure to include important elements of the job when assessing an employee's performance. For example, if we were to assess only the cognitive abilities of an auto mechanic, while ignoring psychomotor abilities, we would have a deficient criterion.

This concept can easily be applied to assessing the performance of students in vocational education. To the extent that our testing omits objectives that are intended to be taught by the course, our testing program is deficient. While this is seldom a major problem at the lower level of cognition, it becomes increasingly apparent as one moves up the hierarchy because of the difficulty of assessing higher-order cognitive objectives. The greatest omission comes, however, in the assessment of behaviors in the noncognitive domains. While some assessment is done in the other three domains, it is usually much more informal and under considerably less standardized conditions than we insist on for assessing cognitive behaviors.

It is hoped, then, that consideration of educational objectives as falling into four domains will help the instructor specify them explicitly rather than ignoring them entirely or hoping that they will somewhere be embedded in the educational experiences to which the student is exposed and that he will somehow learn them. To the extent that this is achieved, the testing program should avoid problems of criterion deficiency.

No attempt is made here to discuss the several taxonomies in detail. The reader is referred to the original reference for that purpose. However, for use in studying Table 23-1, a brief description of each level of the several domains is presented below.

It will be noted that the cognitive domain bears little resemblance to the original cognitive taxonomy. In the author's experience with item-writing committees in industrial education some difficulty has been encountered in communicating the concept of a hierarchy of educational objectives as conceived by the original Bloom committee. A system has been developed, based upon the original taxonomy, which has proved successful in working with industrial education teachers.[4] This system was designed to meet two goals. First, it had to be a system that was easily understood by industrial specialists who were, in general, not familiar with educational theory; and second, it had to ensure a coverage of the levels of cognitive functioning appropriate for the students to be tested. The system, which consists of four levels of objectives, is described below. Items testing for these objectives are presented in the section on testing for Cognitive Objectives. The system, including examples, is presented later in the chapter in its revised form which evolved from two years of work with industrial education committees.

Summary of taxonomies

Cognitive domain (A–D)

Knowledge (*A*). Behaviors which represent knowledge require the repetition of responses that have been practiced in learning experiences previously. After learning, memory is the major requisite to correct performance.

Understanding (*B*). Behaviors which represent understanding require responses in addition to those previously practiced and learned. The additional responses are likely to be interpretations, translations, summarizations, analyses, detection of similarities, detection of differences. At this level tasks do not require solutions other than explorations in meaning.

Application of knowledge (*C*). Behaviors which represent application of knowledge require the use of previously learned responses in the solution of problems. At this level, the type of problem is not new, having been experienced by the student before to the extent that responses necessary to find solutions are more or less routine.

Application of understanding (*D*). At this level the solution requires responses of the understanding level. At least one element of the problem is new to the student and is essential to the solution of the problem. The newness might appear either in the conditions of the problem or in the solution required.

Perceptual domain (E–I; Moore, 1967, pp. 9–10)[5]

Sensation (*E*). "Behavior that indicates awareness of the qualities of a stimulus or of material as perceived through the senses (hue, pitch, odor, etc.). May be further divided into various sensory modalities, visual, auditory, tactile, etc."

Figure perception (*F*). "Behavior that indicates awareness of entity, or what is commonly called a percept (size, form, location, position, etc.). Also awareness of the relationships of parts to each other and to the whole, and awareness of relations between the parts and the background, or between the stimulus and its context. Figure-ground perceptual organization."

Symbol perception (*G*). "Behavior that indicates awareness of percepts in the form of denotative signs having no significance in and of themselves, such as letters, digits, and other signs usually organized as in alphabet and number systems, the relationship among tones in a musical chord or scale, or colors in a visual spectrum, when meanings and form are not considered. The ability to name the percept or assign it to an appropriate class, to indicate similarities and differences between percepts."

Perception of meaning (*H*). "Behavior that indicates awareness of the significance or value of a percept or symbol. The discovery of new relationships or insight into cause and effect relations between symbols or percepts. The abilities to generalize, to understand implications, and to make decisions."

Perception of performance (*I*). "Behavior that indicates sensitive and accurate observation. Diagnostic ability with respect to mechanical or

[4] Prof. J. Clyde Johnson, North Carolina State University, did much of the initial work involved in developing this system.

[5] From "A Proposed Taxonomy of the Perceptual Domain and Some Suggested Applications" by Maxine Ruth Moore. Reprinted by permission of Educational Testing Service, the copyright owner.

electrical systems, medical problems, artistic products, etc. Insight into personal, social, and political situations in which awareness of attitudes, needs, desires, moods, intentions, perceptions, and thoughts of other people and one's self is indicated. Demonstration of a successful analytical or global approach to problem-solving in all areas of endeavor and of artistry and creativity in any medium."

Psychomotor domain (J–N; Simpson, 1966, pp. 135–139)[6]

Perception (*J*). "This is an essential first step in performing a motor act. It is the process of becoming aware of objects, qualities, or relations by way of the sense organs. It is the central portion of the situation-interpretation-action chain leading to purposeful motor activity."

Set (*K*). "Set is a preparatory adjustment or readiness for a particular kind of action or experience."

Guided response (*L*). "This is an early step in the development of skill. Emphasis here is upon the abilities which are components of the more complex skill. Guided response is the overt behavioral act of an individual under the guidance of the instructor. Prerequisite to performance of the act are readiness to respond, in terms of set to produce the overt behavioral act and selection of the appropriate response. . . . Selection of response may be defined as deciding what response must be made in order to satisfy the particular requirements of task performance. There appear to be two major subcategories, imitation and trial and error."

Mechanism (*M*). "Learned response has become habitual. At this level, the learner has achieved a certain confidence and degree of skill in the performance of the act. The act is a part of his repertoire of possible responses to stimuli and the demands of situations where the response is an appropriate one. The response may be more complex than at the preceding level; it may involve some patterning of response in carrying out the task. That is, abilities are combined in action of a skill nature."

Complex overt response (*N*). "At this level, the individual can perform a motor act that is considered complex because of the movement pattern required. At this level, a high degree of skill has been attained. The act can be carried out smoothly and efficiently, that is, with minimum expenditure of time and energy. There are two subcategories: resolution of uncertainty and automatic performance."

Affective domain (O–S; Krathwohl et al., 1964, pp. 176–184)

Receiving (*O*). ". . . We are concerned that the learner be sensitized to the existence of certain phenomena and stimuli; that is, that he be willing to receive or attend to them."

Responding (*P*). "The student is sufficiently motivated that he is not just willing to attend, but perhaps it is correct to say that he is actively attending."

Valuing (*Q*). This behavior shows "that a thing, phenomenon, or behavior has worth" to the learner.

Organization (*R*). "[The] necessity arises for (a) the organization of the values into a system, (b) the determination of the interrelationships among them, and (c) the establishment of the dominant and pervasive ones."

Characterization by a value or value complex (*S*). "At this level of internalization the values . . . are organized into some kind of internally consistent system, [and] have controlled the behavior of the individual for a sufficient time that he has adapted to behaving this way. . . ."

Industrial education viewed in four domains

Several conclusions can be reached by studying the general objectives of industrial education as represented in Table 23-1. One of the most obvious conclusions concerns the differences in objectives for trade training, as represented by auto mechanics, welding, and so forth; technician

[6] From E. J. Simpson. The classification of educational objectives, psychomotor domain. *Illinois Teacher of Home Economics*, 1966, **10**, 110–144. Reprinted by permission of the author.

training as represented by electronics, data processing, and other areas; and industrial arts, the general education component of industrial education. It can be seen that the industrial arts component of industrial education has objectives in all four domains. It is not an objective of industrial arts to achieve the highest level in any domain, but the objectives can appropriately be thought of as encompassing all four domains. While specific objectives in industrial arts vary with the level at which this training is provided, some degree of proficiency in each domain is unquestionably important at each level. Referring to the cognitive, affective, and psychomotor domains, a recent publication concerning industrial arts education states, "Ideally, a student is developing a degree of skill in each of the three classifications when he participates in activity provided in the industrial arts laboratory" (American Vocational Association, 1968, p. 16).

Auto mechanics is an example of training in the trade component of industrial education. It can be seen that the higher degree of proficiency in a more limited area is an objective of training in auto mechanics, as contrasted with greater breadth and less depth in industrial arts. Cognitive factors are learned to a much higher degree in the trades where skill training is important. In addition, considerably more emphasis is placed on psychomotor and perceptual objectives.

In general, the technologies concentrate on cognitive functions almost exclusively. Electronics technology, for example, requires the student to deal with higher-level abstractions and to perform cognitive functions at higher levels in the taxonomy. In many areas of technology today, the psychomotor and perceptual components are minimized, if not entirely disregarded. There is a parallel in this respect between the technologies and the engineering professions, since the latter only a decade or two ago spent much time in conducting shop work that paralleled the study of theory. With the increased body of knowledge required for those in both the technologies and the engineering profession today, much less emphasis is being placed on psychomotor and perceptual objectives.

Another point to be made about Table 23-1 is the predominant emphasis of objectives in the perceptual domain for some fields of industrial education, for example, welding. It is necessary for the successful welder to process information through several of the senses simultaneously to evaluate the accuracy of performance. Visual, auditory, and kinesthetic cues are of utmost importance in successful welding. While there is a degree of psychomotor as well as cognitive performance involved, welding is considered to place very heavy emphasis upon perceptual objectives.

It should be noted that a distinction is made between implicit and explicit objectives in Table 23-1. While this dichotomy is probably an oversimplification, it is certainly true that many educational objectives are stated more explicitly than others. For example, industrial arts education has the explicit objective in grades K through 6 to ". . . develop cooperative attitudes and self reliance through problem-solving situations," and ". . . develop an understanding and appreciation of the dignity of honest work" (American Vocational Association, 1968, p. 12). Such explicit statements of affective objectives are seldom found in trades and technologies. Unquestionably, however, most instructors do have implicit affective objectives in teaching in all subject areas, not just industrial education. It is hard to imagine a dedicated teacher who does not try to modify students' behavior to achieve at least the *Valuing* (Q) level of the affective domain. In fact, the dedication of many teachers to their subject matter would suggest that they strive for even higher levels of this domain.

It can also be seen from Table 23-1 that the affective objectives for trades and technologies do not begin at the lowest level of the domain. It is reasonable to assume that students who enter a trade or technology exhibit affective behaviors at an intermediate level of the hierarchy, probably at the *Responding* (*P*) level. Instructors in these areas would therefore not be expected to concentrate on the lowest level of affective objectives that have to do with responding positively toward auto mechanics. They do, undoubtedly, attempt to achieve affective objectives at a somewhat higher level, hoping to create in their students a more organized value complex toward the particular occupation for which they are studying. While this is seldom stated explicitly as an objective of industrial education programs, much could be gained from doing so. Explicit consideration of such objectives should help the teacher focus consciously on bringing about these behavioral changes by providing appropriate educational experiences.

Specifications for two courses in industrial education

Because of the lag in curriculum development in industrial education, it is possible to single out only those projects discussed previously as being of national significance. Since both of these are in the early experimental stages and since curriculum materials are not generally available for either, the author has chosen not to use them for illustration of testing in industrial education. Instead, he has chosen two courses in industrial education developed in North Carolina, a state recognized as having a relatively advanced program of post high school industrial education.

The North Carolina Department of Community Colleges, which officially began in 1957, consists of over forty community colleges and technical institutes offering programs in post high school industrial education. While other states unquestionably have programs of excellence in industrial education, North Carolina is clearly recognized as one of the leaders in this field. The North Carolina system provides two types of occupational training, one for technical education and one for training in the trades. Technical education consists of two-year programs in such areas as engineering technologies, business and secretarial sciences, nursing, and electronics. Trades education usually consists of one-year programs in curricula such as auto mechanics, drafting, practical nursing, machine shop, and welding.

Within the North Carolina Department of Community Colleges is the Curriculum Laboratory, the purpose of which is to furnish instructional materials for use in all areas of vocational education. The materials may be adapted from those created and in use in other states, or, in the absence of any such existing suitable materials, they are developed by the laboratory. Since the laboratory is established to serve all areas of vocational education and training, its program of service varies according to the needs of each subject-matter area. The laboratory also experiments with visual-aid material and other instructional methods and devices in order to train and advise instructors throughout the state in the use of these modern instructional materials.

The intimate knowledge of members in the Curriculum Laboratory about the various instructional materials available throughout the country, and the cadre of highly trained specialists available for creating new materials, qualifies it as one of the outstanding sources of curriculum materials for industrial education.

Auto mechanics

Course outline Table 23-2, Table of Specifications for Objectives of a Course in Chassis, Suspension, and Braking Systems, shows part of the outline for a course developed by the Curriculum Laboratory of the North Carolina Department of Community Colleges.[7] The first part of the course dealing with steering systems and wheel alignment is presented in detail below for illustration of test construction. The course is designed

1. to help the student master the components of suspension and steering systems and to provide practical job instruction in the adjustment and repair of these systems
2. to help the student understand the construction and operation of automotive brakes and to provide a sequence of service operations designed to develop skill in brake service and repair.

[7] The author would like to express his appreciation to the North Carolina Department of Community Colleges for permission to use this course outline.

TABLE 23-2 TABLE OF SPECIFICATIONS FOR OBJECTIVES OF A COURSE IN CHASSIS, SUSPENSION, AND BRAKING SYSTEMS

	BEHAVIORS													
	Cognitive				*Perceptual*					*Psychomotor*				
	Knowledge	*Understanding*	*Application of knowledge*	*Application of understanding*	*Sensation*	*Figure perception*	*Symbol perception*	*Perception of meaning*	*Perception of performance*	*Perception*	*Set*	*Guided response*	*Mechanism*	*Complex response*
CONTENT	*A*	*B*	*C*	*D*	*E*	*F*	*G*	*H*	*I*	*J*	*K*	*L*	*M*	*N*
1.0 Steering systems														
1.1 Functions of a steering system	X													
1.2 Geometric principles in steering function														
1.21 Camber and caster	X	X												
1.22 Kingpin inclination	X	X												
1.23 Included angle	X	X												
1.24 Toe-in and toe-out	X	X												
1.3 Steering linkages and gears	X	X	X											
1.4 Power steering	X	X	X											
2.0 Front-end alignment														
2.1 Alignment equipment		X	X											
2.2 Preliminary checks														
2.21 Air pressure in tires			X											
2.22 Wheel-bearings wear and adjustment			X					X					X	
2.23 Wheels for run-out			X											
2.24 Steering knuckles and/or ball joints			X					X					X	
2.25 Steering linkage			X	X										
2.26 Wheel balance		X	X		X									
2.27 Shock absorbers and springs		X	X											
2.28 Tracking				X										
2.3 Alignment procedures														
2.31 Check and adjust caster				X								X	X	
2.32 Check and adjust camber				X								X	X	
2.33 Check kingpin inclination				X										
2.34 Check and adjust toe-in			X									X	X	
2.35 Check toe-out			X											
3.0 Etc.														

It can be seen that Table 23-2 presents objectives in the cognitive, perceptual, and psychomotor domains. The measurement of these objectives is covered in the following sections. Objectives in the affective domain are not reflected in this table since, as shown in Table 23-1, they are usually implicit for trades and technologies, and therefore they are seldom assessed. As discussed earlier, such objectives should be stated explicitly; techniques for their evaluation are presented in a later section of this chapter.

The two-way classification used in Table 23-2 shows subject matter in the left-hand margin and behavioral domain and level across the top. An "x" in the table indicates the educational objective appropriate for a given subject-matter content. For example, *A*-1.21 designates knowledge of caster and camber and *L*-2.31 designates the psychomotor ability to adjust caster under the guidance of the instructor (the *Guided response* level).

Summative test specifications Using the outline for the above course a committee of five auto-mechanics instructors, working with a test-construction specialist, developed a table of cognitive specifications for a summative test which is presented as Table 23-3.

The table shows the distribution of emphasis by subject matter and objective considered by the committee to be appropriate to adequately sample student learning. Such a distribution of emphasis is generally achieved by having committee members make independent judgments of the relative emphasis to be placed on each content area. For example, each member might be asked to distribute 100 points among the several content areas in accordance with the distribution of emphasis that he considers appropriate.

It is apparent from Table 23-3 that little emphasis is placed on the highest level of cognitive functioning. Problems with which the auto mechanic is expected to deal in this subject-matter area involve primarily knowledge, understanding, and the application of knowledge to routine problems.

The use of a table of test specifications such as this helps ensure adequate coverage of both subject matter and level of objective. It is particularly useful in helping to avoid the tendency to write all items at the knowledge level.

Electronics

Course outline Table 23-4, Table of Specifications for Objectives of a Course in the Application of Vacuum Tubes and Transistors, presents part of the outline of a course also developed by the North Carolina Curriculum Laboratory. This table is included to illustrate the relative emphasis placed on the different domains by technologies, as contrasted with trades. As emphasized in Table 23-1, the technologies are generally devoted to objectives in the cognitive domain. As mentioned earlier, implicit affective objectives undoubtedly exist, although they are seldom measured formally.

It should be pointed out that Table 23-1 does not reflect the greater emphasis placed upon higher-level cognitive objectives in the technologies as contrasted with the trades. This difference is readily apparent, however, when comparing the course outlines contained in Tables 23-2 and 23-4, and the summative test specifications contained in Tables 23-3 and 23-5.

The differences in cognitive functioning are a reflection of the nature of the work for which the respective educational programs are preparing students. To a large extent, auto mechanics function in a factual, concrete world. On the other hand, electronics technicians deal with complex abstractions which require them to function at higher cognitive levels.

Summative test specifications Table 23-5 presents the specifications for a summative test on the application of vacuum tubes and transistors. These specifications, arrived at by following the same procedure as described for the summative test in auto mechanics, represents the distribution of emphasis considered appropriate for sampling student learning in this course. As

Table 23-3 Summative Test Specifications for a Course in Chassis, Suspension, and Braking Systems (Showing Number of Items by Content and Level)

	Knowledge A	*Understanding* B	*Application of knowledge* C	*Application of understanding* D
I. Chassis and suspension				
A. Fundamentals				
1. Springs and shocks	7	3		
2. Alignment	9	6	1	1
B. Operating principles				
1. Steering mechanisms	2	1		
2. Stabilizer principles	3	5	1	
C. Service and repair				
1. Diagnosis of troubles		7	4	
2. Tool usage	7	1		
3. Alignment techniques	1	1	2	1
4. Steering and balancing	1		1	
II. Braking systems				
A. Fundamental types				
1. Drums and shoes	2	2		
2. Disc	1	2		
3. Hydraulic	4	1		
B. Operating principles				
1. Pressures, mechanical-hydraulic	2	4	7	1
2. Friction coefficients	3	3		
C. Diagnosis and service				
1. Indications of trouble and adjustments	4	5	8	
2. Drum, line, and cylinder repair	2	1	1	
3. Tool and equipment usage	2			
Total test items	50	42	25	3

stated earlier, the higher cognitive functioning required of electronics technicians is reflected in these specifications.

Testing for cognitive objectives (A–D)

As previously discussed, a system for categorizing cognitive objectives in industrial education has been developed. The system provides the instructor with a means of conceptualizing objectives at several levels of cognition for assessing student achievement in various industrial education programs. Examples of how this system has been successfully applied for the two courses outlined in Tables 23-2 and 23-4 are presented below.

TABLE 23-4 TABLE OF SPECIFICATIONS FOR OBJECTIVES OF A COURSE IN THE APPLICATION OF VACUUM TUBES AND TRANSISTORS

CONTENT	BEHAVIORS *Knowledge* *A*	*Understanding* *B*	*Application of knowledge* *C*	*Application of understanding* *D*
1.0 Review of basic amplifiers				
1.1 Common emitter	X	X	X	
1.2 Common collector	X	X	X	
1.3 Common base	X	X	X	
1.4 Common cathode	X	X	X	
1.5 Common plate	X	X	X	
1.6 Common grid	X	X	X	
2.0 Common amplifier configurations				
2.1 Push-pull amplifiers, Class A, B, and C		X		X
2.2 Complementary-symmetry amplifier		X		X
2.3 Paraphase amplifiers		X		X
2.4 Coupling	X	X	X	X
3.0 Detectors and modulators				
3.1 Diode detectors		X	X	X
3.2 Grid detectors		X		
3.3 Plate detectors		X	X	X
3.4 Phase detectors		X		
3.41 Foster-Seeley discriminator	X		X	
3.42 Ratio detector	X		X	
3.5 A.M. modulators			X	
3.51 Low-level and high-level modulation		X	X	
3.52 Grid modulation		X		
3.53 Plate modulation		X	X	
3.6 F.M. modulation			X	
3.61 Reactance modulation		X		
3.62 Phase modulation	X	X	X	
4.0 Special-purpose transistors				
4.1 Tunnel diode	X	X	X	X
4.2 Unijunction transistor	X	X		X
4.3 Control rectifiers	X	X	X	X
5.0 Etc.				

Table 23-5 Summative Test Specifications for a Course in the Application of Vacuum Tubes and Transistors

	Knowledge A	*Understanding* B	*Application of knowledge* C	*Application of understanding* D
I. Application of electronics				
A. Principles of vacuum tubes	3	3	2	4
B. Signal elements	3	3	2	1
C. Active networks				
1. Power supply	2	3	2	
2. Amplifiers	3	2	1	3
D. Detection and modulation				
1. Diodes	1	2	3	3
2. am-fm modulation		3	2	
E. Oscillators				
1. Sinusoidal	3	3		1
2. Nonsinusoidal	1		1	
3. L-R, C-R, L-C-R	3	1	2	3
4. R-C circuits		1	2	2
F. Amplification				
1. Voltage	4	3	3	
2. Current	2	1	2	
3. Power		2	2	
4. Regulation	3	3		
G. Transistors				
1. Junction	4	3	2	
2. Field effect	4	2		
3. Semiconductor diodes	3	3	2	1
H. Special-purpose transistors	3	2	2	1
Total test items	44	40	30	25

Auto mechanics

The following items were designed to measure specific cognitive behaviors contained in Table 23-2. In each case the item is designated by the code used on the table to specify the pertinent behavior (or objective) and subject matter, such as *A*-1.21 for knowledge of caster and camber. The asterisk marks the desired response.

Knowledge (A) Item 1 requires that the student recall the specific definition of negative camber as the inward tilt of the kingpin at the top. In item 2 the student is required to recall the definition of steering-axis inclination as the inward tilt of the center line of the kingpin or ball joint. In both instances no response other than the recall of specific information is required.

A-1.21

1. Negative camber is the
   *a. inward tilt of the kingpin at the top
   b. outward tilt of the kingpin at the top
   c. forward tilt of the kingpin
   d. backward tilt of the kingpin

B-2.27

2. The inward tilt of the center line of the kingpin or ball joints is called
   *a. steering axis inclination
   b. included angle
   c. camber
   d. caster

Understanding (B) At this level of cognition the student is expected to respond by making interpretations, translations, etc., which are in addition to the recall of specific information. In item 3 the student must see the similarity between the design of the front end of the automobile and the geometric principles upon which this design is based. A similar understanding is required with regard to the shock absorber in item 4.

B-1.21

3. In terms of steering geometry the inward tilt of the top of the front wheel from the vertical plane is referred to as
   a. toe-out on turns
   b. positive caster
   c. excess toe-in
   *d. negative camber

B-2.27

4. When the direct-acting shock absorber is compressed or telescoped, fluid passes through the piston orifices into the upper part of the cylinder and also
   *a. out of the reservoir
   b. out of the dust shield
   c. into the reservoir
   d. into the dust shield

Application of knowledge (C) In item 5 the student is required to apply previously learned facts to eliminate the cause of tire squeal. In 6 it is necessary to apply the knowledge about the steering system to arrive at the correct response of disconnecting the linkage from the pitman arm. In both cases the problems are comparatively routine.

C-1.3

5. A complaint is that the tires squeal on turns. The condition that would *not* cause this is
   *a. steering-gear center point not aligned straight ahead
   b. bent steering arm
   c. incorrect toe-in
   d. excessive speed

C-2.25

6. With manual steering gear, hard steering caused by trouble in the steering linkage or in steering gear could be located by
   *a. disconnecting the steering linkage from the pitman arm
   b. disconnecting the linkage at the steering knuckle
   c. jacking up the front end and turning the steering wheel
   d. jacking up one side of the car and checking the gear

Application of understanding (D) In items 7 and 8 the correct response requires that the student have an understanding of principles of operation of suspension and steering systems. In neither item would the student be expected to have experienced this *type* of problem before and in neither case would knowledge alone permit him to select the correct response. Nevertheless, with an understanding of the particular system he should be able to arrive at the correct solution to these previously unexperienced problems.

D-2.31

7. On the type of suspension systems with a single inner support for the lower control arm, changing the length of the strut rod between the lower arm and frame changes
   a. camber angle
   *b. caster angle
   c. axis inclination
   d. toe-out on turns

D-2.25

8. In an automobile with a manual steering gearbox, a design modification is to be made to the gear reduction ratio. The steering characteristic is desired to be slowed, thus the ratio is set at 15/1. As a check on the accuracy of this modification the steering wheel should turn, on an average, from
   a. 3 to 5 turns
   *b. 4 to 6 turns
   c. 5 to 7 turns
   d. 5.5 to 7.5 turns

It should be kept in mind that *all* the above items were constructed by committees consisting of subject-matter specialists and a specialist in test construction. All items were, in the judgment of this committee, considered to be good items. Nevertheless, empirical analysis shows that half of them failed to adequately discriminate among students in a summative test. Actually, the second item in each pair was shown by item analysis not to meet the statistical criteria usually accepted for a summative test where differentiation among students is a prime consideration.

Judgments about the adequacy of items are made on the basis of item analyses which typically yield a difficulty index ($p =$ proportion of students answering the item correctly) and a correlation between the item and the total score (r_{bis}). Generally, items of moderate difficulty (having p values between .30 and .70) are of greatest value in a test, although extreme difficulty levels are necessary in order to make precise discriminations among students at the upper or lower ends of the distribution.

The item-total correlation is an index of the extent to which a given item measures the same thing as the entire test. The higher this correlation (this value can range from -1.00 to $+1.00$), the more assurance one has that the item measures behaviors similar to those contained in the entire test. While this represents an extreme oversimplification of item analysis, it is felt to be sufficient to illustrate the points to be made in this chapter. For a detailed discussion of item analysis the reader is referred to *Test Construction* (Wood, 1960) and *Psychometric Methods* (Guilford, 1954).

It should be pointed out that the above statistical criteria present an incomplete picture of the value of a given item. For example, if all students get a given item correct ($p = 1.00$), that item could well be measuring student learning even though it does not differentiate among students. Essentially, all students can be considered to have achieved mastery of the subject matter contained in such an item. Likewise, a low item-total correlation could be obtained because the particular item shares little in common with the rest of the test. Nevertheless, if that item covers content that is important for the course it should be retained.

In reviewing the parts of items presented above, it should be noted that the reasons why the first item proved good (from a statistical point of view), while the second item did not, are difficult to ascertain. The reasons for the failure of some items to meet the criteria of item analysis may be several. For example, ambiguity in the item stem, poorly worded instructions, and poor item format may all detract from an item's utility in discriminating among students. The extent to which such factors are operating can only be determined through empirical item analysis.

Electronics technology

A series of items designed to measure specific objectives, similar to those presented previously for auto mechanics, is presented below. These items are keyed to the objectives contained in Table 23-4, using the same system as was used for auto mechanics. For example, item 9 was designed to measure knowledge about common-emitter circuits.

As in the case of auto mechanics, two items have been included at each of the four levels of cognition. Again, the first item in each pair has been empirically demonstrated to be a "good" item in terms of its ability to discriminate among students in a summative test. The second item has failed to meet this criterion for inclusion in a summative test.

Knowledge (A)

A-1.1

9. Signal phase reversal occurs in the
   *a. common-emitter circuit
   b. common-base circuit
   c. common-collector circuit
   d. emitter-follower circuit

A-4.1

10. The type of carrier utilized to convey information from the input circuit to the output circuit of a transistor amplifier employing a pnp junction transistor is a (an)
    *a. hole c. proton
    b. electron d. positron

Understanding (B)

B-1.1

11. A given transistor has a collector current which is 99 percent of the emitter current. The β of the transistor is
    a. 0.01 c. 1
    b. 0.99 *d. 99

B-2.1

12. In the design of a transistor multivibrators, the load line should be drawn so that the transistor can operate
    a. as a class A amplifier
    b. as a class B amplifier
    c. as a class C amplifier
    *d. between saturation and cutoff

Application of knowledge (C)

C-2.4

13. Increasing the size of C_c and R_g in an R-C coupling will
    *a. improve low-frequency response
    b. improve high-frequency response
    c. decrease the low-frequency response
    d. increase the drop-off frequency

C-1.1

14. Doubling the value of the load resistance of a common-emitter transistor amplifier utilizing a junction transistor will
    *a. lower the input resistance
    b. increase the input resistance
    c. have no effect upon the input resistance
    d. create a negative input resistance

Application of understanding (D)

D-2.4

15. One half of a 12AX7 having a plate resistance of 62,500 ohms and an μ of 100 volts works into a load resistance of 470 ohms in an R-C coupled amplifier. The voltage gain to the nearest tenth is
    a. 84.0 volts
    b. 84.4 volts
    c. 88.0 volts
    *d. 88.3 volts

D-3.1

16. When the physical distance between the cathode and anode of a diode is 0.1 mm and the anode potential is 50 volts, the transit time is
    *a. 7.15 microseconds
    b. 28.3 milliseconds
    c. 8.7×10^{-9} seconds
    d. 5.32×10^{-4} seconds

The above section dealt with the application of a system for categorizing cognitive objectives for industrial education to specific courses in auto mechanics and electronics. As stated earlier, the system was designed to have general applicability and has been used successfully with committees of subject-matter specialists in a number of fields. The instrument used with these committees, incorporating modifications resulting from several years of use, is presented below together with examples from other areas of industrial education.

Items of a test which measure *Knowledge (A)* require the repetition of responses that have been practiced in learning experiences previously. After learning, memory is the major requisite to correct performance.

Knowledge of data processing card preparation

17. An alphabetic character in the Hollerith card code consists of
    a. one numeric punch
    b. two numeric punches
    c. one zone and one control punch
    *d. one numeric and one zone punch

18. A control punch in a card is used to
    a. define fields
    *b. identify different types of cards
    c. control key punching
    d. prevent punching errors

Knowledge of electronics symbols

19. Identify the following schematic symbols:

    a. capacitor, resistor, coil
    b. condensor, inductor, rheostat
    c. capacitor, coil, potentiometer
    *d. all of the above

Knowledge of electronics equations

20. Ohm's Law is expressed by the following equation:
    a. $W = E/R$
    b. $E = (W/R)\,1/2$
    c. $EI = R$
    *d. $E = IR$

Knowledge of welding materials and equipment

21. The amount of heat generated, and therefore the thickness of the metal which may be welded, will depend on
   a. the amount of oxygen used
   b. the color of the flame
   *c. the size of the torch orifice
   d. the amount of pressure used

Knowledge of machine cutting tools

22. The primary clearance angle on a milling cutter is the angle
   *a. from the cutting edge back toward the gullet
   b. from cutting edge back on the side of the cutter
   c. that forms the tooth on top
   d. that has the same angle as the body of the tooth

Items of a test which measure *Understanding* (*B*) require responses in addition to those previously practiced and learned. The additional responses are likely to be interpretations, translations, summarizations, analyses, detection of similarities, detection of differences, etc. Items at this level do not set tasks which require solutions other than explorations in meaning.

Understanding of computer storage

23. In storage, instruction and data
   a. must be separated by 100 positions of storage
   b. should be grouped by length of field
   c. can occupy the same locations simultaneously
   *d. should be assigned separate areas

Understanding of computer logic

24. A computer can make logical decisions by
   a. comparing
   b. arithmetic results
   c. testing signs or characters
   *d. all of the above

Understanding of welding techniques

25. When welding an inside corner joint, a flame adjustment of a slightly oxidizing nature is used because
   a. the amount of penetration should be kept at a minimum
   b. the inner cone has a tendency to touch the metal
   c. it provides for the unusual amount of contraction
   *d. it is difficult to obtain additional oxygen from the air

Understanding of machine cutting tools

26. Drilling a hole with a drill that has one lip ground longer than the other will produce a hole that is
   *a. oversized
   b. out-of-round
   c. bell-mouthed
   d. undersized

Items of a test which measure *Application of knowledge* (*C*) require the use of previously learned responses in the solution of problems. At this level, the problems are not new, having been experienced by the testee before to the extent that responses which are necessary to find solutions are more or less routine.

Application of knowledge of welding equipment

27. The regulator adjusting screws should always be turned out before opening the cylinder valves to
   a. blow out the hose
   *b. assist in checking leaks
   c. allow some gas to escape
   d. build up sufficient pressure

Application of knowledge of speeds and feeds

28. A milling cutter with 6 teeth is turning at 130 rpm. For a chip load of 0.004, the correct feed in inches per minute would be
   a. 0.312 c. 6.24
   *b. 3.12 d. 9.36

Application of knowledge of electronic circuits

29. A dual trace oscilloscope is connected to points *P* and *Q* in the grounded base amplifier circuit shown below. Select the pattern you would see on the oscilloscope.

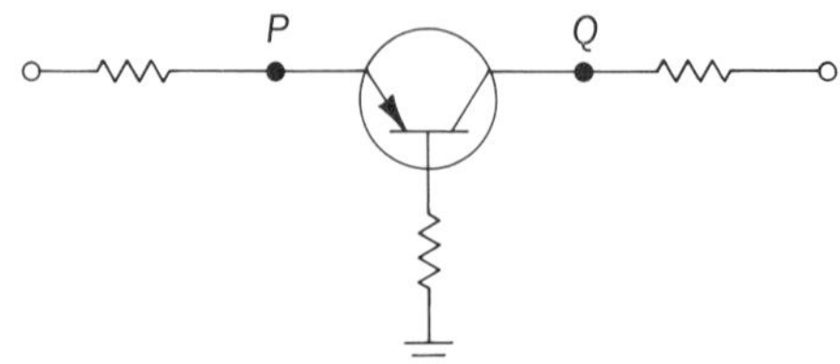

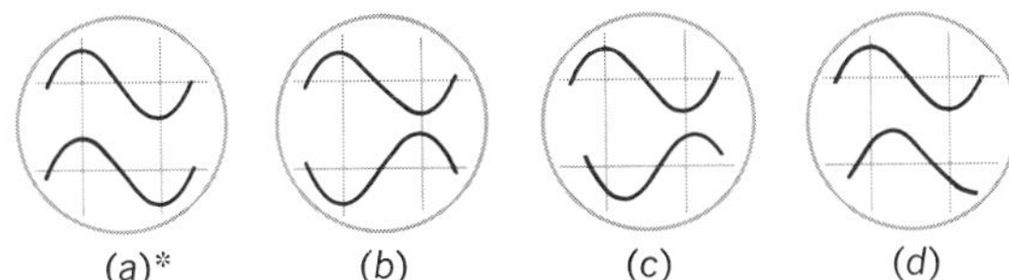

30. Calculate the time constant of the following circuits.

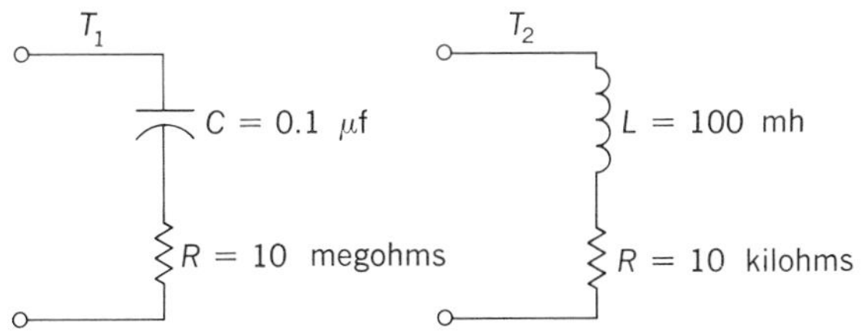

*a. $T_1 = 1$ second, $T_2 = 0.00001$ seconds
b. $T_1 = 1$ second, $T_2 = 10$ seconds
c. $T_1 = 1$ microsecond, $T_2 = 1$ microsecond
d. $T_1 = 1$ millisecond, $T_2 = 1$ millisecond

At the *Application of understanding* (D) level, the solution requires responses of the understanding level. At least one element of the problem is new to the student and is essential to the solution of the problem. The newness might appear in either the conditions of the problem or in the solution required.

Application of understanding of electronic circuits

31. Two meters, M_1 and M_2, are placed in an rf-amplifier circuit as shown. When the tuned circuit in the plate circuit is adjusted to resonant frequency,
a. M_1 will increase, M_2 will decrease
b. M_1 will increase, M_2 will increase
c. M_1 will decrease, M_2 will decrease
*d. M_1 will decrease, M_2 will increase

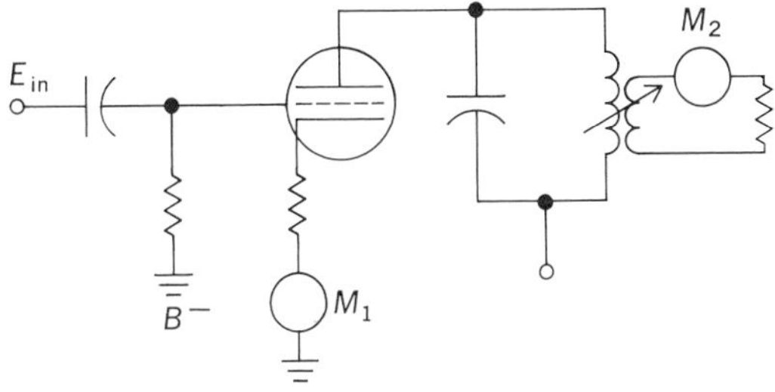

32. Given the following circuit, which of the given statements describes the circuit's operation?

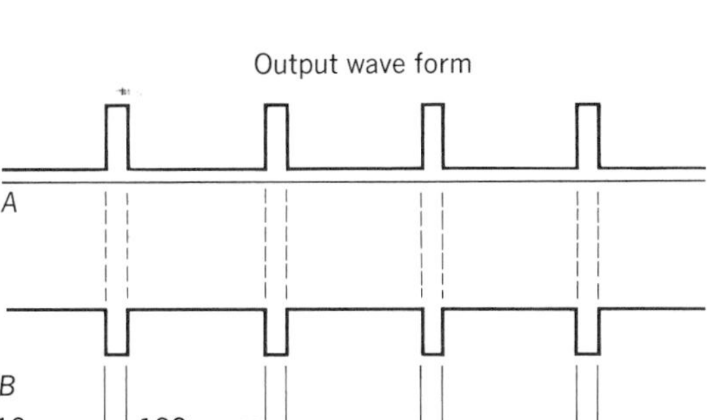

a. The operation is nonsymmetrical.
b. The time constants for C_1R_7 and C_2R_5 are not equal.
c. The period of operation is 110 milliseconds.
*d. All of the above.

Application of understanding of welding techniques

33. As one is welding, an occasional "popping" sound occurs. A check of the gas pressure, the temperature of the torch tip, and the cleanliness of the tip reveal that they are not causing this condition. One may suspect that
*a. the inner cone of the flame is submerged in the puddle
b. the gasses are flowing unevenly
c. the welding rod is becoming overheated
d. the regulator valves are defective

Testing for perceptual objectives (E–I)

As is evident from the early part of this chapter, this author considers the concept of a perceptual domain to be an important one for industrial education. As will be shown below, many of the behavioral changes that occur during training, and that have traditionally been referred to as psychomotor, could be classified more appropriately as perceptual. Several important questions need to be examined, however, before attempting to test for perceptual objectives. First, the question of the extent to which individuals differ at the end of training with respect to a particular objective needs to be examined. For example, the perceptual domain includes certain objectives for radio and television repair such as auditory cues which a serviceman uses in diagnosing a malfunction set. Distinct auditory signals of use to the technician are 60-cycle hum, 120-cycle hum, and 15,750-cycle hum. These and other auditory stimuli used by radio-television repairmen are, however, so distinct from each other that mastery learning is almost assured for all students. Since anyone completing a course in radio-television repair can be expected to distinguish among the several auditory signals, it is not important to test for this ability. Another example in the perceptual domain has to do with the olfactory sense. There are a number of distinct odors, such as a burned-out transformer, that aid the television repairman in diagnosing difficulty. Again, however, these are so distinct that students perform without error in identifying these odors, and testing for them becomes unnecessary.

The second question that needs to be examined, assuming that individual differences in performance are known to exist, is the establishment of reliability in measuring these individual differences. Other things equal, the larger the individual differences, the higher the probability that we can measure them reliably. In the case mentioned above, traditional reliability measures become meaningless. In fact, to the extent that formative testing achieves its objective of ensuring mastery of material, one can expect that traditional reliability measures will be more difficult to demonstrate. However, the causes of unreliability can be many, only one of which is the distribution of talent in the student population. A major problem in establishing reliability of measurement in noncognitive objectives in industrial education has to do with the techniques of measurement. So little work has been done on establishing procedures and associated instrumentation to measure many of these behaviors that reliability is often difficult to demonstrate. Several techniques that have been found successful will be discussed below.

Much could be learned by the study of individual differences in perceptual areas, in addition to testing. For example, in discussions of noncognitive performance with instructors in vocational education, the concept of "feel" is often introduced. When pressed to define this concept, they are usually at a loss. The fact that the concept is difficult to define in conventional terms does not argue against its importance in industrial education, however. Probably a large component of "feel" is tactile-kinesthetic sensitivity, or the sensitivity of the skin, muscles, tendons, etc., to touch and the movement of body members. If more were known about the existence of individual differences in this phenomenon in untrained subjects, about its susceptibility to different training techniques, and about the distribution of individual differences in highly skilled craftsmen, the implication for industrial education would be great.

The separate domain of perception is not clearly distinct from the other three domains, and much overlap exists with psychomotor objectives in industrial education. However, if one thinks of perception as the input side and psychomotor performance as the output side of behavior the distinction becomes somewhat clearer. It is often not the motor aspect of behavior that undergoes a change as a function of training, but rather it is the perceptual aspect that is modified. This is true at least within the context of most jobs with which vocational education is concerned. Individuals undergoing training in vocational programs are not, in most instances, acquiring new responses.

In some training, responses may be modified. For example, the response made by a boxer would not be the same before he began training and after he became proficient at boxing, since substantial changes in the musculature which determine his response would have occurred. It is doubtful, however, that similar changes in the "output mechanisms" of the human occur within vocational training courses, or in fact within most training. For example, the responses involved in manipulating a set of feeler gauges or a micrometer are within the repertoire of individuals who are not mechanics. If this is true, what then occurs during training which makes a man a proficient auto mechanic and distinguishes him from the untrained individual? A mechanic using feeler gauges to adjust the valves or points on an automobile is making very fine sensory discriminations; he is able to feel very small degrees of friction exerted on the gauge. Therefore, since the change which occurs is a perceptual one, to speak of a perceptual objective for auto mechanics in this instance is more appropriate than to speak of a psychomotor objective. To take another example, the driver changing from a standard hydraulic brake system to a power brake system must learn to make the same response to different proprioceptive stimuli. He now has to discriminate finer degrees of feedback and stop responding sooner than he had before.

If this line of argument is a valid one, a major emphasis in industrial education measurement should be devoted to measuring changes that occur in perception as a function of training rather than studying the more traditional motor-performance side of the picture. The problem then could perhaps be more adequately described as one of sensory discrimination or perceptual learning, rather than one of psychomotor performance. The important areas to which we need to direct our attention include individual differences on such variables as kinesthetic sensitivity, tactile sensitivity, and auditory sensitivity as they exist in the various industrial education programs. If these elements of the curriculum can be isolated, they will provide important additional dimensions of performance which are now receiving only incidental attention in much of industrial education and are virtually being ignored in our measurement of student performance.

The literature shows that several authors have attempted to exploit the factor of individual differences on such things as kinesthetic sensitivity. Fitts, for example, suggests that in learning a motor skill the individual learns to respond to interoceptors rather than exteroceptors (Fitts, 1951). In the unskilled individual, external stimuli such as those involved in vision are the input to which the individual responds. In the skilled worker, however, it is the internal kinesthetic cues to which the individual responds. In a study reported by Fleishman and Rich (1963), Fleishman empirically investigated the validity of this idea. He had subjects perform complex psychomotor tasks involving both hands. The task was essentially a two-hand coordination task involving complex target tracking. His hypothesis was that the external cues (vision) are important during early phases of training and the internal cues (kinesthetic feedback) are important during later stages of training. He dichotomized the group at the median on scores of visual ability as measured by a visual orientation test. As predicted, he found that the group with high visual ability showed significantly better performance during the initial stages of training than did the group with low visual ability and that the learning curves converged, since the visual factor became less important with increased training.

The second and related hypothesis had to do with the kinesthetic or internal cues as they related to performance over training trials. In this part of the experiment he used a measure of kinesthetic sensitivity to dichotomize the group into groups of high and low kinesthetic sensitivity. His hypothesis, in this part of the experiment, stated that the two groups should produce curves which diverged. Again, as he predicted, he found that both groups performed at the same level during initial training trials and that, as they successively responded to a greater degree to the internal cues, the group with high kinesthetic sensitivity performed at a higher level than did the group with low kinesthetic sensitivity.

The study by Fleishman is an interesting example of a most profitable line of research. It clearly illustrates the importance of perceptual factors in learning what are traditionally referred to as psychomotor skills. Since a large part of industrial education is concerned with this type of training, greater attention needs to be directed toward the study of perceptual changes and their measurement.

Several examples of testing for perceptual objectives are given below. These have all been undertaken as part of research funded by the U. S. Office of Education Grant No. OEG-0-8-051315-3626(085) to develop instruments to measure achievement in industrial education (see page 903). Examples of testing for perceptual objectives covering several levels of the taxonomy have been included. In some instances it is shown that considerable overlap exists with cognitive factors, while in others there is little or no overlap.

Symbol perception (G)

It is the opinion of instructors in auto mechanics, air-conditioning, machine shop, etc., that one component of the concept of "feel" might be assessed by measuring the ability of students to discriminate very close tolerances, such as one would expect to find in the bearings of different types of machinery. To test this, a series of 1-inch metal plugs was constructed which fit into a 1-inch ring. The plugs varied in size by 2/10,000 of an inch so that the several plugs ranged from "snug" to "loose." The students' task was to rank the series in terms of looseness of fit. Since the task involved the determination of similarities and differences between percepts, it appears to be most appropriately classified as *Symbol perception* (*G*).

It was found that over 95 percent of the students were able to do this task successfully, indicating that mastery had been achieved on this task. While individual differences might have been demonstrated by increasing the difficulty of the task, it was the opinion of instructors that finer discriminations would not be called for by these students on the job.

Perception of meaning (H)

In many fields of industrial education, such as machine shop, farm mechanics, and auto mechanics, the student is expected to make precise absolute judgments while using instruments such as feeler gauges and micrometers. A high degree of tactile-kinesthetic sensitivity is probably the most important factor. Performance on this test is considered to measure objective *H*, *Perception of meaning*. The student must be aware of the significance of varying degrees of friction exerted upon his measuring instrument.

The measurement pod used in the test reported here consisted of fifteen gauge blocks connected so as to provide for four measurements using feeler gauges and four measurements using 1- and 2-inch micrometers. The students' task was to list his answers to the fourth decimal place, which involved interpolation in some of the cases. A time limit was imposed, and the score for the test was the sum of the absolute error expressed to the nearest ten-thousandths of an inch.

This test was found to be highly reliable and to correlate near zero with paper and pencil achievement tests, suggesting that performance on this test is independent of cognitive ability.

Perception of performance (I)

Auto mechanics make extensive use of electronic engine analyzers to diagnose ignition faults in engines, and the ability of the student to identify correctly the cause of the malfunction is considered to be an important facet of his performance. In doing this the student must interpret a visual pattern presented on a CRT. Clearly, this involves both perceptual and cognitive abilities and is included here as an example of overlap among the domains. Because this performance involves both perception and cognition it is more difficult to specify the exact level of perceptual ability that is involved. Probably the visual component of this test is at the *I* level, *Perception of performance*.

The test described here contained a number of malfunctions introduced into the engine analyzer; the students' task was to correctly identify the malfunction. The test had moderately high reliability and low correlations with paper and pencil tests measuring cognition, suggesting moderate overlap.

This test involved the use of an actual engine analyzer and ignition simulator, a situation which makes administration of the test rather difficult. The question arises whether a dynamic presentation using the actual scope is necessary or whether a static version using photographs of the scope would not produce the same results. To test this idea, a static form of the same test was developed and administered to the same students. The static form was found to have a reliability slightly lower than the dynamic form and the pattern of correlations with the cognitive subtests was quite similar for both tests. With improved reliability of this test, these correlations could be expected to increase somewhat, providing empirical evidence that there is some dependence upon cognition as well as perception. With further refinement of the static form of this test, it could probably be made sufficiently reliable that it would serve as an adequate substitute for the dynamic test and thereby eliminate the problem of evaluating student performance on actual equipment.

In many areas of vocational education considerable emphasis is placed upon diagnostic ability. This ability is viewed by many as being the differentiating factor between "good" and "average" students in many fields. At first glance, diagnostic ability might seem to depend entirely on cognitive factors. Yet, while this is recognized as being of considerable importance, it seems that much more is often necessary to make a good diagnostician. For example, the senses of audition, vision, kinesthesis, and olfaction often play a major role in the diagnostic process. A good automotive diagnostician may spend as much time listening to and touching a malfunctioning engine as actually using the numerous mechanical tools available to him. One example of an attempt to develop such a measuring instrument is of particular importance (Swanson, 1968). It involved the development of an auditory diagnostic test for automobile mechanics, and ability classified as objective *I, Perception of performance.*

The choice of the auditory sense was made on several accounts: (1) in discussions with instructors of auto mechanics the consensus of opinion was that the auditory sense is invaluable for diagnostic ability; (2) it is a sense which can be adequately investigated given reasonable resources; (3) it is a sense, unlike smell, taste, or temperature, which can feasibly be tested outside of the laboratory situation. The primary questions to be answered in this study were whether certain diagnostic sounds do discriminate among students, and if so, whether this discrimination is independent of that made by paper and pencil tests.

It should be mentioned that auditory diagnosis is important in many areas of industrial education—auto mechanics, machine shop, radio-television repair, air-conditioning-refrigeration, and agricultural mechanics, to mention just a few. The area of auto mechanics used below illustrates the work which can be done using less conventional testing procedures.

The initial phase of this study was to have auto-mechanic instructors in post high school trade and technical institutions identify sounds which are useful in doing diagnostic work. This was supplemented by obtaining similar information from master mechanics in industry. This initial phase corresponded fairly closely to the delineation of critical areas of cognitive behavior that should be included in a paper and pencil test. Instructors were contacted individually and later brought together as a committee to determine which sounds should be included in such a test.

Since items on any test represent a sampling of the behaviors expected of the student, it was essential that these malfunctions be a sample of sounds found in actual automobiles with which students would eventully work. To ensure that this was the case, items were recorded for Chevrolets, Fords, and Plymouths roughly in proportion to the number of these cars on the road. Recording all makes of automobiles was not feasible, nor was including all engine options for a given make. Therefore, the most widely used engine for each make was selected, for example, the Chevrolet 283-cubic-inch displacement engine.

In the next step, a mechanic was hired to "build in" the malfunctions that had been specified by the committee. This involved such things as inserting a bad connecting-rod bearing into an engine and installing a burned valve. The malfunctioning engine was then recorded using a high-fidelity binaural recording system.

The tape produced consisted of a series of forty-five sounds of malfunctioning parts of an automobile. In consultation with instructors, four alternatives, or possible causes of the malfunction, were constructed for each item in the test. The students' task was to select from the several alternatives the one which correctly identified the malfunction. The entire test was recorded on tape so that it could be administered without benefit of specially trained psychometricians. The tape was played back using a high-fidelity tape recorder and binaural headphones for each student.

An example of an item in this test is for the student to listen to the sound of a bad connecting rod, not knowing, of course, what is causing the sound. He is then asked the following question:

Perception of performance of malfunctioning engine

34. Select, from among the following four alternatives, the cause of the sound you have just heard.
    a. collapsed hydraulic lifter
    b. broken push rod
    *c. bad connecting rod
    d. fan striking another component

The data produced by this test were quite similar to data produced by conventional paper and pencil tests. An item analysis yielded conventional item statistics, such as item difficulties, biserial correlations between the item and the total test score, and proportion responding to each incorrect alternative. The test was shown to have sufficient reliability to warrant further refinement of this technique of measurement, although the original form of the test was not sufficiently reliable to justify its use in making individual decisions regarding student performance. The results of this preliminary study are nevertheless promising.

The test was also shown to differentiate among four groups of auto mechanics having different backgrounds. These included a group of high school students who had little or no knowledge of auto mechanics, a group completing one year of auto mechanics, a group ready to graduate from a two-year program in auto mechanics, and a group of master mechanics who had worked for some years in industry. Furthermore, the fact that this test measured a dimension different from those cognitive factors measured by paper and pencil tests was supported by very low correlations between the two.

A test, similar to the above, is being constructed for measuring the ability of machinists to detect out-of-tolerance conditions during the use of a number of different machines against the background of noise produced in the machine shop.

Testing for psychomotor objectives (J–N)

Unquestionably the greatest amount of work by educators in the area of psychomotor performance has been done in the field of physical education. An excellent review of the work that has been done by psychologists, neurologists, and educators is provided by Cratty (1967). Much of the work that has been undertaken by psychologists has been concerned with motor behavior for which no specific training has been provided. Dimensions of motor behavior that can best be considered as aptitude indices (since no specific training is required) include finger dexterity, manual dexterity, speed of arm movement, etc. While a number of tests have been developed to measure some of these dimensions, they are of little direct value for measuring motor skills taught by specific educational programs. Motor skills tend to be highly specific, thereby making it necessary for the industrial educator to design tests which represent the specific psychomotor objectives of the course. While it might at first appear that a student who has become highly proficient in operating a machine lathe would demonstrate considerable transfer to a drill press, research has shown that this is seldom the case. Since the degree of transfer from one task to another depends upon the extent to which the stimulus conditions and appropriate responses are similar, it is not surprising to find little transfer among tasks within the same subject-matter area.

Even though the high degree of specificity of motor skills does make the task of constructing achievement instruments more difficult, there are many opportunities for the industrial educator who is intimately acquainted with the skills that he wishes to measure to develop tests. Although several examples of tests to measure psychomotor objectives in industrial education are given below, most of the discussion in this section is concerned with the methodological problems of developing such tests.[8]

Educational objectives in the psychomotor domain are of major importance in many areas of industrial education. However, some controversy exists over the importance of psychomotor performance in industrial arts. At least one major school of thought, as represented by the Industrial Arts Curriculum Project, still considers this to be an important part of student learning. Others minimize the role psychomotor performance should play. But even when the belief in psychomotor objectives is upheld in industrial arts, the intent is usually not directed toward achieving a high degree of proficiency. Objectives for industrial arts probably extend to the third level of the taxonomy, *Guided response* (*L*), as indicated in Table 23-1, at which behavior represents the earlier stages in the development of motor skill. It is doubtful that many programs in industrial arts attempt to achieve objectives at the next level, *Mechanism* (*M*), at which the response has become habitual and is performed with a degree of confidence.

By contrast, the skill produced in trade training probably achieves the next two levels of objectives in the hierarchy, *Mechanism* (*M*) and *Complex overt response* (*N*). At the *N* level the individual is performing a complex task accurately, efficiently, and with a high degree of muscular control. It is with these three levels of objectives then, that industrial education is concerned.

Fortunately, many of the psychomotor tasks in industrial education produce products which can be evaluated as evidence of psychomotor skill. Psychomotor tests used to evaluate performance of students, sometimes referred to as work-sample tests, have a high degree of face validity. While face validity in a test is generally desirable, it can have disadvantages. It may create a tendency on the part of the test constructor or test user to ignore characteristics of the test, such as reliability, that would be given more careful attention for other measuring instruments.

In most instances the objective physical measurement of the student's performance is more desirable than subjective evaluation, although in some instances the latter are necessary. Objective indices of the accuracy with which a student performs psychomotor tasks are often available. An example is the accuracy with which a machinist can produce bushings of a given size. To provide a gross measure of accuracy, industrial "go" and "no-go" gauges can be used to see if the bushing is within the acceptable tolerances established by the instructor. Measurement of this sort, however, yields dichotomous data (within tolerance or not within tolerance) which might be less precise than the instructor desires. A higher degree of precision could be obtained by checking the dimension with a micrometer. In general, it is more desirable to have continuous data than to have data that simply say the student is performing at an acceptable or an unacceptable level.

Other objective physical measurements which can be used include the accuracy with which an auto mechanic student can adjust the front end of an automobile for caster, camber, and toe-in (see Table 23-2, cells *M*-2.31, *M*-2.32, *M*-2.34); the strength of a solder joint for a television repair man; the squareness of a wood cut for industrial arts students; etc.

[8] As mentioned earlier in this chapter, a distinction is made between psychomotor objectives and perceptual objectives. The reader should keep in mind that this distinction is an oversimplification in most instances, since student behavior usually contains a component from both domains and much of what is discussed in this section is equally applicable to measurement of objectives in the perceptual domain, and vice versa.

Several examples of objective tests of psychomotor performance at the *Mechanism* (M) level are presented below. This level and level *L*, *Guided response*, are undoubtedly the two levels at which assessment is most appropriate for industrial education. While levels *J* (*Perception*) and *K* (*Set*) are prerequisites for performance at higher levels, formal evaluation of them is seldom necessary.

Mechanism (M)

The Machine Indexing Test was designed to measure psychomotor precision which is developed through machine-shop training and which is necessary to perform certain tasks using precision machine tools. In the machine shop, vertical or horizontal milling machines are used to demonstrate and measure the students' skills. Using only the cross-feed screw, the subject is required to perform a series of ten movements, moving the table in and out according to instructions given verbally by the test administrator. An indicator mounted on the machine reveals to the test administrator the accuracy of the subjects moves, and the score is the total absolute error for all ten moves.

This test of psychomotor ability has high reliability and correlates with subtests of cognitive functioning near zero, suggesting that a different dimension of performance is, in fact, being measured.

The Truing Test is another example of the learned psychomotor ability of machine-shop students at the *Mechanism* level. A plug of convenient diameter is placed in a four-jaw chuck which is mounted in an engine lathe. Prior to the test, the plug is offset $\frac{1}{16}$ inch. The student must perform four tasks in a ten-minute period. He must true the plug to within ± 0.0005 as task 1; task 2 is to offset the plug by $\frac{1}{16}$ inch ± 0.0005; tasks 3 and 4 are the reverse of tasks 1 and 2. These tasks require that the student return the equipment to its original setting, which renders it ready for the next student.

This is a timed test, and the score is the total time required for the student to make the several adjustments. The test assumes that the skill of the student is inversely related to the time required for him to perform the task.

This test is reliable and correlates with subtests of cognitive functioning from zero to very low negative, suggesting again that a different dimension of performance is being measured.

Other techniques for measuring psychomotor objectives

Rating systems While it is generally desirable to use objective rather than subjective evaluation of a student's performance, this is not always possible. In many instances the product produced by the student does not lend itself to physical measurement. An example is the quality of a finished surface on wood. In other situations, the student's work might involve a number of different tasks necessary to produce a finished product, as is the case in many industrial arts projects. In these cases, a number of variables must be taken into account in evaluating the overall quality of the product. One technique that has proved useful in evaluating a student's performance in situations such as these is the use of a rating scale. Since subjective evaluation of performance is subject to a number of different types of error (Ghiselli & Brown, 1955), a well-constructed rating scale, accompanied by explicit instructions of what qualities to look for, usually results in higher reliability than subjective evaluations made without the benefit of such a scale. For example, in one study involving the evaluation of fabric patches (Caveny & Weichelt, 1945) subjective evaluations were found to be no better than chance. In another example, a piece of work produced in the machine shop was resubmitted to the same instructor on several different occasions and each time received a different rating, ranging from 72 to 90 (Dolan & Schulz, 1944). Figure 23-1 presents a sample rating scale for evaluating student performance in woodworking.

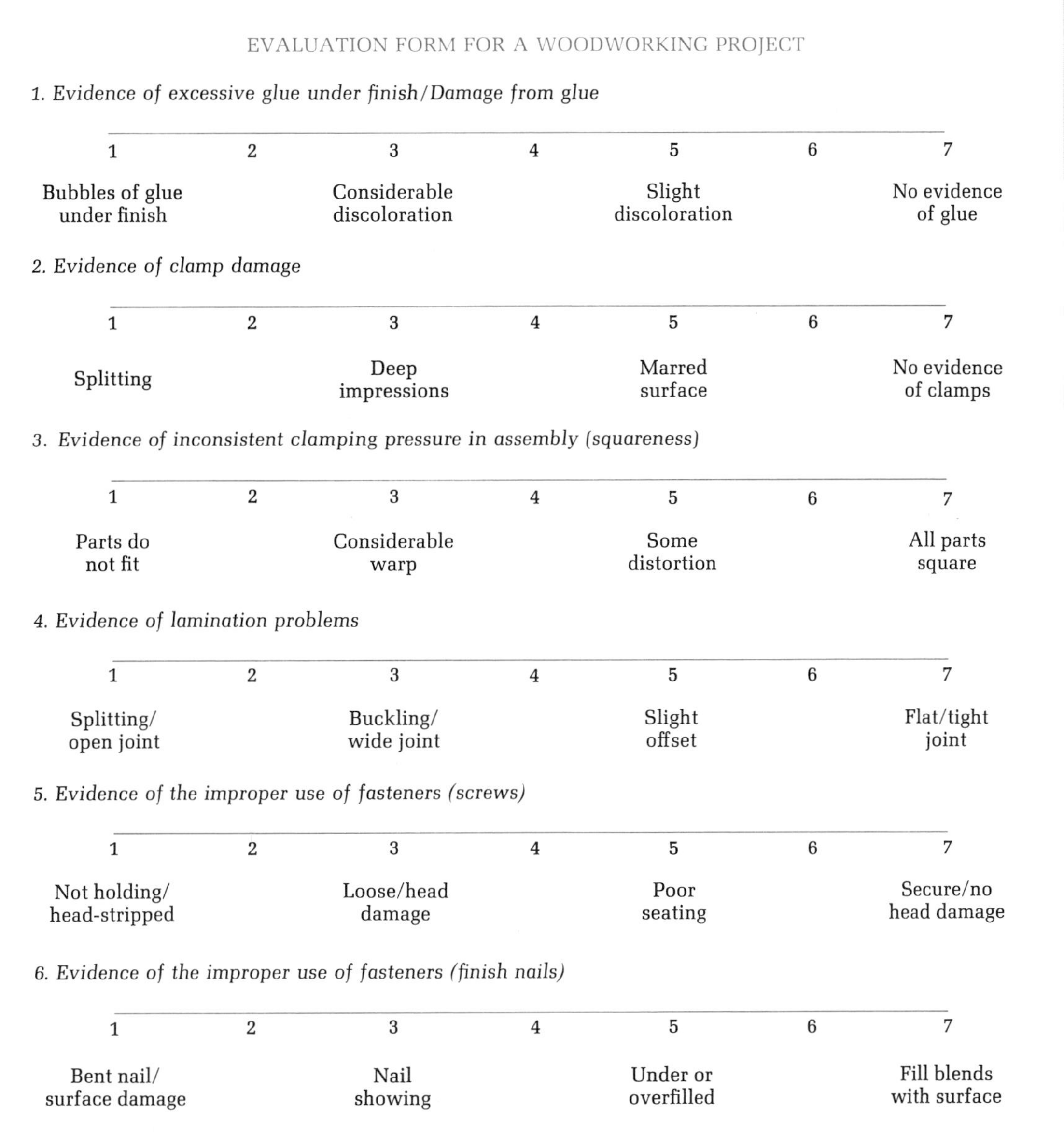
EVALUATION FORM FOR A WOODWORKING PROJECT

1. *Evidence of excessive glue under finish/Damage from glue*

1	2	3	4	5	6	7
Bubbles of glue under finish		Considerable discoloration		Slight discoloration		No evidence of glue

2. *Evidence of clamp damage*

1	2	3	4	5	6	7
Splitting		Deep impressions		Marred surface		No evidence of clamps

3. *Evidence of inconsistent clamping pressure in assembly (squareness)*

1	2	3	4	5	6	7
Parts do not fit		Considerable warp		Some distortion		All parts square

4. *Evidence of lamination problems*

1	2	3	4	5	6	7
Splitting/ open joint		Buckling/ wide joint		Slight offset		Flat/tight joint

5. *Evidence of the improper use of fasteners (screws)*

1	2	3	4	5	6	7
Not holding/ head-stripped		Loose/head damage		Poor seating		Secure/no head damage

6. *Evidence of the improper use of fasteners (finish nails)*

1	2	3	4	5	6	7
Bent nail/ surface damage		Nail showing		Under or overfilled		Fill blends with surface

FIGURE 23-1 Evaluation form for a woodworking project.

The use of a rating system does not necessarily guarantee reliability in the judgment of individual difference in students' performances. Unreliability in making such judgments may come from a number of sources. For example, the selection of a task for evaluation on which students show small individual differences would make it difficult to establish reliability. Other causes of unreliability include inadequate instructions to the rater, lack of training in using these particular rating instruments, and poorly designed instruments. It is therefore important that the instructor empirically demonstrate the reliability of the instrument in the situation for which it was designed. In this instance the most appropriate measure of reliability would be interrater reliability, or the extent to which the ratings of one judge agree with the ratings of another. For a more thorough treatment of rating-scale construction, the reader is referred to *Personnel and Industrial Psychology* (Ghiselli & Brown, 1955).

Comparative standards It has long been recognized that humans make more accurate comparative judgments than they do absolute judgments. In a comparative judgment, the judge has a standard by which to compare the stimulus or object which he is judging. For example, even untrained individuals can make many precise judgments on the loudness of a given tone when a standard for comparison is provided. On the other hand, when no such standard is provided and the individual is required to make an absolute judgment, he can discriminate relatively few degrees of loudness. Research has supported the fact that the human is limited in his ability to make absolute judgments over a wide variety of stimulus conditions to within about seven to nine degrees of the stimulus (Miller, 1956). Much finer discriminations can be made when the judge is provided a standard against which to make his evaluation.

A method which capitalizes on the greater precision of comparative judgments in industrial education is described by Adkins (1947). The procedure for doing this involves the establishment of a series of quality "bench marks" ranging from excellent to poor, which are used by the instructor in evaluating products produced by individual students. A good example of where this method could be applied is the traditional industrial arts laboratory in which it is common to have students produce a series of projects over the period of a school year. While the work produced by these students may involve a number of different behaviors, the ultimate excellence of these projects is often heavily dependent upon their psychomotor ability in the laboratory.

The initial step in constructing such a series of quality bench marks is to identify those products which are not amenable to direct physical measurement and therefore must be evaluated on a somewhat subjective basis. In constructing a scale for a given product, the instructor would select a series of twenty or more samples of this product which range from good to bad. In many instances the actual products produced by students can be used, but it would also be possible for experienced teachers to produce these sample products. The next step is to have several instructors rank these products in order of overall quality. It is necessary to demonstrate that the several instructors do agree on the ranking of the products, that is, that they have high interrater reliability. This can be done by computing the rank-order correlation coefficient between pairs of raters (Siegel, 1956). Obviously, if instructors cannot agree among themselves on which products are good and which are poor, it is unfair to judge students using this system.

The results at this stage of scale development consist of twenty work samples, each of which has been ranked independently by several raters. The next step is to compute the average ranking for each work sample. For example, if work sample A were rated best (a rank of 1) in the group by two raters and second (a rank of 2) in the group by two raters, the average rating would be 1.5. This average ranking provides an index of the overall judged value of this work sample. For example, two work samples could both have an average rank of 10. In one instance, however, the rank of 10 might have been achieved by all raters assigning it that value and in another instance it might have been achieved by ratings of 8, 9, 11, and 12. In the latter case, there is obviously less agreement among raters about the relative standing of that work sample than there was for the first work sample. The first one would clearly be the better choice for inclusion in the final scale.

The final selection of work samples to form the qualitative comparison scale is done as follows. Select samples whose average rank represents approximately equal intervals over the entire range of ratings. (It should be noted that the maximum possible range is determined by the number of samples used. For example, if twenty samples are used, the maximum range of mean ratings is from 1 to 20, and this situation would occur only when all judges agreed on the best and on the poorest quality sample.) At the same time, the samples selected should be chosen from those that show highest agreement among raters as discussed above.

The final product is a series of samples which range from good to poor and on which it has been shown that there is high agreement among raters (interrater reliability). With training in the use of such scales, judges can make highly reliable evaluations of individual student's work by comparing their product with the series of quality bench marks. If desired by the instructor, the mean rating values can be converted to a more convenient scale. For example, a 70 might be assigned to the lowest scale value, and 100 to the highest. Points between these extremes could be prorated to the other samples included in the final scale.

A final check on the reliability of the instrument can be made by correlating the results obtained by two different raters when evaluating the quality of samples produced in a given class.

Special problems in psychomotor testing

Standardized conditions The importance of standardized conditions in testing for psychomotor objectives cannot be overemphasized. Instructions for paper and pencil tests are usually written and are therefore the same for all subjects. They frequently are given orally in tests measuring psychomotor performance. Slight variations in instructions can produce large results in the performance of students. Likewise, since subjects are likely to be tested individually or in small groups, it is more difficult to control factors such as lighting, temperature, and other environmental conditions. Raw materials such as wood and metal should be the same for all students, and above all, any tools or equipment to be used should be of the same type and in the same condition of repair. Since the quality of equipment within a given institution often varies considerably, it is usually better to test all students on the same or identical pieces of equipment.

The accumulation of errors in man-machine systems In much of the testing of psychomotor objectives in industrial education, the individual student is expected to perform on a piece of equipment such as a metal lathe or surface grinder. The student and piece of equipment can be considered jointly as a man-machine system which produces a product. The accuracy of this product is a joint function of the two components of the system, the man and the machine. The importance of the standardization and accuracy of equipment when testing students can best be understood by analyzing how errors, which show up in the final product, accumulate in man-machine systems. A thorough theoretical analysis of how such errors accumulate has been reported by Chapanis (1951).

Two types of error can be identified, and both can be attributed to each component in a system. The two types of error are constant error and variable error. The appropriate measure of constant error is the mean or average of all errors. For example, if a machinist were producing bushings on a machine lathe that were supposed to be 1 inch in diameter and actual measurement of a number of bushings showed the average size to be 1.002 inches in diameter, the constant error would be 0.002 inch.

The most appropriate measure for the variable error is the standard deviation of all errors. In general, the greater the standard deviation, the greater the variability in the product being produced.

Each of these two types of errors can be associated with any component within the system. For example, a machine contributes a constant and variable error, and the human contributes a constant and variable error. Since some error of each type can be associated with each component in the system, the question is how do errors from the various components accumulate in the final product. The rules are simple enough: constant errors add algebraically, and variable errors accumulate according to their squares. Constant errors are of relatively little importance in man-machine systems, regardless of their source within the system, since they can be calibrated out rather easily. For example, if a machinist is consistently producing bushings too large, a minor adjustment to the machine can be made which corrects for this regardless of whether the error is attributable to the operator or the machine. Unfortunately, there is no way of calibrating out the variable error of the system. If the variable error contributed by the machine is small relative to that contributed by the man, there is little reason for concern. For example, if the variable error inherent in the man is equivalent to 40 units (standard deviation = 40), and the variable error inherent in the machine is equivalent to 10 units (standard deviation = 10), representing a ratio of 4 to 1, the variable error of a man and machine together is only 41.23 units.[9] Thus the total error is not much different from that attributable to the man alone. On the other hand, if the variable error inherent in the man is 20 units and that in the machine only 20 units, a ratio of 1 to 1, the error for the man-machine system is 28.28 units, half of which is attributable to the man and half to the machine.

It can be seen, therefore, that as equipment with which the student works has inherent variable error which approaches his own variable error, the equipment contributes significantly to the product which the student produces. If judgments are made comparing students' performance on different machines and the error associated with those two machines varies considerably, erroneous conclusions regarding the relative performance of the students will be reached.

[9] This is derived by computing the square root of the sum of the variances (squared standard deviations) for the man and machine:

$$\text{standard deviation of total error} = \sqrt{40^2 + 10^2} = 41.23$$

Testing for affective objectives (O–S)

As was stated earlier in this chapter and reflected in Table 23-1, affective objectives in industrial education are seldom explicitly stated. The most obvious exception to this is in the field of industrial arts, where an attempt is made to achieve objectives at the lower end of the hierarchy. By contrast, in most areas of trade and technical education, affective objectives are best characterized as implicit and occurring at intermediate stages of the hierarchy. As was stated earlier, it is reasonable for the teacher to assume that most students entering a trade or technical program exhibit behavior at the *Receiving* (O) and *Responding* (P) levels with respect to the particular trade or technology that they have elected. On the other hand, it is equally reasonable to assume that most instructors attempt to achieve objectives at the *Valuing* (Q) and probably the *Organization* (R) levels of the affective hierarchy. The difficulty inherent in explicitly stating affective objectives, and for objectively evaluating their achievement, probably accounts for teachers leaving such objectives at the implicit level. Consideration should, nevertheless, be given to specifying such objectives explicitly.

While it is true that relatively little consideration has been given affective objectives within specific industrial education programs, it is equally true that few other fields of education have at their disposal so many instruments for measuring affective behaviors. The distinction is made here between instruments designed to measure objectives of specific educational programs and instruments that have been designed to measure affective behaviors relating to the choice of an occupation. Much work has been done on the latter question, but it has been an outgrowth of the need existing in the field of counseling and guidance, rather than the need of industrial educators to evaluate specific programs. Since these instruments were developed for purposes other than course evaluation, their applicability to specific educational objectives is somewhat peripheral. Nevertheless, these instruments do have considerable utility in educational programs, and the techniques that they use for measuring student behavior have important implications for the development of other instruments which could be more closely related to specific educational objectives. Some of the major instruments that have been used in vocational counseling will therefore be reviewed in this section, together with a discussion of the techniques of measurement employed by the particular instrument.

Responding (P)

Several instruments have been designed to measure objectives at the responding level of the affective hierarchy. At this level, the authors of the affective domain considered interests as being the most important characteristic. One of the most widely used instruments for assessing occupationally related interests is the Kuder Preference Record (Vocational). While this instrument existed prior to the formulation of the affective domain, it can best be considered as a measure at the responding level. A more recent instrument, the Kuder Preference Record (Occupational), is also available. However, since it was validated in a manner similar to that used in the Strong Vocational Interest Blank discussed below, the Kuder (Vocational) is used here to illustrate a different approach to interest measurement. The student is referred to the *Sixth Mental Measurements Yearbook* (Buros, 1965) for a more detailed discussion of these and other interest inventories.

The Kuder (Vocational) is designed to yield scores indicating a student's interest in each of ten different occupationally related areas: outdoor, mechanical, computational, scientific, persuasive, artistic, literary, musical, social service, and clerical. It can be seen that the scores on this test are not related to specific occupations, as is true of some instruments of this type, but to general areas of activity. These activities in turn can be associated with specific occupations. It is assumed that a student who shows a high interest in the types of activities associated with specific occupations will be more successful in that occupation, assuming that he is able to achieve the cognitive, perceptual, and psychomotor objectives necessary for the occupation, than he would be if he were not interested in those activities.

The manual which accompanies the Kuder provides a "job chart" which helps to call the student's attention to the specific group of occupations most appropriate for his particular profile. It is thereby possible for the teacher or counselor to make the transition from the ten general areas of vocational interests to interest in specific jobs.

The technique of measurement used in the Kuder is to present the student with a set of three activities, each of which belongs to one of the ten categories. The student's task is to select the activity which he likes most and to select the activity which he likes least. The particular combination of activities contained in the various items (triad of activities) varies from one item to the next. For example, in the first item the student might be asked to select from an activity associated with the outdoors, a mechanical activity, and a computational activity. In the next item he might be asked to select from an activity associated with the outdoors, a scientific activity, and an artistic activity. The entire test contains items which require the student to select from a specific activity over each of the other nine for which scores are provided. If a student consistently selects mechanical activities over activities contained in the other nine categories he would receive a high score on mechanical interests. Likewise, if he consistently says that he prefers least those activities which are identified as artistic he would receive a low score on artistic interests. The result produces a profile of interests for the student covering the ten activities assessed by this test. This profile is then related to specific occupations through the job chart mentioned above.

To illustrate how this technique might be applied to evaluating affective objectives within a specific educational program, suppose an automechanic instructor wanted to assess the interest shown by his students in each of several areas.

The following item is an example of how this could be done.

Responding to alternative automotive repair jobs

35. Listed below are three tasks which a mechanic is expected to perform. In the blank space next to the tasks, write an "M" to indicate the one you would like to do *most*, and an "L" for the one you would like to do *least*.
    ___ Perform a valve and ring job
    ___ Trace a short in the electrical system
    ___ Repair a hydraulic brake system

A somewhat different approach to the measurement of affective behaviors that are significant in the choice of an occupation is that found in the Strong Vocational Interest Blank for Men (another version is available for women). While this blank is oriented largely toward the professions rather than toward the occupations with which industrial education is concerned, the techniques of measurement of affective behaviors are applicable and are therefore reviewed in this section.

The philosophy behind the construction of the Strong Vocational Interest Blank (SVIB) is somewhat different from that for the Kuder (Vocational). The approach used by Strong was empirical, rather than rational. In other words, Strong demonstrated that certain interests in activities, people, occupations, school subjects, etc., differed for different occupational groups. For example, if a significantly larger proportion of engineers liked "driving an automobile" than did the population as a whole, this is taken as empirical evidence that driving an automobile is associated with the profession of engineering. While a single activity such as driving an automobile would, of course, not be taken as evidence that a person should become an engineer, the collective interests over the entire scale do provide such evidence. Since the scale contains 400 items, it has been possible through research to show that certain groups of these tend to be preferred more by people in a given occupation than they are by the general population. A person who chooses a similar interest pattern to those in this occupation would, then, be considered more likely to be successful in that occupation than he would in a field where his interest pattern is not like others in the occupation. Again, this assumes that other attributes necessary for success in the occupation, such as intellectual abilities and motivation, are possessed by the individual.

The technique of measurement used in the Strong is different from that used in the Kuder. In the Strong, the student is presented with a series of occupations, school subjects, activities, peculiarities of people, etc., about which he must make judgments. While there are several different types of items in the test, the majority of them require that the student react by indicating whether he likes, is indifferent to, or dislikes the particular occupation, school subjects, etc., that are presented in the item. For example, the student may be required to indicate whether he likes, is indifferent to, or dislikes (1) the idea of being a real estate salesman, (2) the subject of physics, (3) reading detective stories.

The most significant feature of the Strong which has led to its widespread acceptance in the areas of vocational counseling is the extensive use of empirical analysis in establishing the instrument's validity. The research that stands behind this inventory is the result of many years of effort and successive refinements of the instrument. Such an extensive investment in establishing the validity of an instrument is beyond the typical teacher. Nevertheless, the approach is one which is applicable to measuring affective behaviors and on a more modest scale could be applied to educational objectives within specific programs. The typical teacher would probably have to rely more on the content validity and the rationale underlying the items than on extensive empirical data.

An instrument designed to measure interest in occupations which are more appropriate for industrial educators is the Gordon Occupational Check List. This checklist contains a series of 240 activities appropriate for occupations for which less than a college-level education is required. The activities are grouped into the five major categories of business, outdoor, arts, technology, and service. The instrument is designed primarily for use by counselors and has received less empirical study of its validity than either the Strong or Kuder. Since this instrument is relatively new, compared to the above two instruments, it is reasonable to expect that additional research studies will be forthcoming.

The technique for measuring the various activities requires a student to underline the activity that he would like to perform on a job. After he has done this, he is requested to return and indicate those activities that he would like to do the very most. While the technique for administering the instrument is very straightforward, and the instrument has a degree of face validity, additional research is needed. It is of particular significance for industrial education, however, as it represents those activities associated with jobs of less than college-degree requirement, the occupations with which industrial education is concerned.

Valuing (Q)

The next level of the affective hierarchy is the valuing level; it is most closely associated with what has been referred to in traditional psychometrics as attitude measurement. The field of attitude measurement is a very broad one on which a substantial body of research literature has been developed. A thorough treatment of the subject in this chapter is impossible. However, an attempt will be made to introduce the reader to several techniques that are widely used in measuring attitudes and to certain existing instruments that are useful in measuring attitudes of importance in industrial education.

A widely used technique for measuring attitudes is the Thurstone method of equal-appearing intervals (see Woodworth & Schlosberg, 1965, pp. 246–252). The first step involved in constructing a Thurstone scale is to collect a large number of statements dealing with the attitude in question. These should range from positive statements, representing a favorable attitude, to negative statements, representing an unfavorable attitude. An example of such a statement is, "The field of electronics holds the key to the advancement of technology."

Next, a group of judges is asked to sort these statements into a series of categories, usually eleven, which they feel are equally spaced with respect to the underlying attitude. For example, the above statement would be perceived by most judges as reflecting a very positive attitude toward electronics and would be placed in one of the categories toward the upper end of the scale.

Statements for inclusion in the final scale are selected which represent various points on the attitude continuum and on which there is high agreement among the judges. The final scale then consists of a small number of the original items representing different points along the attitude continuum. In using the scale, the respondent is asked to check those items with which he agrees, and his score on the scale is the median value for all items checked.

A second widely used technique for measuring attitudes is the Likert Scale. Using the Likert system, respondents are requested to rate each statement, such as the one given above regarding electronics, according to the following system: strongly approve, approve, undecided, disapprove, and strongly disapprove. These categories are assigned values of 5, 4, 3, 2, and 1, for positively worded items, and the reverse for negatively worded items. Items are selected for inclusion in the final scale which correlate highly with the total score, thus producing a scale which is homogeneous in the sense that it measures a common underlying attitude. Items included in the final scale are scored according to the same five-point system mentioned above, and the score for an individual respondent is the sum of his responses to all items contained in the scale.

The above discussion is an attempt to familiarize the reader with two of the most widely used measurement techniques for attitudes. A thorough treatment of the psychometric problems involved in the measurement of attitudes is beyond the scope of this chapter, and the student is referred to Shaw and Wright's *Scales for the Measurement of Attitudes* (1967) for a more detailed, nontechnical discussion of these problems.

This book also contains a compilation of attitude instruments which have been developed by different authors dealing with attitudes toward a number of subjects. The book draws heavily upon the research literature and provides essential information regarding each of the attitude scales that is reported. For example, the actual instrument is reproduced, a description of the scale is provided, and a description of subjects on which the scale was developed, the method of responding, scoring, reliability and validity, and general comments by the authors regarding the scale are given. Several of the scales included in this book are of potential interest for industrial educators. The book contains instruments for measuring attitudes toward the following subjects: any occupation, labor, union toward management, the company, and the supervisor.

The authors recognize that data supporting the reliability and validity of many of these instruments are insufficient to warrant their use in making individual decisions. They point out that some of the instruments should be used only for research purposes and for group testing because of the lack of such pertinent information. The reader should, therefore, consider carefully the summary of pertinent data which accompany each of the scales in evaluating them for use on an individual testing basis.

Organization (*R*)

The *Organization* level of affective behavior probably represents the highest objective in the hierarchy that is attempted within most of industrial education. At this level the student has internalized a series of values and begun the process which ultimately culminates in the highest level of the affective domain, that being characterized by a value complex which influences his behavior in all aspects of his life (behavior S). At these higher levels the assessment of affective behavior becomes a much more difficult task, even when it is not attempted in relation to specific educational objectives. The problem approaches a complexity requiring the type of insight into the personality of the student which can be accomplished best in a clinical setting and is beyond the scope of most teachers.

Nevertheless, some assessment techniques can be used for measuring behavior at these levels. Rating systems, which were discussed earlier in the chapter, have been designed to measure objectives at this level. It is not uncommon, for example, for rating scales used to evaluate technical competence to include questions such as, "What is the student's dedication to the field of electronics?" The instructor is asked to rate the student on a scale from high to low. As discussed earlier, however, rating systems are subject to a number of different types of errors. Even when the behavior being rated is easily observable, for example, behaviors having to do with quality and quantity of production, the sources of error are a major problem. When the behaviors in question become less easily observed, as is usually the case with behaviors belonging to the affective domain, the problems associated with rating scales are significantly increased.

One technique which overcomes some of the problems associated with rating scales and is appropriate for higher-level affective objectives is peer rating (see Doll & Longo, 1962; Fisk & Cox, 1960; Hollander, 1956; Prien & Lee, 1965; Suci, Vallance, & Glickman, 1954). In peer ratings, each student in a class is asked to nominate several (usually three or four) fellow students who are outstanding with respect to some particular attribute. This technique takes advantage of the fact that interaction among students is often quite close and the students often have an opportunity, for example, in the industrial education laboratory, to observe each other for much greater lengths of time than a single instructor has for each student.

If all students in the class nominate a particular student as being outstanding with respect to the attribute in question, one would conclude that the particular student probably exceeds most members of the class. On the other hand, a student receiving no nominations from his peers would be considered to be at the lower end of the class with respect to the attribute being evaluated.

An example of how peer rating might be used in assessing individual differences among students on higher level affective behaviors is presented below.

Peer Rating for Auto Mechanics

Upon graduation from your program you are considering establishing a garage to service automobiles. Your lack of funds to establish this business alone makes it necessary for you to consider a partner. Nominate the three classmates that you feel show the greatest dedication to the occupation of auto mechanics. You should assume that all of your fellow students have equal competence in terms of their technical ability. Your nomination should be based on the dedication that fellow students have to this occupation since this is the major factor which will ultimately determine the success of your business venture.

1. ____________________
2. ____________________
3. ____________________

The score for particular students using this system is the total number of nominations that they receive from other members of the class. While negative nominations can be used (for example, name the three students that you would least like to enter business with) these are often met with resistance and seem to add little to the overall evaluations.

It should be noted that several methodological problems arise in using this system. For example, direct comparisons from one class to another cannot be made if the class size varies greatly. Since the maximum score a student can get is determined by the number of students in the class, interpretation of the raw score (number of nominations) requires caution. For example, a student receiving ten nominations in a class containing ten students would be quite a different situation than a student receiving ten nominations in a class containing twenty students.

It also should be pointed out that differences in the ability of the total class markedly influence the results. For example, a student receiving ten nominations in an average class of auto mechanics would not be the same as a student receiving ten nominations in a class of ten outstanding students. If one can assume that several classes are equally talented, the number of nominations can be converted into a standard score which takes into account differences in class size and permits comparison across classes. If this assumption cannot be met, interpretation of results should be limited to describing individual differences of students within the particular class in question.

This technique has been used widely in assessing complex affective behaviors in a variety of situations although not as related to specific educational objectives. For example, the author has successfully used this technique in assessing the commitment of Peace Corps volunteers for the overseas work for which they were being trained. Such trainees know that their success in a foreign country is highly dependent upon other volunteers with whom they are working and, in fact, the very well being of a volunteer often is in the hands of his colleagues.

Problems of formative evaluation

A detailed discussion of formative evaluation is presented in Chap. 6, where the philosophical as well as practical distinctions between formative and summative evaluation are discussed. It will be recalled that formative evaluation takes place at the completion of a unit of learning and is designed to determine the degree of mastery that a student has obtained for all elements of learning contained in the unit. It will also be recalled that the elements of learning, as conceived in formative testing, are hierarchical and that test items at each level of the behavior hierarchy should be included in a formative test.

The concept of formative evaluation of student learning is a recent one in the literature regarding testing. In practice, however, the ideas underlying formative evaluation have been employed by teachers in industrial education for many years, and in fact, they outdate the formal discipline of psychometrics as it is known today. In the early master-apprentice relationship, and today in the instructor-student relationship of the laboratory, the process of evaluating the performance of the apprentice or student is essentially a type of formative evaluation. The work of the student is periodically evaluated by the instructor, feedback is provided the student, and remedial work is undertaken until the level of mastery established by the instructor has been reached.

This section contains two examples of formative evaluation in industrial education and presents a generalized model of formative evaluation. It is hoped that this model will help the test constructor conceptualize new units of study in the framework of formative evaluation. The means of applying this model and the data yielded by the model will be discussed in terms of the implications for both students and instructor.

Specifications for a unit in auto mechanics

Table 23-6 presents the Table of Specifications for a Unit on Wheel Alignment for Auto Mechanics. To master this unit successfully, the student must learn the applied geometric concepts underlying the operation of the front end of an automobile, how these concepts are related to the automobile's construction, the consequences of out-of-tolerance conditions in the front end, and how to correct such conditions.

The objectives in Table 23-6, which are keyed to the outline presented in Table 23-2, were arrived at through an analysis of the subject matter that the student is expected to master. For example, in analyzing the unit it can be seen that a knowledge of positive caster is essential for the mastery of this unit. An item measuring this knowledge is:

A-1.21

36. Positive caster is the
    a. inward tilt of the kingpin at the top
    b. outward tilt of the kingpin at the top
    c. forward tilt of the kingpin at the top
    *d. backward tilt of the kingpin at the top

Mastery of this objective is necessary to achieve the next higher level, which deals with an understanding of roll-out on turns, as measured by the following item:

B-1.21

37. Positive caster will tend to cause the car to
    *a. roll-out on turns
    b. lean-in on turns
    c. toe-out on turns
    d. bank on turns

It can also be seen that to obtain objective *C*-1.21, which deals with altering the spindle supports, it is necessary that the student master the concepts of positive and negative caster. An example of how objective *C*-1.21 could be measured is represented by the following item:

C-1.21

38. The top of the front spindle support is tilted toward the rear of the car to obtain
    a. positive camber
    b. negative caster
    *c. positive caster
    d. negative camber

At the *Application of understanding* level (*D*), the problem confronting the student involves elements to which he has not previously been exposed. The following item represents a situation with which auto-mechanic students are seldom confronted. Nevertheless, a thorough understanding of the principles of caster and camber would permit him to solve the problem successfully.

TABLE 23-6 TABLE OF SPECIFICATIONS FOR A UNIT ON WHEEL ALIGNMENT FOR AUTO MECHANICS

A. *Knowledge*	B. *Understanding*	C. *Application of knowledge*	D. *Application of understanding*
1.21 Caster	Steering stability		
1.21 Caster angles		Diagnosis of steering difficulties	Consequences of structural modification
1.21 Positive caster	Roll-out on turns	Altering spindle supports	
1.21 Negative caster			
1.21 Camber	Uneven tire tread wear		
1.21 Camber angle			
1.21 Positive camber			
1.21 Negative camber	Inward tilting of front wheels		
1.2 Steering geometry	Centerline of wheel and kingpin or ball joint		
1.22 Steering axis inclination	Structural faults		Adjustments for absorbing suspension shocks
1.22 Kingpins			
1.22 Ball joints		Adding or removing shims	
1.22 Steering knuckle	Effect of altering angles		
1.23 Toe-in and toe-out	Point of intersection	Adjustment of tie rods	
2.1 Alignment test equipment			

D-1.21

39. On the type of suspension systems with a single inner support for the lower control arm, changing the length of the strut rod between the lower arm and frame changes
    a. camber angle
    *b. caster angle
    c. axis inclination
    d. toe-out on turns

Specifications for a unit in electronics technology

Table 23-7 presents a Table of Specifications for a Unit on Transformers for Electronics. Again, the interrelationships among the several levels of cognitive functioning are represented by lines connecting the objectives. For example, the following item represents the *Application of understanding* level (*D*):

Application of understanding of transformer design

40. To match a 20K-ohm source to an 8-ohm load in a transformer requires a turns ratio of:
    a. 25/1
    *b. 50/1
    c. 250/1
    d. 500/1

To answer this item successfully a student must be able to determine the power transfer (level *C*), understand the effects of turns ratio on voltage (level *B*), and know what is meant by turns ratio (level *A*).

Selection of items for inclusion in formative tests

As was discussed earlier, a major purpose of formative testing is to provide short-term feedback to students and instructors regarding mastery of critical elements in a particular learning unit. This is contrasted with the primary purpose of summative testing, which is to sample those behaviors intended to be taught over an entire course. Furthermore, formative testing is not intended to report results to the student by comparing his performance to other students in the class, but rather to report his mastery of the material contained in the particular learning unit. As stated earlier, such a report to the student should be in terms of the proportion of formative test questions answered correctly.

However, the ease with which students can answer a particular test question correctly is a function of a number of different factors, only one of which is the student's learning. Factors such as wording of the question and the attractiveness of alternatives influence the ease with which a given question can be answered correctly. It is suggested, therefore, that questions to be included in a formative test be selected not only on the basis of relevance for that unit, but also on the basis of their psychometric characteristics. While this is not always possible, it is suggested that questions to be used in formative testing might well be those that have previously been used in summative tests prior to their inclusion in formative tests. This provides the educator with additional information upon which to select test items for inclusion in formative tests and supplements his judgment about the utility of a particular question. If, for example, a question regarding knowledge of a particular fact is considered by the educator to be relevant to a particular unit of instruction, the fact that that question discriminates between students making high and low scores on a summative test (has a high item-total correlation) would provide additional evidence to the test construction in favor of its inclusion in a formative test.

The difficulty level (proportion of students getting the item correct), as determined in the summative test, would provide even further evidence upon which the formative-test constructor might decide to include a particular item. The fact that an item has a difficulty level of .50 (half the students get it correct) in a summative test does not argue against its inclusion in a formative test where the goal is to have approximately 80 to 85 percent of the

TABLE 23-7 TABLE OF SPECIFICATIONS FOR A UNIT ON TRANSFORMERS FOR ELECTRONICS

A. *Knowledge*	B. *Understanding*	C. *Application of knowledge*	D. *Application of understanding*
Function of the transformer	Hysteresis loss	Distortion of current by inphase hysteresis loss	
Eddy currents			
Coil resistance			
Electromagnetism	Magnetic field		
Magnetic flux	Residual magnetism		
Induction, inductance	Incremental inductance		
Mutual inductance	Power transferral	Calculation of inductance with parameter values	
Electromagnetic induction	Pickup and energizing coils		
Self-induction			
Primary, secondary windings	Primary current	Calculation of % efficiency Calculation of terminal voltage	
Turns; ratios	Effects on voltage	Determination of power transfer	Matching source to load
Impedance	Matching	Matching of source impedance Matching source to load impedance	
Coupling	Frequency response curves R-C couplings		
Voltage addition	Combined ac and dc		
Reference point	Phase voltage		Shifting the reference point

students answer correctly. In general, one would expect a question included in a summative test to be considerably more difficult than the same question included in a formative test. Nevertheless, if the instructor feels that the particular question is relevant to adequate mastery of a particular unit of learning, he would be justified in including that item in a formative test and striving for 80 to 85 percent mastery.

A model for formative evaluation

Table 23-8 presents a generalized model of formative evaluation. It can be seen that behavioral objectives at the several levels of cognition are represented on the vertical axis and are designated sequentially with the behavioral-objective category that they are designed to measure. For example, item 1 is the first item of

Table 23-8 Model for Formative Evaluation

	Students 1 2 3 . . . . *n*	$\sum_{1}^{n} X_J$	$\sum_{1}^{n} X_J$	Objectives $\sum_{1}^{n} X_J$	$\sum_{1}^{n} X_J$
		A Knowledge	B Understanding	C Application of knowledge	D Application of understanding
Items	1	X_{11}			
	2	X_{12}			
		X_{13}			
		⋮			
	C	X_{1C}			
	D		X_{1D}		
			⋮		
	F		X_{1F}		
	G			X_{1G}	
				⋮	
	I			X_{1I}	
	J				X_{1J}
	K				X_{1K}
		$\sum_{1}^{C} X_i$	$\sum_{D}^{F} X_i$	$\sum_{G}^{I} X_i$	$\sum_{J}^{K} X_i$

the category designated *Knowledge*, and item C is the last item in that category. Item D designates the first item designed to measure the behavioral objective *Understanding*, and item F is the last item in that category. It should be noted that an entry does not occur in each cell of the matrix. Finally, K represents the total number of items in this particular test.

Table 23-8 also represents individual student's performance on various items in the formative tests. Students are represented on the Z axis and the number in a particular class is designated as n. The levels of cognitive objectives necessary to cover this unit of learning are shown on the horizontal axis. It should be pointed out that the number of objectives, as well as the domains from which they come, might vary both from one curriculum to another and within units of instruction for a given curriculum. For example, one unit might concentrate on objectives that could best be described as lower-level cognitive objectives. Another unit within the same curriculum might include both cognitive and psychomotor objectives.

This conceptual model presents us, then, with a method of looking at the performance of a class on a particular formative test by educational objectives included in the test specifications. Looking at the notation accompanying Table 23-8 one can see that a number of different kinds of information are yielded by such a test. As presented in Table 23-8, the notation $X_{i,J}$ represents the score for any student on any item. It can be seen that the first subscript (lower case) designates the student, and the second subscript (capitals) designates the item. X_{11} represents the score for student 1 on item 1; X_{21} represents the score for student 2 on item 1; X_{12} represents the score for student 1 on item 2, etc. It now becomes possible to write a number of characteristics of this particular test that are important for individual student evaluation and for instructor evaluation.

Student diagnosis One of the major functions performed by formative tests is student diagnosis. Feedback to a student regarding his mastery of the various objectives in a given unit of learning provides him with the various objectives in a given unit of learning provides him with the information necessary to either progress to the next unit or to take remedial measures to obtain mastery. Using the model above, the instructor can provide diagnostic information for each student.

The most general information that could be provided the student would be his overall performance on the formative test. This would be his total score for this particular test and would be represented by the equation:

$\sum_{1}^{K} X_i =$ the sum of all items (1 to K) for student "i" (if items are scored wrong = 0 and right = 1 this quantity becomes the number of items answered correctly and can be converted to a proportion by dividing by K)

If the student's performance on the total test reaches the established criterion of mastery, he would be ready to proceed to the next unit. However, if his performance does not reach this level, the instructor should provide more detailed information to tell the student where his performance is inadequate. More specific information could be provided by reporting the student's performance on each category of behavioral objectives contained in that particular unit.

It can be seen in Table 23-8 that the K items have been broken up into subgroups corresponding to the objective which they are designed to measure. For example, items 1 to C are those items that measure behaviors classified as *Knowledge*, items D to F correspond to behaviors classified as *Understanding*, etc. To represent this algebraically, therefore, the instructor would write $\sum_{1}^{C} X_i/C$ as the expression for the proportion of *Knowledge* items answered correctly by the ith student. The following four quantities represent the level of mastery for the ith student on each category of behavioral objectives.

$\sum_{1}^{C} X_i/C =$ level of mastery for the ith student on *Knowledge* objectives

$\sum_{D}^{F} X_i/F - C =$ level of mastery for the ith student on *Understanding* objectives

$\sum_{G}^{I} X_i/I - F =$ level of mastery for the ith student on *Application of knowledge* objectives

$\sum_{J}^{K} X_i/K - I =$ level of mastery for the ith student on *Application of understanding* objectives

The above information provides the individual student with a "profile of mastery" at each category of objectives. Since these objectives are hierarchical—that is, successful performance at lower levels is a necessary but not sufficient condition for successful performance at higher levels—it can be expected that lack of mastery at lower-level behaviors will prevent successful performance of higher-level behaviors.

If a student fails to reach criterion level in one of the categories of objectives, the next level of feedback that the instructor should provide would include information in individual objectives that the student has failed to master. This, of course, is represented by individual items in a formative test. As discussed in Chap. 6, feedback at this level should be accompanied by sources for remedial work to ensure mastery of that objective. In the model, information at this level is represented below:

$X_{iJ} =$ performance of the ith student on the Jth item

Instructor diagnosis A second major function served by formative tests is diagnosis by the instructor. The most general information that the instructor needs is his overall success in achieving mastery of all objectives with all students. This is represented as follows:

$\sum_{1}^{K} \sum_{1}^{n} X/Kn =$ the average level of mastery for all students over all objectives

If this value falls short of acceptable criterion performance, the instructor should evaluate the performance of his class in more detail. The next step would be to examine his success in achieving mastery for each of the categories of objectives. This can be written as follows:

$\sum_{1}^{C} \sum_{1}^{n} X/Cn =$ the average level of mastery for all students on all *Knowledge* items

$\sum_{D}^{F} \sum_{1}^{n} X/(F - C)(n) =$ the average level of mastery for all students on all *Understanding* items

$\sum_{G}^{I} \sum_{1}^{n} X/(I - F)(n) =$ the average level of mastery for all students on all *Application of knowledge* items

$\sum_{J}^{K} \sum_{1}^{n} X/(K - I)(n) =$ the average level of mastery for all students on all *Application of understanding* items

The above provides the instructor with a "profile of success" in teaching the several categories of behavioral objectives. If the results of this profile suggest that the instructor is failing to achieve criterion performance for a particular category, his next step would be to examine his success on individual objectives in that category. This can be expressed as follows:

$\sum_{1}^{n} X_J/n =$ proportion of students successfully completing the Jth item

As discussed in Chap. 6, failure by the majority of the class to achieve a given objective suggests that the instructor reassess his method of teaching that objective.

The above conceptual model for formative tests provides further information of importance to the instructor. For example, the quality control advantage discussed in Chap. 6 could easily be implemented by the instructor. A series of profiles for a given unit over different classes would indicate his success in teaching that unit with reference to his past successes. A further advantage of this model of formative testing is the relative ease in programming the results for computer processing. All the indices of performances by student and instructor discussed above could be provided easily for any given test. In addition, the references necessary for remedial work to master any objective could be programmed so that the computer printed them out with each individual student's diagnosis. For example, if a student misses an item dealing with caster in the auto-mechanics area, the computer would automatically print out several references to assist him in mastering this concept.

Standardized achievement tests

In reviewing the literature on testing in vocational education, the most obvious conclusion that one can reach is that virtually no work has been done in standardized achievement testing until very recent years. This is in contrast with a very large number of predictive studies in which researchers have attempted to predict achievement from standardized aptitude batteries. Many of these predictive studies have been well designed and carried out. In most cases, they have used tests such as the General Aptitude Test Battery, the Differential Aptitude Test, or the Flanagan Aptitude Classification Test. Each of these batteries has been well standardized and all are accepted as providing a good, comprehensive picture of an individual's aptitude.

Ideally, such prediction studies would rely on objective criteria against which validities could be established. Unfortunately, such objective criteria have seldom been available. Instead of standardized achievement tests, these studies have typically been conducted with teachers' grades, teachers' ratings, or locally produced, and as yet unproven, subject-matter tests. The lack of standardized achievement tests in vocational education has resulted in a severe disadvantage to those involved in this discipline.

There is a substantial interest growing throughout the country in the development of standardized tests for vocational education. This interest has been demonstrated by individual researchers, by state organizations concerned with vocational education, and by several of the national testing services. The interest in this area ranges from concern by individual researchers for better instruments with which to study the process of learning to the interest of national organizations in the certification of individuals in particular technologies. There seems little question that the certification of technicians in many fields will be a reality within the next decade. The upgrading of the technician, to a point approximating the engineer of several years ago, places a burden on that profession to provide some certification of competence. Since these technologies lack the uniformity of instructional programs that exist in university settings, some means of certifying competence is considered a necessity. Standardized achievement tests are one way of accomplishing this.

For a variety of reasons, then, the efforts now going on in the development of standardized instruments for vocational education are only a small beginning to what can be expected over the next decade. There is undoubtedly much work being conducted by individuals in vocational education today which is not generally available to those who are not directly involved in that field. One of the most technically sound programs being presently conducted, for example, is reported only in a locally produced brochure, and information is not generally available through the recognized research journals on testing. The advancement of the state of the art of achievement testing in industrial education could be enhanced considerably if those involved in test development provided for more widespread dissemination of their efforts, such as professional journals devoted to problems of testing.

The Ohio trade and industrial achievement tests

One of the outstanding contributions to standardized achievement testing in vocational education has been made by the state of Ohio. This program was originated in 1958 and represents one of the major efforts toward developing standardized achievement tests in trade and industrial education. For the first five years the program was limited to Ohio. However, since that time a number of other states have participated in this testing program. The program is designed to test the level of achievement for high school students in several trade areas. Additional areas are planned for the program in the future. While the program is not designed specifically around any of the existing taxonomies, it does attempt to have students respond to a number of situations representing a continuum of cognitive complexity.

The program is a well designed one, and in addition to the achievement tests, the Stanford Arithmetic Achievement Test and the California Survey of Mental Maturity are administered to the same students. This provides data which help anchor achievement in specific areas to well-established tests of cognitive functioning. The procedures used to implement this program reflect a high degree of competence in vocational achievement testing. Committees are formed and have representatives from the state supervisory staff, educators of teachers, supervisors of trade and industrial education, selected teachers of the course, and a representative of the testing program. This committee's function is to develop outlines of subject-matter content, to develop questions reflecting the educational objectives of the program, to review the results of experimental testing for individual items, and to revise tests for subsequent use. The Instructional Material Laboratory of the Ohio Trade and Industrial Education Service compiles, publishes, and distributes the tests and handles all scoring, reporting, and evaluation of test results. Details on test validity are reported by the Ohio Trade and Industrial Service, and several types of validity information are presented. For example, validity of content is assured by the formation of committees discussed above. A degree of construction validity is claimed by intercorrelating the tests with others administered at the same time. Concurrent validity with teachers' grades is also reported.

The areas covered to date by this program include machine trades, automotive mechanics, basic electricity, basic electronics, mechanical drafting, and printing. Detailed psychometric characteristics of these tests are reported for both juniors and seniors in high school and include the means, standard deviations, and reliability coefficients for the total tests, although no reliabilities are reported for individual subtests. In addition, this program reports the standard error of measurement as well as intercorrelation of the achievement tests with the standard measures of cognitive functions mentioned above.

A number of related research studies are in process. These have to do with questions such as the background and preparation of teachers, the relationship of expenditure per student and quality programs, and self-concept of trade and industrial teachers. Results of these studies have not been reported in the literature, but they are available from the Instructional Materials Laboratory, The Ohio State University, Columbus, Ohio. The tests appear to be quite comprehensive and involve from 1½ hours of testing for electronics to as much as 6 hours of testing for machinists, draftsmen, and sheet metal workers. The project has taken great care to ensure test security, a problem of considerable importance in achievement testing. Instructors are not allowed to review tests, and the administration of the instruments is handled by someone who is not directly concerned with instruction.

Reliabilities of the total tests in each of the areas mentioned above are quite high. For high school seniors they are as follows: machine trades .95; auto mechanics .96; basic electricity .95; basic electronics .90; mechanical drafting .92; and printing .97.

While this program deals with only a few of the areas with which industrial education is concerned, it probably represents the most extensive effort in achievement test development that is operational today. The Instructional Materials Laboratory, Trade and Industrial Education, The Ohio State University, Columbus, Ohio 43210, administers this program for the State Department of Education, Division of Vocational Education. A service for the administration of these tests is provided by this organization, and the reader is referred to this organization for details regarding the use of these tests. (See Ohio Trade and Industrial Education Service, 1966.)

The University of Illinois achievement tests

With the increased emphasis on vocational education, as reflected in the Vocational Education Act of 1963, the U. S. Office of Education funded a major program to develop achievement tests for post high school education in trades and technologies. This program, on which the author served as principal investigator, was conducted jointly by the University of Illinois and North Carolina State University and was funded for a four-year period ending in June 1970. Preliminary results of this effort are presented below. A detailed report of this project was to be published in the summer of 1970 as a final report on the U. S. Office of Education Grant No. OEG-0-8-051315-3626(085) as well as in journals on educational measurement. The program was designed to assess competence in five trades and two technologies. The five trades include auto mechanics, electrical installation and maintenance, machine shop, radio and television repair, and air-conditioning, heating, and refrigeration. These programs are typically designed as one-year, full-time programs in post high school technical institutes and junior colleges. The two technologies, which are typically two-year post high school programs, are electronics and data processing. Details of the procedure used in developing these instruments will be published as indicated above. Arrangements are currently being made to provide these instruments to educational institutions interested in assessment of proficiency in the several areas covered by this project. A brief description of the tests is presented below.

In the machine trades area, the tests consist of eight parts as follows: hand tools and applications, measuring tools and processes, cutting tools, milling machines, lathes, grinding machines, minor machines, and metallurgy. The subtests contain from twenty-five to eighty items and require between twenty and seventy minutes each. Reliabilities range from .31 to .87 for the subtest and the total test reliability is .95.

For auto mechanics, seven subtests cover engines, fuel systems, electrical systems, chassis and suspensions, brakes, air-conditioning, and power trains. These subtests contain from twenty-five to sixty items and require from twenty to fifty-five minutes per subtest. Reliabilities range from .56 to .89 and total test reliability is .97.

In radio and television servicing, seven subtests include fundamentals of direct current, fundamentals of alternating current, fundamentals of vacuum tubes, semiconductors, circuits, radio, and television. These subtests contain from thirty to seventy items and require twenty-five to fifty minutes. Reliabilities range from .79 to .86 with a total test reliability of .96.

For the curriculum in air-conditioning, heating, and refrigeration, six subtests cover principles of refrigeration, refrigeration applications, controls, air-conditioning, blueprint reading and estimating, and materials tools and safety. They contain from twenty-five to eighty items and require between twenty and seventy-five minutes for administration. Reliabilities range from .62 to .89 with a total test reliability of .95.

The area of electrical installation and maintenance is organized into seven subtests covering basic electrical theory, machines and controls, construction wiring, basic electronic theory, industrial electrical applications, diagnosis of electrical malfunctions, and safety personnel and equipment. These tests contain from twenty-five to forty-five items each and require from twenty-five to fifty minutes for administration. Reliabilities for the subtests range from .70 to .87 with a total test reliability of .94.

The test on electronics technology is organized into six parts consisting of fundamentals of electricity, fundamentals of electronics, instrumentation, application of electronics, special circuitry, and systems analysis. The subtests contain from thirty to forty-five items and require thirty to forty-five minutes for administration. Reliabilities for subtests range from .76 to .86 with a total test reliability of .96.

The second technology covered in this program is data processing. Since data processing has at least two major areas of application, business and scientific, two versions of this test were necessary. Of the five subtests contained in the data-processing area, four were common. The fifth subtest, however, was designed around programming for COBOL for the business application and FORTRAN for the scientific application. The common subtests include data-processing-system fundamentals, statistics, mathematics, and general accounting. Reliabilities range from .71 through .95 on subtests containing from twenty-five to seventy items. The administration time for the subtests range from thirty to sixty minutes. Total test reliability is .97 for scientific data processing and .92 for business data processing.

REFERENCES

Adkins, D. C. *Construction and analysis of achievement tests.* Washington, D.C.: U. S. Civil Service Commission, 1947.

American Vocational Association. *A guide to improving instruction in industrial arts.* Washington, D.C.: AVA, 1968.

Bloom, B. S. (Ed.) *Taxonomy of educational objectives: The classification of educational goals.* Handbook 1. *Cognitive domain.* New York: McKay, 1956.

Brogden, H. E., & Taylor, E. K. The theory and classification of criterion bias. *Educational and Psychological Measurement,* 1950, **10,** 159–186.

Buros, O. K. (Ed.) *The sixth mental measurements yearbook.* Highland Park, N.J.: Gryphon Press, 1965.

Bushnell, D. S. "E. S. '70": For the neglected majority. *Journal of Industrial Arts Education,* 1968, **27**(5), 23–25.

Caveny, C. C., & Weichelt, J. A. Reliability of shop grades. *Industrial Arts and Vocational Education,* 1945, **34,** 233–236.

Chapanis, A. Theory and methods for analyzing errors in man-machine systems. *Annals of the New York Academy of Sciences,* 1951, **51,** 1179–1203.

Cratty, B. J. *Movement behavior and motor learning.* (2nd ed.) Philadelphia: Lea & Febiger, 1967.

Dolan, F. D., & Schulz, H. A. Machine shop grading in ordnance school. *Industrial Arts and Vocational Education,* 1944, **33,** 403–405.

Doll, R. E., & Longo, A. A. Improving the effectiveness of peer ratings. *Personnel Psychology,* 1962, **15,** 215–220.

Face, W. L., & Flug, E. R. New concepts and where they lead. *Industrial Arts and Vocational Education,* 1966, **55**(5), 24–28.

Fisk, D. W., & Cox, J. A., Jr. The consistency of rating by peers. *Journal of Applied Psychology,* 1960, **44,** 11–17.

Fitts, P. M. Engineering psychology and equipment design. In S. S. Stevens (Ed.), *Handbook of experimental psychology.* New York: Wiley, 1951. Pp. 1287–1340.

Fleishman, E. A., & Rich, S. Role of kinesthetic and spatial-visual abilities in perceptual-motor learning. *Journal of Experimental Psychology,* 1963, **66,** 6–11.

Ghiselli, E. E., & Brown, C. W. *Personnel and industrial psychology.* (2nd ed.) New York: McGraw-Hill, 1955.

Guilford, J. P. *Psychometric methods.* (2nd ed.) New York: McGraw-Hill, 1954.

Hollander, E. P. The friendship factor in peer nominations. *Personnel Psychology,* 1956, **9,** 435–447.

Inlow, G. *The emergent in curriculum.* New York: Wiley, 1966.

Krathwohl, D. R., Bloom, B. S., & Masia, B. B. *Taxonomy of educational objectives: The classification of educational goals.* Handbook 2. *Affective domain.* New York: McKay, 1964.

Lux, D. G., Ray, W. E., Stern, J., & Towers, E. R. A rationale and structure for industrial arts subject matter. Unpublished manuscript, Ohio State University, 1966.

Miller, G. A. The magic number seven, plus or minus two: Some limits on our capacity for processing information. *Psychological Review*, 1956, **63**(2), 81–97.

Moore, M. R. *A proposed taxonomy of the perceptual domain and some suggested applications.* (Tech. Rep. No. TDR-67-3.) Princeton, N.J.: Educational Testing Service, August 1967.

Ohio Trade and Industrial Education Service, Instructional Materials Laboratory, Ohio State University. *Trade and industrial education achievement test program.* Columbus: OTIES, 1966.

Olson, J. C. Pittsburgh's OVT program features open-ended occupational education. *School Shop*, 1966, **26**(8), 80–83.

Prien, E. P., & Lee, R. J. Peer ratings and leadership group discussions for evaluation of classroom performance. *Psychological Reports*, 1965, **16,** 59–64.

Shaw, M. E., & Wright, J. M. *Scales for the measurement of attitudes.* New York: McGraw-Hill, 1967.

Siegel, S. *Nonparametric statistics.* New York: McGraw-Hill, 1956.

Simpson, E. J. The classification of educational objectives, psychomotor domain. *Illinois Teacher of Home Economics*, 1966, **10,** 110–144.

Suci, G. J., Vallance, T. R., & Glickman, A. S. *An analysis of peer ratings: I.* (Tech. Bull. No. 54-9) Washington, D.C.: U. S. Bureau of Naval Personnel, 1954.

Swanson, R. A. Auditory Automotive Mechanics Diagnostic Achievement Test. Unpublished doctoral dissertation, University of Illinois, 1968.

Toops, H. A. The criterion. *Educational and Psychological Measurement*, 1944, **4,** 271–297.

Turnquist, C. H. Galaxy approach to education for the world of work. *School Shop*, 1965, **25**(3), 25–27.

U. S. Senate, Committee on Labor and Public Welfare. *Vocational education: The bridge between man and his work.* Washington, D.C.: U. S. Government Printing Office, 1968.

Wood, D. A. *Test construction.* Columbus, Ohio: Merrill, 1960.

Woodworth, R. S., & Schlosberg, H. *Experimental psychology.* (Rev. ed.) New York: Holt, Rinehart and Winston, 1965.

NAME INDEX

SUBJECT INDEX

Page references in **boldface** refer to evaluation illustrations.